EQUITABLE PRINCIPLES OF MARITIME BOUNDARY DELIMITATION

Equity emerged as a powerful symbol of aspired redistribution in international relations. Operationally, it has had limited impact in the Westphalian system of nation states – except for maritime boundary delimitations. This book deals with the role of equity in international law, and offers a detailed case study on maritime boundary delimitation in the context of the enclosure movement in the law of the sea. It assesses treaty law and the impact of the United Nations Convention on the Law of the Sea. It depicts the process of trial and error in the extensive case law of the International Court of Justice and arbitral tribunals and expounds the underlying principles and factors informing the methodology both in adjudication and negotiations. Unlike other books, the main focus is on equity and its implications for legal methodology, in particular offering further guidance in the field of international economic law.

THOMAS COTTIER is a full professor of European and International Economic Law at the University of Bern, Switzerland, and former Managing Director of the World Trade Institute. Much of his professional work has been dedicated to international economic law, in particular international trade regulation, working in the field both as an academic and a negotiator and chair and member of WTO panels.

EQUITABLE PRINCIPLES OF MARITIME BOUNDARY DELIMITATION

The Quest for Distributive Justice
in International Law

THOMAS COTTIER

CAMBRIDGE
UNIVERSITY PRESS

University Printing House, Cambridge CB2 8BS, United Kingdom

Cambridge University Press is part of the University of Cambridge.

It furthers the University's mission by disseminating knowledge in the pursuit of education, learning and research at the highest international levels of excellence.

www.cambridge.org
Information on this title: www.cambridge.org/9781107080171

© Thomas Cottier 2015

This publication is in copyright. Subject to statutory exception and to the provisions of relevant collective licensing agreements, no reproduction of any part may take place without the written permission of Cambridge University Press.

First published 2015

A catalogue record for this publication is available from the British Library

Library of Congress Cataloguing in Publication data
Cottier, Thomas, author.
Equitable principles of maritime boundary delimitation : the quest for distributive justice in international law / Thomas Cottier.
    pages   cm
ISBN 978-1-107-08017-1 (hardback)
1. Maritime boundaries.   I. Title.
KZA1450.C68   2015
341.4′48–dc23
2014035077

ISBN 978-1-107-08017-1 Hardback

Cambridge University Press has no responsibility for the persistence or accuracy of URLs for external or third-party internet websites referred to in this publication, and does not guarantee that any content on such websites is, or will remain, accurate or appropriate.

For Silvia

CONTENTS

List of tables   xviii
List of maps   xix
Preface   xxiii
Acknowledgements   xxvi
Table of cases   xxix
Table of treaties and instruments   xxxiv

Equity revisited: an introduction   1

    I. The renaissance of equity   1
       A. New frontiers   1
       B. Traditional functions and the decline of equity   8
       C. The rebirth of equity in the law of natural resources   16

    II. The quest for global equity   21
       A. The programmatic function of equity   22
       B. The impact of sovereignty and self-determination   25

    III. The legal nature of equity   28
       A. Different layers   28
       B. A source of new legal principles   29
       C. Ambivalence and the need for context   31
       D. The impact of different schools   34

    IV. Conclusion   39

PART I   Context: the enclosure of the seas   43

1   The silent revolution   45

    I. The partition of the seas   45

    II. Conferences, conventions, and customary law   49
       A. UNCLOS I, II and the Geneva Conventions   49

CONTENTS

  B. UNCLOS III and the LOS Convention 50
  C. Multiple sources of law 59
  D. A historical perspective 63

2 **The new maritime zones: evolution and legal foundations** 67

 I. Horizontally shared zones and quasi-territoriality 67
 II. The continental shelf zone 70
  A. Description and development 70
  B. The scope of shelf rights 74
  C. The foundation and legal nature of shelf rights 77
   1. The concept of natural prolongation of the territory of the coastal state 77
   2. Distance: close relationship of the coastal state to offshore marine spaces 92
  D. Summary and conclusions 101
 III. The exclusive economic zone 104
  A. Description and development 104
  B. The foundation and legal nature of EEZ rights 111
   1. Permanent sovereignty over natural resources and the close relationship of the coastal state to offshore marine spaces 111
   2. Customary law 114
  C. The scope of EEZ rights 116
   1. State practice and customary law 116
   2. The LOS Convention 118
 IV. The relationship of the continental shelf and the EEZ 121
  A. Divergencies 121
  B. Convergencies: towards a single homogeneous zone 122
  C. Summary and conclusions 125
   1. Towards a presumption of single maritime boundaries 125
   2. Exceptions: diverging boundaries 128

3 **Distributive effects of the enclosure movement: an assessment of global equity** 130

 I. The quest for global equity in maritime law 130
 II. The allocation of marine spaces 140

A. The main beneficiaries 140
B. The position of land-locked and geographically disadvantaged states 143
   1. Mineral resources 144
   2. Living resources: the concept of equitable surplus allocation 146

III. Developments in fisheries production and market shares 153

IV. Conservation and management – equity towards sustainable use 161

V. Structural limits to equitable sharing in contemporary international law 170

PART II **The new boundaries** 177

4 Approaches to delimitation 179

I. The basic dilemma 179

II. Technical and scientific methods of delimitation 182
   A. Geometrical and geographical methods 183
      1. The method of equidistance or median line 184
      2. The bisector method 191
      3. Perpendicular to the general direction of the coastal line 195
      4. The extrapolation of the land boundary 196
      5. Parallel lines (corridors) 197
      6. Enclaving 197
      7. Annex: problems of scale distortions 198
   B. Geological and ecological methods (natural boundaries) 199
      1. Practical problems of scientific evidence 200
      2. Theoretical and legal issues 202

III. Competing legal approaches to delimitation 204
   A. Four regulatory models 204
      1. The model of juridical vacuum (*ex aequo et bono*) 205
      2. The model of equity and equitable principles 206
      3. The model of residual rules and exceptions (equidistance or median line) 208

4. Equidistance v. equity: the model of agreed equitable solutions based on international law   213

IV. Conclusions   233

5 State practice   236

I. Unilateral acts (proclamations and legislation)   236
   A. Continental shelf   236
   B. Fisheries and exclusive economic zones   238

II. Maritime boundary delimitation agreements   242
   A. Indications in agreements   243
   B. Models and methods applied   244
   C. The impact of the 1958 Shelf Convention equidistance–special circumstances rule   245
   D. Assessment and former studies   246
   E. Protracted negotiations   250

III. The functional approach in co-operation agreements   252
   A. The model of revenue sharing and compensation   257
   B. The model of shared jurisdiction in boundary area pending exploration   258
   C. The model of long-lasting zones overlapping a boundary line   259
   D. The model of common zones under joint administration   261
   E. The potential and limits of co-operation and package deals   266

6 Judicial and conciliatory settlements   271

I. Introductory   271

II. Claims and results in legal proceedings   272
   A. The 1969 *North Sea Continental Shelf* cases   272
   B. The 1977/78 *Anglo-French Channel* arbitration   275
   C. The 1981 *Arbitration concerning the Border between the Emirates of Dubai and Sharjah*   279
   D. The 1982 and 1985 *Tunisia* v. *Libya Continental Shelf* cases   281
   E. The 1984 *Canada* v. *United States Gulf of Maine* case   285
   F. The 1985 *Guinea* v. *Guinea-Bissau* arbitration   290
   G. The 1985 *Libya* v. *Malta Continental Shelf* case   294
   H. The 1992 *Canada* v. *France St. Pierre and Miquelon* arbitration   297

I.   The 1992 *Land, Island and Maritime Frontier Dispute (El Salvador v. Honduras)*   300
J.   The 1993 *Jan Mayen* case *(Denmark v. Norway)*   303
K.   The 1999 *Eritrea v. Yemen* award   306
L.   The 2001 *Case Concerning Maritime Delimitation and Territorial Questions (Qatar v. Bahrain)*   311
M.   The 2002 *Case Concerning the Land and Maritime Boundary (Cameroon v. Nigeria)*   315
N.   The 2006 *Barbados v. Trinidad and Tobago* award   318
O.   The 2007 *Guyana v. Suriname* Award   321
P.   The 2007 *Territorial and Maritime Dispute (Nicaragua v. Honduras)*   324
Q.   The 2009 *Case Concerning the Maritime Delimitation in the Black Sea (Romania v. Ukraine)*   327
R.   The 2012 *Bay of Bengal (Bangladesh v. Myanmar)* case   332
S.   The 2012 *Territorial and Maritime Dispute (Nicaragua v. Colombia)*   336
T.   The 2014 *Maritime Dispute (Peru v. Chile)*   338

III. Claims and Results in Domestic and Quasi-judicial Proceedings   341
   A.   The 1979 United States CEIP Delimitation Recommendations   341
   B.   The 1981 Jan Mayen Ridge Conciliation   344
   C.   The 2002 Arbitration between Newfoundland and Labrador and Nova Scotia   346

IV. Assessment   348
   A.   Individuality of configurations   348
   B.   The importance of the compromis (special agreement)   349
   C.   Claims and the role of equidistance   350
   D.   Geometrical constructions and results   352
   E.   The common basis of equity   352

7 An assessment of customary law   354

I. The state of play in customary law   354
   A.   The prohibition of unilateral delimitation   357
   B.   The absence of a duty to negotiate boundaries   358
   C.   The absence of specific customary rules for shelf and EEZ delimitation   359
      1.   The model of residual rules and exceptions (equidistance–special circumstances)   359

2. The model of equitable principles   363
3. Other methods and legal approaches   365
4. Customary obligation to achieve an equitable solution   365
5. Customary obligation of mutual co-operation?   367

II. The potential and limitation of equidistance   369

PART III **Delimitation based on equity**   373

8 **The rule of equity**   375

I. The rationale of equity and equitable principles   375
   A. Corrective or autonomous equity?   375
   B. The inherent need for underlying values and principles   379
   C. The normative level of equitable principles   381
   D. A closer look at equidistance–special circumstances   381
      1. A clear and simple model?   382
      2. A more predictable model?   385
      3. The shortcomings of an equidistance rule   386
   E. The roots of the controversy: jurisprudence and legal theory   389
   F. The appropriateness of equity   392

II. The evolution of the fundamental norm of equity   394
   A. Roots of the fundamental rule   394
      1. The 1909 *Grisbadarna* arbitration   394
      2. The 1951 *Anglo-Norwegian Fisheries* case   398
   B. 1969: The beginnings   403
   C. 1977: Reducing the rule   404
   D. 1982 and 1984: The victory of discretionary determination   405
   E. 1985: The turning of the tide   409
   F. 1999–2014: The two-step and three-step approach   413
   G. Conclusions   417

III. Legal foundations of the fundamental rule of equity   418
   A. The Truman Proclamation and legal thinking   421
   B. The principle of peaceful settlement of disputes (Article 33 UN Charter)   422
   C. Justice, good faith, and equity in the *North Sea Continental Shelf* cases   423
   D. Judicial legislation   426
   E. Decision-making *ex aequo et bono* in disguise?   430
   F. Subsequent case law   435

1. Paramount foundation in equity   435
2. Foundation in the LOS Convention   437
G. Towards a set of independent equitable principles   438

9   Conceptual issues and the context of equity   440

I. The conceptual task   440
   A. The quest for equitable standards   440
   B. The process in case law   442
   C. Basic conceptual problems   451

II. The impact of underlying concepts, objectives and ideas   453
   A. The relational nature of equity and equitable standards   453
   B. The object of delimitation: resources or marine space?   456
   C. The window of delimitation   459
   D. The issue of natural boundaries   462
      1. The impact of natural prolongation and plate tectonics   463
      2. The impact of ecology (ecosystems)   470
   E. A doctrine of the closest relationship   472
   F. The impact of underlying objectives and values   473

III. The legal environment of equity   475
   A. Pacta sunt servanda   476
      1. Delimitation and related agreements   476
      2. The principle of *uti possidetis*   479
      3. Compromis (special agreement)   482
   B. Historic rights   485
   C. Estoppel and acquiescence   489
   D. Third party interests   491
      1. Substantive claims and rights   491
      2. Procedural claims and rights: intervention or fair hearing ?   494

IV. The political environment of equity and the need for transparency   510

V. Conclusion: essential elements of an equitable solution   512

10   Justiciable standards of equity   515

I. The legal nature of equitable standards   515

A. The requirement of justiciability 515
B. The legal nature of equitable principles and relevant circumstances 518
  1. Equitable principles 518
  2. The nature of relevant circumstances 522
  3. The element of 'equitable solution' 525

II. Equitable standards related to physical geography 525
  A. Standards related to surface coastal configuration 525
    1. The coast dominates the sea (CDS) 526
    2. The principles of non-encroachment and non-cutting-off (NEP, NCP) 530
  B. Equitable principles related to space allocation 538
    1. Equal division of marine space (EDS) 538
  C. The principle of fair and reasonable proportionality (FRP) 541
    1. The relationship to the coastal lengths 542
    2. The problem of specification 543
    3. The field of application 556
    4. Assessment 557
  D. Relevant circumstances related to resource allocation 559
    1. The location of resources 560
    2. The possibility of eco-geographical criteria 563
    3. Inherent limitations to resource allocation in general law of delimitation 564
    4. Improving resource allocation by negotiation and by special agreement (compromis) 567

III. Equitable standards related to conduct and human geography 568
  A. Standards related to conduct of coastal states 568
    1. Relevant circumstance: historical conduct prior to the creation of the legal shelf and the EEZ 571
    2. The principle of recent and contemporary conduct (RCCP) 574
    3. Conclusions 577
  B. Social and economic standards 577
    1. General social and economic interests 578
    2. Specifically related economic interests, in particular to the EEZ, and the principle of viability (VP) 583
    3. The circumstance of cultural and ethnological interests 589

C. National security interests   590
D. Toward a principle of third generational rights   593

IV. Ad hoc concretization of equity by way of special agreement (compromis)   596

11 The methodology of judicial boundary delimitation   602

I. Competing schools of jurisprudence   602
A. Introduction   602
B. Topical jurisprudence   605

II. The programme of delimitation   610
A. Adjudication of legal issues outside the realm of equity   611
B. Defining the window of delimitation   611
C. Adjudication of rights and obligations stemming from treaty law, historical rights, estoppel and acquiescence or any other legal title   613
D. Adjudication of territorial jurisdiction   614

III. The proper methodology of equity   614
A. The beginnings in the courts: the idea of weighing and balancing factors   614
B. Toward a topical, problem-oriented methodology of equity   622
   1. Assessing the type of boundary required or permitted   623
   2. Assessment and adjudication of equitable principles   625
   3. Specification and visualization of principles   625
   4. Vector analysis and co-ordination of boundary lines   626
   5. The corrective impact of relevant circumstances and of the requirement of an equitable result   628
C. The methodological impact of the goal of an equitable apportionment   630
D. Role of technical methods and geometrical constructions   631
E. *Iura novit curia* and the need for structural pairing of substance and procedure   631
F. Conclusions   634

IV. The problem and impact of islands   635
A. Introduction   635
B. Legal issues   638
   1. Basic entitlement to shelf and EEZ   638

CONTENTS

    2. Two categories of islands: constitutive and accessory entitlement 641
  C. Assessment and adjudication of equitable principles 642
    1. The impact of additive islands: ignoring locations 642
    2. Constitutive islands 644
    3. Special circumstances and geometric fixation 644

12 The role of equity in negotiations 645

 I. Introduction 645
 II. The rule of equity and equitable principles in negotiated settlements 647
  A. Mandatory or residual rules? 647
  B. Law and policy in the negotiating process 653
  C. Equity and the methodology of negotiations 654
    1. The role of equitable standards 654
    2. The proper methodology of delimitation in negotiations 655
  D. Conclusion 660
 III. The equitable obligation to negotiate 660
  A. A new dimension of law 660
  B. The duty to negotiate maritime boundary delimitations 663
    1. The scope of obligation 663
    2. The impact of good faith and legitimate expectations 665
    3. The prohibition of acts frustrating negotiations 666
  C. Foundations of the duty to negotiate 672
    1. Issues 672
    2. Specific foundations 672
    3. UN Charter? 674
    4. Customary law: prior consultation 675
    5. Equity 676
  D. Legal effects of violations of the duty to negotiate 679
    1. Compliance and possible reprisals 679
    2. The impact in court proceedings 681
    3. The 1978 *Aegean Continental Shelf* case: an opportunity missed 682
    4. Ordering negotiations 687

Appendix I   *Maritime boundary agreements
             1942–1992*   691
Appendix II   *General maps*   721
Bibliography   747
Index   778

TABLES

3.1　Allocation of EEZ marine space　　141
3.2　Allocation of marine catches　　156
3.3　Distribution of exports of fish products　　157
3.4　Distribution of imports of fish products　　158
5.1　Principles or methods indicated in 120 agreements　　243
5.2　Methods applied and effected in 120 sample agreements effecting 131 applications of methods　　245
5.3　Application of Article 6 of the 1958 Shelf Convention　　246
5.4　Account of methods of delimitation used (Legault/Hankey)　　249
A.1　Maritime boundary agreements 1942–1992　　692

MAPS

1 *North Sea Continental Shelf (Federal Republic of Germany v. Denmark; Federal Republic of Germany v. Netherlands)* Judgment, ICJ Reports 1969, p. 3 at p. 15. A–B: German-Danish Agreement, 9.6.65; C–D: German–Dutch Agreement, 1.12.1964; E–F: Dutch–Danish Agreement, 31.3. 1966, contested by the Federal Republic of Germany. The Court produced guiding principles of delimitation. It was not asked to draw a boundary line.   722
2 *Arbitration Between the United Kingdom of Great Britain and Northern Ireland and the French Republic on the Delimitation of the Continental Shelf*, Decisions of the Court of Arbitration dated 30 June 1977 and 14 March 1978, Command Paper 7438, March 1979, reprinted in 18 ILM, p. 397 at 494.   723
3 *The 1981 Arbitration concerning the Border between the Emirates of Dubai and Sharjah*, E. Lauterpacht and C. J. Greenwood (eds.), *International Law Reports*, vol. 91 (Cambridge University Press, 1993), p. 700.   724
4 *Continental Shelf (Tunisia v. Libyan Arab Jamahiriya)*, Judgment, ICJ Reports 1982, p. 18 at p. 90.   725
5 *Delimitation of the Maritime Boundary in the Gulf of Maine Area (Canada v. United States of America)*, Judgment, ICJ Reports 1984, p. 246 at p. 346.   726
6 *Arbitration Tribunal for the Delimitation of the Maritime Boundary Between Guinea and Guinea-Bissau*, Award of 14 February 1985, transl. in (1986) 25 ILM, p. 251 at p. 307.   727
7 *Continental Shelf (Libyan Arab Jamahiriya v. Malta)*, Judgment, ICJ Reports 1985, p. 13 at p. 54.   728
8 *Court of Arbitration for the Delimitation of Maritime Areas between Canada and France, Case concerning de Delimitation of Maritime Areas between Canada and the French Republic* (1992) 31 ILM p. 1145 at p. 1148.   729
9 *Land, Island and Maritime Frontier Dispute (El Salvador v. Honduras: Nicaragua intervening)*, Judgment, ICJ Reports 1992, p. 351 at p. 587; the map illustrates the Gulf of Fonseca, in the judgment no delimitation of the disputed maritime spaces, whether within or outside the Gulf were made.   730

xx   LIST OF MAPS

10 *Maritime Delimitation in the Area between Greenland and Jan Mayen (Denmark v. Norway)*, Judgment, ICJ Reports 1993, p. 38 at p.80.   731
11 *Permanent Court of Arbitration (PCA): Eritrea–Yemen Arbitration* (Second Stage: Maritime Delimitation) (17 December 1999), www.pca-cpa.org/showpage.asp?pag_id=1160 (last accessed 27 March 2014).   732
12.1 *Maritime Delimitation and Territorial Questions between Qatar and Bahrain*, Merits, Judgment, ICJ Reports 2001, p. 40 at p. 105.   733
12.2 (Enlargement of Map 12.1) *Maritime Delimitation and Territorial Questions between Qatar and Bahrain*, Merits, Judgment, ICJ Reports 2001, p. 40 at p. 106.   734
13 *Land and Maritime Boundary between Cameroon and Nigeria (Cameroon v. Nigeria: Equatorial Guinea intervening)*, Judgment, ICJ Reports 2002, p. 303 at p. 449.   735
14 *Permanent Court of Arbitration (PCA): In The Matter of an Arbitration between Barbados and the Republic of Trinidad and Tobago* (11 April 2006) (2006) 45 ILM, p. 800 at p. 869.   736
15 *Arbitral Tribunal Constituted Pursuant to Article 287, and in Accordance with Annex VII, of the United Nations Convention on the Law of the Sea in the Matter of an Arbitration between Guyana and Suriname*, Award of 17 September 2007, A-5.   737
16.1 *Territorial and Maritime Dispute between Nicaragua and Honduras in the Caribbean Sea (Nicaragua v. Honduras)*, Judgment, ICJ Reports 2007, p. 659 at p. 761.   738
16.2 (Enlargement of Map 16.1) *Territorial and Maritime Dispute between Nicaragua and Honduras in the Caribbean Sea (Nicaragua v. Honduras)*, Judgment, ICJ Reports 2007, p. 659 at p. 762.   739
17.1 *Maritime Delimitation in the Black Sea (Romania v. Ukraine)*, Judgment, ICJ Reports 2009, p. 61 at p. 132.   740
17.2 *Maritime Delimitation in the Black Sea (Romania v. Ukraine)*, Judgment, ICJ Reports 2009, p. 61 at p. 133.   741
18 *Delimitation of the Maritime Boundary in the Bay of Bengal (Bangladesh v. Myanmar)*, Judgment, ITLOS Reports 2012, p. 4 at p. 129.   742
19 *Territorial and Maritime Dispute (Nicaragua v. Colombia)*, Judgment, ICJ Reports 2012, p. 624 at p. 714.   743
20 *Maritime Dispute (Peru v. Chile)*, ICJ Judgment of 27 January 2014, ICJ Reports 2014, p. 66.   744
21 *Conciliation Commission on the Continental Shelf Area between Iceland and Jan Mayen: Report and Recommendations to the Governments of Iceland and Norway*, Report and Recommendations to the Governments of Iceland and Norway of the Conciliation Commission on the Continental Shelf Area between Iceland and Jan Mayen (1981) 20 ILM, p. 797 at p. 828.   745

22 *Arbitration between Newfoundland and Labrador and Nova Scotia Concerning Portions of the Limits of Their Offshore Areas as defined in the Canada-Nova Scotia Offshore Petroleum Resources Accord Implementation Act* and the *Canada-Newfoundland and Atlantic Accord Implementation Act*, Award of the Tribunal in the Second Phase, Ottawa, 26 March 2002, p. 96.   746

PREFACE

The twentieth century witnessed a new generation of national boundaries. Claims of coastal states to the continental shelf and an exclusive economic zone resulted in new entitlements. They called for co-ordination. In delineating these claims, the principle of equity took on a prominent role. Equity, beyond its traditional functions in legal history, emerged in a process of trial and error as the very foundation of the principles and methodology determining the delimitation of overlapping claims to marine space. As a result, it plays in important role in the allocation of marine resources. This field of study allows for insights to be gained into the modern role and function of equity in international law, assessing both the potential and the limitations of distributive justice in the society of nations.

The book undertakes a detailed analysis of the evolution and process of equity in contemporary international law of the sea. It focuses on the relationship of legal rules on delimitation, in particular equidistance, and of equitable principles and relevant factors. It explores the relationship of law and equity in complex individual cases and particular circumstances which do not lend themselves to the application of ready-made, hard and fast legal rules. The operation of maritime boundary delimitation is essentially based upon a genuine rule of equity. It is determined by a number of standards, employing in the final analysis a topical method of weighing and balancing different and competing interests in a methodologically sound manner. The study seeks to further clarify and contribute to the methodology which, in an abundant series of adjudicated and negotiated cases, has been subject to trial and error. No case is like another. Conclusions cannot be readily drawn. And yet, it is submitted that common and shared methodologies, features and consistencies can be identified and further developed. It is hoped that the book will make a contribution in conceptualizing underlying principles and the methodology which eventually may be applied to other fields of law.

The book starts with a review of traditional and contemporary functions of equity in international law, showing not only its complementary and corrective functions, but also the aspirations for justice in international law and relations. Part I of the book addresses the advent of the maritime zones and their limited implications for distributive justice. Part II deals with the new boundaries, reviewing state practice and the abundant case law based upon which the doctrine of equity evolved in a process of trial and error. Part III of the book develops the underlying principles of delimitation, identifies the standards to be taken into account and sets out the methodologies for the adjudication of complex cases and for negotiations.

This book is of interest both to the field of maritime boundary delimitation and to legal theory. It offers a complete analysis of more than fifty years of maritime boundary delimitation and should assist lawyers and diplomats in future negotiations and adjudication of complex cases. For legal theory, it is hoped that it is able to demonstrate that recourse to modern equity essentially entails a constructive approach, building on the underlying foundations of a particular concept, taking into account a host of pertinent factors and interests in a topical manner. The discussion of the relationship of equidistance and of equity offers insights into the relationship of rules and equity. Whether courts depart from the law on the basis of equity, or whether they take equitable principles into account in assessing exceptions to a rule, the process is inherently fact-intensive and creative. It is far removed from the traditions of syllogism and the idea of applying pre-existing rules to a particular fact. Relevant factors and interests need to be identified in a transparent manner and brought to the table and balanced against each other. The legitimacy of the decision depends greatly on the pertinence of reasoning and argumentation. Equity has come a long way from correcting the law, providing foundations and a proper methodology based upon which results are composed, rather than simply found.

Insights from maritime boundary delimitation therefore can also be rendered fruitful not only in related areas but also in other areas addressing fact-intensive issues of distributive justice in international law, even beyond the allocation of natural resources. It may inspire other fields of international law, in particular human rights, trade regulation, investment protection, competition law, and environmental law. In conclusion, equity revisited reveals an innovative method of legal discourse in search of justice and solutions supporting peaceful and friendly relations among nations.

March 2014
Thomas Cottier

ACKNOWLEDGEMENTS

Equity and this project have been companions of mine for much of my professional life. They strongly informed my thinking on law, justice and legal methodology long after my work moved on to include other areas of international law and of European law. The book describes legal developments of law and equity over roughly seventy years of maritime boundary delimitation since the 1940s. The process of doing so, writing intermittently, stretched to a period of no less than three decades of thinking and rethinking a topic which evolved into one of the main areas of practice in international law relating to natural resources.

Inspired by the emerging case law of the International Court of Justice following the 1969 *North Sea Continental Shelf* cases, I was privileged to take up research as a post-doctoral fellow at Wolfson College and the Faculty of Law of the University of Cambridge from 1984 to 1986. I am grateful to the College and the Faculty of Law for hosting me during what became a formative and important period of my life. I sincerely thank Jörg Paul Müller, Emeritus Professor of Constitutional and International Law at the University of Bern, Switzerland. He strongly supported and encouraged me at the time. I am indebted to the Swiss National Research Foundation for support enabling our young family to move to Cambridge, and laying the foundations for additional support for many other projects in the subsequent years of my research. I am grateful to my parents and my late father Paul in particular for sharing part of his salary to make ends meet at the time. I thank my family, Silvia, Annie, Samuel and Maurice for keeping fond memories of the Cambridge years.

I vividly recall discussions with the late Sir Derek William Bowett, Whewell Professor of International Law at the University of Cambridge. His advice, expertise and practical experience in the field were invaluable in conceptualizing and structuring the complexities of the subject matter. He taught me the practice of international law. He encouraged me to focus more on the legal intricacies of maritime boundary delimitation and less so on aspirational dimensions in the political debate on global and intergenerational equity which eventually moved centre stage in work on international economic law. The hospitality of Betty and Derek has remained an example to me and my family. I cherish the memory of discussions with my fellow researcher Esa Passivirta at the old Squire Law Library. Much of what we stand for today was shaped in those days. The two years in Cambridge provided much of the theoretical backbone for my subsequent work, first as a trade negotiator in the GATT Uruguay Round from 1986 to 1993, and subsequently as a full professor of European and International Economic Law at the University of Bern and Managing Director of the World Trade Institute.

During all these subsequent years, work on the project on equity continued steadily, but at a slow pace and in different stages, whenever scarce time allowed for it. The UN Convention on the Law of the Sea, dominating discussions in the 1980s, entered into force in 1994. The case law of the International Court of Justice and of courts of arbitration continued to grow and became one of the most important areas of international litigation next to WTO law (my main area of practice and research today) and investment protection. Without the help from fellows and staff at the Institute of European and International Economic Law and the World Trade Institute of the University of Bern, the project would not have been able to be further developed and completed. I am most grateful for research assistance provided at the time by then doctoral students and research fellows Serge Pannatier, Krista Nadakavukaren Schefer, and Jonas Attenhofer. Their support was critical in editing, updating more recent developments, both in state practice and judicial dispute settlement and the growing body of academic literature on the subject. The work of Jonas has been essential in completing the manuscript over the past two years, incorporating recent case law and developments. Additional persons lent their hands and skills. Beatrice Wettstein retyped an early manuscript. Students at the time, Annie Cottier and Maurice Cottier took on summer jobs checking and completing footnotes. Subsequently, junior research fellows at the Institute, Ruth Peterseil, Christiane Fürst, Raffaela Iseponi, Maya Taylan and Maria Schultheiss assisted in checking and completing footnotes as well as in the compilation of the bibliography. They all moved on into successful careers upon leaving law school, and the book entails fond memories of working with them. Over the years, Susan Plattner reviewed and edited a number of chapters. It laid the foundation of a long-lasting co-operation at the World Trade Institute. Kathrin Rüegsegger kindly compiled the maps. To all these persons, I am immensely grateful. Shortcomings and omissions will remain. They are my own responsibility.

I am grateful to Cambridge University Press for having accepted the manuscript and to the anonymous reviewers for useful critique and suggestions. I am particularly grateful to Joanna Breeze, Sarah E. Green, Deborah Hey, Kim Hughes, Ramya Rangathan and Richard Woodham for all their careful effort and work in producing the book.

Throughout all these years, Silvia my beloved wife has been my companion and main support. She shared all the ups and downs of the project and beyond. To her this work is dedicated: for all we missed and for all we shared.

Bern
March 2014
Thomas Cottier

TABLE OF CASES

Aegean Sea Continental Shelf (Greece v. Turkey), Interim Protection, Order of 11 September 1976, ICJ Reports 1976, p. 3.   62
Aegean Sea Continental Shelf (Greece v. Turkey), Judgment, ICJ Reports 1978, p. 3.   62, 69, 250–251, 468, 683
Application for Revision and Interpretation of the Judgment of 24 February 1982 in the Case concerning the Continental Shelf (Tunisia v. Libyan Arab Jamahiriya) (Tunisia v. Libyan Arab Jamahiriya), Judgment, ICJ Reports 1985, p. 192.   281, 479
Arbitral Tribunal Constituted Pursuant to Article 287, and in Accordance with Annex VII, of the United Nations Convention on the Law of the Sea in the Matter of an Arbitration between Guyana and Suriname, Award of 17 September 2007 (hereinafter Guyana v. Suriname Award), International Court of Arbitration: www.pca-cpa.org/showfile.asp?fil_id=664 (last accessed 18 February 2012).   63, 76, 190, 321
Arbitral Tribunal Constituted Pursuant to Article 287, and in Accordance with Annex VII, of the United Nations Arbitration Between the United Kingdom of Great Britain and Northern Ireland and the French Republic on the Delimitation of the Continental Shelf, Decisions of the Court of Arbitration dated 30 June 1977 and 14 March 1978, Command Paper 7438, March 1979, reprinted in 18 ILM (1979) p. 397.
Arbitration Between Newfoundland and Labrador and Nova Scotia Concerning Portions of the Limits of Their Offshore Areas as defined in the Canada–Nova Scotia Offshore Petroleum Resources Accord Implementation Act and the Canada–Newfoundland and Atlantic Accord Implementation Act, Award of the Tribunal in the Second Phase, Ottawa, 26 March 2002: www.cnsopb.ns.ca/sites/default/files/pdfs/phaseii_award_english.pdf (last accessed February 2014).   346, 746
Arbitration Between the United Kingdom of Great Britain and Northern Ireland and the French Republic on the Delimitation of the Continental Shelf, Decisions of the Court of Arbitration dated 30 June 1977 and 14 March 1978, Command Paper 7438, March 1979, reprinted in 18 ILM 397, 662 (1979).   62, 96, 184, 198, 275, 361, 363, 383, 443, 531, 617, 646, 723
Arbitration Tribunal for the Delimitation of the Maritime Boundary Between Guinea and Guinea-Bissau, Award of 14 February 1985, transl. in (1986) 25 ILM 251.
Award of the Arbitral Tribunal in the First Stage (Territorial Sovereignty and Scope of the Dispute) from 9 October 1998 (hereinafter Award of the First Stage) Reports of International Arbitral Awards, vol XXII p. 209–332, United Nations 2006.   306

Award of the Arbitral Tribunal in the Matter of Arbitration between Barbados and the Republic of Trinidad and Tobago, 11 April 2006 Reports of International Arbitral Awards vol. XXVII pp. 147-251 (United Nations 2008); (2006) 45 ILM 800-869.   318, 362

Award of the Tribunal in the First Stage (Territorial Sovereignty and Scope of Dispute), Permanent Court of Arbitration, Award of 9 October 1998 (2001) 40 ILM 900.   306

Award of the Arbitral Tribunal in the Second Stage (Maritime Delimitation) in the Matter of an Arbitration between Eritrea and Yemen, 17 December 1999 (hereinafter *Eritrea v. Yemen* (Second Stage)) (2001) 40 ILM 983.   62, 306, 533

Barcelona Traction, Light and Power Company, Limited (Belgium v. Spain), Judgment, ICJ Reports 1970, p. 3.   230

Beagle Channel Arbitration, Report and Decision of the Court (1978) 17 ILM 634-79.   322, 533

Canada: *Supreme Court Judgment Concerning Jurisdiction over the Seabed and Subsoil of the Continental Shelf off Newfoundland* (Appeal heard, 22-24 February 1983. Judgment pronounced, 8 March 1984) (1984) 23 ILM 288-319.   79, 85

Case Concerning Maritime Delimitation in the Black Sea (Romania v. Ukraine), Judgment, 3 February 2009, ICJ Reports 2009 p. 61.   187, 194, 327, 358, 363, 449, 524

Case Concerning the Arbitral Award made by the King of Spain on 23 December 1906, Judgment of 18 November 1960, ICJ Reports 1960, p. 192.   524

Case Concerning the Land, Island and Maritime Frontier Dispute (El Salvador v. Honduras) Application by Nicargua for Permission to Intervene, Judgment, 13 September 1990, ICJ Reports 1990, p. 92.   300, 498

Cayuga Indians (Great Britain) v. United States, reprinted in: Reports of International Arbitral Awards, vol. VI, pp. 173-90, 179.   16

Chorzow Factory (Jurisdiction) Case, Permanent Court of International Justice, Series A No. 9, p. 31 (1927).   489

Conciliation Commission on the Continental Shelf Area between Iceland and Jan Mayen: Report and Recommendations to the Governments of Iceland and Norway, Report and Recommendations to the Governments of Iceland and Norway of the Conciliation Commission on the Continental Shelf Area between Iceland and Jan Mayen (1981) 20 ILM 797-842.   260, 344, 745

Continental Shelf (Libyan Arab Jamahiriya v. Malta), Application to Intervene, Judgment, ICJ Reports 1984, p. 3.   62, 295

Continental Shelf (Libyan Arab Jamahiriya v. Malta), Judgment, ICJ Reports 1985, p. 13.   62, 77, 187, 294, 376, 409, 615, 728

Continental Shelf (Tunisia v. Libyan Arab Jamahiriya), Application to Intervene, Judgment, ICJ Reports 1981, p. 3.   62, 281

Continental Shelf (Tunisia v. Libyan Arab Jamahiriya), Judgment, ICJ Reports 1982, p. 18.   62, 74, 186, 240, 281, 358, 376, 479, 617, 653, 725

TABLE OF CASES   xxxi

Court of Arbitration for the Delimitation of Maritime Areas between Canada and France, Case concerning the Delimitation of Maritime Areas between Canada and the French Republic (1992) 31 ILM 1145.
Court of Arbitration for the Delimitation of Maritime Areas between Canada and France: Decision in Case Concerning Delimitation of Maritime Areas, (1992) 31 ILM 1145–48.   62, 197, 298, 466
Delaware v. National Oceanic and Atmospheric Administration, Civil Action No 80-0565 (D.D.C.).   344
Delimitation of the Maritime Boundary in the Gulf of Maine Area (Canada v. United States of America), Judgment, ICJ Reports 1984, p. 246.   61, 68, 183, 239, 248, 285–287, 376, 406, 444, 726
Denmark v. Norway (Jan Mayen), ICJ Reports 1993, p. 53.   349–352, 387, 411, 477, 490, 547, 554–555, 570, 586
Dispute concerning Delimitation of the Maritime Boundary between Bangladesh and Myanmar in the Bay of Bengal (Bangladesh v. Myanmar), Judgment, International Tribunal for the Law of the Sea, 14 March 2012, Case No. 16.   88, 187, 332, 413, 450, 524, 616
East Greenland Case [1933] Permanent Court of International Justice, Series A/B No. 53 (Legal Status of Eastern Greenland).   569
Electricity Company of Sofia and Bulgaria Case, [1939] Permanent Court of International Justice, Series A/B, No. 778, p. 199.   672
Exchange of Greek and Turkish Population Advisory Opinion [1925] Permanent Court of International Justice, Series B No. 20, at p. 24.   648
Fisheries Case (United Kingdom v. Norway), Judgment, ICJ Reports 1951, p. 116.   61, 106, 187
Fisheries Jurisdiction (Federal Republic of Germany v. Iceland), Merits, Judgment, ICJ Reports 1974, p. 175.   61
Fisheries Jurisdiction (United Kingdom v. Iceland), Judgment, ICJ Reports 1973, p. 3.   109, 231, 674
Fisheries Jurisdiction (United Kingdom v. Iceland), Merits, Judgment, ICJ Reports 1974, p. 3.   61, 109–110
Free Zones of Upper Savoy and the District of Gex [1929] Permanent Court of International Justice, Series A No. 22.   673
Frontier Dispute (Burkina Faso v. Republic of Mali), Judgment, ICJ Reports 1986, p. 554, para. 149.   6
Gentini Case, Ven Arb 1093 720, at 715.   521
Judgment on Application for Revision and Interpretation of the Judgment in the Case Concerning the Continental Shelf (Tunisia v. Libyan Arab Jamahiriya) (1986) 25 ILM 152–72.   477
Land and Maritime Boundary between Cameroon and Nigeria (Cameroon v. Nigeria: Equatorial Guinea Intervening), Judgment, ICJ Reports 2002, p. 303.   6, 124, 186, 315, 362, 413–414, 448, 620, 664, 735

Land, Island and Maritime Frontier Dispute (El Salvador v. Honduras), Application to Intervene, Judgment, ICJ Reports 1990, p. 92.   301

Land, Island and Maritime Frontier Dispute (El Salvador v. Honduras: Nicaragua intervening), Judgment, ICJ Reports 1992, p. 351.   301

Louisana v. Luther Hodges, Jr., et al., Civil action No. 79-601-B (M.D. La).   344

Maritime Delimitation and Territorial Questions between Qatar and Bahrain (Qatar v. Bahrain), Merits, Judgment, ICJ Reports 2001, p. 40.   62, 124, 186, 242, 311, 326, 366, 413, 447, 527, 614, 733–734

Maritime Delimitation in the Area between Greenland and Jan Mayen (Denmark v. Norway), Judgment, ICJ Reports 1993, p. 38.   62, 116, 121, 190, 303, 313, 362, 411, 619, 731

Maritime Delimitation in the Black Sea (Romania v. Ukraine), Judgment, ICJ Reports 2009, p. 61.   63, 184, 187, 194, 327, 358, 363, 449, 524

Maritime Dispute (Peru v. Chile), ICJ Judgment of 27 January 2014, ICJ Reports 2014___, (2014) 53 ILM 430.   188, 339, 366, 416, 451, 479, 554, 744

Military and Paramilitary Activities in and against Nicaragua (Nicaragua v. United States of America), Merits, Judgment, ICJ Reports 1986, p. 14.   230, 354–355

Mississippi v. Secretary U. S. Dept. of Commerce et al., Civil action No. 579-0634 (R) Miss.).   344

New South Wales et al v. Commonwealth of Australia (Austl. 1975) 135 Commonwealth Law Reports (CLR) 337, 416.   83

North Sea Continental Shelf (Federal Republic of Germany v. Denmark. Federal Republic of Germany v. Netherlands), Judgment, ICJ Reports 1969, p. 3.   62, 74, 185, 272, 355, 376, 403, 617, 722

Nuclear Tests (Australia v. France) (New Zealand v. France), ICJ Reports 1974, pp. 253, 457.   497, 682

Railway Traffic between Lithuania and Poland 139 [1935] Permanent Court of International Justice, Series A/B No. 42, p. 108.   673

Société Commerciale de Belgique [1939] Permanent Court of International Justice, Series A/B No. 78, p. 160.   648

Petroleum Development (Qatar) v. Ruler of Qatar (1951) reprinted in 18 ILR 161.   73

Petroleum Development Ltd. v. Sheik of Abu Dhabi (1951) reprinted in 18 ILR 144.   73

Reference Re: *Ownership of Off-Shore Mineral Rights* (1967) Supreme Court Reports (SCR) 792, 65 Dominion Law Reports (DLR) 353 (Can. 1968).   82

Report and Recommendations to the Governments of Iceland and Norway of the Conciliation Commission on the Continental Shelf Area between Iceland and Jan Mayen, Washington DC 1981, reprinted in (1981) 20 ILM 797.   82

Scotia case, 14 Wallace 170 [81 US] 1971.   354

Sentence du Tribunal Arbitral Franco-Espagnol en date du 16 novembre 1957 dans L'affaire de l'utilisation des eaux du Lac Lanoux (1958) 62 Revue Générale de Droit International Public 79, transl. (1961) 24 ILR 101, 128.   679

Serbian Loans Case [1929] Permanent Court of Justice, Series A No. 20, at p. 39.   648

Exchange of Greek and Turkish Population Advisory Opinion [1925] Permanent Court of Justice, Series B No. 20, at p. 24   648

Société Commerciale de Belgique Cas, [1939] Permanent Court of International Justice, Series A/B No. 78, at p. 178

South West Africa Cases (Ethiopia v. South Africa, Liberia v. South Africa), Second Phase, Judgment, ICJ Reports 1966, p. 6.   21

State of Louisiana v. State of Mississippi, 202 US 1 (1906).   342

State of New Jersey v. State of Delaware, 291 US 361 (1934).   342

State of New Jersey v. State of Delaware, 295 US 694 (1935).   342

Territorial and Maritime Dispute between Nicaragua and Honduras in the Caribbean Sea (Nicaragua v. Honduras), Judgment, ICJ Reports 2007, p. 659.   63, 183, 192, 324, 362, 413–414, 449, 689

Territorial and Maritime Dispute (Nicaragua v. Colombia), Judgment, ICJ Reports 2012, p. 624.   89, 191, 362, 413, 416, 450, 529

The 1981 Arbitration concerning the Border between the Emirates of Dubai and Sharjah [1993] 91 International Law Reports 549–701.   279, 724

The Diversion of Water from the Meuse (Netherlands v. Belgium), Judgment from 28 June 1937, Permanent Court of International Justice, Series A/B No. 70, 1925, 4–89.   17

The Case of the S. S. Lotus, Judgment [1927] Permanent Court of International Justice, Series A No. 9, p. 12.   483

The Queen v. Keayn, 2 Ex.D. 63 (1876).   82

Trail Smelter Case (United States v. Canada), 16 April 1938 and 11 March 1941, UNIRIAA vol. 3, pp. 1905–82.   17

Tribunal Arbitral pour la délimitation de la frontière maritime Guinée/Guinée-Bissau, Sentence du 14 Février 1985, reprinted in French (the authentic text) in (1985) 89 Revue Générale de Droit International Public, 484.   290, 464, 615

United States Diplomatic and Consular Staff in Tehran (United States of America v. Iran), Judgment, ICJ Reports 1980, p. 3.   230

United States v. Louisiana, 339 US 699 (1947).   72

United States v. Texas, 339 US 707 (1950).   72

TABLE OF TREATIES AND INSTRUMENTS

Agreement for the Implementation of the Provisions of the United Nations Convention on the Law of the Sea of 10 December 1982 relating to the Conservation and Management of Straddling Fish Stocks and Highly Migratory Fish Stocks (Straddling Stocks Agreement), done 8 September 1995, in force 11 December 2001, 2167 UNTS 3, (1995) ILM 1542, (2004) UKTS 19.   53, 119, 166
Agreement on the Resolution of Practical Problems with Respect to Deep Seabed Mining Areas' (1987) 26 ILM 1505–8.   58
Convention on the Law of Non-Navigable Uses of International Watercourses, 21 May 1997, UN Doc. A/51/ 869.   520
Declaration of Montevideo on Law of the Sea, Signed at Montevideo, Uruguay, 8 May 1970 (1970) 10 ILM 1081–3.   109, 112
Proclamation No. 2667, Policy of the United States with Respect to the Natural Resources of the Subsoil and Sea Bed of the Continental Shelf, 28 Oct. 1945' (1965), reprinted in Whiteman, 4 Digest of International Law, 740, 756. For the twin-proclamation on fisheries see 4 Digest of International Law, 954.   72, 207, 237
United Nations Conference on Straddling Fish Stocks and Highly Migratory Fish Stocks: Agreement for the Implementation of the Provisions of the United Nations Conventions of the Law of the Sea of 10 December 1982, Relating to the Conservation and Management of the Straddling Fish Stock and Migratory Fish Stocks (Adopted 4 August 1995; Opened for Signature 4 December 1995) (1995) 34 ILM 1542–80.   53, 119, 166
United Nations Convention on Fishing and Conservation of the Living Resources of the High Seas, Geneva, 29 April 1958, in force 20 March 1966, 599 UNTS 285.   49
United Nations Convention on the Continental Shelf, Geneva, 29 April 1958, in force 10 June 1964, 499 UNTS 311.   49, 85, 209
United Nations Convention on the High Seas, Geneva, 29 April 1958, in force 30 September 1962, 450 UNTS 82.   49
United Nations Convention on the Law of the Sea (Done at Montego Bay, 10 December 1982), UN Doc. A/CONF. 62/122 (1982), done at Montego Bay, 10 Dec. 1982 (1982) 21 ILM 1261–354; United Nations, The Law of the Sea: Official Text of the United Nations Convention on the Law of the Sea with Annexes and Index, Sales No. E.83. V.5 (1983), entered into force on 16 November 1994.   46, 53, 119, 166, 213, 226, 474

United Nations Convention on the Law of the Sea: Understanding of the Preparatory Commission for the International Sea-Bed Authority and for the International Tribunal for the Law of the Sea for Proceeding with Deep Sea-Bed Mining Applications and Revolving Disputes of Overlapping Claims of Mine Sites (Reached during Meeting of 11 August–5 September 1986) (1986) 25 ILM 1326–36.   58

United Nations Convention on the Territorial Sea and the Contiguous Zone, Geneva, 29 April, in force 10 September 1964, 516 UNTS 205.   49, 106, 209, 291, 369

United Nations Preparatory Commission for the International Sea-Bed Authority and for the International Tribunal for the Law of the Sea: Statement of Understanding for Proceeding with deep Sea-Bed Mining Applications (10 April 1987) (1987) 26 ILM 1725–7.   58

United Nations Charter of Economic Rights and Duties of States (12 December 1974) (1975) 14 ILM 251–61.   131

Vienna Convention on the Law of Treaties, UNTS 1155 p. 351, ILM 8 (1969) 679, entered into force 27 January 1980.   474

State practice on maritime boundary delimitation

1–6 New Directions of the Law of the Sea (Robin Churchill et al. (eds.), 1973–1977); 7–11 New Directions in the Law of the Sea (Myron Nordquist et al. (eds.), 1980–1981); 12 ff. *New Directions in the Law of the Sea* (Kenneth R. Simmonds (ed.), London: Oceana Publications, 1983 and subsequent supplements).   236

Benedetto Conforti and Giampiero Francalanci (eds.), *Atlante dei Confini Sottomarini – Atlas of the Seabed Boundaries*, Part I (Milan: Giuffrè, 1979).   236–237, 294

Benedetto Conforti et al. (eds.), *Atlante dei Confini Sottomarini – Atlas of the Seabed Boundaries*, Part II (Milan: Giuffrè, 1987).   236–237

Edward Duncan Brown, *Sea-Bed Energy and Minerals: The International Legal Regime*, 3 vols. (The Hague: Martinus Nijhoff, 1992), vol I: The Continental Shelf.   45, 72, 237, 272

Faraj Abdullah Ahnish (ed.), *The International Law of Maritime Boundaries and the Practice of States in the Mediterranean Sea* (Oxford: Oxford University Press, 1994).   237

Jonathan I. Charney et al. (eds.), *International Maritime Boundaries*, 5 vols. (Dordrecht, Boston MA, The Hague: Martinus Nijhoff, 1993–2005): vols. I and II (Charney and Alexander (eds.), 1993); vol. III (Charney and Alexander (eds.), 1998); vol. IV (Charney and Smith (eds.), 2002); vol. V (Colson and Smith (eds.), 2005) (containing the most comprehensive analysis and evaluation of approximately 180 agreements concluded between 1942 and 2004).   118, 126, 180, 271, 360, 388, 456, 560, 676

National Legislation and Treaties Relating to the Law of the Sea, United Nations Legislative Series, ST/LEG/SER.B/19 (1980); ST/LEG/SER.B/16 (1976).   236

National Legislation on Treaties Relating to the Territorial Sea, the Contiguous Zone, the Continental Shelf and the High Seas and to Fishing Conservation of the

Living Resources of the Sea, United Nations Legislative Series, ST/LEG/SER.B/2, 2 vols. (1951).   236

United Nations: Maritime Space: Maritime Zones and Maritime Delimitation, State practice on the internet, www.un.org/Depts/los/LEGISLATIONANDTREATIES/index.htm.

Equity revisited: an introduction

> The way is equity, the end is justice
>
> *Aroa Mines Case*, Frank Plumley, Umpire, Venezuelan Arbitration of 1903, Ralston's Report p. 385-7

I. The renaissance of equity

A. New frontiers

The enclosure of the seas in the twentieth century silently, but fundamentally, reshaped the geographical allocation of marine resources between coastal states. The partial return to a philosophy of *mare clausum* amounts to the most profound revolution of quasi-territorial jurisdiction of nations over natural resources embedded at sea. The new territorial allocation was prompted by the emergence of the continental shelf doctrine in the 1950s and of the exclusive economic zone (EEZ) in the 1970s, both today codified by the 1982 United Nations Convention on the Law of the Sea. The movement brought about new and fundamental challenges within the Westphalian system of nation states. Claims and responses to maritime resources called for an assessment of the newly emerging customary law and, subsequently, of treaty law. This resulted in the allocation and fine-tuning of jurisdiction and control over mineral resources, including oil and gas, and living resources, in particular fisheries. Allocation resulted in horizontally shared rights over resources, derived from the extension of land masses of coastal states. The doctrine of the continental shelf was based upon the extension of the land mass. Today, the concept of the continental shelf combines the criteria of natural prolongation with that of distance, extending to a minimum of 200 nautical miles (nm). At least within those 200 nm, both the continental shelf and the coincident EEZ rely upon the configuration of the coast. The enclosure movement resolved problems of competing claims under the doctrine of the freedom of the seas. It brought about new rights and responsibilities for coastal states. But it also brought about new and fundamental questions of distributive justice on two principal accounts. Both triggered a renaissance of equity in international law.

Firstly, the foundations of the enclosure movement are, in hindsight, essentially based upon the philosophy of permanent sovereignty over natural resources of coastal states. This assignment of jurisdiction to states over portions of the ocean may allow those to regulate the use of marine resources in an efficient manner and by those who are mostly interested in the matter.[1] At the same time, the allocation of jurisdiction and powers on the basis of geographical features and political boundaries led to a widely uneven distribution of marine resources, which raises fundamental problems of distributive justice and of global equity in contemporary international law. Both, the continental shelf and the EEZ limited the problem of distribution to coastal states, at the exclusion of land-locked and other geographically disadvantaged states. Large coastal states, but also small island states, largely benefited from the movement and acquired jurisdiction over vast expanses of the sea. Isolated islands, even uninhabited ones, enjoyed a renaissance and became of paramount importance as base points delineating maritime jurisdictions of coastal states. As a result, the enclosure movement amounted to a paradigm of unequal allocation of natural resources, often amplifying the jurisdiction of already large nations with extensive coastal margins. The new allocation of resources was meant to overcome the tragedy of the commons[2] and the lack of responsibility for resource management under the previous regime of the high seas and its largely unrestricted freedom of exploitation. The enclosure movement succeeded partly, but also brought about new and unsettled problems. Exploitation of oil and gas resources increased – given enhanced legal security – thus accelerating the depletion of scarce and non-renewable resources. Over-fishing and depletion of livestock was partly reduced and partly enhanced under the new EEZ, depending on the resource management policies of coastal states. While conditions for coastal fisheries in particular improved in some of zones, the granting of licences also became more lucrative and many nations failed to develop adequate

---

[1] Eric Posner and Alan O. Sykes, 'Economic Foundations of the Law of the Sea' (16 December 2009) *University of Chicago Law & Economics*, Olin Working Paper No. 504' (available at SSRN: http://ssrn.com/abstract=1524274); see however, Bernard H. Oxman, 'The Territorial Temptation: A Siren Song at Sea, Centennial Essay' (2006) 100 *American Journal of International Law*, 830, 849.

[2] Garret Hardin, 'The Tragedy of the Commons' (1968) 162 (3859) *Science*, 1243.

means to police and patrol their seas. While the outcome probably would not have been any better absent the advent of the EEZ, it should be noted that it was wrong to assume that territorialization in itself would solve conservation problems in all places.[3] The fate of the remaining high seas and its resources was left to the commons, devoid of sufficient management and governance. It was essentially left on its own under the doctrine of freedom of the seas. That this general economic problem justifies some kind of international regulation of the oceans has been widely recognized.[4] Yet overall, the law of the sea, some thirty years after the adoption of the United Nations Convention on the Law of the Sea, remains a field with ticking time bombs and unresolved issues. It still faces a host of issues relating to distribution other than that of territorial jurisdiction over natural resources. They range from deep seabed mining in the area and related transfers of technology to the co-ordination of communication and extraction of resources; from the compensatory rights of land-locked and geographically disadvantaged states to finding a proper balance in preventing and combating marine pollution, chronic over-fishing and the preservation of biodiversity.

Exploring the foundations of the continental shelf doctrine and of the EEZ thus amounts to a fascinating legal history inquiry into the process of international law, the emergence of new concepts in customary and treaty law, and into the effect they produce. The inquiry takes place within the parameters of the classic international law of co-existence. While co-operation between coastal states can be occasionally found, it is determined by classical precepts, far from current ideas of the law of integration, which tends to remove the importance and relevance of territorial allocations and of political boundaries. It examines the extent to which future problems of the law of the sea can still be managed under traditional precepts, and to what extent new forms and structures of global governance and enhanced integration are called upon.

Secondly, the enclosure movement triggered the need to settle new boundaries in an overall context which does not respond to the ideals of distributive justice for the reasons set out above. Demarcation causes political tensions; the difficulties that arise have still not been resolved

---

[3] See Oxman 2006, n. 1, 849, stating that the environmentalists should have at least exacted a higher price for accommodating the territorial temptation 'before it consolidated its grasp on the living resources of the EEZ'.

[4] See e.g. Robert L. Friedheim, 'A Proper Order for the Oceans: An Agenda for the New Century' in Davor Vidas and Willy Østreng (eds.), *Order for the Oceans at the Turn of the Century* (The Hague: Kluwer, 1999), pp. 537, 539.

after more than half a century. New international tensions, even conflict, may arise. Even when oil and gas extraction has been completed, new uses, such as wind, tidal and biomass energy as well as the potential of carbon storage, will maintain interest in the jurisdiction over the shelf. New claims, partly induced by the melting of the ice cap in the Arctic Circle, have been introduced. The issue of proper allocation of rights and obligations is far from settled. Among all the challenges of distributive justice, the problem of maritime boundary delimitation between adjacent and opposite coastal states perhaps amounts to the most prominent issue. From the legal and methodological point of view, it clearly is the most interesting aspect of distributive justice in the field. This is not only true for the law of the sea, but perhaps for all of international law within the classical body of the law of co-existence of states. True, particular issues of distributive justice, delimitation and sharing of resources have not been alien to international law prior to the enclosure of the seas, in particular relating to the law of water and waterways, or the determination of land boundaries. Yet, compared to the challenges posed by the enclosure movement, they have remained of lesser scope and impact in, and on, international law.

Maritime boundary delimitation became of importance in a manner unprecedented in history. It became the subject of a multitude of bilateral agreements and the foremost occupation of the International Court of Justice (ICJ) and courts of arbitration throughout the second part of the twentieth century. No other field of law, except for trade regulation and investment protection, has been exposed such a significant stream of case law. It is in this field that the quest for distributive justice materialized in its most sophisticated manner. It is here that equity experienced its renaissance and became one of the leading principles in allocating natural resources among nations. Maritime boundary delimitation became the main legal battle field of trial and error in discharging distributive justice among nations before courts of law in a context which overall does not respond to distributive justice but to the vagaries and accidents of geography and political boundaries. It amounts to the main legal test as to whether and to what extent public international law is, in a given and difficult context, able to discharge distributive justice, both among and between generations, given the divergence of states in terms of size, prosperity, power and development operating under the laws of co-existence and of co-operation under the United Nations. It largely tells us to what extent international law has been able to bring about the fair distribution of resources under the inequitable foundations of maritime zones and among unequal nations, and to contribute to sustainable use of resources in the long run. The topic could not be more classical, essentially for three reasons:

Firstly, we deal with a prime field of classical international law. The law of the sea has been at the outset of the law of nations. Many of its concepts were shaped by the need to regulate navigation, commerce and marine spaces. It has nurtured the evolution of international law. Many concepts born in this context have found applications in other areas of international life and law. Findings in the law of the sea continue to have the potential to spill over into other areas of public international law and become of generic importance. They are of general interest to the discipline. This is particularly true for the judicial function, the application of general principles and the role of precedents of courts.

Secondly, boundaries, in general, and both on land and sea, are a paradigm of the law of co-existence. They separate, distinguish, segregate and allocate jurisdictions and control. They are the opposite of integration, which removes such boundaries, and play a reduced role in the law of co-operation. In this era of globalization, it is perhaps worth recalling that political boundaries amount to the most basic and profound expression of the traditional system of nation states and the quest and claim of sovereignty over land, people and natural resources. They are a paradigm of co-existence for humans and states. They are at the core of classical international law and relations. The history of mankind is a history of boundaries. Many wars have been fought over them and many lives lost. From ancient times to the end of World War II and beyond, the struggle for land and resources has largely determined human conduct in the pursuit of power and influence, with law playing just a minor role. It is only since the end of World War II and the completion of decolonization in the 1970s, the end of the Cold War in the 1990s and the decline of ideological battles among industrialized and emerging countries, advances in co-operation, enhanced market access and regional integration in parts of the globe, that the importance of territorial control has somewhat declined and is no longer the primary factor used to determine power and influence. Some boundaries have even been surrendered, leading to unification. The law and policy of co-operation and integration has shifted interests to other forms of securing access and political and economic influence. An open trading system under the auspices of the World Trade Organization (WTO), supported by other organizations and programmes, and by high levels of economic interdependence, has gradually reduced the paramount importance of boundaries. The principle of non-aggression, limiting legitimate war to individual and collective self-defence and perhaps humanitarian intervention, has profoundly reduced the potential for territorial expansion. Governments have found other methods of securing their interests abroad. Yet wars have persisted, not only at a local level, and minorities continue to struggle in pain for self-determination. Land boundary disputes will continue to persist in the struggle by minorities for self-determination, yet overall, the map of nations has largely stabilized and attempts to further change it risk forceful intervention by the international community. In many instances, land boundary disputes will be a matter of completing existing boundary regimes.[5] Despite the obvious deficiencies of many frontiers inherited from colonization, the ICJ held that their modification can hardly be justified, for reasons of stability, on the ground of considerations of equity.[6] Compared to other periods of history, it is safe to say that the nuclear age and the system of multilateral security following World War II has, by and large, stabilized territorial allocations, at least for the time being.

The situation is completely different in the field of marine expanses. Whilst the appropriation of land has stalled, the large-scale taking of marine spaces has emerged instead. Boundary making in the twentieth and twenty-first centuries mainly relates to the seas, an area covering more than 70 per cent of the globe's surface. Once again, appropriation is a matter of securing national sovereignty over resources, and securing power.[7] In fact, as Bernhard Oxman puts it '[t]he territorial temptation thrust seaward with a speed and geographic scope that would be the envy of the most ambitious conquerors in human history'.[8] Again, we are dealing with the core of the classical law of co-existence. Yet, humankind was faced with an entirely new problem, which – fortunately – could not and cannot lawfully be approached using traditional methods of securing sovereignty. The principles of non-aggression and non-intervention preclude the lawful use of occupation by military means or other forms

---

[5] See e.g. *Land and Maritime Boundary between Cameroon and Nigeria (Cameroon v. Nigeria) (Equatorial Guinea Intervening)*, ICJ Reports 2002, p. 303.
[6] *Frontier Dispute (Burkina Faso v. Republic of Mali)*, Judgment, ICJ Reports 1986, p. 554, para. 149.
[7] See generally John R. V. Prescott, *The Maritime Political Boundaries of the World* (London, New York: Methuen, 1985).
[8] Oxman, n. 1, 832.

of coercion. For the first time in modern human history, allocation of resources was bound to take place within and on the basis of law. It is no coincidence that peaceful negotiations and courts of law have played a much more prominent role in shaping the law of marine boundaries than was the case in the field of land boundaries.[9] Successful delimitation reinforces the role of boundaries. Failure to settle them and to find appropriate models of resource management are indications that new approaches will be required, either based upon co-operation and joint exploitation of marine resources or full integration which entirely removes old needs for boundaries and thus the paradigm of mere co-existence. The same may be true for other jurisdictional aspects such as the regulation of navigation, where unilateralism leads to particularly protracted situations

Thirdly, and of main importance in the context of this study, the operation of maritime boundary delimitation in international law emerged on the basis of equity and equitable principles. It gave rise to a renaissance of equity. Initially, no general rules existed on how maritime boundaries should be drawn in disputed cases, and the issues were complicated, given a background of maritime zones which themselves do not respond to ideals of distributive justice. It is here that equity entered the stage and started to work. The quest for distributive justice within a given conceptual framework of the continental shelf doctrine and the EEZ and of the co-existence of coastal states has been answered by the ICJ, courts of arbitration and treaty making by recourse to equity, equitable principles and equitable solutions. The process, in other words, took recourse to the fundamental principles of justice in the life of the law. This has significance far beyond the technical subject of maritime boundary delimitation.

In an inductive process of trial and error, a doctrine and methodology of delimitation emerged, partly in competition with efforts at law-making, and by way of recourse to geographical and predictable principles of delimitation, in particular the principle of equidistance. Different and competing methodologies were developed. Extensive case law and scholarly work offers a fascinating and complex account of trial and error in finding and shaping the rules, factors and methodology of maritime boundary delimitation over the last fifty years. It is

[9] See e.g. the Arbitration for the Brcko Area which took recourse to equitable principles with reference to the case law on maritime boundary delimitation (Arbitral Tribunal for Dispute over Inter-Entity Boundary in Brcko Area ('), para. 88, reprinted in 36 ILM 369 (1997), pp. 427–8.

the most prominent, if not exclusive, field where equity and equitable principles have been developed and applied in a unique series of case law in recent public international law. It will be seen and argued, throughout this book, that its principles and rules essentially rely, in a unique manner, on judge-made law based upon the broad precept of equity. Different schools of thought and jurisprudence are involved. They offer valuable insights into the relationship of equity and the application of strict rules subject to exceptions, and its relationship to decision-making *ex aequo et bono* in accordance with Article 38 of the Statute of the ICJ. Equity developed novel features in terms of legal methodology with a view to combining legal objectivity, fairness and the avoidance of unfettered subjectivity of decisions taken. It profoundly reshapes traditional perceptions of the role of judges and the persistently alleged absence of judge-made law in international relations. In addition, a wide body of international agreements allows the comparison of these judge-made principles with agreed diplomatic solutions and the establishment of a common ground in international law. Finally, it raises the issue of extent to which the international law of the Society of States of the Westphalian system reaches beyond co-existence and is able to venture into domains of distributive justice among nations.

In order to prepare for this, we turn to a brief history of the different functions of equity in legal systems and in international law and introduce a number of theoretical problems at the end of this introduction.

B. *Traditional functions and the decline of equity*

Equity (*équité, Billigkeit*) has been a companion of the law ever since rule-based legal systems emerged. It offers a bridge to justice where the law itself is not able to adequately respond. Equity essentially remedies legal failings and shortcomings. Rules and principles of law are essentially and structurally of a general nature. Their prescriptions predictably apply to future circumstances. They seek to steer and influence future conduct of humans. They create expectations as to lawful conduct and stabilize human relations. Yet, the law is not complete. Sometimes answers are lacking, or the application of the law fails to bring about satisfactory results in line with the moral or ethical values underlying contemporary society. It is here that the companion of the law enters the stage. Aristotle authoritatively described completing and rectifying functions of equity within the law in the *Nicomachean Ethics*:

[A]ll law is universal, but there are some things about which it is not possible to speak correctly in universal terms... So in a situation in which the law speaks universally, but the issue happens to fall outside the universal formula, it is correct to rectify the shortcomings, in other words, the omission and mistake of the lawgiver due to the generality of his statement. Such a rectification corresponds to what the lawgiver himself would have acted if he had known. That is why the equitable is both just and also better than the just in one sense. It is not better than the just in general, but better than the mistake due to the generality. And this is the very nature of the equitable, a rectification of its universality.[10]

The functions of equity, however, are not limited to a static concept of law reflected in Aristotle's conception. It goes beyond completing and corrective functions. All legal systems face the problem that rules and principles that were shaped and developed in the past may no longer be suitable for achieving justice under changing conditions. Moral and ethical attitudes and perceptions change as society changes. Society changes as factual conditions change due to economic or technological developments, which create new regulatory needs. For centuries, equity has served the purpose of facilitating legal adjustment and bringing laws in line with contemporary perceptions of justice and regulatory needs. The function of equity therefore equally entails the advancement of the law in the light of new regulatory needs. It offers a prime response, laying foundations for new developments which eventually find their way into the body of legal institutions.

Historical and comparative studies demonstrate the point. A study published in 1972 and edited by Ralph A. Newman recalls that the functions of equity are inherent to all the world's legal systems.[11] They can be found in Greek law (*Epieidia*), in Roman law (*Aequitas*), but also in the Judaic tradition referred to as justice (*Elohim*) or mercy (*Jhyh*). They can be found in Hindu philosophy in the doctrine of rightousness (*Dharma*), and also in Islamic law (*Istihsan*). The companion is universal, and an inherent ingredient of all law based upon justice and its inherent shortcomings and deficiencies, with a view to responding to new challenges, bringing about change and adjusting to altered circumstances in society to which the law and justice properly have to respond. Albeit the functions exist in different forms, they share a common relationship

---

[10] Aristotle, *Nicomachean Ethics*, trans. Martin Oswald, Book 5 Chapter 10 (New York: Bobbs-Merrill, 1962), pp. 141–2.
[11] Ralph A. Newman (ed.), *Equity in the World's Legal Systems: A Comparative Study* (Brussels: Bruylant, 1972).

to rules and principles, as equity acts and enters the stage under the facts of a particular case, seeking to do justice. Ever since, equity has therefore been an instrument of the judiciary, dealing with human conduct and the specific facts of a particular situation. It inherently entails an active judicial role, either completing or even altering law in the pursuit of ideals of justice and fairness. Equity, in other words, amounts to an important ingredient of the legitimacy of the overall legal system. Without the ability to have recourse to equity, justice may miscarry and the authority of law as the prime organizer of human co-existence and co-operation may be undermined.

From these traditions which reflect the shared and common needs of all legal systems, the Roman law concept of *Aequitas* was most influential as a foundation for equity in Western European law, which, in turn, provided the basis for the development of equity in international law under the Westphalian state system. In 1861, Sir Henry Maine identified legal fiction, equity and legislation to be, in this order, the main drivers of legal change and adaptation to societal developments and need.[12] Legal fiction in a broad sense entails the assumption that law remains unchanged, while in fact it evolves through case law and judicial law-making, the existence of which is carefully denied. Allegedly, judges merely find the law. They do not make the law: 'We do not admit that our tribunals legislate; we imply that they have never legislated, and we maintain that the rules of English common law, with some assistance from the Court of Chancery or from Parliament, are coextensive with the complicated interests of modern society.'[13] The second engine of change, according to Maine, is equity which brought together *jus gentium* and the law of nature. 'I think that they touch and blend through Aequitas, or Equity in its original sense; and here we seem to come to the first appearance in jurisprudence of this famous term, Equity',[14] the essence of which has been proportionate distribution and, based upon that, a sense of levelling: 'I imagine that the word was at first a mere description of that constant *levelling* or removal of irregularities which went on wherever the praetorian system was applied to the cases of foreign litigants.'[15] And it is from here that it developed its ethical content based upon natural law in Roman times and assisted in adapting law in praetorian law, and finally crystallized into rigidity, a process which could

---

[12] Sir Henry Maine, 'Ancient Law' in Ernest Rhys (ed.), *Everyman's Library: History: [no. 734]* (London et al.: Dent, 1917 (reprinted 1977)), p. 15.
[13] Ibid. p. 20.   [14] Ibid. p. 34.   [15] Ibid. p. 34.

equally be observed in English equity centuries later. 'A time always comes at which the moral principles originally adopted have been carried out to all their legitimate consequences, and then the system founded on them becomes as rigid, as unexpansive, and as liable to fall behind moral progress as the sternest code of rules avowedly legal.'[16] Legislation, finally, amounts to the third form of law-making, stemming from an autocratic prince or a parliamentary assembly, owing their force to the binding authority of the legislator which allows adjustment to new realities independent of its principles. 'The legislator, whatever be the actual restraints imposed on it by public opinion, is in theory empowered to impose what obligations it pleases on the members of a community.'[17]

It would seem that this triad of fiction, equity and legislation is inherent to all legal cultures, albeit, of course, in varying combinations. The role of equity was dependent upon, and complementary to, these other law-making functions and instruments of legal progress and adaptation. It therefore did not evolve in a uniform and static manner in different legal constituencies. The functions of equity varied as the underlying legal concept and traditions of fiction and legislation varied. Yet, they shared a common trait of being closely wedded to individual cases and circumstances.[18]

The more rigid the underlying law, the more active the role of equity became. Different concepts emerged. English equity emerged under the rigidity of the common law and constellations of power, leading to the independent and centralized judiciary of the Lord Chancellor. English law witnessed the emergence of an entirely separate legal system under equity, applied in parallel and by different judicial authorities, the task of which also was to secure legal uniformity and centralization (equity courts).[19] Based on a case-by-case approach, new legal institutions such as the trust emerged under this title, responding to new economic and societal needs. In addition, a set of principles, maxims of equity, emerged, constituting essential due process requirements and standards of justice.[20] The two traditions were merged only in the

[16] Ibid. p. 40. [17] Ibid. p. 17. [18] See ibid. p. 11.
[19] Harold G. Hanbury in Jill E. Martin (ed.), *Hanbury & Martin: Modern Equity* (London: Thomson, Sweet and Maxwell, 15th edn., 1997).
[20] These maxims comprise: (i) equity will not suffer a wrong to be without a remedy; (ii) equity follows the law; (iii) he who seeks equity must do equity; (iv) he who comes to equity must come with clean hands; (v) where the equities are equal, the law prevails; (vi) where the equities are equal, the first in time prevails; (vii) equity imputes an intention to fulfil an obligation; (viii) equity regards as done that which ought to be done; (ix) equity is equality; (x) equity looks to the intent rather than the

nineteenth century and became part of one and the same Anglo-Saxon and Anglo-American common law. In other systems, the law was able to absorb most of the change itself. The codification of civil law on the European continent was a response to excessive recourse to equity, which had often been perceived as arbitrary by pre-revolutionary continental European aristocracy.[21] The very idea of codification and democratic legislation emerged as a prime tool of adaptation of positive law and apparently left much less room for broadly defined equitable doctrines. It was generally agreed that equity henceforth be confined to equity *infra legem, praeter legem* and, exceptionally *contra legem*. Civil law was seen to develop in a way that was much less in need of recourse to equity outside the law, due to codification and, subsequently, to the evolution of constitutional law and the process of judicial review of legislation. While English equity thus produced a host of principles and maxims, its counterparts emerged under different titles elsewhere within the law. The role of equity is much more limited in civil law. The classical description of equity *infra, praeter and contra legem* reflects the idea of a complete and codified system, and found its way into international law on the basis of the continental law tradition. Similar conclusions may be drawn from the analysis of other systems of law, albeit that they have been less influential in international law. Under most codes, equity's function remains vague and largely unexplored. Equity, in continental law, was marginalized.

An exception to this is the Swiss Civil Code of 1907. This entails explicit powers to discharge cases by recourse to equity in the absence of existing rules on the subject matter. It laid the foundations for an objective recourse to equity within the law and recognized the powers of courts to legislate in the absence of positive rules. The Swiss Civil Code avoids the fiction of the completeness of codification, often found abroad at the time. In Article 1 para. 2, the judge is called upon to legislate in the absence of existing rules. In a remarkable manner, the legislative function of courts is recognized. The Swiss Civil Code would thus please modern realist schools, emphasizing the law-making functions of the judicial branch in the legal process. While this related to functions *praeter legem*, Article 4 calls upon the judge's exercise of his

---

form; (xi) delay defeats equities; (xii) equity acts in personam, see *Hanbury and Martin*, n. 19, pp. 25–32.

[21] See Georges Boyer, 'La Notion d'équité et son rôle dans la jurisprudence des Parlements' in *Mélanges offerts à Jacques Maury, tome II droit comparé, théorie générale du droit et droit privé* (Paris: Librairie Dalloz et Sirey, 1960), pp. 257–82.

or her discretion in accordance with law and equity (*règles du droit et de l'equité*). Swiss doctrine and the Swiss Supreme Court consider rules and equity to be fully part of the law. It is a matter of rendering an objective, and not a subjective decision. The perception is one of equitable law (*billiges Recht*) which incorporated the concern for individualized justice into rulings based upon the law. Law and equity are perceived as inseparable and not as different spheres of justice. Even in individualized circumstances, the Swiss Civil Code calls upon courts to apply and design criteria which are suitable for generalization and wider application.[22] '*Billigkeit muss das Recht meistern*' (equity masters the law) is an adage to be found on a painted window frame at my Alma Mater in Bern; allegorical figures call upon a non-pendantic, merciful interpretation of the law, taking into account, and in line with, reasonable and widely shared perceptions. In the 1920s Max Rümelin took this allegory as a starting point for his seminal work on equity in Swiss and continental law.[23] Equity, in other words, is part of the legal process, informing the law's interpretation by taking recourse to objective factors and criteria, yet short of formalism and dogmatism, in deciding individual cases. While strict rule-making is alien to equity, it does not exclude the formation of principles comparable to the maxims of equity in English law.[24] Much of what we shall find in the international adjudication of the twentieth century on equity can find a conceptual parallel in the philosophy of equity enshrined in Swiss law. The classical functions of equity, therefore, are essentially defined in relationship to the adaptation and adjustment of the law itself: they change over time and place. Equity has been part of the legal process and needs to be

---

[22] See Arthur Meier-Hayoz (ed.), *Berner Kommentar zum schweizerischen Privatrecht* (Bern: Stämpfli, 1966), Art. 4, pp. 421–42; Henri Deschenaux, 'Richterliches Ermessen' in Max Gutzwiller (ed.), *Einleitung und Personenrecht* (Basel: Helbling Lichtenhahn, 1967), pp. 130–42; Henri Deschenaux, 'Le Traitement de l'équité en droit Suisse' in M. Bridel (ed.), *Recueil des travaux suisses présentés au VIIIe Congrès international de droit comparé* (Basel: Verlag Helbing & Lichtenhahn, 1970), pp. 27–39.

[23] Max Rümelin, *Die Billigkeit im Recht* (Tübingen: Mohr Paul Siebeck, 1921).

[24] 'Jede Art von Regelbildung ist ausgeschlossen. Es lassen sich nur die Umstände anführen, die nach der einen oder andern Seite ins Gewicht fallen ... Soweit die Aufstellung bestimmter Grundsätze und fester Regeln möglich ist, wird man sich immer bemühen, zu solchen zu gelangen. Dahin drängt sowohl das Bedürfnis nach Rechtssicherheit als der Ordnungstrieb des Menschen, sein Streben nach Vernunft-, d.h. planmässigem Handeln. So lehrt uns denn auch die Geschichte, dass innerhalb der Billigkeitsrechtssprechung stets wieder feste Rechtssätze sich gebildet haben. Am deutlichsten zeigt sich dies Bild im englischen Equity-Recht, im Lauf der Zeit ein vollständiges System von *Equity* Sätzen entstanden ist.' Rümelin, n. 23, pp. 60–1.

distinguished from decision-making outside the law, on the basis of powers exceptionally granted to dispose *ex aequo et bono*. It plays a particularly important role in static and rigid concepts of law, particularly in legal systems defined by custom and religion. Equity's effect is different in systems dominated by legislation which are more amendable to reflect social change and needs. As legislation emerged as the prime and frequent response to changing and novel needs, recourse to equity became less pressing. Moreover, principles of law emanating from equity became of an independent and self-standing nature. Constitutional and international law, moreover, assumed corrective functions, mainly by recourse to fundamental rights and human rights.

As legal development progresses, concerns originally voiced under equity are being absorbed and integrated into the law. They no longer belong, strictly speaking, to the realm of equity *infra, praeter* or *contra legem*. They develop into principles and institutions of their own, much as English equity formalized over time and developed into a parallel body of law, complementing common law.[25] The principle of proportionality, of good faith and the protection of legitimate expectations and more particularly of estoppel and acquiescence, the doctrine of abuse of rights, are prime examples of equitable doctrines turned into legal concepts and principles of their own. Once established, there is no longer a need to resort to equity, and, indeed, principles are no longer directly based upon, or related to, equity in terms of legal foundations.

Thus, the process of the constitutionalization of law and states during the eighteenth and nineteenth centuries and the establishment of democratic representation and ongoing legislation was bound to reduce the role and functions of equity. Constitutionalism and the advent of fundamental rights fundamentally altered the equation. During the twentieth century, standards of justice in equity were increasingly replaced by recourse to human rights. Particularly after World War II, human rights emerged as the primary sources and standards of justice. They not only reduced the role of natural justice, but also of equity. In essence, constitutional judicial review under the Bill of Rights no longer made recourse to equity a necessary tool for remedying injustice and to assume the role of distributive justice and levelling in the way perceived by Maine. Law and legislation became subject to specific standards of justice and fairness embodied in the Constitution. The relationship between

---

[25] Hanbury, see n. 19.

constitutional law and equity is hardly discussed in the literature.[26] Yet, it is evident that the former has increasingly absorbed what in previous periods of pre-constitutional times equity was expected and assigned to bring about. Today, the adage of *summum ius summa iniuria* is no longer able to play to its full effect as it is tempered and controlled by human rights and constitutional law. Equity is no longer required to dampen the rigour of the law.

International law increasingly exerts corrective functions in adapting domestic law to international commitments. Human rights provide important yardsticks, albeit they still largely lack effective judicial protection at the international level, except for regional law, such as the European Convention on Human Rights. Principles of non-discrimination can be enforced by the WTO and help to remedy inequitable domestic legislation. In Europe, European Community law emerged as a new and additional corrective layer based upon a new legal system *sui generis*. Checks and balances increasingly extend to multilevels of governance, assuming traditional functions of equity.

It is therefore unsurprising that the incorporation of equitable doctrines into the law, either in legislation or in case law, made the requirement of equity as such almost redundant in recent decades in Western legal systems, as the desired aim could be achieved by other means. There are only a few cases where courts took explicit recourse to equity in domestic jurisdictions, and it is no longer a main concern of legal doctrine. This is true in civil law countries.[27] In a sense it is equally

---

[26] Rare and passing references to the relationship between constitutional law and equity can be found in Mario Rotoni, 'Considerations sur la fonction de l'équité dans un système de droit positif écrit' in *Aspects Nouveaux de la Pensée Juridique : Recueil d'études en hommage à Marc Ancel, vol. I, Etudes de droit privé, de droit public et de droit comparé* (Paris: Editions A. Pedone, 1975), pp. 43, 46; Paul Kirchhof, 'Gesetz und Billigkeit im Abgaberecht' in Norbert Achterberg et al. (eds.), *Recht und Staat im sozialen Wandel, Festschrift für Hans Ulrich Scupin zum 80. Geburtstag* (Berlin: Dunker & Humblot, 1983), pp. 775, 784; Rümelin, n. 23, p. 69 (calling upon the prohibition of arbitrary decisions in the French declaration on human rights as a more suitable foundation than equity in addressing certain problems in administrative law); Oscar Schachter discusses the relationship in the context of natural justice: 'The fact that equity and human rights have come to the forefront in contemporary international law has tended to minimize reference to "natural justice" as an operative concept, but much of its substantive content continues to influence international decisions under those other headings', *International Law in Theory and Practice* (Dordrecht, Boston MA, London: Martinus Nijhoff, 1991), p. 55.

[27] See Joseph Esser, 'Wandlungen von Billigkeit und Billigkeitsrechtssprechung im modernen Privatrecht' and Joachim Gernhuber, 'Die Billigkeit und ihr Preis' in University of Tübingen, Law Faculty, *Summum Ius Summa Iniuria: Individualgerechtigkeit und der Schutz allgemeiner Werte im Rechtsleben* (Tübingen: Mohr, 1963), pp. 22, 224;

true in common law jurisdictions to the extent that we consider the established institutions of English equity as part of modern common law.[28] The area no longer attracts much attention. History has moved on.

C. *The rebirth of equity in the law of natural resources*

Whilst the trend in domestic legal systems has been a decline in the use of equity, for it is no longer used to its fullest extent, it is interesting to observe that the situation is entirely opposite in public international law. International arbitration was frequently asked to decide on the basis of law and equity, and the nineteenth and early twentieth centuries saw a stream of decisions referring to equity which often formed a basis of law in treaties, ever since the 1794 Jay Treaty referred to justice, equity and international law.[29] Perhaps the most important precedent was the *Cayuga Indians* arbitration, granting legal status in equity to a tribe who otherwise would have remained without rights and entitlement.

> When a situation legally so anomalous is presented, recourse must be had to generally recognized principles of justice and fair dealing in order to determine the rights of the individuals involved. The same considerations of equity that have repeatedly been invoked by the courts where strict regard to the legal personality of a corporation would lead to inequitable results or to results contrary to legal policy, may be invoked here. In such cases courts have not hesitated to look behind the legal person and consider the human individuals who were the real beneficiaries.[30]

The arbitrator was Professor Roscoe Pound, who observed a decline in equity as it was increasingly consumed in law, and called for a fight for equity as an ever new port of entry to justice in a positivist legal order: 'Ihering has told us that we must fight for our law. No less must we fight

---

Joachim Gernhuber, 'Die Integrierte Billigkeit' in Joachim Gernhuber (ed.), *Tradition und Fortschritt im Recht, Festschrift zum 500-jährigen Bestehen der Tübinger Juristenfakultät* (Tübingen: J. C. B. Mohr (Paul Siebeck), 1977), p. 193.

[28] See Roscoe Pound, 'The Decadence of Equity' (1905) 5 *Columbia Law Review*, 20–35.

[29] See Karl Strupp, 'Das Recht des internationalen Richters, nach Billigkeit zu entscheiden' in F. Giese and K. Strupp (eds.) *Frankfurter Abhandlungen zum Völkerrecht* (1930), vol. 20, at p. 17; ibid. 'Le Droit du juge international de statuer selon l'équité' (1930) 33 *Recueil des cours de l'Académie de Droit International*. Vladimir-Duro Degan, *L'Equité et le Droit International* (The Hague: Martinus Nijhoff, 1970).

[30] *Cayuga Indians (Great Britain) v. United States*, reprinted in Reports of International Arbitral Awards, Vol. VI, pp. 173–90, 179.

for equity.'[31] The 1909 *Grisbadarna* case,[32] a maritime boundary delimitation case between Norway and Sweden, was decided upon historical patterns of conduct and *uti possidetis*, but was, according to Friedmann, in reality based on balancing the equities of that particular case.[33]

Recourse to equity also was implicit, rather than explicit, in the judgments of the ICJ, perhaps owing to the newly introduced clause of decision-making *ex aequo et bono* which separated law and equity, but was never formally invoked under Article 38 of the Statute of the ICJ. Traces of equity and equitable doctrines can be found in different cases. It was implicit in particular in the reasoning of the 1937 *Water from the Meuse* case.[34] Judge Manley Hudson in his concurring opinion, expounding the doctrine of equity, described the ruling as an application of maxims of equity in international law.[35] It is submitted that the founding precedent of international environmental law, the *Trail Smelter* arbitration,[36] was strongly influenced by considerations of equity.

The interwar period witnesses an increased and explicit interest in equity in legal writings. In the United States, L. B. Orfield published a seminal article on equity in international law in 1930.[37] In Europe, Karl Strupp published his work on equity in international arbitration in 1930,[38] reflecting the weaknesses of the positivist tradition.[39] In 1935,

---

[31] Pound, n. 28, 35.

[32] Arbitral award rendered on 23 October 1909 in the matter of the delimitation of a certain part of the maritime boundary between Norway and Sweden, decided 23 October 1909, reprinted in Hague Court Reports (Scott) 487 (Permanent Court of Arbitration, 1909), for English translations, see ibid, p. 121.

[33] Wolfgang Friedmann, 'The Contribution of English Equity to the Idea of an International Equity Tribunal' in *The New Commonwealth Institute Monographs*, Series B, No. 5 (London: Constable, 1935) at 35; the case is discussed below in Chapter 8(II)(A)(1).

[34] *The Diversion of Water from the Meuse (Netherlands v. Belgium)*, Judgment from 28 June 1937, PCIJ, Series A/B, No. 70, 1925, 4–89.

[35] Ibid., pp. 76–9. Wilfred Jenks considers the case the *locus classicus* of equity of that period, *The Prospects of International Adjudication* (London: Stevens, 1964), pp. 316–427, at p. 322.

[36] *Trail Smelter Case (United States, Canada)*, 16 April 1938 and 11 March 1941, UNIRIAA Vol. 3, pp. 1905–82.

[37] Lester B. Orfield, 'Equity as a Concept of International Law' (1930) 18 *Kentucky Law Journal*, 31.

[38] Karl Strupp, 'Das Recht des internationalen Richters, nach Billigkeit zu entscheiden' in F. Giese and K. Strupp, n. 29; Karl Strupp, 'Le Droit du juge international de statuer selon l'équité' (1930) 33 *Recueil des cours de l'Académie de Droit International*. For a discussion see Christopher R. Rossi, *Equity and International Law: A Legal Realist Approach to International Decisionmaking* (Irvington NY: Transnational Publishers, 1993) pp. 145–8. For further references to authors of this period see also Degan, n. 29, pp. 15–40.

[39] The intellectual effort criticizing positivism in international law was led, at the time, by the Commonwealth Institute; see Norman Bentwisch et al., 'Justice and Equity in the

18   EQUITY REVISITED: AN INTRODUCTION

Max Habicht drew renewed attention to the power to adjudicate *ex aequo et bono*.[40] These efforts culminated in the joint proposal to establish an International Equity Tribunal, based upon principles of co-operation by which decisions reached under distinct and separate positive public international law could be reviewed.[41] The idea was supported at the time by eminent international lawyers within the Commonwealth Institute, A. S. de Bustamante, Karl Strupp, Wolfgang Friedmann and Georg Schwarzenberger. The proposal never saw the light of the day, but equity was able to make a comeback after World War II in legal doctrine.

After the war, Wilfried Jenks offered an extensive review of the case law relating to equity in 1964.[42] Vladimir Degan submitted his analysis of arbitration in 1970,[43] and Charles de Visscher published a book on the subject in 1972.[44] The review of these works shows a wide and diverging view on the topic and the relationship of law and equity in a wide array of topics of international law, ranging from treaty interpretation, unilateral acts, state responsibility, diplomatic protection, procedural law, territorial disputes and natural resources – in particular access to water. While at this point in time – prior to the 1969 *North Sea Continental Shelf* cases – it is fair to say that no consolidated doctrine and approach existed; authors and cases show a clear interest in equity and a common concern for individualized justice (*Einzelfallgerechtigkeit*) being the main feature and function of equity within the body of public international law.

Given the developments in constitutional law, human rights protection and the emergence of general principles of law essentially detached from

---

International Sphere' in *The New Commonwealth Institute Monographs*, Series B, No. 1 (London: Constable, 1936); for a discussion see Rossi n. 38, p. 145.

[40] Max Habicht, 'The Power of the Judge to Give A Decision *Ex Aequo et Bono*' in *The New Commonwealth Institute Monographs*, Series B, No. 2 (London: Constable, 1935).

[41] A. S. de Bustamante and Karl Strupp, 'Proposals for an International Equity Tribunal' in *The New Commonwealth Institute Monographs*, Series B, No. 4 (London: Constable, 1935); Wolfgang Friedmann, 'The Contribution of English Equity to the Idea of an International Equity Tribunal' in *The New Commonwealth Institute Monographs*, Series B, No. 5 (London: Constable, 1935); Georg Schwarzenberger and William Ladd, 'An Examination of an American Proposal for an International Equity Tribunal' in *The New Commonwealth Institute Monographs*, Series B, No. 3 (London: Constable, 1936); see also Rossi, n. 38, p. 146.

[42] Wilfred Jenks, *The Prospects of International Adjudication* (London: Stevens, 1964), pp. 316–427; see also Wilfred Jenks, 'Equity as a Part of the Law Applied by the Permanent Court of International Justice' (1937) 53 *Law Quarterly Review*, 519.

[43] Vladimir-Duro Degan, *L'Equité et le Droit International* (The Hague: Martinus Nijhoff, 1970).

[44] Charles de Visscher, *De L'Equité dans le règlement arbitral ou judiciaire des litiges de droit international public* (Paris: Editions A. Pedone, 1972).

equity, we can understand that the main role of equity in twentieth- and twenty-first-century international law relates to issues such as the allocation of natural resources – a field neither governed by established legal institutions nor human rights. Indeed, it is striking to observe that recourse to equity implicitly or explicitly emerged in the context of allocation of natural resources among nations. It became its prime field of application while most other areas remained untouched by it. The 1951 *Fisheries Jurisdiction* case took into account a number of factors in deciding the case and in many ways anticipated methodologies subsequently developed under the doctrine of equitable principles in the 1969 *North Sea Continental Shelf* cases and subsequent case law by the court and in international arbitration discussed throughout this book.[45] The Helsinki Rules on equitable principles relating to the allocation of non-navigable waters, adopted in 1966 by the International Law Association,[46] introduced the concept of equitable principles relating to resource allocation in Articles IV and V of the instrument. It was subsequently taken up in treaty making by the International Law Commission of the United Nations.[47]

The renaissance of equity in the law of natural resources in the second part of the twentieth century can be partly explained by the fact that the international law of co-existence has remained a primitive system of law, devoid of effective legislative means capable of adjusting to new requirements, values and economic or scientific developments. The lack of a swift and timely legislative response remains one of the main traits of international law. The principles of international law established in the post World War II order, such as the prohibition of the use of force, the principle of non-intervention, the obligations to peaceful settlement of disputes and permanent sovereignty over natural resources, provide the constitutional pillars of world order and contemporary justice, but are often not in a position to settle complex issues on a case-by-case basis. Human rights only emerged in international law after World War II. Even today, they are still far from providing constitutional functions, in the sense that they may alter international and domestic law, assuming the role of equity. The general principles, stemming from equity and maxims of equity, which have found their way into international law and

---

[45] See below, Chapters 4, 6, 8, 11.
[46] See International Law Association (ed.), *Report of the Fifty-second Conference, held at Helsinki, 1966* (London: 1967), pp. 484–532.
[47] The effort resulted in the United Nations Convention on the Law of the Non-Navigational Uses of International Watercourses, adopted by the United Nations General Assembly Resolution 51/229 of 21 May 1997.

practice (good faith, *pacta sunt servanda*, estoppel, acquiescence and others), are not able to address all of the contentious issues that have not been adequately dealt with through customary law or treaty law. Again, as occurred in domestic law centuries before, recourse to equity was needed in order to address new and pressing issues that arose in response to changes in the international community. An answer was found in turning to what will amount to equitable principles as key tools addressing pressing issues of distributive justice.

Recourse to equity in jurisprudence and resource allocation in return triggered renewed interest in the functions of equity in contemporary international law. The reception of civil law concepts of equity *infra*, *praeter* and *contra legem* was basically recognized in international law, as well as by lawyers rooted in the common law tradition, albeit reluctantly.[48] Equity was increasingly applied to the allocation of natural resources. While many scholars deal with equity in the context of maritime boundary delimitation, which will be discussed subsequently, general works on equity comprise the book by Christopher Rossi, stressing the law-making role of courts and tribunals applying equity – very much reminiscent of the fictions of the judicial role expounded by Sir Henry Maine more than a hundred years earlier.[49] Critical legal studies turned to equity in order to demonstrate the generic lack of objectivity of international law and the problem of subjectivity. Koskenniemi's work, first published in 1989, was strongly inspired by the alleged imprecision and vagaries of equity and equitable principles in the jurisprudence of the world's courts.[50] The case law on maritime boundary delimitation – much the subject of this book – gave rise to comprehensive legal opinions on equity in modern international law. Judge Weeramantry developed an extensive treatise on equity in the context of his separate opinion in the 1993 *Jan Mayen* case, essentially expounding the classical functions of equity, *infra*, *praeter* and *contra legem* and its different functions and methodologies in the administration of international justice.[51]

---

[48] See Michael Akehurst, 'Equity and General Principles of Law' (1976) 25 *International and Comparative Law Quarterly*, 801.

[49] Christopher R. Rossi, *Equity and International Law: A Legal Realist Approach to International Decisionmaking* (Irvington, NY: Transnational Publishers, 1993).

[50] Martti Koskenniemi, *From Apology to Utopia: The Structure of International Legal Argument: Reissue with a New Epilogue* (Cambridge University Press, 2005) (originally published by the Finnish Lawyer's Association in 1989).

[51] *Case Concerning the Maritime Delimitation in the Area between Greenland and Jan Mayen (Denmark v. Norway)*, Judgment of 14 June 1993, Separate Opinion of Judge Weeramantry, ICJ Reports 1993, pp. 1, 177–245.

Equity as applied by courts and tribunals, in conclusion, has found its particular place in the context of the allocation of natural resources. It is here that the renaissance took place while other fields of traditional equity, in particular procedural equity, were absorbed into constitutional and international public law by the renaissance of human rights, or developed into self-standing legal principles in customary international law.

II. The quest for global equity

The renaissance of the use of equity in the international law of natural resources inspired a broader movement of taking recourse to equity in the process of decolonization throughout the period of the 1960s to the 1980s and the effort to reshape international law and remedy the flaws of the colonial period. The period and process of decolonization did not merely cause the number of actors and sovereign states on the stage of international law and relations to proliferate. What were formerly largely domestic matters under colonial rule became issues and problems of international law, particularly under the umbrella of the Charter of the United Nations. This created the North–South debate. Colonial experience caused authors from the newly independent states to call for a new international economic order and a new concept of international law built upon a law of co-operation, enshrined in the United Nations Charter, and on broad precepts of equity.[52] The international law of co-existence, largely structured on colonial lines, experienced considerable difficulties in adjusting to the new map and values, and a largely positivist application by and in the ICJ reinforced suspicions at the time.[53] The term and notion of equity, similarly used in economic theory as a counterpart to economic efficiency, became a symbol and code word for new aspirations of justice in international law in order to remedy

---

[52] Prakash Narain Agarwala, *The New International Economic Order: An Overview* (New York: Pergamon Press, 1983); Ram P. Anand, *New States and International Law* (Delhi: Vikas Publishing House, 1972); Mohammed Bedjaoui, *Towards a New International Economic Order* (New York: Holmes and Meier, 1979); Francisco V. Garcia-Amador, 'The Proposed New International Economic Order: An New Approach to the Law Governing Nationalizations and Compensations' (1980) 12 *Lawyer of the Americas*, 1; Kamal Hussein (ed.), *Legal Aspects of the New International Economic Order* (London: Frances Pinter, 1980); see generally Patricia Buirette-Maurau, *La Participation du tiers-monde à l'élaboration du droit international* (Paris: Pichond et Durand-Auzias, 1983).
[53] The controversial ruling of the ICJ in the *South West Africa* cases essentially triggered the debate, *South West Africa Cases (Ethiopia v. South Africa; Liberia v. South Africa)*, Second Phase, Judgment, ICJ Reports 1966, p. 6.

existing inequities in the allocation of wealth, income and opportunities between industrialized and developing countries. It became a basis for the quest of enhanced co-operation and development aid. It firmly established and depicted the issue of distributive justice. True, this age-old theme existed before in international law, as it exists in any legal order. It was, for example, already part of territorial boundary delimitation and the allocation of fishing rights or irrigable water or market shares. Yet, it only now emerged as a global theme considered as affecting the very basics of international law. The symbol of equity helped to establish what Stone called 'in terms at any rate of paper declarations and programs the establishment of standards of human welfare as an area of central guidance'.[54]

A. The programmatic function of equity

Equity assumed an important programmatic and symbolic role beyond and outside the province of law properly speaking. It became synonymous with justice at large. It essentially turned to diplomacy and the process of law-making, seeking to remedy the wrongs of the past. It sought, in other words, to enter the realm of international legislation, beyond its traditional province of the judiciary discussed above. Developing countries sought progress on the basis of national sovereignty and pursued the quest for resource allocation and market access on the basis of equity. Oscar Schachter observed that in 1974, 'the idea of equitable sharing of resources among nations had moved, almost suddenly, to the center of the world's stage'.[55] Important documents such as successive Development Decades, the 1974 Declaration on the Establishment of a New International Economic Order[56] and, in the same year, the Charter of Economic Rights and Duties of States[57] rely upon equity and sovereignty as their prime foundation and the justification for bringing about distributive justice and welfare

---

[54] Julius Stone, 'A Sociological Perspective on International Law' in Roland St. J. Macdonald and Douglas M. Johnston (eds.), *The Structure and Process of International Law* (The Hague et al.: Martinus Nijhoff, 1983), pp. 263, 301, note 66.
[55] Oscar Schachter, *Sharing the World's Resources* (New York: Columbia University Press, 1977), p. vii.
[56] UN General Assembly Resolution 3201 (S-VI) of 1 May 1974 (UN Document A/RES/S-6/3201).
[57] UN General Assembly Resolution 3281 (XXIX) of 12 December 1974 (UN Document A/RES/29/3281).

among nations.[58] The New International Economic Order, combining enhanced market access for developing countries and stronger interventionism at domestic and international levels, aspired to an order 'which shall correct inequalities and redress existing injustices, make it possible to eliminate the widening gap between the developed and the developing countries and ensure steadily accelerating economic and social development in peace and justice for present and future generations'.[59] A debate on a right to development was launched.[60]

Subsequently, the movement for sustainable development and ecology embraced equity. Edith Brown Weiss developed the concept of intergenerational equity.[61] She laid the doctrinal groundwork of what eventually emerged as sustainable development as a prime foundation of international environmental law. In 2002, the International Law Association adopted the ILA *New Delhi Declaration of Principles of International Law Relating to Sustainable Development*, placing the principle of equity at the heart of sustainable development. Principle 2.1 states:

> The principle of equity is central to the attainment of sustainable development. It refers to both *inter-generational equity* (the right of future generations to enjoy a fair level of the common patrimony) and *intra-generational equity* (the right of all peoples within the current generation of fair access to the current generation's entitlement to the Earth's natural resources).[62]

With intergenerational equity, a new and powerful symbol was created. However, equity's role was not confined to the allocation of resources among nations. Excessive and careless exploitation of resources due to technological advances increasingly threatens the balance of nature and has brought about the danger of both the exhaustion of resources and also of substantial damage to natural and human environments. Increasingly, equity has become a symbol, synonymous with sharing the world's resources, not merely amongst existing, but also amongst

---

[58] See P. van Dijk, 'Nature and Function of Equity in International Economic Law' (1986) 7 *Grotiana New Series*, 5.
[59] The Preamble of UNGA Res. 3201 (S-VI).
[60] See e.g. Paul de Vaart, Paul Peters and Erik Denters (eds.), *International Law and Development* (Dordrecht, Boston MA, London: Martinus Nijhoff, 1988).
[61] Edith Brown Weiss, *In Fairness to Future Generations: International Law, Common Patrimony, and Intergenerational Equity* (Tokyo: The United Nations University, 1989); Edith Brown Weiss, 'Our Rights and Obligations to Future Generations for the Environment' (1990) 84 *American Journal of International Law*, 198.
[62] Annex to Resolution 3/2002, Sustainable Development, ILA, *Report of the 70th Conference, New Delhi* (London: ILA, 2002) pp. 22, 26.

future generations within and outside national boundaries. The 1992 United Nations Agenda 21 refers to it as an agenda for change, both in the traditional sense of allocating resources between rich and poor, and also between present and future generations.[63] The term of intergenerational equity was firmly adopted. Similarly, the Convention on Biological Diversity[64] calls for an equitable sharing of genetic resources in this sense.[65] Scientific advances in genetic engineering create new issues of resource allocation between North and South, present and future. Issues of property and expropriation emerge in a new context. Again, equity finds itself at the centre of claims for a better world. There is little doubt that it will serve equally well as a challenger of law and relations in the light of future problems.

Scientific and technological advances since the end of World War II account for a greater importance for the role and function of equity in international law than decolonization. They raised new issues of resource allocation amongst all nations, including resource allocation amongst industrialized countries. Worldwide interaction, ranging from air travel to telecommunications, created the basis for increased globalization and enhanced interdependence of markets. Space travel, for example, required the creation of international space law. Technology allowed for resources to be exploited that previously could not have been. In 'the commons' (areas traditionally viewed as being of common ownership), technological progress resulted in offshore drilling, high seas industrial fishing activities and the potential for deep seabed mining. All of these activities triggered the silent revolution of the law of the sea and fundamentally changed the global map of sovereign rights exercised by nations over such resources. Once again, equity emerged as one of the foundations invoked to settle such allocations. The 1982 Convention on the Law of the Sea (LOS Convention), perhaps the single most important emanation of the aspirational 1974 New International Economic Order, contains no less than thrity-two references to equity, all seeking to provide guidance in resource allocation: twice in the preamble and in Articles 69, 70, 155 and 162; three times in Article 160; once in Articles 59, 74, 76, 82, 83, 140, 161, 163, 266, 269, 274; eight times in the Annexes.

---

[63] See *Report of the United Nations Conference on Environment and Development*, Rio de Janeiro, 3–14 June 1992 (UN Document A/CONF.151/26/Rev.l (Vol. I), Annex II).
[64] Convention on Biological Diversity opened for signature 5 June 1992, 1760 UNTS 79 (entered into force 29 December 1993).
[65] Ibid.Art. 1.

B. The impact of sovereignty and self-determination

At the same time, throughout these periods of development of international law, defence of the newly gained independence and self-determination perpetuated the very classical concept of national sovereignty. It was reinforced by the principle of self-determination and non-interference in domestic affairs. In fact, the quest for a new international law soon resulted in a defence of overwhelmingly traditional concepts, and therefore the core of international law has not fundamentally changed for this reason.[66] As stated at the outset, reliance upon the doctrine of the continental shelf and national sovereignty resulted in a highly uneven distribution of natural resources among coastal states, let alone land-locked countries.[67] The adoption of the principles of permanent sovereignty over natural resources in 1962, rejecting ideas of the common heritage of mankind, was a landmark to this effect.[68] Today, the proponents of new and relaxed approaches to sovereignty, the movement of constitutionalization of international law and the doctrine of multilevel governance, are mainly found among authors of industrialized nations, in order to cope with environmental challenges and the enhanced interdependence of financial systems and markets, in particular within Western Europe with the creation and evolution of the European Community and today the European Union.[69] The evolution of the European Union shaped new attitudes to international law in general in Europe, rethinking some of the classical precepts of international law which still are fiercely defended by countries in the process of

---

[66] See generally Patricia Buirette-Maurau, *La Participation du tiers-monde à l'élaboration du droit international* (Paris: Pichond et Durand-Auzias, 1983).

[67] See Stephen C. Vasciannie, *Land-locked and Geographically Disadvantaged States in the International Law of the Sea* (Oxford: Clarendon Press, 1990), pp. 105–38 (saying that '[t]he failure of the [land-locked and geographically disadvantaged states] to influence the final position on the outer limit of the continental shelf in the [LOS Convention] was almost complete', p. 118).

[68] UN General Assembly Resolution 1803 (XVII) of 14 December 1962 (UN Document A/5217 (1962)).

[69] See Ronald St. John Macdonald and Douglas M. Johnston (eds.), *Towards World Constitutionalism: Issues in the Legal Ordering of the World Community* (Leiden, Boston MA: Martinus Nijhoff Publishers, 2005); Anne Peters, *Elemente einer Theorie der Verfassung Europas* (Berlin: Duncker & Humblot, 2001); Jan Klabbers, Anne Peters and Geir Ulfstein (eds.), *The Constitutionalization of International Law* (Oxford University Press, 2009). John H. Jackson, *Sovereignty, WTO, and Changing Fundamentals of International Law* (Cambridge University Press, 2006); Thomas Cottier and Maya Hertig, 'The Prospects of 21st Century Constitutionalism' (2004) 7 *Max Planck Yearbook of United Nations Law*, 261.

nation-building and those defending their interests on their own and outside a larger and supranational union of states. The classical precepts of international law, based upon sovereignty, independence, non-intervention and international co-operation, are still predominant in shaping international relations at large. In this co-existence of programmatic claims to global equity and of classical precepts of international law based upon sovereignty and independence, the impact of equity, if any, remains indirect most of the time. The quest for global equity influenced the advent of reforms of the GATT[70] when Part IV was introduced in 1966. Special and differential treatment for developing countries emerged and may be considered an outflow of equity in terms of levelling uneven conditions of competition in terms of economic and social development. The General System of Preferences, allowing industrialized countries to unilaterally grant preferences to developing countries, amounts to the most important emanation of efforts purported by UNCTAD,[71] established in 1964. Efforts to co-ordinate official development assistance (ODA) was undertaken within the OECD[72] and led to increased efforts, jointly with the work of multilateral development institutions, in particular the World Bank and regional development banks.

But by and large, efforts at global equity failed to materialize. Efforts to stabilize commodity prizes failed to operate successfully. The set of equitable principles on restricted business practices remained a document of soft law and did not influence the anti-trust practices of industrialized countries. Even today, no ban on export cartels exists. Recourse to global equity resulted in substantial frustration, as expectations created did not materialize. The WTO, founded in 1995 on the basis of the GATT, was built upon the doctrine of progressive liberalization and on principles of non-discrimination and transparency. Differences in levels of development were taken into account in diverging levels of commitment and special and differential treatment. Yet overall, the WTO is built upon the philosophy of a single undertaking and the philosophy to fully integrate developing countries into the global trading system. Obligations, including those on protecting intellectual property rights, were essentially shaped in a uniform manner for all members alike, with some transitional arrangements for developing countries. Equity did not emerge as a leading idea. It indirectly produced distributional effects,

---

[70] General Agreement on Tariffs and Trade, opened for signature 30 October 1947, 55 UNTS 187 (entered into force 29 July 1948).
[71] United Nations Conference on Trade and Development, established in 1964.
[72] Convention on the Organisation for Economic Co-operation and Development, entered into force 30 September 1961.

without taking explicit recourse to equity. Trade liberalization and equal opportunities dismantled colonial structures, brought about growth in industrialized countries and developing countries alike, in particular in newly emerging economies, while it failed to serve least developed countries in significant terms. Their growth rates were left behind and fuelled the powerful quest for the right to development and affirmative action, such as special and differential treatment, preferential market access and aid for trade. Differential treatment with a view to bringing about distributive justice remains an unresolved challenge in trade regulation and calls for new avenues of graduation in law. Today, it may indirectly inform efforts to bring about graduation and a legal regime which is more likely to take into account unequal levels of competitivness and social and economic developments.[73]

Achieving broad goals of global welfare and equity is not a matter of international charity, but of common and shared interests in the light of the 'ticking time bombs' of excessive population, mass migration, poverty and destitution facing many parts of the globe. These goals are essential for stability and world peace. And yet, whilst the goal of sharing resources receives overwhelming support, the methods used to achieve the goal of global equity have been the subject of persistent fundamental controversy. They were somewhat reduced by the collapse of communism and the end of the Cold War in the 1990s, but, even with a move towards market-oriented policies in many countries, fundamental differences over resource allocation still remain. There is no end to history and the struggle for power will continue, significantly defined by power over human and natural resources.

In conclusion, the impact of programmatic equity has remained modest and mainly rhetorical, albeit it has had some indirect influence in shaping international law. To some extent, distributive justice has entered international agreements, yet without profoundly transforming the system as a whole. Equity, in other words, has not played a crucial role, albeit the spirit of it may have influenced and motivated actors. Yet, it has been far from bringing about new general principles and rules of customary international law. It has not brought about new methods of discharging distributive justice in broad terms in public international law. The classic body of public international law is still predominantly shaped by the law of

---

[73] See Thomas Cottier, 'The Legitimacy of WTO Law' in Linda Yueh (ed.), *The Law and Economics of Globalisation. New Challenges for a World in Flux* (Cheltenham: Edward Elgar Publishing, 2009), pp. 11–48; Thomas Cottier, 'From Progressive Liberalization to Progressive Regulation in WTO Law' (2006) 9 *Journal of International Economic Law*, 779.

co-existence. True, the law of the United Nations transformed international law to a law of co-operation in promoting these concerns. Regionalism, in particular the emergence of the European Union, laid the foundations for an international law of integration which, today, is beginning to develop, based upon cosmopolitan values and doctrines of global constitutionalism.[74] Distributive justice, in all this, amounts to an important programme besides the removal of barriers to international trade. Aid for development has become a standard feature in bilateral and multilateral relations. Yet, it has been mainly pursued by means of programmes and finance, rather than through the establishment of new legal principles based upon equity. Human rights, in particular the canon of social and economic rights of the 1948 Universal Declaration of Human Rights and the 1966 United Nations Covenant, replaced equity and underwrote the call for distributive justice. They have largely remained of a programmatic and gradual impact. Subsequently, environmental concerns brought about the doctrine of sustainable development, balancing economic, social and ecological concerns within a magic triangle beyond the idea of intergenerational equity.

III. The legal nature of equity

A. Different layers

A comparison between the global aspirations of equity in reshaping the world order and its functions in dispute settlement, both discussed above, readily reveals that equity operates on different normative levels. Equity as a norm of political and moral aspiration of justice, often powerfully influencing political agendas and perceptions, is beyond the realm of law and the legal sphere, properly speaking.[75] Global justice, in these terms, needs to be distinguished from operational equity, as it finds itself, as an ideal and programme, on a different normative layer which is not accessible in the operation of international law in negotiations and dispute settlement. It lacks the basic qualities of being wedded to a particular context. It influences the law as it influences perceptions of justice, which in return may eventually redefine rights and obligations. To the extent

---

[74] See Gillian Brock and Harry Brighouse (eds.), *The Political Philosophy of Cosmopolitanism* (Cambridge University Press, 2005); Simon Caney, *Justice Beyond Borders: A Global Political Theory* (Oxford University Press, 2005).
[75] The normative difference is clearly expressed in Robert Jennings and Arthur Watts (eds.), *Oppenheim's International Law*, vol. I (London, New York: Longman, 9th edn., 1996), pp. 43–4.

that aspirations of global equity are expressed in declarations and resolutions of international organizations, they form part of soft law. Non-binding in principle, they nevertheless create legitimate expectations as to promised conduct which may find legal protection under the principle of good faith. To the extent that aspirations of global equity enter treaty law, equity may form part of the preamble which should be taken into account in the process of interpreting operational provisions. To the extent that equity enters operational provisions, the legal nature changes. Equity becomes part of the law. It is here that the recourse to equity or to equitable principles or equitable solutions informs subsequent processes of negotiations or dispute settlement in the process of implementing such provisions. On this level, equity also may emerge in customary international law. It may, alternatively, find its way into the law as a general principle of law, forming the starting point, influencing and shaping the law. Yet, whatever the source, the legal operation of equity, it essentially remains wedded to individual circumstances, to negotiations and to judicial settlement and case law. Equity, on all accounts, is inherently wedded to the context and facts of a particular case. The Aristotelian doctrine has prevailed and proven appropriate. Equity cannot operate in a vacuum, but depends upon a particular problem which needs to be solved. Equity operating on high levels of abstraction is bound to remain without guidance and direct impact. The failure of global equity to influence international law profoundly contrasts with its paramount importance in the contained field of maritime boundary delimitation. In other words, while its programmatic functions remained limited, it developed prominently within a particular and precise context. The finding confirms that operational equity, as a legal principle, essentially requires an inductive approach. Ever since equity began to influence the course of law and international law by being applied and used in the context of specific issues within a particular framework, it has worked bottom-up, and thereby contributed to the evolution of individual fields of law.

B. *A source of new legal principles*

Over time, repeated recourse to equity in like or comparable circumstances led and will lead to new principles and rules; at some point, these rules and principles will become part of the law and so will leave the realm of equity properly speaking. As discussed, this holds true for principles of natural justice, specific maxims of equity, proportionality and of protecting good faith and legitimate expectations. Estoppel and acquiescence are examples in point. Whether these principles continue to be part of equity, or whether they have a life of their own, is assessed differently. Principles derived from equity partly continue to be part of equity, partly they are discussed independently henceforth. Oscar Schachter thus distinguishes different manifestations of equity:

(i) equity as a basis of individualized justice tempering the rigours of strict law;
(ii) equity as consideration of fairness, reasonableness and good faith;
(iii) equity as a basis for certain specific principles of legal reasoning, in particular estoppel, unjust enrichment and abuse of rights;
(iv) equitable standards for sharing natural resources;
(v) equity as a broad synonym for distributive justice to justify demands for economic and social arrangements and redistribution of wealth.[76]

Similarly, Thomas Franck in 1995 surveyed the development of equity in the international system from the turn of that century, discussing: (i) equity as an instance of 'law as justice', encompassing such concepts as 'unjust enrichment', estoppel, good faith and acquiescence; and (ii) equity as a mode of introducing justice into resource allocation, distinguished as corrective equity, 'broadly conceived equity' and 'common heritage equity', all the while stressing the difference between equitable decisions and decisions *ex aequo et bono*.[77] Other authors, in particular Jörg Paul Müller, Elisabeth Zoller and Robert Kolb, address the protection of good faith and legitimate expectations independently of equity. These principles operate, according to those authors, in their own right and on their own terms.[78] As a practical matter, the difference is not of substantial importance. Invocation of more specific principles, such as estoppel, no longer depend upon recognition as equitable principles but are principles of law, and of international law, in their own right. At the same time, it is still reasonable to group them under equitable doctrines

---

[76] Oscar Schachter, *International Law in Theory and Practice* (Dordrecht, Boston MA, London: Martinus Nijhoff Publishers, 1991), pp. 50–65, in particular pp. 55–6.
[77] Thomas M. Franck, *Fairness in International Law and Institutions* (Oxford: Clarendon Press, 1995).
[78] See Jörg Paul Müller, *Vertrauensschutz im Völkerrecht* (Köln, Berlin: Carly Heymanns Verlag, 1971); Elisabeth Zoller, *La Bonne foi en droit international public* (Paris: Editions A. Pedone, 1977); Robert Kolb, *La Bonne foi en droit international public: Contribution à l'étude des principes généraux de droit* (Paris: Presse Universitaire de France, 2000), p. 109.

as they often contract positive rights and obligations and continue to exert their corrective functions. It is more important to demarcate equity in terms of justiciable and non-justiciable layers and components. The most important function of equity remains being operative in new territories where rules are lacking or inappropriate for application in a particular context, and yet fair and just answers need to be found.

The study of equity in law, therefore, has to be as specific as possible in order to learn about its nature in contemporary and future international law. This is why an inquiry into the foundations, methods and the scope of allocating marine resources in the process of maritime boundary delimitation becomes of prime and contemporary interest for the future of equity in international law. The subject matter thus offers the possibility and precise context for a detailed inquiry into existing dimensions of distributive justice and equity within co-existence, and within the traditional system of nation states. Its findings will be useful to other areas of law where the renaissance of equity, so far, has not taken place but where enhanced recourse to its methodology may be useful in the future.

C. Ambivalence and the need for context

Yet, even within a narrowly defined field of application, we still are faced with the difficult situation that, on the one hand, equity is clearly established as a symbol and code word for distributive justice in international law. It has become part of many international instruments and provisions, both in force and to be applied. On the other hand, we lack agreement as to its scope and contents of distributive justice. We do not know what it means to a precise degree. In a pluralist, multicultural world of diverging stages of economic development, despite a high degree of interdependence, we cannot hope to achieve consensus by deducing conclusions from elusive and evasive precepts, even within an inductive and bottom-up approach. This is particularly true in international law. The risk of subjectivism and legal uncertainty in the recourse to equity is apparent and amounts to a main argument in favour of per se rules. Selden keeps coming back in different forms and arguments, with his famous quote:

> Equity is a roughish thing; for law we have a measure, know what to trust to Equity is according to the conscience of him that is chancellor, and as that it larger or narrower so is equity. Tis all one, as if they should make the standard for the measure we call a chancellor's foot, what an uncertain

measure this would be! One chancellor has a long foot, another a short foot, a third an indifferent foot tis the same thing is the chancellors conscience.[79]

Every negotiator, judge and scholar dealing with equity at any time faces the problem of objectively defining its contents in specific terms. There are several reasons for this.

Firstly, equity, whilst constituting an established value of justice, is not in a position to readily clarify the approaches, goals, means and methods concerning how and to what point changes need to be brought about in more than general terms. Since its inception, the shape and content of equity have been vague and elusive, falling short of allowing for more specific conclusions that go beyond speculation. More than anything else, Justice Holmes' statement remains accurate with regard to equity: 'A word is not a crystal, transparent and unchanging, it is the skin of a living thought and may vary greatly in colour and content according to the circumstances and time in which it is used.'[80] Little help may be expected from equity as a general principle of law beyond mere generalities. Extensive comparative studies reveal that it means different things in different contexts, legal systems and time periods. Reducing the principles discovered to their common denominator and foundation, Ralph A. Newman expounded upon the moral precepts of good faith, honesty and generosity, and combinations thereof, with the underlying concept of human brotherhood: 'Equity may be described as a way of adjusting the burdens of misfortune arising out of human encounters in accordance with standards of generous and honorable conduct that are commonplace facts of all systems of ethics, morals and religion.' And: 'Equity may be defined as the expression of standards of decent and honorable conduct which are the mark of a morally mature society.'[81]

These ethical precepts affirm the legitimacy of invoking equity in current international law. Yet, they still offer little help towards shaping operational legal principles and concepts of resource allocation. Similarly, the juxtaposition of equity and efficiency in economic theory, if correct at all, does not provide much normative guidance. Equity is perceived as a correcting factor to allocation according to efficiency, but

---

[79] Quoted from Karl Strupp, n. 38, p. 103 (orthography in original).
[80] Oliver Wendell Holmes Jr., as quoted at www.quotationspage.com/quote/29065.html (last accessed 24 October 2009).
[81] Ralph A Newman (ed.), *Equity in the World's Legal Systems: A Comparative Study* (Brussels: Bruylant 1972), pp. 27 and 599, respectively.

little is settled as to what extent such a correction should take place in the process of balancing the scales in international relations. Similarly, the theory of equity in social psychology has not yet reached international relations. This theory is concerned with the effects of different distributional schemes on the human psyche. The main (simplified) tenet of the theory holds that striving to maximize personal outcomes and rewards causes, if not unlimited, then serious threats to the social system. This is therefore counterbalanced by the norms of equity, compliance with which is honoured by society. It indicates the requirement for a counterbalance, but little about specific methods and degrees can yet be found to have been applied to international relations.[82] Finally, similar problems concerning limits to the scope of inquiry into distributive justice are common in moral philosophy. There may be good reasons for discussing such issues, primarily in the context of well-organized society and in a national context.[83] Yet the absence of a common and widely shared view regarding similar problems, as adjusted to international society, results in the search for equity being more troublesome and difficult in the quest for cosmopolitan justice.[84]

Secondly, and given its dependence upon particular circumstances, equity continues to mean different things in different contexts. Each circumstance has to be assessed on its own merits. We are faced with the question of to what extent equity offers predictability and legal security. Is it a matter of gradually developing new rules? Or is it rather the function of equity to remain a blanket norm which allows the addressing of new and novel circumstances which require adjustment?

Thirdly, equity in international law uses different legal systems as its sources of inspiration. Whilst it was seen above that the basic idea and function is shared, emanations of equity vary, as alternative legal systems vary and define the relationship of law and equity differently. Differences in legal traditions and culture, discussed above, loom large and need to be considered. They continue to influence international law.

---

[82] E.g. Leonard Berkowitz and Elaine Walster (eds.), *Equity Theory: Toward a General Theory of Social Interaction* (New York: Academic Press, 1976); David Miller, *Social Justice* (Oxford: Clarendon Press, 1976), emphasizing distributive allocations according to desert.

[83] John Rawls, *A Theory of Justice* (Cambridge MA: Harvard University Press, 1971); John Rawls, *The Law of Peoples* (Cambridge MA: Harvard University Press, 1999).

[84] See Simon Caney, *Justice Beyond Borders: A Global Political Theory* (Oxford University Press, 2005); Gillian Brock and Harry Brighouse (eds.), *The Political Philosophy of Cosmopolitanism* (Cambridge University Press, 2005).

Fourthly, the function and role of equity varies under different legal theories and doctrines.[85] This is an important point to note, as lawyers and jurists (as well as courts) do not always reveal the theoretical underpinnings of their arguments. Equity assumes different functions under the main schools of thought. It is at the crossroads of ethics, morals, natural law and positive law. Its role varies over time, as different theories and schools of law emerge, prevail, change and eventually disappear, superseded by newly emerging theories in a long-term cycle. In his work on law and morals, Roscoe Pound exposed these evolutions and differences at the time.[86] They continued to exist in subsequent periods[87] and persist today under contemporary legal theories. The problem of diverging perceptions even exists when the particular context of equity is well defined, as in maritime boundary delimitation. It will be seen throughout the book that disputations on the role of judges and of equity in relation to pre-defined rules, such as the principle of equidistance and its relationship to equity, equitable principles and equitable results, are essentially rooted in diverging schools of jurisprudence and legal thought.

D. The impact of different schools

Without attempting to assign different authors to different schools and to define and assign clearly distinguishable functions of equity, basic distinctions can be observed. Natural law schools and idealism, recognizing pre-statal rights and obligations, inherently or explicitly accord important functions to equity as a point of entry for the articulation of rights and obligations. Equity essentially serves as a port of entry for religious, ethical, moral and philosophical considerations when interpreting, completing and overruling the rigidity of the existing law. Of course, the fundamental problem remains that, in pluralistic societies, there is no common and generally agreed content of such

---

[85] For a discussion see Rossi, n. 49 p. 12–19.
[86] Roscoe Pound, *Law and Morals* (Littleton CO: Fried B. Rothmann, 1897).
[87] Different schools are discussed in Ronald St. J. Macdonald and Douglas M. Johnston, *The Structure and Process of International Law* (The Hague et al.: Martinus Nijhoff Publishers, 1983), pp. 1–178; e.g. W. L. Morison, 'The Schools Revisited' inibid. at p. 131, lists the natural law school, the historical school of jurisprudence, Austrian positivsm, modern English positivism; the positivism of Hans Kelsen, and sociological jurisprudence. Wolfgang Friedmann, *Legal Theory* (New York: Columbia University Press, 1967), pp. 95–364, distinguished in his seminal work the following classical schools at the time: natural law, philosophical ideals, sociological theories, positivism (including realism), and utilitarianism.

considerations. The advent of human rights in constitutional law and in post World War II international law partly imported such values into positive law and rendered recourse to equity somewhat less elusive. It still may serve as an entry point today, for example when applying pre-statal concepts of natural law to relations among private parties in civil law.

Positivism and neo-positivism inherently limit the functions of equity to operations within the law. This theory does not accept pre-statal concepts of law. All law flows from existing and positive rules and principles. In its formal approaches, there is no room for equity. The pure theory of law, which denies its inherent value, therefore denies any possibility of taking recourse to equity beyond the operation of interpretations within the law as it stands. There is no definitive school of positivism, and its different variants thus accord different roles to equity.

Legal realism, often combining idealism, utilitarianism and sociological schools, essentially stresses the role of decision-makers and decision-making processes and considers them to be of practically higher importance than substantive rules and principles and distinctions of law or non-legal norms. Sociological schools exist in different variations. The American New Haven School of Jurisprudence (McDougal and Lasswell) analyse political and legal processes along a continuum, denying strict boundaries of law and politics, and accept those decisions that are in a position to affect reality as authoritative. This school of thought may be employed in an apologetic manner, simply justifying the outcomes of power relations. At the same time, it is combined with high normative aspirations of human dignity and just world order, and contains high aspirations of justice.[88] In this normative context, equity may serve to import moral and ethical values and seek to bring about what have been described as utopian goals. New Haven has been influential and shaped the minds of many international lawyers who remained within traditional precepts, but accepted the importance of realist and sociological implications to the legal process. In particular, this involves recognition of the active role of judges and recourse to equity being analysed in terms of judicial law-making and legislation. The active role of equity in this process

[88] Myres McDougal, Harold Lasswell and James C. Miller, *The Interpretation of Agreements and World Public Order* (New Haven CT, London: Yale University Press 1967); Myres McDougal and Harold Lasswell, 'The Identification and Appraisal of Diverse Systems of Public Order' (1959) 53 *American Journal of International Law*, 1; Myres S. McDougal, Harold D. Lasswell and Lunch-Chu Chen, *Human Rights and World Public Order* (New Haven CT, London: Yale University Press, 1980).

is recognized and supported. Critical legal studies, inspired by linguistic and sociological de-constructivism, build upon the traditions of legal realism and takes issue with formalism and objectivism.[89] The main tenet of this school denies the existence of natural law and of the objectivity of law. The law is inherently indeterminate. It is not a matter of finding the law. The law has to be shaped in a discursive process, laying out the underlying political values in a transparent manner based upon a liberal and pluralist theory of politics and the state. In the present context, Martti Koskenniemi's seminal work provides a comprehensive framework for the analysis and deconstruction of different legal theories in international law.[90] The analysis of different schools and positions in legal and political science doctrine is of great help in clarifying and deepening insights into fundamental attitudes, angles and perceptions that underlie the use of and recourse to equity, as well as other principles and basic rules of international law. Koskenniemi operates within theories depicting the liberal doctrine of politics underlying international law. This doctrine essentially denies natural law and pre-statal rights. The initial liberal solution, used by Wolff and Vattel, relied upon the state's self-definition. The author argues that 'the international legal argument is constructed upon pluralistic and individualistic ideas ... associated with the liberal doctrine of politics'.[91] In order to solve conflicts that go beyond procedural approaches (negotiations), a viewpoint external to states was needed, and this was often taken from precepts of natural law. According to Koskenniemi, however, this undermines the original liberal assumption.[92] Mere procedural solutions alone cannot suffice as they equally require a normative framework. This framework can thus only be man-made. He therefore essentially relies upon positivism, and addresses problems of the law's

---

[89] See Roberto Mangabeira Unger, *The Critical Legal Studies Movement* (Cambridge MA, London: Harvard University Press, 1983); also in *Essays on Critical Legal Studies Selected from the Pages of the Harvard Law Review* (Cambridge MA: Harvard Law Review Association, 1986), p. 318; see generally Mark Kelman, *A Guide to Critical Legal Studies* (Cambridge MA: Harvard University Press, 1987); Drucilla Cornell, Michel Rosenfeld and David Gray Carlson (eds.), *Deconstruction and the Possibility of Justice* (New York, London: Routledge, 1992).

[90] Koskenniemi, n. 50. In this work, which was first published in 1989, apology stands for law justifying existing power constellations, bare of normativity. Utopia, on the other hand, expresses high normative aspirations independently of factual constellations, cf. Koskenniemi, n. 50, pp. 21, 45, 54, 536–7. While policy-oriented schools (McDougal and Lasswell) are deemed to be on the extreme side of the apologetic spectrum, the pure theory of law (Kelsen) stands for utopia on the other side of the spectrum, with other schools of thought fluctuating in between.

[91] Koskenniemi, n. 50, p. 156.   [92] Ibid., p. 155.

objectivity on this basis. He expounds the relative indeterminacy of law (often using examples relating to equity) and the alleged inability to assess law objectively.[93] Problems can be approached from the perspective of the international community (descending arguments). They can also be addressed from the state's point of view (ascending argument), and the two points of view often produce conflicting results.[94] His main deconstructivist thesis argues that the law is incapable of providing convincing justifications and each solution remains exposed to criticism. Instead of seeking a more determinate system of legal argument, lawyers need to take a stand on political issues without assuming a privileged rationality.[95]

The analysis is based on an assessment of the main theories and schools of thought within the parameters of positivism and the realm of man-made law. They share a common trait in that they accept that the law can be found even in hard cases, but they do so in a different manner. Koskenniemi distinguished four approaches to this effect:[96] The formalistic view (Kelsen) assumes the completeness of the legal system on the basis of the Lotus doctrine. Secondly, the naturalist schools argue that certain material standards are inherent to the law and offer guidance. A third, purposive variant emphasizes that in the absence of positive rules, the decision must either give effect to some legislative purpose, or to some conception of utility or equity.[97] A fourth variant emphasizes the constructive aspects of legal decisions and the autonomous and systemic character of legal concepts, equally assuming material completeness of the law.

Having analysed the relationship of doctrine and practice and the relationship of law and political science further, Koskenniemi introduces another four viewpoints for the assessment of the role of law in international relations:[98]

---

[93] Ibid., pp. 23–24, 60–70.   [94] Ibid., pp. 59–60.
[95] Ibid., p. 69. 'I shall argue, then, that law is incapable of providing convincing justifications to the solution of normative problems. Each proposed solution will remain vulnerable to criticisms which are justified by the system itself. Moreover, depending on which of the systems' two contradictory demands one is led to emphasize, different – indeed contradictory – solutions can be made to seem equally acceptable ... No coherent normative practice arises from the assumptions on which we identify international law ... My suggestion will not be to develop a "more determinate" system of legal argument. Quite the contrary, I believe that lawyers should admit that if they wish to achieve justifications, they have to take a stand on political issues without assuming that there exists a privileged rationality which solves such issues for them.'
[96] Koskenniemi, n. 50, pp. 44–58.   [97] Ibid., p. 48.   [98] Ibid., pp. 184–5.

(i) the rule approach position denies the fluidity of law and politics and stands for an independent and defined, albeit narrow, body of law;
(ii) the policy approach position, reflecting mainly sociological schools, considers law to be normatively weak and broad in scope;
(iii) the sceptical position considers law to be normatively weak and materially restricted; and
(iv) the idealistic position considers law to be normatively strong and materially wide.

These positions are useful for the provision of a framework for our analysis. None of them is immune from criticism from the perspective of the other three. Indeed, according to the author, the rule approach lawyer will be criticized by the policy approach lawyer because the rule approach does not take realities into account and results in the creation of a utopian model.[99] Similarly, sceptical political scientists and economists will be reminded by Henkin that 'almost all nations observe almost all principles of international law and almost all of their obligations almost all of the time'.[100] And legal idealists will be reminded of the law's shortcomings, particularly in the context of political disputes. Doctrines and arguments therefore oscillate within and among these positions, leading to some middle ground. According to Koskenniemi:

> This explains the movement by modern lawyers constantly towards a middle-position – a position from which it would be possible to reject the utopias of those who think the world is or is in a process of becoming a law-regulated community and the apologies of those who engage themselves in law's infinite manipulation in favour of political ends.[101]

It would seem that the research undertaken by Koskenniemi was partially inspired by the renaissance of equity in international law and frequent recourse to it. He frequently refers to the case law of the ICJ. Problems of indeterminacy, conflicting solutions and the inability to assess the law objectively are often exemplified by taking recourse to cases based upon equity and equitable principles. It is premature at this stage to assess whether Koskenniemi's thesis stands the test of detailed analysis of the case law and underlying doctrines and principles. It is the task of this book to undertake such detailed analysis in one particular field of law – maritime boundary delimitation – with a view to assessing the de-constructivist

---

[99] Ibid., p. 185.
[100] Louis Henkin, *How Nations Behave: Law and Foreign Policy* (New York: Columbia University Press, 1979), p. 47.
[101] Koskenniemi, n. 50, p. 186.

thesis. Yet, such detailed examination will show that the scope for 'a more determinate system of legal argument' can be developed in this field, and that Koskenniemi's conclusions are partly based upon a lack of sufficiently detailed analysis of the case law and the underlying legal doctrines and equitable principles. Clearly, equity as a foundation and methodology of maritime boundary delimitation is more than splitting the difference, ex post justification or application of *ex aequo et bono* in disguise. However, his useful framework of classifying different schools of thought and positions makes it clear from the outset that equity is also bound to mean different things in the context of different theories. His work assists in assessing where different views come from and why one or another normative function of equity is preferred in a particular context. The discourse on equity, as with other principles of international law, is exposed to these different schools and positions and fluctuates equally among and between them. Koskonniemi makes a convincing case that it would be futile and incorrect to seek a final and exclusive theory of equity in international law. The underlying assumptions of international law based upon the liberal theory of state and sovereign equality are bound to project a pluralist view. Moreover, there are no intellectual limitations to theorizing about law, even positive law, and bringing about different schools of thought in assessing the normativity and impact of factual relations in between the ranges offered by utopia and apology.

Pluralism, however, does not prevent us from seeking the description and analysis of equity in a particular context and of identifying its foundations, functions and processes as they operate within the legal system of international law – the functions ascribed to equity in diplomacy, in treaty making and, foremost, in adjudication relating to maritime boundary delimitation.

IV. Conclusion

Our thesis is, to conclude this introduction, that much can be learned about the reality and processes of law and equity in a particular and detailed context. This is the goal of this book. And by doing so, it hopes to gain further insights into the real operation of equity and of distributive justice in the law of co-existence. Such analytical work, of course, cannot aspire to find the truth of the matter *per se*. This is not an exercise in natural sciences. Oscillating theories, underlying arguments and decisions continue to render the task complex and difficult. Yet, it is hoped that such a step-by-step analysis will assist in clearing the path, with the aim of achieving a more complete picture and a rational view of the interrelationship of law and equity in this particular field. Much can be learned about the methodologies applied, and methodologies that should be applied, taking the details of the problem into account. It is through this approach that we hope to learn more about the very functions of equity and the judge in contemporary international law relating to maritime boundaries. It is on this basis that insights can be offered into the operation of equity within a specific field of law as well as into the evolution and development of equity in the legal process. Results in substantive law will remain within the bounds of this particular field. Equity means different things in different contexts. Generalizations will only be made with respect to fundamental functions and the methodology developed under the realms of equity. It will be argued that such common ground exists. While the substance of equity is bound to vary from field to field, a methodology of concretization and shaping of equitable standards, and applying such standards in their respective legal and political environments, can be found, which may be helpful in all issues related to resource allocation based on equity.

Modern equity in international law brings a new legal methodology to the table which is of importance far beyond the specific context of maritime boundary delimitation. It offers an approach to complex problems and conflicts, the settlement of which need to be left to assessment case by case, taking into account relevant factors to be determined on the basis of respective foundations of the regulatory field at stake. Such findings on modern equity and its new methodology thus are not only of importance with a view to unsettled boundaries. They may be equally crucial in the face of the new challenges that are emerging with climate change, such as the melting of the polar ice and, with it, the enhanced access to further navigational routes and submarine resources.[102] At the same time the possible rise of sea levels and the ensuing change of coastal configurations loom large and strongly depend upon past experience and findings in the law of distributive justice.[103] But the lessons do not end here. The methodological insights may be applied to other areas of

---

[102] See The Ilulissat Declaration, Adopted by the five States bordering the Arctic Ocean at the Arctic Ocean Conference, Illulisat, Greenland, 28 May 2008, available at http://www.ocean law.org/downloads/arctic/Ilulissat_Declaration.pdf (last accessed 7 September 2014).

[103] On the problem of rising sea levels, see David D. Caron, 'Climate Change, Sea Level Rise and the Coming Uncertainty in Oceanic Boundaries: A Proposal to Avoid Conflict' in Seoung-Yong Hong and Jon M. Van Dyke (eds.), *Maritime Boundary Disputes, Settlement Processes, and the Law of the Sea* (Leiden, Boston: Martinus Nijhoff, 2009).

international economic law relating to the allocation of natural resources, as well as to other areas taking recourse to equity. The methodology expounded in judicial dispute settlement on maritime boundaries may serve as a model whenever treaties and customary law refer to equity. It stands for a particular methodology. Negotiators agreeing on treaty text invoking equity or equitable principles essentially delegate decision-making to further negotiations or dispute settlement in which precedents may play an important role. It implies that the matter is inherently justiciable. The approach is suitable for many areas entailing problems of distributive justice, such as allocation of territorial jurisdiction, the allocation of fresh water rights, navigable rivers and perhaps clean air, the allocation of compensation, the assessment of subsidies, countervailing duty determination in WTO law and anti-trust. Finally, the inquiry will teach and tell us to what extent justice is, and can be, done within the law of nations and to what extent new foundations will be required in global governance in order to address unresolved issues and challenges in bringing about distributive justice.

Accordingly, Part I of this book provides and assesses the particular context of this inquiry into equity: the law of the sea and the enclosure movements and its distributive effects. Part II focuses on the new boundaries which the enclosure of the seas produced. It deals extensively with the emerging role of equity and equitable principles in maritime boundary delimitation in what amounts to the most extensive area of litigation in international law besides trade and investment disputes. Part III conceptualizes the rule of equity and justiciable standards in the present context. It develops a proper methodology both for adjudication and negotiations which may eventually finds its way into other areas of international law.

In essence, this book argues that the rule of equity is able to gradually develop, in the particular field of a regulatory area and context, more specific equitable principles and define relevant circumstances the operation of which allows the bringing about of fair and equitable results beyond the technicalities of positive law or strict rules and exceptions. As a topical methodology, it contributes to the achievement of fair outcomes, given the constraints of the international society of sovereign states in the Westphalian system. It bears the potential to be applied to other and emerging regulatory areas of international law. They can learn from the experience over half a century of maritime boundary delimitation, the process of trial and error, the exceptional wealth of jurisprudence and doctrine, and from the gradual emergence of equitable principles offering guidance in what amounts to an utterly complex field.

PART I

Context: The enclosure of the seas

1

The silent revolution

I. The partition of the seas

Since the end of World War II, the law of the sea has changed profoundly. Nations began to claim jurisdiction over marine resources and to enclose parts of the globe by the end of the 1940s. Within a relatively short period of time, the traditional doctrine of 'freedom of the high seas' lost ground, both with regard to natural resources from the sea and seabed and for communication purposes; yet freedom of the high seas continues to prevail in principle, and freedom of navigation for ships and flight paths for aeroplanes remain unimpaired. A complex, dualistic scheme of both national and supranational jurisdiction over the non-living and living resources in the seas emerged and has continued to develop.[1] The

---

[1] See the substantial body of general literature on the partition of the sea (in alphabetical order): Lewis M. Alexander, 'The Ocean Enclosure Movement' (1983) 20 *San Diego Law Review*, 561; Ram P. Anand (ed.), *The Law of the Sea: Caracas and Beyond* (The Hague: Martinus Nijhoff Publishers, 1980); Ram P. Anand, *Origin and Development of the Law of the Sea, Publications on Ocean Development* (The Hague: Martinus Nijhoff Publishers, 1983), vol. VII; Ram P. Anand, 'Freedom of the Seas: Past, Present and Future' in Rafael G. Girardot et al. (eds.), *New Directions in International Law, Essays in Honour of Wolfgang Abendroth: Festschrift zu seinem 75. Geburtstag* (Frankfurt am Main: Campus Verlag, 1983), p. 215; David Anderson, *Modern Law of the Sea, Selected Essays* (The Hague: Martinus Nijhoff Publishers, 2008); Nisuke Ando et al. (eds.), *Liber Amicorum Judge Shigeru Oda* (The Hague: Kluwer Law International, 2002); Gilbert Apollis, *L'Emprise maritime de l'Etat côtier* (Paris: Editions A. Pedone, 1981); David J. Attard, *The Exclusive Economic Zone in International Law* (Oxford: Clarendon Press, 1987); Daniel Bardonnet and Michel Virally (eds.), *Le Nouveau droit international de la mer* (Paris: Editions A. Pedone, 1983); Ronald P. Barston and Patricia Birnie (eds.), *The Maritime Dimension* (London, Boston: Allen & Unwin, 1980); Edward Duncan Brown, *Sea-Bed Energy and Minerals: The International Legal Regime*, 2 vols. (The Hague: Martinus Nijhoff Publishers, 2001); Edward Duncan Brown, *The International Law of the Sea*, 2 vols. (Aldershot: Dartmouth Publishing, 1994); Edward Duncan Brown, 'Vers une nationalisation ou une internationalisation des espaces marins?' (1990) 61 *Relations Internationales*, 59; Ian Brownlie, *Principles of Public International Law* (Oxford University Press, 2008), pp. 173–246; Lucius Caflisch, 'Les Zones maritimes sous juridiction nationale, leurs limites et leurs délimitations'(1980) 84 *Revue Générale de Droit International Public*, 68;

seas have been divided not only among different nations, but also among different and partially overlapping zones and legal regimes, with divisions now going far beyond the traditional 3-mile territorial limit of national coastal waters. The enclosure movement of the seas evolved

Hugo Caminos (ed.), *Law of the Sea* (Aldershot: Ashgate/Dartmouth, 2001); David D. Caron and Harry N. Scheiber (eds.), *Bringing New Law to Ocean Waters* (Leiden: Martinus Nijhoff Publishers, 2004); Jonathan I. Charney et al., 'Introduction' in Charney et al. (eds.), *International Maritime Boundaries*, 5 vols. (The Hague: Martinus Nijhoff Publishers, 1993–2005), vols. I and II (Charney and Alexander (eds.), 1993), vol. III (Charney and Alexander (eds.), 1998), vol. IV (Charney and Smith (eds.), 2002), vol. V (Colson and Smith (eds.), 2005); vol. I, p. xxiii; Robin R. Churchill and Alan V. Lowe, *The Law of the Sea* (Manchester University Press, 1999); Jean Combacau, *Le Droit international de la mer* (Paris: Presses Universitaires de France, 1985); René-Jean Dupuy, 'Droit de la mer et communauté internationale', in D. Bardonnet (ed.), *Mélanges offerts à Paul Reuter: le droit international: unité et diversité* (Paris: Editions A. Pedone, 1981), p. 221; René-Jean Dupuy, *The Law of the Sea: Current Problems* (Dobbs Ferry NY: Oceana Publications Inc.; Leiden: Sijthoff, 1974); René-Jean Dupuy, *L'Océan partagé* (Paris: Editions A. Pedone, 1979); René-Jean Dupuy and Daniel Vignes (eds.), *A Handbook of the New Law of the Sea* (Dordrecht: Martinus Nijhoff Publishers, 1991); René-Jean Dupuy and Daniel Vignes (eds.), *Traité du nouveau droit de la mer* (Paris: Editions Economica, 1985); Ross D. Eckert, *The Enclosure of Ocean Resources: Economics and the Law of the Sea* (Stanford CA: Hoover Institution Press, 1979); Alex G. Oude Elferink and Donald R. Rothwell (eds.), *Oceans Management in the 21st Century: Institutional Frameworks and Responses* (Leiden: Martinus Nijhoff Publishers, 2004); Jens Evensen, 'The United Nations Convention on the Law of the Seas of December 10, 1982: Its Political and Legal Impact – Present and Future' (1982) 38 *Revue égyptienne de droit international public*, 11–32; David Freestone et al. (eds.), *The Law of the Sea: Progress and Prospects* (Oxford University Press, 2006); Maria Gavouneli, *Functional Jurisdiction in the Law of the Sea* (Leiden: Martinus Nijhoff Publishers, 2007); Allan E. Gotlieb, 'The Impact of Technology on the Development of International Law' (1981) 170 *Recueil des cours* I, 115, 137–147, 156–222; Institute of Public International Law and Relations (ed.), *The Law of the Sea with Emphasis on the Mediterranean Issues, Thesaurus Acroasium* (Thessaloniki: Sakkoulas Publications, 1991), vol. XVII; Institute of Public International Law and Relations (ed.), *The Law of the Sea, Thesaurus Acroasium* (Thessaloniki: Sakkoulas Publications, 1977), vol. VII; S. P. Jagota, 'Recent Developments in the Law of the Sea', in Elisabeth Mann Borgese et al. (eds.), *Ocean Yearbook* (University of Chicago Press Journals, 1989), vol. VII, p. 65; Robert J. Jennings and Arthur Watts (eds.), *Oppenheim's International Law* (Oxford University Press, 1996), vol. I, pp. 709–825; Winrich Kühne, *Das Völkerrecht und die militärische Nutzung des Meeresbodens* (Leiden: Sijthoff, 1975); Marklen I. Lazarev (ed.), *Modernes Seevölkerrecht* (Berlin: Duncker & Humblot, 1987); Alan V. Lowe, 'Reflections on the Waters Changing Conceptions of Property Rights in the Law of the Sea' (1986) 1 *International Journal of Estuarine and Coastal Law*, 1; Myres McDougal and Thomas C. Burke, *The Public Order of the Oceans: A Contemporary International Law of the Sea* (New Haven CT, London: Yale University Press, 1962); Ingo von Münch, *Internationales Seerecht: Seerechtliche Abhandlungen 1958–1982 mit einer Einführung in das internationale Seerecht* (Heidelberg: R. v. Decker Verlag, 1985); Shigeru Oda, *International Law of the Resources of the Sea* (Alphen aan den Rijn: Sijthoff & Noordhoff, 1979); Bernard H. Oxman, 'The Territorial Temptation: A Siren Song at Sea' (2006) 100 *The American Journal of*

through three successive generations of jurisdictional zones: the continental shelf; the exclusive economic zone (EEZ); and the Area. Chapter 2 will describe the first and second of these zones in more detail, while a discussion of the third follows below. The gradual extension of the territorial sea up to 12 nm and the controversial expansion of the contiguous zone are beyond the scope of this book.[2]

Long before the great majority of newly independent countries, both developing and least developed, began gaining influence in international affairs, the legal concept of the continental shelf emerged in the 1950s. Under this concept, the coastal states were entitled to appropriate mineral resources found in the seabed of the shallow waters of the shelves. Oil and gas were the major resources that benefited these privileged states. The outer limit of the concept was not limited and followed the feasibility of technological exploitation. These limits, while comprising today at least 200 nm, are still not properly settled and are subject to new and ongoing claims.

International Law, Centennial Essays, 830; Majorie B. Paulsen (ed.), *Law of the Sea* (New York: Nova Science Publishers Inc., 2007); J. Ashley Roach and Robert W. Smith, *United States Responses to Excessive Maritime Claims* (The Hague: Martinus Nijhoff Publishers, 1996); Clyde Sanger, *Ordering the Oceans: The Making of the Laws of the Sea* (London: Zed Books, 1986); Tullio Scovazzi, 'The Evolution of International Law of the Sea: New Issues, New Challenges' (2000) 286 *Recueil des cours (Académie de Droit International)*, 39; Robert W. Smith, 'Global Maritime Claims'(1989) 20 *Ocean Development & International Law*, 83; Louis B. Sohn and Kristen Gustafson, *Law of the Sea in a Nutshell* (St. Paul MN: West Group, 1984); Yoshifumi Tanaka, *A Dual Approach to Ocean Governance: The Cases of Zonal and Integrated Management in International Law of the Sea* (Farnham: Ashgate Publishing Ltd., 2008); Yoshifumi Tanaka, The International Law of the Sea (Cambridge University Press, 2012); Bo Johnson Theutenberg, *The Evolution of the Law of the Sea* (Dublin: Tycooly International Publishing, 1984); UNFAO (ed.), *The Law of the Sea: Essays in Memory of Jean Carroz* (Rome: UNFAO, 1987); Budislav Vukas, *The Law of the Sea: Selected Writings* (Leiden, Boston MA: Martinus Nijhoff Publishers, 2004); Davor Vidas and Willy Østreng (eds.), *Order for the Oceans at the Turn of the Century* (The Hague: Kluwer Law International, 1999); Per Magnus Wijkman, 'UNCLOS and the Redistribution of Ocean Wealth', 16 *Journal of World Trade Law* (1982), reprinted in Richard Falk et al. (eds.), *International Law: A Contemporary Perspective* (Boulder CO: Westview Press, 1985), p. 598. For further publications see Nikos Papadakis, *International Law of the Sea: A Bibliography* (Dordrecht: Kluwer Academic Publishers, 1980); Uwe Jenisch, *Bibliographie des deutschen Schrifttums zum internationalen Seerecht 1945–1981* (Hamburg: Alfred Metzner Verlag, 1982); Tafsir Malick Ndiaye and Rüdiger Wolfrum (eds.), *Law of the Sea, Environmental Law and Settlement of Disputes: Liber Amicorum Judge Thomas A. Mensah* (Leiden: Martinus Nijhoff Publishers, 2007).

[2] For the evolution of the territorial sea and the contiguous zone (which by now may extend up to 24 miles for purposes of law enforcement) see e.g. Churchill and Lowe, n. 1, pp. 53–80, 101–107; Alan V. Lowe, 'The Development of the Concept of the Contiguous Zone' (1981) 52 *British Yearbook of International Law*, 109.

The second generation evolved from the development of exclusive fishing zones, which eventually grew into the 200 nm exclusive economic zone of coastal states (EEZ) in the 1970s. Under this concept and regime, coastal states appropriated all living and other potential resources within these frontiers. It remains to be seen whether the limits of this zone have yet been reached; the continued process of appropriation may well result in the current 200 nm limit being exceeded. At the same time, a process of territorialization is making itself felt within the 200 nm limit, as states seek to approximate the legal regime of the EEZ to the territorial sea entailing full sovereignty.[3]

Lastly, a third category of zone called 'the Area' emerged in the 1980s, mainly as a result of improvements in prospects to explore deep seabed minerals, particularly manganese nodules. At the time, these strategic resources were mainly located in unstable countries and means to secure supplies during the Cold War years were sought. During the 1960s and 1970s, the concept of this zone was still controversial and the Area gradually evolved through both unilateral and multilateral frameworks.

The main driving forces and the motivation behind the enclosure movement were the concerns by coastal states to protect national economic interests in natural resources, national security and conservation and environmental concerns, all of which increased with improvements in the technological capacity to exploit marine resources.[4] The main impetus leading to the establishment of the continental shelf zones was the preservation of potential offshore drilling and the proceeds thereof, whereas the main stimulus behind the protection of offshore fishing grounds through the creation of the EEZ was over-fishing and exploitation by foreign fishing fleets, at the expense of indigenous industries. In addition to the protection of fishing grounds, this zone also offers prospects of mining, fish farming and tidal energy production to coastal states.

It is important to note that in the creation of the EEZ and in the discussions of the further evolution of the Area, the newly developed countries, at the time particularly the Group of 77, emerged as the main driving force of the enclosure movement. Traditional patterns of

---

[3] See Oxman, 'The Territorial Temptation: A Siren Song at Sea', n. 1.

[4] See in particular Gotlieb, n. 1; D. N. Hutchinson, 'The Seaward Limit to the Continental Shelf Jurisdiction in Customary International Law' (1985) 56 *British Yearbook of International Law*, 111, 123. For an assessment of the economic interests involved, see Jean Vignes, *Le Rôle des intérêts économiques dans l'évolution du droit de la mer* (Geneva: Institut universitaire de hautes études internationales, 1971); Suzette V. Suarez, *The Outer Limits of the Continental Shelf: Legal Aspects of their Establishment* (Berlin: Springer, 2008).

non-appropriation and free access, favouring militarily and economically powerful nations 'irrespective of relative needs for the resource or geographic relationships',[5] were no longer considered acceptable. Thus, since the 1970s, the enclosure movement also became a movement to achieve global distributive justice in the allocation of marine resources between North and South – a quest put forward in terms of and in the name of equity. Whatever the 'equitable' results achieved,[6] the enclosure of the seas perhaps amounted to the most ambitious project of reshaping economic power by legal means in the history of modern international relations.

II. Conferences, conventions, and customary law

The fundamental policy shift from freedom of the seas to their enclosure led to the development of a dynamic diplomatic and law-making process in customary law, treaty law, and judicial settlements.

A. UNCLOS I, II and the Geneva Conventions

The first United Nations Conference on the Law of the Sea (UNCLOS I) and the 1958 Conventions on the Law of the Sea (prepared by the International Law Commission (ILC)) resulted in the initial consolidation of the newly emerging doctrine of the continental shelf in treaty law.[7] However, the conference was unsuccessful in resolving the controversial issues of the breadth of the territorial sea and limits on fisheries.

---

[5] Oscar Schachter, *Sharing the World's Resources* (New York: Columbia University Press, 1977), p. 39.

[6] For an assessment of equity and the distributive effects of the enclosure of the seas see Chapter 3.

[7] Convention on the Continental Shelf, Geneva, 29 April 1958, in force 10 June 1964, 499 UNTS 311; Convention on the High Seas, Geneva, 29 April 1958, in force 30 September 1962, 450 UNTS 82; Convention on the Territorial Sea and the Contiguous Zone, Geneva, 29 April, in force 10 September 1964, 516 UNTS 205. The fourth treaty, the Convention on Fishing and Conservation of the Living Resources of the High Seas, Geneva, 29 April 1958, in force 20 March 1966, 599 UNTS 285, remained virtually without any effects. The 1958 Geneva Conventions established the first successful codification and negotiated development of the law of the seas. Earlier attempts at the pre-war League of Nations 1930 Codification Conference had failed, a fact which indicates that the law of the sea had never achieved sufficient stability even before the great transitions following World War II. For more information on the Conference and its extensive preparations by the Committee of Experts for the Progressive Codification of International Law see, e.g. Gilbert Gidel, *Le Droit international public de la mer*, 3 vols. (Chateauroux: Mellottée, 1932–1934, repr. 1981), vol. III, pp. 141–52.

Follow-up negotiations in 1960 (UNCLOS II) also failed to achieve agreement on these subjects.[8] Despite efforts to codify traditional customary law, protectionist marine policies were rapidly evolving and received increasing support from Latin American states and the growing number of newly independent developing nations who had had little involvement in UNCLOS I and II.[9]

B. UNCLOS III and the LOS Convention

Only a few years after the 1958 Conventions entered into force, new initiatives were taken to renegotiate the law of the sea. Fears that nuclear weapons would be stationed on the seabed, as well as new prospects for the economic exploitation of deep seabed minerals provided the incentives for renewed negotiation. The result was the Third United Nations Conference on the Law of the Sea (UNCLOS III). It was described by former American Secretary of State Henry Kissinger as 'one of the most important, complex and ambitious diplomatic undertakings in history'.[10] Indeed, for almost a decade (1974–1982), the Conference was the most prominent event in the process of international law,[11] perhaps equalled

---

[8] See Second United Nations Conference on the Law of the Sea, *Official Records*, UN Doc. A/CONF. 19/8; Daniel P. O'Connell, *The International Law of the Sea*, 2 vols. (Oxford: Clarendon Press, 1982–1984), vol. I, pp. 163–4.

[9] The Non-Aligned Movement of developing countries started only shortly before the Conference with the 1955 Bandung Conference attended by representatives from twenty-nine mostly newly independent states. It took more formal shape at the 1961 Belgrade Conference and with the foundation of the Group of 77 (amounting to some 125 members) in 1964. For an account of LDC reactions at UNCLOS I see Emmanuel G. Bello, 'International Equity and the Law of the Sea: New Perspectives for Developing Countries' (1980) 13 *Verfassung und Recht in Uebersee*, 201, 203–4.

[10] Quoted from Elliot L. Richardson, 'Dispute Settlement under the Convention on the Law of the Sea' in T. Buergenthal (ed.), *Contemporary Issues in International Law, Essays in Honor of Louis B. John* (Kehl, Strasbourg: N. P. Engel Publisher, 1984), pp. 149, 150.

The importance of the negotiations were highlighted by Sir Robert Jennings at an early stage, in 1972, in the following terms:

> The legal régime of the sea has been a persistently important theme of the law of nations from the beginning; but it has probably never been more dominant than it is at the present time, touching as it does so many of the most vital interests of nations, such as the supply of food and of energy; politically sensitive questions like defence and immigration; and some of the most pressing aspects of pollution and conservation policy.

Sir Robert Jennings, 'A Changing Law of the Sea' (1972) 31 *Cambridge Law Journal*, 32.

[11] The writings on UNCLOS III are abundant, in particular during the 1970s and early 1980s. For an account of the evolution and the process of negotiations see in particular the

only by the successive emphasis on global trade negotiations under the GATT Uruguay Round from 1986–1994, which led to the establishment of the World Trade Organization (WTO). The effects of UNCLOS III go far beyond substantive maritime law. New conference techniques such as the absence of ILC drafts, consensus diplomacy, package deals and off-the-record negotiations, to mention only the most important,

chairman's assessment: Tommy T. B. Koh, 'Negotiating a New World Order for the Sea' (1984) 24 *Virginia Journal of International Law*, 761, 780 ff; Lucius Caflisch, 'La Révision du droit international de la mer' (1973) 29 *Schweizerisches Jahrbuch für Internationales Recht*, 49; John R. Stevenson and Bernard H. Oxman, 'The Preparations for the Law of the Sea Conference' (1974) 68 *American Journal of International Law*, 1; John R. Stevenson and Bernard H. Oxman, 'The Third United Nations Conference on the Law of the Sea: The 1974 Caracas Session' (1975) 69 *American Journal of International Law*, 763; Bernard H. Oxman, 'The Third United Nations Conference on the Law of the Sea: The 1976 New York Session' (1977) 71 *American Journal of International Law*, 247; Bernard H. Oxman, 'The 1977 New York Session' (1978) 72 *American Journal of International Law*, 57; Bernard H. Oxman, 'The Seventh Session (1978)' (1979) 73 *American Journal of International Law*, 1; Bernard H. Oxman, 'The Eighth Session (1979)' (1980) 74 *American Journal of International Law*, 1; Bernard H. Oxman, 'The Ninth Session (1980)' (1981) 75 *American Journal of International Law*, 211; Bernard H. Oxman, 'The Tenth Session (1981)' (1982) 76 *American Journal of International Law*, 1; Bernhard H. Oxman, 'The Third United Nations Conference on the Law of the Sea' in R.-J. Dupuy and D. Vignes (eds.), *A Handbook on the New Law of the Sea* (Dordrecht: Kluwer Academic Publishers, 1991), pp. 163–244; see generally Tono Eitel, 'Seerechtsreform und internationale Politik' (1982) 107 *Archiv des oeffentlichen Rechts*, 216; Guy de Lacharrière, 'La Réforme du droit de la mer et le rôle de la Conférence des Nations Unies' (1980) 84 *Revue Générale de Droit International Public*, 216; Jean-Pierre Lévy, *La Conférences des Nations Unies sur le droit de la mer: Histoire d'une négociation singulière* (Paris: Editions A. Pedone, 1983); Jean Monnier, 'La Troisième Conférence des Nations Unies sur le droit de la mer' (1983) 39 *Schweizerisches Jahrbuch für Internationales Recht*, 1; Evelyne Peyroux, 'Les Etats africains face aux questions actuelles du droit de la mer' (1974) 78 *Revue Générale de Droit International Public*, 623; Manohar Lal Sarin, 'Reflections on the Progress made by the Third United Nations Conference in Developing the Law of the Sea' in R. G. Girardot et al. (eds.), *New Directions in International Law: Essays in Honour of Wolfgang Abendroth: Festschrift zu seinem 75. Geburtstag* (Frankfurt a. M., New York: Campus Verlag, 1982), p. 278; James K. Sebenius, *Negotiating the Law of the Sea* (Harvard University Press, 1984); Alphons Studier (ed.), *Seerechtskonferenz und Dritte Welt* (Munich: Weltforum Verlag, 1980); Budislav Vukas (ed.), *Essays on the Law of the Sea* (University of Zagreb, Faculty of Law, 1985); Wolfgang Graf Vitzthum, 'Auf dem Wege zu einem neuen Meeresvölkerrecht: Zur Rechtslage vor der dritten Seerechtskonferenz' (1973) 16 *Jahrbuch für internationales Recht*, 229; Klaus Dieter Wolf, *Die Dritte Seerechtskonferenz der Vereinten Nationen* (Baden-Baden: Nomos Verlagsgesellschaft, 1981); Bernhard Zuleta, 'The Law of the Sea after Montego Bay' (1983) 20 *San Diego Law Review*, 475.

Documents: The enormous amount of published but rather poorly organized documents of the Conference are available on an electronic database. Conference materials are recollected in *Official Records of the United Nations Conference on the*

52   CONTEXT: THE ENCLOSURE OF THE SEAS

fundamentally challenged traditional modes of the international bargaining process within the United Nations system and elsewhere.[12]
The United Nations Convention on the Law of the Sea (LOS Convention) entered into force on 16 November 1994.[13] It is an impressive achievement within the United Nations, considering the complex disparities of interests between industrialized nations and the least developed countries (LDCs), and the novelty of many issues, particularly deep seabed mining. Although far from perfect and often vague in its wording, the sheer scope and size of the agreement with its

---

Law of the Sea XV vols., UN Doc. A/CONF. 62 (1974–1981). Non-official collections: Renate Platzoeder (ed.), *Third United Nations Conference on the Law of the Sea: Documents*, 7 vols. (Dobbs Ferry NY: Oceana Publications Inc., 1982–1985); Renate Platzoeder (ed.), *Dokumente der Dritten Seerechtskonferenz, 1977 Geneva Session*, 3 vols. (Materialiensammlung der Stiftung Wissenschaft und Politik, 1977); Renate Platzoeder (ed.), *1979 New York Session*, 2 vols. (Dobbs Ferry NY: Oceana Publications, 1979); Renate Platzoeder (ed.), *The 1994 United Nations Convention on the Law of the Sea: Basic Documents with and Introduction* (Dordrecht: Martinus Nijhoff Publishers, 1995). See also, as a helpful source, the published Reports of the United States Delegation to the Third United Nations Conference on the Law of the Sea; M. H. Nordquist and C. H. Park (eds.), *The Law of the Sea Institute, Occasional Papers No. 33* (University of Hawaii Press, 1983).

[12] See e.g. Barry Buzan, 'Negotiation by Consensus: Developments in Technique at the United Nations Conference on the Law of the Sea' (1981) 75 *American Journal of International Law*, 324; Jorge Castañeda, 'La Conférence des Nations Unis sur le droit de la mer et l'avenir de la diplomatie multilaterale' in A. Migliazza et al. (eds.), *International Law at the Time of its Codification: Essays in Honour of Roberto Ago*, 4 vols. (Milan: Giuffrè, 1987), vol. II, pp. 76–85; Jonathan I. Charney, 'Technology and International Negotiations' (1982) 76 *American Journal of International Law*, 78; M. C. M. Pinto, 'Modern Conference Techniques: Insights from Social Psychology and Anthropology' in R. Maconald and D. Johnston (eds.), *The Structure and Process of International Law: Essays in Legal Philosophy, Doctrine and Theory* (The Hague: Nijhoff, 1983), pp. 305, 310–13; Daniel Vignes, 'Will the Third Conference on the Law of the Sea Work According to the Consensus Rule?' (1975) 69 *American Journal of International Law*, 119; Tullio Treves, 'Une Nouvelle technique de la codification du droit international: Le comité de rédaction dans la conférence sur le droit de la mer' (1981) 27 *Annuaire Français de Droit International Public*, 65; Martin Limpert, *Verfahren und Völkerrecht: Völkerrechtliche Probleme des Verfahrens von Kodifikationskonferenzen der Vereinten Nationen* (Berlin: Duncker und Humblot, 1985), pp. 104–21, 160 ff.

[13] 'UN Doc. A/CONF. 62/122 (1982), done at Montego Bay, 10 Dec. 1982' (1982) 21 *International Legal Materials* 1261, United Nations, The Law of the Sea: Official Text of the United Nations Convention on the Law of the Sea with Annexes and Index, Sales No. E.83.V.5 (1983), www.un.org/depts/los/doalos_publications/doalos_publications.htm (last accessed 11 August 2014) (the alternatively proposed name of Montego Bay Convention did not prevail, but see (1984) 78 *American Journal of International Law*, 196). The Convention received its sixtieth ratification on 16 November 1993 and, according to Art. 308, came into force on 16 November 1994.

320 articles and 8 substantial annexes made it a laudable achievement.[14] Since its conclusion the Convention has been complemented and clarified by a number of follow-up resolutions and implementation agreements.[15] During the 12-year period preceding its entry into force, the Convention was far more than just law-in-waiting. Since the Convention's adoption in 1982, it has shaped policies and attitudes to maritime law. It has influenced state practice and international law in many ways and has unequivocally contributed to the evolution of customary law, as anticipated by Philip Allott in 1983:

> The United Nations Convention on the Law of the Sea is a fact. It exists. Whether or not it becomes a fully operational treaty – signed, ratified, in force, widely supported, generally followed – it is and will be the cause of significant effects. Its very existence modifies political, economic, and legal relationships in countless ways whose directions and intensity we can predict only in a most speculative way.[16]

---

[14] The text of the Convention was adopted in New York on 30 April 1982, with 130 states including France and Japan voting in favour, 17 abstentions (15 because of the deep seabed regime: Belgium, Bulgaria, Byelorussia SSR, Czechoslovakia, German Democratic Republic, Federal Republic of Germany, Hungary, Italy, Luxembourg, Mongolia, Netherlands, Poland, Ukrainian SSR, USSR, United Kingdom; Spain and Thailand on other grounds), and 4 states voting against (Israel, Turkey, United States and Venezuela). Reports of the United States Delegation, see n. 10, pp. 592–93, 607–8. The treaty was signed by 119 states when opened for signature at Montego Bay on 10 December 1982 for a period of two years. Three additional states, including Japan, signed on 7 February 1983. See Addendum to Depository Notification C.N.279.1982. Treaties-1 (17 Dec. 1982) and Depository Notification C.N.7.1983.Treaties-1 (23 Feb. 1983). As of 9 December 1984, the closing date for signature, 159 states and other entities had signed and the first 13 countries (Bahamas, Belize, Cuba, Fiji, Egypt, Gambia, Ghana, Ivory Coast, Jamaica, Mexico, Philippines, Senegal, Zambia) and the UN Council for Namibia had ratified the Convention (UN Doc. A/39/647). As of 4 November 2009, 159 states have ratified the LOS Convention.

[15] Namely, the Agreement Relating to the Implementation of Part XI of the United Nations Convention on the Law of the Sea of 10 December 1982, done at New York, 28 July 1994, entered into force 28 July 1996 (A/RES/48/263); and the United Nations Agreement for the Implementation of the Provisions of the United Nations Convention on the Law of the Sea of 10 December 1982 relating to the Conservation and Management of Straddling Fish Stocks and Highly Migratory Fish Stocks, adopted on 4 August 1995, entered into force on 11 December 2001 (A/CONF.164/37). For documentation of UN General Assembly Resolutions and materials, see the website of the Division for Ocean Affairs and the Law of the Sea, Office of Legal Affairs, United Nations, at www.un.org/Depts/los (last accessed 25 September 2014).

[16] Philip Allott, 'Power Sharing in the Law of the Sea' (1983) 77 *American Journal of International Law*, 1. Bernardo Zuleta wrote:

> [T]he longest, most ambitious and most innovative endeavor ever undertaken by the community of nations, and ... whatever the ultimate outcome of this

54   CONTEXT: THE ENCLOSURE OF THE SEAS

Indeed, at the time it was difficult to anticipate the fate of the Convention. The regime of deep seabed mining, negotiated at UNCLOS III throughout the 1970s, became a major stumbling block to ratifications and finally to a timely and rapid entry into force of the Convention. The complex and innovative regulation of Part XI of the Convention combined ideas of supranational control and administration, mixed economy, and considerable differential and preferential treatment for LDCs, essentially being based upon the principles of equity and a common heritage for humankind. The concept faced opposition from industrialized countries, especially the United States, mainly because of conflicts with the established perception of intellectual property protection.[17]

> collective effort, it is evident that international law will never be the same again and that the legal regime for the oceans will certainly not be the customary law of the sea as it existed when it commenced.

'The Impact of the Third UN Conference on the Law of the Sea', in C. Buderi and D. Caron (eds.), *Perspectives on U.S. Policy Toward the Law of the Sea: Prelude to the Final Session of the Third U.N. Conference on the Law of the Sea*, Proceedings of a Symposium held in 1982, The Law of the Sea Institute Occasional Paper No. 35 (Honolulu: Law of the Sea Institute, University of Hawaii, 1985), p. 63.

[17] See Jean-Pierre Quéneudec, 'Les Incertitudes de la nouvelle Convention sur le droit de la mer', in Budislav Vukas (ed.), *Essays on the New Law of the Sea* (University of Zagreb, Faculty of Law, 1985), pp. 47–58 (indicating at the time, and rightly, Part XI and Annexes III and IV as the main area of uncertainty in the Convention:

> elles représentent très largement une anticipation, une préfiguration de l'avenir, qui se concrétisera par le passage à la communauté institutionnelle du fond des mers lorsque sera mise sur pied l'Autorité internationale. Une réelle incertitude pèse cependant sur cette perspective, en raison de l'attitude de refus d'un certain nombre de pays industrialisés principalement intéressés par l'exploitation des fonds marins internationaux.
>
> (ibid. at 47)

See generally Markus G. Schmidt, *Common Heritage or Common Burden? The United States Position on the Development of a Regime for Deep Sea-bed Mining in the Law of the Sea Convention* (Oxford: Clarendon Press, 2001); see also for assessments at the time, Elisabeth Mann Borgese, Aldo E. Chircop and Mahinda Peresa, 'The UN Convention on the Law of the Sea: The Cost of Ratification' in E. Mann Borgese et al. (eds.), *Ocean Yearbook* (University of Chicago Press, 1989), vol. VIII, pp. 1–17; David L. Larson, 'When will the UN Convention on the Law of the Sea Come into Effect?' (1989) 20 *Ocean Development and International Law*, 175 (in 1988, only thirty-five states and one other entity had ratified the Convention); Satya N. Nandan, 'The 1982 UN Convention on the Law of the Sea: At a Crossroad' (1989) 20 *Ocean Development and International Law*, 515.

For discussion of the historic, economic and complex legal problems related to deep seabed mining, see inter alia Samuel L. Bleicher, 'The Law Governing Exploitation of Polymetallic Sulfide Deposits from the Seabed' in T. Buergenthal (ed.), *Contemporary Issues in International Law, Essays in Honor of Louis B. John* (Kehl, Strasbourg: N. P. Engel

The Area amounted to one of the most prominent, most elaborate, and most controversial concretizations of the basic tenets of the 1974 New International Economic Order (NIEO) and the 1975 Charter of Economic Rights and Duties of States.[18] However, Western governments

> Publisher, 1984); Jean-Pierre Beurier and Patrick Cadenat, 'Le Contenu économique des normes juridiques dans le droit de la mer contemporain' (1974) 78 *Revue Générale de Droit International Public*, 575; Boleslav A. Boczek, *The Transfer of Marine Technology to Developing Nations in International Law* (The Law of the Sea Institute, Occasional Paper No. 32, 1982); Edward Duncan Brown, 'Freedom of the High Seas Versus the Common Heritage of Mankind: Fundamental Principles in Conflict' (1983) 20 *San Diego Law Review*, 521; Ian Brownlie, 'Legal Status of Natural Resources in International Law'(1979) 162 *Recueil des cours* I, 245; René-Jean Dupuy (ed.), *The Management of Humanity's Resources: The Law of the Sea*, Workshop 29–31 October 1981, Hague Academy of International Law (The Hague, Boston MA: Martinus Nijhoff Publishers, 1982); Jürgen B. Donges, *The Economics of Deep-Sea Mining* (Berlin: Springer-Verlag, 1985); Jens-Lienhard Gaster, *Der Meeresbodenbergbau unter der hohen See: Neuland des Seevölkerrechts und der nationalen Gesetzgebung* (Cologne: Carl Heymanns Verlag, 1987); the extensive and comprehensive work in French on the subject by Alain-Denis Henchoz, *Réglementations nationales et internationales de l'exploration et de l'exploitation des grands fonds marins* (Zurich: Schulthess Polygraphischer Verlag, 1992); Wilhelm A. Kewening, 'Common Heritage of Mankind – politischer Slogan oder völkerrechtlicher Schlüsselbegriff ?' in I. von Münch (ed.), *Staatsrecht, Völkerrecht, Europarecht* (Berlin, New York: de Gruyter, 1981), p. 385: Alexandre Kiss, 'La Notion du patrimoine commun de l'humanité' (1982) 175 *Recueil des cours*, 99; Theodore G. Kronmiller, *The Lawfulness of Deep Seabed Mining*, 2 vols. (Dobbs Ferry NY: Oceana Publications, 1980); Günther Jaenicke, 'The Legal Status of the International Seabed', in R. Bernhardt et al. (eds.), *Völkerrecht als Rechtsordnung, Internationale Gerichtsbarkeit, Menschenrechte, Festschrift für Hermann Mosler* (Berlin, Heidelberg: Springer Verlag, 1983), p. 429; Alan V. Lowe, 'The International Seabed: A Legacy of Mistrust' (1981) 5 *Marine Policy*, 205; Urs Nef, *Das Recht zum Abbau mineralischer Rohstoffe vom Meeresgrund und Meeresuntergrund unter besonderer Berücksichtigung der Stellung der Schweiz* (Zurich: Schulthess Polygraphischer Verlag, 1974); Roderick C. Ogley, *Internationalizing the Seabed* (Aldershot: Gower, 1985); Ernst U. Petersmann, 'Rechtsprobleme der deutschen Interimsgesetzgebung für den Tiefseebergbau' (1981) 41 *Zeitschrift für ausländisches öffentliches Recht und Völkerrecht*, 257; Kurt M. Shusterich, *Resource Management and the Oceans: The Political Economy of Deep Seabed Mining* (Boulder CO: Westview Press, 1982); Alexandra M. Post, *Deep Sea Mining and the Law of the Sea* (Dordrecht: Martinus Nijhoff Publishers, 1983), pp. 33–56; Manjula R. Shyam, *Metals from the Seabed: Prospects for Mining Polymetallic Nodules by India* (New Delhi: Oxford and IBM, 1982).
>
> [18] This holds true even if a link between the NIEO and UNCLOS III was rarely done for the simple reason that both nationally and internationally different parts of the administration were dealing with trade and development on the one hand, and maritime law on the other. For the NIEO, see the Declaration on the Establishment of a New International Economic Order, GA Res. 3201 (S-VI), 6th Spec. Sess. GAOR (1974) Supp. l (A/9559), and the Charter of Economic Rights and Duties of States (CERDS), GA Res. 3281 (XXIX), 29 GAOR 484 (1975), reprinted in 14 ILM (1975), 251 ff.; see Anton Vratusa, 'Convention on the Law of the Sea in the Light of the Struggle for the New International Economic

refrained from ratifying the Convention in the 1980s when it fell out of line with contemporary thinking. This was largely the result of a considerable shift in mainstream economic policy during this period, with a tendency towards a less interventionist approach and general deregulation.

In 1981, the newly inaugurated Reagan Administration undertook a marine policy review, partly for ideological reasons[19] and partly because of strategic and security concerns.[20] Similar reasons led the United Kingdom and the Federal Republic of Germany to follow the United States' policy.[21]

Order' in B. Vukas (ed.), *Essays on the New Law of the Sea* (University of Zagreb, Faculty of Law, 1985), pp. 17–30. For the overall mixed results of UNCLOS III for LDCs see Chapter 3.

[19] See statement of 2 March 1981 by the US Department of State, quoted by Oxman, *The Tenth Session*, n. 11, at 2. For the foundations and the new approach, see the guiding Republican Party Platform complaining that multilateral negotiations have not sufficiently focused attention on US long-term security requirements:

> A pertinent example of this phenomenon is the Law of the Sea Conference, where negotiations have served to inhibit U.S. exploitation of the sea-bed for its abundant mineral resources. Too much concern has been lavished on nations unable to carry out sea-bed mining with insufficient attention paid to gaining American access to it. A Republican Administration will conduct multilateral negotiations in a manner that reflects America's abilities and resources.

Quoted from David L. Larson, 'The Reagan Administration and the Law of the Sea' (1982) 11 *Ocean Development and International Law*, 297, 298. See also Ann L. Hollick, 'U.S. Foreign Policy and the Law of the Sea' (1981) 17 *Virginia Journal of International Law*, 196.

[20] At the time, it was thought that: 'after approximately the years 1900–2000 most of the world's manganese ore will be found in South Africa and the Soviet Union', Leigh S. Ratiner, 'The Deep Seabed Mining Controversy: A Rejoinder', in C. Buderi and D. Caron (eds.), *Perspectives on U.S. Policy Toward the Law of the Sea: Prelude to the Final Session of the Third U.N. Conference on the Law of the Sea*, Proceedings of a Symposium held in 1982, The Law of the Sea Institute Occasional Paper No. 35 (Honolulu: Law of the Sea Institute, University of Hawaii, 1985), pp. 1438, 1441.

[21] For a comprehensive discussion of the consequences of the Western policy review, including the issue of whether it constituted an act of bad faith negotiations, see the results of a 1984 workshop, Jon M. Van Dyke (ed.), *Consensus and Confrontation: The United States and the Law of the Sea Convention* (Honolulu: The Law of the Sea Institute, University of Hawaii, 1984). For a European perspective see Kenneth R. Simmonds, 'The Community's Declaration upon Signature of the U.N. Convention on the Law of the Sea' (1986) 23 *Common Market Law Review*, 521; Alfred H. A. Soon, 'The Position of the EEC towards the LOS Convention', Proceedings of the 84th Annual Meeting (1990) *American Society of International Law*, 278.

The pressure to achieve a less interventionist regime increased during the early 1980s. In 1980–81, seabed mining industries, concerned about the uncertain future of the protracted UNCLOS negotiations, stepped up their pressure for government action. The United States, the United Kingdom and the Federal Republic of Germany (FRG) enacted interim legislation concerning the deep seabed in order to assure legally secured sites for the industry, which was making an enormous investment into the exploration of deep-sea minerals. This approach was eventually followed by other nations, including France, Japan, the Soviet Union, and Italy.

Though termed interim legislation, the legal protection given to mining sites had little in common with the philosophy of common heritage and its concretization in the 1982 Convention. Apart from levies, which in most cases could (but did not need to) be used for international development of common heritage or other development objectives of LDCs, the regime applied by these states reflected traditional policies of co-existence and free exploitation and marketing of resources.[22] In private negotiations with relevant industries, the FRG, France, Britain, and the United States agreed upon mutual principles of site allocation, dispute settlement and reciprocal recognition of mining sites in the Clarion–Clipperton Zone (Pacific Ocean). Subsequent agreements enlarged the circle of states adopting this 'allocation' approach.[23]

---

[22] Unlike the LOS Convention, allocation of sites basically relies on agreed-upon appropriations co-ordinated among mining states and based on reciprocity. No regulation of markets is planned and no obligations of transfer of technology are acknowledged. The establishment of funds in particular in the US, FRG, French, UK and then-Soviet legislation from levies imposed upon mining activities all take up the idea of common heritage of mankind. However, only France and the FRG prescribed a compulsory use of such funds for the purposes of development of LDCs. See Edward Duncan Brown, 'The Impact of Unilateral Legislation on the Future Legal Regime of Deep-Sea Mining' (1982) 20 *Archiv des Völkerrechts*, 148, 165. For initial national deep seabed legislation see 19 ILM 1003 (1980) (United States). For subsequent regulations see 20 ILM 1228 (1981); 'United States, Department of Commerce National and Atmospheric Administration – Further Regulations on Deep Seabed Mining' 21 ILM 867 (1989); 19 ILM 1330 (1980) (Federal Republic of Germany); 20 ILM 1218 (1981) (United Kingdom); (1982) 21 ILM 808 (France); (1982) 21 ILM 551 (Soviet Union); 22 ILM 102 (1983) (Japan); 24 ILM 983 (1985) (Italy). For a discussion of the US, FRG, UK and French legislation see Brown above; Guy de Lacharrière, 'La Loi française sur l'exploration des ressources minerales des grands fonds marin' (1981) 27 *Annuaire Français de Droit International*, 673; Petersmann, n. 17, 267; Gaster, n. 17.

[23] 'Agreement Concerning Interim Arrangements Relating to Polymetallic Nodules of the Deep Sea Bed' 21 ILM 950 (1982); H. S. Lay et al. (eds.), *New Directions in the Law of the Sea* (looseleaf, Dobbs Ferry NY: Oceana Publications, 1973); Belgium-France-Federal

Simultaneously, efforts continued within the Law of the Sea Preparatory Commission as a second 'official' track, dealing with applications from France, India, Japan, and the Soviet Union.[24] By 1987, the allocation of rights to India was complete, and a bridging agreement was successfully reached when the United States and the Soviet Union indirectly agreed upon allocations of mining sites. Remarkably, with the exception of the Indian site, the zones under national jurisdiction remained confidential, with no disclosures allowed concerning the location or size of the sites under exploration, or regarding exploitation by private consortia and national enterprises.[25]

At the time when the regime of deep seabed mining was negotiated at UNCLOS III (spurred on by the assumption that deep seabed exploitation would be necessary to secure sufficient supplies, particularly of manganese nodules), it was reported that new developments and studies had shown that these operations would not be economically feasible until well into the twenty-first century, if ever.[26] According to a panel report published by prominent US scholars in 1988, UNCLOS IV therefore provided an opportunity to renegotiate the concept of deep seabed mining found in the 1982 Convention and to 'present new opportunities to reach general agreement on the Law of the Sea', which is obviously essential for achieving overall stability and predictability of maritime law.[27]

Republic of Germany-Italy-Japan-Netherlands-United Kingdom-United States: Provisional Understanding regarding Deep Seabed Mining, 3 August 1984, in force 2 September 1984 23 ILM 1354 (1984).

[24] See 'Understanding of the Preparatory Commission for the International Sea-Bed Authority and for the International Tribunal for the Law of the Sea for Proceeding with Deep Sea-Bed Applications and Resolving Disputes of Overlapping Claims of Mine Sites (5 September 1986)' 25 ILM 1326 ff. (1986); Statement of Understanding for Proceeding with Deep Sea-Bed Mining Applications (10 April 1987) 26 ILM 1725 (1987).

[25] See 'Belgium-Canada-Italy-Netherlands-Union of Soviet Socialist Republics: Agreement on the Resolution of Practical Problems with Respect to Deep Seabed Mining Areas, 14 August 1987; Exchange of Notes between the United States and the Soviet Union, 14 August 1987' 26 ILM 1505 ff. (1987) For the allocation of the sites to India see decision of the preparatory Commission of 17 August 1987, pp. 1729–35. While this decision was made public, the exact locations of other sites remain secret in accordance with the Agreement on the Preservation of Confidentiality, pp. 1045.

[26] 'Statement by Expert Panel: Deep Seabed Mining and the 1982 Convention on the Law of the Sea' (1988) 82 *American Journal of International Law*, 363.

[27] Ibid. The Panel recommends that all nations:

1. re-evaluate their requirements for a satisfactory mining regime in light of the changed industrial and economic circumstances; and
2. support measures that would remove the obstacle posed by the deep seabed mining issue to widespread entry into force of a comprehensive Law of the Sea Convention.

In order to achieve universal participation in the Convention, the Secretary-General of the United Nations convened informal consultations in July 1990, which aimed to re-evaluate some aspects of the Area regime and its resources. This consultation process lasted from 1990 to 1994, and resulted in a draft agreement regarding the implementation of Part XI of the LOS Convention. The Agreement was immediately opened for signature following its adoption on 28 July 1994 and entered into force two years later.[28] The LOS Convention has subsequently been ratified by many industrialized countries, including the then European Community (European Union), but not yet the United States.[29]

C. Multiple sources of law

The protracted entry into force of the LOS Convention in 1994 made continued reliance necessary, in the meantime, upon a complex variety of interrelated sources. Apart from existing treaties, the main focus of developments during the last decades has been on customary law developments. An active International Court of Justice (ICJ), amongst other fora, has continued to promote the transformation of the provisions and concepts of the Convention (outside Part XI) into customary law in order to increase stability and security. The LOS Convention has also operated

---

See also Stojan Novakovic, 'Could we have Provided for a better United Nations Convention on the Law of the Sea?' in B. Vukas, *Essays on the New Law of the Sea* (University of Zagreb, 1985), pp. 301, 311–12 (recalling Dutch proposals for joint venture operations in deep seabed mining).

[28] UN Doc. A/48/950 (1994). The Resolution and the Agreement Relating to the Implementation of Part XI of the 1982 Convention of the United Nations Convention on the Law of the Sea is reprinted in: (1994) 9 *The International Journal of Marine and Coastal Law*, 59; 'Accord relatif à l'application de la Partie XI de la Convention des Nations Unis sur le droit de la mer du 10 décembre 1982' (1994) *Revue Générale de Droit International Public*, 837. As of January 2000, ninety-six states (including the EC, 1 April 1998) had signed, and seventy-nine states (including the EC, 1 April 1998) had ratified the Agreement, see http://www.un.org/depts/los/doalos_publications/doalos_publications.htm (last accessed 11 August 2014).

[29] The EC ratified the LOS Convention on 1 April 1998; ratification by the United States is still outstanding, despite the previous administration's voiced intent to join the Convention (see National Security Presidential Directive 66/Homeland Security Presidential Directive 25, 9 January 2009, available at www.uscg.mil); the issue of ratification of the LOS Convention is nevertheless still hotly debated by the US public. See David J. Bedermann, 'The Old Isolationism and the New Law of the Sea: Reflections on Advice and Consent for UNCLOS', (2008) 49 *Harvard International Law Journal Online*, 22, www.harvardilj.org/online/126.

as a catalyst for the development of general international maritime law,[30] working as a source of inspiration for state legislation, practice and adjudication to secure the most coherent body of rules possible in the absence of a comprehensive codification. However, even after the Convention's entry into force, many provisions continue to need concretization in practice and through the judicial process, with a number of complex issues, notably the individual rules and the concept of equitable principles of maritime boundary delimitation, remaining difficult to codify. They continue to depend upon state practice and case law under the LOS Convention.

It is important to recognize that the LOS Convention is much more of a constitution in nature and function than a mere contractual, multilateral agreement. The openness and vagueness of many of the Convention's provisions, combined with the duty to negotiate (*pactum de contrahendo/negotiando*), resemble in many respects the nature of national constitutions as basic laws from which additional instruments will flow and depend. Adjudication related to it will show the particular legal and political features of constitutional thinking and reasoning familiar to us from the practice of Western constitutional courts.[31]

---

[30] Jonathan Charney, 'Progressive Development of Public International Law through International Conferences' in C. Buderi and D. Caron (eds.), *Perspectives on U.S. Policy Toward the Law of the Sea: Prelude to the Final Session of the Third U.N. Conference on the Law of the Sea*, Proceedings of a Symposium held in 1982, The Law of the Sea Institute Occasional Paper No. 35 (Honolulu: Law of the Sea Institute, University of Hawaii, 1985), pp. 88, 90 ('Arguably, contributions to general international law may be the only real value of such a conference'). For a survey of sources of law in maritime law, see Hugo Caminos, 'Sources of the Law of the Sea' in R.-J. Dupuy and D. Vignes (eds.), *A Handbook of the New Law of the Sea*, 2 vols. (Dordrecht: Martinus Nijhoff Publishers 1991), vol. I, pp. 29–140.

[31] On the constitutional nature of the Convention, see Bernard Oxman, 'Interest in Transportation, Energy, and Environment' in C. Buderi and D. Caron (eds.), *Perspectives on U.S. Policy Toward the Law of the Sea: Prelude to the Final Session of the Third U.N. Conference on the Law of the Sea*, Proceedings of a Symposium held in 1982, The Law of the Sea Institute Occasional Paper No. 35 (Honolulu: Law of the Sea Institute, University of Hawaii, 1985), p. 95 ('I do want to emphasize that the Convention on the Law of the Sea should be regarded in many respects as a constitutive document rather than as a settlement'). On the vagueness and ambiguity of the Convention (often inherent to constitutions) see Arvid Pardo, 'An Opportunity Lost', in C. Buderi and D. Caron (eds.), *Perspectives on U.S. Policy Toward the Law of the Sea: Prelude to the Final Session of the Third U.N. Conference on the Law of the Sea*, Proceedings of a Symposium held in 1982, The Law of the Sea Institute Occasional Paper No. 35 (Honolulu: Law of the Sea Institute, University of Hawaii, 1985), pp. 68, 70–72. On dispute settlement, as perceived at the time, see A. O. Adede, 'Prolegomena to the Dispute Settlement Part of the Law of the Sea Convention' (1977) 10 *NYU Journal of International Law and Politics*, 253.

International judicial settlement will continue to fulfil its historical role as an important element both for the progressive development of the law and as an important stabilizer of international relations.

Due to the enclosure movement, cases relating to the allocation of maritime jurisdiction have predominated amongst the cases coming before the ICJ over recent decades. The field emerged as one of the most prominent areas of international dispute settlement, in particular before the ICJ. The dynamics of maritime law also introduced a unique series of cases to ad hoc arbitration and conciliation. These cases not only contribute to, and reshape important aspects of, the law of the sea;[32] they are equally important to the development of international law in general, and particularly to the doctrine of equity. In 1951, the *Anglo-Norwegian Fisheries* case laid down important foundations for the enlargement of the exclusive fishing zones.[33] The 1974 *Fisheries Jurisdiction* cases represented another landmark promoting the advent of the EEZ.[34] The 1984 *Gulf of Maine* case between the United States and Canada[35] was the first judgment by a Chamber of the ICJ dealing with the EEZ, and thus providing authority for the definition and structure of that zone and its relations to the continental shelf, which had first been expounded upon by the Court in the 1969 *North-Sea*

---

[32] See Nagendra Singh, 'Codification and Progressive Development of International Law: The Role of the International Court of Justice' (1978) 18 *American Journal of International Law*, 1, 11–16; Paolo Mengozzi, 'The International Court of Justice. The United Nations Conference and the Law of the Sea' (1972) 3 *Italian Yearbook of International Law*, 92. For a detailed account of the cases, see Chapter 6. They triggered a substantial body of literature, in particular Peter J. Cook and Chris M. Carleton (eds.), *Continental Shelf Limits: The Scientific and Legal Interface* (Oxford University Press, 2000); Robert Kolb, *Case Law on Equitable Maritime Delimitation/Jurisprudence sur les délimitations maritimes selon l'équité; Digest and Commentaries/Répertoire et commentaires* (The Hague: Martinus Nijhoff Publishers, 2003); Nuno Sérgio Marques Antunes, *Towards the Conceptualisation of Maritime Delimitation, Legal and Technical Aspects of a Political Process* (Leiden: Martinus Nijhoff Publishers, 2003); Rainer Lagoni and Daniel Vignes (eds.), *Maritime Delimitation* (Leiden: Martinus Nijhoff Publishers, 2006); Seoung-Yong Hong and Jon M. Van Dyke (eds.), *Maritime Boundary Disputes, Settlement Processes, and the Law of the Sea* (Leiden: Martinus Nijhoff Publishers, 2009).
[33] *Fisheries Case (United Kingdom v. Norway)*, Judgment, ICJ Reports 1951, p. 116. This and subsequent cases are discussed in Chapter 6 and passim.
[34] *Fisheries Jurisdiction (United Kingdom v. Iceland)*, Merits, Judgment, ICJ Reports 1974, p. 3; *Fisheries Jurisdiction (Federal Republic of Germany v. Iceland)*, Merits, Judgment, ICJ Reports 1974, p. 175.
[35] *Case Concerning Delimitation of the Maritime Boundary in the Gulf of Maine Area (Canada v. United States of America)*, Judgment, ICJ Reports 1984, p. 246.

Continental Shelf cases fifteen years earlier.[36] The law of the continental shelf and its delimitation was further refined by the 1978 *Aegean Continental Shelf* case,[37] the 1982 *Tunisia v. Libya Continental Shelf* case[38] and the 1985 *Libya v. Malta Continental Shelf* case,[39] as well as all of the *Intervention* cases,[40] the 1992 *Maritime Frontier Dispute* (El Salvador v. Honduras, Nicaragua intervening)[41] and the 1993 *Jan Mayen* case.[42] Additionally, the 1977 *Anglo-French Channel* arbitration,[43] the 1981 *Dubai v. Sharjah* award (unpublished),[44] the 1985 *Guinea v. Guinea-Bissau* arbitration[45] and the 1992 *St Pierre and Miquelon* Award[46] have made important contributions to the case law prior to the entering into force of the LOS Convention. Since 1994, the case law has been enriched by the 1999 *Eritrea v. Yemen* Award (Second Stage),[47] the 2001 *Qatar v. Bahrain* case,[48] the 2002 *Cameroon v. Nigeria* case,[49] the 2006 *Barbados v. Trinidad and Tobago*

---

[36] *North Sea Continental Shelf (Federal Republic of Germany v. Denmark; Federal Republic of Germany v. Netherlands)*, Judgment, ICJ Reports 1969, p. 3.

[37] *Aegean Sea Continental Shelf (Greece v. Turkey)*, Judgment, ICJ Reports 1978, p. 3; see also *Aegean Sea Continental Shelf (Greece v. Turkey)*, Interim Protection, Order of 11 September 1976, ICJ Reports 1976, p. 3.

[38] *Continental Shelf (Tunisia v. Libyan Arab Jamahiriya)*, Judgment, ICJ Reports 1982, p. 18.

[39] *Continental Shelf (Libyan Arab Jamahiriya v. Malta)*, Judgment, ICJ Reports 1985, p. 13.

[40] *Continental Shelf (Tunisia v. Libyan Arab Jamahiriya)*, Application to Intervene, ICJ Reports 1981, p. 3; *Continental Shelf (Libyan Arab Jamahiriya v. Malta)*, Application to Intervene, Judgment, ICJ Reports 1984.

[41] *Land, Island and Maritime Frontier Dispute (El Salvador v. Honduras: Nicaragua intervening)*, Judgment, ICJ Reports 1992, p. 351.

[42] *Maritime Delimitation in the Area between Greenland and Jan Mayen (Denmark v. Norway)*, Judgment, ICJ Reports 1993, p. 38.

[43] *Arbitration between the United Kingdom of Great Britain and Northern Ireland and the French Republic on the Delimitation of the Continental Shelf* (Judgments of 30 June 1977 and 14 March 1978) reprinted in 18 ILM 397 (1979).

[44] *Award in the Matter of an Arbitration concerning the Border between the Emirates of Dubai and Sharjah* (typescript 1981).

[45] *Tribunal Arbitral pour la délimitation de la frontière maritime Guinée/Guinée-Bissau*, 14 February 1985, (1985) 89 *Revue Générale de Droit International Public*, 484; 'Guinea/Guinea-Bissau: Dispute Concerning Delimitation of the Maritime Boundary' (trans. 1986) 25 ILM 251.

[46] *Court of Arbitration for the Delimitation of Maritime Areas between Canada and France: Decision in Case Concerning Delimitation of Maritime Areas*, (1992) 31 ILM 1145.

[47] 'Award of the Arbitral Tribunal in the Second Stage (Maritime Delimitation) in the Matter of an Arbitration between Eritrea and Yemen (*Eritrea v. Republic of Yemen*) 17 December 1999' reprinted in 40 ILM 983 (2001).

[48] *Maritime Delimitation and Territorial Questions between Qatar and Bahrain (Qatar v. Bahrain)*, Merits, Judgment of 16 March 2001, ICJ Reports 2001, p. 40.

[49] *Land and Maritime Boundary between Cameroon and Nigeria (Cameroon v. Nigeria: Equatorial Guinea Intervening)*, Judgment of 10 October 2010, ICJ Reports 2002, p. 303.

Award,[50] the 2007 *Guyana* v. *Suriname* Award,[51] the 2007 *Nicaragua* v. *Honduras* case,[52] the 2009 *Romania* v. *Ukraine Maritime Delimitation in the Black Sea* case[53] and the 2014 *Maritime Dispute (Chile* v. *Peru)*,[54] which all further enhanced the establishment of a methodology of maritime boundary delimitation and the doctrines of the underlying zones. Finally, conciliation and domestic law courts contributed equally to the law of the new enclosure of the seas and to related long-distance maritime boundary delimitation.[55] Analysis of the aforementioned cases will provide the core material for consideration throughout this book.

D. A historical perspective

From an historical perspective, the ongoing enclosure of the seas amounts to nothing less than a sophisticated renaissance of the doctrine of *mare clausum*, in which the seas were first globally divided. This doctrine prevailed in Europe throughout the seventeenth and eighteenth centuries. Fundamental changes were brought about not so much through the writings of Grotius in the early seventeenth century,[56] as

---

[50] *Award of the Arbitral Tribunal in the Matter of an Arbitration Between Barbados and the Republic of Trinidad and Tobago (Barbados* v. *Republic of Trinidad and Tobago)* 11 April 2006 reprinted in 45 ILM 800 (2006).

[51] *Arbitral Tribunal Constituted Pursuant to Article 287, and in Accordance with Annex VII, of the United Nations Convention on the Law of the Sea in the Matter of an Arbitration between Guyana and Suriname*, Award of 17 September 2007 (hereinafter *Guyana* v. *Suriname* Award). The Award and pleadings are available at www.pca-cpa.org (last accessed 25 September 2014).

[52] *Territorial and Maritime Dispute between Nicaragua and Honduras in the Caribbean Sea (Nicaragua* v. *Honduras)*, Judgment, ICJ Reports 2007, p. 659.

[53] *Maritime Delimitation in the Black Sea (Romania* v. *Ukraine)*, Judgment, ICJ Reports 2009, p. 61.

[54] *Maritime Dispute (Chile* v. *Peru)*, Judgment, ICJ Reports 2014, p. ___ www.icj-cij.org/docket/files/137/17930.pdf (last accessed 17 February 2014).

[55] See Chapter 6(III).

[56] Hugo Grotius, *Mare Liberum (The Freedom of the Seas or the Right which belongs to the Dutch to take part in the East Indian Trade)* (1609) (R. v. Deman Magoffin trans., 1916). As is well known, the book emerged from a legal brief (a work later dismissed by its author 'as a young man's book written out of fierce passion for the Fatherland') in defence and support of claims of the Dutch East India Company which sought to gain rights of free navigation in the Indian Ocean and other Eastern seas and to trade with India and the East Indies politically dominated by Spain and Portugal and commercial monopoly. Some years later, in lawyerly manner, Grotius denied freedom of the seas, claiming and defending a Dutch monopoly of trade with the spice islands against the British. See Ram P. Anand, 'The Influence of History on the Literature of International Law' in

through the shifting balance of power within Europe and rapid economic developments approximately 200 years later. Unlike Asia, which is said to have enjoyed a long tradition of freedom of navigation and unobstructed trade,[57] European policies of *mare liberum* and 'deregulation' only began to prevail in the early nineteenth century, after Britain had established itself as the leading maritime and trading power. Colonialism and expansionism, which followed the industrial revolution, clearly favoured the freedom of the seas.[58] After all, every coastal state is entirely, or to a significant extent, dependent upon navigation through the waters of neighbouring states for access to the rest of the world, as well as for the maintenance of its security interests.[59] But the exhaustibility of resources has always been a major argument against a 'laissez-faire' regime.[60] As O'Connell observed, apart from their intellectual foundations, '(t)he arguments pro and contra the freedom of the seas then and now ... are strikingly similar, and, despite its archaic phrasing, the 17th Century debate is surprisingly contemporary in its character.'[61] The process of enclosing the seas, both now and in the future, is therefore nothing new, and can be seen to reflect the tidal movements of history.

Having said that, however, it is evident that contemporary problems and interests are much more numerous and complex than those facing scholars and statesmen of the seventeenth century: there are more known

R. Macdonald and D. Johnston (eds.), *The Structure and Process of International Law: Essays in Legal Philosophy, Doctrine and Theory* (The Hague, Boston MA: Martinus Nijhoff, 1983), pp. 341, 345–7; H. Gary Knight, *The Life and Works of Hugo Grotius* (London: Sweet & Maxwell, 1925), pp. 80–85, 136–43; see also Hans Klee, *Hugo Grotius and Johannes Selden, Von den geistigen Ursprüngen des Kampfes um die Meeresfreiheit* (Bern: Paul Haupt, 1946).

[57] See Anand, n. 56, p. 343, recalling that Grotius relied on Asian practice in support of *mare liberum*. See also Ram P. Anand, 'Maritime Practices and Custom in South East Asia Until 1600 AD and the Modern Law of the Sea', (1881) *International and Comparative Law Quarterly*, 443–7; and Elizabeth Van Wie Davis, *China and the Law of the Sea Convention* (Lewiston: Edwin Mellen Press, 1995).

[58] For a concise history, see Daniel P. O'Connell in Ivan Shearer (ed.), *The International Law of the Sea*, 2 vols. (Oxford: Clarendon Press, 1982), vol. I, p. 126; see also Anand, *Origin and Development of the Law of the Sea, Publications on Ocean Development*, n. 1, p. 356.

[59] See Oxman, 'The Territorial Temptation: A Siren Song at Sea', n. 1, 837, see also pp. 841–2.

[60] The early theorists of *mare clausum* denied the inexhaustibility of fish resources, while the champions of freedom of the sea, in particular Grotius, argued on the assumption of the inexhaustibility of the sea, as opposed to the limited stocks in lakes and rivers and wild animals on the land. See Douglas M. Johnston, *The International Law of Fisheries: A Framework for Policy-Oriented Inquiries* (New Haven CT, London: Yale University Press, 1965), pp. 157, 170–1, 321–2.

[61] See O'Connell, n. 58, p. 2.

uses of the sea and its resources. Today they extend beyond the exploitation of oil and gas and include energy production (wind and tidal) and genetic resources in the age of biotechnology. States pursue interests of free access and controlled management simultaneously, depending on the resources at stake: economic and military interests may be at variance; the North–South divide introduced new issues of distributive justice and equity, hardly considered before. Ultimately, the enclosure of the seas and their resources remains the most important area of politically and economically feasible national expansion left in the twenty-first century. This provides both an incentive for national ocean-grabbing and a warning to stop it. And it is this diversity of interests and concerns that explains why the contemporary shapes of *mare clausum* cannot be readily compared with the regimes applied in seventeenth-century Europe.

Given the scope, intensity and, in terms of international law, the relatively short period of change, largely during the second part of the twentieth century, the process of enclosing the seas could be seen as something of a revolution. At the same time it has been a silent revolution. Despite the fact that the efforts to reshape the global framework that affects around 71 per cent of the globe became one of the most prominent issues of diplomacy and international law during the 1970s, it is remarkable that all of the fundamental shifts occurred in an almost silent manner. When this process is compared to the arms race during the Cold War, the perception of global warming and environmental degradation, multilateral trade negotiations, war and peace, and other central issues in international relations, the reform of maritime law received comparatively little media coverage and publicity. World public opinion and general debate has been left widely uninformed and remains of little impact in what may appear to be the merely technical and legal issues of maritime law, without much appeal to the international political process. Exceptions may be the recent surge of claims in the South China Sea, in particular relating to the Natuna Islands, the Spratly Islands and the Paracel Islands,[62] and the interest in Arctic Ocean governance where legal uncertainties have surfaced coinciding with the public perception of

---

[62] See Gregory B. Poling, *The South China Sea in Focus: Clarifying the Limits of Maritime Dispute* (Lanham MD, Boulder CO, New York, Toronto, Plymouth UK: Center for Strategic & International Studies, Roman & Littlefield, 2013) available at https://csis.org/files/publication/130717_Poling_SouthChinaSea_Web.pdf (last accessed 4 September 2014).

climate change as demonstrated in the melting of the polar ice.[63] Rarely has a struggle for resources had such an important long-term effect, but yet attained so little attention outside the circles of the governments, professionals and businesses involved.

---

[63] See David D. Caron, 'Climate Change, Sea Level Rise and the Coming Uncertainty in Oceanic Boundaries: A Proposal to Avoid Conflict' in S.-Y. Hong and J. Van Dyke (eds.), *Maritime Boundary Disputes, Settlement Processes and the Law of the Sea* (Leiden, Boston MA: Martinus Nijhoff Publishers, 2009); see also the Ilulissat Declaration, Adopted at the Arctic Conference, Illulisat, Greenland, 28 May 2008, at para. 2, available at www.ocean law.org/downloads/arctic/Ilulissat_Declaration pdf (last accessed 4 September 2014).

2

The new maritime zones: evolution and legal foundations

I. Horizontally shared zones and quasi-territoriality

Before turning to the subject of maritime boundary delimitation properly speaking and the core functions of equity, it seems appropriate to describe and analyse the scope and legal nature of the new zones of the continental shelf and the exclusive economic zone (EEZ) which the silent revolution brought about. Description, development and a legal analysis will be of importance to subsequent discussions of the boundary problem, since equitable principles and the operation of delimitation are influenced by the very foundations, the purpose and the legal nature of the two zones involved. No further discussion of the law of the Area will be provided except those aspects relating to seaward maritime boundary delimitation. The following discussion therefore excludes zones which the United Nations Convention on the Law of the Sea (LOS Convention) placed under supranational jurisdiction but which are in actual fact mainly used on the basis of mutually agreed appropriation of the resources by mining states.

Though different in many respects, the new zones of the continental shelf and the EEZ show important conceptual similarities. Unlike the territorial sea, they constitute zones of partial jurisdiction. This jurisdiction is limited to specific resources and activities. States have exclusive rights to these particular resources from the outset. As a result, these resources can no longer be understood in the traditional terms of *res communis* or *res nullius*, as being open to appropriation on the basis of free access or acquisition under effective and continuous control. At the same time, the exercise of these exclusive rights has to be reconciled with rights shared by other subjects and exercised within the same region, which requires a careful balance of interests. Since the zones are related to specific resources, they do not reflect the established territorial concepts of full sovereignty typical for *terra firma*. They cannot be perceived in terms of the classical distinction between the territorial and the high seas.

It will be seen that the debate on the EEZ was concluded with the broad acceptance that the EEZ possesses a legal nature *sui generis*; a characterization that is equally appropriate for the continental shelf, although jurisdiction over resources is differently allocated in the two zones.

Legally, the zones only assign sovereignty or jurisdiction over those resources within a geographically defined space. As discussed above, this is due to the existence of a wide range of simultaneous, overlapping interests which the law must reconcile. Even after the entry into force of the LOS Convention, the widely shared historical perception of *mare liberum* still influences the question of balancing claims by coastal states for exclusive jurisdiction over non-living and living resources within the continental shelf and the EEZ respectively. What has emerged is a notion of object-related, functional rights and horizontally shared zones (Allott).[1] The Chamber of the ICJ initially expressed this concept in the *Gulf of Maine* case. The Chamber stated that the continental shelf and the EEZ both entail:

> different forms of partial jurisdiction, i.e. the 'sovereign rights' which, under current international law, both treaty-law and general law, coastal States are recognised to have in the marine and submarine areas lying outside the outer limit of their respective territorial seas, up to defined limits.[2]

In other words, a particular state or entity does not have exclusive jurisdiction encompassing all the activities occurring at a particular location outside its territorial seas. Despite vast appropriation by coastal states, oceans and enclosed seas lying outside the territorial sea essentially remain common space, with all the inherent problems of co-ordination, co-existence and co-operation which accompany shared areas. Activities such as fishing, mining or drilling may conflict with commercial or military activities and vice versa. Legally, there are no easy answers as to which group of activities deserves priority over the other.

Politically and historically, the concept of subject-related, functional rights and horizontally shared zones is a compromise, which attempts to

---

[1] Philip Allott coined the term 'horizontally shared zone', Philip Allott, 'Power Sharing in the Law of the Sea' (1983) 77 *The American Journal of International Law*, 1, 15. The notion of functional rights is primarily used with regard to the EEZ, 'in the sense that (the coastal state) can only exercise those powers which are necessary for the total, exclusive, and rational exploitation of resources', J. C. Lupinacci, 'The Legal Status of the Exclusive Economic Zone in the 1982 Convention on the Law of the Sea' in O. F. Vicuña (ed.), *The Exclusive Economic Zone: A Latin American Perspective* (Boulder CO: Westview Press, 1984), p. 109. The notion of functional rights can be applied equally to shelf rights.

[2] *Delimitation of the Maritime Boundary in the Gulf of Maine Area (Canada v. United States of America)*, Judgment, ICJ Reports 1984, p. 265, para. 19.

balance divergent interests among maritime nations. Proposals to expand jurisdiction over marine spaces into all-encompassing rights of coastal states were rejected by marine powers. Historically, their dependency on access to foreign waters outweighed exclusive jurisdictional aspirations in domestic waters.[3] The situation is still similar today, with military powers depending on global mobility and thus the freedom of the seas in the EEZs of other states, as well as the right of transit passage through straits connecting EEZs or the right of archipelagic sea lanes passage.[4] The enclosure movement only progressed further when national claims to establish jurisdiction over natural resources were reconciled with international rights of communication, both civilian and military. However, the existence of such a compromise should not obscure the realization that in practical terms the legal concept of horizontally shared zones closely resembles that of territorial sovereignty.

In the 1978 *Aegean Sea Continental Shelf* case, the International Court of Justice (ICJ) recognized that since the principles used to determine the expanses of the shelf and its delimitation bear a close relationship to the shape of the territory of a coastal state, 'a dispute regarding entitlement to and delimitation of areas of continental shelf tends by its very nature to be one relating to territorial status'.[5] Quite correctly, the Court did not conclude that the shelf is a territorial

---

[3] Bernard H. Oxman, 'The Territorial Temptation: A Siren Song at Sea' (2006) 100 *American Journal of International Law*, 830.
[4] Ibid., 840–1. Both the exercise of collective self-defence and collective security under the United Nations Charter, including enforcement, peacekeeping and humanitarian operations, continue to rest on the assumption of global mobility.Ibid., 840–1 and note 51. Thus far, global mobility is a predicate of the international security system as it exists at present and for the foreseeable future. Seeibid., 840.
[5] *Aegean Sea Continental Shelf (Greece v. Turkey)*, Judgment, ICJ Reports 1978, p. 36, para. 86. The Court was bound to address the issue of the legal status of the continental shelf because of a Greek reservation in accordance with Art. 39, para. 2, General Act for the Pacific Settlement of International Disputes 1928. The reservation excluded jurisdiction of the Court, inter alia, for 'disputes related to the territorial status of Greece, including disputes relating to its rights of sovereignty over its ports and lines of communication', ibid., p. 20, para. 48. Greece (plaintiff) argued that this reservation did not apply since the continental shelf is not a territorial concept. The Court, however, rejected the argument, presumably to avoid a judgment on the merits for political reasons. In a broad, ahistoric and controversial interpretation, it concluded that 'territorial status' is a generic term, which follows new legal developments, including the continental shelf, ibid., pp. 30–8, paras. 71–90. But see also ibid., pp. 62 and 66–71, paras. 10–17 (Judge de Castro in dissent, supporting a narrow interpretation of reservations); Rudolf Bernhardt, 'Das Urteil des internationalen Gerichtshofs im Ägäis-Streit' in I. von Münch and H.-J. Schlochauer (eds.), *Staatsrecht – Völkerrecht – Europarecht: Festschrift für Hans-Jürgen Schlochauer zum 75. Geburtstag am 28. März 1981* (Berlin, New York: Walter de Gruyter, 1981), p. 175

concept *per se*. It is evident from the Court's definition, however, that the problems related to the zone are strikingly similar to those of territoriality and this is particularly true with regard to the delimitation of boundaries. The law has to satisfy similar needs both on land and at sea:

> Whether it is a land frontier or a boundary line in the continental shelf that is in question, the process is essentially the same, and inevitably involves the same element of stability and permanence, and is subject to the rule excluding boundary agreements from fundamental change of circumstances.[6]

It is submitted that, *a fortiori*, the same holds true for the delimitation of the EEZ. To the degree that it overlaps with the shelf, the EEZ encompasses virtually all of the economically interesting activities except for communications (navigation, over-flight, submarine cables and pipelines). Equally, drilling or mining activities by their very nature entail the almost exclusive use of a given geographic area during the time for which these activities are conducted. So, almost inevitably, the allocation of a site for exploitation effectively permits virtually exclusive usage of the ocean space concerned. National legislatures tended to expand their jurisdiction to their benefit when confronted with conflicting interests, so long as no consensual legal regime of the EEZ was established in international law in force. Such decisions led to the voicing of fears of a 'territorialization' of the EEZ.[7] In conclusion, it seems fair to say that the new zones amount to quasi-territorial, national concepts, both practically and politically, despite the absence of full sovereignty exercised by a single subject.

II. The continental shelf zone

A. Description and development

Geographically, the continental shelf consists roughly of the tectonic terraces between continents, islands and the deep seabed (abyssal plains). These terraces are generally conceived as a model of three different zones: the continental shelf itself; the continental slope; and the continental rise.

(opposing dynamic interpretation of the reservation since it may withdraw issues from the Court's jurisdiction that had previously been subjected to it).
[6] See ICJ Reports 1978, pp. 35–6, para. 85.
[7] F. Orrego Vicuña, 'La Zone économique exclusive' (1987) 199 *Recueil des Cours* (1986/IV) 10, 120.

It should be noted, however, that no uniform terminology has been established; these terms are used here in a merely descriptive manner.

(i) The *continental shelf* consists of a relatively narrow and shallow platform with depths generally between 130 m and 200 m (other data speak of 130 m, 72 fathoms on average).[8] In some places it is as shallow as 50 m, in others as deep as 500 m. The shelf covers approximately 7.5 per cent (7.6 per cent) of all submarine soil which in itself amounts to some 18 per cent of the globe's *terra firma* and 5 per cent of the overall surface. Comprising 11 million square miles (27 million km2), the combined area of shelves equal the size of the entire African continent. Together, the shelf and slope form the continental terrace.

(ii) Adjacent to the terrace and linked by the shelf edge, the *continental slope* descends at an average angle of 3 to 4 degrees to depths of 1,500 m to 3,500 m (others: 1,500 m, 2,000 m on average). This zone extends 40 km to 50 km seaward.

(iii) The *continental rise* makes a gentle decline seaward from its border with the continental slope. The rise reaches the deep seabed at depths of 15,000 feet to 17,000 feet or 1,500 m to 5,000 m according to others (5,000 m on average). The terrace plus the rise constitute the continental margin.

While the concept of the shelf originally only referred to the first zone mentioned, the term now generally includes all three. Strictly speaking, it would therefore be appropriate to refer to a continental margin zone (CMZ). However, the traditional term shows considerable persistence, remaining constant while its contents change. The wider notion of the continental shelf is now firmly established in law and was restated in Article 76 of the LOS Convention.

The discovery and technological exploitability of offshore gas and oil deposits in the continental shelves incited claims of national jurisdiction over the soil and subsoil of these parts of the high seas, as coastal states

---

[8] Data from Ross D. Eckert, *The Enclosure of Ocean Resources: Economics and the Law of the Sea* (Stanford CA: Hoover Institution Press, 1979), pp. 20–1. Figures in brackets from Ulf-Dieter Klemm, 'Die seewärtige Grenze des Festlandsockels. Geschichte, Entwicklung und lex lata eines seevölkerrechtlichen Grundproblems' in H. Mosler and R. Bernhardt (eds.), *Beiträge zum ausländischen öffentlichen Recht und Völkerrecht, Band 68* (Berlin, Heidelberg, New York: Springer, 1976), pp. 5–6; Bernd Rüster, *Die Rechtsordnung des Festlandsockels* (Berlin: Duncker und Humblot, 1977), p. 83. Daniel Patrick O'Connell (I. A. Shearer, ed.), *The International Law of the Sea*, 2 vols. (Oxford: Clarendon Press, 1982–84), vol. I, pp. 443–4.

sought to secure control over these resources and the revenues they would bring, as well as seeking to protect them from 'foreign' exploitation.[9] Though not the first claim of its kind,[10] the 1945 Truman Proclamation[11] is generally considered to be the starting point of the

[9] Ibid., and Edward Duncan Brown, *Sea-Bed Energy and Minerals: The International Legal Regime*, 2 vols. (The Hague: Martinus Nijhoff Publishers, 1992), vol. I; Edward Duncan Brown, *The Legal Regime of Hydrospace*, published under the auspices of the London Institute of World Affairs (London: Stevens, 1971), pp. 3–78; Robin R. Churchill and Alan V. Lowe, *The Law of the Sea* (Manchester University Press, 1983), pp. 108–22; René-Jean Dupuy, 'The Sea under National Competence' in René-Jean Dupuy and Daniel Vignes (eds.), *A Handbook on the New Law of the Sea*, 2 vols. (Dordrecht: Martinus Nijhoff, 1991), vol. I, pp. 247–308; Emmanuel Gounaris (Günther Doeker, ed.), *Die völkerrechtliche und aussenpolitische Bedeutung der Kontinentalshelf-Doktrin in der Staatenpraxis Griechenlands, der Bundesrepublik Deutschland und der Deutschen Demokratischen Republik* (Frankfurt am Main, Bern, Las Vegas NV: Peter Lang, 1979); Emmanuel Gounaris, 'The Extension and Delimitation of Sea Areas Under the Sovereignty, Sovereign Rights and Jurisdiction of Coastal States' in B. Vukas (ed.), *Essays on the New Law of the Sea* (University of Zagreb, 1985), pp. 85–98; D. N. Hutchinson, 'The Seaward Limit to the Continental Shelf Jurisdiction in Customary International Law' (1986) 56 *British Yearbook of International Law*, 111; Marcus L. Jewett, 'The Evolution of the Legal Regime of the Continental Shelf' (1984) 22 *Canadian Yearbook of International Law*, 153; Myres S. McDougal and William T. Burke, *The Public Order of the Oceans* (New Haven CT, London: Yale University Press, 1962), pp. 630–729; Jean-François Pulvenis, 'The Continental Shelf Definition and Rules Applicable to Resources' in René-Jean Dupuy and Daniel Vignes (eds.), *A Handbook on the New Law of the Sea*, 2 vols. (Dordrecht: Martinus Nijhoff, 1991), vol. I, pp. 315–75; Vicente M. Rangel, 'Le Plateau Continental dans la Convention de 1982 sur le Droit de la Mer' (1985) 194 *Recueil des Cours*, 267; see Rüster, n. 8. Peter N. Swan, *Ocean Oil and Gas Drilling and the Law* (Dobbs Ferry NY: Oceana Publications, 1979); Charles Vallée, *Le Plateau Continental dans le droit positif actuel* (Paris: Editions A. Pedone, 1971).

[10] The first claims date back to the beginning of the twentieth century. In 1916, Odon de Buen, a Portuguese lawyer, claimed the extension of territorial seas to the shelf in view of the rich fisheries in its shallow waters. See Jacques Vigne, *Le Rôle des intérêts économiques dans l'évolution du droit de la mer* (Geneva: Institut Universitaire Des Hautes Etudes Internationales, 1971), p. 32. Among the first manifestations of claims related to the exploitation of mineral resources were those to extended zones by Louisiana and Texas in the early 1940s. Compare *United States v. Louisiana*, 339 US 699 (1947), *United States v. Texas*, 339 US 707 (1950) (both cases without mentioning the shelf doctrine); and the 1942 Boundary Agreement between the United Kingdom, on behalf of Trinidad and Tobago, and Venezuela 'Related to the Submarine Areas' of the Gulf of Paria, 205 LNTS 122. See also E. J. Cosford, 'The Continental Shelf 1910–1945' (1958) 4 *McGill Law Journal*, 245; F. V. Garcia-Amador, 'The Latin American Contribution to the Development of the Law of the Sea' (1974) 68 *American Journal of International Law*, 33; see Rüster, n. 8, p. 133 ff. For an account of declarations see also *Maritime Dispute (Chile v. Peru)*, Judgment of 27 January 2014, ICJ Rep 2014 ___ para. 112 ss.

[11] 'Proclamation No. 2667, Policy of the United States with Respect to the Natural Resources of the Subsoil and Sea Bed of the Continental Shelf, 28 Oct. 1945' (1965), reprinted in Marjorie M. Whiteman, *Digest of International Law* (Paris: Editions du Centre National

post-war enclosure movement.[12] As a policy in the tradition of the *Monroe doctrine*, it reflected the traditional interests and attitudes of the United States as a regional power, at the time. Its impact on international law, however, showed the emergence of the United States as the dominant power of the post-war years. Rarely has a single, unilateral statement by an individual state exerted such an influence on legal developments. Many states were immediately encouraged by the US policy to proclaim similar aspirations during the 1950s and 1960s,[13] leading to the perception of instant customary law.[14] Significantly enough, the proclamation has later prevented the United States from protesting effectively against the much more comprehensive claims for full and territorial sovereignty by Latin American states in the 1950s.[15] Many years later, such claims eventually resulted in the compromise of the 200-mile EEZ being reached.

The concept of the continental shelf was established in customary international law within a remarkably short period of time. The interests of coastal states were widely concordant, at the expense of land- and shelf-locked states, which largely failed to influence the development of the law in this field.[16] Moreover, unilateral legislation by pioneering states tended to increase competition in shelf areas that were as yet unregulated, consequently developing into a snowball effect.

Even in 1951, the *Abu Dhabi* arbitration still concluded that 'there are in this field so many ragged ends and unfilled blanks, so much that is merely tentative and exploratory.'[17] Comparable views prevailed at the

---

de la Recherche Scientifique, 1963–1973), vol. IV, 740, 756. For the twin proclamation on fisheries see 4 *Digest of International Law*, 954. For text see text accompanying n. 37.

[12] See the account of the proclamation by the ICJ in *Maritime Boundary Dispute (Peru v. Chile)*, Judgment of 27 January 2014, ICJ Reports 2014, ___, para. 113–15; Makhdoom Ali Khan, 'The Juridical Concept of the Continental Shelf' (1985) 38 *Pakistan Horizon*, 21.

[13] See e.g. Jewett, n. 9, pp. 157–64; see also Ali A. El-Hakim, *The Middle Eastern States and the Law of the Sea* (Manchester University Press, 1979), p. 31 ff.

[14] Restatement (third) of the Foreign Relations Law of the United States § 102 reporters' note 2 (1987).

[15] See Ann L. Hollick, 'U.S. Ocean Policy: The Truman Proclamation' (1981) 17 *Virginia Journal of International Law*, 23; Ann L. Hollick, 'U.S. Foreign Policy and the Law of the Sea' (1981) 17 *Virginia Journal of International Law*, 196.

[16] Stephen C. Vascianne, *Land Locked and Geographically Disadvantaged States in the International Law of the Sea* (Oxford: Clarendon Press, 1990), pp. 109–11.

[17] *Petroleum Development Ltd. v. Sheik of Abu Dhabi* (1951), reprinted in 18 *International Law Reports*, 144, 155. See also *Petroleum Development (Qatar) v. Ruler of Qatar* (1951), reprinted in 18 *International Law Reports*, 161.

time within the International Law Commission (ILC)[18] and the International Law Association (ILA).[19] By the time of the first United Nations Conference on the Law of the Sea (UNCLOS I) in 1958, the customary nature of the concept was still somewhat controversial, and the conference dealt with it neither as a matter of codification nor of law-in-making.[20] The ambiguity of the state of the law in 1958 was expressed by the ICJ when it held that the first three Articles of the 1958 Shelf Convention had been 'regarded as reflecting, or as crystallising, received or at least emergent rules of customary international law relative to the continental shelf'.[21] By the late 1960s, however, the concept of the continental shelf was clearly established within general international law.[22]

B. The scope of shelf rights

The legal concept of the continental shelf vests exclusive rights to explore and exploit the natural, non-movable resources on and in the soil of the shelf in the coastal state.[23] As discussed before, these rights do not establish exclusive and territorial sovereignty over the soil. Activities which are not related to these resources, such as military surveillance and monitoring installations, are allowed, so long as they are compatible with the exercise of the coastal state's rights to exploit the shelf.[24]

---

[18] See (1950) *Yearbook of the International Law Commission* II, 50; (1951) *Yearbook of the International Law Commission* II, 100; see Jewett, n. 9, p. 164.

[19] See ILA, 'Report of the Fifty-Sixth Conference', Edinburgh, 1954, 425, 434, para. 16 (majority of Committee 'not prepared to say that there exists any customary practice on the subject which qualifies to be generally accepted as law').

[20] See Zdenek J. Slouka, *International Custom and the Continental Shelf* (The Hague: Martinus Nijhoff, 1968); Jewett, n. 9, p. 169.

[21] *North Sea Continental Shelf (Federal Republic of Germany v. Denmark; Federal Republic of Germany v. Netherlands)*, Judgment, ICJ Reports 1969, p. 39, para. 63.

[22] See Hutchinson, n. 9 pp. 111, 118 (late 1960s); *Continental Shelf (Tunisia v. Libyan Arab Jamahiriya)*, Judgment, ICJ Reports 1982, p. 182, para. 247, Shigeru Oda ('firmly established by the late 1960s'). Churchill and Lowe, n. 9, p. 111, however, consider the shelf to have been firmly established in international law by 1958. The matter was certainly no longer controversial by the time of the 1969 *North Sea Continental Shelf* case.

[23] Art. 2 Shelf Convention, Arts. 77, 81 LOS Convention. For a discussion of the negotiations of coastal state jurisdiction at UNCLOS III see Rangel, n. 9, pp. 326–36.

[24] Art. 78(2) LOS Convention. Lawful activities of states other than the coastal state relate to navigation and over-flights, cables and pipelines, subject to possible security zones of a maximum of 500 m, Arts. 60(5), 80; Rangel, n. 9, pp. 330–1 and 336–41.The use of the shelf (and the EEZ) for military purposes remains controversial.

So far, practical interest has focused mainly upon oil and gas deposits within 200 nm from the coasts where the majority of offshore oil and gas deposits (87 per cent in 1977, subject to further discoveries) have been reported.[25] The economic importance of the shelves has steadily increased; in 1985, offshore exploitation amounted to 30 per cent of land-based drilling. This figure was expected to rise to about 50 per cent by 1990, and then even more considerably due to technological progress towards the end of the twentieth century.[26] In addition to oil and gas (hydrocarbons), the continental shelf zone includes numerous opportunities for dredging for sand and gravel,[27] for setting out sedentary fisheries (such as sponge and pearls),[28] for exploiting phosphates used in fertilizers,[29] and for mining valuable polymetallic nodules which act as placer deposits of heavy metals (containing metals such as titanium, tin, zirconium, and pools of brine in the subsoil containing lead, zinc, gold and silver),[30] as well as for the exploitation of genetic resources, the potential uses and value of which have emerged in recent years. Commensurate with the gradual decline of oil and gas exploitation, the interest has equally shifted to the use of the continental shelf for wind and tidal energy installations in the quest for sustainable energy production.[31] The shelf is not only a suitable location because of its generally

---

[25] Robert Krueger and Myron H. Nordquist, 'The Evolution of the 200-mile Exclusive Economic Zone: State Practice in the Pacific Basin' (1979) 19 *Virginia Journal of International Law*, 321 (quoting Claude-Albert Colliard, 'Tendances actuelles du droit de la mer' (1977) 195 *Après Demain*).
[26] See Rangel, n. 9, p. 194.   [27] Ibid.
[28] Art. 2(4) Shelf Convention, Arts. 68, 77(4) LOS Convention. Though of marginal interest, historic exploitation of sponge-banks can be relevant in the delimitation of the shelf between neighbouring states. In the *Tunisia v. Libya Continental Shelf* case, a modus vivendi boundary, drawn for the purposes of sedentary fishing in 1919, was given essential weight, ICJ Reports 1982, n. 22, p. 70, para. 93. For a long time, there was controversy over whether or not crabs and lobsters are part of shelf exploitation. The matter was resolved with the advent of the overlapping EEZ. See Churchill and Lowe, n. 9, p. 119. On this problem, see S. V. Scott, 'The Inclusion of Sedentary Fisheries within the Continental Shelf Doctrine' (1992) 41 *International and Comparative Law Quarterly*, 788.
[29] See Klemm, n. 8, p. 9.
[30] Containing, inter alia, nickel, cobalt, molybdenum, copper and, in particular, manganese. For a discussion of the production, use and markets of these metals, most of which are important ingredients in steel production, see e.g. Alexandra M. Post, *Deep Sea Mining and the Law of the Sea* (The Hague: Martinus Nijhoff Publishers, 1983), pp. 45–65.
[31] See generally David Kenneth Leary, *International Law and the Genetic Resources of the Deep Sea* (Leiden: Brill, 2007); e.g. K. H. Brink, D. C. Chapman and G. R. Halliwell Jr., 'A Stochastic Model for Wind-Driven Currents Over the Continental Shelf' (1987) 92(C2) *J. Geophys. Res.*, 1783.

shallow waters, but also because it entails legal security in terms of allocation of property rights and jurisdiction.

The exercise of shelf rights and their relationship with the concept of freedom of the high seas has arisen without substantial difficulties, although conflicts between drilling activities and fishing could arise. Within the EEZ, however, such conflicts are increasingly withdrawn from international law and 'nationalized' instead. Remaining disputes have to be settled on the basis of a mutual balance of interests, under the principle of the reasonable exercise of maritime rights.[32] Likewise, disputes may arise, where exploratory drilling is used in order to assess the potential of a hitherto undelimited continental shelf. Such drilling was conducted by one state, Guyana, in shelf areas disputed by neighbouring Suriname. With regard to the obligation of making every effort not to hamper or jeopardize the reaching of a final agreement (Article 83(3) UNCLOS), the 2007 *Guyana* v. *Suriname* Tribunal held that '[a] distinction [has] to be made between activities of the kind that lead to a permanent physical change, such as exploitation of oil and gas reserves, and those that do not, such as seismic exploration.'[33] The Tribunal noted that the distinction thus adopted is consistent with the jurisprudence of international courts and tribunals on interim measures.[34] The exploratory drilling in the disputed area, as licensed by Guyana, fell into the class of permanent physical damage and thus violated the obligation.[35]

Major legal uncertainties and difficulties still remain. Practical problems relate to the temporal and geographical limits of the shelf rights. For example, at what point in history were shelf rights vested in coastal states? This question is of particular importance when considering existing historic rights and human conduct, and the relationship of the continental shelf and the EEZ. Major difficulties have also arisen as to the geographical extent of shelf rights. How far seaward do they expand, under general international law dictates? Finally, of

---

[32] Art. 2(2) High Seas Convention; Arts. 3–5 Shelf Convention; Arts. 78(2), 87(2) LOS Convention.

[33] *Arbitral Tribunal Constituted Pursuant to Article 287, and in Accordance with Annex VII, of the United Nations Convention on the Law of the Sea in the Matter of an Arbitration between Guyana and Suriname* (henceforth *Guyana* v. *Suriname*), Award of 17 September 2007, available at www.pca-cpa.org (last accessed 25 September 2014), para. 467.

[34] See *Guyana* v. *Suriname* Award, n. 33, para. 468, referring to the ICJ's decision in the *Aegean Sea* case, which distinguished between activities of a transitory character and activities that risk irreparable prejudice to the position of the other party.

[35] See *Guyana* v. *Suriname* Award, n. 33, para. 477.

course, there is the main question addressed by this study: what are the relevant equitable principles, factors, and criteria for the delimitation of rights between adjacent or opposite coastal states and what are their foundations? How can distributional justice be achieved in the field? The discussion of and answers to these issues depend to a great extent on the legal nature and foundation of the continental shelf itself.

C. *The foundation and legal nature of shelf rights*

The foundations and legal nature of the legal concept of the continental shelf have, for practical purposes, been discussed mainly in the context of maritime boundary delimitation. Indeed, a determination of legal foundations is essential in shaping the principles and rules of delimitation, and thus the substance of equity in this field. Findings have been influential on the results of delimitation. At the same time, the process of delimitation and the idea or concept of equity equally influenced the legal nature of the shelf. What we find is a dialectical relationship[36] between legal foundations and approaches to delimitation. Nevertheless, it seems useful to start with a discussion of the nature of shelf rights before entering the boundary problem.

As to the foundation of shelf rights, two basic approaches can be identified. An early foundation and justification was based on the *natural* relationship between the territory of the coastal state and the shelf. A more recent foundation is '*man-made*'. The latter approach emerged in the process of complex maritime boundary delimitation and was strongly reinforced by the advent of the 200-mile EEZ and the Area. It will be argued that it ultimately relies upon the closeness or intensity of the relationship between the resources and the coastal state involved.

1. The concept of natural prolongation of the territory of the coastal state

a. Recourse to natural law   The Truman Proclamation stated a number of reasons in support of the exercise of national jurisdiction over the

---

[36] As the ICJ put it in *Continental Shelf (Libyan Arab Jamahiriya v. Malta)*, Judgment, ICJ Reports 1985, p. 30, para. 27: 'That the questions of entitlement and of definition of continental shelf, on the one hand, and of delimitation of continental shelf on the other, are not only distinct but are also complementary is self-evident. The legal basis of that which is to be delimited, and of entitlement to it, cannot be other than pertinent to that delimitation.'

continental shelf by coastal states. After invoking the need for new resources, for taking advantage of the emerging exploitability of offshore resources, and the interest in prudent conservation and utilization, the new claim was ultimately justified by recourse to reasonableness and contiguity:

> (I)t is the view of the Government of the United States that the exercise of jurisdiction over the natural resources of the subsoil and sea bed of the continental shelf by the contiguous nation is reasonable and just, since the effectiveness of measures to utilise or conserve these resources would be contingent upon cooperation and protection from the shore, since the continental shelf may be regarded as an extension of the land-mass of the coastal nation and thus naturally appurtenant to it, since these resources frequently form a seaward extension of a pool or deposit lying within the territory, and since self-protection compels the coastal nation to keep close watch over activities off its shores which are of the nature necessary for utilisation of these resources.[37]

In the *North Sea* cases, the ICJ relied heavily upon parts of the Truman Proclamation. The ICJ held that this policy statement 'must be considered as having propounded the rules of law in this field'.[38] For reasons stated in the proclamation, the Court chose to emphasize and elaborate on the argument of the shelf as a natural extension of land territory. The ultimate legitimacy of jurisdiction over the shelf and 'the most fundamental of all the rules relating to the continental shelf' rely, according to the Court, upon a natural, inherent and territorial link between land-mass and shelf. Therefore, it held:

> that the rights of the coastal State, in respect to that area of continental shelf that constitutes a natural prolongation of its land territory into and under the sea, exist *ipso facto* and *ab initio* by virtue of its sovereignty over the land. Further, the sea rights are an extension of territorial rights, permitting an exercise of sovereign rights over the shelf for the purpose of exploring the seabed and exploiting its natural resources. In short, there is an inherent right. Its existence can be declared (and many states have done this) but does not need to be constituted.[39]

---

[37] See Hutchinson, n. 9, 756. It may also be of interest that President Roosevelt spoke of a 'rule of common sense', Memorandum of 9 June 1943, see Hutchinson, n. 9, 947. A memorandum from 3 July 1945, prepared by the late Professor W. W. Bishop Jr., argued that the coastal states are 'clearly the logical government to assert and exercise jurisdiction', see Hutchinson, n. 9, 755. It should be recalled that in the beginning of claims to shelf jurisdiction, the justification of the legal title was intimately linked to the practicability of seabed exploitation from fixed installations relatively close to the shore, making a clear link to the coastal state apparent, see Hutchinson, n. 9, 129.
[38] ICJ Reports 1969, p. 47, para. 86.   [39] Hutchinson, n. 9, p. 22, para. 19.

The doctrine of natural prolongation, inherent jurisdiction or *ipso iure* title, as the Court also called it,[40] was confirmed in subsequent case law.[41] It became an essential element of the definition of the continental shelf in Article 76(1) of the 1982 Convention besides a minimum legal expanse of 200 nm.[42] Though not yet an expressed element in the definition of Article 1 of the 1958 Shelf Convention, the related independence of existing rights from acquisition and occupation can be already found in Article 2(3) of that instrument, and was later restated by Article 77(3) of the 1982 Convention.[43] It is well established in customary law that the rights exist independently from any historic title based on occupation, acquisition or express proclamation. In contrast to other zones, this is often thought to constitute a particular feature of shelf rights, and to justify a continued independent existence of the continental shelf zone even within the 200 nm of the EEZ. Despite early doubts about the continued existence of the continental shelf concept within a state's 200 nm EEZ, it became clear that the latter does not absorb the former and that both co-exist with significant elements in common arising from the fact that, within 200 nm of a state's base lines, distance provides the practical basis for the entitlement to each of them (Articles 56 and 76 UNCLOS).[44] While within the EEZ, distance is the sole basis of the coastal state's entitlement to both the seabed and subsoil and the superjacent waters, the definition of the continental shelf in Article 76 assigns complementary roles to the concepts of natural prolongation and of distance as the basis for shelf entitlement.

---

[40] ICJ Reports 1969 31, para. 43:
    What confers the ipso iure title which international law attributes to the coastal State in respect of its continental shelf, is the fact that the submarine areas concerned may be deemed to be actually part of the territory over which the coastal State already has dominion – in the sense that, although covered with water, they are a prolongation or continuation of that territory, an extension of it under the sea.

[41] ICJ Reports 1978, p. 36, para. 86; ICJ Reports 1982, p. 48, para. 48; p. 74, para. 100.

[42] The provision says: 'The continental shelf of a coastal State comprises the seabed and subsoil of the submarine areas that extend beyond its territorial sea throughout the natural prolongation of its land territory to the outer edge of the continental margin' (emphasis added). On the impact of the 1969 judgment on this formulation see Rangel, n. 9.

[43] 'The rights of the coastal State over the continental shelf do not depend on occupation, effective or notional, or on any express proclamation.'

[44] ICJ Reports 1985, p. 13, as recalled in the Permanent Court of Arbitration (PCA), *In The Matter of an Arbitration between Barbados and the Republic of Trinidad and Tobago* (11 April 2006) 45 ILM 800 (2006), para. 226.

80   CONTEXT: THE ENCLOSURE OF THE SEAS

The predominant theory of *ipso iure* shelf rights, independent of proclamation and occupation, dates back to the early controversy over the nature of shelf rights. At that time, doctrinal views were split. One view was a concept based on the assertion by occupation and a *res nullius* qualification of shelf resources.[45] The other concept anticipated the idea of common heritage by claiming shelf resources to be *res communis*, subject to some form of international control.[46]

The idea of *ipso iure* rights emerged in order to protect the interests of coastal states, which, at the time, were not yet in a position either to engage in active occupation, or to prevent others from establishing offshore installations in front of their coasts. For such protective reasons, particularly favoured among Latin American states, the concept of *ipso iure* finally prevailed at the ILC, albeit without full discussion and reasoning.[47]

It was Hersch Lauterpacht who provided the theoretical basis for the doctrine of *ipso iure* rights. He rejected the occupation approach as unrealistic in terms of the seabed, and proposed that the title of the coastal state rely instead upon physical contiguity. Thus, while the shelf physically constitutes the platform upon which the continent rests, the coastal state should have the right to its proceeds.[48] In terms of the Truman Proclamation and subsequent cases, the title *ipso iure* of continental shelf jurisdiction thus relies on the fact of natural prolongation. From the point of view of legal theory, the doctrine of natural prolongation, inherent jurisdiction, and *ipso iure* title is of considerable significance. In essence, it seems to be nothing short of a genuine concept of natural law. The doctrine of natural prolongation may well be considered as constituting the most prominent example of the ahistorical school of jurisprudence in the field of international law in the second half

---

[45] For references see Jewett, n. 9, pp. 171–2; Sir Cecil Hurst, 'Whose is the Bed of the Sea' (1923) 4 *British Yearbook of International Law*, 42; F. A. Vallat, 'The Continental Shelf' (1946) 23 *British Yearbook of International Law*, 333, 334.
[46] See Jewett, n. 9, p. 176, quoting Scelle and Gidel.
[47] Jewett, n. 9, p. 166 writes:
> The preference for this alternative of rights ipso iure, as against occupation of a res nullius, does not emerge from the summary records as a clearly reasoned preference. But it is evident that the Commission was unhappy with the idea of occupation, in part because of the rather notional form it would take in respect of the seabed and in part because it might operate against states which were not able to engage in 'occupation' because of their lack of technology.
[48] Hersch Lauterpacht, 'Sovereignty over Submarine Areas' (1950) 27 *British Yearbook of International Law*, 376, 424.

of twentieth century. Though hardly recognized as such, it shows some typical characteristics and problems of natural law. Under the doctrine of natural prolongation, rights over the shelf may be considered to be pre-existent and inalienable in law. They are conceived to appertain to states from the outset. The Court concluded from this doctrine that jurisdictional boundaries merely need to be *found* from negotiations or judicial decisions. Boundaries are not created by the human mind. As the Court said in 1969:

> Delimitation is a process which involves establishing the boundaries of an area already, in principle, appertaining to the coastal State and not the determination *de novo* of such an area.[49]

Such a statement immediately raises the question of how shelf rights relate to other rights exercised in a particular region. A historical definition leaves considerable uncertainty about the temporal dimensions of shelf rights. It is the essence of natural prolongation that rights and obligations related to the shelf do not emerge in an historical process, as customary law does. Rather, these rights are inherent to the subject, and therefore pre-existing. Does it follow that shelf rights deploy retroactive effects? Jurisdiction may be considered to date back to the Pleistocene ice age (when the shelves are thought to have been formed), or any time afterwards. This issue is of relevance to the relationship among different shelf rights and resources, such as oil exploitation and historic sponge-banks, or between resource entitlements coinciding in a particular area, such as historic fisheries and potential drilling areas. It can also be important in matters of state succession. The legal nature of shelf rights is critical for determining the outcome of such conflicts.

b. The customary nature of shelf rights In international litigation, the problems of temporal scope and of the relationship of shelf rights to other uses of the sea have not yet emerged as a decisive issue. However, it has manifested itself in the context of federal state litigation where both the central state and the member state claim jurisdiction over the shelf. In a dispute between the federal government of Canada and Newfoundland the answer depended, inter alia, on the issue of whether shelf rights existed in international law prior to the Province joining the Federation, in March 1949. In 1983, the Newfoundland Court of

---

[49] ICJ Reports 1969 p. 22, para. 18 (emphasis added).

Appeal gave its opinion *In Reference to Mineral and Other Natural Resources of the Continental Shelf*:

> The phrase 'ipso facto and ab initio' used by the [International Court of Justice], may be interpreted as meaning that the rights in international law extend back in geological time, as suggested by D.P. O'Connell, or to when sovereignty over the land mass was first established and recognized, or to when submarine areas in question became exploitable as a result of modern developments of science and technology, or, more specifically, to when these areas become the object of active interest of States. In our opinion, the last is the most logical and is in accord with British practice at the time.[50]

However, the Canadian Supreme Court took a different view. In the 1984 *Newfoundland Continental Shelf Reference advisory opinion*, the Court rejected claims primarily on grounds of constitutional law (lack of incorporation).[51] Yet, it also dealt with the issue in terms of international law. The Court construed '*ab initio*' as referring to the time when the concept of the continental shelf emerged in customary law. Further, no retroactive effects are inherent to the rights of exploitation, which only came into being after 1949. Consequently, such rights do not apply to Newfoundland. In the Court's words:

> The development of customary or conventional international law is, by definition, the development of new law. There is no concept in international law of discovering law that always was. In our view, continental shelf rights have no retroactive application to a time before they were recognized by international law.[52]

---

[50] 145 Dominion Law Reports, 3d. 9, 39 (Can 1983). The Court, in particular, referred to the 1942 Gulf of Paria agreement, see n. 10, and the British-sponsored continental shelf proclamations of the Gulf States. The Court found, based on that evidence, that the shelf rights were established prior to adherence of Newfoundland to the Confederation in 1949. However, it denied title on constitutional grounds.

[51] 'Judgment of 8 March 1984' reprinted in (1984) 23 ILM 288. See also the 1967 'Reference Re: Ownership of Off-Shore Mineral Rights' (1967) *Supreme Court Reports*, p. 792, (1968) 65 *Dominion Law Reports*, p. 353 (Can). In this case, the Court held that both the territorial sea and continental shelf off the Province of British Columbia appertain to Canada. See (1968) 65 *Dominion Law Reports*, pp. 375 and 376–81 (mainly relying on the controversial English common law rule that the realm of property rights end at the low water mark). *The Queen* v. *Keayn* 2 Ex. D. 63 (1876)). For a discussion of the case and its background see Geoffrey Marston, 'The Newfoundland Offshore Jurisdictional Dispute' (1984) 18 *Journal of World Trade Law*, 335. See Jewett, n. 9, pp. 153–7; L. L. Herman, 'The New Foundland Offshore Mineral Rights References: An Imperfect Mingling of International and Municipal Law' (1984) 22 *Canadian Yearbook of International Law*, 194.

[52] Above n. 51 p. 318.

The Court also referred to an opinion by Australian Chief Justice Gibbs of the Supreme Court that illustrates the underlying dispute between ahistorical, natural and customary law developments. Justice Gibbs took a realistic, historical point of view. His view supports the continental shelf as a new concept, which emerged from customary international law:

> To say the rights of coastal States in respect of the continental shelf existed from the beginning of time may or may not be correct as a matter of legal theory. In fact, however, the rights now recognized represent the response of international law to modern developments of science and technology, which permit the sea-bed to be exploited in a way which it was quite impossible for governments or lawyers of earlier centuries to anticipate. In this matter, arguments of history are stronger than those of logic... These rights, if theoretically inherent in the sovereignty of coastal States, were in fact the result of the operation of a new legal principle.[53]

Gibbs' opinion expresses a sound view, one compatible with the jurisprudence of the ICJ. There was no issue of retroactivity in the *North Sea* cases. Although the opinion of the Court can be read, prima facie, in favour of natural, retroactive rights, there is no evidence that the Court meant that the notion of inherent rights be understood as dating back eternally prior to adoption in customary law.[54] Instead, it stated that the Truman Proclamation 'came to be regarded as the starting point of the positive law on the subject'.[55] The judgment goes on to explicitly state that, '[t]he doctrine of the continental shelf is a recent instance of encroachment on maritime expanses which, during the greater part of history, appertained to no-one.'[56] In the *Tunisia* v. *Libya* case, the Court again expressed, obiter dictum, its view that respect for historic rights possibly conflicts with shelf rights.[57] Such statements imply a historic

---

[53] Dissenting opinion, *New South Wales et al v. Commonwealth of Australia* (Austl. 1975) 135 *Commonwealth Law Reports*, 337, 416, quoted by the Canadian Supreme Court, n. 51, p. 318. In this case, the six member states of the Australian Commonwealth challenged federal legislation of 1973 which established jurisdiction of the federal government over the territorial sea and the continental shelf. Based on *The Queen* v. *Keyn*, see n. 51. The majority fully upheld the statute; Gibbs, J. dissented on grounds that too much weight was given to the controversial common law precedent. He considered internal and territorial seas to be under the jurisdiction of the member states. See *Queen* v. *Keyn*, n. 51, p. 414. See also Geoffrey Marston, 'Federal Disputes over Offshore Submerged Lands' (1977) 11 *Journal of World Trade Law*, 184.
[54] See also Judge Oda, dissenting opinion ICJ Reports 1982, p. 191, para. 57; Jewett, n. 9, pp. 187–8.
[55] ICJ Reports 1969, p. 32–3, para. 47.   [56] ICJ Reports 1969, p. 51, para. 96.
[57] ICJ Reports 1982, p. 73, para. 100 ('Historic titles must enjoy respect and be preserved as they have always been by long usage').

concept and are hardly compatible with notions of pre-existing rights that have always applied.

Since the existence of shelf rights as such were not at issue in the above-mentioned cases, the Court was not obliged to make a clear statement on the relationship of such rights to customary law. While the Court did refuse to recognize Article 6 of the Shelf Convention (equidistance rule) as a part of customary law,[58] it remained silent on the question whether the entitlement itself existed as a matter of custom. The doctrine of natural prolongation and *ipso iure* entitlement, however, should not conceal the fact that the Court did not work on the basis of natural law. Logically, having qualified Articles 1 to 3 of the Shelf Convention to be at least emerging customary law in 1958,[59] the Court's view of the concept would still be one of customary, rather than natural, law when the process was completed in the late 1960s. The history of the continental shelf clearly shows that it was a cumulative process of claims and responses, which eventually led to the recognition of coastal states' rights.[60] By 1969, it was apparently clear that such rights existed, and the Court merely qualified their nature when the concept became accepted in customary international law. Emphasis on inherent rights *ipso facto*, *de jure* and *ab initio* therefore merely reflects the doctrinal dispute, in the early stages of the concept, whether or not the shelf is subject to occupation and rights to active acquisition.[61]

In conclusion, shelf rights are rights of customary international law. *Ipso iure* entitlement has only existed since the concept was established in customary law. However, because this qualification brought rights into effect immediately, without the need for proclamation and claim, customary law deploys partially retroactive effects back to the late 1960s, the point at which the rights became a matter of international law.

c. **The functions of natural prolongation** The *North Sea* cases may give the impression that the doctrine of natural prolongation was primarily developed by the Court in order to counter the theory of *de novo*, fair and equitable apportionment of the shelf areas in dispute, or that it was used to prevent what otherwise could be thought to be an unprincipled delimitation similar or identical to decision-making *ex aequo et bono*, and to dismiss delimitation based on a rule of equidistance or adjacency.[62] These were, however, not the intentions for

---

[58] ICJ Reports 1969, pp. 42–6, paras. 70–81.
[59] See above n. 20.
[60] For a review of early claims see Jewett, n. 9.
[61] Rüster, n. 8, pp. 192–204.
[62] ICJ Reports 1969, pp. 32–3, para 47.

using this doctrine. As will be seen, the subsequent process of trial and error proved natural prolongation to be largely irrelevant for delimitation of the shelf between states even before the 200-mile exclusive economic zone emerged.[63] Instead, there are two essential functions: establishing *ipso iure* title and determining the seaward expansion of the continental shelf.

The first function has already been discussed. Natural prolongation primarily served to establish *ipso iure* title in order to avoid the need and dangers of acquisition by proclamation and occupation. Its prime function was to exclude 'foreign' nations from offshore drilling in front of a coastal state.[64]

The second function is a more recent one. The doctrine of natural prolongation became important with respect to the determination of the seaward expanses of the national continental shelves. In this role, it serves the purpose of preventing further expansion and appropriation of the deep seabed under the test of exploitability of Article 1 of the 1958 Shelf Convention.[65] When the test of exploitability (i.e. the decision not to delimit the maximum outer reach) was adopted, future drilling activities were still expected to remain limited to coastal regions.[66] Technical progress, however, allowed drilling in an ever-increasing seaward direction, eventually including all of the margin area and even beyond.[67] The prospects of deep seabed mining, which emerged in the 1960s, changed the situation even further, and far-reaching expansion under the exploitability test could not be excluded.

---

[63] See Chapter 9(D)(1).   [64] Above text accompanying nn. 37–39.
[65] This provision did not define an outer limit of the national shelf but left the boundary to technical exploitability. Art. 1 1958 Convention on the Continental Shelf, Geneva, 29 April 1958, in force 10 June 1964, 499 UNTS 311, reads:
> For the purpose of these articles, the term 'continental shelf' is used as referring (a) to the seabed and subsoil of the submarine areas adjacent to the coast but outside the area of the territorial sea, to a depth of 200 metres or beyond that limit, to where the depth of the superjacent waters admits of the exploitation of the natural resources of the said areas; (b) to the seabed and subsoil of similar submarine areas adjacent to the coasts of islands.
[66] See above n. 31 in fine. For a close analysis of the history and function of the exploitability test see Hutchinson, n. 9, 123–40.
[67] 'The exploitability formula was suitable for those countries which have a developed technology of sea-bed and subsoil exploitation at their disposal. However, it should be noted that this criterion is not reliable when technologies change rapidly because the outer limit of the shelf also changes with them', Davorin Rudolf, 'Some Remarks about the Provisions Concerning the Continental Shelf in the UN Convention on the Law of the Sea' in B. Vukas (ed.), *Essays on the New Law of the Sea* (University of Zagreb, 1985), p. 143.

At the time of the *North Sea Continental Shelf* cases, political efforts to prevent such developments were in full swing and the concept of common heritage was in the making.[68] Scientists were replacing former definitions of the shelf, based on bathymetry (Article 1 of the 1958 Convention on the Continental Shelf) by natural prolongation.[69] The new concept was the perfect aide to contain encroachment of the shelf. On the one hand, it allowed for expansion to the edge of the continental margin, which was by then technically exploitable. On the other hand, it excluded potential resources outside the margin from further nationalization. There could have been no more suitable occasion to legalize the new concept than in the *North Sea* judgment, which came at the dawn of a new conference on the law of the sea.[70] Whatever the Court's intention at the time, it is clear that the 1969 decision significantly influenced the shaping of Article 76 of the 1982 Convention.[71] We face the awkward situation that the doctrine of natural prolongation is firmly established as a foundation of *ipso iure* entitlement, but its second, more recent function of defining the outer limit has remained unclear, both in treaty and in customary law. Although the doctrine of natural prolongation is firmly established in law, operational effects in treaty law with regard to the outer limit of the shelf beyond 200 nm are difficult to assess in light of the complex geological and geophysical requisites of Article 76 of the LOS Convention. Though delimitation remains in principle a matter for the coastal state to decide, the Convention provides interesting procedural machinery for the unilateral establishment of the proper limits. Under the LOS Convention, states are obliged to submit proposals to the Commission on the Limits of

---

[68] At the time, the landmark Declaration of Principles Governing the Sea-Bed and the Ocean Floor, and the Subsoil Thereof, beyond the Limits of the National Jurisdiction, GA Res. 2749 (XXV), adopted in 1970 by a vote of 108 to 0 and 14 abstentions, 25 GAOR Supp. (No. 28) at 28, (1970) 10 ILM 220, was being prepared at the United Nations.

[69] See O'Connell, n. 8, p. 447, referring to a 1969 geological symposium on the international regime of the seabed in Rome, and other sources.

[70] This dimension of the judgment was discussed early on by R. Y. Jennings, 'The Limits of the Continental Shelf Jurisdiction: Some Possible Implications of the North Sea Case' (1969) 19 *International & Comparative Law Quarterly*, 826. For the then existing controversy on the proper expanses of the shelf see e.g. 'The Henkin-Finlay dispute' (1969) 63 *American Journal of International Law*, 54; (1979) *American Journal of International Law*, 42 and 62. Louis Henkin argued in favour of a narrow definition along the 200 nm isobath, while Luke W. Finlay, representing the industry, was in favour of the more extensive interpretation of Art. 1 Shelf Convention, which eventually prevailed, and arguably included all the continental margin.

[71] See Rangel, n. 9, p. 346, the notion of natural prolongation 'fut la conséquence et la répercussion de l'arrêt du 20 février 1969 à la Conférence'.

the Continental Shelf (CLCS), regulated by Article 76(8) LOS and Annex II of the Convention.[72] Delimitations by coastal states must be based upon recommendations of the Commission and cannot, despite formal unilateralism, achieve binding effects without such consent (Article 76(8)).[73] According to Article 76(8) of the Convention, the outer limits established by the coastal state on the basis of the recommendations of the Commission shall be final and binding.

However, Article 76(10) prevents this provision from being invoked by a coastal state to argue that any further change to such outer limit lines is excluded in areas of overlapping continental shelf claims. Article 76(10) provides that '[t]he provisions of this article [Article 76] are without prejudice to the question of delimitation of the continental shelf between States with opposite or adjacent coasts'. The implications of Article 76(10) are addressed in the Rules of Procedure of the CLCS.[74] Rule 46(1) provides:

> In case there is a dispute in the delimitation of the continental shelf between opposite or adjacent States or in other cases of unresolved land or maritime disputes, submissions may be made and shall be considered in accordance with Annex I to these Rules.

Paragraph 5 of Annex I provides that the Commission will not consider and qualify a submission in cases where a land or maritime dispute exists unless all states that are parties to the dispute have given their prior consent. The submission before the Commission and its recommendations shall not prejudice the position of states which are parties to the land or maritime dispute. In similar words, Rule 46(2) provides that '[t]he actions of the Commission shall not prejudice matters relating to the delimitation of boundaries between States'.

---

[72] Art. 4 of Annex II of the 1982 LOS Convention provides that:
Where a coastal State intends to establish, in accordance with article 76, the outer limits of its continental shelf beyond 200 nautical miles, it shall submit particulars of such limits to the Commission along with supporting scientific and technical data as soon as possible but in any case within 10 years of the entry into force of this Convention for that State.

[73] 'Second Report of the Committee on Legal Issues of the Outer Continental Shelf' in *International Law Association Report of the Seventy-Second Conference* (London: ILA, 2006) (hereinafter ILA, Second Report), pp. 15–16. 'The limits of the shelf established by the coastal State on the basis of these recommendations shall be final and binding' (emphasis added). See also Allott (1983), n. 1, 1, 17–19.

[74] Rules of Procedure of the Commission on the Limits of the Continental Shelf, 17 April 2008 (CLCS/40/Rev.1), available at www.un.org/Depts/los/clcs_new/commission_rules.htm (last accessed 28 September 2010).

In the light of this provision, other states should in principle accept the consideration of a submission by a coastal state that raises issues of delimitation of the continental shelf, as its consideration and subsequent recommendations will not prejudice their rights.[75] State practice seems to confirm that states in general have accepted the consideration of a submission by a coastal state involving the delimitation of the continental shelf between neighbouring states.[76]

Accordingly, the question arises, if any subsequent judicial dispute settlement in the matter of a delimitation of competing claims of coastal states should consider the matter of the existence of an outer continental shelf anew. The delimitation of the outer continental shelf between opposite or adjacent states shall in – accordance with Article 76(10) – not be prejudiced by the work of the CLCS. This was also the view held, in principle and for the first time, by the Tribunal in *Barbados v. Trinidad and Tobago*.[77] So far only one contentious delimitation issue concerning the competing claims to an outer continental shelf has been decided.[78]

When dealing with the delimitation of the outer continental shelf beyond 200 nm, the International Tribunal for the Law of the Sea (ITLOS) held in *Bangladesh v. Myanmar* that UNCLOS in its Articles 76, 77 and 83 treats the continental shelf as a single unit, without any distinction being made between the shelf within 200 nm and the shelf beyond that limit and that, therefore, it had 'jurisdiction to delimit the continental shelf in its entirety'.[79] Myanmar opposed the jurisdiction of the Tribunal over the delimitation of the shelf beyond 200 nm in this particular case. The Tribunal phrased the question before it in this way: 'whether, in the circumstances of this case, it is appropriate to exercise that jurisdiction'.[80] It decided that it was competent to delimit the continental shelf beyond 200 nm, pointing out that such delimitation would not encroach upon the functions of the CLCS.[81] The Tribunal stated the corollary to Article 76(8), namely that its adjudicative delimitation function is without prejudice to the establishment of the outer

---

[75] ILA, Second Report, n. 73, p. 19. [76] ILA, Second Report, n 73, p. 19, n. 18.
[77] This was held by the Tribunal only in principle, since, ultimately, it did not have to decide matters as pertaining to the outer continental shelf (*Barbados v. Trinidad and Tobago*, n. 44, para. 368).
[78] *Dispute concerning Delimitation of the Maritime Boundary between Bangladesh and Myanmar in the Bay of Bengal (Bangladesh v. Myanmar)*, Judgment, International Tribunal for the Law of the Sea, 14 March 2012, Case No. 16, para. 462.
[79] Ibid., paras. 361, 363. [80] Ibid., para. 363. [81] Ibid., para. 393.

limits of the continental shelf.[82] Both Bangladesh and Myanmar had made submissions to the CLCS. Bangladesh had not given its consent to consideration of Myanmar's submission by the CLCS.[83] The Tribunal therefore held that not to exercise its jurisdiction over the dispute relating to the continental shelf beyond 200 nm would not only fail to resolve a long-standing dispute, but also would not be conducive to the efficient operation of the Convention, even running contrary to the object and purpose of the Convention.[84] It continued that inaction in the present case, by the Commission and the Tribunal, would leave the parties in a position where they may be unable to benefit fully from their rights under the Convention.[85]

Bangladesh argued that natural prolongation was the primary criterion in establishing an entitlement to an extended continental shelf and that consequently Myanmar had no such entitlement due to a discontinuity between that state's land mass and the seabed of the Bay of Bengal beyond 200 nm. The Tribunal rejected this argument and instead held that entitlement to a continental shelf depended on satisfying the criteria of Article 76(4) UNCLOS.[86] It noted that the floor of the Bay of Bengal was covered by sediment and that each state could claim a continental shelf beyond 200 nm based on the thickness of sedimentary rocks criterion in Article 76(4)(a)(i).[87] With respect to the method of delimitation of this overlap, the Tribunal observed that Article 83 UNCLOS does not distinguish between delimitation within 200 nm and beyond 200 nm and that '[a]ccordingly, the equidistance–relevant circumstances method continues to apply for the delimitation of the continental shelf beyond 200 nm'.[88]

The ICJ in the case of *Nicaragua* v. *Colombia* distinguished the shortly preceding decision of ITLOS in *Bangladesh* v. *Myanmar* because of the unique circumstances of sedimentary rocks on the seafloor of the Bay of Bengal. This circumstance enabled the ITLOS in accordance with UNCLOS to delimit the overlapping shelf claims of the parties. The ICJ recalled that in the *Bangladesh* v. *Myanmar* judgment the ITLOS did not, however, determine the outer limits of the continental shelf beyond 200 nm.[89] The ICJ refused to adjudicate upon Nicaragua's claim to an extended continental shelf beyond 200 nm, finding that Nicaragua had not established that its continental margin extended far enough to

---
[82] Ibid., para. 394. [83] Ibid., paras. 387–9. [84] Ibid., para. 391–2.
[85] Ibid., para. 392. [86] Ibid., para. 437. [87] Ibid., paras. 444–6, 449
[88] Ibid., paras. 454–5.
[89] *Territorial and Maritime Dispute (Nicaragua v. Colombia)*, Judgment, ICJ Reports 2012, p. 624, para. 125.

overlap with Colombia's 200 nm continental shelf entitlement. It also stated that Nicaragua had not met its obligation under Article 76 UNCLOS to submit an extended continental shelf claim to the CLCS.[90] The ICJ also said that Colombia's non-party status did not alter Nicaragua's obligation towards the Convention. It made no reference to an obligation under customary law, but instead based its reasoning on the object and purpose of the Convention as manifested in its preamble.[91] This reasoning may be influenced by an emerging constitutional understanding of UNCLOS and the mechanisms and organs it established. However, the refusal to delimit a shelf in an adjudicative setting with reference to the proceedings before the CLCS leaves open the question whether the outcome of a submission to the CLCS is determinative for the delimitation of the outer continental shelf in a contentious case.

The dichotomy between 'final and binding' recommendations and the 'without prejudice' clause has accordingly not yet been resolved. It seems clear, from the ITLOS ruling in *Bangladesh Myanmar*, however, that absent a recommendation by the CLCS but in the presence of sufficient evidence by a party with respect to its natural prolongation in accordance with the Article 76 requirements, or in circumstances of obvious overlaps – such as in the Bay of Bengal – a ruling on the delimitation of the continental shelf beyond 200 nm is not precluded.

Any future court or tribunal entrusted with the delimitation of the outer continental shelf will thus be faced with a difficult assessment of the law applicable to a shelf extending beyond 200 nm. The scientific definition of such a shelf as contained in Article 76 is without prejudice to a delimitation between opposite or adjacent states by virtue of Article 76(10). Neither is Article 76 universally applicable or accepted as an expression of customary law. It could be expected that at a minimum, an outer continental shelf must not be allowed to trump a competing shelf within the latter's customary 200 nm expanse.[92] In order to delimit two overlapping continental shelves, a court or tribunal may nevertheless find it necessary to invoke scientific requirements, such as those of Article

---

[90] Ibid., paras. 126 ff., 129.   [91] Ibid., para. 126.
[92] This has been contradicted, however, by the ruling in *Bangladesh* v. *Myanmar*, where the extension of the adjusted single boundary line beyond 200 nm produced an area that is further away than 200 nm from one state (Bangladesh), but within 200 nm of the state on the other side of the boundary (Myanmar) (*Bangladesh* v. *Myanmar*, n. 78, paras. 463–4, 471–4). Although the Tribunal held that this line left intact the claims to the superjacent waters by Myanmar within 200 nm in that area, the resulting boundary does encroach upon Myanmar's continental shelf within 200 nm (ibid., paras. 471–4).

76 – independently or in connection with any existing findings of the CLCS. However, it is not clear how a court or tribunal would handle the scientific requirements in more complex circumstances than that in the Bay of Bengal – both in light of the difficult interpretation of scientific data and the restricted accessibility[93] of the data used by the CLCS for its recommendation.[94] Judges may nevertheless find such recourse suitable in the absence of consistent state practice and opinio iuris for the establishment of continental shelves extending beyond 200 nm.

As to customary law, it is still unsettled whether natural prolongation has eventually overridden the test of exploitability as defined by the 1958 Convention. Parties to this Convention, but not the LOS Convention, may argue that the test of exploitability still supersedes. On the one hand, they may claim that exploration and exploitation may extend as far as technically possible, even reaching into the deep seabed, as long as no conflict with existing deep seabed mining rights results. On the other hand, it is doubtful whether the test of exploitability was ever meant to expand beyond the continental margin, given the fact that the 1958 Convention defined the shelf on the basis of adjacency to the coast – itself an indication of natural prolongation.[95] Further, exploitability has not been used to justify national claims to deep seabed mining. These have largely relied upon the doctrine of the high seas, independent of the continental shelf and any relationship to the coastal state.[96] Yet, general developments since the 1960s have fundamentally changed the idea of freedom of the high seas and unlimited national exploitation of the seabed with the emergence of the concept of common heritage. It may therefore be unfeasible to assume unlimited exploitability under the concept of freedom of the high seas. Hutchinson, who carefully examined the question of seaward delimitation in 1985, concluded that the rule of exploitability (Article 1 of the 1958 Convention), which became part of general international law in the late 1960s, has probably ceased to be part

---

[93] Rules of Procedures Annex III, 11(3).
[94] John E. Noyes, 'Judicial and Arbitral Proceedings and the Outer Limits of the Continental Shelf' (2009) 42 *Vanderbilt Journal of Transnational Law*, 1211, 1249–52.
[95] Art. 1, see Chapter 1, n. 6.
[96] Claims for unilateral appropriation of deep seabed mining sites in national legislation is based on doctrines of freedom of the high seas and of *res communis*, independent of relationship to the coastal state; titles are perceived to be acquired either based on prescription, occupation or 'historical consolidation'. See Brown, *The Legal Regime of Hydrospace*, n. 9, pp. 82–6. Edward Duncan Brown, 'Freedom of the High Seas Versus the Common Heritage of Mankind: Fundamental Principles in Conflict' (1983) 20 *San Diego Law Review*, 521, 527.

of customary law, although it remains significant as a norm among parties to the Convention.[97] At the same time, Article 76 of the 1982 Convention is not yet clearly a part of customary law. Whether this vacuum in customary law will gradually be filled by Article 76, and whether natural prolongation will emerge 'as a clear and authoritative guide for future State practice',[98] is largely dependent upon universal recognition of the 1982 Convention itself and on the clarification of the provisions of Article 76(3)–(8) relating to the scientific concept of natural prolongation.

2. Distance: close relationship of the coastal state to offshore marine spaces

a. From natural prolongation to distance Although nominally the doctrine of natural prolongation of the territory of coastal states emerged as the prime foundation of shelf rights, it has not been very useful in solving practical problems in operational terms. Delimitation of the shelf between adjacent and opposite states and the determination of the outer limits of the shelf have increasingly relied upon different foundations. This is hardly surprising, given that most cases relate to the delimitation of more or less uniform shelves in relatively narrow areas, such as the North Sea, the Anglo-French Channel, the Mediterranean Sea, the Gulf of Maine, the Persian Gulf or the Red Sea. The advent of the EEZ and the Area made it necessary to achieve a more precise co-ordination between the two zones. Bilateral continental shelf boundaries up to 200 nm are characterized by coastal geography or – to a lesser degree – 'man-made' elements. At the same time, the unilateral delineation of the outer limits of the continental shelf opposite the Area relies exclusively on natural features of the seabed and subsoil (Article 76(3–6) UNCLOS). Likewise, the subsequent recommendations by the CLCS – concerning the final limits of continental shelf bordering on the Area – are made on the basis of geological and geomorphological factors alone.[99]

The task of reconciling the conflicting interests of national jurisdiction over the shelf and the common Area and accommodation of the shelf with the new EEZ brought about substantial modifications to the rule of using naturally defined boundaries. The definition of the zones was an issue of vital importance to the whole idea of common heritage, and

---

[97] See Brown, *Sea-Bed Energy and Minerals*, vol. I, n. 9, p. 187.   [98] Ibid. p. 188.
[99] See Annex II UNCLOS. See further the Commission's website for past recommendations, rules of procedure and scientific and technical guidelines, available at www.un.org/Depts/los/clcs_new/clcs_home (last accessed 5 September 2014).

agreement was extremely difficult to achieve.[100] Not surprisingly, the regulatory scheme resulting from UNCLOS III was rather complex. In essence, the 1982 Convention provides three models of delimitation, reflecting the great variety of geographical circumstances and special interests, in particular those of states with broad continental margins.[101] The three models are as follows:

(i) In accordance with the EEZ, the shelf has a minimum expansion of 200 nm (Article 76(1)). Thus, jurisdiction over soil and subsoil exists even if there is no continental margin in geological terms (as in the case of Chile).
(ii) The maximum breadth extends to 350 nm or to the 2,500 m isobath plus 100 nm, whichever is more advantageous to the coastal state concerned (Article 76(5)).
(iii) Finally, within minimum and maximum ranges, the shelf is defined on the basis of natural prolongation of the land mass and extends to the outer limit of the continental margin (Article 76(1)). In the operation of establishing the outer edge of the continental margin beyond 200 nm, the Convention again provides the coastal state with alternative methods from which to choose (Article 76(4)). It is here that the CLCS, as discussed above, has to be involved.

With natural prolongation being only one among several distance-related criteria to delimit the shelf, Article 76 of the Convention also implies a partly new legal nature and foundation of the continental shelf. Minimal distances of 200 nm and independent of natural features cannot be explained in terms of natural prolongation. The same holds true for the maximum ranges of 350 nm and 100 nm from the 2,500 metre isobath. This issue was addressed by the ICJ in the 1985 *Libya* v. *Malta Continental Shelf* case. Malta strongly relied upon the impact of the EEZ. It argued that the importance of the 'distance principle', relevant to the EEZ, is equally applicable to the shelf, thus detaching the concept of the shelf from any criterion of the physical prolongation.[102] Libya, on the

---

[100] See e.g. Bernhard H. Oxman, 'The Third United Nations Conference on the Law of the Sea: The Eighth Session (1979)' (1980) 74 *American Journal of International Law*, 1; Bernhard H. Oxman, 'The Third United Nations Conference on the Law of the Sea: The Ninth Session (1980)' (1981) 75 *American Journal of International Law*, 2, 227–31. For further reports see Chapter 1, n. 11.
[101] The regime of Art. 76 relies upon the so-called Irish Formula, taking into account the large shelf of Ireland. Annex II of the LOS Convention was shaped to suit the particular interests of Sri Lanka, see Rangel, n. 9, p. 349 ff.
[102] ICJ Reports 1985, n. 36, p. 32, para. 31.

other hand, emphasized natural prolongation as the sole method of establishing title in customary law.[103] The Court combined the two views. Based on the close interrelationship of the shelf and the EEZ and the fact that the latter has emerged in customary law, it held that natural prolongation of the shelf is now partially defined by distance from the shore, independent of any physical features of the seabed and subsoil:

> Although the institutions of the continental shelf and the exclusive economic zone are different and distinct, the rights which the exclusive economic zone entails over the sea-bed of the zone are defined by reference to the regime laid down for the continental shelf. Although there can be continental shelf where there is no exclusive economic zone, there cannot be an exclusive economic zone without a corresponding continental shelf. It follows that, for judicial and practical reasons, the distance criterion must now apply to the continental shelf as well as to the exclusive economic zone: and this quite apart from the provision of distance in paragraph 1 of Article 76. This is not to suggest that the idea of natural prolongation has now been superseded by that of distance. What it means is that where the continental shelf does extend as far as 200 miles from the shore, natural prolongation, which in spite of its physical origins has throughout its history become more and more a complex and juridical concept, is in part defined by distance from the shore, irrespective of the physical nature of the intervening sea-bed and subsoil. The concepts of natural prolongation and of distance are therefore not opposed but complementary; and both remain essential elements of the juridical concept of the continental shelf.[104]

According to the judgment, shelf rights still rely upon natural prolongation when it says that natural prolongation is in part defined by distance from the shore. On the other hand, the last sentence quoted above indicates that the Court considers natural prolongation and distance as separate, but complementary, concepts. This second view seems appropriate. Up to a distance of 200 nm, the Court acknowledges the existence of shelf rights independent of any physical features. Shelf rights exist in law even if no shelf exists physically. Therefore, title no longer relies upon natural prolongation in such cases. Without explicitly saying so, the Court has in effect accepted the minimal distance of 200 nm as defined in Article 76 of the 1982 LOS Convention as a matter of customary international law.[105] An inner and outer shelf – the latter still

---

[103] See ICJ Reports 1985, p. 32, para. 32.   [104] See ICJ Reports 1985, p. 32, para. 34.
[105] See also Vascianne, n. 16, p. 140.

partly relying on natural prolongation – can now be distinguished, as proposed by Judge Oda.[106] Taking up an argument proposed by Malta, the Court also accepted 'distance' as the foundation and title of rights related to the inner shelf, independent of physical features.

There can be little doubt that this distance limit has passed into the corpus of general international law. In the *Libya* v. *Malta* case, the ICJ accepted the Maltese argument that, as a result of the UNCLOS III process, and, in particular, the evolution of the EEZ concept, the distance principle as reflected in Article 76(1) had achieved customary status.[107] The Court added that this does not mean that the concept of natural prolongation had been superseded by that of distance in configurations beyond 200 nm.[108]

b. From distance to closeness of relationship of offshore spaces to the coastal state   Pragmatically, and at first sight, the idea or the 'principle of distance' from the shore of the coastal state provides the new legal foundation for rights over the inner shelf. However, distance is actually the effect of a principle rather than a principle itself; it is instrumental and mechanical and cannot in itself be a foundation in a sense comparable to natural prolongation. The two are not operating at the same level, and the idea, concept and foundation behind distance still need to be defined. Such foundations are not easy to detect. Whilst they existed from the very beginning, they were hardly noted. State practice did not discuss them, but implicitly relied upon them. Without naming them, the foundations behind the principle of distance emerged gradually and were made concrete through case law relating to maritime boundary delimitation. The *Libya* v. *Malta Continental Shelf* case does not therefore provide an entirely new approach.[109] It merely completes a long evolution towards a second and more operational foundation of shelf rights, which commenced with the *Anglo-French Channel* arbitration, and was accelerated by the advent of the EEZ.

---

[106] ICJ Reports 1985, p. 155, para. 58 (dissenting opinion).
[107] ICJ Reports 1985, p. 33, para. 34.   [108] Ibid.
[109] See also Judge Mbaye, separate opinion, ICJ Reports 1985, pp. 93–9 (arguing that the distance principle is an emanation of the legal concept, as opposed to the physical concept, of natural prolongation).

The Court of Arbitration struggled with the concept of natural prolongation in the context of delimiting the single, coherent, continental shelf of the Channel area, and emphasized that the continental shelf is essentially a juridical concept rather than a natural one:

> The question for the Court to decide, however, is what areas of the continental shelf are to be considered as legally the natural prolongation of the Channel Islands rather than of the mainland of France. In international law, as the United Kingdom emphasised in its pleadings, the concept of the continental shelf is a juridical concept which connotes the natural prolongation under the sea not of a continent of geographical land mass but the land territory of each State. And the very fact that in international law the continental shelf is a juridical concept means that its scope and the conditions for its application are not determined exclusively by the physical facts of geography but also by legal rules.[110]

The juridical nature of the shelf has been emphasized in subsequent cases, including the *Libya* v. *Malta* judgment when it said (as quoted above) that the shelf 'in spite of its physical origins has become more and more a complex and juridical concept'. To some extent, this is a misleading perception. In international law, the shelf has, from the very outset, been a legally defined concept that emerged in customary law in a process of claims and responses. The Court confirmed this view when it said in the last sentence of the *Libya* v. *Malta* judgment quoted that both distance and natural prolongation are parts of the juridical concept. However, what is really meant, in accordance with the Channel arbitration, is that the foundation based on natural prolongation has been gradually amended by a positivist, man-made definition of the shelf, both in a seaward direction for the purpose of its delimitation opposite the Area and between coastal states appertaining to one more or less homogeneous shelf.

The 'distance principle' is one of the instrumental rules that emerged from the 'juridical', or man-made, concept of the shelf. Again, the distance principle is not a foundation and title in its own right, but rather a rule derived from another principle. Tracing it back, this principle first of all relies on coastal configurations. Under the rule defined by distance, seaward delimitation basically relies upon the shape and contours of the

---

[110] 'Arbitration between the United Kingdom of Great Britain and Northern Ireland and the French Republic on the Delimitation of the Continental Shelf' (Judgments of 30 June 1977 and 14 March 1978) para. 191, reprinted in (1979) 18 ILM 397.

coasts of a particular area and upon base lines derived therefrom. These delimitations project the coastline of the coastal state, independently of subsoil and seabed.

It is submitted that this purely geographical concept cannot be a title and foundation of its own. Unlike the natural connection of the land mass and the continental shelf, it does not provide any justification of shelf rights. Pure geography does not explain why shelf rights should expand in accordance with coastal configurations. Like distance, it is again merely instrumental. The projection of coastal configuration and geography instead must stem from a basic foundation. It is evident that this foundation too is man-made, and in that sense a 'juridical' justification, but as it has not been expounded by the Court and doctrine[111] the basic foundation remains unclear and unsettled.

It should be recalled that the Truman Proclamation, which was seen to provide the basic foundation of the shelf, does not refer only to natural prolongation. A more general relationship between marine areas and their resources and the coastal state is equally, if not more, relevant than natural features. The proclamation also stated that: 'self-protection compels the coastal state to keep close watch over activities off its shores which are of the nature necessary for utilisation of these resources'.[112] While natural prolongation, as referred to in the proclamation, became the prime title for shelf rights in international law, this second and more 'political' part of the proclamation relating to offshore positioning and the close relationship of resources has remained unused, with the possible exception of the emphasis upon adjacency found in Article 1 of the 1958 Shelf Convention.

Although natural prolongation provided a suitable argument for the justification of the Proclamation's claim, the pivotal point was that where there were resources ready for exploitation off a coastal state's shores, these should be protected from foreign infringement. In the final analysis, the rationale behind exerting jurisdiction and control is based on the fact that the coastal state is acknowledged to have a *relatively closer relationship* to offshore spaces than all other states and the international community as a whole. In general, the closer to the coast, the more legitimate is the claim for quasi-territorial control, protection, and national exploitation of the resources under the water. Such a relatively

---

[111] It appears that doctrine has been mainly concerned with the legal status of the 200 nm continental shelf and its relation to the EEZ, and not with foundations as such. See Hutchinson, n. 9, 164–72; Rangel, n. 9, pp. 345–6.

[112] Full text above, n. 37, see also text accompanying n. 11.

close relationship provides the essential foundation of shelf rights. This is also the true foundation and rationale behind the doctrine of *ipso facto* and *ab initio* rights, which was established by means of natural prolongation, but which aimed to protect a special relationship. It may be recalled that the ILC never adopted a requirement for the existence of a physical shelf.[113] This may confirm that the protection of a special and close relationship was the ultimate, overriding interest. Moreover, it is interesting to observe that even authors who favoured the doctrine of *res nullius* and acquisition accepted the avoidance of foreign activities in front of a coastal state at the time.[114] This is therefore common ground to all the major doctrines concerning the continental shelf.

As a main foundation, the closeness of the relationship of offshore spaces to the coastal state is also supported by Article 82 of the 1982 LOS Convention, which prescribes payments or contributions in kind for the exploitation of shelf rights beyond the 200 nm zone, i.e. of the outer shelf. Such payments, which commence after five years and are subject to annual increases of up to 7 per cent of the production after twelve years (net importing developing countries exempted), indicate a perception of a gradually decreasing right to the full exploitation of the shelf linked to distance. In other words, there seems to be a geographical relationship between the resources and the coastal state. This provision bridges exclusive national exploitation of the inner shelf and the sharing of resources of the deep seabed. Its operation, of course, fully depends upon the Convention, and of the regime related to the Area in particular. It is not part of customary law, since it envisages a further modification of natural prolongation as the present basis of exclusive shelf rights, which may well exceed 200 nm, given the geological structures. However, such provisions indicate that it is ultimately the degree of intensity of the relationship of offshore resources to the coastal state which is the decisive factor.

c. **Beyond geography** Geographical distance emerges as a prime instrument for translating the concept of the close relationship into operational terms. The central question remains whether geographical distance is the sole criterion used to define the relationship between a

---

[113] See (1950) *Yearbook of the International Law Commission* II, 51–2,; Jewett, n. 9, p. 165.
[114] See Vallat, n. 45, pp. 333, 334 ('A State may find it embarrassing to have mining installations of another State a short distance outside its territorial waters').

coastal state and the use of marine resources. It is difficult to give conclusive answers in abstract terms based on the foundations discussed. At this point, the concept of the continental shelf is influenced by practical reasoning and the results of cases of delimitation. It will be seen that factors other than the geographical and the physical have been, and must continue to be, taken into account despite declining support in more recent case law. Ultimately, we are dealing with relationships between states, which are therefore defined by humans behind them. Such relationships have always been influenced by various parameters; historical, political, cultural and economic. The closeness or intensity of relationships between states and marine spaces are consequently equally influenced by such factors. This goes some way towards explaining why approaches that are exclusively based on geographical or natural features sometimes fall short. They cannot solve complex problems and do not produce equitable and acceptable results in complex cases, and analysis of state practice and judicial settlement further illustrates this point, which is essential to the establishment of the principles of equity in the present field.[115]

The concept of a close relationship is therefore not identical to adjacency or contiguity, as traditionally perceived in an exclusively geographical or physical sense. Close relationship means that spaces and their resources are not allocated using exclusively natural criteria, such as distance. The degree of overall intensity of the relationship between particular states and particular marine spaces emerges as a guiding criterion. It is not limited to particular physical intensity due to the fact of natural prolongation.[116] Instead, the relevant test is which of the coastal states involved shows the closest relationship to a particular area, taking into account all relevant circumstances. The problem is not that factors other than natural or physical must be taken into account, but rather whether or not there is a *numerus clausus* of relevant circumstances and interests and how they relate to geographical considerations. This issue requires further examination.[117]

---

[115] See Chapters 5 and 6.
[116] See Lauterpacht who defined 'the different, and apparently more intense, degree of unity' by the fact that the shelf provides the physical platform upon which the continent rests. Above n. 48.
[117] See Chapters 10 and 11.

100　CONTEXT: THE ENCLOSURE OF THE SEAS

d. **Relationship to permanent sovereignty over natural resources** The concept of close relationship of the coastal state to marine spaces may be considered as emanating from the principle of permanent sovereignty over natural resources. In general terms, it expresses the very same protectionist goals as the founding Truman Proclamation: the avoidance of foreign domination and control over resources to which the coastal state claims a closer relationship and entitlement *ipso iure* and *ab initio*. Legally, there are two reasons for this connection.

Firstly, the principle of close relationship was explicitly applied to the newly emerging rights of coastal states over the soil and subsoil of the continental shelf by the 1962 Resolution 1803 (XVIII) on Permanent Sovereignty over Natural Resources. This resolution was passed with an overwhelming majority.[118]

Secondly, the 'distance principle' was adopted by the Court in the *Libya* v. *Malta Continental Shelf* case mainly because of the existence of the new concept of the 200 nm EEZ in customary international law. In fact, it may be argued that the Court undertook to delimit EEZs, although none had been proclaimed by the two parties to the dispute, and that the special agreement clearly charged the Court to announce the relevant principles of delimitation related to the continental shelves.[119] Evidently, the Court seized this opportunity to clarify the interrelationship between the shelf and the EEZ, and its findings provide a valuable precedent for the formation of a uniform concept of a single homogeneous maritime zone and a uniform set of principles of maritime boundary delimitation.[120] Whether or not this was convincing in this particular case may be left as an open question. It is only important to note at this point that the 200 nm EEZ strongly relies upon the principle of permanent sovereignty, as will be discussed shortly.

It is submitted, however, that even if permanent sovereignty over natural resources is the ultimate foundation of both rights over the continental margin and of rights over the EEZ, the concept of a close and special relationship of the coastal state to marine spaces may provide a somewhat better foundation in operational terms. Though admittedly vague and in need of further specification, it expresses the idea and man-made concept underlying rights over the continental shelf better

---

[118] Resolution 1803 (XVIII), 17 GAOR, Supp. 17, UN Doc. A/5217, at p. 15, adopted 14 December 1962, 87 in favour, France and South Africa against and the Soviet Union abstaining.
[119] Art. I of the Special Agreement, see ICJ Reports 1985, p. 16 para. 2.
[120] See Chapter 2(IV).

than the broad, abstract and still controversial notion of permanent sovereignty.

D. Summary and conclusions

The preceding analysis submits that the continental shelf is a matter of customary, rather than natural, law. It came into operation through an historical process of claims and responses during the mid 1950s. From there, it found its way to confirmation in treaty law, and by the late 1960s it was firmly established in customary law. The principle that shelves need not be actively occupied, effectively or nominally, or proclaimed based on the idea of natural prolongation may resemble natural law. However, this principle also has a basis in customary law, deploying partial and limited retroactive effects.

Confusion regarding the legal nature of shelf rights stems from the fact that in 1969, the Court exclusively relied upon the natural law arguments of the Truman Proclamation. As a new claim, that instrument necessarily had to invoke an 'original, natural, and exclusive (in short a vested) right to the continental shelf', as the Court described the chief doctrine it enunciated.[121] In 1945, coastal states desiring jurisdiction over the continental shelf enunciated the theory that the shelf is an extension of the land mass and thus naturally appurtenant. With regard to claims, establishing a link to the well-recognized territoriality principle was the chief function of natural prolongation at the time.[122]

The true nature of the shelf in customary law only gradually became apparent. After the shelf became firmly established in international law, it was no longer necessary to rely so heavily on natural prolongation. Although continuously reaffirmed as a foundation of shelf rights, the concept of natural prolongation gradually developed into a man-made concept. Difficulties to delimit the continental shelf between coastal

---

[121] ICJ Reports 1969, pp. 32–3, para. 47.
[122] See Derrick W. Bowett, 'Jurisdiction: Changing Patterns of Authority over Activities and Resources' in R. Macdonald and D. Johnston (eds.), *The Structure and Process of International Law: Essays in Legal Philosophy, Doctrine and Theory* (The Hague: Martinus Nijhoff, 1983), pp. 555, 558:

> It is ... clear that states have relied essentially on the territorial principle to support jurisdiction necessary to protect their interests in resources actually located outside their territory but conceded by international law to be within the control of state. The continental shelf doctrine, for example, developed as an assertion of jurisdictional rights, not an assertion of new territorial rights.

states on the basis of natural prolongation and the advent of new zones (the EEZ and the Area) accelerated this process. Still valid as a fundamental justification for the rights and delimitation of the outer limits towards the deep seabed, prolongation was gradually amended by a strictly legal concept of the continental shelf. The basis of this concept was already expressed in the Truman Proclamation as the will to self-protection and maintenance of national control over offshore resources. It relies upon the argument that coastal states have a closer relationship to offshore marine areas than other states. Such a relationship is not exclusively defined in geographical terms, but takes into account other factors as well. As a whole, the concept emanates from the principle of permanent sovereignty over natural resources. Unfortunately, these man-made foundations behind the claim were never explicitly applied, but nevertheless can be determined to be the true basis of delimitation practices which rely (on the surface and somewhat confusingly) partly upon the doctrine of natural prolongation and partly upon a 'distance principle'.

From this analysis, a number of conclusions that are relevant to the problem of boundary delimitation may be drawn even at this early stage of the inquiry. They are of basic importance for the future establishment of equity as a basis for maritime boundary delimitation, as they provide a conceptual framework:

(i) Firstly, the delimitation of maritime boundaries is an eminently creative act. As the Chamber of the Court said in the *Gulf of Maine* case in 1984 (in contrast with its findings in 1969):

> It must, however, be emphasised that a delimitation, whether of a maritime boundary or a land boundary, is a legal-political operation, and that it is not the case that where a natural boundary is discernible, the political boundary necessarily has to follow the same line.[123]

Despite the fact that coastal states do not have to claim or occupy the shelf, although a state's title exists, it is effectively dormant as, since the concept emerged in customary law, actual determination of spaces and delimitation of boundaries is in reality the appropriation of newly and recently attributed jurisdictions. It is not merely a matter of finding what already exists in theory or nature.

(ii) Secondly, since shelf rights are a matter of customary, and therefore fairly recent, man-made law, delimitation cannot rely exclusively

---

[123] ICJ Reports 1984, p. 277, para. 56.

upon rules and principles related to the very concept of the shelf. Human conduct in the area is just as relevant, particularly in relation to pre-existing historic rights.

(iii) Thirdly, since the doctrine of the continental shelf relies upon the intensity or closeness of the relationship between the coastal state and offshore marine spaces, delimitation between states cannot rely exclusively upon the natural features of the seabed and coastal configurations. Definition of the doctrine of the shelf is not merely a matter of geographical distances and contiguity; it may be equally defined in terms of historical, political, cultural and economic criteria. Therefore, the definition of which non-geographic elements are equally legitimate and equally constitutive for closeness of the relationship in the light of equity is a task of the utmost importance.

(iv) Fourthly, it is important to emphasize the ICJ's crucial role in shaping doctrines related to the continental shelf. The ICJ shows the characteristics of an activist, law-making court willing to promote the law. It is striking how easily the Court transformed the very foundations of claims to the shelf into law during the *North Sea* cases. What was argued as being an inherent, natural right, 'reasonable and just' and the basic contention of the United States proclamation, implicitly came to constitute the ultimate foundation of the Court's own doctrine of natural prolongation and inherent rights.

Though the Court elaborated specifically on the requirements of customary law in this case,[124] the doctrine of inherent rights and natural prolongation was established without any reference to customary law. Instead, the Court implicitly relied upon natural law. In fact, on close examination the doctrine constituted a creative act of judicial legislation inspired by the Truman Proclamation.

Similar patterns of judicial activism can be observed from the second landmark case of *Libya* v. *Malta*. The acceptance of a 200 nm distance principle, amending natural prolongation, was strongly inspired by the definition of Article 76 of the 1982 Convention. The justification based on the EEZ, however, cannot conceal the fact that this step, taken in a case purely related to the shelf, was an act of judicial legislation, with no application of the relevant tests of customary law. An implied desire to transform the 1982 Convention into general international law cannot be concealed. It will be seen that this judicial policy not only relates to the

---

[124] ICJ Reports 1969, pp. 41–5, paras. 70–80 (question denied whether Art. 6 Shelf Convention and equidistance emerged into customary law).

shaping of the overall concepts of the shelf, but also to equity and the rules and principles of maritime boundary delimitation.

Finally, the preceding analysis of the foundations and rationale behind the continental shelf raises issues as to what extent these foundations are different from those of the EEZ. Are there two different concepts, or rather a single uniform zone up to a distance of 200 nm? The answer to this question will be provided after the following analysis of the exclusive economic zone.

III. The exclusive economic zone

A. Description and development

The second, more recent and equally fundamental change in the law of maritime resources relates to jurisdiction over offshore resources found in the water column beyond the territorial sea and contiguous zone. It led to the concept of the EEZ, an area adjacent to the territorial sea and not exceeding 200 nm measured from the base lines from which the breadth of the territorial sea is measured.[125] This zone comprises the jurisdiction

---

[125] Writings on the EEZ were abundant in the 1970s and 1980s. For a history and comprehensive analysis see David J. Attard, *The Exclusive Economic Zone in International Law* (Oxford: Clarendon Press, 1987), pp. 3–9; Winston Conrad Extavour, *The Exclusive Economic Zone: A Study of the Evolution and Progressive Development of the International Law of the Sea* (Geneva: Institut universitaire de hautes études internationales, 1978); Eduardo Ferrero Costa, *El nuevo derecho del mar: el Perú y las 200 millas* (Lima: Pontificia Universidad Católica del Perú, 1979); Lothar Gündling, *Die Zweihundert-Seemeilen Wirtschaftszone: Enstehung eines neuen Regimes des Meeresvölkerrechts* (Berlin, New York: Springer, 1999); Krueger and Nordquist, n. 25, 321; Albert W. Koers, *International Regulation of Marine Fisheries: A Study of Regional Fisheries Organizations* (West Byfleet: Fishing News Books, 1973); see Vicuña, n. 7. See also J. E. Carroz, 'Les Problèmes de la pêche à la Conférence sur le droit de la mer et dans la pratique des Etats' (1980) 84 *Revue Générale de Droit International Public*, 705; Sigheru Oda, 'Fisheries under the United Nations Convention on the Law of the Sea' (1983) 77 *American Journal of International Law*, 739; Horace B. Robertson, 'Navigation in the Exclusive Economic Zone' (1984) 24 *Virginia Journal of International Law*, 835; Geir Ulfstein, '200 Mile Zones and Fisheries Management' (1983) 52 *Nordisk Tidsskrift for International Ret*, 3; Jorge Vargas, 'The Legal Nature of the Patrimonial Sea: A First Step towards the Definition of the Exclusive Economic Zone' (1979) 22 *German Yearbook of International Law*, 142; Wolfgang Graf Vitzthum, *Die Plünderung der Meere: Ein gemeinsames Erbe wird zerstückelt* (Frankfurt: Fischer Verlag, 1981). See also reports and discussions by the ILA Committee on the Exclusive Economic Zone, ILA Report of the Sixtieth Conference, Montreal 1982, 303–324 (1983); ILA Report of the Sixty-Fifth Conference, Paris 1984, 183–307 (1985). For national legislation see United Nations, *Division for Affairs of the Law of the Sea, The Law of the Sea: National Legislation on the Exclusive Economic Zone* (1993).

over all natural resources, living and non-living. Unlike the shelf, the new zone is much more clearly defined. Contemporary legal problems focus upon the legal nature of the zone, the contents of rights, the scope of jurisdiction, and the relationship of the established continental shelf doctrine. They are less concerned with the seaward expanses and the very foundation and nature involved.

The introduction and deployment of large and sophisticated distant-water fleets, equipped with efficient gear and on-board capacity to process and conserve catches, caused serious problems of over-fishing within the rich grounds of the shallow waters covering the continental shelves where, in fact, 95 per cent of the seas' yield is harvested within a range of 200 nm offshore from the continents and islands.[126] The problem arose in the 1940s and became aggravated in the 1960s, yet attempts to restore and control the balance of the basis of international law co-operation with a global perspective largely failed.[127] Freedom of the high seas led to a highly uneven distribution of global fish resources. It was reported that in 1979, at the time when the EEZ was emerging globally, and with a total of 137 independent coastal states, more than 50 per cent of the global catch was attributable to 6 major fishing nations (China, Japan, Norway, Peru, USA and the former USSR), and 75 per cent was from the leading 16 countries.[128] At the time, another report concerning distribution in 1976 spoke of 60 per cent catches by Japan and the Soviet Union alone, and 80 per cent by the 9 leading fishing nations, mostly by means of distant-water fleets.[129]

In many coastal states, local industries were threatened or had their future development restricted. This situation encouraged protectionist

---

[126] UN Food and Agriculture Organization (FAO), *Report of the FAO World Conference on Fisheries Management and Development* (Rome 1994), Appendix D, p. 1.

[127] UNCLOS I and II were not able to solve the problems caused by claims to an extended territorial seas and the introduction of fishing limits. Moreover, the 1958 Convention on Fishing and Conservation was only signed by thirty-seven states and remained virtually ineffective. For references see Chapter 1, n. 7. On this issue, see William T. Burke, *The New International Law of Fisheries: UNCLOS 1982 and Beyond* (Oxford: Clarendon Press, 1994).

[128] Ram P. Anand, 'Freedom of the Sea: Past, Present and Future' in Rafael Cutiérrez Giradot et al. (eds.), *New Directions in International Law: Essays in Honour of Wolfgang Abendroth: Festschrift zu seinem 75. Geburtstag* (Frankfurt am Main: Campus Verlag, 1982), p. 215 ff., 267; see also Ram P. Anand, 'The Politics of a New Legal Order for Fisheries' (1980) 11 *Ocean Development & International Law*, 265.

[129] Vladimir Kaczynski, 'Distant Water Fisheries and the 200 Mile Economic Zone' 44, *Occasional Paper No. 34* (Honolulu: The Law of the Sea Institute, 1983). According to this report, distant-water fleets harvested up to 80 per cent in the North-east Pacific, North-west Pacific and West African Waters.

fishing policies. One of the instruments applied by states, which was used to achieve increased protection, was the introduction of straight base lines, which resulted in a seaward expansion of territorial fishing zones. Although it was ultimately decided upon grounds that mainly related to the parties' conduct, the 1951 *Anglo-Norwegian Fisheries* case was an important landmark case in this area. For the first time, the Court acknowledged the legitimacy of social and economic factors in relation to the needs of coastal industries and communities – an argument which was submitted by Norway.[130] This was long before the advent of the concept of sustainable use of natural resources.

The consistency of straight base lines with international law was later confirmed in treaty law and considerably expanded the territorial seas of coastal states.[131] However, it did not respond sufficiently to the problems caused by over-fishing on the basis of the principle of freedom of the sea. Neither did efforts at conventional allocation of catches achieve the goal of conservation and prudent management. The framework in existence at this time, of some twenty regional fisheries management agreements, has not succeeded in achieving an overall balance. Most of them merely assume consultative and other 'non-bite' functions. Many opportunities to provide for an effective and equitable international conservation policy, as was much advocated in the 1960s,[132] as well as a more even distribution of

---

[130] *Fisheries Case (United Kingdom v. Norway)*, Judgment, ICJ Reports 1951, p. 142; See also 1 Pleadings at 219ff. For further discussion of the case and the criterion of economical needs see Chapter 8.

[131] See Art. 4 1958 Convention on the Territorial Sea and the Contiguous Zone, done 29 April, entered into force on 10 September 1964, 516 UNTS 205; Art. 7 LOS Convention. The possibility of drawing straight base lines where coasts 'possess a multitude of deep inlets, or when coasts are bordered by a myriad of islands which appear to be an extension of the land' (John R. V. Prescott) has sometimes led to abuse of such possibilities and undue extension of territorial seas to as much as 24 nm. Prescott, 'Straight Baselines: Theory and Practice' (typescript), paper presented at the 19th Annual Conference of the Law of the Sea Institute, Cardiff, 24–27 July 1985, p. 38 (on file with the author), writes:

> Straight baselines have been drawn along coasts which are neither deeply intended nor fringed with islands. While it is known that the United States of America has been diligent in drawing attention to these infractions, and, where necessary, in asserting their rights of navigation, which have been infringed, observers are left with the impression that some countries have cheated with success.

[132] See Koers, n 125, p. 271 ff. Today, the following argument, first made in 1965, reads like distant historical hope – or utopia, Douglas M. Johnston, *The International Law of Fisheries. A Framework for Policy-Oriented Inquiries* (New Haven CT, London: Yale University Press, 1987), p. 463:

revenue, were missed.[133] Once again, answers were sought through the mechanism of unilaterally declaring exclusive zones. The goals of conservation and sound management, as well as security revenues, began to be pursued irreversibly by means of nationalization and particularization of the water columns off the coasts, which were rich in fish.

The movement to protect and preserve living resources from exploitation by 'foreign' fishing nations by means of exclusive zones originated in the Americas. It can be traced from as far back as the 1889 US legislation for the protection of seals in the Bering Sea, which was held to be completely inconsistent with international law at the time,[134] to the more recent, but never implemented, 1945 Truman Proclamation on Fisheries, which claimed the right to establish 'explicitly bounded conservation zones'.[135] The driving force, however, was exerted by a number of Latin American states.[136] After World War II, they

> The future of the World's resources is more important than the future of familiar legal concepts. National economic interests are, or can become, complementary to one another. The needs of any one state are substantially the same as those of others. By understanding this, governments can adopt a world community perspective that in no way impairs the national interests. Short-term sacrifices would be involved, but these, if rationally planned, would become instruments to secure more firmly based and more enduring benefits.

[133] Apart from the International Whaling Commission, fisheries on the high seas are being co-ordinated and harmonization is being sought on a regional basis. By February 1993, there were thirty-one agreements in force, some of them established within the framework of the FAO. See FAO, *Activities of Regional Fishery Bodies and Other International Organizations Concerned with Fisheries*, Fisheries Circular No. 807 Rev. 1 (1993). With the exception of the EEZ, however, none of these agreements delegates effective powers of management and conservation on the international level. The agreements mainly provide for consultation, recommendation, research, co-ordination and harmonization. See Jean E. Carroz, 'Institutional Aspects of Fishery Management Under the New Regime of the Oceans' (1984) 21 *San Diego Law Review,* 513 (including a survey on existing marine fishery bodies at pp. 553–40). For earlier accounts of international co-operation in fisheries see Francis T. Christy and Anthony Scott, *The Common Wealth in Ocean Fisheries* (Baltimore: Johns Hopkins Press, London: Oxford University Press, 1965), p. 192 ff.; Johnston, n. 132, p. 358 ff.

[134] *Anglo-American Fur Seal Arbitration*, Moore, 1 Arbitrations 755.

[135] Policy of the United States with Respect to Coastal Fisheries in Certain Areas of the High Seas, reprinted in Whiteman, n. 11, pp. 954–5; see also Extavour, n. 125, pp. 67–8.

[136] See e.g. Attard, n. 125, pp. 3–9; Ferrero, n. 125, and the review of this book by Richard Bath (1982) 76 *American Journal of International Law,* 691. F. V. Garcia-Amador, 'The Origins of the Concept of an Exclusive Economic Zone: Latin American Practice and Legislation' in D. J. Attard, *The Exclusive Economic Zone in International Law* (Oxford: Clarendon Press, 1987), pp. 7–26; Ann L. Hollick, 'U.S. Foreign Policy and the Law of the Sea' (1981) 17 *Virginia Journal of International Law,* 196; L. D. M. Nelson, 'The Patrimonial Sea' (1973) 22 *International Comparative Law Quarterly,* 668.

continued to push for extended national jurisdiction over marine space and resources and the establishment of what was called the patrimonial sea. The 1947 Chilean Presidential Declaration,[137] the Peruvian Executive Decree 871 of 1947,[138] and the 1952 Santiago Agreement between Chile, Ecuador and Peru are amongst the landmarks along the path towards expanded national sovereignty over living marine resources.[139] The concept pursued was one of an expanded territorial sea of 200 nm, limiting rights of communication to mere innocent passage.[140]

However, due to the resistance of established maritime powers, territorialist attempts to change international law through the process of claims and responses failed for many years. Since the concept of the patrimonial sea envisaged not merely control over resources, but also included full jurisdiction, it has never been acceptable to marine powers interested in free navigation and communications. They first refused to expand territorial seas beyond 3 miles, and later beyond the present 12-mile limit. A clear expression of the unchanged policies of naval powers was shown through the United States' rejection of Libyan claims to extend full jurisdiction in the Gulf of Sidra up to a 'line of death' (latitude 32° 30' N) beyond 12 miles from the coast, and their use of force against armed attacks in such waters, which had been claimed as territorial waters by Libya in 1986.[141]

The persistent rejection of claims for full sovereignty, however, did not block further development. The situation first began to change in the 1970s, when some of the Latin American states adopted a more moderate approach, which caused a split into two schools of thought (the

---

[137] Reprinted in Laws and Regulations on the Regime of the High Seas, United Legislative Series, LSt/LEG/SER.B/1, at 6 (1951) [hereinafter LST/LEG/SER.B/1 (1951)].
[138] Attard, n. 125, p. 5; Garcia-Amador, n. 136, p. 20, both also mentioning similar legislation by Costa Rica (Decree Law 116 of 27 July 1947).
[139] Signed at the First Conference on the Exploitation and Conservation of the Maritime Resources of the South Pacific, Santiago, 18 August 1952, reprinted in H. S. Lay et al. (eds.), *New Directions in the Law of the Sea* (looseleaf, Dobbs Ferry NY: Oceana Publications, 1973), vol. 1, p. 231.
[140] Lupinacci, n. 1, pp. 75–6 (the Santiago Declaration differed in that respect from the preceding Chilean and Peruvian Instruments, which still referred to freedom of navigation).
[141] After the sixth US fleet was unsuccessfully attacked by Libyan SAM 5 missiles, freedom of navigation was asserted by the sinking of at least three Libyan patrol boats on 24 March 1986, and two attacks on SAM 5 missiles on Libyan territory, *The Economist*, 29 March 1986, p. 37; for US justification (self-defence against military attacks, Art. 51 UN Charter) see (1986) 80 *American Journal of International Law*, 634 at the end.

territorialists versus the patrimonialists), who were still competing at the beginning of UNCLOS III. While those in the territorialist camp continued to press for a 200-mile territorial sea entailing full sovereignty, the patrimonialists gradually changed their aspirations towards the conception of horizontally shared jurisdictions for the coastal states and the community as a whole as a means of power sharing. The Declaration of Montevideo in 1970[142] and the Declaration of Santo Domingo in 1972[143] developed and proposed a concept of the patrimonial sea that established both the coastal states' exclusive rights over all resources and also their jurisdiction over maritime research and pollution control, but which, unlike earlier definitions, reserved community rights of communications (freedom of navigation, over flight and installation of cables and pipelines) outside a 12-mile territorial sea. Comparable aspirations were developed by Asian and African States;[144] and Kenya submitted first draft proposals for the so-called EEZ to the United Nations in preparation of UNCLOS III in 1972.[145] The term replaced the notion, but not yet the content, of the patrimonial sea.[146] The movement gathered further momentum from the findings of the ICJ in the 1974 *Fisheries Jurisdiction* cases.[147] Although not rendering judgment '*sub specie legis ferenda*',[148] and though denying the lawfulness of a unilaterally imposed exclusive 50-mile fishing zone, the Court acknowledged preferential fishing rights of Iceland beyond the limits

---

[142] The Declaration of Montevideo on Law of the Sea (1970) 10 ILM, 1081. See also Declaration of Latin American States on the Law of the Sea, 8 August 1970, (Lima Declaration), 1 *New Directions*, 237.

[143] Specialized Conference of Caribbean Countries Concerning the Problems of the Sea: Declaration of Santo Domingo (1972) 11 ILM, 892 ff. See also Inter-American Judicial Committee Resolution on the Law of the Sea, 10 September 1971, 11 ILM 984.

[144] See Conclusions in the General Report of the African States Regional Seminar on the Law of the Sea, held in Yaounde, 20–30 June 1972, reprinted in 1 *New Directions*, 250; see also Council of Ministers of the Organization of African Unity (OAU), Resolution on Fisheries, June 1971, reprinted in S. Oda, *The International Law of the Ocean Development* (Leiden: A. W. Sijthoff International Publishing Company, 1972), p. 362.

[145] Draft Articles on Exclusive Economic Zone Concept, UN Doc. A/AC. 138/S.C.ii/L.10, reprinted in (1973) 12 ILM 33. See generally Evelyne Peyroux, 'Les Etats africains face aux questions actuelles du droit de la mer' (1974) 78 *Revue Générale de Droit International Public*, 623.

[146] Colombia, Mexico and Venezuela presented draft articles including references to the patrimonial sea that resemble the Santiago Declaration. They later agreed to use the majority term of the EEZ. See Lupinacci, n. 1, pp. 91–2.

[147] *Fisheries Jurisdiction (United Kingdom v. Iceland)*, Merits, Judgment, ICJ Reports 1974, p. 3. See also Judge Nervo (Mexico) dissenting in the 1973 judgment, arguing in favour of the legal existence of the patrimonial sea, *Fisheries Jurisdiction (United Kingdom v. Iceland)*, Judgment, ICJ Reports 1973, p. 44.

[148] ICJ Reports 1974, pp. 23–4, para. 53.

of an agreed 12-mile exclusive fishing zone, due to Iceland's economic dependence on fisheries.[149]

Clearly, however, it was UNCLOS III that exerted the most important educational and catalytic effect. During the Conference, a great number of states declared exclusive jurisdiction over living resources within a 200 nm zone. This policy was adopted not only by developing states, but also within a remarkably short period by states with traditionally strong interests in long-distance water fisheries, including the EEC countries, Japan, Norway, Spain (before joining the EEC), the USA and the USSR.[150] The trend toward exclusive jurisdiction was no longer reversible. As before, a snowball effect practically forced states to go along with the new enclosure movement to protect the remaining international and free fishing grounds from careless depletion and exhaustion. The region of the Falklands provides an excellent example as to how much overall regulation was needed, once a number of shelves were no longer freely accessible to long-distance fishing. A dual system with just some isolated fish-rich areas remaining open to free exploitation cannot be sustained in the long run.[151]

---

[149] *Fisheries Jurisdiction (United Kingdom v. Iceland)*, Merits, Judgment, ICJ Reports 1974, p. 3; see Robin R. Churchill, 'The Fisheries Jurisdiction Cases: The Contribution of the International Court of Justice to the Debate on Coastal States' (1975) 24 ICLQ, 92. See Chapter 10(III)(B) and for the equitable duty to negotiate Chapter 12(III)(C)(5).

[150] For a table of legislation see Attard, n. 125. With regard to the EEC, the 200 nm fishing zone is an internal matter of the Community and delimitation with other states – unlike the continental shelf – and is therefore the responsibility of the EEC. See 'Council Resolution on certain External Aspects of the creation of a 200-mile Fishing Zone in the Community with Effect from 1 January 1977' reprinted in (1976) 15 ILM, 1425; see e.g. Daniel Vignes, 'La Création dans la Communauté au cours de l'automne 1976 et de l'hiver 1977, d'une zone de pêche s'étendant jusqu'à deux cent milles' in Mélanges F. Dehousse (ed.), *La Construction Européenne*, 2 vols. (Paris: F. Nathan, 1979), vol. II, p. 323; Albert W. Koers, 'The External Authority of the EEC in regard to Marine Fisheries' (1977) 14 *Common Market Law Review*, 268. In 1983, the Community adopted a new fishery policy, which provides for a common system of conservation, structural measures, organization of the market and a joint foreign policy. Council Regulation (EEC) No. 177/83 of 25 January 1983, establishing a Community System for the Conservation and Management of Fishery Resources, OJ (1983) L24 1–13. See also Robin R. Churchill, *The EEC's Contribution to 'State' Practice in the Field of Fisheries* (typescript); Tullio Treves, *The EC, the UN and the Law of the Sea* (typescript), both papers presented at the 19th Annual Conference of the Law of the Sea Institute, Cardiff, 25–27 July 1985.

[151] Fishing activities around the Falklands before a protective zone was established provide an illustration of depletion in unprotected waters. The press reported that in 1984, an average of 63 factory ships, mostly from Eastern Europe (e.g. 51 Polish, 32 Russian, 9 East German, 4 Spanish and 7 Japanese in April 1984) logged a total of 3,557 fishing days in what are still high seas off the Falklands. More ships, in particular Japanese ones, were

With UNCLOS III progressing, it became clear that the concept of a comprehensive EEZ would emerge, rather than zones limited to fish conservation and management. In accordance with these developments, many states further expanded the scope of their jurisdiction. By 1983, fifty-six states had established EEZs whereas thirty-six states still preferred to continue to limit the exercise of their jurisdiction to fisheries.[152] By the end of 1989, the numbers had reached 79 and 16, respectively.[153]

B. The foundation and legal nature of EEZ rights

1. Permanent sovereignty over natural resources and the close relationship of the coastal state to offshore marine spaces

Unlike the law of the continental shelf, the foundations of rights related to the EEZ have so far only caused negligible dispute or concern. The issue has not generated a great deal of interest, either in doctrine or in case law. Instead, discussions have mainly focused upon the question of whether the EEZ has become part of customary law and on relationships with the territorial and high seas.

With little attention paid to legal foundations as such, the motivation, the *ratio legis* behind the concept, was left widely ignored in legal discussions.[154] This may well be because there has never been a debate on natural law and prolongation with respect to this zone. Nevertheless, it seems useful to search for the foundations of the new concept beyond the problem of adoption in

---

expected to come in 1985. 'The figures ... disclose a picture of unrestricted, legalised plunder of a scale not so far appreciated in Britain', 'Foreign Fleets Depleting Falklands Fish Stocks', *The Guardian*, 10 December 1984, p. 28, referring to a Royal Navy Report. In May 1985, a report spoke of 200 ships, with a record of 300, earlier in the season. The fleet amounted to 8,000 men, and the value of total annual catches was estimated at £200 million. Although the Falklands government pressed for unilateral fishing limits for protection and in order to raise revenues, the UK government was reluctant. Qualms were reported to 'centre round Argentine sensitivities and, more notably, dread of confrontation with a Russian vessel which refused to observe the limit. The Government's current tack is to try for a multinational conservation policy but little hope is held out', 'Multinational "Task Force" Invades the Falklands', *The Guardian*, 30 May 1985, p. 4.

[152] Lewis M. Alexander, 'The Ocean Enclosure Movement' (1983) 20 *San Diego Law Review*, 561, 568, 590–1, Tables 2, 3.
[153] Donat Pharand, 'The Law of the Sea: An Overview' in Donat Pharand and Umberto Leanza (eds.), *The Continental Shelf and the Exclusive Economic Zone* (The Hague: Martinus Nijhoff, 1993), p. 10.
[154] See Pharand, n. 153.

customary or treaty law, as these are essential for the definition of EEZ rights, the determination of the relationship of the EEZ and the continental shelf zone, and of the principles and rules of boundary delimitation.

An analysis of the legal foundations and nature of the EEZ shows a pattern similar to that which occurred under the shelf concept, although elements of natural law never became as prominent The long and troublesome detours based on natural concepts were carefully avoided under the EEZ. There is no privilege of rights existing *ab initio*, and the establishment of EEZ rights – unlike shelf rights – depends on proclamation. The EEZ emerged, from the very beginning, as a juridical, i.e. solely man-made, concept. Yet in the final analysis, in common with the shelf, its main foundations and justifications are the close relationship of offshore natural resources to the coastal state and the concept of permanent sovereignty over natural resources.

The 1945 Truman Proclamation, that claimed the right to establish exclusive conservation zones, did not rely upon justice (as its twin proclamation of the shelf) but rather on equity. Whether this distinction was purposely phrased in this way remains an open question. Clearly, however, the policy does show strong corrective elements, and thus represents the traditional functions of equity, so it may be that in this sense, the instruments preferred to call upon equity rather than justice, thus justifying the establishment of rights of the coastal state over offshore living resources needing protection. The Proclamation stated:

> (T)here is an urgent need to protect coastal fishery resources from destructive exploitation, having due regard to conditions peculiar to each region and situation and to the special rights and equities of the coastal State and any other State which may have established a legitimate interest therein.[155]

More recently, Latin American claims have sought more specific foundations, taking advantage of general developments in the law of resources brought about by developing nations. As a foundation of exclusive rights within the patrimonial sea, the Declaration of Montevideo invoked the principle of sovereign rights of states over natural resources.[156] This principle was restated by the Lima Declaration[157] and by the Kenya draft articles on the EEZ.[158]

Reference to the principle of sovereignty over natural resources, as applied to maritime riches, formerly *res communis*, provides an

---

[155] Above n. 111 pp. 752, 755.   [156] Above n. 142, p. 108.   [157] Above n. 142, p. 237.
[158] Above n. 118.

interesting example of the scope of legal dynamics and expansion of principles. At the time when the concept of sovereignty over natural resources emerged with regard to land-based and offshore mineral resources, they were often under the control of, and subject to exploitation by, foreign enterprise and capital. As indicated, the founding Resolution in 1962 (1803 (XVIII)), which dealt with Permanent Sovereignty over Natural Resources, implied new rights over the soil and subsoil of the continental shelf only. In accordance with the contemporary law of the sea, no reference was or could be made to living resources.

The situation eventually changed in the next decade, with the 1973 GA Resolution 3171 (XXVIII) on Permanent Sovereignty over Natural Resources explicitly including sovereignty over the water column. In its first paragraph, the resolution

> (s)trongly reaffirms the inalienable rights of States to permanent sovereignty over all their natural resources, on land within their international boundaries as well as those of the sea-bed and the subsoil thereof within their national jurisdiction and in the superjacent waters.[159]

Though it was phrased as a confirmation only, and left the determination of the expanses of jurisdiction open, this resolution indicated a gradually emerging consensus towards the extension of national jurisdiction over the living resources of the sea, based upon the doctrine of permanent sovereignty over natural resources.

With the advent of the doctrine of sustainable social and economic development and enhanced consideration of environmental and ecological concerns gaining importance since the Stockholm principles of 1972[160] and the 1992 Rio Declaration[161] and instruments, a contemporary foundation of the EEZ should additionally be sought along these principles. Chapter 3 of this book will describe the detrimental effects of many of the EEZs upon fishing policies under current practices and

---

[159] 28 GAOR, Supp. 30, UN Doc. A/9080, p. 3, adopted 17 Dec. 1973 (emphasis added), 108 in favour, UK against, 16 abstentions (including France, FRG, Japan and USA) but for different reasons than the law of the sea (mainly issues of expropriation and compensation).

[160] UN Environment Programme (UNEP), Declaration of the United Nations Conference on the Human Environment, Stockholm, 16 June 1972, www.unep.org/Documents.Multilingual/Default.asp?documentid=97&articleid=1503 (last accessed 28 January 2012).

[161] UNEP, Rio Declaration on Environment and Development, 14 June 1992, www.unep.org/Documents.Multilingual/Default.asp?documentid=78&articleid=1163 (last accessed 28 January 2012).

administration. A contemporary foundation for the EEZ, relying upon the requirement for sustainable resource management within appropriated and controlled fishing zones, will assist in the promotion of badly needed policies of conservation and enhanced co-operation among coastal states. The EEZ can no longer be exclusively justified by the needs of local and coastal fisheries. It has to rely increasingly upon, and can be justified to some extent by, the idea that the zone is used to benefit the careful and prudential management of living resources and global commons.

With regard to the discussion of the relationship of the EEZ and the continental shelf, we note that both concepts shared similar philosophical foundations. Though much weaker and better disguised in the case of the continental shelf, permanent sovereignty over natural resources is a common basis for both of the zones. With regard to this common basis, it is submitted that the EEZ is even more closely tied to the idea that jurisdiction over its resources ultimately relies upon a special and close relationship of the coastal state to offshore marine spaces. This is so because distance from the coast has been the decisive element of the concept from the very outset.

2. Customary law

In operational terms, the EEZ emerged as a matter of customary law, as the continental shelf zone had before. Equity, justice and the concept of permanent sovereignty have helped to promote the new zone, just like the idea of natural prolongation has helped to promote the continental shelf zone. But these principles could not by themselves provide a legal basis to establish the zone in international law, as the *Fisheries Jurisdiction* cases have shown.[162] Instead, the process of claims and favourite responses in state practice was once again decisive.

---

[162] In 1974, the Court implied such philosophical foundations to be justifications of claims, not the law, when it commented on efforts to establish 200 miles of fisheries zones: 'The Court is also aware of present endeavours, pursued under the auspices of the United Nations ... which must be regarded as manifestations of the views and opinions of individual States and as vehicles of their aspirations, rather than as expressing principles of existing law.' ICJ Reports 1974, p. 24, para. 53. For a view directly founding the EEZ upon the principle of permanent sovereignty see Vargas, n. 125, 161 (stating that the EEZ 'was created as a political and legal extension of the coastal State's sovereign rights over its natural resources [emphasis added]'). It should be added that neither Art. 2 of the 1975 Charter of Economic Rights and Duties of States (CERDS), GA Res. 3281 (XXIX), 29 GAOR 484 (1975), reprinted in (1975) 14 ILM 251 ss nor Art. 3(e) of the 1974 Declaration on the Establishment of a New International Economic Order, GA Res. 3201

With regard to the timing of this process, it is fair to say that the first and preliminary extension had become established by the middle of the 1970s, while the latter took more years to develop. Presumably by the early 1980s, but certainly by 1985, the right of a coastal state to claim comprehensive jurisdiction over all natural resources within a 200 nm zone were no longer opposable.[163] In 1982, the ICJ endorsed the concept of the EEZ, and obiter dictum, tentatively held it to be part of general international law.[164] Though at the time the Court's view was hardly substantiated, it was certainly in line with subsequent developments and trends. Western criticism[165] was soon overridden by the subsequent adoption of the EEZ by traditional defenders of the high seas. For example, the United States recognized and proclaimed the EEZ (without changing their existing regulations) in the 1983 'Reagan Proclamation'.[166] The former Soviet Union[167] and the United Kingdom[168] followed suit in 1984.

(S-VI), 6th Spec. Sess. GAOR (1974) Supp. 1 (A/9559), further specified the scope of natural resources under national sovereignty, but remained vague and flexible. In particular, no reference was made to marine living resources as was the case for minerals and common heritage in Art. 29 of CERDS. All this suggests, in accordance with the Court, that permanent sovereignty served as a political and philosophical and not a legally operational basis for the EEZ.

[163] Although Latin American states proclaimed 200 nm zones much earlier, it is difficult to establish the legal validity of the concept on the basis of regional custom prior to the date indicated. But see Extavour, n. 125, pp. 285–95, and Vicuña, n. 7, pp. 130–1 (EEZ as established in customary law at least by 1982 and even before when consensus was reached at UNCLOS III). Since the fishing grounds concerned are far beyond regional importance and intensively frequented by long-distance fleets from overseas, acquiescence would have been required by a considerable number of major fishing nations.

[164] ICJ Reports 1982, p. 74, para. 100 ('the concept of the exclusive economic zone, which may be regarded as part of modern international law'); see also separate opinion of Judge Jimenez de Aréchaga, ICJ Reports 1982, p. 115, para. 54. Judge Oda, in his dissenting opinion, raised the issue whether the case should have been dealt with in the light of the EEZ, given its rapid evolution in customary law. He wrote: 'Throughout the history of international law, scarcely any other major concept has ever stood on the threshold of acceptance within such a short period', ICJ Reports 1982, p. 228, para. 120.

[165] Panel, ICJ Decision on the Kibya–Tunisia Continental Shelf Case, Remarks by Ted L. Stein (1982) 76 *American Society of International Law Proceedings*, 161, 164.

[166] Proclamation No. 5030, 'Exclusive Economic Zone of the United States' 10 March 1983 reprinted in (1983) 77 *American Journal of International Law*, 619, 621; (1983) 22 ILM 461.

[167] On Soviet legislation on the EEZ see Barbara Kwiatkoswka, 'New Soviet Legislation on the 200 Mile Economic Zone and Certain Problems of Evolution of Customary Law' (1986) 33 *The Netherlands International Law Review*, 24.

[168] (1984) 55 *British Yearbook of International Law*, 557.

As noted earlier, in 1985 the ICJ left no doubt that the EEZ was by then firmly established in international law: 'It is incontestable in the Court's view that ... the institution of the exclusive economic zone ... is shown by the practice of States to have become part of customary law.'[169] Even though the *Libya* v. *Malta Continental Shelf* case did not concern the delimitation of EEZs and the Court's assessment remains without the provision of empirical evidence, the judgment is no longer a matter of obiter dicta. The very existence of the legal concept of the EEZ commands the delimitation of the shelf up to a distance of 200 nm from the base lines of the coastal states.

C. The scope of EEZ rights

1. State practice and customary law

Concordant evolution and widespread support for the 200 nm zone and subsequent ratifications of the 1982 Convention cannot conceal the fact that the precise contents of the EEZ are as yet unsettled in state practice and customary law. Although established in customary law as a matter of principle,[170] a uniform and consistent international regime is likely to emerge only with the universal acceptance of the multilaterally agreed regime of the EEZ in Part V of the 1982 Convention. While the main problems of the shelf relate to the nature of shelf rights, those of the EEZ concern the scope of rights and obligations in customary law. The predominant qualification of the novel zone as being a zone *sui generis*[171] opened up a wide spectrum of different solutions. In the 1980s, the state of national law was still far from uniform. The EEZ, claiming full jurisdiction over natural resources emerged alongside existing fishing zones, which were characterized, despite being largely equivalent to the EEZ, by a limited jurisdiction over biological resources.[172]

---

[169] ICJ Reports 1985, p. 33, para. 34. For an implicit recognition of the EEZ see also the 'La Bretagne Award': Jean Maurice Arbour, 'L'Affaire du Chalutier-Usine "La Bretagne" ou les droits de l'Etat côtier dans sa zone économique exclusive' (1986) 24 *Canadian Yearbook of International Law*, 61

[170] ILA, 'Report of the Sixty-Second Conference held at Seoul, August 24th to August 30th 1986', p. 328. See also *Maritime Delimitation in the Area between Greenland and Jan Mayen (Denmark* v. *Norway)*, Judgment, ICJ Reports 1993, p. 38, para 77 at 59.

[171] See S. Rawa Rao, 'EEZ Concept under the New Law of the Sea Convention: Basic Framework for another Approach' (1985) 24 *International Journal of Innovation and Learning*, 102, 104 (*sui generis* regime).

[172] Jean-Pierre Quéneudec, 'Les Rapports entre zone de pêche et zone économique exclusive' (1989) 32 *German Yearbook of International Law*, 138.

At the time of UNCLOS III, state practice and unilateral legislation exhibited a great variety of regulatory schemes,[173] with claims and regulations ranging from the 200nm territorial sea concept to jurisdiction which is limited to management and conservation of fisheries. Even with regard to living resources there was no consensus on how far exactly exclusive rights should extend. For example, the United States did not include the jurisdiction to prescribe over highly migratory species under its concept of the EEZ. The view prevailed that its own long distance fishing interests and the very nature of the subject involved require international agreement and management.[174] Equally, it has maintained that scientific research should remain free.[175] In contrast, the weaker states prevailing at UNCLOS III, claimed full jurisdiction over all activities and resources within the zone. As a rule, it appears that national legislation regarding the EEZ has tended to expand national jurisdiction, and the possibility that the zone will generally develop towards a territorial concept through the gradual assertion of authority by coastal states cannot be excluded.[176] The comprehensive regulation of the EEZ in Part V of the 1982 Convention has influenced progress in this area as a matter of fact and by its very existence, but the uniform regime that will eventually emerge in customary international law need not coincide with the provisions of the Convention.[177] Therefore, the precise determination of EEZ rights will continue to depend on a close analysis of state practice and national legislation, particularly in the absence of universal

---

[173] See Vicuña, n. 7, pp. 110–20; see also Reynaldo Galindo Pohl, 'The Exclusive Economic Zone in the Light of Negotiations of the Third United Nations Conference on the Law of the Sea' in F. O. Vicuña (ed.), *The Exclusive Economic Zone: A Latin American Perspective* (Boulder CO: Westview Press, 1984), pp. 31 and 57.

[174] The 176 Fishery Conservation and Management Act (FCMA, 16 United States Code paras. 1801–1857, 22 United States Code, paras. 1972–1973) excluded jurisdiction over tuna. The Act provides for non-recognition of foreign claims and allows sanctions (import prohibition) against states seeking to enforce exclusive jurisdiction against US tuna vessels. Sec. 202(e), 205. See William T. Burke, 'U.S. Fishery Management and the New Law of the Sea' (1982) 76 *American Journal of International Law*, 24, 41–5. The 1983 Reagan Proclamation, adopting the EEZ, above n. 166, did not change this policy.

[175] Burke, n. 174, p. 49.

[176] Vicuña, n. 7 p. 120, quoting Carroz:
    un examen attentif des législations nationales et des accords internationaux recents semble indiquer que les Etats sont parfois sélectifs dans le choix des principes et qu'ils tendent à retenir ceux qui renforcent leur jurisdiction.

[177] See also Judge Oda, dissenting opinion, ICJ Reports 1982, pp. 228, 230, paras. 120, 125.

ratification.[178] For the purposes of this study, a short review of the EEZ as defined by the Convention will have to suffice.

2. The LOS Convention

At UNCLOS III, a great deal of attention was also paid to the relationship of the EEZ with the territorial sea and to the high seas. This subject, in accordance with the history of the zone, was among the most controversial topics at UNCLOS III. At the conference, the territorialists considered the EEZ to be a part of the territorial sea. Subject to some exceptions, a second view (mainly supported by those interested in the freedom of marine communications), defined the concept of the EEZ as part of the high seas, subject to special rights of the coastal sea over natural resources.

A third view, which defined the EEZ as a functional zone *sui generis*, emerged as a compromise.[179] Thus, yet again, the traditional, dualistic concept of the law of the sea was enlarged by a third and intermediate concept. The scope of EEZ rights, which will be discussed shortly, has to be defined in its own terms. It cannot be drawn from a presumption in favour of either the territorial sea or of the high seas resources, as, in fact, neither of these presumptions prevailed. The LOS Convention defines the EEZ as 'an area beyond and adjacent to the territorial sea' (Article 55) and not exceeding 200 nm measured from the base lines of the territorial sea (Article 57). The provisions of the Convention are mostly concerned with exploitation, conservation and management of the living resources of the water column (Article 61–73). This reflects the fact that the concept emerged from its established predecessor, the 200 nm exclusive fishing zone. However, the EEZ is no longer confined by this limit. The new zone establishes the comprehensive jurisdiction and responsibilities of the coastal state. Article 56(1)(a) defines the main rights, jurisdiction and duties as follows:

---

[178] Note that David Anderson speaks of a quasi-universal status of the 1982 Convention. See David Anderson, 'Developments in Maritime Boundary Law and Practice' in Jonathan I. Charney et al. (eds.), *International Maritime Boundaries*, 5 vols. (The Hague: Martinus Nijhoff Publishers, 2005), vols. I and II (Charney and Alexander (eds.), 1993), vol. III (Charney and Alexander (eds.), 1998), vol. IV (Charney and Smith (eds.), 2002), vol. V (Colson and Smith (eds.), 2005); vol. V, p. 3202.

[179] See e.g. Attard, n. 125, p. 62; Lupinacci, n. 1, p. 105; Arias Schreiber, 'The Exclusive Economic Zone: Its Legal Nature and the Problem of Military Uses' in O. F. Vicuña, *The Exclusive Economic Zone Latin American Perspective* (Boulder CO: Westview Press, 1984), pp. 123, 127; Churchill and Lowe, n. 9, p. 130; Vicuña, n. 1, pp. 28 and 53.

1. In the EEZ, the coastal State has:

   (a) sovereign rights for the purpose of exploring and exploiting, conserving and managing the natural resources, whether living or non-living, of the sea-bed and subsoil and the superjacent waters, and with regard to other activities for the economic exploitation and exploration of the zone, such as the production of energy from the water, currents and winds.[180]

Most of the provisions flow from the governing principle of exclusive jurisdiction over natural resources, such as the provisions concerning artificial islands and constructions (Article 60), conservation, management and utilization of living resources (Articles 61 and 62) and jurisdiction to enforce (Article 73). Under the Convention, even subjects that necessarily and *ratione naturae* or *ratione materiae* require inter-zonal regulation remain under national jurisdiction. However, under the Convention, states find themselves under a legal obligation to co-operate by agreement in the management of migratory species, by means of bilateral or multilateral agreements, as appropriate (Articles 65–67). Shortly after the Convention entered into force, some of its provisions on living resources were clarified and enforced by the 1995 UN Fish Stocks Agreement.[181] The Agreement's regulations apply both to international waters and to national EEZs. The Agreement sets out a precautionary approach to the conservation and management of straddling fish stocks and highly migratory fish stocks by regulating the catch of deep-water and migratory species, including tuna, swordfish and cod stocks. Supranational organizations are certainly among possible options for future monitoring, yet there is as yet no obligation to delegate authority to such a degree.[182] Further, the new and innovative conventional rights of land-locked and geographically disadvantaged states over

---

[180] Art. 56(a), (b) further establishes jurisdiction of the coastal state over (i) the establishment and use of artificial islands, installations and structures; (ii) marine scientific research; and (iii) protection and preservation of the marine environment (pollution control).

[181] Agreement for the Implementation of the Provisions of the United Nations Convention on the Law of the Sea of 10 December 1992 relating to the Conservation and Management of Straddling Fish Stocks and Highly Migratory Fish Stocks.

[182] For a model of monitoring by a joint commission see the 1985 US–Canadian treaty on pacific salmon, discussed by Joy A. Yanagida, 'The Pacific Salmon Treaty' (1987) 81 *American Journal of International Law*, 577.

surplus catches (Articles 69 and 70) do not affect the coastal state's full jurisdiction over natural resources.[183]

Besides establishing sovereign rights over natural resources and reflecting the concept of limited and horizontally shared jurisdictions, the Convention explicitly reserves the rights of third states that relate to communications in the high seas. Article 58 provides that all states enjoy freedom of navigation, over-flight, and the laying of submarine cables and pipelines, and 'other internationally lawful uses of the seas related to these freedoms, such as those associated with the operation of ships, aircraft and submarine cables and pipelines,' as referred to in Article 87, and therefore to limitations of such rights as expressed in Articles 87(2) and 88 to 115. In reality, balancing the interests of the coastal state against the international community's navigational interests may pose a number of problems. The very nature of the EEZ only allows for restrictions on navigation in exceptional and compelling circumstances, e.g. where the unimpaired exploitation of fish stocks is of vital importance to the national well being of small coastal nations and restrictions are essential for effective resource management.[184]

Despite such interlinking, the Convention does not exhaustively address all the relevant issues of possible conflicts of jurisdiction. Implicit restrictions of communication relate to pollution control and the existence of artificial islands and installations.[185] Other areas of potential conflict, such as the problem of underwater listening devices for submarine activities, the recovery of wrecks beyond the contiguous zone and jurisdiction over buoys for scientific, research remain unsettled.[186] The Convention provides in Article 59 that such conflicts

> should be resolved on the basis of equity and in the light of all the relevant circumstances, taking into account the respective importance of the interests involved to the parties as well as to the international community as a whole.

Reliance on such an open and flexible principle, based on equity and all the relevant circumstances of a particular case, is an interesting concept, which, as will be seen, largely resembles the approach used in maritime boundary delimitation. Methodological experiences from that field are

---

[183] These articles are briefly discussed in Chapter 3(II)(B)(2) and Chapter 4(E)(III).
[184] William T. Burke, 'Exclusive Fisheries Zones and Freedom of Navigation' (1983) 20 *San Diego Law Review*, 595, 600; Robertson, n. 125, p. 893.
[185] See Churchill and Lowe, n. 9, p. 134.   [186] See ibid., p. 136.

therefore of value in the context of adjudicating conflicts of jurisdiction under Article 59 of the Convention.

IV. The relationship of the continental shelf and the EEZ

Comprehensive jurisdiction over virtually all of the economically exploitable resources within 200 nm offshore, in particular the inclusion of the soil and subsoil, leaves the relationship of the EEZ and the continental shelf somewhat unclear, for some even a mystery.[187] In the *Jan Mayen* case, the ICJ did not provide an answer to the question of the relationship between the continental shelf and the fishery zone:

> Whatever that relationship may be, the Court takes note that the parties adopt in that respect the same position, in that they see no objection, for the settlement of the present dispute, to the boundary of the fishery zones being determined by the law governing the exclusive economic zone, which is customary law.[188]

Rational clarification of this uncertainty is not only a matter of general interest. It is especially important with regard to maritime boundary delimitation of the shelf and the EEZ. It is important to know whether we are dealing with two different and independent concepts, therefore allowing for separate boundaries, or identical or partly overlapping concepts, which therefore require fully identical or partly identical boundaries, respectively.

A. Divergencies

It is generally agreed among writers that the shelf and the EEZ are independent and discrete, and yet interrelated and complementary, concepts.[189] The nature of the shelf as a title *ipso facto* and *ab initio* based on natural prolongation is considered to constitute a major difference from the EEZ. Diverging historical development, different both in their scope of jurisdiction and in the concept of surplus catch entitlements – which

---

[187] E.g. Allott 1983, n. 1, 1, 14 ('The mystery of the relationship between the continental shelf and EEZ').
[188] *Maritime Delimitation in the Area between Greenland and Jan Mayen (Denmark v. Norway)*, Judgment, ICJ Reports 1993, p. 59, para. 47.
[189] Attard, n. 125, pp. 136–45; Churchill and Lowe, n. 9, p. 111; Vicuña, n. 7, pp. 65–7, 124; ILA 1982 Report, n. 125, p. 310 ('duality of concepts'). For the history of UNCLOS III negotiations on this issue see Rangel, n. 9, pp. 308–11 (early efforts at replacement and absorption of the shelf zone into the EEZ failed due to the resistance of states with large shelves extending beyond 200 nm based on the criterion of natural prolongation).

are absent in the shelf – are additional disparities which seem to deny the possibility of either consumption of the shelf by the EEZ or the establishment of a single new type of maritime zone.[190]

The very fact that continental shelf zones may continue to exist without an explicitly proclaimed EEZ and that the seaward expanses of the two zones vary considerably make it apparent that the concept of the shelf zone has not been absorbed by the more recent concept of the EEZ. The existence of two separate titles in the 1982 Convention, for the shelf in Part VI, and for the EEZ in Part V of the Convention, respectively, confirms the point. The Convention provides for the legal, but in practice rather transitory, option of exercising shelf rights without adopting an EEZ, as was true in the *Gulf of Maine* and the *Libya* v. *Malta Continental Shelf* cases. Special provisions for the continental shelf remain indispensable, since the geographic scope of that zone is defined on different standards. As discussed, the continental shelf may well exceed the 200 nm limits of the EEZ. Beyond 200 nm from the coast, the shelf is referred to as 'outer continental shelf' or 'extended continental shelf'. The Tribunal in *Barbados* v. *Trinidad and Tobago* recalled that a shelf may exist beyond 200 nm by dismissing the term 'extended continental shelf' as chosen by the parties in favour of the term 'outer continental shelf', saying that the continental shelf is not being extended.[191]

B. Convergencies: towards a single homogeneous zone

The separate existence of the two zones does not exclude the possibility that in the future they may partly merge and form a uniform and homogeneous zone within the expanses of 200 nm. To that extent, a new EEZ, if proclaimed and established, would fully incorporate an independent regime of the continental shelf zone. There are a number of arguments in support of such partial absorption:

Firstly, it should be noted that the foundations of the two concepts, as discussed above, support the idea of a homogeneous zone; they merely appear to differ at a fundamental level. In the final analysis both, in our view, rely upon the close relationship of the coastal state to offshore marine spaces. Ultimately, both can be traced back to the idea of a close and special relationship of coastal states to offshore areas and the concept of permanent sovereignty over natural resources. The doctrine of *ipso iure* rights and jurisdiction *ab initio* did not establish a fundamental

---

[190] See Attard, n. 125, p. 141.   [191] *Barbados* v. *Trinidad and Tobago*, n. 44, para. 65.

difference. It served the purpose of preventing occupation and exploitation by states other than the coastal state. It therefore assumed the function of permanent sovereignty over natural resources, which, as a concept, emerged only later and became the prime foundation of the EEZ. In addition, it is doubtful whether the conceptual difference between the necessity of a proclamation of the EEZ and the dispensation of such an act with regard to the shelf is actually of any practical significance: since the water column outside the territorial sea is traditionally part of the high seas, the water column is not open to occupation anyway. A similar construction was not necessary in order to achieve an equal degree of protection for the EEZ. Any unlawful attempts to appropriate could be easily met by protests, and proclamation of the EEZ is possible at any time. The protection of the interests and aspirations of coastal states is therefore sufficient. In practical terms, this amounts to the same effect as the concept of *ipso iure* rights, and makes this doctrine dispensable under the principle of permanent sovereignty over natural resources which applies to the shelf as well as to the EEZ.

Secondly, the EEZ includes full jurisdiction over shelf rights. While the shelf can exist independently, the EEZ necessarily includes the continental shelf. As the Court phrased it: 'there can be a continental shelf where there is no exclusive economic zone, [but] there cannot be an exclusive economic zone without a corresponding continental shelf.'[192] It is important to note that up to the 200 nm limit, the existence of the EEZ is no longer dependent upon the existence of a shelf in a physical sense. Thus, to the extent of 200 nm, the doctrine of natural prolongation as legal title to the shelf no longer applies under the definition of Article 76 of the 1982 Convention.[193] Shelf rights therefore directly rely upon the EEZ.

Thirdly, the relationship of the two zones may be best perceived in historical terms. It is not a logical relationship, and it is doubtful whether the concept of two overlapping zones would have become established if the enclosure of the seas had been a planned exercise, rather than an evolutionary process. Nevertheless, the law must endeavour to accommodate the two existing concepts in the best way possible. In the 1982 Convention, this was achieved through a close interrelationship and cross-references of provisions related to the EEZ and the shelf. The

---

[192] ICJ Reports 1985, p. 33, para. 34.
[193] See Yoshifumi Tanaka, *Predictability and Flexibility in the Law of Maritime Delimitation* (Oxford: Hart, 2006), p. 140, noting that natural prolongation still serves as a legal title for the continental shelf beyond 200 nm under Art. 76 of the 1982 Convention (at n. 24).

relationship works both ways. Provisions concerning the shelf are declared applicable to the EEZ. Part VI as a whole is declared applicable within the EEZ by Article 56(3). Article 56(3) requires EEZ rights related to the seabed and subsoil to be exercised in accordance with Part VI. *Vice versa*, provisions on the EEZ are held applicable to the shelf. For example, rules on artificial installations are located within Part V of the EEZ (Article 60) and are referred to in Part VI (Article 80) as applicable *mutatis mutandis* in the continental shelf zone.

The case law and state practice on maritime delimitation has approximated the two zones by the use of single boundary lines. The Court in *Qatar* v. *Bahrain* observed that the concept of a single maritime boundary stems not from multilateral treaty law but from state practice, and that it finds its explanation in the desire of states to establish one uninterrupted boundary line delimiting the various – partially coincident – zones appertaining to them.[194] The Tribunal in *Guyana* v. *Suriname* recalled that while the regimes are separate, a single maritime boundary avoids the difficult practical problems that could arise were one party to have rights over the water column and the other rights over the seabed and subsoil below that water column.[195]

In addition to the preceding arguments, which support the view of partial absorption whenever an EEZ is declared and established, it should be recalled that there is an additional undeclared creeping absorption of the traditional shelf through the concept of the EEZ. The adoption of the 'distance principle' declared applicable to the shelf by the Court, as discussed previously,[196] demonstrates that a shelf zone, even if it exists independently, is increasingly defined by, and inseparable from, criteria established for the EEZ. This is true with respect to delimitation between adjacent and opposite coasts that are less than 400 nm apart. In this scenario, present international law ultimately defines the expanse of shelf zones on the basis of the more comprehensive concept of the EEZ. It will be seen that the traditional geomorphological criteria of the shelf, which relate to natural prolongation are no longer applied within 200 nm from the coast.[197]

---

[194] *Maritime Delimitation and Territorial Questions between Qatar and Bahrain (Qatar v. Bahrain)*, Merits, Judgment, ICJ Reports 2001, p. 40, para. 173, as recalled in *Land and Maritime Boundary between Cameroon and Nigeria (Cameroon v. Nigeria: Equatorial Guinea intervening)*, Judgment, ICJ Reports 2002, p. 303, para. 286 and *Guyana v. Suriname* Award n. 33 at para. 334.
[195] *Guyana v. Suriname*, ibid., para. 334.   [196] Above text accompanying nn. 71 and 72.
[197] Chapter 9 and Chapter 10(II)(A).

All this suggests that in the long run, the continental shelf will play an independent role only to the extent that it reaches beyond 200 nm as based on the criteria set forth in Article 76 relating to the 'outer continental shelf'.[198]

C. Summary and conclusions

The shelf and the EEZ show considerable convergence in terms of *ratio legis*, foundations and evolution through customary law. Differences in legal construction are mainly explained by the subsequent historical and conceptual evolution of the two zones, but do not preclude the strong influence of the EEZ on the shelf and the absorption of the latter by the EEZ within the 200 nm expanse of that zone.

What does this mean for the subject of maritime boundary delimitation and the evolution and application of delimitation rules? Firstly, conclusions drawn with respect to the shelf apply equally to the EEZ. Boundary delimitation is an active, creative legal and political process and business. Criteria and factors applicable to the process cannot be limited to merely geographical considerations, since the concepts and ideas underlying the new zones are man-made, and not required by nature. Secondly, courts have to assume a similarly active role in the process of shaping the rules of boundary delimitation related to the EEZ, as to the continental shelf.[199]

1. Towards a presumption of single maritime boundaries

It is submitted that the prevailing convergence and similarities of the shelf and the EEZ, and the evolution toward a single homogeneous zone, call for a principle of identical boundary lines. The jurisdiction over the

---

[198] See Chapter 3(II)(B)(1)/Chapter 4(B)(2). Attention may be drawn at this point to the fact that in the *Gulf of Maine* case, parties already took the possibility of single maritime boundaries (shelf/fishery zone) for granted – an assumption not refuted by the Court, ICJ Reports 1984, see n. 2, p. 267, para. 27:

[T]he Chamber must observe that the Parties have simply taken it for granted that it would be possible, both legally and materially, to draw a single boundary for two different jurisdictions. They have not put forward any arguments in support of this assumption The Chamber, for its part, is of the opinion that there is certainly no rule of international law to the contrary, and, in the present case, there is no material impossibility in drawing a boundary of this kind.

[199] Chapter 1(II)(D).

seabed and sub-soil and the water column within 200 nm should likewise be identical. State practice supports such a proposal. In the 1993 Volume I of the seminal work *International Maritime Boundaries*, Colson[200] examined the interaction of continental shelf and EEZ boundaries. He found four groups of treaties:

1. in more than half of all agreements, no information is available as to whether the continental shelf boundary also applies to EEZ jurisdiction;
2. a second group of cases formally evolved into particular EEZ boundaries. This was the case in the practice of the former Soviet Union and of Australia;
3. a third group informally applies continental shelf boundaries to the EEZ. Colson observed that a substantial number of agreements and states operate under this model; and that states generally have not regarded the evolution from the continental shelf regime to that of the EEZ as bearing upon the location of their agreed boundaries;
4. a fourth group relates to cases where continental shelf boundaries do not always become EEZ boundaries and where different lines are used.

Colson concluded that the analysis 'confirm[s] the belief that, in general, states, for either practical or legal reasons, take the view there is no advantage to opening an argument with a neighbouring state that new factors require that the delimitation of the exclusive economic zone be different from their continental shelf boundary'.[201]

Since 1970, most boundaries have been negotiated as all-purpose boundaries.[202] From a practical point of view, taking into account the needs of ocean management and dispute prevention, it is difficult to conceive of any other solution. It is submitted that already by the ultimate similarities between the foundations of the two concepts, there needs to be a presumption of uniform boundaries of the EEZ and the continental shelf zone within 200 nm. Colson even argued that with the consolidation of the law of the sea and acceptance of the EEZ 'we may see a gradual

---

[200] David A. Colson, 'The Legal Regime of Maritime Boundary Agreements' in Jonathan I. Charney et al. (eds.), *International Maritime Boundaries*, 5 vols. (The Hague: Martinus Nijhoff Publishers, 1993–2005), vols. I and II (Charney and Alexander (eds.), 1993), vol. III (Charney and Alexander (eds.), 1998), vol. IV (Charney and Smith (eds.), 2002), vol. V (Colson and Smith (eds.), 2005); vol. I, p. 41.
[201] Ibid. pp. 41, 45–8, 51 at 47.   [202] Ibid. p. 48.

turning away from the delimitations of so-called all-purpose maritime boundaries to delimitations which are labelled specifically as boundaries of the exclusive economic zone'.[203]

In fact, the trend in state practice and jurisprudence since Colson's 1993 study favours EEZ and continental shelf delimitations by single maritime boundaries. In the 2005 *International Maritime Boundaries* Volume V, McRae and Yacouba observe a developing unity of the regimes within 200 nm as demonstrated by the fact that no agreement has been concluded in the period under consideration that delimits the water column alone, and only three agreements relating solely to the seabed within 200 nm.[204] But they also conclude that despite the clear trend in favour of an all-purpose or single maritime boundary, it appears that states still have not fully adapted to the unified concept of an EEZ in view of their continuing practice to describe boundaries that delimit the area within 200 nm as EEZ and continental shelf boundaries.[205]

With regard to maritime delimitation, similar criteria and rules should in principle apply to the process of delimitation up to 200 nm. Whatever the precise content of principles applicable, they need to respond to the purpose and foundations of rights over the seabed and subsoil as well as over marine spaces. The Chamber of the ICJ in the *Gulf of Maine* case, which considered for the first time the issues related to a single maritime boundary delimitation, stated:

> a delimitation by a single line ... i.e., a delimitation which has to apply at one and the same time to the continental shelf and to the superjacent water column can only be carried out by the application of a criterion, or combination of criteria, which does not give preferential treatment to one of these two objects to the detriment of the other, and at the same time is such as to be equally suitable to the division of either of them ... it can be foreseen that with the gradual adoption by the majority of maritime States of an exclusive economic zone and, consequently, an increasingly general demand for single delimitation, so as to avoid as far as possible the disadvantages inherent in a plurality of separate delimitations, preference will henceforth inevitably be given to criteria that, because of their more neutral character, are best suited for use in a multi-purpose delimitation.[206]

---

[203] Ibid. p. 51.
[204] Cissé Yacouba and Donald McRae, 'The Legal Regime of Maritime Boundary Agreements' in Charney et. al., *International Maritime Boundaries*, n. 200, vol. V (Colson and Smith), p. 3281.
[205] Yacouba and McRae, ibid. pp. 3290, 3304.   [206] ICJ Reports 1984, p. 327, para. 194.

With regard to the principles applicable, the Chamber continued that 'it is, accordingly, towards an application to the present case of criteria more especially derived from geography that it feels bound to turn'.[207] It is submitted, however, that criteria and factors applicable to the process cannot be limited to merely geographical considerations due to the concepts and ideas underlying the zones which are shared by the EEZ and the continental shelf, as already shown. The identity of these man-made legal foundations of the zones allows for largely uniform applications, and therefore the adoption of similar methods and criteria of delimitation. The identical formulations of boundary delimitation for the shelf [Article 83(1)] and of the EEZ [Article 74(1)] confirm such a view. Indeed today it may be said that there is evidence of a common link between the two maritime spaces for delimitation purposes as they all seem to be delimited by common principles regardless of their differing legal regime.[208]

2. Exceptions: diverging boundaries

The principle or possible presumption, of single maritime boundaries does not exclude exceptions allowing for diverging boundaries.[209] Since both zones are man-made, delimitation requires specific human conduct related to the areas in dispute to be taken into account. The difference in the historical evolution of the zones may lead to non-identical boundaries of jurisdiction over shelf rights and over living and tidal resources. Historical or conventional rights or particular needs may have developed or may have been agreed upon. Where they exist, they should be respected and taken into account. Also, it may be necessary to consider circumstances relevant only to particular resources, and irrelevant to others. Taking them into account may lead to different boundary lines.[210]

The possibility of different, specifically resource-related boundaries is inherent to the concept of the EEZ, because it covers a variety of ocean uses with different historical backgrounds. Partial absorption of the shelf by the EEZ therefore does not necessarily prescribe single maritime boundaries. Maintaining the duality of the shelf and the EEZ in order to allow for non-identical boundaries is not necessarily a conceptual

---

[207] ICJ Reports 1984, p. 327, para. 195.   [208] See Yacouba and McRae, n. 204, p. 3290.
[209] For examples see Colson, n. 200, pp. 47–8.   [210] For examples see Chapter 5(II).

necessity, as has been argued by others.[211] In the ultimate result, differences between absorption and duality may not be significant, except in the fact that diverging boundaries need to be well reasoned and exceptional under the principle of a homogeneous 200 nm zone.

---

[211] Attard, n. 125, p. 139 ('The fusing of the two institutions would suggest that there was little or no possibility of having separate boundaries for the EEZ and the shelf. A single EEZ boundary, covering the shelf and its superjacent waters, would have to be drawn').

3

Distributive effects of the enclosure movement: an assessment of global equity

I. The quest for global equity in maritime law

With a view to preparing the ground for rules and principles on maritime boundary delimitation, it is essential to consider the global distributive effects of the new law of the sea, particularly those of the continental shelf and the EEZ. Global, 'macro-economic' distributive effects and the changes brought about by these concepts may be relevant in the succeeding process of 'micro-economic' maritime boundary delimitation between states. Both levels operate with elusive notions of equity, and it is yet unclear how they interrelate. A brief study of distributive effects in law and the economics of the enclosure of the seas is therefore necessary to define the scope of equity in the context of maritime boundary delimitation. It prepares the ground for the clarification of the relationship of what may be called global equity in the law of the sea and the use of equity in maritime boundary delimitation in subsequent chapters of this book.

The history of the enclosure movement reveals that the EEZ and the Area became an important part of the movement for a new international economic order (NIEO) from the 1970s to the 1980s. While the legal concept of the shelf emerged from policies put forth by industrial and colonial powers, the subsequent developments of the EEZ and the Area – under the concept of common heritage – were largely promoted by developing countries (LDCs) under the flag of equity, with the hope of achieving fundamental changes in the allocation of income, wealth and resources. In the 1970s, UNCLOS III became a central operation in the pursuit of power sharing and of distributive justice or global equity:

> The developing countries have found that the international conferences on the law of the sea provide them with a unique opportunity for ensuring that their own ideas and needs are borne in mind in the formulation of the

rules of international law and that the rules are formulated on the basis of equity.[1]

Indeed, commensurate with the global functions of equity described in the Introduction to this book, equity became a catchword at UNCLOS III, inspired by the frequent use of the term in instruments related to NIEO, which itself relied upon equity as one of its main principles.[2] Equitable goals were framed at UNCLOS III and expressed by the 1982 LOS Convention. The Preamble calls, inter alia, for 'the equitable and efficient utilization' of resources. It directly links the Convention to the goal of realizing a just and equitable international economic order, which takes into account the interests and needs of mankind as a whole and, in particular, the special interests and needs of developing countries, whether coastal or land-locked.[3] The wording of the agreement refers to equity in a number of important articles, mainly those relating to the allocation and distribution of marine resources.[4] While the rejection of the complex interventionist regime of the Area by western states frustrated the negotiated regime of deep seabed mining (and therefore a potential of resource allocation perceived as equitable), it is evident that the rapid development of the EEZ into customary international law, complementing the previously established continental shelf zone, ranks amongst the most significant and influential achievements of the former efforts for new international economic relations based on equity.[5] The

---

[1] Emmanuel G. Bello, 'International Equity and the Law of the Sea: New Perspectives for Developing Countries' (1980) 13 *Verfassung und Recht in Uebersee,* 201. See also Kamal Hossein (ed.), *Legal Aspects of the New International Economic Order* (London, New York: Pinter, 1980), pp. 160-93.

[2] Introduction, section II; Werner Stocker, *Das Prinzip des Common Heritage of Mankind als Ausdruck des Staatengemeinschaftsinteresses im Völkerrecht* (Zurich: Schultheiss, 1993), pp. 124-39.

[3] Preamble, paras. 2 and 3. See also Anton Vratusa, 'Convention on the Law of the Sea in the Light of the Struggle for the New International Economic Order' in B. Vukas (ed.), *Essays on the New Law of the Sea* (University of Zagreb, Faculty of Law, 1985), pp. 17-30; Rüdiger Wolfrum, 'Die UN-Seerechtskonvention in der Perspective der Neuen Weltwirtschaftsordnung' in Jost Delbrück (ed.), *Das neue Seerecht. Internationale und nationale Perspektiven* (Berlin: Duncker & Humblot, 1984), p. 97.

[4] See Arts. 59, 69(3), 70(1), 70(3)(d), 74, 83, 140(2), 160(2)(d), 162(2)(o)(i), 163(4), 269(b), 274(a) of UNCLOS.

[5] Paradoxically, the EEZ and living maritime resources were often absent in discussions and documents related to the UN Conference on Trade and Development (UNCTAD) and NIEO, at least at an earlier stage. For example, the 1974 United Nations Charter of Economic Rights and Duties of States, GA Res. 3281 (XXIX), refers to the deep seabed mining in Art. 29, but not to other equally important aspects of marine resource allocation. The fact of separate development and treatment was attributed to the law of the sea as a

legal result of the enclosure movement considerably reshaped the allocation of jurisdiction over the resources located within some 36 to 40 per cent of the globe's surface.

The continental shelf reserves exclusive rights of exploitation of oil, gas and other sedentary resources. It allows for the establishment of fixed and floating installations facilitating the extraction of these resources. The shelf has generated enormous revenues with all the resultant well-documented implications for the world economy, past, present and future. With decolonization, offshore oil and gas resources became an essential resource of many coastal developing countries and emerging economies. It expanded the basis for fiscal revenues and economic growth of coastal states, including developing and emerging economies. Offshore drilling of oil and gas became a mainstay in the exploitation of these resources, supplementing land-based drilling. A number of developing and emerging economies significantly improved their shares in global production. The process was not without major distributional tensions. The 1982 Falklands/Malvinas War between Argentina and the United Kingdom amounts to the most prominent incidence involving claims based upon the enclosure movement.[6] The potential for exploitation is at the heart of unresolved distributional disputes among developing countries over sovereignty and jurisdiction over strategic islands, such as the Spratly Islands in the South China Sea involving the People's Republic of China, Taiwan, Brunei, Malaysia, the Philippines and Vietnam. Technological development of deep water oil and gas drilling in recent years further expanded the prospects, but also enhanced the risk of environmental damage, fully realized with the 2010 oil spill caused by the BP platform Deepwater Horizon in the Gulf of Mexico. It massively destroyed natural habitats for wildlife, threatening the fishing industry and tourism along the US coast. The incident was a major setback for deep-water mining and is bound to trigger stricter regulation of the extracting industry around the world.[7]

---

highly specialized topic and specialization within national administrations. Elisabeth Mann Borgese, 'The New International Economic Order and the Law of the Sea' (1977) 14 *San Diego Law Review*, 584. Sometimes the law of the sea was entirely absent in research on NIEO. See e.g. Otto Kimminich, 'Das Völkerrecht und die Neue Weltwirtschaftsordnung' (1982) 20 *Archiv für Völkerrecht*, 2.

[6] See Michael A. Morris, 'Maritime Geopolitics in Latin America' (1986) V(1) *Political Geography Quarterly*, 43.

[7] See the US government report resulting from the explosion on 20 April 2012, 'On Scene Coordinator Report Deepwater Horizon Oil Spill' (undated) www.uscg.mil/foia/docs/dwh/fosc_dwh_report.pdf (last accessed 25 September 2014).

While the exploitation of non-renewable resources on the shelves may be depleted within the next few generations, the continental shelf remains of great importance as a legal framework for offshore installations for renewable energy production by means of wave, wind and tidal energy. It allows for fixed installations on the seabed and exploitation of renewable energy. Both the continental shelf and the EEZ offer an important legal framework in particular for wave[8] and wind energy,[9] requiring appropriate installations at sea, while tidal energy so far seems to operate closer to shores. Energy parks are increasing in territorial seas and across the expanses of the continental shelf, and wind and wave technology is increasingly applied.[10] There is also a potential for solar energy at sea, albeit it would somewhat more limited.[11] These technologies offer coastal states the opportunity to promote large-scale exploitation as a substitute for, and alternative to, forms of decarbonated energy production which disturb natural environments and ecosystems on a large scale (hydroelectric dams), pose potential health hazards, or establish a dependence upon foreign supplies (atomic energy). Wind and wave energy generated at sea and located within the shallow waters of the continental shelf and the EEZ is of growing importance in coming decades.[12] Coastal states again enjoy considerable advantages in this respect in comparison to

---

[8] See e.g. *Technology White Paper on Wave Energy Potential on the U.S. Outer Continental Shelf*, Minerals Management Service Renewable Energy and Alternate Use Program, US Department of the Interior (2006), at www.boem.gov/uploadedFiles/BOEM/Renewable_Energy_Program/Renewable_Energy_Guide/Technology%20White%20Paper%20on%20Wind%20Energy%20Potential%20on%20the%20OCS.pdf (last accessed 25 September 2014).

[9] 'The U.S. Department of Energy (DOE) estimates that more than 900,000 MW2 (close to the total current installed US electrical capacity) of potential wind energy exists off the coasts of the United States, often near major population centers, where energy costs are high and land-based wind development opportunities are limited', *Technology White Paper on Wind Energy Potential on the U.S. Outer Continental Shelf*, Minerals Management Service Renewable Energy and Alternate Use Program US Department of the Interior (2006) at p. 2, available at www.boem.gov/uploadedFiles/BOEM/Renewable_Energy_Program/Renewable_Energy_Guide/Technology%20White%20Paper%20on%20Wind%20Energy%20Potential%20on%20the%20OCS.pdf (last accessed 25 September 2014).

[10] See e.g. List of Off-Shore Wind Forms in the North Sea, http://en.wikipedia.org/wiki/List_of_offshore_wind_farms_in_the_North_Sea (last accessed 29 January 2012).

[11] See Technology White Paper on Solar Energy Potential on the US Outer Continental Shelf, Minerals Management Service Renewable Energy and Alternate Use Program, US Department of the Interior (2006), available at www.boem.gov/uploadedFiles/BOEM/Renewable_Energy_Program/Renewable_Energy_Guide/Technology%20White%20Paper%20on%20Wind%20Energy%20Potential%20on%20the%20OCS.pdf (last accessed 25 September 2014).

[12] The application of the technology using tidal steam generators or dynamic tidal power on the continental shelf and the EZZ still seem to be in the early stages of development. The

land-locked countries. Benefits will largely accrue to coastal states that are able to produce for their own needs with the additional opportunity to export electricity in combination with large-scale water storage in often distant hydropower installations. Developments in modern technology allow for the transportation of electricity with much lower losses than before. The modern law of natural resources of the sea may look considerably different in fifty years from now.

The EEZ in its own right continues to provide the most valuable renewable resources to coastal and island states. Foremost, the EEZ has a strong and long lasting impact on fisheries and global nutrition. It was the driving force in bringing about national jurisdiction in the 1970s and 1980s. It remains of particular and lasting importance to the issue of global equity and the right to food. It thus deserves particular attention for the purpose of assessing the past and current effects of the enclosure movement on distributive justice.

Fish plays a significant role in feeding the world's population. In developing countries, a large proportion of the population receives most of its animal protein from fish. The share of fish protein in total animal protein expenditure is higher for lower income groups.[13] In 1997, between 13.8 per cent and 16.5 per cent of the total average global intake of animal protein was attributable to fish while the relative contribution of fish to total animal protein varies greatly from country to country. For example, it amounts to around 15 to 25 per cent in Egypt, Morocco, Oman and Yemen; it is higher in Sub-Saharan Africa, with the share exceeding 50 per cent in some of the

---

costs of installing the necessary equipment at sea has thwarted most attempts to generate energy. Researchers have been focusing on land-based installations, such as the Norwegian projects of using a 'multiresonant oscillating water column'. The device uses the sea's motion to push water up and down, thereby forcing air through a turbine. Another approach leads incoming waves through a channel into a reservoir from which it flows back through conventional turbines. See *The Economist*, 13 July 1985, p. 78; Maureen O'C. Walker and Murray A. Bloom, 'Ocean Thermal Energy Conversion: The Codification of a Potential Technology' (1981) 14 *Vanderbilt Journal of Transnational Law*, 509. So far, tidal plants operate in coastal areas using barrages. The world's largest plant, the Sihwa Lake Tidal Power Station with a total power output capacity of 254 MW, was opened in 2011 in South Korea, surpassing the La Rance Plant in France, opened in 1966 with a capacity of 240 MW, Neil Ford, 'Tidal Power Primed for Breakthrough', *International Water Power & Dam Construction*, www.waterpowermagazine.com/story.asp?sc=2052179 (last accessed 29 January 2012).

[13] FAO, *Marine Fisheries and the Law of the Sea: A Decade of Change*, FAO Fisheries Circular No. 853 (1992), p. 34. See also FAO, *The State of World Aquaculture 2006*, FAO Fisheries Technical Paper No. 500 (Rome 2006), p. 42.

DISTRIBUTIVE EFFECTS OF THE ENCLOSURE MOVEMENT   135

poorest countries.[14] There were high expectations at the time of UNCLOS III that the marine environment could produce as much, or even more than, the land, by means of aquaculture and fish farming.[15] Indeed, the total food fish supply and consumption grew at a rate of 3.6 per cent per year from 1961 to 1997, outpacing population growth. The per capita availability of fish and fish products nearly doubled in those forty years, from 9 kg to 16 kg.[16] In 1996, the World Bank predicted that demand for food would double over the following 30 years as the world's population would exceed 8 billion people.[17] With sound management of resources, the sea offers a real prospect and hope for achieving sufficient long-term, and more evenly distributed, food production. It is hoped that the sea could become an essential resource in the fight against hunger (which currently still affects some 1 billion people) if access to marine food supplies is secured for land-locked and least developed countries (LDCs) and eating habits are adjusted.

Moreover, increasing the production and consumption of seafood in developing countries may constitute an essential element in building self-sufficient regional food supplies and could contribute to food security in the age of climate change and the need for structural adjustment and adaptation. Between 1960 and 1990, an increase in the real price of fish was matched by an increase in fish production at a compound rate of 3.4 per cent per year throughout this period.[18] In fact, between 1975 and 1996, the total worldwide fish production grew from 66.4 million tons to 121 million tons.[19] The use of fish as a source of food in developing countries has risen rapidly from the 1970s to the 1990s at a rate of 4 per cent per year, compared with an increase of only 1.6 per cent per year for developed countries.[20] Developing countries are expected to remain net exporters of fish overall, but rising domestic demand is expected to result in a smaller percentage being exported.[21] At the same time, there also

---

[14] FAO, *Marine Fisheries and the Law of the Sea*, n. 13, p. 35. WHO, *Diet, Nutrition and the Prevention of Chronic Diseases: Report of a Joint WHO/FAO Expert Consultation'*, WHO Technical Report Series, 916 (Geneva, 28 January–1 February 2002), p. 22; FAO, *The State of World Aquaculture 2006*, n. 13, p. 39.

[15] The Brandt Commission considered the EEZ to be a major change in the battle against hunger, provided developing countries find sufficient co-operation. The Independent Commission of Development Issues, *North-South: A Programme for Survival 96-97* (1980).

[16] WHO, *Diet, Nutrition and the Prevention of Chronic Diseases*, n. 14, p. 22.

[17] World Bank, *From Vision to Action in the Rural Sector* (Washington DC: World Bank Group, 1996), p. 66.

[18] FAO, *The State of World Fisheries and Aquaculture 1998* (Rome, 1998), p. 81.

[19] Ibid.   [20] FAO, *Marine Fisheries and the Law of the Sea*, n. 13, p. 34.

[21] See FAO, *The State of World Aquaculture 2006*, n. 13, p. 45.

seems to be an increase in consumption of fish and fish products in the EU and the United States of America as well as in many other regions of the world.[22]

In this process, fish farming within the jurisdiction of coastal waters and the EEZ assumed an important role. Overall, world fisheries production has stagnated since the 1970s.[23] Most of the world's natural fishing areas apparently reached their maximum potential for fisheries production, with a majority of stocks being fully exploited, and substantial increases in total catch are therefore unlikely. This contrasts with the tremendous growth in world aquaculture during the last fifty years – particularly in Asia.[24] The significant growth in aquaculture output (which recorded an annual increase of 11.8 per cent in the period 1984 to 1996) has contributed decisively to this rapid growth.[25] While capture fisheries production stopped growing around the mid-1980s, aquaculture output has maintained an average annual growth rate of 8.7 per cent worldwide (excluding China, 6.5 per cent) since 1970.[26] Growth in aquaculture may thus offset part of the reduction and depletion of the ocean catch of fish. Increasingly, aquaculture contributes to regional food security, such as in the Near East and North Africa.[27] The increasing use of domestic fisheries helps to lessen the dependence of net food importers on foreign food supplies. Within the WTO framework, it could help to further discourage the production of excessive agricultural surpluses by developed countries, which has not only led to aggressive, heavily subsidized and distortive food export policies,[28] but also poses an ecological

---

[22] FAO, *The State of World Fisheries and Aquaculture 2008* (Rome, 2009), p. 47. See, however, FAO, *The State of World Aquaculture 2006*, n. 13, p. 45.

[23] WHO, *Diet, Nutrition and the Prevention of Chronic Diseases*, n. 14, p. 22.

[24] See FAO, *The State of World Aquaculture 2006*, n. 13, p. 5.   [25] Ibid., p. 81.

[26] Ibid., p 17.

[27] According to the FAO, aquaculture contributed just 4.5% of fish production for the entire region in 1994, rising to 18.7% in 2003. Furthermore, for several emerging producer countries, aquaculture did not contribute to national food security in 1994, but did so in 2003 (FAO, *The State of World Aquaculture 2006*, n. 13, p. 42).

[28] Reduction and increased discipline on farm subsidies and dismantling of trade barriers (to the benefit of comparative advantage) emerged as a key issue of the GATT Uruguay Round, launched in 1986 by the Ministerial Declaration of Punta del Este of 20 September 1986; Ministerial Declaration on the Uruguay Round, (1987) 33 *GATT, Basic Instruments and Selected Decisions* 19, 24. Negotiations resulted in the 1995 WTO Agreement on Agriculture which brought about tariffication of existing quantitative restrictions and commitments to reduce production subsidies while allowing for decoupled direct payments, see Melaku Desta, *The Law of International Trade in Agricultural Products* (The Hague: Kluwer Law International, 2002); Ricardo Mélendez-Oriz et al. (eds.), *Agricultural Subsidies in the WTO Green Box* (Cambridge University Press, 2009). The Doha

threat through increased soil erosion. In short, the sea could help us to achieve a better balance in the state of global wealth and contribute towards sustainable development. Conceptually, the 200 nm EEZ may considerably promote these redistributive goals. Exclusive jurisdiction provides a stable foundation and legal framework for fish farming and an incentive for joint-venture production, including transfers of technology, experience and know-how in the field of production, food processing and management of conservation and marine research. In addition, the ability to grant access by agreement and to license fishing rights generates additional revenue for coastal states.[29]

However, the EEZ does not by itself guarantee responsible management and conservation. The enclosure of the seas does not inherently solve the problem of global commons. It has not halted or even reversed depletion. It might have reinforced it. It is not a guarantee for sound marine management. The pursuit of marine research and conservation has not become easier or more effective under split jurisdictions in a highly particularized sea.[30] The effect of the regime upon the successful and prudent management of migratory species remains open to question. In many regions, exploitation continues to endanger living resources. Enhanced fish farming bears the risk of enhanced infections of fish stocks and causes new sanitary and phytosanitary challenges. The prospects of revenue from the granting of licences may override the concerns of prudent and long-term conservation. It is equally evident that the new

---

Development Declaration of December 2001 pledged to further reduce production subsidies and to eliminate export subsidies, see www.wto.org/english/tratop_e/agric_e/negoti_e.htm (last accessed 17 February 2012). Subject to the overall conclusion of the Agenda, agreement to phase out export subsidies in agriculture by 2015 was achieved at the Hong Kong ministerial meeting, Ministerial Declaration 18 December 2005 para 6, WT/Min (05) Dec, www.wto.org/english/thewto_e/minist_e/min05_e/final_text_e.htm (last accessed 17 February 2012). It still awaits implementation despite substantial offers on the part of the EU on tariff reductions, it was not possible to reach agreement by the end of 2014.

[29] For an analysis of agreements see Jean E. Carroz and Michel Savini, *The Practice of Coastal States Regarding Foreign Access to Fisheries Resources*, FAO Fisheries Report No. 293 (1983), p. 43 (listing some 280 agreements concluded between 1975 and 1982). A recent example on revenues is the important 1988 *EEC–Morocco access agreement*, stipulating ECU 70 million per annum, including support in marine research. The agreement operates for four years and allows for reduction or expansion of fishing rights by 5%, depending on the needs of the Moroccan fleet, (1988) 21 *Bulletin der Europäischen Gemeinschaften* 2, 68.

[30] See Part XIII LOS Convention; Alfred H. A. Soons, *Marine Scientific Research and the Law of the Sea* (Deventer, Boston MA: Kluwer Law and Taxation Publishers, 1982).

regime risks the instigation of protectionist policies that will benefit non-competitive national fishing industries. The borderline between protectionism and restriction for the purpose of conserving stocks is a delicate one. Subsidies granted to the fishing industry in the wake of the enclosure movement not only distort competition, but are a main cause of over-exploitation and depletion. The reduction of subsidies granted to fisheries is of key importance in combating depletion. This clearly amounts to an important win–win balancing of trade and environmental concerns. Efforts to reduce fisheries subsidies at the WTO are on the agenda of the Doha Development Agenda and new disciplines are being sought with support measures rendered conditional upon the adoption and approval by the Food and Agriculture Organization of the United Nations (FAO) of appropriate resource management and conservation measures.[31] Margret Young stresses the importance of linking WTO disciplines and other fora and agreement in an effort of regime integration in order to achieve effective policies to preserve and protect fish stocks and endangered marine species, such as sea turtles or dolphins and seals.[32]

Moreover, bilateral access agreements may increase discrimination and violations of the principle of the most favoured nation treatment (MFN) of Article I of the General Agreement on Tariffs and Trade

---

[31] See in particular Anja von Moltke (ed.), *Fisheries Subsidies, Sustainable Development and the WTO* (London, Washington DC: Earthscan, 2011). The 2001 Ministerial Declaration mandates Members 'to clarify and improve WTO disciplines on fisheries subsidies, taking into account the importance of this sector to developing countries' (para. 28, 20 November 2001). Much progress has been achieved since the negotiations were launched, but have not been completed by 2014, see Fabrizio Meliadò, 'Fisheries Management Standards in the WTO Fisheries Subsidies Talks: Learning How to Discipline Environmental PPMs?' (2012) 46(5) *Journal of World Trade*,, available at SSRN: http://ssrn.com/abstract=2002241 (last accessed 9 September 2014). Negotiations essentially seek to link the granting of subsidies under WTO law to notification of fisheries management systems to FAO and to monitoring, see www.wto.org/english/tratop_e/rulesneg_e/fish_e/fish_intro_e.htm (last accessed 17 February 2012). Results have not been achieved by 2014.

[32] Margaret A. Young, *Trading Fish, Saving Fish* (Cambridge University Press 2011). For an example of difficulties in distinguishing economic protection and protection of resources see *United States – Import Prohibition of Certain Shrimp and Shrimp Products*, Report of the Appellate Body, WT/DS58/AB/R (12 October 1998) and *United States – Measures concerning the Importation, Marketing and Sale of Tuna and Tuna Products*, Report of the Appellate Body, WT/DS381 (16 May 2012), European Communities – Measures Prohibiting the Importation and Marketing of Seal Products, Report of the Panel, (WT/DS400, WT/DS401 25 November 2013, appealed).

(GATT 1994).[33] Remedies to avoid artificially low definitions of total allowable catches (TAC) by coastal states (thus excluding foreign fleets from harvesting surpluses), and the elimination of discriminatory practices in the supply of services to fishing vessels or in participation in joint ventures, were sought in exchange for the liberalization of market access by developed countries.[34] Quite apart from any economic problems, the struggle for access to foreign fishing grounds may generate political tensions between marine powers.[35] Finally, the new jurisdiction expands the arsenal of economic sanctions to be used for political ends, in particular by allowing for the withdrawal of fishing rights. All this may increase international tensions and pose a threat to the peaceful and prudent use of the seas and co-existence in ocean management.

Thus, there is the potential for both beneficial and detrimental developments to occur. Some thirty-five years after the gradual advent of the EEZ, the assessment of the long-term effects of the enclosure movement with respect to living resources is still an open issue. Environmental issues have become increasingly significant during this time. It was hoped that according national jurisdiction would improve the conservation and management of resources and reduce the over-fishing of resources that had formerly been freely accessible. However, work which has been undertaken by the FAO shows that marine capture fisheries resources are usually considered close to full exploitation worldwide with about half of them fully exploited, one-quarter over-exploited, depleted or recovering from depletion, and one-quarter only with some capacity for expansion.[36] In other words, the vast majority of stocks are exploited at, or beyond, maximum sustainable yield. Whether the outcome of the geographically defined

---

[33] Cf. *Canada – Measures Affecting Exports of Unprocessed Herring and Salmon*, Report of the Panel of 29 November 1987, GATT Doc L/6268, adopted by the Council on 22 March 1988, Minutes of Meeting, GATT Doc. C/M/218 p. 7.

[34] See e.g. Communication from the European Communities, GATT Doc. MTN/GNG/NG3/Wll, 12 February 1988, p. 4. Before the Round, the problem had already been discussed by a Working Group. *Problèmes du commerce de certains produits provenants des ressources naturelles*, Report of 25 October 1985, GATT Doc. L/5895.

[35] For example, a commercial access agreement between the USSR and Kiribati (Gilbert Islands) caused American concerns for 'Soviet build up in the Pacific', *The Guardian*, 16 July 1985.

[36] FAO, *Review of the State of World Marine Fishery Resources*, FAO Fisheries Technical Paper No. 457 (Rome 2005), 6–14.

allocation of marine space will be the redistribution of resources that will assist in the process of LDCs' social and economic development has been a controversial issue from the outset. As was stated in a report by the FAO:

> The establishment of 200-mile Exclusive Economic Zones (EEZs) constitutes an accident of geography and has only limited relevance to the achievement of a more equitable distribution of wealth. Its most important function has been to provide coastal States with the authority to manage the resources within the zones.[37]

For an assessment of distributive effects, it is important to distinguish between the allocation of marine spaces to individual nations and the overall distribution of resources in a North–South context. The first aspect can be clearly evaluated and shows traits of inequity. The second is a longer-term process, but it seems to reveal a beneficial trend in terms of global equity.

II. The allocation of marine spaces

A. The main beneficiaries

The allocation of marine spaces on the basis of geographically and geologically defined foundations and definitions of the shelf and the EEZ inherently benefits large coastal states. It equally benefits island states, regardless of their size.[38] Since the major industrialized states range among large coastal nations, large areas are not allocated to LDCs and therefore not to those who had lobbied most strongly for enclosure. Indeed, more than half of the fifteen biggest beneficiaries are developed countries, led by the EU – due to French and British jurisdiction over overseas territories. Table 3.1 reflects the situation with respect to the EEZ.[39]

---

[37] FAO, above n. 8, p. 3; on this issue see Lawrence Juda, 'World Marine Fish Catch in the Age of Exclusive Economic Zones and Exclusive Fishery Zones' (1991) 22 *Ocean Development & International Law*, 1.
[38] But see Art. 121(3) LOS Convention, excluding rocks and requiring a potential of human habitation or economic life as essential to the notion of island.
[39] The source of the data for the coastal lengths presented is the CIA World Fact Book, available at https://www.cia.gov/library/publications/the-world-factbook/fields/print_2060.html (last accessed 9 September 2014); the source of the data for the EEZ areas is the Sea Around Us Project, available at www.seaaroundus.org/eez/ (last accessed 29 January 2012).

Table 3.1. Allocation of EEZ marine space

State	Coastal length[40] kilometres (a)	Coastal length[40] Nautical miles	EEZ Thousand square kilometres (b)	EEZ Thousand square nautical miles
EU (27)[41]	65,993	35,570	25,000	7,289
Belgium	67	35	3.45	1
Bulgaria	354	191		
Cyprus	648	349		
Denmark	7,314	3,947	107.58	31.36
Estonia	3,794	2,045	39.94	11.6
Finland	1,126	608	90.82	26.48
France (metropolitan)	3,427	1,849	334.60	97.55
Germany	2,389	1,289	57.25	16.69
Greece	13,676	7,380	494.60	144.19
Ireland	1,448	781	410.53	119.68
Italy	7,600	4101	537.93	158.21
Latvia	498	268	32.02	9.33
Lithuania	90	49	6.10	1.77
Malta	197	106	55.55	16.19

[40] It is duly noted that according to Mandelbrot, the measured length of a coast depends on the scale of measurement (Benoît Mandelbrot, 'How Long is the Coast of Britain? Statistical Self-similarity and Fractional Dimension' (1967) 156 *Science*, 636:

Seacoast shapes are examples of highly involved curves with the property that – in a statistical sense – each portion can be considered a reduced-scale image of the whole. This property will be referred to as 'statistical self-similarity'. The concept of 'length' is usually meaningless for geographical curves. They can be considered superpositions of features of widely scattered characteristic sizes; as even finer features are taken into account, the total measured length increases, and there is usually no clear-cut gap or crossover, between the realm of geography and details with which geography need not be concerned.

[41] Excluding landlocked members: Austria, Czech Republic, Hungary, Luxembourg, Slovakia.

Table 3.1. (*cont.*)

State	Coastal length kilometres (a)	Coastal length Nautical miles	EEZ Thousand square kilometres (b)	EEZ Thousand square nautical miles
Netherlands	451	243	63.91	18.63
Poland	440	237	31.60	9.21
Portugal	1,793	968	322.19	93.93
Spain	4,964	2,679	551.87	160.89
Romania	225	121	20.59	6.00
Slovenia	47	25	0.18	0.05
Sweden	3,218	1,736	170.08	49.58
UK	12,429	6,707	773.67	225.55
USA (mainland and Alaska)	19,924	10,751	6,219.15	1,813.16
Indonesia	54,716	29,525	6,079.36	1,772.40
New Zealand	15,134	8166	4,101.63	1,195.81
Australia	25,760	13,900	6,362.93	1,855.08
Russia	37,653	20,318	8,095.86	2,360.30
Japan	29,751	16,054	4,469.02	1,302.92
Brazil	7,491	4,042	3,179.69	927.02
Canada	243,791	131,551	6,006.15	1,751.06
Mexico	9,330	5,035	3,269.38	953.17
Kiribati	1,143	617	3,437.34	1002.13
Papua New Guinea	5,152	2,780	2,396.21	698.60
Chile	6,435	3,472	2,009.29	585.79
Norway	21,925	11,831	1,395.75	406.92
India (mainland)	7,000	3,777	1,630.35	475.32
China	14,500	7,824	2,285.87	666.43

(a) 1 km = 0.539 nm, 1 nm = 1.8532 km
(b) 1 square km = 3.43 square nm

From this perspective, it can be argued that the goals of global equity and redistribution of resources, wealth and power have largely failed.[42] Moreover, the LOS Convention did not succeed in adopting a global perspective, as it largely ignores the legitimate claims and interests of land-locked and geographically disadvantaged states regarding access to the mineral and living resources of the shelf and the EEZ. A study of claims and responses provides a telling account of the limits to global equity within a system of nation states.

B. *The position of land-locked and geographically disadvantaged states*

About one-third of all states represented at UNCLOS III belonged to the group of thirty-one land-locked countries (LLCs) and an additional number of geographically disadvantaged countries (GDCs).[43] In matters of maritime law, these are the least powerful countries; those belonging at the time to the developing world are often also the poorest and least developed nations. The achievements and failures of this group may therefore be among the strongest indicators of the extent to which equity, and the general idea of distributive justice that it embraces in the overall maritime context, can deploy a normative effect in the global process of law-making.

While the LOS Convention significantly improves the right to communication of LLCs, with respect to access to the sea and transit

---

[42] See e.g. Lewis M. Alexander in a book review (1980) 74 *American Journal of International Law*, 725, 726: 'In the view of [the majority of states], was the exclusive economic zone concept really such a good idea?'

[43] Art. 70(2) LOS Convention defines geographically disadvantaged states as coastal states, including states bordering enclosed or semi-enclosed seas, whose geographical situation makes them dependent upon the exploitation of the EEZ of other states in the subregion or region for adequate supplies of fish for the nutritional purposes of their populations or parts thereof, and coastal states which can claim no EEZ of their own. Land-locked states are states without a sea-coast, Art. 124(1)(a) LOS Convention. See Helmut Tuerk and Gerhard Hafner, 'The Land-Locked Countries and the United Nations Convention on the Law of the Sea' in B. Vukas, *Essays on the New Law of the Sea*, n. 3, pp. 58–70, 67; for critical assessments see Stephen C. Vasciannie, *Land Locked and Geographically Disadvantaged States in the International Law of the Sea* (Oxford: Clarendon Press, 1990); A. Mpai Sinjela, 'Land-locked States Rights in the Exclusive Economic Zone from the Perspective of the UN Convention on the Law of the Sea: A Historical Evaluation' (1989) 20 *Ocean Development & International Law*, 63; Ibrahim J. Wani, 'An Evaluation of the Convention on the Law of the Sea from the Perspective of the Landlocked States' (1982) 22 *Virginia Journal of International Law*, 627.

through coastal states,[44] far less has been achieved at the level of the allocation and distribution of natural resources, which can be exploited from the continental shelf and the EEZ. The coastal states that constitute the majority are quite successful in defending their privileges against such aspirations.

1. Mineral resources

Attempts by LLCs to obtain legal rights of participation in the exploitation of the continental shelves in their respective region have failed completely. The Group of LLCs and GDCs submitted a variety of proposals relating to such rights of access at UNCLOS III, but coastal states were not even prepared to approach such participation on a non-mandatory basis. For example, Austrian-sponsored proposals in 1976 sought to introduce rights of participation of land-locked states in the exploration and exploitation of the regional continental shelves either beyond the 200-metre isobath or beyond a 50-mile limit in a seaward direction. This proposal would have imposed a general duty to promote such participation, to be implemented by 'equitable arrangements', during specific joint ventures.[45] Subsequent compromise proposals merely spoke of coastal states 'granting such participation',[46] but even these failed.

The proposals by the Group to establish a Common Heritage Fund (CHF), which was sponsored by Nepal in 1978, also failed to materialize.[47] The project was further expounded by the Group for the Common Heritage Funds in 1980.[48] It sought to extend the idea of common heritage to all mineral resources beyond the 12-mile territorial sea. Without challenging the national jurisdiction of coastal states over the shelf and the EEZ, it proposed, in essence, an obligation by coastal states to make payments and contributions in kind for their exploitation of

---

[44] Part X LOS Convention. Unlike the 1965 Convention on Transit Trade of Land-Locked States, reprinted in (1965) 4 ILM 957, the new regime in the LOS Convention no longer relies upon reciprocity. Art. 125(1) entails a right of access to and from the sea and freedom of transit through the territory of the transit states to LLCs.

[45] Draft proposal on Art. 63 ISNT II (11 April 1976), reproduced in 4 *The Third United Nations Conference on the Law of the Sea*, pp. 323–4.

[46] Compromise text by Austria of 28 April 1976, ibid. at p. 325.

[47] See statement by the Nepal delegate, *Official Records* vol. IX 88–89 (106th mtg, 19 May 1978); and Letter dated 5 May 1978 from the representative of Nepal to the President of the Conference, UN Doc. A/CONF. 62/65, ibid. at p. 175–9 (incl. draft articles on CHF).

[48] Background Paper on the Common Heritage Fund Proposal (12 February 1980) submitted by Nepal, Austria, Singapore, Uganda, Upper Volta, Zambia and Bolivia, reproduced in 4 *The Third United Nations Conference on the Law of the Sea*, 528–31. See also UN Doc. A/CONF. 62/91 (19 Sept 1979); A/CONF. 62/91 Corr. 1 (15 Oct 1979).

mineral resources within the EEZ and the continental shelf. Rates were to be defined by the Authority of the Area. They were estimated at US$5 billion per annum. As well as supporting international deep sea mining, the revenue would primarily have been used to make disbursements 'on the basis of equitable sharing criteria' to the least developed states and the land-locked amongst them.[49]

In a forum of so many competing national interests, the arguments of these 'have-nots' towards enhanced distributive justice had little chance of being heard and taken seriously by coastal states. Ultimately, the concessions to land-locked and shelf-locked states settled at a much lower level. As far as mineral resources are concerned, the concept of the EEZ (including shelf rights) clearly prevailed as a truly exclusive, national zone. States' contributions to the community only start beyond the 200-mile limit indicated before. Article 82 of the LOS Convention does provide for payments and contributions in kind from the exploitation of the continental shelf between the 200-mile minimum and the outer limit of the continental margin, as defined by the complex regime of Article 76. The obligations of those coastal states that enjoy the privileges of extended natural shelves integrate the exclusively national benefits of the EEZ and the common resources of the Area. To some extent, they mitigate the effect of natural privileges to the community's benefit. No contributions are due during the first five years of operation of gas, oil, or nodule exploitation, however, the contribution amounts to 1 per cent of value or volume during the sixth year and gradually increases on an annual basis until a ceiling of 7 per cent is reached after twelve years of production.[50] This is hardly an impressive amount, but more substantial schemes of redistribution were clearly rejected during

---

[49] Draft Amendment Art. 56(4)(c) to ICNT/Rev. 1, above n. 45, p. 528. Reasons put forward in support of this enlarged concept of redistribution included the following considerations, p. 530:

1. The CHF Proposal is a real and substantial move in the direction of the New International Economic Order.
2. Rich nations should support the Proposal as a sound technique for promoting Third World development.
3. The CHF Proposal is a move to restore equity in a treaty draft, which is weighed overwhelmingly on the side of the rich nations and a small number of poor ones.
4. Under ICNT/Rev. 1 ten nations will get over one half of all the EEZ in the world. Only one of those ten is a poor country. The other 150 nations must share the rest.
5. The Proposal insists that some of the really valuable ocean wealth, i.e. the offshore mineral wealth, must be shared. It is estimated that the at least 90 percent of all seabed oil and gas is within the EEZ.

[50] Art. 82(2) LOS Convention.

UNCLOS III.[51] In addition, developing coastal states that are net importers of the commodity concerned are exempt from such contributions.[52] Moreover, benefits will have to be shared among coastal and land-locked developing countries, with the latter given only minimally preferential consideration:

> The payments or contributions shall be made through the Authority, which shall distribute them to States Parties to this Convention, on the basis of equitable sharing criteria, taking into account the interests and needs of developing States, particularly the least developed and the land-locked among them.[53]

A similar, though less obvious, neglect of the needs and interests of LLCs and GDCs developed in the field of living resources.

2. Living resources: the concept of equitable surplus allocation

The concept of the freedom of the high seas in the fishing industry has been particularly vital to geographically disadvantaged states. However limited its own waters, direct connection to the sea provided a GDC with sufficient access to local or distant fishing grounds. The evolution of the EEZ dramatically impaired these traditional rights. Even though they were primarily developed to cope with the problem of long-distance fishing industries, EEZs simultaneously threaten the livelihood of local fisheries, communities and seafood suppliers in states which happen to be short on extensive coasts which border the seas, and thus are less privileged by nature.

These detrimental effects of the EEZ were of considerable concern to many of the LDCs and LLCs at UNCLOS III. The marine have-nots made considerable efforts and exerted pressure on coastal states to retain access to the fish-rich zones. These countries sought to achieve some sort of redistributive justice, including at the very least a controlled phasing-out of the traditional rights of GDCs. The matter was, and is likely to remain, of great concern to most coastal states as well as to GDCs, LLCs among the developing countries and LDCs. Many LDCs on either side are seeking to expand fishing industries and the nutritional basis for their

---

[51] See proposals by Sri Lanka which sought to impose a much more onerous scheme on industrialized nations (4% in first 5 years, 8% in next five years, 17% during the next ten years, and 15% thereafter). LDCs were exempted, and other LDCs were to pay a quarter. NG 6/6 (10 April 1979), reproduced in 2 *Dokumente der Dritten Seerechtskonferenz, Genfer Session 1979*, p. 637.
[52] Art. 82(3) LOS Convention.   [53] Art. 84(4) LOS Convention.

populations.[54] This problem emerged as one of the core issues of the Conference and was dealt with in a special Negotiating Group 4. Unlike other topics, the problem of access to the EEZ primarily emerged as a dispute within the Group of 77.

Up to the Revised Single Negotiating Text of 1976, draft proposals provided for LLCs and GDCs to have genuine rights of access to the EEZ.[55] Coastal states however, were not prepared to accept such a far-reaching infringement of their newly expanded sovereignty over their coasts' living resources. During the course of negotiations, these rights were substantially reduced. For the following reasons, the 'rights' and 'entitlements' of Articles 69 and 70 of the LOS Convention are merely nominal, and not legally effective. Without bargaining chips and powers, they can hardly be realized as a matter of right and entitlement for these six reasons:

(i) Access rights are limited to those parts of surplus catches that are equal to the difference between the allowable and effective yield exploited by the coastal state, its nationals and affiliates. Articles 69(1) and 70(1) provide for LLCs and GDCs respectively, that:

> 1. Land-locked States [States with special geographical characteristics] shall have the right to participate, on an equitable basis, in the exploitation of an appropriate part of the surplus of the living resources of the exclusive economic zones of coastal States of the same subregion or region, taking into account the relevant economic and geographical circumstances of all

---

[54] The idea of access by LLCs, yet unknown to the Latin American concept of Patrimonial Sea, see below nn. 111–12, was originally introduced by land-locked African states. It remained a major concern of LDCs and some Eastern European states. In Western Europe, the issue is of less practical importance to land-locked, industrialized nations, such as Austria and Switzerland. Moreover, it is dealt with in the EEC as an internal problem. For an account of negotiations in Negotiating Group 4 see Bernard H. Oxman, 'The Seventh Session (1978)' (1979) 73 *American Journal of International Law*, 1, 16–18.

[55] Art. 58 (and 59) RSNT/Part II (6 May 1976) said:
 1. Land-locked States shall have the right to participate in the exploration and exploitation of the living resources of the exclusive economic zones of adjoining coastal States on an equitable basis, taking into account all the relevant economic and geographical circumstances of all the States concerned. The terms and conditions of such participation shall be determined by the States concerned through bilateral, subregional or regional agreements. Developed land-locked States shall, however, be entitled to exercise their rights only within the exclusive economic zone of adjoining coastal States.
Reprinted in 1 *The Third United Nations Conference on the Law of the Sea* 214, 215, identical Arts. 57–58 ISNT/Part II (7 May 1975) p. 30.

the States concerned and in conformity with the provisions of this article and of articles 61 and 62.

(ii) Surplus rights are not specifically reserved for LLCs and GDCs. Article 62(2) allows access to be granted to any other state, although it requires the coastal states to pay particular attention to the rights of land-locked and geographically disadvantaged (developing) states in the region. These rights have to be realized through the use of agreements, and the Convention offers a number of interesting criteria to be taken into account and used as guidelines in the process of sharing and allocating fishing rights. Articles 69(2) and 70(3) provide:

> The terms and modalities of such participation shall be established by the States concerned through bilateral, subregional or regional agreements taking into account, inter alia:
>
> (a) the need to avoid effects detrimental to fishing communities or fishing industries of the coastal State;
> (b) the extent to which the land-locked [geographically disadvantaged] State, in accordance with the provisions of this article, is participating or is entitled to participate under existing bilateral, subregional or regional agreements in the exploitation of the living resources of the exclusive economic zones of other States;
> (c) the extent to which other land-locked States and geographically disadvantaged States [and vice versa] are participating in the exploitation of the living resources of the exclusive economic zone of the coastal State and the consequent need to avoid a particular burden for any single coastal State or a part of it;
> (d) the nutritional needs of the population of the respective States.

The application of such factors was, at the time, a new and innovative approach to guide negotiations on this subject.[56] However, it has remained unclear to what extent such factors can truly influence the process and assist the achievement of balanced results. Significantly, states remain free to introduce additional, and unlimited, considerations. In particular, and as is explicitly referred to in Article 62(3), coastal states are able to emphasize their own national interests as, for example, they are defined in section 201(3) of the US Fishery Conservation and Management Act (FMCA).[57] This Act, as

---

[56] See also Chapter 7.
[57] 16 USC sec. 1108–1857; 22 USC sec. 1972–1973. See William T. Burke, 'U.S. Fishery Management and the New Law of the Sea' (1982) 76 *American Journal of International Law*, 24, 37, n. 39.

amended in 1980, emphasizes a number of factors related to the interests of the industry (such as existence or non-existence of tariff or non-tariff barriers on US fish products, and contribution to the development of US fisheries by imports), of policing (compliance), and of research (co-operation). It considers traditional fishing activities and the needs of the applicant state. Again, the list provided is not exhaustive and contains a catchall phrase that allows for virtually any political interest to be taken into account, including those not necessarily linked to fisheries. Therefore, whilst coastal states cannot deny access to surplus catches under the Convention, they are nevertheless in a position to minimize the scope of such rights if national interests so require.

(iii) The long-term prospects of rights and entitlement to surplus fishing remain unclear at best. According to the text of Articles 69(3) and 70(4), a new situation emerges when the coastal state 'approaches a point which would enable it to harvest the entire allowable catch'. When this occurs, these provisions prescribe that states 'shall co-operate in the establishment of equitable arrangements', applying the same set of factors related to the rights and entitlement of the first place. Thus the Convention provides for renegotiations of catch allocations; and, what was a right of access to surpluses under the Convention turns, it seems, into a mere duty to co-operate. The practical significance is difficult to assess. New agreements only appear possible for developing LLCs and GDCs,[58] and those qualifying under the provision find themselves in a rather weak and uncomfortable position. Since the basic rights extend merely to surplus catches, LLCs and GDCs now have to negotiate without such foundations; new settlements become a matter of mere bilateral treaty law and of a contractual relationship.

Arguably, coastal states remain under an obligation to negotiate such agreements with developing states. But it is far from clear whether their obligation includes a duty to reach an agreement under this particular provision. Based on the general law of negotiation, which is discussed below, the answer seems to be negative.[59] Moreover, Article 62(3), which seems to address access of states to the EEZ

---

[58] Arts. 69(3) and 70(4) explicitly restrict further participation to developing states. Moreover, developed land-locked, or geographically disadvantaged, states are limited to surplus within the EEZ of developed states of the same region or subregion, Art. 69(4) and 70(5).
[59] See Chapter 7.

other than under the surplus regime, does not provide any preferential treatment to LLCs and GDCs. Unlike in Article 62(2), they are no longer given special emphasis, but rather they are merely referred to amongst other factors such as national interests and, in general, the needs of the region's developing states. Thus, it seems compatible for coastal states to exclude further participation of LLCs and GDCs; as long as the reasons for such exclusion are stated, the coastal state will fulfil its obligation.[60] Instead of securing long-term access for LLCs and GDCs, Articles 69(3) and 70(4) primarily exert negative functions: they prevent the creation of acquired rights. All the legal benefits and the future opportunities go to the coastal states.

(iv) The determination of exactly what constitutes the allowable catch (albeit effected on a scientific basis), is entirely left to the coastal state (Article 61(1)). '[S]overeign rights' over living resources within the EEZ (Article 56(1)(a)) imply a considerable amount of discretionary power, which allows varying policies of conservation and standards of exploitability to be applied. It is unlikely that any developing state would define the figure for their allowable catch as being much beyond the capacity it can absorb itself, either by its own industry or (even more limiting to developing LLCs and GDCs), through means of third party contractors. The Convention leaves coastal states free to market their resources virtually unimpaired. Article 62(4)(a) provides for licensing and implicitly for joint ventures with developed and experienced distant-water fishing industries. Moreover, Article 254 does not grant LLCs and GDCs secured rights to undertake marine research in regional waters.

According to the Report of the Chairman of Negotiating Group 4, which adopted Articles 69 and 70 after intensive negotiation at the 1978 Geneva Session, the achievement of full capacity to harvest all the allowable yield in Articles 69(3) and 70(4) was designed to deal with the expansion of capacity by 'joint venture or other similar arrangements with third parties', and not the capacity of the coastal state 'of its own'.[61] Given the over-capacity of the long-distance fishing fleets of industrialized nations, it would hardly be surprising

---

[60] See Geir Ulfstein, '200 Mile Zones and Fisheries Management' (1983) 52 *Nordisk Tideskrift for International Ret*, 3, 20–2.

[61] NG4/10 and Annex A (NG4/9/Rev.2, in *Third Conference on the Law of the Sea. Reports of the Committees and Negotiating Groups on negotiations at the Seventh Session contained in a single document, both for recording purposes and for the convenience*

if developing coastal states are already in a position to exploit their resources to the full extent (if not able to continue to deplete them) through lucrative licensing and joint-ventures.[62] Both are efficient instruments for developing their own fishing technology and know-how and generating state revenues. There can be little doubt that long-distance fishing industries can afford to pay a better price than many poor LLCs or GDCs. As the determination of fees is entirely left to the coastal state in Article 62(4)(a), the possibility cannot be excluded that revenue policies will further impair the access of poor countries to the living resources of their neighbours' exclusive zones. In many cases, access rights were likely to be obsolete even before the Convention entered into force.

(v) Developments detrimental to the interests of developing LLCs and GDCs are all the more likely to occur because these countries, unlike the coastal states, are prevented from marketing or transferring their surplus rights under Article 72(1) of the Convention:

> Rights provided under articles 69 and 70 to exploit resources shall not be directly or indirectly transferred to third States or their nationals by lease or license, by establishing joint ventures or in any other manner which has the effect of such transfer unless otherwise agreed by the States concerned.

Clearly, this establishes the most significant imbalance between coastal states and land-locked or geographically disadvantaged states. Without the possibility of joint ventures, it is difficult to see how the LLCs and GDCs can develop their own industries and effectively use their rights in competition with the coastal state. Article 72(1) makes the whole scheme a doubtful concept, to say the least.

(vi) The land-locked and geographically disadvantaged states did not succeed in establishing compulsory third-party legal dispute settlement measures. Article 297(3)(b)(iii) allows coastal states to exempt the sensitive and complex issue of surplus allocation from legal proceedings. For obvious reasons, many coastal states will opt for

---

of delegations, 19 May 1978, at 71, 72, quoted from Bernard H. Oxman 'The Seventh Session (1978)' (1979) 73 *American Journal of International Law*, 1, 17–18.

[62] In fact, joint-venture agreements have been increasing. In a typical pattern, coastal fishermen retain the exclusive rights to harvest and sell their catches to foreign processing ships at sea. Vladimir Kaczynski, 'Distant Water Fisheries and the 200 Mile Economic Zone' 44, *Occasional Paper No. 34* (Honolulu: The Law of the Sea Institute, 1983) p. 39.

exclusion. Without legal remedies, the rights and aspirations of LLCs and GDCs, however dependent on marine food resources they may be, vanish into thin air with all the rational factors that must be taken into account under the Convention.

In short, the basic flaws and deficiencies of Articles 69 and 70 are that LLCs and GDCs lack any effective and lasting rights of access to the EEZ under the Convention. Entitlement is more nominal than effective. Given the very one-sided prohibition against marketing their surplus rights, it is more than doubtful whether these countries can exercise these rights at all, much less as time progresses, without additional bargaining powers and possible trade-offs that they can offer the coastal state. In short, it is difficult to accept the proposition, submitted by the Chairman of Negotiating Group 4, that the regime adopted provides a 'fair and reasonable' solution.[63] As one observer stated:

> [t]he conclusion to be drawn concerning the rights of land-locked states is that not much was gained by them in the resources of the EEZ. They lost their rights in the area now known as the EEZ (which was part of the high seas prior to the conclusion of the convention), as well as in the resources thereof. What they gained was 'the right to participate', 'on an equitable basis', in exploiting the appropriate part of the living resources of the EEZ. But this right is compounded by a string of conditions, whose implementation is vested in the coastal states.[64]

Indeed, in law and in fact, land-locked and geographically disadvantaged states, many of them amongst the poorest nations, once more are the losers in the race for jurisdiction over resources. Ironically, they pay the highest price for what was achieved in the name of equity and a new international economic order. It seems that nothing more has been achieved than a transitory regulation that provides the basis for bilateral or regional phase-out agreements between coastal states, LLCs and GDCs. It is possible that state practice will follow similar patterns to those seen after the extension of fishing zones in the 1960s. The fishing activities of nationals in areas that are now under exclusive jurisdiction have not found recognition as historic rights, but were gradually phased out.[65] At the same time, and providing a degree of hope, there is also some evidence that developments may take new and innovative routes,

---

[63] UNCLOS, 10 *Official Records* at p. 89.   [64] Sinjela, n. 43, p.75.
[65] See David W. Windley, 'International Practice Regarding Traditional Fishing Privileges of Foreign Fishermen in Zones of Extended Maritime Jurisdiction' (1969) 63 *American Journal of International Law*, 490.

DISTRIBUTIVE EFFECTS OF THE ENCLOSURE MOVEMENT   153

despite a legally unfavourable regime towards land-locked and geographically disadvantaged states. New models appeared after the closing of UNCLOS III in Western Africa where the integration and participation of land-locked and geographically disadvantaged states is of particular importance and a true test of the viability of the concept of surplus allocation under the LOS Convention.[66] It is recalled that the Member States of the Convention are obliged to exercise their rights in good faith (Article 300). This principle is bound to influence the exercise of the rights of coastal states in consideration of the needs and legitimate expectations of land-locked countries.[67]

III. Developments in fisheries production and market shares

Based on an assessment of the inequitable elements discussed, it may be readily concluded that the enclosure movement and the new law of the sea is a complete failure, incapable of achieving long-term community goals of global welfare and development. Arvid Pardo, one of the founding fathers of UNCLOS III, of a community approach, and of a comprehensive concept of common heritage, expressed pessimistic views and disappointment:

> It is clear from what I said that I consider the new Convention on the Law of the Sea as fatally flawed. A truly historic opportunity has been lost to mold the legal framework governing man's activities in the marine resources for the benefit of all.[68]

---

[66] A 1984 multilateral agreement relating to the regional development of fisheries in the Gulf of Guinea, perhaps establishing the first application of Art. 70 LOS Convention, not only includes coastal states (Equatorial Guinea, Gabon, Sao Tome e Principe, Congo) but also (influential) Zaire and potentially other land-locked states. Also, it was reported that Mali, Niger and Upper Volta and three coastal states were negotiating the establishment of a joint company for fishing operations. See William R. Edeson, 'Types of Agreements for Exploitation of EEZ Fisheries', Paper presented at the 19th Annual Conference of the Law of the Sea, Cardiff, 24–27 July 1985 (typescript), p. 9; Jean E. Carroz and Michel Savini, 'Les Accords de pêches conclus par les Etats africains riverains de l'Atlantique' (1983) 23 *Annuaire Français de Droit International*, 675.
[67] See also Surya Prasad Subedi, 'The Marine Fishery Rights of Land-locked States with Particular Reference to the EEZ' (1987) 2 *International Journal of Estuary and Coastal Law*, 4, 227, 238.
[68] Arvid Pardo, 'An Opportunity Lost' in C. Buderi and D. Caron (eds.), *Perspectives on U.S. Policy Toward the Law of the Sea: Prelude to the Final Session of the Third U.N. Conference on the Law of the Sea*, Proceedings of a Symposium held in 1982, The Law of the Sea Institute Occasional Paper No. 35 (Honolulu: Law of the Sea Institute, University of Hawaii, 1985), p. 77. See also Arvid Pardo, 'The Convention on the Law of the Sea: A Preliminary Appraisal' (1983) 20 *San Diego Law Review*, 489. Arvid Pardo, a former ambassador of Malta, considerably influenced the advent of UNCLOS III with an historic

Whilst the full play of natural advantages and disadvantages, and the failure to recognize the effective and meaningful participation by land-locked and geographically disadvantaged states supports such a conclusion, the enclosure nevertheless offers considerable redistributive effects to the benefit of developing countries. It is not sufficient to merely consider the geographical distribution of marine spaces among the largest coastal states and the island states.

Overall, it is evident that the majority of the total area was allocated to the jurisdiction of developing countries. But the main shift and effect of this revolution has not been felt so much through the allocation of space *per se*, but rather has been the fact that what had previously been free fishing grounds were no longer freely accessible to the large fishing fleets of developed countries. Greater restrictions have been placed upon developed countries in terms of access, as well as conservation measures, than for fleets from LDCs, which were either not yet in existence or not operating globally to the same extent. This has been reflected in world fish production figures. Given statistical methods, it is not possible to precisely identify the share of catches within the EEZ. It is estimated that some 90 per cent of all occur within EEZs.

Developing countries as well as low-income food-deficit countries (LIFDCs) have been increasing their marine catch at a considerable rate.[69] Developing countries, which accounted for 27 per cent of the world's catch in 1950, accounted for more than half of the total by the 1990s.[70] LIFDCs exceeded marine catches of developed countries for the first time in 2003, due to strong growth in Asian operations and a decline in developing country catches.[71] China, it is worth noting, trebled its production between the mid-1980s and the mid-1990s. Also since the mid-1980s, catches from developed countries remained roughly stable only in individual cases but continually decreased overall:[72] China and

---

speech given at the UN in 1967, establishing the doctrine of common heritage in UN debate and subsequent developments. (1967) GAOR, 22th Session First Committee, 1515th and 1516th meeting, UN Doc. A/C.1/PV. 1515 and 1516. See also Arvid Pardo, 'Whose is the Bed of the Sea?' (1968) 62 *American Society of International Law Proceed.*, 216.

[69] Source: FAO, *FishStat Plus – Universal Software for Fishery Statistical Time Series, Capture Production 1950–2008* (Rome, 2010).

[70] FAO, *Marine Fisheries and the Law of the Sea*, n. 13, 10.

[71] Counting marine *and* inland captures, LIFDCs exceeded catches of developed countries already in 1997, due to the strong growth of Latin American and Asian operations (see FAO, *FishStat Plus – Universal Software for Fishery Statistical Time Series*, n. 69).

[72] FAO, *FishStat Plus – Universal Software for Fishery Statistical Time Series*, n. 69.

Peru remain the leading fishing nations in terms of marine captures (16 per cent and 8.2 per cent of the global catches in 2008). Since the early 1990s, Japan's catches have fallen from 9.6 per cent to 5.4 per cent of global capture.[73] Table 3.2 indicates marine captures in thousand metric tons in the years 1986, 1997 and 2008, covering an exemplary recent period of twenty-three years.

Similar effects can be observed with respect to exports and imports. The expansion in fish exports by developing countries exceeded that of developed countries throughout the 1970s and 1980s. In 2006, exports by developing countries accounted for 49 per cent of world exports of fish and fish products in value terms.[74] Developing countries are net fish exporters. Developing country net exports have increased significantly in recent decades, growing from US$ 1.8 billion in 1976 to US$ 7.2 billion in 1984, to US$ 16.7 billion in 1996 and reaching US$ 24.6 billion in 2006.[75] Developed countries have consistently accounted for a very high proportion of total world imports, representing 88 per cent of the total value in 1970, 86 per cent in 1989 and still 80 per cent in 2006.[76] Japan, the United States and the EU are the major markets, with a total share of 72 per cent of the total import value in 2006.[77] Japan's share of the value of total imports rose to over 30 per cent in 1996 – reflecting the decline in its own catch of edible fish – but it has shown a negative average annual growth rate of 2 per cent between 1996 and 2006, and its share of world total imports was only 16 per cent in 2006.[78] Still, Japan, as well as Europe and North America are characterized by a fishery trade deficit.[79]

Since 2002, China has been the world's largest exporter of fish and fish products, having further consolidated its leading position in recent years. In the period from 1996 to 2006, Chinese exports grew at an average annual rate of 12.1 per cent, while those of Vietnam grew at 20.9 per cent, in a world export market showing overall growth.[80] China has also

---

[73] See ibid., pp. 10–11.
[74] FAO, *The State of World Fisheries and Aquaculture 2008*, (Rome 2009), p. 48.
[75] Ibid., p. 49.   [76] Ibid., p. 49.   [77] Ibid., p. 49.
[78] Ibid., pp. 48–49; FAO, *Marine Fisheries and the Law of the Sea*, n. 13, 26.
[79] FAO, *The State of World Fisheries and Aquaculture 2008*', n. 74, pp. 50, 53.
[80] Although some weakening in demand was registered in late 2007 and early 2008 as a result of the financial crisis. The long-term trend for trade in fish is, however, positive, with a rising share of production from both developed and developing countries reaching international markets (FAO, *The State of World Fisheries and Aquaculture 2008*, n. 74, pp. 45, 47, 48.

Table 3.2. *Allocation of marine catches*

	Marine captures		
	1985	1997	2008
	(in thousand metric tons)		
Economic classification			
Global marine captures	73,753,440.1	86,945,514.3	80,579,531.2
Developing countries or areas, other than LDCs	32,158,129.3	53,130,402.8	52,754,779.1
Developed countries or areas	40,021,595.8	31,262,755.8	23,600,631.6
LDCs	1,549,127.0	2,391,209.7	4,164,712.5
Economic groups, continents, countries, geographic regions, custom groups			
Other	24,588.0	161,146.0	59,408.0
Asia	28,848,609.1	38,708,387.5	40,604,351.3
LIFDCs	11,803,251.6	25,527,812.4	28,345,504.2
Latin America and the Caribbean	13,536,346.2	18,859,735.4	15,845,668.5
Net food-importing developing countries	7,372,639.5	13,081,092.8	14,178,048.0
China	3,696,706.0	12,959,117.0	12,908,916.0
Northern Europe	7,544,305.0	9,424,439.0	6,545,992.0
EU	7,815,248.3	7,469,633.4	5,055,394.2
Africa	2,722,807.9	4,081,791.3	4,765,603.4
USA	4,645,588.5	5,016,523.8	4,332,433.1
Japan	10,827,191.0	5,982,591.4	4,321,923.6
Former USSR area	9,783,496.0	5,098,222.0	3,834,826.0
Eastern Europe	916,831.0	5,172,904.0	3,501,601.0
Sub-Saharan Africa	2,035,146.0	2,967,201.8	3,343,333.5
Arctic Sea	9,783,496.0	4,461,643.0	3,177,125.0
Western Europe	1,528,027.4	1,353,327.5	1,138,576.8
Oceania	494,763.0	1,126,478.6	1,100,547.3
South Africa	797,608.0	525,094.0	654,553.0
Israel	12,667.0	3,728.0	2,595.0
Land-locked developing countries	500.0	–	–

experienced a significant increase in its fish imports in the decade from 1996 to 2006, when it became the sixth-largest importer. This growth has been particularly noticeable since the country's accession to the WTO in late 2001, as a consequence of which it lowered import duties on fish and fish products.[81] LIFDCs play a growing role in the trade in fish and fishery products. In 1976, their exports accounted for 10 per cent of the total value of fish exports. This share expanded to 12 per cent in 1986, 17 per cent in 1996 and 20 per cent in 2006.[82] Tables 3.3 and 3.4 demonstrate imports and exports by value in million US dollars, in the years 1985, 1996 and 2006.[83]

Table 3.3. *Distribution of exports of fish products*

Exports	1985	1996	2006
	(in million US$)		
Economic classification			
Global	17,132,302	53,386,937	86,573,370
Developed countries or areas	9,747,245	26,987,283	43,814,801
Developing countries or areas other than LDCs	6,911,830	24,976,177	40,585,324
LDCs	473,227	1,423,477	2,173,245
Economic groups, continents, countries, custom groups			
Asia	5,141,274	17,194,698	29,169,447
European Union	3,593,775	11,720,111	21,837,097
LIFDCs	1,889,931	9,193,247	17,519,390
China	267,916	2,955,499	9,150,328
Norway	922,460	3,434,073	5,543,705
Thailand	675,063	4,120,443	5,275,349
United States of America	1,162,372	3,263,358	4,190,109
Africa	766,958	2,552,723	3,930,519
Vietnam	73,989	503,552	3,379,955
Japan	854,365	745,173	1,456,604

[81] See FAO, *The State of World Fisheries and Aquaculture 2008*, n. 74, p. 47. With the accession of China and Vietnam to the WTO (in 2001 and 2007, respectively), all the major fish producing, importing and exporting countries are now members of the organization, with the exception of the Russian Federation.
[82] FAO, *The State of World Fisheries and Aquaculture 2008*, n. 74, p. 49.
[83] Source: FAO, *FishStat Plus – Universal Software for Fishery Statistical Time Series*, n. 69.

Table 3.4. *Distribution of imports of fish products*

Imports	1985	1996	2006
		(in million US$)	
Economic classification			
Global	19,490,690	58,026,974	91,230,805
Developed countries or areas	16,277,402	48,335,392	72,655,621
Developing countries or areas other than LDCs	3,008,725	9,507,701	17,960,678
LDCs	204,563	183,881	614,506
Economic groups, continents, countries, custom groups			
European Union	6,101,514	20,250,366	37,847,206
Asia	7,149,867	24,961,663	29,052,862
Japan	4,852,280	17,287,999	14,258,699
United States of America	4,051,794	7,162,307	13,399,709
LIFDCs	709,667	2,548,287	6,549,835
China	95,390	1,200,992	4,188,548
Africa	641,918	1,097,395	2,052,672
Thailand	138,312	841,085	1,573,958
Norway	70,871	539,989	851,543
Vietnam	–	6,416	302,425

It can be noted, therefore, that fishing operations of LIFDCs in the period examined produced a substantial trade surplus while industrialized countries showed an increased trade deficit. In addition, it should be recalled that access and fishing agreements generate additional revenue for LDCs but are not included in the data concerning fishing operations. To conclude, the trend is contrary to the developments in agriculture, where the 1980s witnessed a considerable stagnation of export growth rates in LDCs and developed countries alike.[84]

---

[84] See e.g. ibid., 1–17 for data covering 1985 and 1986.

The EEZ brought about equally significant shifts in the structure of the industry. Initially, the enclosure of the 200-mile zone encouraged new developments in high seas fishing. In particular, planned economies put considerable emphasis onto developing hitherto unconventional resources of the high seas. For example, the former Soviet Union emerged in the 1970s as the pioneer in the krill (planktonic crustaceans) fishing industry, although the significant catches achieved in the early 1980s had substantially dropped by the 1990s.[85] Extensive exploitation of krill and other resources, and the fishing of the Antarctic region by a number of states, particularly Japan and the former Soviet Union, was making up for what had been lost in the traditionally international fishing grounds of the former high seas.[86] The extent of present day fishing operations, however, is threatening the natural balance in these areas, endangering the livelihood of many dependent species. The result is that the Antarctic region is actually footing the bill for the more efficient conservation and regulation of other areas. The price of leaving Antarctica out of UNCLOS III is being paid for by the environment.

The new regime has also changed traditional patterns to a considerable extent. The evidence shows a substantial decrease in long-distance fishing operations, in particular those of Western industries. Distant-water marine fisheries catches rose strongly through the 1960s to reach over 8 million tonnes in 1975 or 16 per cent of marine capture fisheries production. However, the proportion of production from this source then stabilized to 11 per cent from 1980 to 1990, before it declined dramatically in the 1990s (just over 4 per cent in 1995). The fall in production in the 1990s was largely due to lower catches by the Russian Federation, Japan and the former

---

[85] Krill fishing started in the 1972–73 season. Catches reached a maximum of more than 500,000 tons in 1981–82. However, they substantially dropped in the following years due to problems in processing krill and to shifts to finfishing. From 1985–86 to 1990–91, catches amounted to 350,000–400,000 tons. They started to decline again in the 1991–92 season and collapsed to 87,000 tons in 1992–93. For economic reasons, Russian and Ukrainian trawlers had to cease fishing long before the end of the season, explaining this sharp decline. Given the low market value, the high costs of fuel, the high level of fishing technology required and the high material cost of the trawl fishery, the krill catch is likely to remain low for a number of years. Karl-Hermann Kock, 'Fishing and Conservation in Southern Waters' (1994) 30 *Polar Record*, 3–22.

[86] See e.g. Giulio Pontecorvo, 'The Economics of the Resources of Antarctica' in Jonathan I. Charney (ed.), *The New Nationalism and the Use of Common Spaces* (Totowa NJ: Allanheld, Osmun, 1982), 155, 162. By the 1992–93 season, about 3 million tons of finfish, 4.9 million tons of krill and 300 tons of crabs had been taken form the Southern Ocean. Since 1990, however, total catches have substantially dropped.

maritime Soviet Republics (Estonia, Georgia, Latvia, Lithuania and the Ukraine).[87] The result was overcapacity in Europe and Northern America. This gradually had to be reduced, involving expensive structural adjustment measures.[88] Indeed, the marked decline in production for the Russian Federation and the former Soviet Republics has been principally due to the implementation of market reforms and the resulting industry restructuring.

On the other hand, fleets in developing countries are likely to further increase their relative share, a process supported by joint venture operations and transfers of technology linked to access agreements. Consistent with established marine capture trends, the bulk of inland and marine aquaculture production in 2008 came from developing countries, with two-thirds of inland capture and almost 90 per cent of aquaculture production coming from Asia.[89] China accounted for more than 60 per cent of world aquaculture production in 2008, although the growth rate of its aquaculture production has recently declined to 5.8 per cent from 17.3 per cent in the 1980s and 14.3 per cent in the 1990s.[90] The contribution of LIFDCs to aquaculture production has continuously increased at an average annual growth rate of around 20 per cent between 1990 and 2008. This contrasts with the rate of non-LIFDCs, being around 9 per cent in the same period.[91] This real growth in the aquaculture fisheries sector could reflect the application of technological transfer by developing countries and certainly reflects the increased utilization of alternative fisheries resources.

Developments and trends in fishing are influenced and determined by a large number of factors. It is a highly complex structure which makes it difficult to define the exact impact of the EEZ, past, present and future, on the industry. However, the significant changes in economic allocation of

---

[87] FAO, *The State of World Fisheries and Aquaculture*, n. 74. The report is published biannually, see also FAO, *The State of World Fisheries and Aquaculture* (Rome, 2010), available at www.fao.org/docrep/013/i1820e/i1820e00.htm (last accessed 29 January 2010).

[88] In 1989, the FAO reported that the annual operating deficit is estimated to be approximately US$54 billion; FAO, *Marine Fisheries and the Law of the Sea*, n. 13, 19. In the EEC, for example, the shifts require substantial structural adjustment programmes in order to secure soft landings of a declining industry. A programme was adopted in 1986 that reduces the capacity of all member states in order to establish a better equilibrium of means and available resources. In 1987, the programme involved subsidies of a total of ECU 94.1 million for the construction and modernization of vessels and for the development of fisheries in territorial waters and by aquaculture. Regulation of 18 December 1986, 22 *Bulletin der Europäischen Gemeinschaften* 12–1987, p. 82.

[89] FAO, *FishStat Plus – Universal Software for Fishery Statistical Time Series*, n. 69. Figures for aquaculture harvests include fish, crustaceans, molluscs etc.

[90] See FAO, *The State of World Fisheries and Aquaculture 2008*, n. 74, pp. 17–18.

[91] FAO, *FishStat Plus – Universal Software for Fishery Statistical Time Series*, n. 69.

catches and landings, the activities on the high seas and competition for access to Antarctica all indicate that while the concept of the EEZ may not be the exclusive cause of, it is a major contributor to the structural changes occurring within the fishing industry.

IV. Conservation and management – equity towards sustainable use

The more recent structural changes having an impact on the fishing industry, reflected in the light of chronic over-fishing by a plethora of international initiatives throughout recent decades, are concerned with the conservation and management of fishery resources. This raises the problem of equity for future generations.

From the perspective of global equity, the enclosure of the seas by coastal states is neither entirely inequitable, nor is it entirely equitable. From the point of view of distributive justice, it may best be described as a mixed blessing. On one hand, the allocation of marine spaces, position and increasing trade surpluses in fisheries can be seen to benefit developing countries, partly due to the EEZ. On the other hand, these shifts are largely being achieved through growth in the industry and increased exploitation of the seas. The basic pattern of redistribution by growth risks over-exploitation and careless, shortsighted benefits. This pattern may be equitable to future generations so long as such exploitation cares for effective conservation and management. It is inequitable to the extent that the potential for growth is abused (by over-fishing, pollution) at the expense of nature and future uses by subsequent generations.

Unfortunately, the opportunities presented by the EEZ for the facilitation of rational exploitation of fisheries which were anticipated in 1982 when UNCLOS was negotiated have not been realized. The evidence available today shows the world's marine fish resources to be in a worse condition now than they were some thirty years ago. The growth of marine capture fisheries does not contradict the basic assertion by the FAO that over 70 per cent of the world's marine capture fisheries by the mid-1990s were fully exploited, over-exploited or in a state of recovery, so that the potential for increasing yields from marine capture fisheries in the longer term is extremely limited.[92]

---

[92] FAO, *Review of the State of World Marine Fishery Resources*, FAO Fisheries Circular No. 885 (1994), p. 136; FAO, *Global Fishery Production in 1994* (Rome, 1996), p. 6.

The mixed record in terms of equity shows that classical elements of international law and relations, perceived merely as a practical association of states, largely prevailed at the expense of purposive and shared community goals. However, it can be argued that the need for a global effort in the implementation of effective national and international conservation and management measures towards sustainable fishery resources for the international community and future generations surely provides such a commonly shared goal. Yet, it is evident that the concept of the EEZ has not, of itself, guaranteed responsible management and conservation. Indeed, it appears that longer-term considerations relating to sustainable utilization of fisheries have been traded off in favour of shorter-term productivity and financial gains.[93] It is important to note that the goals of equity are no longer limited to distributive justice among existing generations. Given the dangers of over-exploitation on the path of growth to achieve redistribution, future generations' shares must not be ignored. Whether we conceive such shares in terms of rights of future generations (third generation human rights),[94] or soft law,[95] or whether they are realized in terms of state

---

[93] FAO, *Review of the State of World Marine Fishery Resources*, n. 36, pp. 6–14; see already the World Conservation Union, United Nations Environment Programme and World Wide Fund for Nature, *Caring for the Earth – A Strategy for Sustainable Living* (Gland: IUCN/UNEP/WWF, 1991), p. 55.

[94] See K. Vasak (of UNESCO), 'For the Third Generation of Human Rights: The Rights of Solidarity', Inaugural Lecture to the Tenth Study Session of the International Institute of Human Rights, Strasbourg, 2–27 July 1979, the founding attempt to conceive the big contemporary issues of development, peace, communications, common heritage and ecology in terms of (elusive) human rights. For a critical assessment in particular of the concept of human rights of generations see Philip Alston, 'A Third Generation of Solidarity Rights: Progressive Development of Obfuscation of International Human Rights Law?' (1982) 29 *Netherlands International Law Review*, 307, 316–18; Peter Saladin and Christoph Zenger, *Rechte Künftiger Generationen* (Basel/Frankfurt am Main: Helbing & Lichtenhahn, 1988), p. 71. The concept has been mainly discussed with respect to the controversial (hardly justifiable) right to development, proposed by the UN Commission on Human Rights, ECOSOC OR (1985) Supp. 2 at 87–8, and contained in Art. 22 of the African Charter on Human and Peoples' Rights, reprinted in Paul Sieghart, *The International Law of Human Rights* (Oxford University Press, 1983), p. 375. See e.g. Héctor Gros Espiell, 'The Right of Development as a Human Right' (1981) 16 *Texas International Law Journal*, 189. For a critical assessment see e.g. Christian Tomuschat, 'Das Recht auf Entwicklung' (1982) 25 *German Yearbook of International Law*, 85; Walter Kälin, 'Verfassungsgrundsätze der schweizerischen Aussenpolitik' (1986) 105 *Zeitschrift für Schweiz. Recht II*, 251, 311–12.

[95] See in particular UNGA Res. 37/7 *World Charter for Nature*, 37 GAOR (1982) Supp. 51 at 17, proclaiming inter alia in Art. I:

responsibility,[96] concerns relating to conservation and prudent management of renewable and non-renewable natural resources at sea and elsewhere are becoming a pressing problem and part of global equity.

The lack of proper fisheries conservation and management is a problem affecting all capture fisheries in both developing and developed countries, and impacting on present and future generations. Considerations of global equity are evident in the way that this issue has been more recently addressed. There are many complex reasons that may explain why the conservation and management efforts made since the establishment of the EEZ have not succeeded, despite the wide international acceptance of UNCLOS. These have been described as including: a reluctance by some governments to commit themselves politically to the industrial restrictions and restructuring programs necessary to achieve rationalization; the continuation of subsidies to the fishing industry, either directly or indirectly to associated industries; poor control of fleets by states, leading to high incidences of unauthorized fishing; a lack of real commitment to international co-operation; limited mandates for some fisheries bodies; a reluctance by some countries to heed scientific advice concerning conservation and management; decreased attention on the managers of local area fisheries and the fishing communities they serve; industry resistance to the introduction of limited entry and output restrictions; and a lack of technical and financial capacity on the part of some developing countries to implement and monitor fisheries conservation and management measures.[97]

1. Nature shall be respected and its essential processes shall not be impaired.
   ...
4. Ecosystems and organisms, as well as the land, marine and atmospheric resources that are utilized by man, shall be managed to achieve and maintain optimum sustainable productivity, but not in such a way as to endanger the integrity of those other ecosystems or species with which they coexist.

[96] See Draft Article 19 on state responsibility defining, inter alia, as an international crime violation of an international obligation of essential importance for the safeguarding and preservation of the human environment, such as those prohibiting massive pollution of the atmosphere or of the seas. *Yearbook of the International Law Commission* 1976.

[97] David J. Doulman, 'An Overview of World Fisheries: Challenges and Prospects for Achieving Sustainable Resource Use' (1996), unpublished paper given as keynote speech at the FAO conference, 'A Return to Abundant Seas: Management of Fisheries and the Ocean Environment'. See also FAO, *The State of World Fisheries and Aquaculture 1995*, n. 74, p. 57.

164 CONTEXT: THE ENCLOSURE OF THE SEAS

Governments and the international community have not ignored this problem. Attempts were, and still are, being made to address it, by means of international co-operation, which thus transgresses the law of co-existence enshrined in the concept of exclusive maritime zones. For example, the creation of the North Atlantic Salmon Conservation Organization (NASCO) in 1982 replaced a series of bilateral agreements and was a reaction to the dramatic decline of salmon stocks in the North Atlantic.[98] Fishing beyond 12 miles of the coast was prohibited (except for the Faroe Islands and West Greenland, where limits extend to 200 miles and up to 40 miles from the coast respectively). The Convention also barred northern Norwegian Sea fishing. An international council and three regional commissions monitor the operation of the agreement. Early experiences were characterized by a difficulty in achieving a consensus on conservation measures (quotas, season's closures). The structures provided by international law did not allow the urgent measures that needed to be taken.

Another relatively early effort to address conservation and management issues occurred during, but outside and in the shadows of, UNCLOS III, when the so-called Consultative Parties under the 1959 Antarctic Treaty engaged in negotiations concerning the conservation and management of living resources.[99] Efforts resulted in the 1980 Convention on the Conservation of Antarctic Marine Living Resources (CCAMLR).[100] Although the agreement contains innovative ecosystem

---

[98] For further details see Jill L. Bubier, 'International Management of Atlantic Salmon. Equitable Sharing and Building Consensus' (1988) 19 *Ocean Development & International Law*, 35, 38.

[99] The Antarctic Treaty of 1 Dec. 1959, in force since 23 June 1961 (402 UNTS 71) primarily seeks to co-ordinate scientific research on the yet unknown, frozen continent that became of increasing interest after the first large-scale research operations in 1957–58 (International Geophysical Year). It 'freezes' national claims, made by Argentina, Australia, Chile, France, New Zealand, Norway, and the UK, and prevents military uses, nuclear explosions, and the disposal of radioactive waste in the area south of 60° Latitude. Original parties (Argentina, Australia, Belgium, Chile, France, Japan, New Zealand, Norway, South Africa, USSR, UK, USA) and later-joining parties (Poland, Germany, Brazil, India, Uruguay, China, Italy, Spain, Sweden, Finland, Korea, Peru, Ecuador and the Netherlands) constitute the club of Consultative Parties who, to the exclusion of other parties to the Treaty, determine Antarctic policies under the agreement. The task includes, inter alia, 'preservation and conservation of living resources', Art. IX(1)f). See e.g. Serge Pannatier, *L'Antarctique et la protection internationale de l'environnement* (Zurich: Schulthess, 1994), pp. 105–97; Emilio J. Sahurie, *The International Law of Antarctica* (Dordrecht: Martinus Nijhoff, 1992); Sir Arthur Watts, *International Law and the Antarctic Treaty System* (Cambridge: Grotius Publications Ltd, 1992).

[100] 'Conference on the Conservation of Antarctic Marine Living Resources, Canberra, 7–20 May 1980 Final Act, in force 7 April 1982', reprinted in (1980) 19 ILM, 837 ff. On this

conservation standards,[101] no sufficiently strong regime of international control and management was achieved, mainly due to resistance by the former Soviet Union and Japan, as representatives of the major krill industries.[102] Again, the existing framework was not very effective during its first years of operation. However, since 1990 this situation has changed. The CCAMLR set a precautionary catch limit of 1.5 million tons of krill per year in 1991, thus recognizing at an early stage the need for preventive measures to be taken when faced with scientific uncertainty. Bottom trawling has been prohibited in the Atlantic sector of the Southern Ocean in order to protect species and benthic assemblages by catch limitations; fishing is strictly limited by the setting of strict total allowable catches, and additional conservation measures, including mesh size regulations, closed areas and closed seasons, and by-catch provisions have also been successfully implemented. Finally, as of 1991, state members who are considering initiating a new fishery must notify the Commission in advance and must provide it with the information that would allow it to take a reasonable decision.

In an effort to strengthen fisheries conservation and management, and address the issues noted above (with the exception of the subsidy issue), there have been a number of international initiatives in the period examined,[103] including: the 1992 United Nations Conference on Environment and Development (UNCED), which

---

Convention, see Matthew Howard, 'The Convention on the Conservation of Antarctic Marine Living Resources: A Five-Year Review' (1989) 38 *International & Comparative Law Quarterly*, 104; Pannatier, n. 99, pp. 127–56.

[101] See the 'principles of conservation' of the Convention on the Conservation of Antarctic Marine Living Resources, Art. II(3): (a) no decrease of population below levels which ensure its stable recruitment; (b) maintenance of relationship between harvested, dependent and related populations and restoration of depleted populations; (c) prevention of changes of minimisation of risks of changes in the marine ecosystem which are not potentially reversible over two or three decades.

[102] Agreement of these governments to ecological standards was paid for by the requirement of consensus in the International Commission in matters of substance, effectually veto powers. See n. 101, Art. XII. See James N. Barnes, 'The Emerging Convention on the Conservation of Antarctic Marine Living Resources: An Attempt to Meet the New Realities of the Resource Exploitation in the Southern Oceans' in J. I. Charney (ed.), *The New Nationalism and the Use of Common Spaces* (Totowa NJ: Allanheld, Osmun, 1982), pp. 239, 262; See also F. M. Auburn, *Antarctic Law and Politics* (London: C. Hurst & Co., 1982); Rainer Lagoni, 'Antarctica: German Activities and Problems of Jurisdiction of Marine Areas' (1980) 23 *German Yearbook of International Law*, 392.

[103] Cf. OECD, Short History of International Actions and Initiatives against IUU Fishing Activities, www.oecd.org/document/24/0,3343,en_2649_33901_23460248_1_1_1_1,00.html (last accessed 29 January 2012).

brought fisheries issues to the forefront of media attention; the 1992 Declaration on Environment and Development (the Rio Declaration);[104] the United Nations Agenda 21: Program of Action for Sustainable Development, adopted at UNCED;[105] the FAO 1993 Agreement to Promote Compliance with International Conservation and Management by Fishing Vessels on the High Seas;[106] the FAO 1995 Rome Consensus on World Fisheries;[107] the FAO 1995 Code of Conduct for Responsible Fisheries;[108] the 1995 Kyoto Declaration and Plan of Action on the Sustainable Contribution of Fisheries to Food Security;[109] the United Nations 1995 Agreement for the Implementation of the Provision of the UNCLOS of 10 December 1982 Relating to the Conservation and Management of Straddling Fish Stocks and Highly Migratory Fish Stocks (Straddling Stocks Agreement);[110] and the FAO 1999 Rome Declaration on the Implementation of the Code of Conduct for Responsible Fisheries.[111]

The Straddling Stocks Agreement, in particular, set an important precedent for the conservation and management of high seas fisheries generally, which is significantly closer to achieving the objective of ensuring fisheries exploitation in a manner fully consistent with sustainable development. In particular the Straddling Stocks Agreement reflects the international acceptance by the 1990s that conservation and management are linked to sustainable use and development, as opposed to mere 'utilization' as in UNCLOS.[112]

The experience of the CCAMLR was an important consideration, which contributed to the ultimate adoption of the 'precautionary

---

[104] www.unep.org/Documents.Multilingual/Default.asp?documentid=78&articleid=1163 (last accessed 29 January 2012).
[105] www.un.org/esa/dsd/agenda21/ (last accessed 29 January 2012).
[106] www.fao.org/docrep/meeting/003/x3130m/X3130E00.HTM (last accessed 29 January 2012).
[107] www.fao.org/DOCREP/006/AC441E/AC441E00.HTM (last accessed 29 January 2012).
[108] www.fao.org/docrep/005/v9878e/v9878e00.HTM (last accessed 29 January 2012).
[109] www.un.org/esa/documents/ecosoc/cn17/1996/ecn171996-29.htm (last accessed 29 January 2012).
[110] The United Nations Agreement for the Implementation of the Provisions of the United Nations Convention on the Law of the Sea of 10 December 1982, Relating to the Conservation and Management of Straddling Fish Stocks and Highly Migratory Fish Stocks. In force 11 December 2001 (the 'Straddling Stocks' Agreement) at www.un.org/depts/los/convention_agreements/convention_overview_fish_stocks.htm (last accessed 29 January 2012).
[111] www.fao.org/DOCREP/005/X2220E/X2220E00.HTM (last accessed 29 January 2012).
[112] Francisco Orrego Vicuña, *The Changing International Law of High Seas Fisheries* (Cambridge University Press, 1999), pp. 145, 147.

approach' in the Straddling Stocks Agreement.[113] The precautionary approach (detailed in the Straddling Stocks Agreement, the FAO Code of Conduct and the FAO Technical Guidelines for Responsible Fisheries)[114] is a concept previously used in other industries, such as the pharmaceutical industry. It is applied where there is a high degree of uncertainty concerning the impact of fishing on a resource and, in effect, encourages caution and restraint in adopting methods where their impact is unknown.

One of the important advances achieved by the application of the precautionary approach to the conservation and management of high seas fisheries is that the measures to be adopted by states are based on much more specific criteria and guidelines to ensure their effectiveness. The Straddling Stocks Agreement therefore creates universal standards towards a common international goal that is focused on the needs of future generations. The FAO Code of Conduct identifies in its objectives that the principles underlying these standards need to, in accordance with international law, take into account all relevant biological, technological, economic, social, environmental and commercial aspects.[115] As such it demonstrates a very balanced approach, allowing room for equitable considerations. The FAO Technical Guidelines for Responsible Fisheries more particularly describe the precautionary approach as involving the application of 'prudent foresight' requiring, inter alia, 'consideration of the needs of future generations and avoidance of changes that are not potentially reversible'.[116] The 1999 International Plan of Action for the Management of Fishing Capacity, which addresses the issue of excess fishing capacity as identified in the FAO Code of Conduct, also specifically refers to equity in its description of the immediate objective of the International Plan of Action – being for the achievement worldwide of 'an efficient, equitable and transparent management of fishing capacity'.[117]

Importantly, the Straddling Stocks Agreement also demonstrates a further reversal away from the traditional freedom to fish the high seas to increased regulation in support of conservation and management measures. For example, there are compliance and enforcement

---

[113] 'Straddling Stocks' Agreement, above n. 110, Art. 6.
[114] FAO, *FAO Precautionary Approach to Capture Fisheries and Species Introductions*, FAO Technical Guidelines for Responsible Fisheries (1996).
[115] The FAO 1995 Code of Conduct for Responsible Fisheries, Art. 2(a).
[116] FAO, *FAO Precautionary Approach to Capture Fisheries and Species Introductions*, n. 114, para. 6 (a), p. 6.
[117] FAO, *International Plan of Action for the Management of Fishing Capacity* (1999), Art. 7.

provisions that include the boarding and inspection of vessels on the high seas.[118] Also, because the Agreement requires that the conservation and management measures for straddling and highly migratory fish stocks are compatible in the high seas with those adopted under national jurisdiction in adjacent areas,[119] it could be said to have created a creeping national jurisdiction. Such extension of the national jurisdiction, however, is justified on the basis of the international goal of global equity. Thus, whilst it builds on the adoption of the EEZ and the extension of national jurisdiction to prevent the depletion of ocean resources in UNCLOS, it does so in recognition of the fact that the conservation measures required for the sustainable use of fishery resources are in the best interests of the international community and the more fundamental rights of future generations. Accordingly, by adopting this more balanced perspective of international law, the Straddling Stocks Agreement seeks to guard against long-term inequity for future generations.

It is interesting that in the context of the international community's action to implement conservation and management measures in fisheries, the capacity of developing countries is given special attention in a number of these international instruments. For example, Part VII of the Straddling Stocks Agreement recognizes the special requirements of developing states, requiring states to co-operate with developing states and identifying special assistance to be given in this regard;[120] Agenda 21 addresses the capacity building of developing countries in Chapter 17; the Rome Consensus urges governments and international organizations to assist developing countries in their fisheries conservation and management efforts and the FAO Code of Conduct recognizes the special needs of developing countries in Article 5.

Despite the level of international initiative demonstrated over the past decades and the emerging focus on global equity in this context, there are still major challenges facing governments, groups of states and the international community if the sustainable utilization of world fisheries is to be achieved. The long-term viability of the fishing industry is closely related to the implementation of effective fisheries conservation and management that will sustain fisheries in the long run. This requires the national support of responsible fishing practices and the implementation of regulatory measures geared towards reducing excessive fishing effort and excess fleet capacity, therefore requiring the rationalization of

---

[118] Straddling Stocks Agreement, n. 110, Arts. 21 and 22. [119] Ibid., Art. 7.2.
[120] Ibid., Arts. 24, 25 and 26.

the fisheries sector. Some of the major issues associated with rationalization of the fisheries sector, in particular, require governments to make politically unpopular decisions (such as the abolition or reduction of subsidies).

This raises the fundamental problem of the extent to which these reforms can reasonably be expected to fit into the present system of competing nation states. The enclosure movement suggests that there are inherent limits to the increased sharing and reallocation of resources under the present system of nation states. It provides evidence that equity applied in a system based upon sovereign equality of states so different in size and power can be of only limited distributive effects. The experience of NIEO, linking equity and sovereign equality, provides further proof of the system's inherent limits. General developments and developments in the law of the sea both provide further evidence that the classical concept of state sovereignty is still a major stumbling block to expanded concepts of global justice and welfare.[121]

The outcome of UNCLOS III, the enclosure movement, and NIEO in general, reflect the present system of nation states. States' individual interests are defined on the basis of national considerations, pressures from national lobbies and policies adopted by governments dependent upon national constituencies. The results achieved are logical and rational under the system from the point of view of realpolitik. The legal exclusion of land-locked states and geographically disadvantaged states from offshore mineral resources, the de facto exclusion of them from fisheries within the 200-mile EEZ, and the allocation of spaces on the basis of geographically defined concepts benefiting large coastal states, is a rational result of the variety of different vectors and pressures at work. At the same time, it demonstrates the limits of sharing and

---

[121] This has been a constant tenet of the writings by Richard A. Falk, here in relation to the law of the sea: 'Statist imperatives have been in the foreground of the ocean negotiations, exhibiting the extent to which each government seeks the best possible deal for its country regardless of effects on other less favoured states. This kind of statism implies that there is no real prospect of getting a progressive distributive arrangement based on relative societal need, but each state will bargain for its "fair share" based on its size, ingenuity and capability.' *The End of World Order: Essays on Normative International Relations* (New York: Holmes & Meier, 1983), p. 258. On the limiting impact of sovereignty and statism on sharing and redistribution see also Julius Stone, *Visions of World Order: Between State Power and Human Justice* (Baltimore MD and London: The Johns Hopkins University Press, 1984), pp. 33–40; see also Wolfgang Friedmann, *The Changing Structure of International Law* (London: Stevens & Sons, 1964), p. 35 ('The Anachronism of National Sovereignty').

distributive justice in contemporary international law and relations. Such limitations are inherent to the system which operates on the basis of competing national interests, all of which seek maximum satisfaction. The developments through claims and counterclaims, negotiations, and finally results, are defined in terms of promoting national jurisdiction, sovereignty and control over resources. Evidently, under this system, global considerations based on the needs of individual countries and of distributive justice have not emerged in the law of the sea.

V. Structural limits to equitable sharing in contemporary international law

In conclusion, maritime law and the enclosure movement reflect traditional patterns of international law. It is characterized by notions of classical co-existence and delimitation of national spheres of jurisdiction, rather than co-operation, let alone integration. The global allocation of marine spaces is highly uneven among coastal states, let alone landlocked countries, which remain without rights and protection. Oil and gas revenues are highly uneven, and, despite the enclosure of the seas, fisheries management faces the tragedy of the commons. Accordingly, ideas of distributive justice, developed in and for national societies, are far less prevalent here than within developed industrial countries in the persistent age of 'social democratic consensus'[122] and even times of neo-liberal government since the 1980s (starting with President Reagan's policy review of the law of the sea abolishing the Area and solidarity) up to the recent financial and debt crisis at the outset of the twenty-first century. Such differences have been the subject of a long-standing debate. For Nardin and, more recently, Goldsmith and Posner, there are limits to sharing due to a much lower degree of international organization of international society when compared with national societies.[123] For

---

[122] Ralf Dahrendorf uses the term social-democratic consensus to describe the largely fulfilled programme of the modern welfare state in western society, *Lebenschancen: Anläufe zur sozialen und politischen Theorie* (Frankfurt a.M.: Suhrkamp, 1979), p. 147.

[123] Terry Nardin, *Law, Morality, and the Relations of States* (Princeton University Press, 1983); without denying that redistributive policies might strengthen the foundations of a rule-based international order, they are clearly subordinated to what the author defines as morality, i.e. the non-partial application of non-partial rules of international conduct. The theory, inspired by conservative theories of the minimal state (in particular Michael Oakeshott, *On Human Conduct* (Oxford University Press, 1996)) therefore relies upon the principles of sovereign equality within the present system of nation states. It remains within the classical concept of law as a constraint on individual

Macdonald and Stone, the structure of classical and contemporary international law still lacks the sophistication, integration, constitutional elements and thinking which, in national contexts, are essential for achieving more even distributions of power, including taxation, and mutual controls by constitutional checks and balances.[124] Theories concerning distributive justice in international law are still much less developed, and cannot easily draw from, purposive theories, principles and practices developed within a municipal context.[125] It follows that notions of distributive justice and global equity within this system remain of a more limited scope than in centrally or federally structured nation states.

While Rawls argues that principles of fairness and justice, for such reasons, cannot be transposed and translated into international law and relations,[126] others fail to accept a fundamental divide between the realms of domestic and international relations of humans. The problem of distributive justice in international law and relations necessarily involves issues of global equity and the search for world order models, transgressing the central concept of the nation state as much as traditional international law.[127] Falk believes that substantial progress in the practice of

   purposes rather than an instrument for the pursuit of shared purposes, Jack L. Goldsmith and Eric A Posner, *The Limits of International Law* (Oxford University Press, 2005).
[124] Theories on justice have been predominantly concerned with well-organized societies. They remain parochial and hardly attempt to cope with the pressing problems of global equity. See John Rawls, *A Theory of Justice* (Cambridge MA: Harvard University Press, 1999 revised edition), pp. 376–91 (reducing reflexion to the then-timely problem of conscientious draft resistance); see critique by Anthony D'Amato, *A Descriptive and Normative Analysis of Law* (Dordrecht: Martinus Nijhoff Publishers, 1984), p. 259 ('[T]he problem of international law may be a lot more complex, and the issue of justice among nations more intractable than philosophers generally assume'). Equal limitations to national frameworks can be found, e.g., in Bruce A. Ackerman, *Social Justice in the Liberal State* (New Haven CT: Yale University Press, 1980); Robert Nozick, *Anarchy, State and Utopia* (Oxford: Blackwell Publishing, 1977), p. 279 (not even within his minimal state utopia of 'the best of worlds'); see also Kai Nielsen, *Equality and Liberty: A Defense of Radical Egalitarianism* (Totowa NJ: Rowman & Allanheld, 1985); David Miller, *Social Justice* (Oxford: Clarendon Press, 2002); Wojciech Sadursky, *Giving Desert its Due: Social Justice and Legal Theory* (Dordrecht: D. Reidel Publishing, 1985). For theories of global justice see below nn. 127 to 136.
[125] See Ronald MacDonald et al. (eds.), *The International Law and Policy of Human Welfare* (Alphen aan den Rijn: Sijthoff and Noordhoff, 1978); Julius Stone, 'Approaches to the Notion of Justice of International Justice' in Richard A. Falk and Cyril E. Black (eds.), *The Future of the International Legal Order: Trends and Patterns* (Princeton University Press, 1969), vol. I, p. 372.
[126] John Rawls, *The Law of Peoples* (Cambridge MA: Harvard University Press, 1999).
[127] See in this context research efforts undertaken within the concept of World Order Model Projects (WOMP) of the World Policy Institute (formerly the Institute for World Order). The project, inspired by Richard Falk, achieved transnational participation by

global justice requires not only new perceptions and attitudes (global citizenship) but also new functional approaches to governmental structures at all levels: supranational (including both global and regional), national, and local.[128] In effect what is sought is an appropriate regulatory theory for coping, inter alia, with the complex problems of an international community that transgresses the limited goals of a mere practical association. Caney, in a more recent cosmopolitan theory of justice, does not recognize a basic difference between the national and international realm.[129] The growing theory of the constitutionalization of international law, inspired by conceptual developments of human rights protection and advanced regulation of international trade within the WTO, works towards perceptions of multilevel or multilayered governance, from local, sub-national, national regional to global spheres.[130] The doctrine of multi-level

---

scholars associated with the principal regions of the world. It works on the assumption of agreed values of global humanism: 'minimization of collective violence, maximization of economic well-being, maximization of political and social justice, and maximization of ecological quality', Richard Falk, 'Contending Approaches to World Order' in Richard A. Falk et al. (eds.), *Studies on A Just World Order: Toward A Just World Order* (Boulder CO: Westview Press, 1982), p. 146 ff., at p. 161.

[128] 'The state is too large for human governance, and yet too small to cope functionally with the planetary agenda. Overcoming the predominance of the state presupposes a dialectical unfolding toward values that are on the one hand more communal and personally felt and produce decentralization and values, that, on the other hand, are more universal and functionally successful and, as such, require greater centralization of organizing structures.' Falk (1983), n. 121, p. 246. Thus, there is no prerogative for supranationalism. See also Falk (1982), n. 127, p. 3. On functionalism as applied to international law and relations see R. J. Vincent, 'The Functions of Functionalism in International Relations' (1973) 26 *The Yearbook of World Affairs*, 332, 339 (allocation of authority not according to the principle of state sovereignty, but according to the principle of function based on human, not statist, need and well-being). Importantly, legal and functionalist approaches are only one facet in an overall interdisciplinary strategy that includes, according to Falk, psychological preconditions (group loyalties, identity etc). Falk (1983), n. 121, pp. 65 and 171, respectively ('Feeling, thinking, and acting from a planetary perspective is what world order politics is increasingly about').

[129] See Simon Caney, *Justice Beyond Borders: A Global Political Theory* (Oxford University Press, 2006); Gillian Brock and Harry Brighouse (eds.), *The Political Philosophy of Cosmopolitanism* (Cambridge University Press, 2005); Kwame Anthony Appiah, *Cosmopolitanism: Ethics in a World of Strangers* (New York: W.W. Norton & Company, 2006).

[130] See Ronald St. John MacDonald and Douglas M. Johnston (eds.), *Towards World Constitutionalism: Issues in the Legal Ordering of the World Community* (Leiden: Martinus Nijhoff Publishers, 2005); Anne Peters and Klaus Armingeon (eds.), 'Symposium: Global Constitutionalism – Process and Substance' (2009) 16 *Indiana Journal of Global Legal Studies*, 385; Jan Klabbers, Anne Peters and Geir Ulfstein, *The Constitutionalization of International Law* (Oxford University Press, 2009).

governance and of a Five Storey House argues that essential factors of legitimacy, such as the rule of law, human rights and democracy, are present on all layers alike but vary in degree.[131] The same holds true for the basic distinctions. There is no fundamental divide between domestic community and international society.[132] Governance essentially is a matter of allocating regulatory functions to appropriate levels of governance with a view to produce appropriate public goods. Co-existence, co-operation and integration exist on all layers, albeit to a different degree. In the present context of the enclosure movement and boundary delimitation, it will be interesting to observe that the same principles and rules apply both in international relations and in a domestic context. There is no fundamental difference.[133] Likewise, efforts at co-operation are not limited to federal relations but extend to the realm of international relations in the law of the sea.[134]

Accordingly, there also is no fundamental divide in terms of distributive justice. It is neither uniform, nor excluded, at different layers of governance, but varies in degree. Levels of integration and community vary, but are equally possible on all layers alike. From this perspective, international law – or global law – is open to integration beyond co-existence and co-operation. It is open to distributive justice and reallocation of resources, and thus to a broader and more intense recourse and potential of equity than under classical perceptions of the international law of co-existence. The frameworks of cosmopolitanism, of constitutionalization and multilevel governance create the fundamentals and perspectives of long-term developments

---

Christian Joerges and Ernst Ulrich Petersmann (eds.), *Constitutionalism, Multilevel Trade Governance and Social Regulation* (Oxford: Hart Publishing, 2nd edn., 2011).

[131] Thomas Cottier and Maya Hertig, 'The Prospects of 21st Century Constitutionalism' (2003) 7 *Max Planck Yearbook of United Nations Law*, 261; Thomas Cottier, 'Multilayered Governance, Pluralism and Moral Conflict' (2009) 16 *Indiana Journal of Global Legal Studies*, 647. Thomas Cottier, 'Towards a Five Storey House' in Christian Joerges and Ernst-Ulrich Petermann (eds.), *Constitutionalism, Multilevel Trade Governance and International Economic Law* (Oxford, Portland OR: Hart Publishing, 2011), pp. 495–532.

[132] The basic distinction of *Gesellschaft* (Society) and *Gemeinschaft* (Community) proposed by Toennies, *Gemeinschaft und Gesellschaft* (1887), is equally applied to international relations. It labels two opposite classical practical and purposive patterns of human association: the society constraining individuals with different and possibly incompatible purposes; and the community co-ordinating shared and joint purposes. See René-Jean Dupuy, 'Communauté Internationale et Disparité de Developpement' (1979)165 *Recueil des cours de l'Académie de Droit International* IV 9, 21.

[133] See US CEIP Delimitation Recommendations in Chapter 6(III)(A).

[134] See modes of co-operation in the management of maritime zones in Chapter 5(III).

in international law. It may gradually influence the shaping and application of international law. It will influence the content and scope of global equity over time. Indeed, the contemporary situation does not render rethinking of global structures unnecessary. It is a long-term process that, accelerated by an increasingly integrated world economy and communications network, may gradually change the perceptions and attitudes of national constituencies in light of the obvious stumbling blocks to successful solution of pressing global problems posed by national sovereignties. Politics and diplomacy will change in turn. The conceptual distinction between society and community may vanish, as joint co-operation and shared purposes may become essential to the pursuit and survival of individual goals. In the present context, they may eventually lead to joint management of marine resources, leaving maritime boundaries behind for the sake of more than minimal global equity, being necessary for peace and effective long-term conservation.

Yet, this will take time, education and new generations facing global challenges.[135] In a multipolar world of many still-emerging nations, the perspective of common heritage is still a utopian vision. It may first give way to the doctrine of common concern and shared responsibility. The present world and society of states is a long way from questioning the paradigm of national sovereignty, at least on a global scale. Developing countries are still consolidating the national sovereignty that was gained with decolonization.[136] Apart from regional integration in Europe, functionalist concepts of limited supranationalism, to prepare the ground for increased sharing and higher degrees of global equity, are sought only as far as they increase potential shares, such as deep seabed mining. Otherwise, they are refuted for fear that the newly gained independence of LDCs would be lost and replaced by sophisticated forms of superpower

---

[135] See also Quincy Wright, 'The Foundations of a Universal International System' in Ram P. Anand (ed.), *Asian States and the Development of International Law* (Delhi: Vikas Publications, 1972) pp. 145, 151: 'an enduring change of the international system can be effected peacefully only by a gradual process of education that establishes a general awareness of the existing and emerging conditions of the world and reveals the inadequacy of the existing international system to deal with foreseeable problems.'

[136] Rajni Kothari, an Indian author working within WOMP, insists: 'But it is not possible to move towards [a new state system] without first going through the dialectic based on a counter-assertion of national and regional identities and solidarities through a new collation of power comprising hitherto submerged political and economic entities, both in the Third World and elsewhere.' *Towards A Just World* in R. Falk et al. (eds.), *Studies on a Just World Order: Toward a Just World Order* (Boulder CO: Westview Press, 1982), p. 566 ff., 585.

predominance.[137] Smaller developed countries share such concerns. Equally, developed countries in general are extremely reluctant to pass sovereignty to supranational bodies because, although legitimate claims for democratic rules are difficult to deny, they would inevitably reduce control over vital interests. There is no doubt that, short of a major catastrophe, traditional patterns of international law will prevail for decades.[138]

Any study about maritime boundary delimitation necessarily and humbly relies on the present system of nation states. It is a study of the law of co-existence par excellence. It is a topic as classic as it can get in international law. Boundaries are obstacles to co-operation. They are anathema to integration of the law, which seeks to overcome them. Notions of equity, applicable in this context, cannot fundamentally depart from the logic of a systemic framework defined in terms of geographical and geological definitions of national zones. They cannot fundamentally alter the inequitable allocation and unfair distribution of resources. They operate in a confined province of the law. At a different level, the task still remains a difficult one. What are the appropriate scope and functions of it within a partly inequitable setting? How can justice be done in such circumstances? To what extent can it correct the inequities that the basic concept of the shelf and the EEZ produces in individual cases? Is there room, and to what extent, for the consideration of global equity and, in particular, of sharing on the basis of need? Can or should maritime boundary law promote long-term structural changes in the global system? Can this be achieved both in negotiated and judicial settlement? We shall return to these questions in Part III after an examination of existing methods and approaches to maritime boundary delimitation in theory, adjudication and state practice.

---

[137] See e.g. Hedley Bull, *The State's Positive Role in World Affairs* in R. Falk et al. (eds.), *Studies on A Just World Order: Toward A Just World Order* (Boulder CO: Westview Press, 1982), p. 60 ff., 71: 'It is by insisting upon their privileges of sovereignty that [LDCs] are able to defend their newly won independence against the foreign tutelage implicit in such basic phrases such as "basic human needs" or (more sinister still) humanitarian intervention.' See also Hedley Bull, *The Anarchical Society, A Study of Order in World Politics* (New York: Columbia University Press, 2002); see also Wladyslaw J. Stankiewicz (ed.), *In Defense of Sovereignty* (New York: Oxford University Press, 1969).

[138] Little has changed over the last thirty years, see Falk (1982), n. 127, pp. 171, 533 (world government solutions not likely to be achieved under present conditions except in the aftermath of a global catastrophe such as World War III or a major ecological crisis).

PART II

The new boundaries

4

Approaches to delimitation

I. The basic dilemma

The establishment of continental shelf zones and exclusive economic zones (EEZs) considerably increased the number and length of the maritime boundaries between coastal states. A 1983 survey identified some 376 international maritime boundaries between 137 coastal states around the globe.[1] In 1988, the US Department of State gave a figure of 412 demarcations required.[2] Eventually, additional boundaries arose due to the advent of new states and the breaking-up of the Soviet Union. Yet another generation of boundaries will result from climate change and accessibility to resources in the Arctic waters. Moreover, many of the already agreed boundaries relate only to the continental shelf and may be subject to review and renegotiation in the context of EEZ delimitation. Given the political and economic sensitivity of international boundary delimitation, guiding rules and principles on the subject remain as essential as before. The task has become even more difficult with the enclosure movement expanding its scope from territorial seas to EEZ and ultimately to continental shelves up to and beyond 200 nautical miles (nm).

Ever since the first attempts to formulate general rules on the subject in the 1930 Hague Codification Conference, and despite a substantial number of publications on the subject,[3] the issue of the appropriate rules and

---

[1] Robert W. Smith, *A Geographical Primer to Maritime Boundary-Making* (1983) 12 *Ocean Development & International Law* 1, 3. Blake puts the number at between 353 and 376, Gerald H. Blake, 'Worldwide Maritime Boundary Delimitation; The State of Play' in Gerald H. Blake (ed.), *Maritime Boundaries and Ocean Resources* (New York: Routledge, 1987), vol. VII. For an excellent discussion of pending and future boundary problems in different areas of the globe see John R. Victor Prescott, *The Maritime Political Boundaries of the World* (London: Methuen, 1986).

[2] US Department of State, *Limits in the Seas No 108, Maritime Boundaries of the World* (1st rev., 1988).

[3] For references see Ted L. Mc Dorman, Kenneth P. Beauchamp and Douglas M. Johnston (eds.), *Maritime Boundary Delimitation: An Annotated Bibliography* (Boston MA: Lexington Press, 1983); Prescott, n. 1; S. P. Jagota, *Maritime Boundary* (Dordrecht: Martinus Nijhoff

principles applicable to maritime boundary delimitation has remained a controversial issue of the law of the sea. This problem was further aggravated by the enclosure of the seas and the large-scale partitioning of ocean spaces. At the Third United Nations Conference on the Law of the Sea (UNCLOS III), maritime boundary delimitation between coastal states ranked amongst the most difficult and contentious issues. The difficulty has lain in finding and agreeing upon clear and predictable rules of delimitation, which, at the same time, enable justice to be achieved. An old dilemma of law has found yet another example in point.

On the one hand, states are interested in framing general and predictable rules for maritime boundary delimitation because of political and economic sensitivity related to boundary problems. It is in the interests of the international community as a whole that clear, precise and effective standards are developed based upon which boundary problems can be solved and, if need be, adjudicated on peacefully. In addition, small and less powerful nations derive protection from such rules against the expansionist aspirations of their stronger neighbours. On the other hand, each case of delimitation between states has its own individual characteristics due to the particular features of the coastal configurations, configurations of islands, seabed geomorphology, particularities of the water column (habitat of living resources), and finally the social, economic and legal backgrounds of the states and regions concerned. Importantly, states negotiate general rules on the basis of their particular and pre-existing coastal configurations. Of course, they press for those rules that are of the utmost advantage for

1985); Prosper Weil, *Perspectives du droit de la délimitation maritime* (Paris: Editions A. Pedone, 1988), 311–19. Peter J. Cook and Chris M. Carleton (eds.), *Continental Shelf Limits: The Scientific and Legal Interface* (Oxford University Press, 2000); Robert Kolb, *Case Law on Equitable Maritime Delimitation/Jurisprudence sur les délimitations maritimes selon l'équité; Digest and Commentaries/Répertoire et commentaires* (The Hague: Martinus Nijhoff Publishers, 2003); Nuno Sérgio Marques Antunes, *Towards the Conceptualisation of Maritime Delimitation, Legal and Technical Aspects of a Political Process* (Leiden: Martinus Nijhoff Publishers, 2003); Rainer Lagoni and Daniel Vignes (eds.), *Maritime Delimitation* (Leiden: Martinus Nijhoff Publishers, 2006); Yoshifumi Tanaka, *Predictability and Flexibility in the Law of Maritime Delimitation* (Oxford: Hart, 2006); Seoung-Yong Hong and Jon M. Van Dyke (eds.), *Maritime Boundary Disputes, Settlement Processes, and the Law of the Sea* (Leiden: Martinus Nijhoff Publishers, 2009); Pål Jakob Aasen, *The Law of Maritime Delimitation and the Russian-Norwegian Maritime Boundary Dispute*; Jonathan I. Charney et al. (eds.), *International Maritime Boundaries*, 5 vols. (The Hague: Martinus Nijhoff Publishers, 1993–2005), vols. I and II (Charney and Alexander (eds.), 1993), vol. III (Charney and Alexander (eds.), 1998), vol. IV (Charney and Smith (eds.), 2002), vol. V (Colson and Smith (eds.), 2005); FNI Report 1/2010, Fridtjof Nansen Institute: Lysaker, Norway 2010, p. 77, www.fni.no/doc&pdf/FNI-R0110.pdf (last accessed 20 September 2014).

their own geographical profile. As their interests are defined on the basis of a stable and pre-existing situation, it is generally not of concern to them, with regard to their own maritime zones, to find truly general rules that would be applicable to all situations, because such rules could potentially work to their disadvantage. In other words, states do not have an interest in finding generally balanced rules that provide for adequate and intermediate solutions in both favourable and unfavourable cases and under different circumstances. They have no basic interest in having specific rules providing complete or even partial security and safeguards for as yet unknown future situations. The following summary of a statement by the chairman of the Second Committee of UNCLOS III illustrates this particular aspect of states' defined and stable interests. Made in 1974, it anticipates the great difficulties that are inherently linked to the achievement of agreement on the rules related to long-distance boundaries between states in the second half of the Conference:

> The Chairman explained that, although the aim of the Third United Nations Conference on the law of the sea was to consider and to adopt general rules, every delegation was free to refer to its won special geographic situation and also, where appropriate, exercise its rights to reply in order to explain its own situation.[4]

This situation, and the tension between the multitude of defined interests and the will to find general rules on the subject, is evident throughout the history of maritime boundary law. Long-range boundaries, however, have considerably increased the problems and added new dimensions to it. The experience gained from the delimitation of internal waters and the 3-mile territorial sea, and from the demarcation in narrow straits and bays, remains important, but is limited in terms of guidance. 'Irregularities' in coastal configurations or islands produce an increasing and multiplying impact in the context of long-distance boundaries. They render the formulation and application of general rules much more difficult. In addition, it should be recalled that the problem of co-existing and overlapping zones from different historical origins further complicates the task of formulating precise rules on the subject. Rules must take into account that the principle and presumption of a 200-mile, all-purpose boundary of the shelf and the EEZ, suggested previously,[5] may not always lead to appropriate arrangements.

---

[4] Summary Records of the Second Committee, 4th Mtg (1974), 2 *Official Records* at 104.
[5] See Chapter 2(IV).

The existence of clearly defined and country-specific interests of individual coastal states, on the one hand, and the need to define general rules on the subject in order to prevent and control what may escalate into sensitive international conflicts, on the other hand, defines the bottom line of the problem explored by this book. Such a dichotomy of interests poses a dilemma that is difficult to overcome. It will be seen that the recourse to equity has its roots in that very dilemma. It is in the interests of legal theory and law in general to scrutinize the processes and approaches adopted in maritime boundary law, for the simple reason that the dilemma we find in maritime boundary law is not unique and can also be found in many other areas. Therefore, the solutions developed may, *mutatis mutandis*, equally provide guidance to regulation of other areas. They are of general interest to the theory of law, methodology and jurisprudence.

II. Technical and scientific methods of delimitation

Before turning to the *legal* approaches to maritime boundary delimitation, it is useful to become familiar with the existing technical and scientific methods for maritime delimitation. Unlike mere *ad hoc* constructions, these methods are open to regular and repeated application.[6] As geometrical, mathematical, geographical, geological, or ecological methods, they do not in themselves express legal rules or principles of international law. It is important to emphasize this distinction, as it has sometimes been blurred. Equally, these methods can be distinguished from factors and circumstances which the law requires be taken into account during the process of delimitation.[7] However, scientific methods are valid candidates for adoption as rules of conventional law or customary international law through state practice and *opinio iuris*. It has been argued that existing state practice in the

---

[6] Any approach to delimitation claiming to be a method necessarily implies a normative, albeit not necessarily a legal, element. It means establishing a boundary in accordance with a systematic procedure. It is an application of a technical rule. International law of boundary delimitation, however, uses the term in a much wider and confusing way. Any *ad hoc* construction of geographical lines, parallelograms, etc., are labelled 'methods' or 'systems', although they lack elements of a systematic and generalizable content, and often no distinction is made between technical and legal methods. In such cases, it would be more appropriate to speak of *ad hoc* constructions for which the cases provide numerous examples. See e.g. Leonard H. Legault and Blair Hankey, 'Method, Oppositeness and Adjacency, and Proportionality in Maritime Boundary Delimitation' in Charney et al., *International Maritime Boundaries*, n. 3, vol. I, pp. 203–15.

[7] See Chapters 8–10.

delimitation of opposite coasts is sufficient to generate customary law.[8] At a minimum, scientific methods provide a reservoir from which rule-making can draw inspiration.

A. Geometrical and geographical methods

Over the course of time, geographers and lawyers have developed a number of geometrical methods of maritime boundary delimitation.[9] At present, established scientific or technical methods of practical importance are limited to geographical, surface-related operations, with the method of equidistance, or median line, being the most prominent approach. But equidistance is not the sole method available and used. The *Gulf of Maine* Chamber of the International Court of Justice (ICJ) recalled a list of additional methods proposed by a committee of experts to the International Law Commission (ILC) in 1953: drawing a line that runs perpendicular to the general direction of the coast; extending an existing delimitation of the territorial waters; or the extension of the final segment of the general direction of the land boundary. In *Nicaragua* v. *Honduras*, the Court used a bisector method to define the larger part of the boundary line.[10] For the treatment of islands, state practice and case law developed additional methods amounting to technical rules: the drawing of parallel lines and the method of enclaving.[11] Although these technical methods are not exhaustive,[12] they nevertheless include the major approaches used in state practice and adjudication, alone or in combination. Additional techniques that have been applied relate to the descriptive definition of the boundary line, either by linking points of

---

[8] See Yoshifumi Tanaka, *Predictability and Flexibility in the Law of Maritime Delimitation* (Oxford: Hart, 2006), p. 136.

[9] For an historical review see Sang-Myon Rhee, 'Sea Boundary Delimitation between States Before World War II' (1982) 76 *American Journal of International Law*, 555; see generally Nuno Sérgio Marques Antunes, *Towards the Conceptualisation of Maritime Delimitation: Legal and Technical Aspects of a Political Process* (Leiden: Brill Academic Publishers, 2003), pp. 147–75.

[10] *Territorial and Maritime Dispute between Nicaragua and Honduras in the Caribbean Sea (Nicaragua* v. *Honduras)*, Judgment, ICJ Reports 2007, paras. 283–98.

[11] See Legault and Hankey, n. 6, pp. 212–14.

[12] *Delimitation of the Maritime Boundary in the Gulf of Maine Area (Canada* v. *United States of America)*, Judgment, ICJ Reports 1984, p. 313, para. 159, referring to the Report of the Committee of Experts of the ILC, which served as a basis of rule-making in the 1950s. See 'Rapport du Comité d'experts sur certaines questions d'ordre technique concernant la mer territorial' (1953) *Yearbook of the International Law Commission*, Vol. II, p. 77 ff., 79. See also Marques Antunes, n. 9, pp. 147–75.

intersection of lines of longitude and latitude or by defining them in parallels of longitude or latitude.[13] These, however, are not methods in a proper sense, as they serve the purpose of describing, rather than finding, a boundary line.

1. The method of equidistance or median line

a. **The technique**   The most prominent and widely applied geometrical method of delimitation between adjacent and opposite states is the method of equidistance, or the median line.[14] It was developed and introduced by Whittemore Boggs, mainly for the delimitation of North America's Great Lakes. It eventually expanded to situations of lateral constellations (median line) and was applied in international delimitations.[15]

Unlike other methods discussed later, equidistance fully relies upon and continuously considers the varying landscapes of the coastlines of the states involved. Coast and islands are the determinants. The result is the production of a single line, either as a median between opposite states, or as an equidistant line between adjacent states. Geometrically, the segments of the median between opposite states are established by the perpendiculars bisecting the lines linking the closest corresponding points of the base lines of each state, from which the breadth of the territorial sea is measured. The median line follows the perpendiculars at the point of their intersections.[16] The technique of lateral boundaries between adjacent states, on the other hand, draws an intercept along the coastline of each state, radiating from the terminus of the common

---

[13] For the application of parallels of latitude in African and Latin American state practice, see Appendix I, Table A.1, Nos. 2, 3, 50, 51, 53, 55, 56, 57, 84.

[14] No legal consequences flow from the use of the terms 'median line' and 'equidistance line', since the method of delimitation is the same for both. The different terms are merely used to differentiate between the line of delimitation for opposite and adjacent coasts, respectively (*Maritime Delimitation in the Black Sea (Romania v. Ukraine)*, Judgment, ICJ Reports 2009, p. 101, para. 116).

[15] See S. Whittemore Boggs, 'Delimitation of Seaward Areas under National Jurisdiction' (1951) 45 *American Journal of International Law*, 240. For technical aspects see also Robert D. Hodgson and E. John Cooper, 'The Technical Delimitation of a Modern Equidistant Boundary' (1976) 3 *Ocean Development & International Law*, 361; Cook and Carleton, n. 3, and the Arbitration Between the United Kingdom of Great Britain and Northern Ireland and the French Republic on the Delimitation of the Continental Shelf, Decisions of the Court of Arbitration dated 30 June 1977 and 14 March 1978, Command Paper 7438, March 1979, reprinted in 18 ILM 397, 662 (1979) at 481(hereinafter the *Anglo-French Channel* arbitration).

[16] See Hodgson and Cooper, n. 15, 364–5.

land-boundary at the coast. A standard description, first provided by Shalowitz, indicates the geometrical operation that follows:

> Arcs are then swung seaward from corresponding intercepts with radii equal to the distance between them. The intersections of corresponding arcs form points on the lateral boundary, each of which is by construction equidistant from corresponding points on the coastline of each state.[17]

In both adjacent and opposite configurations and in intermediate situations, the varying shape of the coastal configurations can thereby be continuously taken into account. Computer programmes, developed since the 1970s, permit the median or equidistance line to be located quickly and with great accuracy.[18] For practical reasons, the resulting lines are often simplified and modified in final arrangements.[19]

b. Determination of base points The course and direction of an equidistance and median line essentially depends upon the location and fixation of base points. Determination of such points is an operation undertaken by coastal states, taking into account the legal nature of the zone. It raises legal issues in terms of powers to unilaterally determine such points in contentious cases. The case law offers some guidance both on substance and on the role of courts.

Determination of base points is to be based upon the principle that 'the land dominates the sea'.[20] The Court in the *North Sea Continental Shelf* cases held that 'since the land is the legal source of the power which a State may exercise over territorial extensions to seaward, it must first be clearly established what features do in fact constitute [seaward] extensions'; adding that '[a]bove all is this the case when what is involved is no longer areas of sea, such as the contiguous zone, but stretches of submerged land; for the legal régime of the continental shelf is that of a soil and a subsoil, two words evocative of the land and not of the sea'.[21] In order to choose the base points for the establishment of the provisional

---

[17] Aaron L. Shalowitz and Michael W. Reed, *Shore and Sea Boundaries*, 3 vols. (Washington DC: Office of Coast Survey, National Oceanic and Atmospheric Administration, 1962), Vol. I, p. 235, note 60; Edward Duncan Brown, *The Legal Regime of Hydrospace* (London: Stevens for the Institute of World Affairs, 1971) p. 73.
[18] Hodgson and Cooper, n. 15, 384–7; 1978 *Anglo-French Channel Arbitration*, n. 15, p. 481, paras. 50–2.
[19] For state practice see Chapter 5 and Appendix I.
[20] *North Sea Continental Shelf (Federal Republic of Germany v. Denmark; Federal Republic of Germany v. Netherlands)*, Judgment, ICJ Reports 1969, p. 42, para. 96.
[21] ICJ Reports 1969, p. 42, para. 96.

equidistance line, it is important to determine the coasts of one state, the projections of which overlap with that of another state.[22] These are the coasts which are considered 'relevant coasts' for the construction of the equidistance line.[23] Conversely, the submarine extension of any part of the coast of one party which, because of its geographic situation, cannot overlap with the extension of the coast of the other is to be excluded from consideration for the placement of a base point.[24] This operation is succinct with a view to establishing maritime boundaries. It needs to be distinguished from determining the base line for the purpose of measuring the breadth of the continental shelf and the EEZ. These are considered to be 'two different issues'.[25]

Identification of the relevant coasts calls for the exercise of judgment in assessing the actual coastal geography.[26] The Court in the *North Sea Continental Shelf* case held that no 'markedly pronounced [coastal] configurations can be ignored'.[27] The Court in *Romania v. Ukraine* held that those base points on the relevant coasts should be chosen which 'mark a significant change in the direction of the coast, in such a way that the geometrical figure formed by the line connecting all these points reflects the general direction of the coastlines'.[28]

Once the base points are fixed, the delimitation line could be said to be mathematically determined.[29] However, for the precise selection of base points, several geographical peculiarities have to be considered on a case-by-case basis. In addition, it can be seen that the case law has already

---

[22] ICJ Reports 2009, p. 89, para. 77, 'because the task of delimitation consists in resolving the overlapping claims by drawing a line of separation of the maritime areas concerned'.

[23] See *Maritime Delimitation and Territorial Questions between Qatar and Bahrain (Qatar v. Bahrain)*, Merits, Judgment, ICJ Reports 2001, p. 94, para. 178; *Land and Maritime Boundary between Cameroon and Nigeria (Cameroon v. Nigeria: Equatorial Guinea intervening)*, Judgment, ICJ Reports 2002, p. 442, para. 290.

[24] *Continental Shelf (Tunisia v. Libyan Arab Jamahiriya)*, Judgment, ICJ Reports 1982, p. 61, para. 75, as recalled in ICJ Reports 2009, p. 95, para. 99.

[25] ICJ Reports 2009, p. 108, p. 747, para. 137.   [26] ICJ Reports 2007, p. 92, para. 289.

[27] ICJ Reports 1969, p. 42, para. 96.

[28] ICJ Reports 2009, p. 105, para. 127. The Court also held that attention must be paid to those protuberant coastal points situated nearest to the area to be delimited (ICJ Reports 2009, p. 101, para. 117). In this respect the Court called for a choice of points which are 'appropriate' (ICJ Reports 2009, p. 105, para. 127) or 'most appropriate' (ICJ Reports 2009, p. 101, para. 117). The Court did not exclude the consideration in principle of a dyke built on the coastline, holding that the 'geographical reality covers not only the physical elements produced by geodynamics and the movements of the sea, but also any other material factors that are present' (ICJ Reports 2009, p. 105, paras. 130, 131).

[29] H. W. A. Thirlway, 'The Law and Procedure of the International Court of Justice: Part Five' (1994) 64 *British Yearbook of International Law*, 41.

applied a particular set of considerations at the stage of constructing the provisional boundary line – which deviates from strict equidistance. These are the consideration or disregard of islands, the award of only 'half-effect' to islands or the projection of coastal length ratios onto the equidistance line, as will be shown in the following. Accordingly, a degree of judicial discretion already applies in the construction of the equidistance line. Contrary to the ICJ's statement in *Cameroon* v. *Nigeria*, recent practice shows that the consideration is not limited to relevant circumstances which are considered at the second stage of the delimitation exercise.[30] The ICJ in *Romania* v. *Ukraine* considered it 'inappropriate' to place a base point on Serpent's Island – possibly with an equitable solution already in mind.[31] It may occur that considerations based upon equity are already being made in the selection of base points and subsequently repeated in the consideration of relevant circumstances, rendering the second step obsolete.[32] The statement of the Court in *Romania* v. *Ukraine* that the provisional equidistance line is 'plotted on strictly geometrical criteria on the basis of objective data' therefore seems doubtful.[33] Nevertheless, a line thus adopted depends heavily on the physical geography of the coast.[34]

The determination of base points essentially is a matter pertaining to coastal states, based upon the legal foundations set out above. In contentious cases, it is for courts to review and determine these points. A court's choice of base points does not have to follow the base lines as determined by the parties.[35] The court in *Romania* v. *Ukraine* stated that it 'should not base itself solely on the choice of base points made by one of [the] parties'.[36] Recalling the Court in *Romania* v. *Ukraine*, the Tribunal in *Bangladesh* v.

---

[30] See, however, ICJ Reports 2002, p. 443, para. 295.
[31] *Case Concerning Maritime Delimitation in the Black Sea (Romania v. Ukraine)*, Judgment, 3 February 2009, ICJ Reports 2009, p. 61, para. 149.
[32] *Dispute concerning Delimitation of the Maritime Boundary between Bangladesh and Myanmar in the Bay of Bengal (Bangladesh v. Myanmar)*, Judgment, 14 March 2012, para. 265, pp. 318–19, available on the website of the ITLOS at www.itlos.org/index.php?id=108#c964. See also Robin R. Churchill, 'The *Bangladesh/Myanmar* Case: Continuity and Novelty in the Law of Maritime Boundary Delimitation' (2012) 1 *Cambridge Journal of International and Comparative Law*, 1, 137–52, at 144.
[33] ICJ Reports 2009, p. 101, para. 118.   [34] ICJ Reports 2009, p. 101, p. 101, para. 117.
[35] '[T]he baselines as determined by coastal States are not *per se* identical with the points chosen on a coast to make it possible to calculate the area of continental shelf appertaining to that State' (*Continental Shelf (Libyan Arab Jamahiriya v. Malta)*, Judgment, ICJ Reports 1985, p. 48, para. 64).
[36] ICJ Reports 2009, p. 108, para. 137; in this respect it may be recalled that 'the delimitation of sea areas has always an international aspect' (*Fisheries Case (United Kingdom v. Norway)*, Judgment, ICJ Reports 1951, p. 132).

Myanmar observed that, 'while coastal States are entitled to determine their base points for the purpose of delimitation, the Tribunal is not obliged ... to accept base points indicated by either or both of the them'.[37]

Even where a court does not reconsider a party's unilateral base lines in full detail, it would still assess which base points can be used for the construction of the equidistance line.[38] The Court in *Romania v. Ukraine* stressed that a court 'must, when delimiting the continental shelf and exclusive economic zones, select base points by reference to the physical geography of the relevant coasts'.[39] Similarly, the Tribunal in *Bangladesh v. Myanmar* stated that it should select base points 'on the basis of the geographical facts of the case'.[40] The geography in question must be that which prevails at the time of delimitation.[41] In the boundary dispute between Chile and Peru, the ICJ sought a balanced definition of base points. Due to the relative proximity of Point A to the Peruvian coast, the Court held that only those base points on the Peruvian coast which are more than 80 nm from Point A can be matched with points at an equivalent distance on the Chilean coast.[42]

From the above it can be concluded that a state is unable to secure the extent of its claims to maritime areas by the unilateral determination of base lines when it comes to a contentious delimitation case. Since a court will choose its own base points, such unilateral base lines have no binding legal effect on judicial review and construction of the equidistance line. This is an important observation in the context of uncertainty about rising sea levels, as points fixed today may shift in due course. States may thus have an interest in fixing maritime boundaries as soon as possible on the basis of presently accepted base lines.[43]

---

[37] *Bangladesh v. Myanmar*, n. 32, para. 264.
[38] See *Arbitration Award between the Government of the State of Eritrea and the Government of the Republic of Yemen of the Abitral Tribunal in the Second Stage of the Proceedings (Maritime Delimitation)*, 16 October 1998, www.pca-cpa.org/showfile.asp?fil_id=459 (last accessed 30 January 2012), para. 142; interestingly, the Tribunal chose the outer edge of a fringe of islands as a base point, although Yemen did not make a claim to a straight base line (para. 151).
[39] ICJ Reports 2009, p. 108, para. 137: 'the Court will have in mind considerations relating to both parties' coastlines when choosing its own base points' (para. 117, emphasis added).
[40] *Bangladesh v. Myanmar*, n. 32, para. 264.   [41] ICJ Reports 2009, p. 106, para. 131.
[42] *Maritime Dispute (Peru v. Chile)*, ICJ Judgment of 27 January 2014, ICJ Reports 2014 ___ para. 185 (see Appendix II, Map 3).
[43] David D. Caron, 'Climate Change, Sea Level Rise and the Coming Uncertainty in Oceanic Boundaries: A Proposal to Avoid Conflict' in Seoung-Yong Hong and Jon Van Dyke (eds.), *Maritime Boundary Disputes, Settlement Processes, and the Law of the Sea* (Leiden, Boston MA: Martinus Nijhoff Publishers, 2009), pp. 1, 17.

c. **Modification of base points (half-effect to islands)** Despite the accuracy of the equidistance method, important issues of discretion and consideration, beyond mere geometry and mathematical computation, remain. Obviously, the choice of base points, used to establish the foundations of the entire operation, is of utmost importance to the definition. Disputes may arise over whether a particular base point may be taken into account or not.[44] This problem often arises where islands are in front of coastal lines that, if taken as base points, considerably influence the equidistance or median line independent of their size and importance. One technique to reduce the effect of islands consists of giving them only half-effect. It was described by the 1977 *Anglo-French Channel* arbitration:

> The method of giving half-effect consists in delimiting the line equidistant between the two coasts, first, without the use of the offshore island as a base-point and, secondly, with its use as a base point; a boundary giving half-effect to the island is then the line drawn mid-way between those equidistance lines.[45]

The half-effect method has been applied in a number of decisions and awards, including the 1977 *Anglo-French Channel* arbitration, the 1982 *Tunisia* v. *Libya Continental Shelf* case and the 1984 *Gulf of Maine* case, in order to correct what were considered to be the inequitable effects of islands.[46] Similarly, reduced effect was given to the island of Qit'at Jaradah in the 2001 *Qatar* v. *Bahrain* case.[47] The effect of islands will be further discussed in legal terms and in relation to equity.[48]

---

[44] See e.g. the argument on the legality of taking into account the Eddystone Rock as a base point in the 1977 *Anglo-French Channel* arbitration above, n. 15, 68–76, paras. 122–44, pp. 431–5.

[45] See *Anglo-French Channel* arbitration, n. 15, 117, para. 251, p. 455. Note, however, that in order to treat equally all insular features off the mainland coasts, it has been suggested that it would have been preferable to use a bisector line computed in relation to the angle formed between the equidistance line from the mainland coasts, and an equidistance line between the Scillies and Ushant, see Marques Antunes, n. 9, p. 78. 'What the expert did was to draw a line giving "less-than-half-effect" to the Scillies', corresponding to a 'miscalculation of what the Tribunal demanded in the reasoning ... a "material error"', see Marques Antunes, n. 9, p. 596.

[46] ICJ Reports 1982, p. 89, para. 129; ICJ Reports 1984, p. 336, para. 222. For example, in state practice see Appendix I, Table A.1, Nos. 17, 25, 28; Derrick W. Bowett, 'The Arbitration between the United Kingdom and France concerning the Continental Shelf Boundary in the English Channel and South Western Approaches' (1979) 49 *British Yearbook of International Law*, 1, 21.

[47] ICJ Reports 2001, p. 104, para. 219. See also Marques Antunes, n. 9, p. 160.

[48] See Chapter 11(IV).

d. Projecting the ratio of coastal lengths   Yet another geographically and mathematically defined method that has been applied to influence the boundary line calculates the ratio of the lengths of the coasts of the states involved within the relevant area of delimitation or the 'relevant coasts' of the parties. It is discussed within the method of equidistance, as it often serves as a corrective device to it. It should be noted here that the 'relevant coasts' which are considered for evaluating coastal ratios do not necessarily coincide with that coast which is considered 'relevant' for the choice of base points and the construction of the equidistance line.[49]

In the delimitation of bays, the ratio has been applied to the closing line of the gulf, thereby defining the intersection with the boundary line and its general seaward direction This approach was first applied by the 1974 Spanish–French agreement on the delimitation of the Bay of Biscay.[50] It was also used by the Chamber during the *Gulf of Maine* case, to define the second segment of the boundary between the points where the two states' coasts were nearest. The median line was shifted in proportion to the ratio of the coastal lengths (US:Canada 1.38:1) to the United States' benefit:

> The ratio between the coastal fronts of the United States and Canada on the Gulf of Maine ... should be reflected in the location of the second segment of the delimitation line. For this purpose the Chamber considers

---

[49] The 2007 Tribunal in *Guyana v. Suriname* – in line with Guyana's claim – regarded it as 'logical and appropriate' to regard as relevant coasts, for the question of proportionality, those coastlines between the outermost points along the base line controlling the direction of the equidistance line out to 200 nm, *Arbitral Award Constituted Pursuant to Article 387, and in Accordance with Annex VII, of the United Nations Convention on the Law of the Sea in the Matter of an Arbitration between Guyana and Suriname*, Award of 17 September 2007 (hereinafter *Guyana v. Suriname* Award), paras. 345, 352, www.pca-cpa.org/showpage.asp?pag_id=1147 (last accessed 30 January 2012). The same approach had been taken earlier by the Court in the 1993 *Jan Mayen* case for the delimitation of the opposite coasts of Greenland and the island of Jan Mayen (*Maritime Delimitation in the Area between Greenland and Jan Mayen (Denmark v. Norway)*, Judgment, ICJ Reports 1993, p. 68, para. 67), and implicitly by the Court in the 2002 *Cameroon v. Nigeria* case in a delimitation of adjacent coasts (ICJ Reports 2002, p. 442, para. 291, p. 446, para. 301). In contrast – and also in a situation of opposite coasts – the 2006 Tribunal in *Barbados v. Trinidad and Tobago* was not persuaded that base points should have a determinative role in defining what the relevant coastal frontages are for the question of coastal ratios. It held that although base points have a role in effecting the delimitation and in the drawing of the provisional equidistance line, the 'relevant coastal frontages are not strictly a function of the location of basepoints', *Arbitral Tribunal constituted pursuant to Art. 287, and in accordance with Annex VII, of the United Nations Convention on the Law of the Sea, in the matter of arbitration between Barbados and the Republic of Trinidad and Tobago*, Award of the Tribunal, 11 April 2006, see www.pca-cpa.org/showpage.asp?pag_id=1147 (last accessed 30 January 2012), para 329. For the issue of relevant costs see Chapter 10.

[50] Reprinted in St/LEG/SER. B/19 445, below, Appendix I, Table A.1, No. 41.

that the appropriate method should be to apply the ratio selected to a line drawn across the Gulf where the coasts of Nova Scotia and Massachusetts are nearest to each other ... In the view of the Chamber it would then be proper to shift the median line drawn initially between the opposite and the quasi-parallel lines ... in such a way as to reflect this ratio along the line Cape Cod–Cheboque Point.[51]

Similarly, the Court in *Nicaragua v. Colombia* adjusted the median line to take account of the disparity in coastal lengths between the parties. The disparity in question was 8.2:1 in Nicaragua's favour.[52] The Court found the disparity in coastal lengths to be 'so marked as to justify a significant shift'.[53] The Court consequently weighted the effect of the base points onto the median line in a ratio of 3:1 in favour of the Nicaraguan base points.[54] A ratio that would have been even more favourable to Nicaragua, and thus closer to the coastal length ratio, seems to have been rejected because it would have cut across the 12 nm territorial sea around any of the Colombian islands.[55]

The mathematical calculation of the ratio of coastal lengths provides a particular crystallization of the legal principle of proportionality that will be discussed later. The two are not identical, and it is important to emphasize that the exact calculation of coastal ratios is a technical method and not a legal principle.[56]

2. The bisector method

a. The technique Similar to the method of equidistance, the bisector method seeks to approximate the relationship between two parties' relevant coasts. While equidistance approximates the coastal relationship by designating pairs of base points, the bisector method does so on the basis of a pair of straight lines drawn between two points on the coast of each of the states. The bisector of the angle formed by these lines may ultimately be adopted as the boundary line. Thus, a bisector line is in principle an equidistance line based upon a 'flattened coasts'.[57] In the

---

[51] ICJ Reports 1984, p. 94, para. 222.
[52] *Territorial and Maritime Dispute (Nicaragua v. Colombia)*, Judgment, ICJ Reports 2012, p. 659, available at www.icj-cij.org (hereinafter Nicaragua v. Colombia), para. 211.
[53] Ibid., para. 233.   [54] Ibid., para. 234.   [55] Ibid., para. 233.
[56] See ICJ Reports 1985, p. 45, para. 58, as recalled in ICJ Reports 1993, p. 69, para. 69, Barbados v. Trinidad and Tobago, n. 49 at para. 237 and ICJ Reports 2009, p. 116, para. 166. See also ICJ Reports 1985, p. 164 (dissenting opinion Oda). See further Chapter 6.
[57] Marques Antunes, n. 9, p. 163, noting that this holds true only if the line starts from the vertex of the angle to be bisected, i.e. the point of intersection between the straight lines on the states' coasts. See Judge Oda's critique of the employment of a bisector in the first

words of the Court in *Nicaragua* v. *Honduras*, it is the macro-geography of the coastline which is taken into consideration.[58] In other words, the bisector method simplifies coastal geography to the highest degree possible.[59] Accordingly, where the bisector method is to be applied, care must be taken to avoid 'completely refashioning nature'.[60] Identifying the straight lines on each state's coast calls for the exercise of judgment in assessing the actual coastal geography.[61]

b. **The circumstances of its application**   In accordance with the case law, recourse to the bisector method is only used if, for geographical circumstances, the equidistance method is unsuitable.

In *Nicaragua* v. *Honduras*, the Court noted that the equidistance method is widely used in the practice of maritime delimitation, holding that 'it has a certain intrinsic value because of its scientific character and the relative ease with which it can be applied'.[62] However, the Court added, 'the equidistance method does not automatically have priority over other methods of delimitation and, in particular circumstances, there may be factors which make the application of the equidistance method inappropriate'.[63] The geographical and geomorphological circumstances near the ending of the land boundary made the Court call for a special circumstance 'in which it cannot apply the equidistance principle'.[64] The Court thus made an exception to the equidistance method, as provided for by Article 15 for the delimitation of the territorial sea. On this point, the Court noted that 'nothing in the wording of Article 15 suggests that geomorphological problems are per se precluded from being "special circumstances" within the meaning of the exception, nor that such "special circumstances" may only be used as a corrective element to a line already drawn'.[65] It added that at the same time equidistance remains the rule.[66]

The special circumstance in *Nicaragua* v. *Honduras* was constituted by the ending of the land boundary, which is a sharply convex territorial projection abutting a concave coastline on either side to the north and

---

segment of the boundary line in the *Gulf of Maine* case (ICJ Reports 1985, p. 166, dissenting opinion Oda).

[58] *Territorial and Maritime Dispute between Nicaragua and Honduras in the Caribbean Sea (Nicaragua* v. *Honduras), Judgment,* ICJ Reports 2007, pp. 659, 747, para. 289.
[59] Marques Antunes, n. 9, p. 163.
[60] ICJ Reports 2007, p. 747, para. 289, referring to ICJ Reports 1969, p. 49, para. 91.
[61] Ibid.   [62] ICJ Reports 2007, p. 86 para 272.   [63] Ibid.   [64] Ibid., para. 281.
[65] Ibid., para 280.   [66] Ibid., para. 281.

south-west. The Court noted that, given these geographical configurations, the pair of base points to be identified on either bank of the river mouth would assume considerable importance in constructing an equidistance line, especially as it travels out from the coast. It continued that due to the close proximity of these base points to each other, any variation or error in situating them would become disproportionately magnified in the resulting equidistance line.[67] The Court held that by employing the bisector method, a minor deviation in the exact position of endpoints, which are at a reasonable distance from the shared point, would have only a relatively minor influence on the course of the entire coastal front line.[68] The straight lines finally employed by the Court[69] hinge at a historically agreed point near the land boundary – the so-called '1962 point' – and run north-west to Honduras' Punta Patuca and south to Nicaragua's Wouhnta.[70] The bisector of the angle thus created used the 1962 Point as its vertex. The Court's bisector, which bisected only the relevant parts of the mainland coasts, taking no account of offshore islands, ran to the north of the Honduran islands, thereby placing them on Nicaragua's side of the bisector line. The Court then turned to the separate task of delimiting the waters around and between the islands north and south of the bisector line. Thus the Court left the delimitation line based on the relevant mainland coasts behind it and turned to maritime delimitation between the islands.[71] In line with both parties' argument, the Court granted all four islands in dispute a territorial sea. It used the 12 nm arc and equidistance methods to delimit around and between the islands.[72] Accordingly, the ultimate boundary line follows the bisector until it reaches the territorial seas of each island. From there the line traces the 12 nm arc around the islands' territorial seas. Where that line meets the overlapping territorial seas of Bobel Cay, Port Royal Cay and South Cay (Honduras) and Edinburgh Cay (Nicaragua), it traces the median line between these islands, until it reaches the bisector line again.[73]

The ICJ's invocation of special circumstances and the resulting application of the bisector method to the larger part of the boundary between Nicaragua and Honduras, contrasts with an award in an arbitration between Guyana and Suriname rendered shortly before. In *Guyana* v.

---

[67] Ibid., para. 277.   [68] Ibid., para. 294.   [69] Ibid.
[70] Ibid., para. 298. The Court considered whether the relevant coasts faced the disputed area, whether the relevant coasts were long enough to 'account properly for the coastal configuration in the disputed area', and whether the linear approximation of the relevant coasts would cut off significant portions of territory, thereby depriving them of the effect of the delimitation, ibid. paras. 295–8.
[71] Ibid., 299–304.   [72] Ibid., para. 305.   [73] Ibid., para. 321(3).

Suriname, the Tribunal clearly discarded the bisector method claimed by Suriname.[74] The Tribunal held that:

> the general configuration of the maritime area to be delimited does not present the type of geographical peculiarities which could lead the Tribunal to adopt a methodology at variance with that which has been practised by international courts and tribunals during the last two decades. Such peculiarities may, however, be taken into account as relevant circumstances, for the purpose, if necessary, of adjusting or shifting the provisional delimitation line.[75]

The Court in *Romania* v. *Ukraine* held that those methods should be used that are 'geometrically objective' and also 'appropriate for the geography of the area' in which the delimitation is to take place.[76] The Court added that an equidistance line will be drawn 'unless there are compelling reasons that make this unfeasible in the particular case'.[77] It ultimately chose the equidistance and median line techniques as the appropriate methods of delimitation for the geography of the Romanian and Ukrainian coastal features.[78] The Court referred to the judgment in *Nicaragua* v. *Honduras*, where the bisector method was applied in geographical circumstances unsuitable for the standard equidistance method.[79]

In *Bangladesh* v. *Myanmar*, the ITLOS Tribunal rejected Bangladesh's proposal of a bisector method, since the geographical circumstances did not warrant a deviation from the standard equidistance method.[80] Namely, the relevant coast of Myanmar as determined by the Tribunal would have resulted in an angle that would have failed to give adequate effect to the southward projection of the coast of Bangladesh.[81] However, the Tribunal observed that 'the issue of which method should be followed in drawing the maritime delimitation line should be considered in light of the circumstances of each case' and that '[t]he goal of achieving an equitable result must be the paramount consideration guiding the action of the Tribunal in this connection'.[82] Interestingly, the Tribunal ended up adjusting the equidistance line in the EEZ and continental shelf so that it followed the same 215° azimuth as the angle bisector which Bangladesh had proposed.[83] Ultimately, thus, it was only the geography close to the

---

[74] *Guyana* v. *Suriname* Award, n. 49, para. 261.   [75] Ibid., para. 372.
[76] *Case Concerning Maritime Delimitation in the Black Sea (Romania* v. *Ukraine)*, Judgment, 3 February 2009; ICJ Reports 2009. p. 61, 101 para. 116.
[77] Ibid.   [78] Ibid., paras. 119, 127–49, 153–4.   [79] ICJ Reports 2009, p. 101, para 116.
[80] *Bangladesh* v. *Myanmar*, n. 32, paras. 213–17, 220, 234–7.   [81] Ibid., para. 237.
[82] Ibid., para. 235.   [83] Ibid., paras. 217, 334, 340.

land boundary that made the angle bisector unsuitable, and only for the delimitation of the territorial sea.

The application of the bisector method in *Nicaragua v. Honduras* allows for more flexibility in the choice of method in future delimitations.[84] This is true despite the ICJ's statement that equidistance remains the rule,[85] and despite the Tribunal's rejection in *Guyana v. Suriname*, the ICJ's rejection in *Romania v. Ukraine* and ITLOS' rejection in *Bangladesh v. Myanmar* to take recourse to the bisector method under the geographical circumstances of those particular cases. It remains true that 'the equidistance method does not automatically have priority over other methods of delimitation'[86] and that 'the method to be followed should be one that, under the prevailing geographic realities and the particular circumstances of each case, can lead to an equitable result'.[87]

Where the geographical circumstances of a case are particularly unstable and unpredictable, recourse must be available to a method which approximates the coastal relationship to a more general degree. Such a situation of unpredictable coastal features are likely to emerge should sea levels rise to a substantial degree due to climate change.

3. Perpendicular to the general direction of the coastal line

The application of the perpendicular is a particular case of the general method of the bisector.[88] The perpendicular is applied between adjacent states by drawing a seaward line perpendicular to the general direction of the coastal line at the point where the land boundary reaches the sea. A perpendicular is thus the bisector of an angle of 90 degrees with its vertex at the point where the land boundary meets the line representing the general direction of the coast.

The method is also closely related to equidistance and produces comparable results where there are straight coastlines or long base lines enclosing bays and estuaries. While drawing the perpendicular itself is a simple operation, the main problems and uncertainties lie in establishing the general direction of the coastal lines. Questions arise as to which parts of the coasts – national or regional – should be taken into account. Equally, it is possible to define the line in many different ways. No particular method prevails. Solutions may be tailored individually by suitable geometrical constructions.

---

[84] Coalter G. Lathrop, 'Territorial and Maritime Dispute Between Nicaragua and Honduras in the Caribbean Sea (Nicaragua v. Honduras)' (2009) 102 AJIL 113, 118.
[85] *Nicaragua v. Honduras*, n. 52 para. 281.   [86] Ibid., para. 272.
[87] *Bangladesh v. Myanmar*, n. 32, para. 235.   [88] Marques Antunes, n. 3, p. 163.

In the 1985 *Guinea* v. *Guinea-Bissau* arbitration, the Court applied the perpendicular method, which had rarely been used, although it was recognized by the World Court in 1982.[89] The Court defined the general direction of the coastal line in regional terms. Then it took into account the entire West African coast, because a 'window' limited to the states in dispute would have produced a distorted result, as the coast of the two states is concave, while the entire regional coast is convex.[90] Since long-distance maritime boundaries potentially affect third parties, this is a reasonable view. The longer a boundary line, the more necessary it is to rely upon a regional perspective for the application of this method.

The Court indicated several methods of establishing the general direction. The direction could be based either on the arc of a circle based on two extreme points of the region,[91] or it could rely upon the protruding angles of a polygon linking prominent regional points. The latter method opens up the possibility of different configurations.[92] The Court finally relied upon what it called the 'maritime facade' by drawing a regional straight line from two prominent points in neighbouring Senegal and Sierra Leone.[93] This solution certainly has the advantage of being simpler than the polygon approach, which remains unclear, since the establishment of the resulting single rectangular line is not explained.

4. The extrapolation of the land boundary

Maritime boundaries can be established by extending the general direction of the common territorial boundary in a seaward direction. It can use the thrust of the common boundary or define the general direction of the basis of a segment close to the sea. This method, which in effect relies upon the expanse, location and relationship of the state territories, has hardly been used. It remained without support by writers and the ILC,

---

[89] Rare examples found are the 1972 Brazil–Uruguay Boundary Agreement, reprinted in 13 ILM 251 (1973), Appendix I, Table A.1, No. 35, the Burma–Siam territorial sea delimitation, and three Belgium–France delimitations of a customs surveillance zone. See YILC 1953 II 82, 89. The ICJ confirmed the concept, *obiter dictum* in the *Tunisia* v. *Libya Continental Shelf* case, 1982 ICJ Reports 85, para. 120.

[90] 'Guinea v. Guinea-Bissau: Dispute Concerning Delimitation of the Maritime Boundary' (1986) 25 ILM 251–307, 297, para. 108.

[91] Ibid. para. 109.   [92] Ibid.

[93] Ibid. para. 110 (297–8), linking Alamdias Point (Senegal) and Cape Shilling (Sierra Leone).

even in cases of the territorial sea.[94] Nevertheless, the ICJ held *obiter dictum* that, inter alia, the concept of prolongation of the general direction of the land boundary is a valid method, and may be used by states.[95]

The same approach is possible for establishing the general direction of existing sea boundaries, in particular that of the territorial sea. No application of this method, included in the list by the 1953 committee of experts, could be found. Indeed, a general direction of merely 3 miles was hardly a sufficient base for extrapolation of a long-distance maritime boundary. The extension of the territorial sea to 12 mile may improve the situation. In most cases, however, continuation of the boundary will result from the application of the method of equidistance, in a pure or a modified form.

5. Parallel lines (corridors)

Apart from the modification of base points (half-effect) and the projection of the ratio of respective coastal lengths, the use of parallel lines offers yet another method for coping with the cutting-off effects produced by the convergence of equidistant lines in front of the coast of one of the parties.[96] Instead of an ad hoc modification of equidistance, two parallel straight lines are employed. This method was used in place of the equidistant lines method in the Franco-Monaco Agreement of 1984[97] and the Domenica–France Agreement of 1987[98] to avoid cutting-off. It was most prominently employed in the *St. Pierre and Miquelon* Award to avoid disproportionate seaward allocations to a dependent island close to the Canadian mainland.[99] It can be seen as a technical method, in that one of the lines is defined by its parallelism to the other, e.g. a perpendicular line to a coastal line. Nothing is said about the breadth of the corridors, which are either defined by the frontal coastline or by discretionary considerations.

6. Enclaving

The final method particularly relates to the treatment of dependant islands and often causes modification from equidistance or median

---

[94] See André Gidel *Le Droit international public de la mer*, 3 vols. (Chateauroux: Mellottée, 1932–1934, repr. Topos Verlag AG Vaduz, 1981); Report of the Committee of Experts on the Territorial Sea, YILC 1953 II 77, 79.
[95] 1982 ICJ Reports 85, para. 120.   [96] See Legault and Hankey, n. 6, p. 214.
[97] *International Maritime Boundaries*, n. 3, Report 8-3.   [98] Ibid., Report 2-15.
[99] *Court of Arbitration for the Delimitation of Maritime Areas between Canada and France: Decision in Case Concerning Delimitation of Maritime Areas*, 31 ILM 1145 (1992).

lines, or any other method used. Enclaving consists of establishing a boundary based upon arcs of circles *drawn from appropriate headlands*. The line is established by linking the intersecting arcs drawn from subsequent headpoints. In practice, the breadth of such circles has usually been 3 or 12 nm representing the territorial sea, or 13 nm granting an additional jurisdiction in the context of a continental shelf or EEZ delimitation.[100]

Enclaving may establish either a full enclave or a semi-enclave. The full enclave is employed in cases where the island is situated on the 'wrong side' of the median.[101] The semi-enclave is used when the island is close to the median, but situated on its 'right side'.[102] In all cases, enclaving substantially reduces the maritime space allocation that would otherwise result from applying the equidistance method.

7. Annex: problems of scale distortions

Finally, the technical problem of scale distortion or scale errors should be briefly addressed. It is a problem inherent to all technical methods of delimitation and, according to Beazley, the extensive survey of maritime boundary agreements by the ASIL Project showed that little is known about the extent to which technical issues were considered during negotiations. Even in recent agreements, the problem has not been adequately addressed.[103] The employment of plane geometry, using navigational charts and straight lines (loxodromes), is practical because of its simplicity, but it does not take into account the curvature of the globe as geodesic lines do. The use of one or the other method may amount to quite substantial differences in space allocation, as the 1977 *Anglo-French*

---

[100] See Legault and Hankey, n. 6 p. 212–13.

[101] E.g. *Arbitration Between the United Kingdom of Great Britain and Northern Ireland and the French Republic on the Delimitation of the Continental Shelf, Decisions of the Court of Arbitration dated 30 June 1977 and 14 March 1978*, Command Paper 7438, March 1979, reprinted in 18 ILM (1979), see also Australia–Papua New Guinea Agreement, International Maritime Boundaries, n. 3, Report 5-3; e.g. in the case of the insular features of Quitasueño and Serrana in *Nicaragua v. Colombia*, n. 52, para. 238.

[102] E.g., Italy–Yugoslavia Continental Shelf Agreement of 8 January 1968; *International Maritime Boundaries*, n. 3, Report 8-7(1) (islands of Pelagruz and Pianosa, 12 nm); Italy–Tunisia of 20 August 1971, *International Maritime Boundaries*, Report 8-6 (Pantelleria, Linosa, Lampedusa, 13 nm, and Italian Lampione, 12 nm). For further agreements, see Legault and Hankey, n. 6, p. 213; e.g. in *Nicaragua v. Honduras*, n. 58, para. 305; for the South Cay of Alburquerque Cays and the East-Southeast Cays in *Nicaragua v. Colombia*, n. 52, para. 237; and for St. Martin's island in *Bangladesh v. Myanmar*, n 32, para. 337.

[103] Peter B. Beazley, 'Technical Considerations in Maritime Delimitation' in Charney et al., *International Maritime Boundaries*, n. 3, vol. II (Charney and Alexander (eds.)), pp. 243–62.

Channel arbitration shows.[104] The advanced use of computer technology, rather than manual establishment of lines (plotting) increasingly allows for the avoidance of such difficulties from the outset. It is important to address this problem when the basis of negotiations or third party settlements is established. Otherwise, follow-up problems may arise protracting the settlement of the dispute. It is of utmost importance to deal carefully with technical issues, and in particular to define and adopt shared vertical data (Chart Datum) for low-water lines and shared horizontal datums (Geodetic Datum) for the definition of geographical co-ordinates, in particular the Point of Origin, i.e. the point from which all features of the survey are derived. In order to define a maritime boundary line with accuracy, the co-ordinates must be associated with a particular common datum, and its relationship to other data of the region must be known, together with the risk of deviation. (An example of a deviation of up to 1.5 kilometres was reported for an Indian Ocean island.[105])

B. Geological and ecological methods (natural boundaries)

The methods of delimitation discussed so far share a common reliance upon geographical features (i.e. the contours of the coastal configuration or the territorial expanses of the states concerned) or upon existing man-made land boundaries. Instead of surface geography, methods may rely upon characteristic elements and qualities of the seabed and the water column, independent of territorial, surface-related configurations. The concept of *Thalweg*, defining river boundaries by the middle of navigable water (thus allowing both entities to exercise navigation), is a classical example in point.[106]

Given the scientific definition of the shelf as a natural prolongation of the land mass to the edge of the continental margin,[107] it could be anticipated that scientific methods of delimitation would primarily rely upon geological features and define boundaries in accordance with them.

---

[104] In this case, the use of loxodromes instead of geodesic lines produced distortions of approximately 6 nm at a distance of 200 nm to the disadvantage of the United Kingdom. See the 1978 award, n. 101, pp. 169, 479, para. 40. Although the use of geodesic lines in delimitation is increasing, the Court of Arbitration did not correct the distortion since neither method is compulsory under customary international law and loxodromes are not obsolete. Ibid., p. 491, para. 105.

[105] Beazley n. 103, p. 248.

[106] On the issue of river boundaries, see Schröter, *Les Systèmes de délimitation dans les fleuves internationaux* (1982) AFDI 948.

[107] See Chapter 2.

Interruptions of the abyssal plate (tranches, different tectonics, etc.) could provide a basis of delimitation. The approach corresponds to territorial boundary delimitation to the extent that it relies upon rivers and mountains (water divides) in order to define the borderline. A similar approach is conceivable with respect to the EEZ and the water column. For the purposes of effective resource conservation and management, boundaries could be sought to separate different ecological systems, thereby preserving their unity. In the *Gulf of Maine* case, the United States argued that the area in dispute shows three different ecological systems (Gulf of Maine basin, Scotian Shelf, and Georges Bank) that are separated by natural boundaries, in particular along the Northeast Channel, a shallow geomorphological trough.[108] Although this case was not a delimitation of an EEZ in a legal sense, similar arguments for a combined natural boundary, or separate natural boundaries, of the shelf and the water column could apply to the EEZ as such.

The courts have never ruled out this approach of natural boundaries as a matter of principle. Indeed, it will be seen that geophysical factors influence delimitations which are primarily based on geographical methods.[109] Still, it has not yet led to established methods of commanding *per se* delimitation for a number of practical and theoretical reasons. For the moment, we are only concerned with methods of delimitation *per se*, as *alternatives* to geographical approaches.

1. Practical problems of scientific evidence

Geological methods have caused much controversy and confusion. They did not produce operational methods of delimitation for reasons that have already been partly discussed and which will be further elaborated.[110] Except for two agreements relating to the Timor Trough (Australia–Indonesia),[111] the features of the seabed have not been the deciding factor, because most delimitations deal with a single, and more or less coherent, tectonic shelf. In the absence of clear-cut natural boundaries of different shelves, scientific arguments about tectonics

---

[108] See 1982 ICJ Reports 49/50, paras. 51–2.   [109] See Chapter 9.
[110] See Chapters 2, 6, 9 *et passim*.
[111] 1972 Australia–Indonesia Agreement (Timor and Arafura Seas), *International Maritime Boundaries*, n. 3, report No. 6-2(2) at 1207–18; 1989 Australia–Indonesia (Timor Gap), ibid., No. 6-2(5) at 1245–1328. See also Keith Highet, 'The Use of Geophysical Factors in the Delimitation of Maritime Boundaries' in Charney et al., *International Maritime Boundaries*, n. 3, vol. I (Charney and Alexander), pp. 163, 187 ('The two agreements are the only ones that really adopted a significant geophysical feature of the sea-bottom as an indicator of the boundary or as a component of its determination').

tend to become Homeric. The lack of agreed-upon scientific paradigms and the competition amongst tectonic theories often allow experts and parties to adopt doctrines suitable for the support of their claims and leave courts without much guidance. In addition, significant features may be absent altogether, ruling out any natural boundary from the outset. The situation may be different with regard to the exact location of mineral deposits. Geologists can often indicate their expanses. When this is the case, the deposits themselves could serve as a basis for the delimitation of natural boundaries. However, the location of deposits is not always exactly known in advance, so delimitation, which is as important for the regulation of exploration as for exploitation, would suffer substantial delays.

Similar problems of evidence also arise within the context of ecosystems. Even the largely accepted scientific fact of the Georges Bank system was challenged by Canada on the ground that the system itself is part of a continuous oceanic system belonging to the Nova Scotian (and therefore Canadian) 'biogeographical province'.[112] From a practical point of view, therefore, the lack of a consolidated theory and evidence in marine sciences presents major problems for geological and ecological methods. Again, definable ecosystems may be absent in the area of delimitation, ruling out the application of natural boundaries from the outset.

Such problems of evidence largely reduce the possibility of the successful application of genuine methods related to natural boundaries. After various unfruitful experiences with tectonics ('essays in geopoetry' as Judge Jimenez de Aréchaga recalled[113]), the Chamber of the ICJ adopted the extremely high standard of proof 'beyond all doubt' with respect to ecological facts.[114] This standard not only makes delimitation on the basis of scientific evidence almost impossible, but it also discourages parties from submitting expensive, elaborate and controversial scientific evidence in support of their claims. Moreover, the Chamber in fact denied the possibility of stable natural boundaries in the fluctuating environment of the oceans:

---

[112] 1984 ICJ Reports 275, para. 50.
[113] Separate opinion, 1982 ICJ Reports 110, para. 38, quoting John Noble Wilford, *The Mapmakers* (1st edn., 1981, now revised 2nd edn., New York: Vintage Books, 2001), p. 292.
[114] 1984 ICJ Reports 276, para. 53 ('however, the result [of the scientific hearings] was not such as to clear away all doubt, at least as regards certain of the technical aspects debated').

The Chamber is not however convinced of the possibility of discerning any genuine, sure and stable 'natural boundary' in so fluctuating an environment as the water of the ocean, their flora and fauna. It has thus reached the conviction that it would be vain to seek, in data derived from biogeography of the waters covering certain areas of sea-bed, any element sufficient to confer the property of a stable natural boundary.[115]

Based on such findings, ecological boundaries as such are hardly a practical option. They are refuted for similar practical reasons as the geological approaches to maritime boundary delimitation before.[116]

2. Theoretical and legal issues

Problems related to the delimitation of natural boundaries, however, reach beyond the issue of evidence. Perhaps what is more important are the theoretical and legal complications of delimitation. These relate to the very conceptual foundations of the shelf and the EEZ.

Conceptually, natural sea boundaries between adjacent and opposite states are at variance with the EEZ, including the soil, the subsoil and the water column. Natural boundaries are also increasingly at variance with the law of the shelf. The evolution of the shelf, culminating in minimal expanses of 200 nm, makes natural boundaries obsolete within this range. As discussed, the concept of natural prolongation operates only in a seaward direction. It is here that it is essential to develop methods of delimiting natural boundaries along the edge of the continental margin under Article 76 of the LOS Convention. Within 200 nm, both the EEZ and the shelf are determined by distance. Therefore, geographical methods relying upon configuration of the land mass, rather than the structure of the soil and subsoil of the sea, basically dispose of this issue. From this perspective, it is astonishing that the 1989 Australia–Indonesia Agreement still partly relies upon the Timor Trough, despite invoking the LOS Convention in its preamble.[117] However, it should be noted that

---

[115] Ibid., para. 54.
[116] Cf. David A. Colson, 'Environmental Factors: Are They Relevant to Delimitation', paper presented at the 19th Annual Conference of the Law of the Sea Institute, 24–27 July 1985; Cardiff, (typescript) concluding:

> I do not find the treatment, on balance, unreasonable, particularly from the perspective of judicial policy. The Chamber dealt with the United States' natural boundary argument as if to say that it did not want to open up this new area of the law to the same type of inconclusive scientific debate that had come out of the Court's reference to natural prolongation in 1969.

Ibid., at 9.
[117] Above at n. 111.

this Agreement merely completed the 1971 Agreement and only determines the boundary in a provisional manner, in combination with the establishment of a zone of co-operation, which clearly mitigates the effect of the natural boundary.[118] The Agreement, therefore, cannot be considered as a revival of the geophysical boundary idea.

Moreover, methods of delimitation based on the location of resources, whilst economically feasible, would be at variance with traditional concepts and perceptions of the shelf. Delimitation based on the allocation of deposits (as we find it in the later generation of the Area with respect to manganese nodules) has not been permitted, due to the fact that the foundation of the concept of the continental shelf concerns the closeness of the relationship between coastal states and marine spaces, with definitions based on geographical considerations (tectonic expanses and distances), and in the absence of distributive justice and the goal of global equity in resource allocation.[119] Under the present definition of the EEZ, the same holds true for the location of living resources. The zone aims at the allocation of marine spaces, not at the particular pools and units and entities of resources therein. Reliance upon methods guided by the location of resources would therefore imply a major departure from established concepts.

However, the foregoing does not mean that the exclusion of methods which define purely natural boundaries at sea between adjacent and opposite states completely excludes taking into account geological and ecological considerations. It is reasonable to consider existing shapes, location and the natural boundaries of mineral resources in order to prevent jurisdictional problems.[120] The same is true with regard to living resources in order to achieve effective management and conservation. States are free to draw ecological and geological boundaries in agreements, modifying or even disregarding geography. During adjudication, the room to manoeuvre is more limited. But it will be seen that even here there is scope for geological and ecological considerations to be considered as relevant factors within the existing geographically defined concepts of the shelf and the EEZ. So, in combination with other factors, they may exert some influence on the course of defining the boundary lines as a matter of law and legal methodology.

---

[118] Cf. Report No 6-2(5), *2 International Maritime Boundaries*, n. 3, pp. 1245 –51.
[119] Chapter 3.
[120] In fact, Highet, n. 111, p. 194, concluded that in approximately one-third of all delimitations by agreement, geomorphological and geological factors have played a role; for further discussion of state practice, see Chapter 5.

III. Competing legal approaches to delimitation

A. Four regulatory models

Four principal regulatory models characterize the history of maritime boundary law. They are all reflected in case law and efforts at codification. They may be labelled:

1. the model of juridical vacuum;
2. the model of equitable principles;
3. the model of residual rules and exceptions; and finally
4. the model of equitable solutions based on international law.

All four models contain elements of equity, and it is for this very reason that maritime boundary law is of significant interest to legal theory, methodology and jurisprudence. All the models also utilize the scientific methods discussed above, but use them in very different methodological ways.

The first and third models reflect classical approaches of international law (and law in general) either by leaving the matter open to discretion and without rules, or by establishing residual rules that are applied procedurally in the case of legal dispute settlement by third party procedures. Both approaches leave ample room for the adoption of any negotiated solutions within the limits of the law of treaties. In model 3, parties may or may not refer to residual rules, which need not be applied during negotiation, but which in fact often provide a starting point and deploy effects with a view to a possible third party settlement. The second model, however, is intended to be applied both in negotiations and in dispute settlement. It does not rely upon a concept of specific rules and exceptions, but rather on broad principles to be respected in maritime boundary delimitation. Finally, the fourth model, which emerged from UNCLOS III, is entirely result-oriented. Without defining any particular rules or principles, it is close to the first model, yet is still intended to operate within the realms of international law. It will be argued that, whilst the paramount goal of achieving an equitable solution is a compulsory element of this approach, it does not contain any mandatory rules or principles to be applied in the negotiations. The four models compete with each other. While model 1 was formally abandoned, models 2, 3, and 4 continue to operate, leaving a difficult and complex situation in the law.

1. The model of juridical vacuum (*ex aequo et bono*)

Given the intrinsically individual character of each case of delimitation, the matter may be entirely left to negotiation and agreement. In the case of a third party settlement, the decision is primarily based on past human conduct (including agreements, historical rights, acquiescence, estoppel), and therefore international law in general. It is necessarily based on discretion where these elements do not solve the case. This model is an application of the decision-making *ex aequo et bono* as expressed by Article 38(2) of the Statute of the International Court of Justice.[121]

The model of judicial vacuum or decision-making *ex aequo et bono* in maritime boundary law prevailed at the 1930 Hague Codification Conference and during its preparatory work, with respect to the delimitation of the territorial sea between adjacent and opposite states. Although at the time there was considerable doctrinal support for a rule of delimitation based on the technical method of taking the perpendicular to the general direction of the coast (equidistance was not yet invented), the conference did not adopt this method as a legal rule. The view was expressed by one of the rapporteurs of the preparatory Committee of Experts in 1926, namely that – failing historic rights and considerations:

> [i]t would be better to arrange for the conclusion of a special agreement between States concerned, or for a settlement of the matter by arbitration or an ordinary tribunal, than to lay down an immutable principle.[122]

The UN Secretary General recommended a similar approach of judicial vacuum after World War II with regard to the then-emerging concept of the continental shelf:

> In short, the allotment should be made by agreement between the States concerned or by amicable arbitration, rather than by means of hard and fast rules for which the time is not yet ripe.[123]

---

[121] 'This provision shall not prejudice the power of the Court to decide a case ex aequo et bono, if the parties agree thereto.' ICJ, Acts and Documents concerning the Organization of the Court, No. 1 (1947).

[122] *Memorandum by Walter Schuecking*, in Report of the Subcommittee of the Committee of Experts for the Progressive Development of International Law, League of Nations, Doc. C. 44 M. 21, 1926 V. 10, at 16; Rhee, n. 6, p. 575.

[123] UN Doc. A/CN.4/32, referred to in YILC 1951 I 288, para 1. Bernd Rüster, *Die Rechtsordnung des Festlandsockels* (Berlin: Duncker und Humblot, 1977), p. 357, reports that the author of this advice was André Gidel, one of the authorities on contemporary maritime law.

This advice was taken up by the ILC in an early draft, after no agreement was found within the commission on proposals referring to the median line. Article 7 of the first draft on the delimitation of the continental shelf in effect proposed an approach based upon delimitation *ex aequo et bono*, that, failing agreement between the parties:

> [t]wo or more States to whose territories the same continental shelf is contiguous should establish boundaries by agreement. Failing agreement, the parties are under an obligation to have the boundaries fixed by arbitration.[124]

This proposal of compulsory arbitration reflects a strong preference for procedural obligations within the Commission. Procedural rules should be substituted for substantive rules.[125] Governments, however, largely rejected this approach. As in other areas, decision-making *ex aequo et bono*, particularly if linked to compulsory arbitration, has never been popular with governments.[126] They were not prepared to leave ample discretion to a third party and thereby lose control over the matter. Since early attempts failed to adopt an open-ended model, the option of juridical vacuum was abandoned. It has never been revived, at least not formally.

2. The model of equity and equitable principles

The drafters of the 1945 Truman Proclamation faced the juridical vacuum in international maritime boundary law and, moreover, a completely new and legally unsettled doctrine of the continental shelf, without any guidance in state practice or adjudication on long-distance maritime boundaries. In that situation, they referred to equity and equitable principles as a guiding tool and the foundation of the lateral delimitations of the shelf. The relevant part of the Proclamation reads:

---

[124] YILC 1951 II 141. Cf. also ibid. 1953 II 216, para. 81.
[125] Some members of the Commission even called for an obligation to reach mutual agreement, YILC 1951 II 287, para. 122 (Hudson referring to Brierly); see also R. Young, 'The International Law Commission and the Continental Shelf' (1952) 46 AJIL 123, supporting the ILC's approach as:

> a wise appreciation of the impossibility of laying down any universal rule ...
> Each situation is unique, and can be solved satisfactorily only in the lights of its own facts and the particular interests there involved.

Ibid., p. 126. For a discussion see Etienne Grisel, 'The Lateral Boundaries of the Continental Shelf and the Judgment of the International Court of Justice in the North Sea Continental Shelf cases' (1970) 64 AJIL 562, 566.

[126] Grisel, ibid., p. 566.

In cases where the continental shelf extends to the shores of another State, or is shared with an adjacent State, the boundary shall be determined by the United States and the state concerned in accordance with equitable principles.[127]

Neither the Proclamation nor any accompanying materials reveal the intended content of equitable principles in more specific terms. On the face of it, they appear to be a Delphic and elusive concept which, indeed, may be hardly discernible from settlements in a juridical vacuum and on the basis of the pre-war model of *ex aequo et bono*. It seems, however, that the approach was conceived from the outset as a legal approach, emphasizing a case-by-case method. According to the late Professor Bishop, who served on the team preparing this landmark document, the formula intended to 'encourage states to reach agreement based on a sense of fairness, by employing the most appropriate method or methods "case by case" in the area concerned'.[128] Although a statement *ex post facto*, it reveals *in nuce* the essential normative content of the model.

The approach starts from the pre-war model of decision-making *ex aequo et bono*, but is perceived from the outset as being a legal and principled approach operating within the realms of international law. Those principles are therefore to be applied as a matter of law. Boundary delimitation is no longer a matter of discretion. Further, international law principles should also guide negotiations and negotiated settlements. States are not free to adopt solutions that are incompatible with equitable principles.[129]

The model of equitable principles was adopted by the ICJ in the 1969 *North Sea Continental Shelf* case. It has dominated the case law ever since, despite increased reliance on residual rules in recent developments. Part II of this book will examine the approach in more detail, in particular with regard to the content and methodology of equitable principles governing and guiding maritime boundary delimitation under this

---

[127] 'Proclamation No. 2667, Policy of the United States with Respect to the Natural Resources of the Subsoil and Sea Bed of the Continental Shelf, 28 Oct. 1945' (1965), reprinted in Marjorie M. Whiteman, *Digest of International Law* (Paris: Editions du Centre National de la Recherche Scientifique, 1963–1973), vol. IV, pp. 740, 756. For the twin-proclamation on fisheries see *Digest of International Law*, vol. IV, pp. 954, 757.

[128] Interview quoted in Sang-Myon Rhee, 'Equitable Solutions to the Maritime Boundary Dispute Between the United States and Canada in the Gulf of Maine' (1981) 75 AJIL 590, 591, note 3.

[129] This was a reassuring aspect since the continental shelf was, at the time of the Truman Proclamation, an object of unilateral claim by the United States. The concept of equitable principles was a matter of self-imposed discipline on unilateral delimitations.

model. It will be seen that the model implies a new and particular methodology. It is a model whereby a solution is composed based on the application of different principles or building blocks. It differs fundamentally as an approach from the model of residual rules that follows.

3. The model of residual rules and exceptions (equidistance or median line)

The traditional alternative to legal vacuum in international law, of course, is the establishment of residual rules to be applied in case of third party settlement, after failing, or pending agreement to the contrary. In essence, such a model declares one particular scientific method to be applied as a matter of law, with or without exceptions. Thus, there are two types of residual rules to consider: strict residual rules and flexible residual rules.

a. **Strict residual rules** This type of residual rule provides for a single, and therefore strict or 'hard and fast', rule to be applied in case negotiations fail. A court of law or arbitration, or conciliation in accordance with the law, is therefore left with no choice but to apply the rule without exception and modulation. In maritime boundary law, for example, such an approach was chosen in the 1964 European Fisheries Convention[130] for the purpose of delimitation of the newly introduced six mile fishing zone measured from the base lines of the territorial sea. The method of equidistance became a hard and fast rule of law in Article 7 of the Convention:

> Where the coasts of two Contracting Parties are opposite or adjacent to each other, neither of them are entitled, failing agreement between them to the contrary, to establish a fisheries regime beyond the median line, every point of which is equidistant from the nearest point of the low water lines of the coast of the Contracting Parties concerned.

The model has the obvious advantage of great clarity and predictability. But it is also rigid and may face the problems depicted by the adage of *summum ius – summa injuria* – the main motive for recourse to corrective equity. It is therefore doubtful whether it helps to solve disputes that may arise, for example, over the existence and impact of historic fishing rights. If states disagree about delimitation, it is mainly because they cannot accept a median or equidistance line. With a model that leaves no room for alternative solutions, it is very likely that states will refrain from

---

[130] Fisheries Convention, done at London, on 9 March 1964, New Directions I 41; ST/LEG. SER. B/15 at 862.

submitting the matter to arbitration if agreement fails. The model can only be applied in a multilateral agreement to the extent that all participants can agree, based on a preliminary appraisal of their interests, upon a median or equidistance line. In other words, it can only be applied in a regional context to clearly predictable cases. As a result, the rule itself is a settlement of particular cases, providing *ex ante* for particular boundary lines. It is not as suitable a foundation for the future process of delimitation as a model that combines equidistance and equity.

b. The model of strict residual rules subject to exceptions The third model and approach to the problem follows the classical legal pattern of establishing a general rule and yet at the same time providing for exceptions whenever the application of the general rule does not produce acceptable results.

This pattern prevailed in the codification of rules on delimitation of the territorial sea and of the continental shelf in the 1958 Convention on the Territorial Sea and the Contiguous Zone and the Convention on the Continental Shelf, respectively.[131] Both conventions use equidistance as the legally binding residual method of delimitation of maritime boundaries between adjacent or opposite states. However, this rule is subject to exceptions that are described by a vague formula and by reference to special circumstances. Except for historic titles in territorial waters, such exceptional circumstances are not further elaborated. They therefore leave ample discretion to a court of law in a judicial settlement of the boundary. Article 12(1) of the Territorial Sea Convention (restated with minor textual modifications in Article 15 LOS Convention) reads:

> Where the coasts of two states are opposite or adjacent to each other, neither of the two States is entitled, failing agreement between them to the contrary, to extend its territorial sea beyond the median line every point of which is equidistant from the nearest points on the baselines from which the territorial sea is measured. The provision of this paragraph shall not apply, however, where it is necessary by reasons of historic title or other special circumstances to delimit the territorial sea of the two States in a way that is at variance with this provision.

Similarly, relevant sections of Article 6 of the Continental Shelf Convention read:

---

[131] Convention on the Territorial Sea and the Contiguous Zone, Geneva, 29 April, in force 10 September 1964, 516 UNTS 205; Convention on the Continental Shelf, Geneva, 29 April 1958, in force 10 June 1964, 499 UNTS 311.

1. Where the same continental shelf is adjacent to the territories of two or more States whose coasts are opposite each other, the boundary of the continental shelf appertaining to such States shall be determined by agreement between them. In the absence of agreement, and unless another boundary line is justified by special circumstances, the boundary is the median line, every point of which is equidistant from the nearest points of the baselines from which the breadth of the territorial sea of each State is measured.
2. Where the same continental shelf is adjacent to the territories of two adjacent States, the boundary of the continental shelf shall be determined by agreement between them. In the absence of agreement, and unless another boundary line is justified by special circumstances, the boundary shall be determined by application of the principle of equidistance from the nearest points of the baselines from which the breadth of the territorial sea of each State is measured.

The preparatory work behind both provisions reveals the emphasis given to the escape clause of special circumstances. In the course of its deliberations and drafts, the ILC became increasingly aware of the fact that the general rule of equidistance will not always produce acceptable results. While possible exceptions to the rule of territorial sea delimitation were originally indicated by reference to the application of equidistance in general, the final project bears explicit language of application of equidistance unless another boundary line is justified by special circumstances.[132] The ILC noted that such circumstances 'would probably necessitate frequent departures from the mathematical median line'.[133] A fortiori such departures would substantially increase in the context of the continental shelf with its generally much longer boundary lines. The ILC was clearly ambiguous about the usefulness of the equidistance method which it had transferred to shelf delimitation from application to the territorial sea in an 'almost impromptu and contingent manner', as the ICJ later observed.[134] On the one hand, the Commission stressed the

---

[132] See draft Art. 13, YILC 1952 II 38, and Art. 12, ibid. II 1956, 271; Art. 72, ibid., at 300. The need for exceptions was also expressed by the Advisory Committee of Experts. It recommended equidistance for the territorial sea and – without further elaboration – also for the continental shelf. But it added: 'Dans certains cas, cette méthode (recte méthode) ne permettra pas d'aboutir à une solution équitable, laquelle devra alors être recherchée dans des négociations', YILC 1953 II 77, 79. Cf. also 1969 ICJ Rep. 33-6, paras. 48-55. For an account of the legislative work of the ILC see also Grisel, n. 125, p. 565 et seq.

[133] YILC 1965 II 271.   [134] 1969 ICJ Reports 35, para. 53.

major principle for equidistance.[135] On the other, elasticity was emphasized, without a general principle being mentioned further.[136] In its final comment, the Commission concluded:

> As in the case of the boundaries of the territorial sea, provisions must be made for departures necessitated by any exceptional configuration of the coast, as well as the presence of islands or navigable channels. This scenario can arise fairly often, so that the rule adopted is fairly elastic.[137]

The model of residual rule subject to exception, and the elasticity inherent to it, shows that the rule set out cannot act as anything other than a preliminary guide. Whether or not special circumstances are present and need to be taken into account requires an underlying normative framework upon which claims to exceptions can be evaluated and adjudicated. Under the model, there is still a need to know the underlying criteria of appropriate maritime boundary delimitation. This is the model's basic flaw, and the reason for the continuing controversy over its usefulness. Discussions and applications show that it ultimately refers to the notion of equity and equitable principles for guidance.

At UNCLOS I, the fairly elastic rule-exception model was strongly disputed, both for territorial sea and continental shelf delimitations. For some delegations, the model was too vague, and they stressed the difficulties in construing the notion of special circumstances. For example, the delegation of former Yugoslavia is reported to have rejected the proposal with regard to continental shelf delimitation on the following ground:

> [The] last criterion ... namely, that a different solution might be justified by special circumstances, was unacceptable on legal grounds. It was both vague and arbitrary, and likely to give rise to misunderstanding and disagreement. The question was where and how such special circumstances were enumerated in international law and who could be charged with interpreting their application.[138]

Other delegations, which finally prevailed, insisted on the necessity of a flexible approach, as exemplified by the British delegate, Sir Gerald Fitzmaurice. With respect even to the territorial sea, and explicitly referring to equity, he said that:

---

[135] YILC 1953 II 216 para. 82.   [136] Ibid., para. 83.   [137] YILC 1956 II 300.
[138] [1958] 6 *Official Records* 91. For a discussion of the conference see generally Whiteman, *Digest of International Law*, vol. IV, n. 127, pp. 914–17; Marjorie Whiteman, 'Conference on the Law of the Sea: Convention on the Continental Shelf' (1958) 52 AJIL 629, 650–4.

he appreciated the arguments of some representatives in favour of deleting the reference to special circumstances ... but his delegation had doubted the wisdom of doing so ... It was admittedly a weakness that there was no definition of special circumstances so that their existence might be disputed. Nevertheless, special circumstances did exist which, for reasons of equity or because of the configuration of a particular coast, might make it difficult to accept the true median line as the actual line of delimitation between two territorial seas. There might be a navigation channel, for instance, which was not in the middle of a strait but to one side of it, or went from one side to the other; or the situation might be complicated by small islands. His delegation therefore felt that it would be too rigid to specify that the median line must be adhered regardless of special circumstances.[139]

Within a model of rules and exceptions, it would seem that the rule or principle itself is of predominant importance, and that it would subject exceptions or special circumstances to strict requirements or disciplines. While this is possible for delimitation of 3-mile territorial seas,[140] subsequent applications of the model confirmed the need for flexibility predicted by the ILC. The standard relationship of rule and special circumstances of subordination of exceptions to the rule was left behind. They became of equal normative importance and developed a relationship of co-ordination. The leading case, the 1977 *Anglo-French Channel* arbitration, stressed the aspect of flexibility. Article 6(1) and (2) of the 1958 Shelf Convention was construed as a combined equidistance–special circumstances rule, which pursues the goal of achieving an equitable solution of the dispute.[141] Recourse to equity, equitable principles and equitable solutions within this model shows that it is inherently linked to the concept of equity. In long-distance boundaries it is equally dependant on the concretization of equitable principles.

---

[139] [1958] 3 *Official Records* 189, para. 36 (emphasis added). Hardly consistent, the same delegation rejected the very same formula as applied to the continental shelf, [1958] 6 *Official Record* 93, para 1, and faced opposing views from the US and Italian delegation, among others. Ibid. 93, paras. 5, 21, 95.

[140] Evidence presented to the ICJ did not confirm the need for frequent departure from the rule in the context of a 3 nmterritorial sea as predicted by the ILC. The Court concluded that: 'the distorting effects of lateral equidistance lines under certain conditions of coastal configurations are nevertheless comparatively small within the limits of the territorial waters', 1969 ICJ Reports 38, para. 59. See also ibid. 19, para. 8.

   It is doubtful whether similar conclusions could be drawn with regard to the 12-mile territorial sea nowadays.

[141] See Chapter 6(II)(B).

4. Equidistance v. equity: the model of agreed equitable solutions based on international law

a. The history of Articles 74 and 83 of the LOS Convention Given the basic dilemma of rule-making in the present context, it is hardly surprising that the subject of long-range maritime boundary delimitation was, again, among the most controversial and contentious subjects at UNCLOS III. With more than fifty states having unresolved continental shelf maritime boundaries, and delimitation of the EEZ still unsettled by most coastal states, at the time, a special negotiating group (NG 7) was established in 1978. It was commissioned to examine and seek agreement on this particular hard-core issue of the Conference, including a regulation of appropriate interim measures and third party settlement.[142]

Without much difficulty, NG 7 and the Conference restated the model of residual rule (equidistance) subject to exceptions (special circumstances) for the delimitation of the territorial seas.[143] Although the extension of the territorial waters up to 12 nm (Article 3) is likely to increase the relevance of special circumstances, and therefore the concept of equity, states nevertheless agreed that this model is likely to serve their interests the best. No special provision was adopted for delimitations of

---

[142] UN Doc. A/CONF. 62/61, 10 *Official Records* 1 *et seq.*, concerning Arts. 15, 74, 75, 83, 84, 297(1)(a) Informal Negotiating Composite Text (ICNT). See generally Andronico O. Adede, 'Toward the Formulation of the Rule of Delimitation of Sea Boundaries Between States with Adjacent and Opposite Coasts' (1979) 19 *Virginia Journal of International Law* 207; Lucius Caflisch, 'The Delimitation of Marine Spaces Between States with Opposite or Adjacent Coasts' (1981) 1 *Anuario de Derecho Internacional Publico*, 85; Jens Evensen, 'The United Nations Convention on the Law of the Sea of December 10 1982: Its Political and Legal Impact – Present and Future' (1982) 38 *Revue égyptienne de droit international public*, 11, 23–6; Paul C. Irwin, 'Settlement of Maritime Boundary Disputes: An Analysis of the Law of the Sea Negotiations' (1980) 8 *Ocean Development and International Law*, 105; E. J. Manner, 'Settlement of Sea-Boundary Delimitation Disputes According to the Provisions of the 1982 Law of the Sea Convention' in J. Makarcyk (ed.), *Essays in International Law in Honour of Judge Manfred Lachs* (Dordrecht: Martinus Nijhoff Publishers, 1984), pp. 625, 631–38; subsequent reports by Oxman, (see Chapter 1, n. 11); Janusz Symonides, 'Delimitation of Maritime Areas between the States with Opposite and Adjacent Coasts' (1984) 13 *Polish Yearbook of International Law* 19, 21–46; Budislav Vukas, 'The LOS Convention and the Sea Boundary Delimitation' in B. Vukas (ed.), *Essays in the New Law of the Sea* (Zagreb: Sveučilišnanaklada Liber, 1985), pp. 147–85 (including a historical account of UNCLOS I–III). See also the scholarly review of the negotiations by Judge Oda, *Tunisia v. Libya Continental Shelf case*, 1982 ICJ Reports 234, paras. 131–45 (dissenting opinion).

[143] See Second Committee, Summary Reports, 57th mtg. (1979) 11 *Official Records* 57, 59; Adede, n. 142, at 209; MASH, 'The Boundary Provisions of the United Nations Convention on the Law of the Sea' in *National and International Boundaries* (Institute of Public Int'l Law and Int'l Relations of Thessoloniki ed., 1985), pp. 233, 243.

the contiguous zone up to 24 nm. A lacuna was left by the Conference in this respect.[144] No reference was made in Article 33 LOS Convention to the question of whether delimitation should be effected in accordance with Article 15. The exclusive reference to the continental shelf and the EEZ in the controversial debate on long-distance boundaries and the absence of recorded discussions on the subject seem to imply that the model of Article 15 would basically apply to the contiguous zone, if a problem of single delimitation of contiguous zones should ever occur. In most cases, however, the boundary of the zone will coincide with the EEZ delimitation and be absorbed.[145] Therefore, Article 15 only applies in cases where states refrain from establishing EEZs or where they adopt schemes of joint administration and co-operation.

The main attention and preoccupation of the group, of course, was paid to the problem of determining appropriate rules for the delimitation of the continental shelf and the EEZ. Based upon different formulas in the Main Trends,[146] the Informal Single Negotiating Text (ISNT) suggested a compromise formula, using both model 2 and model 3. The text contained a reference to equitable principles and to equidistance as the favoured method. Articles 61(1) (EEZ) and 70(1) (Continental Shelf) read:

> The delimitation of the exclusive economic zone/the continental shelf between adjacent or opposite States shall be effected by agreement in accordance with equitable principles, employing, where appropriate, the median or equidistance line, and taking account of all the relevant circumstances.[147]

This formula was upheld during subsequent drafts, the Revised Single Negotiating Text (RSNT) Part II of 1976,[148] the Informal Composite Negotiating Text (ICNT) of 1977, and its first revision.[149] Though it first seemed that the formula would be successful,[150] discussions about the

---

[144] Evensen, n. 142, p. 26; Caflisch, n. 142, p. 91.   [145] Caflisch, ibid.
[146] The Main Trends proposed four different formulas reflecting and combining existent approaches of equidistance and equity. UN Doc. A/CONF. 62/C.2./WP.1 (1974), reprinted in R. Platzoeder (ed.), *The United Nations Conference on the Law of the Sea* 4 vols. (Dobbs Ferry NY: Oceana Publications, 1982-85) (hereinafter Platzoeder), pp. 3, 42–3.
[147] UN Doc. A/CONF. 62/WP8 Part II (7 May 1975), reprinted in Platzoeder, pp. 30, 31–2.
[148] UN Doc. A/CONF.62/WP8/Rev. 1/Part II (6 March 1976); Platzoeder, n. 146, pp. 215–16, 219.
[149] UN Doc. A/CONF.62/WP10 (July 15, 1977), Platzoeder, n. 146 p. 317–18; and –Rev 1, ibid. at 420, 423–4.
[150] Cf. the following statement by the Chairman of the 2nd Committee:
> On the issue of delimitation of the exclusive economic zone and the continental shelf between adjacent or opposite states an extensive exchange of views took

subject at the seventh session resulted in a rejection of the proposition. It was deemed unacceptable for both groups of interests (sometimes called schools of thought[151]), which either favoured model 2 (equitable principles) or model 3 (equidistance). The equidistance group (the Bahamas Group of 24) rejected the proposal because equidistance was merely mentioned as a scientific method. Instead, the Group proposed a draft based on a model of equidistance – special circumstances.[152] On the other hand, the equitable principles group (the Algerian Group of 32) considered explicit reference to equidistance to be an inappropriate privilege of a single method and contrary to the multimethod approach inherent to the model.[153] The Chairman summarized the issue, and the interrelationship of the conflicting views, as follows:

---

    place. A close study of discussion, bearing in mind the rule of silence, revealed support for the thrust of the article in the single negotiating text.
RSNT, Part II, Text Presented by the Chairman of the Second Committee, Introductory Note, UN Doc. A/CONF.62/WP8/Rev 1 Part II, reprinted in Platzoeder, n. 146, pp. 184–5.

[151] 1982 ICJ Reports 237–238 (dissenting opinion Oda). Both groups were perhaps less concerned, as at UNCLOS II, with methodological purity and more with national interests. While equidistant rules suited the interests of the first group, the second group sought to preserve the largest possible degree of discretionary power under the Convention.

[152] Informal proposal by Bahamas, Barbados, Canada, Colombia, Cyprus, Democratic Yemen, Gambia, Greece, Guyana, Italy, Japan, Kuwait, Malta, Norway, Spain, Sweden, United Arab Emirates, United Kingdom and Yugoslavia (later joined by Cape Verde, Chile, Denmark, Guinea-Bissau and Portugal):
    The delimitation of the Exclusive Economic Zone/Continental Shelf between adjacent or opposite States shall be effected by agreement employing, as a general principle, the median or equidistance line, taking into account any special circumstances where this is justified.
NG 7/2, reprinted in Adede, n. 142, pp. 212–13; Oda, n. 142, p. 238. Cf. also the great number of individual proposals submitted to the Conference, 3 *Official Records* 183 et seq.

[153] Informal proposal by Algeria, Bangladesh, Benin, Burundi, Congo, France, Iraq, Ireland, Ivory Coast, Kenya, Liberia, Libya, Madagascar, Maldives, Mali, Mauritania, Morocco, Nicaragua, Nigeria, Pakistan, Papua New Guinea, Poland, Romania, Senegal, Syria, Somalia, Turkey, Venezuela and Vietnam:
    The delimitation of the Exclusive Economic Zone (or Continental Shelf) between adjacent or/and opposite States shall be effected by agreement, in accordance with equitable principles taking into account all relevant circumstances and employing any methods, where appropriate, to lead to an equitable solution.
NG 7/10, reprinted ibid.

One of the most difficult problems the Negotiating Group has to solve refers to the relation between equitable principles and the equidistance line (some prefer to speak of a method, others of a principle of equidistance) as elements of the definition of delimitation criteria. Although it is generally admitted that the delimitation agreement should be concluded with a view of reaching an equitable solution, and often the employment of the median or equidistance line appears in accordance with equitable principles, the question of 'preference' has, so far, proved too hard to be solved. At this stage of the negotiations the necessary compromise might be within reach, if the Group could agree on a neutral formula.[154]

Based upon informal discussions within NG 7, the Chairman of the Group presented a new compromise formula[155] that was eventually included in ICNT Rev. 2 of 1980.[156] After the Group had refused to include an explicit, but presumably useless, reference to the principle of equality of states, the most significant novel feature of the proposal was a general reference to international law. Draft Articles 74(1) and 83(1) read:

> The delimitation of the exclusive economic zone/continental shelf between States with opposite or adjacent coasts shall be effected by agreement in conformity with international law. Such an agreement shall be in accordance with equitable principles, employing the median or equidistance line, where appropriate, and taking into account of all circumstances prevailing in the area concerned.[157]

This text was not satisfactory to either interest group and was greeted 'with cries of anguish'.[158] Except for the wording, it is difficult to say what substantive changes were made by the new proposal. Subsequent discussions, now under increasing pressure from parties outside the two interest groups, finally led to a formula that was included in the Draft Convention of 28 August 1981.[159] It remained unchanged. Articles 74(1) and 83(1) of the LOS Convention show an identical formulation and read as follows:

> The delimitation of the exclusive economic zone/the continental shelf between States with opposite or adjacent coasts shall be effected by

---

[154] Statement by the Chairman, NG7/26 (March 26, 1979), reprinted in Stiftung für Wissenschaft und Politik, 2 Dokumente der Dritten Seerechtskonferenz der Vereinigten Nationen, Genfer Session 1979, 645–646 (R. Platzoeder ed., 1979).
[155] See in particular Report of the Chairman of Negotiating Group 7, UN Doc. A/CONF. 62/L.47 (24 March 1980) 8 *Official Records* 76. For prior developments and reports see 12 *Official Records* 107, 10 *Official Records* 170.
[156] UN Doc. A/CONF. 62/WP.10/Rev. 2 (11 April 1980).   [157] Ibid., at 48, 51.
[158] Bernard H. Oxman 'The Ninth Session (1980)' (1981) 75 *American Journal of International Law*, 211, 231.
[159] UN Doc. A/CONF. 62/WP. 10/Rev. 3 (22 September 1980).

agreement on the basis of international law as referred to in Article 38 of the Statute of the International Court of Justice, in order to achieve an equitable solution.[160]

The text was secretly worked out by the Irish and Spanish delegations, representing the two groups, and the Fiji Islands, representing the Chair of NG 7. It was an emergency solution in the final hours, and was made available to delegations only a few days before the termination of the Conference. The proposal was hastily adopted for the sake of concluding the Conference, but at the time was hardly considered satisfactory from any point of view or interest.[161]

b. The interpretation of Articles 74(1) and 83(1) of the LOS Convention On the surface, Articles 74(1) and 83(1) of the LOS Convention seem fairly clear. They contain a three-step programme: first, delimitation shall be effected by agreement; second, such agreement shall be based on international law; and third, the result achieved has to provide an equitable solution. Yet, due to the reference to both international law and an equitable solution, the model is much more complex than may appear at first glance.

The provisions do not contain any clear decision on the substantive rules of maritime boundary delimitation. The general law of maritime boundary law is still controversial and the concept of equitable solutions is elusive and without any normative guidance for specific settlement of disputes. From that perspective, the provisions are hardly more than a face-saving device, papering over differences, and drafted in order to secure the overall successful conclusion of the diplomatic conference. The dispute between the schools of thought of equidistance and equitable principles remains. The replacement of any reference to either school by calling upon international law and the requirement of an equitable solution provided a solution that put off facing the complex issue and left it to later attempts at codification, perhaps at a future UNCLOS IV. For such reasons, commentators have widely considered the provisions of long-distance maritime boundaries to be a diplomatic quick fix, which, void of any substance, is a useless and unworkable approach and model.[162] That view is certainly correct to the extent that clear, precise,

---

[160] Platzoeder, vol. II, n. 146, p. 224, 227–8.
[161] Bernard H. Oxman 'The Tenth Session (1981)' (1982) 76 *American Journal of International Law*, 1, 14, 15.
[162] See e.g. Prosper Weil, 'A Propos du droit coutumier en matière de délimitation maritime' in *International Law at the Time of Its Codification, Essays in Honour of*

and directly applicable rules were expected from the conference. It is different if another perspective is chosen.

A somewhat closer analysis of the provisions, however, reveals that there is more substance than generally expected at first glance. The key to a meaningful interpretation is provided if the provisions are no longer considered in traditional terms of directly operational rules and settlement, ready for direct application. It will be seen that the provisions assume different functions and elements that reflect what we shall call the constitutional approach of the Convention in many of its parts and provisions. Partly these functions allow for clear conclusions, described in the two following subparagraphs. Partly they pose complex but interesting problems, particularly with respect to the mandatory or residual nature of the provisions, the relationship of international law and equitable solutions. They also raise issues related to the relationship of the LOS Convention, general international law, other conventions, and implementing delimitation agreements.

In accordance with the principles set forth in Articles 31 and 32 of the Vienna Convention on the Law of Treaties, the interpretation of Articles 74 and 83 mainly depends on the wording and its ordinary meaning, the purpose, and legitimate expectations (good faith). The context of the provisions and their systemic relationship to other articles of the Convention are of particular importance. Also, it will be seen that the case law on maritime boundary delimitation has been of significant influence on the negotiating process of UNCLOS III and the wording of the Articles 74(1) and 83(1).[163] Finally, the *travaux préparatoires* and the history of the negotiations, albeit largely undisclosed and off the record, assist the interpretation to the extent that the competing schools show common values. Still, these are clearly subsidiary elements to be used for interpretation only if no meaningful result is reached on the basis of wording and context.

Roberto Ago (Milan, Dott.: A. Guiffrè Editore, 1987), vol. II, pp. 535, 537 ('La pauvreté extrême de leur contenu matériel'); P. Alexiades, 'The Search for a Panacea for Maritime Boundary Settlement: Equity or Equidistance?' in (1985) *National and International Boundaries*, 813, 815 ('Any formula whereby delimitation will proceed "on the basis of international law ... in order to achieve an equitable solution" seems both superfluous and unworkable'); David J. Attard, *The Exclusive Economic Zone in International Law* (Oxford: Clarendon Press, 1987), p. 223 ('All efforts to produce an effective formula, which did not tilt to one side or another, failed').

[163] See Chapter 6 et passim.

(i) A uniform concept for shelf and EEZ boundaries

The Convention provides a single and uniform concept for both the continental shelf and the EEZ. The wording of both provisions is similar. The concept of Articles 74(1) and 83(1) does not necessarily imply that continental shelf boundaries and EEZ boundaries have to be identical in a particular case. The application of international law under the provisions may produce different lines. However, the identical formulation of the applicable models suggests an absorption of the continental shelf by the EEZ within a 200 nm limit (wherever declared) and the presumption of a single and uniform boundary under the Convention, as found in customary law.[164] This observation has been confirmed by the ruling in *Bangladesh* v. *Myanmar*, where the extension of the adjusted single boundary line beyond 200 nm produced an area that is beyond 200 nm from one state (Bangladesh), but within 200 nm of the state on the other side of the boundary (Myanmar).[165] The Tribunal thus held that the boundary abutting the grey zone delimited the continental shelf only, but did not 'otherwise limit Myanmar's rights with respect to' the EEZ, notably as regards the superjacent waters.[166] Thus, the seabed of the grey area ended up as Bangladesh's continental shelf and the superjacent waters Myanmar's EEZ. The Tribunal left it to each state, to 'exercise its rights and perform its duties with due regard to the rights and duties of the other'.[167]

(ii) The exclusion of unilateral settlement

The Convention prescribes that delimitation shall be effected primarily by agreement. The provisions therefore contain an obligation to negotiate. They establish a *pactum de negotiando*. It does not, however, include an obligation to reach agreement at any cost (*pactum de contrahendo*). Although a literal reading of Articles 74(1) and 83(1) seems to imply that delimitation must be reached by agreement only, it follows from paragraphs 2 of the provisions and general international law that avenues of third party settlements are equally open, failing an agreement.[168]

While the Conference failed to establish compulsory judicial settlement,[169] the dispute should nevertheless be resolved by judicial

---

[164] Chapter 2(IV).   [165] *Bangladesh* v. *Myanmar*, n. 32, paras. 463-4.
[166] Ibid., paras. 471-4.   [167] Ibid., para. 475.
[168] Art. 33 UN Charter; Art. 279 LOS Convention.
[169] For a drafting history of provisions related to dispute settlement of maritime boundary disputes see A. O. Adede, *The System for Settlement of Disputes under the United Nations Convention on the Law of the Sea* (Dordrecht, Boston MA: Martinus Nijhoff, 1987), pp. 165-84; Manner n. 142, pp. 634-8.

settlement. At least under Annex V of the Convention, a dispute is subjected to compulsory conciliation, upon the request of another party under Article 298. Parties rejecting compulsory dispute settlement are therefore under an obligation to negotiate on the basis of results proposed by the commission of conciliation. They are exempted from compulsory conciliation only to the extent that the dispute necessarily involves the concurrent consideration of any unsettled dispute concerning sovereignty or other rights over continental or insular land territory, or if the sea boundary delimitation was settled or is to be settled in accordance with a special bilateral or multilateral agreement binding upon these parties.[170]

Whatever approach states choose in a particular case, it clearly follows that any unilateral determination or abrogation of boundaries of the continental shelf or the EEZ is void under this model. Unilateral claims cannot establish lawful boundaries to neighbouring states. Early experiences with unilateral settlements in the context of the shelf therefore cannot be repeated in the context of the EEZ.[171] This does not exclude tacit agreement by acquiescence, but consent of the parties affected is an essential requirement under these provisions. The result is consistent with general international law and the overall purpose of the Convention.[172] The preamble explicitly states that all matters of maritime law should be settled in a spirit of mutual understanding and co-operation. Also, the principle of negotiated settlement has never been controversial; throughout the Conference, and in accordance with contemporary state practice, it has been understood that maritime boundary delimitation has to be effected jointly by the states concerned.[173]

(iii) Residual or mandatory rules?

A first difficulty relates to the question of whether the model of UNCLOS III is one of residual or mandatory rules. The reference to international law and the goal of an equitable solution in Articles 74(1) and 83(1) seems to suggest that substantive rules (whatever they are) have to be respected and implemented in negotiations as much as in adjudicated settlements on a compulsory basis. Indeed, the intention to link negotiations to substantive standards of law seems to be an essential feature of this

---

[170] Art. 298(1)(a)(i) and (iii); Adede, ibid., pp. 180-2; Manner n. 142, 180-2; Manner, n. 142, pp. 635.
[171] For early unilateral state practice see Chapter 5.
[172] The duty to negotiate and to seek settlement by agreement in customary maritime boundary law is discussed in Chapters 7 and 12.
[173] Cf. proposals of the two competing groups above at n. 152 and n. 153.

model shared with the original concept of the equitable principles of the Truman Proclamation in model 2. States should no longer be free to adopt just any solution under the LOS Convention, but rather they should be bound by substantive standards. Conceptually, this departs from the model of residual rules under the 1958 Convention on the continental shelf.

The failure to achieve directly operational rules, however, has somewhat reduced the realization of mandatory links of negotiations to particular rules. By referring to the much broader notions of international law and equitable solutions, instead of equitable principles or equidistance–special circumstances, the goal was only partly achieved. A closer analysis in the context of other relevant provisions reveals that the application of equitable principles or the equidistance–special circumstances rule remains residual, while the goal and objective of an equitable result is a mandatory requirement to be respected under the Convention in each and every case.

(iv) The requirement to apply international law in negotiations

The idea of negotiations based on law, and thus without the traditional full discretion of parties, was an essential element of negotiations at UNCLOS III. Increased discipline and guidance should be provided not only for judicial settlement, but also for the process and result of negotiated settlements. The text in Articles 74(1) and 83(1) LOS Convention clearly states that delimitation 'shall be effected by agreement on the basis of international law'. The same intention was inherent to the proposals set forth by the competing schools. Both of them sought agreement either based on equidistance or equitable principles.[174] The link was not limited to the formula finally adopted. It can therefore be concluded from the incidents of drafting history available that this element is commonly shared. There was consensus on the point that maritime boundary delimitation must be in accordance with international law. This implies various approaches.

For the first school of thought, reference to international law establishes the link to existing agreements, namely the equidistance–special circumstances model of Article 6 of the 1958 Continental Shelf Convention. For the other school, the formula was not merely linked to the 'application' of international law, but also included the goal and objective of an equitable solution. This reflects the linkage to the principles developed in case law, in particular those cases decided by the ICJ. It

---

[174] Ibid.

is for that reason that explicit reference to Article 38 was insisted upon. Agreements should not depart from the law applied by The Hague Court.[175] It may be expected that referring to and incorporating international law into a treaty may give rise to difficult issues. The rules on boundary delimitation cover the same subject matter as the previously established rules of general law and treaty law (*in pari materiae*). It might be argued that the newer provisions should replace the older ones under general principle of *lex posterior derogat lege priori*. Yet, in the international law of treaties, and unlike many municipal systems, the *lex posterior* rule only applies if there is a conflicting rule.[176] Here this is not the case, as the broad language of Articles 74(1) and 83(1) covers all existing legal models except that of strict equidistance. Moreover, the Convention itself does not stipulate the replacement of the 1958 Conventions. Article 311 prescribes that the LOS Convention prevails over the 1958 Conventions, but that does not mean it replaces them.[177] The Article further states that rights and obligations arising under other agreements, which are not inconsistent with the 1982 Convention, remain unimpaired. It even allows parties to derogate from the Convention, provided this is compatible with the object, purpose and basic principles of this agreement, and that third party rights are not impaired. International agreements expressly permitted under the Convention are not affected. A particular reservation to that principle is only made in Article 311(6) with respect to the common heritage of humankind – a principle that must not be amended.

The Convention therefore explicitly regulates the relationship to existing conventional rules *pari materiae*. The reference to international law in Articles 74(1) and 83(1) not only includes a reference to customary law, but also to Article 6 of the 1958 Convention. Parties to the 1982 Convention and the 1958 Convention are therefore entitled to effect delimitation on the basis of the model of equidistance–special circumstances. Similarly, a court of law adjudicating disputes among such parties has to rely upon that model, unless the parties agree otherwise.

---

[175] Manner, n. 142, p. 639.
[176] See Donald E. Karl, 'Treaties, Conflicts Between Them (1984) 7 EPIL 467, 468; cf. Vienna Convention on the Law of Treaties, Art. 30.
[177] See also Caflischn. 142, 99 (note 61); Manner, n. 142, 640 (either approach possible, but text is leaning toward equitable principles). Symonides, n. 142 38, however, argues that the Convention excludes the application of the model of equidistance – special circumstances. This view in 1984 inaccurately implies that Arts. 74(1) and 83(1) only refer to customary law. It also fails to realize the impact of Art. 311.

Article 293(1) obliges a Court to apply all law not incompatible with this Convention. The result is confirmed by Articles 74(4) and 83(4): where there is an agreement in force between the parties, delimitation shall be effected in accordance with that instrument.

The reference to international law in Articles 74(1) and 83(1), however, includes all sources of law as expressed by Article 38 of the ICJ Statute. It not only includes multilateral agreements and customary law, but also general principles and case law. It equally includes bilateral agreements. Such *ad hoc* agreements (*pactum de negotiando or contrahendo*) are as much a part of international law as referred to in Articles 74(1) and 83(1). Moreover, Article 311(3) of the Convention *expressis verbis* authorizes states to modify or suspend their provisions by agreement, provided that such derogations are not incompatible with the object, purpose and basic principles of the Convention, and that third party rights are preserved. The provision will be discussed shortly, but it can readily be seen that neither of the main competing models incorporated into international law emerged as a basic principle of the Convention in the sense of Article 311(3). This is due to the simple fact that no consensus was found on that matter. It is therefore submitted that states effectively remain free to adopt any approach by consent. They are not limited to established rules and concepts. They may agree to adopt a principled and rule-based approach in accordance with state practice or co-operative schemes, or they may introduce particular considerations not inherent to the body of generally accepted law. States may even agree to resolve the dispute on the basis of *ex aequo et bono* on the grounds that the agreement to agree or a compromise is equally a part of international law. It may be argued that this is a formal argument, yet in Article 293(2), the Convention itself retains the possibility of referring to decisions of this kind. If this model is possible for arbitration, it is difficult to see why parties could not, *a fortiori*, pursue this approach in negotiations as well.

In conclusion, parties remain largely free to choose any agreed approach under the Convention. That is the effect of such a broad reference to the sources of international law as such. They are neither limited to equidistance–special circumstances nor to the model of equitable principles. The Convention therefore does not prescribe mandatory rules as to the application of particular models of delimitation. The models apply as residual rules in negotiations and judicial settlement, provided no agreement was reached to the contrary. Consequently, they apply in default. It is difficult to say whether this effect was in fact intended or even considered by the drafters of the last-minute compromise. It may well be that the will to oblige parties to the Convention to reach settlements in accordance either with the rule of equidistance or the concept of equitable principles remained unimpaired. The language finally adopted, however, and its reading in the context of the provisions discussed, does not allow the exclusion of ad hoc settlements based on agreements among the parties not necessarily consistent with the models of equitable principles or equidistance-special circumstances.[178]

(v) The requirement of equitable solution and respect of third party rights
The situation is different with respect to the third element of the formula, the requirement of an equitable solution. The reference to international law in Articles 74(1) and 83(1) is merely instrumental. It has to be applied, whatever its contents and at the exclusion of unilateral settlement, in order to achieve an equitable solution. Such finality is the most significant feature of the model adopted at UNCLOS III. The goal of achieving an equitable solution is paramount – a perception which also influenced contemporary case law. Being an essential part of the consensus reached, it is submitted that this element, unlike conventional or general international law referred to in the provisions, is the very mandatory element required in all maritime boundary delimitation. Article 311(3) confirms this view. The provision, mentioned before, does not allow for mutually agreed-upon modifications of the objective or purpose of basic principles of the Convention, or for the impairment of third party rights:

Two or more parties to this Convention may conclude agreements modifying or suspending its provisions, applicable solely to the relations between them, provided that such agreements do not relate to those provisions of this Convention, derogation from which is incompatible with the effective execution of the object and the purpose of the Convention, and provided, further, that such agreement shall not affect the application of the basic principles embodied in this Convention and that the provisions of such agreements do not affect the enjoyment by other states parties of their rights or the performance of their obligations under this Convention.

---

[178] See also Rainer Lagoni, 'Interim Measures Pending Maritime Delimitation Agreements' (1984) 78 AJIL 348 ('Only if there is no agreement in force between [the parties] is one referred by paragraph 1 to the principles and rules of delimitation of general international law').

Given the importance of the subject of maritime boundary delimitation at UNCLOS III and for maritime law in general, the achievement of equitable solutions is certainly at the very core of the Convention. It belongs, inter alia, to the prime objectives and purposes of the treaty. It may even be considered to be a fundamental principle of the Convention from which no derogation is allowed. It is paramount. The results achieved, much more than the methods by which they are achieved, are of major interest to the international community and the preservation of peace and justice. For the same world public interests, solutions must not impair third party rights under Article 311(2), in accordance with the principle of *pacta tertiis nec prosunt nec nocent* and the case law. While solutions may be achieved under different titles and models, these purposes and goals are mandatory. The discretionary power of negotiating parties is therefore restricted and subject to the Convention. Parties are no longer free to adopt just any (perhaps inequitable) solution, as they could under a fully residual model. The Convention defines a framework, albeit a vague and broad one. It contains a certain limitation to the freedom of contract. This again is not without any effect on the notion of international law as referred to in Articles 74(1) and 83(1).

The principle of equitable solution stemming from the 1982 Convention cannot be entirely separated from the application of international law. There is conflict between a purely residual rule of Article 6 of the 1958 Convention, and the purpose and goal of equitable solutions. To that extent, the Convention overrides pre-existing freedom of contract by means of Article 311(1). It prevails over international law as far as it is not compatible with the goal of equitable solutions. The conflict may be a theoretical one and without any practical impact. Nevertheless, parties to both the 1958 and the 1982 Conventions are bound to respect the goal of equitable solution whatever the scope of equity will be. There is no room for deviation from this objective under Articles 74(4) and 83(4). Unfortunately, the mandatory character and impact of the objective of an equitable solution depends upon its specification. The norm suffers by the very fact that the notion of equity and an equitable solution are inevitably vague and elusive in the abstract. The wider it is, the larger the discretionary powers remain. The more precise it is, the less scope it allows for variation. The normative weight, and with it any practical importance of a mandatory rule, will therefore depend heavily on whether an operational concretization of the notion can be found.

In conclusion, coastal states are no longer free to adopt any solution on the basis of interests and bargaining powers under this model. The

Convention leaves freedom of contract with respect to the application of international law. However, states do remain free to adopt agreed-upon, different and innovative schemes that are not necessarily consistent with the rules and principles a court of law would have to apply short of an explicit mandate to the contrary. The Convention does not exclude solutions found on the basis of non-legal considerations, as long as the overall result remains within the scope of equity.

(vi) Law and equitable solution: a complex relationship
The relationship of international law to the goal of equitable solutions in Articles 74(1) and 83(1) raises a number of additional, intriguing methodological issues. The problem is of particular importance in negotiations and judicial settlements.

On the one hand, delimitation on the basis of international law implies the application of rules and principles, whatever their precise context. The usual, and pure, operation of the law is one of implementing norms to a particular set of facts. In theory, the result is achieved by this very operation. Articles 74(1) and 83(1) seem to support it when international law is to be applied 'in order to achieve an equitable solution': it implies that the application of international law will produce such a result. It is not simply a matter of defining a particular result, which is then justified by an appropriate application of rules and exceptions.

On the other hand, it is difficult to see why the Convention would then need to emphasize the mandatory goal of an equitable solution, if it merely follows from the operation and process of applying the law. Is it merely a rhetorical reference, since all law aims at justice and equitable solutions?[179] The question is of even more importance since the concept of an equitable solution is the mandatory part to be achieved by this model. This obligation to achieve an equitable result may now even be regarded as part of customary law.[180]

---

[179] Such is the understanding of Jens Evensen, 'The United Nations Convention on the Law of the Seas of December 10, 1982: Its Political and Legal Impact – Present and Future' (1982) 38 *Revue égyptienne de droit international public*, 11, 25. ('Basically, it is the aim of all negotiations, agreements and lawsuits to reach solutions that are equitable').

[180] Marques Antunes, above n. 9, p. 415; David Anderson, 'Developments in Maritime Boundary Law and Practice' in Charney et al. (eds.), *International Maritime Boundaries*, n. 3, vol. V (Colson and Smith (eds.)), pp. 3197–222; see also Chapter 5.

The modification of Article 6 of the 1958 Convention, if applied under the LOS Convention (the requirement to reach an equitable result even if no rule is applied in bilateral agreement), suggests that the result to be achieved is not without any impact on the methods and rules of delimitation to be applied. Yet, the relationship of rules and principles of international law, either conventional or customary, to the concept of an equitable result can hardly be established in the abstract. It depends on the content and density of both these rules and principles and the meaning of equity. Provided that the applicable rules are fairly strict (e.g. the notion of special circumstances would be well defined), and the concept of equitable solution vague, there is hardly a feedback by equity. On the other hand, if rules and principles are vague, but the concept of equitable solutions is well defined, the application of rules is practically defined by the result. In other words, the weight of each element is of importance. It is therefore necessary to examine both sides of the concept in order to define their relationship. A study of the case law will provide further insights into the complex and dialectical relationship of rules, principles and results. It will provide further insight into whether the model of the LOS Convention is one of result-oriented or rule-oriented justice.

c. **Towards a constitutional approach** The model of equitable solution based on international law provides a framework upon which individual boundaries should be agreed to within legal guidelines, the breadth of which still requires definition in more detail. These are mandatory requirements to be respected in subsequent, implementing treaties (*traités exécutoires*). Articles 74(1) and 83(1) are meaningful if, and only if, they are understood and read as norms of a higher rank than specific boundary delimitation agreements. Although the general law of international treaties does not (yet) know a general hierarchy of sources and different treaties, different ranking is nevertheless possible in terms of conventional law.[181] States may decide that a particular instrument prevails over others. Article 311 of the LOS Convention expresses such a will. This is equally implied by Articles 74(1) and 83(1) and preceding drafts, when agreements have to be concluded on the basis of international law, defined in very broad terms,

---

[181] See *Free Zone Case*, PCIJ, Series A No. 22, p. 13; Suzanne Bastid, *Les Traités dans la vie internationale. Conclusion et effets* (Paris: Économica, 1985), p. 163, ('la tendence à ne considérer qu'une hiérachie peut exister entre les traités'). But see Paul Jean-Marie Reuter, *Introduction au droit des traités* (Paris: Armand Colin, 1972), pp. 119–20 ('en effet, il n'y a pas techniquement de traités ayant une valeur supérieure aux autres, la forme constituante n'existe pas en droit international public').

and have to reach an equitable result. The concept is equivalent to Article 103(3) of the UN Charter, establishing the predominance of the Convention over any other treaty.[182]

Without a constitutional understanding, the provisions of Articles 74(1) and 83(1) are indeed meaningless and nonsensical. How could a norm refer to international law, present and future, including the equidistance–special circumstances rule of Article 6 of the 1958 Shelf Convention, or the case law, if itself it would propound the basic substantive rule of law? Calling upon international law in such a norm is itself nonsensical from a traditional perspective.[183] Would it not, under Article 30 of the Vienna Convention on the Law of Treaties, replace any former agreement on the same and identical matter (*pari materiae*), since formally different, and therefore conflicting, rules on the same subject are proposed? Therefore, like the UN Charter, the LOS Convention is a constitutional instrument. Many of its provisions, including those on long-distance maritime boundaries, are not directly operational in the sense that they provide specific rules that do not need any further decision and implementation The provisions are not simply contractual norms in a classical sense; nor are they a settlement in a classical sense, ready for direct application.[184] Instead the provisions delegate decision-making powers.[185] In effect, the provisions are norms of delegation, both to states and to courts or commissions of conciliation More than in the models discussed above, their main function is to allocate authority

---

[182] In the event of a conflict between the obligation of the members of the UN and the present Charter and their obligations under any other international agreement, their obligation under the present charter shall prevail.
   See also Art. 73(2) Vienna Convention on the Consular Relations, which establishes the supremacy of the Convention over bilateral agreements. See Bastid, n. 181, p. 164.

[183] Philip Allott, 'Power Sharing in the Law of the Sea' (1983) 77 *American Journal of International Law*, 1, 22.

[184] Allott, n. 183, p. 22; Bernhard H. Oxman, 'Interests in Transportation, Energy and Environment' in C. Buderi and D. Caron (eds.), *Perspectives on U.S. Policy Toward the Law of the Sea: Prelude to the Final Session of the Third UN Conference on the Law of the Sea*, Proceedings of a Symposium held in 1982, The Law of the Sea Institute Occasional Paper No. 35 (Honolulu: Law of the Sea Institute, University of Hawaii, 1985), p. 95:
   You may be aware of the very famous dictum delivered by the Supreme Court of the United States: 'It is, after all, a constitution that we are expounding'. I do want to emphasize that the Convention on the Law of the Sea should be regarded in many respects as a constitutive document rather than as a settlement.

[185] Allot, n. 184 p. 22.

within a broad framework, which was set out earlier, containing the following basic decisions:

- Delimitation must not be effected unilaterally. Primarily, it has to be sought by agreement, thus including a duty to negotiate in good faith.
- Delimitations are legal operations. They either rely upon existing rules and principles in conventional or customary law, general principles, and specific rights; or upon approaches that have been deliberately and consensually chosen by the parties.
- At any rate, results have to provide equitable solutions. This, as well as the duty to negotiate in good faith and respect of third party rights, is mandatory.

The functions of these principles contained in Articles 74(1) and 83(1) are comparable to those we find in domestic constitutional law: allocation of authority and setting broad principles (such as due process of law or human rights standards) or programmatic targets. They all share the need for specification and individualization in a process which often is at the same time law-applying and law-making, either by legislators, constitutional courts, or other decision makers operating within the realm of the constitution It is also for such reasons that the notion of international law as referred to in Articles 74(1) and 83(1) need not be read in an excessively strict manner. The constitutional character of such reference allows emergent trends and developments to be taken into account, short of making them a part of customary law in a strict sense.[186] The practice of the ICJ will confirm such a broader perception.[187] The constitutional concept also clarifies the mandatory character of the principles discussed before. They prevail over other instruments due to their higher conventional ranking. This is not an application of *jus cogens*, although the term is sometimes – and hardly accurately – used in the context of treaties (consensual *jus cogens*).[188]

The concept of *jus cogens*, as distinct from conventional ranking, is limited to rules of general international law, such as the prohibition of the use of force, basic human rights, and the prohibition of torture and

---

[186] Ibid., speaking in this context (somewhat far reaching) of international law as a 'symbolic formula', including material found in formative sources (such as prenormative state practice, judicial decisions and general principles of law).
[187] Chapters 6, 8, 9–11 et passim.
[188] Georg Schwarzenberger, 'Equity in International Law' (1972) *The Yearbook of World Affairs*, 346, 365.

genocide.[189] Today, the general law of maritime boundaries certainly does not form a part of it. Authors maintain that states are not under any constraint to apply the rules of maritime boundary law as a matter of *jus cogens*, but remain free to adopt any solution under contemporary customary law.[190] Thus it can hardly be a question of norms having effects *ergo omnes*.[191] A member of the international community that is not particularly affected therefore cannot challenge inequitable boundaries between two states. It cannot, of course, be totally excluded that the law and principles of maritime boundary delimitation will become part of *jus cogens*, although this does seem unlikely. The rules, albeit important for the global order and for resources, are hardly so fundamental that any violation renders a decision void *ab initio*. Instead, impairments of a conventional norm of higher ranking obey general rules on state responsibility for violation of international agreements. The LOS Convention does not provide specific rules on the legal effects of violations. Therefore, the general rules on restitution *in integrum*, compensation, reprisals and retorsion are the main remedies. In a bilateral relation, a remedy may be applied if one state unilaterally declares a boundary line, persistently refuses to negotiate in good faith and, finally, refuses to submit the case to mandatory conciliation or arbitration.

---

[189] See *Military and Paramilitary Activities in and against Nicaragua (Nicaragua v. United States of America)*, Merits, Judgment, ICJ Reports 1986, pp. 14, 100, para. 190; *Barcelona Traction, Light and Power Company, Limited (Belgium v. Spain)*, Judgment, ICJ Reports 1970, pp. 3., 32, para. 34; *United States Diplomatic and Consular Staff in Tehran (United States of America v. Iran)*, Judgment, ICJ Reports 1980, pp. 3, 42, para. 91.

See generally e.g. Maria Rita Saulle, 'Jus Cogens and Human Rights' in Università di Genova et al. (eds.), *International Law at the Time of its Codification, Essays in Honour of Roberto Ago*, vol. II, n. 192, pp. 385–96; Hermann Mosler, 'Ius Cogens im Völkerrecht' (1968) 25 *Schweizerisches Jahrbuch für Internationales Recht*, 9; Levan Alexidze, 'Legal Nature of Ius Cogens in Contemporary Law' (1981) III (172) *Recueil des cours*, 219; Giorgio Gaja, 'Jus Cogens Beyond the Vienna Convention' (1981) III (172) *Recueil des cours*, 271; Juan Manuel Gomez Robledo, 'Le ius cogens international: sa genèse, sa nature, ses fonctions' (1981) III (172) *Recueil des cours*, 9; F. A. Mann, 'The Doctrine of Jus Cogens in International Law' in H. Ehmke et al. (eds.), *Festschrift für Ulrich Scheuner zum 70. Geburtstag* (Berlin: Duncker & Humblot, 1973), pp. 399–418.

[190] Weil, n. 162, pp. 535, 548; Jiménez de Aréchaga, 'The Conception of Equity in Maritime Delimitation' in Università di Genova et al. (eds.), *II International Law at the Time of its Codification, Essays in Honour of Roberto Ago* (Milan: Giuffré, 1987), pp. 229, 233.

[191] See Jochen Frowein, 'Die Verpflichtungen erga omnes im Völkerrecht und ihre Durchsetzung' in Rudolf Bernhardt et al. (eds.), *Völkerrecht als Rechtsordnung, Internationale Gerichtsbarkeit, Menschenrechte, Festschrift für Hermann Mosler* (Berlin, Heidelberg: Springer, 1983), pp. 241, 261.

Once an agreement has been reached, the rules on state responsibility may still be invoked by third states if the agreement does not respect the aspirations and claims of that state. Since Article 311(3) explicitly reserves the rights of third parties, delimitations allegedly violating such rights are subject to challenge by third parties affected (*pacta tertiis nec prosunt noc nocent*).[192] The impact of the principle, as well as of Articles 34 to 38 of the Vienna Convention on the Law of the Treaties, are still to be explored. Beyond the obvious case that two states cannot divide areas to which they are not entitled,[193] it is difficult to anticipate all the situations affectingthird party rights affected. Historic fishing rights could be harmed by a particular agreement. Potential access might be impaired. The law of land boundaries hardly knows this kind of problem, and it is well established that the international community generally respects boundaries settled among states in law. With the concept of horizontally shared jurisdiction, delimitation of boundaries has become much more complex. It is no longer necessarily a matter exclusively between two adjacent or opposite neighbouring states.

Under a constitutional doctrine of prevailing agreements, measures available do not nullify an agreement inconsistent with the constitutional framework of the LOS Convention *ab initio*. They do not eliminate an inequitable boundary inconsistent with the provisions of the Convention. A successful challenge merely deploys effects *ex nunc*. Nullification *ab initio* only takes place if one of the situations provided for in Articles 46 to 52 of the Vienna Convention on the Law of Treaties can be shown to exist by the complainant state. In this context, the invalidity *ab initio* of coerced agreements concluded under the use or threat of force in violation of the principles set forth in the United Nations Charter (Articles 2(4) and 51) may be of particular interest.[194] The rule, however, is of limited effect in the present context, as it is of limited retroactivity. In particular, land boundaries established by peace treaties, often essential in the context of modern maritime boundaries, can only be challenged if they were established either after the entry into

---

[192] See generally reports by Christian Tomuschat, Hanspeter Neuhold and Jan Kropholler, *Völkerrechtlicher Vertrag und Drittstaaten (Treaties and Third States): Referate und Thesen mit Diskussion with English summaries of the reports* (Heidelberg: Müller, 1988), p. 179.
[193] See Chapter 11.
[194] See also *Fisheries Jurisdiction (United Kingdom v. Iceland)*, Judgment, ICJ Reports 1973, p. 3, 59.

force of the Convention (27 January 1980) or after the prior, but still blurry, date of emergence of the prohibition of coerced agreements in customary law dating back to the early 1930s (a date, however, that has not been authoritatively established).[195] Also, it should be recalled that the principle of *uti possidetis* in regional territorial boundary law considerably reduces the potential of the exercise of Article 52.[196] As a result, the provision may primarily be effective *pro futuro*, i.e. for the many future EEZ delimitations. Here, it may indeed operate as an important procedural safeguard against excessive political or economic pressures, although the inclusion of such pressures is controversial.[197] Still, it supports the adoption of equitable solutions, and, at the least, deters grossly inequitable boundary delimitations.

The paramount importance of an equitable solution carries with it the danger that the model of the LOS Convention in effect turns into a fully discretionary concept *ex aequo et bono* within the law. Whether this is in fact the case needs further examination. It will be seen that the constitutional and programmatic goal of equitable solutions does not exclude the emergence of guiding rules and principles that provide a framework in

---

[195] See e.g. Bastid, n. 181, p. 96. It is generally accepted to start with the adoption of the 1932 Simpson Doctrine, Quincy Wright, 'The Simson Note of January 7, 1932'(1932) 26 *American Journal of International Law*, 342; it was clearly established by Arts. 2(4) and 51 of the UN Charter, the Friendly Relations Declaration, Res. 2625 (XXV) of 1970 and the Definition of Aggression, Res. 3314 (XXIX) of 1974; Alfred Verdross and Bruno Simma, *Universelles Völkerrecht: Theorie und Praxis* (Berlin: Duncker & Humblot, 2010), p. 380; Reuter, n. 181, p. 150.

[196] See the *Guinea* v. *Guinea-Bissau* case (1986) 25 ILM 251, p. 271, para. 40, invoking the principle and referring to the 1964 Declaration of the Heads of State and Heads of Government of the Organization of African Unity declaring that all Member States pledged to 'respect the boundaries existing at the time they reached their independence'. The tribunal left open the controversial issue whether *uti possidetis* equally applies to existing maritime boundaries, since none was in existence in that particular case. *Guinea* v. *Guinea-Bissau* case ibid., p. 288, para. 85.

[197] Although a motion by developing countries to include an explicit reference of political and economic pressure was rejected at the Vienna Conference, the Final Act contains a declaration condemning 'the threat or use of pressure in any form, whether military, political or economic' in order to press a state into agreement. *Official Records*, Documents of the Conference, UN Doc. A/CONF. 39/11/Add. 2 p. 285. Also, the preamble of the Convention reaffirms the principle of free consent. See Verdross and Simma, n. 195, p. 381.

The problem is that negotiations are often linked to political or economic bargaining. Particular advantages are used as bargaining chips and incentives to achieve agreement. It may therefore be argued that at least excessive and unrelated political and economic pressures exerted to achieve agreement may give rise to nullification.

terms of methodology and substance. Indeed, it will be argued that the body of law has already made considerable normative achievements. The structure of the provisions of the LOS Convention concerning long-distance maritime boundary delimitation not only shows an emerging constitutional concept, but also reflects the deficiencies that are still looming large. It is evident that states stopped half way and left an imperfect constitutional approach, despite the wording finally adopted. The rejection of compulsory jurisdiction over maritime boundary delimitation by most members of the equitable principles group shows how little constitutional thinking has entered practical diplomacy.[198] Indeed, there is a particular need for procedural safeguards in order to achieve equitable results where norms remain vague and open under constitutional doctrine. In addition, all problems related to third party rights and interests and the authoritative application of the Vienna Convention on the Law of Treaties and state responsibility in the field ultimately require compulsory dispute settlement procedures. Without them, a constitutional approach necessarily remains *lex imperfecta*. The LOS Convention of 1982 emerged as a hybrid between traditional patterns of state sovereignty and an emerging constitutional thinking in international law. With a view toward making Articles 74(1) and 83(1) and their inherent goals operational, it is hoped that states will opt for compulsory judicial settlement when acceding to the Convention

IV. Conclusions

The field of long-distance maritime boundary delimitation shows a considerable range of different scientific, technical and legal approaches. Scientific and technical methods extend from strictly geometrical concepts to those involving a considerable amount of discretion A similar range exists with respect to legal approaches, the normativity of which varies considerably. Possibilities range from strict rules, such as mandatory equidistance, to the model of decision-making *ex aequo et bono* based on conferred authority. Although there is a general preference for the model of equidistance–special circumstances and the model of equitable principles, UNCLOS III showed that in the context of codification, none of the models prevailed. Instead, norms of constitutional character

---

[198] Compulsory jurisdiction was largely rejected both by the equitable principles group and by many socialist states that, following a long tradition, stressed the pre-eminence of national sovereignty. See Adede, n. 142, p. 182, and Manner, n. 142, p. 634.

emerged which provide a broad conceptual framework for delimitation, both in procedural and substantive terms. A consensus emerged that the solution must be equitable, regardless of the technical method and legal model applied.

The content and specification of equity and equitable solutions therefore emerges as a central tenet of maritime boundary law. Under any of the models except for strict equidistance, it is necessary to define and learn what the notion of equity should and can be in this field of law. Without clear perceptions of what it means, states and decision makers cannot define what constitutes a solution *ex aequo et bono* under model 1, special circumstances under model 2, equitable principles under model 3, or finally what the appropriate rules of international law are under the model of mandatory equitable solutions based on international law. Given the parameters of highly individualized disputes and constellations, the relative novelty of long-range maritime boundary delimitation, the experiences of UNCLOS I to III and, finally, the constitutional wording of Articles 74(1) and 83(1) of the Convention, the international law of shelf and EEZ boundary delimitation is not yet fully codifiable in terms of a settlement. The result of UNCLOS III, unsatisfactory as it is in respect to specific rules of delimitation, demonstrates that there are areas where the law has to develop, in state practice and judicial decisions on a case-by-case basis. Perhaps, one day, more precise rules will be framed on the basis of experience gained in a process of trial and error. Alternatively, it may lead to a conclusion that any attempt at too specific a codification is not wise. After all, a constitutional approach, contained in Articles 74(1) and 83(1) and 311, may well prove to be more appropriate in a multilateral, global instrument. Instead of having detailed substantive rules, it may be more advisable to improve the constitutional remedies and develop the matter from *lex imperfecta* into a concept that effectively protects all relevant interests. It may be wise to leave the body of substantive rules without attempts to codify them in detailed terms. Given the basic dilemma of rule-making in the present context, efforts at codification should focus on the amelioration of the constitutional setting: this includes the elimination of decision-making *ex aequo et bono* which is not compatible with a legal approach. It would also require a clarification of the relationship of existing agreements, multilateral and bilateral, with the framework of the constitution. Last but not least, it would require the introduction of compulsory dispute settlement in order to achieve a balance of procedural safeguards and necessarily broad substantive rules on the subject.

The following examination of state practice and judicial decisions provides the foundation for an assessment of the concretization of the meaning both of rules of international law and of equitable solutions in the present context. It will examine what has been considered fair and just, and which of the operational models have been mainly used and adopted in general international law, exclusively or in combination. It is hoped that the analysis will provide a basis for more precise and guiding prescriptions, which may gradually fill in the blanks of delegated authority of Articles 74(1) and 83(1) of the LOS Convention.

5

State practice

I. Unilateral acts (proclamations and legislation)

In the process of claims and responses, unilateral practice and acts of states are of importance in assessing the status of methods of delimitation. This chapter analyses the period from 1942 to 1992, comprehensively covering the formative stage of the continental shelf doctrine and of the EEZ. This prepares the ground for assessing state practice and customary international law in Chapter 7, taking into account the record of judicial settlement discussed in Chapter 6.

A. Continental shelf

Unilateral practice and acts reflect two of the three models discussed prior to UNCLOS III. While many documents do not explicitly address the principles and methods of delimitation applied, others refer to the models of equitable principles and the concept of equidistance-special circumstances, albeit with different weight and significance.[1] In no case

---

[1] For state practice on maritime boundary law see generally the seminal five-volume work initiated by Jonathan I. Charney: Jonathan I. Charney et al. (eds.), *International Maritime Boundaries*, 5 vols. (The Hague: Martinus Nijhoff Publishers, 1993–2005), vols. I and II (Charney and Alexander (eds.), 1993), vol. III (Charney and Alexander (eds.), 1998), vol. IV (Charney and Smith (eds.), 2002), vol. V (Colson and Smith (eds.), 2005) (containing the most comprehensive analysis and evaluation of approximately 180 agreements concluded between 1942 and 2004); see also, National Legislation and Treaties Relating to the Law of the Sea, United Nations Legislative Series, ST/LEG/SER.B/19 (1980); ST/LEG/SER. B/16 (1976); National Legislation on Treaties Relating to the Territorial Sea, the Contiguous Zone, the Continental Shelf and the High Seas and to Fishing Conservation of the Living Resources of the Sea, United Nations Legislative Series, ST/LEG/SER.B/2, 2 vols. (1951); Robin Churchill et al. (eds.), *New Directions of the Law of the Sea* (London: Oceana Publications, 1973–1977), vols. I-VI; Myron Nordquist et al. (eds.), *New Directions in the Law of the Sea* (London: Oceana Publications, 1980–1981), vols. VII-XI; Kenneth R. Simmonds (ed.), *New Directions in the Law of the Sea* (London: Oceana Publications, 1983 and subsequent supplements), vols. XII ff.; Benedetto Conforti and Giampiero Francalanci (eds.), *Atlante dei Confini Sottomarini* –

was the concept of the legal vacuum *(ex aequo et bono)* found to be formally applied.

(i) Given the early uncertainty of the law on maritime boundary delimitation during the 1950s, it is hardly surprising that most of the post World War II proclamations on the shelf did not address the issue of boundary delimitation at all, or merely referred to settlement by agreement. They did not indicate any standards of delimitation. The 1964 declaration of the Federal Republic of Germany on the continental shelf is an example it point. It refers to international agreement[2] and thus implicitly to general international law to the extent that boundaries will be settled in court.

(ii) Several states, although not many, explicitly referred to equidistance or the median line. Iraq is an example in point.[3] Norway claimed rights of exploration and exploitation of the soil and the subsoil 'within as well as outside the maritime boundaries otherwise applicable, but not beyond the median line in relation to other States'.[4] Another form of reference to the median line was used in terms of a residual rule by Italy to be applied pending agreement.[5] This approach was adopted by all states whose proclamations or laws explicitly referred to Article 6 of the 1958 Continental Shelf Convention.[6]

(iii) Several early texts took up the concept of equitable principles, founded by the 1945 Truman Proclamation.[7] One example includes

---

Atlas of the Seabed Boundaries, Part I (Milan: Giuffrè, 1979); Benedetto Conforti et al. (eds.), *Atlante dei Confini Sottomarini – Atlas of the Seabed Boundaries,* Part II (Milan: Giuffrè, 1987); Faraj Abdullah Ahnish (ed.), *The International Law of Maritime Boundaries and the Practice of States in the Mediterranean Sea* (Oxford University Press, 1994); Edward Duncan Brown, *Sea-Bed Energy and Minerals: The International Legal Regime,* 3 vols. (The Hague: Martinus Nijhoff, 1992), vol I: The Continental Shelf.

[2] '1. ... The detailed delimitation of the German continental shelf in relation to the continental shelf of foreign states shall be subject of agreement with those States.' National Legislation and Treaties related to the Law of the Sea, United Nations Legislative Series, ST/LEG/SER.B/15, 351 (1970).

[3] Proclamation of 10 April 1958, 'adherence to international practice ... and to the principle of equidistance'. See ST/LEG/SER.B/15, n. 2, p. 369.

[4] Act of 21 June 1963 Relating to Exploration and Exploitation of Submarine Natural Resources. ST/LEG/SER.B/15, n. 2, p. 363.

[5] Act No. 613 of 21 July 1967, Article 1(3). ST/LEG/SER.B/15, n. 2, p. 370.

[6] Declaration of 23 October 1968, p. 772. See also United Nations Legislative Series, ST/LEG/SER.B/18, pp. 153–4 (1976), including the German Democratic Republic, Denmark, Poland and the USSR on the Baltic Sea.

[7] 'Proclamation No. 2667, Policy of the United States with Respect to the Natural Resources of the Subsoil and Sea Bed of the Continental Shelf, 28 Oct. 1945', reprinted in Marjorie M. Whiteman, *Digest of International Law* (Washington DC: Government Printing Office,

the British sponsored 1949 Proclamation by the Arabian Gulf States.[8] This document, however, substantially differs from the United States' precedent to the extent that delimitation was not to be settled by agreement. Instead, it was to be settled unilaterally, as the Abu Dhabi Proclamation said, 'on equitable principles by us after consultation with the [Bahrain] neighbouring states'.[9] One of the proclamations employed the term 'just principles',[10] which is related to the model of equity. The term was later equally used in proclamations by Iran[11] and the Philippines.[12]

B. Fisheries and exclusive economic zones

The problem of boundary delimitation and the standards applicable more frequently were addressed in proclamations and laws relating to the establishment of the EEZ or exclusive fishing zones up to 200 nm. These proclamations and laws reflect an increasing experience in the field, particularly accelerated by the rulings of the ICJ and debates at UNCLOS III during the 1970s. Again, the review reveals a great variety of different approaches. They are no longer limited to the three models discussed prior to UNCLOS III. There are also examples invoking international law as a basis for delimitation. While most proclamations and laws rely upon delimitation by agreement, there are still a number of cases calling upon unilateral determination. The following groups may be distinguished:

(i) Texts calling for a solution by negotiations and agreement, yet without indicating any guiding principles or methods of delimitation. Examples include the economic zone declared by France,[13] the Federal Republic of Germany,[14]

1965), vol. IV, pp. 740, 756. For the twin-proclamation on fisheries see ibid., 954, United Nations Legislative Series ST/LEG/SER.B, 38 (1951).

[8] See proclamations by Saudi Arabia, Ajman, Bahrain, Dubai, Kuwait, Qatar, Ras al Khaimah, all using 'equitable principles'. ST/LEG/SER.B/15, n. 2, pp. 22–27. For analysis see e.g. Ali A. El Hakim, *The Middle Eastern States and the Law of the Sea* (Manchester University Press, 1979), p. 31 ff.; Husain M. Al-Baharna, *The Arabian Gulf States, Their Legal and Political Status and their International Problems* (Beirut: Librairie du Liban, 1975), p. 278 ff.

[9] ST/LEG/SER.B/15, n. 2, p. 22.
[10] Proclamation by Bahrain, ST/LEG/SER.B/15, n. 2, p. 25.
[11] Delimitation 'conformément aux règles de l'équité', ST/LEG/SER.B/15, n. 2, p. 366.
[12] Determination 'in accordance with legal and equitable principles', ST/LEG/SER.B/15, n. 2, p. 422.
[13] Decree No. 77–130 of 11 February, 1977, Churchill et al., *New Directions*, vol. V, n. 1, p. 303.
[14] Proclamation of 21 December 1976, ST/LEG/SER.B/19, n. 1, pp. 211–12.

Mexico[15] and Venezuela.[16] Closely related to this model are texts that refer to the United Nations Charter, or regional instruments, in order to stress the need for peaceful settlement, yet again without indicating any substantive principles or methods to be applied. This approach was utilized by the Declaration of Santo Domingo[17] and during the African States Regional Seminar on the Law of the Sea.[18]

(ii) Texts defining the boundary unilaterally by means of co-ordinates of longitude and latitude. This approach, without indicating any principles of delimitation, has been applied by a number of states, using different methods of definition: Canada,[19] Ireland,[20] the United States (in the Gulf of Maine area),[21] Maldives[22] and Mexico.[23] The Seychelles defined their boundary by reference to charts,[24] and Kenya unilaterally made its delimitation by using a parallel of latitude.[25]

(iii) Texts referring to the equidistance or the median line to be applied as a mandatory rule. Such cases include:

---

[15] Art. 27 of the Mexican Constitution, as amended by Decree of 26 January 1976, ST/LEG/SER.B/19, n. 1, pp. 232, 234.

[16] Law Establishing a 200 Nautical Miles Outer Limit of the Territorial Sea of Venezuela, 26 July 1978, Article 2(2). Nordquist et al. (ed.), *New Directions*, vol. VIII, n. 1, p. 29; ST/LEG/SER.B/19, n. 1, p. 261.

[17] Declaration on the Continental Shelf, para 4; Churchill et al., *New Directions*, n. 1, vol. I, p. 247.

[18] Conclusions in the General Report of the African States Regional Seminar on the Law of the Sea, Yaounde, 20–30 June 1972, paras. 6 and 7; Churchill et al., *New Directions*, n. 1, vol. I, p. 250.

[19] Fishing Zones of Canada (Zones 4 and 6) Order (1976), (1976) 15 ILM, 1372 ff, including the Gulf of Maine; see *Delimitation of the Maritime Boundary in the Gulf of Maine Area (Canada v. United States of America)*, Judgment, ICJ Reports 1984, 284, para. 71; Arctic Pollution Prevention Act (1970), ST/LEG/SER.B/16, n. 1, p. 183.

[20] Maritime Jurisdiction (Exclusive Fishery Limits) Order (1976) (corresponding, according to Art. 4 to an 'equitable equidistant line'), ST/LEG/SER.B/19, n. 1, p. 213.

[21] Federal Register of 4 November 1976; see ICJ Reports 1984, p. 284, para. 70.

[22] Law No. 30/76 of 5 December 1976 relating to the Exclusive Economic Zone of the Republic of Maldives, Art. 11, ST/LEG/SER.B/19, n. 1, pp. 230–1. The agreement between India and the Maldives was signed later, on 28 December 1976. See Appendix I, Table A.1, No. 60, in Charney et al., *International Maritime Boundaries*, n. 1, vol. II (Charney and Alexander), Report Number 6-8.

[23] Decree of 4 June 1976 Establishing the Outer Limit of the EEZ of Mexico, ST/LEG/SER.B/19, n. 1, p. 235. The maritime boundary Agreement between Cuba and Mexico was only signed later, on 26 July 1976. See Appendix I, Table A.1, No. 58, in Charney et al., *International Maritime Boundaries*, n. 1, vol. I (Charney and Alexander), Report Number 2-8.

[24] The Exclusive Economic Zone Order 1978, ST/LEG/SER.B/19, n. 1, pp. 230–1.

[25] Proclamation by the President of the Republic of Kenya of 28 February 1979, Article 1(a) and (b), ST/LEG/SER.B/19, n. 1, pp. 228–9.

Fiji,[26] Norway,[27] Morocco,[28] New Zealand[29] and the Soviet Union, specifying particular geographical areas of application.[30]

(iv) Texts referring to equidistance or the median line to be applied as a residual rule, pending or failing agreement to the contrary. Such cases include: Barbados,[31] Comoros,[32] Denmark,[33] Guyana,[34] German Democratic Republic,[35] Iceland,[36] India,[37] Japan,[38] Nigeria,[39] Portugal,[40] Spain[41] and Yemen.[42] These states follow the model of the 1958 Continental Shelf Convention.

[26] The Fiji Marine Space Act of 1977, Art. 3(3) and (4). Nordquist et al. (eds.), *New Directions*, vol. VII, n. 1, p. 391.
[27] Law No. 91 of 17 December 1976, Relating to the Economic Zone of Norway, Art. 1(2), ST/LEG/SER.B/19, n. 1, p. 241('not beyond the median line').
[28] Moroccan Law (Dahir) No. 1-81, 8 April 1981, Art. 11; referred to by Judge ad hoc Jens Evensen, dissenting opinion, *Continental Shelf (Tunisia v. Libyan Arab Jamahiriya)*, Judgment, ICJ Reports 1982, p. 285, para. 7.
[29] New Zealand Territorial Sea and Exclusive Zone Act, No 28, 1977, Sec. 9(2)(a), Nordquist et al. (eds.), *New Directions*, vol. VII, n. 1, p. 440; ST/LEG/SER.B/19, n. 1, p. 240.
[30] Decision No. 1963 of 24 February 1977 of the Council of Ministers of the USSR on the Introduction of Provisional Measures to Protect the Living Resources and Regulate Fishing in the Areas of the Pacific and Arctic Oceans Adjacent to the Coast of the USSR, ST/LEG/SER.B/19, n. 1, p. 255 (an exception was made for the historical boundaries based on the Russian–American Treaty of 18 (30) March 1867 in the Bering and Chukotsk Seas and the Arctic Ocean).
[31] Marine Boundaries and Jurisdiction Act 1978-3, Art. 3(3) and (4), Nordquist et al. (eds.), *New Directions*, vol. VII, n. 1, p. 337.
[32] Ordinance No. 76–038 of 15 June 1976, Art. 3, ST/LEG/SER.B/19, n. 1, pp. 15–16.
[33] Act No. 507 of December 1976, Art. 1(2), ST/LEG/SER.B/19, n. 1, p. 192 ('failing agreement to the contrary').
[34] Maritime Boundaries Act, No. 10, June 1977, Art. 35, ST/LEG/SER.B/19, n. 1, p. 41.
[35] Decree of 22 December 1977 (concerning the Baltic Sea), Art. 2(1), ST/LEG/SER.B/19, n. 1, p. 206.
[36] Law No. 41 of 1 June 1979 concerning the Territorial Sea, the Economic Zone and the Continental Shelf, Art. 7, ST/LEG/SER.B/19, n. 1, pp. 43, 45. See also 'Iceland: Law Concerning the Territorial Sea, The Economic Zone and the Continental Shelf' (1979) 18 ILM, 1504.
[37] The Territorial Waters, Continental Shelf, Exclusive Economic Zone and other Maritime Zones Act 1976, Art. 9(1); Churchill et al., *New Directions*, vol V, n. 1, pp. 305, 313; ST/LEG/SER.B/19, n. 1, pp. 47, 52.
[38] Law No. 31 of 2 May 1977, Art. 3(2) and (3), ST/LEG/SER.B/19, n. 1, p. 215.
[39] Exclusive Economic Zone Decree 1978, No. 28, Art. 1(2), Nordquist et al. (eds.), *New Directions*, vol. VII, n. 1, p. 474.
[40] Act No. 33/77 of 28 May 1977, Art. 2(2), Nordquist et al. (eds.), *New Directions*, vol. VIII, n. 1, p. 19, ST/LEG/SER.B/19, n. 1, p. 93.
[41] Law 15/1978 of 20 February, Art. 2; Nordquist et al. (eds.), *New Directions*, vol. VIII, n. 1, p. 19, ST/LEG/SER.B/19, n. 1, pp. 250–1.
[42] Act No. 45 of 17 December 1977, sec. v. Art. 17; Nordquist et al. (eds.), *New Directions*, vol. VII, n. 1, p. 57, ST/LEG/SER.B/19 n. 1, pp. 21, 25.

(v) Texts referring to equitable principles as the foundation of delimitation to be applied. The only document found, however, which explicitly restated that model was the 1983 Reagan Proclamation on the Exclusive Economic Zone, that reaffirmed the approach of the 1945 Truman Proclamation as the modern approach in the United States:

> In cases where the maritime boundary with a neighboring state remains to be determined, the boundary of the Exclusive Economic Zone shall be determined by the United States and the other States concerned in accordance with equitable principles.[43]

In the light of the prominence of this model in international law, it is remarkable that proclamations did not use it more frequently.

(vi) Texts referring to international law in general as a basis for delimitation. This model was chosen by Kenya in its draft articles on the EEZ (in combination with a reference to the United Nations Charter and regional organizations).[44] It was also employed by the Bahamas[45] and Vietnam (including a reference to the respect of independence and sovereignty as a basis for settlement).[46]

In conclusion, unilateral state practice both on the shelf and the EEZ predominantly shows a preference for delimitation by agreement. The model of legal vacuum has never been invoked. Where substantive rules are mentioned, unilateral state practice developed, in quantitative terms, a preference for the model of equidistance–special circumstances (residual or mandatory) while examples that use the concept of equitable principles remained a minority. No support could be found in the period under review for the concept of delimitation based on international law in order to achieve an equitable solution. Since the predominant references to equidistance–special circumstances were made prior to the adoption of Articles 74(1) and 83(1) of the LOS Convention, they cannot be read as supporting a customary adoption of that model in state practice; such a process was frustrated by the adoption of the model of equitable solution in the multilateral negotiations of UNCLOS III.

---

[43] Proclamation No 5030, entitled 'Exclusive Economic Zone of the United States of America' (10 March 1983) (1983)77 *American Journal of International Law*, 619, 622, (1983) 22 ILM 461.
[44] UN Doc. A/AC. 138/S/C/II/L.10. (1972), Art. VIII; (1973) 12 ILM 33.
[45] Bahamas Fisheries Resources (Jurisdiction and Conservation) Act 1977, Sec. 11, ST/LEG/SER.B/19, n. 1, pp. 179, 184.
[46] Socialist Republic of Vietnam Statement on the Territorial Sea, The Contiguous Zone, the Exclusive Economic Zone, and the Continental Shelf of Vietnam, 12 May 1977; para. 7, Nordquist et al. (eds.), *New Directions*, vol. VIII, n. 1, p. 36.

II. Maritime boundary delimitation agreements

The following analysis relies upon a sample of 120 long-distance maritime boundary agreements (excluding territorial sea or contiguous zone delimitations, as well as the establishment of purely joint or common zones), which were concluded between 1942 and 1992. They establish a total of 132 boundaries and are listed in Appendix I of the present study.[47] Subsequent agreements are not systematically taken into account in this study.[48] The period and numbers available are believed to be sufficiently representative for the forming stage of customary international law.

Fifty-eight of these agreements exclusively relate to the continental shelf. Forty-two agreements relate to the water column, including fishing zones or EEZs. Finally, twenty-one agreements delimitate an all-purpose, overall maritime boundary, which includes the soil and the water column, providing that an EEZ had been declared.[49] With the development of the EEZ, agreements increasingly opted to adopt such all-purpose boundaries.[50] In the 2001 *Qatar/Bahrain* case, the ICJ observed that the concept of a single maritime boundary stems from state practice.[51] This trend is likely to continue for the reasons already discussed.[52]

---

[47] The sample of agreements is based on the compilation presented by Canada at the ICJ in the 1984 *Gulf of Maine* case. Annexes to the Reply submitted by Canada, Pleadings, vol. I, State Practice, 12 December 1983, a collection presented by counsel for Libya in the 1984 *Libya–Tunisia Continental Shelf* case, Pleadings, as well as Conforti and Francalanci, *Atlas of the Seabed Boundaries*, Part I, n. 1 and Conforti et al., *Atlas of the Seabed Boundaries*, Part II, n. 1; and Limits in the Seas (The Office of the US Geographer, ed. 1969); and Charney et al., *International Maritime Boundaries*, n. 1.

[48] For an updated list of Agreements cf. Wikipedia, List of Maritime Boundary Treaties, http://en.wikipedia.org/wiki/List_of_maritime_boundary_treaties (last accessed February 2012).

[49] It may be remembered that the EEZ, unlike the continental shelf zone, requires an act of will to be established, see Chapter 2(III).

[50] All-purpose boundaries were often negotiated between the United States and its neighbours, the Gulf of Maine boundary being the most prominent example. See Mark B. Feldman and David A. Colson, 'The Maritime Boundaries of the United States' (1981) 75 *American Journal of International Law*, 729, 742; Edward J. Collins and Martin Rogoff, 'The International Law of Maritime Boundary Delimitation' (1982) 34 *Maine Law Review*, 1, 14–24.

[51] *Maritime Delimitation and Territorial Questions between Qatar and Bahrain (Qatar v. Bahrain)*, Merits, Judgment, ICJ Reports 2001, p. 93, para. 173.

[52] Anderson observed in 2005 that '[s]ome older agreements relating solely to the continental shelf remain in force, but the only new ones having this limited scope relate to areas beyond the 200 n.m. limit' (David H. Anderson, 'Developments in Maritime Boundary Law and Practice' in Charney and Alexander, *International Maritime Boundaries*, n. 1, vol. V (Colson and Smith), pp. 3197, 3210). However, states still

Tables 5.1, 5.2 and 5.3 flow from an analysis of the agreements from 1942 to 1992 from three perspectives. With a view toward assessing the practical importance and impact of different models and methods of delimitation, indications in agreements as well as effective applications are considered. Also, the impact of the 1958 Shelf Convention is examined.

A. Indications in agreements

Table 5.1 shows a quantitative distribution of models and methods called upon in the sample agreements: 98 of the 120 agreements contain an explicit indication of a particular model (positive indication); 36 treaties remain silent (negative indication); 14 agreements contain two different references.[53] Altogether, 134 indications (positive and negative) were found.

Table 5.1. *Principles or methods indicated in 120 agreements*

None	36 (26.9%)
Equidistance (incl. minor modifications)	23 (17.2%)
Median line (incl. minor modifications)	22 (16.4%)
Equity	20 (14.9%)
Parallel of latitude	12 (10%)
Straight line/Azimuth	11 (8.2%)
Perpendicular to coastal line	1 (0.7%)
Others (ad hoc constructions)	9 (6.7%)
Total indications	134 (100%)

refer to the EEZ and the continental shelf when they establish single maritime boundaries up to 200 nm as separate regimes (Cissé Yacouba and Donald McRae, 'The Legal Regime of Maritime Boundary Agreements', in Charney et al., ibid., pp. 3285–7). This may be due to caution on behalf of states, which might have future claims of continental shelves beyond 200 nm in mind, since the definition of the continental shelf in Art. 76 UNCLOS refers to 'the sea-bed and subsoil of the submarine areas that extend beyond the territorial sea', including thereby the area within 200 nm as well as the area outside 200 nm.

[53] The difference between the number of agreements (120) and number of indications (134, positive and negative) is explained by the fact that 14 agreements contain 2 indications (see Appendix I, Table A.1, Nos. 21, 29, 36, 42, 57, 63, 65, 81, 83, 85, 90, 95, 100, 114).

The absence of any indication of method in almost one-third of all agreements does not imply the absence of a particular method applied. Agreements may simply contain the results of the negotiations, and parties may well have worked on the basis of an agreed-upon method. Table 5.1 indicates that equidistance and the median line are clearly the most prominent methods invoked, together used in a total of 45 agreements (33.6 per cent). These are followed by equity or equitable principles in 20 agreements (14.9 per cent). The latter have been referred to mostly in the more recent years under review, presumably due to the educational process of UNCLOS III. Between 1978 and 1991, 16 of 53 agreements (30.2 per cent) call upon equity in one form or another. However, recourse to equity is not necessarily meant to exclude delimitation on the basis of equidistance, if this method would produce an equitable result.[54] Since equity or equitable principles are a broader concept than equidistance, and may include it, indications in agreements are not conclusive for the determination of the actual use of the different approaches. It nevertheless shows that if states chose to indicate a method, they most frequently named the median or equidistance line, leaving equity in an increasingly important minority. Other methods clearly appear less frequently.

B. Models and methods applied

More important and significant than the principles and methods invoked by the agreements are the results achieved and effected by them. The analysis in Table 5.2 based on the maps reproduced in Appendix II shows the distribution and application of different legal models and methods applied in 120 sample agreements. Given the fact

---

[54] See e.g. The French–Tonga Agreement of 11 November 1980, Conforti et al., *Atlas of the Seabed Boundaries*, Part II, n. 1, p. 119; Charney et al., *International Maritime Boundaries*, n. 1, vol. I (Charney and Alexander), Report Number 5-8, which states in the preamble:
> Le Gouvernement de Tonga ayant proposé que cette délimitation soit effectuée selon la méthode de l'équidistance; le Gouvernement français ayant accepté cette proposition, conforme dans le cas présent à l'application de principes équitables.

See also the French-Santa Lucia agreement of 4 March 1981, Charney et al., *International Maritime Boundaries*, n. 1, vol. I (Charney and Alexander), Report Number 2-10 (with the two governments: 'Considérant que l'application de la méthode de l'équidistance constitue dans ce cas un mode équitable de délimitation').

Table 5.2. *Methods applied and effected in 120 sample agreements effecting 131 applications of methods*

Method	Opposite	Adjacent	Mixed	Total
Equidistance	27 (38%)	4 (16%)	20 (57.1%)	51 (38.9%)
Equidistance (mod.)	22 (31%)	4 (16%)	3 (8.6%)	29 (22.1%)
Non-equidistant	22 (31%)	17 (68%)	12 (34.3%)	51 (39.0%)
Total	71 (100%)	25 (100%)	35 (100%)	131

that 10 agreements apply 2 models[55] and 1 agreement applies to 3,[56] a total of 131 applications resulted.

Table 5.2 shows that equidistance was applied (either strictly or in a modified form) in more than half of all the delimitations effected (61 per cent). Fifty-one agreements (39 per cent) relied on non-equidistant delimitations. Attention should be paid to the fact that non-equidistant methods clearly prevail over equidistance in geographical configurations of adjacent coasts. The sample suggests that equidistance has been most successful in opposite and mixed configurations, employed respectively in 69 per cent and 65.7 per cent of all cases. Simultaneously, non-equidistant methods prevailed in 68 per cent of all adjacent cases, and showed a considerable presence in mixed configurations (34.3 per cent). Taken together, these results suggest that delimitation with adjacent or mixed coastal constellations often requires particular solutions that cannot rely upon the mathematics of equidistance.

C. The impact of the 1958 Shelf Convention equidistance–special circumstances rule

It may be of some interest to evaluate the impact of Article 6 of the 1958 Convention on the Continental Shelf for the parties to that agreement. Looking at 111 agreements concluded among the parties since the Convention entered into force on 10 June 1964, 42 agreements delimitating 45 boundaries were completed. This amounts to a total of 40.5 per cent of all maritime boundary agreements and to 77.6 per cent of the 58 agreements of the sample strictly relating to the continental shelf.

---

[55] Nine of the sample agreements establish two different boundaries (see Appendix I, Table A.1, Nos. 29, 59, 70, 101, 102, 105, 107, 108 and 113); one of them applies to different segments of the line (see No. 42).

[56] See Appendix I, Table A.1, No. 112.

Table 5.3. *Application of Article 6 of the 1958 Shelf Convention*

Method	1	2	3	4
Strict equidistance	22	48.9%	19.8%	37.9%
Equidistance modified	8	17.8%	7.2%	13.8%
Agreed, non-equidistance	15	33.3%	13.5%	25.9%
Total	45	100%	40.5%	77.6%

1. Percentage of agreements concluded under the Convention.
2. Percentage of total of 111 boundary agreements concluded since the entry into force of the Convention (1964–1991).
3. Percentage of all maritime boundary agreements since the entry into force of the Convention (1964–1991).
4. Percentage of total of 58 agreements exclusively related to shelf delimitation since the entry into force of the Convention (1964–1991).

Table 5.3 indicates that the combined equidistance–special circumstances rule of the 1958 Convention is of considerable importance, but that it has not clearly emerged as the dominant factor in maritime boundary delimitation. Between 1964 and 1992, equidistance (strict or modified) under the Convention has been applied in 51.7 per cent of all continental shelf delimitations and in 27 per cent of all maritime boundary agreements (including EEZ and all-purpose boundaries).[57] Although conceived merely as a residual rule, equidistance was applied in two-thirds of all delimitations under the 1958 Convention. This fact shows that states can indeed achieve negotiated settlements under particular rules of international law in a considerable number of scenarios. Further, it is evident that the 1958 Convention also served as an example to states that were not parties to the instrument. It certainly stimulated the use of equidistance, which served in 80 out of a total 131 cases (61 per cent) of delimitation, as Table 5.2 indicates.

D. Assessment and former studies

The present evaluation, of course, does not achieve more than a rough approximation. Models and methods applied cannot be coded and

---

[57] The indications of percentage result from additions of positions 1 and 2 of col. 3, col. 2 and col. 1, respectively, of Table 5.3. A relatively small overall impact of Art. 6 of the 1958 Shelf Convention was also found by S. P. Jagota, 'Maritime Boundary' (1981) 171 *Recueil des cours* II, 85, 131–2; Sang-Myon Rhee, 'Equitable Solutions to the Maritime Boundary Dispute between the United States and Canada in the Gulf of Maine' (1981) 75 *American Journal of International Law*, 590, 605–6.

evaluated very precisely in quantitative terms: firstly, because a considerable number (one-third) of all settlements are purely negotiated solutions, which do not indicate any principles or methods applied; and secondly, because what appears on the map to be an application of a particular method may in fact be a purely negotiated solution, a result of a *quid pro quo* based on political expediency, as the history of the 1978 US–Mexican agreement indicates.[58] Most negotiations are, at least for academic purposes, off the record. The intentions of states are therefore difficult to assess.

Given the imponderable nature of these uncertainties, it may be useful to compare results achieved here with previous studies of the subject. They generally show a higher percentage of agreements based on equidistance than this study. Compared to each other, however, assessments vary considerably. This is not only due to the fact that the problem of imponderables always exists. Variations are also due to the different samples and time periods chosen. Nevertheless, overall, the findings of others reaffirm the results found above.

A review of fifty agreements on the continental shelf by Rüster, published in 1977, concluded that some forty agreements examined rely on the median or equidistance line (80 per cent). Only ten were 'negotiated' solutions (20 per cent).[59]

Gounaris concluded in the same year that from a total of sixty-six continental shelf boundary agreements, twenty-eight (42.4 per cent) applied equidistance and twenty-two (33.3 per cent) apply modified equidistance methods, while only three agreements (3.5 per cent) rely upon equity, twelve agreements (18.2 per cent) used other methods, and one treaty was without any positive indication.[60] The same author found in 1980 a total of seventy-three agreements, of which thirty (41.1 per

---

[58] The agreement favoured the United States in the Pacific by using US islands as base points. Mexico is favoured in the Gulf of Mexico by using small Mexican islands as base points. The Treaty, signed 4 May 1978, 'Mexico–United-States: Four Bilateral Agreements' (1978) 17 ILM, 1056; Charney et al., *International Maritime Boundaries*, n. 1, vol. I (Charney and Alexander), Report Number 1-5, however, was later withdrawn from consideration by the US Senate, and a new study on hydrocarbon resources in the Gulf was ordered, Feldman and Colson, n. 50, 743–4.

[59] Bernd Rüster, *Die Rechtsordnung des Festlandsockels* (Berlin: Duncker und Humblot, 1977), p. 399 et seq.

[60] Emmanuel Gounaris, 'Die Aufteilung des Festlandsockels unter dem Adriatischen und Ionischen Meer zwischen Griechenland und Italien vom 24.5.1977 und die Internationale Praxis' (1978) 31 *Revue hellénique de droit international*, 191.

cent) relied on equidistance, 22 (30.1 per cent) on modified equidistance, and seventeen agreements (23.3 per cent) relied on other methods.[61]

In a 1985 study, Jagota concluded from a sample of seventy-five agreements that forty-eight (64 per cent) applied equidistance, seventeen (22.7 per cent) rely on a modified equidistance line, and only ten (13.3 per cent) are 'negotiated' solutions.[62] An expanded version covering a hundred agreements (twelve of which deal with the territorial sea and four establish joint or common zones) shows a total of sixty-four median or equidistance boundaries, eighteen modified median lines, fourteen non-equidistant (negotiated) solutions and four joint or common zones.[63]

An evaluation of state practice by Canada in the Gulf of Maine argued in support of equidistance, showing that forty-four agreements (45.4 per cent) rely on strict or simplified equidistance (four between adjacent, sixteen between opposite and twenty-four in mixed constellations), twenty-four agreements (24.7 per cent) were considered using a modified equidistance line, with only twenty agreements (29.9 per cent) being non-equidistant.[64] The United States, in opposing a strict application of equidistance, argued that merely 37 per cent of all agreements in force were based exclusively upon a strict application of equidistance.[65]

The most comprehensive analysis, based upon detailed reports from 134 agreements effected by the project of the American Society of International Law was presented by Leonard Legault and Blair Hankey in 1993. The results of their analyses are summarized in Table 5.4.[66]

In 2006 Tanaka concluded on the basis of the same material, but short of distinguishing strict and modified applications of the method, that 83 per cent of all continental shelf delimitation between opposite coasts are based upon equidistance, and 46 per cent of agreements in adjacent configurations. In hybrid cases, the method was used in 88 per cent of cases. Single maritime boundaries in opposite configurations were found to rely upon equidistance in 82 per cent and in adjacent configurations in 50 per cent of the agreements. In hybrid cases, he found 90 per cent of all purpose boundary agreements to be based upon equidistance. On the

---

[61] Emmanuel Gounaris, 'The Delimitation of the Continental Shelf of Islands: Some Obervations' (1980) 33 *Revue hellénique de droit international* 111.
[62] See Jagota, n. 57, 131.   [63] See ibid., p. 122.   [64] Canadian Reply, n. 47, pp. 23–34.
[65] *Delimitation of the Maritime Boundary in the Gulf of Maine Area (Canada v. United States of America)*, Counter Memorial of the United States of America, 28 June 1983, Pleadings p. 145, para. 217.
[66] Leonard H. Legault and Blair Hankey, 'Method, Oppositeness and Adjacency, and Proportionality in Maritime Boundary Delimitation' in Charney et al., *International Maritime Boundaries*, n. 1, vol. I (Charney and Alexander), pp. 203, 215–17.

Table 5.4. *Account of methods of delimitation used (Legault/Hankey)*

Method	General	Opposite	Mixed	Adjacent
Equidistance	103 (77%)	55 (89%)	37 (86%)	12 (40%)
Strict/simplified	63 (47%)	28 (45%)	29 (67%)	6 (20%)
Modified	40 (30%)	27 (43%)	8 (19%)	6 (20%)
Other methods	42 (31%)	8 (13%)	13 (30%)	20 (67%)
Mixed methods (Eq./parallels of lat.)			16 (14%)	8 (27%)

The relatively high percentage of agreements based on equidistance in this study may be partly explained by the inclusion of territorial boundaries in several of the 134 agreements taken into account.

whole, maritime delimitations taking into account the continental shelf and the territorial sea amount to 83 per cent of the agreements in opposite constellations, and 51 per cent in adjacent agreements to be based upon equidistance.[67]

A comparison of the results of the different studies suggests that the conclusions found in the present examination are roughly appropriate. Equidistance is mainly applied in opposite and mixed configurations, while adjacent coastal configurations are often dealt with on the basis of different methods. For those, as well as for modified equidistance, additional guidance is required that goes beyond the method of equidistance.

This analysis concludes that the widespread perception of a strongly predominant, almost exclusive use of the combined equidistance–special circumstances rule, as codified in Article 6 of the 1958 Shelf Convention, has not been supported by state practice. There are clearly more agreements than generally thought which refer to methods other than equidistance.[68] Whatever the percentages in detail, and regardless of possible fluctuations, it should be emphasized that the application of strict mathematical equidistance or median line methods did not produce acceptable results for the coastal states in 50 to 60 per cent of all the agreements examined. Other considerations prevailed in these

---

[67] Yoshifumi Tanaka, *Predictability and Flexibility in the Law of Maritime Delimitation* (Cambridge University Press, 2006) pp. 134–5.
[68] But see e.g. Elisabeth Zoller, arguing that practically all agreements have used the model of equidistance–special circumstances in one way or another to establish the boundary line. Elisabeth Zoller, 'Recherche sur les méthodes de délimitation du plateau continental: à propos de l'Affaire Tunisie/Libye' (1982) 86 *Revue generale de droit international public*, 645, 673.

delimitations. Since negotiations need not rely upon principled arguments, it often cannot be said which specific criteria governments actually used.[69]

E. Protracted negotiations

Besides successfully concluded agreements, it is of equal interest to look at state practice in difficult negotiations. There are a number of disputes that have been pending for many years and decades. Unsettled negotiations in Europe, for example, still include boundary delimitations between Poland and Denmark, between Sweden and Denmark in the Baltic Sea,[70] and the case of Greece and Turkey in the Mediterranean, despite agreed procedures for negotiations and litigation before the ICJ in 1978.[71] Other negotiations were concluded after great difficulties, in particular in the Barents Sea between Russia (the former Soviet Union) and Norway, only settled in 2010.[72] There are, of course, many different reasons that cause the complexity, protraction, or even the failure, of maritime boundary delimitation at great political and economic cost. The overall relationship of the states concerned is certainly an important factor. While friendly relations and mutual trust ease the way for negotiated solutions of complex cases, tensions, distrust or hostility

---

[69] The ASIL study has considerably expanded the knowledge made available to the community on motivation and factors determining single lines in the 137 agreements. Nevertheless, the study concluded that in particular political, strategic and historic factors often remain undisclosed in the agreements and remain within the diplomatic process in hidden agendas. See Charney, 'Introduction' in Charney et al., *International Maritime Boundaries*, n. 1, vol. I (Charney and Alexander), p. xxxv; Bernard H. Oxman, 'Political, Strategic, and Historical Considerations' in Charney et al., *International Maritime Boundaries*, n. 1, vol. I (Charney and Alexander), pp. 3–40, in particular pp. 24, 25; p. 13 ('It is often difficult to discern what, if any, effect political considerations had on the location of an agreed maritime boundary'); p. 39 ('It is often difficult to demonstrate what particular influence political factors have on the precise location of a specific boundary').

[70] See Erik Franck, 'Baltic Sea Boundaries' in Charney et al., *International Maritime Boundaries*, n. 1, vol. V (Colson and Smith), p. 3508.

[71] Greece–Turkey: Agreement on Procedures for Negotiation of Aegean Continental Shelf Issue (Done at Berne, 11 November 1976) (1977) 16 ILM 13; *Aegean Sea Continental Shelf (Greece v. Turkey)*, Judgment, ICJ Reports 1978, p. 3. See Chapter 12.

[72] See Pål Jakob Aasen, 'The Law of Maritime Delimitation and the Russian–Norwegian Maritime Boundary Dispute', Fridtjof Nansen Institute, February 2010, www.fni.no/publ/marine.html#pja (last accessed 1 February 2012). The boundary was eventually settled by agreement on 27 April 2010, Denis Dyomkin, Gwladys Fouche, 'UPDATE 1 – Russia and Norway reach Barents Sea border deal, 27 April 2010 *Reuters*, www.reuters.com/article/idUSLDE63Q14D20100427?type=marketsNews (last accessed 27 April 2010); Wikipidia, n. 48.

may prevent the solution even under simple geographical configurations.[73] There is some evidence that the model of equidistance, as applied as a rule of delimitation in negotiations, plays a significant part in these failures on a technical level. Equidistance tends to frustrate other approaches and models, particularly schemes of co-operation, because it tends to prejudice negotiations. States are inclined not only to start negotiations on the basis of equidistance, but then to stick to it as a basis for a settlement without flexibility. Typically, one party, relying on the widespread use of equidistance in state practice, invokes this method and then shows little readiness to discuss other approaches or substantial modifications claimed by the other party under the title of special circumstances. Thus, while one party sticks to the narrow line of equidistance, the other is left without much guidance, and is therefore in a weaker negotiating position. This tends to result in its subsequent withdrawal from the negotiating process, as the weaker party then prefers to leave the dispute unresolved. Examples of this dynamic are easily found in history. In one instance it was reported that no agreement was reached in the Baltic Sea between Norway and the Soviet Union (Russia) because Norway insisted on applying a strict equidistance approach and the Soviet Union claimed, under special circumstances, a more westerly boundary due to their important naval facilities at Kola Peninsula.[74] Similarly, negotiations between Greece and Turkey, pending for many years, broke down because of Greece's insistence on the median line, taking full account of the Greek islands.[75] In the dispute between Canada and France over the maritime areas around the Island of St. Pierre et Miquelon, France at first insisted on the application of strict equidistance. It is reported that a provisional agreement was only reached in 1972, after this claim was modified in return for substantial special access

---

[73] John R. Prescott, *The Maritime Political Boundaries of the World* (London: Methuen, 2004), pp. 384–92; see also the assessments of the general relationships of any states concerned in the reports in Charney et al., *International Maritime Boundaries*, 5 vols., n. 1.

[74] For a detailed account see Aason, n. 72; Kim Traavik and Willy Ostreng, 'Security and Ocean Law: Norway and the Soviet Union in the Barents Sea' (1977) 4 *Ocean Development & International Law*, 343; Willy Ostreng, 'Norwegen und die Sowjetunion in der Barentsee' (1980) 35 *Europa Archiv*, 711. In 1987, it was reported that Norwegian satellite-controlled exploration buoys disappeared, allegedly removed by the Soviet Union, *Neue Zürcher Zeitung*, 3 September 1987, No. 203, p. 3 col. 3.

[75] See Prescott, n. 73, pp. 215 ff.; see *Aegean Sea Continental Shelf (Greece v. Turkey)*, Judgment, ICJ Reports 1978, p. 45, para. 109.

rights off the Canadian coast and in the Gulf of St Lawrence.[76] Negotiations, however, failed with regard to the boundaries off the south and west coasts, and it was necessary to revert to arbitration.

In conclusion, equidistance and the median line are successful approaches as long as both or all of the parties involved regard their interests to be sufficiently protected by this model, and negotiations are limited to smaller or larger modifications of that line. However, in cases of fundamental differences, the approaches tend to act as catalysts of logjams and breakdowns. Thus, what is on the face of it a clear and well-defined legal model at times rather complicates the process of maritime boundary negotiations and settlement.[77] In shaping appropriate approaches, legal principles and rules of maritime boundary delimitation, it will therefore be appropriate to take into account not merely quantitative elements, but also the qualitative elements of the different models. In addition to the findings that more than half of all agreements somehow deviate from equidistance, due account must be given to the primary goal that legal principles and rules should be able to assist foremost in the solution of complex cases and protracted negotiations.

III. The functional approach in co-operation agreements

Schemes of co-operation are a significant aspect of state practice related to the allocation of marine resources. Pioneered by the Arabian Gulf states, the concept of co-operation in the exploitation of mineral and living resources is more advanced in treaty practice than legal discussions on general maritime boundary law seem to suggest.[78] Agreements

---

[76] See Clive R. Symmons, 'The Canadian 200 mile Fishery Limit and the Delimitation of Maritime Zones around St. Pierre and Miquelon' (1980) 12 *Ottawa Law Review*, 145; *Anglo-French Channel* arbitration, Chapter I, notes 39, 88, para. 77; Charney et al., *International Maritime Boundaries*, n. 1, vol. I (Charney and Alexander), Report Number 1-2, pp. 387, 389.

[77] The point is further elaborated in Chapter 6 et passim.

[78] For the most part, general treatises on maritime boundaries have not dealt with co-operation arrangements and their implementation in a very systematic manner; cf. Jagota, n. 57; Prescott n. 73; Marques Antunes, *Towards the Conceptualisation of Maritime Delimitation: Legal and Technical Aspects of a Political Process* (Leiden: Brill Academic Publishers, 2003); see, however, Yoshifumi Tanaka, *Predictability and Flexibility in the Law of Maritime Delimitation*, (Oxford: Hart, 2006). More specifically see Thomas A. Mensah, 'Joint Development Zones as an Alternative Dispute Settlement Approach in Maritime Boundary Delimitation' in Rainer Lagoni and Daniel Vignes (eds.), *Maritime Delimitation* (Leiden: Martinus Nijhoff 2006), p. 143; Sun Pyo Kim, *Maritime Delimitation and Interim Arrangements in North East Asia* (Dordrecht: Martinus

contain various forms of co-operation, such as joint development zones[79] (13 out of 120 agreements at the end of 1991[80] and around 20 out of 180 agreements by 2004[81]), the more numerous provisions dealing with the unity of deposit problem,[82] as well as various other forms of co-operation.[83] A study by Colson, published in 1993, identified schemes of co-operation in two-thirds of the 137 agreements examined.[84] At least half of the agreements concluded between 1993 and 2005 included some form of co-operative arrangement.[85] The trend towards schemes of co-operation continues despite a traditional preference for boundary delimitation agreements.[86] The following survey focuses on state practice until 1992. References are made where appropriate in light of subsequent developments and judicial activity.

Traditionally, doctrine and case law have approached boundary delimitation as a problem of drawing lines and of separating jurisdictions. Indeed, one author pointed out that the idea of frontier areas of co-operation almost necessarily causes negative reactions because it is contrary to all international law development, which has traditionally aimed at clear and precise lines separating different jurisdictions of states.[87] The ideal of precise lines also prevails with respect to boundaries in the 1982 Convention. True, this agreement does focus on the co-operation inherently necessary to protect the migratory species within

---

Nijhoff, 2004); David H. Anderson, 'Strategies for Dispute Resolution: Negotiating Joint Agreements' in Gerald H. Blake et al. (eds.), *Boundaries and Energy: Problems and Prospects* (London: Kluwer, 1998), p. 473.

[79] For definitions of the term 'joint development', see Mensah, n. 78, pp. 146–7.

[80] Barbara Kwiatkowska, 'Economic and Environmental Considerations in Maritime Boundary Delimitations' in Charney and et al., *International Maritime Boundaries*, n. 1, vol. I (Charney and Alexander), pp. 87–8.

[81] Anderson, n. 52, p. 3216.

[82] In 1993 around 45 agreements could be found which contained what was termed 'resource deposit clauses' (Barbara Kwiatkowska, n. 80, pp. 75, 87) or 'unitisation provisions', respectively (David A. Colson, 'The Legal Regime of Maritime Boundary Agreements' in Charney et al., *International Maritime Boundaries*, n. 1, vol. I (Charney and Alexander), pp. 41, 55–6). See further Cissé Yacouba and Donald McRae (eds.), 'The Legal Regime of Maritime Boundary Agreements' in Charney et al., *International Maritime Boundaries*, n. 1, vol. V (Colson and Smith), pp. 3281, 3291–3.

[83] The point made by Colson in 1993, that there is no limit to the kinds of understandings that parties may reach in the context of maritime boundary agreements, was reinforced in the period to 2005, Yacouba and McRae, n. 82, pp. 3281, 3297, citing Colson, n. 82, pp. 41, 60.

[84] Colson, n. 82, pp. 41, 55–6.   [85] Yacouba and McRae, n. 82, p. 3291.

[86] See Mensah, n. 78, p. 145.

[87] Claude Blumann, 'Frontières et limites' in Société française de droit international colloque de Poitiers, *La Frontière* (Paris: Editions A. Pedone, 1980), 3, 25.

the EEZ of different states (Articles 63 to 69), and upon the co-operation implied by the (weak) rights of land-locked and geographically disadvantaged states to equitable access to surplus catches of the region (Articles 69 and 70).[88] Yet, in the context of allocation of marine spaces and jurisdiction, the rules of the Convention fully adhere to the concept of delimitation, and therefore to neatly separated zones of national jurisdiction. Co-operation is limited to interim arrangements pending the final settlement of the dispute (Articles 74(3) and 83(3)). Thus, the traditional concept of the peaceful co-existence of States still prevails, notwithstanding the overall 'spirit of mutual understanding and co-operation' invoked by the preamble and inherent to many provisions of the Convention, particularly those relating to common heritage and deep seabed mining. State practice with models of durable and lasting co-operation in the boundary area has not yet been sufficiently reflected and encouraged in the multilateral framework of the law of the sea.

It was reported at the end of the twentieth century that the ratio of joint development agreements to all types of maritime boundary delimitation agreements amounts to a ratio of 1:10.[89] Most of these agreements relate to solving the problem of sharing units of deposits of oil and gas within areas claimed by both parties within an overall operation of maritime boundary delimitation. In 1999, Ong extensively analysed state practice and identified three different models.[90] The first model, rarely applied in recent time, allocates the unit of deposits to one of the states and grants rights of sharing the proceeds. This model entails minimal co-operation and leaves one of the states with legal security to obtain its fair share. The second model consists of establishing compulsory joint ventures between the interested states and their national and other nominated companies in the designated area of joint exploitation. The third model, finally, establishes joint institutions for the administration and management of the zone as described by the examples above. It entails the highest level and form of co-operation. According to Ong, joint development zones have been gaining ground in recent decades, in particular in the North Sea, the Persian Gulf, the East China Sea, the South China Sea and the Carribean Sea.[91] As the lack of an agreement over disputed uniform deposits allows one state to block exploration and exploitation by another

---

[88] See Chapter 3(II)(B).
[89] Anderson, n. 78, p. 474; David M. Ong, 'Joint Development of Common Offshore Oil and Gas Deposits: "Mere" State Practice or Customary International Law?' (1999) 93 *American Journal of International Law*, 771, 793.
[90] Ong, n. 89, p. 787–92.   [91] Ibid., pp. 795 and 797.

state, co-operation is often necessary to start exploitation short of delimitation, at least on a provisional basis. Pending delimitation, such co-operation is required under the LOS Convention for continental shelf rights.[92] In the view of the Tribunal in *Guyana* v. *Suriname*, the obligation to enable provisional utilization:

> constitutes an implicit acknowledgment of the importance of avoiding the suspension of economic development in a disputed maritime area, as long as such activities do not affect the reaching of a final agreement. Such arrangements promote the realisation of one of the objectives of the Convention, the equitable and efficient utilisation of the resources of the seas and oceans.[93]

Beyond the three models described above, existing bilateral co-operation treaties regarding mineral and living marine resources show a wide range of different elements and approaches. They all go beyond mere delimitation of a boundary line. Indeed, they sometimes even replace them. State practice can best be grouped in four models, which are not meant to be exhaustive.[94]

The first model offers compensation and revenue sharing in order to mitigate the effects of uneven geographic allocations of resources. The

---

[92] Art. 83(3) LOS Convention.

[93] *Arbitral Award Constituted Pursuant to Article 387, and in Accordance with Annex VII, of the United Nations Convention on the Law of the Sea, between Guyana and Suriname*, Award of 17 September 2007, (hereinafter *Guyana* v. *Suriname* Award), International Court of Arbitration: www.pca-cpa.org/showpage.asp?pag_id=1147 (last accessed 30 January 2012), para. 460; with reference to Mensah, n. 78, p. 143, and the 1982 Convention's preamble.

[94] In 1993, Kwiatkowska found the following three groupings of agreements containing joint development schemes: (1) four agreements applying to previously established boundaries; (2) five agreements accompanying new bilateral boundary agreements; (3) five agreements reached pending the final settlement of a boundary (n. 80, 88). Also in 1993, Colson grouped those agreements containing co-operative clauses into three broad categories: (1) agreements containing general or best effort provisions on co-operation; (2) agreements containing provisions that deal with the unity of deposit problem; (3) agreements which set out even more specific rules of a co-operative nature (Colson, n. 82, pp. 41, 55). Subsequent studies engaged by the ASIL project covering the time-span from 1993 to 2005 again identified several categories of co-operative arrangements. Yacouba and McRae identified the following: (1) agreements that acknowledge the cross-boundary unity of deposit problem and providing for co-operation; (2) agreements that provide for a joint development area or other form of joint arrangement; (3) agreements providing for other forms of co-operation (Yacouba and McRae, n. 82, p. 3291); while Anderson classified provisional arrangements into five types: (1) joint development of mineral resources; (2) special areas for fisheries; (3) provisional boundaries; (4) bilateral co-operation and third states; (5) co-ordinated patrols in undelimited waters (Anderson, n. 52, p. 3216).

second model of provisional co-operation provides for joint jurisdiction over the boundary area during exploration with a view toward reaching further definite agreements on delimitation. The third model establishes lasting common zones overlapping established boundaries. The fourth model establishes schemes of joint administration that work either with or without a common boundary.[95]

The models may be applied in any combination imaginable. But whatever the specific contents of co-operation, all these agreements share a common trait: there is more to maritime boundary law than finding a single line. As in matters of territorial boundaries, they demonstrate that delimitation is not merely a matter of fixing a particular line of demarcation, but rather is a problem of regulating overall boundary areas and transboundary problems in an equitable manner. As such it increasingly transgresses the traditional perceptions of mere rights and obligations of good neighbourliness.[96] The same is equally true for marine spaces. Both with regard to mineral and living resources, there are issues of transboundary administration and co-ordination which need to be addressed and cannot be solved by a single line of demarcation.

To the extent that bilateral boundary agreements employ schemes of co-operation, they add to the list of non-equidistant solutions. Whatever method of delimitation is used, it is amended or even substituted by

---

[95] Rainer Lagoni (Rapporteur of the ILA International Committee on the Exclusive Economic Zone), 'Report on Joint Development of Non-Living Resources in the Exclusive Economic Zone', in ILA, Report of the Sixty-Third Conference (Warsaw, 1988), pp. 510–55; Hazel Fox et al. (eds.), *Joint Development of Offshore Oil and Gas: A Model Agreement for States for Joint Development with Explanatory Commentary* (London: British Institute of International and Comparative Law, 1989); Kwiatkowska, n. 80.

[96] See e.g. Rainer Bothe, 'Zusammenarbeit statt Grenzziehung: Neue Wege zur 'Lösung' von Grenzstreitigkeiten' in Rudolf Bernhardt (ed.), *Deutsche Landesreferate zum öffentlichen Recht und Völkerrecht* (Heidelberg: Müller, 1982), p. 247; Blumann, n. 87.

The need for co-operation at boundaries is particularly evident in the context of the EEC or in the context of economic regions crossed by international boundaries. See Patrick Daillier, *La Coopération européenne en matière douanière* (Paris: Frontière, 1980), pp. 225–52; see e.g. the French–German–Swiss Agreement of 5 March 1975 (establishing a tripartite intergovernmental commission for the upper Rhine area (*regio basiliensis*); the exchange of letters between France and Switzerland establishing a comparable commission for the Geneva area.

See generally Alexandre Kiss, 'La Frontière-coopération' in Société française de droit international colloque de Poitiers, *La Frontière* (Paris: Editions A. Pedone, 1980), pp. 183–223. The author concludes that transboundary co-operation is increasingly becoming a necessity in the relations of neighbouring states. See Kiss, n. 96, p. 222. See also René-Jean Dupuy, 'La Coopération régionale transfrontalière du droit international' (1977) 23 *Annuaire français de droit international*, 837.

schemes that cannot be explained in terms of geographic proximity to coastal configurations. Even an equidistant boundary amended by an overlapping zone is no longer an equidistant line, strict or modified. The zone fundamentally affects the patterns of distribution. Or it was only possible to draw a particular line (equidistant or not) because additional elements were added to the settlement. Co-operation agreements including boundary lines therefore are often package deals.

A. *The model of revenue sharing and compensation*

Unbalanced economic effects resulting from a particular boundary delimitation may be mitigated by compensating one or both parties under a scheme of revenue sharing. Legally, this is not yet a model of co-operation. Economically, however, it produces comparable effects. The 1958 Agreement between Saudi Arabia and Bahrain is a good example. This agreement provides for a hexagonal zone located within the continental shelf of Saudi Arabia.[97] Revenues from the zone, however, are shared equally with Bahrain. A similar agreement between Abu Dhabi and Qatar provides for equal rights of ownership and shared revenues in the oil field of Al Bunduq, although the field is geographically located on the continental shelf of Abu Dhabi and was agreed to be exploited by an Abu Dhabi corporation in accordance with the terms of its concession (Articles 6 and 7).[98] A variation on the pure two-way shared resource areas was the 1989 Agreement between Australia and Indonesia (Timor Gap).[99] There, the parties established a coffin-shaped common zone of co-operation within three segments A–B–C. The middle part, A, was subjected to joint administration and equal sharing of the benefits of the exploitation of petroleum resources (see section D below).

---

[97] Bahrain–Saudi Boundary Agreement of 22 February 1958, ST/LEG/SER.B/16, n. 1, p. 409 (1976); Charney et al., *International Maritime Boundaries*, n. 1, vol. II (Charney and Alexander), Report Number 7-3.

On Middle East state practice related to maritime boundaries see generally Charles G. MacDonald (ed.), *Iran, Saudi Arabia and the Law of the Sea: Political Interaction and Legal Development in the Persian Gulf* (Westport: Greenwood Press, 1980); El Hakim, n. 8.

[98] Agreement on Settlement of Maritime Boundary Lines and Sovereign Rights Over Islands between Qatar and Abu Dhabi of 30 March 1969, ST/LEG/SER.B/16, n. 1, 403; Charney et al., *International Maritime Boundaries*, n. 1, vol. II (Charney and Alexander), Report Number 7-9.

[99] 'Treaty between Australia and the Republic of Indonesia on the Zone of Cooperation in an Area between the Indonesian Province of East Timor and Northern Australia, 11 December 1989' (1990) 29 ILM 469; Charney et al., *International Maritime Boundaries*, n. 1, vol. II (Charney and Alexander), Report Number 6-2(2).

Zones B and C established mutual rights to 10 per cent of the revenues from the exploitation of resources in their respective segments (Income Tax by Indonesia and Gross Revenue Tax by Australia).[100]

B. The model of shared jurisdiction in boundary area pending exploration

A number of agreements on continental shelf delimitation include a formula pledging future agreement ('seek to reach agreement') on *prospective* common deposits in the boundary area.[101] The formula, so-called resource deposit clauses, was coined in the 1965 Anglo-Norwegian Agreement[102] and used in many later agreements. It was successfully applied and implemented by the subsequent Frigg Gas Field Agreement between the two countries concerned.[103] It provides

---

[100] See in particular Art. 2 of the Agreement, in Charney et al., *International Maritime Boundaries*, n. 1, vol. II (Charney and Alexander), Report Number 6-2(5), pp. 1245, 1259.

[101] For a list see Kwiatkowska, n. 80, p. 87;, n. 82, p. 55; Ted L. McDorman et al. (ed.), *Maritime Boundary Delimitation: An Annotated Bibliography* (Boston MA: Lexington Press, 1983), p. 157 ff.; Bernd Rüster, n. 59, pp. 407–8.

[102] See Agreement between the Government of the United Kingdom of Great Britain and Northern Ireland and the Government of the Kingdom of Norway Relating to the Delimitation of the Continental Shelf between the Two Countries, 10 March 1965, Art. 4. The agreement reads:

> If any single geological petroleum structure or petroleum field, or any single geological structure or field of any other mineral deposit, including sand or gravel, extends across the dividing line and the part of such structure or field which is situated on one side of the dividing line is exploitable, wholly or in part, from the other side of the dividing line, the Contracting Parties shall, in consultation with the licencees, if any, seek to reach agreement as to the manner in which the structure or field shall be most effectively exploited and the manner in which the proceeds deriving therefrom shall be apportioned.

551 UNTS 214, in Charney et al., *International Maritime Boundaries*, n. 1, vol. II (Charney and Alexander), Report Number 9-15.

On this and the following see also Rainer Lagoni, 'Oil and Gas Deposits across National Frontiers' (1979) 73 *American Journal of International Law*, 215, 229 ff.; Robert S. Reid, 'Petroleum Development in Areas of International Seabed Boundary Disputes: Means for Resolution' (1984/5) 3 *Oil & Gas Law & Taxation Review*, 214.

[103] Reprinted in Churchill et al., *New Directions*, n. 1, vol. V, pp. 398–412. See J. C. Woodliffe, 'International Unitisation of an Offshore Gas Field' (1977) 25 *The International and Comparative Law Quarterly*, 338; William T. Onorato, 'Apportionment of an International Common Petroleum Deposit' (1977) 25 *The International and Comparative Law Quarterly*, 324 et seq.; Rüster, n. 59, p. 407.

for joint exploration and exploitation by a single concessionaire and for revenue sharing in a proportion of 60 per cent (UK) and 40 per cent (Norway), according to the existing demarcation of the shelf. For technical reasons, such common deposits that overlap the boundary have to be explored and exploited in a combined and simultaneous effort. Pending exploration, the model necessarily implies joint and shared jurisdiction over such operations.

As indicated, these and other modalities of interim agreements, pending a dispute over final allocation of living and non-living resources, have been addressed by Articles 74(3) and 83(3) of the 1982 LOS Convention. These provisions provide that pending an agreement on delimitation, 'the States concerned, in a spirit of understanding and co-operation, shall make every effort' to enter into provisional arrangements without prejudging the final delimitation. There is a duty to co-operate on an interim basis, until final agreement is reached.[104] The Tribunal in *Guyana v. Suriname* held that the first obligation contained in Articles 74(3) and 83(3) is designed to promote interim regimes and practical measures that could pave the way for provisional utilization of disputed areas pending delimitation.[105] Indeed, the Tribunal held that the 1982 Convention imposes an obligation on parties to a dispute to 'make every effort' to reach provisional arrangements for joint exploitation of mineral resources that straddle the boundary.[106] It added that this obligation imposes on the parties 'a duty to negotiate in good faith'.[107]

C. *The model of long-lasting zones overlapping a boundary line*

It is difficult to see why co-operation should be limited to interim agreement. Indeed, the practice of co-operation makes a significant step forwards in agreements establishing a lasting common zone of exploration or exploitation. Such zones may overlap a boundary. They supplement the line, and secure equal or equitable access and a balanced exploitation of resources the exact location of which is often unknown. Such zones thereby mitigate the uncertainty of potential advantages and

---

[104] See Elliott L. Richardson, 'Jan Mayen in Perspective' (1988) 82 *American Journal of International Law*, 443, 454; Rainer Lagoni, 'Interim Measures Pending Maritime Boundary Delimitation Agreements' (1984) 78 *American Journal of International Law*, 345, 355 (obligation to reach agreement in good faith is often paraphrased an obligation to co-operate).
[105] *Guyana v. Suriname* Award, n. 93, para. 460.   [106] Ibid., paras. 463–4.
[107] Ibid. para. 461.

disadvantages of a particular boundary line and cope with the problem of overlapping deposits.

This type of common developing zone was established between France and Spain in the Bay of Biscay to encourage equal distribution of the resources within the zone among national companies.[108] The agreement provides for co-ordinated exploitation and equal sharing of the resources found in the zone.[109] The landmark agreement between Iceland and Norway on the area of the Jan Mayen Ridge also provides, as proposed by a conciliation commission, for joint exploration and exploitation of the zone.[110] Under this agreement, each of the parties is entitled to a basic share of 25 per cent of the proceeds from the partner's area at the other side of the EEZ boundary line crossing the zone.[111] In these cases, the establishment of a common zone made delineating a boundary acceptable to both parties, despite the uncertainties in the location of mineral resources.

The 1977 (interim) Reciprocal Fisheries Agreement between Canada and the United States is another example of the variations on boundary zones. This agreement provided for harmonious sharing, mutual access and joint management of transboundary stocks, research and fishing, for an area extending 20 nm from the median line. The parties agreed to grant mutual access to the other's part of the zone, to exchange results and co-ordinate research on living resources, and to provide information about catches. Remarkably, although the US and Canada even agreed to co-operate in matters of policing the boundary area, the agreement does not establish a joint administration.[112]

---

[108] Convention entre le Gouvernement de la République française et le Gouvernement de l'Etat espagnol sur la délimitation des plateaux continentaux des deux Etats dans le Golfe de Gascogne (Golfe de Biscaye), ST/LET/SER.B/19, 445 (1980) in Charney et al., *International Maritime Boundaries*, n. 1, vol. II (Charney and Alexander), Report Number 9-2, Arts. 3, 4 and Annex II. For a comment see José Luis de Azcarraga de Bustamante, 'España suscribe, con Francia e Italia, Dos Convenios sobre Delimitación de sus Plataformas Submarinales Comunas' (1985) 28 *Rivista Española de Derecho Internacional*, 131.

[109] ST/LET/SER.B/19 (1980), n. 108, Art. 3, Annex II.

[110] 'Agreement between Norway and Iceland on the Continental Shelf in the Area between Iceland and Jan Mayen 22 October 1982'(1982) 21 ILM 681 in Charney et al., *International Maritime Boundaries*, n. 1, vol. II (Charney and Alexander), Report Number 9-4. See also Conciliation Commission on the Continental Shelf Area Between Iceland and Jan Mayen: Report and Recommendations to the Governments of Iceland and Norway, May/June 1981, 20 ILM 797 (1981). See also Richardson, n. 104. The report is discussed in Chapter 6.

[111] Ibid. (1982) 21 ILM 681 Arts. 5 and 6.

[112] A subsequent solution reached, the 1979 Agreement between the Governments of the United States and of the Government of Canada on East Coast Fishery Resources,

The 1978 agreement between Australia and Papua New Guinea relies on a comparable, but much more elaborate, concept of co-operation.[113] In order to protect the traditional way of life of the islanders of the Torres Strait, the agreement established a large 'Protected Zone' overlapping the separate and not identical boundaries of the continental shelf and of the water column (Article 10). The treaty obliges both parties to take legislative or other action to preserve the marine environment, fauna and flora in their respective part of the zone. At the time, a ten-year prohibition against drilling activities was also required (Article 15). As in the US–Canada Agreement from the previous year, the Australian and Papua New Guinea negotiators established no authority beyond an advisory function. A similar scheme operates with regard to fisheries within that zone (Articles 20 to 28). These agreements provided for the sharing of catches in the zone on a 25 per cent/75 per cent basis, for preferential rights on surplus, and for mutual recognition of licences. Implementation and enforcement is sought by co-operation in inspection activities, consultation on harmonization of national regulations, and prosecution in the courts of the nationality of the vessel concerned.

D. The model of common zones under joint administration

The concept of joint administration of boundary areas has a long tradition in the context of rivers.[114] This idea of *condominium* as applied to marine spaces was proposed by J. C. Bluntschli in the nineteenth

---

reprinted in Nordquist et al. (eds.), *New Directions*, vol. IX, n. 1, p. 157, and in Charney et al., *International Maritime Boundaries*, n. 1, vol. I (Charney and Alexander), Report Number 1-3, was not ratified by the US Senate, Rhee, n. 57, 592–5.

[113] Treaty between Australia and the Independent State of Papua New Guinea concerning Sovereignty and Maritime Boundaries in the Area between the two Countries, including the Area known as Torres Strait, and related Matters, 18 December 1978, (1979) 18 ILM 291; Conforti et al., *Atlas of the Seabed Boundaries*, Part II, n. 1, p. 89; Charney et al., *International Maritime Boundaries*, n. 1, vol. I (Charney and Alexander), Report Number 5-3. See Henry Burmester, 'The Torres Strait Treaty: Ocean Boundary Delimitation by Agreement' (1982) 76 *American Journal of International Law*, 321 (it came into force on 15 February 1985).

[114] Joint administration of common rivers forming national boundaries were among the first international administrative institutions in the nineteenth century, sometimes even vested with supranational powers, such as the Donau Commission. See e.g. Ignaz Seidl-Hohenveldern (ed.), *Das Recht der Internationalen Organisationen einschliesslich der Supranationalen Gemeinschaften* (Cologne, Berlin, Bonn, Munich: Carl Heymann, 1972), 275 ff.; Derek W. Bowett, *The Law of International Institutions* (London: Steven & Sons, 1982).

century.[115] The idea was realized with the advent of the exploitation of the continental shelf.[116] Whether or not a common boundary exists, shared jurisdiction and joint administration in fact replaces the need for boundary lines and relegates their importance in practical terms to second rank.

Co-operation agreements establishing joint administration of the common area sometimes completely replaced the need for a boundary line. For example, the agreement between Saudi Arabia and Sudan established a common zone of exploitation beyond the 1000 m isobath in the Red Sea.[117] The two states 'have equal sovereign rights in the Common Zone' (Article VI) which is entirely administered by a joint commission vested with full and broad powers (Article VII). The agreement does not explicitly indicate the shares of each state. Presumably they are 50 per cent for each, discounting Saudi Arabia's costs of financing the operation of the joint commission (Article XII).[118]

In the case of Japan and South Korea, in 1974 the establishment of a formally interim joint development zone, to be in force for at least fifty years, allowed the parties to suspend the delimitation of a boundary line in the southern parts of adjacent waters without impending joint research and exploitation efforts in the development zone and its different subdivisions.[119] The agreement provides for joint operating agreements by the concessionaires of both parties (Article V). The operation is placed under the jurisdiction of a joint commission (Articles XXIV and XXV). Finally,

---

[115] Johann Caspar Bluntschli, *Das Moderne Völkerrecht der Civilisierten Staaten als Rechtsbuch dargestellt* (1861), Art. 303. See also Sang-Myon Rhee, 'Sea Boundary Delimitation between States Before World War II' (1982) 76 *American Journal of International Law*, 555, 560.

[116] For extensive analysis see Ong, n. 89, p. 771; Anderson, n. 78, p. 473.

[117] Agreement between Sudan and Saudi Arabia Relating to the Joint Exploitation of the Natural Resources of the Seabed and the Subsoil of the Red Sea in the Common Zone, 16 May 1974, ST/LEG/SER.B/18, 452 (1976).

[118] The area has not been exploited under the agreement, however, and its current status is unclear (Chris M. Carleton, 'Red Sea/Persian Gulf Maritime Boundaries' in Charney et al., *International Maritime Boundaries*, n. 1, vol. V (Colson and Smith), pp. 3467, 3470).

[119] Agreement between Japan and the Republic of Korea concerning Joint Development of the Southern Part of the Continental Shelf Adjacent to the Two Countries, 5 February 1974, Churchill et al., *New Directions*, vol. IV, n. 1, p. 117; Conforti and Francalanci, *Atlas of the Seabed Boundaries*, Part I, n. 1, p. 151; Charney et al., *International Maritime Boundaries*, n. 1, vol. I (Charney and Alexander), Report Number 5-12. In 1998 the two parties entered into a fisheries agreement that created a joint fishing area in the waters disputed between them in the Sea of Japan and a joint-use zone around the disputed islets known as Dokdo in Korean and Takeshima in Japanese (the agreement is reproduced in Kim, n. 78, p. 327).

the concessionaire of each party is entitled to equal shares of revenues and allocation of expenses (Article IX).

The 1973 boundary agreement between Uruguay and Argentina introduced and pioneered elaborate schemes of co-operation both in the common Rio de la Plata Estuary and the 200 nm EEZ in seaward direction. The agreement is based on strict reciprocity and equality.[120] The Estuary was divided for the exploitation of the soil and subsoil (Article 41), but with respect to fishing (and navigation), each state is entitled to operate within the entire Estuary. A joint administrative commission, vested with rights to prescribe, enacts, inter alia, regulations on scientific research, prevention and control of pollution, and conservation of living resources (Article 66). Co-operation also extends to the 200 nm EEZ. Here, a boundary line was drawn based on equidistance by acres of a circumference of 200 nm measured from the points at the Estuary of the two states (Article 73). The treaty, however, established a common fishing zone (Article 73, or zone of common interest, Article 79), which extensively overlaps the common boundary line. The agreement provides for equitable sharing of the catches (Article 74), the allocation to be determined by a joint technical committee (Articles 80 to 84). This body enjoys powers comparable to, though not identical with, those of the Estuary administrative commission.

Besides establishing zones of mutual revenue participation, the 1989 Australia–Indonesia Timor Gap Agreement, created an 'Area A' within the zone subject to common and joint administration.[121] This zone was supervized by a ministerial council and a joint authority, with equal representation from both states.[122] According to Article 2(2)(a):

> In Area A, there shall be joint control by the Contracting States of the exploration for and exploitation of petroleum resources, aimed at achieving optimum commercial utilisation thereof and equal sharing between the two Contracting States of the benefits of the exploitation of petroleum resources, as provided for in this Treaty.

The 1989 Treaty was signed to close the Timor Gap, open since 1972 between two sections of the Australian–Indonesian seabed line. Together

---

[120] Treaty of the Rio de la Plata and its Maritime Boundary, 19 November 1973, (1974) 13 ILM 251 ff.; Charney et al., *International Maritime Boundaries*, n. 1, vol. I (Charney and Alexander), Report Number 3-2.

[121] A 'functionally sophisticated approach' according to the words of Douglas M. Johnston (ed.), *The Theory and History of Ocean Boundary-Making* (Montreal: McGill–Queen's University Press, 1988), p. 219.

[122] N. 99, Arts. 3 and 5(2).

with the subsequent agreements mentioned earlier, it amounts to compensation for the boundary which was prejudged by two lines established in 1972 on the basis of geomorphology.[123] These lines were fixed in accordance with the traditional definition of the shelf based on the theory of natural prolongation and, as such, were outdated by the LOS Convention's definition of the shelf. The creation of the 'coffin-shaped' scheme and the eventual unitization of the resources lying in the disputed zones therefore were held to amount to an *equitable remedy* in that situation.[124]

The 2002 Timor Sea Treaty[125] established a similar scheme of co-operation, albeit with a sharing of the exploitation proceeds in a ratio of 9:1 in favour of East Timor (Article 4(a)). The Timor Sea Treaty also established a three-tiered joint administrative structure consisting of a Designated Authority, a Joint Commission and a Ministerial Council. The Designated Authority is responsible for the day-to-day regulation and management of petroleum activities (Article 6(b)). Its work is overseen by the Joint Commission (Article 6(c)(i)), which also establishes the policies and regulations relating to petroleum activities in the relevant zone. According to Article 6(c)(i), the Joint Commission consists of commissioners appointed by Australia and East Timor, with East Timor being allowed to appoint one more commissioner than Australia. The Ministerial Council consists of an equal number of Ministers from Australia and East Timor and considers any matter relating to the operation of this Treaty – such as dispute resolution – that is referred to it by one of the parties (Article 6(d)(i), (ii)).

In 2002, Australia and East Timor[126] signed the Timor Sea Treaty.[127] The Timor Sea Treaty applies only in Area A of the Zone of Co-operation

---

[123] Charney et al., *International Maritime Boundaries*, n. 1, vol. II (Charney and Alexander), Report Number 6-2(2).

[124] The background of the 1989 Timor Gap Agreement is well developed by Richard D. Lumb, 'The Delimitation of Maritime Boundaries in the Timor Sea' (1981) *Australian Yearbook of International Law 1981*, 72.

[125] Timor Sea Treaty between the Government of East Timor and the Government of Australia, 20 May 2002, entered into force 2 April 2003; see Report Number 6-20(1) and (2) in Charney et al., *International Maritime Boundaries*, n. 1, vol. V (Colson and Smith), p. 3806.

[126] Negotiation of the Timor Sea Treaty prior to the independence of East Timor was conducted between Australia and the United Nations Transitional Administration in East Timor (UNTAET), marking the first instance that a United Nations body was given sole responsibility for managing a territory during its transition to statehood, including the competence to enter into international agreements on behalf of the peoples of East Timor (see Security Council Res. 1272 (1999) of 25 October 1999).

[127] Timor Sea Treaty between the Government of East Timor and the Government of Australia, 20 May 2002, entered into force 2 April 2003; see Report Number 6-20 (1)

as described under the Timor Gap Treaty of 1989, and which was now called Joint Petroleum Development Area (JPDA).[128] All petroleum activities within this zone are to be carried out through a contract between the Designated Authority and a limited liability corporation or other such entity.[129] While in this respect, the Timor Sea Treaty is similar to the earlier terms of the Timor Gap Treaty, the two instruments differ markedly in the allocation of the share of the products. While in the 1989 Timor Gap Treaty petroleum exploitation in this Area was split equally, the 2002 Timor Sea Treaty gives East Timor a 90 per cent share and Australia a 10 per cent share of production, respectively.[130] It was known at the time of the signing of the Timor Sea Treaty that the Sunrise and Troubadour fields, collectively known as Greater Sunrise, lie partially (20.1 per cent) within the waters of the JPDA and partly (79.9 per cent) in the waters outside the eastern boundary of the JPDA claimed by Australia.[131] Under the Treaty, East Timor would get 90 per cent of the 20.1 per cent of the Greater Sunrise field lying within the JPDA and thus only an overall share of some 18 per cent of that field. Soon after signing the Treaty, the two states thus initiated negotiations that led to an agreement in 2003 to exploit the reserves in these fields in an integrated manner.[132] The Australia–East Timor unitization agreement provides for the development of straddling reserves as a unit by a single unit operator. It is unique, in that the reserves do not lie across a maritime boundary between two states but straddle the limit between a joint development area and the jurisdictional waters of a state.[133] Since the unitization agreement alone would have allocated only about 18 per cent of the Greater Sunrise fields to East Timor, and in light of East Timor's arguments with respect to the correct application of international law to the maritime delimitation in the region (the fields are lying closer to East

---

and (2) in Charney et al., *International Maritime Boundaries*, n. 1, vol. V (Colson and Smith), p. 3806.

[128] See Art. 3 and Annex A of the Timor Sea Treaty in Charney et al., *International Maritime Boundaries*, n. 1, vol. V (Colson and Smith), pp. 3832, 3845. Area B and Area C are now under the full sovereignty of Australia and East Timor respectively and are no longer subject to joint development (n. 127, p. 3812).

[129] Art. 3(c), n. 127, p. 3832.   [130] Art. 4, n. 127.

[131] Charney et al., *International Maritime Boundaries*, n. 1, vol. V (Colson and Smith), Report Number 6-20 (3), p. 3867.

[132] Agreement between the Government of Australia and the Government of the Democratic Republic of Timor-Leste relating to the Unitisation of the Sunrise and Troubadour Fields (Dili, 6 March 2003, in force 23 February 2007 [2007] Australian Treaty Series 11).

[133] See n. 131, p. 3869.

Timor than to Australia, according to surface geography) the two parties entered into yet another agreement in 2006.[134] Under this agreement, both countries share the upstream revenue from the Greater Sunrise field on a 50:50 basis (Article 5(1)) measured at arm's length (Article 5(2)).

E. *The potential and limits of co-operation and package deals*

There is evidence that the adoption of co-operative approaches to the problem of allocation of marine spaces has allowed parties to achieve agreements that would not have been possible on the basis of mere co-existence. In the cases of the Australia–Papua New Guinea and Australia–Indonesia Agreements, the common boundaries as established could not have been agreed to without simultaneously creating the overlapping zone of co-operation. The classical approach to maritime boundary delimitation failed. Settlement was only reached after negotiations included the concept of co-operation. As Burmester put it:

> the final result only occurred after a breakdown in the negotiations. The rigid and single-focus approach of the initial round of negotiations, where attention was primarily given to the drawing of a single maritime boundary, did not lead to productive solutions. It was only after the adoption of an imaginative, broadly focused approach that a solution acceptable to all parties concerned – not just governments, but the peoples themselves – was achieved.[135]

Similarly, the same approach in the Australia–Indonesia Timor Gap Agreement took effect after the breakdown of consecutive attempts to settle the boundary delimitation in line with the 1971 Agreement which favours Australia on the basis of natural prolongation. 'After fruitless negotiations at various times after 1975, attention became focused on the concept of a joint zone of cooperation.'[136] There is no doubt that the 1989 Timor Gap Agreement was inspired by the Papua New Guinea Agreement. The history of the Jan Mayen conciliation and agreement is another case in point. The establishment of an overlapping zone solved a dispute entrenched in arguments pro and contra the doctrine of natural

---

[134] Treaty between Australia and the Democratic Republic of Timor-Leste on Certain Maritime Arrangements in the Timor Sea (Sydney, 12 January 2006, in force 23 February 2007 [2007] Australian Treaty Series 12).
[135] Burmester, n. 113, 328.
[136] John R. Prescott in Charney et al., *International Maritime Boundaries*, n. 1, vol. II (Charney and Alexander), Report Number 6-2(5), p. 1245.

prolongation.[137] The Spanish–French agreement in the Gulf of Biscay is yet another example where the problem of yet unknown resources was solved by the adoption of joint and co-operative schemes.

These examples teach important lessons. Firstly, they show that the adoption of a wider approach to the problem of delimitation may help overcome the logjams in negotiations that solely focused on the boundary line. Including mutual access to the respective zones or rights to shares of revenues, their prospects enlarge the scope of negotiations and therefore the room for manoeuvring, compromise and equitable solutions. The adoption early on in negotiations of a 'without prejudice' clause may enhance mutual trust for entering into co-operation agreements of a provisional nature pending the final delimitation.[138] Without prejudice clauses are explicitly mandated for provisional arrangements in Articles 74(3) and 83(3) of the 1982 Convention.[139]

Secondly, the examples show that co-operation agreements reduce the risks of unfavourable delimitation by a court ruling which have been limited so far to drawing boundary lines. The Gulf of Maine is a case in point. Had the United States Senate agreed to the 1979 United States–Canadian Fisheries Agreement, the *Gulf of Maine* case could have been limited to the continental shelf. New England fishing industries would now be better served under a scheme of co-operation. As Richardson put it:

> Although joint management was the obvious and sensible way of resolving the boundary dispute between the United States and Canada in the Gulf of Maine, a 1979 fishing agreement signed by both countries was rejected by the Senate under pressure from the New England fishing lobby. The two countries thus were obliged to submit the division of one of the most important fishing areas in the world to the International Court of Justice on the basis of a complex and sometimes inconsistent or conflicting geological, geomorphological and ecological data. The Court's delineation of a single maritime boundary was disappointing to the United States, which thereby lost access to part of the Georges Bank, with the consequent disruption of the fishing patterns followed by New England fishermen for more than 300 years ... In his analysis of the Gulf of Maine case, an American commentator expressed the hope that '[t]he Gulf of Maine Case will stand as an example of how

---

[137] Iceland invoked the doctrine of natural prolongation and claimed a continental shelf beyond the 200 nm zone agreed on living resources. See (1981) 20 ILM 797, n. 110; see Richardson, n. 104, 444, and Chapter 6.
[138] Anderson, n. 78, pp. 476–7.
[139] 'Such agreements shall be without prejudice to the final delimitation'.

not to proceed in a delimitation dispute, and that nations will follow the much wiser alternative chosen in The Jan Mayen Case.[140]

Apart from limiting risks inherent to third party settlement of a single boundary line, the need for co-operation agreements is also likely to increase for substantive reasons. With the advent of the EEZ, yet another dimension of complexity was added to the process of negotiations. Problems increased with the second generation of the maritime revolution. Mere delimitation of national zones of jurisdiction over living and non-living resources will often not be sufficient.

Firstly, stocks do not respect human boundaries. Successful management and conservation, particularly of migrating species, requires transboundary arrangements and co-operation. Articles 63 to 69 of the LOS Convention provide the necessary framework for bilateral or multilateral arrangements. It may well be that these obligations can best be realized by means of common zones which overlap or even replace boundary lines, and put the area under joint administration and joint jurisdiction.

Secondly, existing and settled boundaries of the shelf are likely to prejudice the establishment of EEZ boundaries, given the undisputed advantages of a single boundary. However, shelf boundaries will not always fit.[141] It may well be that they should be renegotiated in order to achieve an all-purpose boundary that is equally suitable for the purposes of equitable allocation of living resources. The creation of common zones or other schemes of co-operation having comparable effects, may allow states to overcome such problems. The actual and potential disadvantages of the existing line can be compensated for by schemes of joint administration, mutual access and revenue sharing. It may allow existing shelf boundaries to remain, turning them into all-purpose boundaries even if they cut through an ecological system. The establishment of a common zone covering that system could preserve the interests of all parties and help them accept the boundary as it stands for all purposes.

Co-operation therefore opens up promising new avenues to the equitable allocation of marine resources and to dispute settlement. Equitable solutions no longer need be achieved solely by the difficult task of determining a single boundary line. Co-operation allows for creative approaches, something a focus on a single line simply cannot

---

[140] N. 104, pp. 451–2, referring to Robert S. Reid, 'Gulf of Maine – A Disappointing First in the Delimitation of a Single Maritime Boundary' (1985) 25 *Virginia Journal of International Law*, 521, 605 (emphasis in original, footnotes omitted). The Gulf of Maine case is discussed in Chapter 6.

[141] See Chapter 2(IV)(B).

provide. Co-operation should not be seen merely as a second-best solution, as Prescott suggests,[142] but rather as a valid approach to achieving equitable solutions. It helps, within the limits of global equity in maritime law discussed earlier,[143] to achieve balanced results between the parties involved.

Of course, the approach can only be successful if the necessary foundation, mutual trust, and the spirit of co-operation are present. If agreement on boundaries is difficult or impossible to achieve in a hostile climate, *a fortiori* it is difficult or even impossible to establish forms of co-operation, let alone joint administration, under such circumstances. Co-operation is not suitable in all cases. If the area involves sensitive security issues, and relations of states are strictly based on co-existence, the co-operation approach is the wrong one. Richardson points to the fact that co-operation in fact requires the adaptability of resources to joint management, the likelihood of co-operative relationship between the states concerned, and their willingness to share control and technology.[144] Under these parameters, and based on the experience of the Jan Mayen agreement, he suggests a number of areas with long-lasting disputes that may be suitable for a co-operative approach: the Bering Sea (US–Russia); the Beaufort Sea (US–Canada); the Rockhall Faroe Plateau (UK–Ireland–Denmark),[145] and the Paracels and Spratly Islands in the South China Sea.[146] On the other hand, the dispute in the Barents Sea (Norway–Russia) seemed hardly suitable for joint administration for a long time due to the strategic interests of the former Soviet Union because of the proximity to its naval base on the Kola Peninsula.[147] For Richardson, co-operative schemes seem similarly unlikely to solve the long-standing conflict between Greece and Turkey in the Aegean Sea. It may be argued, however, that this case will become a

---

[142] See Prescott, n. 73, p. 86. Joint zones are generally less satisfactory than a single line, the special administrative arrangements they require are often inconvenient and expensive, but they are certainly preferable to unfriendly relations which might otherwise fester because of an unresolved dispute over seas and seabed.
[143] Chapter 3.   [144] See Richardson, n. 104, 454.
[145] A Memorandum from 27 February 1989 by the Icelandic Prime Minister to the British Prime Minister proposed the establishment of a joint development between the UK, Ireland, Denmark and Iceland in the Hatton–Rockall area, Kwiatkowska, n. 80, p. 88, note 51 in fine. See also on potential zones of joint development Fox et al. (eds.), n. 95, pp. 155–80.
[146] Kwiatkowska, n. 80, p. 75.
[147] Ibid. See also Willy Ostreng, 'Regional Delimitation Arrangements in the Arctic Seas: Cases of Precedence?' (1986) 10 *Marine Policy*, 132, 143.

candidate for co-operative approaches in the long run.[148] Both states are members of NATO and share a customs union with the EU. Although the problem of Cyprus cannot be ignored, it may be balanced by a shared interest in effective and peaceful exploitation of resources. Co-operation may overcome the blocking issue of equidistance and base lines that have so far prevented the parties from successful delimitation. Moreover, the aspirations of Turkey for membership in the EU may promote better conditions for co-operation and gradually remove old animosities.

It should be noted that under the 1982 Convention, states are free to adopt any creative scheme of co-operation and joint administration, with or without the transfer of jurisdiction. They may even create regional supranational organizations. The Convention does not exclude co-operation agreements in matters of maritime boundary delimitation. As explained previously, such agreements are also part of international law as referred to in Articles 74(1) and 83(1). This is even more so since they offer increased chances of fulfilling the mandatory requirement of an overall equitable solution.[149]

---

[148] See also Barbara Kwiatkowska, 'Maritime Boundary Delimitation between Opposite and Adjacent States in the New Law of the Sea – Some Implications for the Aegean' in *The Aegean Issues, Problems and Prospects* (Ankara: Foreign Policy Institute, 1989) 181, pp. 203–4.

[149] Chapter 4(III)(4).

6

Judicial and conciliatory settlements

I. Introductory

Maritime boundary delimitations determined by judicial or quasi-judicial proceedings are necessarily and generally complex and difficult. After all, the matter had not been successfully settled by means of negotiations and escalated into an international dispute. The results achieved in such cases are therefore of paramount importance for shaping appropriate legal methods and rules on the subject upon which adjudication needs to rely. Delimitations to be resolved in judicial proceedings are the ultimate test of the feasibility of such rules, because it is here that they have to prove their viability and practicability in controversial configurations.

Unlike other areas of international law relating to resource allocation, maritime boundary law has developed a relatively rich body of judicial and important quasi-judicial settlements over the last four decades. Next to the jurisprudence of the World Trade Organization (WTO) since 1995 and the settlement of investment disputes both within and outside the International Convention for the Settlement of Investment Disputes (ICSID Convention), maritime boundary delimitation amounts to the most important field of ligitation in contemporary public international law. As of 1993, twenty delimitations had been submitted to judicial settlement.[1] By January 2014, at least ten additional disputes have been settled by the International Court of Justice (ICJ) or arbitral tribunals.[2] Maritime boundary delimitation emerged as a main preoccupation of the ICJ. The case law not only contributes to the law of maritime boundaries, but in a very substantial way to international law in general. Once again,

---

[1] Jonathan I. Charney, 'Introduction', in Jonathan I. Charney et al. (eds.), *International Maritime Boundaries*, 5 vols. (The Hague: Martinus Nijhoff Publishers, 1993–2005), vols. I and II (Charney and Alexander (eds.), 1993), vol. III (Charney and Alexander (eds.), 1998), vol. IV (Charney and Smith (eds.), 2002), vol. V (Colson and Smith (eds.), 2005); vol. I (Charney and Alexander), p. xxvii.

[2] See section II below (K–T).

the law of the sea spearheads general developments. Some of the cases became landmarks, engendering wide discussion way beyond the realm of maritime law.

The present chapter seeks to offer in chronological order brief summaries of the pertinent cases and provides a bibliography of the literature discussing them. Particular attention is paid at this point to the factual configurations causing the problem, the terms of reference and special agreements, the claims of the parties and the methods applied in resolving the dispute. It summarizes the results achieved. Together with the negotiations at UNCLOS III and state practice, these results provide an important basis for subsequent discussion and evaluation of different methods and legal approaches, particularly equidistance and equitable principles. Legal foundations, principles, rules, and the reasoning of the courts and conciliatory commissions will be discussed in greater detail in Part III. The following discussion of cases distinguishes between judicial and conciliatory proceedings. It covers the period of forty-five years, from 1969 to 2014 in chronological order.

II. Claims and results in legal proceedings

A. *The 1969* North Sea Continental Shelf *cases*[3]

The facts of these founding landmark cases are well known: the coastal line along Denmark, the Federal Republic of Germany and the

---

[3] *North Sea Continental Shelf (Federal Republic of Germany v. Denmark; Federal Republic of Germany v. Netherlands)*, Judgment, ICJ Reports 1969, p. 3; Appendix II, Map 1. The landmark case was widely discussed; see generally: F. M. Auburn, 'The North Sea Continental Shelf Boundary Settlement' (1973) 16 *Archiv des Völkerrechts*, 28; E. Jiménez de Azcárraga, 'La Sentencia del Tribunal Internacional de Justicia sobre los casos de la plataforma continental del Mar del Norte' (1969) 21 *Revista Española de Drecho Internacional*, 349; S. Bilge, 'Le Nouveau rôle des principes équitables en droit international' in Emanuel Diez et al. (eds.), *Festschrift für R. Bindschedler,Botschafter, Professor Dr. iur., zum 65. Geburtstag am 8. Juli 1980* (Bern: Stämpfli, 1980), pp. 105, 112; Edward Duncan Brown, *Sea-Bed Energy and Minerals: The International Legal Regime*, 2 vols. (The Hague: Martinus Nijhoff Publishers, 2001), vol. I, p. 50 ff.; Edward Duncan Brown, *The Legal Regime of Hydrospace* (London: Stevens for the London Institute of World Affairs, 1971), pp. 41–78; Edward Duncan Brown, 'The North Sea Continental Shelf Cases' (1970) 23 *Current Legal Problems*, 187; François Eustache, 'L'Affaire du plateau continental de la mer du Nord' (1970) 74 *Revue Générale de Droit International Public*, 591; Wolfgang Friedmann, 'The North Sea Continental Shelf Cases – A Critique' (1970) 64 *American Journal of International Law*, 229; Etienne Grisel, 'The Lateral Boundaries of the Continental Shelf and the Judgment of the International Court of

Netherlands is concave with an almost rectangular angle of the German coast situated between the other countries. It was this particularity that caused the difficulties in the delimitation of the common and largely homogeneous continental shelf of the North Sea. The Federal Republic of Germany entered into agreements with the Netherlands and Denmark in 1964 and 1965 respectively, on the delimitation of small parts of the common shelf outside territorial waters. These delimitations were mainly based on equidistance.[4] Beyond these mini-treaties, however, no settlement was achieved and negotiations broke down. The Netherlands and

Justice in the North Sea Continental Shelf Cases' (1970) 64 *American Journal of International Law*, 526; Edvard Hambro and Arthur W. Rovine, *The Case Law of the International Court of Justice* (Leiden: A.W: Sijthoft, 1972), vol. VI-B 1967–1970; S. P. Jagota, *Maritime Boundary* (The Hague: Martinus Nijhoff Publishers, 1985), pp. 127–39; Robert Y. Jennings, 'The Limits of Continental Shelf Jurisdiction: Some Possible Implications of the North Sea Case Judgment' (1969) 18 *International and Comparative Law Quarterly*, 819; Jack Lang, *Le Plateau continental de la mer du Nord: l'arrêt de la Cour de Justice, 20 février 1969* (Paris: Collection Bibliothèque de droit international, LGDJ, 1988); Krystyna Marek, 'Le Problème des sources du droit international dans l'arrêt sur le plateau continental de la mer du Nord' (1970) 6 *Revue Belge de Droit International*, 44; Philippe Manin, 'Le Juge international et la règle générale' (1976) 80 *Revue Générale de Droit International Public*, 7; Eberhard Menzel, 'Der Festlandsockel der Bundesrepublik Deutschland und das Urteil des Internationalen Gerichtshofes vom 20. Februar 1969' (1969) 14 *Jahrbuch für Internationales Recht*, 13; François Monconduit, 'Affaire du plateau continental de la mer du Nord' (1969) 15 *Annuaire Français de Droit International*, 213; Edward McWhinney, *The World Court and the Contemporary International Law Making Process* (Alphen aan den Rijn: Sithoff & Noordhoff, 1979); F. Münch, 'Das Urteil des IGH vom 20.2.1969 über den deutschen Anteil am Festlandsockel der Nordsee' (1969) 29 *Zeitschrift für ausländisches öffentliches Recht und Völkerrecht*, 455; Tomas Rothpfeffer, 'Equity in the North Sea Continental Shelf Cases' (1972) 42 *Nordisk Tidskrift for International Ret*, 93; Bernd Rüster, *Die Rechtsordnung des Festlandsockels* (Berlin: Duncker und Humblot, 1977), p. 372 ff.; André Reynaud, *Les Différends du plateau continental de la mer du Nord devant la Cour internationale de justice: La volonté, la nature, et le droit* (Paris: LGDJ/Montchrestien, 1975); Francis Rigaldies, 'La Délimitation du plateau continental entre Etats voisins' (1976) 14 *Canadian Yearbook of International Law*, p. 141; Charles Vallée, *Le Plateau continental dans le droit positif actuel* (Paris: Editions A. Pedone, 1971), p. 273 ff.; Marek, Krystyna, 'Le Problème des sources du droit international dans l'arrêt sur le plateau continental de la mer du Nord' (1970) 6 *Revue Belge de Droit International*, 44; Wilhelm Wengler, 'Die Abgrenzung des Festlandsockels zwischen benachbarten Staaten' (1969) 22 *Neue Juristische Wochenschrift*, 965; Charney et al., *International Maritime Boundaries*, n. 1, vol. II (Charney and Alexander), Report Number 9-8, p. 1801, Report Number 9-11, p. 1835.

[4] Treaty Between the Kingdom of the Netherlands and the Federal Republic of Germany Concerning the Lateral Delimitation of the Continental Shelf in the Vicinity of the Coast, signed 1 December 1964, 550 UNTS 123; Agreement Between the Kingdom of Denmark and the Federal Republic of Germany Concerning the Delimitation in the Coastal Regions of the Continental Shelf of the North Sea, signed 9 June 1965, 650 UNTS 91.

Denmark both insisted on the application of equidistance as the governing principle for the delimitation of the entire boundary. The Federal Republic refused to use such a principle on the ground that it would result in an unacceptably limited shelf zone due to the overall concavity of the coastal configuration. It would cause the boundaries of Denmark and the Netherlands to intersect at a substantial distance from the common boundary cross point of the shelves of the United Kingdom, the Netherlands and Denmark, close to the centre of the North Sea. Some 13,000 square kilometres were in contention.[5]

The matter was submitted to the ICJ in 1965, based on a tripartite protocol and corresponding bilateral special agreements concluded between the Federal Republic and the others. The parties did not ask the Court to delineate the boundary. Rather, they asked it to expound the 'principles and rules of international law ... applicable to the delimitation' between the parties in dispute.[6] Before the Court, the Netherlands and Denmark again argued that equidistance should mandatorily apply as a rule of law.[7] The Federal Republic, on the other hand, argued that the correct rule to apply under the circumstances of the case is one that would result in the allocation of a 'just and equitable share' of the available continental shelf to all the coastal states.[8] Such allocation should be based upon the proportions of the coastal lengths or the sea frontage. It emphasized that this approach was not a matter of delimitation *ex aequo et bono*. Instead, the Federal Republic relied upon the philosophical concept of *justitia distributiva*, known to each legal system. In particular, the Federal Republic denied the legal nature of equidistance and complained about the 'cut-off' effect caused by applying this method in the present case.[9]

The Court refuted the contentions and arguments of both parties. The concept of *distributive justice*, or just and equitable apportionment, was rejected on grounds that the case was not about apportionment, but about delimitation of the shelf. The shelf, said the Court, already *ipso facto* and *ab initio*, belongs to coastal states as a matter of natural prolongation of the land territory.[10] The Court went on to reject the mandatory application of equidistance.[11] Instead, the Court relied on the

---

[5] Münch, n. 3, p. 458.   [6] ICJ Reports 1969, p. 7.
[7] ICJ Reports 1969, p. 20, para. 13.   [8] ICJ Reports 1969, p. 21, para. 16.
[9] ICJ Reports 1969, p. 21, para. 15.
[10] ICJ Reports 1969, pp. 22–3, paras. 18–20; p. 31, para. 43.
[11] ICJ Reports 1969, pp. 43–4, para. 75; p. 44, para. 77; p. 46–7, paras. 81–2.

model of equity and equitable principles, as introduced by the 1945 Truman Proclamation.[12] It developed the model of equity and equitable principles and set forth a number of criteria and factors to be taken into account by the parties as a matter of legal obligation in subsequent negotiations: the general configuration of the coasts of the parties; the physical and geological structure and location of natural resources of the shelf involved; the element of a reasonable degree of proportionality between the continental shelf areas appertaining to the coastal state; and the length of each state's coast measured in the general direction of the coastline.[13]

The Court did not suggest a particular line or *ad hoc* construction for the boundary. In 1971, the three states achieved a practical compromise based on non-equidistance.[14] The negotiated boundaries extended the 'German corridor' to the middle of the North Sea while respecting the already-existing areas under exploitation (in particular the promising Dan-Field) at the northern boundary with Denmark.

B. The 1977/78 Anglo-French Channel *arbitration*

The delimitation of the continental shelf in the English Channel and its western approaches in the Atlantic area posed problems during negotiations preceding this landmark arbitration[15] for two reasons. Firstly, the

---

[12] ICJ Reports 1969, p. 32, para. 47 ('the starting point of the positive law of the subject'); ICJ Reports 1969, p. 47, para. 86 ('must be considered as having propounded the rules of law in this field'). For a discussion of the proclamation see Chapter 2 and Chapter 4 (III)(A)(2).
[13] ICJ Reports 1969, pp. 47–54, paras. 83–101. For detailed discussion see Part III.
[14] Agreement between the Federal Republic of Germany and the Kingdom of Denmark Concerning the Delimitation of the Continental Shelf Under the North Sea, done 28 January 1971, St/LEG/SER.B/16 224 (1976); Agreement Between the Kingdom of the Netherlands and the Federal Republic of Germany Concerning the Delimitation of the Continental Shelf Under the North Sea, done 28 January 1971, ibid., p. 419; the extension of the German shelf required a delimitation with the United Kingdom, Agreement Between the United Kingdom of Great Britain and Northern Ireland and the Federal Republic of Germany Relating to the Delimitation of the Continental Shelf Under the North Sea Between the Two Countries, done 25 November 1972, 880 UNTS 185. The agreements represent a political compromise. See D. von Schenk, 'Die Verträge zur Abgrenzung des Festlandsockels unter der Nordsee zwischen der Bundesrepublik Deutschland, Dänemark und den Niederlanden nach dem Urteil des Internationalen Gerichtshofes vom 20. Februar 1969' (1970) *Jahrbuch für Internationales Recht*, 379.
[15] Arbitration Between the United Kingdom of Great Britain and Northern Ireland and the French Republic on the Delimitation of the Continental Shelf, Decisions of the Court of Arbitration dated 30 June 1977 and 14 March 1978, Command Paper 7438, March 1979, reprinted in 18 ILM (1979), 397 (hereinafter Award); Appendix II, Map 2. For general

English Channel Islands, under British sovereignty for purposes of foreign relations, consist of an archipelagic formation of four main groups with the principle islands of Alderney, Guernsey, Jersey, Sark, Herm and Jethon. The islands are situated off the coast of France, the closest, the island of Ecrehos, being only 6.6 miles from the continent. Geologically, the islands are both linked to the English mainland by a basic continuity of the shelf, and also separated from it by a the trough of Hurd Deep, a trench of some 100 metres running a few miles north of the islands in south-westerly direction for some 80 miles. Secondly, in the western part (or the western approaches or Atlantic area), both states show atypical coastal configurations in the sense that they are neither in a clearly opposite nor in a clearly adjacent constellation. Moreover, both parties have islands: the Scilly Isles off the Cornish coast and the island of Ushant (Quessant) off the Brest peninsula. As possible base points, both groups of islands could strongly influence the direction of the western boundary extending into the Atlantic Ocean.

Negotiations between France and the United Kingdom took place between 1970 and 1974 and reached a partial agreement.[16] However, they failed to settle a boundary in the area 30 minutes west of the Greenwich meridian as far as the 1,000 metre isobath in the Atlantic region. The case was submitted by Special Agreement to a Court of

---

discussion see Derek W. Bowett, 'The Arbitration Between the United Kingdom and France Concerning the Continental Shelf Boundary in the English Channel and South-Western Approaches' (1978) 49 *British Yearbook of International Law*, 1; M. D. Blecher, 'Equitable Delimitation of Continental Shelf' (1979) 73 *American Journal of International Law*, 60; Edward Duncan Brown, 'The Anglo-French Continental Shelf Case' (1979) 16 *San Diego Law Review*, 461; Brown, n. 3, p. 88 ff.; David A. Colson, 'The United Kingdom-France Continental Shelf Arbitration' (1978) 72 *American Journal of International Law*, 95; David A. Colson, 'The United Kingdom-France Continental Shelf Arbitration: Interpretative Decision of March 1978' (1979) 73 *American Journal of International Law*, 112; J. G. Merills, 'The United Kingdom-France Continental Shelf Arbitration' (1980) 10 *California Western International Law Journal*, 314; Jean-Pierre Quéneudec, 'L'Affaire de la délimitation du plateau continental entre la France et le Royaume Uni' (1979) 83 *Revue Générale de Droit International Public*, 53; Bernd Rüster, 'Das britisch-französische Schiedsverfahren über die Abgrenzung des Festlandsockels: Die Entscheidungen vom 30. Juni 1977 und vom 14. März 1978' (1978) 40 *Zeitschrift für ausländisches öffentliches Recht und Völkerrecht*; Elisabeth Zoller, 'L'Affaire de la délimitation du plateau continental entre la République française et le Royaume-Uni de Grande-Bretagne et d'Irlande du Nord' (1977) 28 *Annuaire Français de Droit International*, 359; Charney et al., *International Maritime Boundaries*, n. 1, vol. II (Charney and Alexander), p. 1735, Report Number 9-3.

[16] For a map see Quéneudec, n. 15, p. 54.

Arbitration.[17] Unlike in the *North Sea* cases, these parties asked for a final delimitation of the continental shelf boundary.

Britain argued that the Channel Islands are to be taken into full account under Article 6 of the 1958 Shelf Convention and that the requirements for considering special circumstances were not met. The Islands' entitlement to a shelf was stressed, in accordance with Article 1(b) of the Convention. The United Kingdom further claimed a strict median line fully embracing the islands in a deep loop towards the French coast, linking the shelf of the islands with that of the English mainland.[18] France, on the other hand, argued that the islands should be completely ignored when drawing a median line in the Channel. Instead, the line should be measured from the French and English coasts.[19] With regard to the south-western approaches (or the Atlantic area), the United Kingdom argued that the two coasts were opposite, and that no proof existed to justify the use of special circumstances to depart from the median line. Full effect should be given to both the Scilly Islands and the Island of Ushant, leaving the result similar to that under customary law. The United Kingdom went on to assert that if the median line were to be departed from, this could only be done by relying on the natural boundary of the Hurd Deep Fault Zone, a continuation of the Hurd Deep to the south-west and south of the median line.[20]

France, on the other side, proposed a median line consisting of a line bisecting the general directions of the coastlines of the English and the French coasts (*lignes de lissages*). It argued that neither paragraph 1 nor 2 of Article 6 of the 1958 Shelf Convention would apply, as the situation is neither one of opposite nor adjacent coasts in the Atlantic area.[21]

In making its decision, the Court of Arbitration essentially adopted the French position. Relying upon the doctrine set forth by the *North Sea*

---

[17] Art. 2(1)(2) of the special agreement reads:
What is the course of the boundary (or boundaries) between the portions of the continental shelf appertaining to the United Kingdom and the Channel Islands and to the French Republic, respectively, westward of 30 minutes west of the Greenwich Meridian as far as the 1,000 metre isobath?
Award, n. 15, p. 6.
[18] Award, n. 15, p. 76, para. 146, and submissions, p. 14, para. 3(d) [404]; 20, para. 3(d).
[19] Award, n. 15, p. 76, para. 146 and submissions, p. 11, para. B(a); p. 17, para. B(a); Bowett, n. 15, p. 7.
[20] Award, n. 15, p. 99, para. 210, submissions, p. 14; submissions, p. 20, para. 3(a); Bowett, n. 15, p. 10.
[21] Award, n. 15, p. 98, para. 207, submissions, p. 12; submissions, p. 18, para. B(b).

cases, the Court applied the model of equity and equitable principles.[22] It declined to apply the rule of equidistance–special circumstance of Article 6 of the 1958 Shelf Convention due to a French reservation made at its accession to the agreement. The Court drew a median line without taking into account the Channel Islands, but granted them a 12-mile territorial sea toward the median line, leaving undefined the extension of that zone toward the French coast.[23]

In the Atlantic area, the Court adopted its own proposition of giving half-effect to both the Scilly Isles and Ushant.[24] It drew a straight boundary line roughly in the middle of the lines as proposed by the two parties to the dispute.[25] An additional award in March 1978 completed and clarified the base points from which the territorial sea of the Channel Islands has to be measured.[26]

A British petition to modify the straight loxodrome boundary line in the Atlantic into a geodesic line was declined.[27] The disputed line had been drawn by the technical experts of the Court on the basis of a mercator navigational chart by means of plane geometry. This resulted

---

[22] Submissions, n. 15, pp. 31–50, paras. 29–74.

[23] In 1965, when acceding to the Shelf Convention, France made what the Court held to be a reservation which included the application of Art. 6 in areas beyond the 200 m isobath and in the Bay of Biscay and Granville, the areas of Dover, the North Sea off the French coast, and therefore included the area in dispute (p. 33, para. 33). The UK in 1954, rejected such a reservation concerning Art. 6, saying they were 'unable to accept' it (p. 34, para. 34 at the end). The result was complete disagreement over whether this legal conflict rendered the treaty not being in force and operation between the parties (French position, p. 35, para. 36; p. 44, para. 57) or whether it invalidated the reservation (UK position, pp. 3738, paras. 41–3; p. 44, para. 58). In its opinion of general importance to the law of reservations to multilateral treaties, the Court held that Art. 6 does not apply for the reservation as it extends geographically (pp. 44–5, paras. 59–61). This ruling resulted in the application of what the Court held to be the customary law of equitable principles in the Channel area (p. 50, para. 74). In the Atlantic area, Art. 6 was held applicable for interesting reasons. The parties had agreed, in the course of their negotiations, on a French proposal to extend the delimitation from the 200 m isobath to the 1,000 m isobath. The Court found it relevant that during these negotiations no suggestion was made to exclude the application of Art. 6 altogether (p. 49, para. 73). In effect, the negotiations were found to include a tacit withdrawal of the 200 m isobath reservation and a subsequent tacit agreement between the parties to rely upon Art. 6. This provided an opportunity to the Court to discuss and clarify the relationship of the model of rule – exception in Art. 6 and the concept of equitable principles, discussed below in Chapters 8–12.

[24] Award, n. 15, pp. 95–6, paras. 201–3. The Court did not find itself to have jurisdiction under Art. 2(1) of the Special Agreement to delimit the seabed boundary between the Channel Islands and the French mainland, p. 28, para. 20.

[25] Award, n. 15, p. 117, para. 251.   [26] Ibid., p. 118, para. 254.

[27] Ibid., pp. 162–6, paras. 31–7.

in distortions of approximately 4 miles at the 1,000 meter isobath and several miles at the 200-mile limit, at the expense of the United Kingdom's shelf.[28]

C. The 1981 Arbitration concerning the Border between the Emirates of Dubai and Sharjah

The coastal facade of the two federate states of the United Arab Emirates in the Persian Gulf engaged in this arbitration[29] does not show major peculiarities except for the island of Abu Musa, a territory of the Emirate of Sharjah having more than 800 inhabitants. This island is situated approximately 35 nm offshore, in the middle of the Gulf. The coast of the Federation extends 240 nm from Qatar to Oman. The coastline from the boundary of Abu Dhabi and Dubai to the boundary of Sharjah and Oman in the south extends 41 nm.

The Court of Arbitration was requested to delimitate both the land border and the maritime boundary of the homogeneous continental shelf of the two federate states. The case involved the analysis of complex historical facts and conduct of the parties. With respect to the land boundary in particular, delimitation was necessary to allocate the formerly nomadic, borderless territory for the purpose of oil extraction. While the land boundary is not of interest in the present context, the arguments and decisions with regard to the maritime boundary are an important contribution to the emerging case law on our subject.

Dubai and Sharjah requested the Court to decide the case in accordance with international law. Neither of the parties were signatories to the 1958 Shelf Conventions, and the 1949 British-sponsored declarations stipulated that future delimitations be made in accordance with the model of equitable principles.[30] Sharjah primarily claimed a boundary based on former conduct and historical title of a 312-degree rhumb line (i.e. a line cutting the meridians at the same angle) from the land boundary, in accordance with a British proposal from 1956. In fact, that line had been a simplified equidistance line ignoring Abu Musa. Subsidiarily, Sharjah claimed an equidistance line taking into account special circumstances, in particular the amount of marine space (territorial and shelf) allocated to the two states in federacy.

---

[28] Ibid., pp. 182–94, paras. 85–113.
[29] (1993) 91 ILR 549; Appendix II, Map 3; D. W. Bowett, 'The Dubai/Sharjah Boundary Arbitration' (1994) 65 BYIL, 103.
[30] Chapter 5(I)(A).

Given the position of, and its jurisdiction over, the island of Abu Musa, Sharjah first claimed to give full effect to the island. This position was later changed to half-effect when it was seen that a full-effect boundary would cut into existing oil fields that were under Dubai's jurisdiction (Fateh Field). However, no effect should be given to the outermost permanent harbour constructions, as this would benefit Dubai. Dubai also claimed the application of equidistance, but without giving any effect to the island. Dubai reasoned that Abu Musa was too remote from the coastline and too close to the equidistance line between the parties, and that giving effect to it would constitute an encroachment on the natural prolongation of its land boundary. Conversely, Dubai argued, full effect should be given to the harbour constructions when establishing relevant base lines.

The Court of Arbitration established the land boundary based on conduct and historical title at the extremity of the Al Mamzer peninsula. It did not consider the proposal of 312-degree rhumb line, which relied on a different terminus of the land boundary and therefore could not be of relevance. The Court then proceeded to delimit the maritime boundary in accordance with customary international law. In doing so, the Court also heavily took into account the relevant provisions of the 1958 Conventions and the then-existing draft proposals of UNCLOS III that relied upon the equitable principles approach.[31] In accordance with law and practice, the history of Article 8 of the 1958 Territorial Sea and the Contiguous Zone, and Article 5 of the 1980 Draft Convention, the Court affirmed the inclusion of the outermost permanent harbour works of both parties, denying that this would lead to inequitable results. Relying on the *North Sea* cases and the *Anglo-French Channel* arbitration, the Court also found that equidistance should apply without taking into account the island of Abu Musa. For that purpose, it relied upon calculations of allocation of marine spaces. It argued that giving half-effect to the island would result in a disproportionate and exaggerated entitlement to marine space by Sharjah. The Court established a boundary by equidistance beginning from the land boundary until it intersects with the 12-mile territorial sea of that island, and continuing to the unsettled boundary with Iran. As a result, no continental shelf was allocated to the inhabited island of Abu Musa, and Dubai was made the clear winner of the case.

[31] Chapter 4(III)(A)(4).

D. The 1982 and 1985 Tunisia v. Libya Continental Shelf cases

The geography of the area of delimitation in this case[32] is characterized by a large triangular indentation of the North African coast between Ras Kaboudia, Tunisia and Ras Tajoura, Libya. The area of the common land boundary is fairly even and straight in the direction of the coastline. Further north-west, though, the island of Jerba (Jazirat Jarbah), the significant concavity of the Gulf of Gabes (Kalij Qabis), the almost rectangular change of direction of the coast within the Gulf, and finally the archipelago of the Kerkennah Islands (Juzur Qarquanna) are prominent features of the area. These constitute the complicating geographical elements that led to this dispute.

---

[32] *Continental Shelf (Tunisia v. Libyan Arab Jamahiriya)*, Judgment, ICJ Reports 1982, p. 18; *Application for Revision and Interpretation of the Judgment of 24 February 1982 in the Case concerning the Continental Shelf (Tunisia v. Libyan Arab Jamahiriya) (Tunisia v. Libyan Arab Jamahiriya)*, Judgment, ICJ Reports 1985, p. 192; Appendix II, Map 4. For general discussion see American Society of International Law, 'Workshop on ICJ Decision in the Libya-Tunisia Continental Shelf Case' (1982) 76 *American Society of International Law Proceedings*, 150 (with contributions from Charney, Feldman, Rhee and Stein); Romualdo Bermejo, 'Les Principes équitables et les délimitations des zones maritimes: analyse des affaires Tunisie/Jamahariya Arabe Libyenne et du Golfe du Maine' (1988) 1 *Hague Yearbook of International Law*, 59; Brown (1992), n. 3, pp. 139 ff.; Edward Duncan Brown, 'The Tunisia/Libya Continental Shelf Case: A Missed Opportunity' (1983) 7 *Marine Policy*, 142; Donna R. Christie, 'From the Shoals of the Ras Kaboudia to the Shores of Tripoli: The Tunisia/Libya Continental Shelf Boundary Delimitation' (1983) 13 *Georgia Journal of International and Comparative Law*, 1; Emmanuel Decaux, 'L'Arrêt de la Cour internationale de justice dans l'affaire du plateau continental (Tunisie/Libye)' (1982) 28 *Annuaire Français de Droit International*, 357; Mark B. Feldman, 'The Tunisia-Libya Continental Shelf Case: Geographic Justice or Judicial Compromise?' (1983) 77 *American Journal of International Law*, 219; Jagota, n. 3, pp. 168–206; Lawrence L. Herman, 'The Court Giveth and the Court Taketh Away: An Analysis of the Tunisia-Libya Continental Shelf Case' (1984) 33 *International and Comparative Law Quarterly*, 825; Note, 'International Court of Justice Judgment of February 24, 1982: Case Concerning the Continental Shelf (Tunisia/Libya Arab Jamahiriya)' (1983) 4 *Ocean Yearbook*, 515; Karin Oellers-Fram, 'Die Entscheidung des IGH zur Abgrenzung des Festlandsockels zwischen Tunesien und Libyen: eine Abkehr von der bisherigen Rechtssprechung?' (1982) 42 *Zeitschrift für ausländisches öffentliches Recht und Völkerrecht* V, 804; Jean-Pierre Quéneudec, 'Note sur l'arrêt de la Cour internationale de justice relatif à la délimitation du plateau continental entre la Tunisie et la Libye' (1981) 27 *Annuaire Français de Droit International*, 203; Wilhelm Wengler, 'Der internationale Gerichtshof und die Angrenzung des Meeresbodens im Mittelmeer' (1982) *Neue Juristische Wochenschrift* 1198; Elisabeth Zoller, 'Recherches sur les méthodes de délimitation du plateau continental: à propos de l'affaire Tunisie-Libye' (1982) 86 *Revue Générale de Droit International Public*, 645; Charney et al., *International Maritime Boundaries*, n. 1, vol. II, (Charney and Alexander), p. 1649, Report Number 8-8.

Tunisia and Libya both granted offshore oil concessions in the boundary area since 1964 and 1968, respectively, but did so without a delimitation of the shelf. Until 1972, both states took into account a 26-degree line when they granted concessions, as this line had been used since 1913 (and more formally since 1919) as a *modus vivendi* for purposes of offshore fishing activities. In 1974, a Tunisian concession applied equidistance, while Libya continued to draw the area of the concession along the 26-degree line. The result was an overlapping of claims in an area 50 miles from the coast. In 1977, following mutual protests and cursory diplomatic intercourse, the matter was submitted to the ICJ. In the special agreement, the Court was asked to declare the principles and rules of international law which may be applied for the delimitation, taking into account equitable principles and relevant circumstances, as well as the then 'recent trends' recognized at UNCLOS III. The Court was not asked to draw a boundary line itself, but was to formulate its order sufficiently precisely so as to allow a technical delimitation by experts without any difficulties.[33] Neither state was a party to the 1958 Shelf Convention. Both viewed equidistance as an unsuitable approach under the particular configuration of the case. Instead, both parties to the dispute primarily relied on geological and geomorphological evidence and theories, in the application of the principle of natural prolongation as expounded by the Court in the 1969 *North Sea* cases.

Tunisia argued that the area in dispute, the Pellagian Sea, is an easterly extension of 'submerged Tunisia' in geological terms.[34] Relying on minor geological features (ridges, furrows) and, in a second line of arguments, on geography and geometrical constructions, Tunisia claimed a so-called sheaf of lines that extended within a range of 60 to 63 degrees east-north-east.[35] At the same time, based on an historic title of sponge fishing, Tunisia claimed the entire Gulf of Gabes as its territorial sea to the 50 metre isobath, and delimited against Libya by a 45 degree line (*zénith verticale*) established for the purposes of maritime surveillance.[36]

Libya, on the other hand, relied upon the then-recently developed theory of plate tectonics that characterized the shelf off the Libyan

---

[33] ICJ Reports 1982, p. 21, para. 2.
[34] ICJ Reports 1982, p. 52, para. 58; p. 55, para. 62; p. 73, para. 99.
[35] *Continental Shelf (Tunisia v. Libyan Arab Jamahiriya)*, Memorial of Tunisia, 27 May 1980, pp. 199–200, pp. 205–8; ICJ Reports 1982, p. 81, map 2; Feldman, n. 32, 224.
[36] Tunisian Memorial, submission 2, p. 187, quoted in ICJ Reports 1982, see n. 34, p. 26, para. 15.

coast as a 'northward thrust' of the African land mass.[37] Under this theory, Libya claimed a boundary in a northward direction in a first segment. A second segment reflected the coastline of Tunisia and extended parallel to the general direction of that coast without taking into account the archipelago of the Kerkennahs.[38]

The Court dismissed the geological and geomorphological facts as irrelevant.[39] Instead, it relied on geographical considerations[40] and human factors relating to the previous conduct of the parties.[41] The judgment separated the boundary area into two sectors. The first, closer to the land, begins at the outer limit of the territorial sea. It follows the traditional line of *modus vivendi* of approximately 26 degrees east of north, linking the intersection of the land boundary at Ras Ajdir and the co-ordinate 33° 55' N, 12° E, accepted as being the south-western point of a Libyan concession (a fact later disputed in 1985[42]).

A second sector reflects the radical change of the coastline in the Gulf of Gabes. The maritime boundary runs at a bearing of approximately 52 degrees to the meridian. This line was established as a parallel to a line drawn from the most westerly point of the Gulf of Gabes, bisecting an angle formed by a line from that point to Ras Kaboudia and a line drawn from the same point along the Kerkennah Islands. It thereby gave half-effect to that archipelago.[43] The line ran seaward without delimitation, given the fact that the boundary between Libya and Malta was still pending. The result appears as an intermediate solution between the claims of the parties, but the judgment provided a boundary line leaving practically no discretion for further negotiations of the parties.

There was disagreement over whether a correct understanding of the special agreement should include the task of precisely specifying the practical method of application of the relevant principles and rules. The Court found its task to be somewhere between the *North Sea* cases

---

[37] ICJ Reports 1982, p. 52, para. 57. See also Libyan Memorial, Submission 5, quoted in ICJ Reports 1982, p. 29, para 15.
[38] Libyan Counter-Memorial, submissions 6 and 7, quoted in ICJ Reports 1982, p. 31, para. 15, see also p. 81, map 2.
[39] ICJ Reports 1982, pp. 50-8, paras. 51-68, 80.
[40] ICJ Reports 1982, pp. 61-5, paras. 73-81.
[41] ICJ Reports 1982, pp. 65-71, 83-5, paras. 82-96, 117-19. See Chapter 9.
[42] See text accompanying n. 50 ss.
[43] ICJ Reports 1982, pp. 92-3, para. 133 (operative part) and, in particular, at p. 85, para. 121; p. 89, para. 129; p. 90, map 3.

and the *Channel* arbitration.[44] It construed the compromise rather extensively, in such a way that the only remaining negotiations could be for the technical details of implementation.[45] Indeed, the first segment was precisely defined by linking two specific points. The second segment was defined at a bearing of 52 degrees to the meridian, and only the exact base points to construct such a line were left to the parties to define.

Libya objected to the Court playing an activist role. This is one of the reasons why no agreement was reached following the judgment. Neither was Tunisia content with the result achieved. In 1984 it filed an application for revision in accordance with Article 61 and for an interpretation based on Article 60 of the Statute of the ICJ. It requested a correction of the judgment, but did not challenge the basic methods and approach applied by the Court in 1982. Tunisia argued that the point 33° 55' E, 12° N did not accurately define the westerly limits of Libyan concessions. The line of approximately 26 degrees to the north created overlaps. This, it argued, was contrary to the rationale of the ruling, which should correspond to the angle of the north-western boundary of existing Libyan concessions and align on the south-eastern boundary of Tunisian oil concessions. It asked the Court to replace that point with the co-ordinates; 33° 50' 17" N, 11° 59' 53" E, the real south-western corner of the relevant Libyan concession, resulting in a line of 24° 75' 03" east of north, instead of 26 degrees.

Moreover, Tunisia sought a judicial declaration that the most westerly point of the Tunisian coastline between Ras Kaboudia and Ras Ajdir be the base point of the most westerly point on the shore lines (low-water mark) of the Gulf of Gabes at 34° 05' 20" N (Cartage). Subsidiarily, it requested the Court to order an expert survey.[46] Libya argued the inadmissibility of the revision on substantive and jurisdictional grounds.[47]

The Court unanimously rejected the arguments of Tunisia on several grounds. Although it is quite evident that the 1982 Court was not aware of the true boundaries of the oil concessions and that the overlaps were created unintentionally,[48] the existence of a new fact was denied, since Tunisia could have presented it to the Court on the basis of existing materials.[49] Moreover, the Court stated that the point in dispute was not

---

[44] Charney, ASIL Proceedings, n. 32, p. 154–5 ('Splitting the difference was the Court's prime objective').
[45] ICJ Reports 1982, p. 38, para. 25.   [46] ICJ Reports 1985, pp. 195–6, para. 6.
[47] ICJ Reports 1985, pp. 195–6, para. 6.
[48] ICJ Reports 1985, p. 236, para. 2 (Judge Oda, separate opinion).
[49] ICJ Reports 1985, p. 205, para. 23.

a decisive factor for Article 61 of the ICJ Statute. The line of approximately 26 degrees east of the meridian primarily reflects the de facto maritime limit respected by the parties prior to 1974 and an element of a reasonable degree of proportionality.[50] The Court, however, accepted the job of clarifying the most westerly point of the Gulf of Gabes, but reconfirmed that its determination was a matter to be defined by experts in accordance with the 1982 judgment. It denied its authority to order an expert survey.[51]

In 1988, Libya and Tunisia signed three agreements: one concerning the implementation of the 1982 ICJ judgment; one creating a joint venture for oil research and exploitation; and one on the financing of joint projects by percentage of oil revenues.[52]

E. The 1984 Canada v. United States Gulf of Maine case

The Gulf of Maine forms a significant indentation of the North American eastern coast. It is framed in a roughly rectangular shape by the coast and bays of Massachussetts, the coast of Maine, and the south-western coast of Nova Scotia. Contiguous to the Gulf lies the Bay of Fundy, defined at its northern expanses by the coast of New Brunswick and the northern coast of Nova Scotia. The land boundary between Canada and the United States reaches the Gulf in its most northern part, following the Saint Croix River and ending in the Grand Manan Channel, close to Grand Manan Island. In a seaward direction, the significant features of the George Bank in the south and the Brown's Bank off the southern coast of Nova Scotia can be found, each separated from the other by the Northeast Channel.

All these areas, including the Bay of Fundy, comprised the area in dispute in this leading case.[53] Its soil and subsoil are essentially

---

[50] ICJ Reports 1985, p. 210, para. 35.
[51] ICJ Reports 1985, p. 221-7, paras. 53-63; pp. 227-9, paras. 64-8.
[52] Charney et al., *International Maritime Boundaries*, n. 1, vol. II (Charney and Alexander), p. 1663 Report Number 8-9.
[53] *Delimitation of the Maritime Boundary in the Gulf of Maine Area (Canada v. United States of America)*, Judgment, ICJ Reports 1984, p. 246; Appendix II, Map 5. The case attracted considerable pretrial attention. For general discussion see S. H. Amin, 'Law of Continental Shelf Delimitation: The Gulf Example' (1980) 27 *Netherlands International Law Review*, 335; Brown (1999), n. 3, p. 226 ff.; L. E. Clain, 'Gulf of Maine – A Disappointing First in the Delimitation of a Single Maritime Boundary' (1985) 25 *Virginia Journal of International Law*, 521; John Cooper, 'Delimitation of the Maritime Boundary in the Gulf of Maine Area' (1986) 16 *Ocean Development & International Law*, 59; Emmanuel Decaux, 'L'Arrêt de la Chambre de La Cour Internationale de Justice sur l'affaire de la délimitation de la frontière maritime dans le

continuous, without significant geological features or particularities.[54] The water column provides a large habitat for living resources, particularly on the Georges Bank. Unlike the geological structure, the ecological characteristics of the area were fiercely disputed by Canada and the United States. This conflict centred around whether there are different and discernible ecological systems in the Gulf, on the Nova Scotian Shelf and, in particular, on the Georges Bank, separated by the South and Northeast Channels from other systems.[55]

The dispute arose in 1964 as a matter of continental shelf delimitation, when the United States issued exploratory drilling permits on the Georges Bank, and Canada did so in the Gulf. The case has a history of long and protracted, but ultimately unsuccessful, negotiations.[56] It was characterized by two basic positions. Until 1977, Canada claimed a strict equidistance line cutting across the Georges Bank. The United States, on the other hand, claimed the entire area of the Georges Bank ever since, as a natural prolongation of the US land mass and territory.[57]

Golfe du Maine (Canada/Etats-Unis)' (1984) 19 *Annuaire Français de Droit International*, 304. Mark B. Feldman and David A. Colson, 'The Maritime Boundary of the United States' (1981) 75 *American Journal of International Law*, 729, 754; Jagota, n. 3, p. 290; L. H. Legault and Blair Hankey, 'From Sea to Seabed: The Single Maritime Boundary in the Gulf of Maine Case' (1984) 22 *Canadian Yearbook of International Law*, 267; Donald M. McRae, 'Adjudication of Maritime Boundary in the Gulf of Maine' (1979) 17 *Canadian Yearbook of International Law*. 292; Donald M. McRae, 'Proportionality and the Gulf of Maine Maritime Boundary Dispute' (1981) 19 *Canadian Yearbook of International Law*, 287; Donald M. McRae, 'The Gulf of Maine Case: The Written Proceedings' (1983) 21 *Canadian Yearbook of International Law*, 266; Sang-Myon Rhee, 'Equitable Solutions to the Maritime Boundary Dispute between the United States and Canada in the Gulf of Maine' (1981) 75 *American Journal of International Law*, 590; Sang-Myon Rhee, 'The Application of Equitable Principles to Resolve the United States – Canada Dispute over East Coast Fishery Resources'(1980) 21 *Harvard International Law Journal*, 667; Jan Schneider, 'The Gulf of Maine Case: The Nature of an Equitable Result' (1985) 79 *American Journal of International Law*, 539; David Van der Zwaag, *The Fish Feud: The U.S. and Canadian Boundary Dispute* (Lexington KY, Toronto: Lexington Books, 1983); David A. Colson, 'Litigating Maritime Boundary Disputes at the International Level – One Perspective', in D. G. Dallmeyer and L. De Vorsey (eds.), *Rights to Oceanic Resources* (Dordrecht: Martinus Nijhoff Publishers,1989), p. 75 (an interesting assessment of the negotiations and a lawyer's experience in that case); Charney et al., *International Maritime Boundaries*, n. 1, vol. I (Charney and Alexander), p. 401, Report Number 1-3.

[54] ICJ Reports 1984, p. 273–4, paras. 44, 45.
[55] ICJ Reports 1984, p. 275–6, paras. 50, 51. See also US submission B(1)(a)(b), US submission, p. 258, para. 12 and restated in subsequent submissions to the Court.
[56] See pre-trial publications above, n. 56; e.g. Rhee (1981), n. 56, 602.
[57] ICJ Reports 1984, p. 278–83, paras. 60–8, 74.

A new dimension complicated the matter in 1976, when both parties proclaimed 200 nm exclusive fishing zones.[58] The dispute now extended to the water column. The Interim Fisheries Agreement operated from July 1977 to June 1978.[59] Based upon a joint report of 1977, an elaborate co-operative treaty on fisheries was reached in March 1979, including an agreement to submit the boundary dispute to a Chamber of the ICJ.[60] When the United States Senate withdrew the *Agreement on East Coast Fisheries Resources* from consideration in March 1981, the matter was submitted to a Chamber of the ICJ in November 1981.[61]

The special agreement fixed a starting point (A) for delimitation within the Gulf, and a triangular area adjacent to it in a south-easterly direction off the Georges Bank, as the area defining the range of possible end points. The Chamber was requested to make a decision, which would be final and binding upon the parties, as to the exact course and location of a single all-purpose boundary 'in accordance with the principles and rules of international law'.[62]

The main interest of both parties was clearly focused on the Georges Bank. The United States was primarily concerned with the fisheries jurisdiction, whereas Canada's main focus remained on the non-living resources of the Bank.[63] The preoccupations of the parties are reflected by the respective delimitations envisaged. The final application by the United States claimed a line perpendicular to the Maine coast at Point A, proceeding in rectangular segments through the Northeast Channel, applying what the Court described as an 'ecological method',[64] in order

---

[58] ICJ Reports 1984, p. 282, para. 68; see McRae, n. 55, pp. 292–4.
[59] ICJ Reports 1984, p. 283, para. 69.   [60] ICJ Reports 1984, pp. 286–7, para. 75.
[61] ICJ Reports 1984, p. 287, para. 76. It was the first case using the new instrument of an appointed Chamber of the Court in accordance with Arts. 26(2) and 31 of the ICJ Statute and the Treaty to Submit to Binding Dispute Settlement of the Delimitation of the Maritime Boundary in the Gulf of Maine Area, signed 29 March 1979. See also Elisabeth Zoller, 'La Première constitution d'une Chambre spéciale par la Cour internationale de justice: Observations sur l'ordonnance du 20 janvier 1982'(1982) 86 *Revue Générale de Droit International Public*, 305.
[62] Special Agreement Article II(1), ICJ Reports 1984, p. 253, para. 5. See also map 1 at 269.
[63] ICJ Reports 1984, p. 283, para. 70:
It is important to stress that, within the dual dimension characterising the dispute between the two states following the Proclamation by each of them of an exclusive fishery zone, the United States attributed importance in particular to the fishing aspect, whilst Canada long continued to give priority to the original aspect, i.e., the continental shelf.
[64] ICJ Reports 1984, pp. 57–61.

to preserve the vitality of the ecosystem and particularly that of the fish stocks of the entire Georges Bank.[65] The United States stressed the historical use of the Bank, which had been almost exclusively by the United States fishing industry. They also pointed to the serious effects of depletion of stocks that would occur if a single national management scheme for the conservation of the Bank was not implemented.[66]

Canada, on the other hand, claimed a line of modified equidistance, which discounted (under the influence of the 1977 Channel Arbitration) the US peninsula of Cape Code and the islands of Nantucket and Martha's Vineyard. Their argument would shift the median closer to the US coast.[67] The Canadians justified their claim by reliance on adjacency;[68] on estoppel grounded on the United States' early acquiescence to their use of the area;[69] and on the socio-economic impact on the (dependent) fishing industry of Nova Scotia.[70]

The Chamber rejected the application of Article 6 of the 1958 Shelf Convention, to which both states were parties, on grounds that the object of the dispute was an all-purpose boundary.[71] Also, the legal relevance of arguments based on conduct was refuted under the facts of the

---

[65] See ICJ Reports 1984, map 3 at 289 and 284–5, 287, paras. 73 and 77. See in particular the United States Memorial, ICJ Reports 1984, p. 258, para. 12, lit. A(1)(b): 'The principle that the delimitation facilitates conservation and management or resources of the area,' and lit. B(2)(a) and (b):

That the relevant environmental circumstances in the area include:

(a) The three separate and identifiable ecological regimes associated, respectively, with the Gulf of Maine Basin, Georges Bank and the Scotian Shelf; and

(b) The Northeast Channel as the natural boundary dividing not only separate and identifiable ecological regimes of Georges Bank and the Scotian Shelf, but also most of the commercially important fish stocks associated with each such regime.

For discussion of the approach see Part III, Chapter 9. The formerly proposed line of delimitation, as proclaimed unilaterally by the United States in 1976 (Fed. Reg. of November 4, 1976) was based on an equidistance–special circumstances approach, following the thalweg in the North Eastern Channel. See ICJ Reports 1984, map 2 at 285 and 283–4, para. 70.

[66] ICJ Reports 1984, pp. 277–8, para. 58. For the claim of exclusive historical use see p. 259, para. 12 US Memorial lit. B(3)(a)–(c) (restated in subsequent submissions).

[67] ICJ Reports 1984, p. 284, para. 71; map 3 at 289.

[68] ICJ Reports 1984, p. 296, para. 102.

[69] ICJ Reports 1984, pp. 304, 310, paras. 127, 128, 149.

[70] ICJ Reports 1984, pp. 277–8, para. 58.

[71] ICJ Reports 1984, pp. 301–3, paras. 118–24.

case.[72] The Chamber relied exclusively on geographical configurations and geometrical methods for the construction of the boundary line.[73] Socio-economic, historic and ecological factors were only considered for the purposes of a final test of the equitableness of results achieved in the Georges Bank area.[74]

The Chamber reached a decision to declare a boundary consisting of three segments. Based on the perception of the Gulf of Maine as a rectangular indentation,[75] the first segment (A–B) was established as a bisector of the lines along the Maine coast (Cape Elisabeth to the international land boundary), and from the latter point, the Cape Sable along the south-west coast of Nova Scotia.[76]

The second segment (B–C) consists of a median line, intersecting with the first segment and modified by calculations of proportionality of the respective coastal lengths. It runs between the roughly parallel and opposite coasts of Massachusetts and Nova Scotia as its base lines.[77] However, since the 'back' of the Gulf is entirely United States' territory, the Court shifted the median to the north, enlarging the US share of the Gulf in proportion to the two parties' coastal lengths in the area of delimitation. The Chamber also took into account the Bay of Fundy, except waters within 12 nm. Initially, the Chamber reached a proportion of 284:206 miles, i.e. a factor of 1.38:1 in favour of the United States. This ratio was then modified to take account of the fact that the Chamber had given only half-effect to the Seal Islands off the coast of Nova Scotia. This reduced the proportion to 1.32:1 on the closing line of the Gulf between its closest points on each side, Cape Cod and Cheboque Point on Nova Scotia. As in the French–Spanish Agreement in the Gulf of Biscay,[78] this line finally determined, in the ratio indicated, the end point of the second segment.[79]

The third segment (C–D) was entirely defined by its starting point on the closing line, constructed, as in the Argentina–Uruguay Agreement,[80] as a perpendicular to the closing line, cutting through the Georges Bank roughly in a ratio of 3:1, and reaching the endpoint (D) in the triangular

---

[72] ICJ Reports 1984, pp. 303–12, paras. 126–54.
[73] ICJ Reports 1984, pp. 327–8, paras. 194–6.
[74] ICJ Reports 1984, pp. 278, para. 59 in fine; paras. 232–41.
[75] ICJ Reports 1984, pp. 268–71, paras. 29–34.
[76] ICJ Reports 1984, pp. 331–2, 333, paras. 209, 213.
[77] ICJ Reports 1984, pp. 333–4, paras. 214, 216. [78] See Chapter 4.
[79] ICJ Reports, pp. 335–57, paras. 221–3. [80] See Chapter 5.

prescribed by the special agreement.[81] This solution, again, is a compromise between the claims of the parties to the dispute.[82]

F. The 1985 Guinea v. Guinea-Bissau arbitration

For the most part, the West African coast from Senegal to Sierra Leone is convex. The intermediate coastal front of Guinea-Bissau, Guinea and Sierra Leone, informing this arbitration,[83] is somewhat concave[84] – a configuration not unlike that of the frontal coasts dealt with in the *North Sea Continental Shelf* cases. In western Africa, this concavity posed problems of enclavement to Guinea's disadvantage, as it is situated between two other states. Other particularities of the West African coast, and especially that of Guinea-Bissau, are the largely scattered coastline and the large number of islands. Some of the islands are merely separated from the mainland by narrow sea channels, and others are further out. The mainly uninhabited Bijagos Islands off Guinea-Bissau extend from 2 nm to 37 nm. Further to the south, the islands of Poiloa, Samba, Sene and Alcatrez are scattered over shallow areas. The homogeneity of the shelf was not in dispute among the parties.[85]

The *Guinea/Guinea-Bissau* case has a long and complicated history rooted in the colonial past.[86] Although Portugal had first granted oil concessions to a foreign company off the Guinean coast in 1958, commercial exploitation never began in the boundary area, due to the insecurity of the unsettled boundary. Upon its independence from France, Guinea established lateral limits on the territorial sea of 130 nm

---

[81] ICJ Reports 1984, pp. 337–9, paras. 224–9. [82] See map 3 at 289 and map 4 at 346.
[83] Tribunal Arbitral pour la délimitation de la frontière maritime Guinée/Guinée-Bissau, Sentence du 14 Février 1985, reprinted in French (the authentic text) in (1985) 89 *Revue Générale de Droit International Public*, 484; 'Arbitration Tribunal for the Delimitation of the Maritime Boundary Between Guinea and Guinea-Bissau, Award of 14 February 1985', transl. in (1986) 25 ILM 251 (the 1985 *Guinea v. Guinea-Bissau* arbitration; hereinafter Award); Appendix II, Map 6. The Tribunal was composed of judges of the ICJ, Lachs (President), Mbaye, and Bedjaoui. For general discussion of the case see Brown (1999), n. 3, p. 279; Armel Kerrest, 'Note sur la Sentence du Tribunal Arbitral pour la délimitation de la frontière maritime Guinée/Guinée/Bissau' (1988) 3 *Espaces et Ressources Maritimes* 175, 176; K. A. McLlarky, 'Guinea/Ginea-Bissau: Disputes Concerning Delimitation of Maritime Boundary, February 14, 1985' (1987) *Maryland Journal of International Law and Trade*, 93; Charney et al., *International Maritime Boundaries*, n. 1, vol. I (Charney and Alexander), p. 857, Report Number 4-3.
[84] See Award, n. 83, pp. 294–5, para. 103. [85] See ibid., p. 264, para. 19.
[86] See ibid., pp. 266–70, paras. 26–36. For the background of the long and hostile history of the dispute see Kerrest, n. 87, 177–80, and R. A. Pietrowski, 'Introductory Note' of ILM to the Award, n. 83, p. 251.

in 1964, and expanded them to 200 nm in 1965 along the parallel latitude of 10° 56' 42". Portugal considered such a boundary to be illegal. It argued, instead, for a line of equidistance inspired by Article 12 of the 1958 Convention on the Territorial Sea and the Contiguous Zone. Moreover, Portugal established a base line system partly extending beyond the unilateral boundary decreed along the parallel latitude of 10° 56' 42" by Guinea, a base line that was never disputed.

Upon independence in 1974, Guinea-Bissau enacted a territorial sea of 150 nm. That marked the beginning of the dispute. Guinea first offered the idea of joint development of the disputed areas, a proposal rejected by Guinea-Bissau. Later, Guinea proposed settling the boundary following the *thalweg* of River Cajet, the Pilots Pass, and a parallel of 10° 40'N latitude, in accordance with the final paragraph of Article I of a 1886 convention between France and Portugal which had settled the territorial boundary between the two provinces at the time.[87] Again, Guinea-Bissau rejected the offer.

In 1980, after unsuccessful talks, Guinea unilaterally enacted a maritime boundary on the basis of that agreement. At the same time, it reduced the territorial sea to 12 nm and proclaimed a 200 nm EEZ with the low-water mark as a base line. Guinea-Bissau first proposed an azimuth of 225 degrees drawn from the Pilots Pass. In 1981, claims by Guinea-Bissau were expanded, now requesting a line of equidistance measured from the base lines of both parties.[88]

Upon the failure of further negotiations, the parties agreed to submit the matter to a Tribunal in 1982. The special agreement requested that the Tribunal decide, according to the relevant rules of international law, the course of the boundary between the maritime territories appertaining respectively to the Republic of Guinea-Bissau and the People's Revolutionary Republic of Guinea.[89] Given the importance of the 1886 Convention to this case, the Tribunal was requested to construe the relevant provisions of the Convention and the protocols and documents annexed to it. Guinea argued that the Convention determined a general maritime boundary.[90] Guinea-Bissau disagreed, claiming a line of equidistance taking full account of its islands,[91] but prepared, as it

---

[87] Convention relative à la délimitation des possessions françaises et portugaises dans l'Afrique occidentale, of 12 May 1986, see Award, n. 83, pp. 273–5, para. 45.
[88] Award, n. 83, p. 269 paras. 34–5. [89] Special Agreement, Art. II, Award, at para. 1.
[90] Ibid., Award, n. 83, pp. 261–3, paras. 16–17. [91] Ibid., p. 269, para. 35.

followed from the reasoning of the Tribunal, to accept a modified equidistance line.[92]

The Tribunal concluded that the 1886 Convention, subsequent practice and conduct were limited to defining territorial boundaries, and did not include maritime delimitation.[93] The Tribunal therefore had to define the maritime boundary based on customary law. Based on the model of equitable solution as defined in Article 76(1) and 83(1) of the 1982 LOS Convention,[94] the Court rejected both the Guinean claim to draw a parallel of latitude and the contention of Guinea-Bissau to establish the boundary in accordance with equidistance. Instead, the Tribunal applied *curia novit iura* and developed its own method of delimitation. The resulting boundary has three segments.

The determination of the inner segment, close to the coast, mainly relied upon the conduct of the parties. Following the thalweg of the Cajet River, but without defining it precisely due to natural shifts which may occur,[95] the boundary starts from the intersection of the thalweg and the meridian of 15° 06' 30" west longitude along the line as defined by the 1886 treaty ('the southern limit'). This is not as a matter of conventional title, but was used because that line has been respected by the parties in practice since 1958.[96] It follows the Pilots Pass from the mouth of the Cajet River and the parallel of 10° 40' north latitude as far as the island of Alcatrez.[97]

A second segment was established by extension of the territorial sea from the island of Alcatrez to 12 nm in westerly direction, because the 'southern limit' would otherwise result in a territorial sea of only 2.25 nm.[98]

---

[92] Ibid., p. 293, para. 99.
[93] Ibid., pp. 270–88, paras. 37–84. In addition, it may be said that the 1886 treaty could hardly anticipate the evolution of the law of the sea and therefore the extension of the territorial seas and, in particular, the evolution of the shelf and the EEZ, almost a century later in the post-World War II period of international law. At the time, the territorial sea did not exceed 3 nm. See Chapter 1(II)(C). Moreover, a rejected French proposal to delimit the territorial waters at the time shows that the 1886 treaty could not, even if sea boundaries were included, extend beyond the then contemporary notion of the territorial sea. Award, n. 83, pp. 285 and 287, paras. 74 and 80.
[94] Ibid., Award, n. 83, p. 289, para. 88.   [95] See ibid., pp. 303–4, para. 129.
[96] Ibid., p. 295, para. 105:
Until 1958, this limit was not breached by France or Portugal during activities concerned with the installations and maintenance of beacons and buoys, the laying of certain submarine cables, the control of navigation in peace and war, customs patrols etc.
[97] Ibid., Award, n. 83, p. 298, para. 111(a).   [98] See ibid., p. 298, para. 111(a).

The third segment consists of a straight line starting at the end point of the second segment at a bearing of 236 degrees. It was established '*grosso modo*' as a perpendicular to a straight line drawn from Almadies Point in Senegal to Cape Shilling in Sierra Leone.[99] The line reflects the general thrust of the regional facade of the West African coast. It does not follow the coastal line of the two parties in dispute and runs through a considerable part of the interior of their territories.

By crafting such a line, the Tribunal developed a novel perspective. It took into account the entire region of the West African coast and facade, including the two neighbouring states to the north and south, Senegal and Sierra Leone, as a foundation for delimitation. It seems the line was adopted for its simplicity, after the Tribunal had first examined other and more complicated *ad hoc* constructions, which were partly of a regional macro-geographic dimension, and partly of a micro-geographic dimension limited to the territories of the two parties in dispute.[100]

Once again, the boundary established for the outer segment of the disputed area was lying in the middle of the contentions of the two parties to the dispute. The result was tested *ex post* by considering it under the aspect of proportionality. The Tribunal thereby did not take into account all of the islands. The coastal islands and the Bijagos Archipelago were included, but the more southerly islands scattered over the shallow areas (Poilao, Samba, Sene) were not.[101] As a result, the coastal length of both states happened to amount to exactly the same figure – 154 miles.[102] This neutralized any need to correct the established boundary line.

Finally, the Tribunal considered that the line adopted satisfied the security interests of the parties.[103] While the Tribunal refused to take into account developmental needs and circumstances, it recommended that the parties establish formal efforts at co-operation within the boundary area in order to respond to the developing needs of both.[104] The Award removed the uncertainty which had impeded the development of commercial exploitation. In 1986, the Presidents of Guinea and Guinea-Bissau announced that they would co-operate in the development of the offshore resources of their respective countries.[105]

---

[99] Ibid., p. 298, para. 111(b).
[100] Ibid., p. 297, para. 109. For discussion of the method applied and those examined see Chapter 3(II)(A)(2).
[101] Ibid., pp. 291–2, 292–3, paras. 95, 97.   [102] Ibid., p. 292–3, 301, paras. 97, 120.
[103] Ibid., p. 302, para. 124.   [104] Ibid., p. 301–2, paras. 121–3.
[105] Ibid. and Pietrowski, 'Introductory note', n. 86, p. 251.

G. The 1985 Libya v. Malta Continental Shelf case

The geographical configuration of this case is unique.[106] For the first time in the history of judicial settlement, the parties were situated with fully opposite coasts in a classical textbook relationship. However, the coasts are of significantly unequal lengths, somewhat reminiscent of David and Goliath. The sovereign state of Malta consists of a group of small islands encompassing some 305 square kilometres (Malta, Gozo, Comino, Cominotto, and the uninhabited rock of Fifla). The islands are oriented in a north-west–south-east direction and extend for a distance of 44.5 kilometres. Libya's territory comprises 1,775,500 square kilometres and has a coastal length of more than 1,700 kilometres between Ras Ajdir and Port Pardia. The south-east corner of Malta lies 340 kilometres (183 nm) north of the nearest point of the Libyan coast.[107]

The dispute arose in the early 1970s. Malta insisted on a delimitation based on unmodified equidistance (median line), whereas Libya pursued a line further to the north. This line, however, was rejected as 'an inequitable yardstick completely unacceptable to the Government of Malta'.[108] In 1974, after negotiations had failed, Malta granted concessions for the exploration of the continental shelf to TEXACO Malta Inc. The concessions lay 40 miles south of the islands between the latitudes of 34° 26' S and 35° 06' N, an area considered by Libya to be north of the median line.[109] Libya protested against such exploration to the extent they occurred south of latitude 34° 54'.[110]

---

[106] *Continental Shelf (Libyan Arab Jamahiriya v. Malta)*, Judgment, ICJ Reports 1985, p. 13; Appendix II, Map 7; For general discussion see Brown (1999), n. 3, p. 262; Edward Duncan Brown, 'The Libya-Malta Continental Shelf Case (1985)' in Bin Cheng and E. D. Brown (eds.), *Contemporary Problems of International Law: Essays in Honour of G. Schwarzenberger on his Eightieth Birthday* (London: Stevens, 1988), pp. 3–18; Benedetto Conforti, 'L'Arrêt de la Cour internationale de justice dans l'affaire de la délimitation du plateau continental entre la Libye et Malte' (1986) *Revue Générale de droit international public*, 313; Umberto Leanza, 'La controversia tra Libia, Malta ed Italia sulla delimitazione della piattaforma continentale nel Mediterraneo centrale' in Umberto Leanza (ed.), *Nuovi saggi di diritto del mare* (Turin: Giapricelli impr., 1988), p. 83; Ted L. McDorman, 'The Libya-Malta Case: Opposite States Confront the Court' (1986) 24 *Canadian Yearbook of International Law*, 335; U. Villani, 'Gli interessi dell'Italia sulla piattaforma continentale del Mediterraneo centrale e la controversia tra Libia e Malta' (1984) *Studi marittimi*, 85.

[107] ICJ Reports 1985, pp. 20–2, paras. 15, 16.

[108] Message from the Prime Minister of Malta to the Chairman of the Revolutionary Command Council of the Libyan Arab Republic of 23 April 1973, reprinted in: Official Documents about the Malta/Libya Dispute on the Dividing Line of the Continental Shelf, Malta 35 (1980) (hereinafter Official Documents).

[109] Official Documents, n. 108, p. 40.   [110] Official Documents, n. 108, p. 42.

By 1976, the parties had signed a special agreement to submit the matter to the ICJ.[111] The agreement, however, was not ratified by Libya at that time. The application based on the special agreement was only filed by both parties on 19 July 1982, after the Court had handed down its judgment in the *Tunisia v. Libya Continental Shelf* case.[112] When Italy applied for permission to intervene, further protraction occurred. The Court refused this request by a judgment of 21 March 1984.[113]

As in the *Tunisia v. Libya* case, and in accordance with Libyan policies, the parties to the special agreement did not request the Court to define a precise boundary line. Rather, the Court only had to decide '[w]hat principles and rules of international law are applicable to the delimitation of the area of the continental shelf' and appertain to each of the parties. Nevertheless, to satisfy Malta, the Court was also to state 'how in practice such principles and rules can be applied by the two Parties in this particular case in order that they may without difficulty delimit such areas by an agreement'.[114] In practical terms, the mandate again required the Court to indicate a fairly precise line, leaving merely technical aspects to be solved by subsequent negotiations.[115] The case was limited to the delimitation of the shelf. Neither of the parties had proclaimed an EEZ, although Malta had enacted a 25 nm exclusive fishery zone at the time.[116]

Libya essentially relied upon the model of equity and equitable principles to achieve an equitable solution. It argued the case on a number of asserted circumstances: natural prolongation, geological features, geography, and proportionality. It particularly stressed the inequality of coastal lengths.[117] Malta, on the other hand, argued that delimitation based on the method of unmodified equidistance (median line) provides an equitable solution. It claimed that such equidistance should be measured from the base lines of Malta and the low-water marks of the coast of Libya.[118] In support of this line, Malta made arguments related to

---

[111] Official Documents, n. 114, p. 44; ICJ Reports 1985, p. 16, para. 2. For Maltese diplomatic notes protesting the protraction of ratification of the Special Agreement by Libya see Official Documents, n. 108, pp. 51–6.
[112] ICJ Reports 1985, p. 15, para. 1.
[113] *Continental Shelf (Libyan Arab Jamahiriya v. Malta)*, Application to Intervene, Judgment, ICJ Reports 1984, p. 3.
[114] Special Agreement, Art. I, ICJ Reports 1985, p. 16, para. 1.
[115] For the interpretation of the Agreement see ICJ Reports 1985, pp. 23–6, paras. 19–21 (asserting the binding force of the judgment).
[116] ICJ Reports 1985, p. 22, para. 17.
[117] ICJ Reports 1985, p. 18, para. 11, p. 43, para. 55.
[118] ICJ Reports 1985, p. 19, para. 12, Memorial (ii).

national security, economic development, the political independence of the island[119] and the principle of equality of states.[120]

Faced with the arguments of the parties, the Court first set out the relevant area of delimitation. Here, it took into account the interests of third parties, particularly those communicated by Italy in the proceedings of the intervention case and which by then were well known to the Court.[121] In order to avoid any prejudice to still pending boundaries, the Court limited the relevant area to start meridians of 13° 50' E and 15° 10' E, respectively.[122]

After examination of the relevant sources of law, the Court found that the case should be decided on the basis of customary international law.[123] However, it granted considerable weight to the rules propounded by the LOS Convention (not yet in force) and considered the distance principle inherent to the definition of the shelf in Article 76(1) to be decisive. The approach it applied was a combination of equitable principles and equitable solution[124] based on entitlement determined by reason of distance.[125] The Court entirely dismissed the Libyan arguments relating to geology not only on principle, but also due to the lack of sufficient evidence in this case.[126] Furthermore, in line with its purely geographical approach, it rejected arguments relating to security and economic development.[127] The Court held the median line to be an appropriate starting point in such opposite constellations.[128] For its computation, the Court did not take into account the rock of Fifla as a base point.[129]

However, the Court then found that the line had to be adjusted northward for a number of reasons. Firstly, because it relied on a comparison of the relevant coastal lengths of Malta (24 miles) and the Libyan coast from Ras Ajdir to Ras Zarruq (192 miles),[130] whilst refusing to apply a strict test of proportionality to such lengths from a regional perspective for such a limited area of delimitation.[131] Secondly, it held from the same perspective that this case also entails a delimitation between the northern and southern littoral of the Mediterranean, with Malta merely being a minor feature of the northern seaboard.[132] Thirdly, the Court took into

---

[119] ICJ Reports 1985, p. 42, paras. 52, 53.   [120] ICJ Reports 1985, pp. 42–3, para. 54.
[121] The problem of intervention is discussed in Chapter 9.
[122] ICJ Reports 1985, p. 26, para. 22, maps 2 and 27.
[123] ICJ Reports 1985, p. 29, para. 26.
[124] ICJ Reports 1985, pp. 29–31, paras. 27–30, p. 47, para. 62. See also Chapter 8.
[125] Part I, Chapter 2(II)(C)(2).   [126] ICJ Reports 1985, pp. 34–7, paras. 35–41.
[127] ICJ Reports 1985, pp. 41–3, paras. 51, 52.   [128] ICJ Reports 1985, p. 47, para. 62.
[129] ICJ Reports 1985, p. 48, para. 64.   [130] ICJ Reports 1985, p. 50, para. 68.
[131] ICJ Reports 1985, pp. 53–5, paras. 74, 75.   [132] ICJ Reports 1985, p. 50, para. 69.

account that the relevant base points of Malta, even disregarding the islet of Fifla, are all situated on the south-western coast of Malta and do not reflect the receding westerly coast of the island.[133]

For its determination of the final line, the Court first established an auxiliary median of the coast of Sicily and Libya, which intersects the meridian 15° 10' E (the easterly end of the segment of delimitation) at the approximate latitude of 34° 36' N. The median of Malta and Libya intersects the same meridian at 34° 12' N, amounting to a difference of 24' of latitude. The Court concluded that a shift of 24' N would be the extreme limit of a shift in northward direction. In fact, it would ignore the island of Malta. This could neither be done under the hypothesis that Malta was Italian territory, nor, *a fortiori*, an independent state. Therefore, the shift had to amount to less than 24' of latitude. Taking into account the relevant circumstances discussed, it shifted the median in northward direction through 18' of latitude (i.e. three-quarters of the extreme limit). This resulted in an intersection of the meridian at 15° 10' E at 34° 30' N whilst leaving it to the parties to define the exact position of the final line.[134]

When compared to the original claims that the parties had set forth in diplomatic intercourse during the 1970s, it can be seen that once again the Court's decision lies within the original negotiating positions of the parties. While Malta failed to reach its original lines of concessions granted by some 4' and the median by 18', Libya's original claims to jurisdiction of the shelf in this particular area fell short by 24'.[135] In 1986, an agreement was concluded which defined the exact co-ordinates of the boundary line, closely following the Court's ruling.[136]

H. *The 1992* Canada v. France St. Pierre and Miquelon *arbitration*

An arbitral award on 10 June 1992 brought the rather long-standing dispute concerning Canada and France on the maritime delimitation

---

[133] ICJ Reports 1985, p. 50, para. 70; see also ICJ Reports 1985, pp. 52–3, para. 73.
[134] ICJ Reports 1985, p. 51–3, paras. 72, 73; see ICJ Reports 1985, p. 54, map 2.
[135] Compared to the latitude 34° 30' N found by the Court, Malta, in 1974, claimed a line at 34° 26' latitude, and Libya, in 1975, of 34° 54' latitude in the relevant area (between longitudes 14° 50' (14° 49') W and 15° 32' E). Official Documents, n. 114, pp. 40, 42–3.
[136] Agreement Implementing Article III of the Special Agreement and the Judgment of the International Court of Justice, done 10 October 1986, reprinted in B. Conforti et al., *Atlas of the Seabed Boundaries*, Part II, n. 1, pp. 29, 31 (map).

around the French Islands of St. Pierre and Miquelon to an end.[137] The area within which the delimitation was to occur is situated south of the Canadian island of Newfoundland and east of the coast of Nova Scotia. These coasts, together with the opening of the Gulf of St. Lawrence, form a marked concavity, in which the two islands of St. Pierre and Miquelon are located.

In this area, the continental shelf is a geological continuum. To the east and south-east of Newfoundland, the 200 metre isobath extends to a distance of nearly 250 nm from the coast. It is characterized by a series of banks (*plateaux*) collectively known as the Grand Banks of Newfoundland, amongst which lies the St. Pierre Bank, traditional fishing grounds of both Canadian and French trawlers.

Since 1966, the parties had been unable to settle their dispute by negotiations. Whilst France kept arguing in favour of a delimitation based on the principle of equidistance, Canada maintained that the rule of 'special circumstances' was to be applied in the area. The extension of maritime jurisdiction in the area by both parties in response to developments affecting the law of the sea during the 1970s emphasized the seriousness of the dispute and made the need for its settlement more urgent. Negotiations relating to fisheries had been more successful, with each party granting the other equal access for fishing vessels along its coasts. A document allotting the annual catch that French trawlers were permitted to take in Canadian waters during the period 1981–1986 was signed in 1980. Unfortunately, however, the application of this document gave rise to a new dispute between the two states.

On 30 March 1989, with the assistance of a mediator, Canada and France eventually agreed on temporary quotas for French fishermen for the period 1989–1991, and, on the same day, the two states agreed to submit their delimitation dispute to a Court of Arbitration. The Court was asked to 'establish a single delimitation which shall govern upon all rights and jurisdiction which the Parties may exercise under

---

[137] Court of Arbitration for the Delimitation of Maritime Areas between Canada and France: Decision in Case Concerning Delimitation of Maritime Areas, 31 ILM 1145; Appendix II, Map 8. For general discussion see Jonathan I. Charney, 'Progress in International Maritime Boundary Delimitation Law' (1994) 88 *American Journal of International Law*, 227; H. Dipla, 'La Sentence arbitrale du 10 juin 1992 en l'affaire de la délimitation des espaces maritimes entre le Canada et la France'(1994) *Journal du droit international*, 653; Hélène Ruiz-Fabri, 'Sur la délimitation des espaces maritimes entre le Canada et la France. Sentence arbitrale du 10 juin 1992' (1993) 97 *Revue Générale de Droit International Public*, 67.

international law in these maritime areas'.[138] Both parties substantially agreed on the identification of the relevant area. They differed, however, in their identification of the relevant coasts and their relative lengths.

Canada sought to deprive St. Pierre and Miquelon of any of the economic zone and continental shelf, and to award the two islands only a belt of 12 nm. According to the Canadians, a solution based on equidistance would encroach upon what was the natural prolongation of its territory. Canada also opposed the much greater land mass of Nova Scotia to the exiguity of the French islands. Proportionality, they argued, should be taken into account and the great disparity in the total length to the relevant coasts should lead to the rejection of the method based on equidistance. Finally, Canada asserted that St. Pierre and Miquelon do not constitute an independent state, and therefore should be given a diminished treatment.

France relied on two basic principles to claim an extensive EEZ around St. Pierre and Miquelon: the sovereign equality of states; and the principle of the equal capacity of islands and mainland countries to generate maritime areas.

Rejecting the solutions proposed by both parties, the Court formulated its own solution. It created two sectors around St. Pierre and Miquelon: the western seaward projection and the south-south-east projection. For the first sector, the Court found it 'reasonable and equitable' to grant the French islands a 12 nm territorial sea and an additional 12 nm zone, noting that it is unavoidable that any seaward extension of the French coasts beyond their territorial sea would cause some degree of encroachment and cut off the seaward projection towards the south from points located in the southern shore of Newfoundland.[139]

For the second sector, the Court awarded St. Pierre and Miquelon 'a frontal seaward projection towards the south until it reaches the outer limit of 200 nautical miles'.[140] The arbitrators felt that the coastal opening of the French islands towards the south appeared unobstructed by any opposite Canadian claims. The 10.5 nm width of this corridor corresponded to the distance between the meridians passing through the easternmost point of the island of St. Pierre and the westernmost point of the island of Miquelon respectively, measured at the mean latitude of

---

[138] Agreement Establishing a Court of Arbitration for the Purpose of Carrying out the Delimitation of Maritime Areas between France and Canada, signed on 30 March 1989, Art. 2.
[139] See text of the Award, 31 ILM 1145, p. 1169, para. 67.
[140] Text of the Award, ibid., p. 1170, para. 70.

these two points.[141] It is worth noting that the Award was rendered by a three-to-two vote. The two arbitrators who had been appointed by the parties voted against it.

I. The 1992 Land, Island and Maritime Frontier Dispute (El Salvador v. Honduras)

The *El Salvador* v. *Honduras* case was primarily concerned with a dispute over the land boundary between the two states.[142] It also involved the legal status of the Gulf of Fonseca, which 'lies on the Pacific coast of Central America, opening to the ocean in a generally south westerly direction'.[143] Three states surround it: El Salvador to the north-west; Nicaragua to the south-east; and Honduras in between. The two parties and the intervening state, Nicaragua, came into existence with the break-up of the Spanish Empire in Central America. It was then accepted that the new international boundaries should be determined by the application of the principle generally accepted in Spanish America of the *uti possidetis juris*, whereby the boundaries would follow the colonial administrative boundaries.[144] The issue then became the determination of where those boundaries actually lay.

The maritime boundary dispute between El Salvador and Honduras manifested in 1884. For almost a century, various negotiations had taken place, but had not achieved any results. The two states reached an agreement regarding the major part of the land boundary only in 1972, leaving six sectors remaining to be settled.

In the General Peace Treaty, signed and ratified by El Salvador and Honduras in 1980, the delimitation of the frontier line in the remaining six sectors was entrusted to a Joint Frontier Commission, which was also

---

[141] Ibid., para. 71.
[142] *Land, Island and Maritime Frontier Dispute (El Salvador* v. *Honduras: Nicaragua intervening)*, Judgment, ICJ Reports 1992, p. 351; *Case concerning the Land, Island and Maritime Frontier Dispute (El Salvador* v. *Honduras)*, Application by Nicaragua for Permission to Intervene, Judgment of 13 September 1990, ICJ Reports 1990, p. 92 (cf. Chapter 9); Appendix II, Map 9. For general discussion see Charney (1994), n. 137, 227; Laurent Lucchini, 'L'Arrêt de Chambre de la CIJ dans le différend Honduras/Salvador. Aspects insulaires et maritimes' (1992) *Annuaire Français de Droit International*, 427; Malcolm N. Shaw, 'Case Concerning the Land, Island and Maritime Frontier Dispute (El Salvador/Honduras: Nicaragua Intervening), Judgment of 11 September 1992' (1993) 42 *International and Comparative Law Quarterly*, 929; Brigitte Stern, 'Chronique de la Cour internationale de justice' (1993) *Journal de droit international*, 684.
[143] ICJ Reports 1992, p. 586, para. 382. [144] ICJ Reports 1992, p. 380, para. 28.

charged to 'determine the legal situation of the islands and the maritime spaces'.[145] Articles 31 and 32 of the General Peace Treaty provided that if, upon the expiry of a five-year period, total agreement had not been reached on the frontier dispute, the parties would jointly submit their controversy to decision by the ICJ.

Due to the failure of the Joint Frontier Commission to fulfil its mandate, on 24 May 1986 the parties signed the Special Agreement submitting their dispute to a Chamber of the ICJ. As El Salvador and Honduras had also agreed to set up a Special Demarcation Commission, the Chamber immediately indicated that its duty was 'to give such indications of the line of the frontier in the disputed sectors as will enable the Special Demarcation Commission to demarcate it by a technical operation'.[146] The intervention of Nicaragua in the proceedings was granted by a Judgment of the Chamber on 13 September 1990.[147] According to El Salvador, 'the Chamber ha[d] no jurisdiction to effect any delimitations of the maritime spaces'.[148] The waters of the Gulf of Fonseca were subject to a condominium in favour of the three coastal states of the Gulf, so delimitation would be inappropriate. Honduras opposed this argument and argued that 'within the Gulf there is a community of interests which both permits of and necessitates a judicial delimitation'.[149]

Using the traditional rules of interpretation of Article 31 of the Vienna Convention on the Law of Treaties, the Chamber was unable to accept the arguments put forward by Honduras and found that there was no indication in the Special Agreement which would require delimitation. Its task was limited to the determination of the juridical status of the maritime spaces. To fulfil its mandate, the Chamber investigated the different factors able to clarify the juridical status of the waters of the Gulf of Fonseca. It firstly analysed the geography and the history, and was able to confirm that, according to the views of both parties, of the intervening state, and of commentators, 'it is an historic bay, and that the waters of it are accordingly historic waters'.[150]

The historic bay is governed by a special regime established over the centuries. Discovered in 1522, the Gulf of Fonseca was under Spanish jurisdiction until the three actual riparian states gained their

---

[145] ICJ Reports 1992, p. 383, para. 37. [146] ICJ Reports 1992, p. 386, para. 39.
[147] *Land, Island and Maritime Frontier Dispute (El Salvador v. Honduras)*, Application to Intervene, Judgment, ICJ Reports 1990, p. 92
[148] ICJ Reports 1992, p. 582, para. 372. [149] ICJ Reports 1992, p. 582, para. 372.
[150] ICJ Reports 1992, p. 585, para. 383.

independence in 1821. Thus, the rights of the three coastal states in this region were acquired by succession from Spain. What was the legal status of the Gulf waters in 1821? This question was at stake in 1917 in a case between El Salvador and Nicaragua before the Central American Court of Justice. The 1917 judgment gave a clear answer to the questions relating to both the legal status of the Gulf waters and to the respective rights of the coastal states:

> The legal status of the Gulf of Fonseca having been recognised by this Court to be that of a historic bay possessed of the characteristics of a closed sea, the three riparian States of El Salvador, Honduras and Nicaragua are, therefore, recognised as co-owners of its waters.[151]

El Salvador and Honduras were diametrically opposed about the correctness of this part of the judgment. While the former approved the condominium concept, the latter argued against it, relying mainly on the fact that it was not a party to the case and so could not be bound by that decision. The position of the Chamber on that problem was clear: it would take the 1917 judgment into account as a relevant precedent decision of a Court but not as *res judicata* between the parties to the present dispute.

The conclusion of the Chamber on the particular regime of the Gulf of Fonseca was very similar to the one expressed in the 1917 judgment: '[T]he Gulf waters, other than the 3-mile maritime belts, are historic waters and subject to a joint sovereignty of the three coastal States.'[152] The Chamber justified its conclusion by saying that the Gulf waters had not been divided during the greater part of their history and it added that '[a] joint succession of the three States to the maritime area seems in these circumstances to be the logical outcome of the principle of *uti possidetis juris* itself'.[153] Honduras' argument, according to which the Gulf of Fonseca would not be a condominium but only a 'community of interests', was rejected by the Chamber on the basis that 'a condominium is almost an ideal juridical embodiment of the community of interest's requirements'.[154] Therefore, if those waters were to be divided, this would require the participation of all three states together in the creation of a suitable regime.

The closing line of the Bay was easy to determine. It links Punta Amapala to Punta Cosiguina and has been recognized by the three coastal states in practice. This line represents the ocean limit, and the Chamber

---

[151] ICJ Reports 1992, pp. 596–7, para. 397. [152] ICJ Reports 1992, p. 601, para. 404.
[153] ICJ Reports 1992, p. 602, para. 405. [154] ICJ Reports 1992, p. 602, para. 407.

came logically to the conclusion that it also marks 'the baseline for whatever regime lies beyond it'.[155]

The waters inside this line cannot be strictly considered to be internal waters, as this term would imply complication if applied to a pluri-state historic bay. Practical necessities require rights of passage through the whole Gulf. 'The Gulf waters are therefore, if indeed internal waters, internal waters subject to a special and particular regime, not only of joint sovereignty but of rights of passage.'[156] This meant that the rights of Honduras could not be confined to the back of the Gulf, but that they extend up to the closing line.

The final question the Chamber had to deal with related to the legal status of the waters outside the Gulf. In 1917, these waters all belonged to the high sea. This situation has since changed – the law of the sea has created new maritime zones and there could be no question that this law was now also applicable to the area of the Gulf of Fonseca. Since the legal situation on the landward side of the closing line is one of joint sovereignty, it follows that all three joint sovereigns must have entitlement outside the closing line to the territorial sea, continental shelf and EEZ.[157] The Chamber added that any division into three separate zones remains, as inside the Gulf, a matter for the three states to decide between themselves.

J. The 1993 Jan Mayen case (Denmark v. Norway)

The whole maritime area disputed in this case by Denmark and Norway lies in the Atlantic Ocean north of the Arctic Circle.[158] Jan Mayen is a small, unpopulated Norwegian island, located north of Iceland and 250 nm seaward of the eastern coast of Greenland. Sovereignty over Greenland appertains to Norway. In 1980, Denmark decided to extend

---

[155] ICJ Reports 1992, p. 604, para. 411.   [156] ICJ Reports 1992, p. 605, para. 412.
[157] ICJ Reports 1992, p. 608, para. 420.
[158] *Maritime Delimitation in the Area between Greenland and Jan Mayen (Denmark v. Norway)*, Judgment, ICJ Reports 1993, p. 38; Appendix II, Map 10. For general discussion see Charney (1994), n. 143, 227; R. R. Churchill, 'The Greenland-Jan Mayen Case and Significance for the International Law of Maritime Boundary Delimitation' (1994) 9 *International Journal of Marine and Coastal Law*, 1; E. Decaux, 'L'Affaire de la délimitation maritime dans la région située entre le Groënland et Jan Mayen (Danemark c. Norvège) arrêt de la C.I.J. du 14 juin 1993' (1993) *Annuaire Français de Droit International*, 495; Malcolm D. Evans, 'Case Concerning Maritime Delimitation in the Area between Greenland and Jan Mayen (*Denmark v. Norway*)' (1994) 43 *International and Comparative Law Quarterly*, 697.

the fishing zone off the eastern coast of Greenland north of latitude 67° N, to 200 nm. However, vis-à-vis Jan Mayen, the Danish Executive Order stipulated that fisheries jurisdiction would not immediately be exercised beyond the median line. In the same year, the Norwegian Government issued a decree, which established a 200 nm fishing zone around Jan Mayen. In relation to Greenland, this decree also specified that the zone would not extend beyond the median line. Until 31 August 1981, the two parties exercised their fishery jurisdiction over areas separated by the median line.

In 1988, the dispute arising out of this situation was *unilaterally* brought before the ICJ by Denmark. This country sought a full 200 nm fishing zone off the east coast of Greenland, whilst Norway claimed only the area located at the eastern side of the median line between Greenland and Jan Mayen. The parties differed on the nature of the task conferred upon the Court. Denmark asked the Tribunal to draw 'a single line of delimitation of the fishery zone and continental shelf area', whereas Norway only requested the Court to declare 'the basis of delimitation' and leave the precise delimitation to negotiation between the parties. It suggested that there were two delimitation lines: a median line for the continental shelf, and a median line for the fishing zone, which, although they coincided, remained conceptually distinct.

The Court referred to the *Gulf of Maine* case and decided that it could not draw a single maritime boundary because the parties had not agreed to this. Therefore it would have to deal separately with the delimitations of the continental shelf and of the fishing zone. The Court explained that the drawing of a single line or two coincident lines did not amount to the same thing. The two lines, even if they should coincide, stemmed from different strands of the applicable law, Article 6 of the 1958 Continental Shelf Convention for the continental shelf boundary and customary international law for the fishing zone boundary.[159]

Norway first argued that a bilateral agreement of 1965[160] had already established a delimitation between Jan Mayen and Greenland. This treaty, together with the 1958 Convention on the Continental Shelf, declared the median line to be the boundary of the continental shelf of the parties. According to Norway, the practice of the parties respecting fishing zones had to be seen as a recognition of existing continental shelf

---

[159] This was and so far remains the only case to which the ICJ was able to apply Art. 6 of the 1958 Convention on the Continental Shelf.

[160] Denmark/Norway 1965 Agreement relating to the Delimitation of the Continental Shelf, 634 UNTS 71.

boundaries and as being applicable to the exercise of fishery jurisdiction. Denmark replied that, despite its apparent generality, Article 1 of the 1965 Treaty was only applicable to the part of the North Sea located between the mainland territories of both parties.

The Court, following the Danish argument, found the 1965 treaty inapplicable to the current dispute. The Court also decided that the conduct of the parties concerning the continental shelf boundary and the fishing zone did not lead to the conclusion that the median line constitutes the delimitation between Greenland and Jan Mayen.

As a first step in the delimitation process, the Court found it appropriate to have recourse to a provisionally drawn median line. It would then look at the circumstances commanding any adjustments to that line. A first factor brought up by Denmark was the great disparity between the lengths of the relevant coasts. The Court determined that the ratio between the relevant coasts of Jan Mayen and Greenland was approximately 1:9. Such disproportion, according to Denmark, should lead to a delimitation line that would grant Greenland a maritime zone of 200 nm. Norway replied that proportionality is not an independent principle of delimitation but only a test of the equitableness of a result arrived at by other means. After a careful examination, the Court considered that 'the differences in length of the respective coasts of the Parties are so significant that this feature must be taken into consideration during the delimitation operation'.[161] Therefore, the median line should be adjusted and located much closer to the coast of Jan Mayen. This did not mean that the boundary line had to be drawn 200 nm from the coast of eastern Greenland. The coast of Jan Mayen could also generate a potential title to the maritime areas recognized by customary law. To disregard this fact would be contrary to the demands of equity.

With regard to fishing, the median line appeared to be too far west for Denmark, which, if the final maritime delimitation remained with the median line, would have been deprived of equitable access to the maritime resources of the area. This was another reason to shift the boundary line eastward. As the presence of ice does not affect access to the fishing resources of the area, the Court felt that it could ignore this circumstance. Finally, looking at the conduct of the parties concerning the relevant area, the Court reached the conclusion that this did not constitute an element that could influence the process of delimitation in the present case. All this led the Court to the general conclusion that the provisionally drawn

[161] ICJ Reports 1993, p. 68, para. 68.

median line ought to be adjusted so as to grant Denmark a larger area of maritime space. The delimitation line was drawn in such a way as to leave to the parties with only those matters strictly relating to the negotiable hydrographic technicalities.

In order to draw the final delimitation line, the Court divided the whole area of overlapping claims into three zones. Zone 1, the main fishing area, was divided into two equal parts so as to secure to both parties equitable access to the fishing resources. Zones 2 and 3 were split in a way that favoured Jan Mayen. The Court found that this solution both met the requirements of equity and did not give too great a weight to the circumstance of the marked disparity in coastal lengths.

K. The 1999 Eritrea v. Yemen *Award*

On 17 December 1999, the Arbitral Tribunal, established by Eritrea and Yemen by Agreement of 3 October 1996, delivered the second award in a trial containing two stages.[162] As agreed by the parties, the first award addressed territorial sovereignty and the scope of the dispute,[163] and the second award, of main interest here, addressed maritime delimitation.

Eritrea and Yemen face each other across the narrowing southern end of the Red Sea containing numerous insular features. The traditional fishing regime in the region around certain islands was to be perpetuated according to the first stage of the Award,[164] but the details of the regime remained disputed among the parties in the second stage of the Award.

Article 2 of the Arbitration Agreement provided that in determining the maritime boundary, the Tribunal has to take 'into account the opinion it will have formed on questions of territorial sovereignty, the LOS Convention, and any other pertinent factor'.[165] The requirement to take into account the LOS Convention is important because Eritrea was not a party to that Convention. As to other pertinent factors, the Tribunal adopted a broad concept, including various factors that are generally recognized as being relevant to the process of delimitation, such as

---

[162] *Award of the Arbitral Tribunal in the Second Stage (Maritime Delimitation) in the Matter of an Arbitration between Eritrea and Yemen* from 17 December 1999 (hereinafter Award in the Second Stage) Reports of International Arbitrational Awards, vol. XXII, 335–410 (United Nations 2006); Appendix II, Map 11.

[163] Award of the Arbitral Tribunal in the First Stage (Territorial Sovereignty and Scope of the Dispute) from 9 October 1998 (hereinafter Award of the First Stage) Reports of International Arbitral Awards, vol. XXII, pp. 209–332, United Nations 2006.

[164] Award in the First Stage, n. 163, para. 526 and dispositif Art. 527(vi).

[165] Award in the Second Stage, n. 162, Annex 1, Art. 2(3).

proportionality, non-encroachment, the presence of islands and any other factors that might affect the equities of the particular situation.[166] The Tribunal also stated that it is a generally accepted view that between opposite states the median or equidistance line normally provides an equitable boundary in accordance with the requirements of the Convention.[167] Both parties claimed a boundary constructed on the equidistance method, although based on different points of departure and resulting in very different lines.[168]

The Tribunal held that the international boundary shall be a single all-purpose boundary which is a median line and that it should, as far as practicable, be a median line between the opposite mainland coastlines. The Tribunal noted at this point that it had occasion to observe in its 1998 Award on Sovereignty[169] that the offshore petroleum contracts entered into by Yemen, and by Ethiopia and by Eritrea, 'lend a measure of support to a median line between the opposite coasts of Eritrea and Yemen, drawn without regard to the islands, dividing the respective jurisdiction of the Parties'. The Tribunal noted, however, that this was not the same as saying that the maritime boundary now to be drawn should be drawn throughout its length entirely without regard to the islands whose sovereignty had only been determined by the 1998 Award.[170]

For the purpose of measuring the equidistance in accordance with the definition in Article 15 of the 1982 Convention, the Tribunal agreed with Eritrea that the base line should be the low-water line as laid down by a 'general international rule' in the 1982 Convention's Article 5.[171]

In the northern part of the boundary, the Tribunal was confronted with Eritrea's Dahlak group of islands. The Tribunal held the Dahlak Islands to be a 'carpet' of islands and islets, the larger of which have a considerable population, and therefore a typical example of a group of islands that forms an integral part of the general coastal configuration. The Tribunal thus followed that the waters inside the island system are internal or national waters and that the base line of the territorial sea is to be found at the external fringe of the island system.[172] While the parties agreed in principle to draw a straight base line, as described in Article 7 of the 1982 Convention, the base points for this line were disputed.

---

[166] Ibid., para. 130.   [167] Ibid., para. 131.   [168] Ibid., para. 131.
[169] Ibid., para. 438.   [170] Ibid., para. 83; see also para. 132.
[171] Ibid., para. 135. The Yemen claim was that, in view of prior Eritrean national legislation the Tribunal should measure the median line boundary from the high-water line instead of the low-water line along the Eritrean coast (Award in the First Stage, n. 173, para. 134).
[172] Award in the Second Stage, n. 162, para. 139.

Eritrea suggested an insular feature called the 'Negileh Rock', which lies further out than some larger but still small and uninhabited islets. Yemen objected to the use of this feature by reason of the fact that this feature is a reef and, moreover, one which appears not to be above water at any state of the tide. The Tribunal held a reef that is not also a low-tide elevation to be out of the question as a base point by virtue of Articles 6 and 7(4) of the Convention.[173]

Yemen for its part employed several smaller islands in front of its coast as controlling base points. The Tribunal held that these islands do not constitute a part of Yemen's mainland coast. It stated that 'their barren and inhospitable nature and their position well out to sea' mean that they should not be taken into consideration in computing the boundary line.[174] For these reasons, the Tribunal did not give the single island of al-Tayr and the island group of al-Zubayr any effect upon the median line.[175] Instead, the Tribunal used as base points for this part of the Yemen coast 'a considerable scattering of islands and islets' which are the beginning of a large area of coastal islands and reefs, extending northward, and ultimately forming part of a large island cluster off the coast of Saudi Arabia.[176] It therefore employed the westernmost extremity of the relatively large, inhabited and important island of Kamaran off this part of the Yemen coast as a base point. The Tribunal held this island to form, together with the mainland, an important bay and that therefore there could be no doubt that these features are integral to the coast of Yemen and part of it.[177] The Tribunal further used as base points the islets to the north-west named Uqban and Kutama, since they were held to be part of an intricate system of islands, islets and reefs which guard the coast. In the view of the Tribunal, this constituted a 'fringe system' of the kind contemplated by Article 7 of the 1982 Convention.[178]

In the middle stretch of the maritime boundary to be delimited there was the added problem of overlapping territorial seas generated by the Yemeni islands of Zuqar and Hanish, and by the Eritrean islands of the Haycocks and South West Rocks, respectively. Yemen suggested leaving the Eritrean islands in this area isolated outside and beyond the 12 nm territorial sea measured from the high-water line of the mainland coast. Yet, the Tribunal recalled that any island, however small, and even rocks, provided they are above the water at high tide, generate a territorial sea of

---

[173] Ibid., paras. 143–6.   [174] Ibid., para. 147.
[175] Ibid., para. 148. The island of al-Tayr and the island group of al-Zubayr were attributed by the 1998 Award to the Sovereignty of Yemen.
[176] Ibid., para. 149.   [177] Ibid., para. 150.   [178] Ibid., para. 151.

up to 12 nm.[179] Accordingly, the Tribunal held a chain of islands which are less than 24 nm apart to generate a continuous band of territorial sea (so-called 'leap-frogging'[180]), and applied this concept up to, and including, the Eritrean South West Rocks.[181] In the resulting area of overlapping territorial seas – no more than 4 or 5 nmwide – between the Eritrean South West Rocks and the Haycock group of islands on the one hand, and the Yemen islands of the Hanish group on the other – the Tribunal applied the median line.[182]

With respect to the boundary endpoints, the Tribunal was cautious of potential claims by third parties.[183] With regard to the principle of proportionality, the Tribunal refused to consider that part of the Eritrean coast which does not lie opposite the Yemeni coast.[184] Considering the resulting ratios of coastal lengths (Yemen:Eritrea; 1:1.31); and of water areas (1:1.09), the Tribunal held that the line of delimitation chosen did not result in disproportion.[185]

With respect to fisheries, the Tribunal further clarified the conclusions of the 1998 Award on Sovereignty concerning the perpetuation of the traditional fishing regime in the region, including free access and enjoyment for the fishermen of both countries around several groups of islands, which were attributed, in that same Award, to Yemen.[186] The Tribunal clarified that the 'perpetuation of traditional fishing rights' is neither an entitlement to common resources nor a shared right in them. But it held that it entitles fishermen of both parties to engage in artisanal fishing around the islands which came under the sovereignty of Yemen.[187]

---

[179] Ibid., para. 155, referring to Art. 121.2 of the 1982 Convention.
[180] Award in the Second Stage, n. 162, para. 156.
[181] Ibid., para. 155. See also Chapter 4 and Chapter 10.
[182] Award in the Second Stage, n. 162, paras. 158–9.
[183] Ibid., para. 136. With regard to the northern end of the boundary, the Kingdom of Saudi Arabia had written to the Registrar of the Tribunal on 31 August 1997 pointing out that its boundaries with Yemen were disputed (Award in the First Stage, n. 163, para. 44).
[184] Award in the Second Stage, n. 162, para. 167. The point where the Eritrean coast ceased to be opposite that of Yemen was identified by the intersection on the Eritrean coast of a line starting at the northern end of the Yemeni land boundary and drawn at a right angle to the general direction of that coast (Award in the First Stage, n. 173, para. 167)
[185] Award in the Second Stage, n. 162, para. 168.
[186] Award in the First Stage, n. 163, para. 526 and dispositif para. 527(vi) as reaffirmed by the Award in the Second Stage, n. 162, paras. 62–9 and 87–112.
[187] Award in the Second Stage, n. 162, para. 103. For the definition of artisanal fishing rights, see para. 106. As an integral element of the traditional fishing regime, the Tribunal also recognized 'certain associated rights': the free passage of fishermen between both coasts and the islands and entitlement to enter the relevant ports and sell the catches there.

The parties' arguments and evidence with respect to fisheries were not given any effect upon the delimitation line. In the view of the Tribunal, neither party had demonstrated that the boundary line proposed by the other party would produce 'catastrophic' or inequitable effect on its own fishing activity and the population's economic dependence thereupon.[188] Because regional fishing was equally important to both parties, it held that the fishing practices were not germane to the task of arriving at a line of delimitation.[189]

The Tribunal in *Eritrea v. Yemen* strived to preserve existing fishing patterns in the region for the benefit of the lives and livelihoods of the poor and industrious order of artisanal fishermen. It held in the first stage of the Award, concerning questions of territorial sovereignty, that sovereignty over the islands in the case 'entails the perpetuation of the traditional fishing regime in the region'.[190] The Tribunal thus held that Yemen shall – in the exercise of the sovereignty over the islands attributed to it – ensure that the traditional fishing regime of free access and enjoyment for the fishermen of both Eritrea and Yemen shall be preserved.[191] In the second stage of the Award concerning maritime delimitation, the Tribunal clarified that the traditional fishing regime was neither an entitlement in common to resources nor a shared right in them. The traditional fishing regime merely entitles both Eritrean and Yemeni fishermen to engage in 'artisanal fishing',[192] including the exercise of certain 'associated rights',[193] around the islands which were attributed to Yemen in the first stage of the Award. The Tribunal stressed that the traditional fishing regime is not limited by the normal rules on access to foreign maritime zones specified under the 1982 Convention, nor is it to be limited by reference to claimed past patterns of fishing.[194]

> With regard to the latter entitlement, the Tribunal emphasized the non-discriminatory treatment in the ports and within the markets themselves, in so far as cleaning, storing and marketing is concerned (Award in the Second Stage, n. 171, para. 107). See also Chapter 5.

[188] Award in the Second Stage, n. 162, paras. 50–1, 59–60, 74.
[189] Ibid., paras. 62–3. See also Chapter 10.
[190] Ibid., para 526 and dispositif, para. vi.
[191] Ibid.
[192] The term was employed in contrast to 'industrial fishing', Award in the Second Stage, n. 162, para 106.
[193] Such as unimpeded passage through waters and non-discriminatory access to each other's domestic ports and market places as well as recourse to a traditional dispute settlement mechanism confined to artisanal fishing disputes, Award in the Second Stage, n. 162, para 107.
[194] Award in the Second Stage, n. 162, para. 109. The preservation of existing fishing patterns has been provided for in recent boundary agreements, see David Anderson,

L. The 2001 Case Concerning Maritime Delimitation and Territorial Questions (Qatar v. Bahrain)

On 16 March 2001, the ICJ ruled on the merits in a case including maritime delimitation and territorial questions between Qatar and Bahrain.[195] The case was brought by Qatar on 8 July 1991. The proceedings were the longest in the history of the Court.

The geographical setting of the region comprises the Qatar peninsula and a number of islands and islets off the western coast of Qatar and the eastern coast of the main island of Bahrain. Key insular features for the determination of the maritime boundary were disputed. Pursuant to valid agreements between the parties, the Court was 'to decide any matter of territorial right or other title or interest which may be a matter of difference between them; and to draw a single maritime boundary between their respective maritime areas of seabed, subsoil and superjacent waters'.[196] The parties also agreed that the Court should render its decision in accordance with international law. Neither Bahrain nor Qatar was a party to the 1958 Geneva Conventions and only Bahrain to the 1982 Convention, but both parties agreed that 'most of the provisions of the 1982 Convention which were relevant for the case reflect customary law'.[197]

In delimiting the maritime boundary the Court followed a sectoral approach. In the southern sector, it had to delimit the territorial seas.[198] In the northern part, it had to carry out a delimitation of the continental shelf and EEZ.[199] Concerning the territorial seas, the Court considered Article 15 of the 1982 Convention to be customary international law.[200] In order to draw a provisional equidistance line and to measure the breadth of the territorial sea, the Court noted that the base lines needed to be determined – which neither party had done.[201] The Court therefore first had to determine the relevant coasts of the parties on which the base lines and the pertinent base points were to be located.[202]

Bahrain claimed to be a de facto archipelagic state, holding that to reduce the State of Bahrain to only a limited number of islands would be a refashioning of geography. However, since Bahrain had not made this

---

'Developments in Maritime Boundary Law and Practice' in Charney et al., *International Maritime Boundaries*, n. 1, vol. V (Colson and Smith), pp. 3197, 3218.

[195] *Maritime Delimitation and Territorial Questions between Qatar and Bahrain (Qatar v. Bahrain)*, Merits, Judgment, ICJ Reports 2001, p. 40; Appendix II, Maps 12.1 and 12.2.
[196] ICJ Reports 2001, p. 63 para. 67. [197] ICJ Reports 2001, p. 91 para. 167.
[198] ICJ Reports 2001, p. 91 para. 169. [199] ICJ Reports 2001, p. 91 para. 170.
[200] ICJ Reports 2001, p. 94 para. 176. See also Chapter 7.
[201] ICJ Reports 2001, p. 94 para. 177. [202] ICJ Reports 2001, p. 97 para. 184.

claim one of its formal submissions, the Court refused to draw straight archipelagic base lines joining the outermost points of the outermost islands and drying reefs of the archipelago.[203] It also refused Bahrain the right to employ (ordinary) straight base lines, holding that this is an exceptional method which must be applied restrictively. In the view of the Court, Bahrain does not have a coastline which is deeply indented and cut into. Neither did the maritime features east of Bahrain's main islands qualify as a fringe of islands in the immediate vicinity of the coast, although they were considered to be part of the overall geographical configuration. The Court held that the islands concerned are relatively small in number and that, in the present case, it is only possible to speak of a 'cluster of islands' or an 'island system' if Bahrain's main islands are included in that concept. Thus each maritime feature had to have its individual effect for the determination of the base lines.[204]

The presence of numerous insular features made the process of delimitation especially challenging. The low-tide elevation of Fasht ad Dibal lies in the overlapping territorial seas of both states. Qatar maintained that Fasht ad Dibal cannot be appropriated, while Bahrain contended that low-tide elevations by their very nature were territory, and therefore could be appropriated.[205] The Court held that the decisive question is whether a state can acquire sovereignty by appropriation over a low-tide elevation which lies at the same time within the breadth of the territorial seas of two states.[206] Despite the absence of international treaty law and uniform state practice on the question, the Court followed from a number of rules established in the law of the sea that there was no assumption that low-tide elevations are territory in the same sense as islands.[207] The Court, for example, named the absence of a territorial sea of its own of a low-tide elevation lying beyond the limits of the territorial sea.[208] Consequently, the Court dismissed low-tide elevations which are situated in the zone of overlapping claims both for the use of their low-water line as a base line and for the purpose of drawing the equidistance line.[209]

---

[203] ICJ Reports 2001, p. 96 paras. 180–1, 183.
[204] ICJ Reports 2001, p. 103 paras. 212–5.   [205] ICJ Reports 2001, p. 100, para. 200.
[206] ICJ Reports 2001, p. 101 paras. 203–4. The question arises only in the context of overlapping territorial seas. The Court noted that there is no doubt that a coastal state has sovereignty over low-tide elevations which are situated only within its own territorial sea, since it has sovereignty over the territorial sea itself (ICJ Reports 2001, p. 101, para. 204).
[207] ICJ Reports 2001, p. 101, paras. 205, 206.   [208] ICJ Reports 2001, p. 102, para. 207.
[209] ICJ Reports 2001, p. 102, para. 209.

The Court qualified the maritime feature of Qit'at Jaradah as an island which is above water at high tide and thus held that Qit'at Jaradah should be taken into consideration for the drawing of the equidistance line.[210] The Court reasoned that in the case of very small islands such as Qit'at Jaradah, activities like the construction of navigational aids by Bahrain must be considered sufficient to support a claim of sovereignty.[211] Qit'at Jaradah was thus allowed to shift the boundary line closer to Qatar.[212]

With regard to the maritime feature of Fasht al Azm, the Court did not determine whether it was to be regarded as part of Bahrain's Sitrah Island or as a mere low-tide elevation.[213] The question was relevant for the choice of a base point. But since the Court did not determine the state of Fasht al Azm, it chose the unusual method of provisionally drawing two equidistance lines reflecting the two hypotheses.[214] The Court found both hypothetical equidistance lines to be inappropriate for achieving an equitable result: the first in view of the fact that less than 20 per cent of the surface of this island are permanently above water and that it would thus place the boundary disproportionately close to Qatar's mainland coast; the second because it would brush Fasht Al Azm. In the view of the Court, these special circumstances justified choosing a delimitation line passing between Fasht al Azm and Qit'at ash Shajarah.[215]

The Court next considered the question of the 'tiny island'[216] of Qit'at Jaradah again, which it had attributed to Bahrain.[217] The Court observed that the island is situated about midway between the main island of Bahrain and the Qatar peninsula. It held that to place a base point on

---

[210] ICJ Reports 2001, p. 99, para. 195.
[211] ICJ Reports 2001, p. 99, para. 197. In this context the Court cited the Permanent Court of International Justice in the *Legal Status of Eastern Greenland* case that:

> It is impossible to read the records of the decisions in cases as to territorial sovereignty without observing that in many cases the tribunal has been satisfied with very little in the way of the actual exercise of sovereign rights, provided that the other State could not make out a superior claim.

PCIJ, Series AIB, No. 53, p. 46, ICJ Reports 2001, p. 99, para. 198.

[212] See text accompanying notes 217 and 218 below for the exact degree of influence on the boundary line which was granted to Qit'at Jaradah.
[213] ICJ Reports 2001, p. 98, para. 190. The Court had been unable to establish whether a permanent passage separating Sitrah Island from Fasht al Azm existed before reclamation works were undertaken by Bahrain in 1982.
[214] ICJ Reports 2001, p. 104, paras. 216. See Appendix II, Maps 3, 4, 5 and 6.
[215] ICJ Reports 2001, p. 104, para. 217, citing the *Case concerning Maritime Delimitation in the Area between Greenland and Jan Mayen (Denmark v. Norway)*, Judgment, ICJ Reports 1993, p. 60, para. 50, p. 62, para. 54; ICJ Reports 2001, p. 104, para. 218.
[216] ICJ Reports 2001, p. 104, para. 219.   [217] ICJ Reports 2001, p. 99, para. 197.

Qit'at Jaradah would give a disproportionate effect to this insignificant maritime feature. The Court thus drew a delimitation line passing immediately to the east of Qit'at Jaradah.[218] In order to determine the course of the delimitation line near the low-tide elevation of Fasht ad Dibal, the Court had to consider the influence of Fasht al Azm once again. The Court observed that under both hypotheses as to the status of the maritime feature of Fash al Azm the situation was nearly the same. Namely, that Fasht ad Dibal would fall either largely or totally onto the Qatari side of the equidistance line. The Court therefore drew the boundary line between Qit'at Jaradah and Fasht ad Dibal. Since Fasht ad Dibal was thus situated in the territorial sea of Qatar, it fell for that reason under the sovereignty of that state.[219]

In the southern sector, the Court adopted a simplified line delimiting the territorial seas around the Hawar Islands. Because of the line thus adopted, Qatar's maritime zones to the north and south of Bahrain's Hawar Islands were connected only by the channel separating the Hawar Islands from the Qatar peninsula. Since this channel is little suited for navigation, the Court emphasized each state's right under customary international law of innocent passage through the other state's territorial waters.[220]

In the northern sector, the Court regarded the coasts to be rather comparable to adjacent coasts.[221] In this part of the delimitation area, it had to draw a single maritime boundary covering both the continental shelf and the EEZ.[222] The Court thus noted that 'preference will henceforth inevitably be given to criteria that, because of their more neutral character, are best suited for use in a multi-purpose delimitation'.[223] It held it to be in accord with its own precedents to begin with the median line as a provisional line and then to ask whether special circumstances require any adjustment or shifting of that line in order to achieve an equitable result.[224]

---

[218] ICJ Reports 2001, p. 104, para. 219. The Court cited similar situations where it had sometimes been led to eliminate the disproportionate effect of small islands (*North Sea Continental Shelf*, ICJ Reports 1969, p. 36, para. 57; *Continental Shelf (Libyan Arab Jamahiriya v. Malta)*, ICJ Reports 1985, p. 48, para. 64).
[219] ICJ Reports 2001, p. 109, para. 220.   [220] ICJ Reports 2001, p. 109, paras. 221, 223.
[221] ICJ Reports 2001, p. 91, para. 170.   [222] ICJ Reports 2001, p. 91, paras. 170, 224.
[223] ICJ Reports 2001, p. 110, para. 225, citing *Gulf of Maine*, ICJ Reports 1984, p. 327, para. 194.
[224] ICJ Reports 2001, p. 110, paras. 227–30, with reference to *Jan Mayen*, ICJ Reports 1993, p. 61–2, paras. 51, 55. The Court noted that the equidistance-special circumstances rule, which is applicable to the delimitation of the territorial sea, and the equitable principles-relevant circumstances rule, as it has been developed since 1958 through case law and

The Court dismissed the activity of pearling as a relevant circumstance in Bahrain's favour, since the activity was traditionally considered as a right that was common to the coastal population in the Gulf.[225] It also dismissed the marginal disparity in length of the coastal fronts of the parties as to necessitate an adjustment of the equidistance line.[226] The Court disregarded in the northern sector the insular feature of Fasht al Jarim – 'a remote projection of Bahrain's coastline', 'located well out to sea'.[227] The Court noted that 'considerations of equity require that [it] have no effect in determining the boundary line'.[228]

M. The 2002 Case Concerning the Land and Maritime Boundary (Cameroon v. Nigeria)

In 1994, Cameroon filed an application with the ICJ instituting proceedings against Nigeria in a dispute concerning the question of sovereignty over the peninsula of Bakassi. In this case, Cameroon also asked the Court to determine the course of the maritime boundary between the two states, whose coastlines are adjacent and lie in the Gulf of Guinea.[229] The Gulf of Guinea, which is concave in character at the level of the Cameroonian and Nigerian coastlines, is bounded by other states, in particular by Equatorial Guinea, whose Bioko Island lies opposite the parties' coastlines. Equatorial Guinea has thus been granted permission to intervene, as a non-party intervener.[230] In 2002 the ICJ decided the case including the course of the maritime boundary between the two states. The parties had agreed that the Court should rule on the question of maritime delimitation in accordance with international law. Both Cameroon and Nigeria were parties to the 1982 Convention.[231]

In delimiting the maritime boundary, the Court first addressed the sector from the mouth of the Akwayave River up to a so-called Point G.[232] Cameroon claimed that this sector has been delimited by valid international agreements between the parties.[233] It asked the Court

---

state practice with regard to the delimitation of the continental shelf and the EEZ, are closely interrelated (ICJ Reports 2001, see para. 231); see further Chapters 7 and 9.

[225] ICJ Reports 2001, p. 235, paras. 235-6.   [226] ICJ Reports 2001, p. 114, para. 243.
[227] ICJ Reports 2001, p. 114, paras. 247, 248.   [228] ICJ Reports 2001, p. 115, para. 248.
[229] *Land and Maritime Boundary between Cameroon and Nigeria (Cameroon v. Nigeria: Equatorial Guinea intervening)*, Judgment, ICJ Reports 2002, p. 303; Appendix II, Map 13.
[230] ICJ Reports 2002, p. 314, para. 18. See also Chapter 9.
[231] ICJ Reports 2002, p. 440, para. 285.   [232] ICJ Reports 2002, p. 425, para. 247.
[233] Namely, the Anglo-German Agreement of 11 March 1913, the Cameroon–Nigeria Agreement of 4 April 1971, comprising the Yaoundé II Declaration and the appended

merely to confirm that delimitation.[234] The Court agreed with Cameroon by finding that the international instruments invoked by Cameroon established the course of the maritime boundary in that sector.[235]

The Court then turned to the sector of the maritime boundary beyond Point G and outside the territorial sea limit, where no agreement existed between the two parties. The Court recalled that Articles 74 and 83 of the 1982 Convention formed the applicable law. The Court also recalled that these provisions called for the achievement of an equitable solution.[236] It further noted that the parties agreed that the delimitation should be effected by a single boundary line.[237] The Court then pointed out that it had on various occasions made it clear what the applicable criteria, principles and rules of delimitation are when a line covering several zones of coincident jurisdictions is to be determined. It held that they are expressed in the so-called equitable principles–relevant circumstances method, a method which, in its view, is very similar to the equidistance–special circumstances method applicable in delimitation of the territorial sea, and which thus involves first drawing an equidistance line and then considering whether there are factors ('relevant circumstances') calling for the adjustment or shifting of that line in order to achieve an equitable result.[238]

In order to draw the equidistance line, the Court first had to define the relevant coastlines and to locate the base points for the construction of that line.[239] It chose two land-based anchorage points as the sole base points for the construction of the equidistance line. These points – West Point and East Point – are the most southerly points on the low-water line for Nigeria and Cameroon to either side of the bay formed by the estuaries of the Akwayafe and Cross Rivers.[240]

The Court next considered the relevant circumstances.[241] It felt bound to stress in this connection that delimiting with a concern to achieving an equitable result, as required by current international law, is not the same

---

Chart 3433, and the Maroua Declaration of 1 June 1975; See ICJ Reports 2002, p. 431, para 268.
[234] ICJ Reports 2002, p. 425, paras. 248–53, 260.
[235] ICJ Reports 2002, p. 428, paras. 261–7 and in particular 268. See also Chapter 9.
[236] ICJ Reports 2002, p. 440, para. 285.   [237] ICJ Reports 2002, p. 440, para. 286.
[238] ICJ Reports 2002, p. 441, para. 288. See also Chapter 8 and Chapter 9.
[239] ICJ Reports 2002, p. 442, para. 290.
[240] ICJ Reports 2002, p. 443, para. 292; West Point and East Point are determined in the 1994 edition of British Admiralty Chart 3433.
[241] ICJ Reports 2002, p. 443, para. 293, citing *Libyan Arab Jamahiriya* v. *Malta*, ICJ Reports 1985, n. 106, p. 47, para. 63.

as delimiting in equity. The Court continued that its jurisprudence shows that, in disputes relating to maritime delimitation, equity is not a method of delimitation, but solely an aim that should be borne in mind in effecting the delimitation.[242] The Court also noted that 'the geographical configuration of the maritime areas that the Court is called upon to delimit is a given. It is not an element open to modification by the Court but a fact on the basis of which the Court must effect the delimitation'.[243]

Cameroon pointed out that if the Court drew a strict equidistance line, it would be entitled to practically no EEZ or continental shelf.[244] Cameroon alleged that the concavity of the Gulf of Guinea in general and of its own coastline in particular created its own virtual enclavement which should constitute a special circumstance.[245] The Court, however, held that Cameroon's coastline exhibited its concavity mainly in that part which faces Bioko Island and not the coast of Nigeria and that therefore it is not relevant to the maritime delimitation between Cameroon and Nigeria.[246] Thus the configuration of the coastlines within the area to be delimited did not exhibit a particular concavity which would call for an adjustment of the equidistance line.[247]

The Court likewise dismissed Cameroon's call for shifting the equidistance line on the basis of proportionality.[248] The Court recalled that Cameroon's relevant coast must exclude that part which faces Bioko Island, and that therefore no disparity of coastal lengths results.[249]

Cameroon also pointed to the presence of Bioko Island, which belongs to Equatorial Guinea but lies closer to Cameroon's coast. Cameroon submitted that the presence of Bioko Island constitutes a special circumstance requiring an adjustment of the equidistance line.[250] The Court observed that islands have sometimes been taken into account as a relevant circumstance in delimitation when such islands lay within the zone to be delimited and fell under the sovereignty of one of the parties. It added, however, that the effect of Bioko Island on the seaward projection of Cameroon's coastal front was an issue between Cameroon and

---

[242] ICJ Reports 2002, p. 443, para. 294. See also Chapter 8.
[243] ICJ Reports 2002, p. 443, para. 295, recalling the *North Sea Continental Shelf* cases, n. 3, para. 91.
[244] ICJ Reports 2002, p. 432, para. 271. [245] ICJ Reports 2002, p. 445, para. 296.
[246] ICJ Reports 2002, p. 496, paras. 291, 297; see Appendix II, Map 11. See also Chapter 9.
[247] ICJ Reports 2002, p. 291, para. 297. [248] ICJ Reports 2002, p 446, paras. 300, 301.
[249] ICJ Reports 2002, p. 442, paras. 291, 301.
[250] ICJ Reports 2002, p. 433, paras. 272 and 274–5.

Equatorial Guinea, and was not relevant to the issue of the maritime delimitation between Cameroon and Nigeria.[251]

Contrary to Nigeria's argument with respect to oil practices, the Court did not consider the conduct of the parties concerning oil concessions as a relevant circumstance absent express or tacit agreement.[252]

Having found no other reasons that might have called for an adjustment of the equidistance line, the Court finally decided that the equidistance line represents an equitable result for the delimitation of the area in respect of which it had jurisdiction to give a ruling.[253] The *Cameroon v. Nigeria* case was the first case between adjacent states in which the ICJ applied the equidistance line without modification. The equidistance line, however, could not be extended very far, since the Court could not take a decision which might have affected rights of other parties. It therefore did not specify the location of a tripoint where the maritime boundary between Cameroon and Nigeria meets the claims of Equatorial Guinea.[254]

N. The 2006 Barbados v. Trinidad and Tobago *award*

The Tribunal in *Barbados v. Trinidad and Tobago* issued its Award on 11 April 2006 in an arbitration relating to the delimitation of the EEZ and the continental shelf under the LOS Convention.[255] The arbitral proceedings had been initiated by Barbados on 16 February 2004 pursuant to Part XV and the Tribunal was constituted in accordance with Annex VII of the LOS Convention.

The islands of Trinidad and Tobago lie off the north-east coast of South America. Trinidad and Venezuela are, at their closest, a little over 7 nm apart. The island of Barbados consists of a single island with a surface area of 441 square kilometres lying 116 nm north-east of Tobago.[256] The Republic of Trinidad and Tobago is made up of the island of Trinidad, with an area of 4,828 square kilometres and the island of Tobago with an area of 300 square kilometres, lying 19 nm to the north-east. A number of much smaller islands also lie close to those two

---

[251] ICJ Reports 2002, p. 446, para. 299.
[252] ICJ Reports 2002, p. 447, paras. 304–6. See also Chapter 10.
[253] ICJ Reports 2002, p. 448, paras. 305–6.   [254] ICJ Reports 2002, p. 421, para. 238.
[255] *Award of the Arbitral Tribunal in the Matter of Arbitration between Barbados and the Republic of Trinidad and Tobago*, 11 April 2006 (hereinafter *Barbados v. Trinidad and Tobago* Award), Reports of International Arbitral Awards vol. XXVII p. 147–251 (United Nations 2008), see also International Court of Arbitration: www.pca-cpa.org/showpage.asp?pag_id=1152 (last accessed 17 February 2012); Appendix II, Map 14.
[256] Barbados/Trinidad and Tobago Award, n. 255, para. 43.

main islands. Therefore, Trinidad and Tobago has declared itself an 'archipelagic state' pursuant to the provisions of the LOS Convention.[257]

By domestic legislation, both countries established their 12 nm territorial sea and 200 nm EEZ.[258] Trinidad and Tobago's legislation displayed a preference for delimitation 'on the basis of international law in order to achieve an equitable solution'.[259] In contrast, Barbados' legislation favoured delimitation by equidistance between Barbados and another state, in the absence of agreement.[260]

Before drawing the single maritime boundary, the Tribunal appraised and reinforced the modern application of the law and process of equitable maritime delimitation by the ICJ and prior arbitral tribunals.[261] It emphasized the need for predictability and stability within the rule of law and the need for flexibility in the outcome – implying a certain degree of judicial discretion.[262] The Tribunal confirmed the observation of prior case law that the equitable principles–relevant circumstances rule as codified in Articles 74 and 83 of the LOS Convention and concerning the EEZ and continental shelf produces much the same result as the equidistance–special circumstances rule as retained in the Convention's Article 15 concerning the territorial sea.[263] In this respect the Tribunal employed a two-stage process of drawing a provisional single boundary median line and then considering whether that boundary must be adjusted in the light of relevant circumstances in order to achieve an equitable result.[264] With respect to the relevant circumstances applicable to a single boundary delimitation, it stressed the primary role of neutral criteria of a geographical character.[265]

In the western sector, the parties disputed access to fisheries. The Tribunal did not accept Barbados' suggestion to adjust the provisional equidistance line so as to ensure equitable access to fisheries for the Barbadian population, as the ICJ had done in the *Jan Mayen* judgment by virtue of applying the *Gulf of Maine* exception of 'catastrophic repercussions'.[266] It noted that it is altogether exceptional to determine a maritime boundary on the basis of traditional fishing on the high

---

[257] Ibid., para. 44. [258] Ibid., paras. 47, 95.
[259] Ibid., para. 95, quoting section 15 of Trinidad and Tobago's 1986 domestic legislation.
[260] Barbados/Trinidad and Tobago Award, n. 255, para. 302, quoting section 3(3) of Barbados' 1987 domestic legislation.
[261] Ibid., paras. 219–45. [262] Ibid., paras. 232, 243–4. See also Chapter 8.
[263] Ibid., para. 305, citing *Cameroon v. Nigeria*, above n. 240, para. 288. See also Chapter 8.
[264] Ibid., para. 242. See also Chapter 9. [265] Ibid., para. 228.
[266] Ibid., para. 241, quoting the exception of *Gulf of Maine*; and paras. 264–71.

seas by one of the parties.[267] Having rejected the adjustment of the provisional boundary line, the Tribunal considered itself also barred from ruling upon the access rights of Barbados to waters that now fell into Trinidad and Tobago's EEZ.[268] The Tribunal, however, did call upon the parties both to negotiate in good faith and to conclude an agreement providing for non-exclusive fishery access on mutually acceptable conditions.[269]

In the eastern sector, the Tribunal had to determine a single boundary line.[270] With respect to relevant circumstances in the area, the Tribunal dismissed both parties' hydrocarbon activities.[271] In addition, it recalled the ICJ decision in *Cameroon* v. *Nigeria* that oil wells are not in themselves to be considered as relevant circumstances, unless based on express or tacit agreement between the parties.[272] Thus neither the parties' activities nor the subsequent responses thereto constituted a factor that had to be taken into account in the drawing of an equitable delimitation line.[273]

With respect to coastal lengths, the Tribunal held that:

> broad coastal frontages of the island of Trinidad and of the island of Tobago as well as the resulting disparity in coastal lengths between the Parties, are relevant circumstances to be taken into account in effecting the delimitation as these frontages are clearly abutting upon the disputed area of overlapping claims.[274]

The Tribunal held that since there was no magic formula of where precisely to adjust the equidistance line, it was here that discretion must be exercised within the limits set out by the applicable law.[275] The Tribunal adjusted the last segment of the provisional equidistance line, while being mindful that, as far as possible, there should be no cut-off effects arising from the delimitation and that the line as drawn

---

[267] Ibid., para. 267. See also Chapter 10.
[268] Such a solution had, however, been found in *Eritrea* v. *Yemen*. But the Tribunal stated that the *Eritrea* v. *Yemen* solution was devised in the specific context of awarding sovereignty and with a view to excluding fisheries from affecting the boundary (Barbados/Trinidad and Tobago Award, n. 255, paras. 277–83). Furthermore, the Tribunal concurred with Trinidad's argument that Barbados' fishing off Tobago did not amount to traditional, artisanal fishery but rather to large-scale semi-industrial operations (paras. 254 and 266).
[269] Barbados/Trinidad and Tobago Award, n. 255, paras. 284–93. [270] Ibid., paras. 298.
[271] Ibid., para. 241. See also Chapter 10.
[272] Ibid., paras. 361–64, citing *Cameroon* v. *Nigeria*, n. 229, para. 304.
[273] Barbados/Trinidad and Tobago Award, n. 255, para. 366.
[274] Ibid., para. 255, 334. See also Chapter 10. [275] Ibid., para. 373.

avoids the encroachment that would result from an unadjusted equidistance line.[276]

The Tribunal was cautious not to prejudice any potential claim by a third party in respect of which it had no jurisdiction.[277] The Tribunal ended the boundary at the point where it intersects with the boundary agreed in 1990 between Trinidad and Tobago and Venezuela.[278]

O. The 2007 Guyana v. Suriname *Award*

The Tribunal, established under Annex VII of the LOS Convention, issued its Award in the dispute between Guyana and Suriname on 17 September 2007.[279] The award concerns the delimitation of the parties' maritime boundary as well as the lawfulness of various acts committed by the parties in the disputed maritime area.

Guyana and Suriname are situated on the north-east coast of the South American continent. They have adjacent coastlines, separated by the mouth of the Corentyne River. Guyana gained independence from the United Kingdom in 1966, while Suriname gained independence from the Netherlands in 1975.

The arbitration proceedings were initiated by Guyana under Part XV, Section 2 of the Convention in February 2004, following unsuccessful negotiation triggered by the so-called CGX incident. The CGX incident occurred in June 2000. An oil exploration fleet on behalf of CGX Resources Inc. and operating under a Guyanese concession was ordered by the Surinamese navy to leave the disputed maritime area and was escorted away by two Surinamese patrol boats.[280] In this respect the Tribunal also considered and ruled on allegations by Guyana that Suriname had engaged in the unlawful use or threat of force. It also considered the parties' obligations under Articles 74(3) and 83(3) of the Convention with respect to negotiations appending delimitation of the EEZ and the continental shelf.[281]

With respect to the delimitation of the territorial sea, the Tribunal noted that international courts and tribunals are not constrained by a

---

[276] Ibid., paras. 374–5. [277] Ibid., para. 218. [278] Ibid., paras. 345–6.
[279] *Arbitral Tribunal Constituted Pursuant to Article 287, and in Accordance with Annex VII, of the United Nations Convention on the Law of the Sea in the Matter of an Arbitration between Guyana and Suriname*, Award of 17 September 2007 (hereinafter *Guyana v. Suriname* Award), International Court of Arbitration: www.pca-cpa.org/showfile.asp?fil_id=664 (last accessed 18 February 2012); Appendix II, Map 15.
[280] Ibid., paras. 150–1. [281] See Chapter 12.

finite list of special circumstances.[282] Rather they should examine 'every particular factor' of a case which might suggest an adjustment or shifting of the equidistance line, thereby consulting also previous decided cases and the practice of states.[283] The Tribunal thus found that navigational interests may constitute special circumstances justifying deviation from the median line.[284] It held in accordance with the *Beagle Channel* Tribunal[285] that factors such as 'convenience, navigability, and the desirability of enabling each Party so far as possible to navigate in its own waters', should be taken into account.[286] The Tribunal also found that the record amply supports Suriname's conclusion that the predecessors of the parties agreed upon a N 10° E delimitation line for the reason that all of the Corentyne River was to be Suriname's territory and that the 10° line provided appropriate access through Suriname's territorial sea to the western channel of the Corentyne River.[287]

However, the 10° line was established between the parties only from the starting point to the 3 nm limit.[288] Suriname argued that the N 10° E line should be extended up to the modern 12 nm territorial sea limit by virtue of the doctrine of inter-temporal law.[289] The Tribunal, however, held that the only special circumstances which would call for a deviation from the equidistance line was the circumstance of navigation and control over the approaches to the Corentyne River, which did not apply beyond 3 nm seawards, and therefore rejected an automatic extension of the 10° line.[290] The Tribunal ultimately drew a straight line from the 3 nm limit of the 10° line to the 12 nm limit where the single boundary equidistance line determined by the Tribunal to delimit the continental shelves and EEZs of the parties begins.[291]

For the delimitation of the EEZ and continental shelf, the parties agreed that the Tribunal should draw a single maritime boundary.[292] With respect to the method of delimitation, the Tribunal held that in the course of the last two decades international courts and tribunals have

---

[282] *Guyana* v. *Suriname* Award, n. 279, paras. 298, 302. See also Chapter 11.
[283] Ibid., para. 303, citing *Jan Mayen*, ICJ Reports 1993, paras. 54, 58.
[284] Ibid., paras. 301, 304.
[285] Beagle Channel Arbitration, Report and Decision of the Court (1978) 17 ILM, 634, 673.
[286] *Guyana* v. *Suriname* Award, n. 279, para. 305.   [287] Ibid., para. 306.
[288] Ibid., para. 307.
[289] Ibid., paras. 286–7. Suriname relied on the finding of the ICJ in the *Aegean Sea* case that a Guyana/Suriname agreement 'must be interpreted in accordance with the rules of international law as they exist today' (para. 286).
[290] Ibid., para. 314.   [291] Ibid., para. 315.   [292] Ibid., paras. 213, 218.

come to embrace a clear role for equidistance. It continued that this role consists of a two-step approach of drawing a provisional equidistance line and then adjusting that line to reflect special or relevant circumstances.[293]

The parties were in disagreement with regard to the relevant coasts for the purpose of delimitation. In Guyana's view the relevant coastlines were those between the outermost points along the base line controlling the direction of the equidistance line to a distance of 200 nm, because these coastal base points define the limits of each party's area of legal entitlement.[294] Suriname argued that the relevant coasts were those that faced onto, or abutted, the area to be delimited. This meant that the relevant coasts were only those that extend to a point where the coasts faced away from the area to be delimited.[295] The Tribunal adopted Guyana's approach, by stating that it seems 'logical and appropriate' to treat as relevant the coasts of the parties which generate 'the complete course' of the provisional equidistance line.[296]

The Tribunal found that the geographical configuration of the relevant coastlines did not present any marked concavity or convexity nor any other circumstance that would justify an adjustment or shifting of the provisional equidistance line.[297] While both parties agreed that geography was of 'fundamental importance', Guyana also claimed the relevance of the conduct of the parties concerning the oil concession practice, which dated back nearly fifty years.[298] Guyana claimed that the oil concessions were based on a serious and good faith effort to identify a historical equidistance line, thus reflecting a de facto pattern of

---

[293] Ibid., para. 335. See also Chapter 11.   [294] Ibid., para. 345.   [295] Ibid., para. 349.
[296] Ibid., para. 352. By rejecting Suriname's approach, the Tribunal turned away from the approach taken in the Barbados/Trinidad and Tobago Award where the Tribunal concluded that 'what matters is whether [coastal frontages] abut as a whole upon the disputed area by a radial or directional presence relevant to the delimitation, not whether they contribute base points to the drawing of an equidistance line' (Barbados/Trinidad and Tobago Award, n. 255, para. 331). This issue is likely to remain highly contentious in future delimitation contexts, including for the question of proportionality. See Stephen Fietta, 'Guyana/Suriname Award' (2008) 102(1) *American Journal of International Law,* 119, note 14, 127.
[297] *Guyana v. Suriname* Award, n. 279, para. 377. In their written and oral pleadings, both parties agreed that there were no coastal features that rendered the coastline extraordinary and that the coastal geography is 'unremarkable' (para. 375). Nevertheless, Suriname invoked a cut-off effect, caused by a combination of Suriname's concave and Guyana's convex coastlines which made the equidistance line encroach upon Suriname's coast (para. 360). Meanwhile, Guyana claimed an exaggerated effect of the base points placed on the headland of Suriname's Hermina Bank (para. 366).
[298] Ibid., paras. 357, 378.

acceptance that its proposed line of delimitation has long been treated as the valid equidistance line.[299] The Tribunal, however, found no evidence of any express or tacit agreement between the parties and therefore refused to take the parties' oil practice into account in the delimitation of the maritime boundary.[300]

The Tribunal concluded that there were no relevant circumstances in the EEZ or continental shelf zone which would require it to adjust the provisional equidistance line which it described as starting from the 12 nm limit of the territorial sea boundary, extending to the 200 nm limit.[301]

P. The 2007 Territorial and Maritime Dispute (Nicaragua v. Honduras)

On 8 October 2007, the ICJ determined a single maritime boundary between Nicaragua and Honduras.[302] Nicaragua had requested the ICJ, on 8 December 1999, to 'determine the course of the single maritime boundary between the areas of territorial sea, continental shelf and exclusive economic zone appertaining respectively to Nicaragua and Honduras, in accordance with equitable principles and relevant circumstances recognised by general international law as applicable to such a delimitation of a single maritime boundary' in the Caribbean Sea.[303] The case was brought to the Court by Nicaragua on the basis of the American Treaty of Pacific Settlement (the Pact of Bogotá) and Article 36(2) of the ICJ Statute.[304]

Nicaragua and Honduras are adjacent states that share a land boundary stretching across the isthmus of Central America from the Pacific Ocean in the west to the Caribbean Sea in the east. The eastern sector of Nicaragua and Honduras' land boundary follows the thalweg, or deepest channel, of the River Coco and terminates in the mouth of the River Coco on the delta referred to as Cape Gracias a Dios. The eastern part of the land boundary is subject to a historical dispute between the parties. A mixed boundary commission installed by the 1894 Gámez-Bonilla

---

[299] Ibid., para. 378.   [300] Ibid., para. 390. See also Chapter 10.
[301] Ibid., paras. 392, 399, 400(b). The Tribunal also checked the relevant coastal lengths for proportionality and came up with nearly the same ratio of relevant areas (Guyana 51%: Suriname 49%) as well as for coastal frontages (Guyana 54%: Suriname 46%) (para. 392).
[302] *Territorial and Maritime Dispute between Nicaragua and Honduras in the Caribbean Sea (Nicaragua v. Honduras)*, Judgment, ICJ Reports 2007, pp. 659, 760, paras. 321(2) and (3); Appendix II, Maps 16.1 and 16.2.
[303] ICJ Reports 2007, p. 666, para. 17.   [304] ICJ Reports 2007, p. 663, para. 1.

Treaty[305] was unable to agree on the demarcation of the eastern two-thirds of the land boundary. The parties, pursuant to the treaty, had submitted their dispute over the outstanding portion of the boundary to arbitration by the King of Spain, who rendered his Award in 1906. In 1960 the ICJ found that the 1906 Award was valid and binding in that it fixed the common boundary point on the coast of the Atlantic at the mouth of the river Coco and that Nicaragua was under an obligation to give effect to it.[306] In order to implement the 1906 Award, the co-ordinates of the land boundary terminus in the mouth of the River Coco were subsequently fixed by a second boundary commission in 1962.[307]

During the present proceedings, Nicaragua raised the question of sovereignty over several small islands lying within the area of overlapping maritime claims.[308] This late-coming claim by Nicaragua was found by the Court to be admissible for being 'inherent in the original claim relating to maritime delimitation'.[309] In order to determine sovereignty over the islands, the Court considered the arguments and evidence presented by the parties with respect to the principle of *uti possidetis iuris*, the evidentiary value of maps, recognition by third states, and post-colonial *effectivités*.[310] The Court found that the post-colonial *effectivités* presented by Honduras evidenced an 'intention and will to act as sovereign' and that they 'constitute a modest but real display of authority over the four islands'.[311] Honduras had shown that on the islands it has applied and enforced its civil and criminal law, has regulated immigration, fisheries activities and has exercised its authority in respect of public works.[312] The Court found that Honduras was sovereign over the islands of Bobel Cay, Savanna Cay, Port Royal Cay, and South Cay.[313]

The Court encountered difficulties at the land boundary terminus in the identification of suitable base points for the construction of a provisional equidistance line. The problems were caused by the unstable geomorphology at the mouth of the River Coco. The Court noted that

---

[305] 1894 Gámez-Bonilla Treaty; a translation of the Treaty appears in Arbitral Award Made by the King of Spain on 23 December 1906 *(Honduras v. Nicaragua)*, 1960 ICJ Reports 192, 199 (18 November).
[306] ICJ Reports 2007, p. 677, paras. 45–6. [307] ICJ Reports 2007, p. 677, para. 47.
[308] ICJ Reports 2007, p. 694, paras. 105–7 and para. 127.
[309] ICJ Reports 2007, p. 697, para. 115.
[310] ICJ Reports 2007, p. 704, para 146–226. See also Chapter 9.
[311] ICJ Reports 2007, p. 721, paras. 208, 272.
[312] ICJ Reports 2007, p. 713, paras. 176–207.
[313] ICJ Reports 2007, p. 721, paras. 208, 227 and p. 760, operative para. 321(1).

the parties agreed that 'the sediment carried to and deposited at sea by the River Coco have caused its delta, as well as the coastline to the north and south of the Cape, to exhibit a very active morpho-dynamism' and that 'thus continued accretion at the Cape might render any equidistance line so constructed today arbitrary and unreasonable in the near future'.[314] Due to the problem of identifying base points for the construction of an equidistance line, the Court chose the angle bisector method to delimit the maritime areas.[315] The Court pointed out the practical advantages of the bisector method where a minor deviation in the exact position of endpoints, which are at a reasonable distance from the shared point, will have only a relatively minor influence on the course of the entire coastal front line.[316]

Before opting for the bisector method, the Court noted with respect to the method of delimitation in the territorial sea that to draw a provisional equidistance line and adjust it in the light of special circumstances is the most 'logical and widely practised approach' and that equidistance has a certain intrinsic value because of its scientific character and the relative ease with which it can be applied.[317] But the Court explained that the difficulties at the land boundary constituted a special circumstance in themselves in the territorial sea as provided for in Article 15 of the Convention 'in which it cannot apply the equidistance principle'.[318] It added that at the same time equidistance would remain the rule.[319] The Court noted that neither party had as its main argument a call for a provisional equidistance line as the most suitable method of delimitation.[320]

With respect to the starting point of the maritime boundary, the Court noted the unpredictable situation at the land boundary terminus, including the temporary and unpredictable formation of small islands in the mouth of the River Coco.[321] The Court solved this problem by leaving un-delimited the first 3 nm of the territorial sea boundary.[322] The Court requested that the parties negotiate in good faith the course of this un-delimited portion from the endpoint of the land boundary as

---

[314] ICJ Reports 2007, p. 742, para. 277.   [315] See Chapter 4.
[316] ICJ Reports 2007, p. 748, para. 294.
[317] ICJ Reports 2007, p. 741, paras. 272 and 268 citing *Maritime Delimitation and Territorial Questions between Qatar and Bahrain (Qatar v. Bahrain)*, Merits, Judgment, ICJ Reports 2001, p. 94, para. 176.
[318] ICJ Reports 2007, p. 745, para. 281. See Chapter 4.
[319] ICJ Reports 2007, p. 745, para. 281.   [320] ICJ Reports 2007, p. 742, para. 275.
[321] ICJ Reports 2007, p. 754, para. 310.   [322] ICJ Reports 2007, p. 756, para. 311.

described by the 1906 Award to the starting point of the maritime boundary.[323]

The Court in *Nicaragua v. Honduras* disregarded the offshore islands for the construction of the bisector, treating the delimitation around the islands as a separate task. The bisector thus ran to the north of the Honduran islands, thereby placing them on Nicaragua's side of the delimitation line. The Court then turned to the separate task of delimiting the waters around and between the islands north and south of the bisector line.[324] The Court used the 12 nm arc and equidistance methods to delimit around and between the opposite-facing offshore islands.[325] Accordingly the Court drew a delimitation line following along the bisector until it reached the outer limit of the 12 nm territorial sea of Honduras' Bobel Cay. From there the line traces the 12 nm arc around the islands' territorial seas. Where that line meets the overlapping territorial seas of Bobel Cay, Port Royal Cay and South Cay (Honduras) and Edinburgh Cay (Nicaragua), it traces the median line between these islands, until it reaches the bisector line again.[326] Thereafter the line continues along that azimuth until it reaches the area where the rights of third states, namely Jamaica and Columbia, may be affected.[327]

Q. The 2009 Case concerning Maritime Delimitation in the Black Sea (Romania v. Ukraine)

On 3 February 2009, the ICJ delivered its judgment in the *Maritime Delimitation in the Black Sea* case.[328] The proceedings were instituted in 2004 by Romania against Ukraine (prior to the annexation of the peninsula by Russia in 2014) concerning the delimitation of the continental shelf and the EEZ of Romania and Ukraine in the Black Sea.[329]

The area within which the Court carried out the delimitation is located in the north-western part of the Black Sea.[330] The Black Sea is an enclosed sea bordered by several states. The Crimean Peninsula extends southward from Ukraine's mainland into the Black Sea.[331] The Court also

---

[323] ICJ Reports 2007, p. 756, paras. 311, 321(4). See also Chapter 12.
[324] ICJ Reports 2007, p. 749, paras. 299–304.   [325] ICJ Reports 2007, p. 752, para. 305.
[326] ICJ Reports 2007, p. 760, para. 321(3). See Chapter 4 and Chapter 11.
[327] ICJ Reports 2007, p. 760, para. 321(3).
[328] *Case Concerning Maritime Delimitation in the Black Sea (Romania v. Ukraine)*, Judgment, 3 February 2009, ICJ Reports 2009, p. 61; Appendix II, Maps 17.1 and 17.2.
[329] ICJ Reports 2009, p. 64, para. 1.   [330] ICJ Reports 2009, p. 68, para. 14.
[331] ICJ Reports 2009, p. 68, para. 15.

noted that there is a natural feature called Serpents' Island, lying in the north-western part of the Black Sea, approximately 20 nm to the east of the Danube delta. Serpents' Island is above water at high tide and has a circumference of approximately 2,000 m.[332] At stake in the disputed maritime area were extensive reported reserves of natural gas and crude oil.[333]

The jurisdiction of the Court was founded on Article 36(1) and paragraph 4(h) of the Additional Agreement which was concluded with reference to Article 2 of the Treaty on the Relations of Good Neighbourliness and Co-operation between Romania and Ukraine, dating from 1997.[334] The Court noted that the parties agreed at the time of filing of the Application by Romania that it has jurisdiction to decide the case.[335] Romania requested the Court 'to draw in accordance with the international law, and specifically the criteria laid down in Article 4 of the Additional Agreement, a single maritime boundary between the continental shelf and the exclusive economic zones of the two States in the Black Sea'.[336] The Court found that there was no agreement in force between the parties that already delimited their EEZs and continental shelf zones.[337] Both Romania and Ukraine are parties to the LOS Convention. Articles 74 and 83 thus were the provisions relevant to the present case.[338]

The parties agreed that the whole Romanian coast constituted the relevant coast for the purpose of delimitation since it abuts the area of delimitation.[339] In considering the relevant coast of Ukraine, the Court recalled two principles which underpinned its jurisprudence on relevant coasts: first, that the 'land dominates the sea', meaning that coastal projections in the seaward direction generate maritime claims;[340] and second, that the coast relevant for delimitation must generate projections which overlap with projections from the coast of the other party.

---

[332] ICJ Reports 2009, p. 69 para. 16.
[333] See http://uk.reuters.com/article/idUKL222156420090203 (last accessed 7 July 2009).
[334] ICJ Reports 2009, pp. 64, 70, paras. 1, 20. According to para. 4 of the Additional Agreement, the parties 'shall negotiate an Agreement on the delimitation of the continental shelf and the exclusive economic zones in the Black Sea' (ICJ Reports 2009, p. 70, para. 18). Paragraph 4 continues that '[i]f these negotiations shall not determine the conclusion of the above-mentioned agreement in a reasonable period of time, but not later than 2 years since their initiation' either party could submit the matter to the ICJ (para. 20). The negotiations on the delimitation of the continental shelf and EEZ opened in January 1998 and lasted for six years without a result (para. 21).
[335] ICJ Reports 2009, p. 71, para. 22.   [336] ICJ Reports 2009, p. 66, para. 11.
[337] ICJ Reports 2009, p. 89, para. 76. See Chapter 9.
[338] ICJ Reports 2009, p. 74, para. 31.   [339] ICJ Reports 2009, p. 93, para. 88.
[340] ICJ Reports 2009, p. 95, para. 99, citing *North Sea Continental Shelf* cases, n. 3, para. 96.

Consequently, the Court excluded from consideration the coasts of Karkinits'ka Gulf, since they are facing each other rather than projecting on Romania's coast in the area to be delimited.[341] Following the exclusion from the relevant coastline of Karkinits'ka Gulf, the Court drew a closing line over the entrance of Karkinits'ka Gulf. The Court noted that it found it 'useful to do so with respect to such a significant feature as Karkinits'ka Gulf, in order to make clear both what coasts will not be under consideration and what waters will not be regarded as falling within the relevant area'. Furthermore, the Court did not include this line in the calculation of the total length of the Ukrainian relevant coasts. It held that the line 'replaces' the coasts of Karkinits'ka Gulf which do not themselves generate any entitlement to the EEZ and continental shelf and that therefore the closing line could not generate any entitlement either.[342]

Regarding the methodology of delimitation the Court stated that it proceeds in 'defined stages' which in recent decades have been 'specified with precision'.[343] The Court stated that once the provisional equidistance line has been drawn in the first stage, it shall then consider in the second stage 'whether there are factors calling for the adjustment or shifting of that line in order to achieve an 'equitable result''.[344]

In order to draw a provisional equidistance line, the Court noted that it had to identify those points on the parties' relevant coasts which mark a significant change in the direction of the coastline so that the resulting provisional equidistance line takes due account of the coastal geography.[345] The first base point under consideration lay on the Sacalin Peninsula and was disputed by Ukraine, which described the peninsula as a spit of sand. However, the Court observed that the peninsula belongs to the Romanian mainland and is permanently above sea level. The Court held that 'the geomorphological features of the peninsula and its possibly sandy nature have no bearing on the elements of its physical geography which are relevant for maritime delimitation'.[346] In another part of the Romanian coast, the Court had to choose a base point either at the seaward end of the 7.5 km long Sulina Dyke or at the end where it adjoins the mainland.[347] The

---

[341] ICJ Reports 2009, p. 97, para. 100.   [342] Ibid.
[343] ICJ Reports 2009, p. 101, paras. 115–16.
[344] ICJ Reports 2009 p. 101, paras. 120–1 and 155, citing *Cameroon v. Nigeria*, n. 299, at para. 288. See Chapter 9 and Chapter 11.
[345] ICJ Reports 2009, p. 105, para. 127. See Chapter 4.
[346] ICJ Reports 2009, p. 105, para. 129.   [347] ICJ Reports 2009, p. 105, para. 130.

Court held that the geographical reality of the coast covered 'any material factors that are present' and not only naturally accumulated physical elements.[348] With reference to the negotiating history, the Court found that it could proceed on a case-by-case basis with respect to the necessity of mitigating any excessive length of harbour works in the sense of Article 11.[349] The Court finally pointed out that, irrespective of its length, no convincing evidence had been presented that this dyke served any direct purpose in port activities. Accordingly, the Court discarded the seaward end of the Sulina dyke for the choice of a base point.[350] The Court instead chose the landward end of the Sulina dyke, where it joins the Romanian mainland, saying that this has the advantage of 'not giving greater importance to an installation than to the physical geography of the landmass'.[351]

With regard to Ukrainian base points, the Court paid specific attention to Serpents' Island. The Court observed that there have been instances where a cluster or fringe of islands has been considered as part of a state's coast.[352] The Court noted, however, that Serpents' Island lies alone and some 20 nm away from the mainland, and is not one of a cluster of fringe islands constituting 'the coast' of Ukraine. It added that including Serpent's Island into the relevant coast would be a refashioning of geography. Accordingly, the Court discarded Serpents' Island for the placement of a base point.[353] With respect to relevant circumstances, the Court rejected the disproportion between the parties' coastal lengths of 1:2.8 (Romania to Ukraine) for not being 'particularly marked'.[354]

The parties disagreed about the proper characterization of Serpents' Island and the role this maritime feature should play in the delimitation

---

[348] ICJ Reports 2009, p. 106, para. 131. [349] ICJ Reports 2009, p. 106, paras. 133–4.
[350] ICJ Reports 2009, p. 108, para. 138.
[351] ICJ Reports 2009, p. 108, paras. 139–40. Romania had previously used the seaward end of the Sulina dyke as a base point when delimiting the territorial sea. Therefore the Court also observed that the issue of determining the base line for the purpose of measuring the breadth of the continental shelf and the EEZ and the issue of identifying base points for drawing an equidistance/median line for the purpose of delimiting the continental shelf and the EEZ between adjacent/opposite states are two different issues. In the first case, the coastal state, in conformity with the 1982 Convention, may determine the relevant base points. In the second case, the delimitation of the maritime areas involving two or more states, the Court should not base itself solely on the choice of base points made by one of those parties. The Court must, when delimiting the continental shelf and EEZ, select base points by reference to the physical geography of the relevant coasts (ICJ Reports 2009, p. 108, para. 137).
[352] ICJ Reports 2009, p. 109, para. 149, citing *Eritrea and Yemen*, n. 171, paras. 139–46.
[353] Ibid.   [354] ICJ Reports 2009, p. 116, paras. 164, 168. See Chapter 10.

of the parties' EEZ and continental shelf.[355] The Court recalled its refusal to choose Serpents' Island as a base point, before noting that the presence of the island does not call for an adjustment of the provisional equidistance line, since any maritime entitlements potentially generated by it would in any case be fully subsumed by other maritime entitlements of Ukraine. Therefore, it held that it did not need to consider whether Serpents' Island is a rock or an island, falling under paragraphs 2 or 3 of Article 121 of the Convention.[356] The Court thus gave no effect to Serpent's Island other than the 12 nm arc of territorial seas as attributed pursuant to agreements between the parties.[357] The delimitation line near Serpent's Island thus traces the 12 nm arc around Serpents' Island until it intersects with the line equidistant from Romania's and Ukraine's adjacent coasts.[358]

Ukraine argued that its oil-related activities are relevant circumstances.[359] The Court, however, noted that Ukraine did not rely on state activities in order to prove a tacit agreement or *modus vivendi* between the parties regarding a potential maritime boundary.[360] Therefore the Court did not award any particular role to the state activities for this maritime delimitation.[361] The Court held that the equidistance line fully respected the legitimate security interests of either party. It thus merely observed that 'legitimate security considerations of the parties may play a role in determining the final delimitation line'.[362]

In a third step, the Court turned to check that the line it arrived at would not allocate significantly disproportionate areas compared to the respective coastal lengths.[363] The Court recalled that maritime areas are not to be assigned in proportion to length of respective coastlines, but that the Court will apply an ex post facto test of equitableness of the delimitation line it has arrived at.[364] It stated that the assessment of what constitutes significant disproportionality 'remains in each case a matter for the Court's appreciation, which it will exercise by reference to the overall geography of the area'.[365] The Court noted that the ratio of the

---

[355] ICJ Reports 2009, p. 120, para. 179.
[356] ICJ Reports 2009, p. 122, para. 187.
[357] ICJ Reports 2009, p. 123, para. 188.
[358] ICJ Reports 2009, p. 128, para. 206.
[359] ICJ Reports 2009, p. 123, para. 190.
[360] ICJ Reports 2009, p. 125, para. 197.
[361] ICJ Reports 2009, p. 125, para. 198, recalling the Tribunal in *Barbados v. Trinidad and Tobago*, that '[r]esource-related criteria have been treated more cautiously by the decisions of international Courts and tribunals, which have not generally applied this factor as a relevant circumstance' (Barbados/Trinidad and Tobago Award, n. 267, para. 241).
[362] ICJ Reports 2009, p. 128, para. 204.
[363] See Chapter 10.
[364] ICJ Reports 2009, p. 129, para. 211, citing *Guinea v. Guinea-Bissau*, n. 83 paras. 94–5.
[365] ICJ Reports 2009, p. 129, para. 213.

respective coastal lengths of the parties is approximately 1:2.8 and the ratio of the relevant area between Romania and Ukraine is approximately 1:2.1 and that the line as constructed thus required no alteration.[366] The Court ended the maritime boundary at the point beyond which the interests of third states may be affected.[367]

R. The 2012 Bay of Bengal (Bangladesh v. Myanmar) case

The International Tribunal for the Law of the Sea (ITLOS) rendered its first maritime delimitation judgment in a dispute between Bangladesh and Myanmar on 14 March 2012.[368]

Bangladesh is located in the north-east corner of the Bay of Bengal. It has a markedly concave coastline and thus faces a cut-off effect vis-à-vis its neighbours Myanmar and India. In this respect, the geographic setting is much reminiscent of the one in the *North Sea Continental Shelf* cases. Bangladesh began maritime boundary negotiations with Myanmar in 1974, but ultimately decided to unilaterally initiate proceedings under UNCLOS in 2009.[369] Since no party had originally made a declaration under Article 287 UNCLOS, the case initially proceeded as an Annex VII arbitration but was later transferred to ITLOS, following a proposal by Myanmar and subsequent declarations by both parties.[370]

The Tribunal was asked to delimit the territorial sea; the EEZ and continental shelves as a single maritime boundary; and the outer continental shelf beyond 200 nm. It proceeded in three separate tasks.[371]

For the delimitation of the territorial sea boundary, the geography in the immediate vicinity of the terminus of the land boundary deserved attention. The land boundary terminates at the mouth of the Naaf River. The coastlines on either side are relatively straight. Lying off the mouth of the Naaf River and extending roughly parallel to the coast of Myanmar is St. Martin's Island, which belongs to Bangladesh. The island lies a few miles off the land boundary, is about 5 kilometres long,

---

[366] ICJ Reports 2009, p. 130, paras. 215–16. [367] ICJ Reports 2009, p. 130, para. 218.
[368] *Dispute concerning Delimitation of the Maritime Boundary between Bangladesh and Myanmar in the Bay of Bengal (Bangladesh v. Myanmar)*, Judgment of 14 March 2012, available on the ITLOS website at www.itlos.org/fileadmin/itlos/documents/cases/case_no_16/1-C16_Judgment_14_02_2012.pdf; Appendix II, Map 18.
[369] Ibid., paras. 1, 39.   [370] Ibid., paras. 1–4.   [371] Ibid., paras. 179–81.

has a population of about 7,000 and a relatively significant tourist and fishery industry.[372]

Myanmar argued that St. Martin's Island was a special circumstance to be considered under the model of equidistance–special circumstances in accordance with Article 15 UNCLOS.[373] It stated that the island would be on the 'wrong side' of an equidistance line drawn between the mainland coasts of Bangladesh and Myanmar.[374] The Tribunal rejected this argument, stating that '[w]hile it is not unprecedented in case law for islands to be given less than full effect in the delimitation of the territorial sea, the islands subject to such treatment are usually "insignificant maritime features"'.[375] It found St. Martin's Island to be a significant maritime feature by virtue of its size, population and the economic activities connected with it, and therefore gave it full effect in drawing the delimitation line in the territorial sea.[376] Accordingly, the equidistance line was drawn starting in the mouth of the Naaf River, proceeding equidistant between the parties' mainland coasts for a short distance, before turning south-eastwards and equidistant between the mainland coast of Myanmar and the coast of Bangladesh's St. Martin's Island out to the 12 nm limit.[377]

For the delimitation of the single maritime boundary, the ITLOS endorsed the three-step methodology as expounded by previous judgments and arbitral awards.[378] The Tribunal rejected Bangladesh's proposal of a bisector method, since the circumstances did not warrant a deviation from the standard equidistance method.[379] The Tribunal also rejected placing a base point on Bangladesh's St. Martin's Island, in order not to block the seaward projection of Myanmar's coast.[380]

Myanmar argued that there were no relevant circumstances requiring an adjustment of the equidistance line.[381] Bangladesh, however, argued that such circumstances do exist, inter alia, in the concavity of its coastline and the presence of St. Martin's Island.[382] The Tribunal held that St. Martin's Island was not a relevant circumstance, since the distorting effect of an island, as already observed at the stage of selecting

---

[372] Ibid., paras. 143–4, 314.   [373] Ibid., para. 131.   [374] Ibid., para. 134.
[375] Ibid., para. 151, referring to Qit'at Jaradah, a 'very small island, uninhabited and without any vegetation' (ibid.) in *Qatar* v. *Bahrain* (n. 195, para. 219).
[376] *Bangladesh* v. *Myanmar*, n. 368, paras. 151–2.   [377] Ibid., para. 157–69.
[378] Ibid., paras. 239–40.   [379] Ibid., paras. 213–17, 220, 234–7.
[380] Ibid., para. 265, citing the ICJ in *Romania* v. *Ukraine* (n. 328, para. 149).
[381] Ibid., para. 278.   [382] Ibid., para. 276.

base points, 'may increase substantially as the line moves beyond 12 nm from the coast'.[383] With respect to the concavity of Bangladesh's coast, the Tribunal noted that there are various possible adjustments that could be made to produce an equitable result.[384] It applied the adjustment from the point 'where the equidistance line begins to cut off the southward projection of the coast of Bangladesh'.[385] From this point, the boundary was to follow the azimuth of 215° – the same angle that Bangladesh's proposed bisector would have followed – up to the 200 nm limit, so as to avoid cutting off the seaward projection of the coasts of either Bangladesh or Myanmar.[386] The Tribunal set the starting point of the single maritime boundary at the intersection of a 12 nm territorial sea arc around St. Martin's Island.[387] Thus, the island was semi-enclaved with a territorial sea inside Myanmar's EEZ and continental shelf.

Turning to the delimitation of the outer continental shelf beyond 200 nm, the ITLOS noted that UNCLOS in its Articles 76, 77 and 83 treats the continental shelf as a single unit, without any distinction being made between the shelf within 200 nm and the shelf beyond that limit and that, therefore, it had 'jurisdiction to delimit the continental shelf in its entirety'.[388] Myanmar opposed the jurisdiction of the Tribunal over the delimitation of the shelf beyond 200 nm in this particular case, but not in general. The Tribunal phrased the question before it: 'whether, in the circumstances of this case, it is appropriate to exercise that jurisdiction'.[389] It decided that it was competent to delimit the continental shelf beyond 200 nm, pointing out that such delimitation would not encroach upon the functions of the Commission on the Limits of the Continental Shelf (CLCS).[390] It held that not to exercise its jurisdiction over the dispute relating to the continental shelf beyond 200 nm would not only fail to resolve a long-standing dispute, but would also not be conducive to the efficient operation of the Convention, even running contrary to the object and purpose of the Convention.[391] It continued that inaction in the present case, by the Commission and the Tribunal, would leave the parties in a position where they may be unable to benefit fully from their rights under the Convention.[392]

Bangladesh argued that natural prolongation was the primary criterion in establishing an entitlement to an extended continental

---

[383] Ibid., para. 318. [384] Ibid., para. 327. [385] Ibid., para. 331.
[386] Ibid., paras. 334–5. [387] Ibid., para. 337. [388] Ibid., paras. 361, 363.
[389] Ibid., para. 363. [390] Ibid., para. 393. [391] Ibid., para. 391–2.
[392] Ibid., para. 392.

shelf and that consequently Myanmar had no such entitlement due to a discontinuity between that state's land mass and the seabed of the Bay of Bengal beyond 200 nm. The Tribunal rejected this argument and instead held that entitlement to a continental shelf of both parties was a given since the whole Bay of Bengal was covered by sediment, fulfilling the requirement of Article 76(4)(a)(i).[393] With respect to the method of delimitation of this overlap, the Tribunal observed that Article 83 UNCLOS does not distinguish between delimitation within 200 nm and beyond 200 nm and that '[a]ccordingly, the equidistance/relevant circumstances method continues to apply for the delimitation of the continental shelf beyond 200 nm'.[394] Consequently, the concavity of Bangladesh's coastline continued to be a relevant circumstance and the Tribunal extended the single maritime boundary line beyond 200 nm until it reached the area where the rights of third states might be affected.[395]

The result of the extended single maritime boundary was the establishment on Bangladesh's side of the boundary of what the Tribunal called a 'grey area'. Such a 'grey area' exists where, due to the adjustment of the equidistance line, an area on one state's side of the boundary is beyond 200 nm from that state (Bangladesh), but within 200 nm of the state on the other side of the boundary (Myanmar).[396] The Tribunal held that the boundary abutting the grey zone delimited the continental shelf only, but did not 'otherwise limit Myanmar's rights with respect to' the EEZ, notably as regards the superjacent waters.[397] Thus, the seabed of the grey area ended up being Bangladesh's continental shelf and the superjacent waters Myanmar's EEZ. The Tribunal left it to each state to 'exercise its rights and perform its duties with due regard to the rights and duties of the other'.[398]

Applying the disproportionality test, the Tribunal found that the ratio of the relevant coasts of the parties was 1:1.42 and that the relevant area was divided between the parties in the ratio of 1:1.54 – both in favour of Myanmar.[399] The Tribunal found that the relationship between those two ratios reflected an equitable solution without additional adjustment of the equidistance line.[400]

---

[393] Ibid., paras. 437, 444–6, 449.   [394] Ibid., paras. 454–5.   [395] Ibid., para. 461–2.
[396] Ibid., para. 463–4.   [397] Ibid., paras. 471–4.   [398] Ibid., para. 475.
[399] Ibid., paras. 202, 204, 205, 477, 498–9.   [400] Ibid., para. 499.

S. The 2012 Territorial and Maritime Dispute (Nicaragua v. Colombia)

In its judgment of 13 December 2007, regarding Colombia's preliminary objections,[401] the Court had unanimously ruled that it had jurisdiction pursuant to the 'Pact of Bogota'[402] to adjudicate upon sovereignty over some of the disputed maritime features between the parties as well as upon the dispute concerning the maritime delimitation between them.[403] For the judgment on the merits,[404] the delimitation was to be exercised according to customary law, with Colombia not being a party to UNCLOS.[405]

The area of delimitation between Nicaragua and Colombia lies in the western Caribbean Sea. The delimitation to be effected by the Court in its judgment on the merits was not between two mainland coasts, but between Nicaragua's mainland coast and several Colombian insular features. The Colombian islands are scattered across over 100 nm in front of the Nicaraguan coastline – approximately 100 nm away from Nicaragua and more than 350 nm from the Colombian mainland.[406]

Sovereignty over a number of the small islands, cays and banks was disputed between the parties.[407] The Court unanimously awarded sovereignty over all of these insular features to Colombia.[408] Consequently, Nicaragua argued that it would be cut off, or blocked, from the maritime areas into which its coastline projects, by the effect of the small Colombian island territories. It argued that Colombia's approach treated the western coasts of Alburquerque Cays, San Andrés, Providencia, Santa Catalina and Serrana as a wall blocking Nicaragua's access to its maritime entitlements.[409]

With respect to its methodology, the Court confirmed the established judicial practice of a three-step delimitation process.[410] The Court thus

---

[401] *Territorial and Maritime Dispute (Nicaragua v. Colombia)*, Preliminary Objections, 2007 ICJ Reports, p. 832.
[402] American Treaty on Pacific Settlement, vol. 30 UNTS 55, 30 April 1948 (hereinafter 'Pact of Bogota').
[403] The Court found that a treaty between the parties from 1928 and its 1930 protocol had settled sovereignty only over the insular features of San Andrés, Providencia and Catalina, which where thus settled issues within the meaning of Article XXXI of the Pact of Bogota (*Nicaragua v. Colombia*, Preliminary Objections, n. 403, 876).
[404] *Territorial and Maritime Dispute (Nicaragua v. Colombia)*, Judgment of 19 November 2012, ICJ Rep. 2012 p. 624; Appendix II, Map 19.
[405] Ibid., para. 141.   [406] Ibid., paras. 18–24, 215.   [407] Ibid., para. 24.
[408] Ibid., paras. 103, 251.   [409] Ibid., para. 212.   [410] Ibid., paras. 190–4.

had to determine the relevant coasts of the parties in order to draw a median line as a first step and for the purpose of comparing coastal lengths with the maritime areas awarded on each side as a third and final step.[411] The relevant coast of Nicaragua for the purpose of establishing a base line and measuring the breadth of maritime entitlements comprised some fringing insular features. For the purpose of measuring the relevant coast, the Court disregarded the west-facing coastlines of those fringing insular features, as well as a south-facing part of the Nicaraguan mainland coast that does not project into the area of overlapping claims.[412] The relevant Colombian coast for matters of bilateral delimitation with Nicaragua was comprised only of the insular features that are within 200 nm of Nicaragua and not the Colombian mainland, which is more than 400 nm away from Nicaragua's coast.

Of the Colombian insular features,[413] the whole coastline was considered relevant for purposes of measuring that state's relevant coast, since even their eastern-facing coasts projected into waters of overlapping claims within 200 nm from the Nicaraguan coast.[414] This was in line with the Court's view that the area lying east of the Colombian insular features is relevant to the delimitation and should not cut off all projection of maritime entitlements by the Nicaraguan coast lying to the west of the Colombian islands.[415]

Cutting off the substantial eastward projection of the Nicaraguan coastline would have been the effect of an unmodified median line generated by the Colombian insular features. Nicaragua instead suggested enclaving the Colombian islands with 12 nm territorial seas.[416] The Court had drawn its provisional median line using as base points only the major insular features of Colombia and the fringing insular features of the Nicaraguan coast.[417] Two notable Colombian features that were disregarded for the purpose of constructing the median line were Quitasueño and Serrana.[418]

While Colombia was satisfied with the provisional median line, Nicaragua was not.[419] The Court found with Nicaragua that the ratio of relevant coastal lengths of 1:8.2 in favour of Nicaragua warranted adjustment of the provisional median line – especially given the overlapping maritime areas to the east of the Colombian islands.[420] Similarly, the

---

[411] Ibid., para. 141.   [412] Ibid., paras. 145, 201.
[413] Namely, San Andrés, Providencia and Santa Catalina Islands, and Alburquerque, East-Southeast Cays, Roncador and Serrana Cays.
[414] *Nicaragua* v. *Colombia*, n. 404, paras. 151f.   [415] Ibid., paras. 215, 236.
[416] Ibid., para. 206.   [417] Ibid., paras. 201, 203.   [418] Ibid., para. 202.
[419] Ibid., para. 206.   [420] Ibid., para. 211.

Court refused to allow the Colombian insular features to cut off entirely the projections of the Nicaraguan coast in this area.[421] However, the Court stressed that, conversely, neither should the Nicaraguan projections on the eastern side of the Colombian islands be allowed to cut off the entitlements of those maritime features.[422]

In the area between the Colombian islands and the Nicaraguan mainland, the Court found the disparity in coastal lengths to be 'so marked as to justify a significant shift'.[423] The Court accordingly weighted the effect of the base points onto the median line in a ratio of 3:1 in favour of the Nicaraguan base points.[424] East of the median line, the Court constructed a corridor so as to allow San Andrés and Providencia to project eastward to the 200 nm limit. The corridor is largely defined by two lines running along parallels of latitude.[425] The two features of Quitasueño and Serrana that had already been disregarded as base points now lay north of the corridor and were instead enclaved with territorial seas.[426]

Applying its well-established disproportionality test in the last step of the delimitation exercise, the Court calculated that the relevant areas between the parties had been divided in a ratio of approximately 1:3.44 in Nicaragua's favour. Comparing this ratio to the 1:8.2 ratio with respect to coastal lengths, also in Nicaragua's favour, the Court held the ratio to be of no marked disproportion.[427] The resulting delimitation was thus found by the Court to be an equitable result.[428] The Court did not adjudicate upon Nicaragua's claim to an extended continental shelf beyond 200 nm, finding that Nicaragua had not established that its continental margin extended far enough to overlap with Colombia's 200 nm continental shelf entitlement and that it had not met its obligation under Article 76 UNCLOS to submit an extended continental shelf claim to the Commission on the Outer Limits of the Continental Shelf.[429]

T. The 2014 Maritime Dispute (Peru v. Chile)

On 16 January 2008, the Republic of Peru filed an application instituting proceedings against the Republic of Chile with respect to maritime

---

[421] Ibid., para. 215.   [422] Ibid., para. 216.   [423] Ibid., para. 233.
[424] Ibid., para. 234.   [425] Ibid., para. 236.   [426] Ibid., para. 238.
[427] Ibid., para. 243, 245.
[428] Ibid., para. 247. The judgment was, however, strongly objected to by Colombia (see e.g. Paul S. Reichler, 'A Case of Equitable Maritime Delimitation: Nicaragua and Colombia in the Western Caribbean Sea' (2013) 2(3) *Revista Tribuna Internacional*, 129.
[429] *Nicaragua v. Colombia*, n. 404, paras. 126 ff., 129.

delimitation[430] leading to a judgment on the merits in 2014.[431] Chile is a party to UNCLOS but Peru is not.[432] In the area of delimitation, the coast of Peru runs in a north-west direction from the land boundary on the Pacific coast, and the coast of Chile generally follows a north–south direction.[433] The land boundary between Peru and Chile had been fixed in the 1929 Treaty of Lima. The Court noted that in 1947 both parties unilaterally proclaimed certain maritime rights extending 200 nm from their coasts. The Court recalled that in subsequent years Chile, Ecuador and Peru negotiated twelve instruments to which the parties made reference in the present proceedings. The case thus is mainly concerned with treaty interpretation, but also applies customary rules on maritime boundary delimitation.

The parties took fundamentally different positions in this case. Peru argued that no agreed maritime boundary existed between the two countries and asked the Court to draw a boundary line using the equidistance method. Chile, however, contended that the 1952 Santiago Declaration established an international maritime boundary along the parallel of latitude passing through the land boundary terminus and extending to at least 200 nm.[434] Neither party claimed an extended continental shelf in the area under review.[435] The Court observed that the 1952 Santiago Declaration lacked express reference to and therefore did not establish a delimitation line between the zones generated by the continental coasts of the parties.[436] Likewise, the Court found that the 1954 Special Maritime Frontier Zone Agreement acknowledged the existence of a maritime boundary, but only with reference to a prior existing tacit agreement. The 1954 Agreement, however, did not indicate what the precise extent of the boundary was under the tacit agreement.[437] Likewise, the 1968–1969 lighthouse arrangements indicate that a maritime boundary extending along the parallel beyond 12 nm existed, but they did not indicate the extent and nature of that maritime boundary.[438] The Court was able to determine that the existing boundary as referred to by the above-mentioned instruments was a single maritime boundary if the instruments are interpreted in the context of the 1947 Proclamations and the 1952 Santiago Declaration.[439] With respect to the extent of the

---

[430] *Maritime Dispute (Peru v. Chile)*, ICJ Judgment of 27 January 2014; Appendix II, Map 20.
[431] Ibid., paras. 1–15.   [432] Ibid., para. 178.
[433] Ibid., paras. 16–21 (see also Appendix II, Map 20).   [434] Ibid., paras. 22–3.
[435] Ibid., para. 178.   [436] Ibid., paras. 45–70.   [437] Ibid., paras. 71–95.
[438] Ibid., paras. 96–9.   [439] Ibid., paras. 100–2.

existing boundary, the Court concluded on the basis mainly of the fishing activities of the parties at that time – which were conducted up to a seaward distance of some 60 nm – that the boundary along the parallel could not extend beyond 80 nm from its starting point.[440]

For the delimitation of the boundary beyond 80 nm from the coast (Point A), the Court proceeded on the basis of the provisions of Articles 74(1) and 83(1) UNCLOS, which the Court recalled to reflect customary international law and which required the finding of an equitable solution.[441] With reference to its now well-established case law, the Court recalled that the methodology it usually employs in seeking an equitable solution involves three stages. In the first, it constructs a provisional equidistance line unless there are compelling reasons preventing that. At the second stage, it considers whether there are relevant circumstances which may call for an adjustment of that line to achieve an equitable result. At the third stage, the Court conducts a disproportionality test in which it assesses whether the effect of the line, as adjusted, is such that the parties' respective shares of the relevant area are markedly disproportionate to the lengths of their relevant coasts.[442]

Peru argued for the establishment of a provisional equidistance line and contended that there were no special circumstances calling for an adjustment of that line, which represented an equitable result.[443] Chile advanced no arguments on this matter. Its position throughout the proceedings was that the parties had already delimited the whole maritime area in dispute, by agreement, in 1952, and that, accordingly, no maritime delimitation should be performed by the Court.[444]

In line with its established methodology, the Court proceeded to the construction of a provisional equidistance line, which starts at the endpoint of the existing maritime boundary (Point A).[445] The Court first selected appropriate base points. The provisional equidistance line constructed runs in a general south-westerly direction, until it reaches the 200 nm limit measured from the Chilean base lines (Point B).[446] After Point B, the 200 nm limits of the parties' maritime entitlements delimited on the basis of equidistance no longer overlap. The Court finally observed that, from Point B, the 200 nm limit of Chile's maritime entitlement runs in a generally southward direction. The final segment of the maritime

---

[440] Ibid., paras. 103–51.
[441] Ibid., para. 179 (with reference to *Qatar* v. *Bahrain*, n. 195, para. 167 and *Nicaragua* v. *Colombia*, n. 401, para. 139).
[442] Ibid., para. 180.   [443] Ibid., para. 181.   [444] Ibid., para. 182.
[445] Ibid., para. 184.   [446] Ibid., para. 186.

boundary therefore proceeds from Point B to Point C, where the 200 nm limits of the parties' maritime entitlements intersect.[447]

The Court held that there were no relevant circumstances calling for an adjustment of the provisional equidistance line.[448]

Finally, the Court performed the disproportionality test for the purpose of assessing 'the equitable nature of the result'.[449] The Court recalled that in some instances in the past, because of the practical difficulties arising from the particular circumstances of the case, it has not undertaken that calculation.[450] The Court also recalled that the calculation under the disproportionality test does not purport to be precise and is approximate: '[t]he object of delimitation is to achieve a delimitation that is equitable, not an equal apportionment of maritime areas'.[451] It followed that in such cases, the Court engages in a broad assessment of disproportionality. The Court concluded that no significant disproportion is evident, such as would call into question the equitable nature of the provisional equidistance line.[452] The Court accordingly delimited the maritime zones between the parties from Point A along the equidistance line to Point B, and then along the 200 nm limit measured from the Chilean base lines to Point C.[453]

III. Claims and results in domestic and quasi-judicial proceedings

A. The 1979 United States CEIP Delimitation Recommendations

The 1976 United States Coastal Energy Impact Program (CEIP)[454] was introduced to alleviate the burdens of offshore resource activities on the coastal states of the United States. The distribution of federal subsidies depended, inter alia, on the criteria of adjacency of the drilling activities to the states. Adjacency itself was to be determined according to already existing or future maritime boundaries to be settled for the purposes of the CEIP. Negotiations between states on boundary delimitation failed in five cases.[455] In response, federal authorities commissioned a panel of three consultants to propose and recommend delimitation lines in these cases.[456] The consultants were to determine the boundaries on the basis

---

[447] Ibid., para. 190.   [448] Ibid., para. 191.   [449] Ibid., para. 192.
[450] Ibid., para. 193 (with reference to *Libya* v. *Malta*, n. 106, para. 74).
[451] Ibid., (with reference to *Romania* v. *Ukraine*, n. 328, para. 111).
[452] Ibid., para. 194.   [453] Ibid., para. 195 (see also Appendix II, Map 4).
[454] 16 USC sec. 1451 (1979).
[455] The contentious cases were: (i) Louisiana/Mississippi; (ii) Maryland/Delaware; (iii) Delaware/New Jersey; (iv) New Jersey/New York; and (v) New York/Rhode Island.
[456] The panel was composed of R. R. Baxter, J. I. Charney and H. Orlin.

of existing interstate compact agreements, judicial decisions as sources of domestic law, and on the basis of international law, in particular Article 12 of the 1958 Territorial Sea Convention, Article 6 of the 1958 Continental Shelf Convention (equidistance–special circumstances), and the precedents of the *North Sea Continental Shelf* cases and the *Anglo-French Channel* arbitration.

The five cases show the application of a variety of different legal sources.[457] The consultants found that delimitation between New York and New Jersey and between New York and Rhode Island should rely on the interstate compact agreements of 1987 and 1942 respectively, and therefore on the basis of principles applied in these agreements as required by CEIP law. However, the panel did not acknowledge a 1975 'agreement' between Delaware and New Jersey, because of inconclusive conduct (implied authority, estoppel and acquiescence).[458] Instead, the boundary was to be established on the basis of a 1935 Supreme Court decision.[459] Equally, a 1906 decision of that Court provided the basis for the delimitation of the Louisiana–Mississippi boundary.[460]

Only a seaward boundary existed in the 1942 New York–Rhode Island agreement, as in the other four cases delimitation was either lateral *(New Jersey v. Delaware* case, and therefore not applicable to CEIP), or terminated relatively close to the shore in accordance with the then-existing limitations of the territorial sea to 3 nm. Application of legal principles of delimitation of these agreements was difficult to find, since

---

[457] The recommendations were not published at the time. The following summary relies upon the analysis by Jonathan I. Charney, 'The Delimitation of Ocean Boundaries' in L. De Vorsey and D. Dallmeyer (eds.), *Rights to Oceanic Resources* (Dordrecht: Martinus Nijhoff Publishers, 1989), p. 25; Jonathan I. Charney, 'The Delimitation of Lateral Seaward Boundaries between States in a Domestic Context' (1981) 75 *American Journal of International Law*, 12, at 28; and by Donna R. Christie, 'Coastal Energy Impact Program Boundaries on the Atlantic Coast: A Study of the Law Applicable to Lateral Seaward Boundaries' (1979) 19 *Virginia Journal of International Law*, 841. On other areas of US maritime boundary and in particular litigation on historic waters and base lines between states and the United States see Patricia T. Barmeyer, 'Litigation of State Maritime Boundary Disputes' in L. De Vorsey and D. G. Dallmeyer (eds.), *Rights to Oceanic Resources* (Dordrecht: Martinus Nijhoff Publishers, 1989), pp. 53–9; and Michael W. Reed, 'Litigating Maritime Boundary Disputes: The Federal Perspective' in L. De Vorsey and D. G. Dallmeyer (eds.), *Rights to Oceanic Resources* (Dordrecht: Martinus Nijhoff Publishers 1989), pp. 61–3.

[458] Jonathan Charney, 'The Delimitation of Lateral Seaward Boundaries between States in a Domestic Context' (1981) 75 *American Journal of International Law* 12, at 48, note 47.

[459] *State of New Jersey v. State of Delaware* 295 US 694 (1935); *State of New Jersey v. State of Delaware* 291 US 361 (1934).

[460] *State of Louisiana v. State of Mississippi* 202 US 1 (1906).

they constituted political *quid pro quo* agreements. Equally, it was found that the thalweg rule, as applied in the 1906 Supreme Court delimitation, was not suitable for the establishment of seaward boundaries. The New York–New Jersey agreement reflected an equal partition of spaces. It was construed as applying a modified equidistance line, a method also found in the New York–Rhode Island agreement.

The consultants therefore concluded that modified equidistance provided the basis for the two later agreements. In the more complex cases of the Louisiana–Mississippi and the New Jersey–Delaware delimitations, they applied the model of equidistance–special circumstances. In accordance with existing precedents, this model was used as a unitary rule, not giving preference to equidistance over special circumstances or other equitable principles.[461]

In the case of the Louisiana–Mississippi delimitation, the consultants considered a number of factors, in particular geography and proportionality, whilst rejecting geology and socioeconomic factors. The analysis, guided by equity, led to the partial exclusion of minor protrusions with significant effects and the small, uninhabited Chandeleur Islands, for the purpose of establishing the basis for an equidistance line.[462] In the Delaware–New Jersey delimitation, the consultants found the concavity to be a classic case of a special circumstance to be partially taken into consideration.[463] Disregarding the agreement of Delaware and Maryland,[464] they established a straight line closing the Hereford Inlet–Ocean City Inlet to establish the basis of an equidistance line.

In both of these cases, the consultants invented and applied a technical method[465] that resulted in giving half-effect to the sum of special circumstances identified. Firstly, a mathematical equidistance line was established, taking into account all geographical features. Secondly, an equidistance line that was extremely favourable to the state that was adversely affected geographically was established, substantially ignoring the disadvantageous features. Thirdly, the recommended line was located halfway between the two auxiliary lines.[466]

The federal government implemented the consultants' recommendations. Louisiana and Mississippi initially considered challenging the delimitation in Court, but the litigation was terminated and no agreement on a maritime boundary for the purposes of CEIP was

---

[461] Charney, n. 458 at 35. [462] Ibid., at 53–7. [463] Ibid., at 57–61.
[464] Ibid., at 37 (application of principle that a third state cannot be bound by an agreement between other states).
[465] Above Chapter 3(II)(A)(1)(b). [466] Charney, n. 458, at 64.

established.[467] Delaware did challenge the procedure used by the United States, but, on appeal from the judgment of the District Court upholding the United States' determination, the case was dismissed by the Court of Appeal upon the suggestion of the defendant. Thus, four of the delimitations determined from the five conventions cases (except Louisiana–Mississippi) still stand.

B. The 1981 Jan Mayen Ridge Conciliation

Jan Mayen is a volcanically active island 53 kilometres long and having a 15 to 20 kilometre maximum width in its northern part. The total area of the island is only 773 square kilometres. It is situated at the northern end of the Jan Mayen Ridge, at a distance of 540 kilometres (292 miles) from Iceland in a roughly north–north-easterly direction. The island is under Norwegian sovereignty.

The delimitation of a maritime boundary in the area caused difficulties because Iceland claimed rights over the continental shelf beyond the 200 nm outer limit of the EEZ, encompassing large parts of the Jan Mayen Ridge and its still largely unexplored mineral resources. Norway agreed to a full 200 nm Icelandic EEZ, but it rejected claims to the continental shelf beyond that (non-median) line.

The parties agreed to submit the matter to a Conciliation Commission. The panel was composed of three members.[468] It rendered its report in 1981.[469] Article 9 of the agreement of 28 May 1980 provided for a non-binding advisory conciliation with an obligation that the parties must

---

[467] *Louisana v. Luther Hodges, Jr., et al.*, Civil action No. 79-601-B (M.D. La); *Mississippi v. Secretary U.S. Dept. of Commerce et al.*, Civil action No. 579-0634 (R) Miss.); *Delaware v. National Oceanic and Atmospheric Administration*, Civil Action No. 80-0565 (D.D.C.); Charney, n. 478, at 28–9.

[468] Members of the panel: E. L. Richardson (Chairman), H. G. Andersen (conciliator for Iceland) and J. Evenson (conciliator for Norway).

[469] 'Report and Recommendations to the Governments of Iceland and Norway of the Conciliation Commission on the Continental Shelf Area between Iceland and Jan Mayen, Washington D.C. 1981' (undated), reprinted in (1981) 20 ILM 797 (hereinafter Report); Appendix II, Map 21. For general discussion see Robin R. Churchill, 'Maritime Delimitation in the Jan Mayen area' (1985) 9 *Marine Policy*, 16; Jens Evensen, 'La Délimitation du plateau continental entre le Norvège et l'Islande dans le secteur de Jan Mayen' (1983) 27 *Annuaire Français de Droit International*, 738; Erik A. Grahl-Madsen, 'Økonomisk sone rundt Jan Mayen?' (1980) 49 *Nordisk tidsskrift for international ret*, 3; Emmanuel Gounaris, 'The Delimitation of the Continental Shelf of Jan Mayen' (1983) 24 *Archiv des Völkerrechts*, 492; Elliott L. Richardson, 'Jan Mayen in Perspective' (1988) 82 *American Journal of International Law*, 443; Charney et al., *International Maritime Boundaries*, n. 1, vol. II (Charney and Alexander), p. 1755, Report Number 9-4, p. 799.

'pay reasonable regard' to the recommendations of the Commission. The Commission was not mandated to decide the shelf boundary in accordance with international law. Instead, Article 9 provided that:

> [t]he Commission shall take into account Iceland's strong economic interests in these sea areas, the existing geographical AND geological factors and other special circumstances.

Nevertheless, the Commission adopted a 'lawyerly approach', taking into account the case law and state practice in order to achieve an equitable solution for the questions concerned.[470]

Based upon the scientific evidence incorporated in the report, the Commission found that the concept of natural prolongation would not constitute a suitable approach in this case.[471]

Instead of mere delimitation of the shelf in terms of traditional co-existence and demarcation, the Commission proposed[472] co-operation arrangements and the establishment of an area of joint development, to cover substantially all of the hydrocarbon potentials in the area. The zone has been divided by the agreed 200 nm EEZ boundary for jurisdictional purposes, into the northern Norwegian shelf (32,750 square kilometres) and the southern Icelandic shelf (12,725 square kilometres).[473] However, the two zones have been closely linked for the process of exploration and exploitation throughout the three stages of pre-drilling, drilling, and development, in a manner that reflects the financial and developmental backgrounds of the parties and the size of their respective zones.

The Norwegian authorities (the Petroleum Directorate) recommended that pre-drilling exploration should be carried out in the northern part and, through joint ventures and common plans of the two governments, also in the Icelandic zone,[474] with the cost of such operations being born by Norway. However, it was proposed that the profits from the sale of the resultant survey data to oil companies would be shared.[475] Subsequent drilling contracts with private or state-owned companies should be negotiated through joint venture arrangements between the two parties and the corporations. Iceland should have the right to acquire shares of control and interest up to 25 per cent in the northern (Norwegian) shelf. It may assume such rights from the beginning or after drilling activities prove to be economically feasible.[476] Norway should be in a position to acquire similar, although not identical, rights in the southern (Icelandic)

---

[470] Report, n. 469, p. 823. [471] Ibid., p. 822. [472] Above Chapter 5.
[473] Report, n. 488, p. 836. [474] Ibid., p. 829 ff. [475] Ibid., pp. 830–1, 841.
[476] Ibid., pp. 831, 836, 838.

part.[477] It was proposed that the two states should also make investments in the third, development stage of the project in similar proportions.[478]

The Commission's proposals were highly successful and were fully adopted in the 1981 Continental Shelf Agreement between Norway and Iceland.[479]

C. The 2002 Arbitration between Newfoundland and Labrador and Nova Scotia

Offshore natural resources pertain, in accordance with Canadian constitutional law, to the provinces. Efforts to assign these resources date back to the 1960s, but failed in relations between the east coast provinces of Newfoundland and Labrador, on the one hand, and Nova Scotia, on the other hand. Based upon the dispute settlement provisions of the Newfoundland Atlantic Accord Implementation Act and the Canada–Nova Scotia Offshore Petroleum Resources Implementation Act (so-called Accords Acts), the Tribunal was called upon to define the offshore maritime boundary between the parties to the dispute within the respective offshore areas of the Canada's continental shelf.[480] The federal Accords Act, in its provisions on dispute settlement, referred to 'the principles of international law governing maritime boundary delimitation, with such modifications as the circumstances require.'[481] The Tribunal thus applied

---

[477] A difference reflecting the more dependent position of Iceland is shown by the provision that Iceland is not, unlike Norway in this area of jurisdiction, obliged to seek so-called 'carried interests arrangements' with contracting oil companies. Report, n. 488, pp. 833, 837, 842–3. This means that Norway may well be obliged to carry up to 25% of the potential losses from unsuccessful drilling operations in the Icelandic shelf, provided that the corporations are not willing to carry these losses, and Norway acquires rights in the Icelandic shelf.

[478] Report, n. 469, p. 838.

[479] 'Agreement between Norway and Iceland on the Continental Shelf in the Area between Iceland and Jan Mayen, done 22 October 1981' reprinted in (1982) 21 ILM 1222.

[480] Arbitration between Newfoundland and Labrador and Nova Scotia Concerning Portions of the Limits of Their Offshore Areas as defined in the Canada-Nova Scotia Offshore Petroleum Resources Accord Implementation Act and the Canada-Newfoundland and Atlantic Accord Implementation Act, Award of the Tribunal in the Second Phase, Ottawa, March 26, 2002 (hereinafter Award), www.cnsopb.ns.ca/sites/default/files/pdfs/phaseii_award_fnglish.pdf (last accessed February 2014); Appendix II, Map 22. Coalter G. Lathrop, 'Newfoundland and Labrador–Nova Scotia: The Latest "International" Maritime Boundary (April 10, 2002)' (2003) 34 *Ocean Development & International Law*, 83; Valerie Hughes, 'Nova Scotia – Newfoundland Dispute over Offshore Areas: The Delimitation Phase' (2002) XK *Canadian Yearbook of International Law*, 373.

[481] Award, n. 480, para. 2.1, p. 28.

international law by reference and in analogy and fully drew from existing sources and practices in international law.

The dispute arose in the context of the *Gulf of Maine* case between the United States and Canada, and the *St. Pierre and Miquelon* arbitration between France and Canada which were settled in 1984 and in 1992, respectively. The Tribunal was instructed to act in two phases. The first phase found that no agreement, either explicit or implicit, existed among the parties as to the allocation of offshore resources and spaces. The second phase turned to the delimitation of the boundary. While the Tribunal held in its first award that the governing provision, at least *prima facie*, is Article 6 of the 1958 Geneva Convention on the Continental Shelf, the parties submitted that the matter should be settled in accordance with the principles developed in case law and Article 83 of the LOS Convention (to which Canada, at the time, was not a signatory). The Tribunal adopted a combination of these different sources:

> The apparent contrast between these two articles has been attenuated bysubsequent practice and caselaw. On the one hand, the 'special circumstances' of Article 6 of the 1958 *Geneva Convention* have rather readily been found to exist, and to be not very different from the 'relevant circumstances' of Article 83; moreover, the underlying aim of achieving an equitable result, the focus of Article 83 and customary international law, has also tended to suffuse the consideration of Article 6. On the other hand, in the application of Article 83or of the customary international law principle of equitable delimitation since *Libya/Malta*, courts and tribunals, notably the International Court, have normally begun by considering an equidistance line and adjusting that line in accordance with relevant considerations in each case.[482]

Upon assssing and dismissing claims based upon conduct and alleged aquiescence,[483] the Tribunal accordingly set out to apply equidistance as a practical method:

> The Tribunal will first address the question of the choice of a practical method that will assure an equitable result in the particular circumstances of this case. That choice is not difficult to determine. Since the Parties are to be treated as being bound by Article 6 of the 1958 *Geneva Convention*, it is appropriate for the Tribunal to begin with the construction of a provisional equidistance line and to determine whether it requires adjustment in the light of special circumstances. The Tribunal would note, however, that its approach would have been precisely the same in applying customary international law or Article 83 of the *1982 Law of the Sea Convention*.[484]

---

[482] Ibid., para. 2.27, p. 41. [483] Cf. ibid., paras. 3.2–3.18, pp. 49–59.
[484] Ibid., para. 5.2, p. 85

The Tribunal accordingly adopted an equistance line for the Inner Area, simplifying it with a straight line between turning points 2016 and 2017 and without taking into account special circumstances.[485] Similarly, it established a provisional equidistance line for the Outer Area from the closing line of the Inner Area to the outer edge of the continental margin. The Tribunal discarded any impact of the conduct of the parties, but took into account the cut-off effect of Sable Island to the detriment of Nova Scotia. It discussed the impact of half-effect, concluding that this would not be sufficient, and disregarded the island altogether.[486] Finally, the Tribunal refrained from applying a proportionality test in light of the problem that the parties could not agree in defining the relevant area of delimitation and in light of the 'impressionism' such an operation often entails. Nevertheless, the Tribunal offered a calculation in conclusion which resulted in a coastal rate of 52 per cent for Nova Scotia and of 48 per cent for Newfoundland and Labrador.[487]

IV. Assessment

An assessment of the cases and conciliations at this stage of the inquiry allows for a number of observations.

A. Individuality of configurations

Each of the cases discussed, covering a representative period of forty-five years of judicial experience in maritime boundary delimitation, demonstrate highly unique characteristics. This confirms the basic difficulty of finding appropriate rules that are capable of covering them all in a satisfactory manner.[488] The cases differ in terms of both case history and geographical configurations. They reflect an unlimited variety of nature in terms of geographical configurations. At best, comparable configurations could be found with respect to three features. The first is the concavity of coasts and their effect on maritime spaces allocated to the state situated between two neighbouring states. The precedent of the *North Sea Continental Shelf* cases was of guiding importance to the *New Jersey Delaware* CEIP delimitation, the *Bangladesh/Myanmar* case, and, implicitly, to the *Guinea/Guinea-Bissau* arbitration. Second, the impact of islands or protrusions on the maritime boundary gave rise to special

---

[485] Ibid., para 5.7, p. 88. [486] Ibid., para. 5.15, pp. 91, 92. [487] Ibid,. para. 5.19, p. 94.
[488] See Chapter 3(I).

treatment of them in most cases, with the exceptions of the *North Sea* cases, the New York CEIP delimitations and the *Guyana/Suriname* arbitration, where no islands or protrusions were involved. Third, a majority of cases, with the exception of the CEIP delimitations, the *Guinea/Guinea-Bissau* arbitration, the *Guyana/Suriname* arbitration and partly the *Barbados/Trinidad and Tobago* arbitration, relate to relatively narrow or closed maritime configurations, and all of them to largely uniform shelves. Perhaps the most striking common feature of the cases is that geology was not decisive in any of them. Otherwise, each case presented its own and new problems.

B. The importance of the compromis (special agreement)

Cases were brought under different terms of references. Proceedings were brought by unilateral applications in the case of *Denmark v. Norway (Jan Mayen)* and partly in *Qatar v. Bahrain, Romania v. Ukraine* and *Nicaragua v. Colombia* (with jurisdiction essentially relying upon an earlier agreement). More recent cases were instituted pursuant to Part XV of the 1982 LOS Convention and are governed by the Convention's relevant provisions, most notably Article 288. The main body of case law, however, relies upon cases brought under special and diverging terms of reference in an agreed compromise or special agreement. These instruments define the task and power ascribed to the judicial or conciliatory body. Interestingly, domestic disputes are referred to international law, as in the US CEIP delimitation and the *Newfoundland, Labrador and Nova Scotia* arbitration. Four types of compromises may be distinguished: first, a mandate to indicate relevant principles to be taken into account in further negotiations, as in the *North Sea* cases; second, a final determination of the boundary, as in the *Channel Arbitration*, the *Gulf of Maine* case, the *Guinea v. Guinea-Bissau* arbitration and the *St. Pierre and Miquelon* arbitration, and in all cases from the 1999 *Eritrea v. Yemen* Award to the 2012 *Nicaragua v. Colombia* ruling of the ICJ and the 2014 *Maritime Dispute* between Peru and Chile; third, an intermediate solution envisaging indications of the boundary which may be implemented by the parties, a solution leading to political difficulties, as the *Tunisia v. Libya* delimitation shows. It almost necessarily ends up with fairly precise prescriptions by the Court, leaving little room for the parties to negotiate, as the *Libya v. Malta* case shows. Finally, recommendations may be given as to the proper boundary to provide further guidance in negotiations. This approach is typical for conciliations and expert advisory panels, as found in the *Jan Mayen* conciliation and CEIP delimitations.

According to the respective compromis, delimitations also rely upon different sources of law. The special agreements range from the inclusion of domestic, statutory or interstate compact law, to customary international law, or international law, as the CEIP delimitation and *Qatar* v. *Bahrain* shows. International cases commonly refer to delimitation in accordance with the principles of international law. An exception are those cases where both states are parties to the LOS Convention, namely the proceedings before tribunals which were established under the Convention itself and where the applicable law is governed by Article 293. Another exception was the *Jan Mayen* conciliation, which did not bind the commission to law but specifically commissioned it to take into account particular economic factors of emerging treaty law, and interests of development. A particular feature of that conciliation consisted of the reference to 'recent trends' in the 1980s, i.e. the then-existing drafts of the UNCLOS III Conference, which, in the *Tunisia* v. *Libya* case practically excluded the use of equidistance and considerably increased the influence of the LOS Convention even before the multilateral agreement was in force. Only in its later *Denmark* v. *Norway (Jan Mayen)* judgment could the Court apply Article 6 of the 1958 Continental Shelf Convention.

In conclusion, it is important to take into account the particularities of the special agreement when cases and the legal reasoning of the Courts are compared. Parties have considerably influenced the course of the decision with the content of special agreements, in particular in the earlier stages of the case law prior to the entry into force of the LOS Convention.[489]

C. *Claims and the role of equidistance*

With respect to claims, the initial cases showed a common trait to the effect that one of the parties argued in favour of an equidistance or median line, whilst the other parties mainly relied on different methods and approaches. An exception to that was the *Tunisia* v. *Libya* case where both parties agreed that equidistance was an inappropriate solution. The cases since the 1990s reveal an approval on behalf of the parties of equidistance at least as a starting point – possibly in light of the increasingly consistent case law in this respect. The focus of the parties has thus shifted to disputing the employment of particular base

---

[489] For further discussion see Chapter 9.

points and invoking relevant circumstances and equitable principles that would call for an adjustment to strict equidistance. Despite the employment of equidistance, the lines employed by each party still differ markedly and frequently call for considerations of special circumstances.

The predominance of claims for equidistance highlights the overall importance of this method. The same holds true for recourse to equidistance in a number of judicial and conciliatory settlements discussed, in particular the *Anglo-French Channel* arbitration, the *Gulf of Maine* case, the *Libya* v. *Malta* case, two CEIP delimitations, the *Jan Mayen* case, the *Newfoundland, Labrador and Nova Scotia* abritration and most subsequent adjudications – most prominently the *Cameroon* v. *Nigeria* case and the *Maritime Dispute* between Peru and Chile. The cases, however, also show that strict equidistance without modification has rarely been adopted by the Courts. The *Cameroon* v. *Nigeria* case and the *Maritime Dispute* are the only exceptions in point. The *New York–Jersey* and the *New York–Rhode Island* cases came close to the application of strict equidistance; however it should be recalled that this was primarily due to the expansion of principles inherent to the existing state compact agreements. The *Guyana* v. *Suriname* arbitration experienced only a minor deviation from strict equidistance. In the *Anglo-French Channel* arbitration, the *Dubai* v. *Sharjah* arbitration, the *Gulf of Maine* case, the *Malta* v. *Libya* case, the *Denmark* v. *Norway (Jan Mayen)* case, the *Delaware–New Jersey* case, the *Mississippi–Louisiana* case, the *Eritrea* v. *Yemen* arbitration, the *Qatar* v. *Bahrain* case and the *Romania* v. *Ukraine* case, equidistance was modified, mainly by corrections for the impact of islands or protrusions. In the *Barbados* v. *Trinidad and Tobago* arbitration and the *Nicaragua* v. *Colombia* case, the deviation from equidistance was mainly based on the disproportion of coastal lengths. The *North Sea* cases, parts of the *Anglo-French Channel* arbitration, the *Tunisia* v. *Libya* cases, the *Guinea* v. *Guinea-Bissau* arbitration, the *St. Pierre and Miquelon* arbitration and the *Bangladesh* v. *Myanmar* case relied on lines other than equidistance. The *Nicaragua* v. *Honduras* case drew a bisector line, which in parts took account of islands lying in its course.

In summary, equidistance can be seen to have served as a starting point in many cases, particularly since the 1990s, however with major modifications to the strict principle in almost all of them. Five cases used other methods and two employed a combination of equidistance and other methods for different segments.

D. Geometrical constructions and results

The cases show a considerable number of different and imaginative *ad hoc* constructions of final, non-equidistant boundary lines. They bear little resemblance to one another, as the maps in Appendix II illustrate. They were used either to modify equidistance or to construe an *ad hoc* line. It can already be seen at this stage that *ad hoc* lines, often divided into different segments, do not contain any inherent normative logic or necessity. The reason why one particular construction was used rather than another is difficult to discover in most cases. Comparing the results achieved with the claims of the parties, the *North Sea* cases, the *Anglo-French Channel* arbitration, the *Dubai* v. *Sharjah* arbitration, the *St. Pierre and Miquelon* arbitration, the *Eritrea* v. *Yemen* arbitration, the *Qatar* v. *Bahrain* case, the *Cameroon* v. *Nigeria* case, the *Barbados* v. *Trinidad and Tobago* arbitration, the *Nicaragua* v. *Honduras* case, the *Romania* v. *Ukraine* case and the *Nicaragua* v. *Colombia* case, demonstrate a clear preponderance to the benefit of one of the parties. A winning party can be found in the *North Sea* cases (at least conceptually), in the *Anglo-French Channel* arbitration (France), and foremost in the *Dubai* v. *Sharjah* arbitration (Dubai). In other cases, the solutions better reflect the middle ground of the parties' claims. This may be particularly true for the *Tunisia* v. *Libya, Gulf of Maine, Guinea* v. *Guinea-Bissau, Libya* v. *Malta, Denmark* v. *Norway (Jan Mayen)*, the *Newfoundland, Labrador and Nova Scotia* arbitration and *Bangladesh* v. *Myanmar* cases, the *Guyana* v. *Suriname* arbitration and the *Maritime Dispute* between Peru and Chile. The *Jan Mayen* conciliation was able to find a solution that satisfied both parties and, in particular, the development needs of Iceland, yet fell short of granting the entire area claimed to Iceland.

To summarize, it can be seen that the overall picture is a mixed one and not all that clear; it would, however, certainly be wrong to conclude that judicial delimitation merely generally splits the difference between the original claims submitted by the parties.

E. The common basis of equity

Given the disparities and individual character of each of the cases, it is striking that all the international disputes, in some form or another (to be explored in more detail in Part III of this study) rely on the model of equity as a common basis of delimitation.[490] The concept of equitable principles developed by the Court in the *North Sea Continental Shelf* cases has been reflected in all subsequent cases and was further elaborated under the impact of the UNCLOS III and the concept of equitable solutions. It includes equidistance and other methods, as the above results demonstrate. All the international cases from the 1980s contain the normative elements of a combined approach of equitable principles and equitable solutions, with the exception of the *Guinea* v. *Guinea-Bissau* arbitration, which particularly emphasized the normative element of an equitable solution under the influence of the 1982 Convention. The case law since the 1993 *Jan Mayen* case has proceeded in two steps, starting with the establishment of a provisional equidistance line. Equitable principles, however, still serve to test the strictness of the equidistance method against the requirement of achieving an equitable solution.

---

[490] See also Louis B. Sohn, concluding a survey:

[P]recedent by precedent, equity has become an important factor in the determination of the maritime boundary, and new rules are slowly emerging, which are likely to crystalise soon, especially if the anticipated numerous disputes find their way into international tribunals.

Louis B. Sohn, 'Exploring New Potentials in Maritime Boundary Dispute Settlement', in L. De Vorsey and D. Dallmeyer (eds.), *Rights to Oceanic Resources* (Dordrecht: Martinus Nijhoff Publishers, 1989), pp. 153, 163.

7

An assessment of customary law

The review of negotiations at UNCLOS III on maritime boundary delimitation and the factual analysis of state practice and of the case law in the preceding chapters allows for a number of conclusions. They relate to the legal nature of bilateral settlements, the different methods of delimitation of boundaries and the legal approaches to customary and general public international law. The analysis of state practice also allows for a combined assessment of the practical implications of the methods of delimitation and in particular that of equidistance. The analysis is of importance with a view to determining, in subsequent chapters, the role and impact of equity as a principle of law and foundation of maritime boundary law. This chapter discusses to what extent rules relating to maritime boundary delimitation and co-operation can be found in customary law. It finds that there is little evidence to this effect. Normative concepts outside of treaty law will need to be found elsewhere.

I. The state of play in customary law

The law of the sea has always played a significant role in the process of the formation of customary international law and the shaping of criteria for the assessment of customary rules as distinct from mere usage.[1] Fundamental principles of the freedom of the sea and navigation were established in customary law and remain of some importance, despite subsequent codification in agreements.[2] UNCLOS III today is recognized to a large extent as customary law. The same holds true for the enclosure of the seas. Indeed,

---

[1] See e.g. *The Scotia Case*, 14 Wallace [81 US] 170 (1871) *The Paquete Habana* 175 US 677 (1900); *The Lotus Case*, Series A No. 10 (1927). See generally Jörg Paul Müller and Luzius Wildhaber, *Praxis des Völkerrechts* (Bern: Stämpfli, 2nd edn., 2001), pp. 13–39.

[2] Subsequent codification of customary law in treaty law does not end its existence in customary law, even among parties to the agreement, see *Military and Paramilitary Activities in and against Nicaragua (Nicaragua v. United States)*, ICJ Reports 1986, pp. 14, 93.

the evolution of the legal concepts of the continental shelf and the EEZ rank among the most prominent examples of recent developments in customary international law. They emerged in a close interrelationship with multilateral treaty-making at UNCLOS II and III[3] and a series of court cases relating to maritime boundary delimitation described in Chapter 6. The findings will also be of importance to other issues of allocation of natural resources and distributive justice in public international law.

The ICJ addressed the criteria of customary law in the 1951 *Anglo-Norwegian Fisheries* case[4] and the *North Sea* cases,[5] when it examined the legal status of Article 6 of the 1958 Continental Shelf Convention. The Court affirmed the well-established requirements for the existence of a rule in customary law: the norm has to be of a rule-making type (norm-creating character). It must be able to form the basis of a general rule of law; the evidence of state practice must demonstrate that if the norm has only been in use for a short period of time, the practice, including that of states whose interests are especially affected, 'should have been extensive and virtually uniform in the sense of the provision invoked'.[6] Finally, such practice has to have been exercised by governments in the belief that they are applying the rule as a matter of obligation in international law (*opinio juris sive necessitatis*).[7] In *Libya* v. *Malta*, the Court confirmed that customary law must be 'looked [at] primarily in the actual practice and *opinio juris* of States'.[8]

As to state practice, it is accepted that there is no need to establish full consistency and complete adherence. In *Military and Paramilitary Activities in and against Nicaragua*, the Court held that 'for a rule to be established in customary law, the corresponding practice must not be in absolutely rigorous conformity with the rule', and that it is sufficient that 'States should, in general be consistent with such rules, and that instances of State conduct inconsistent with a given rule should generally be treated as breaches of that rule, not as indications of the recognition of a new rule'.[9] State practice therefore requires a regular pattern of conduct to be

---

[3] See Chapter 2(II)(C)(1)(b).
[4] *Fisheries Case (United Kingdom* v. *Norway)* ICJ Reports 1951, p. 116. See in particular Jörg Paul Müller, *Vertrauensschutz im Völkerrecht, Beiträge zum ausländischen öffentlichen Recht und Völkerrecht* (Cologne, Berlin, Bonn: Heymann, 1971), pp. 89–91.
[5] See *North Sea Continental Shelf (Federal Republic of Germany* v. *Denmark; Federal Republic of Germany* v. *Netherlands)*, Judgment, ICJ Reports 1969, pp. 41–2, para. 72.
[6] ICJ Reports 1969, p. 43, para. 74.   [7] ICJ Reports 1969, p. 44, para. 77.
[8] ICJ Reports 1985, p. 29, para. 27, affirmed in 'Threat or Use of Nuclear Weapons Advisory Opinion' ICJ Reports 1996, pp. 226, 253.
[9] *Nicaragua* v. *United States*, n. 2, pp. 14, 98, para. 186.

shown, any departure from which regularly causes some reaction on the part of the international community. Again, the reaction provides evidence that such conduct is considered to be a matter of lawfully required conduct, and thus of *opinio juris* on behalf of the reacting states.

Given the highly subjective nature of the element of *opinio juris*, and thus a shared perception that the conduct is required as a matter of legal rights and obligations, it is a requirement that is often difficult to establish through means of explicit evidence. Governments may undertake to make statements or express views to this effect in international instruments, particularly in resolutions of international bodies.[10] However, ultimately, it is not a matter of providing evidence of explicit expressions of will. Nor is it mere reliance upon state conduct as a matter of factual evidence in a process of claims, response, acceptance and rejection.[11] Instead, in accordance with the principle of good faith in inter-state relations, it is the regularity and uniformity of the application of the rule that allows a third party to perceive it as being part of the body of law and to conclude that the norm is being applied as a matter of legal obligation.[12] Whether or not conduct amounts to a rule of customary law depends upon the legitimate expectations of an addressee rather than on the subjective perception of the conducting state.[13] The process of claims, responses and state conduct in

---

[10] It is recognized that *opinio juris* may be assessed and even deduced 'though with all due caution' on the basis of the conduct of governments in international fora, in particular in support of, or opposition to, UN General Assembly resolutions, *Nicaragua v. United States*, n. 2, pp. 99, 100, para. 188.

[11] But see Myres McDougal, 'The Hydrogen Bomb Tests and the International Law of the Sea' (1955) 49 *American Journal of International Law*, 356.

[12] Müller, n. 4, p. 85:

> The practice has to show such constancy that a detached observer may perceive it as an expression of regularity (*Gesetzmässigkeit*), or in other words, that such an observer may or should expect a similar conduct in the future. A subject of international law may therefore successfully invoke a rule of customary law if the expectation seems legitimate that the conduct of another state or other states, considering all circumstances of the case, will be in conformity with the conduct practised so far. (trans. by the author).

[13] The psychology of informal norm-making in international relations need not be dealt with extensively in this context. Attention may be drawn to the jurisprudence developed by Oscar Schachter, 'Toward a Theory of International Obligation' in S. Schwebel (ed.), *The Effectiveness of International Law* (Leiden, Dobbs Ferry NY: Oceana Publications, 1971), pp. 9, 16, 30. Schachter relied upon the New Haven Approach of McDougal and Lasswell ('attitudes, expectations perceptions and probable compliance' ranging among the major constituting factors of international obligations in a process of demand and responses), but relies, as Müller does, above, n. 12, more strongly on the norm-making effects of patterns of conduct as they create legitimate expectations.

AN ASSESSMENT OF CUSTOMARY LAW 357

customary law-making is therefore essentially based on a need to honour the stabilizing principle of conduct in good faith. As a fundamental principle of international law, it also informs the formative process of customary law.[14]

In the present context, the requirements of a norm-creating character, uniform conduct and *opinio juris sive necessitatis* in terms of protecting legitimate expectations induced by conduct, allow for three major conclusions: the prohibition of unilateral delimitation; the absence of a duty to negotiate settlements; and the non-existence of any particular method of delimitation in customary international law.

A. *The prohibition of unilateral delimitation*

The sample of delimitation agreements examined in Chapter 5 clearly shows that delimitation has been overwhelmingly exercised in bilateral and, more rarely, plurilateral operations. Moreover, negotiations at UNCLOS III suggest that delimitation cannot be effected unilaterally as a matter of customary law. There has to be at least a meaningful bilateral effort to reach a boundary by peaceful means.

The requirement of bipartisan delimitation was never challenged in UNCLOS III. It can be found in all the drafts on maritime boundary delimitation, in the provisions of Articles 74(1) and 83(1),[15] and in the fact that maritime boundary delimitation is subject to compulsory conciliation under Annex V of the Convention – albeit with the possibility of exceptions.[16] The requirements of the norm-creating character of such an obligation, state practice and *opinio juris* are therefore sufficiently established. This confirms the view established by the ICJ in 1969 that delimitation must be the object of an agreement between two or more parties,[17] unlike the law of seaward delimitation, which

---

[14] The relationship of good faith, legitimate expectations and equity is discussed in the Introduction to this book.
[15] See Chapter 3(III)(4).
[16] LOS Convention, Art. 298(1)(a) (option to exempt maritime boundary disputes under Arts. 15, 74 and 83 from compulsory proceedings entailing binding decisions, provided that such states accept, after unsuccessful negotiation and upon request, submission of the matter to conciliation under Annex V).
[17] ICJ Reports 1969, p. 47, para. 85. Somewhat paradoxically, the early Arab proclamations in support of the Truman Proclamation which the Court considered to be the basis of that rule, p. 47, para. 86; see Chapter 5(I)(A). envisaged unilateral delimitation after consultations. See Judge Koretsky, dissenting opinion, ICJ Reports 1969, pp. 167–8. In practice, however, Arab delimitations all occurred by agreement, and support the rule which was

still relies on unilateral delimitation in accordance with general international law.[18]

B. *The absence of a duty to negotiate boundaries*

The question arises as to whether the customary rule prohibiting unilateral delimitation necessarily implies, as a corollary, an obligation to negotiate an agreed settlement. The cases show that courts have paid attention to the conduct of the parties prior to the dispute. Such attention suggests that boundary delimitation can be effected without formal negotiations, in a process of claims and responses. Unilateral action relating to delimitation is possible, albeit that it has often been met with protest. But if it is not protested against, such unilateral action may result in tacit bilateral boundary delimitation agreement due to acquiescence.

---

clearly confirmed in subsequent cases. See ICJ Reports 1982, p. 52, para. 87; ICJ Reports 1982, p. 66, para. 87; see also ICJ Reports 1985, p. 39, para. 46 ('The duty of Parties to seek first a delimitation by agreement').

The rule was most clearly expressed in ICJ Reports 1984, p. 299, para. 112(1):

No maritime delimitation between States with opposite or adjacent coasts may be effected unilaterally by one of those States. Such delimitation must be sought and effected by means of an agreement, following negotiations conducted in good faith and with the genuine intention of achieving a positive result.

[18] See the *Fisheries Case*, ICJ Reports 1951, p. 132, restated in the 1974 *Fisheries Jurisdiction Case*, ICJ Reports 1974, p. 22, para. 49, and cited in *Case Concerning Maritime Delimitation in the Black Sea (Romania v. Ukraine)*, Judgment, 3 February 2009; ICJ Reports 2009. p. 61, p. 108 para 137. The principle was stated in the *Fisheries Case* as follows:

The delimitation of sea areas has always an international aspect; it cannot be dependent merely upon the will of the coastal State as expressed in municipal law. Although it is true that the Act of delimitation is necessarily a unilateral Act, because only the coastal State is competent to undertake it, the validity of delimitation with regard to other States depends upon international law.

Inappropriately, the statement was also restated in *Continental Shelf (Tunisia v. Libyan Arab Jamahiriya)*, Judgment, ICJ Reports 1982, pp. 18, 66, para. 87, to confirm the prohibition of unilateral settlement. Unilateral settlement, however, is not excluded by that very statement under general international law. The possibility of a unilateral settlement of the outer limit of the shelf is restricted under the LOS Convention. With the Area as defined by the LOS Convention, determination of the outer limit of the continental shelf beyond 200 nm will be subject to recommendations by the Commission established under Art. 76(8) and Annex II of the Convention. Prescriptions on payments for exploitation of the shelf beyond 200 miles are described above Chapter 2(II)(C)(2).

Given such considerations and the importance paid in the case law to the prior conduct of the parties, it is difficult to conclude that states are under an explicit obligation to negotiate in customary law. Parties are merely under an obligation to pursue the matter bilaterally. However, they may do so by recourse to processes other than negotiation, such as conciliation, arbitration or judicial settlement from the very beginning, without engaging in extensive negotiations.[19] An explicit obligation to negotiate, however, exists under treaty law, both under the 1958 Convention and the LOS Convention. The Tribunal in *Guyana v. Suriname* held that Articles 74(3) and 83(3) of the LOS Convention impose on the parties a duty to negotiate in good faith.[20] Whether or not such obligations also exist in customary law, as the ICJ held in the 1969 *North Sea Continental Shelf* cases and the 1974 *Fisheries Juridiction* case,[21] calls for further examination. It will be submitted that the obligation relies upon the principle of equity.[22]

C. The absence of specific customary rules for shelf and EEZ delimitation

1. The model of residual rules and exceptions (equidistance–special circumstances)

In 1969 the ICJ, expounding on the three central tenets of customary law, concluded that the conventional rule of equidistance–special circumstances from Article 6 of the 1958 Shelf Convention had not developed into customary law. At the time, the Court relied on an examination of

---

[19] ICJ Reports 1969, pp. 3, 36, para. 55 ('delimitation should ... be carried out by agreement (or by reference to arbitration').
[20] *Arbitral Award constituted pursuant to Art. 387, and in accordance with Annex VII, of the United Nations Convention on the Law of the Sea, between Guyana and Suriname*, Award of 17 September 2007 (hereinafter *Guyana v. Suriname* Award), International Court of Arbitration: www.pca-cpa.org/showfile.asp?fil_id=664 (last accessed 18 February 2012), para 461. The Tribunal reasoned that:
  Indeed, the inclusion in Articles 74(3) and 83(3) of the phrase 'in a spirit of understanding and cooperation' indicates the drafters' intent to require of the parties a conciliatory approach to negotiations, pursuant to which they would be prepared to make concessions in the pursuit of a provisional arrangement. Such an approach is particularly to be expected of the parties in view of the fact that any provisional arrangements arrived at are by definition temporary and will be without prejudice to the final delimitation.
[21] ICJ Reports 1969, p. 48, para. 86; ICJ Reports 1974, pp. 32–4, paras. 73–78; see also above, n. 4.
[22] Chapter 12(III).

fifteen agreements. Briefly, it held that these agreements did not sufficiently reflect state practice; rather than being a rule of law, equidistance–special circumstances was nothing more than a method for the delimitation of boundaries, particularly for those who were not parties to the 1958 Convention, and that there was no evidence that states applied equidistance as a matter of obligation.[23] This finding has remained unchanged, despite the fact that many more long-distance maritime boundaries have been settled in the mean time. It is extremely difficult to draw clear inferences from treaty practice since motivation, expectations and *opinio juris* are rarely on public record, despite the comprehensive analysis of state practice discussed in Chapter 5 and available through such projects as that initially directed by Jonathan Charney and Lewis Alexander.[24]

Firstly, the actual use of methods other than equidistance or equidistance–special circumstances in some 40 per cent of the sample treaties examined shows a lack of sufficiently developed state practice to support a customary law character of equidistance.[25] Secondly, it is highly

---

[23] ICJ Reports 1969, pp. 37–45, paras. 60–81. There was ample agreement among commentators that there was not sufficient state practice at the time to support equidistance as a rule of customary law.

[24] Jonathan I. Charney et al. (eds.), *International Maritime Boundaries*, 5 vols. (The Hague: Martinus Nijhoff Publishers, 1993–2005); see in particular Bernard Oxman, 'Political, Strategic, and Historic Consideration' in ibid., vol. I (Charney and Alexander), pp. 3–40; and Jonathan I. Charney, 'Introduction' in ibid., vol. I, at xxiii, xxxv on such considerations:

> [Oxman's] was a rather difficult assignment because these are particularly broad, undefined, and cross-cutting subjects. In addition, states are not likely to admit that such factors independently influenced the delimitation and/or the related management regime.

See also Prosper Weil, 'Geographic Considerations in Maritime Delimitation' in ibid., vol. I (Charney and Alexander), n. 24, pp. 115, 121–2:

> Th[e] inherent difficulty faced by an objective assessment of state practice is compounded by the fact that more often than not it is impossible to identify with any certainty which considerations lie behind any specific agreed boundary. Even an apparently equidistant line does not always speak of itself; there are different varieties of equidistance. Many so-called equidistant boundaries are such only in a general sense. Every time quasi- or modified equidistance has been preferred by the parties to strict equidistance, some factor other than geography, pure and simple, has obviously come into play. On the other hand and quite to the opposite, some agreements which announce explicitly a given method (e.g. equidistance) draw a line which does not actually match that method.

[25] See Chapter 5(II). See also Jonathan I. Charney, 'The Delimitation of Ocean Boundaries' in D. G. Dallmeyer and L. De Vorsey Jr. (eds.), *Rights to Oceanic Resources* (Dordrecht: Martinus Nijhoff, 1989).

relevant that some 35 per cent of the sample indicated the use of methods other than equidistance. This suggests that equidistance rules are not perceived as legal rules, but rather are seen merely as methods of delimitation; methods, moreover, that can be replaced by others where it is advantageous to do so. During the highly controversial negotiations at UNCLOS III on the core issues of maritime boundary delimitation, there were positive signs that equidistance has not been perceived as an appropriate rule of law. At the time, a significant number of states (the Algerian Group of 32)[26] refused to adopt the model of residual rules and exceptions of equidistance–special circumstances. They probably will continue to do so, based upon their particular geographical configuration and economic interests at stake. There is no indication that they have accepted the model as a rule of customary law.

Finally, without knowing the states' motivation for using equidistance or equidistance–special circumstances in the approximately 60 per cent of the sample agreements which relied upon this approach, the number on its own cannot lead to the conclusion that states would apply equidistance as a matter of legal obligations. None of the three elements necessary to establish a customary international law are present for the equidistance rule of delimitation, and it seems that the equidistance rule expressed in Article 6 of the 1958 Shelf Convention was not even gradually moving into that realm. This view is shared by Prosper Weil:

> It is clear in this area that while one may safely speak of trends, no clear-cut practice, and *a fortiori* no customary rule, has emerged as regards the influence that oppositeness and adjacency may have on maritime boundary delimitation.[27]

These findings confirm the initial perception of the ICJ in the *North Sea Continental Shelf* cases that equidistance is neither inherent to natural prolongation nor to customary law.[28] Courts have frequently taken recourse to equidistance as methodological starting point, yet without recognizing it as a legal and mandatory norm.[29] The ICJ confirmed this in *Nicaragua* v. *Honduras* as follows:

---

[26] See Chapter 4(III)(A), text accompanying n. 153. [27] Weil, n. 24, p. 126.
[28] ICJ Reports 1969, p. 35, para. 55 and above n. 23.
[29] *Arbitration Between the United Kingdom of Great Britain and Northern Ireland and the French Republic on the Delimitation of the Continental Shelf*, Decisions of the Court of Arbitration dated 30 June 1977 and 14 March 1978, Command Paper 7438, March 1979, reprinted in 18 ILM 397, 662 (1979) p. 424 para. 85; *Case concerning the Continental Shelf (Tunisia* v. *Libyan Arab Jamahiriya)*, ICJ Reports 1982, pp. 78–80, paras. 109, 110; ICJ Reports 1984, p. 297, para. 107; *Continental Shelf (Libyan Arab Jamahiriya* v. *Malta)*,

The jurisprudence of the Court sets out the reasons why the equidistance method is widely used in the practice of maritime delimitation: it has a certain intrinsic value because of its scientific character and the relative ease with which it can be applied. However, the equidistance method does not automatically have priority over other methods of delimitation and, in particular circumstances, there may be factors which make the application of the equidistance method inappropriate.[30]

Likewise, the observation by the ICJ in *Nicaragua* v. *Colombia* that the parties agreed that 'the provisions [of UNCLOS] relating to the delimitation of the exclusive economic zone and the continental shelf reflect customary international law'[31] cannot be taken to mean that a specific method of delimitation – including equidistance – is prescribed by customary law. However, the same is no longer true for the delimitation of the territorial sea. The ICJ in *Qatar* v. *Bahrain* held that the equidistance method as expressed in Article 15 of the LOS Convention amounts to a customary rule of delimitation in the territorial sea.[32] In the same and following judgments, the Court also tended to assimilate the equidistance – special circumstances rule for the delimitation of the territorial sea with the equitable principles–relevant circumstances rule for the delimitation of the EEZ and continental shelf.[33] However, the Court in *Qatar* v. *Bahrain*, applying customary international law, did explicitly elaborate on the legal nature of the equidistance–special circumstances rule that it applied to the delimitation of the EEZ and continental shelf, but instead relied on its own

Judgment, ICJ Reports 1985, p. 13, pp. 37–8, paras. 42–4; *Guinea/Guinea-Bissau: Dispute Concerning Delimitation oft the Maritime Boundary* (1986) 25 ILM 251, 294, para. 102; *Maritime Delimitation in the Area between Greenland and Jan Mayen (Denmark v. Norway)*, Judgment, ICJ Reports 1993, p. 38, pp. 59–60, paras. 49–50. *Eritrea–Yemen Arbitration (Second Stage: Maritime Delimitation)* (17 December 1999) (2001) 40 ILM 983–1019, paras. 131–2; *Qatar v. Bahrain*, n. 33, p. 40, para. 230; *Land and Maritime Boundary between Cameroon and Nigeria (Cameroon v. Nigeria: Equatorial Guinea intervening)*, Judgment, ICJ Reports 2002, p. 303, para. 288; *Guyana v. Suriname Award*, n. 21, para. 335; *Award of the Arbitral Tribunal in the Matter of Arbitration between Barbados and the Republic of Trinidad and Tobago*, 11 April 2006, Reports of International Arbitral Awards vol. XXVII, pp. 147–251 (United Nations 2008), para. 242; *Romania v. Ukraine*, n. 35, p. 61, paras. 115–21.

[30] *Territorial and Maritime Dispute between Nicaragua and Honduras in the Caribbean Sea (Nicaragua v. Honduras)*, Judgment, ICJ Reports 2007, pp. 659, 741, para. 272.

[31] *Territorial and Maritime Dispute (Nicaragua v. Colombia)*, Judgment, ICJ Reports 2012, p. 624, para. 114.

[32] *Maritime Delimitation and Territorial Questions between Qatar and Bahrain (Qatar v. Bahrain)*, Merits, Judgment, ICJ Reports 2001, pp. 40, 94, para. 176.

[33] Ibid., p. 111, para. 231; confirmed in *Land and Maritime Boundary between Cameroon and Nigeria (Cameroon v. Nigeria: Equatorial Guinea intervening)*, Judgment, ICJ Reports 2002, p. 303, para. 288; *Nicaragua v. Honduras*, n. 31, para. 271.

precedents which mandated a two-step approach.[34] The approval of equidistance–special circumstances as a rule of customary law in territorial sea delimitations can be explained by the fact that substantial deviations and adjustments are less likely due to much shorter distances and expanses of boundaries involved. Equidistance offers the potential of a solid starting point and thus is suitable as a legal norm for the purpose of delimitation of the 12 nm territorial sea.

In conclusion and regarding the shelf and the EZZ, the model of equidistance–special circumstances has remained a treaty-based rule. In general public international law and under the LOS Convention, so far, it is a mere method of delimitation for the shelf and the EEZ. Whether or not equidistance should become a legal rule of general international law *de lege ferenda* will be discussed in Part III.

2. The model of equitable principles

The examination of UNCLOS III and state practice allows for similar conclusions as were found in relation to customary law regarding the model of equity and equitable principles. The ICJ held in 1969, without further empirical analysis of state practice, that the concept of delimitation in accordance with equitable principles put forth by the 1945 Truman Proclamation was: 'the starting point of the positive law on the subject', and has 'underlain all the subsequent history of the subject'.[35] Moreover, 'from the beginning [it has] reflected the *opinio juris* in the matter of delimitation'.[36] Such reference to *opinio juris* suggests that, from the outset, the model of equitable principles was considered a part of the body of contemporary customary law. Subsequent cases have gone some way towards confirming that view.[37]

---

[34] Ibid., n. 33 p. 110 paras. 227–30. Initially, however, the Court had noted that it would 'determine the rules and principles of customary law to be applied to the delimitation of the Parties' continental shelves and their exclusive economic zones', '[o]nce it has delimited the territorial seas belonging to the Parties' (para. 176). The Court in *Case Concerning Maritime Delimitation in the Black Sea (Romania v. Ukraine)*, Judgment, 3 February 2009, ICJ Reports 2009, pp. 61, 101, paras. 115–21, relied more explicitly on precedents when it applied this two-step approach.

[35] ICJ Reports 1969, pp. 32–3, para. 47.   [36] ICJ Reports 1969, pp. 46–7, para. 85.

[37] *Arbitration Between the United Kingdom of Great Britain and Northern Ireland and the French Republic on the Delimitation of the Continental Shelf*, Decisions of the Court of Arbitration dated 30 June 1977 and 14 March 1978, Command Paper 7438, March 1979, reprinted in 18 ILM 397, 662 (1979) (hereinafter the *Anglo-French Channel* arbitration), paras. 65, 74, 75, 97, 148; *The Gulf of Maine Case*, ICJ Reports 1984, p. 300, paras. 113–14 ('the fundamental norm of customary international law governing maritime delimitation'). The model of equitable principles was equally qualified in terms of customary law

In state practice, the frequent absence of any indication of the approaches and methods applied in the final text of maritime boundary agreements once again makes an assessment of *opinio juris* difficult. It may be argued that the overwhelming use of equidistance or modified equidistance in some 60 per cent of the sample agreements invites the conclusion that delimitation is based upon equitable principles expressed in terms of equidistance or modified equidistance. However, the controversial negotiations at UNCLOS III, which led to a strong body of opinion (the Bahamas Group of 24) rejecting, and probably continuing to refuse, a rule of equitable principles, does not allow such a conclusion on a uniform perception of *opinio juris*. Moreover, it was noted that only 18 out of 109 indications in the sample agreements (16.5 per cent) refer to equity. This is less than can be found for the median and equidistant line, each showing 20 indications (18.3 per cent). Therefore, it is difficult to conclude that there is sufficient expression of *opinio juris*, particularly after the equidistance and median line methods were not found to form part of customary law. There is ample agreement among authors on the subject that there was insufficient evidence to establish customary law, and that the Court indeed applied very different standards of scrutiny in establishing equity and equitable principles in customary law whilst respecting the existence of equidistance in practice.[38] According to Charney, the surveys contained in his study of maritime boundaries support the conclusion that no normative principle of international law has developed that would mandate the specific location of any maritime boundary line. State practice varies substantially. Due to the unlimited geographical and other circumstances that influence the settlements, no binding rule that would be sufficiently determinative to enable the prediction of the location of a maritime boundary with any degree of

---

in the *Dubai* v. *Sharjah* arbitration and the *Guinea* v. *Guinea-Bissau* arbitration, para. 87 (equitable solution). For other foundations see Chapter 8.

[38] See e.g. Edward Duncan Brown, *The Legal Regime of Hydrospace* (London: Stevens for the London Institute of World Affairs, 1971), pp. 49, 70; Jack Lang, *Le Plateau continental de la mer du Nord: l'arrêt de la Cour internationale de justice, 20 février 1969* (Paris: Collection Bibliothéque de droit international, LGDJ, 1988), pp. 80, 101, also 129; Tomas Rothpfeffer, 'Equity in the North Sea Continental Shelf Cases' (1972) 42 *Nordisk Tidskrift for International Ret*, 97, 101; Bernd Rüster, *Die Rechtsordnung des Festlandsockels* (Berlin: Duncker und Humblot, 1977), p. 393. In support of customary law, however, see Suat Bilge, 'Le Nouveau rôle des principes équitables en droit international' in E. Diez, *Festschrift für R. Bindschedler zum 65. Geburtstag am 8. Juli 1980* (Bern: Stämpfli, 1980), p. 114.

precision is likely to evolve in the near future.[39] He adds, '[p]erhaps, this is due to the fact that negotiators have acted without knowledge of the practice throughout the world'.[40] Perhaps. But it is also reasonable to think that even with full knowledge of state practice, it is unlikely that any clear trend with regard to a particular rule will emerge. The full collection of treaties now available is indeed an important source of inspiration in particular cases, but it further reduces the possibility of drawing any conclusions about customary law, due to the great variety of existing situations.

The situation is completely different in case law. The brief summaries in Chapter 6 show a uniform picture of reference to equity, equitable principles, and/or equitable solutions since the 1969 *North Sea* cases expounded the law. While the terminology of the method of delimitation applied may vary from equitable principles–relevant circumstances to equidistance–special circumstances, the consideration of equitable principles is inherent to the process of delimitation under all methods. The practice of courts contributes to the body of general international law, but cannot, strictly speaking, provide a formative element of customary law. It will therefore be necessary to establish and define the proper legal qualifications.[41]

3. Other methods and legal approaches

It is evident that, *a fortiori*, other methods and approaches discussed and partly applied in state practice also do not form part of customary law. The percentage of applications of parallels of latitude, straight lines/azimuth, perpendiculars to the coastline,[42] or any other *ad hoc* construction, clearly does not demonstrate sufficient state practice either in indications or in application.

4. Customary obligation to achieve an equitable solution

In addition to the obligation of achieving an agreed-upon or peaceful settlement of the boundary, involving the affected parties at the exclusion of unilateral delimitation, there was also consensus on a second element among the schools of thought expressed at UNCLOS III: it was equally uncontroversial that, regardless of the means applied, delimitation should result in an equitable solution.[43] The consensus suggests that

---

[39] Jonathan Charney, 'Introduction', in Charney et al., *International Maritime Boundaries*, n. 24, vol. I, p. xlii.
[40] Ibid., at p. xliii.   [41] See Part III, Chapter 8.
[42] The methods are described in Chapter 4(II).   [43] See Chapter 4(III)(4).

this principle, as broad and undefined as it is, expresses the necessary *opinio juris* required for the establishment of a rule of customary law. Antunes and Anderson successfully argued that the obligation to achieve an equitable result must now be regarded as part of customary law.[44] The ICJ recognized Articles 74(1) and 83(1) respectively expressing customary law in 2001. It was restated in 2014 in the *Maritime Boundary Dispute*:[45]

> The Court proceeds on the basis of the provisions of Articles 74, paragraph 1, and 83, paragraph 1, of UNCLOS which, as the Court has recognized, reflect customary international law (*Maritime Delimitation and Territorial Questions between Qatar and Bahrain (Qatar v. Bahrain), Merits, Judgment, I.C.J. Reports 2001*, p. 91, para. 167; *Territorial and Maritime Dispute(Nicaragua v. Colombia), Judgment, I.C.J. Reports 2012 (II)*, p. 674, para. 139). The texts of these provisions are identical, the only difference being that Article 74 refers to the exclusive economic zone and Article 83 to the continental shelf. They read as follows:
> 'The delimitation of the exclusive economic zone [continental shelf] between States with opposite or adjacent coasts shall be effected by agreement on the basis of international law, as referred to in Article 38 of the Statute of the International Court of Justice, in order to achieve an equitable solution.'

These provisions, while addressing the goal of international negotiations, thus are equally used to form the customary law basis for adjudication by the Court. It provides the foundation for delimitation based upon the method of equidistance–special circumstances in more recent case law. It should be noted that the wording of these provisions provides guidance for political negotiations, but does not address legal dispute settlement properly speaking. Two problems arise.

Firstly, it is doubtful whether the goal of an equitable solution is sufficiently precise to meet the requirements of a norm-creating character. In the absence of established principles of delimitation in customary law, the concept of an equitable solution indeed provides little guidance. At best it may avoid the imposition of grossly unfair agreements that obviously neglect the interests of one of the parties in the sense of *pacta leonida*. But,

---

[44] Nuno S. Antunes, *Towards the Conceptualisation of Maritime Delimitation, Legal and Technical Aspects of a Political Process* (Leiden: Martinus Nijhoff Publishers, 2003) p. 415; David Anderson, 'Developments in Maritime Boundary Law and Practice' in Charney et al., *International Maritime Boundaries*, n. 24, vol. V (Colson and Smith), pp. 3197–222, 3212.

[45] *Maritime Dispute (Peru v. Chile)*, Judgment of 27 January 2014, ICJ Reports 2014 ___ para. 179.

in order to achieve any truly operational meaning, it requires specification through the establishment of underlying and guiding principles; equitable principles that were seen to have been absent in customary law so far.

Secondly, the affirmation of a rule or principle of equitable solution in customary law would require some overwhelming evidence that the rule is actually applied in state practice, i.e. that negotiations are engaged in on the basis of international law and that the results achieved in negotiations are equitable. It is practically impossible to determine to what extent international law is actually applied in negotiations on maritime boundary delimitation. As to the results, the samples examined do not appear grossly inequitable. Yet, are they all equitable? An answer to this question is not possible without more precisely defined guiding principles of law. The problem of assessing state practice suggests that this kind of a principle is not suitable for customary law on its own. And even if recognized in customary international law, the goal of an equitable solution does not provide sufficient guidance. It is not justiciable and depends upon further specification in judge-made law on the basis of equitable principles. The matter needs further discussion in Part III of this book.

5. Customary obligation of mutual co-operation?

Finally, the question arises to what extent obligations of co-operation developed, in particular in configurations of overlapping resources. The concept of joint development of resources that straddle a boundary gained judicial attention in the *Eritrea* v. *Yemen* Award in the second stage. The Tribunal held that 'having regard to the maritime boundary established by this Award, the Parties are bound to inform one another and to consult one another on any oil and gas and other mineral resources that may be discovered that straddle the single maritime boundary between them or that lie in its immediate vicinity'.[46] It continued that 'the body of State practice in the exploitation of resources that straddle maritime boundaries import that Eritrea and Yemen should give every consideration to the shared or joint or unitised exploitation of any such resources'.[47] The above findings by the Tribunal in *Eritrea* v. *Yemen* seem to suggest that the practice of seeking co-operation where resources straddle a boundary is about to acquire customary law character.[48]

---

[46] Award in the Second Stage, n. 30, para. 86.   [47] Ibid.
[48] Anderson, n. 45, p. 3217; See also W. Michael Reisman, 'Eritrea-Yemen Arbitration (Award, Phase II: Maritime Delimitation)' (2000) 94 *American Journal of International Law*, 721, 735. See also Chapter 6(II)(K).

It is quite another issue to what extent a court of law may take into account the concept of co-operation when charged with determining a maritime boundary line. In an area that has traditionally been concerned with a strict separation of jurisdiction under the concept of peaceful co-existence of states, little, if any, judicial experience is available related to co-operation beyond recognition of historical rights and of condominium.[49] Moreover, it is evident that the establishment of schemes of co-operation is an eminently creative and hand-tailored operation, which seems accessible to general rules of law to, at most, a limited extent. Based upon his detailed analysis of state practice, Ong submitted in 1999 that states are under a customary law obligation to co-operate in the context of sharing uniform deposits.[50] The fact that one state may block exploration and exploitation practically compels states to co-operate in such circumstances to prevent the postponement of drilling operations. Despite difficulties to proof *opinio juris*, an inherent obligation to co-operate can be built upon. The *Eritrea* v. *Yemen* Award Second Phase and the assessments by Anderson and Reisman confirm this finding.[51] Courts of law may rely upon it and thus act accordingly in the process of delimiting maritime zones. With regard to uniform deposits and straddling stocks, common zones of joint administration could be contemplated as part of the equitable solution which the court is bound to find. Beyond this point of dealing with uniform deposits and shared resources, the model of common zones under joint administration, replacing the need for maritime boundary delimitation, is an option states may choose without being obliged to do so.

For the time being, failing agreement, it is certainly more appropriate for disputing states to call upon conciliation. It enjoys larger discretion than a court of law. In the Jan Mayen conciliation, the commission was required to 'take into account Iceland's strong economic interests in these sea areas', but was generally entitled to take into account all aspects it felt relevant.[52] Without being bound by law, conciliation commissions are in a much better position than courts to work out and propose schemes of

---

[49] See *Land, Island and Maritime Frontier Dispute (El Salvador* v. *Honduras: Nicaragua intervening)*, Judgment, ICJ Reports 1992, p. 351, Chapter 6 (II)(P).

[50] David M. Ong, 'Joint Development of Common Offshore Oil and Gas Deposits: "Mere" State Practice or Customary International Law?' (1999) 93 AJIL 771, 801–4.

[51] See above n. 49.

[52] Art. 9 of the Conciliation Agreement between Iceland and Norway of 28 May 1980, (1981) 20 ILM 797, 799, speaks of a 'broad scope of considerations,'

co-operation. It should be noted however, that a carefully drawn special agreement may charge a court of law to decide upon appropriate schemes of co-operation, provided the issues in dispute are well defined. Moreover, with an ongoing use of co-operation schemes in state practice, it may well be that general duties of transboundary co-operation will expand in future customary international law, enlarging the present, still modest, legal standards relating to duties of co-operation.

II. The potential and limitation of equidistance

The overwhelming application of equidistance, strictly or simplified in some 39 per cent (51 of 131 delimitations) or in a modified form in some 22 per cent (29 of 131 delimitations) of the sample agreements reviewed in Chapter 5[53] provides sufficient evidence that the method is highly capable of bringing about successful delimitations in a large number of geographical configurations.[54] The same amount of some 39 per cent (51 of 131 delimitations) of the sample agreements discussed in Chapter 5 referred to methods other than equidistance. And it was seen that equidistance was less prominent in case law, albeit it was often used as a starting point.[55] The focus shifts to special circumstances with the increasing complexity of the case, requiring a different approach. The following stages may be distinguished.

The evidence clearly suggests that the examination of boundary problems and negotiations should start on the basis of equidistance or median lines, unless the parties agree at the outset to rely on a different, equally simple method, such as parallels of latitude in accordance with regional preferences. Under Article 12(1) of the 1958 Convention on the Territorial Sea and Contiguous Zone and Article 15 of the LOS Convention, equidistance is a legally mandatory approach to

---

[53] Chapter 5(II), Table 5.2.
[54] This was particularly emphasized in the *Malta* v. *Libya Case*, ICJ Reports 1985, p. 38, para. 44 ('it is impressive evidence that the equidistance method can in many different situations yield an equitable result'), and for configurations of opposite coasts as a preliminary line. *Malta* v. *Libya Case*, ICJ Reports 1985, p. 47, para. 62 ('most judicious manner of proceeding with a view to an eventual achievement of an equitable result'); *Anglo-French Channel* arbitration, see n. 21, p. 294, para. 95. See also Charney, 'Introduction'in Charney et al., *International Maritime Boundaries*, n. 25, vol. I, p. xliv.
  Second, the equidistance line will be considered in most circumstances as a basis for analyzing the boundary situation. It may very well be used in some form or variant to generate the boundary line itself.
[55] Chapter 6(IV)(C), and above n. 29.

negotiations for delimitations of the territorial sea. It was seen that the same is true for the delimitation of the territorial sea under customary law.[56] For delimitation of the continental shelf under the 1958 Convention, equidistance as a residual rule does not oblige the parties to rely upon it.[57] Practical experience, however, strongly suggests using equidistance as a methodological starting point and exploring how far agreement can be achieved on such a basis. At its best, equidistance may prove to be a sufficient foundation for agreeing on boundaries of either the continental shelf or the EEZ by diplomacy, at relatively low financial and political cost. The prohibition of a unilateral settlement provides a certain balance of negotiating powers, even between partners who are unequal in terms of political or economic impact. The weaker state is in a position to decline a settlement if its interests are not sufficiently taken into account. Under the LOS Convention it may even enjoy the right to submit the matter to compulsory conciliation. This right, of course, deploys significant preventive effects. The considerable percentage of successfully concluded agreements starting with equidistance and partly modifying it suggests that this method sufficiently takes care of economic and political interests in a great number of delimitations. It seems possible to propose and achieve a simplification or modification of the equidistance line that is mainly based on political judgment, without necessarily relying upon a detailed analysis and discussion of maritime boundary law. Equidistance therefore provides an extremely helpful starting point of the operation, as Lauterpacht had already pointed out in the very early days of maritime boundary law.[58]

Often, however, configurations are more complex and cannot be sufficiently dealt with by equidistance for a number of reasons. During the diplomatic process, evidence shows that negotiating positions are predominantly shaped on the basis of political and economic interests. These interests, in turn, are often decisively influenced by the organized private interests and lobbies of the industries affected. This does not imply that the law is not taken into consideration at this stage. However, it is mainly invoked in order to strengthen a negotiating position that was

---

[56] *Qatar v. Bahrain*, n. 32, para. 176.
[57] The text of Art. 6 clearly states that equidistance or special circumstances apply 'in the absence of an agreement'. See Chapter 4(III)(A)(3).
[58] Hersch Lauterpacht, 'Sovereignty Over Submarine Areas' (1950) 27 *British Yearbook of International Law*, 410. See also Jens Evensen, dissenting opinion, ICJ Reports 1982, p. 290 ff., para. 12. (dissenting opinion Evensen, stating that equity requires equidistance principle as a starting point); ICJ Reports 1982, p. 319.

primarily shaped in accordance with political and economic interests and needs. Whether or not the result of a negotiation is acceptable to a government depends much more on political and economic considerations than it does on the law. A result is acceptable if it sufficiently respects the bottom line set for the main economic and political claims. In order to achieve a goal, diplomacy applies pragmatic approaches. The situation is no different from that in the delimitation of land boundaries or any other negotiation. Solutions are sought on the basis of bargaining chips, negotiating power, and trade-offs.

Once solutions based on equidistance, modified in a process of give and take, *quid pro quo*, or any other simple method such as parallels of latitude, can no longer be achieved by diplomacy, the process reaches a more complex stage. Protraction then becomes a frequent feature. Based on the experience of state practice, it is suggested that parties in such circumstances first seek to solve the matter through co-operation agreements, provided the political climate allows for such schemes. Co-operative agreements either allow the matter of boundary delimitation to remain unsettled or, if the scheme allows for mutually conceded rights of exploitation in each of the areas allocated, they render a boundary less important in economic terms. There is no legal limit to imaginative agreements besides the LOS Convention's obligation to achieve an overall equitable result. The body of general law is still of minor importance at this stage. This facilitates negotiating a solution.

If a settlement based on equidistance, on any other simple method or on the basis of co-operation fails, it is at this stage that the law begins to play an increasingly important role, possibly with a view to submitting the matter to adjudication. Economically, a settlement is required for the long-term relations of the parties and the health of the industries concerned. It is a matter of creating legal security based upon which exploitation can be legally organized. Unsettled allocations of marine spaces and the uncertainties linked to it discourage investments for the exploitation of the shelf and give rise to political problems. The same is true with regard to fishing communities and their constituencies in the context of EEZ delimitations. Governments cannot afford to leave these matters unresolved for years or decades, and where they do so (such as in the case of Greece and Turkey), this goes hand in hand with difficult and volatile relations.

It was seen that some of the most contentious cases reaching the courts are characterized by one of the parties insisting upon equidistance and the other denying the feasibility of this method. Generally, the second party either invokes a different method or calls upon the existence of special circumstances, including history. The main task of the court in such cases is to decide on the existence and impact of the special circumstances. It is at this stage that the concept of equidistance or any specific geometrical method of delimitation is no longer of service. The potential of equidistance as a pragmatic starting point is exhausted and the more fundamental legal issues of delimitation now have to be addressed. While there are many good reasons to support the application of equidistance, it is for these reasons that neither strict equidistance nor fixed modifications taking proportionality into account, such as combining equidistance and proportionality (*equiratio*), can provide the basis for a legal regime which is capable of settling complex and protracted cases for which the law has to be prepared. Attempts to re-establish equidistance as a rule of law have failed to sufficiently address this crucial point.[59] There are no easy solutions, and the approaches developed so far are open to much criticism. But flaws and difficulties cannot be simply remedied by taking recourse to a particular method. The law is bound to be more complex as it faces complex cases in adjudication.

---

[59] See Phaedon John Kozyris, 'Lifting the Veils of Equity in Maritime Entitlement: Equidistance with Proportionality around Islands' (1998) 26 *Denver Journal of International Law and Policy*, 319; Yoshifumi Tanaka, *Predictability and Flexibility in the Law of Maritime Delimitation* (Oxford, Portland OR: Hart Publishers, 2006), pp. 148–9.

PART III

Delimitation based on equity

8

The rule of equity

I. The rationale of equity and equitable principles

A. Corrective or autonomous equity?

We have found that the model of rules and exceptions based on equidistance has been fairly successful as a starting point in some 60 per cent of all delimitations. Yet, ever since the *North Sea Continental Shelf* cases, the courts have consistently adhered to the model of equity and equitable principles and denied equidistance as a rule of customary law, except for delimitations of the territorial sea. There is still considerable debate about the proper rules for maritime boundary delimitation: should equidistance or equitable principles be applied with a view to achieving an equitable solution? And, if equitable principles are applied, should this take the form of corrective equity or of an independent, autonomous function of equity in this field of law?

After UNCLOS III, this key issue of the Conference[1] largely disappeared from the political arena. It mainly continues as a dispute within the legal community, involving fundamental issues of legal and regulatory theory. Different schools argue about which of the models is best suited to securing a peaceful settlement of the world's long-distance maritime boundaries. There is also debate over whether this goal should be pursued on the basis of strict rules or with a more open-textured approach. The problem is one of optimizing the level of precision and of the density and predictability of international law, and the chances of successful dispute settlement within a setting of highly individualistic configurations. The debate is therefore one that is of general importance to the theory of international law, extending far beyond the scope of maritime boundary delimitation. It is a structural problem of general interest to jurisprudence and legal theory.

---

[1] See Chapter 4(III)(A)(4).

Since 1969, the rejection of the equidistance–special circumstances model as a rule of general international law and the adoption of a more flexible approach based on equity, equitable principles and, today, on the basis of equitable solutions by the ICJ and courts of arbitration, has been controversial and the subject of profound criticism by both dissenting judges[2] and scholars that adhere to the school of equidistance–special circumstances.[3] At least in part, the discussion is based

---

[2] See e.g. *North Sea Continental Shelf (Federal Republic of Germany v. Denmark; Federal Republic of Germany v. Netherlands)*, Judgment, ICJ Reports 1969, p. 3, p. 171 (dissenting opinion Tanaka) p. 197 (dissenting opinion Morelli), p. 218 (dissenting opinion Lachs), p. 241 (dissenting opinion Sorenson); *Case Concerning the Continental Shelf (Tunisia v. Libyan Arab Jamahiriya)*, Judgment, ICJ Reports 1982, p. 18, p. 290 (dissenting opinion Gros, Oda, Evensen); *Delimitation of the Maritime Boundary in the Gulf of Maine Area (Canada v. United States of America)*, Judgment, ICJ Reports 1984, p. 246, p. 360 (dissenting opinion Gros); *Continental Shelf (Libyan Arab Jamahiriya v. Malta)*, Judgment, ICJ Reports 1985, p. 13, p. 127 (dissenting opinion Oda).

[3] See in particular Edward Duncan Brown, *The Legal Regime of Hydrospace* (London: Stevens for the London Institute of World Affairs, 1971); Edward Duncan Brown, 'The Anglo-French Continental Shelf Case' (1979) 16 *San Diego Law Review*, 461, 498, 505; Edward Duncan Brown, 'The Tunisia-Libya Continental Shelf Case – A Missed Opportunity' (1983) 7 *Marine Policy*, 142; Robin R. Churchill, 'The Greenland-Jan Mayen Case and its Significance for the International Law of Maritime Boundary Delimitation' (1994) 9 *International Journal of Marine and Coastal Law*, 1, 27–8; Edward Collins and Martin A. Rogoff, 'The International Law of Maritime Boundary Delimitation' (1982) 34 *Maine Law Review*, 1, 33 (suggesting a rule of equidistance-proportionality); Emmanuel Decaux, 'L'Arrêt de la Cour internationale de justice dans l'affaire du Plateau Continental (Tunisie/Libye)' (1982) 28 *Annuaire Français de Droit International*, 357, 373–5; Emmanuel Decaux, 'L'Arrêt de la Chambre de la Cour internationale de justice dans l'affaire de la délimitation de la frontière maritime dans le Golf du Maine (Canada/Etats-Unis)' (1984) 19 *Annuaire Français de Droit International*, 304, 339; Emmanuel Decaux, 'L'Affaire de la délimitation maritime dans la région située entre le Groënland et Jan Mayen (Danemark c. Norvège) arrêt de la C.I.J. du 14 juin 1993' (1993) 39 *Annuaire Français de Droit International*, 495, 503; Elisabeth Zoller, 'Recherches sur les méthodes de délimitation du plateau continental: à propos de l'affaire Tunisie/Libye' (1982) 86 *Revue Générale de Droit International Public*, 645, 668–78. See also Prosper Weil, *Perspectives du droit de la délimitation maritime* (Paris: Editions A. Pedone, 1988), pp. 54, 64, 216–22, 301–7 (equidistance as legally mandatory starting point but subject to correction on the basis of equitable principles and special circumstances); Prosper Weil,'Des Espaces maritimes aux territoires maritimes: vers une conception territorialiste de la délimitation maritime' in *Droit international au service de la paix, de la justice et du développement: Mélanges Michel Virally* (Paris: Editions A. Pedone, 1991), pp. 501–11; Phaedon John Kozyris, 'Lifting the Veil of Equity in Maritime Entitlements: Equidistance with Proportionality around the Islands' (1998) 26 *Denver Journal of International Law and Policy*, 319 (equidistance combined with proportionality: equiratio); Yoshifumi Tanaka, *Predictability and Flexibility in the Law of Maritime Delimitation* (Oxford and Portland OR: Hart Publishers, 2006) pp. 147–8.

on an incorrect assumption that equidistance is applied in some form or another in substantially all maritime boundary delimitation agreements and that therefore it is a rule of customary law.[4] These authors argue that the model of equidistance–special circumstances is a paradigm of relatively strict law, and that in the interests of peaceful settlement and limited discretion and exceptions, it provides a much more suitable legal approach for delimitation than equity. It is argued that this approach provides better guidance, stability and predictability,[5] whereas using equitable principles actually amounts to arbitrary decision-making *ex aequo et bono*.[6] This supposedly invites states to lay claims and fosters disputes which would be unlikely under a model of strict rules and strictly defined exceptions. With the advent of the EEZ and the overruling of the doctrine of natural prolongation, particularly in the 1985 *Malta* v. *Libya* case, this school has argued that equidistance, which is subject to exceptions on the basis of corrective equity, has become the most appropriate rule of delimitation in light of the theory of adjacency and of the distance principle as the founding titles of the continental shelf zone and the EEZ.[7]

Despite the undisputed great practical importance of the method of equidistance and its standardized recourse in more recent litigation, this chapter does not follow the school that advocates a legal rule of equidistance–special circumstances. Instead, I refer to reasons set

---

[4] See e.g. Brown, *The Legal Regime of Hydrospace*, n. 3, p. 370, and Zoller, n. 3, 673:

> C'est la seule [the rule of equidistance–special circumstances] qui permette de 'coller' à la réalité naturelle des choses et c'est la raison pour laquelle pratiquement tous les accords de délimitation passés entre Etats l'ont utilisée d'une manière ou d'une autre pour tracer matériellement la ligne de délimitation. Il s'agit donc d'une règle qui correspond à la pratique des Etats.

[5] Brown, *The Legal Regime of Hydrospace*, n. 3, p. 70; Decaux, 'L'Affaire de la délimitation maritime dans la région située entre le Groënland et Jan Mayen', n. 3, 495–6; Shigeru Oda, ICJ Reports 1985, p. 160, para. 67 (dissenting opinion); ICJ Reports 1982, p. 260, para. 165; Tanaka n. 3, pp. 148–9.

[6] See the comment of Judge Schwebel on distributive justice: 'If what is lawful in maritime delimitation by the Court is what is equitable, and if what is equitable is as variable as the weather in The Hague, then this innovation may be seen as, and it may be, as defensible and desirable as another', ICJ Reports 1993, p. 120 (separate opinion).

[7] In particular Weil, *Perspectives du droit de la délimitation maritime*, n. 3, pp. 86–90; Weil, 31 ILM 1197 (1992) (dissenting opinion); ICJ Reports 1985, pp. 150–163, paras. 49–70 (Oda's dissenting opinion entitled: 'The "Equidistance/Special-Circumstances" Rule in Terms of the 200-Mile Distance Criterion').

forth in previous chapters of this book. I argue and affirm that in the final analysis, equity assumes an independent, autonomous function in maritime boundary law, in accordance with the idea of the fundamental rule of equity adopted by the courts. Equity forms the very foundation of the rule. It may therefore be called the model of delimitation based upon equity as a lead-rule, as expressed by Judge Aréchaga. It is clearly different from traditional perceptions of corrective equity described in the introduction to this book:

> This conception of equity, not as a correction or moderation of a non-existent rule of law, but of a 'lead rule' well adapted to the shape of the situation to be measured, is the one which solves the fundamental dilemma arising in all cases of continental shelf delimitation: the need to maintain consistency and uniformity in the legal principles and rules applicable to a series of situations which are characterised by their multiple diversity.[8]

It is submitted that the model of equity and equitable principles is more suitable to pursuing the goals of fair and equitable maritime boundary delimitation by the judicial branch than a concept of a rule of equidistance subject to exceptions on the basis of corrective equity. Thus, in what is sometimes called a 'religious war' between the two schools of thought,[9] I side with the school of equity. The reasons relate to the need for underlying principles, and to the complexity of contentious delimitation both in substance and as a political and legal process. The view is based on the cases and materials examined in Part II, and finally on legal theory and jurisprudence which support delimitation based on equity in maritime boundary law. At the same time, this does not mean simply endorsing the law and approaches developed by the courts. It is important to remember that the support of delimitation based on equity and equitable principles does not preclude the search for ways and means to reduce the gap between the schools, helping to draw this this intellectual dispute to a conclusion. In the interest of the law and optimal chances for the successful prevention and settlement of disputes for the numerous delimitations still to be undertaken, it is important to seek a bridging of viewpoints. The first step consists in discussing the underlying and shared values of the different schools.

---

[8] ICJ Reports 1982, p. 106, para. 26 (dissenting opinion Aréchaga).
[9] Weil, *Perspectives du droit de la délimitation maritime*, n. 3, p. 17 ('l'enjeu de véritables guerres de religion juridiques').

B. The inherent need for underlying values and principles

Any delimitation process starting from a particular practical method of delimitation, such as equidistance or parallels of latitude, or any other geometric approach that relies on the coastal configuration in dispute and ultimately reaching legal settlement in the courts, inherently focuses upon exceptions and deviations from such methods. This is of the utmost importance. Under approaches relying on the model of rules and exceptions, it becomes essential at this stage to define the scope and impact of such exceptions in more precise legal terms, so as to provide the basis for a legal delimitation. Such exceptions cannot be defined on their own. They require recourse to the more fundamental ideas and concepts of the relevant zones, and therefore to the more fundamental issues of delimitation. Exceptions cannot be dealt with without an underlying network of reference points from which the success of deviation from a particular method can be measured.

The underlying rationale of the concept of exceptions or special circumstances is a perception that there are normal situations and abnormal special situations, or exceptional situations. Mental distinctions of normal and irregular situations merely project what we conceive of, and evaluate as, normal or natural.[10] In this context, a natural coast would be one for which the application of equidistance (or any other method) produces a result that is not in need of adaptation and modification. We tend to assume, as a matter of unreflected feelings, a particular result or a range of possible results which are considered to be lawful and equitable. The model of equidistance–special circumstances therefore presumes the existence of normal situations in nature. But what is an unnatural situation in nature? There is no such thing in nature by definition. There cannot be an 'unnatural' coastal configuration, just as there cannot be 'irregular' islands situated off a coast. As Friedmann pointed out:

> To speak of a particular form of coastline as unnatural is simply not capable of rational generalisation.[11]

The problem, therefore, is that nature itself does not provide any clues as to when and to what extent special circumstances should take effect. In

---

[10] For essential reliance on 'normal' and 'exceptional' geographical circumstances see ICJ Reports 1985, see p. 160, para. 67 (dissenting opinion Oda).
[11] Wolfgang Friedmann, 'The North Sea Continental Shelf Cases – A Critique' (1969) 64 *American Journal of International Law*, 229, 237.

other words, the method of equidistance–special circumstances is not self-explanatory. Whether or not special circumstances exist depends entirely on human value judgments. Such assessments then function as the basis for making decisions in claims invoking special circumstances. They are indispensable under any method or legal approach, including where equidistance–special circumstances is established as a prime or residual rule. An exception only exists for the extreme models of *ex aequo et bono* or strict rules (without exceptions). It can be seen at this point that there is a need for underlying ideas, values and principles of maritime boundary law, broad as they may be, so that the lawfulness of a claim and the parties' responses, and of any method and *ad hoc* construction, can be intellectually examined. Without such principles, there is no way to rationalize and review the subjective feelings in the use of special circumstances.

It is important to emphasize that the need for underlying principles exists under any approach to delimitation, except under decision-making *ex aequo et bono* or strict rules without exceptions. Specifically, the need for underlying principles exists where exceptions to equidistance are sought to remain well-defined on the basis of corrective equity. Exceptions cannot be defined rationally without an appropriate normative background. This is true even if they are limited to geographical or natural features, as originally envisaged by Article 6 of the 1958 Shelf Convention, and expanded by the 1977 Channel arbitration. A normative background becomes even more indispensable if the exceptions are extended to encompass the features of natural and human geography.

The school of equidistance does not deny the need for underlying principles or criteria. The difference is one of methodology rather than substance. Whilst the underlying principles play a primary role under the model of equity and equitable principles, they serve as a mandatory legal starting point for equidistance and are then used to examine possible exceptions.[12] The need for underlying principles under both schools, indeed any method of legal delimitation, is a shared element of the two schools of thought. It is an important *acquis*.[13] But it also shows that the principles cannot be directly compared to equidistance because they assume a different normative level and function.

[12] See in particular Weil, *Perspectives du droit de la délimitation maritime*, n. 3, pp. 221–93 (engaging in a comprehensive analysis of equitable principles serving as a foundation for correction of equidistance as the line of departure).
[13] Ibid., n. 3, pp. 195–9.

C. The normative level of equitable principles

The need for underlying principles also helps in understanding that the approach taken by the courts – regulation by reference to equity and equitable principles – is conceptually very different from more specific models, such as the rule of equidistance–special circumstances embodied in Article 6 of the 1958 Shelf Convention or Article 15 of the LOS Convention with respect to the delimitation of the territorial seas. This is true even if equidistance serves as an initial step in the delimitation exercise. The two approaches cannot be directly compared. Regulation by equity is the broader and more fundamental approach. It includes the model of equidistance–special circumstances.[14] But equidistance–special circumstances cannot be legally applied without an underlying set of principles of delimitation indicating the standards upon which a judgment can be made of whether 'special' or 'relevant' circumstances deviating from equidistance are present. This is exactly what the regulation by equity and equitable principles is trying to develop. Therefore it is not appropriate to let the two models compete. They are not placed on the same normative level.

Discussions at UNCLOS III, as well as much of the debate in literature and dissenting opinions, largely fail to recognize the fundamental conceptual difference in terms of normative levels of the two approaches to delimitation. The high rate of successfully concluded negotiations starting from equidistance on the one hand, and a broader and more complex rule of equity applied by the courts on the other, is not a contradiction. Differences consistently result from the fact that only negotiations that have failed reach the courts, making it necessary to refer to a more sophisticated set of rules.

D. A closer look at equidistance–special circumstances

A closer look at the equidistance–special circumstances model reveals that, in reality, the model does not provide a simpler and more manageable approach to delimitation than the rule of equity. To a large extent the problems encountered under this model are the same as those resulting from delimitation based on equity, or regulation by equity, particularly

---

[14] See also Oda's dissenting opinion: 'the method of equidistance has never been proposed as a counter-concept to the rule of equity and ... this method has been considered by adjudicators to lie well within the framework of the rule of equity', ICJ Reports 1985, p. 129, para. 7.

regarding the set of relevant circumstances and therefore of predictability. No decisive advantages arise under this aspect. The contrary is true. For the following reasons, it is submitted that equidistance–special circumstances is not suitable for coping with complex and hard cases which tend to reach judicial settlement in the end.

1. A clear and simple model?

The model of equidistance–special circumstances is an approach that relies upon the idea of surface geography. The contours of the coasts, including the position of islands, are the determinant factors. Contrary to the ILC's predictions, exceptions to equidistance under the special circumstances rule were conceived to be narrowly defined under the 1958 Shelf Convention, when the traditional corrective concept of equity was applied. It was generally thought that a model that had been successful for the then 3-mile territorial sea could simply be transposed to the expanses of the shelf as a residual rule. The materials of UNCLOS I show the negotiators' concern that exceptions which were too wide would actually erode the governing principle of equidistance.[15] Arguments made before the ICJ in the *North Sea* cases confirm that this was a shared concern. The narrow construction of exceptions under the 1958 Convention was one of the reasons why the counsels of the Federal Republic of Germany, including Professor Oda,[16] rejected equidistance as a rule at the time. There are also indications that such an interpretation caused the majority of the Court to deny equidistance as a rule of customary law in 1969.[17]

It is not merely a coincidence that the first case bound to apply the equidistance–special circumstances model to delimitation under Article 6 of the 1958 Shelf Convention considerably expanded the concept of exceptions to equidistance. In the *Anglo-French Channel* arbitration, considerations unrelated to surface geography, such as the legal status

---

[15] See Chapter 4(III)(A)(3) text accompanying n. 138.
[16] Pleadings 1969, vol. II, p. 57. See also Shigeru Oda, 'Proposals for Revising the Convention on the Continental Shelf' (1968) 7 *Columbia Journal of Transnational Law*, 1, 24–25 (stating, with a view to the North Sea problem: 'Does the equidistant line necessarily reflect the most reasonable solution in all cases? In point of fact, conditions in different parts of the world are too varied to justify the categorical adoption of the equidistant line as a rule for boundaries. Those cases where the equidistant line offers the reasonable solution are likely to arise less frequently than others, so that exceptions may be more numerous than the rule.')
[17] See in particular the analysis by Judge ad hoc Sorenson, dissenting opinion, ICJ Reports 1969, pp. 254–5 and Judge Morelli, dissenting opinion, ICJ Reports 1969, pp. 208–9, para. 13 (requiring a 'particular serious discrepancy' for deviation from equidistance).

of islands and the economic and security concerns introduced by the parties, were discussed and partially taken into account.[18] The models of equidistance and equitable principles were virtually merged under the specific facts of the case. Summing up, the Court of Arbitration stated:

> In short, the role of the 'special circumstances' condition in Article 6 is to ensure an equitable delimitation; and the combined 'equidistance–special circumstances rule', in effect, gives particular expression to a general norm that, failing agreement, the boundary between States abutting on the same continental shelf is to be determined on equitable principles.[19]

This Court conceived that the difference between the models was a reflection of differences of approach and terminology rather than of substance.[20] Why then, despite a sceptical doctrine and a successful use of equidistance in state practice, did the Court depart from the traditional view of the 1958 Shelf Convention when faced with the particular facts of the case? Why did it depart from what seems to be a perfectly rational four-point rule (agreement–equidistance–special circumstances–equitable solution), which seems to be a classical realization of equity, as well as being a predictable rule that is considered to ensure real fairness between the neighbouring coastal states? It may be argued that such a merger of the two models was entirely wrong and has unnecessarily undermined the rule of Article 6 of the 1958 Shelf Convention.[21] It may have been undertaken simply to reconcile the position of the parties in dispute, or even to send a signal to the rather sterile debate and stalemate at

---

[18] *Arbitration between the United Kingdom of Great Britain and Northern Ireland and the French Republic on the Delimitation of the Continental Shelf*, Decisions of the Courts of Arbitration dated 30 June 1977 and 14 March 1978, reprinted in 18 ILM (1979), 397, para. 70 (hereinafter Channel Award).
Ibid., paras. paras. 97 and 148; Derek W. Bowett, 'The Arbitration between the United Kingdom and France Concerning the Continental Shelf Boundary in the English Channel and South-Western Approaches' (1978) 49 *British Yearbook of International Law*, 1, 4–6; Zoller, n. 3, 372–85; Brown, 'The Anglo-French Continental Shelf Case', n. 3, p. 497.
[19] See Channel Award, ibid., para. 148.
[20] In particular Weil, *Perspectives du droit de la délimitation maritime*, n. 3, pp. 159–60. See also the declaration of Judge Briggs, Channel Award, n. 18, pp. 457, 460, stating 'that the rule of positive law expressed in Article 6 will be eroded by its identification with subjective equitable principles, permitting attempts by the Court to redress inequities of geography'. A narrow interpretation was also argued by the UK, including a special burden of proof for the party invoking an exception. See Channel Award, n. 18, p. 67. See also Brown, 'The Anglo-French Continental Shelf Case', n. 3, pp. 496 ff., 505–6, 521; Bowett, n. 18, p. 6 (emphasizing the far-reaching impact of the assimilation to equitable principles).
[21] See Chapter 4(III)(A)(4)(a).

UNCLOS III on the subject at the time.[22] However, it is submitted that the combined approach taken was inherently necessary for coping with the complexity of the case.

The cases and materials examined in Part II show that, in fact, maritime boundary delimitation is not limited to aspects of surface geography. The negotiating positions of states are defined by a multitude of additional factors, such as location and quality of resources, economic and social impacts, and security interests. Given the interests at stake, the evidence shows that the process of maritime boundary delimitation, like any delimitation of boundaries between states, is a complex, multifaceted and multifactor business. Furthermore, both natural and human geography are inherently involved.

Maintaining a conceptual and fundamental difference between the two models of equitable principles and equidistance only makes sense if the rule of equidistance–special circumstances under Article 6 of the 1958 Shelf Convention (or possibly customary law) is made less complex by limiting legitimate exceptions under corrective equity, as was originally intended and advocated by Judge Oda.[23] But such a limitation as not been realistic, given the complexity of the issues, claims, interests and arguments involved in most of the cases adjudicated over the last forty-five years since 1969. In fact, the wing of the equidistance school represented by Professor Weil does not make any fundamental distinction between the two models in addressing the factors, criteria and principles discussed as essentially the same problems under both schools of thought.[24] Yet, under an intact rule of geographical equidistance, there must be clear limits to the extent that such factors can be taken into account. If the difficulties of achieving effective limits could be overcome, that would be an advantage from the point of view of legal certainty. At the same time, respect has to be paid to the complexity of the cases considered. The more aspects related to human geography (such as history, social and economic interests, and the conduct or negotiating positions of states) are taken into account, the less we can rely upon equidistance–special circumstances, and the more a comprehensive framework of underlying equitable principles expounding underlying values is essential. The matter therefore depends upon the catalogue of factors and interests to be taken into account in maritime boundary delimitation.

[22] Brown, 'The Anglo-French Continental Shelf Case', n. 3, pp. 497, 500–5.
[23] See Oda, ICJ Reports 1985, p. 161, para. 68 ('Considering geography as the sole factor to be employed for the discussion of the continental shelf').
[24] Weil, *Perspectives du droit de la délimitation maritime*, n. 3, pp. 221–87.

2. A more predictable model?

One of the great assets of equidistance is generally believed to be its inherent predictability. Provided that base lines and base points are settled, equidistance geometrically produces a clearly defined mathematical result. This was recognized as being a major advantage over the rule of equity. After arguing in favour of strict equidistance under a theory of narrow interpretation of special circumstances under Article 6 of the 1958 Shelf Convention, Judge Sorenson wrote in his dissent in 1969:

> The delimitation of maritime areas between neighbouring States is a matter which may quite often cause disagreement and give rise to international disputes. In accordance with the function of law in the international community, the rules of international law should be so framed and construed as to reduce such causes of disagreement and dispute to a minimum. The clearer the rule, and the more automatic its application, the less the seed of discord is sown.[25]

He therefore disagreed with the model of equity:

> [I]f the delimitation is to be governed by a principle of equity, considerable legal uncertainty will ensue, and that in a field where legal certainty is in the interest not only of the international community, but also – on balance – of the States directly concerned.[26]

The problem is that a rule of equidistance equally includes the corrective element of special circumstances. The method cannot be looked at in isolation, but rather the entire norm has to be taken into account when judging its virtues of predictability. It is doubtful whether effective differences exist, given the fact that the rule has to deal with the same set of criteria and factors causing possible deviations from the starting line of equidistance. The price would be a limitation of such factors at the cost of the ability of the rule to deal with all the complexities of the case. It is submitted that such limitation would decrease, rather than increase, the potential of the rule of delimitation.[27] The truth of the matter is that the apparent predictability and efficiency of

---

[25] ICJ Reports 1969, p. 256.   [26] ICJ Reports 1969, p. 257.
[27] See also François Monconduit, 'Affaire du Plateau continental de la mer du Nord' (1969) 15 *Annuaire Français de Droit International,* 213, 244 (responding to Judge Sorenson), affirming the following question: 'Mais ne peut-on pas répondre que, tout au contraire, la réalisation de l'équité, permettant de satisfaire, autant qu'il est possible, les intérêts contradictoires de plusieurs Etats, est la meilleure garantie contre l'apparition de différends?' See also Tomas Rothpfeffer, 'Equity in the North Sea Continental Shelf Cases' (1972) 42 *Nordisk Tideskrift for International Ret,* 81, 119.

the rule of equidistance only exist at first sight. A more detailed investigation reveals problems similar to those existing under a more sophisticated rule of equity.

Predictability and stability are among the most important functions of law. The prevention of disputes, and particularly of international legal disputes which are costly to tax-payers and politicians, decreases to the extent that rules become flexible or are absent. Such a situation is also contrary to the interests of smaller and politically weaker states, because the settlement of disputes is increasingly either defined by bargaining power or exposed to the unlimited discretion of courts, which may cause problems in the acceptance of the results. It is not a matter of questioning the ideal of the predictability of rules in general and specifically in maritime boundary law. The rules have to be defined as precisely as possible. The problem lies in developing the optimal density and precision of the lead-rule of equity and of the underlying principles of delimitation. Much work still lies ahead. Presently, the rule of equity is far from mature. Except for the basic principles, most aspects of the rule of equity are unsettled, be it the concept and number of equitable principles or be it the role of special circumstances of the methodology, including the inherent duty to negotiate. All efforts should now be undertaken to develop the concept and to conceptualize the doctrine towards a more mature and stable pattern that is capable of exerting optimal predictability and certainty of the law and, at the same time, of achieving fair and equitable results.

3. The shortcomings of an equidistance rule

So far, it has been difficult to discern the fundamental difference between the two schools. Both require underlying principles and elaborate criteria to deal with complex cases, and the predictability of both is ultimately reliant upon the optimal precision of underlying principles and criteria. It is submitted that the main difference between the two relies on an additional dimension: the impact of delimitation on the political–legal process. It is here that the true shortcomings of equidistance become apparent.

Most of the difficulties in reconciling the rational and successful model of equidistance in state practice with the model of equity and equitable principles stem from the fact that the process of delimitation is not considered *in extenso*, i.e. from the beginning of negotiations to the deadlock and then on to the implementation of a judicial decision that either sets a final boundary line or sets out a mandatory guide for further negotiations. If the judicial phase is considered in isolation, as lawyers tend to do, it is difficult to raise any objections to a rule of equidistance in line with the statements made by Judge Sorenson quoted above. It clearly is the single most important and practically simple method of delimitation. The importance of equidistance as a starting point has already been emphasized. But what if agreement cannot be reached on the basis of this method? By their nature, the cases that are likely to reach a court of law are of this kind, in particular in adjacent coastal configurations. Equidistance, pure or modified, often was incapable of bringing about a mutually acceptable equitable solution.

Legal rules on delimitation serve two purposes at two different stages. Firstly, they should be able to influence the negotiating process from the very beginning. Starting with equidistance as a practical method, or even a procedural obligation, they have to provide an argument to claim or reject deviations from the line in the negotiating process. Secondly, residual rules have to be provided for the legal settlement of complex cases that ultimately reach the courts. Residual rules of general international law must therefore be shaped in order to deal with cases where equidistance led to major problems and deadlocks in the negotiating process. They also have to fit the worst-case scenario of failed negotiations.[28] In short, they need to be able to cope with hard cases. A sunshine rule cannot achieve this goal.

After failed negotiations, parties may take different attitudes toward the method of equidistance. Essentially, three scenarios are conceivable and have been illustrated in practice and discussed in Part II:

1. Parties A and B agree that equidistance is an acceptable starting point, but disagree on particular exceptions (e.g. *Malta* v. *Libya* case, *Eritrea* v. *Yemen* Award).
2. Party A claims an equidistance line. Party B rejects, or ignores, equidistance as an appropriate approach (e.g. *North Sea* cases, *Gulf of Maine* case, *Denmark* v. *Norway (Jan Mayen)* case, *Bangladesh* v. *Myanmar* case, *Nicaragua* v. *Colombia* case, *Maritime Dispute (Peru.v. Chile)* case).

---

[28] For an excellent analysis of transgression from the diplomatic to the judicial process, from negotiation to advocacy, and its consequences, see David A. Colson, 'Litigating Maritime Boundary Disputes at the International Level – One Perspective' in D. Dallmeyer and L. De Vorsey (eds.), *Rights to Oceanic Resources* (Dordrecht: Martinus Nijhoff, 1989), p. 75.

3. Parties A and B agree that equidistance does not provide a suitable line according to their interests (e.g. *Tunisia* v. *Libya* case, *Nicaragua* v. *Honduras* case).

The law of maritime boundary delimitation has to be able to cope with all three cases. Consequently, all three need a set of underlying principles. Case 1 is perfectly suited to a court decision on the basis of equidistance, since the issue is limited to a problem of deviation. The method as such is not controversial. Cases 2 and 3 are more difficult.

Under a rule of equidistance, Party A claiming equidistance would enjoy the benefit of the rule. Even if exceptions are not subject to the burden of proof, pleading exceptions to the rule always remains de facto an uphill battle. The court case may end with a correction to, rather than a fundamental deviation from, equidistance. This may not be acceptable to Party B. Or, the court case may end with a fundamentally different line, because it found that equidistance was not suitable under the facts of the case. This result may be unacceptable for Party A, because, after all, equidistance is the rule of law. In the third scenario, the danger of such an outcome is doubled. A ruling based on a rule of equidistance, which the court is obliged to implement due to its mandatory nature, could well be unsatisfactory to both parties.

Under a rule of law that does not prescribe a particular method, the court is in a better position to avoid such situations. Of course, it remains possible that governments will nevertheless be prepared to accept and implement a case that is clearly lost. But it seems reasonable to adopt a course of action that at least avoids hazards of this kind as much as possible, i.e. by relying on methods other than equidistance. There still remain ample factors that may incite a party to refuse compliance. It is exactly for such reasons that, in the terms of Legault and Hankey:

> [e]quidistance has been largely spurned in judicial proceedings because it is the hard cases that end up in litigation, and in the hard cases pure equidistance will seldom, if ever, produce an equitable result. Many of the boundaries not yet settled are probably hard cases in this sense, although many others, including some where equidistance may be acceptable to all parties, remain undelimited because of the absence of economic or other motives for an early settlement, or because of technical charting and datum problems.[29]

---

[29] Leonard H. Legault and Blair Hankey, 'Method, Oppositeness and Adjacency, and Proportionality in Maritime Boundary Delimitation' in Jonathan I. Charney et al. (eds.), *International Maritime Boundaries*, 5 vols. (The Hague: Martinus Nijhoff Publishers, 1993–2005), vol. I (Charney and Alexander), pp. 203, 205.

E. The roots of the controversy: jurisprudence and legal theory

The problem of the appropriate concept of delimitation involves basic issues of legal theory and jurisprudence. It asks the fundamental question of whether courts should take into account the attitudes of parties and their probable compliance, and consequently the prospects of effective implementation and dispute settlement when deciding a case of boundary delimitation. Leaving aside or taking into account the perceptions, attitudes, expectations and probable compliance of the parties involves a fundamental legal question of jurisprudence and legal theory: should the ambience of the legal case and the surrounding realities be a legal concern? Obviously, there is much less room to consider such social factors under equidistance than there is under the rule of equity. It is submitted that the controversy between the equidistance and equitable principles schools reflects nothing short of fundamental divergences in jurisprudence and approach to law. Such differences may be decreased (as in the *Channel Arbitration*), but not fundamentally overcome.

In the *Tunisia* v. *Libya* case, for example, the special agreement did not categorically exclude the application of equidistance. However, both parties argued against the application of the method in the particular case. The majority of the court then held that '[t]he Court must take this firmly expressed view of the parties into account'.[30] Consequently, while it did not explicitly exclude equidistance, in practical terms it ruled it out from the outset. By doing so, the Court took into account the expectations and probable compliance of the parties. While Quéneudec did not think it would be a bad thing to take into account the climate of the particular case,[31] not everyone agreed with the majority's decision. Judges Evensen, Gros and Oda objected on these grounds;[32] Decaux argued that the Court should have taken up equidistance after it had rejected natural prolongation (the main basis of the parties' claims[33]) and

---

[30] ICJ Reports 1982, p. 79, para. 110.
[31] Jean-Pierre Quéneudec, 'L'Affaire de la délimitation du plateau continental entre la France et le Royaume Uni' (1979) 83 *Revue Générale de Droit International Public*, 53, 103 ('Néanmoins, chaque problème de délimitation étant singulier, il n'était peut-être pas mauvais qu'un Tribunal d'arbitrage insistât sur la nécessité d'apprécier avant tout le 'climat' général d'une situation particulière.')
[32] See ICJ Reports 1985, pp. 294, 295–6, 301, para. 270.
[33] See Emmanuel Decaux, 'L'Arrêt de la Chambre de la Cour internationale de justice dans l'affaire de la délimitation de la frontière maritime dans le Golf du Maine (Canada/Etats-Unis)', n. 3, 373.

Zoller held the Court's policy to please the parties to be unworthy of any legal comment.[34]

These divergent comments are telling. They highlight two fundamentally different perceptions of the legal process and law in international relations. On the one side, the majority of the Court implies a perception of law and the legal process reflective of the surrounding realities of the case, including the psychology of the parties and their attitudes. The prospects of compliance with the judgment by the parties, and thus the factor of acceptance of the result, are a major concern in its thinking. Without saying so, the majority adhered to legal realism in a broad sense.

The critics show a purer and stricter position on the perception of law. This perception insists on applying the law irrespective of the political environment of the case. To those holding this view, issues such as the probable compliance and acceptance of results are not considered to be of legitimate legal concern. Instead, such factors are seen as an excuse for pleasing the parties, and this engenders the erosion of law toward mere conciliation. The critics imply that the binding force of the judgment is sufficient in itself to bring the parties into compliance. The position reflects a strong Kelsenian belief in a pure theory of law in international relations.

Explicitly confessed attitudes toward the law and legal process in international law are rare. They do not appear in the findings, and even individual opinions hardly deal with these subjects. They remain a matter of underlying thinking and legal education. It is therefore also difficult to pin them down and conclusively relate different schools of thought in maritime boundary law to different schools of jurisprudence in precise terms. Yet it seems fair to say that the rule of equity and equitable principles reflects a tendency toward a realist jurisprudence,[35] while the

---

[34] Zoller, n. 3, 675–6 ('Que la Cour n'applique pas cette méthode [équidistance] par crainte de déplaire aux Parties, c'est un choix qui n'appelle pas de commentaires *juridiques*').

[35] See the particularly realist attitudes linked to equity in Judge Jessup's separate opinion in the *North Sea Continental Shelf* cases, providing a detailed factual analysis of interests involved. See ICJ Reports 1969, pp. 79–83. See also his following statement: 'I am quite cognisant of the fact that the general economy of the Court's Judgment did not conduce to the inclusion of detailed, and largely factual, analysis which I have considered it appropriate to set forth in this separate opinion, but I believe that what is stated here, even if it is not considered to reveal an emerging rule of international law, may at least be regarded as an elaboration of the factors to be taken into account in the negotiations now to be undertaken by the Parties. Beyond that, I hope it may contribute to further understanding of the principles of equity, which, in the words of Judge Manley O. Hudson, are "part of international law which it [the Court] must apply"', ICJ Reports 1969, pp. 83–4.

advocates of a mandatory rule of equidistance–special circumstances are closer to a positivist perception of law abstaining from the social and political context of a case. Thus, it is not a coincidence that the majority of the court ruling out an equidistant line which was *contre coeur* to the parties instead advocated the concept of equity in 1982. On the other hand, judges and authors insisting on equidistance are likely to equally reject such attitudes.[36] The differences therefore reflect fundamental differences in legal theory and jurisprudence which were set out in the Introduction to this book.

To achieve an effective dispute settlement which is ultimately also respected and realized, it is essential that rules of maritime boundary delimitation are framed on the basis of a realist perception of the law. Attitudes, perceptions, probable compliance and acceptance of a judgment by the parties are essential elements that cannot be ignored. Rules cannot be shaped and applied without regard to social realities. There has to be a constant comparison of our view of the rule to reality.[37] A realist approach bears such social factors in mind as a matter of legitimate legal consideration[38] and seeks to make them transparent.

Consideration of such attitudes is especially required in the present context of complex legal operations if residual rules and legal dispute settlement are to remain attractive for governments. To some extent, this is necessary in all legal systems that depend more on persuasion and acceptance than on Austinian enforcement. But in the imperfect system of international law, where peaceful enforcement is generally weak, and is fully dependent on voluntary compliance by the governments affected, it becomes absolutely essential. All this does not mean that rules should make way for unfettered judicial discretion. It does not mean advocating a return to voluntarism. A realist approach does not mean simply relying

---

[36] In particular Weil, *Perspectives du droit de la délimitation maritime*, n. 3. (who does not address the problem of failed negotiations on the basis of equidistance). Zoller implicitly argued the case of excluding social facts in the rule-making process when she denied, in a different context, good faith being a legal, not merely a moral, principle of international law, see Elisabeth Zoller, *La Bonne foi en droit international public* (Paris: Editions A. Pedone, 1977). The difference between a realist and purist approach in the context of good faith is elaborated by Michel Virally, 'Review Essay: Good Faith in Public International Law' (1983) 77 *American Journal of International Law*, 130, 133. It may apply, *mutatis mutandis*, also in this context.

[37] Karl Engisch, *Logische Studien zur Gesetzesanwendung* (Heidelberg: Carl Winter Universitätsverlag, 1963), p. 15.

[38] Dietrich Schindler, *Verfassungsrecht und soziale Struktur* (Zurich: Schulthess Polygraphischer Verlag AG, 1970), p. 92.

on specific claims, expectations and attitudes of the parties. This would be fully at variance with the idea of a rule-oriented approach to delimitation, and would lead to settlement nothing short of *ex aequo et bono*. Realism must develop a range of principles related to substance and human conduct, which under this approach may be argued and taken into account. The task of optimal predictability, as discussed before, remains essential.

Which is the appropriate approach that should be taken in working toward these goals? The lesson to learn from the complexity of materials and cases discussed, and the conclusion to be drawn from the arguments put forward, is that a rule of equidistance–special circumstances, despite its practical importance in the negotiation phases, is not a mandatory starting-point for a suitable legal foundation. Corrective equity cannot sufficiently cope with the realities of complex cases at a post-negotiation stage. State practice, attempts at codification at UNCLOS III and the experience of the courts prove that long-distance maritime boundary delimitation between adjacent or opposite states is not successfully codifiable under traditional approaches to regulation (unlike the territorial sea). A broader approach is required: the rule of equity and equitable principles.

Despite a process of trial and error that will be discussed in more detail, and a lack of sufficient conceptualization and concretization, it is promising that the equity approach has not done too badly so far. The concerns voiced by Judge Sorenson have not materialized. Experience using the rule of equity has neither caused an inflation of disputes nor frustrated the process of legal settlement of maritime boundaries. Indeed, the contrary is actually occurring. It is fascinating to observe that states are calling upon the judicial branch of dispute settlement despite, and perhaps because of, an approach to delimitation essentially based on equity that is still open-ended. Contrary to the fears that had been expressed, its subjectivity and vagueness have not exerted chilling effects on governments to call upon third-party adjudication in international relations.

F. The appropriateness of equity

Logically, the established need for more sophisticated underlying principles does not necessarily imply the model of equity. The application of equitable principles and/or equitable solutions is not the sole legal approach to delimitation conceivable in complex cases. It may be argued that the reference to equity, and therefore the regulation of maritime boundary delimitation based on it, is merely accidental, because those who drafted the Truman Proclamation discussed in Part I found it convenient to resort to such an elusive concept. They might have called upon justice or fairness without changing the substance; instead, equity only makes sense in the traditional perception of corrective equity.

Whatever the history of the Proclamation, in the present context equity is used in line with its overall broad function in the legal process of law-making, even if this does not correspond to established notions of corrective equity *infra legem*. In 1945, no established underlying principles of delimitation existed. The legal concept of the continental shelf was still emerging, and little was known about the possible implications of the evolving legal nature of the shelf on maritime boundary delimitation. There was no law in place, while new challenges had to be addressed and met. Recourse to equity, therefore, was perfectly suitable and in accordance with historical functions of the concept in the main legal systems. It offered a foundation in law based upon which a body of principles and rules would eventually emerge and develop. It was equitable principles that provided a basis for the long-term development of more specific underlying principles over time on a case-by-case basis. They provided a first answer to a novel problem and its basic dilemma between predictability and justice, serving as a starting point in response to the long-term need of underlying principles which other specific legal approaches (and particularly those embodying specific geometrical methods), have not been able to satisfy, given the complexity and variety of human circumstances and geographical configurations involved in the delimitations of the new boundaries. Equity has opened the door for a constructive normative framework, which, from the very beginning, has searched for, and relied upon, essential, and otherwise unspoken, principles of long-distance maritime boundaries.

In a period of great transition and silent maritime revolutions, in a field of highly individualized cases, the rule of equity is a suitable approach for the development of a more consolidated set of broad rules and principles that may crystallize over time as experience with other examples of equity law is gained. At the same time, it will avoid the shortcomings of hard and fast rules, which are not capable of doing justice to more complex cases of delimitation. Recourse to equity, therefore, was appropriate in the Truman Declaration. And ever since, it has dominated the law of maritime boundary delimitation.

II. The evolution of the fundamental norm of equity

At the outset, the concept of equity and of equitable principles in maritime boundary delimitation has been a highly elusive concept. It serves as an umbrella for very different perceptions of what an equitable delimitation should be. The very broad and general idea has to be gradually developed into more precise operational principles.

The first step in this direction is the formulation of the basic approach, or of the fundamental rule, in order to provide a first concretization of equity in the present context. Each of the cases briefly reviewed in Part II has contributed to the body of law and specification of the concept in a process of trial and error. The process and results of UNCLOS III were of equal importance. The evolution of the fundamental norm of maritime boundary delimitation shows different competing traits and schools of thought within the concept of equitable principles. Typically, two approaches are distinguished: a concept which is rule-oriented; and a concept which is result-oriented, although in practice these two concepts are intertwined.

More than sixty years of history of long-distance maritime boundary law has shown pendulum-like shifts from a tentative rule-oriented approach towards result-oriented thinking, and back to a more elaborate rule-oriented jurisprudence. The following examination shows the tentative, almost experimental development of normative elements by jurisprudence. It took forty years from the Truman Proclamation until the 1985 *Libya* v. *Malta* case, for the Court to *legally* define the equitable principles as such to be applied in the process of delimitation.

A. Roots of the fundamental rule

1. The 1909 *Grisbadarna* Arbitration

The maritime boundary treaty of 1661 between Norway and Denmark, following the 1658 Peace Treaty of Roskilde, set the maritime boundary at a distance that was roughly equal between the Norwegian island of Tisler and the Swedish island of Koster. When the two countries, united by the cession of Norway to Sweden in 1815, separated again at the end of the nineteenth century, the boundary problem once again became an issue of practical importance. Norway and Sweden were able to agree on delimitation mainly along the median line up to a point (point no. 18), but beyond that there was disagreement. The major cause of dispute was the ownership of the rich fishing grounds of Grisbadarna and the Skjöttegrunden banks, both situated within the territorial sea.

The parties requested that the newly founded Permanent Court of Arbitration at The Hague would settle the matter.[39] That Court was asked to rely on existing treaty law (the boundary treaty of 1661) and to make a decision by '[t]aking into account the circumstances of fact and the principles of international law'.[40] Both parties claimed, based on different constructions, the entire Grisbadarna Bank, and Sweden additionally claimed almost the whole of Skjöttegrunden. The Court found the treaty law inconclusive, and the Award allocated the whole of the Bank to Sweden, and all of Skjöttegrunden to Norway. The Court reached its solution by applying a line perpendicular to the general direction of the coast, and then modifying it from 20 degrees to 19 degrees in a westerly direction, in order to omit the admitted inconvenience of cutting through an important bank.[41]

Superficially, the Court seemed to rely upon a strict rule, subject to modification, and therefore on a traditional rule/exception model. It held that a line perpendicular to the general direction of the coast constituted the leading rule of delimitation of the seventeenth century 'in accord with the ideas of the seventeenth century and with the notions of law prevailing at that time',[42] i.e. when the underlying boundary agreement of 1661 was negotiated. Such a reference is an early example of the doctrine of intertemporal law as applied by the Court.[43] The correction from 20 to 19 degrees, however, was justified by the Tribunal on the grounds of the historic and actual conduct of the parties in the areas concerned, and in particular on fishing and related activities:

> [A] demarcation which would assign the Grisbadarna to Sweden is supported by all of several circumstances of fact which were pointed out during the discussion and of which the following are the principle ones:
>
> (a) The circumstance that lobster fishing in the shoals of Grisbadarna has been carried on for a much longer time, to a much larger extent, and

---

[39] Decided 23 October 1909, reprinted in Hague Ct. Reports (Scott) 487 (Permanent Court of Arbitration 1909), transl. in English, see p. 121. For a recent review see e.g. Sang-Myon Rhee, 'Sea Boundary Delimitation between States before World War II' (1982) 76 *American Journal of International Law,* 555, 566–71 (with further references); Collins and Rogoff, above n. 3, 56–68.

[40] Agreement for Arbitration, Art. 3, Hague Ct. Rep. (Scott) 134, and also 123.

[41] See ibid., p. 129.   [42] Ibid.

[43] Elias Olufemi, 'The Doctrine of Intertemporal Law' (1980) 74 *American Journal of International Law,* 285, 289–90.

by a much larger number of fishermen by the subjects of Sweden than by the subjects of Norway.

(b) The circumstance that Sweden has performed various acts in the Grisbadarna region, especially of late, owing to her conviction that these regions were Swedish, as, for instance, the placing of beacons, the measurement of the sea, and the installations of a light-boat, being acts which involved considerable expense and in doing which she not only thought that she was exercising her right but even more that she was performing her duty; whereas Norway, according to her own admission, showed much less solicitude in this region in these various regards.[44]

The Court also continued to stress the economic importance of the fishing activities to the Swedish communities on the island of Koster:

> Lobster fishing is much the most important fishing on the Grisbadarna banks, this fishing being the very thing that gives the banks their value as fisheries.[45]

From such considerations and circumstances, the Court concluded that the Swedes almost certainly used the banks of Grisbadarna 'much earlier and more effectively than the Norwegians'.[46] Conversely, there was evidence that the Norwegians deployed fishing activities on the bank of Skjöttegrunde 'in a comparatively more effective manner than at Grisbadarna'.[47]

It is very likely that these circumstances played a far more decisive and constructive role in the judgment than mere correction and mitigation of a general rule of the perpendicular to the general direction of the coast. There is no evidence, either within or outside the judgment, that this particular method dominated maritime boundary delimitation in the seventeenth century,[48] and it is doubtful whether the case really is a prominent example of the doctrine of intertemporal law. A more probable scenario is that the facts of historic and actual conduct constituted the essentials of the judgment and delimitation. This is highlighted by the expression of what later became known in the *North Sea* cases as the Grisbadarna Principle.[49] This principle reflects the normative power of facts, particularly with respect to private interests:

---

[44] Hague Ct. Rep., see n. 40, p. 130.   [45] Ibid.   [46] Ibid., p. 131.   [47] Ibid., p. 132.
[48] See Rhee, n. 39, pp. 569–70.
[49] ICJ Reports 1969, pp. 80–1 (Judge Jessup's separate opinion stating that the Grisbadarna principle should be taken into account as an additional criterion in the process of future negotiations). Indeed, the facts of already existing oil fields largely influenced the boundaries in the final settlement.

[I]t is a settled principle of the law of nations that a state of things which actually exists and has existed for a long time should be changed as little as possible; and [t]his rule is specially applicable in a case of private interests which, if once neglected, can not be effectively safeguarded by any manner of sacrifice on the part of the Government of which the interested parties are subject.[50]

Moreover, the Court emphasized considerations of Norwegian acquiescence to Swedish activities[51] as creating settled expectations on the part of Sweden. It further supports the allocation of the Bank to Sweden on the basis of good faith and equity.[52] All this indicates that historic and contemporary conduct was the Court's primary motivation, and that the perpendicular was found *ex post* to provide a suitable method, as opposed to being applied as rule, in order to achieve the result.[53]

From this perspective, the *Grisbadarna* Award constitutes an important early precedent of the fundamental rule based on equity. The significance of the case from the point of view of contemporary maritime boundary delimitation lies in its use of factual circumstances in order to draw the boundary line.[54] Although from a perspective of contemporary international law, the particular conduct of the parties in this case amounts to title in its own right (acquiescence),[55] the predominance of factual considerations and principles related to conduct may well provide a root of the concept of equitable principles and relevant circumstances, both of which form the essential part of the fundamental rule. Regardless of whether the Grisbadarna factors are called 'equitable considerations'[56]

---

[50] Hague Ct. Rep., see above n. 40, p. 130.

[51] Ibid., p. 131 (stationing of light-boats was done by Sweden 'without meeting any protest and even at the initiative of Norway').

[52] Ibid., p. 131. For discussion of this perhaps most important aspect of the case, see Jörg Paul Müller, *Vertrauensschutz im Völkerrecht, Beiträge zum ausländischen öffentlichen Recht und Völkerrecht* (Cologne, Berlin, Bonn: Heymann, 1971), p. 42.

[53] See also Strupp, who expressed the view that the case was decided on a factual basis. Karl Strupp, 'Der Streitfall zwischen Schweden und Norwegen' in W. Schücking (ed.), *Das Werk vom Haag, die gerichtlichen Entscheidungen* (1917), p. 124. Rhee, n. 40, p. 570, on the other hand, suggests that the award was probably based on the general principles of law regarding division of rivers and lakes prevailing in Europe in the seventeenth century, as well as on doctrinal suggestions by contemporary writers such as Pufendorf.

[54] See Collins and Rogoff, n. 3, p. 57.   [55] See also Chapter 9(III)(C).

[56] Charles De Visscher, *De l'équité dans le règlement arbitral ou judiciaire des litiges en droit international public* (Paris: Editions A. Pedone, 1972), p. 31 (arguing that the Grisbadarna principle was, at the time, a mere 'considération équitable', and later developed into the principle of effectiveness. The Court, however, formulated this principle quite stringently, and it is doubtful whether the Court in fact intended to develop it on the basis of equity, rather than law in its own perception.

or an 'equitable remedy',[57] it is certainly appropriate to link them to equity. The case shows an early, albeit still disguised, regulation by equity and good faith.

2. The 1951 *Anglo-Norwegian Fisheries* case

Forty-two years after the Grisbadarna Arbitration, Norway was again involved in the Hague, this time before the ICJ.[58] In this eminent case, the Court dealt indirectly with the delimitation of seaward boundaries of the territorial sea, in particular with the problem of straight base lines that extended beyond a length of ten nm in closing bays, basins and fjords along the 1,500 kilometres of the scattered Norwegian coast ('skjaergaard'). At issue were the expanses of the Norwegian internal waters and territorial sea (at the time, 4 nm) as defined by base lines, some of which running up to 44 kilometres and some reaching far into the sea.

The real issue was whether Norway was entitled to such extensive, unilaterally defined internal and territorial (and therefore exclusive) fishing zones under international law.[59] All this came at a time when the first claims to the patrimonial sea were about to emerge in Latin America,[60] and the idea of preferential or exclusive fishing zones had by no means been established, let alone accepted, in international law under the doctrine of freedom of the seas.[61] The ICJ did not find a strict rule of customary international law prohibiting straight base lines beyond 10 nm, as it was urged to do by the United Kingdom. Yet the Court continued to develop 'certain principles' and 'criteria' of geographical and economic content to be applied as guidelines and to be respected in order to achieve the accommodation of the parties' interests in the present field of international relations. It did this without explicit reference to the *Grisbadarna* case:

> It does not at all follow that, in the absence of rules having the technically precise character alleged by the United Kingdom Government, the delimitation undertaken by the Norwegian Government in 1935 is not subject to certain principles which make it possible to judge as to its validity under international law. The delimitation of sea areas has always an international aspect; it cannot be dependent merely upon the will of the coastal State as expressed in its municipal law. Although it is true that the act of

---

[57] Rhee, n. 39, p. 571.
[58] *Fisheries Case (United Kingdom v. Norway)*, ICJ Reports 1951, pp. 116 ff.
[59] Ibid., pp. 198–9 (dissenting opinion Read).   [60] See Chapter 2(III).
[61] See e.g. J. P. A. François, 2nd. Rep. *Yearbook of the International Law Commission* (New York: United Nations, 1951), vol. II, p. 93, para. 119.

delimitation is necessarily a unilateral act, because only the coastal State is competent to undertake it, the validity of the delimitation with regard to other States depends upon international law.

In this connection, certain basic considerations, inherent in the nature of the territorial sea, bring to light certain criteria which, though not entirely precise, can provide courts with an adequate basis for their decisions, which can be adapted to the diverse facts in question.[62]

The Court then continued to set forth three basic, non-exclusive considerations to be respected, namely: the close dependence of the territorial sea upon the land domain; the close relationship of sea areas and land formations; and, finally, economic interests:

Among these considerations, some reference must be made to the close dependence of the territorial sea upon the land domain. It is the land which confers upon the coastal State a right to the waters off its coasts. It follows that while such a State must be allowed the latitude necessary in order to be able to adapt its delimitation to practical needs and local requirements, the drawing of base-lines must not depart to any appreciable extent from the general direction of the coast.

Another fundamental consideration, of particular importance in this case, is the more or less close relationship existing between certain areas and the land formations which divide or surround them. The real question raised in the choice of base-lines is in effect whether certain sea areas lying within these lines are sufficiently closely linked to the domain to be subject to the regime of internal waters ...

Finally, there is one consideration not to be overlooked, the scope of which extends beyond purely geographical factors: that of certain economic interests peculiar to a region, the reality and importance of which are clearly evidenced by a long usage.[63]

This passage gives rise to several observations of interest in the present context. Firstly, they relate to the motivation of the Court to develop such principles or considerations. The underlying rationale is that the delimitation of marine spaces is inherently a problem of international relations. Therefore, according to the Court, it cannot be left entirely to unilateral regulation. The judgment implies that there must be some standards (albeit not necessarily strict rules) regarding the subject in international law. This attitude and perception of the Court reflects a gradual change in the understanding of international law, moving away from a strictly positivist view, towards prescriptive and creative, less prohibiting perceptions of international law, observable since the end of World War II and the founding of the United Nations. The *Fisheries* case, and not the

---

[62] ICJ Reports 1951, pp. 132–3.   [63] ICJ Reports 1951, p. 133.

North Sea Continental Shelf cases in 1969, signalled the evolution of such perceptions within the judiciary. Although the *Fisheries* case judgment did not mention equity as its basis, this case provides the best explanation of why equity came into prominence in subsequent, comparable configurations of international relations which are equally characterized by a lack of rules to settle the legal problems involved.

Secondly, the factors and criteria or principles expounded in this case are closely linked to the concept of the territorial sea. The criteria were derived from the principle that territorial waters must follow the general direction of the coast.[64] Indeed, the geographic criteria set forth by the judgment express the close relationship between land and sea and anticipate what would later be expressed in the context of the continental shelf and the EEZ as the principle that the coast dominates the sea.[65] Similarly, the consideration of the Court relating to economic interests also derives from the closeness of relationship between the land and sea. The concepts of internal and territorial waters have included the purpose of protecting local fisheries ever since. In the final analysis, principles and criteria are developed and shaped in the light of the underlying function and rationale of the zone. It will be seen that the same approach dominates, and should dominate, delimitation of the shelf and the EEZ under the fundamental rule of equity.[66]

Thirdly, a most interesting aspect of the above quotation is the methodological implications of the judgment. The Court emphasized the flexibility of principles and criteria as distinct from traditional perceptions of law as a set of strict rules. Nevertheless, they establish a framework for decision-making and for guiding courts in the process of evaluating the lawfulness of particular base lines as established by unilateral acts. Again, this appears to be an expression of a fundamentally new approach to legal reasoning in international law, before only found implicitly in the *Grisbadarna* case.

This novelty is prominently reflected in Judge McNair's dissent, which has been called upon by opponents of the equitable principles approach ever since.[67] After expressing sympathy for the cause of Norwegian coastal fisheries that were threatened under the then ongoing

---

[64] ICJ Reports 1951, p. 129 ('The principle that the belt of territorial waters must follow the general direction of the coast makes it possible to fix certain criteria').
[65] See Chapter 10.   [66] See Chapter 9.
[67] See e.g. Judge Koretsky, dissenting opinion, *North Sea Continental Shelf* cases, ICJ Reports 1969, p. 166; Judge Gros, dissenting opinion, *Gulf of Maine* case, ICJ Reports 1984, p. 361, para. 3.

development towards high seas industrial factory fishing,[68] the judge rejected the idea that considerations of economic and other social interests were subjective elements without foundations in law:

> In my opinion the manipulation of the limits of territorial waters for the purpose of protecting economic and other social interests has no justification in law; moreover, the approbation of such a practice would have a dangerous tendency in that it would encourage States to adopt a subjective appreciation of their rights instead of conforming to a common international standard.[69]

In the legal operation of the judgment, the geographical and economic criteria and principles played a much more limited role than the general statement of the Court implies. In explicit terms, they were only applied in the final consideration of the compatibility of the 1935 Decree with the already established and accepted system of straight base lines in the particular area of the Lopphavet Basin. The geographic principle stipulating that base lines need to follow the general direction of the coast was, in fact, reduced to a test of reasonableness or arbitrariness, operating only in cases of 'manifest abuse'.[70] The principle was furthermore subjected to historic title, originating under the doctrine of *mare clausum*, on vital needs of the population, and attested by very ancient and peaceful use.[71]

The central issue as to whether the Norwegian system of straight base lines itself was in conformity and compatible with international law was not decided on the basis of principles and considerations set forth in the new approach. Rather, it was decided on grounds based on historic conduct and interaction of communication of the parties and other states concerned. The Court found that Norway had consistently applied her system of straight base lines and had not been challenged by other states before the 1935 regulation was enacted, despite their knowledge of it.[72] In other words, the international community had acquiesced to the system of straight base lines which was gradually accepted as customary law.

---

[68] ICJ Reports 1951, p. 158. See also Chapter 2(III) (on the evolution of the EEZ).
[69] ICJ Reports 1951, p. 169.   [70] ICJ Reports 1951, p. 142.
[71] ICJ Reports 1951, p. 142 ('Such [fishing] rights, founded on the vital needs of the population and attested by very ancient and peaceful usage, may legitimately be taken into account in drawing a line which, moreover, appears to the Court to have been kept within the bounds of what is moderate and reasonable.')
[72] The Court did not accept the UK's argument of not having had any knowledge in the light of British interests and concerns as a marine power. Ibid., p. 139.
   But see the dissenting opinions of Judges McNair and Read, ibid., pp. 180 and 200, respectively.

The *Fisheries* case primarily stands for the importance of good faith, claims and responses, and settled expectations in the historical process of forming customary international law along the lines submitted by the New Haven school of jurisprudence.[73] Compared to the decisive importance of conduct, the newly developed reference to principles and criteria of delimitation set forth by the judgment almost appears to be *obiter dicta*, although there can be little doubt that the economic interests vigorously argued by Norway were not without impact in the context of historical rights,[74] as well as on subsequent developments in treaty law. The aspect of economic interests was introduced in the 1958 Convention on the Territorial Sea,[75] and restated with minor changes in Article 7(5) LOS Convention for the purpose of base line determination.

It may be because of these qualities of mere *dictum* that subsequent cases, and in particular the *North Sea* cases, did not explicitly refer to the principles and considerations of the judgment as a precedent. Perhaps the 1969 Court did not want to emphasize historical conduct, given the relative novelty of the continental shelf concept.[76] Whatever the reasons, the *Fisheries* judgment nevertheless contains *in nuce* substantial parts of the new, flexible approach to the problem of international marine resource allocation. It does so, as in *Grisbadarna*, without referring to equity as such. In contemporary terms, however, the approach developed corresponds to the concept of equitable principles. The case provides a precedent for regulation by equity.[77] It laid the foundations for the increased reference to equity by the ICJ in the following decades. In hindsight, Judge Jennings was correct when he pointed to the fact that

---

[73] For discussion of these aspects see Müller, n. 52, pp. 77, 92–4, 101; Myres S. McDougal and Harold D. Lasswell, *The Public Order of the Oceans: A Contemporary International Law of the Sea* (New Haven CT, London: New Haven Press, 1987).

[74] Particularly in northern Norway, about half of the population was dependent upon coastal fisheries at the time, according to the Norwegian Counter Memorial. See 1 Pleadings 219, 216.

[75] 515 UNTS 205, Art. 4(4).

[76] Charney submits that the omitted references in the 1969 case were not unintentional because the Court did not want to emphasize historical conduct but rather the underlying normative concept of equity, Jonathan I. Charney, 'Ocean Boundaries between Nations: A Theory for Progress' (1984) 78 *American Journal of International Law*, 582, 593. This explanation seems to ignore that the *Fisheries* case also contained comparable normative concepts, and that the 1969 case closely examined issues of conduct of the parties. The reason why the Court declined to refer to the 1951 case remains unclear.

[77] See also Shabtai Rosenne, *The International Court of Justice: An Essay in Political and Legal Theory* (Leiden: A.W. Sijthoff, Uitgeversmaatschappij N.V., 1957), pp. 427–8 (particularly emphasizing the 'pressing necessity for a device' which takes into consideration geographic and economic factors).

'the effect of that decision in loosening the grip of the old law of sea boundaries can hardly be overestimated'.[78]

B. 1969: The beginnings

The fundamental rule as expounded by the ICJ in the *North Sea Continental Shelf* cases consists of two major elements in accordance with the Truman Proclamation: (i) delimitation has to be effected by *agreement*; and (ii) such agreement has to rely upon *equitable principles*:

> those principles being that delimitation must be the object of agreement between the States concerned, and that such agreement must be arrived at in accordance with equitable principles.[79]

These two elements have provided the basis of maritime boundary law ever since.

Additional elements vary from case to case. In the *North Sea* cases, a third element was indirectly added, in the sense that the Court considered that the importance of an equitable result based on the concept of natural prolongation was held to establish title to the continental shelf rights and therefore was not encroachable. A fourth element prescribed that, failing agreement, remaining areas of overlap are to be divided into equal parts. A full elaboration of the fundamental norm of the 1969 Court can be found in the operational part of the judgment:

> (1) delimitation is to be effected by agreement in accordance with equitable principles, and taking into account of all the relevant circumstances, in such a way as to leave as much as possible to each Party all those parts of the continental shelf that constitute a natural prolongation of its land territory into and under the sea, without encroachment on the natural prolongation of the land territory of the other;
> (2) if, in the application of the preceding sub-paragraph, the delimitation leaves to the Parties areas that overlap, these are to be divided between them in agreed proportions or, failing agreement, equally unless they decide on a regime of joint jurisdiction, use, or exploitation for the zones of overlap or any part of them.[80]

The Court did not formulate specific equitable principles as such to be applied as a matter of law, despite the fundamental rule it adopted

---

[78] Robert J. Jennings, 'A Changing Law of the Sea' (1972) 31 *Cambridge Law Journal*, 32, 34.
[79] *North Sea Continental Shelf (Federal Republic of Germany v. Denmark/Netherlands)*, Judgment, ICJ Reports 1969, p. 47, para. 85, Chapter 6(II)(A).
[80] ICJ Reports 1969, p. 53, para. 101.

from the Truman Proclamation. Instead, it emphasized the importance of an equitable result to be achieved by the application of unnamed principles and relevant circumstances. At the same time, the Court conceded that the achievement of an equitable result is a truism; and the problem is above all one of defining the means whereby the delimitation can be carried out in such a way as to be recognized as being equitable.[81]

The Court therefore defined a number of *factors*. It made an effort to establish normative elements allowing for the achievement of an equitable result. It seems that the *North Sea* judgment sought to strike a careful balance between result-oriented and rule-oriented jurisprudence. Despite the elaboration of a considerable number of factors, the rule-oriented side of this decision is still highly tentative. The factors were not given the compelling legal value of equitable principles. This may be explained as the Court's belief that guidance should merely provide for further negotiations and that no judicial administration needs to take place. But it may also stem from the fact that the Court had just entered new territory to be explored in more detail before equitable principles of a legal nature can be defined.

C. 1977: Reducing the rule

The *Anglo-French Channel* arbitration restated the rule established by the *North Sea Continental Shelf* Court without further reasoning. It coined the term of 'the *fundamental norm* that the delimitation must be in accordance with equitable principles'.[82]

The Award, however, narrowed the norm in two ways. Firstly, it was explicitly limited to cases of delimitation of the *same* shelf. This may already be found as inherent to the 1969 decision, since that case was also dealing with a uniform shelf of the parties in dispute. The second element is of greater importance: it turned equitable principles into residual rules, departing from the mandatory fundamental rule contained in the Truman Proclamation. The Court exempted agreed solutions from being bound by equitable principles, and compulsory application was legally limited to judicial settlement. It explicitly stated a general norm that, failing agreement, the boundary between states abutting the same continental shelf is to be determined on equitable principles.[83]

---

[81] ICJ Reports 1969, p. 50, para. 92.
[82] *Channel Award*, n. 18, 18 ILM 397, pp. 426–7, para. 97 (emphasis added).
[83] Ibid., p. 421, para. 70.

This definition reflects a movement of the model of equitable principles closer to the residual rule of equidistance and special circumstances of Article 6 of the 1958 Shelf Convention.[84] The Court took pains to narrow the differences between the effects of the two approaches. On the side of equidistance, this was achieved by defining Article 6 not as a model of rule and exception, but rather as a combined rule. In practice, this relieves a party from bearing the burden of proof, usually linked to the invocation of exceptions of special circumstances, but left it to the Court to decide to weigh the evidence and find an appropriate solution. Indeed, the Court continued to apply similar considerations under both models, and it concluded that, at least under the particular facts of the case, 'the result is the same'.[85]

The convergence of the two models in this case finds two explanations. Firstly, it helped to narrow the opposing views of the parties as to the application of conventional or general international law.[86] Secondly, the Award may also have intended to make a contribution to what the judges considered a false and politicized debate over equidistance versus equity at UNCLOS III. As a result, the fundamental norm established by the *North Sea* Court was only superficially restated. Its scope considerably changed. The question remained open over the extent to which this was merely due to the particular facts of the case, involving a dispute over the application of conventional rules and the task of bringing about a final determination of the boundary, and was not followed by subsequent implementing negotiations.

D.   1982 and 1984: The victory of discretionary determination

In the 1982 *Tunisia* v. *Libya Continental Shelf* case, the fundamental rule of equity was further developed. Again new elements were added, this time under the influence of UNCLOS III and the mandate to take into account 'new accepted trends'.[87] The operational part of the decision essentially relies upon the basic norm of the *North Sea* cases.[88] However, under the influence of the 1981 compromise proposal by the Chairman of special negotiating group NG 7 of UNCLOS III (that became the present text of Article 83 LOS Convention[89]), it was the achievement of an 'equitable result' that now became paramount. The Court particularly

---

[84] See Chapter 7(I)(C)(1).   [85] 18 ILM 397, n. 18, p. 425, para. 87.
[86] See Chapter 6(II)(B).
[87] ICJ Reports 1982, p. 23, para. 3, Art. 1. See also Chapter 6(II)(D).
[88] Ibid., p. 92, para. 133 A(1).   [89] See Chapter 4; ICJ Reports 1982, p. 49, para. 49.

stressed its case-by-case approach in its very last paragraph and cautioned against 'overconceptualizing' the application of equitable principles.[90] The Court considerably enhanced the concept of result-oriented justice of the fundamental rule: 'The principles and rules applicable to the delimitation of continental shelf areas are those which are appropriate to bring about an equitable result.' In full:

> The result of the application of equitable principles must be equitable. This terminology, which is generally used, is not entirely satisfactory because it employs the term equitable to characterise both the result to be achieved and the means to be applied to reach this result. It is, however, the result which is predominant; the principles are subordinate to the goal. The equitableness of a principle must be assessed in the light of its usefulness for the purpose of arriving at an equitable result. It is not every such principle which is in itself equitable; it may acquire this quality by reference to the equitableness of the solution. The principles to be indicated by the Court have to be selected according to their appropriateness for reaching an equitable result. From this consideration it follows that the term 'equitable principles' cannot be interpreted in the abstract; it refers back to the principles and rules which may be appropriate in order to achieve an equitable result.[91]

This trend toward a discretionary approach to maritime boundary delimitation under the rule of equity was further strengthened by the reasoning of the Chamber of the ICJ in the *Gulf of Maine* case.[92] In that case, both parties agreed on the fundamental rule to be applied. They both argued, albeit using somewhat different formulations, that the boundary requires determination on the basis of international law in conformity with equitable principles, and must take into account all relevant circumstances in the area concerned to achieve an equitable result or solution.[93] Moreover, both parties put forth a number of varying principles and circumstances. This also reflects the fact that for the first time it was a matter of delimitating an all-purpose boundary, which could not be determined solely on the basis of established principles related to the continental shelf.[94]

---

[90] 1982 ICJ Rep 1982, p. 92, para 137 ('Clearly, each continental shelf case in dispute should be considered and judged on its own merits, having regard to its peculiar circumstances; therefore, no attempt should be made here to overconceptualise the application of the principles and rules relating to the continental shelf ["essayer d'élaborer toute une construction abstraite"]'. See also ICJ Reports 1969, p. 100, para. 53.
[91] ICJ Reports 1982, p. 59, para. 70.
[92] *Delimitation of the Maritime Boundary in the Gulf of Maine (Canada v. United States of America)*, Judgment, ICJ Reports 1984, p. 246.
[93] ICJ Reports 1984, p. 293 para 99. See also Chapter 6(II)(E).
[94] ICJ Reports 1984, pp. 296–8, paras. 103–9.

The novelty of the problem and the widely varying views among the parties may have led this Court to downplay the normative significance of equitable principles. The Chamber thus preferred the term of *equitable criteria* or *ideas* rather than principles, and held that these are themselves not principles and rules of international law.[95] Given the variety of arguments and principles or criteria proposed by the parties to be applied, the Chamber held that general international law would only contain a 'limited set of norms for ensuring the co-existence and vital co-operation of the members of the international community'.[96] This limited set of rules was defined as containing (referring particularly to the *North Sea* cases): (i) the prohibition of unilateral settlement; and (ii) the obligation to effect delimitation on the basis of equitable criteria and practical methods capable of ensuring an equitable result:

> (1) No maritime delimitation between States with opposite or adjacent coasts may be effected unilaterally by one of those States. Such delimitation must be sought and effected by means of an agreement, following negotiations conducted in good faith and with the genuine intention of achieving a positive result. Where, however, such agreement cannot be achieved, delimitation should be effected by recourse to a third party possessing the necessary competence.
>
> (2) In either case, delimitation is to be effected by the application of equitable criteria and by the use of practical methods capable of ensuring, with regard to the geographic configuration of the area and other relevant circumstances, an equitable result.[97]

This formulation of the fundamental rule has been the most result-oriented one. It eliminated almost any rule-orientation and turned delimitation into a fully discretionary operation. Judge Gros concluded in his dissent that it actually turned the ICJ into a 'court of equity whose decisions are being shaped by its political or economic views of the moment'.[98]

Phrasing the substantive rule of equity in such an open-ended manner and leaving ample discretion to any court, however, was not necessarily intended to pre-empt refinement of the rule in the future

---

[95] ICJ Reports 1984, p. 292, para. 89; p. 298, para. 110; p. 303, para. 123.
[96] ICJ Reports 1984, p. 299, para. 111.   [97] ICJ Reports 1984, para 112(1) and (2).
[98] ICJ Reports 1984, p. 388, para. 47.

process of the law. However, the Chamber repeatedly stated that more detailed rules are not suitable at the present stage, especially in a new and still unconsolidated field such as that involving the quite recent extension of the claims of states to areas that until recently were zones of the high seas.[99] This prospect, though, does not change the fact that the Chamber missed an opportunity to make a substantive contribution to the refinement of the law and adapt it to the requirements of an all-purpose boundary; the fundamental rule as adopted lagged behind the formulation proposed by the parties to the dispute.

The Court of Arbitration in the *Guinea/Guinea-Bissau* case closely followed the new precedent of the *Gulf of Maine* case. It restated the wide-open, discretionary approach, emphasizing the predominant goal of achieving an equitable result. Citing only the *Gulf of Maine* case, it held that:

> international customary law can provide, in a matter like that of the present Award, 'only a few basic legal principles which lay down guidelines to be followed with a view to reaching an essential objective' *(ICJ Reports 1984, p. 290, paragraph 81)*. For the Tribunal, the essential objective consists of finding an equitable solution with reference to the provisions of Article 74, paragraph 1, and Article 83, paragraph 1, of the Convention of 10 December 1982 on the Law of the Sea. This is a rule of international law which is recognised by the Parties and which compels recognition by the Tribunal.[100]

The Tribunal then added:

> However, in each particular case, its application requires recourse to factors and the application of methods which the Tribunal is empowered to select.[101]

This addition to a purely result-oriented approach through the legal requirement of the application of other factors may be seen as a subtle first indication of a reversion of the evolution of the law back to a more rule-oriented approach. Indeed, it will be seen that the Tribunal applied a number of important factors, such as non-cutting off and non-encroachment, in its reasoning,[102] although discretionary reasoning still largely prevailed.

---

[99] ICJ Reports 1984, p. 299, para. 111; see also p. 290, para. 81.
[100] *Guinea/Guinea-Bissau: Dispute Concerning Delimitation of the Maritime Boundary* (1986) 25 ILM 251–307, 289, para. 88, Chapter 6(II)(F).
[101] Ibid.   [102] See Chapter 9.

E. 1985: The turning of the tide

In the process of trial and error, the tide turned with the 1985 *Libya* v. *Malta Continental Shelf* case.[103] The discretionary and result-oriented approach by the courts, reinforced by the last-minute compromise results of UNCLOS III, had been widely criticized since the *North Sea* cases began to develop the case law, both by scholars and by dissenting judges within the ICJ[104] who advocate the equidistance–special circumstances model. Efforts by the court to find a more principled approach were favoured in this case by the fact that the issue was limited to a continental shelf boundary. Moreover, the configuration of opposite states rendered the problem much less complex than in previous cases.

The changing of the tide to a more rule-oriented approach is indicated by a number of the Court's statements. They reiterate, in accordance with the parties, the substantive fundamental rule of equity that the delimitation of a continental shelf boundary must be effected by the application of equitable principles in all relevant circumstances in order to achieve an equitable result.[105] The fundamental goal of achieving an equitable solution is not dismissed, but the decision no longer predominantly adheres to a result-oriented approach. The *Libya* v. *Malta* Court referred primarily to the 1982 *Tunisia* v. *Libya* case. This in itself may have been a first indication that the concept of equitable criteria, void of any legal normativity, was dismissed by the case. A stronger indication to that effect can be found in the Court's emphasis on the importance of consistency and predictability in the rules of maritime boundary law and of the consequent need for underlying principles:

> Thus the justice of which equity is an emanation, is not abstract justice but justice according to the rule of law; which is to say that its application should display consistency and a degree of predictability; even though it looks with particularity to the peculiar circumstances of an instant case, it also looks beyond it to principles of more general application.[106]

Unlike the *Gulf of Maine* case and the *Guinea* v. *Guinea-Bissau* arbitration, and indeed unlike all previous cases, the Court finally acknowledged such principles to be principles of international law. In the following statement, they were even held fully applicable to delimitation by agreement, and therefore to the diplomatic process, in accordance with the

---

[103] *Continental Shelf (Libyan Arab Jamahiriya* v. *Malta)*, Judgment, ICJ Reports 1985, p. 13; Chapter 6(II)(G).
[104] See above n. 2. [105] ICJ Reports 1985, p. 38, para. 45.
[106] ICJ Reports 1985, p. 39, para. 45.

intention of the Truman Proclamation. Although the court also held that there are no legal limits to the considerations states may take into account in the negotiating process,[107] it reinforced the overall importance of such principles. The Court named a number of such principles as examples, indicating that it did not intend to provide an exhaustive set of rules. All of the principles referred to had already been developed in previous cases, not with legal qualifications, but as mere factors, ideas or criteria.

> The normative character of equitable principles applied as a part of general international law is important because these principles govern not only delimitation by adjudication or arbitration, but also, and indeed primarily, the duty of Parties to seek first a delimitation by agreement, which is also to seek an equitable result. That equitable principles are expressed in terms of general application, is immediately apparent from a glance at some well known examples: the principle that there is to be no question of refashioning geography, or compensating for the inequalities of nature; the related principle of non-encroachment by one party on the natural prolongation of the other, which is no more than the negative expression of the positive rule that the coastal state enjoys sovereign rights over the continental shelf off its coasts to the full extent authorised by international law in the relevant circumstances; the principle that although all States are equal before the law and are entitled to equal treatment, 'equity does not necessarily imply equality' *(ICJ Reports 1969, p. 49, para. 91)*, nor does it seek to make equal what nature has made unequal; and the principle that there can be no question of distributive justice.[108]

Finally, the rule-orientation of the Court's reasoning can be found in an effort to contain the type of considerations to those which ought to be taken into account in law by tying them closely to the legal concept of the continental shelf as it was described in Part I of this book:

> Yet although there may be no legal limit to the considerations that States may take into account, this can hardly be true for a court applying equitable procedures. For a court, although there is assuredly no closed list of considerations, it is evident that only those that are pertinent to the institution of the continental shelf as it has developed within the law, and to the application of equitable principles to its delimitation, will qualify for inclusion. Otherwise, the legal concept of continental shelf could itself be fundamentally changed by introduction of considerations strange to its nature.[109]

The rule-oriented approach of the *Malta* v. *Libya* Court was elaborated with respect to the delimitation of the continental shelf. The Court was

---
[107] ICJ Reports 1985, p. 40, para. 48.   [108] ICJ Reports 1985, pp. 39–40, para. 46.
[109] ICJ Reports 1985, p. 40, para. 48.

not given the task of establishing an all-purpose boundary, although it has been seen that the new concept of the EEZ significantly influenced the thinking of the Court.[110] The shelf and the EEZ are, indeed, closely intertwined, and there is no reason from the point of view of legal theory and methodology to apply a different approach with regard to the establishment of an EEZ boundary or an all-purpose boundary.[111]

In the *St. Pierre and Miquelon* award, the parties agreed that the fundamental rule to be applied in the case requires the delimitation to be effected in accordance with equitable principles, or equitable criteria, taking account of all the relevant circumstances in order to achieve an equitable result.[112] This formula is very much in line with the one which can be found in the *Libya* v. *Malta* case and that was introduced in the *Gulf of Maine* case. The Court, however, immediately added that: 'the underlying premise of this fundamental norm is the emphasis on equity and the rejection of any obligatory method'.[113] The exact meaning of this last sentence is not clear. It seems that the Court wanted to retain complete freedom to formulate its own solution, only allowing itself to be bound to the achievement of an equitable result. As in the *Gulf of Maine* case, the Court did not even accept considering that the principles put forward by the parties provided a starting point for the delimitation. It therefore decided to formulate its own solution, which turned out to be totally unpredictable and inconsistent with the rule of law. This decision, therefore, can be seen as a step backwards, in that it again turned to the result-oriented jurisprudence of the early 1980s.

For the first time, in the *Denmark* v. *Norway (Jan Mayen)* case, the ICJ had a case before it to which the 1958 Shelf Convention was directly applicable.[114] The Court was not only required to delimit the continental shelf of both parties, but it was also asked to delimit their respective fishing zones. As there was no agreement between the parties for a single delimitation line, the Court decided that it would freely examine the two strands of the applicable law: Article 6 of the 1958 Convention for the continental shelf boundary; and customary law for the delimitation of the

---

[110] See Chapter 2(III)(B).
[111] See *Land, Island and Maritime Frontier Dispute (El Salvador* v. *Honduras: Nicaragua intervening)*, Judgment, ICJ Reports 1992, p. 351.
[112] 'Court of Arbitration for the Delimitation of Maritime Areas between Canada and France, Case concerning de Delimitation of Maritime Areas between Canada and the French Republic' (1992) 31 ILM 1163, para. 38; see Chapter 6(II)(H).
[113] Ibid.
[114] *Maritime Delimitation in the Area between Greenland and Jan Mayen (Denmark* v. *Norway)*, Judgment, ICJ Reports 1993, p. 38, see Chapter 6(II)(J).

fishing zone. However, as acknowledged in the *Libya* v. *Malta* case, the continental shelf and the EEZ are linked together in modern law.[115] The Court was therefore able to state:

> The fact that it is the 1958 Convention which applies to the continental shelf delimitation in this case does not mean that Article 6 thereof can be interpreted and applied either without reference to customary law on the subject, or wholly independently of the fact that a fishery zone boundary is also in question in these waters. The Anglo-French Court of Arbitration in 1977 placed Article 6 of the 1958 Convention in the perspective of customary law in the much quoted passage of its Decision that:
>
>> the combined 'equidistance–special circumstances rule', in effect, gives particular expression to a general norm that, failing agreement, the boundary between States abutting on the same continental shelf is to be determined on equitable principles. (United Nations, *Reports of International Arbitral Award (RIAA)*, Vol. XVIII, p. 45, para. 70).
>
> If the equidistance–special circumstances rule of the 1958 Convention is, in the light of this 1977 Decision, to be regarded as expressing a general norm based on equitable principles, it must be difficult to find any material difference – at any rate in regard to delimitation between opposite coasts – between the effect of Article 6 and the effect of the customary rule which also requires a delimitation based on equitable principles.[116]

Looking at the facts of the case in the light of the applicable law, the Court came to the conclusion that '[i]t thus appears that, both for the continental shelf and for the fishery zones in this case, it is proper to begin the process of delimitation by a median line provisionally drawn'.[117]

With the aim of achieving an equitable solution, the Court then went on to examine each factor of the case that might suggest an adjustment or shifting of the provisionally drawn line.[118] This, however, did not mean that the Court went back to its result-oriented jurisprudence. In fact, it made clear that:

> A court called upon to give a judgment declaratory of the delimitation of a maritime boundary, and *a fortiori* a court called upon to effect a delimitation, will therefore have to determine 'the relative weight to be accorded to different considerations' in each case; to this end, it will consider not only 'the circumstances of the case' but also previous decided cases and the practice of States. In this respect the Court recalls the need, referred to in

---

[115] ICJ Reports 1985, p. 33, para. 33.
[116] ICJ Reports 1993, p. 58, para. 46.
[117] ICJ Reports 1993, p. 62, para. 53.
[118] ICJ Reports 1993, p. 62, para. 54.

the *Libya/Malta* case, for 'consistency and a degree of predictability' *(I.C.J. Reports* 1985, p. 39, para. 45).[119]

F. 1999–2014: The two-step and three-step approach

Subsequent developments to *Jan Mayen* case are characterized by developing what may be called a two-step approach, adopting equidistance as a starting point of delimitation, and followed by the application of equitable principles with a view to achieving an overall equitable result.[120] These developments occurred in applying Articles 74 and 83 of the UNCLOS Convention which increasingly applied to maritime boundary delimitation. In the *Black Sea* case, the ICJ, under the heading of delimitation methodology, held that, in accordance with the Court's settled jurisprudence, the delimitation exercise proceeds in well defined steps.[121] A third stage was explicitly added in the 2009 *Delimitation in the Black Sea* case when the overall result was checked under the angle of avoiding disproportional results.[122] The three-step approach applies between

---

[119] ICJ Reports 1993, pp. 63–4, para. 58.
[120] The pertinent decisions, summarized in section II(B), include *Permanent Court Arbitration (PCA): Eritrea–Yemen Arbitration (Second Stage: Maritime Delimitation) (17 December 1999)* (2001) 40 ILM 983–1019 *(Eritrea v. Yemen)*; *Maritime Delimitation and Territorial Questions between Qatar and Bahrain (Qatar v. Bahrain)*, Merits, Judgment, ICJ Reports 2001, p. 40 *(Qatar v. Bahrain)*; *Land and Maritime Boundary between Cameroon and Nigeria (Cameroon v. Nigeria: Equatorial Guinea intervening)*, Judgment, ICJ Reports 2002, p. 303; *Permanent Court of Arbitration (PCA): In The Matter of an Arbitration between Barbados and the Republic of Trinidad and Tobago (April 11, 2006)* (2006) 45 ILM 800–69 *(Barbados v. Trinidad and Tobago)*; *Arbitral Tribunal Constituted Pursuant to Article 287, and in Accordance with Annex VII, of the United Nations Convention on the Law of the Sea in the Matter of an Arbitration between Guyana and Suriname*, Award of 17 September 2007 (hereinafter *Guyana v. Suriname* Award), International Court of Arbitration: www.pca-cpa.org/showfile.asp?fil_id=664 (last accessed 18 February 2012); *Territorial and Maritime Dispute between Nicaragua and Honduras in the Caribbean Sea (Nicaragua v. Honduras)*, Judgment, ICJ Reports 2007, p. 659, with the only difference in *Nicaragua v. Honduras* being that the provisionally established boundary line in that case was constructed according to the bisector method and not the equidistance method (ibid., para. 287); *Dispute concerning Delimitation of the Maritime Boundary between Bangladesh and Myanmar in the Bay of Bengal (Bangladesh v. Myanmar)*, Judgment, International Tribunal for the Law of the Sea, 14 March 2012, Case No. 16, paras. 233, 240; *Territorial and Maritime Dispute (Nicaragua v. Colombia)*, Judgment, ICJ Reports 2012, p. 624, paras. 190–4.
[121] *Maritime Delimitation in the Black Sea (Romania v. Ukraine)*, Judgment, ICJ Reports 2009, pp. 61, 101, para 115.
[122] ICJ Reports 2009, pp. 102, 103, paras. 120–2.

adjacent as well as opposite coasts.[123] It may also apply where the line to be drawn covers several zones of coincident jurisdictions.[124]

The Court describes the three steps as follows in the *Black Sea Maritime Boundary Delimitation* case:

> 118. In keeping with its settled jurisprudence on maritime delimitation, the first stage of the Court's approach is to establish the provisional equidistance line. At this initial stage of the construction of the provisional equidistance line the Court is not yet concerned with any relevant circumstances that may obtain and the line is plotted on strictly geometrical criteria on the basis of objective data.
>
> ...
>
> 120. The course of the final line should result in an equitable solution (Articles 74 and 83 of UNCLOS). Therefore, the Court will at the next, second stage consider whether there are factors calling for the adjustment or shifting of the provisional equidistance line in order to achieve an equitable result (*Land and Maritime Boundary between Cameroon and Nigeria (Cameroon v. Nigeria: Equatorial Guinea intervening), Judgment, I.C.J. Reports 2002*, p. 441, para. 288). The Court has also made clear that when the line to be drawn covers several zones of coincident jurisdictions, 'the so-called equitable principles/relevant circumstances method may usefully be applied, as in these maritime zones this method is also suited to achieving an equitable result' (*Territorial and Maritime Dispute between Nicaragua and Honduras in the Caribbean Sea (Nicaragua v. Honduras), Judgment, I.C.J. Reports 2007 (II)*, p. 741, para. 271).
>
> ...
>
> 122. Finally, and at a third stage, the Court will verify that the line (a provisional equidistance line which may or may not have been adjusted by taking into account the relevant circumstances) does not, as it stands, lead to an inequitable result by reason of any marked disproportion between the ratio of the respective coastal lengths and the ratio between the relevant maritime area of each State by reference to the delimitation line (see paragraphs 214–215). A final check for an equitable outcome entails a confirmation that no great disproportionality of maritime areas is evident by comparison to the ratio of coastal lengths.

---

[123] See *Cameroon v. Nigeria*, n. 120, paras. 286, 288–90, where the Court for the first time applied the then two-step approach in a case of adjacent coasts; as recalled by the Tribunal in *Guyana v. Suriname* Award, n. 120, para. 338. Previously thereto, the Court in *Qatar v. Bahrain* used the same approach to delimit the northern sector of the maritime boundary between Qatar and Bahrain 'where the coasts of the two States are no longer opposite to each other but are rather comparable to adjacent coasts' (para. 170.)

[124] See *Qatar v. Bahrain*, n. 120, paras. 224–30; *Cameroon v. Nigeria*, n. 120, para. 288; *Guyana v. Suriname* Award, n. 120, para. 334; see also ICJ Report 2007 p. 741 para. 271.

THE RULE OF EQUITY 415

The three-step approach emphasizes equidistance as a starting point, subject to modification on the basis of factors or relevant circumstances, and without excluding equitable principles as an alternative method. The relationship of these components remains unclear. The Tribunal in *Barbados v. Trinidad and Tobago* referred in 2006 to the two-step approach which applies to the delimitation of the continental shelf and the EEZ as the 'equidistance/relevant circumstances' principle.[125] The same approach had previously been termed by the Court in *Qatar v. Bahrain* and *Cameroon v. Nigeria* as the 'equitable principles/relevant circumstances' rule, as it has been developed since 1958 in case law and state practice with regard to the delimitation of the continental shelf and the EEZ.[126] In 2007, the Tribunal in *Guyana v. Suriname* found that the case law of the previous two decades, as well as state practice, have come to embrace a clear role for equidistance as the first step in the delimitation exercise.[127] But already the Courts in *Qatar v. Bahrain* and in *Cameroon v. Nigeria* said that the 'equitable principles/relevant circumstances' approach is 'closely interrelated' with or 'very similar' to the 'equidistance/special circumstances' rule, which is applicable in particular to the delimitation of the territorial sea.[128] The Tribunal in *Barbados v. Trinidad and Tobago* confirmed this view and noted that only 'occasionally there has been a distinction made' between the method applied to the delimitation of the territorial sea and the approach characterizing the delimitation of the EEZ and the continental shelf under Articles 74 and 83 UNCLOS.[129] The Tribunal added that the similarity of the two processes stems from the 'common need to ensure an equitable result'.[130] The approach was confirmed in the *Maritime Dispute (Peru v. Chile)* in 2014. The ICJ held that delimitation is based upon the application of Articles 74(1) and 83(1) UNCLOS as a matter of customary law and continued:

---

[125] *Barbados v. Trinidad and Tobago*, n. 120, para. 242.
[126] *Qatar v. Bahrain*, n. 120, para. 231.
[127] *Guyana v. Suriname* Award, n. 120, para. 335, 342.
[128] *Qatar v. Bahrain*, n. 120, para. 231. *Cameroon v. Nigeria*, n. 120, para. 288, see ICJ Reports 2007, p. 741, para 271.
[129] *Barbados v. Trinidad and Tobago*, n. 120, para. 305.
[130] Ibid., para. 305. See also the Court in *Jan Mayen*, stating that there is inevitably a tendency towards assimilation between the special circumstances under Art. 6 of the 1958 Convention and relevant circumstances under customary law, since both are intended to enable the achievement of an equitable result, ICJ Reports 1993, p. 62, para. 56. (*Jan Mayen*, para. 56).

The methodology which the Court usually employs in seeking an equitable solution involves three stages. In the first, it constructs a provisional equidistance line unless there are compelling reasons preventing that. At the second stage, it considers whether there are relevant circumstances which may call for an adjustment of that line to achieve an equitable result. At the third stage, the Court conducts a disproportionality test in which it assesses whether the effect of the line, as adjusted, is such that the Parties' respective shares of the relevant area are markedly disproportionate to the lengths of their relevant coasts (*Maritime Delimitation in the Black Sea (Romania v. Ukraine), Judgment, I.C.J. Reports 2009*, pp. 101–103, paras. 115–122; *Territorial and Maritime Dispute (Nicaragua v. Colombia), Judgment, I.C.J. Reports 2012 (II)*, pp. 695–696, paras. 190–193).[131]

Such prominence of equidistance, subject to corrective factors and a final check of disproportionality in the third step, suggests a departure from equity towards a strict rule-based approach based upon equidistance. The Court in *Cameroon* v. *Nigeria* stressed the rule-orientation of the approach, saying that delimiting with a concern to achieve an equitable result is not the same as delimiting in equity.[132] It noted that, 'equity is not a method of delimitation, but solely an aim that should be borne in mind in effecting the delimitation'.[133] These developments are strongly related to Articles 74 and 83 UNCLOS, which stress the requirement of achieving an overall equitable result. Equity, in other words, is being limited to secure an overall fair result, but no longer plays an important role in terms of methodology.

Yet, a closer examination reveals that for the reasons stated at the outset of this chapter, the three-step approach cannot dispense with an inquiry into the underlying normative concepts and principles informing maritime boundary delimitations beyond equidistance and relevant circumstances. True, the application of equidistance and of equitable principles will often produce the same results in configurations of opposite costs.[134] Yet this does not alter the finding that maritime boundary delimitation depends upon the identification of underlying normative equitable principles based upon which deviations from equidistance and avoidance of disproportionate results can be assessed. The role of equity

---

[131] *Maritime Dispute (Peru v. Chile)*, Judgment of 27 January 2014, ICJ Reports 2014 ___ para. 180.
[132] *Cameroon v. Nigeria*, n. 120, para. 294.   [133] Ibid., para. 294.
[134] In *Jan Mayen*, the Court held: 'It cannot be surprising if an equidistance–special circumstances rule produces much the same result as an equitable principles–relevant circumstances rule in the case of opposite coasts, whether in the case of a delimitation of a continental shelf, of fishery zone, or of an all purpose boundary', ICJ Reports 1993, p. 62, para. 56.

and equitable principles in law has not been diminished. Delimitation on the basis of Articles 74 and 83 UNCLOS continues to depend upon legal principles to be identified. The Tribunal in *Barbados v. Trinidad and Tobago* called the provisional equidistance line merely a 'hypothesis and a practical starting point' and described Articles 74(1) and 83(1) UNCLOS as:

> [an] apparently simple and imprecise formula [which] allows in fact for a broad consideration of the legal rules embodied in treaties and customary law as pertinent to the delimitation between the parties, and allows as well for the consideration of general principles of international law and the contributions that the decisions of international courts and tribunals and learned writers have made to the understanding and interpretation of this body of legal rules.[135]

The basic relationship of equidistance and equity thus has not changed with recent case law. Under the three-step approach, equity and equitable principles do not find themselves on the same normative level as equidistance and therefore cannot be mingled. It remains necessary to identify the underlying principles more precisely and how they relate to factors and relevant circumstances to be taken into account in the following chapters of the book.

Instead, the three-step approach developed in recent case law remains a matter of legal methodology, rather than applying competing rules to a set of facts.[136] It reaffirms that equidistance essentially is employed as a practical starting point in the methodology of maritime boundary delimitation. It does not render redundant the quest for the underlying fundamental norm and equitable principles. Whether or not they are applied from the outset, or within a second or third step, long-distance maritime boundary delimitation conceptually relies upon them. Any application of equidistance inherently needs to respond and comply with underlying equitable principles. They comprise the core of the fundamental rule.

G. Conclusions

Based on the evolution of the fundamental norm during the process of trial and error since 1969, it seems possible to draft a somewhat more comprehensive fundamental norm. This norm should reflect the fact that

---
[135] *Barbados v. Trinidad and Tobago*, n. 120, para. 222.
[136] But see Tanaka n. 3, pp. 148–9, concluding that equidistance is suitable as a rule of law both in opposite and adjacent configurations.

delimitation must not be unilateral. Preferably, delimitation should be effected by agreement, without excluding informal agreement, acquiescence and other forms of peaceful settlement of international disputes, including conciliation, arbitration and judicial settlement. Consent is the common denominator.

In substance, delimitation should be effected in accordance with equitable principles that are part of the law. There should be scope to take the relevant circumstances of the particular case into account. Technical methods, in particular equidistance, should be used in order to implement and refine the application of equitable principles and the effects of relevant circumstances. Altogether, the operation should achieve an equitable result.

Subject to further refinement at a later stage,[137] we may conclude:

> The delimitation of the continental shelf, the EEZ or other zones of comparable function and expansion, between States with opposite or adjacent coasts shall be effected by consent. Such delimitation shall be in accordance with equitable principles, taking into account all relevant circumstances of the particular case and using appropriate technical methods, in order to achieve an equitable solution.

It is one of the most striking features of the fundamental norm of equity that it also applies in negotiations. Unlike the ruling and perception of the 1977 Channel Arbitration and Article 6 of the 1958 Shelf Convention, the application of equitable principles is not merely a residual rule. The rule of equity and equitable principles of delimitation in maritime boundary law is much more: it is a constitutional rule governing all avenues and methods of delimitation. The approach is not limited to the conventional rule contained in the LOS Convention,[138] but is part of general international law. We thus turn to its foundations.

III. Legal foundations of the fundamental rule of equity

It is submitted that the fundamental rule of delimitation by consent on the basis of equitable principles provides the underlying foundation of delimitations and is by now firmly established in substance in international law. Introduced as a precedent in the *North Sea* cases and subjected to extremely critical reviews of the concept initially,[139] by the time the

---

[137] See Chapter 10.   [138] See Chapter 4(III)(A)(4).
[139] For general reviews of critical comments on equity, at the time, see Bernd Rüster, *Die Rechtsordnung des Festlandsockels* (Berlin: Duncker und Humblot, 1977), p. 389 ff.;

1977 *Channel Arbitration* decision was handed down, the rule was taken for granted.[140] It has been accepted in customary or general international law without much discussion ever since.[141] In a field of much legal uncertainty, it was only natural that lawyers and governments were interested in stabilizing the law to the greatest possible extent, as constant challenges to the foundations of the rule would make the task of delimitation even more difficult. Since the 1982 *Tunisia* v. *Libya* case, states submitting their boundary disputes to judicial settlement have been in agreement on the basic approach of the fundamental rule, while the content of the rule has remained disputed. The advent of the LOS Convention and the three-step approach in recent case law under Articles 74 and 83 of the agreement, emphasizing equidistance as a starting point, offers a contractual, positivist foundation of rules for the delimitation of all maritime zones. Yet, it does not alter the need for guiding and underlying normative principles in complex cases.

Today, an inquiry into the foundations of the fundamental norm may then be of no more than historical interest, as Lauterpacht suggested in 1977.[142] Nevertheless, a critical examination of the different foundations

Rothpfeffer, n. 27, pp. 107–8. We find some of the most critical views, most of them originating in French legal thinking: 'Enfin, les conclusions de la Cour concernant l'équite sont susceptibles de devenir une source de confusion plus que de clarté', Charles Vallée, *Le Plateau continental dans le droit positif actuel* (Paris: Editions A. Pedone, 1971), p. 273 ss, p. 292; 'Loin de clarifier le débat, le recours à l'équité contribue donc à l'obscurcir', François Eustache, 'L'Affaire du plateau continental de la mer du Nord' (1970) 74 *Revue Générale de Droit International Public*, 591, 632; 'L'exégèse d'un tel texte se révèle un jeu intellectuel d'une stérilité totale', Krystina Marek, 'Le Problème des sources du droit international dans l'arrêt sur le plateau continental de la mer du Nord' (1970) 6 *Revue Belge de Droit International*, 44, 71.

[140] Indeed: 'le Tribunal n'a nulle part abordé le problème des conditions de formation de ce nouveau droit coutumier', Jean-Pierre Quéneudec, 'L'Affaire de la délimitation du plateau continental entre la France et le Royaume Uni' (1979) 83 *Revue Générale de Droit International Public*, 53, 70.

[141] Authors were more interested in the practical problem of shaping and applying equitable principles, e.g. Derek W. Bowett, 'The Arbitration Between the United Kingdom and France Concerning the Continental Shelf Boundary in the English Channel and South-Western Approaches'(1978) 49 *British Yearbook of International Law*, 1; M. D. Blecher, 'Equitable Delimitation of Continental Shelf' (1979) 73 *American Journal of International Law*, 60; Brown, 'The Anglo-French Continental Shelf Case', n. 3, 461. Continued interest in foundations can, however, be found in Charney, n. 76, 582 ff.; Rothpfeffer, n. 27, 95–103.

[142] Elihu Lauterpacht, 'Equity, Evasion, Equivocation and Evolution in International Law' (1977–1978) *Proceedings and Commentaries Report of the American Branch of the International Law Association*, 1, at 3 (suggesting that the Court only relied on customary law).

and their evolution some forty-five years after they were established by the ICJ is of continuing theoretical and practical interest. Such examination provides insights into the process in international law. The relationships between different sources of law and their foundations have an impact on the proper specification and definition of equitable principles. Whether or not the fundamental rule is inherent to the concepts of the continental shelf and the EEZ, or any other zone, whether in the final analysis it is a matter of customary law, of general principles, or a matter of judge-made law, may not be without an effect on the scope of equitable principles. Finally, an examination is of a general interest with regard to the process of international law.

The key to, and good starting point for, the inquiry into the legal foundations can be found in the much-quoted paragraph 85 of the 1969 *North Sea Continental Shelf* cases. The Court not only expounded the main contents of the fundamental rule, but also indicated relevant sources of the law of equitable principles:

> It emerges from the history of the development of the legal régime of the continental shelf, which has been reviewed earlier, that the essential reason why the equidistance method is not to be regarded as a rule of law is that, if it were to be compulsorily applied in all situations, this would not be consonant with certain basic legal notions which, as has been observed in paragraphs 48 and 55, have from the beginning reflected the *opinio juris* in the matter of delimitation; those principles being that delimitation must be the object of agreement between the States concerned, and that such agreement must be arrived at in accordance with equitable principles. On a foundation of very general precepts of justice and good faith, actual rules of law are here involved which govern the delimitation of adjacent continental shelves – that is to say, rules binding upon States for all delimitations; – in short, it is not a question of applying equity simply as a matter of abstract justice, but of applying a rule of law which itself requires the application of equitable principles, in accordance with the ideas which have always underlain the development of the legal régime of the continental shelf in this field, namely:
>
> (a) the parties are under an obligation to enter into negotiations with a view to arriving at an agreement, and not merely to go through a formal process of negotiation as a sort of prior condition for the automatic application of a certain method of delimitation in the absence of agreement; they are under an obligation so to conduct themselves that the negotiations are meaningful, which will not be the case when either of them insists upon its own position without contemplating any modification of it;

(b) the parties are under an obligation to act in such a way that, in the particular case, and taking all the circumstances into account, equitable principles are applied, – for this purpose the equidistance method can be used, but other methods exist and may be employed, alone or in combination, according to the areas involved;

(c) for the reasons given in paragraphs 43 and 44, the continental shelf of any State must be the natural prolongation of its land territory and must not encroach upon what is the natural prolongation of the territory of another State.[143]

Thus, the fundamental rule of delimitation by agreement and in accordance with equitable principles is linked to a variety of sources. They are interrelated and not easy to discern.

A. The Truman Proclamation and legal thinking

The Court in the *North Sea Continental Shelf* cases held, in paragraph 85, that the fundamental rule of equity is inherent to 'certain basic legal notions' of delimitation. By referring to paragraphs 48 (recte 47) and 55 of the judgment, the Court relates these 'notions' to two major sources: the Truman Proclamation and the International Law Commission (ILC).

Firstly, the Court relied heavily upon the 1945 Truman Proclamation, which had formally introduced the concept of equitable principles into state practice.[144] The Proclamation was given 'a special status'[145] and was 'considered of having propounded the rules of law in this field'.[146] This conclusion was based on the perception and assessment that 'the two concepts – delimitation by mutual agreement and delimitation in accordance with equitable principles – have underlain all the subsequent history of the subject'.[147] Equally, the court relied upon the legal thinking of the ILC on the subject, as set forth in paragraphs 48 to 55 of the judgment.

The Court avoided qualifying *expressis verbis* these sources of law in 1969. Yet, given the references to state practice[148] and the emphasis of *opinio juris*,[149] it is likely that the fundamental rule of equity was conceived from the very beginning to be a rule of customary law. Qualifications to this effect without further elaboration in subsequent cases, particularly the 1977 *Channel Arbitration*,[150] confirm that view.

---

[143] ICJ Reports 1969, pp. 46–7, para. 85.
[144] See Chapter 4(III)(A)(2).
[145] ICJ Reports 1969, p. 33, para. 47.
[146] ICJ Reports 1969, p. 48, para. 86.
[147] ICJ Reports 1969, p. 47, para. 33.
[148] ICJ Reports 1969, p. 34, para. 47 in fine.
[149] ICJ Reports 1969, p. 46, para. 85.
[150] Channel Award, n. 18, para. 62.

In the light of the above examination of state practice,[151] the status of customary law of the fundamental rule of equity only exists for one part of the rule. There is no doubt that the obligation to seek agreement, or maybe to better the prohibition of unilateral delimitation, is firmly established in state practice and legal thinking, even if it was seen that early declarations of Arab states following the Truman Proclamation paradoxically claimed unilateral delimitation.[152] But the Court stated, in agreement with a majority of commentators, that by the end of the 1960s there still had not been either a sufficient body of practice or sufficient legal thinking to establish the model of equitable principles in customary law, the more so since the Court adopted in the very same case fairly stringent requirements and criteria on customary law (extensive and virtually uniform application, general recognition as a rule of law or legal obligation).[153]

In addition, it is doubtful whether in 1969 the legal thinking or *opinio juris* on a subject could be limited to the views expressed by the members of the ILC or even the body as a whole. Since *opinio juris* is an essential element upon which the legitimate expectations of particular conduct are based, it is essential that *opinio juris* is primarily expressed by governments. This does not imply excluding the work and views of the ILC; the Court's reference to the Commission in 1969 has greatly helped to shape equity[154] and to enhance the importance of this body. But such views on their own cannot suffice to fulfil the requirement of *opinio juris*. Both under a traditional, voluntary approach to customary law and under an approach based on legitimate expectations, expressions by governments themselves, responsible for the conduct of foreign affairs, remain essential.

B. The principle of peaceful settlement of disputes (Article 33 UN Charter)

In order to sustain the legal requirement of delimitation by agreement (the first part of the fundamental rule), the Court, in addition to the Truman Proclamation, invoked the general principle of peaceful settlement of disputes, inter alia, by means of international negotiations. The

---

[151] See Chapter 7.
[152] See Chapter 5(I)(A). See also ICJ Reports 1969, pp. 167–8 (dissenting opinion Koretsky).
[153] ICJ Reports 1969, p. 44, para. 74.
[154] See Müller, n. 52, p. 85, note 297 (*opinio juris* was an essential element in shaping the content of justice in the *North Sea* cases).

Court argued that the fundamental rule in that respect 'merely constitutes a special application of a principle which underlies all international relations, and which is moreover recognised in Article 33 of the Charter of the United Nations'.[155]

Given the fact that the parties to the 1969 *North Sea Continental Shelf* cases actually were engaged in a dispute, it was feasible to invoke the principle in that particular case. However, it is a different question whether the principle of peaceful settlement can provide a sufficient basis for a prohibition of unilateral delimitation as such. The principle inherently requires the existence of a dispute. It does not apply prior to the existence of a dispute, and it is perfectly conceivable that a maritime boundary would be unilaterally established without necessarily causing an international dispute. For example, the 1951 *Anglo-Norwegian Fisheries* case, affirmed by the 1974 *Fisheries Jurisdiction* cases, did not exclude a unilateral delimitation of seaward boundaries, provided that such delimitation was based on international law.[156]

The fundamental rule of equity which requires agreed settlement by means of negotiation or any other method – but at least acquiescence – in the context of maritime boundary delimitation between opposite or adjacent states, is therefore a more stringent rule than the general principle of peaceful settlement of disputes as expressed in Article 33 of the UN Charter. Consequently, the rule cannot only rely on this principle, but has to find a more specific foundation.

C. *Justice, good faith and equity in the North Sea Continental Shelf cases*

It may be that it was due to fairly weak evidence supporting the customary law justification of the substantive part of the fundamental rule of equity (delimitation in accordance with equitable principles) that the Court felt compelled to invoke a number of additional sources in paragraph 85 of the *North Sea* judgment. Thus, the legal concept of

---

[155] ICJ Reports 1969, p. 47, para. 86.
[156] ICJ Reports 1951, p. 132; ICJ Reports 1974, p. 23, para. 49: 'The delimitation of sea areas has always an international aspect; it cannot be dependent merely upon the will of the coastal State as expressed in its municipal law. Although it is true that the act of delimitation is necessarily a unilateral act, because only the coastal State is competent to undertake it, the validity of the delimitation with regard to other States depends upon international law.' Reference was made to this statement in the *Tunisia* v. *Libya* case, ICJ Reports 1982, p. 67, para. 87.

delimitation, the 'actual rules of law involved', was also held to rely upon 'a foundation of very general precepts of justice and good faith'. To the Court, this meant 'in short' that equity does not apply simply as a matter of abstract justice, but rather applies in accordance with the underlying principles of the continental shelf.

This reasoning by the Court has been the subject of a great deal of criticism from commentators, who felt that it uses overbroad and misleading language.[157] It may, however, be understood if justice and good faith are not expected to provide operational, formal sources of law, but rather material sources of inspiration, similar to those that helped frame the approach adopted by the Truman Proclamation, that was itself held by the Court to be the operational source of law.

Similarly, it seems that equity in paragraph 85 was equally meant to apply as a source of inspiration for justice, together with the underlying ideas of the continental shelf (in particular the ideas of agreed delimitation, consideration of relevant circumstances, respect of natural prolongation, and non-encroachment), rather than as a formal source of law. However, it is not clear whether the Court in 1969 intended to limit the general concept of equity to such functions as mere inspiration, or whether the Court's idea was to extend the basis of the fundamental rule beyond positive law. The following statement is ambiguous. It seems to refer simultaneously to equity as an additional source of law and also to exclude such independent functions at the same time:

> The Court comes next to the rule of equity. The legal basis of that rule in the particular case of the delimitation of the continental shelf has already been stated. It must however be noted that the rule also rests on a broader basis. Whatever the legal reasoning of a court of justice, its decisions must by definition be just, and therefore in that sense equitable. Nevertheless, when mention is made of a court dispensing justice or declaring the law, what is meant is that the decision finds its objective justification in considerations lying not outside but within the rules, and in this field it is precisely a rule of law that calls for the application of equitable principles. There is consequently no question in this case of any decision *ex aequo et bono*.[158]

---

[157] E.g. Brown, *The Legal Regime of Hydrospace*, n. 3, p. 70 ('It is submitted that the Court's Judgment suffers from an excess of deductive reasoning from vague premises'); Rothpfeffer, n. 27, p.109 ('misleadingly euphemistic' and having the doubtful consequence of endowing certain claims with moral superiority within a system being far apart from just sharing of resources').

[158] ICJ Reports 1969, p. 48, para. 88.

Perhaps it is not surprising that interpretations of this statement varied considerably amongst authors at the time. Differing views were expressed as to the function of equity in this context and its relationship to traditional perceptions of equity.[159] As a result, Brown considered it to be equity *infra* or *secundum legem*.[160] Friedmann argued that this is equity *contra legem*.[161] For Lauterpacht this was a law-making exercise,[162] while Bilge argued that it is neither *infra* nor *contra legem*, but instead is the application of a rule of customary law.[163]

It is evident that the main purpose of this paragraph was to refute contentions that, without the parties' authorization, the Court renders a decision *ex aequo et bono*. Perhaps it would then follow that equity would not add to the sources of positive law except for its traditional function as an instrument of interpretation (equity *infra legem*). From that perspective, it is misleading to invoke equity as a means of providing an additional, broader basis for the fundamental rule.

However, when viewed from a different angle, the very purpose of this paragraph could be seen to be the establishment of the principle of equity as an independent source of law. The concurring opinion by Judge Ammoun affirmed such a role for equity in much more explicit terms, characterizing it as an instrument to fill the lacuna caused by the absence of specific rules on maritime boundary delimitation.[164] Even without saying so, the court actually did just that. Given the fundamental rule of delimitation in accordance with equitable principles (Truman Proclamation), it could be expected that the Court would elaborate such equitable principles in more detail. Yet, it is telling that once the rule of equity was established, the Court refrained from shaping such normative principles and instead continued to elaborate on what it called factors relevant in the case. Such factors solely rely upon equity and are specifications thereof:

> it would ... be insufficient simply to rely on the rule of equity without giving some degree of indication as to the possible ways in which it might be applied in the present case.[165]

---

[159] See Introduction, I(B).
[160] See Brown, *The Legal Regime of Hydrospace*, n. 3, p. 196.
[161] Friedmann, n. 11, p. 236.   [162] Lauterpacht, n. 142.
[163] S. Bilge, 'Le Nouveau rôle des principes équitables en droit international' in E. Diez et al. (eds.), *Festschrift für R. Bindschedler* (Bern: Stämpfli, 1980), p. 105, p. 117.
[164] ICJ Reports 1969, pp. 132–6 (separate opinion, Judge Ammound).
[165] ICJ Reports 1969, p. 50, para. 92.

The fact that the Court at this stage did not speak of equitable principles in their own right, as the Truman Proclamation would suggest, but rather spoke only of factors and considerations, equally suggests that the rule of equity was already the essential source of law that operated in the *North Sea* cases.

D. Judicial legislation

Although there are indications that equitable principles were considered to be part of customary law in 1969, the Court carefully avoided explicitly stating this. Neither did the Court clarify whether it also meant to derive the fundamental rule from 'the broader basis' of equity in order to apply it as a general principle of law in accordance with Article 38(1)(c) of the ICJ Statute, as Judge Ammoun suggested in his elaborate separate opinion.[166]

Such ambiguity, and the evolution and establishment of the fundamental rule of delimitation in the North Sea and subsequent cases, amounts to a paradigm of the Court's role in shaping international law, and therefore of its judicial activism, faced with the pending and complex international disputes before it. The Court was confronted with a situation that did not allow for qualification of the foundations of the fundamental rule in precise terms. Given the lack of applicable customary and treaty law, the Court was theoretically left to apply general principles of law and related precedents and to rely on doctrine expressed by jurists. However, at the time, neither of these resources was clearly pertinent.

In the context of equity, the Court referred to the advisory opinion of *Judgments of the Administrative Tribunal of the I.L.O. Upon Complaints Against Unesco*[167] and the *Corfu Channel* case.[168] These references, however, merely show that the allocation of compensation based on reasonableness rather than on specific rules (even if applying the term *ex aequo et bono* in the context of compensation) does not imply an intention to depart from the principles of law.[169] The precedents support the proposition that reasonable decisions remain within the ambit of the law, even though there are areas of law not governed by specific rules.

Such precedents certainly support the view that the fundamental rule can be a legal concept. But they do not help to establish it as a rule of maritime boundary law. They help even less to shape particular equitable

---

[166] ICJ Reports 1969, pp. 132–43.   [167] ICJ Reports 1956, p. 86
[168] ICJ Reports 1949, p. 4.   [169] ICJ Reports 1969, p. 49, para. 88.

principles. Astonishingly enough, the 1909 *Grisbadarna* case and the 1951 *Anglo/Norwegian Fisheries Jurisdiction* case that could have helped to do so, remained without any reference.[170] Finally, apart from using the work of the ILC, the Court followed its practice of not referring to legal doctrine and particular authors. Indeed, the concept of equitable principles was not a predominant approach in legal writing at the time, unlike in the interwar period.[171] At the time, legal thinking was shaped instead by the positivist model of equidistance–special circumstances contained in Article 6 of the Shelf Convention.

With respect to established sources of law in Article 38(1) of the Statute, the conclusion that the Court faced major difficulties in attaching the fundamental rule to the canon of established sources of international law in a conclusive manner is inevitable. The shaping and specification of the substantive part of the fundamental rule involved a significant degree of judicial activism and judicial legislation.[172] In a process of trial and error, the Court set out to develop the law of maritime boundary delimitation based on a broad principle of equity; attempting to satisfy the needs of international relations of states which had been left without sufficient guidance to settle complex cases in a relatively new field of international allocation of resources.

The phenomenon of judicial activism and legislation is not unique to the problem of long-distance maritime boundary delimitation. Judicial landmarks often exhibit the characteristics of deliberate decisions to break new ground, displaying the qualities and virtues of meticulous, evolutionary reasoning within the existing fabric of law and well-established precedents. This phenomenon can be readily observed in constitutional law, particularly when courts refer to broad concepts, such as justice or equity.[173]

The same is true in international law. The process of developing rules and principles for the delimitation of the new boundaries reinforces the fact that, to quote Brierly: 'the act of the Court is a creative act despite our

---

[170] Cf. section II(A) in this chapter.   [171] See Introduction to this book.
[172] In particular Rothpfeffer, see n. 27, p. 91 ('One must go outside the practice of the PCIJ and the ICJ to find parallels to the North Sea Continental Shelf cases').
[173] See e.g. the landmark case *Brown* v. *Board of Education*, 349 US 294, 300 (1955) (strongly relying upon equity to set a new course: ('Traditionally, equity has been characterised by a practical flexibility in shaping its remedies and by a facility for adjusting and reconciling public and private needs. These cases ... call for the exercise of these traditional attributes of equity power').

conspiracy to represent it as something else',[174] and that a clear distinction in the application of different sources of law is often difficult to make.[175] Customary law and general principles of law, as much as the general principles of international law, often overlap and are mutually supportive in the establishment of the legitimacy of a normative concept. Moreover, transitions from morality to law are equally fluent. The business of maritime boundary delimitation confirms the findings of Lauterpacht, who said of the judicial process: 'The imperceptible process in which the judicial decision ceases to be an application of existing law and becomes a source of law for the future is almost a religious mystery.'[176] The process reaffirms the importance of case law as a stabilizer in the emergence of the law from broad precepts of justice and equity into the fabric of law. Reviewing the history of the cases related to maritime boundary delimitation, Judge Cardozo's famous dictum about the twilight existence of emerging legal norms in *New Jersey* v. *Delaware* comes to mind:

> International law or the law that governs between States, has at times, like the common law within States, a twilight existence during which it is hardly distinguishable from morality or justice, till at length the *imprimatur* of a court attests to it jural quality.[177]

Indeed, the emergence of the fundamental rule of law on the delimitation of the new boundaries out of ambiguities into a well-established fundamental rule that was no longer challenged is one of the most illustrative examples of the process of law and equity during the recent history of international law. It provides a deeper insight into the mysteries of the law-making process by the judicial branch of international law and relations, which remains unimpaired, even during times of paramount

---

[174] James L. Brierly, 'The Judicial Settlement of International Disputes' in J. L. Brierly, H. Lauterpacht and C. H. M. Waldock, *The Basis of Obligation in International Law* (Oxford: Clarendon Press, 1958), p. 98.

[175] See C. Wilfred Jenks, *The Prospects of International Adjudication* (London: Stevens & Sons, 1964), p. 264 ('Custom as a basis of legal obligation neither can be nor should be rigidly separated from general principles of law, equity, public policy and practical convenience').

[176] Hersch Lauterpacht, *The Development of International Law by the International Court* (London: Stevens & Sons, 1958, reprinted 1982), p. 21.

[177] *New Jersey* v. *Delaware*, 291 US 383 (1983); Oscar Schachter, 'Creativity and Objectivity in International Tribunals' in R. Bernhardt, W. K. Geck, G. Jaenicke and H. Steinberger (eds.), *Völkerrecht als Rechtsordnung, internationale Gerichtsbarkeit, Menschenrechte, Festschrift für Hermann Mosler* (Berlin, Heidelberg, New York: Springer Verlag, 1983), p. 46.

positivist, treaty law, as the main source of contemporary international law. In the era of human rights, enshrined as basic standards and benchmarks of justice and often codified in international agreements or constitutions, courts do not find it necessary to take recourse to justice and equity as a prime source of orientation and legitimacy. Where such standards do not exist, as in the case of international maritime resource allocation, the process of judicial law-making inherently relies on and is inspired by the concept of justice or equity in the context of a particular setting.

The evolution of equity into a prime source of the fundamental rule is an interesting phenomenon. Normally, the law evolves the other way round. Starting out as general principles, it eventually finds more concise foundations in treaty law or customary law. The reverse process in maritime boundary law may have four explanations. Firstly, the Court's primary foundation of the fundamental rule of equity on customary law was significantly weakened by critical reviews. It could hardly serve as a solid foundation. Secondly, the concept of natural prolongation, one of the main ideas underlying the *North Sea* reasoning, failed to develop into a decisive concept in subsequent cases.[178] This further weakened existing foundations. Thirdly, the debates at UNCLOS III and the evolution toward a result-oriented approach in the Convention reinforced a trend to de-link the fundamental rule from close ties to the concept of the continental shelf. Finally, the evolution of the EEZ required new foundations. The fundamental norm related to this new zone could not rely directly upon the Truman Proclamation on the shelf. Significantly, the twin declaration on fishery zones at the time, as well as all subsequent declarations on the EEZ or related zones (with the exception of the 1983 Reagan Proclamation), contained no references to the equitable principles of delimitation.[179]

If the Court, instead of looking for positivist sources, had been able to rely from the beginning more directly on equity as a general principle of law, it would have been possible to avoid the confusions which were caused by insufficient evidence provided by customary law. Calling upon equity as the prime source of law and the justification of equitable principles would have provided a more transparent reflection of what the Court was in fact doing.

---

[178] See Chapter 6.
[179] See Chapter 6(I)(B); Marjorie M. Whiteman, *Digest of International Law* (Paris: Editions du Centre National de la Recherche Scientifique, 1963–1973), vol. IV, pp. 954–5.

E. Decision-making ex aequo et bono *in disguise?*

Given the high degree of creative judicial contribution to maritime boundary delimitation and the difficulties in attributing the foundation of equitable principles consistently to one or more sources within the narrow framework of Article 38(1) of the ICJ Statute, the question arises as to whether equitable principles are relying upon paragraph 2 of this Article. If they are, then the Court is producing decisions *ex aequo et bono*, contrary to its repeated assurances otherwise. Neither the Permanent Court of Justice (PCIJ) nor the ICJ have ever explicitly relied upon paragraph 2. One must ask, however, if the judges in the *North Sea Continental Shelf* cases and subsequent cases actually ruled *ex aequo et bono* under the guise of legal operation and interpretation, as the critical reviews continue to argue?

The *North Sea Continental Shelf* judgment created considerable confusion; there are almost as many different views as there are comments on the case. Many of the reactions to the judgment's legal foundations and the fundamental rule, though, were negative at the outset. Commentators emphasized the novelty of the concept, which was without precedent in international law.[180] It was argued that the Court had exceeded its authority by stating normative criteria about how delimitation should be undertaken.[181] It was further argued that the Court had in reality handed down a decision *ex aequo et bono* under the guise of legal operation and interpretation,[182] or – to similar effect – that the equitable principles were void of any normative character, merely indicating the goal to be achieved.[183]

In and outside the Court, the fiercest objections to the Court's rulings were expressed by judges and authors arguing the case of equidistance–special circumstances as the appropriate and established customary rule of delimitation. From this perspective, the role of equity can merely be one of mitigating the harsh edges of the main

---

[180] Rothpfeffer, n. 27, p. 91.   [181] Marek, n. 139, p. 71.
[182] Friedmann, n. 11, p. 236. See also Judge Tanaka, ICJ Reports 1969 p. 197 (dissenting opinion Tanaka): 'It may be said that the Court's answer amounts to the suggestion that [the parties] settle their dispute by negotiations according to *ex aequo et bono* without any indication as to what are the principles and rules of international law, namely judicial principles and rules vested with obligatory power rather than considerations of expediency – factors and criteria – which are not incorporated in the legal norm and which the Parties did not request to answer.'
[183] Etienne Grisel, 'The Lateral Boundaries of the Continental Shelf and the Judgment of the International Court of Justice in the North Sea Continental Shelf Cases' (1970) 64 *American Journal of International Law* 526, 589.

rule. It cannot be considered a foundation of the rule itself. Critical objections to the Court's approach increased to the extent that the fundamental rule shifted toward a more result-oriented rule. With this evolution, in particular by the *Tunisia v. Libya* Court and the *Gulf of Maine* Chamber, and again by the *St. Pierre and Miquelon* Tribunal of Arbitration, characterizations of the judgments as being an application of *ex aequo et bono*, both in fact and result *a fortiori*, increased. In subsequent cases, these characterizations were most authoritatively expressed by Judges Gros, Oda and Weil in their dissenting opinions.

Judge Gros argued that the 1982 decision is contrary to the more contained concept of equity adopted in 1969. What the Court did, Gros proposes, intrinsically amounts to *ex aequo et bono*; a mere compromise, as opposed to equity. According to him, the only circumstances in which equidistance should not be applied are when it would produce 'extraordinary, unnatural or unreasonable results'.[184] Gros' critique culminates in the rhetorical question: 'is it still a conception of equity?'[185] This line of persistent objections continued in 1984.[186]

Similarly, Judge Oda has repeatedly (although not right from the outset) insisted on the appropriateness of the equidistance–special circumstances rule. He also frames his criticism of the view of his brethren in scholarly dissenting opinions.[187] According to Judge Oda, equitable principles cannot be rules and principles of law, but rather are truisms, stating that the Court has to achieve an equitable solution.[188] In 1985, he restated this view. Again Oda claimed that the equidistance–special circumstances rule, as suggested in the 1958 Conventions, still remains the basic rule for the delimitation of the continental shelf[189] and that equity cannot apply except within this rule.[190]

---

[184] ICJ Reports 1982, p. 149, para. 12, referring to ICJ Reports 1969, p. 24, para. 24.
[185] ICJ Reports 1982, at p. 152, para. 17 in fine.
[186] Dissenting opinion, ICJ Reports 1984, p. 388, para. 47 ff.: ('The course taken since February 1982 has been to indulge in equity beyond the law, detached from any established rules, based solely on whatever each group of judges seized of a case declares itself able and free to appreciate in accordance with its political or economic views of the moment'). See in particular his dissenting opinion in ICJ Reports 1984, p. 361, para. 3 and para. 31 (1982 judgment amounted to sudden change in case law); p. 377, para. 27 (subjectivity of equity); p. 378, para. 28 (incorporation of 1872 dissent); p. 383, para. 38 (equity in the meaning of the 1969 and 1977 cases was rejected); p. 385, para. 41 (present concept of equity leads to government of judges).
[187] ICJ Reports 1982, p. 260, para. 165.   [188] ICJ Reports 1982, p. 255, para. 155.
[189] ICJ Reports 1985, p. 160, para. 67.   [190] ICJ Reports 1985, p. 159, paras. 65–6.

Judge Weil's essential reason for voting against the Decision of the *St. Pierre and Miquelon* Court of Arbitration was that 'the delimitation in the strange form of mushroom which is its result does not seem to me to be founded "on the basis of law"'.[191] After showing the problems arising out of the application of the equitable principles used by the Court of Arbitration, he came to the conclusion that:

> It must nevertheless be realised that accommodating the interests of the Parties is an inherent requirement of the fundamental norm of an equitable result; one may even ask oneself whether the attribution to each Party of a 'just and equitable share of the space involved' (*1969 ICJ Rep. 21, para. 17*) – which is what the courts since 1969 have asserted that they did not wish to do – was not included in the fundamental norm as an embryo in the egg.[192]

In general terms, the problem involved goes to the heart of what constitutes a legal operation in international relations, as distinct from other forms of interactions and settlement of disputes, in particular negotiations and conciliation, or decision-making by a court on the basis of Article 38(2) ICJ Statute. Nothing less than the relationship of law and *ex aequo et bono* are implied.

Neither the notion of law, nor of *ex aequo et bono* are clearly defined in international law. Article 38 of the Statute of the PCIJ was deliberately framed on the basis of the positivist distinction between law and decision-making *ex aequo et bono*. Equity as a specific principle was explicitly excluded.[193] In the *Free Zone* case, the majority of the Court declined to construe the law to include functions of judicial law-making, without explicit reference to *ex aequo et bono*. Thus, under the impression of this case, *ex aequo* was essentially perceived as 'a species of legislative activity'.[194] Article 28 of the General Act of 26 September 1928, which introduced compulsory arbitration between Members of the League of Nations, provided for decision-making *ex aequo et bono* where rules of law were absent.[195] This affirms that *ex aequo* was historically conceived to be a legislative function.

There is no doubt that the Court sought to establish factors that could be applied generally, rather than being limited to the particular case. Indeed, subsequent cases show that the fundamental rule of equity, albeit

---

[191] See n. 112, (1992) 31 ILM 1197, para. 2.
[192] See n. 112, (1992) 31 ILM 1212–13, para. 26.   [193] See Jenks, n. 175, p. 320.
[194] Lauterpacht, see n. 142, p. 213; see also Jenks, n. 175, p. 321.
[195] See de Visscher, n. 56, p. 22.

THE RULE OF EQUITY 433

changed in an evolutionary process, relied upon the legislative findings of the 1969 *North Sea* cases.

From a narrow perspective of the traditional perceptions of the judicial function, defined in terms of the application of law – and limited to that function – it may be argued that the creative approach taken by the *North Sea* Court was *ultra vires* and therefore necessarily turned the result into a decision *ex aequo et bono* without the necessary consent of the parties. On the other hand, taking into account the creative role which the ICJ and its predecessor have played in the process of international law, it is doubtful whether such a conclusion is still accurate in light of the overall practice of the Court and tribunals. No case of applying *non licet* is known to this writer; courts have never refused to decline judgment due to a lack of existing rules. Indeed, maritime boundary law is by no means the only field of 'judicial legislation through the application of general principles of law'.[196] But courts often use their quasi-legislative powers in these other fields without causing commentators to qualify such activities as decision-making *ex aequo et bono* or being *ultra vires*.

It seems, then, that the problem of *ex aequo et bono* in maritime boundary law was largely reinforced by the explicit references to it in the context of equity. Why has the active role of the Court only created a problem in this instance and not in other ones? It is submitted that this is due to the more fundamental changes in the fabric of international law since the Statute of the ICJ was framed under the predominant doctrines of positivism. Since the positivist concept of international law became dominant, general principles such as good faith and equity have been accepted as a part of international law as such.[197] With these principles inside the body of law, legislative functions became almost inherent to the work of the courts when they shaped and further elaborated concepts derived from such principles. Acquiescence and estoppel are examples in point. Both rely on good faith and equity.[198] In addition, constitutional

---

[196] Lauterpacht, n. 142, p. 158 ss.
[197] See in particular Manley O. Hudson, *International Tribunals, Past and Future* (Washington: Carnegie Endowment for International Peace, 1944), p. 103; see Jenks, n. 175, p. 321.
[198] See in particular the *Gulf of Maine* case, ICJ Reports 1984, p. 305, para. 130 ('The Chamber observes that in any case the concepts of acquiescence and estoppel, irrespective of the status accorded to them by international law, both follow from the fundamental principles of good faith and equity'); see also Hersch Lauterpacht, 'International Law' in E. Lauterpacht (ed.), *Collected Papers of Hersch Lauterpacht* (Cambridge University Press, 1970), p. 257 (estoppel is an 'equitable principle'); Müller, n. 52, pp. 9, 41 (the content of the doctrine of estoppel and acquiescence both essentially rely

and broad principles, contained in the UN Charter, became part of the law, leaving room for much judicial interpretation. The same is true for the advent of human rights protection in international law, all of which need interpretation beyond the letter of the law. Although there can be no free-wheeling judicial legislation, there is *per se* more room for judicial activism within the fabric of contemporary international law than previously.

Applying equity to fill the gaps between rules of maritime boundary law is therefore a paradigm of the Court's broad legislative powers. The evolution and broadening of international law cannot be without effect on the notion of *ex aequo et bono* within the law. The essence of it no longer is rule-making, but is a decision made without applying or shaping general rules of law. It stands for the proposition of discretionary decisions on the basis of compromise, morality and the opportunity of 'utilité pratique' and '*bonum*', as de Visscher says.[199] It implies a dispensation from applying the law and the task to achieve a just and satisfactory result. In the context of maritime boundary law, this means that an *ad hoc* judgment that the Court feels will result in acceptable distributive justice for both the parties concerned will be implied. It is the paradigm of a result-oriented operation. *Ex aequo et bono* is therefore not bound by legal considerations. Nor is it bound by the application and interpretation of rules, or even by the shaping of rules on the basis of broad principles, which have to meet the test of generalization and further application in subsequent situations.

A general qualification of the activity of the Court in maritime boundary law therefore depends on the particular notion of *ex aequo et bono* applied. Given the fact that there were no established rules in customary law concerning delimitation of the new boundaries in 1969, the Court necessarily had to engage in rule-making. If decision-making is perceived as judicial legislation, the *North Sea* cases indeed amounted to decision-making *ex aequo et bono*. If decision-making *ex aequo et bono* is defined in narrow terms outside and without regard to the law, however, the rule-making activity of the Court cannot be discretionary decision-making.

Instead, the elaboration of the fundamental rule of equitable principles and of criteria applicable to delimitation based on all the sources of law cited, including the underlying ideas of the continental shelf in the *North*

---

upon the idea of protecting good faith); Vladimir D. Degan, *L'Équité en droit international* (The Hague: Martinus Nijhoff, 1970), p. 194 (radix of estoppel in equity).

[199] De Visscher, n. 56, pp. 23, 26.

Sea cases, do not amount to *ex aequo et bono*, since these criteria are capable of being applied in other cases as well. They were of a legislative nature even if the factors were shaped on the basis of, and influenced by, the particular facts of the case.

Whether or not subsequent cases amount to *ex aequo et bono*, it is only at this stage that the approaches taken by the courts can be examined in each case. It is therefore not possible to define in abstract terms whether maritime boundary delimitation effected by the Courts since 1969 amounts to decision-making *ex aequo et bono*. Answers depend on the reasoning in each case. The distinction between legal and extra-legal operations much more depends on a test of whether the Court adopts a reasoned, principled and methodological approach, based on established or newly developed general rules and principles which could enjoy general application. To the extent that judgments adopt solutions on an *ad hoc* basis in order to reach a balanced, practical and acceptable result, but still fall short of applying rules and principles that can be generalized, the decision is, in fact, one of *ex aequo et bono*.

In conclusion, it is not possible to allocate the application of equitable principles to decision-making *ex aequo et bono* at the outset and to characterize the model of equidistance–special circumstances as belonging *per se* to the realm of law and equity. Both may be applied by law, and both may take into account factors, considerations or special circumstances outside the realm of law. Answers depend on the quality of each judgment and its reasoning. It will be seen that the record is a mixed one. The decisions show both rule-oriented and discretionary elements.[200]

F. Subsequent case law

1. Paramount foundation in equity

Whatever the function of equity in the *North Sea Continental Shelf* cases, it is most interesting that equity eventually developed into the sole and paramount source of law of the fundamental rule and of equitable principles in subsequent decisions of the ICJ until the provisions of the LOS Convention became operative in due course upon the entry into force in 1982 of the agreement.

While the 1977 *Channel Arbitration* simply qualified equitable principles in terms of customary law,[201] the 1982 *Tunisia* v. *Libya* case seems to suggest an identity of equity and equitable principles. It is worth noting

---

[200] See above, para. II and Chapter 9.   [201] See e.g. Channel Arbitration, n. 18, para. 97.

that in the following paragraph from the *Tunisia* v. *Libya* case, the equitable principles are dealt with absent any separation from equity as an emanation of justice:

> Equity as a legal concept is a direct emanation of the idea of justice. The Court whose task is by definition to administer justice is bound to apply it. In the course of the history of legal systems the term 'equity' has been used to define various legal concepts. It was often contrasted with the rigid rules of positive law, the severity of which had to be mitigated in order to do justice. In general, this contrast has no parallel in the development of international law; the legal concept of equity is a general principle directly applicable as law. Moreover, when applying positive international law, a court may choose among several possible interpretations of the law the one which appears in the light of the circumstances of the case, to be closest to the requirements of justice. Application of equitable principles is to be distinguished from a decision *ex aequo et bono*. The Court can take such a decision only on condition that the Parties agree (Art. 38, para. 2, of the Statute), and the Court is then freed from the strict application of legal rules in order to bring about an appropriate settlement. The task of the Court in the present case is quite different: it is bound to apply equitable principles as part of international law, and to balance up the various considerations which it regards as relevant in order to produce an equitable result. While it is clear that no rigid rules exist as to the exact weight to be attached to each element in the case, this is very far from being an exercise of discretion or conciliation; nor is it an operation of distributive justice.[202]

This paragraph, which one author concluded to be 'une glose assez embarrassée sur la notion d'équité en droit international',[203] serves, together with the 1969 cases, to help distinguish the legal concept of equity from decision-making *ex aequo et bono*. Unlike existing precedent however, in this case equity also constitutes the principal foundation of the fundamental rule. References to the *North Sea* cases mainly relate to the notion of the continental shelf, and particularly to the concept of natural prolongation.[204] But these precedents were not taken into account for the refinement and reinforcement of the existing foundations of equitable principles. The same is true for the Court's consideration and subsequent state practice, legal thinking, and in particular developments within the UNCLOS III 'accepted trends' that the Court was obliged to

---

[202] ICJ Reports 1982, p. 60, para. 71.
[203] See Decaux, 'L'Arrêt de la Chambre de la Cour internationale de justice dans l'affaire de la délimitation de la frontière maritime dans le Golf du Maine (Canada/Etats-Unis)', n. 3, p. 357.
[204] ICJ Reports 1982, pp. 43–9, paras. 36–50.

take into account by the Special Agreement and also did *proprio motu* in the process of newly emerging customary law.[205]

After the notion of natural prolongation (a main idea in the *North Sea* cases and a starting point for both parties in this case) turned out to be irrelevant in the present case, the rules and principles of delimitation were left to rely solely on the principle of equity emanating from the idea of justice. It is perhaps not a coincidence that the new foundation corresponds with the more flexible result-oriented approach described above.[206]

The 1984 *Gulf of Maine* case equally seems to base its concept of equitable criteria directly on equity. The concept of equity as a lead-rule (Aréchaga) proliferated. The Chamber held that:

> any agreement or other equivalent solution should involve the application of equitable criteria, namely criteria derived from equity – whether they are designated 'principles' or criteria.[207]

In 1985, the Court reaffirmed its obligation to apply equity as a direct emanation of justice, as expounded in the 1982 case.[208] However, the Court also restated the more restricted concept of equity from the *North Sea* cases, as linked to the underlying ideas of the continental shelf.[209] The attempt to return to the roots of legal foundation corresponds to the shift toward a more rule-oriented approach.

2. Foundation in the LOS Convention

Under the LOS Convention, the legal foundations for maritime boundary delimitation are part of positive law with Articles 74 and 83 of the Convention. No longer, in most cases, is there a need to rely upon the fundamental rule of equity in addressing maritime boundary delimitation. The issue is no longer discussed, and decisions merely refer to the applicable law.[210] Reference to international law as well as the requirement of achieving equitable results, however, continues to incorporate the body of law developing on the basis of the fundamental rule prior to the operation of these provisions. Equity continues to play an important role and foundation in the search of equitable principles applicable within the LOS Convention.

The 2002 *Cameroon* v. *Nigeria* case set the stage for a rules-based approach under the maxim of the equitable result (Articles 74 and

---

[205] ICJ Reports 1982, p. 38, para. 24.   [206] Chapter 6 and above, para. II.
[207] ICJ Reports 1984, p. 292, para. 89.   [208] ICJ Reports 1985, p. 39, para. 45.
[209] ICJ Reports 1985, referring to para. 85.   [210] E.g. ICJ Reports 2009, p. 74 para. 31.

83 UNCLOS), but recalled equity as the legal foundation. In this connection, the Court stressed that:

> delimiting with a concern to achieving an equitable result, as required by current international law, is not the same as delimiting in equity. The Court's jurisprudence shows that, in disputes relating to maritime delimitation, equity is not a method of delimitation, but solely an aim that should be borne in mind in effecting the delimitation.[211]

The Tribunal in the 2006 *Barbados* v. *Trinidad and Tobago* Arbitration summarized the emergence of the rules-based approach as captured in UNCLOS and prevalent in the case law of the last decade. First, the Tribunal held that:

> Since the very outset, courts and tribunals have taken into consideration elements of equity in reaching a determination of a boundary line over maritime areas. This is also the approach stipulated by UNCLOS Articles 74 and 83, in conjunction with the broad reference to international law.[212]

But the Tribunal then also held that equitable considerations *per se* are an imprecise concept in light of the need for stability and certainty in the outcome of the legal process.[213] It thus states that:

> The search for predictable, objectively determined criteria for delimitation, as opposed to subjective findings lacking precise legal or methodological bases, emphasised that the role of equity lies within and not beyond the law.[214]

The Tribunal recalled that this search for an approach that would accommodate both the need for predictability and stability within the rule of law and the need for flexibility in the outcome that could meet the requirements of equity resulted in the identification of a variety of criteria and methods of delimitation.[215] It concluded that '[c]ertainty, equity, and stability are thus integral parts of the process of delimitation'.[216]

G. Towards a set of independent equitable principles

The 1985 *Libya* v. *Malta* case, as indicated before, acknowledged the normative character of equitable principles as applied as a matter of international law for the first time. These principles, mentioned in

---

[211] *Cameroon v. Nigeria*, n. 120, para. 294.
[212] *Barbados/Trinidad and Tobago*, n. 120, para. 229.   [213] Ibid., para. 230.
[214] Ibid., referring to *Libya v. Malta*, p. 13.
[215] *Barbados/Trinidad and Tobago*, n. 120, para. 232.   [216] Ibid., para. 244.

terms of examples, still depend on the foundation of the principle of equity in this case. Could they become principles of their own, independent sources of law of maritime boundary delimitation on their own terms and in their own right? Could they render the principle of equity dispensable as a proper source of law in the present context?

In the process of legal development by trial and error, it is perfectly conceivable that equitable principles transcend their original source, the principle of equity, and develop the general law of the new maritime boundaries into more operational rules that are directly applicable. Historically, such a process corresponds to the functions of equity in English law that provided a basis for new and gradually more specific rules that responded to new societal needs, which the more rigid system of common law was not able to produce. Whether or not such a process is possible very much depends on the quality of the equitable principles. Whether or not they are or may become primary sources of law of delimitation depends on their ability to provide operational rules and a methodology to apply them in a coherent way.

The next chapters seek to identify and shape a set of such principles that will provide the basis for more specific rules on maritime boundary delimitation in future international law.

9

Conceptual issues and the context of equity

I. The conceptual task

A. The quest for equitable standards

The fundamental rule of delimitation, essentially based on equity, is a legal concept. It is meant to provide an approach to maritime boundary delimitation in general public international law that is different from delimitation *ex aequo et bono*. Chapter 8 demonstrates that it is a rule of judge-made law which was eventually incorporated into the positive law of the Convention on the Law of the Sea. The courts have emphasized the legal quality being the essence of delimitation by equity in the present context of maritime boundary delimitation. Yet, the fundamental rule merely offers a starting point. Inherently, the substance of it – delimitation in accordance with equitable principles taking into account all relevant circumstances in order to achieve an equitable result – has to be defined and shaped in more concrete terms in order to qualify as a legally operational concept. In turn, equitable standards (encompassing equitable principles, circumstances, criteria and factors) need to be defined. The mutual relationship of such standards needs clarification. A proper methodology has to be developed in order to apply such standards under the facts of each particular case.

Indeed, the long-term viability and efficiency of the still fragile, judge-made rule of equity fully depends, as a legal concept, upon whether it brings about a number of defined and settled normative and operational standards capable of reducing overly broad discretion and subjectivism to an optimal degree, whatever their form, terminology and normative levels. Comparable to the evolution of equity in English law, the fundamental rule needs to develop into operational standards. Likewise, in international maritime boundary law, it has to achieve a stage of maturity where it effectively provides guidance in diplomatic negotiations and shows qualities of increased predictability in judicial settlements. A discussion of the evolution and sources of the zones and the fundamental rule shows that the law of delimitation cannot merely rely upon broad notions of justice, fairness and good faith. As the Court held in 1969:

> It is a truism to say that the determination of the maritime boundary must be equitable; rather is the problem above all one of defining the means whereby the delimitation can be carried out in such a way as to be recognised as equitable ... [I]t would ... be insufficient simply to rely on the rule of equity without giving some degree of indication as to the possible ways in which it might be applied in the present case.[1]

This programme, set out in the 1969 *North Sea* cases, which involves the tentative finding and giving of 'some degree of indication' is still in evolution. The present three-step approach still leaves unresolved the relationship of equitable principles, circumstances and factors to be taken into account. The process has not yet been completed and perhaps will never be. The problem aptly defined by the Court entails both the search for the means with respect to substance and to the methodology of delimitation. It is a matter of finding equitable standards and applying them to the particularities of each case of delimitation in a consistent manner. Equitable principles and criteria have to be framed, as closely as possible, in terms of the underlying concepts and purposes of the respective maritime zones of the continental shelf and the EEZ, respectively. Such reliance on the functions may require different factors to be taken into account. For example, geological factors may be relevant to the former, and ecological factors to the latter, while surface geography may serve the two at the same time. However, this does not mean that the principles, criteria, factors and other guidelines relevant to the process of delimitation can simply be derived from these concepts. The underlying notions only provide a starting point, and the framing of operational factors and rules is an extensively creative process. At the same time, the experience and assessment of strict rules and the failed attempts to codify such rules in maritime boundary law teaches us that the operation cannot lead to a set of strict rules comparable to mathematical equidistance, as is sometimes suggested. Such a result, again, would inevitably call for exceptions, undermining the rules as such. In other words: workable principles, guidelines, criteria or factors should be aspired to, rather than overly detailed rules. Specification in the present context still remains essentially linked to the particularities of each case.

---

[1] *North Sea Continental Shelf Cases (Federal Republic of Germany v. Denmark; Federal Republic of Germany v. Netherlands)*, ICJ Reports 1969, p. 50, para. 92.

Regulation by equity remains fact-intensive. At the same time, the normative potential of equity should not be underestimated. The required degree of flexibility must not discourage efforts to substantiate the rule of equity to an optimal degree. Equity is perfectly capable of developing, over time and perhaps in a process of trial and error, a set of normative standards that may ultimately even become independent from the source of equity.

The process of making, shaping and using equitable standards in maritime boundary law is therefore more aptly understood as a process of conceptualization and specification of equitable principles and standards. It is neither a process simply of law-making nor of merely applying the law, but instead is a combination of both. This renders the issue of relevance and importance way beyond maritime boundary delimitation. It entails a legal methodology which is capable of radiating into other areas of law where precedents and judicial work has remained absent or much more fragmented. Yet, since equity as such is the most elusive legal concept and abstract point of reference in all legal systems, national and international, conceptualization and specification are even more important here than elsewhere. The task entails a number of objectives. It comprises not merely the shaping and making of equitable principles and standards, but also the clarification of their form, normative levels and mutual interactions, as well as other elements operative in maritime boundary delimitation, such as existing titles, including third party rights. Broadly speaking, it comprises the development of a coherent general system and methodology of maritime boundary delimitation based on the fundamental rule of equity. Specification, on the other hand, is a somewhat narrower term. It is used here to encompass the use of equitable principles and standards in a particular case. This operation entails both elements of application and creation of the law, and the results of this operation feed back at the conceptual level. The terms are inherently intertwined.

B. The process in case law

A review of the case law shows that the process of conceptualization and specification is well under way in maritime boundary law; but it is far from being completed in a process of trial and error. It has shown a very slow, tentative and reluctant evolution throughout more than sixty-five years since the 1945 Truman Proclamation. Yet, it demonstrates some progress toward more substantive principles and standards as experience has increased. Through a process of trial and error, there has been a movement towards situating the set of legal principles within the legal concept of the respective zone. It is no longer fully open-ended, at least in the case of judicial settlements.[2] Future experience may refine the relevant principles even further.

Equally, attitudes of the ICJ and its Chambers toward a general conceptualization of equity have evolved over time. Given the novelty of the matter, a case-by-case approach was emphasized in 1969. The judgment cautioned against the desire to 'over systematize' or 'over conceptualize' the application of equitable principles.[3] The Court held that states are actually free to adopt any criteria: 'In fact, there is no legal limit to the considerations which states may take into account for the purpose of making sure that they apply equitable procedures'.[4] At the same time, the Court elaborated quite a comprehensive list of factors, considerations, ideas and elements, without using uniform connotations, that were more or less loosely related to the general principle of natural prolongation and domination of the land over the sea: the geology of the shelf; geographical configuration; the unity of deposits; a reasonable degree of proportionality; and an equal division of overlapping areas.[5] The operative part of the judgment, which instructed the parties to participate in further negotiations, obliged them to effect delimitation 'in accordance with equitable principles, taking account of all the relevant circumstances'.[6] The Court refrained from developing a coherent method and from defining the legal relationship of equitable principles and relevant circumstances. Subsequent cases did not seek to improve and systematically stabilize the tentative approach of 1969. The cases brought additional

---

[2] ICJ Reports 1969, p. 50, para. 92, *Arbitration between the United Kingdom of Great Britain and Northern Ireland and the French Republic on the Delimitation of the Continental Shelf, Decisions of the Court of Arbitration dated June 30, 1977 and 14 March 1978*, Command Paper 7438, March 1978, reprinted in 18 ILM (1979), 397 (hereinafter Channel Award), para. 245; *Case Concerning the Continental Shelf (Libyan Arab Jamahiriya v. Malta)*, ICJ Reports 1985, p. 40, para. 47 ('there is 'assuredly no closed list of considerations'), as recalled in *Arbitral Tribunal Constituted Pursuant to Article 287, and in Accordance with Annex VII, of the United Nations Convention on the Law of the Sea in the Matter of an Arbitration between Guyana and Suriname*, Award of 17 September 2007 (hereinafter *Guyana v. Suriname*), International Court of Arbitration: www.pca-cpa.org/showfile.asp?fil_id=664, (last accessed 18 February 2012) para. 302 ('International courts and tribunals are not constrained by a finite list of special circumstances'). For the role of equitable principles in negotiations, see Chapter 12.
[3] ICJ Reports 1969, p. 53, para. 100.   [4] ICJ Reports 1969, p. 51, para. 93.
[5] ICJ Reports 1969, pp. 52–3, paras. 95–9.
[6] ICJ Reports 1969, p. 54, para. 101 C(1) and (2).

factors and considerations into the discussion, such as the economic, political and security interests in the 1977 Channel Arbitration.[7]

Under the influence of the equitable solution approach, emerging during UNCLOS III, this open philosophy was further enhanced in 1982. The Court initially declined to develop a more systematic approach:

> Clearly, each continental shelf case in dispute should be considered and judged on its own merits, having regard to its peculiar circumstances; therefore, no attempt should be made to over-conceptualize the application of the principles and rules relating to the continental shelf.[8]

This attitude was still equally implicit in the 1984 *Gulf of Maine* case, being limited to a very broad fundamental norm in negotiations as well as in dispute settlement:

> delimitation is to be effected by the application of equitable criteria and by the use of practical methods of ensuring, with regard to the geographic configuration of the areas and other relevant circumstances, an equitable result.[9]

The Chamber declined to conceptualize the relationship of equitable principles and circumstances with different factors, essentially upon their finding that no customary law has yet emerged in the new field of long-distance maritime boundary delimitation:

> In customary international law, it is not a body of detailed rules that should be looked for which in fact comprises a limited set of norms for ensuring the co-existence and vital co-operation of the members of the international community, together with a set of customary rules whose presence in the *opinio juris* of States can be tested by introduction based on the analysis of a sufficiently extensive and convincing practice, and not by deduction from preconceived ideas. It is therefore unrewarding, especially in a new and still unconsolidated field like that involving the quite recent extension of the claims of States to areas which were until yesterday zones of the high seas, to look to general international law to provide a ready-made set of rules that can be used for solving any delimitation

---

[7] Channel Award, n. 2, paras. 162, para. 184 ss. See also Elihu Lauterpacht, 'Equity, Evasion, Equivocation and Evolution in International Law' in Proceedings and Commentaries, Report of the American Branch of the International Law Association 1977/1978, p. 1 ('It is to be noted that the factors are not identical with those which were identified in the *North Sea Continental Shelf* case and in some important respect go wider than those factors').

[8] *Case Concerning the Continental Shelf (Tunisia v. Libyan Arab Jamahiriya)*. ICJ Reports 1982, p. 92, para. 132.

[9] *Case Concerning Delimitation of the Maritime Boundary in the Gulf of Maine Area (Canada v. United States of America)* ICJ Reports 1984, p. 299, para. 112.

CONCEPTUAL ISSUES AND THE CONTEXT OF EQUITY   445

problems that arise. A more useful course is to seek a better formulation of the fundamental norm.[10]

Up until 1984, courts operated under the influence of UNCLOS III, and thus refrained from conceptualizing the fundamental rule of equity. At the time, Charney observed that the classical process of law-making development, which permits further refinement of the norm and which ultimately leads to a strict rule of law, had not yet occurred.[11] Significantly, with the shift in position back towards a more rule-oriented approach, as discussed in Chapter 8, judicial attitudes changed, and the reluctance to adopt a normative concept of equitable principles was finally abandoned in the 1985 *Libya* v. *Malta* case and in the *Denmark* v. *Norway (Jan Mayen)* case, if not in practical application, then at least at a theoretical level.

After stressing the legal requirement of consistency and a degree of predictability, the ICJ approached equitable principles as a normative or prescriptive concept, which is relevant both for negotiations and dispute settlement. For the first time, a fairly comprehensive list of equitable principles was listed in 1985, although their relationship to relevant circumstances still remains unclear:

> The *normative* character of equitable principles applied as a part of general international law is important because these principles govern not only delimitation by adjudication or arbitration, but also, and indeed primarily, the duty of Parties to firstly seek delimitation by agreement, which is also an equitable result. The fact that equitable principles are expressed in terms of *general application*, is immediately apparent from a glance at some well-known examples: the principle that there is not to be a question of refashioning geography, or compensating for the inequalities of nature; the related principle of non-encroachment by one party on the natural prolongation of the other (which is no more than a negative expression of the positive rule that the coastal State enjoys sovereign rights over the continental shelf off its coasts to the full extent authorised by international law in the relevant circumstances); the principle of respect to all such relevant circumstances; the principle that although all States are equal before the law and are entitled to equal treatment, 'equity does not imply equality' (*ICJ Reports 1969, p. 49 para. 91*), nor does it seek to make equal what nature has made unequal; and the principle that there can be no question of distributive justice.[12]

---

[10] ICJ Reports 1984, p 299, para 111.
[11] Jonathan I. Charney, 'Ocean Boundaries between Nations: A Theory for Progress' (1984) 78 *American Journal of International Law*, 582, 593.
[12] *Case Concerning the Continental Shelf (Libya Arab Jamahiriya* v. *Malta)*, ICJ Reports 1985, p. 39, para. 46 (emphasis added).

Moreover, the Court emphasized that while courts are not limited to a restricted list of considerations, only those that are pertinent and related to the concept of the maritime zone can be considered in law:

> Yet, although there may be no absolute legal limit to the considerations that States may take into account, this can hardly be true for a court when applying equitable procedures. Although there is assuredly no closed list of considerations, it is evident that a court may only take into account those that are pertinent to the institutions of the continental shelf as it has developed *within the law*, and to the application of equitable principles to its delimitation. Otherwise, the legal concept of continental shelf could itself be fundamentally changed by the introduction of considerations strange to its nature.[13]

Another fact is also significant and shows a process of gradual conceptualization of the fundamental rule of equity. Although from the very beginning of the 1945 Truman Proclamation this was expressed in terms of equitable principles, the courts, for some forty years, did not seek to define such principles in legal terms. They preferred notional concepts such as factors, or – even less normatively – criteria.[14] However, in 1985, such factors and criteria were clearly given a legal, normative value by being called equitable principles.[15] Yet, they still were merely referred to in terms of non-exhaustive examples, and their relationship to special circumstances, among other issues, remained a mystery.

Some of these considerations were reflected in the 1993 *Jan Mayen* case, within the application of Article 6 of the 1958 Continental Shelf Convention.[16] Restating the convergence of customary law and treaty law in the field expounded by the 1977 Channel Arbitration,[17] the Court worked from a median line and took into account a number of the principles described below in Chapter 10, However, the Court again preferred to variously call these *factors* or *principles*, or simply addressed them as considerations, without further clarifying the relationship of these notions.[18] In subsequent case law,

---

[13] ICJ Reports 1985, p. 40, para. 48 (emphasis added), as recalled in *Guyana v. Suriname* Award, n. 2, para. 303.
[14] ICJ Reports 1984, p. 300, paras. 112, 110 and 113.
[15] ICJ Reports 1985, p. 39, para. 46.
[16] *Case Concerning Maritime Boundary Delimitation in the Area Between Greenland and Jan Mayen (Denmark v. Norway)*, ICJ Reports 1993, p. 63 para. 57.
[17] ICJ Reports 1993, p. 62, para. 56.
[18] ICJ Reports 1993, p. 67, para. 66 (factor), p. 68, para. 67 (principle) for proportionality, p. 70, para. 72 (factor of overlapping claims), p. 71, para. 75–6 consideration of economic

the Court undertook to clarify the relationship of equitable principles, relevant circumstances and equidistance. It gradually turned to a model which adopted equidistance as a methodological starting point, yet without qualifying it as a rule or legal principle for single purpose boundaries.

The ICJ in the 2001 *Qatar v. Bahrain* case followed the approach of the preceding judgment in the 1993 *Jan Mayen* case by firstly and provisionally drawing an equidistance line and then considering whether there were circumstances which must lead to an adjustment of that line.[19] The Court called the approach for the delimitation of the EEZ and the continental shelf the 'equitable principles/relevant circumstances rule, as it has been developed since 1958 in case-law and State practice'.[20] The Court noted that the equitable principles–relevant circumstances rule is closely interrelated with the equidistance–special circumstances rule, which is applicable in particular to the delimitation of the territorial sea.[21]

The Court in a second step examined whether there are circumstances which might make it necessary to adjust the equidistance line in order to achieve an equitable result.[22] The court had to establish a single boundary. It recalled the *Gulf of Maine* Chamber, which held that that in order to avoid the disadvantages inherent in a plurality of separate delimitations, preference should be given to criteria which, because of their more neutral character, are best suited for use in a multipurpose delimitation. The Court also referred to the view in the *Tunisia v. Libya* case that greater importance must be attributed to elements, such as distance from the coast, which are common to both EEZ and the continental shelf.[23]

In the 2002 *Cameroon v. Nigeria* case, the ICJ held, with reference to its own jurisprudence from *Qatar v. Bahrain* and *Jan Mayen*, that:

> The Court has on various occasions made it clear what the applicable criteria, principles and rules of delimitation are when a line covering several zones of coincident jurisdictions is to be determined. They are expressed in the so-called equitable principles/relevant circumstances

---

factors (access to fisheries), p. 72, para. 77 (factor of geophysical character), p. 74, para. 80 (in fine socio-economic factors as circumstances).

[19] *Maritime Delimitation and Territorial Questions between Qatar and Bahrain (Qatar v. Bahrain)*, Merits, Judgment, ICJ Reports 2001, pp. 40, 110, paras. 227–30.
[20] ICJ Reports 2001, p. 110, para. 231.   [21] ICJ Reports 2001, p. 110, para. 231.
[22] ICJ Reports 2001, p. 110, para. 232.   [23] ICJ Reports 2001, p. 110, paras. 225–6.

method. This method, which is very similar to the equidistance/special circumstances method applicable in delimitation of the territorial sea, involves first drawing an equidistance line, then considering whether there are factors calling for the adjustment or shifting of that line in order to achieve an 'equitable result'.[24]

The Tribunal in the 2006 *Barbados* v. *Trinidad and Tobago* arbitration confirmed the two-step approach and held that:

> While a convenient starting point, equidistance alone will in many circumstances not ensure an equitable result in the light of the peculiarities of each specific case. The second step accordingly requires the examination of this provisional line in the light of relevant circumstances, which are case specific, so as to determine whether it is necessary to adjust the provisional equidistance line in order to achieve an equitable result.[25] ... Certainty is thus combined with the need for an equitable result.[26]

The Tribunal stressed the rule-orientation of its approach of equitable principles–relevant circumstances with the following words:

> The process of achieving an equitable result is thus constrained by legal principle, in particular in respect of the factors that may be taken into account. It is furthermore necessary that the delimitation be consistent with legal principle as established in decided cases, in order that States in other disputes be assisted in the negotiations in search of an equitable solution that are required by Articles 74 or 83 of the Convention.[27]

The 2007 Tribunal in *Guyana* v. *Suriname* confirmed the two-step approach taken since the 1993 *Jan Mayen* case.[28] It called the considerations of the second step 'special or relevant circumstances'.[29] The initial differentiation between the terms 'special circumstances' stemming from Article 6 of the 1958 Shelf Convention and 'relevant circumstances' stemming from customary law seems to have definitely become obsolete, since they are both intended to enable the achievement of an equitable result.[30] The same is true for the methods of equidistance–special circumstances in the territorial sea and equitable principles–relevant

---

[24] *Land and Maritime Boundary between Cameroon and Nigeria (Cameroon* v. *Nigeria: Equatorial Guinea intervening)*, Judgment, ICJ Reports 2002, p. 303, p. 441, para. 288.
[25] Permanent Court of Arbitration (PCA): In The Matter of an Arbitration between Barbados and the Republic of Trinidad and Tobago (11 April 2006) (2006) 45 ILM 800–869 (hereinafter *Barbados* v. *Trinidad and Tobago*), para. 242.
[26] Ibid.   [27] Ibid., para. 243.   [28] *Guyana* v. *Suriname Award*, n. 2, paras. 335, 342.
[29] Ibid., para. 335.
[30] See already *Case Concerning Maritime Boundary Delimitation in the Area Between Greenland and Jan Mayen (Denmark* v. *Norway)*, ICJ Reports 1993. p. 63, para. 56.

CONCEPTUAL ISSUES AND THE CONTEXT OF EQUITY 449

circumstances for the delimitation of the continental shelf and EEZ, which are both intended to achieve an equitable result.[31]

It is worth mentioning that while delimiting the territorial sea, the Tribunal in *Guyana* v. *Suriname* recalled the 1977 *Anglo-French Channel* arbitration which 'took the approach that the notion of special circumstances generally refers to equitable considerations rather than a notion of defined or limited categories of circumstances'. The Tribunal confirmed the view in *Barbados* v. *Trinidad and Tobago* that special circumstances are case specific.[32] But the Tribunal also recalled the 'requirement of achieving a stable legal outcome' and that '[c]ertainty, equity, and stability are thus integral parts of the process of delimitation'.[33] In this respect, the Tribunal in *Guyana* v. *Suriname*, like the Tribunal in *Barbados* v. *Trinidad and Tobago*, stressed the rule-orientation of the fundamental approach by stating that reference should be paid to international jurisprudence and state practice.[34]

In the 2009 *Romania* v. *Ukraine* case, the court was able to hold that in the delimitation of the continental shelf or the EEZ or both zones together, 'the Court proceeds in defined stages'[35] – 'in keeping with its settled jurisprudence on maritime delimitation'.[36] With reference to its own practice, the Court termed the approach applicable to single boundary delimitations as the equitable principles–relevant circumstances method.[37] Also consistent with its own practice, the Court held that because '[the] final line should result in an equitable solution (Articles 74 and 83 of UNCLOS) the Court will at the ... second stage consider whether there are factors calling for the adjustment or shifting of the provisional equidistance line in order to achieve an equitable result.[38] The Court added that '[s]uch factors have usually been referred to in the jurisprudence of the Court, since the North Sea Continental Shelf ... cases, as the relevant circumstances'.[39] Without explicitly referring to its rules-based understanding of the concept of equitable principles, the

---

[31] *Qatar* v. *Bahrain*, n. 19, para. 231, *Cameroon* v. *Nigeria*, n. 24, para. 288, *Barbados* v. *Trinidad and Tobago*, n. 25, para. 305.
[32] *Guyana* v. *Suriname Award*, n. 2, para. 303.   [33] Ibid., paras. 334, 341.
[34] Ibid., paras. 303, 334.
[35] *Case Concerning Maritime Delimitation in the Black Sea (Romania* v. *Ukraine)*, Judgment, 3 February 2009, ICJ Reports 2009, pp. 61, 101 para. 115. See also Chapter 8(II)(F).
[36] Ibid., para. 118.
[37] Ibid., para. 120, citing *Territorial and Maritime Dispute between Nicaragua and Honduras in the Caribbean Sea (Nicaragua* v. *Honduras)*, Judgment, ICJ Reports 2007, p. 659, para. 271.
[38] Ibid., citing *Cameroon* v. *Nigeria*, n. 24, para. 288.   [39] Ibid., p. 112, para. 155.

Court relied on its own jurisprudence and that of arbitral tribunals in the consideration of relevant circumstances.[40] It added a third step, checking whether results achieved avoid disproportionate allocations of marine space under a broadly termed principle of proportionality.

The ITLOS adopted the three-step test from *Romania v. Ukraine* and likewise referred to it as the equidistance–relevant circumstances method in *Bangladesh v. Myanmar*.[41] The Tribunal stated that in applying this method, it takes into account the jurisprudence of international courts and tribunals.[42] The Tribunal noted:

> Over time, the absence of a settled method of delimitation prompted increased interest in enhancing the objectivity and predictability of the process. The varied geographic situations addressed in the early cases nevertheless confirmed that, even if the pendulum had swung too far away from the objective precision of equidistance, the use of equidistance alone could not ensure an equitable solution in each and every case. A method of delimitation suitable for general use would need to combine its constraints on subjectivity with the flexibility necessary to accommodate circumstances in a particular case that are relevant to maritime delimitation.[43]

It stated that, if it finds 'any relevant circumstances requiring adjustment of the provisional equidistance line ... it will make an adjustment that produces an equitable result'.[44] Turning to the delimitation exercise, it stated similarly that it would 'consider whether there are factors in the present case that may be considered relevant circumstances, calling for an adjustment of that line with a view to achieving an equitable solution'.[45]

The ICJ in *Nicaragua v. Colombia* further consolidated its three-step approach for the delimitation of the EEZ and continental shelf, calling it its 'standard method'.[46] It recalled from *Libya v. Malta* and *Romania v. Ukraine* that it 'has made clear on a number of occasions that the methodology which it will normally employ when called upon to effect a delimitation between overlapping continental shelf and exclusive economic zone entitlements involves proceeding in three stages'.[47] It also

---

[40] Ibid., p. 116 ss, paras. 63–168, 185, 198, 204.
[41] *Dispute concerning Delimitation of the Maritime Boundary between Bangladesh and Myanmar in the Bay of Bengal (Bangladesh v. Myanmar)*, Judgement, International Tribunal for the Law of the Sea, 14 March 2012, Case No. 16,, paras. 233, 239.
[42] Ibid., para. 240.   [43] Ibid., para. 228.   [44] Ibid., para. 240.   [45] Ibid., para. 275.
[46] *Territorial and Maritime Dispute (Nicaragua v. Colombia)*, Judgment, ICJ Reports 2012, p. 624, para. 199.
[47] Ibid., para. 190.

cautioned, however, that '[t]he three-stage process is not, of course, to be applied in a mechanical fashion and the Court has recognized that it will not be appropriate in every case to begin with a provisional equidistance/median line'.[48] With reference to *Libya* v. *Malta* and *Romania* v. *Ukraine*, it recalled that, '[i]n the second stage, the Court considers whether there are any relevant circumstances which may call for an adjustment or shifting of the provisional equidistance/median line so as to achieve an equitable result. If it concludes that such circumstances are present, it establishes a different boundary which usually entails such adjustment or shifting of the equidistance/median line as is necessary to take account of those circumstances'.[49]

While special circumstances are invoked and present in most contentious cases, the 2014 *Maritime Boundary Dispute (Peru v. Chile)* dispensed the case without taking recourse to them. Neither Peru nor Chile claimed special circumstances and the Court did not consider any in determining a boundary which was strongly influenced by existing treaty obligations.[50]

In case law and state practice, relevant circumstances were developed predominantly in single boundary delimitations.[51] Their development and current state are examined below in Chapter 10. In conclusion, while equidistance emerged as a prime step in the methodology of maritime boundary delimitation, the essence of the rule of equity as a basic norm is reflected in principles and standards to be applied in order to achieve an equitable result. Jurisprudence, in other words, confirms what was found in previous chapters in determining the relationship of law and equidistance and equitable principles. The identification of these principles and standards amounts to the main challenge before us in search of equitable solutions in the settlement of complex and protracted cases under the fundamental rule of equity.

C. *Basic conceptual problems*

The process of conceptualization and specification through a history of trial and error reflects the substantial difficulties that are inherent when coming to grips with a fundamental norm as elusive as equity.

---

[48] Ibid., para. 194.   [49] Ibid., para. 192.
[50] *Maritime Dispute (Peru v. Chile)*, Judgment of 27 January 2014, ICJ Rep___ paras. 181, 182, 191.
[51] See *Barbados* v. *Trinidad and Tobago*, n. 25, para. 235; *Guyana* v. *Suriname* Award, n. 2, para. 334; ICJ Reports 101, para. 115.

Developing a coherent system of equitable standards able to respond to the equities of different geographical, economic and political configurations is arduous and difficult to achieve in case law, which by its very nature has to focus on one specific dispute and cannot easily formulate an entire system. But the conceptualization of equity poses difficult legal and methodological issues in any doctrinal attempt to develop a coherent system and set of equitable standards.

What is the legal nature and content of equitable principles and standards? Is it possible to identify them with a reasonable degree of precision? As much as it is necessary to go beyond equidistance and elaborate underlying standards of delimitation, it is necessary to draw on the concepts, objectives and underlying values of the respective zones in order to seek answers and shape the values of the respective zones in order to seek answers and form and organize such standards on delimitation. Equity, and references to it in legal texts, cannot be construed in itself. It requires a precise context. Yet, some of the substantial difficulties in conceptualizing and concretizing equitable standards witnessed over the last forty-five years stem from the very fact that such underlying values have not yet been clearly and sufficiently defined, let alone generally accepted. Discussion has largely been dominated by the quest for appropriate methods of delimitation, as demonstrated by the debate on equidistance versus equitable principles. Mostly, the situation has been either that underlying values have been taken for granted and left without expression, or the reduction of the problem to specific values is difficult to achieve. Before turning to operational standards, it will therefore be necessary to address the impact of underlying interests, objectives and values, which ultimately should be respected during the process of delimitation. They form an essential, underlying part of the environment in which the rule of equity operates within the process of delimitation of the different zones.

Similarly, conceptual issues concerning the legal environment in which equity operates have to be dealt with. How does equity relate to other legal rules and principles of international law which equally affect, and sometimes even determine, boundary delimitation? Moreover, how does it relate to the political environment and the overall goal of achieving an equitable result?

Conceptually difficult questions concern the interdependence and interaction of equitable standards. Should there be a normative distinction between equitable principles and relevant circumstances, factors or criteria? Are they simply different terms for the same type of normative standard? Is there a hierarchy, or are they to be found and placed on the same normative level? Should there be a *numerus clausus*, an exhaustive list in order to assure a legal operation and to avoid discretionary and unprincipled decision-making *ex aequo et bono*? Should answers to that basic issue be the same for both judicial and negotiated settlement of boundaries? What effect would equitable standards being justiciable in legal dispute settlement have? What does justiciability mean in the present context? On the other hand, what should the proper meaning of equity during negotiations be, as opposed to during the judicial process? Moreover, are equitable standards for the continental shelf and the EEZ identical? Finally, how do equitable standards relate to the concept of an equitable solution that is equally part of the fundamental rule? What is the appropriate methodology for putting all of these elements into operation?

The following paragraphs and chapters of Part III offer an attempt to address these questions as well as others. Sometimes they are presented in terms of legal theory, sometimes in terms of conclusions, depending on the factual materials and arguments developed at the respective stages of this study of equity. Before turning to the substance of equity in Chapter 10, it is essential to discuss the context of equity in some detail.

II. The impact of underlying concepts, objectives and ideas

A. The relational nature of equity and equitable standards

The rule of equity does not operate in a legal vacuum. Conceptualization and concretization have to draw upon and take into account the legal foundations, underlying ideas, objectives and values inherent to the legal concepts of the continental shelf and the EEZ. The analysis of the history and evolution of the respective zones in Part I revealed a number of underlying ideas, objectives and values that are much less community-oriented than the preamble of the LOS Convention suggests.[52] Overall, it

---

[52] In particular paras. 4 and 5 of the preamble of the 1982 LOS Convention:

> *Recognising* the desirability of establishing, through this Convention, with due regard to the sovereignty of States, a legal order for the seas and oceans which will facilitate international communication, and will promote the peaceful uses of the seas and oceans, the equitable and efficient utilisation of their resources, the conservation of their living resources, and the study, protection of the marine environment.

was concluded that the maritime revolution and its values and objectives are more closely linked to the classical concepts of sovereign nations and an international society than to the idea of a global community. The continental shelf and the EEZ zones serve to promote the national interests of coastal states. Nevertheless, by exerting national jurisdiction, they also offer the possibility of fostering global community interests to some extent by effectively policing the zones in the absence of global management policies. In addition, the concept of horizontally shared jurisdictions, short of a territorial concept, seeks to realize the value and objective of free communications within the zones. Both types of zones assert national jurisdiction to prevent foreign exploitation, to control exploitation and management, and to reap fiscal revenues from licensing the exploitation of living and non-living resources. There also are more specific purposes. Historically, jurisdiction over the continental shelf also serves national security interests by prohibiting the stationing of weapons and, arguably, intelligence equipment. The EEZ, on the other hand, historically includes the protection of traditional local fishing industries and the livelihood of coastal populations. Moreover, it is dedicated to the efficient management and conservation of living resources that, at least historically, have been absent from the functions of the shelf.

Both in law and in fact, the concepts of the continental shelf and the EEZ are essentially defined in geographical and physical terms. From the outset, entitlement is limited to coastal states. In accordance with protectionist and conservationist values, the title ultimately relies on the principles of sovereign equality and the permanent relationship of a state to the resources located in the respective zone. It is true that such closeness is primarily defined in geographical terms, as is shown by zones being defined by distance and the essentially geographic concept of equidistance in state practice. However, importantly, closeness is not limited to physical proximity, adjacency or distance. Closeness of relationship may also be expressed in historical, political, economic or other terms relating to human activities. Such an understanding perhaps provides the most important valuational basis for an equitable

> *Bearing in mind* that the achievement of these goals will contribute to the realisation of a just and equitable international economic order which takes into account the interests and needs of mankind as a whole, and in particular, the special interests and needs of developing countries, whether coastal or land-locked.

sharing of resources amongst competing coastal states. This same closeness of relationship, however, also results in the uneven global distribution of resources, depending on the size of the coastal state. Thus the concept equally stands for a partly inequitable situation, when viewed from a global perspective.

Given such a valuational network, it becomes possible at this point to narrow the scope of equity within the present context. Equity cannot be defined in the abstract in operational terms. We are left with either explicit or implicit perceptions of justice and morality, of the good and the bad, all too often allowing for different conclusions in a pluralistic global society. In the context of existing law and legal references and the application of justice and equity, therefore, the notions have to be discussed and applied within the framework of the particular field in which their effects should be deployed.

In maritime boundary delimitation, justice and equity cannot transgress the basic framework of nationalized maritime zones. The same holds true for the rule of equity and equitable standards. It operates, as seen in Chapter 3, in an inherently unfair and inequitable environment which allocated resources on accidental geographical contours and the largely varying sizes of coastal states and the location of islands. This is what the ICJ meant when it repeatedly stated that it is not a matter of applying equity as a matter of abstract justice, that equity does not necessarily imply equality, and that it is not a matter of 'totally refashioning geography'.[53] Equally, this is what is meant by the Courts' consistent rejection of the concept of delimitation as a matter of abstract distributive justice between the states during delimitation, although the result may actually come close to this.

All this reflects the fact that justice or equity in the present context of maritime boundary delimitation is no longer justice or equity on an abstract moral or philosophical level. It is relational justice and equity. Although still fairly elusive and vague, it clearly applies within a concept, in a particular geographical and historical context. There are only limited opportunities to mitigate the fundamental inequities of this system in general law, unless a solution is deliberately sought as a mutually agreed policy on the basis of a special agreement, as it was for example, in the case of the *Jan Mayen* conciliation.[54] The rule of equity, therefore, does not represent a passport to pursue unfettered

---

[53] 1969 ICJ Reports, p. 50, para. 91.   [54] See Chapter 6(III)(B).

goals of global equity (the allocation of resources on the basis of developmental, social and economic need), in an abstract and independent manner, beyond the limits and constraints of the system of nation states and the concepts of the continental shelf and the EEZ. Indeed, and whether we like it or not, the rule of equity operates within a context which was itself found to be inequitable – despite the Preamble and aspirations of the LOS Convention calling upon the 'needs of mankind as a whole and of developing countries'. The protectionist allocation of marine spaces and resources largely on the basis of coastal configurations, and therefore dependent upon an accident of nature, is at the expense of states with short coasts, and can even operate to the total exclusion of land-locked states without regard to their state of economic developments and need for resources.[55] Respect for such constraints makes the difference to allocation of resources *ex aequo et bono* and any unprincipled subjectivism of distributive justice clear.

B. The object of delimitation: resources or marine space?

A detailed study of state practice confirmed that governments are primarily interested in economically advantageous allocations of resources (non-living and living: oil; gas; metalliferous deposits or manganese nodules; and sedentary and, in particular, transitory fisheries) when negotiating maritime boundaries and as parties to legal dispute settlement.[56] Today, they are increasingly interested in opportunities to use marine spaces for energy-sustainable energy production (wind, wave and solar energy) and access to the sea's biological gene pool. Space is primarily relevant with regard to national security interests, which, it should be recalled, contributed equally to the evolution of the legal concept of the continental shelf. It follows from the historical motivation and economic purposes of the shelf and the EEZ that such prime interests in resource allocation are perfectly legitimate. Equally, the Preamble of the LOS Convention aspires to a marine order that facilitates 'equitable share and efficient utilisation of their resources', and not so much to space allocation as such. In the *North Sea Continental Shelf* cases, the

---

[55] See Chapter 3.
[56] See Barbara Kwiatkowska, 'Economic and Environmental Considerations in Maritime Boundary Delimitations' in Jonathan I. Charney et al. (eds.), *International Maritime Boundaries*, 5 vols. (The Hague: Martinus Nijhoff Publishers, 1993–2005), vol. I (Charney and Alexander), pp. 75–113.

CONCEPTUAL ISSUES AND THE CONTEXT OF EQUITY   457

Court clearly stated that access to resources is 'the very object' of delimitation.[57]

From a realist perspective, there is no need to hide this fact behind all sorts of geographical or human-related arguments, as often seems to be the case in the process of delimitation. As Judge Jessup put it in his 1969 opinion (after he had given a detailed analysis of the pertinent interests involved):

> It is apparent from the above extracts that the problem of the exploitation of the *oil and gas resources* of the continental shelf of the North Sea was in front of the minds of the Parties but that none of them was prepared to base its case squarely on consideration of this factor, preferring to argue on other legal principles which are sometimes advanced with almost academic detachment from realities.[58]

The same, of course, is true for the resources of the water column. Parties have been primarily interested in the quality and amount of fish stock, and arguments related to surface allocation are framed and submitted with a view to achieving an optimal allocation of stock.[59] They are interested in using the water column for energy production (wave, biomass), while the continental shelf remains important for fixed installations to this effect. Why, then, have arguments and approaches to delimitation not been based more directly on the underlying economic interests at stake?

Refraining from squarely basing a case on resource allocation may have deeper roots than a simple reluctance to offer full transparency over the underlying economic interests. While the *economic* objective of resource allocation of delimitation is evident, the *legal* concepts of the shelf and the EEZ are clearly founded upon spatial concepts. From the beginning of natural prolongation, to minimal distances of 200 nm, both the shelf and the EEZ have depended upon geophysical or geographical features. Entitlement to these zones exists independently of whether and to what extent and quality mineral resources exist in the tectonic plates or fisheries in the water column. This was the very essence of the 1969 *North Sea* judgment, in which the Court rejected the German distributional doctrine of a fair and equitable share of resources, as much as it rejected equidistance as a rule in customary law based upon the spatial concepts of natural prolongation and *ipso facto* and *ab initio* entitlement. Charney expressed the same opinion:

---

[57] ICJ Reports 1969, p. 51, para. 97.   [58] ICJ Reports 1969, separate opinion at p. 72.
[59] Cf. ICJ Reports 1993, p. 71, paras. 118–20 (separate opinion Schwebel).

> In my opinion, the general rejection of considerations other than coastal geography in maritime boundary delimitation cases is the preferable course. The reintroduction of other considerations, albeit in a limited and indirect way, in the Jan Mayen Judgment is unfortunate and likely to encourage greater conflict and uncertainty. It may slow the evolution of a more stable law. Natural resource, environmental and similar concerns may be best addressed on their own merits in light of, but apart from, the boundary delimitation.[60]

Within the legal concept, delimitation is therefore primarily concerned with spatial issues. Relevant principles and circumstances therefore have to be sought on a spatial basis in the first place. Equitable principles of delimitation are thus necessarily principles of space allocation. Indeed, they are the prime operational sources for delimitation, ignoring any underlying goals of resource allocation. It will be seen that problems of scientific evidence and the limited justiciability of direct resource allocation in judicial settlements form a major argument supporting this conceptual view.

In conclusion, delimitation primarily involves spatial allocation. There are inherent conceptual limitations to directly addressing and relying upon economic resource allocation. Yet, we still are faced with the interesting phenomenon that, politically, the ultimate goals and purposes of delimitation are at variance with its underlying concepts. Future delimitations in the Arctic in particular will demonstrate this. States are primarily interested in the location and potential of resources, much more than spatial allocation. Conceptually, a question arises over the extent to which the two elements can be combined. A careful examination will be necessary when determining the extent to which resource allocation may be taken into account. It may already be anticipated that the answer will show that there are inherent limits to space allocation, as delimitation may still result in a grossly unfair and unjust allocation of resources.[61] But this is just another aspect of the fact that the legal concept of equity and the fundamental rule operate within an imperfect and partly inequitable environment. If the divergence between the object and goal is too large on the facts of a specific case, alternative approaches to delimitation, such as joint zones of common management, may be required.[62]

---

[60] Jonanathan I. Charney, 'Progress in International Maritime Boundary Delimitation Law' (1994) 88 *American Journal of International Law*, 240.
[61] Cf. Chapter 10(II)(B).   [62] Cf. Chapters 5(III), and 10(II)(D)(4) and (IV).

C. The window of delimitation

In line with the relational nature of equity that operates within a partly inequitable system and which cannot redress the basic inequities of the concept of the shelf and the EEZ, the operation of delimitation generally does not encompass *per se* the entire allocation of spaces to a coastal state. This may have been the case for the Federal Republic of Germany in the *North Sea Continental Shelf* cases, but usually delimitation only concerns parts of the marine area or resources claimed by a coastal state. Equity and equitable principles are not only not given the task of bringing about an overall distribution of marine resources that is globally equitable, but they are also not expected to achieve an allocation of marine space which is equitable overall. This is an important insight into the operational and conceptual limitations of equity in resource-related disputes. Three aspects are of importance here.

Firstly, where one of the parties already enjoys jurisdiction over other non-disputed areas *vis-à-vis* the other party, in principle this cannot be taken into account in terms of compensation. Equally, any actual or potential entitlement *vis-à-vis* a third state has no influence on the allocation of the marine spaces. The 1977 *Channel Arbitration* emphasized 'that no inference may be drawn from [the] decision' with regard to the prospective delimitation between the United Kingdom and the Republic of Ireland.[63] And vice versa, the features of the dispute with Ireland were held not to affect the delimitation in the Channel area.[64] In particular, the United Kingdom argued an analogy with the tripartite situation of the *North Sea* cases in vain, and was not eligible for any compensation in its dispute with France, in view of its narrow shelf with Ireland.[65] Similarly, the ICJ in *Cameroon v. Nigeria* refused to compensate Cameroon for the fact that the presence of a third state's island (Equatorial Guinea's) blocked the seaward projection of its coast. The Gulf of Guinea, which is already concave in character at the level of the Cameroonian and Nigerian coastlines, contains in addition the presence of Equatorial Guinea's Bioko Island, which lies opposite the two states' coastlines. The Court gave no effect in any step of the delimitation exercise to that part of the Cameroonian coast which lies behind Bioko Island, stating that it cannot be treated as facing Nigeria. The Court thus considered irrelevant for the question of delimitation between Cameroon and Nigeria this substantial part of the Cameroonian coast behind Bioko

---

[63] Channel Award, n. 2, para. 28.   [64] Ibid., para. 236.   [65] Ibid., para. 24.

Island where the maritime rights of Cameroon and Equatorial Guinea had not yet been determined.[66]

Secondly, parties can only deal with overlapping areas that unquestionably belong to one or the other. As the Court stated in 1982:

> The need for delimitation of areas of continental shelf between the Parties can only arise within the submarine region in which claims by them to the exercise of sovereign rights are legally possible according to international law. Those claims relate, as far as the areas near the coast are concerned, to regions which undoubtedly appertain to the one or the other Party.[67]

Hence, delimitation is confined to mutual claims over overlapping areas. Therefore, the task of equity is a narrow one in geographical terms: involving the achievement of an equitable result within the area in dispute between the states concerned. It only involves the zone of mutual interference (*zône de chevauchement*) which all of the parties concerned are legally entitled to claim by virtue of the 200 nm extension of the shelf (or beyond) and the EEZ. The operation of delimitation – or of 'mutual amputation of claims' (Weil)[68] – takes place within this area. It is limited to it. The ITLOS in the *Bangladesh* v. *Myanmar* case did not entirely stick to this maxim. It held that for the purpose of determining any disproportionality in respect of areas allocated to the parties, the relevant area should include maritime areas subject to the overlapping entitlements of the parties to the present case.[69] But it continued that the fact that a third party may claim the same maritime area does not prevent its inclusion in the relevant maritime area for the purposes of the disproportionality test.[70]

Thirdly, the relevant area of delimitation is defined not only by the claims of the parties involved, but also to a considerable extent by the rights or claims of third parties. These can exert a considerably limiting or expanding effect. It is a well-established rule that bilateral or judicial settlements between two parties must not prejudice the rights of non-participating third states. This fundamental principle goes beyond the concepts and objectives of the zones themselves. It is an essential part of the legal environment to be discussed separately.[71]

---

[66] ICJ Reports 2002, p. 442, para. 291; see also Appendix II, Map 13.
[67] ICJ Reports 1982, p. 42, para. 34.
[68] Prosper Weil, *Perspectives du droit de la delimitation maritime* (Paris: Editions A. Pedone, 1988); Weil, 'Geographic Considerations in Maritime Delimitation' in Charney et al., *International Maritime Boundaries*, vol. I, n. 56, pp. 115.
[69] *Bangladesh* v. *Myanmar*, n. 41, para. 493.   [70] Ibid., para. 494.
[71] See Chapter 9(III)(D).

The practical definition of the relevant zone, or the window of delimitation, as it may be called, is not without practical difficulties, particularly with regard to defining the relevant coasts and islands, as well as to finding the appropriate means of establishing third party interests. But whatever the difficulties, such definition is an indispensable first step in the process of delimitation. Facts, entitlement and expectations that fall outside the zone are not relevant for the purposes of this operation. At least where judicial settlement is involved, considerations of macro-geography outside the relevant zone are beyond the scope and reach of equitable standards.

All this does not mean that the disputed areas are necessarily small in size. This may sometimes be the case, for example, in semi-enclosed or enclosed seas such as the Mediterranean. However, zones may also extend for long distances into open oceanic space, as is the case, for example, with the American or African coasts. But legally speaking, these areas remain limited in scope. The standards apply, so to speak, to micro-geography. It is within a local or regional dimension that they have to produce an equitable result. Limitation to micro-geography is also of importance from the point of view of justiciability. The definition of, and limitation to, the relevant area in dispute is important to keeping the matter manageable in negotiations. The larger an area in dispute, the more complex the interests involved, and the more difficult it becomes to achieve agreement. Therefore the reduction of the relevant area to the smallest possible scope is essential for legal settlement. The definition of the area in dispute, if possible by the parties in the special agreement, is a necessary prerequisite in order to prepare the ground for the application of equitable standards. For example, without the limitation to the relevant area in the Pelagian Sea between Ras Kaboudia and Ras Tajoura in the *Tunisia* v. *Libya* case,[72] the limitation of the dispute to the Gulf of Maine area to the exclusion of other spaces in the *Gulf of Maine* case,[73] or the description of the relevant area in the *St. Pierre and Miquelon* arbitration,[74] the *Romania* v. *Ukraine* case[75] and the *Nicaragua* v. *Colombia* case,[76] it would not have been possible to apply the principle of proportionality, whatever its precise contents.

---

[72] ICJ Reports 1982, p. 31, para. 130, and map at para. 75.
[73] ICJ Reports 1984, p. 268, paras. 29 ff.
[74] *Court of Arbitration for the Delimitation of Maritime Areas between Canada and France, Case concerning de Delimitation of Maritime Areas between Canada and the French Republic* (1992) 31 ILM 1159–60, paras. 18–23.
[75] *Romania* v. *Ukraine*, n. 35, para. 110.   [76] *Nicaragua* v. *Honduras*, n. 37, para. 158.

D. The issue of natural boundaries

The function and role of equity in maritime boundary law is strongly influenced and dependent on a particular key issue: the extent to which boundaries can be drawn and defined *ex ante* by natural features that necessarily leave no room for delimitation based on equitable standards within the fundamental rule. Equity does not need to apply to the extent that natural features, such as troughs, channels and plate tectonics of the shelf and the structure of the water column, and ecological systems in particular, are fundamental in the finding and establishing of boundaries of the shelf and the EEZ. Natural features that determine the course of a boundary are more than equitable standards; they are elements that are inherent to the definition and scope of the respective zone. In terms of methodology, they invariably determine a line and are not subject to the typical elements of balancing different equitable standards inherent to the concept of equity in this context. Natural features and natural boundaries, therefore, are part of the context and environment of equity, and not a question of equitable delimitation as such. It is essential to make this distinction and to clarify their impact before the study turns to the concretization of equity.

The issue of naturally defined boundaries shows a long and complex history. It became a classical case of trial and error in international law. The early, natural definition of the shelf and the concept of natural prolongation and entitlement *ab initio* and *ipso facto* invited and gave rise to a long and arduous debate on natural boundaries based on plate tectonics. Similar arguments based on the concept of ecological systems were put forward with respect to the water column and the EEZ. Whilst allowing for the theoretical possibility of natural boundaries, courts have so far not relied upon the natural features of the seabed and the water column. Indeed, it will be seen that the possibility remains rather exceptional.[77] To the extent that the possibilities of relying upon nature lessened, the relevance and importance of equity as the main pillar for delimitation increased. This does not deny the fact that natural features of the seabed and the water column, and in particular the location of resources, remain of some influence in the process of delimitation. But to that effect they apply within the concept of equity, and therefore amongst other competing standards.

---

[77] See Chapter 10(II)(D).

CONCEPTUAL ISSUES AND THE CONTEXT OF EQUITY   463

1. The impact of natural prolongation and plate tectonics

The physical context of equity is not necessarily limited to surface-related features, such as coastal configurations and the position and size of islands. Features related to the seabed and subsoil in continental shelf delimitations could also significantly influence it. Indeed, given the evolution and history of the first generation of new zones, one would assume that geological features play a significant role in the process of delimitation. The matter has been one of great controversy and confusion, and efforts to find an appropriate place for such features within the methodology of delimitation have been an interesting process of trial and error, reflecting gradually changing attitudes towards and perceptions of the maritime zones over the years. It is necessary to clarify the potential impact at this stage before the study turns to the concretization of equity.

a. **The decline of plate tectonics**   Under the doctrine of natural prolongation, which was paramount in the early days of the legal shelf concept discussed in Chapter 2, it is evident that claims to the shelf only extend to the geological shelf that constitutes the prolongation of the territory and landmass of the coastal states. Physical features that intersect the continuity of the shelf necessarily cause claims to halt at such features. Troughs may therefore establish natural boundaries, which are inherent to the early legal concept of the shelf. Thus, the *North Sea* Court held in famous dicta that, while ignored by the previously agreed delimitation based on equidistance, the shelf areas in the North Sea are separated from the Norwegian Shelf by the 80 to 100 kilometre trough. Without attempting to pronounce on the status of that feature, the Court notes that the areas of shelf in the North Sea that are separated from the Norwegian coast by this trough cannot in any physical sense be said to be adjacent to it, nor to be its natural prolongation.[78] As in the dictum on the Norwegian Trough, physical features of the seabed have remained without any impact in almost all delimitations between opposite and adjacent states. With the exception of the 1971 Australia–Indonesia agreement, which drew the boundary along the Timor Trench, removing the median at the expense of Indonesia,[79] it seems that plate tectonics have not been taken into account in negotiated settlements. In case law, geological features have only had an impact on the location and unity of

[78] ICJ Reports 1969, p. 33, para. 45.
[79] Agreement between Australia and Indonesia establishing Certain Seabed Boundaries, 18 May 1971, 10 ILM 830 (1971). See also Appendix I, Table A.1, No. 29.

resources, which is a different problem. In all cases so far, delimitation has involved the process of delimiting a legally single, coherent and continuous shelf. In other words, none of the cases to date have led to a limitation of the window of overlapping claims by virtue of discontinuity of the shelf.

While plate tectonics were not yet an issue in the *North Sea* cases, the *Anglo-French Channel* arbitration eight years later failed to take into account the so called 'Deep Hurd' and the 'Hurd Deep Fault Zone' put before the Court for consideration by the United Kingdom.[80] The *Gulf of Maine* Chamber declined to draw the boundary along a line separating Brown's and the Georges Bank for lack of conclusive evidence that the Northeast Channel does not interrupt the continuity of the shelf. The ICJ rejected arguments related to bathymetry due to the insignificance of the features presented.[81] The CEIP delimitation courts did the same with arguments that were in favour of taking into account a 'trench' in the Pearl River.[82] Similar conclusions can be found in the *Guinea* v. *Guinea-Bissau* arbitration, where the Court refused to take into account what it considered to be underwater troughs of too little importance to be taken into account.[83]

In *Libya* v. *Malta*, the first case of shelf delimitation involving opposite states, the Court finally ruled out the relevance of geology as a matter of principle, because overlapping claims remained within an area of less than 400 nm.[84] In other words, within the scope of the 200 nm expanse, entitlement exists independent of any geological features on the basis of a distance principle. In cases involving adjacent states, such conclusions have not yet been drawn as a matter of principle.

These results strongly contrast with the volume and intensity of arguments and with the expensive evidence and expert views related to plate

---

[80] Channel Award, n. 2, paras. 104–9.   [81] ICJ Reports 1984, pp. 273–5, paras. 44–7.
[82] Jonathan I. Charney, 'The Delimitation of Lateral Seaward Boundaries between States in a Domestic Context' (1981) 75 *American Journal of International Law*, 28–53.
[83] *Tribunal Arbitral pour la délimitation de la frontière maritime Guinée/Guinée-Bissau, Sentence du 14 Février 1985*, reprinted in French (the authentic text) in (1985) 89 Revue Générale de Droit International Public, 530–1, para. 113.
[84] ICJ Reports 1982, p. 33, para. 34; see also separate opinion Judge MBaye, p. 94: 'The development of the law of the sea, especially since 1958, has shown a tendency to extend the concept of the continental shelf and to attach it increasingly to legal principles, and to detach it ever more surely from its physical origins, whether geological or geomorphological. Moreover, the indisputable connection between the continental shelf and the exclusive economic zone argues in favour of a purely legal approach to the former which is henceforward to be primarily defined in terms of a certain distance rather than by the physiography of the sea-bed and its subsoil.'

tectonics that were submitted by parties on the basis of abstract statements of judicial dicta, such as that concerning the Norwegian Trough in the *North Sea* cases. There has been a significant discrepancy from the outset between the amount of effort exerted on arguments related to geology and the effect that such arguments have had. This provides a classical example of trial and error during the process of finding appropriate legal concepts, characterized at first by a surge and then a decline in the number of surface-related arguments. Indeed, since the birth of the legal concepts of the shelf and the EEZ, delimitation has developed a clear predominance over surface-related standards of delimitation. Since the ICJ recognized and adopted the 200 nm minimum rule in the *Tunisia* v. *Libya* case, it is evident that the scope of application for plate tectonics has been strongly reduced. A number of factors would appear to indicate that the exclusion of plate tectonics has been part of judicial policy over the years:

1. The uniformity of findings may be accidental, in the sense that the cases that have so far been submitted to the courts did not happen to show physical discontinuities of the shelf. The explicit reasoning of the courts supports this idea. However, a different thought may well lie behind this reasoning. The multitude of theories and scientific arguments in existence suggest that there are no generally accepted theories of plate tectonics upon which courts could rely. The matter largely remains a matter of scientific opinion. The 1982 *Tunisia* v. *Libya* case provides an example in point, with Judge Aréchaga quoting the term of 'essay in geopoetry'.[85] Indeed, the plate tectonics issue poses serious problems of evidence, but there is also a deeper problem for the courts. There are serious doubts as to whether courts of law have sufficient resources to deal competently and in an authoritative manner with issues belonging to the realm of natural science and, hence, whether plate tectonics are justiciable and manageable by courts at all. Experts on geology and the evolution of plate tectonics frequently disagree, and courts would be faced with the impossible task of assessing conflicting geological theories. The constant denial of a sufficient degree of prominence of features invoked may stem by implication from the fact of the limited justiciability of these matters.
2. The problem of evidence is particularly serious in the light of the impact that plate-tectonic features of the continental shelf may have.

[85] ICJ Report 1982, p. 110 (separate opinion Aréchaga), quoting John Noble Wilford, *The Mapmakers*, (1st edn. 1981, now revised 2nd edn., New York: Vintage Books, 2001), p. 292.

Whether or not the area to be delimited deals with a uniform shelf or two disconnected shelves depends on existing geological features. Discontinuity, in fact, establishes a boundary on the basis of a single geological feature. Thus, plate tectonics absolutely define the window of delimitation, leaving no flexibility for the operation of equitable standards. It is conceivable that courts sought to refrain from such absolute conclusions by denying evidence based on plate tectonics any role in the delimitation process.

3. Finally, delimitation in accordance with claims based on the features of the seabed are difficult to reconcile with the coincident expanse of the EEZ which is independent of the nature of the seabed. Such delimitation could require the establishment of different boundaries for the shelf and the EEZ. It would be contrary to the overall trend of state practice to converge the two zones and to adopt all-purpose boundaries. In the *St. Pierre and Miquelon* Award, the Court made clear that:

> [i]t should not be forgotten, either, that the physical structure of the sea-bed ceases to be important when the object, as in this case, is to establish a single, all purpose delimitation both of the sea-bed and the superjacent waters.[86]

Nevertheless, the fact that prominent plate tectonics may play an important role in future delimitations between adjacent states cannot be completely ruled out, although with the current trend toward all-purpose boundaries, they may be overwhelmed by the underlying entitlement to claims to the EEZ. There might be configurations in adjacent cases where prominent tectonic structures define a boundary, or parts of it, in terms of natural prolongation. If, to take a hypothetical example, a significant trough ran at an angle less than 90 degrees from the land in a seaward direction, it could divide the shelves, but would not impair claims to the EEZ in seaward direction. Either two boundaries would have to be drawn, or, for practical reasons, a single boundary ignoring the trough. A conclusive answer would imply a geological analysis of all possible boundaries. It seems safe to say, however, that such a case would be exceptional. Where parties agree to draw a single boundary line, the influence of plate tectonics is inherently excluded. In other cases, the parties should seek agreement as to whether or not the delimitation process should take these features into account.

---

[86] Court of Arbitration for the Delimitation of Maritime Areas between Canada and France: Decision in Case Concerning Delimitation of Maritime Areas, 31 (1992) ILM 1145, p. 1156 para 47.

At any rate, it is important from a legal point of view to emphasize the fact that plate tectonics have to be dealt with independently of delimitation in accordance with equitable principles and relevant circumstances. They either include or exclude a claim to the shelf by a particular coastal state, and in fact define the boundary line in the affirmative of a geological discontinuity. Much of the confusion surrounding natural prolongation stems from the fact that the question of plate tectonics has been considered under the heading of equitable standards or relevant circumstances, and argued for or considered by the courts from this perspective. Geological features, however, cannot be dealt with on this level. They have to be considered at the same time as the expanse of basic entitlement is decided upon, and it can be decided that either they will prevent further entitlement, or not. *Tertium non datur.* It is inconsistent for geophysical features of the seabed to influence the boundary in one way or another in a totally fluid manner, as is typical for the balancing methodology under equitable principles and relevant circumstances. This is not a new insight; nothing demonstrates this better than Article 6 of the 1958 Shelf Convention. The rule of equidistance only applies to delimitation of the *same* continental shelf, appertaining to opposite or adjacent states. The same is true for other applicable methods, including those contained in the fundamental rule of equity in general international law.

b. The irrelevance of natural prolongation The main function of natural prolongation was viewed as the establishment of rights *ipso facto* and *ab initio*, thereby excluding acquisition or occupation of shelf areas other than by the respective coastal state. Natural prolongation is still relevant for delimitations of the seaward boundary under the LOS Convention.[87] In addition to the decline in importance of plate tectonics for contentious delimitation, natural prolongation ceased to provide the legal basis for the delimitation of and within a coherent shelf. As the case law evolved, the view of the Courts gradually shifted away from natural prolongation and towards a perception of delimitation as an active legal–political operation.

Throughout the *North Sea* cases, the rejection of both equidistance as a mandatory rule and the doctrine of equitable shares, as well as the establishment of the principles of non-cutting-off and

---

[87] See Chapter 2(II)(C).

non-encroachment, were primarily founded upon, and justified by, the doctrine of natural prolongation. The continental shelf and the slope were defined as a natural prolongation of the land territory. In essence, it was conceived as a submarine, territorial concept, closely reliant upon the geological and geomorphological structure of the seabed. As the Court said, 'The continental shelf is, by definition, an area physically extending the territory of most coastal states'.[88] Article 6 of the 1958 Shelf Convention implies a similar concept when equidistance is limited in its application to areas of the *same* shelf. At the time, natural prolongation was conceived much more as an expression of a geological and geomorphological structure of the seabed, than as a geographical and surface-related extension of the thrust of the mainland in a seaward direction. Even if the *North Sea* cases would allow for a different reading,[89] states and the legal community at the time generally shared a territorial perception of natural prolongation.[90] This view became decisive in the *Aegean Continental Shelf* case[91] and was reflected in subsequent cases.

However, the concept of natural prolongation created more problems than it was able to settle in the context of basically uniform shelves, as is highlighted by the *Anglo-French Channel* arbitration.[92] The move towards viewing delimitation as a task of a legal, rather than physical, definition of natural prolongation[93] reflects this analysis. In *Tunisia* v. *Libya* in 1982, the ICJ held that natural prolongation was not applicable, due to the continuity of the shelf.[94] It was generally discarded to the benefit of more human-related factors, particularly the historic conduct of the parties.[95] The general decline of natural prolongation continued, as

---

[88] ICJ Reports 1969, p. 52, para. 95.
[89] ICJ Reports 1969, pp. 109–18, paras. 37–64 (separate opinion Aréchaga).
[90] Derek W. Bowett, 'Jurisdiction: Changing Patterns of Authority over Activities and Resources' in R. St. J. Macdonald and D. M. Johnston (eds.), *The Structure and Process of International Law: Essays in Legal Philosophy, Doctrine and Theory* (Dordrecht: Martinus Nijhoff Publishers, 1983), p. 555: 'It is equally clear that states have relied essentially on the territorial principle to support the jurisdiction necessary to protect their interest in resources actually located outside their territory but conceded in international law to be within the control of the state.'
[91] *Aegean Sea Continental Shelf (Greece v. Turkey)*, Judgment, ICJ Reports 1978, p. 3.
[92] Channel Award, n. 2, p. 52, para. 79. [93] Ibid., pp. 92–3, paras. 191–4.
[94] ICJ Reports 1982, pp. 66–7, paras. 57–8.
[95] See also Emmanuel Decaux, 'L'Arrêt de la Cour internationale de justice dans l'affaire du plateau continental (Tunisie/Libye)' (1982) 28 *Annuaire Français de Droit International*, 364–71; and Elisabeth Zoller, 'Recherches sur les méthodes de délimitation du plateau continental: à propos de l'affaire Tunisie-Libye' (1982) 86 *Revue Générale de Droit*

was demonstrated in the *Gulf of Maine* case. In this case, the principle was left unapplied to a consistent shelf, primarily due to the establishment of an all-purpose boundary. The Chamber clearly stressed, *obiter dictum*, completing the turn of the Channel arbitration, that delimitation is a legal–political operation that does not necessarily follow natural patterns:

> It must, however, be emphasised that a delimitation, whether of a maritime boundary or of a land boundary, is a legal-political operation, and that it is not the case that where a natural boundary is discernible, the political delimitation must necessarily follow the same line.[96]

After this point, delimitation clearly became a surface-related operation, unless a natural separation existed from a factual viewpoint between the shelves of the parties in dispute. The *Guinea* v. *Guinea-Bissau* arbitration affirmed this finding. The case further clarified the fact that natural prolongation does not apply within the minimal 200 nm expanse.[97] Similarly, the ICJ in *Malta* v. *Libya* implicitly denounced the application of natural prolongation within such expanses in opposite configurations.[98] The *St. Pierre and Miquelon* Court of Arbitration made clear that the concept of natural prolongation, in spite of its physical origins, has become an increasingly complex juridical concept and confirmed its practical application with the advent of the EEZ:

> [T]he physical structure of the sea-bed ceases to be important when the object, as in this case, is to establish a single, all purpose delimitation both of the sea-bed and the superjacent waters.[99]

Case law thus marks a clear turn towards surface-related criteria, leaving the doctrine of natural prolongation to apply only where a natural separation does exist from a factual point of view between the respective

---

International Public, pp. 655–6 (critical on such departure from the *North Sea* doctrine. 'En décidant de prendre en compte toutes les circonstances et surtout en les détachant de l'assise physique à laquelle elles étaient détachées en 1969, la Cour s'est engagé dans uns voie dangereuse'. It should be recalled that the development towards a juridical notion of the shelf was already completed in the 1977 Channel Arbitration, see Channel Award, n. 2, para. 191. See also Elisabeth Zoller 'L'Affaire de la délimitation du plateau continental entre la République française et le Royaume-Uni de Grande-Bretagne et d'Irlande du Nord' (1977) 28 *Annuaire Français de Droit International*, 391–2.

[96] ICJ Reports 1984, p. 277, para. 56.
[97] *Arbitration Tribunal for the Delimitation of the Maritime Boundary Between Guinea and Guinea-Bissau*, Award of 14 February 1985, transl. in (1986) 25 ILM 251 (hereinafter *Guinea/Guinea-Bissau* arbitration), p. 530, para. 115. But also para. 116 (affirming the juridical nature of the concept). It is, however, doubtful whether para. 91 is correct in saying that all zones rely upon natural prolongation.
[98] ICJ Reports 1985, p. 33, paras. 34, 36 and 40.   [99] N. 86, p. 1165, para. 47.

platforms of the parties in dispute.[100] Natural prolongation therefore only plays a role where neighbouring states happen to be separated by two geologically succinct shelves, which is apparently a rare, but nevertheless possible, configuration. It is doubtful whether natural prolongation and geology will ever play an important role in the delimitation between opposite and adjacent states.[101] It does not figure prominently in state practice and treaty negotiations.[102]

c. Conclusion   In conclusion, natural prolongation and geomorphology are relevant only in very exceptional cases of delimitation between coastal states. It is important to emphasize the fact that plate tectonics are not part of the rule of equity, but are constitutive of the expanse of claims, and therefore of boundaries *per se*. As with the window of delimitation, they form part of the context of equity, i.e. they influence equity, but are not part of it.

As to the delimitation of coherent, uniform shelves, natural prolongation is no longer of any importance. This reiterates the need for a different, underlying entitlement. A doctrine and foundation are required to allow for the assessment of decisions over which of the competing claims in an area has a better title in the process of a political–legal delimitation. The theory of close relationship, established in Part I, will provide a starting point for further analysis.

2. The impact of ecology (ecosystems)

In the delimitation of the EEZ, the ecology of the water column may provide arguments and problems that are comparable to those that natural prolongation and geology provide in the field of shelf delimitation. Before the decline of plate tectonics, it seemed natural and evident that the structure of the water column would provide factors and criteria that would be equally relevant for equitable delimitation.[103] An

---

[100] ICJ Reports 1984, p. 275, para. 47; ICJ Reports 1982, p. 64, para. 80.
[101] But see Jonathan I. Charney, Proceedings of the American Society of International Law 1982, pp. 154, 158 (geology can make an important contribution).
[102] Edward Collins and Martin Rogoff, 'The International Law of Maritime Boundary Delimitation' (1982) 34 *Maine Law Review*, 1, 19. See also Charney, 'The Delimitation of Lateral Seaward Boundaries between States in a Domestic Context', n. 82, 28 at 53–4.
[103] As Colson put it: 'If one asked a group of international lawyers a few years ago if they thought that the first delimitation of a 200 nautical mile zone maritime boundary would stress new elements of legal relevance for delimitation, I feel safe in asserting that most persons would have answered yes. And, I believe, that they would have said that environmental factors would attain such a role', David A. Colson, 'Environmental

ecological system is formed from the specific features of a particular area, including: the species living there; the interaction of different resources; the texture of the water column as regards biological composition; the food chain; hydraulic circulation; temperature; salinity; density; vertical stratification; and tidal activity. Such systems arguably form distinct units with invisible natural boundaries requiring coherent management, conservation and exploitation.

In the 1984 *Gulf of Maine* case, the United States submitted extensive scientific evidence to the effect that the food chains of the Gulf of Maine basin, the Georges Bank (linked to that of the Nantucket Shoals) and the Scotian Shelf constituted distinct and separate ecological systems. The United States therefore concluded that the Northeast Channel between the Scotian Shelf (the German Bank and Brown's Banks) constituted the most important recognizable natural boundary between these different ecological systems, 'forming a line of separation within the area in the case of most of its commercially important fish stocks'.[104] The US' scientific evidence and arguments were challenged by Canada, and the Chamber (applying strict standards of proof),[105] which was not convinced by the theory of different ecosystems, assumed a general unity of the water column within the window of delimitation.[106]

Whether or not such a finding by the Chamber was correct in accepted terms of marine biology cannot be assessed here. From a legal perspective, however, the question that arises concerns whether ecosystems (i.e. natural features of the water column) are eligible to determine a boundary under the legal concept of the EEZ on exclusive grounds. Unlike the situation with the shelf, the 200 nm zone has been an essentially space-related concept from the beginning. The outer limits are exclusively defined by distance from coastal configurations and islands. There is no parallelism with the geological definition of expanses of the shelf which, in exceptional cases, may define a natural boundary between coastal states both in opposite or adjacent configurations. Therefore, ecosystems, even if established, cannot *per se* qualify as a criterion by which to define a boundary line. It also seems that the argument for ecosystems in the *Gulf of Maine* case supported the argument of boundaries defined by the channels.

Factors: Are they relevant to Delimitation?', Paper presented at the 19th Conference of the Law of the Sea Institute, 24–27 July 1985, Cardiff, Wales, p. 1 (on file with author).
[104] ICJ Reports 1984, p. 276, para. 51.   [105] ICJ Reports 1984, p. 277, para. 53 in fine.
[106] ICJ Reports 1984, p. 277, para. 55.

The Chamber did not approach the problem in basic terms, but produced similar effects when dealing with ecosystems, stressing, as seen before, the fact that delimitation is essentially a 'legal–political operation'.[107] This is inherently at variance with any concept of *ex ante* naturally defined boundaries which, incidentally, would have been very much to the United States' benefit in their claim for the whole of Georges Bank. Indeed, Georges Bank – the very object in dispute – was divided,[108] and the parties were reminded of their long tradition of 'friendly and fruitful co-operation in maritime matters' with regard to the problem of coherent management, conservation and exploitation of the rich fishing grounds.[109]

E. A doctrine of the closest relationship

It follows from the concepts and definitions of the shelf and the EEZ that delimitation is an operation that is limited to coastal states that are entitled to claim rights over space and resources. The definition of the window of delimitation is not only a matter of assessing areas which are in dispute among the parties, but is also primarily a matter of whether they are both entitled to claim the area and resources on the basis of the definitions of the shelf and the EEZ.

The question arises over which of the parties has a superior right over the claimed areas within the window of delimitation. It is submitted that the underlying foundation (analysed in Part I of this study) both of the shelf and the EEZ constitutes the most important normative value by which to decide this question. It was concluded that, based on the principle of permanent sovereignty over natural resources, entitlement over space and resources ultimately relies on the idea that the coastal state has a close relationship to them. Geographic equidistance equally reflects this underlying concept as the main competing approach to delimitation. Both schools of thought share a common perception and this may therefore be considered to have been clearly established. Significantly, however, such closeness is not merely defined in geographical terms (contiguity, proximity, distance), but may equally be defined in terms of human geography, such as economics, politics or historical relationships as is relevant to the particular facts of each configuration.

---

[107] ICJ Reports 1984, p. 277, para. 56.   [108] See Chapter 6(II)(E).
[109] ICJ Reports 1984 p. 343, para. 240.

The issue involved in delimitation therefore concerns which of the parties involved demonstrates the closest relationships to all of the factors in a particular area and the resources in dispute. Close relationship emerges as the most fundamental test of resource and spatial allocation within the concepts of the shelf and EEZ (closest relation test: CRT). In ligation, the CRT test often materializes in giving half-way or no effect to islands when drawing equidistance-based boundaries, or in avoiding the cut-off effects of particular geographical features.[110] Of course, the question may be difficult to answer in a particular case and there will always be grey areas, which in the end need decision-making either by agreement or by a court of law. In the latter case, such decisions have to be justified with arguments based on physical (geographical, rarely geological) or human (economic, political or historical) considerations. The influence of underlying objectives and values offers additional help in the rationalization and achievement of a reasoned delimitation. In this process, it may appear under the facts of a particular case that the test provides different answers to the question of closeness of relationship to the shelf and the EEZ. A different relationship to mineral resources, on the one hand, and living resources, on the other, indicates that the result of the process can end up with different boundaries for two zones, thereby optimizing the underlying values without taking practical problems into account.

F. The impact of underlying objectives and values

Beyond entitlement based on the closest relationship, the rule of equity seeks to realize the underlying values and objectives of the zones and their functions. They are of particular importance for the purpose of fine-tuning a boundary that has been drawn for the time being on the basis of the CRT.

Each national zone that is delimited should be in a position to function in accordance with its purpose and goals. Delimitation is therefore a process of optimizing, in all areas, the values and goals discussed above. Obviously, different values and goals compete against one another, and rational decisions need to be made in favour of one or the other zone and coastal state. Clearly, the process entails an operation of balancing values. Given its relational nature, the rule of equity cannot be shaped without taking into account the goals, purposes, history and legal

---

[110] Cf. Chapter 10(II)(A)(2), Chapter 11(IV).

foundations of the respective zones. Article 30(1) of the Vienna Convention on the Law of Treaties (VCLT) refers, inter alia, to the goals and purposes of interpretation. Article 32(a) allows recourse to be taken to the *travaux préparatoires*, and thus the legislative history of an agreement, to the extent that interpretation in accordance with the elements contained in Article 31 leaves the meaning of the provisions ambiguous or unclear.[111] The elusiveness of the notion of equity renders the primary elements, and particularly the wording, ordinary meaning and context, rather useless and circular. The same problem arises in the interpretation of the fundamental rule. The inclusion of materials and the legislative history may therefore be appropriate for the interpretation of equity both in treaty and, *mutatis mutandis*, for the fundamental rule of delimitation in general international law.

While the 1958 Shelf Convention[112] is silent due to the absence of a preamble, the purpose and goal of the shelf and the EEZ are at least partly stated in explicit terms in the 1982 LOS Convention. The Preamble calls upon the establishment of a legal order of the seas by this Convention:

> which would facilitate international communication and promote their peaceful uses, the equitable share and efficient utilisation of their resources, the study, protection and preservation of the marine environment and the conservation of the living resources thereof.[113]

Such explicitly stated purposes already provide some guidance, albeit minimal, as to the interpretation of the conventional rules as well as of fundamental norms. All delimitations must promote the efficient utilization and preservation of the marine environment and conservation of living resources without impeding communications. For example, where a boundary crosses a particular oil deposit, it is difficult to see how, short of co-operation between the parties, the boundary would facilitate the management and exploitation of these resources and serve the function of dispute prevention that is inherent to the law. Likewise, a boundary that cuts through an area that requires the comprehensive and uniform conservation and management of living resources in the region would hardly respect the purpose of improved marine conservation and protection from over-fishing that is envisaged by the EEZ. It would be equally difficult to uphold the goal of unimpaired naval

---

[111] Vienna Convention on the Law of Treaties 1969, 1155 UNTS 336.
[112] Convention on the Continental Shelf 1958, 7302 UNTS 499.
[113] United Nations Convention on the Law of the Sea (Done at Montego Bay, December 10, 1982) (1982) 21 ILM 1261–354.

communication in a situation where access to a particular harbour leads exclusively through waters whose resources are subject to the jurisdiction of a different state, for the obvious reason of potential disputes about conflicting priorities.

Beyond these general elements, it seems difficult to draw further requirements for delimitation from the purposes that were explicitly stated. This is particularly true for the idea of equitable share that is contained in the Preamble of the LOS Convention. Since it refers to equity as such, nothing can be won for the interpretation of equity itself. Further insight may be achieved on the basis of the conceptual elements discussed above, and additional guidance may be found in the values inherent to the shelf and the EEZ that were discussed throughout Part I of this study: control of the exploitation and management of resources, both mineral and living; increasing fiscal revenues; the preservation of national security interests on the shelf; and the protection of local fishing industries. An equitable delimitation has to respect these values for the parties involved and seek the optimal allocation of resources under the facts of the particular case.

It was seen that these objectives and values are not identical for the shelf and the EEZ. Such differences may lead to the evolution of different equitable standards. It will therefore be necessary to examine whether or not each applies equally to both zones of horizontally shared jurisdiction. They may differ under the same fundamental rule of equity. In addition to the existence of relationships of varying proximity to mineral and living resources in a particular area, equity may also exceptionally suggest differing boundary lines for the shelf and the EEZ for these reasons.

III. The legal environment of equity

It is important to reiterate the fact that equity, of course, is not the only legally relevant source of maritime boundary delimitation. Delimitation is equally, if not predominantly, reliant upon treaty law, as well as on general rules and on principles of international law. Although in a way all of the context of equity discussed could be considered to form part of the legal environment of equity, this chapter limits such an environment to prominent legal norms, which are of importance to delimitation outside the concept of equitable standards of maritime boundary law. Other than principles such as permanent sovereignty over national resources, the sovereign equality of states, or the principle of proportionality, which need further specification within the concepts of the shelf and the EEZ, these norms can be readily applied, independent of the subject matter under consideration. To the extent to which they apply, there is theoretically no longer any room for equity to play a role. In fact, the situation is comparable with the window of delimitation and geology that has been discussed previously. If such a norm applies, it may largely dispose of the case. From a methodological point of view, it is therefore necessary to deal with the legal environment before delimitation based on equity can be addressed.

It will be seen that the factual conditions necessary for applying general legal principles such as estoppel are often not sufficiently met. Yet it is interesting to observe that some of them nevertheless exert spillover effects upon the delimitation process at a sub-legal level. Even where such legal principles do not apply in a strict sense, they may influence delimitation within the concept of equity to the extent that conduct of the parties is taken into account. Therefore, legal principles can be seen not only as important neighbours to equity, but also to exert an indirect influence on the substance of equity, equitable principles and relevant circumstances. Such spillover effects will be dealt with in Chapter 10.

A. *Pacta sunt servanda*

1. Delimitation and related agreements

Delimitation often involves the application and interpretation of international agreements. Such agreements are to be honoured under the fundamental principle of *pacta sunt servanda* that is enshrined in Article 26 VCLT. Contentious cases may be entirely constrained to issues of treaty law and interpretation, particularly where agreements concerning delimitation of the shelf, the EEZ or fishery zones have been concluded and now give rise to different interpretations. Sometimes, treaties pre-date the post-World War II maritime revolution's influence, or even determine the boundaries of the new zones. Treaties related to the delimitation of narrow straits may inherently cover the new shelf and EEZ rights, due to the fact that the areas have long been part of historic internal waters and the territorial sea.[114] Sometimes, whether or not the scope of a particular treaty applies to the subject matter and area in

---

[114] E.g. 'The US–Russian Treaty of 1867 effecting the cessation of Alaska with respect to the Bering and Chuchki Seas and North Pacific Ocean' (1981) 75 *American Journal of International Law*, see n. 11, p. 751.

CONCEPTUAL ISSUES AND THE CONTEXT OF EQUITY 477

dispute is a controversial issue. Similar problems may arise with respect to arbitral awards.[115]

More commonly, however, treaty law will be just one of several aspects of a case, and will not entirely dispose of the dispute on delimitation. Often it only affects particular issues of the case, such as land boundaries in coastal areas, sovereignty over islands, delimitation of the territorial sea, or perhaps also the boundaries of the contiguous zone. Treaties that were concluded before the evolution and establishment of the new zones in customary international law often do not cover the subject matter of the shelf and the EEZ. Long-distance maritime boundary delimitation, therefore, regularly involves new issues and requires creative activities during negotiations or in court.

The *Guinea/Guinea-Bissau* arbitration is a good example of the need to fit an old treaty to new international maritime law. A substantial part of this award was dedicated to a decision concerning whether the 1886 Convention between France and Portugal, including its annexes and protocols, established a maritime boundary between the two former colonies.[116] The Court argued *in extenso* that there was no intention at the time to establish a maritime boundary of the territorial sea,[117] and intentions were merely limited to the establishment of a land boundary. Another example can be found in the *Denmark v. Norway (Jan Mayen)* case. The ICJ had to determine to what extent the case was disposed of by the alleged application of a 1965 Maritime Boundary Treaty between Denmark and Norway. Norway relied on Article 1 of that Treaty to argue for the equidistance line to form the limit between the small island of Jan Mayen and the great land mass of Greenland. Denmark contested this interpretation, claiming that the provision was only applicable to the North Sea maritime boundary. Upon construing the agreement, the Court found that the treaty did not apply to the disputed area.[118]

In the *Cameroon v. Nigeria* case, Nigeria disputed the validity of prior agreements establishing the maritime boundary from the mouth of the Akwayafe River up to a point G.[119] The Court agreed with Cameroon that

---

[115] E.g. *Arbitral Award of 31 July 1989 (Guinea-Bissau v. Senegal)*, Judgment, ICJ Reports 1991, p. 53.
[116] Art. 2 procès-verbal, 'International Court of Justice: Judgment on Application for Revision and Interpretation of the Judgment in the Case Concerning the Continental Shelf (Tunisia/Libyan Arab Jamahiriya)' 25 (1986) ILM, 155–6, paras. 44–82 of the Award dealing with the treaty issue, see also Chapter 6(II)(F).
[117] Ibid., pp. 155–6, paras. 63–82.   [118] ICJ Reports 1993, pp. 48–53, paras. 22–32.
[119] ICJ Reports 2002, p. 303, 449, map no. 12.

the Anglo-German Agreement of 11 March 1913, the Yaoundé II Declaration of 4 April 1971 and the Maroua Declaration of 1 June 1975 are binding on Nigeria and establish the maritime boundary up to and including point G.[120] In *Guyana v. Suriname*, the Tribunal found that the record amply supports Suriname's conclusion that the predecessors of the parties agreed upon a N 10°E delimitation line for the reason that all of the Corentyne River was to be Suriname's territory and that the 10° line provided appropriate access through Suriname's territorial sea to the western channel of the Corentyne River.[121] However, the 10° line was established between the parties only from the starting point to the 3 nm limit.[122] Suriname argued that the N 10°E line should be extended up to the modern 12 nm territorial sea limit by virtue of the doctrine of intertemporal law.[123] The Tribunal, however, held that the only special circumstances which would call for a deviation from the equidistance line was the circumstance of navigation and control over the approaches to the Corentyne River, which did not apply beyond 3 nm seawards, and therefore rejected an automatic extension of the 10° line.[124] The Tribunal ultimately drew a straight line from the 3 nm limit of the 10° line to the 12nm limit where the single boundary equidistance line determined by the Tribunal to delimit the continental shelves and EEZs of the parties begins.[125]

In *Romania v. Ukraine*, the Court concluded from a pre-existing delimitation agreement that it relates only to the demarcation of the state border between Romania and the USSR, which around Serpents' Island followed the 12 nm limit of the territorial sea. Therefore, the USSR did not forfeit its entitlement beyond the 12 nm limit of its territorial sea with respect to any other maritime zones. Consequently, the Court held that there was no agreement in force between Romania and Ukraine delimiting between them the EEZ and the continental shelf.[126]

In *Maritime Dispute (Peru v. Chile)*, much of the case depended upon the application and interpretation of existing treaties and instruments of the parties to the dispute. While Peru argued that there are no treaty obligations in place, Chile contended that the boundary had been established by the 1952 Santiago Declaration and subsequent treaty law. Upon

---

[120] Ibid., p. 425 ss, paras. 248, 261, 268.
[121] *Guyana v. Suriname* Award, n. 2, para. 306.   [122] Ibid., para. 307.
[123] Ibid., paras. 286–7. Suriname relied on the finding of the ICJ in the *Aegean Sea* case that an agreement 'must be interpreted in accordance with the rules of international law as they exist today' (para. 286).
[124] Ibid., para. 314.   [125] Ibid., para. 315.   [126] ICJ Report 2009, p. 89, para. 76.

assessing treaty law, unilateral acts and state practice, the Court found an agreed maritime boundary extending to 80 nm along the parallel from the starting point, but not beyond.[127] The latter was left to judicial determination.

Finally, it should be recalled that maritime boundary agreements that are concluded after a court of law has rendered its judgment may either complete delimitation or deviate from it. Although a judgment is binding, nothing can prevent the parties from renegotiating a settlement, in much the same way as they are free to revise negotiated delimitations by a treaty superseding the special agreement, provided they remain within the bounds of an equitable solution.[128]

2. The principle of *uti possidetis*

Uti possidetis juris was originally applied in Latin American land boundary disputes.[129] In essence, the principle stipulates that the boundaries of newly created states should be those of the former colonies.[130] In post-World War II decolonization, it found prominent expression in the setting of the African continent's post-colonial boundaries. Rather than being a general principle, it flows from informal and formal agreements reached by African states. Pledged by the states of the Organization of African Unity (OAU) in 1964, it assures the existence, direction and positioning of those former colonial land boundaries that were in existence at the time the states reached independence.[131] For the sake of legal security and the prevention of tribal and international disputes, the principle does not allow arguments over the lawfulness of existing colonial boundaries by the succeeding independent state. The principle was later further generalized and incorporated in the 1978 Vienna Convention on

---

[127] *Maritime Dispute (Peru v. Chile)*, Judgment of 27 January 2014, ICJ Reports___ paras. 24–151.

[128] See *Application for Revision and Interpretation of the Judgment of 24 February 1982 in the Case concerning the Continental Shelf (Tunisia v. Libyan Arab Jamahiriya)*, Judgment, ICJ Reports 1985, pp. 192, 219, para. 48 (parties 'may of course still reach mutual agreement upon a delimitation that does not correspond to that decision').

[129] John R. V. Prescott, *Political Frontiers and Boundaries* (London: Routledge, 1990), pp. 102, 105–6, 199–200.

[130] Ibid., pp. 199–200.

[131] Proclaimed in Cairo on 21 July 1963, reaffirming para. III(3) of the Charter of the Organization of African Unity (OAU Charter of 25 May 1963) (respect for the sovereignty and territorial integrity of each state and for its inalienable right to independent existence).

Succession of States in Respect of Treaties (Article 11),[132] and therefore also applies to states party to this Convention, independent of their geographical location.

The *Guinea/Guinea-Bissau* award held these provisions to reflect customary international law of state succession and therefore to be in operation independently of the entry into force and membership to this Convention.[133] Today, it may therefore be considered as an established principle of general international law and a concretization of *pacta sunt servanda* in the context of colonial transition of international agreements. But to what extent does it also apply to maritime boundaries and, in particular, to the delimitation of the shelf and the EEZ?

Uti possidetis is certainly relevant to the extent that the principle determines the location and direction of land boundaries at the shore with legal security, and thereby defines boundaries of internal waters (to the extent established) and the starting point of the territorial sea and the new maritime zones. However, from a legal point of view, it is not entirely clear whether the principle of *uti possidetis* also applies more specifically to maritime boundaries *per se*. When the issue was raised in the *Guinea/Guinea-Bissau* arbitration, the Court held that *uti possidetis* would only be relevant if the boundary was defined by the 1886 agreement. This was held not to be the case in this scenario and no further elaboration was required.[134] Similarly in the 2007 *Nicaragua/Honduras* case, the Court accepted the *uti possidetis juris* principle's general validity in a maritime delimitation dispute, but it rejected Honduras' *uti possidetis* argument with respect to a particular boundary line.[135] The Court found that a 1906 Arbitral Award, which indeed was based on the *uti possidetis juris* principle, did not deal with the maritime delimitation between Nicaragua and Honduras and that it did not confirm a maritime boundary between them along the 15th parallel.[136] Both decisions imply that the principle does not apply to delimitation other than in formal, and perhaps also in informal, agreements or decisions.

However, the principle, at least as a regional principle, is not necessarily limited to such sources. It refers to those boundaries that were in existence at the time of independence, and not to forms of boundary

---

[132] Done at Vienna on 23 August 1978. Entered into force on 6 November 1996. United Nations, Treaty Series, vol. 1946, p. 3.
[133] *Arbitration Tribunal for the Delimitation of the Maritime Boundary between Guinea and Guinea-Bissau*, Award of 14 February 1985, reprinted in 25 (1986) ILM, pp. 252, 271.
[134] Ibid.   [135] ICJ Reports 2007, p. 727 ss, paras. 229–36.
[136] ICJ Reports 2007, p. 727, para. 235.

delimitation by way of agreement or judgment. Boundaries may have been established on the basis of conduct through a process of claims and counterclaims, involving prescription and acquiescence, that will be discussed shortly. The principle should therefore also cover such titles, provided it can be shown that they were already established and clearly accepted at the time independence was gained. There is no reason why *uti possidetis* should not also apply to maritime boundaries. The purposes of stabilization and legal security that are pursued by the principle are equally valid and relevant in this context. However, as the concept of the shelf and the EEZ emerged only during and after the process of decolonization in most instances, this principle remains of limited impact. In practical terms, it is of importance mainly with regard to internal and 3-mile territorial waters for the simple reason that the jurisdiction of coastal states and their boundaries were already established under colonial rule. In the 1992 case, *Maritime Frontier Dispute (El Salvador v. Honduras, Nicaragua Intervening)*, the ICJ made clear that *uti possidetis* may be applied 'to the waters of the Gulf as well as to the land'.[137] The evolution of the shelf and the process of decolonization overlap greatly with regard to continental shelf boundaries, and few boundaries were established before independence. This is even truer with respect to the EEZ, which only emerged in the early 1980s. Each instance of delimitation therefore requires a careful comparison of boundary delimitation and dates of independence.

Finally, it may be argued that the principle cannot be applied to delimitations that were proclaimed unilaterally before the concepts of the shelf and the EEZ became part of customary international law. Unlike the situation that occurred in the area of territorial boundaries, legal title to undertake such allocations was still lacking. This interesting problem, however, is a general one, and is specifically related to state succession. Early agreements and claims, important in the evolution towards customary law, cannot be, and never were, considered null and void due to lack of jurisdiction. The subject matter was not one prohibited by *jus cogens* (if known at all, at the time), and agreements between parties are valid. The absence of jurisdiction merely rendered these agreements non-opposable to third states and their drilling or fishing activities, so long as the concept was not accepted among all the parties affected by the treaty or, ultimately, by means of customary law. Once this step was achieved,

---

[137] ICJ Reports 1992, p. 589, para. 386. See also Charney, 'Progress in International Maritime Boundary Delimitation Law', n. 60, pp. 234–5.

third parties could no longer insist on former rights, but were limited to the defence of third party rights as neighbouring coastal states. Since *uti possidetis* only relates to the delimiting states and not to third parties, it lawfully covers all agreements or delimitations by the conduct of former colonial powers.

In conclusion, the principle of *uti possidetis* applies to those boundaries that were in existence at the date of independence, but not to ones that only emerged after that date. As to agreements which were concluded before independence and even before the shelf became part of customary law, the principle would not allow such boundaries to be challenged, on the basis that they were concluded by the predecessor, even if it produced an inequitable result from a contemporary perspective. An agreement to undertake peaceful renegotiations or a special authorization by the court to ignore the principle in the compromise, remain the only alternatives that enable the allocation of marine resources formerly imposed under the principle of *uti possidetis juris* to be changed. Delimitation of the more recent EEZ and the practical feasibility of achieving all-purpose boundaries provide a useful rationale for doing so in such cases. Once again, it is important to emphasize that equity does not apply where a boundary is disposed of by *uti possidetis*.

3. Compromis (special agreement)

A very important element that is responsible for shaping the legal environment of equity in delimitation by judicial or conciliatory means are the special agreements or compromis based upon which a case is submitted to a court of law, tribunal, or to a person or panel for conciliation. Special agreements may either request a definition of relevant principles and rules of delimitation[138] or the establishment of a final boundary line fully or partly within an agreed-upon window of delimitation.[139]

Special agreements set forth important parameters, upon which a legal decision or conciliation is bound to operate. Usually the compromis reflects the state of negotiations between the parties that failed to settle the boundary. Parties may nevertheless have been able to agree upon approaches or special considerations, or even to have settled parts of the boundary or at least target areas, as the *Gulf of Maine* agreement

---

[138] E.g. *North Sea Continental Shelf Cases*, ICJ Reports 1969, p. 3; *Tunisia* v. *Libya* case, ICJ Reports 1982, p. 18.

[139] E.g. 1977 Channel Award, n. 2; *Gulf of Maine* case, ICJ Reports 1984, p. 246; *Libya* v. *Malta* case, ICJ Reports 1985, p. 4; *St. Pierre and Miquelon* Arbitration, n. 86.

shows.[140] The theoretical possibility of requesting delimitation *ex aequo et bono* demonstrates that such agreements in fact may completely define the method of delimitation. The same holds true where parties agree to apply specific technical methods, such as equidistance. There is wide scope for creativity. An agreement may, for example, mandate a court or panel to focus its attention particularly on the economic dependence of one or both parties on particular resources,[141] or to the location of resources.

An important decision relates to whether or not delimitation should establish an all-purpose boundary or separate, special boundaries, related to the shelf or the EEZ. Such a decision may still be of importance for the specification of equity in a particular case. This is true despite the general tendency in case law towards neutral criteria of a geographical nature, since these criteria have been mainly developed in the context of all-purpose boundaries. States might also agree that zones of joint venture and co-operation should be established, thus requiring a task to be undertaken that goes beyond what a court of law could do at this stage of development of international maritime boundary law. Nothing stands in the way of parties requiring such a scheme. The *Jan Mayen* commission, although not stating it in law, showed that such a task could be justiciable. Requirements set forth in special agreements may be grouped in two basic categories: the first concerns the legal environment of equity, in the sense that it defines the scope and task of delimitation; and the second operates within the rule of equity, to the extent that the parties agree on the particular emphasis of equitable standards or circumstances, effectively limiting the court's discretion. This influences the methodology of delimitation in equity. Due to these agreements, the role of courts differs between different cases, as their task varies considerably – a fact that must be taken into account when precedents are compared.

In accordance with the *Lotus* case, it follows from the principle of *pacta sunt servanda* that a court has to rely upon the terms of the agreement rather than on the conclusions of the parties.[142] As the Court said in 1950, '[t]he consent of States, parties to a dispute, is

---

[140] ICJ Reports 1984, p. 246.
[141] E.g. ' the commission shall take into account Iceland's strong economic interests in these sea areas', Art. 9(3), *Fisheries Jurisdiction Case (United Kingdom v. Iceland)*, ICJ Reports 1974, p. 3.
[142] 'The Lotus Case'; No. 10, *The Case of the S.S. Lotus*, Judgment No. 9, *Permanent Court of International Justice*, Series A, p. 12.

the basis of the Court's jurisdiction in contentious cases'.[143] The courts have shown close adherence to the agreements. Controversies over the proper delimitation between the parties were decided on the basis of special agreements, taking into account the pleadings of the parties.[144] In the *Tunisia/Libya* case, the enumeration of 'equitable principles, relevant circumstances which characterise the area' and 'the new accented trends' at UNCLOS III[145] strongly influenced the Court.[146]

Similarly, a revision of the judgment rendered has to take place on the basis of the terms of the special agreement.[147] Equally, the Chamber accepted the task of establishing a single maritime boundary as a 'fact' in the 1984 *Gulf of Maine* case[148] without discussing the legal foundations of the concept – an approach strongly objected to by Judge Gros.[149] While this certainly was a missed opportunity for clarifying the relationship of the shelf and the EEZ,[150] there can be no doubt that the parties could lawfully require the Chamber to address this task, as they may emphasize other elements in the process of delimitation.

Are there limitations to strict adherence by the courts to the terms of special agreements? Despite *pacta sunt servanda*, the possibility that there are such limitations cannot be ruled out. A compromise may prescribe a window of delimitation or parameters within which it encroaches upon the claims or rights of third parties which the court has to respect under the principle that an agreement must not harm third party rights (*pactum tertiis nec prosunt nec nocent*).[151] Or, an agreement achieved under diplomatic pressure may limit a court's discretion to such an extent that close adherence to the terms inevitably ends in an inequitable result, whatever methods and criteria are applied. These two examples demonstrate that special agreements are subject to overriding principles and rules either of general international law or treaty law (VCLT), as well as to basic principles of maritime boundary delimitation.

---

[143] ICJ Reports 1950, p. 71, restated in ICJ Reports 1985, p. 216, para. 43.
[144] ICJ Reports 1982, pp. 39–40, paras. 25–30. See also Judge Aréchaga ICJ Reports 1982, p. 101, para. 5 (separate opinion).
[145] Art. 1 (2) Agreement, ICJ 1982 Reports, para. 23.
[146] Art. 1 (2) Agreement, ICJ 1982 Reports, p. 37, para. 23.
[147] See ICJ Reports 1985, pp. 214–50, paras. 41–50 (relation of compromise to Art. 60 ICJ Statute).
[148] ICJ Reports 1984, pp. 326–7, paras. 192–4.
[149] ICJ Reports 1984, p. 363, paras. 6–7 (dissenting opinion).
[150] See Collins and Rogoff, n. 102.   [151] See Chapter 12(II)(C)(2).

Although not part of *jus cogens*, it should be recalled that the principles on delimitation set forth in Articles 74 and 83 of the LOS Convention are of a constitutional nature.[152] The overall goal of achieving an equitable solution, broad as it is, cannot be waived in negotiations or even more so in adjudicated solutions. It is submitted that the same holds true with respect to the fundamental rule in customary international law. No agreement can request a court to achieve inequitable solutions that would be at variance with accepted standards of maritime boundary delimitation.

B. Historic rights

The relative novelty of the shelf and the EEZ significantly reduces the impact of the fundamental concept of historic rights in the present chapter of maritime boundary law. But there is no doubt that historic rights apply as much as they do to territorial boundaries, and they may be of particular importance in close proximity to the coast. The *Tunisia* v. *Libya* Court clearly held that 'historic rights must enjoy respect and be preserved as they have always been by long usage'.[153]

Historic rights played an important, perhaps even decisive, role in the 1909 *Grisbadarna* case and the 1951 *Anglo-Norwegian Fisheries* case.[154] Such an impact, however, so far has not materialized in cases related to the delimitation of the shelf and the EEZ. Historic rights were argued with respect to maritime activities and patterns, and in particular drilling and sedentary and mobile fisheries, but were held not to be decisive and disposing by the courts.[155] The *Tunisia* v. *Libya* Court did not find it necessary to decide the issue because historic rights, as claimed by Tunisia, were not affected by the line that was finally drawn by the court.[156] Equally, in the *Gulf of Maine* case, the issue of historical presence, 'somewhat akin to the invocation of historic rights, though that expression has not been used',[157] was examined only *ex post* the denomination. It did not, at least legally, influence delimitation. US claims that were based on former conduct (navigation, assistance, research, defence)[158] and preferential situations due to such activities and fishing patterns were held not to be relevant and could not be given

---

[152] See Chapter 4(III)(A)(4).   [153] ICJ Reports 1982, p. 73, para. 100.
[154] *Fisheries Case (United Kingdom* v. *Norway)*, ICJ Reports 1951, para. 116.
[155] ICJ Reports 1982, p. 71, paras. 97–100.   [156] ICJ Reports 1982, p. 77, para. 105.
[157] ICJ Reports 1982, pp. 340–1, para. 233.   [158] ICJ Reports 1982.

'decisive weight',[159] even though one judge considered Georges Bank 'as American as apple pie'.[160]

The question of whether historical rights affect delimitation of the new zones at all is a difficult and controversial one. The historical understanding of the legal concept of the shelf belonging *ipso facto* and *ab initio* to the coastal state[161] implies that such rights already exist and are merely waiting to be activated, thus frustrating any evolution of historic title related to these zones. A categorical denial of historic rights, as expressed by Judges Gros and Oda in the *Tunisia* v. *Libya* case, seems to suggest such an approach.[162] On the other hand, historic title was considered possible by Judge Aréchaga,[163] and also found to exist by Judge Ago.[164] The fact that the Court suggested that matters may be different in the context of the EEZ (not invoked by parties) suggests that the majority of the court thought historic rights irrelevant in the context of the shelf. Although not held relevant to the case, the *Gulf of Maine* Chamber implied that historic rights are not relevant as a matter of principle and cannot be decisive:

> Clearly, whatever preferential situation the United States may previously have enjoyed, this cannot constitute in itself a valid ground for its own claiming the incorporation into its own exclusive fishing zone of any area which, in law, has become part of Canada's.[165]

The reasoning rather begs the question. Whether or not the particular area has indeed become part of the Canadian jurisdiction is the very issue of historical rights. The problem cannot be dismissed in summary terms. Neither would predomination or subjection *in abstracto* of such rights provide a satisfactory answer. Conclusive answers have to rely upon the legal nature of the shelf and the EEZ and the doctrine of intertemporal law.

From a historical perspective of the shelf, which only emerged in customary law in the early 1960s, it follows that the existence of historical rights cannot be excluded. *A fortiori*, the same is true for the EEZ, because

---

[159] ICJ Reports 1982, p. 241, para. 235, paras. 234-7; para. 146 (distinguishing case from *Grisbadarna* (not territorial waters, but recent jurisdiction only). See also Chapter 11(III)(A).
[160] ICJ Reports 1982, p. 353 (separate opinion Schwebel).   [161] Chapter 2.
[162] ICJ Reports 1982, p. 211 para. 88, para. 104 (dissenting opinion Oda), p. 159 para. 20 (dissenting opinion Gros).
[163] ICJ Reports 1982, p. 122-3, paras. 79-80 (separate opinion Aréchaga).
[164] ICJ Reports 1982, p. 97, para. 4 (separate opinion Ago).
[165] ICJ Reports 1984, p. 342, para. 235 in fine.

CONCEPTUAL ISSUES AND THE CONTEXT OF EQUITY 487

fishing patterns are more ancient than activities related to the shelf, with the possible exception of sedentary fishing. Historic rights, however, only relate to matters that, in the history of maritime law, were lawfully open to jurisdiction and entitlement of coastal states at the time. This implies the difficult issue of consecutive legal orders in maritime law. It therefore has to be dealt with on the basis of intertemporal law, which was perhaps most prominently developed by Judge Huber in the *Las Palmas* arbitration as a two-step approach. A distinction is made between the creation of, and the contemporary exercise of, historic rights:

> As regards the question which of different legal systems prevailing at successive periods is to be applied in a particular case (the so called intertemporal law), a distinction must be made between the creation of rights and the exercise of rights. The same principle which subjects the act creative of a right to the law in force at the time the right arises, demands that the existence of the right, in other words its continued manifestation, shall follow the conditions required by the evolution of a law.[166]

An historical analysis must therefore discuss the existence of alleged historic titles over maritime expanses on the basis of the then-existing contemporary law, as the Court did in the *Grisbadarna* case regarding the alleged predominance of the perpendicular to the general direction of the coast in the seventeenth century.[167] Historic rights may rely upon *mare clausum*, prevailing until the end of the eighteenth century, and, for later periods, they may rely upon acquiescence to encroachment of the High Seas, as in the 1951 *Fisheries* case. The doctrine of the High Seas and of *res communis* or *nullius* did not pre-empt the expansion of national jurisdiction over the shelf and the EEZ at large: and it also did not pre-empt local encroachments, either by explicit or implied consent of the other states affected.

Under the second test of intertemporal law, however, it needs to be shown that these rights have been continuously exercised until present times. This requirement was not fulfilled with regard to sedentary rights beyond the 26-degree line in the 1982 case. It was also no longer met in the *Gulf of Maine* case, given the increased Canadian activities during the previous fifteen years. In the *Maritime Frontier Dispute (El Salvador*

---

[166] *Island of Palmas case (Netherlands* v. *United States)*, 2 United Nations Reports of International Arbitral Awards, p. 831, 845; see also Olufemi Elias, 'The Doctrine of Intertemporal Law' (1980) 74 *American Journal of International Law*, see n 11, 285, 286.

[167] Decided 23 October 1909, reprinted in Hague Ct. Reports (Scott) 487 (Permanent Court of Arbitration 1909), transl. in English, see p. 121. See Chapter 8(II)(A)(1).

v. *Honduras, Nicaragua Intervening)*, the ICJ had to discern the legal status of the waters of the Gulf of Fonseca. It soon established that the Gulf, being surrounded by the three states, is not a juridical bay, because according to both Article 4 of the 1958 Convention on the Continental Shelf and Article 10 of the 1982 LOS Convention, such a bay can only be found on the coast of one state. To determine the legal status of these waters, the ICJ recognized that:

> It is clearly necessary, therefore, to investigate the particular history of the Gulf of Fonseca, to discover what is the regime of that Gulf resulting there from; especially as the Court in the same Judgment also said: 'Historic titles must enjoy respect and be preserved as they have always been by long usage' (*ICJ Reports 1982, p. 73*). Moreover, the particular historic regime established by practice must be especially important in a pluri-state bay; a kind of bay for which there are notoriously no agreed and codified general rules of the kind so well established for single-State bay.[168]

After a detailed investigation, the Court came to the conclusion that the Gulf of Fonseca was an historic bay and that 'the essential juridical status of these waters is the same as that of internal waters, since they are claimed *à titre de souverain* and, though subject to certain rights of passage, they are not territorial sea'.[169]

This issue of historic rights thus needs careful examination on a case-by-case basis. To the extent that requirements of intertemporal law are fulfilled, historic rights must indeed be recognized in accordance with the general statement made by the Court in 1982. The lack of express reference to historic rights as it exists in the context of the territorial sea in the 1958 Shelf Convention, as well as in Articles 74 and 83 LOS Convention, does not oppose the application of general principles of intertemporal law and the concept of historic rights. To the extent that such rights exist, they reduce the scope and concretization of equity. They are yet another important contextual element of equity in the legal environment. However, they must be distinguished from considerations of conduct within the concept of equity. It will be seen that although the courts declined to recognize historic rights as such, patterns of former conduct did influence their decisions on a sub-legal basis within the rule of equity where the threshold of legal entitlement was not considered to have been met.[170]

---

[168] ICJ Reports 1992, p. 589, para. 384.   [169] ICJ Reports 1992, p. 605, para. 412.
[170] See Chapter 10(III)(A).

C. Estoppel and acquiescence

The principles of estoppel (preclusion) and acquiescence constitute yet another pair of important elements of the legal environment of equity in maritime boundary law. Stemming from the broad principle of good faith and the general principle of equity,[171] estoppel and acquiescence developed into fairly precise rules in case law.[172]

Although views on the content and precise scope of these concepts are not uniform, ranging from broad to narrow definitions, the contemporary concept of estoppel contains the following elements: a party invoking estoppel against another subject of international law must have been induced to undertake legally relevant action, or abstain from such action, by relying in good faith on clear and unambiguous representations by that subject. In addition, such reliance must prejudice the addressee of representation, causing harm to the addressee or bringing about advantages to the party that made the representation. Typically, that party is barred, ('estopped' or precluded) from successfully adopting differing subsequent statements and positions, without regard to their truth and accuracy. The notion is related to, but different from the broader concept *venire contra factum proprium*.[173]

Acquiescence, on the other hand, stands for the proposition of binding effects caused by passiveness and inaction with respect to claims by another subject of international law, which usually calls for protest in order to assert, preserve, or safeguard rights and claims. *(Qui tacet consentire videtur si loqui debuisset ac potuisset)*. The far-reaching impact of acquiescence of creating legal rights and obligations by silence and inaction has an important stabilising effect on international relations.

The two principles have often been invoked in the context of maritime boundary delimitation (as well as elsewhere), the *North Sea* cases providing one of the most elaborate opinions ever on the doctrine of estoppel.[174] The same argument has regularly been offered in

---

[171] ICJ Reports 1984, p. 305, para. 130: 'The Chamber observes that in any case, the concepts of acquiescence and estoppel, irrespective of their status accorded to them by international law, both follow from the fundamental principles of good faith and equity.'

[172] See Wilfred Jenks, *The Prospects of International Adjudication* (London: Stevens & Sons, 1964), pp. 328, 336; Thomas Cottier and Jörg Paul Müller, 'Estoppel', *Max Planck Encyclopaedia of Public International Law* (Oxford University Press, 2012).

[173] See *Chorzow Factory (Jurisdiction)* Case, PCIJ, Series A No. 9, p. 31 (1927).

[174] ICJ Reports 1969, p. 25, paras. 28, p. 26, para. 30.

subsequent delimitation cases.[175] Indeed, estoppel and acquiescence are perhaps more important than historic rights, because they allow conduct related to more recent periods during which the shelf and the EEZ were already established in law to be taken into account. But again, courts so far have not found that the facts presented satisfied the precise requirements of either estoppel or acquiescence. None of the judgments so far has found this type of conduct to dispose of delimitation and therefore establishment of the boundary line. This, on the one hand, provides welcome evidence that the doctrines are applied in a rather strict manner. On the other hand, it indicates that estoppel and acquiescence, as much as other legal principles, may not be readily applied because they would strongly prejudice delimitation at the expense of equity and its more flexible standards to be discussed in Chapter 10.

There is no reason why the general principles should not apply in maritime boundary law.[176] In fact, as elsewhere, the application of estoppel and acquiescence encourages states to settle their boundaries by agreement or judicial settlement in order to avoid creeping jurisdictions on the basis of informal claims and counterclaims that may lead to conflict. Perhaps one objection to full application of estoppel and acquiescence, provided factual requirements are fulfilled, may flow from the constitutional function of the LOS Convention. Once in force and applied, the requirement of achieving a solution that is equitable overall pre-empts delimitations based on principles which, *in casu* would not meet this overriding requirement. In practice, this may remain a hypothetical case. Yet, the implicit goal of achieving an equitable solution may well have induced the courts to apply strict requirements of estoppel and acquiescence, in order to gain more leeway in taking human behaviour into account in terms of equity. It will be seen in Chapter 10(III) that the conduct of governments and other relevant actors, albeit falling short of creating legal rights and obligations, influences delimitation on a sub-legal level within the concept of equity, similar to its relation to historic rights.

---

[175] See *Tunisia* v. *Libya* case, ICJ Reports 1982, p. 83, para. 118; see Mark B. Feldman, 'The Tunisia-Libya Continental Shelf case: Geographic Justice or Judicial Compromise?' (1983) 77 *American Journal of International Law*, 233–4; *Tunisia* v. *Libya* Revision case, ICJ Reports 1985, p. 213, para. 38; *Libya* v. *Malta*, Intervention by Italy, ICJ Reports 1984, para. 25; *Gulf of Maine* case, ICJ Reports 1984, pp. 303–4, paras. 124–6; *Guinea* v. *Guinea-Bissau*, n. 133, p. 282, para. 66; *Denmark* v. *Norway (Jan Mayen)*, ICJ Reports 1993, p. 53, para. 33; *Guyana* v. *Suriname Award*, n. 2, para. 282.

[176] But see Feldman, n. 175, 234.

D. *Third party interests and rights*

1. Substantive claims

The claims and rights of neighbouring third party coastal states form a further important part of the legal environment of equity. To the extent that they deploy effects within the window of delimitation, they are of considerable influence. Such rights may already be defined by an international agreement or adjudication, which can provide guidance in the process of delimitation between the parties in dispute. More often, unfortunately, such rights are not yet settled, and claims are contested. Delimitation must not encroach upon what can be lawfully claimed by the third state (*pacta tertiis nec nocent nec prosunt*).[177] The problem of respecting this principle is particularly acute in closed seas. It may result in the delimitation of extremely small segments, as the example of the *Libya* v. *Malta* case shows. Moreover, it poses methodological problems of evidence and the proper way to hear third parties in defence of their existing or prospective rights. It is therefore evident that third parties and their actual or potential rights to marine spaces strongly affect the operation of equity.

Within the law of maritime boundary delimitation, the principle of non-interference with third party rights is well settled, and the case law on this point is clear. The principle is one of general international law, expressed, inter alia, by Article 34 of the VCLT and Article 59 of the ICJ Statute. States have no jurisdiction to deal and reach agreement *erga omnes* with regard to alleged rights of third states. The agreement of March 1966 between Denmark and the Netherlands, for example, was claimed to be valid *erga omnes*, but was held by the *North Sea* Court to be not opposable to the Federal Republic of Germany because the Federal Republic had not been included in the agreement.[178] Equally, in the CEIP delimitation, existing agreements with third states of the Union were not considered.[179] This also implies that the qualification of a particular

---

[177] See generally Christine Chinkin, *Third Parties in International Law* (Oxford University Press, 1993). In the present context cf. Alex G. Oude Elferink, 'Third Stats in Maritime Boundary Delimitation Cases: Too Big a Role, Too Small a Role, or Both?' in Aldo Chircop, Ted L. Dorman, Susan J. Rolston (eds.), *The Future of Ocean Regime Building: Essays in Tribute to Douglas M. Johnston* (Leiden: Martinus Nijhoff Publishers, 2000), p. 611.

[178] ICJ Reports 1969, p. 4, para. 5, map 3, line E–F, at 28–9.

[179] Charney, 'The Delimitation of Lateral Seaward Boundaries between States in a Domestic Context', n. 82, p. 37.

feature, such as the effects attributed to a particular island, cannot prejudice its prospective role in the context of a separate delimitation with another neighbouring state.[180]

Similarly, Courts have no jurisdiction over claims and potential rights of third parties. This was clearly expressed in the *Tunisia* v. *Libya* case. There the Court said 'the rights of other States bordering on the Pelagian Sea which may be claimed ... must not be prejudged by the decision in the present case'.[181] In the complex configurations of the Mediterranean Sea, with many coastal states competing for marine spaces, third party rights led to an open-ended extension of the boundary line in a north-eastward direction.[182] Thus, the allocation of space was left open. For similar reasons, the boundary line defined in the 1985 *Libya* v. *Malta* case was limited to a relatively small segment, giving no final answers to the spaces allocated to each of the parties.[183] Third party rights and interests influenced the *Guinea* v. *Guinea-Bissau* arbitration in quite a different manner. The fact that the tribunal took the entire coastline of the West African coast into account, transgressing the territories of the parties in order to establish its 'base line' for delimitation, clearly reflects the will to take into account third party rights in the region. As the Tribunal held:

> A delimitation designed to obtain an equitable result cannot ignore the other delimitations already made or still to be made in the region.[184]

The Tribunal continued:

> In order for the delimitation between the two Guineas to be suitable for equitable integration into the existing delimitation of the West African Region, as well as into future delimitations which it would be reasonable to imagine (from consideration of the equitable principles and most likely assumptions), it is necessary to consider how all of these delimitations fit in with the general configuration of the West African coastline, and what deductions should be drawn from this in relation to the precise area concerned in the present delimitation.[185]

---

[180] Mark B. Feldman and David A. Colson, 'The Maritime Boundaries of the United States' (1981) 75 *American Journal of International Law*, pp. 743, 748.
[181] ICJ Reports 1982, p. 62, para. 75 in fine, see also p. 91, para. 143.
[182] ICJ Reports 1982, para. 133 C(3) in fine.
[183] ICJ Reports 1985, pp. 24–8, paras. 20–3. [184] 25 ILM 1986, p. 291, para. 93.
[185] 25 ILM 1986, p. 297, para. 109.

Courts and Tribunals from the 1999 *Eritrea/Yemen* award to the 2009 *Romania/Ukraine* judgment have consistently been careful not to extend the boundaries into areas where the rights of third parties apply.[186]

The consideration of third party rights and interests is of great importance to the authority of a court or tribunal to state the law. It may be argued that they should be bound exclusively by the submissions and motions of the parties. The rights of third parties, however, necessarily impose the principle of *iura novit curia* in matters of maritime boundary law wherever such third party interests are involved. If the parties choose a common ground at the expense of a third party, the court needs to remedy this. Thus, in the *Guinea/Guinea-Bissau* case, the Tribunal did not adopt the position of either party, and instead relied upon an approach that took the shape of the whole of West African coast and the entire region into account.[187] Third party interests and rights further confirm the existence of judicial activism during the process of maritime boundary delimitation.

While the need to take third party rights and expectations into account is not controversial, the legal nature of such interests is. Judge Jennings qualifies them as a relevant circumstance within the framework of the fundamental rule when he argued in his dissent to the 1984 *Intervention* case:

> In determining any continental shelf boundary it is necessary to draw attention to all relevant circumstances, and it is difficult to imagine a more relevant circumstance than the legal rights of a geographically immediate neighbour.[188]

From the point of view of methodology, it is doubtful whether third party rights are limited to existence only under the title of relevant circumstances and therefore within the concept of equity. Rather, it seems that they should instead be defined, whenever possible, at the outset of the dispute, at the point when the relevant area and frame are defined. From this perspective, these rights are clearly more than mere circumstances. They belong to the legal framework that defines the basic parameters of the case.

---

[186] *Eritrea v. Yemen*, n. 120, para. 164; *Qatar v. Bahrain*, n. 19, para. 221; *Cameroon v. Nigeria*, ICJ Reports 2002, p. 443, para. 292; *Barbados v. Trinidad and Tobago*, n. 25, para. 381; *Nicaragua v. Honduras* ICJ Reports 2007, p. 759–60, para. 320; *Romania v. Ukraine*, ICJ Rep 2009, p. 120, para. 177; *Bangladesh v. Myanmar*, n. 41, para. 462; *Nicaragua v. Colombia*, n. 46, paras. 160–5.
[187] *Guinea v. Guinea-Bissau*, 25 ILM 1986, pp. 296–297, paras. 107–8.
[188] *Intervention case*, ICJ Reports 1984, p. 158, para. 29 (dissenting opinion Jennings).

They contribute to defining the window of the dispute. Third party rights and expectations should therefore be considered as a part of the legal environment of delimitation. This could even apply in constellations such as that found in the *Guinea* v. *Guinea-Bissau* case (where the larger environment was eventually taken into account), instead of defining the region as the relevant area to be considered from the outset. The chapter on methodology will therefore argue that determination of such rights should be amongst the first issues to be addressed in judicial reasoning.[189]

2. Procedural claims and rights: intervention or fair hearing?

a. **The need for participation of third parties**   While the principles of third party claims and rights, non-interference, and the need for a separate evaluation and geographical limitation for each window of delimitation are theoretically clear, the distinction of non-encroachment on, and abstinence from, the respect of third party rights is often difficult to achieve in practical terms. Boundaries that are settled either by way of agreement or judicial decision are very likely to exert an impact on the subsequent processes of boundary delimitation in the region. Even where third party rights are being respected, the settlement influences the bargaining positions and legal arguments of the states concerned. This is particularly true for judicial settlements, given the legal authority of judgments by the ICJ and its Chambers or of the International Tribunal for the Law of the Sea. Moreover, because maritime boundary law is, to a large extent, a matter of case law, a precedent almost necessarily influences subsequent delimitation, even where the Court succeeds in not prejudicing third party rights. For example, the Court in the 1982 *Tunisia* v. *Libya* case had to adopt a hypothetical seaward limit of the Libyan and Tunisian shelves for the purposes of calculating proportionality.[190] This line was likely to influence subsequent delimitations, since a major deviation from it would disturb the proportionality achieved between the two parties. Particularly in closed seas and gulfs with more than two coastal states in the region, it is evident that there is a close interrelationship between different boundary lines and legal regimes. Indeed, together they form a regional system, which requires close co-ordination in order to achieve an overall equitable result for all coastal states in the region concerned.[191]

[189] Chapter 11.   [190] ICJ Reports 1982, p. 91, paras. 130–1.
[191] See also Jonathan I. Charney, 'Technology and International Negotiations' (1982) 76 *American Journal of International Law*, 78. Proceedings 156 (1982) (boundaries that appear equitable in a two-party context may be inequitable once third parties take their share of the area).

Evidently, bilateral approaches to boundary delimitation in such configurations can be highly fragmentary and in that sense deficient. From the point of view of regional equity, it would therefore be advisable to undertake comprehensive plurilateral negotiations and to seek a multilateral boundary agreement that encompasses all riparian states and boundaries of the region. In theory, a similar approach should also be sought for conciliatory and judicial dispute settlements. Unfortunately, reality tells a different story. The need for delimitation often arises in the light of specific problems based upon practical economic interests in disputed areas. Novel expectations and the successful exploration of potential resources draws attention to claims where, before, there was no need to undertake delimitation. Such needs often arise in a bilateral context, and it is no coincidence that trilateral or plurilateral agreements have remained the exception.[192] As for judicial settlement, apart from the *North Sea* cases, most cases have been of a purely bilateral nature, even where a clear regional context is given.

A particular problem is that existing procedures before the ICJ, as well as before arbitral bodies, have been shaped by a long tradition of bilateral disputes. Cantered around a two party adversarial system, judicial procedures are not designed to absorb the complexity of more than two main points of view. Plurilateral procedures can work, so long as the parties can be grouped in two major camps or classes, each of them sharing basic interests and points of view. The *North Sea* cases, again, provide an example in point. The Netherlands and Denmark both shared the view that delimitation should be undertaken on the basis of equidistance, while Germany, on the other hand, insisted on a different approach based upon equitable principles.

Procedures where more than two basic points of view are presented inevitably become very complex, and the adversarial principle may be difficult to uphold in all points. Moreover, it may be exceedingly difficult to negotiate special agreements that could satisfy all of the parties involved. As a result, such cases are not likely to reach the courts in the first place. Again, it is not a coincidence that judicial disputes so far have regularly worked on a bilateral basis, even where the boundaries to be drawn are evidently part of an overall regional network, and remedies have been sought by recourse to the institution of third party intervention under the Statute of the ICJ.

---

[192] See listing of agreements in Appendix 1.

b. **The dilemmas of third party intervention** Under Article 63 of the ICJ Statute, third parties are entitled to intervene, provided they are parties to a multilateral convention in dispute. The right relies on the idea that such parties have an inherent interest in how their obligations are construed by the Court.[193] The instrument in fact recognizes the wide impact the case law of the Court has in the development of international law. It shows that the possibility of influencing the interpretation of legal principles, in particular by the major powers, was a main incentive for introducing what became Article 63.[194]

Paragraph 2 provides that the interpretation given by the Court's judgment to a provision of a convention is also binding upon the intervening state, therefore replacing the operation of Article 59, which formally limits legal effects to the parties concerned. The *Haya de la Torre* case held that an intervening state therefore becomes a party to the dispute under Article 63.[195] Such an effect may at the same time explain why the method of intervention under Article 63 has not been widely used by interested parties.[196] In the field of maritime boundary law, this provision has not yet been invoked, e.g. under the existing 1958 Continental Shelf Convention. With the entry into force of the LOS Convention, it is possible that the provision may be used in order to influence the evolution of the case law on maritime boundary delimitation under the broadly textured language of Articles 74(1) and 76(1) of the Convention. Yet again, third parties may prefer to refrain from doing so because of the binding effects that are also foreseen under Article 32 of Annex VI of the LOS Convention.

---

[193] See John T. Miller, 'Intervention in Proceedings before the International Court of Justice' in L. Gross (ed.), *The Future of the International Court of Justice* (Dobbs Ferry NY: Oceana, 1976), vol. II, pp. 550, 551.

[194] See report by Mr. Bourgois on the Permanent Court of Justice, adopted by the Council on 27 October 1920, which expresses the underlying motivation: '[I]t might happen that a case appearing unimportant in itself might be submitted to the jurisdiction of the Court, and that the Court might take a decision on this case, laying down certain principles of international law which, if they were applied to other countries, would completely modify the principles of the traditional law of this country, and which might therefore have serious consequences.' League of Nations, PCIJ, Documents concerning the action taken by the Council of the League of Nations under Article 14 of the Covenant and the adoption by the Assembly of the Statute of the Permanent Court, League of Nations, Official Journal No. 8 12, 50 (1920).

[195] ICJ Reports 1951, p. 72; Miller, n. 193, p. 552.

[196] Apart from the *Haye de la Torre* case, ibid., the only case reported is the Polish intervention in *S.S. Wimbledon*, PCIJ, see n. 173, Series A No. 1 at 18; Miller, see n. 193, p. 553.

For the time being, intervention by third parties has relied on Article 62 of the ICJ Statute. Unlike Article 63, this provision does not grant a right to intervene, but leaves decisions largely to the discretion of the Court. Until the advent of maritime boundary disputes, the provision had remained largely untested and unexplored.[197] Many issues of interpretation were open, including the appropriate legal position of the intervener, its relationship to the parties, and the binding nature of the judgment.

The last two decades of the twentieth century, however, produced three major cases and extensive individual opinions on the subject, clarifying the requirements and scope of intervention to some extent in a controversial process of trial and error. Again, the law of the sea made a substantial contribution, which is of general interest to all international law. With regard to the *Tunisia* v. *Libya* dispute, at the beginning of 1981 Malta sought permission to intervene based upon Article 62. In April 1981, the Court dismissed the request,[198] and proceeded to deliver its judgment on the merits in 1982. Similarly, a request by Italy to obtain permission to intervene in the *Libya* v. *Malta* case was dismissed in March 1984.[199]

Both decisions were highly controversial in the court and triggered abundant writing on the subject.[200] The ensuing debate and discussions

---

[197] There was only one application which, however, remained undecided. The Government of Fiji requested permission to intervene in the *Nuclear Tests* cases (*New Zealand* v. *France*), but the decision was deferred by order of 12 July 1973, until the basic question of jurisdiction was settled which never became necessary. Miller, see n. 193, p. 555.

[198] *Case Concerning the Continental Shelf (Tunisia* v. *Libyan Arab Jamahiriya)*, Application by Malta for Permission to Intervene, Judgment of 14 April 1981, ICJ Reports 1982, p. 3 ff.

[199] *Case Concerning the Continental Shelf (Libyan Arab Jamahiriya* v. *Malta)*, Application by Italy for Permission to Intervene, Judgment of 21 March 1984, ICJ Reports 1984, p. 4 ff.

[200] See e.g. Giovanni Cellamore, 'Intervento in causa davanti alle Corte internazionale di giustizia e lien jurisdictionel tra interveniente e parti originale del processo' (1983) 66 *Rivista di diritto internazionale*, 291; Decaux, 'L'Arrêt de la Cour internationale de justice dans l'affaire du plateau continental (Tunisie/Libye)', n. 95, 177; Emmanuel Decaux 'L'Arrêt de la Cour internationale de justice sur la requête de l'Italie à fin d'intervention dans l'affaire du Plateau continental entre la Libye et Malte' (1984) 29 *Annuaire Français de Droit International*, 282; Eduardo Jiménez de Azcárraga, 'Intervention under Article 62 of the Statute of the International Court of Justice' in R. Bernhardt (ed.), *Völkerrecht als internationale Rechtsordnung, Internationale Gerichtsbarkeit, Menschenrechte, Festschrift Mosler* (Berlin, Heidelberg, New York: Springer Verlag, 1983), p. 453; T. O. Elias, 'The Limits of the Right of Intervention in a Case Before the International Court of Justice' in R. Bernhardt, *Völkerrecht als Rechtsordnung – Internationale Gerichtsbarkeit – Menschenrechte: Festschrift für Hermann Mosler* (Berlin, Heidelberg,

helped to clarify the issues and allowed the *El Salvador/Honduras* Chamber (after the Court had affirmed its jurisdiction on the matter in February 1990[201]) to decide on the request of Nicaragua to intervene. In September 1990, the Chamber granted permission to intervene with respect to the issue of the legal regime of the three states in the Gulf of Fonseca, but dismissed the request with regard to the other aspects, particularly the interpretation of relevant legal and equitable principles.[202]

In the 2002 *Cameroon* v. *Nigeria* case, the Court unanimously granted Equatorial Guinea permission to intervene in the case, pursuant to Article 62 of the ICJ Statute, to the extent, in the manner and for the purposes set out in its application for permission to intervene.[203] The application had been filed in June 1999 and was granted by an order of the Court in October 1999. In the view of the Court, Equatorial Guinea had sufficiently established that it had an interest of a legal nature which could have been affected by any judgment which the Court might have handed down for the purpose of determining the maritime boundary between Cameroon and Nigeria.[204] Neither of the parties objected to the application by Equatorial Guinea for permission to intervene being granted.[205]

In the *Nicaragua* v. *Colombia* case, the Court denied Costa Rica permission to intervene. It held that 'a third State's interest will, as a matter of principle, be protected by the Court, without it defining with specificity the geographical limits of an area where that interest may come into play'.[206] It continued that Costa Rica's interest of a

---

New York: Springer Verlag, 1983), p. 159; Shigeru Oda, 'Intervention in the International Court of Justice' in R. Bernhardt, *Völkerrecht als Rechtsordnung – Internationale Gerichtsbarkeit – Menschenrechte: Festschrift für Hermann Mosler* (Berlin, Heidelberg, New York: Springer, 1983), p. 629; Wolfgang Fritzemeyer, *Die Intervention vor dem Internationalen Gerichtshof: Eine internationale verfahrensrechtliche Untersuchung auf rechtsvergleichender Grundlage* (Baden-Baden: Nomos Verlagsgesellschaft, 1984); Philip C. Jessup, 'Intervention in the International Court of Justice' (1981) 75 *American Journal of International Law*, 903; V. Morelli, 'Note sull' intervento nel processo internazionale' (1982) 67 *Rivista di diritto internazionale*, 805.

[201] *Case Concerning the Land, Island and Maritime Frontier Dispute (El Salvador v. Honduras), Application for Permission to Intervene*, Order of 28 February 1990, ICJ Reports 1990, p. 3 (hereinafter the Nicaraguan Intervention Order).

[202] Ibid., for the request see in particular p. 108, para. 37.

[203] *Land and Maritime Boundary between Cameroon and Nigeria, Application to Intervene*, Order of 21 October 1999, ICJ Reports 1999, p. 1029, at para. 18(1).

[204] ICJ Reports 1999, p. 203, para. 13.   [205] ICJ Reports 1999, p. 203, para. 12.

[206] *Territorial and Maritime Dispute (Nicaragua v. Colombia), Application by Costa Rica for Permission to Intervene*, Judgment of 4 May 2011, para. 86.

CONCEPTUAL ISSUES AND THE CONTEXT OF EQUITY 499

legal nature may only be affected if the maritime boundary between Nicaragua and Colombia were to be extended beyond a certain latitude southwards, where it reaches an area in which the interests of a legal nature of third states may be involved.[207] In the judgment on the merits, the Court avoided such an extension of the maritime boundary.[208] The Court emphasized that this protection is to be accorded to any third state, whether intervening or not. It recalled its judgment in *Cameroon v. Nigeria*, where it had adopted the same position with regard to Equatorial Guinea, which had intervened as a non-party, and to Sao Tome and Principe, which had not.[209]

According to Article 81 of the Rules of the Court,[210] recourse to Article 62 of the ICJ Statute is subject to four requirements, one of a procedural and three of a substantive nature. Article 81(1) prescribes that the intervention has to be filed as soon as possible, but no later than the closure of the written proceedings of the parties. It follows that there is neither a need for a definition of a dispute in prior negotiations before the application can be made, nor for prior negotiations, as will be seen to be otherwise required under the procedural obligations of equity for the original parties.

As to substance, Article 62 was specified as follows in the Rules of the Court, as revised in 1978:

(a) the interest of a legal nature which the state applying to intervene considers may be affected by the decision in that case;
(b) the precise object of the intervention;
(c) any basis of jurisdiction which is claimed to exist as between the state applying to intervene and the parties to the case.[211]

The third substantive element (c) was the object of intense controversy until the 1990 decision on the Nicaraguan intervention. Although not formally decided in 1984,[212] it seems that a majority of the court felt bound to the consensual principle of international adjudication. Thus, the jurisdictional link was construed in the sense of a necessary consent

---
[207] Ibid., para. 89.   [208] Ibid., paras. 160–5.
[209] Ibid., para. 86, citing *Cameroon v. Nigeria*, para. 238.
[210] ICJ, Rules of Court (1978) adopted on 14 April 1978 and entered into force on 1 July 1978, available at www.ICJ-cij.org.
[211] Art. 81(2) Rules of the Court, reprinted in ICJ Reports 1990, p. 107, para. 36.
[212] ICJ Reports 1984, p. 28, para. 45.

by the parties to the intervention of a third party.[213] Such a requirement would lead in most cases to a dismissal of the request, since intervention regularly disturbs the carefully established balance between the parties upon which they agreed to submit the dispute to judicial settlement.[214] Indeed, all maritime boundary cases so far, except *Cameroon v. Nigeria*, do show opposition to the intervention by at least one of the parties.[215] 'Since third-party dispute settlement procedures requires the consent of the participating parties, a liberal approach to third-state intervention is unlikely'.[216] In other words, intervention in the International Court would 'inevitably atrophy'.[217] It inherently renders the instrument of little practical use in international litigation.

Indeed, there is an intrinsic tension between a consensual basis of jurisdiction in international disputes that is based upon special agreement, and the concept of intervention that stems from compulsory jurisdiction in domestic law. An instrument of intervention, as intended by the drafters of the Statute, diminishes the states' control over a dispute. It affects the balance negotiated in the special agreement and, if applied in

---

[213] See ICJ Reports 1981, p. 35, para. 20 ('The Court at the same time thinks it proper to state that it has necessarily and at all times to be sensible of the limits of its jurisdiction conferred upon it by its Statute and by the Parties to the case before it'); ICJ Reports 1984, p. 20, para. 31; p. 22, para. 34; and in particular para. 35 (denying that Art. 62 itself constitutes a basis of jurisdiction since this would deviate from the principles of consent, reciprocity and equality of states).

See also separate opinion of Judge Mbaye, ICJ Reports 1984, p. 41 (inviolability of the principle of consensualism); Judge Aréchaga, separate opinion at p. 59, para. 12, p. 60, para. 16, p. 61, para. 20, p. 66, para. 31, p. 68, para. 36; 462 (with further references on this matter which has been controversial ever since).

No direct consent required by Judges Sette Camara, dissenting opinion, ICJ Reports 1984, p. 88, para. 83; Schwebel, dissenting opinion, ICJ Reports 1984, p. 139, para. 18 ff.; Ago, dissenting opinion, ICJ Reports 1984, p. 120, para. 8; Jennings, dissenting opinion, ICJ Reports 1984, p. 156, para. 24 ff.; Oda, dissenting opinion, 1984, ICJ Reports 1993, para. 7 ff.

[214] See Elias, 'The Limits of the Right of Intervention in a Case Before the International Court of Justice', n. 200, p. 165 ('an intrusion or interference'); Azcárraga, 'Intervention under Article 62 of the Statute of the International Court of Justice', n. 200, p. 455. (In the 1981 intervention case 'the Court was confronted with an unprecedented situation of a prospective litigant who attempted to infiltrate the judicial proceedings between two parties.')

[215] All parties rejected an intervention in the 1981 and 1984 cases. See ICJ Reports 1981, pp. 15, 16 paras. 10 and 11; ICJ Reports 1984, pp. 8, 9, paras. 9, 11; pp. 14–16, paras. 19–24; pp. 17–18, paras. 25–7.

The intervention was partly accepted by Honduras, but fully rejected by El Salvador. ICJ Reports 1990, p. 99, paras. 19, 20.

[216] Charney, 'Progress in International Maritime Boundary Delimitation Law', n. 60, p. 251.

[217] Oda, dissenting opinion, ICJ Reports 1981, p. 27, para. 9; ICJ Reports 1984, p. 94, para. 8.

liberal terms, could frustrate recourse to the Court in the long run.[218] Such negative repercussions may well induce states to turn firstly to *ad hoc* arbitration that allows for the intervention to be excluded by third states from the outset. A judicial policy 'to prefer a prudent confinement within the sheltered precincts of a purely bilateral, and relativist notion of its task', which was strongly deplored by Judge Ago,[219] may be well understood from that perspective. Moreover, there are unexpressed fears of interventionism by major powers. It is perhaps not a coincidence that judges from industrialized countries have been more in favour of a liberal approach than those from developing nations. The problem provides yet another example of the fact that there are no easy analogies to be drawn from domestic civil law or common law procedures, or of any other legal system, to the realm of an imperfect international legal order, which still largely relies on voluntary compliance. On the other hand, a strictly legal interpretation that takes historic materials into account,[220] including comparisons with Article 63 of the Statute, the location of Article 62 outside Chapter II on the competence of the Court, and the opinions of eminent jurists,[221] convincingly demonstrates that intervention is a matter of inherent jurisdiction. Therefore, it is independent of consent in a particular case. Indeed, such independence is the very essence of the instrument, and it is difficult to see how it could otherwise work in contentious cases.

Both under Article 62 and Article 63, the requirement for a jurisdictional link cannot be more than indirect, relying on adherence to the Statute of the Court and its implied recognition that third countries may seek and be granted permission to intervene under certain circumstances. This is particularly evident in maritime boundary cases. The Court is bound to take third party rights into account as a matter of legal obligation. It is difficult to see how a third party can be denied permission to intervene because the main parties do not agree to it, therefore rendering the task of the Court in assessing such third party rights more difficult. Substance and procedural aspects cannot reasonably be separated. The 1990 Nicaraguan

---

[218] See also Charney, 'Progress in International Maritime Boundary Delimitation Law', n. 60, 251.
[219] Dissenting opinion, ICJ Reports 1984, p. 131, para 22.
[220] See in particular the analysis of the *travaux préparatoires* by Judge Oda, dissenting opinion, ICJ Reports, p. 91 ff.
[221] See in particular dissenting opinion Judge Schwebel, ICJ Reports 1984, pp. 140-2, paras. 22-5 (quoting Fitzmaurice, Hudson, Kelsen and Elias). But see also Judge Aréchaga for different views, p. 462 in favour of consent (Anzilotti, Huber).

intervention case, therefore, decided the 'vexed question' of the valid jurisdictional link[222] when the Chamber held:

> The competence of the Court in this matter of intervention is not, like its competence to hear and determine the dispute referred to it, derived from the consent of the parties to the case, but from the consent given by them, in becoming parties to the Court's Statute, to the Court's exercise of its powers conferred by the Statute. There is no need to interpret the reference in Article 36, paragraph 1, of the Statute to 'treaties in force' to include the Statute itself. Acceptance of the Statute entails acceptance of the competence conferred on the Court by Article 62. Thus the Court has the competence to permit an intervention, even though it may have been opposed by one or both of the parties to the case; as the Court stated in 1984, 'the opposition [to an intervention] of the parties to a case is, though very important, no more than one element to be taken into account by the Court' (*ICJ Reports 1984, p. 28, para 46*). The nature of the competence thus created by Article 62 of the Statute is definable by reference to the object and purpose of intervention, as this appears from Article 62 of the Statute.[223]

Much of the underlying concern behind the view in support of direct consent is related to the problem of the legal nature and legal effect of the intervention. To the extent that the third party indeed becomes a full party to the dispute, as generally construed,[224] the provisions would clearly be prone to exert the sort of negative effects that were discussed previously.

It seems that the refusal to grant permission in the Maltese and Italian cases relied upon the notion that these parties would indeed need to become full parties to the dispute within the existing dispute. Malta's request to intervene was, at least partially, dismissed because it was held not to seek intervention as a full party obliged under the judgment, but rather as a 'direct yet limited form of participation', deemed incompatible with Article 62.[225] On the other hand, the

---

[222] ICJ Reports 1990, p. 132, para 94; ICJ Reports 1984, p. 28, para. 45.
[223] ICJ Reports 1990, p. 133, para. 96. The Court followed the views expressed in particular by the dissent of Judge Ago in the *Case Concerning the Continental Shelf (Libyan Arab Jamhiriya v. Malta)* Application by Italy for Permission to Intervene, Judgment of 21 March 1984, ICJ Reports 1984, pp. 4, 119–20, paras. 8–10
[224] See Miller, n. 193, p. 555 (referring to the English text of Art. 62 of the Statute of the PCIJ, see n. 173, which, unlike the French text, referred to 'third party').
The drafters of the Statute of the ICJ deleted such reference as 'misleading', yet without any intention to change the meaning. See Oda, n. 200, p. 639.
[225] ICJ Reports 1981, pp. 19–20, paras. 33–4. But see separate opinion of Judge Schwebel, ICJ Reports 1981, pp. 19–20, para. 38.

Court held in 1984 that Italy's intervention, which claimed 'nothing less than respect for its sovereign rights over certain areas of the continental shelf in issue in the present dispute', amounted to a new dispute, and obliged the Court to define Italy's rights as being beyond the scope of a genuine intervention.[226] As Judge Jennings put it, Malta asked for too little, and Italy for too much.[227]

The rationale of both decisions by the Court's majority can only be explained under the assumption that the intervening state would become a full party to the dispute. Therefore, the third party has to find exactly the right specificity, having a valid claim, but at the same time without introducing new issues to the original dispute. The widely diverging views held by the Court led to further evolution of the law, and clarification again came about in the 1990 decision. Without much elaboration, the Chamber held that Article 62 does not establish the intervening state as a party to the dispute. The matter is closely linked to the problem of consent. While the Court denied the need for direct jurisdictional links to the parties in dispute, at the same time it held that becoming a full party couldn't be reconciled with the basic principle of consent governing international dispute settlement. The Chamber said:

> If an intervener were held to become a party to a case merely as a consequence of being permitted to intervene in it, this would be a very considerable departure from [the] principle of consensual jurisdiction ... It is therefore clear that a State which is allowed to intervene in a case does not, by reason only of being an intervener, become also a party to the case. It is true, conversely, that, provided that there be the necessary consent by the parties to the case, the intervener is not prevented by reason of that status from itself becoming a party to the case.[228]

The Chamber struck a careful balance between the principle of implied consent and by limiting the scope of this principle to the effect that consent inherent to Article 62 does not amount to the status of a party to the dispute. Therefore, by virtue of Article 59, the third party will also not be bound by the judgment. The solution appears to represent a proper and functional reading of the instrument in the context of international litigation among sovereign states. Again, the conclusion relates to the careful balance inherent to the reaching of a compromise between two parties and the potentially detrimental effects of full intervention in

---

[226] ICJ Reports 1984, p. 11, para. 15, p. 21, para. 33, p. 25, para. 41.
[227] Ibid., dissenting opinion, p. 150 para. 7.   [228] ICJ Reports 1990, p. 134, para. 99.

accordance with Article 63 or Article 32 of Annex VI of the LOS Convention would entail. With this interpretation, Article 62 may become a more widely used instrument while remaining tolerable to parties who submitted their case to the ICJ.

However, it should also be noted that this interpretation given to the instrument in the context of maritime boundary delimitation fundamentally changes the concept of intervention as it is traditionally conceived, both in domestic and international law. In fact, intervention is limited to the level that it has always been at in maritime boundary disputes: a fair hearing of the third parties by the court. The Chamber held that the object (in the sense of Article 82(2)(c) of the Rules of the Court) of informing the Court cannot be said to be an improper one, and is in accordance with the function of intervention:

> It seems to the Chamber however that it is perfectly proper, and indeed the purpose of intervention, for an intervener to inform the Chamber of what it regards as its rights or interests, in order to ensure that no legal interests may be 'affected' without the intervener being heard.[229]

c. *Amicus curiae* **rights and legitimate interests** It is submitted that the construction of Article 62 – short of requiring direct jurisdictional links, but also having binding effects of the judgment to the intervener – has moved the substance of Article 62 somewhat toward the concept of *amicus curiae* contained in Article 66. This institution is limited to procedures on advisory opinions and cannot be invoked in contentious cases between states. Without explicitly saying so, the Chamber has in effect brought the functions of Articles 62 and 66 *mutatis mutandis* into a closer relationship. An interested party should take the opportunity to fully inform the Court about potential implications for it, which thereby assists in the process of establishing the proper window of delimitation.

The proximity of the two instruments in practical effect is evidenced by the paradoxical fact that, whether or not it was formally granted, all applications succeed in fully informing the Court about relevant third party interests; and the Court takes these into account even when intervention is formally denied.[230] As Judge Nagendra Singh bluntly

---

[229] ICJ Reports 1990, p. 130, para. 90; but see ICJ Reports 1984, p. 25, para. 40 (denying the Court's information to be a legally relevant consideration).

[230] See as a result the very limited boundary drawn in the *Libya* v. *Malta* case, Chapter 6(II)(G).

CONCEPTUAL ISSUES AND THE CONTEXT OF EQUITY 505

put it in the Italian case: 'The purpose of warning the Court as to the area of Italian concerns has indeed been totally fulfilled.'[231] The goal of third states to forewarn the Court, therefore, can be achieved independently of formal intervention. Charney reaches the same conclusion:

> In a sense, the ICJ promotes greater involvement by excluding areas claimed by third states from consideration. This practice could be seen as de facto making an interested third state a necessary party, and might encourage states in the future to include closely related third states in the dispute settlement process.[232]

Although states act and intervene to preserve self-interests, their role is nevertheless comparable to that of a friend of the Court, indicating sensitivities that need to be taken into account in order not to pre-empt an equitable solution in other parts of the maritime region concerned. Whatever the formal requirements, interested third states are therefore likely to use Article 62 procedures to submit all relevant issues to the court in order to preserve their interests, whether their concerns are of a legal or factual nature. Therefore, the new assignment of intervention under this provision cannot reasonably remain without impact on the notion of a legal interest set forth in the provision and in the Rules of the Court. In the 1990 case, however, such conclusions had not yet been drawn.

While it significantly changed the traditional underlying paradigm of intervention, the *El Salvador* v. *Honduras* Chamber still adhered to an extremely limited interpretation of the notion of legal interest. Despite a new policy and philosophy (no direct jurisdictional link, no party status and information as a proper objective), the Chamber, before addressing these issues, affirmed the existing standards on legal interests that were established in the Malta and Italian intervention cases.[233] It restated the fact that a third state's interest in the general legal rules and principles, including equitable principles, does not suffice for intervention.[234] The intervening state clearly has to indicate the legal interests which may be affected, and bears the burden of proof to that effect.[235] In the end,

---

[231] Separate opinion, ICJ Reports, p. 33, para. (i); ICJ Reports, p. 33, para 32: 'There can be no doubt that the Court has now been made fully aware of Italian interests and where they lie so that there should be no possibility of it even inadvertently encroaching upon or undermining Italian claims and interests in this case.'
[232] Charney, 'Progress in International Maritime Boundary Delimitation Law', n. 60, 251.
[233] ICJ Reports 1990, p. 124, para. 76.   [234] ICJ Reports 1990, p 126, para. 82.
[235] ICJ Reports 1990, p. 117, para. 61, p. 118, para. 62.

the Chamber denied that Nicaragua had a legal interest in the concretization of legal and equitable principles, in the legal situation of the islands, in the delimitation of waters of the Gulf of Fonseca between El Salvador and Honduras, or in the legal situation outside the Gulf, including any decision on the entitlement of or the delimitation between the parties.[236]

The Chamber limited its permission for Nicaragua to intervene to the legal regime of the waters within the Gulf. The Court reasoned that a decision in favour of the Salvadoran contention of a trilateral condominium, or in favour of the Honduran contention of a community of interests, or a finding that none of them exists, affects the legal interests of Nicaragua as a participator in the relevant regime. Indeed, that interest is so strong, that the issue arose as to whether the question did not really amount to the very subject matter of the decision, which the Chamber would not be allowed to make without Nicaragua's participation under the standards of the *Gold Coin* case.[237] The Chamber answered with a negative, but acknowledged that a finding on the merits that held there was no such condominium opposable to Honduras would also amount to a finding denying a condominium with respect to Nicaragua.[238]

It is difficult to see how this issue does not amount to the very subject matter of the main judgment. In fact, it may be argued that the Court effectively applied the *Gold Coin* case standards, not to abstain from ruling, but as a test to determine and limit the scope of intervention. This narrow interpretation is difficult to reconcile with explicit affirmations that the third party is not under an obligation to demonstrate its rights to be protected[239] and that the objective of being heard and informing the court is a proper goal of intervention.[240] But foremost, it is submitted that such a narrow interpretation is reasonable only to the extent that the intervening party would become a party to the dispute and is therefore bound by the decision. This is no longer the case, at least in the field of maritime boundary law.

The role of a quasi-*amicus curiae* need not be restricted to issues where a third party is in a position to demonstrate that the question may not be solved without it necessarily being involved. This was the case with regard to the issue of joint jurisdiction including Nicaragua, in the Gulf

---

[236] ICJ Reports 1990, p. 136, para. 104. [237] ICJ Reports 1990, p. 122, para. 73.
[238] ICJ Reports 1990, p. 123, para. 74.   [239] ICJ Reports 1990, p. 129, para. 87.
[240] ICJ Reports 1990, p. 130, para. 90.

of Fonseca. Limitation of intervention and fair hearing on the matter of joint jurisdiction in the Gulf, whilst excluding any advice on the application of relevant principles of law and equity in the area, is too restrictive with regard to the overall interests of Nicaragua in the region concerned. Instead, the requirement of a legal interest should be read so as to intend the exclusion of an abstract interest in the interpretation of such rules and principles (as is, however, allowed under Article 63), and the requirement of an interest which is clearly more intensive than that of any other third state that is not directly affected by virtue of the geographical constellation.

It should be recalled that the very purpose of requiring a legal interest, as evidenced by the *travaux préparatoires*, is the exclusion of third party intervention which is motivated by mere political interests. It is worth recalling the 1920 report by the drafting committee, which emphasized the requirement of a legitimate interest in order to exclude political intervention:

> It is for the Court to decide whether the interest is legitimate and consequently whether the intervention is admissible. To refuse all rights of intervention might have unfortunate results. The essential point is to limit it to cases in which an interest of a legal nature can be shown, so that political intervention will be excluded and to give the Court the right of decision.[241]

The notion of legal interests was therefore used as a synonym for legitimate interests, which is not identical to the notion of legal interests that was construed in a narrow sense by the 1990 Chamber. In order to qualify, it is not necessary that an actual right or entitlement be at stake. The term of legitimate interests is broader, also covering interests of a factual nature. A requirement of legitimate interests, moreover, reflects the fact that a strict separation of legal and factual interests is extremely difficult to achieve, as experience in other contexts, particularly related to due process and fair hearing, shows.

The Court may, in this context, draw from the wide experience made with third party interventions in the context of GATT and now the WTO dispute settlement procedure, which ranks amongst the most successful and frequently used instruments for international dispute settlement. Third parties are entitled to intervene in a hearing to the extent that they can show a significant interest in the matter. Admission by the dispute resolution panel does not depend on distinctions between legal

---

[241] Quoted from Oda, n. 200, p. 635.

and factual or economic interests.[242] Experience shows that such distinctions are extremely difficult to make, particularly at an early stage of what should remain a preliminary, procedural decision. The standards applied should not anticipate a decision on the merits, which would often be needed if the test strictly relied upon legally defined interests. In the end, it is the intensity of interests, beyond a general nature, that should set the appropriate standards for qualification to be heard under the facts of a particular case. An intervening state should be required to demonstrate that the decision might have effects beyond the general interest that the international community might share in the case.

On such a basis, it is submitted that any neighbouring state of the region inherently fulfils the requirement of a legal interest. From this perspective, it is evident that both the Malta and Italian intervention petitions should have been granted in accordance with the dissenting opinions, as, indeed, they informally were, since their positions were largely reflected on the merits in subsequent decisions. In accordance with Judge Oda, the Chamber should also have granted Nicaragua permission to intervene with regard to jurisdiction over the islands and maritime spaces in and outside the Gulf, and therefore also with regard to a potential delimitation.[243] This would necessarily also entail the possibility of being heard with regard to the proper interpretation and concretization of law, and in particular the rule of equity, in the region. Under the hypothesis that the Chamber should dismiss the existence of a common regime, it is difficult to see how it could define the boundaries within the Gulf without knowledge of the Nicaraguan claims. Equally, any decision on Honduras' claims for an EEZ and a shelf zone in front of the Gulf cannot be made without affecting Nicaraguan claims to the expanses of its zones in the region, since it would seem that the allocation of such zones would entail the creation of some sort of a corridor to the benefit of Honduras and not solely at the expense of El Salvador.

As in the previous Malta intervention case, permission was also denied because the Chamber found that Nicaragua had not sufficiently specified its interests in the application to intervene.[244] Perhaps the case

---

[242] See Art. 10 of the Understanding on Rules and Procedures Governing the Settlement of Disputes, World Trade Organization, *The Legal Texts* (Cambridge University Press, 1999), p. 362. Third party participation in WTO dispute settlement is frequent and a standard method of participating in the shaping of precedents relevant for the multilateral trading system.
[243] Separate opinion, ICJ Reports 1990, p. 144 (conclusions).
[244] ICJ Reports 1990, p. 123, para. 74; p. 124, para. 76; p. 128, para. 87.

for intervention would have been more compelling had Nicaragua submitted a hypothetical boundary line. Yet, is the application for intervention the appropriate procedural stage to ask for such specificity? Following the present policy of the Court, future cases will take pains to present more precise contentions under different scenarios of the case. This will further protract and complicate the process of decision-making, since judgments about intervention will increasingly have to develop the merits of the case in hypothetical terms without prejudicing the final decision.

From a procedural point of view, the standards required should equally not be too high. They should be in line with the wording of Article 62, which only asks for legal interests that may, and not necessarily will, affect third party rights, as Judge Oda also pointed out.[245] More detailed perceptions of the intervening state should be presented in subsequent written statements and oral presentations. Since there is no right to intervene or to be heard under Article 62, the Court may even decide on admission of specific issues on a case-by-case basis as proceedings evolve in accordance with the informational needs of the Court.

Moreover, it follows from the discretionary nature of the hearing that the Court is not under an obligation to explicitly consider and reflect all presentations by third parties, as is the case under a right to be heard. A liberal interpretation of legal interests is the best possible option, since the Court may well look to it under its discretionary powers under Article 62 paragraph 2 to prohibit intervening states from jeopardizing and unduly protracting the settlement of dispute by means of unduly excessive arguments. This safeguard should suffice to avoid the negative repercussions which otherwise may deter states from using dispute settlement under the Statute of the ICJ.

Finally, a more liberal approach to the notion of legal interests would not only decrease the complexity and duration of decision-making on permission or refusal of intervention, and therefore accelerate the process of reaching the merits of the case, it would also increase the transparency of the process, thereby enhancing the chances that the result attained will be politically acceptable to the intervening state and its political constituencies, as well as to the parties. Nothing is gained from the point of view of peaceful settlement if a judgment will not be complied with, because claims eventually voiced by a third riparian state upset the balance

---

[245] ICJ Reports 1990, pp. 140–1 (separate opinion).

achieved by the Court in the first place, or render it politically difficult for one of the parties to honour its international commitments under the binding force of the judgment.

IV. The political environment of equity and the need for transparency

Besides the relational nature of equity, underlying concepts, objectives and values of the shelf and the EEZ, and the legal environment of equity, maritime boundary delimitation is always situated in a particular political context. This is apparent in the process of negotiations, and perhaps even more so in the follow-up of non-conclusive negotiations, i.e. in cases submitted by parties to judicial or quasi-judicial settlement. Indeed, the political importance of such disputes will regularly be increased after negotiations to reach agreement on the merits have failed.

Submissions to judicial settlement tend to involve major political decisions at the higher echelon, which naturally attracts great public attention and media coverage. It politicizes the water. Constituencies may increase efforts to influence the position of parties. They may carefully monitor the process. As David Colson, an experienced negotiator and litigator, assessing the *Gulf of Maine* case, put it:

> this is a very political process. It is not an academic process that can achieve results just because we think it is the best thing to do. If you cannot convince your political system that it is the best thing to do, you have got nothing.[246]

To what extent is and should a particular political environment be relevant to the process of delimitation? The answer is an easy one with respect to the process of negotiations. Evidently, negotiating positions will primarily be shaped by political and economic interests, and solutions will be sought that will satisfy such interests on both sides. The conclusion of an agreement with such qualities arrived at under reasonably fair conditions, i.e. the absence of duress, coercion and massive pressure, will by its very nature generally qualify as an equitable solution within the meaning of Articles 74 and 83 of the LOS Convention. Parties are not subject to any limitations with respect to

---

[246] In Lewis M. Alexander, *The Gulf of Maine Case: An International Discussion* (Washington DC: American Society of International Law, 1988), p. 79.

the arguments and interests tabled. And it was to this that the ICJ referred when it held that: 'In fact, there is no legal limit to the considerations which States may take into account of for the purpose of making sure that they apply equitable procedures' in the process of delimitation.[247]

The problem is more difficult with respect to judicial settlement. Judges, of course, are fully aware of the political context and the sensitivities of the case, and of the underlying interests driving the parties and their counsels. As Colson says: 'Judges are politicians. International judges often have had a whole lifetime of experience in their own foreign ministries as diplomats, politicians, and lawyers.'[248] The fundamental and difficult question arises to what extent the political environment of a case and expediency can and should be legitimately taken into account in an open and transparent manner in judicial proceedings and settlement in accordance with the law. There are differences in the perceptions of jurisprudence underlying the dispute between the equidistance–special circumstances rule and the concept of equity and equitable principles that has already been addressed. The model of a strict rule and exceptions, particularly where limited to geographically motivated exceptions, is generally advocated from a strictly legal background that seeks to exclude, or at least to limit and control, the temptations of using and applying implied arguments of political expediency. The realist conception underlying the model of equity implies, beyond logical arguments already developed, the acknowledgement of more flexibility. The question of the political environment can only be raised legitimately under this approach, since political expediency or the acceptability of results as such, hardly qualifies as a special circumstance.

The question is whether it should be made part of the overall methodology. The problem is a delicate one. On the one hand, it would be unrealistic to produce results that run an apparent risk of being rejected by one of the parties, given the political environment of a case. The genuine function of settling an international and political dispute and the preservation of peaceful intercourse could not be maintained. On the other hand, focusing on the political environment tends to reduce the function of rules and principles and to develop into unprincipled decision-making *ex aequo et bono*, which is ultimately governed by standards of acceptability as the guiding idea. The stricter the

[247] ICJ Reports 1969, p. 50, para. 93.   [248] Colson, n. 246, p. 84.

rules and the more limited the exceptions, the more such dangers of implicit and unexpressed expediency disguised as special circumstances exist.

The dilemma can be only solved by means of a sufficiently elaborate set of principles and relevant circumstances that can be taken into account as part of the law. They must also be in a position to take the political environment of the case into account in an inherently creative act and operation. Courts should clearly express and analyse the political environment, and deal with it in a transparent manner, instead of using it in disguise by means of a more or less convincing application of technical methods, for example, by giving half-effect short of a reasoned statement. Explicit language with respect to these interests is essential in bringing about understanding and improving the acceptability of a ruling by the constituencies concerned. For the purpose of political implementation, judgments have to be 'sold' domestically. Judgments also entail an educational function. Thus, they need to be written in such a way that enables the interested public to fully understand why its political concerns have or have not been taken into account in order to achieve an equitable solution. Silence is a bad guide. A transparent judgment dealing with the political environment facilitates the important task of the post-judgment phase.[249]

The political environment inherent to each case reinforces the importance of what may be called the human geography of each case. The task of full discussion of political and economic interests can and should take place within the objectives and underlying values set out above. These elements also define the scope of legitimate interests to be considered. They prevent excessive politicization which would result from taking into account interests unrelated to these objectives and values, inevitably leading into the realm of decision-making *ex aequo et bono* outside the rule of law. An appropriate methodology needs to be developed which is able to deal with legitimate economic and political concerns in a principled and systematic manner.

V. Conclusion: essential elements of an equitable solution

The preceding analysis of the relational nature of equity, the concepts of the shelf and the EEZ, objectives and underlying values, and the legal and political environment, allows for the definition of the essential elements

---

[249] Ibid. p. 53.

of an equitable solution of delimitation, in abstract terms. It is recalled that the requirement of an equitable solution is part of the fundamental rule in general international law as incorporated in Articles 74 and 83 of the LOS Convention's constitutional rule of maritime boundary delimitation.

An equitable solution or result consists of a boundary line that relies on the conceptual and valuational elements discussed above. Within the window of delimitation, the allocation of space and resources is based on a test of closest relationship. Such a relationship is defined mainly in geographical terms, but also by considerations of efficient management and conservation of resources, fiscal revenues, preservation of security interests, the preservation of free naval communication, and the protection of the livelihood of coastal fishing communities, an element which may also include aspects of political and cultural identity. An equitable solution, furthermore, has to respect existing rights and obligations in the area of delimitation. This includes the principles of *pacta sunt servanda*, *uti possidetis*, historic rights, the principles of estoppel and acquiescence, and third party rights and claims. Equitable solutions also have to take the political environment of the particular delimitation into account. This is reflected in the economic, political and cultural interests of the parties, which form part of the analysis within the test of closest relationship. To the extent that conduct does not amount to an existing legal title, it may form a part of the considerations within the political environment, and thereby influence the delimitation nevertheless.

Evidently, the process of delimitation based on the essential elements is not conclusive *per se* unless it is an exceptionally clear case. The operation entails a great deal of overlapping values, which can legitimately be invoked by either party to the delimitation. It requires creative and active decision-making during negotiations, conciliation and judicial settlement. Ultimately, an overall result that takes the essential elements into account in a transparent and reasoned manner must be achieved. In a negotiated settlement, the overall result is equitable if it is achieved without duress and is voluntarily accepted. In conciliation, the result has to be acceptable to the parties; if it is rejected by one of them, then the exercise was futile.

In judicial dispute settlement, the operation should produce a result with which, from the point of view of the political environment, parties can be reasonably expected to comply. Unlike a conciliated or negotiated settlement, this does not mean that the result has to be acceptable or accepted, respectively. Acceptance by, and acceptability to, the parties cannot be the goal, because then any delimitation which falls short of fulfilling a defined position or fall-back position would hardly meet the requirement of an equitable solution. The operation would then become one of political expediency and pure decision-making *ex aequo et bono*. What is required under the rule of equity is a result that a non-partisan observer would consider acceptable in light of the general body of law, including state practice and case law, and the particular facts of the case.

10

Justiciable standards of equity

I. The legal nature of equitable standards

A. *The requirement of justiciability*

The conceptualization and specification of the fundamental rule of maritime boundary delimitation and of equitable standards (hitherto variously labelled equitable principles, relevant circumstances, criteria, factors or rules) has to result in the formulation of operational standards. These standards need to be of such a nature that they are legally enforceable by judges in a rational and transparent manner.

During the process of negotiation, parties may invoke any argument they choose and put forward reflections and considerations that do not necessarily need to conform to such specifications. We return to this dimension in Chapter 12, where the role of equity in the negotiating process is discussed. The situation is different with respect to judicial settlements. Here, a need arises for a limitation of the scope and number of equitable standards. In order to achieve a legally operable delimitation, the standards must be manageable by courts, using only the limited tools with which judges are equipped. Standards, in other words, need to be justiciable. Justiciability stands for the proposition that conceptualization and specification remain within the province of reasoned and transparent decision-making based on law. Thus, it cannot involve major discretionary decisions for which the courts neither have the necessary legitimacy, nor the authority in the international system, or in any political system. Equity, as a legal concept, is therefore bound to operate on the basis of justiciable standards only.

In the present context, it is worth recalling that decision-making *ex aequo et bono* transgresses the boundary of a legal operation. It is not a justiciable standard as described. It entails high levels of discretionary and creative powers beyond the limits of the law that the parties concerned agreed to vest in the court because this seems to be the best avenue for promoting their mutual interests of peaceful dispute settlement under the particular circumstances of the case. Judges, in this form, simply replace the political process under the assumption and understanding that parties are willing to accept the outcome. Political power is vested in them with a view to discharging governments from full responsibility for the results achieved. Of course, extra legal decisions, including *ex aequo et bono*, are perfectly capable of being rational and intelligible. They should be, and need to be, with a view to successful implementation. But, as in negotiated settlements or solutions found on the basis of conciliation, this is not necessarily the same type of rationality and transparency as is inherent to the operation of the law and judicial settlement. It may take arguments and considerations into account that legal methodology and the confinement of the law does not allow for. Not surprisingly, it was seen that, unlike in the case of equity, powers to decide overtly on the basis of *ex aequo et bono* are hardly ever granted to a court of law.[1]

The problem of justiciability of legal standards is not peculiar to the operation of equity. International law courts may be confronted with the application of programmatic norms, albeit cases of *non-liquet* are rare, if not non-existent. Courts of law need to deal with a problem submitted, whatever the quality and density of applicable norms, unless it turns into decision-making *ex aequo et bono* to which they may not be authorized. International courts hardly ever reach this limit. The rules and principles of international law are broadly termed and allow courts to operate within a broad margin and a broad concept of justiciability. The need to introduce equity courts, expounded in the interwar period in the age of positivism, did not materialize in international law under the umbrella of the United Nations.[2] Justiciability of international law, including equity, is not a practical problem, but taken for granted.

More frequently, domestic courts are confronted with the problem of justiciability in interpreting and applying international agreements. The determination of whether a specific rule has direct (self-executing) effect entails an investigation as to whether the subject matter is amenable to judicial decision-making, i.e. whether it belongs to the province of the courts or needs to be left to political and democratic discretionary legislation and decision-making. Often, the question is assessed on the basis of whether the norm is sufficiently precise and thus in a position to provide guidance to the courts. Yet, courts are also perfectly capable of

---

[1] See Chapter 4(III)(A)(1).   [2] See Introduction, section I(C).

construing open-textured norms and legal principles. The application and interpretation of human rights and fundamental rights are an example in point. In the final analysis, it is not the structure of a norm which is decisive, but whether courts of law, by way of their procedures and compositions, are best suited to deal with the matter.[3] Whatever the form of the standard at stake, it is a matter of assessing whether the issue belongs to the province of the courts and of judicial settlement or whether it inherently requires political action by government and parliament. In a constitutional context, this has to be assessed by taking into account the balance of powers and of checks and balances. Courts play different roles in different constitutional structures, and single and uniform answers cannot be provided, except where the justiciability of standards is explicitly prescribed by specific treaty law. This is, however, exceptional.

Even under narrowly defined terms of justiciability, the breadth and elusiveness of equity *per se* do not therefore render the concept unsuitable for the legal operation. These attributes do not remove it *a priori* from justiciability and the province of the courts. On the contrary, the history and role of equity in different legal systems shows that equity has been a judicial instrument *par excellence* in addressing new challenges and change. It often provided first answers to new problems.[4] Whether or not equity remains within the law or turns into disguised decision-making *ex aequo et bono* depends on whether a court of law operates on the basis of principled argumentation, i.e. on the basis of pre-existing and identifiable legal standards and criteria. This does not necessarily exclude standards that allow for political considerations to be taken into account. Indeed, the term 'political decision', following a classical distinction of legal and political disputes, is deliberately not

---

[3] This author has particularly addressed the problem in the context of WTO law, see Thomas Cottier and Krista N. Schefer, 'The Relationship between WTO Law, Regional Law and National Law' (1998) 1 *Journal of International Economic Law*, 83; Thomas Cottier, 'A Theory of Direct Effect in Global Law' in A. von Bogdandy et al (eds.), *European Integration and International Co-ordination, Studies in Transnational Law in Honour of Claus-Dieter Ehlermann* (The Hague: Kluwer International, 2002), p. 99; Thomas Cottier, 'International Trade Law: The Impact of Justiciability and Separations of Powers in EC Law' (2009) 5 *European Constitutional Law Review*, 307. The problem is dealt with from the particular angle of Swiss law in Thomas Cottier, Albert Achermann, Daniel Wüger and Valentin Zellweger, *Der Staatsvertrag im schweizerischen Verfassungsrecht* (Bern: Stämpfli, 2001); Daniel Wüger, *Anwendbarkeit und Justiziabilität völkerrechtlicher Normen im schweizerischen Recht: Grundlagen, Methoden und Kriterien* (Bern: Stämpfli, 2005).
[4] See Introduction to this book.

used in this context. It was seen that all delimitations, like most legal operations, take place within a political environment. All decisions, especially those of resource allocation, are, in a wider sense, decisions of a political nature. The test, therefore, is not so much legal or political, but principled or discretionary, or even arbitrary in the original meaning of term: i.e. decision-making according to unfettered human will. From this perspective, a first qualification to bear in mind is that the only standards and criteria that can qualify as equitable standards within the fundamental rule provide sufficient guidance to the judge. Thus, justiciability would exclude from the outset any criteria that are not conclusive in terms of evidence, or those that entail considerations that exceed the limited task normally allocated to judicial settlement. It will be seen that standards related to geology, ecology or global equity are to a large extent of just such a non-justiciable nature. But, contrary to the line of reasoning which generally denies the justiciability of maritime boundary delimitation on the basis of equity, it is possible to develop a set of operational standards that are fully justiciable and provide the basis for delimitation based upon the fundamental rule of equity.

B. The legal nature of equitable principles and relevant circumstances

A second problem that must be addressed from the outset relates to the notions of standards that have so far been randomly applied and used without clarifying their classification or mutual relationship. Linguistic evolution from mere factors to criteria and, finally, to equitable principles and relevant circumstances in case law, has not clarified this type of normative problem. In fact, the terms can reasonably be given different normative meanings at the outset. We distinguish, under the overall umbrella of equitable standards, the notions of equitable principles and relevant circumstances. They assume different functions. Moreover, they need to be distinguished from the notion of equitable solutions.

1. Equitable principles

Any reference to principles in international law risks causing considerable confusion. The problem is that there is no coherent doctrine or perception of principles in international law, and in law in general. Principles are commonly discussed within the meaning of Article 38, paragraph 1(c) of the ICJ Statute, which allows the court to apply general principles recognized by civilized nations as a formal source of law. These principles are generally conceived of as shared principles, commonly applied in different legal systems. The principle of equity, as such, is one such shared principle.[5]

It is obvious, however, that the equitable principles of maritime boundary delimitation are not identical to this concept of legal principles. They cannot be found primarily in domestic law. A maritime boundary, as the ICJ put it in the context of its jurisdiction, 'has always an international aspect'.[6] True, it can be seen that delimitations take place within the jurisdiction of a state. But there would hardly be a sufficient number of sea or lake boundaries to be delimited between different entities of sovereign (federal) states in order to effectively build such a body of law beyond a source of inspiration. Rather, they are imported to domestic law from international law and applied in analogy within federacies. Indeed, where they were applied in a domestic context, it was by direct or indirect application of international law, as in the CEIP delimitation, or the *Dubai/Sharjah* arbitration within the United Arab Emirates.[7] In other words, equitable principles are of a different nature than general principles of domestic law.

There is yet another obstacle. The notion of principle is increasingly applied on a separate normative level in international law. Outside the established system of legal sources, as expressed by Article 38 of the ICJ Statute, principles of a constitutional function and nature exist in international law. The principles of sovereign equality, self-determination, permanent sovereignty over natural resources, non-aggression, non-intervention, and peaceful settlement of disputes, many of them enshrined in the Charter of the United Nations, are of a fundamental quality and importance to the actual system of international law. They influence the concept of maritime zones and the shaping of equitable principles of delimitation, such as permanent sovereignty over natural resources and sovereign equality. But unlike equitable principles, they are part of treaty or customary law and are of a far more general and fundamental nature, as they apply to all fields of international relations.

Therefore, equitable principles do not correspond to established normative perceptions and levels of principles that generally exist in international law. They are neither general principles of law, nor

---

[5] See Ralph A. Newman, 'The General Principles of Equity' in R. A. Newman (ed.), *Equity in the World's Legal Systems: A Comparative Study* (Brussels: Bruylant, 1973), p. 595; cf. also Introduction to this book.
[6] ICJ Reports 1951, p. 132.
[7] For references and discussion of these delimitations, see Chapter 6.

constitutional principles of international law, but principles *sui generis*. The notion is a specific one, related to a particular context and subject matter. Comparable principles of this normative type may also be found in other regulatory areas of resource allocation, e.g. equitable principles relating to the allocation and use of water.[8]

Nevertheless, equitable principles are able to share the normative nature and quality of principles in law. They share the quality of providing guidance when confronted with a particular set of facts. They inherently point in a particular direction. The fundamental rule of equitable principles implies in general terms that delimitation is not a matter of applying strict rules, such as equidistance, but of principles – as it says.

There is a general normative difference between principles and rules, although in practical terms this may often be rather fluid. Categorization offered by Dworkin is useful in the present context. He distinguishes standards, principles, policies and rules. While rules depict positive legal norms, policies set out economic and social goals to be achieved. Principles are standards which need to be observed, not because they secure political, social and economic goals, but because compliance is a requirement of justice and fairness or some other dimension of morality.[9]

> The difference between legal principles and legal rules is a logical distinction. Both sets of standards point to particular decisions about legal obligations in particular circumstances, but they differ in the character of the direction they give. Rules are applicable in an all-or-nothing fashion. If the facts a rule stipulates are given, then either the rule is valid, in which case the answer it supplies must be accepted, or it is not, in which case it contributes nothing to the decision ... A principle like 'No man may profit from his own wrong' does not even purport to set out conditions that make its application necessary. Rather, it states a reason that argues in one direction, but does not necessitate a particular decision ... The first difference between rules and principles entails another. Principles have a dimension that rules do not – the dimension of weight and importance. When principles intersect ... one who must resolve the conflict has to take into account the relative weight of each. This cannot be, of course, an exact measurement, and the judgement that a particular principle of policy is more important than another will often be a controversial one. Nevertheless, it is an integral part of the

---

[8] See in particular the Convention on the Law of Non-Navigable Uses of International Watercourses, 21 May 1997, UN Doc. A/51/869; Edith Brown Weiss, 'Water Transfers and International Trade Law' in Edith Brown Weiss, Laurence Boisson de Chazournes and Nathalie Bernasconi-Osterwalder (eds.), *Fresh Water and International Economic Law* (Oxford University Press, 2005), p. 63.
[9] Ronald Dworkin, *Taking Rights Seriously* (St. Louis, MO: San Val, 1978), p. 22.

concept of a principle that it has this dimension, that it makes sense to ask how important or how weighty it is.[10]

The difference between principles and rules thus is one of normative density.[11] In the normative process, starting from ideas and morality to the establishment of applicable rules, principles occupy a middle ground.[12] They are more precise than ideas, but less specific than rules applicable in an operation of subsumption of particular facts. Legal principles are not suitable to the established distinction between law-making and law-applying. Broad as they are, they necessarily possess the potential to cause diverging results when applied to a particular set of facts. Perhaps, as a minimum, they do not express more than, as a tribunal once stated, 'general truth, which guides our action, serves as a theoretical basis of the various acts of life'.[13] But even as such a minimum, principles provide guidance to the course of action. They provide positive indications of justice and, if they fail to be respected, they indicate where injustice looms large. They inherently have a normative content, which requires concretization in a creative act. They essentially imply a topical method which calls for pertinent consideration of facts in the process of specification.[14] This process may eventually, but not necessarily, lead to the elaboration of ever more precise legal norms in an evolutionary process of refinement in case law. Again, the history of constitutional law in many countries is analogous to the process of equity. The case law on fundamental rights – generally nothing more than principles – gradually produced a rich body of detailed rules that became part of the unwritten law of the land, or found entry into successive codification, but it is a body that remains open for further elaboration and concretization as new societal regulatory problems and needs arise.

---

[10] Ibid., pp. 24, 26–7.
[11] See Sir Robert Jennings, 'The Principles Governing Marine Boundaries' in Kay Hailbronner (ed.), *Staat und Völkerrechtsordnung, Festschrift für Karl Doering* (Berlin, Heidelberg, New York, London, Tokyo, Hong Kong: Springer, 1989), pp. 397, 398–400.
[12] See Josef Esser, *Grundsatz und Norm in der richterlichen Fortbildung des Privatrechts* (Tübingen: Mohr, 1990); Josef Esser, *Vorverständnis und Methodenwahl in der Rechtsfindung: Rationalitätsgrundlagen richterlicher Entscheidungspraxis* (Frankfurt am Main: Athenäum-Fischer-Taschenbuch-Verlag, 1972); Karl Larenz, *Richtiges Recht: Grundzüge einer Rechtsethik* (Munich: Beck Verlag, 1979): Franz Bydlinski, *Juristische Methodenlehre und Rechtsbegriff* (Vienna, New York: Springer, 1982), pp. 132–3).
[13] *Gentini Case*, Ven Arb 1093 720, p. 715 (Umpire quoting Bourgignon & Bergerol's Dictionnaire of Synonymes); Bin Cheng, *General Principles of International Law As Applied By International Courts and Tribunals* (London: Stevens, 1994), pp. 24, 376.
[14] See Chapter 11.

It is important to emphasize that the process of specification of legal principles is a process of law. In other words, it is a normative process. Starting from broad precepts, the shaping of the principles is an evolutionary process, which has to build upon insights from past experiences. It is not a matter of applying such principles in a completely independent manner from case to case. Even if precedents do not amount to *stare decisis* in international law, they need to be taken into account and parties have and shall inevitably argue on the basis of existing concretizations.

The same qualifications also apply to equitable principles in the field of maritime boundaries. Given the inherent individuality of each delimitation and the established and demonstrated inability of strict rules such as equidistance to solve complex cases, equitable principles, at least at the outset, cannot be anything but fairly broad principles. They cannot be applied in a technical sense, but are used for guidance, broadly indicating a direction of action. As such, they require concretization in each case. In due course, new and more precise contents may arise and enrich the content of principles, but they will always remain short of strict, hard and fast rules.

In conclusion, equitable principles are an appropriate normative tool with which to approach the problem of delimitation. They should be able to establish norms that provide guidance without needing to become strict rules. Equitable principles form the basic framework and structure for delimitation. In this quality they differ from relevant circumstances, which provide the second, factual element of the substantive fundamental rule of delimitation.

2. The nature of relevant circumstances

The courts and doctrine[15] to date have hardly made a distinction between equitable principles and relevant circumstances, using the terms interchangeably. Under the rule of Article 6 of the 1958 Shelf Convention, the special circumstances exception necessarily includes all considerations that induce deviations from the general rule of equidistance. Yet, under the fundamental rule of equity, the lack of a precise definition of equitable principles has led to decisive considerations being made in the 1982 *Tunisia* v. *Libya* case either under the term of factors, criteria, or special or relevant circumstances.[16] Also, it is not clear whether relevant circumstances

---

[15] This is the case even for the most comprehensive analysis of state practice, including judicial settlements, see Jonathan I. Charney et al. (eds.), *International Maritime Boundaries*, 5 vols. (The Hague: Martinus Nijhoff Publishers, 1993–2005).

[16] ICJ Reports 1982, p. 60, para. 72.

are limited to those characterizing the area in dispute, as in the 1982 *Tunisia v. Libya* case,[17] or whether the notion may also address circumstances not necessarily linked to geographic or natural particularities, as with the general formulations in the *North Sea* cases (taking into account all the relevant circumstances)[18] and the *Gulf of Maine* case ('with regard to the geographic configuration of the area and other relevant circumstances'[19]) suggest. The 1985 *Libya/Malta* case offered yet another concept when the judgment said that equitable principles have to be applied 'in all the relevant circumstances'.[20] The French text suggests an independent function of relevant circumstances when it said that equitable principles are applied 'en tenant compte de toutes les circonstances pertinentes'.[21] Yet another concept seems to underlie the equitable principle enunciated by the Court, that coastal states enjoy 'sovereign rights over the continental shelf off its coasts to the full extent authorised by international law in the relevant circumstances' – a principle considered as being the positive expression of non-encroachment.[22] Finally, the judgment adds 'the principle of respect due to all such relevant circumstances'.[23]

In the *Jan Mayen* case, the ICJ had to apply both Article 6 of the 1958 Shelf Convention and customary law. When called upon to examine each particular factor of the case which could influence an adjustment of the median line that was provisionally drawn in order to start the process of delimitation, the Court stated that:

> although it is a matter of categories which are different in origin and in name, there is inevitably a tendency towards assimilation between the special circumstances of Article 6 of the 1958 Convention and the relevant circumstances under customary law, and this is only because they both are intended to enable the achievement of an equitable result.[24]

It is submitted that equitable principles and relevant circumstances should be conceptually separated. They serve different functions within the fundamental rule. Equitable principles are inherently normative and are able to provide basic guidance in all cases of delimitation, eventually leading to further refinement as the case law is formed. On the other hand, in my view, relevant circumstances are primarily of a factual nature. They reflect the particular facts of a case, such as the size of an

---

[17] Imposed by special agreement; ibid. at 23, Art. 1.
[18] ICJ Reports 1969, p 53, para. 101(1). [19] ICJ Reports 1984, p. 300, para. 112(2).
[20] ICJ Reports 1985, p. 38, para. 45. [21] ICJ Reports 1985, p 38, para. 45.
[22] ICJ Reports 1985, p. 39, para. 46. [23] ICJ Reports 1985, p. 39, para. 46.
[24] ICJ Reports 1993, p. 62, para. 56.

island, its population, the degree of dependence of local fisheries on particular areas, patterns of conduct that fall short of strictly legal impact, the location and riches of resources, and so on. Facts as such do not *per se* have any normative content. Nor do they provide guidance *per se*. Rather, in the first place they are facts of nature and life. Why, then, and in what way are they relevant?

Normative effects of special factual circumstances are primarily based on the third element of the fundamental rule, as the Court's statement above confirms: the obligation to achieve an overall equitable result. To this effect, the factual matrix and its elements influence the process and impact on the boundary. Within the framework of equitable principles, relevant circumstances therefore respond to the need for additional flexibility in each case. They assist the process of finding appropriate and equitable results in each case of delimitation. They encapsulate a function and concept of equity somewhat different from the equity inherent to equitable principles.

However, it is possible that such circumstances may develop into principles if particular features – e.g. the impact of islands off the coast – consistently deploy a similar or comparable effect on boundary line placement over time. Such a development might be discernible from the similar treatment by the ICJ of Serpent's Island in *Romania v. Ukraine* and by ITLOS of St. Martin's island in *Bangladesh v. Myanmar*, with respect to their impact on the construction of the delimitation line in the EEZ and continental shelf.[25] By consistent treatment in case law, the existence of these features may develop a normative nature of some precedential value. Similarly, the fact that resources form a coherent system may lead to a principle that the unity of systems should be preserved in light of efficient resource management. It is for such reasons that a strict separation of principles and relevant circumstances is not easily achieved in practice and, again, there is a blurring of the line. It is for that reason that the general term of 'standards' is suggested to encompass both categories, despite their normative differences.

In conclusion, and as a conceptual guideline, the term 'equitable principles' will be used to depict normative, guiding elements, while

---

[25] *Case Concerning Maritime Delimitation in the Black Sea (Romania v. Ukraine)*, Judgment, 3 February 2009, ICJ Reports 2009, p. 61, p. 109, para. 149; *Dispute concerning Delimitation of the Maritime Boundary between Bangladesh and Myanmar in the Bay of Bengal (Bangladesh v. Myanmar)*, Judgment, International Tribunal for the Law of the Sea, 14 March 2012, Case No. 16, para. 265.

'relevant circumstances' captures the factual matrix relevant to achieving the normative goal of an overall equitable solution.

3. The element of 'equitable solution'

From the point of view developed so far, it can be seen that the third element of the fundamental rule – equitable solution – is not in itself a justiciable standard. Rather, it describes a result. It does not provide sufficient guidance on its own, even though it is of a normative content. Under the LOS Convention, equitable solution is the overall constitutional obligation to fulfil whatever method is used in adjudication. Negotiated solutions comply with it if they are arrived at bilaterally or plurilaterally without undue pressure or duress, and while respecting third party rights.

Under the fundamental rule of equity in general international law of maritime boundary delimitation, an equitable solution results from the specification of equitable principles and a consideration of relevant circumstances in the light of the concepts, objectives and underlying values of the zones. We sought to describe this at the end of Chapter 9. Perhaps this is as far as this requirement can be described in substance, as there always remains a meta-juridical element, similar to the overall goal of justice, which is open to capturing the feelings and intuition of negotiators and judges in the process of delimitation.

The role that the concept of an equitable solution can assume in law lies, at best, on a different methodological level. It may be used to shape an appropriate methodology of delimitation. The goal of an equitable solution helps to keep in mind that the methodology of delimitation (the process itself) equally has to be equitable and shaped in a manner that allows for an equitable result within the overall goals and purposes of the respective maritime zones. It will provide the basis for balancing different principles and circumstances in a principled manner in Chapter 11. But first, we turn to the discussion and identification of the different equitable standards.

II. Equitable standards related to physical geography

A. Standards related to surface coastal configuration

The history, definition and rationale of the respective zones, which have been enhanced by the geographical definition of the shelf under the LOS Convention (and which abandoned geophysical determination in a seaward direction within 200 nm), have all led to geography's dominant position amongst the relevant circumstances applied.[26] It does not come as a surprise that a close analysis of state practice revealed that geographic considerations have played a paramount role in maritime boundary delimitation. The overwhelming role of geographic considerations and the infinite variety of influences these considerations have exerted on these delimitations are the main lessons that may be drawn from the practice of states. It cannot be concealed, however, that to a certain extent these were foregone conclusions.[27] It is, however, surprising that the underlying principles have not been fully worked out; the debate has been stuck too often in the overall equity–equidistance dispute and left to elements of relevant circumstances and thus did not move far enough to set out the basic principles of delimitation at stake in sufficient clarity. This is what the following paragraphs seek to achieve in a systematic manner.

1. The coast dominates the sea (CDS)

Ever since the encroachment of the seas began with the 3-mile territorial sea (the cannon ball rule), its expanses and boundaries and the allocation of maritime zones and resources have been significantly influenced by the land and coastal configuration, including islands entitled to a shelf and states with an EEZ. The general rationale and foundation of the zones, and the close relationship of such states to the sea, makes it quite evident why the allocation of marine space has closely followed the coastal configuration ever since. The rationale also remains essential even where, for practical purposes, the coastal facade is simplified by means of straight base lines. These should follow the contours of the coastal line as closely as possible, as the more such lines deviate from the natural line, and thus the more they artificially enlarge territorial waters, the more they are subject to objections.[28]

The courts have consistently emphasized the importance of the land and coastal configuration for the purposes of maritime boundary delimitation in terms of an equitable principle (or 'a classical formula'[29]), stating that

---

[26] See Keith Highet, 'The Use of Geophysical Factors in the Delimitation of Maritime Boundaries' in. Charney et al., *International Maritime Boundaries*, n. 15, vol I (Charney and Alexander), pp. 163, 177.

[27] Prosper Weil, 'Geographic Considerations in Maritime Delimitation' in Charney et al., *International Maritime Boundaries*, n. 15, vol. I (Charney and Alexander), pp. 115, 130.

[28] See Chapter 4.   [29] ICJ Reports 1984, p. 312, para. 157.

the 'land dominated the sea'.[30] The principle dates back to before the time of continental shelf and EEZ delimitations, emerging in seventeenth-century law and finding expression in the *Grisbadarna* case. The Court of Arbitration called upon the 'fundamental principles of the law of nations, both ancient and modern, in accordance with which the maritime territory is an essential appurtenance of the land territory'.[31] Before being formulated in the *Continental Shelf* cases in terms of explicit equity, the 1951 *Anglo-Norwegian Fisheries* case expounded '[t]he principle that the belt of territorial waters must follow the general direction of the coast' as a basis for elaboration of a number of criteria for effecting the delimitation.[32] The principle of the land dominating the sea was extended to the contiguous zone by the 1969 *Continental Shelf* cases, and to the continental shelf[33] as a basis for taking geographical factors into account.[34] Finally, by way of establishing a single all-purpose boundary, it reached the EEZ by the 1984 *Gulf of Maine* case.[35]

The classical and often restated formula that it is the *land* that dominates the sea reflects the underlying philosophy of maritime boundary delimitation. It equally contains and absorbs what is sometimes depicted as an independent legal principle 'that there is to be no question of refashioning geography or compensating for the inequalities of nature'.[36] With the fundamental principle that the land dominates the sea, there is no need for these statements to go beyond the realm of ideas in order to illustrate the overall underlying philosophy of delimitation, and its inherent limitations. These concepts are emanations of the classical international law of co-existence and of formal equality of states. The starting point based on geographical factors reflects the large factual difference of states. It explains the widely diverging sizes of marine spaces

---

[30] Ibid.; *Maritime Delimitation and Territorial Questions between Qatar and Bahrain (Qatar v. Bahrain)*, Merits, Judgment, ICJ Reports 2001, para. 185; *Land, Island and Maritime Frontier Dispute (El Salvador v. Honduras: Nicaragua intervening)*, Judgment, ICJ Reports 1992, p. 351, paras. 113, 126; *Romania v. Ukraine*, n. 25, para. 77.

[31] *Grisbardarna Arbitration (Norway v. Denmark)*, decided 23 October, 1909, reprinted in Hague Ct. Reports (Scott) 487 (Permanent Court of Arbitration 1909), transl. in English, see p. 121, at 127. See also ibid. at 129. For a summary see Chapter 8(II)(A)(1).

[32] ICJ Reports 1951, p. 129.   [33] ICJ Reports 1969, p. 52, para. 96.

[34] ICJ Reports 1969, pp. 30, 32, paras. 39, 40, 43. See also ICJ Reports 1982, p. 61, para. 73.

[35] ICJ Reports 1984, p. 312, para. 157; ICJ Reports 1984, p. 338, para. 226.

[36] ICJ Reports 1985, p. 36, para. 46; *Arbitral Tribunal Constituted Pursuant to Article 287, and in Accordance with Annex VII, of the United Nations Convention on the Law of the Sea in the Matter of an Arbitration between Guyana and Suriname*, Award of 17 September 2007 (hereinafter *Guyana v. Suriname* Award), International Court of Arbitration: www.pca-cpa.org/showfile.asp?fil_id=664 (last visited 18 Feburary 2012), para. 374.

allocated to different coastal states, and thus the very relational nature of equity which operates within this classical paradigm, stripped of any inherent obligations to co-operate or even to integrate different marine spaces. As a corollary, it ignores, at least in macro-geographical terms, the absence of any global distributive justice in this field. Fundamental differences in allocation of resources and wealth are not addressed. Many of the unresolved problems, in particular in the field of management of fisheries, are inherent to this basic philosophy.

Within these basic precepts of classical international law, *the land dominates the sea*, however, is unnecessarily broad as a legal, equitable principle. Thus it is susceptible to further refinement and definition. The terminology that uses land as the starting point suggests that the land mass of the coastal state exerts an impact on the allocation of marine resources. However, this is actually inaccurate. The land mass was important for the establishment and legitimization of the doctrine of the continental shelf,[37] but it never played a decisive role in the process of maritime boundary delimitation. In the *Tunisia* v. *Libya* case, in applying the concept of natural prolongation, Libya argued that the terrestrial reference is the continental land mass, and not the 'incidental or accidental direction' of any particular coast.[38] This argument was rejected by the Court, who held that the coast of the territory is the decisive factor. It said, '[t]he geographic correlation between coast and submerged areas off the coast is the basis of the coastal State's legal title', referring at the same time to the principle that the land dominates the sea.[39] Although the *Guinea/Guinea-Bissau* arbitration held that the maritime zones are the prolongations of the land territories,[40] it concluded that the land mass of each state 'does not constitute a relevant factor' for delimitation.[41] Instead:

> A State with a fairly small land area may well be justified in claiming a more extensive maritime territory than a larger country. Everything depends on the respective maritime facades and their formations.[42]

The principle therefore says that it is the *coast* or *the coastal configuration* that dominates the sea – the land mass or the hinterland, its comparative size, and its general thrust is not relevant.

---

[37] See Chapter 2.   [38] ICJ Reports 1982, pp. 44–5, para. 40.
[39] ICJ Reports 1982, p. 61, para. 73.
[40] *Arbitration Tribunal for the Delimitation of the Maritime Boundary between Guinea and Guinea-Bissau*, Award of 14 February 1985, 25 ILM 290 (1986) para. 91 (hereinafter *Guinea* v. *Guinea-Bissau*).
[41] Ibid., p. 301, para. 119.   [42] Ibid.

The *Malta/Libya* case confirmed that view, much to the benefit of smaller independent islands which, by their very nature, have much smaller land masses than continental coastal states.[43] In the *St. Pierre and Miquelon* arbitration, France claimed a large maritime area on the basis of the principle of equal capacity of islands and mainland to generate maritime areas,[44] and in the *Denmark/Norway (Jan Mayen)* case, the tiny Norwegian island was awarded quite a large maritime area in comparison with the much greater land mass of Greenland. Similarly, the Colombian islands that generated the boundary with Nicaragua are small compared with Nicaragua's mainland coast, scattered across a large area and far removed from the Colombian mainland.[45] It is therefore accurate to speak of the principle that *the coast dominates the sea* (CDS principle). There is no need to take recourse to a principle that the land dominates the sea. This is limited to an underlying philosophy that sets the stage and informs operational principles of delimitation.

This conclusion corresponds to the decline into irrelevance of the doctrine of natural prolongation for the purpose of establishing boundaries between adjacent states.[46] It also corresponds to the increased relevance of distance brought about by UNCLOS III. Finally, it corresponds to state practice. As examples such as Chile show, the title and expanse of the continental shelf has been fully independent of the size of the land mass, relying on the length and configuration of the coast since the new seaward definition of the continental shelf under the LOS Convention, comprising, in conjunction with the EEZ, an extension of at least 200 nm.[47] The relationship of the coastal state to the sea today is exclusively defined in law on the basis of its coastal configuration, both with respect to the outer limits and with respect to delimitation with neighbouring and opposite states.

Even with this clarification, the CDS principle remains extremely broad. It may be for that reason that the 1985 *Libya* v. *Malta* case did not mention it in its non-exclusive list of equitable principles.[48] Indeed, the principle may be further elaborated and divided into somewhat more operational principles for the purposes of maritime boundary

---

[43] ICJ Reports 1985, pp. 40–1, para. 49; See also ICJ Reports 1985, p. 49, para. 66.
[44] 'Court of Arbitration for the Delimitation of Maritime Areas between Canada and France, Case concerning de Delimitation of Maritime Areas between Canada and the French Republic' 31 ILM 1164 (1985), para. 43.
[45] *Territorial and Maritime Dispute (Nicaragua* v. *Colombia)*, ICJ Reports 2012, p. 624, paras. 18–24, 215.
[46] See Chapter 2. [47] See Chapter 2. [48] ICJ Reports 1985, p. 39, para. 46.

delimitation: non-encroachment (NEP); non-cutting-off (NCP); and proportionality. We discuss them consecutively.

2. The principles of non-encroachment and non-cutting-off (NEP, NCP)

Maritime boundary delimitation is a process of allocating overlapping claims that the states concerned legitimately claim on the basis of an existing relationship to the marine areas in dispute. Each of the parties will argue that it has a closer relationship based on geography or other considerations. The closer the area in dispute to the coast of a state, the more that state will dominate this maritime area. This is logical, reasonable and fully in accordance with the concept of closer relationship, the true foundation of the shelf and the EEZ discussed in Chapter 2, as well as with the CDS principle. At some stage, however, it is evident that claims by one of the parties can no longer be overriding, as they collide with the equally legitimate claims of another coastal state. Once there is a clearly closer relationship by one state, the non-encroachment principle (NEP) or, as a corollary, the non-cutting-off principle (NCP), arises to shape the principle of CDS in the process of delimitation. Introduced by Germany in the 1969 *North Sea Continental Shelf* case,[49] the principle of non-cutting-off was taken up by the Court in the context of the then-founding principle of natural prolongation.[50] It was later exchanged for the term of non-encroachment.[51] Both principles are by now well established in the case law.

The crux of the matter is to define more precisely when and where such encroachment or cut-offs take place. While it is easy to agree that this is the case, the closer a boundary line lies to the coast, therefore infringing upon the special relationship and CDP, the more difficult it is to precisely define the point or line of encroachment or cut-off.

a. **Case law** In the *North Sea* cases, NEP was founded upon the concept of natural prolongation, and the decision consequently stipulated that delimitation must not encroach upon areas constituting such natural prolongation.[52] It is difficult to tell to what extent this principle exerted an influence on the eventual negotiations and the establishment of the German Corridor. Since agreement on delimitation in the coastal

---

[49] ICJ Reports 1969, p. 22, para. 15. [50] ICJ Reports 1969, p. 32, para. 44.
[51] ICJ Reports 1969, p. 48, para. 85, litt. c. [52] ICJ Reports 1969, p. 32, paras. 43–4.

areas based on equidistance already existed between the parties to the dispute, it may be argued that application of equidistance in the outer and controversial areas was considered contrary to NEP and NCP. Such a view corresponds to that of Judge Aréchaga, to whom non-encroachment constitutes the modern and original sense of natural prolongation.[53] On the other hand, the areas in dispute clearly showed qualities of legitimately overlapping claims that were insufficiently close to the coast of one of the parties. Here, NEP and NCP reach their limits. Indeed, the German Corridor was allocated under the principle of proportionality, to be discussed shortly, which is more suitable for dealing with such overlapping claims.

Subsequent cases reaffirm such a view in result. Partly, they apply NEP and NCP implicitly, partly the principles are invoked explicitly, but all cases apply them in areas much closer to the coastal configuration of one of the parties. The purpose of the principles is to avoid having a boundary run through areas that must be considered to be within the vicinity of a coastal state.

The 1977 *Channel Arbitration* contains the famous, but nevertheless somewhat helpless, statement that the Channel Islands are 'on the wrong side' of the mid-Channel median.[54] This 'rationale' led, without further reasoning, to their non-inclusion in the determination of the median boundary.[55] There is, of course, no way to argue that an island is simply in the wrong location, since this assumes an answer to the very point in issue, i.e. whether they should influence the allocation of shelf rights.[56] In fact, the NEP or NCP was applied, since giving effect to the islands would have created enclaves encroaching upon waters very close to the French coast.

Another implicit application of NEP and NCP can be found in the CEIP delimitation between Mississippi and Louisiana. The discounting of the banks and associated land areas in the Mississippi Delta and the Chadeleur Islands constitutes special circumstances, since their effect on equidistance would be inequitable to Mississippi. Most likely, such a

---

[53] ICJ Reports 1982, p. 119, para. 69 (separate opinion Aréchaga).
[54] 'Arbitration between the United Kingdom of Great Britain and Northern Ireland and the French Republic on the Delimitation of the Continental Shelf' 18 ILM 397 (1979), p. 444, para. 199
[55] Ibid., pp. 444–5, para. 202.
[56] See Derek W. Bowett, 'The Arbitration between the United Kingdom and France concerning the Continental Shelf Boundary in the English Channel and South-Western Approaches' (1978) 49 *British Yearbook of International Law*, 1, 17.

discount took place because otherwise the boundary would encroach upon Mississippi, running too close along its coast and islands.[57]

In the *Gulf of Maine* case, the Court explicitly referred to NCP in order to reject a US proposal to establish a perpendicular boundary in the first segment, since such a boundary 'would intersect Grand Manan island and what is more the Nova Scotia peninsula, cutting off part of its territory'.[58]

The first prominent explicit application of this principle so far is found in the *Guinea/Guinea-Bissau* arbitration. Due to the concave configuration of the coast, the methods proposed by the parties were rejected and an *ad hoc* construction was adopted instead, in order to avoid the cut-off effects of marine areas situated in the vicinity of the coasts.[59] The Court of Arbitration decided that encroachment exists if a coastal state would not have jurisdiction over areas 'unquestionably situated opposite and in the vicinity of their coasts'. In fuller elaboration, the Court held:

> What are the effects of such a circumstance [of concavity]? Between two adjacent countries, whatever method of delimitation is chosen, the likelihood is that both will lose certain maritime areas which are unquestionably situated opposite and in the vicinity of their coasts. This is the cut-off effect. Where equidistance is concerned, the Tribunal, which as we have seen is confronted here with two lines of equidistance, is forced to accept that both would have serious drawbacks in the present case. In the vicinity of the coast, they would give exaggerated importance to certain insignificant features of the coastline, producing a cut-off effect which would satisfy no equitable principle and which the Tribunal could not approve.[60]

In the *St. Pierre and Miquelon* award, both the Court of Arbitration and the parties to the dispute explicitly acknowledged that any delimitation involves some mutual cut-off and encroachment.[61] In its decision, the Court granted the two French islands areas that did not 'encroach upon or cut off a parallel frontal projection of the adjacent segments of the Newfoundland southern coast'.[62]

The Tribunal in *Eritrea v. Yemen* rejected Yemen's suggestion to enclave the Eritrean insular features called Haycocks and South West Rocks with a 12 nm territorial sea in a part of narrow seas between the

---

[57] Jonathan I. Charney, 'The Delimitation of Lateral Seaward Boundaries between States in a Domestic Context' (1981) 75 *American Journal of International Law*, 28, 55, 56, map at 44.
[58] ICJ Reports 1984, p. 318, para. 171.   [59] See Chapter 6(II)(F).
[60] *Guinea v. Guinea-Bissau*, n. 40, p. 295, para. 103. See also p. 293, para. 100, and p. 296, para. 107 (with respect to the parallel of latitude of 10° 40′).
[61] See n. 44, 31 ILM 1169, para. 67.   [62] Ibid., para. 70.

two states.[63] The Tribunal mentioned the 'obvious impracticality of establishing limited enclaves around islands and navigational hazards in the immediate neighbourhood of a main international shipping lane', and held that, in any case, the Eritrean insular features in this area were entitled to extend the mainland coast territorial sea beyond the limit of 12 nm from the mainland coast (so-called 'leap-frogging').[64] The Tribunal added:

> If any further reason were needed to reject the Yemen suggestion of enclaving the Eritrean islands in this area beyond a limit of 12 miles from the high-water line of the mainland coast, it may be found in the principle of non-encroachment which was described by Judge Lachs in the *Guinea/Guinea-Bissau* Award in the following terms: 'As stated in the award, our principal concern has been to avoid, by one means or another, one of the Parties finding itself faced with the exercise of rights, opposite to and in the immediate vicinity of its coast, which might interfere with its right to development or put its security at risk.'[65]

The Tribunal in *Guyana* v. *Suriname* in effect applied the principle of non-cutting-off in the territorial sea. For the first 3 nm of the boundary line, the Tribunal chose a line which avoids cutting off Suriname's access to the Corentyne River. Suriname contended that the need to control the approach to the Corentyne River, as territorial waters, for reasons of administrative and navigational efficiencies, constituted a special circumstance under Article 15 of the LOS Convention.[66] The Tribunal held in accordance with the *Beagle Channel*[67] Tribunal's finding that factors such as 'convenience, navigability, and the desirability of enabling each Party so far as possible to navigate in its own waters', should be taken into account.[68] The established practice of navigation in the western channel thus constituted a special circumstance requiring the adjustment of the equidistance line over the first 3 nm of the territorial sea boundary.[69]

In the 2002 *Newfoundland, Labrador and Nova Scotia* arbitration, the Tribunal explicitly invoked NEP and NCP in assessing the impact of islands and the region. Based upon the following assessment, Sable Island off the coast of Nova Scotia was completely ignored:

> Another significant concern relates to the cut-off effect that the provisional line has on the southwest coast of Newfoundland. Although giving

---

[63] *Award of the Arbitral Tribunal in the Second Stage (Maritime Delimitation) in the Matter between Eritrea and Yemen*, 17 Dec. 1999, (2001) 40 ILM 983, paras. 154, 155.
[64] Ibid., paras. 155, 156. See also Chapter 4. [65] Ibid., para. 157.
[66] *Guyana* v. *Suriname* Award, n. 36, para 285.
[67] 'Beagle Channel Arbitration, Report and Decision of the Court' 17 ILM (1978), pp. 634, 673.
[68] *Guyana* v. *Suriname* Award, n. 36, para. 305.   [69] Ibid., para. 306.

half effect to Sable Island reduces the cut-off effect, the Tribunal considers that it should be further reduced in some limited measure. While agreeing that it is especially important to ensure that a delimitation line does not come 'too close' to the coast of one of the states concerned, the Tribunal is not persuaded by Nova Scotia's argument that the cut-off effect necessarily becomes irrelevant as the distance from the coast increases. As the International Court stated in *Libya/Malta*, the principle of non-encroachment 'is no more than the negative expression of the positive rule that the coastal State enjoys sovereign rights over the continental shelf off its coasts to the full extent authorized by international law in the relevant circumstances'.[70]

In the *Bangladesh/Myanmar* case, the ITLOS observed that 'the coast of Bangladesh, seen as a whole, is manifestly concave'.[71] In fact, the setting of Bangladesh's coast resembled that of the coast of the Federal Republic of Germany in the *North Sea* cases.[72] The Tribunal noted that while concavity *per se* is not necessarily a relevant circumstance, it becomes one where the equidistance line produces a cut-off effect on the maritime entitlement of one state as a result of the concavity of the coast.[73] In the case at hand, the provisional equidistance line as construed by the Tribunal did produce a cut-off effect on the maritime projection of Bangladesh and would have resulted in an inequitable solution, if left unadjusted.[74] The Tribunal held with reference to the *North Sea Continental Shelf* cases that the result of a concave coast on such a line would only be exacerbated the further that line proceeds away from the coast.[75] Consequently, the Tribunal found the concavity of Bangladesh's coast to be a relevant circumstance requiring an adjustment of the provisional equidistance line.[76] Turning to the adjustment of the equidistance line, the Tribunal took the position that, while an adjustment must be made to its provisional equidistance line:

> an equitable solution requires, in light of the coastal geography of the Parties, that this be done in a balanced way so as to avoid drawing a line having a converse distorting effect on the seaward projection of Myanmar's coastal façade.[77]

---

[70] *Newfoundland and Labrador and Nova Scotia Arbitration*, para. 5.15 (footnotes omitted).
[71] *Bangladesh* v. *Myanmar*, n. 25
[72] The Federal Republic of Germany specifically invoked the geographical situation of Bangladesh (then East Pakistan) to illustrate the effect of a concave coast on the equidistance line (ICJ Pleadings, *North Sea Continental Shelf, Vol. I*, p. 42).
[73] *Bangladesh* v. *Myanmar*, n. 25, para. 292.   [74] Ibid., para. 293.   [75] Ibid., para. 294.
[76] Ibid., para. 297.   [77] Ibid., para. 325.

Citing the ICJ in *Romania* v. *Ukraine*, the ITLOS held that the relevant coasts of the parties should produce their effects 'in a reasonable and mutually balanced way'.[78]

The Tribunal noted that there were various adjustments that could be made within the relevant legal constraints to produce an equitable result.[79] It decided that, in view of the geographic circumstances, the provisional equidistance line is to be deflected at the point where it begins to cut off the seaward projection of the Bangladesh coast.[80] Since the projection southward from the coast of Bangladesh continues throughout the delimitation area, the Tribunal found a continuing need to avoid cut-off effects on this projection.[81] The Tribunal accordingly replaced the single boundary equidistance line by a geodetic line starting at an azimuth of 215°. It observed that any shift of this azimuth would produce a line that either does not adequately remedy the cut-off effect on the southward projection of the coast of Bangladesh, or produces a cut-off effect on the seaward projection of Myanmar's coast.[82]

Noting that the delimitation method for the continental shelf within and beyond 200 nm is the same, it stated that the concavity of the coast has a continuing effect as a relevant circumstance beyond 200 nm.[83] The Tribunal therefore decides that the adjusted single boundary line continues in the same direction beyond the 200 nm limit of Bangladesh until it reaches the area where the rights of third states may be affected.[84]

In *Nicaragua* v. *Colombia*, Nicaragua argued that Colombia's approach treated the western coasts of Alburquerque Cays, San Andrés, Providencia, Santa Catalina and Serrana as a wall blocking all access for Nicaragua to the substantial area between the east coasts of those islands and the line 200 nm from the Nicaraguan base lines. According to Nicaragua, this was an area to which it was entitled by virtue of the natural projection of its coast.[85] Accordingly, Nicaragua contended that one of the most important principles of the international law of maritime delimitation is that, so far as possible, a state should not be cut off, or blocked, from the maritime areas into which its coastline projects, particularly by the effect of small island territories.[86] The Court agreed with Nicaragua that the area lying east of the Colombian insular features is relevant to the delimitation and should not cut off all projection of

---

[78] Ibid., para. 326, citing *Romania* v. *Ukraine* (para. 201).   [79] Ibid., para. 327.
[80] Ibid., para. 329.   [81] Ibid., para. 333.   [82] Ibid., para. 334.
[83] Ibid., paras. 455, 461.   [84] Ibid., para. 462.
[85] *Nicaragua* v. *Colombia*, n. 45, para. 212.   [86] Ibid.

maritime entitlements by the Nicaraguan coast lying to the west of the Colombian islands.[87]

The Court avoided a cut-off partly through its initial construction of the median line and partly by determining the remaining course of the boundary. Cutting off the substantial eastward projection of the Nicaraguan coastline would have been the effect of an unmodified median line generated by all the Colombian insular features. The Court instead drew a provisional median line using as base points only the major insular features of Colombia and the fringing insular features of the Nicaraguan coast.[88] Two notable Colombian features that were disregarded for the purpose of constructing the median line were Quitasueño and Serrana, thus reducing the extension of the line in the northern part.[89]

The Court thus refused to allow the Colombian insular features to cut off entirely the projections of the Nicaraguan coast in this area.[90] But the Court stressed that, conversely, neither should the Nicaraguan projections on the eastern side of the Colombian islands be allowed to cut off the entitlements of those maritime features.[91] The Court thus rejected the Nicaraguan proposal to enclave the Colombian islands within the 12 nm territorial seas.[92] The Court instead constructed a corridor turning immediately east along lines of latitude from the southern and northern ends of the median line towards the 200 nm limit – leaving only the two insular features of Quitaseño and Serrana outside the resulting Colombian maritime corridor.[93] The Court held this solution to be equitable, recalling that a median line should avoid completely cutting off either party from the areas into which its coasts project.[94]

b. Vicinity and the preservation of security interests The cases confirm that vicinity is therefore an essential criterion within the NEP and NCP. Behind the geographical concept, we find that the ultimate purpose of the two equitable principles is the preservation of security interests. It should be recalled that the underlying policy behind the Truman Proclamation consisted of taking action against future 'encroachment by foreign nationals' over offshore resources.[95] Materials related to the Truman Proclamation show that concerns of encroachment were not

---

[87] Ibid., paras. 215, 236, 244. [88] Ibid., paras. 201, 203. [89] Ibid., para. 202.
[90] Ibid., para. 215. [91] Ibid., para. 216. [92] Ibid., paras. 206, 230, 244.
[93] Ibid., para. 236. [94] Ibid., paras. 216, 236.
[95] See Ann L. Hollick, 'U.S. Ocean Policy: The Truman Proclamation' (1976) 17 *Virginia Journal of International Law*, 23, 38. See Chapter 1.

limited to the control over both mineral and living resources, but also encompassed the realization of offshore security interests. It seems that these interests provided the main test that could be used to define the point of encroachment as points 'sufficiently near the coast to impair or endanger' security interests:

> In the exercise of its rights of self-protection and as a matter of national defense, the United States could not view without serious concern any attempt by a foreign power or the nationals thereof to exploit the resources of the continental shelf off the coast of the United States, at points sufficiently near the coast to impair or endanger its security, unless such activities were undertaken with its approval.[96]

Therefore, security interests cannot be reduced to national security in a military sense. As envisaged by the founding Truman Proclamation, they include a broader notion of security. Security of the local fishing industry based upon established zones, for example, would surely also be included. The *Anglo-French Channel* Court held that the boundary 'must not ... be so drawn as to allow the continental shelf of the French Republic to encroach upon the 12 mile fishery zone of the Channel islands'.[97] They also include labour and environmental security, which may require control and jurisdiction over offshore drilling operations. Finally, the notion also includes respect for existing operations under historic or quasi-historic title. Accordingly, the 1982 *Tunisia/Libya* Court held that the boundary must not 'encroach upon the historic rights area',[98] and in the *Abu Dhabi* arbitration, Sharjah offered half-effect to the island of Abu Musa because it conceded that full-effect equidistance would encroach upon Dubai's existing oil field. The Tribunal in *Eritrea* v. *Yemen* rejected enclavement of insular features in a narrow sea, mentioning security reasons and navigational hazards.[99] Access to a navigational channel and enabling each party so far as possible to navigate in its own waters was a factor in *Guyana* v. *Suriname*.[100] In *Nicaragua* v. *Colombia*, both parties invoked security and law enforcement considerations in relation to the appropriate course of the maritime boundary.[101] The Court said that it had recognized that legitimate security concerns might be a

---

[96] Reprinted in: Marjorie Whiteman, *Digest of International Law* (Paris: Editions du Centre de la Recherche Scientifique, 1963–1973), vol. IV, p. 755.
[97] N. 54, p. 444, para. 202.
[98] ICJ Reports 1982, p. 76, para. 101. See also section III below.
[99] *Eritrea* v. *Yemen*, n. 63, paras. 155, 157.   [100] *Guyana* v. *Suriname*, n. 36, para. 304.
[101] *Nicaragua* v. *Colombia*, n. 85, para. 221.

relevant consideration if a maritime delimitation was effected particularly near to the coast of a state and that it would bear this consideration in mind in determining what adjustment to make to the provisional median line or in what way that line should be shifted.[102]

Attempting to qualify non-encroachment to the same extent, it may therefore be submitted that a maritime boundary, whatever method of delimitation is chosen, must not impair or endanger security interests in a broader sense. Except in the cases of narrow streets and rivers (*thalweg*), this would imply that boundaries must certainly not reduce the scope of the territorial sea and the contiguous zone, as these are by their very definitions zones primarily established for reasons of security and policing. 'Vicinity' in the context of maritime boundary delimitation would therefore comprise at least 12 to 24 nm. This is a distance from shore upon which a long-distance boundary should not encroach or interfere.

These numbers, however, should not be taken in absolute terms. Recalling that principles are not strict rules, NEP and NCP cannot and should not be applied arithmetically. In each case, an assessment needs to be made of what the relevant security interests are, and therefore what the relevant area of vicinity is. At a minimum, besides the rule of the territorial sea and the contiguous zone, it may also be said that encroachment would take place if the boundary would not run approximately perpendicular to the coast. State practice confirms this, in that most territorial sea boundaries applying equidistance in the vicinity to produce lines to this effect.

B. Equitable principles related to space allocation

1. Equal division of marine space (EDS)

The practical importance and prominence of the CDS, NEP and NCP principles, as well as the concept of proportionality to be addressed shortly, have somewhat overshadowed and displaced a principle that deserves to be stated and discussed here as a starting point: the principle of equal division of marine space (EDS) within a defined window of delimitation. The *Gulf of Maine* Chamber held that within the geographic setting of a case, mainly defined by the geography of the coast (to which political aspects may be added), an equal division of marine areas should be envisaged:

> Within this framework, it is inevitable that the Chamber's basic choice should favour a criterion long held to be equitable as it is simple, namely

---

[102] Ibid., para. 222.

that in principle, while leaving regard to the special circumstances of the case, one should aim at an equal division of areas where the maritime projections of the coasts of the States between which delimitation is to be effected converge or overlap.[103]

The relatively minor operational role of EDS in case law so far is due to the fact that delimitation in contentious cases is complex, determined not merely by a single basic standard, but on quite a number of standards. However, this should not disguise the fact that it does reflect an important goal of the fundamental rule of equity. Ideally, delimitation should achieve an equal division of marine space within the coastal configurations defining the overall window of overlapping claims based on entitlement of two or more coastal states. Equal division is more than a criterion, and, in fact, nothing stands in the way of it being qualified as a normative principle. It is certainly equivalent to other principles discussed in this chapter, and the 1984 Chamber even seemed to attribute to it a higher normative level when it considered equal division a 'basic criterion' and the corrections due to the particularities and characteristics as effected by means of 'auxiliary criteria'.[104] Whether or not there is and should be a hierarchy of principles within a proper methodology of the fundamental rule remains to be seen.[105] It is safe to say, however, that the equal division of overlapping space clearly belongs to the family of equitable principles of maritime boundary delimitation.

The principle of equal division relies on a number of underlying rationales. It reflects the fundamental concept of equality inherent to the law in general. The constitutional principle of sovereign equality of states prescribes, in the absence of principles and circumstances to the contrary, that spaces and the resources therein need to be allocated equally. In ideal conditions, equal sharing is the very realization of equality and of equity alike. Equal sharing also flows from the concept of a close relationship of coastal states to marine spaces and resources. In the absence of other principles and circumstances further influencing the degree of such closeness, it leads to equal division, because none of the parties can claim a superior right to the space or resources therein. The conceptual definitions of the EEZ and, as a minimum, of the shelf in terms of distance (200 nm), further supports the principle of equal division of overlapping claims. Finally, it corresponds to the finding that delimitation is primarily an allocation of space, and not an allocation of the resources within that space.

---

[103] ICJ Reports 1984, p. 327, para. 195. [104] ICJ Reports 1984, p. 328, para. 196.
[105] See Chapter 11.

In practice, the principle of equal division has been important to the delimitation of opposite coasts, as is demonstrated by states' overwhelming use of the median line or equidistance in such configurations.[106] The median line is successful because it largely reflects the principle of equal division.

Particular evidence of such close connection is provided by the New York–New Jersey boundary agreement. Delimiting the Raritan Bay (mainly an opposite configuration), the parties sought to achieve an equal division of the waters. A ratio of 1:1.17 was achieved by a line that the report thought was best analysed in terms of equidistance.[107] It is telling that here, in a federal context which requires particularly careful balancing of the equities among federal states of a union, particular attention was paid to EDS (or at least to its effects).

There is general agreement that the method of equidistance in opposite cases causes many fewer difficulties than in adjacent configurations. This was, *obiter dictum*, emphasized in the *North Sea* cases[108] and reaffirmed on the merits in the 1977 *Anglo-French Channel* arbitration. All the modifications of equidistance in the latter case, and in particular the complete neglect of the Channel Islands for the purposes of establishing the median line, show that EDS was the leading idea. Modifications of the median line and the application of other methods, such as using a bisector in the first segment of the *Gulf of Maine* boundary,[109] likewise served the goal of equal division. Whether or not small features such as 'islets, rocks, [and] minor coastal projections'[110] are to be taken into account is equally influenced by EDS, as is apparent in the *Romania* v. *Ukraine* and *Nicaragua* v. *Colombia* cases.[111] The principle, therefore, is an important modifier of any strictly geometrical approaches based on the exact geography of a case.[112]

In adjacent and combined adjacent and opposite configurations, EDS is closely related to the principle of fair and reasonable proportionality, to be discussed shortly. The relationship is rarely expounded in explicit terms. The Court in *Romania* v. *Ukraine* introduced what it called the

---

[106] See Leonard Legault and Blair Hankey, 'Method, Oppositeness, and Proportionality in Maritime Boundary Delimitation' in Charney et al., *International Maritime Boundaries*, n. 15, vol. I (Charney and Alexander), pp. 203, 215–16.
[107] See Charney, 'The Delimitation of Lateral Seaward Boundaries between States in a Domestic Context', n. 57, 28, 48–9.
[108] ICJ Reports 1969, p. 57, para. 36.   [109] ICJ Reports 1984, p. 332, para. 210.
[110] ICJ Reports 1969, p. 36, para. 57.
[111] ICJ Reports 2009, p. 109, para. 149; ICJ Reports, p. 75, para. 202.
[112] ICJ Reports 1984, p. 329–30, para. 201.

'disproportionality test' as a third step in the delimitation exercise in order to test – *ex post facto* – the equitableness of the delimitation line it has arrived at through the first step of constructing an equidistance line and the second step of applying equitable principles.[113] In doing so, the Court made it clear that:

> The purpose of delimitation is not to apportion equal shares of the area, nor indeed proportional shares. The test of disproportionality is not in itself a method of delimitation. It is rather a means of checking whether the delimitation line arrived at by other means needs adjustment because of a significant disproportionality in the ratios between the maritime areas which would fall to one party or other by virtue of the delimitation line arrived at by other means, and the lengths of their respective coasts.[114]

At first sight, this finding seems to exclude the application of EDS in adjacent and combined cases. Yet, the emphasis on the relationship of the coastal lengths ultimately serves the same purpose and seeks to assess *ex post* whether EDS is achieved within a defined area of delimitation. Recourse to proportionality in its different forms and methods does not exclude EDS. It will be seen that it offers a specification of this principle particular in adjacent configurations.

EDS seems to imply that the overall goal of delimitation is to compromise and to split the difference amongst the parties. Evidence shows that overall results can sometimes be seen in such a light. However, it would be wrong to assume that the principle of equal division implies a judicial policy to the effect of splitting the difference. This is particularly evident where EDS – or the disproportionality test – is applied in the form of a test of equitableness in the last step of the delimitation exercise. The influence of other standards or relevant circumstances may well lead to results that cannot be explained in terms of compromise. Equity does not necessarily imply equality. The concepts, the objectives and the values of the zones, as well as other principles inherent to the rule of equity, confirm this ancient trait of equity in law.[115] This is especially true for proportionality.

C. *The principle of fair and reasonable proportionality (FRP)*

Beside the principles of non-encroachment and non-cutting off of areas in the vicinity of a coastal state, proportionality emerged as perhaps the

---

[113] ICJ Reports 2009, p. 129, para. 211, citing *Guinea v. Guinea-Bissau*, at paras. 94–5.
[114] Ibid., para. 110.   [115] See the Introduction to this book.

most prominent and influential explicit tool of maritime boundary delimitation related to physical geography in case law.[116] Much more attention has been paid to it than to the principle of equal division. Proportionality clearly qualifies as an equitable principle in the terms defined above. *Per se* it exerts a normative effect. Difficulties in finding specific concretization conducive to general application do not impair this quality. In normative terms, the principle is operationally equal to CDS, NEP, NCP and EDS.

1. The relationship to coastal lengths

The principle of proportionality establishes a working relationship between the coastal lengths of the parties in dispute in the relevant area and of the marine spaces allocated to them. In essence, the boundary line should result in an allocation of the continental shelf and of the EEZ that correlates proportionally to the lengths of the parties' coastlines within the window of delimitation.

In law, the general idea of proportionality stems from a number of sources. It relates, as does proportionality in general, to the general principle of equality requiring equal treatment for equal, and different treatment for different, facts. Proportional equality is an expression of *suum cuique* and thereby inherent to the idea of justice in general terms. It may also be allocated to equity for the same reasons and as a direct function thereof.[117]

In the more specific context of maritime boundary law, proportionality was sometimes considered inherent to the notion of a natural prolongation.[118] Today, it relies more on the relative nature of equity, the closeness of the relationship and the principle of permanent sovereignty over natural resources, which were identified as the main sources of entitlement to both the shelf and the EEZ. While all these general sources and roots of proportionality are correct, the principle is most closely related to, and is a direct concretization of, the principle that the coast dominates the sea. It expresses the basic geographic impact of the coast at configuration on the allocation of marine resources. The close link is reflected by the ruling in the 1982 *Tunisia/Libya* case that proportionality effectively relies upon the coastal configuration, and not on the simplified base lines drawn for the determination of internal

---

[116] See Legault and Hankey, n. 106, pp. 217–21 ('Proportionality is fundamental to the law of maritime delimitation').
[117] ICJ Reports 1982, p. 76, para. 104.
[118] ICJ Reports 1969, pp. 58–9 (separate opinion Bustamante).

waters and the outer limits of the shelf and EEZ. Equally, it is reflected in findings that the relevant area for the purposes of considering proportionality normally includes the internal waters and territorial waters.[119]

2. The problem of specification

The general idea and the foundations of proportionality in maritime boundary law are fairly clear. The situation is quite different with respect to the operational and precise function and position of proportionality within the basic rule and equitable principles. The details of the principle are confusing and far from settled with respect to practical implementation, normativity and methodology. What is equally controversial is whether the principle can and should be applied to all configurations without producing inequitable results. A brief survey of the case law and doctrine shows a wide spectrum of divergences. There are striking differences between abstract statements, specification and the effective influence of the principle in the judgments.

Introduced by the Federal Republic of Germany as a key element of the doctrine of fair and equitable sharing (competing against the rule of equidistance) in the *North Sea* cases, proportionality emerged as a factor to be taken into account to correct an 'unacceptable', disproportionate delimitation due to the concavity of the North Sea coast.[120] Among the factors to be taken into account was the Court's formulation of proportionality:

> the element of a reasonable degree of proportionality, which a delimitation carried out in accordance with equitable principles ought to bring about between the extent of the continental shelf areas appertaining to the coastal State and the length of its coast measured in the general direction of the coastline, account being taken for this purpose of the effects, actual or prospective, of any other continental shelf delimitation between adjacent States in the same region.[121]

Despite rejection of the doctrine of fair sharing, proportionality emerged as the most influential factor opposing equidistance to that effect, when the German Corridor was eventually negotiated.

---

[119] ICJ Reports 1982, p. 76, para. 104.
[120] ICJ Reports 1969, p. 50, para. 91; ICJ Reports 1969, p. 52, para. 98. For an account of the development of proportionality before the Court, see Donald McRae, 'Proportionality and the Gulf of Maine Maritime Boundary Dispute' (1981) 19 *Canadian Yearbook of International Law*, 287, 291.
[121] ICJ Reports 1969, p. 54, para. 101D(3).

The *Anglo-French Channel* Court of Arbitration was bound to apply and construe proportionality for the first time in a judicial settlement of the boundary line. The judgment provides no detailed analysis and comparisons of the coastal lengths at issue, and the principle was construed in a very broad manner – excluding all mathematical, 'nice calculations' of proportionality of coasts and marine spaces allocated. The Court held that proportionality as defined above would not apply in all cases, but is particularly suited to configurations of concave coasts.[122] In the context of opposite coasts, as were then in dispute, proportionality was broadly construed in such a way as to avoid a boundary which would not reflect the general configuration of the coast due to particular individual features producing distorting effects:

> The concept of 'proportionality' merely expresses the criterion or factor by which it may be determined whether such a distortion results in an inequitable delimitation of the continental shelf as between the coastal States concerned. The factor of proportionality may appear in the form of the ratio between the areas of continental shelf or the EEZ to the lengths of the respective coastlines, as in the North Sea Continental Shelf cases. But it may also appear, and more usually does so, as a factor for determining the reasonable or unreasonable; the equitable or inequitable, effects of particular geographical features or configurations upon the course of an equidistance-line boundary.[123]

As a result, the Court of Arbitration reduced proportionality to a rule of reason and a test to avoid arbitrary disproportionality contrary to equity. Stating that delimitation is not a matter of apportioning or sharing out, nor of completely refashioning nature, but rather of applying the fundamental principle of natural prolongation, the idea of proportionality between coastal lengths and marine spaces was in fact explicitly rejected.

> In short, it is disproportion rather than any general principle of proportionality which is the relevant criterion or factor. The equitable delimitation is not ... a question of apportioning – sharing out – the continental shelf amongst the States abutting upon it. Nor is it a question of simply assigning to them areas of the shelf in proportion to the length of their coastlines; for to do this would be to substitute for the delimitation of boundaries a distributive apportionment of shares ... Proportionality, therefore is to be used as a criterion or factor relevant in evaluating the

---

[122] N. 54, p. 427, para. 99.   [123] Ibid., pp. 197, 427, para. 100.

equities of certain geographical situations, not as a general principle providing an independent source of rights to areas of continental shelf.[124]

While the stating of such a broad principle received praise as a welcome clarification of the law,[125] it is interesting to observe that the *Anglo-French Channel* Court hardly lived up to such commendation when it invoked proportionality in order to justify the mere half-effect given to the Scilly and Ushant islands to the benefit of France.[126] Under a true test of disproportionality, it is hardly convincing to characterize these important features as distortions. In fact, the Court applied a stricter test of proportionality.[127] The new standard therefore contributed considerably to a result-oriented and discretionary approach at the time that allowed for the construing of proportionality in almost any manner. This makes it difficult to distinguish from decision-making *ex aequo et bono*.

The abstract formulation of the Award, however, did not fail to influence the ICJ. The philosophy of avoiding mere disproportionality was in effect implicitly applied in the 1982 *Tunisia* v. *Libya* case, corresponding to the result-oriented and discretionary approach at the time. The Court conceived of proportionality as a final test for checking the results arrived at on the basis of other criteria.[128] The method used to establish the lines of outer delimitation was rather arbitrary and no more than an indication of rough proportionality, despite the use of 'exact' numbers. Nevertheless, it seems that a minority still thought proportionality was being applied too strictly.[129]

The *Gulf of Maine* case further added to the evidence of how unsettled the concept of proportionality still is. It formally adhered to the theory of proportionality as a test for checking a provisional delimitation.[130] The Chamber considered the element of coastal length relations not to be a

---

[124] Ibid., p. 397, 427, para. 101.
[125] Derek Bowett, 'The Arbitration Between the United Kingdom and France Concerning the Continental Shelf Boundary in the English Channel and South-Western Approaches'(1978) 49 *British Yearbook of International Law*, 1,17.
[126] N. 54, p. 455, paras. 249–50.
[127] See also Bowett, n. 125, pp. 12, 21 ff.; M. D. Blecher, 'Equitable Delimitation of Continental Shelf' (1979) *American Journal of International Law*, 76–77 ('It looks as though "proportionality" as defined in the North Sea cases, although rejected as a governing principle, has not been forgotten').
[128] ICJ Reports 1982, p. 91, para. 130.
[129] See Judge Gros dissenting opinion, p. 152, para. 17; Judge Evensen dissenting opinion, p. 131, para. 23; Judge Oda dissenting opinion, p. 269, para. 181; Judge Aréchaga at 139, para. 122 (speaking of an 'overall evaluation of fairness and proportionality' in his separate opinion).
[130] ICJ Reports 1984, p. 323, para. 185.

method or independent factor, but merely to be an auxiliary criterion and a corrective device to the basic criterion of equal division.[131] Paradoxically, however, proportionality became the essential constructive element for the second segment of the boundary.[132] The exact relationship of the respective coastal lengths was employed to define the intersection of the second segment on the closing line of the bay. It was therefore also of eminent importance for the third segment crossing the Georges Bank. The basic ratio calculated (US: Canada = 284:206 or 1.38:1) was slightly modified by giving half-effect to some islands (resulting 1.32:1),[133] but did not change the paramount impact of the approach. The decisive importance, far beyond that of a final test, may also be seen from the fact that the methods of computing the relevant coastal lengths remained extremely controversial.[134]

Proportionality not only assumed a paramount role of avoiding disproportionality in litigation. It was also applied in a completely new manner which finds a precedent only in the Gulf of Biscay Treaty.[135] It is no longer directly concerned with the relationship of spaces allocated, but rather constitutes an innovative geometrical method, assuming, without further elaboration, that it will produce an equitable relationship between coastal lengths and marine spaces.

The 1985 *Malta* v. *Libya* case shows yet another approach to proportionality. Faced with delimitation between opposite states merely within a small segment, due to third party interests, in principle the Court did not rule out the application of an *ex post* test of proportionality. Yet, it held that the determination of the relevant coasts 'is so much at large that virtually any variant could be chosen'.[136] Moreover, the small segment in delimitation would render the test unrealistic. Instead, the Court considered the marked difference of the respective coastal lengths of the parties (Malta:Libya = 24:192 measured by base lines) to fit under the heading of special circumstances. It led to the shifting of the median line to the benefit of Libya, but independent of any calculations of spatial ratios. Unlike proportionality, the Court held this to be an operation within the construction of the boundary, and therefore *ex ante*.[137] Moreover, it did not require any calculations of the coastal relationships, because the marked difference *per se* established a relevant circumstance

---

[131] ICJ Reports 1984, p. 327, para. 196; ICJ Reports 1984, p. 334, para. 218.
[132] See also ICJ Reports 1982, p. 164, para. 26 (dissenting opinion Oda).
[133] ICJ Reports 1984, pp. 334–7, paras. 217–22.   [134] See Chapter 10(II)(C)(1).
[135] ST/LEG/SER 19 at 445.   [136] ICJ Reports 1985, p. 53, para. 74.
[137] ICJ Reports 1985, p. 49, para. 66.

to be taken into account.[138] Moreover, it argued that even if the proportionality test was not applied, the line gives a result which seems to the Court to meet the requirements of the test of proportionality, and more generally to be equitable, taking into account all relevant circumstances.[139]

In the *St. Pierre and Miquelon* arbitration, the Tribunal applied a quantified proportionality test based on the *Tunisia/Libya* model. Again, the method used was arbitrary, as was clearly pointed out by French arbitrator Weil in his dissenting opinion:

> After all, one may question whether there is any real difference between a quantified proportionality test as used in the Decision and proportionality as a direct delimitation criterion. What would happen if the proportionality test indicated an unreasonable disproportion between the ratios of coastal lengths and those of areas? Would the judge or arbitrator then be bound, in order to arrive at a more proportionate result, to adjust the line which he states he has arrived at by other methods? A negative reply would deprive the proportionality test of all significance. An affirmative reply would be tantamount to converting proportionality into the dominant principle of delimitation. It may perhaps be said that an unfavourable test is unlikely and has never occurred, but is not this precisely because the data on which the arithmetical test is based are in reality selected so as to confirm a predetermined result?[140]

In the *Denmark* v. *Norway (Jan Mayen)* case, the ICJ found that the substantial disproportion in the coastline lengths of Greenland (524 kilometres) and of Jan Mayen (57.8 kilometres) constituted a relevant circumstance to be taken into consideration in drawing a boundary line closer to Jan Mayen than the equidistance line.[141] The Court, however, made clear that:

> taking account of the disparity of coastal lengths does not mean a direct and mathematical application of the relationship between the length of the coastal front of eastern Greenland and that of Jan Mayen.[142]

This part of the judgment led Charney to the conclusion that '[b]y drafting a solution that produced a division of the water so different from the coastline proportions (1:9), the Court seems to have diminished the importance of proportionality'.[143]

---

[138] ICJ Reports 1985, p. 49, para. 67.   [139] ICJ Reports 1985, p. 56, para. 78.
[140] N 44, para. 25.   [141] ICJ Reports 1993, pp. 68–9, paras. 68–9.
[142] ICJ Reports 1993, p. 69, para. 69.
[143] Jonathan I. Charney, 'Progress in International Maritime Boundary Delimitation Law' (1992) 88 *American Journal of International Law*, 243.

In the 2002 judgment in *Cameroon* v. *Nigeria*, proportionality was treated as a *factor* in the second step of the delimitation exercise which would ensure that the provisional equidistance line as drawn in the first step is adjusted, if necessary, so as to reflect an equitable result. The Court held that:

> a substantial difference in the lengths of the parties' respective coastlines may be a factor to be taken into consideration in order to adjust or shift the provisional delimitation line.[144]

The Court did not, however, find a difference in coastal lengths that would have called for an adjustment of the equidistance line.[145]

The Tribunal in the 2006 *Barbados/Trinidad and Tobago* arbitration considered coastal lengths as a relevant circumstance to be applied as a last factor in the delimitation exercise. At the outset it noted that '[t]he question of coastal length has come to have a particular significance in the process of delimitation'.[146] It also said that:

> the decisions of international courts and tribunals have on various occasions considered the influence of coastal frontages and lengths in maritime delimitation and it is well accepted that disparities in coastal lengths can be taken into account to this end, particularly if such disparities are significant.[147]

The Tribunal made clear, however, that this does not mean that the ratio of the parties' relative coastal lengths would require that delimitation should be based on that ratio or that any mathematical calculation of the boundary line should apply.[148] In the words of the Tribunal, '[p]roportionality is a broader concept, it is a sense of proportionality, against which the Tribunal can test the position resulting from the provisional application of the line that it has drawn'.[149]

The Tribunal also held that proportionality as a relevant circumstance is not a question of determining the equitable nature of a delimitation as a function of the ratio of the lengths of the coasts in comparison with that of the areas generated by the maritime projection of the points of the coast.[150] Neither is it a question of 'splitting

---

[144] ICJ Reports 2002, p. 303, para. 301.   [145] Ibid., p. 303, para. 301.
[146] Permanent Court of Arbitration: In the matter of an arbitration between Barbados and the Republic of Trinidad and Tobago (11 April 2006), 45 ILM 800, para. 236 (*Barbados* v. *Trinidad and Tobago*), para. 236.
[147] Ibid., para. 237.   [148] Ibid., para. 236.   [149] Ibid., para. 376.
[150] Ibid., para. 237, referring to the judgment in *Jan Mayen*, at para. 68, which itself referred to the judgment in *Libya* v. *Malta*, at para. 59.

the difference' or 'refashioning geography'.[151] Rather, in the view of the Tribunal:

> the real role of proportionality is one in which the presence of different lengths of coastlines needs to be taken into account so as to prevent an end result that might be 'disproportionate' and hence inequitable. In this context, proportionality becomes the last stage of the test of the equity of a delimitation. It serves to check the line of delimitation that might have been arrived at in consideration of various other factors, so as to ensure that the end result is equitable.[152]

The Tribunal found that an adjustment of the equidistance line was necessary due to 'the existence of the significant coastal frontage of Trinidad and Tobago' – without reference to the much smaller coastline of Barbados.[153] The significant coastal frontage of the island of Trinidad had not been given any influence on the equidistance line.[154] The Tribunal next had to consider where precisely the adjustment should take place. It held:

> There are no magic formulas for making such a determination and it is here that the Tribunal's discretion must be exercised within the limits set out by the applicable law.[155]

It should be recalled that the delimitation between Barbados and Trinidad and Tobago concerned opposite coasts. However, in those maritime areas where the equidistance line was adjusted, the delimitation could have just as well been one between adjacent coasts, similar to the situation in the *Qatar v. Bahrain* case.[156] The Tribunal therefore held relevant for the question of proportionality that part of Trinidad's coast which did not produce base points for the equidistance line, but which nevertheless abuts the area of delimitation. The Tribunal stated that it would be inequitable to ignore that particular coastal frontage.[157] It therefore included that part of Trinidad's coast in the consideration of proportionality in this second step of the delimitation exercise which is concerned with relevant circumstances.

In contrast to the *Barbados/Trinidad and Tobago* Award, the Tribunal in the 2007 *Guyana v. Suriname* Award applied a proportionality test only as a last test after the application of any relevant circumstances.

---

[151] *Barbados v. Trinidad and Tobago*, n. 146, paras. 237, 338, referring to the judgment in the *North Sea Continental Shelf* cases, para. 91.
[152] Ibid., para. 240; see also ibid., para. 337.   [153] Ibid., paras, 371–2.
[154] Ibid., para. 372.   [155] Ibid., para. 373.   [156] See *Qatar v. Bahrain*, n. 30, para. 170.
[157] *Barbados v. Trinidad and Tobago*, n. 146, para. 372.

Moreover, the proportionality test which the Tribunal applied was one of comparing the ratios of coastal lengths with that of maritime areas.[158] The Tribunal came up with nearly the same ratio of relevant areas (Guyana 51 per cent:Suriname 49 per cent) as for coastal frontages (Guyana 54 per cent:Suriname 46 per cent).[159]

The situation did not become much clearer with the subsequent consolidation of a two-step approach to the delimitation exercise. Courts and Tribunals inconsistently applied proportionality between coastal lengths and/or a test of disproportionality which compares the ratios between the coastal lengths and the maritime areas.

The 2009 judgment in *Romania* v. *Ukraine* included the consideration of proportionality as a relevant circumstance and in addition as a 'disproportionality test' which it applied in a separate third and last step of the delimitation exercise. The ruling made a clear distinction between proportionality as a relevant circumstance and as a final test of comparing the ratios of coastal lengths to that of maritime areas. It applied a test of proportionality also in the second step of the delimitation exercise, terming the pertinent relevant circumstance 'disproportion between lengths of coasts'.[160] That final test compares the ratios between the coastal lengths and the maritime areas as partitioned by an equidistance line which may or may not have been adjusted in consideration of relevant circumstances.

Assessing the disproportion between lengths of coasts as a relevant circumstance in the second step of the delimitation exercise, the Court still recalled once again that '[t]here is no principle of proportionality as such which bears on the initial establishment of the equidistance line'.[161] The Court continued:

> Where disparities in the lengths of coasts are particularly marked, the Court may choose to treat that fact of geography as a relevant circumstance that would require some adjustments to the provisional equidistance line to be made.[162]

The Court also rejected any direct and mathematical application of the coastal ratios upon the delimitation.[163] The Court found no particularly

---

[158] Ibid., para. 392.   [159] *Guyana* v. *Suriname* Award, n. 36, para. 392.
[160] ICJ Reports 2009, p. 61, paras. 158–8.
[161] Ibid., para. 163, recalling the Court in the *North Sea Continental Shelf* cases that delimitation in an equitable manner is not the same thing as the apportionment of areas (para. 18).
[162] *Romania* v. *Ukraine*, paras. 164, 165, referring to the judgment in *Cameroon* v. *Nigeria* at para. 301.
[163] Ibid., para. 166, referring to the judgments in *Jan Mayen* at para. 69 and *Libya* v. *Malta* at para. 58.

marked disparities between the relevant coasts of Ukraine and Romania that would have required it to adjust the provisional equidistance line at this juncture.[164] Interestingly, the Court in *Romania v. Ukraine* assessed the 'disproportion between lengths of coasts' as the first of several relevant circumstances.[165] Having considered the relevant circumstances, the Court then turned to the third and final step of the delimitation exercise – the disproportionality test, referred to in the context of EDS above.[166] The test, according to the Court, does not amount to a method of delimitation, but merely serves as an *ex post facto* review of whether the delimitation line arrived at by other means needs adjustment because of a significant disproportionality in the ratios between the lengths of the coasts and the maritime areas attributed to the parties by virtue of the delimitation line as hitherto determined.[167] When checking the coastal lengths against the maritime areas apportioned, the Court in *Romania v. Ukraine* held that:

> This checking can only be approximate. Diverse techniques have in the past been used for assessing coastal lengths, with no clear requirements of international law having been shown as to whether the real coastline should be followed, or baselines used, or whether or not coasts relating to internal waters should be excluded.[168]

It further observed that – with respect to the ratio – various tribunals, and the Court itself, have drawn different conclusions over the years as to what ratio between coastal lengths and maritime apportionments would constitute an inequitable disproportionality and that:

> [t]his remains in each case a matter for the Court's appreciation, which it will exercise by reference to the overall geography of the area.[169]

The Court eventually measured the coasts according to their general direction, excluding coastlines alongside waters lying behind gulfs or deep inlets. The controversial calculation resulted in a ratio of the respective coastal lengths for Romania and Ukraine of approximately 1:2.8 and a ratio of the relevant areas of approximately 1:2.1 – which the Court held to be equitable.[170]

---

[164] Ibid., para. 168.   [165] See ibid., paras. 158–204.
[166] Above text accompanying n. 114.
[167] ICJ Reports 2009, p. 61, paras. 210–11, with reference to the *Anglo-French Continental Shelf* case, at para. 101 and the *Guinea v. Guinea-Bissau* award, at paras. 94–5.
[168] Ibid., para. 212.   [169] Ibid., para. 213.   [170] Ibid., paras. 214–16.

The ITLOS Tribunal, in its first judgment on maritime delimitation delimitation in *Bangladesh v. Myanmar*, adopted the three-step methodology[171] as described in the *Romania v. Ukraine* case. The comparison of coastal lengths was, however, only an issue in the final examination of any disproportion between the coastlines and the maritime areas apportioned.[172] At the outset, the Tribunal held that the areas accruing to each party are those areas located within the relevant area, namely 'the area of overlapping entitlements of the Parties that is relevant to [the] delimitation'.[173] The ITLOS noted – probably with similar notions by the ICJ and arbitral tribunals in mind – that 'mathematical precision is not required in the calculation of either the relevant coasts or the relevant area'.[174] One question was what account should be taken of the fact that the size of the area accruing to Bangladesh could be affected by the location of its eventual boundary with India. On this point, the ITLOS decided simply that 'the fact that a third party may claim the same maritime area does not prevent its inclusion in the relevant maritime area for the purposes of the disproportionality test'.[175] The Tribunal found that the ratio of the relevant coasts of the parties was 1:1.42 and that the relevant area was divided between the parties in the ratio of 1:1.54 – both in favour of Myanmar.[176] The Tribunal consequently found that there was no 'significant disproportion in the allocation of maritime areas to the Parties relative to the respective lengths of their coasts that would require the shifting of the adjusted equidistance line in order to ensure an equitable solution'.[177]

The Court in *Nicaragua v. Colombia* considered the disparity in coastal lengths between the parties a relevant circumstance that necessitated adjustment of the median line. The disparity in question was 8.2:1 in Nicaragua's favour.[178] With reference to its prior case law, the Court found the disparity in coastal lengths to be 'so marked as to justify a significant shift'.[179] The Court consequently weighted the effect of the respective base points onto the median line in a ratio of 3:1 in favour of the Nicaraguan base points.[180] The Court noted that the provisional median line, as favoured by Colombia, would have left Colombia in possession of 'a markedly larger portion of the relevant area than that accorded to Nicaragua, notwithstanding the fact that Nicaragua has a far

---

[171] *Bangladesh v. Myanmar*, n. 25, paras. 239–40.   [172] Ibid., para. 477.   [173] Ibid.
[174] Ibid.   [175] Ibid., para. 494.   [176] Ibid., paras. 202, 204, 205, 498–499.
[177] Ibid., para. 499.   [178] *Nicaragua v. Colombia*, n. 45, para. 211.
[179] Ibid., paras. 211, 233.   [180] Ibid., para. 234.

longer relevant coast'.[181] A ratio that would have been even more favourable to Nicaragua, and thus closer to the coastal length ratio, seems to have been rejected because it would have cut across the 12 nm territorial sea around any of the Colombian islands.[182]

A second measure for the mitigation of the disparity of coastal lengths had to do with the start and endpoint of the median line. The Court noted:

> While the simplified weighted line represents a shifting of the provisional median line which goes some way towards reflecting the disparity in coastal lengths, it would, if extended [at either end] still leave Colombia with a significantly larger share of the relevant area than that accorded to Nicaragua, notwithstanding the fact that Nicaragua's relevant coast is more than eight times the length of Colombia's relevant coast.[183]

The Court found that this would give insufficient weight to the relevant circumstance of proportionality. As a result, the Court continued the boundary line out to the line 200 nm from the Nicaraguan base lines along lines of latitude. It did so not only by reference to proportionality, but in a combined consideration of that relevant circumstance and the relevant circumstance of the overall geography – namely to avoid a cutting-off effect.[184] The Court held that an equitable result requires this turn of the boundary.[185]

It is worth noting that to turn the boundary line at the northern extreme is essentially a result of disregarding the two insular features of Quitaseño and Serrano in the construction of the median line and of enclaving them instead with territorial seas.[186]

In its by now established practice to run a disproportionality test in a third step of the delimitation exercise, the Court nevertheless cautioned, again by reference to *Libya v. Malta*, that it is not applying a principle of strict proportionality.[187] It held that '[m]aritime delimitation is not designed to produce a correlation between the lengths of the Parties' relevant coasts and their respective shares of the relevant area'.[188] It recalled the ITLOS Tribunal in *Bangladesh v. Myanmar*, which spoke of checking for 'significant disproportion'.[189] The idea being 'to ensure that there is not a disproportion so gross as to "taint" the result and render it inequitable'.[190]

---

[181] Ibid., para. 229. [182] Ibid., para. 233. [183] Ibid., para. 236.
[184] Ibid., para. 236; see the discussion under section II(A)(2) above.
[185] *Nicaragua v. Colombia*, n. 45, para. 236. [186] Ibid., para. 238.
[187] Ibid., para. 240, citing *Libya v. Malta*, para. 58. [188] Ibid., para. 240.
[189] *Bangladesh v. Myanmar*, n. 25, para. 499.
[190] *Nicaragua v. Colombia*, n. 45, para. 242.

Having calculated the ratio of relevant coasts between the parties to be approximately 1:8.2,[191] the Court was now able to compare this to the relevant areas which it had divided in a ratio of approximately 1:3.44 – both in Nicaragua's favour.[192] Considering whether this disproportion is 'so great as to render the result inequitable',[193] the Court recalled prior cases,[194] but cautioned also that '[w]hether any disproportion is so great as to have that effect is not a question capable of being answered by reference to any mathematical formula but is a matter which can be answered only in the light of all the circumstances of the particular case'.[195] Looking back at how it arrived at the division of the maritime areas in this case, the Court recalled that the delimitation line was 'designed to ensure that neither State suffered from a "cut-off" effect'[196] and that the resulting allocation of maritime space was thus equitable.[197]

The 2014 *Maritime Dispute* between Peru and Chile applied proportionality in a very limited manner, also due to the fact that the boundary line started 80 nm offshore. The Court briefly note that 'no significant disproportion is evident', limiting its third test to practical irrelevance in this case.[198]

In sum, the case law does not show a uniform and coherent application of proportionality. It offers a number of precedents for a number of different geographical configurations: concavity; semi-enclosed bays with opposite and adjacent coasts; adjacent and opposite configurations. For comparable cases, each may provide some guidance in negotiations and adjudication. Some of the cases deal with proportionality as a factor. Some deal with it as a relevant circumstance. Some seek mathematical relations. Others are limited to broad comparison and relations. The test is not mandatory. In the *Newfoundland, Labrador and Nova Scotia* arbitration, the test was rejected by the Tribunal due to difficulties with defining the relevant area and to avoid imprecision and 'impressionism'. It was merely added a hypothetical test.[199] More recent cases, in

---

[191] Ibid., para. 153.   [192] Ibid., para. 243.   [193] Ibid.
[194] Ibid., para. 245, recalling *Libya v. Malta*; and ibid., para. 246, recalling *Denmark v. Norway (Jan Mayen)*.
[195] Ibid., para. 242.   [196] Ibid., para. 244.   [197] Ibid., para. 247.
[198] *Maritime Dispute (Peru v. Chile)*, ICJ Judgment of 27 January 2014, ICJ Reports 2014___, para. 194.
[199] *Arbitration between Newfoundland and Labrador and Nova Scotia Concerning Portions of the Limits of Their Offshore Areas as defined in the Canada-Nova Scotia Offshore Petroleum Resources Accord Implementation Act and the Canada-Newfoundland and Atlantic Accord Implementation Act*, Award of the Tribunal in the Second Phase, Ottawa,

particular on adjacent configurations, conceive it as an *ex post* review of results achieved in the process of delimitation. Yet, in the light of the broad standards applied in the *Channel* arbitration, the *Tunisia/Libya* case, the *St. Pierre and Miquelon* award, the *Barbados/Trinidad and Tobago* award and the de facto constructive uses of proportionality in the *Gulf of Maine* case, the *Denmark* v. *Norway (Jan Mayen)* case and the *Nicaragua/Colombia* case, the shifting of the median line might as well be construed as an *ex ante* application of the proportionality principle. Indeed, the Court in *Libya* v. *Malta* recognized the close relationship of the two concepts.[200] State practice does not, at any rate, clearly distinguish between *ex ante* and *ex post* assessments of proportionality. In both instances, the methods applied are not fundamentally different and generally operate without precision. The same is true for state practice and treaty making. As Legault and Hankey observed:

> The evidence in the individual reports suggests that in state practice, as in the jurisprudence, the use of proportionality is often more subjective and impressionistic than precise. Where mathematical formulas have been advanced in the course of the negotiations, the evidence has not, for obvious reasons, been made publicly available. To do so would furnish potential critics with powerful ammunitions to criticise politically sensitive boundaries that frequently represent compromise solutions.[201]

It is submitted that there is nothing more than a broad and shared principle that may say that there should be a roughly fair and reasonable relationship between the coastal length and the marine spaces allocated. It is no more than a rule of thumb. Nevertheless, it is suitable as a legal principle and should be observed in appropriate terms in all cases alike. It may be employed *ex ante* in shaping appropriate methods in a particular case (in particular in opposite configurations) – to the extent proportionality applies to opposite conconfigurations, a problem discussed shortly. It may be used *ex post* in order to review whether an overall equitable result is achieved. As a legal principle, it opens different avenues by which the goals of proportionality can be secured.

26 March 2002, paras. 5.18, 5.19, www.cnsopb.ns.ca/sites/default/files/pdfs/phaseii_award_english.pdf (last accessed February 2014).

[200] ICJ Reports 1985, p. 49, para. 66. The two operations are neither mutually exclusive, nor so closely identified with each other that the one would necessarily render the other supererogatory.

[201] Legault and Hankey, n. 106, p. 219.

3. The field of application

Beyond the difficulties in shaping the principle, it is controversial whether or not proportionality should indeed apply to opposite coastal configurations. The field of application of the principle is not settled. The *Libya v. Malta* judgment suggests it should apply, although it was seen that the respective lengths of the coast were taken into account under a different title than that of proportionality.[202] Similarly, the Tribunal in *Barbados v. Trinidad and Tobago* merely held that 'the existence of the significant coastal frontage of Trinidad and Tobago' is a relevant circumstance which requires adjustment of the equidistance line.[203] The Court in *Nicaragua v. Colombia* applied proportionality in the western sector of the delimitation area, where the coasts are clearly opposite, as well as in the eastern section, where the relationship of the coasts is arguably a combination of adjacency and oppositeness.[204]

It may be argued that proportionality emanates from the principle of equal division or sharing within the window of delimitation. The concept of justice, however, requires that factual differences be taken into account to avoid equal treatment of unequal facts. Such a doctrine would require taking different coastal lengths into account in both adjacent and opposite configurations. Applying proportionality to opposite coasts, however, is difficult to reconcile with the success of the median line in state practice and the broad consensus that this method generally provides equitable results in such configurations. Applying proportionality would require a comparison of the respective lengths of the opposite coastal facades and correcting the median, and therefore an equal division, to the benefit of the coastal state with the longer facade. Except for the *Libya v. Malta* and *Nicaragua v. Colombia* cases, which dealt with one and several islands, respectively, this has not been the practice in case law of opposite configurations. The *Barbados/Trinidad and Tobago* arbitration included two island states and three main islands, but the equidistance line was adjusted with reference only to the exceptionally large coast of the island of Trinidad, which had had no influence on the equidistance line in the first stage of the delimitation. The *Denmark/Norway (Jan Mayen)* case also involved an island. According to Judge Schwebel, the solution found by the Court which resulted in attributing almost three-quarters of the

---

[202] Text accompanying n. 136.
[203] *Barbados v. Trinidad and Tobago*, n. 146, paras. 371–2.
[204] Paul S. Reichler, 'A Case of Equitable Maritime Delimitation: Nicaragua and Colombia in the Western Caribbean Sea' (2013) 2(3) *Revista Tribuna Internacional*, 129–60, at 146.

total area of overlapping potential entitlements to Denmark, 'may tend to encourage immoderate and discourage moderate claims in future'.[205]

It should be recalled that the CDS principle essentially relates to configurations of adjacent states. With respect to seaward expansion of both the continental shelf and the EEZ, the law does not distinguish between large and small coastal states. Entitlement relies partly on natural features and partly on distance on equal terms for all coastal states, independent of coastal lengths. The principle of sovereign equality fully applies.

The relational nature of equity essentially relates to differences in the size of adjacent states. Based upon entitlement, it is therefore inconsistent to apply proportionality in a seaward direction, as such an application would produce curious results. If three adjacent states, the middle with only a small coastal facade, face a large state opposite them, the median line would have to be shifted not only toward the smaller state, but, in addition, even further to the smallest of them located in the middle. Such a result may be justified by the fundamental inequity of maritime zones, but it is doubtful whether such inequity should be amplified by applying proportionality in opposite cases. Proportionality therefore should apply to such configurations.

Independent of the coastal lengths of the respective coasts, delimitation instead should be primarily guided by the principle of equal division.[206] This does not exclude other principles from having an influence on where the boundary will be set. It may still be necessary to shift the median line, but this will be for reasons other than proportionality, such as unity of resource systems, conduct and protection of livelihood or because of the need to interlink and connect boundaries with existing or emerging lines in the region.

4. Assessment

Some cases suggest that proportionality is a precise and well-defined criterion and test; almost a rule in nature. In reality, proportionality has never been applied in mathematical terms. Even where coastal relationships were calculated, the judgments do not show any evidence that comparable studies on respective areas expressed quantitatively were taken into account. Nor is there such evidence in state practice. Often it is not possible to compute the overall size of space appertaining to one

---

[205] ICJ Reports 1993, p. 127 (separate opinion Schwebel).
[206] See also ibid. Judge Schwebel.

state, since not all of the necessary boundaries have been established, or the outer limit of the zone still remains to be determined in a different procedure. For such reasons, it has always been a rather broad principle of overall proportionality which, it seems, the judges decide upon intuitively by looking at the maps, perhaps more guided by reflections of political acceptability than of geographical proportions. The projection of the specific ratio of coastal lengths to the closing line still remains a highly discretionary approach, since no such projection is required by law. It has always been a principle that is actively applied in order to maintain an overall proportionality, beyond merely avoiding arbitrary disproportion. It necessarily encompasses a considerable degree of discretion on the part of the Courts. Recalling the wording of the 1969 judgment and recalling that equitable principles rather than mathematical rules are required, the reality of the cases are better than the abstract statements of the law which were developed but not realized for good reasons.

The disparity may be overcome by returning to a broader notion of proportionality, such as the one expressed by the *North Sea* Court in 1969 and partly taken up by the Court in the 2009 *Romania/Ukraine* case. If further elaborated in future cases, proportionality may become more than a pseudo-mathematical technique by which results reached on other grounds are rationalized.[207] What is required is a reasonable degree (not a mathematical relationship) of proportionality, based on the extent of the maritime areas appertaining to a party and the lengths of its coast measured by the general direction (rather than a mathematical computation) of the coastal lengths of the respective states and the taking into account of any potential or actual effects of any other boundaries with third states in the region. It is important to stress the quality as a principle and not as a strict rule. It is exactly the nature of fair and reasonable proportionality that allows qualification of the concept as a legal principle in line with the general description given, beyond being a mere concept, a factor or criterion. As a specification of the CDS principle, it is not at the disposition of the parties and the Court, but has to be included and considered in all *legal* operations of maritime boundary delimitation related to the shelf or the EEZ between adjacent coastal states.

Is it possible to further refine the general concept of proportionality within this perception? While leaving it as a broad principle, guidance

---

[207] See also Charney, n. 143, 242.

could still be improved. The relationship between coastal length and marine spaces has not yet been sufficiently developed. Given that the underlying objective of the zone is to achieve equitable allocation of space in the first place, the ratio of coastal lengths and square mile allocation could be developed as a tool at least to check *ex post* whether an equitable boundary was achieved. This method, which was perhaps used in the Raritan Bay delimitation, allows for evaluation of the equity of different technical methods of delimitation under discussion in a case, provided that the overall space to be allocated can be reasonably determined and does not have to be left open because of third party claims that are as yet unsettled. Again, it would not be a matter of achieving mathematical computation and relationships, but one of preserving a relationship that is reasonable overall between the coastal lengths and spaces allocated under this important principle. Negotiators or courts should first define the approximate ratio of coastal lengths, and then proceed to seek, study and compare different technical methods that allocate a proportional area of space in specified units. Technical studies should therefore examine the size of the allocations under different methods.

D. Relevant circumstances related to resource allocation

Given the overwhelming importance of natural resources as the prime objective of delimitation and the underlying attention paid to it,[208] the question arises as to whether, even within the primarily spatial concepts of the shelf and the EEZ, resources could not themselves be the object of central equitable principles or relevant circumstances upon which delimitation should rely, as much as on principles related to surface geography. This would respond to an observation that legal arguments are sometimes advanced with almost academic detachment from reality, ignoring the very purpose of obtaining permanent sovereignty, control and jurisdiction over natural resources as the prime goal of maritime boundary delimitation. It would also contribute to the effect that judicial decisions and reasoning directly confront, as well as expressing the real underlying issues of delimitation that are important in achieving the goal of transparency and in improving conditions for successful implementation of results in the political environment of delimitation.[209]

The spatial concepts of the shelf and the EEZ and the finding that delimitation is not just a matter of sharing resources equitably, do not

---

[208] See Chapter 9(II)(B).   [209] See Chapter 9(IV).

necessarily exclude location and quality of resources from being the object of equitable standards which influence the process of delimitation and may possibly alter lines that are otherwise established on the basis of geographic, surface-related and additional conduct-related principles. Equally, this is not excluded by the fact that, in the same way as geology, the location of resources (particularly ecosystems) can hardly ever establish a natural boundary in an essentially political and legal process.[210] However, the focus on location of resources may lead to the argument that geology and geomorphology should gain relevance again, since they are linked to the location of currently exploitable natural resources, such as hydrocarbons.[211] But unlike other principles, standards related to the location of resources have not developed much beyond abstract statements in case law. As natural, realistic and evident as it seems to focus on the location of resources in order to achieve an equitable result, conceptual and practical problems do arise, particularly in the context of legal dispute settlement.

1. The location of resources

a. Unity of deposits In 1969, the ICJ gave some consideration to the impact of the unity of deposits in the area of delimitation. The location of resources as such was not considered decisive for the boundary line, already anticipating, *in nuce*, later developments with regard to the issue of natural boundaries. The Court only dealt with the situation of a boundary running across a uniform deposit. It did not consider 'that unity of deposits constitutes anything more than a factual element which it is reasonable to take into consideration in the course of negotiations for a delimitation'.[212] The matter, therefore, was left to negotiations, without indicating any clear normative content of such a factor. However, by referring to existing agreements in the area, the Court certainly had in mind schemes of co-operation and joint exploitation for such cases.[213]

---

[210] See Chapter9(II)(D)(2).
[211] Jonathan I. Charney, 'International Maritime Boundaries for the Continental Shelf: The Relevance of Natural Prolongation' in Nisuke Ando, Edward McWhinney and Rüdiger Wolfrum (eds.), *Liber Amicorum Judge Shigeru Oda* (The Hague: Kluwer Law International, 2002), pp. 1011, 1028.
[212] ICJ Reports 1969, p. 53, para. 97.
[213] ICJ Reports 1969, p. 53, para. 97. See also William T. Onorato, 'Apportionment of an International Common Petroleum Deposit' (1968) 17 *International and Comparative Law Quarterly*, 85.

b. Existing oil wells and concessions Beyond unity of deposits, a further reference to allocation of resources can be found in the 1982 *Tunisia* v. *Libya* case, this time with a potential impact on the boundary line. The location of existing oil wells was considered to be a potential factor to be taken into account. While in this judgment the location of oil wells remained without practical effect, the Court held *obiter dictum*:

> As to the presence of oil-wells in an area to be delimited, it may, depending on the facts, be an element to be taken into account in the process of weighing all relevant factors to achieve an equitable result.[214]

Efforts by Tunisia in 1985 to revise the boundary line based on the fact that the 1982 judgment unintentionally created overlaps of existing oil concessions failed for procedural reasons.[215] In substance, the argument nevertheless showed that, at the time, the location of resources, at least in terms of existing concessions, was basically relevant, and should be taken into account. Perhaps the argument related to existing oil wells, as much as that of fishing grounds, is more closely related to human conduct and the Grisbadarna principle, since it does not essentially rely upon the location of resources but rather on human activities.[216]

In the *St. Pierre and Miquelon* award, the Court of Arbitration did not consider, despite Canada's impressive demonstration with computer-assisted charts of resource location, that the potential for mineral resources had an impact on the delimitation process, and rejected any conclusion to that effect.[217]

In recent case law, oil wells and concessions have ceased to be of relevance for the position of the boundary. They are nevertheless regularly argued by the parties and examined by Courts and Tribunals.

The Court in the 2002 *Cameroon* v. *Nigeria* case – having reviewed the case law of courts and tribunals – held:

> Overall, it follows from the jurisprudence that, although the existence of an express or tacit agreement between the parties on the siting of their respective oil concessions may indicate a consensus on the maritime areas to which they are entitled, oil concessions and oil wells are not in themselves to be considered as relevant circumstances justifying the adjustment or shifting of the provisional delimitation line. Only if they

---

[214] ICJ Reports 1982, p. 78, para. 107. Judge Eversen pointed to the fact that the Court failed to take into account the location of wells, ICJ Reports 1982, p. 318, para. 26 (dissenting opinion).
[215] See Chapter 6(II)(D) in fine.   [216] See Chapter 10(III).
[217] See n. 44, paras. 89–91.

are based on express or tacit agreement between the parties may they be taken into account.[218]

The Court found no agreement between the parties regarding oil concessions. Accordingly, the oil practice of the parties was not a factor to be taken into account for the maritime delimitation in this case.[219]

In the 2002 *Newfoundland, Labrador and Nova Scotia* arbitration, the Tribunal did not exclude taking into account the location of resources, while the task of the delimitation clearly is not one of equitably sharing offshore resources:

> True, to have regard to the location of potential resources stands in some tension with the often-repeated statement that a court engaged in maritime delimitation is not sharing out an undivided whole. For the reasons explained already, this Tribunal is in no different position in dividing the continental shelf of Canada between the two Parties to the purposes of the *Accord Acts*. Thus, it is not the Tribunal's function to share out equitably any offshore resource, actual or hypothetical, irrespective of its location. On the other hand, the effect of any proposed line on the allocation of resources is, in the Tribunal's view, a matter it can properly take into account among other factors.[220]

Examining possible relevant circumstances, the Tribunal in the 2006 *Barbados* v. *Trinidad and Tobago* award held in general terms that:

> Resource-related criteria have been treated more cautiously by the decisions of international courts and tribunals, which have not generally applied this factor as a relevant circumstance.[221]

In accordance with the arguments of the parties, the Tribunal looked at the practice of oil concessions in terms of estoppel and acquiescence but did not find sufficient evidence to that effect.[222] With respect to oil wells it held that the finding in *Cameroon* v. *Nigeria* applied to this case as well, that 'oil wells are not in themselves to be considered as relevant circumstances, unless based on express or tacit agreement between the parties'.[223]

In *Guyana* v. *Suriname*, the Tribunal stated:

> The cases reveal a marked reluctance of international courts and tribunals to accord significance to the oil practice of the parties in the determination of the delimitation line.[224]

---

[218] *Cameroon* v. *Nigeria*, n. 144, para. 304.   [219] Ibid., para. 304.
[220] *Newfoundland, Labrador and Nova Scotia* arbitration, n. 199, para. 3.21, referring to *North See Continental Shelf* cases, ICJ Rep 1969, para. 18, p. 21.
[221] *Barbados* v. *Trinidad and Tobago*, n. 146, para. 241.   [222] Ibid., para. 363.
[223] Ibid., para. 364.   [224] *Guyana* v. *Suriname* Award, n. 36, para. 390.

The Tribunal referred to the Court in *Cameroon* v. *Nigeria* and stated that it is 'guided by this jurisprudence'. Examining the practice of the parties with regard to oil concessions and oil wells, the Tribunal found no evidence of any agreement between the parties regarding such practice, with the consequence that the oil practice of the parties could not be taken into account.[225]

The Court in *Romania* v. *Ukraine* rejected oil concessions as being a relevant circumstance with reference to the Tribunal in *Barbados* v. *Trinidad and Tobago*, which had observed that '[r]esource-related criteria have been treated more cautiously by the decisions of international courts and tribunals, which have not generally applied this factor as a relevant circumstance'.[226]

The Court in *Nicaragua* v. *Colombia* referred to *Romania* v. *Ukraine* and repeated the dictum from *Barbados* v. *Trinidad and Tobago* when finding that the case did not present issues of access to natural resources so exceptional as to warrant it treating them as a relevant consideration. Both parties had raised the question of equitable access to natural resources, but neither offered evidence of particular circumstances that the Court considered had to be treated as relevant.[227]

2. The possibility of eco-geographical criteria

Despite rejection of natural boundaries based on ecology, the *Gulf of Maine* Chamber did not rule out the impact of eco-geographic criteria or standards. It rendered them subject to the particular facts of the case, but was not any more specific than that:

> the advantages and disadvantages of a particular criterion and a particular method cannot be assessed and judged in the abstract but only with reference to their application to a specific situation.[228]

The statement leaves wide open the extent to which aspects related to ecology could have an impact on future cases, but again, it was without practical impact on the case in hand.[229] The Court's main purpose was perhaps to leave the door ajar for future developments in the field. Would it and should it be possible to take into account the particular needs of conservation management beyond the effects given to unity of deposits? Would the statement allow for the evolution of particular schemes

---

[225] Ibid., para. 390.
[226] ICJ Reports 2009, p. 61, para. 198, citing *Barbados* v. *Trinidad and Tobago* 241.
[227] ICJ Reports 2012, p. 624, para. 223. [228] ICJ Reports 1984, p. 319, para. 174.
[229] See ICJ Reports 1984, p. 373, para. 19 in fine (dissenting opinion Oda).

beyond boundary delimitation, even taking into account third generational rights?[230]

3. Inherent limitations to resource allocation in general law of delimitation

Overall, the location of deposits has not so far played a role in delimitation, in accordance with the limited role of geomorphology.[231] The potential, particularly of eco-geographical standards, is more open. Unity of deposits is without direct impact on the boundary line. Oil wells and concessions are likely to exert only marginal corrections of a line adopted on the basis of surface-related standards, and have to be based on explicit agreement by the parties rather than on standards related to location as such.

The concept of delimitation in case law works from the implied assumption that the equitable allocation of spaces inherently and equally leads to equitable allocation of actual and potential resources, and therefore generally satisfies the main interests in dispute. While this may often be the case, it is nevertheless conceivable that a boundary line drawn upon a specification of equitable principles related to space allocation would result in an uneven allocation of resources within the window of delimitation because they happen to be found to an overwhelming extent within the area allocated to one of the parties. Should the real location and quality of resources be taken into account beyond minimal corrections in such cases? Would it not be necessary to do so in order to take into account the underlying realities of interests, and therefore as a prerequisite for successful solutions and dispute settlement? Indeed, this has been the very idea behind the allocations realized in the *Jan Mayen* conciliation[232] and a number of agreements operating with joint zones of administration, exploration and exploitation.[233] From this perspective, it seems realistic that the location of resources and riches should be taken into account. More or less reluctantly, a number of judges and authors expressed their views to that effect,[234]

---

[230] See section III(D) in this chapter.   [231] See also Highet, n. 26, p. 164.
[232] See Chapter 6(II)(J).   [233] See section II(D)(4) in this chapter.
[234] See in particular President Y. Rivero's separate opinion, ICJ Reports 1969, p. 60, para. 5 (expressing the view that taking into account the location of deposits during negotiations constitutes, on the one hand, a 'disturbing factor to the detriment of equity'; on the other hand, he continued, the judge cannot ignore the realities of social and economic interests; he concluded that the shelf is in principle not subject to the location of resources 'unless decisive circumstances so require', without indicating, however, what such circumstances may be). Other judges gave more weight to the location of resources:

provided that the location of resources is known. The findings of the *Newfoundland* arbitration, quoted above, offers appropriate guidance to this effect, allowing the location of resources to be taken into account as a factor, while not as the objective of delimitation.

The importance of actual resource allocation and the possibility of a substantially uneven allocation of resources in a geographically equitable delimitation raise the issue of whether location of resources should be more than a factual element to consider, and thus be developed into an equitable principle of its own to compete on an equal basis with geographical and other principles. From a general point of view of justice and general equity, this is a tempting objective. For a number of reasons, however, this objective is extremely difficult to achieve, at least in legal dispute settlement, and it is no coincidence that the case law so far has remained embryonic with respect to standards of resource allocation. There are both conceptual and practical difficulties.

Firstly, it should be recalled that delimitation is not a matter of simply allocating equitable and fair shares of resources. This doctrine, strongly advocated by the Federal Republic of Germany in the *North Sea* cases,[235] was rejected at that time on grounds of its inconsistency with the concept of natural prolongation and *ipso facto* and *ab initio* entitlement.[236] With the decline of natural prolongation, these arguments are no longer pertinent. The rise of minimal expanses and, foremost, the foundations of entitlement submitted in the present study, are based on the closest relationship of a coastal state to space and resources.[237] These foundations also contain inherent limitations on the possibility of taking into account the location of resources in a legal operation of delimitation. Unlike space, resources as such, their location and their quality do not establish any particular natural relationship to a particular coastal state. Only human conduct and geography related to such resources in their

---

ICJ Reports 1969, p. 256 (dissenting opinion of Judge Sorenson, affirming the consideration of the location of resources if the location is known); see also ICJ Reports 1969, p. 72 (separate opinion Jessup); ICJ Reports 1982, p. 322 (dissenting opinion Eversen); Blecher, n. 127, 60, 65 (affirming that delimitation may well be affected by natural resources).

[235] See ICJ Reports 1969, p. 9; 1 Pleadings 1968 30–6, a reply particularly relating the doctrine of equitable share to resources as a principle of 'inherent, self-evident, and necessary validity'. Ibid., at 393.

[236] ICJ Reports 1969, pp. 22–3, paras. 18–20; ICJ Reports 1969, p. 31, para. 43; see Chapter 6(II)(A). See also Common Rejoinder of Denmark and the Netherlands, *North Sea Continental Shelf* cases, 1 Pleadings 463–4.

[237] See Chapter 9(II)(E).

location are able to do so. Indeed, this is the rationale for taking existing wells or concessions, or living resources due to human conduct and patterns of exploitation, into account. Under the doctrine of close relationship, the location and quality of resources is only relevant to the extent that it is linked with human geography.

Secondly, since delimitation is not simply a matter of achieving distributive justice *ex aequo et bono*, but essentially relies upon the geographical concepts of the shelf and the EEZ, it cannot simply be a matter of sharing resources within the window of delimitation at the outset. Allocation of resources should therefore basically follow spatial allocation essentially achieved on the basis of principles related to the geographic, surface-related principles of CDS, NEP, NCP, EDS and FRP, as well as to human geography. It essentially remains linked to surface geography. Any standard related to resource allocation would have to start from this premise and should be able to remedy distortions of the assumption that spatial allocation also leads to equitable resource allocation.

In theory, an equitable principle in which the allocation of resources should be roughly proportional to spatial delimitation based on surface-related principles could be coined. Delimitation would therefore firstly require an allocation of space; secondly, a calculation of spatial allocation; thirdly, an assessment of resource allocation; and fourthly, based upon comparison, a shifting of the tentative boundary line to remedy existing disproportions between the two assessments. A principle of roughly proportional resource allocation would therefore remain dependent on principles related to geographical space allocation. At best, it could be a principle of secondary rank from a point of view of methodology.

Thirdly, such a four-step operation of assessing roughly proportional resource allocation would entail a considerable number of practical difficulties which may not always be overcome. While calculations of spatial areas seem possible, the same is much more difficult with respect to the location, quality and quantity of living and non-living resources. Clear evidence is required,[238] but this is difficult to establish in most cases, because neither the quantitative amount of actual, nor potential, resources is available at the time of delimitation.[239] The consideration of resources

---

[238] In 1984, the *Gulf of Maine* Chamber required almost prohibitively high standards of evidence for ecological arguments with respect to natural boundaries. See ICJ Reports 1984, p. 277, para. 53 ('the result was not such as to clear away all doubt').

[239] The Federal Republic of Germany, pleading in the *North Sea* cases for the inclusion of resources into the doctrine of just and equitable share, upon interrogation by Judge Jessup, conceded the impracticability of the argument as long as necessary data and

again raises difficult issues of justiciability. For such reasons, a principle of resource allocation will be of very limited practical use, despite the underlying importance of its goal. There is a danger that the experiences that occurred when geological and ecological evidence was presented in courts would be repeated: endless, expensive and inconclusive debate and argument.[240] Principles of equitable resource allocation *per se* would again be prone to what were called essays in geopoetry or ecopoetry.[241]

Finally, resource allocation as a principle would soon conflict with the common practice of establishing, for obvious practical purposes, uniform and single boundaries both for the shelf and the EEZ.[242] Fair apportionment, based on proportional space allocation, would often require different lines for the shelf and the EEZ, since different types of resources in many instances are unlikely to be found in similar concentrations in similar areas. The possibility of drawing different lines still leaves the option of considering resource allocation. If, however, parties agree in the special agreement to ask for a single line, this prevents the court from taking it into account, as the example of the *Gulf of Maine* case shows.

For such reasons, no principle of proportional allocation of resources should be introduced. The location, quality and quantity of resources are bound to be, at best, relevant factual circumstances that cannot exert major changes in spatial allocations except when linked to, or based on, human geography.[243]

4. Improving resource allocation by negotiation and by special agreement (compromis)

The legal process based on the fundamental rule of equity is faced with the paradox that the objective of delimitation – equitable allocation of extractable resources – is itself not suitable for serving as a basis of adjudication. Conceptual limitations and, more significantly, practical problems related

---

evidence are lacking. See Pleadings, 4 Nov. 1968 C.R. 68–69 at 2–3; François Monconduit, 'L'Affaire du plateau continental de la Mer du Nord' (1969) 15 *Annuaire Français de Droit International*, 213, 243.

[240] See Charney, n. 211, pp. 1011, 1028.   [241] See section III below.
[242] The Court in *Qatar* v. *Bahrain* observed that the concept of a single maritime boundary stems not from multilateral treaty law but from state practice, and that it finds its explanation in the desire of states to establish one uninterrupted boundary line delimiting the various – partially coincident – zones appertaining to them (*Qatar* v. *Bahrain*, n. 30, para. 173, as recalled in *Guyana* v. *Suriname* Award, n. 36, at para. 334). While the regimes are separate, a single maritime boundary avoids the difficult practical problems that could arise were one party to have rights over the water column and the other rights over the seabed and subsoil below that water column (*Guyana* v. *Suriname* Award, n. 36, para. 334).
[243] See section III below.

to fact-finding and evidence are major impediments. There is a price to pay for equity being developed and concretized as a legal concept. Perhaps this problem of resource allocation demonstrates most aptly the limitations of legal settlement and, foremost, those of the concept of boundaries as such.

In the process of negotiations, such limitations do not exist, at least in theory. Parties are free to take into account the location of resources to a much wider degree than in legal dispute settlement based on the fundamental rule. They may agree that solutions should primarily reflect and focus upon resource allocation, rather than on space. The examples from state practice already referred to above show that states have chosen this approach rather than a legalistic one.

Ultimately, solutions may result in the establishment of joint zones of exploration, exploitation and administration. To the extent that parties wish to submit the matter to dispute settlement on a basis that takes into account allocation of resources, they are in a position to do so by requesting the court to adjudicate based on *ex aequo et bono* or by means of agreeing on appropriate provisions in the special agreement or compromise. Again, the *Jan Mayen* conciliation is an example in point. The limitations of the law can be overcome by giving the courts or quasi-judicial bodies a special mandate to that effect. The practical problem is that states benefiting from a privileged allocation of resources on the basis of general law will often be reluctant to make such concessions in the first place, and will do so only in exchange for another advantage. The fundamental limitations of the law to take into account the location and abundance of resources in a particular area feed back to the original definition of negotiating positions. The problem, it will be seen, can only be overcome in the long term with the evolution of new and more functional concepts in law that allow the courts to avoid drawing boundary lines and to establish joint zones, even without a special mandate by the parties.[244]

III. Equitable standards related to conduct and human geography

A. *Standards related to conduct of coastal states*

It was seen in Chapter 9 that entitlement based on historic rights and inter-temporal law, as well as the doctrines of estoppel and acquiescence, may form an important part of the legal environment of equity and

---

[244] See Chapter 5(III).

cannot be excluded from exerting a decisive influence on delimitations.[245] Unlike the field of territorial boundaries, however,[246] legal requirements to that effect are rarely met in the context of shelf and EEZ delimitation. Except for the denial of a pre-existing boundary based on particular conduct in the *Guinea/Guinea-Bissau* arbitration,[247] no case establishing boundaries on such legal grounds was found. Instead, the ICJ denied a German obligation based on acquiescence or estoppel in the *North Sea* cases.[248] In the *Tunisia/Libya* case, neither unilateral acts,[249] nor a *modus vivendi*,[250] nor factually observed lines of granted drilling concessions,[251] nor fishing patterns were held to amount to legal rights and obligations *per se* under the facts of the case as assessed by a majority of the Court.[252] Equally, the *Gulf of Maine* Chamber rejected Canadian contentions of US conduct amounting to acquiescence and estoppel, and therefore a binding line of delimitation.[253] Similarly, the Court found itself unable to discern historical rights or 'any pattern of

---

[245] See Chapter 9(III)(C).
[246] For the operation of estoppel and acquiescence, see in particular *East Greenland Case*, PCIJ, Series A/B No. 53 (Legal Status of Eastern Greenland); *Temple of Preah Vihear Case*, Merits, ICJ Reports 1962, pp. 13, 32 ff.; 'Indo-Pakistan Western Boundary Case' 7 ILM, 667 (1968); *Award of Her Majesty Queen Elizabeth II for the Arbitration of a Controversy between the Argentine Republic and the Republic of Chile concerning certain Parts of the Boundary between their Territories*, Court of Arbitration, 24 November 1966 (London: HM Stationery Office, 1966), partly reprinted in 'Chile: Constitutional Amendment Concerning Natural Resources and their Nationalization' 10 ILM 1067 (1971); generally, and for further relevant cases, see J. P. Müller, *Vertrauensschutz im Völkerrecht* (Cologne: Heymann, 1971), pp. 13–27, 39–67. Thomas Cottier and Jörg Paul Müller, 'Estoppel', *Max Planck Encyclopedia of Public International Law* (Oxford University Press, 2012). See also Chapter 9(III)(C).
[247] The Tribunal construed the absence of protest by France when Portugal granted oil concessions in 1958 as evidence that no maritime boundary had been established by the 'Southern limit' before. *Guinea v. Guinea-Bissau*, n. 40, paras. 26, 63.
[248] ICJ Reports 1969, p. 26–7, paras. 27–30.
[249] ICJ Reports 1982, p. 66–9, paras. 87–92.   [250] ICJ Reports 1982, p. 70, para. 95.
[251] ICJ Reports 1982, p. 118, para. 84.
[252] The case shows how blurry the line may be, as well as how subject it can be to discretionary evaluation. Judge Ago argued that there was a genuine maritime boundary prior to decolonization, and that the facts correspond to a proper situation of acquiescence, ICJ Reports 1982, p. 96, paras. 3, 4. Judge Oda disagreed on the grounds that mutual dissatisfaction with such a line induced the parties to submit the dispute for settlement by the Court, ICJ Reports 1982, p. 254, para. 177 (dissenting opinion Oda). Charney, argued that the finding of the Court rather encourages conflict than peace settlement, since states will keep the line in conflict in order to avoid its qualification as a legally accepted boundary. Jonathan I Charney, Proceedings of the American Society of International Law vol. 76 (1982), p. 156–7.
[253] ICJ Reports 1984, pp. 310–11, paras. 149–51.

conduct of either side sufficiently unequivocal' to constitute acquiescence in the 1985 *Libya v. Malta* case.[254] The Tribunal in *Barbados v. Trinidad and Tobago* did not find activity of determinative legal significance by Barbados – namely seismic surveys or oil concessions and patrolling – which would have been sufficient to establish estoppel or acquiescence on the part of Trinidad and Tobago.[255] The Court in *Nicaragua v. Colombia* did not consider that the conduct of the parties was 'so exceptional as to amount to a relevant circumstance which itself requires it to adjust or shift the provisional median line' delimiting the EEZ and continental shelf. That Court held that it cannot be ruled out that conduct might need to be taken into account as a relevant circumstance in an appropriate case, but that the jurisprudence of the Court and of arbitral tribunals showed that conduct will not normally have such an effect.[256] Equally, the Tribunal in the *Newfoundland, Labrador and Novia Scotia* arbitration carefully examined the conduct of the parties, but found no evidence sufficient to establish acquiescence or tacit agreement.[257]

The striking aspect of conduct related to the respective zone and its purpose is, however, that without crystallizing into legal titles and obligations, conduct emerged as an important standard within the fundamental rule of equity. This standard was given due consideration amongst other equitable standards during the process of delimitation. To the same extent that geological features and natural submarine boundaries and geology have decreased, the relevance of human conduct has emerged once more, affirming, from a particular angle, the legal and political nature of maritime boundary delimitation in search of what parties may consider to be an equitable boundary in the light of their mutual conduct. As the Court said in 1982:

> it is evident that the Court must take into account whatever indices are available of the line or lines which the Parties themselves may have considered equitable or acted upon as such – if only as an interim solution affecting part only of the areas to be delimited.[258]

Even if short of amounting to independent legal title, human conduct therefore constitutes a standard amongst the others *within* equity, on a

---

[254] ICJ Reports 1985, pp. 28–9, paras. 24, 25.
[255] *Barbados v. Trinidad and Tobago*, n. 146, para. 363.
[256] *Nicaragua v. Colombia*, n. 45, para. 320, referring to *Denmark v. Norway (Jan Mayen)*, para. 86; ICJ Reports 2002, p. 303, para 304; ICJ Reports 2009, p. 61, para 198; *Barbados v. Trinidad and Tobago*, para. 269; and *Guyana v. Suriname* Award, n. 36, paras. 378–91.
[257] *Newfoundland, Labrador and Nova Scotia* arbitration, paras. 3.2–3.18, pp. 49–59.
[258] ICJ Reports 1982, p. 84, para. 118; see also ICJ Reports 1982, p. 65, para. 81.

sub-legal level.[259] In other words, it is not necessary to meet the legal requirements of historic rights, estoppel or acquiescence in order for human conduct to play a potential role in delimitation. Conduct has evidently become a more flexible concept in equity, and the difficulty that must be solved arises over when it should exert such an impact within the fundamental rule. In a similar way as with historic rights,[260] there is also on this normative level an inherent tension between the relatively new and novel legal concepts of the shelf and the EEZ, introduced just short of customary law within a few years, and considerations of human conduct, which tend to cover longer periods. The fact that a maritime revolution has taken place in the meantime does not allow the application of an unfettered *Grisbadarna* Principle in this context; i.e. short of established historic rights, acquiescence or estoppel, the state of things which actually exist and have existed for a long time[261] cannot readily prevail over the entitlement created by the marine revolution of the shelf and the EEZ. The law is not settled, and it is difficult to draw clear lines between relevant and irrelevant conduct with the fundamental rule. Perhaps a distinction between historic conduct, on the one hand, and recent or contemporary conduct, on the other, may provide further guidance.

1. Relevant circumstance: historical conduct prior to the creation of the legal shelf and the EEZ

The case law on conduct dating before the creation of the shelf and the EEZ shows diverging assessments as to the impact on the new boundaries.

In the *Tunisia* v. *Libya* case, the Court took into account, inter alia, a de facto maritime boundary which was practised between France and Italy, the former colonial powers of Tunisia and Libya, respectively. The boundary related to fisheries, and in particular sponge fishing, and gradually emerged as a 'sort of *modus vivendi*' observed by the parties.[262] The line runs perpendicular to the coast, at an angle of approximately 26 degrees to the north. That boundary was not the sole ground that was important for the adoption of exactly that angle and line as a shelf boundary, but it certainly influenced the Court's delimitation,[263] and it shows the impact that existing patterns of conduct have.

---

[259] See ICJ Reports 1982, pp. 64–5, para. 81 (the Court appears to define conduct as one of the relevant circumstances).
[260] See Chapter 9(III)(B).   [261] See Chapter 8(II)(A)(1).
[262] See ICJ Reports 1982, pp. 93–4, para. 70. For a detailed recollection of the diplomatic history see ICJ Reports 1982, pp. 122–9, paras. 77–95 (separate opinion Aréchaga).
[263] See ICJ Reports 1982, p. 119, para. 84.

Another dimension of historic conduct in that case was related to fishing practices and other maritime activities that were not directly related to a specific boundary line, but, instead, to the acquisition and occupation of marine spaces beyond the territorial sea.

Such arguments were put forth by Tunisia claiming historic rights on the basis of long-established conduct.[264] Whilst in principle, accepting the relevance of historic rights,[265] the Court did not find it necessary to pass judgment on the issue in this case, since the method and line finally adopted (perpendicular to the general coastline) did not encroach upon these alleged historic rights, whatever the validity of their title.[266] Similarly, it was held to be irrelevant for the calculations of proportionality, because historic rights did not correlate to internal and territorial waters as defined by Tunisian base lines, and the test of proportionality was based on the coastal configuration rather than on these contended base lines.[267] However, it is submitted that the Court nevertheless considered these arguments concerning historic conduct and chose, based on several considerations, a solution which was largely compatible with these historic claims and accommodated prior conduct. Again, conduct, whatever its precise legal qualification, emerged as a relevant consideration among others in equity. It is likely that it implicitly influenced the final outcome of the dispute.

Findings perhaps closest to, but short of, historic rights based on conduct or acquiescence can be found it the *Guinea* v. *Guinea-Bissau* case, where the Court relied upon long-accepted practices to recognize the 'southern limit' for the first segment of the new boundary.[268] Again, the Court did not rely upon such conduct as a legal title in order to define the boundary. Instead, together with the coincidence of that line with the land boundary, it established the basis required to take that line into account as a factor.[269]

On the other hand, in the *Gulf of Maine* case, attempts to establish an equidistance or median line as a result of *modus vivendi* between the US and Canada failed to be accepted by the Chamber, for good reason. The

---

[264] ICJ Reports 1982, p. 62, paras. 76, 71, 97.
[265] ICJ Reports 1982, p. 73, para. 100; see Chapter 9(III)(B).
[266] With the exception of spaces between the 26 degree line and the 45 degree *zénith verticale* (ZV) beyond the 50 metre isobaths, ICJ Reports 1982, p. 76, para. 105.
[267] ICJ Reports 1982, p. 75, para. 102; ICJ Reports, p. 76, para. 104.
[268] *Guinea* v. *Guinea-Bissau*, n. 40, at 295, para. 105.
[269] Ibid., at 296, para. 106 in fine.

Chamber not only found insufficient evidence to support such a claim, but it also considered such conduct as was demonstrated to have been engaged in for 'too brief' a time (1965–1972) to qualify as a *modus vivendi* along the median line and through the Georges Bank comparable to the one between Tunisia and Libya.[270] Comparable arguments made by the United States to those on historic rights in the 1982 *Tunisia v. Libya* case were rejected, and historic conduct was not only denied in terms of legal entitlement, but also did not exert any influence in terms of an equitable standard in this case.[271]

The differences between the three cases may indicate the point at which the line between relevant and irrelevant conduct within equity may be drawn. It is submitted that there are essentially two factors:

Firstly, relevant conduct in the *Tunisia/Libya* case did not represent a fundamental conflict with equitable delimitation based on standards related to surface geography. The *modus vivendi* lay in the realm of what was also considered an equitable result from a geographical point of view. Equally, the 'southern limit', adopted in the first segment, did not fundamentally affect geographical equities in the *Guinea/Guinea-Bissau* arbitration. On the other hand, claims based on conduct in the *Gulf of Maine* case were at variance with geographical equity. Decisive, or at least considerable, weight attributed to US claims would have resulted in a substantial shifting of the boundary, resulting in the allocation of the entire object in dispute (the Georges Bank) to the United States. This may also explain why the Chamber thought it necessary to rule out any impact of historical conduct in a broad, general manner.

Secondly, there are differences in evidence. Observation of the *modus vivendi* under the facts of the *Tunisia/Libya* and *Guinea/Guinea-Bissau* cases was much more conclusive than under the *Gulf of Maine* case. Canadian activities during the preceding twenty years in what formerly were clearly US-dominated fisheries frustrated conduct-related arguments put forward by the United States. The circumstances required the ruling out of not only historic title on the basis of inter-temporal law,[272] but also that of the relevance of such conduct under equitable standards.

The case law seems to suggest that historic conduct falling short of historic rights, estoppel or acquiescence, exerts only a minimal impact in

---

[270] ICJ Reports 1984, pp. 310–11, paras. 149–51.
[271] ICJ Reports 1984, pp. 341–2, paras. 235–7; see also Chapter 9(III)(B).
[272] See Chapter 6(II)(E).

the sense that it cannot fundamentally alter a line arrived at on the basis of surface-related principles. The impact is further weakened by the fact that clear and unequivocal historic evidence is sometimes difficult to produce. At best, such conduct may exert limited corrective effects. It is therefore of nothing more than a factual nature and should be defined as a relevant circumstance.

2. The principle of recent and contemporary conduct (RCCP)

Recent and contemporary conduct related to the purposes of the respective zones, after they emerged in customary law, are of greater, albeit not exclusive,[273] practical importance than historical conduct within the rule of equity. In the *Tunisia* v. *Libya* case, the fact that parties had granted oil concessions since 1966, while observing de facto a particular line of delimitation in the disputed area, was considered 'a circumstance of great relevance'.[274] This de facto line played a significant role, more significant than historic conduct, in the adoption of the first segment of 26 degrees, approximately perpendicular to the coast. Even under the broad and general dismissal of conduct in the *Gulf of Maine* case, contemporary conduct may be seen to be more important than past practices. Although the Chamber rejected, under its primarily geographical approach, the adoption of an equitable principle requiring that a boundary should ensure the status quo of existing patterns of activities and exploitation,[275] such patterns were nevertheless taken into account. It seems that recent developments of Canadian fisheries within the fifteen years preceding the judgment played an implicit role. Assessing and reviewing the geographically defined boundary across the Georges Bank, the Chamber reassured the parties that existing patterns are not impaired:

> Canada may still be sure of very nearly all the major locations of its catches ... Conversely, the localities in which same sedentary species have been traditionally fished by the United States ... will lie entirely on the United States' side of the dividing line.[276]

---

[273] The *Gulf of Maine* Chamber correctly rejected Canadian contentions that such relevant conduct be limited to the period after decisions to establish the EEZ were taken by both parties, ICJ Reports 1982, p. 341, para. 235.
[274] ICJ Reports 1982, p. 71, para. 96; ICJ Reports 1982, p. 83, para. 117 ('highly relevant').
[275] ICJ Reports 1984, p. 341, para. 234.
[276] ICJ Reports 1984, p. 343, para. 238. Similar observations were made for lobster fishing, ICJ Reports 1984, p. 343, para. 238.

The extent to which contemporary conduct and patterns of exploitation were taken into account and informally anticipated by the Chamber when the boundary was established on a geographical basis, cannot be assessed. Yet, it is not likely to be a mere coincidence that the geographical solution adopted in Georges Bank very closely reflects the parties' recent patterns of conduct. In fact, it may be argued that these patterns emerged as a main standard for delimitation, and it should have been taken into account appropriately in the first place. This does not mean that contemporary conduct preceding the dispute should be given priority and therefore establish a principle of status quo. But, with a view towards achieving transparent reasoning, contemporary conduct should be explicitly analysed and introduced as an equitable standard to be balanced against other standards. Evidently, the more a negotiated solution or a judgment is in line with the existing patterns of conduct and exploitation by parties and their constituencies, the more successful implementation is assured.

Recent and contemporary conduct should therefore be taken into account explicitly, and deviations based on conduct need careful and recorded reasoning. Conduct must not be a hidden political agenda of courts, veiled by purely geographical or technical consideration and operation. It must be discussed and form part of the overall result, one way or the other, in explicit terms.

Significantly, relevant conduct in equity needs to show consistent patterns of good faith over a number of years preceding the dispute. Short-term conduct with a view to improving negotiating positions or creating a beneficial impact on the balance of equities cannot form part of RCCP. The principle must not favour and honour coastal states that merely increase their presence in order to achieve larger shares of spaces in delimitation once the decisions to claim and establish a zone are made. The rule of equity must not encourage ocean grabbing vis-à-vis neighbouring states. It is therefore essential to discuss and define the relevant time span that should legitimately be considered.

The ITLOS in *Bangladesh* v. *Myanmar* rejected Bangladesh's argument that there was a tacit or de facto agreement on the territorial sea boundary resulting from the consistent conduct of the parties over three decades, finding that there was no compelling evidence to this effect.[277] The Tribunal was neither convinced by Bangladesh's argument that Myanmar was estopped from denying that there was any territorial sea

---

[277] *Bangladesh* v. *Myanmar*, n. 25, paras. 112–18.

boundary other than that set out in an instrument from 1974. It held that there was no indication that Myanmar's conduct caused Bangladesh to change its position to its detriment or suffer some prejudice in reliance on such conduct, as required for a claim of estoppel.[278]

Unlike general historic conduct, recent and contemporary conduct is related to the respective zone. The relevant time span for delimitation under RCCP should therefore begin with the emergence of the relevant zone in customary international law. This dates back to former centuries with regard to internal waters and to the nineteenth century with regard to the territorial seas. As to the shelf, the late 1950s set the starting point,[279] while the EEZ only emerged in the early 1980s.[280] The conduct that should be relevant includes all of that which occurs up until it is met with protest from the other party, therefore at the latest when a dispute arises. After that point in time, changing patterns of conduct should no longer be considered relevant, since they are often too closely related to the dispute itself to give an accurate indication of mutual assessment of conduct by the parties or their nationals. Moreover, changing patterns that occur after the establishment of claims to the respective zone could be made with a view to substantiating and improving the basis for the expansion of claims and should thus be treated in a similar manner.

Within the concept of equity of boundary delimitation of the shelf and the EEZ, it is submitted that taking such conduct into account as one standard amongst others amounts to a slight modification of the *Grisbadarna* principle. The actual state of affairs during the relevant time span is to be taken into account, but not in an exclusively decisive manner. What was a prime, and perhaps exclusively operative, concept in a delimitation of internal and territorial waters, has to share its impact with other normative principles, such as proportionality, brought into operation with the maritime revolution. Consideration of the *Grisbadarna* principle, as modified, as a mere standard among others within the concepts of the shelf and the EEZ, still allows an equitable principle of RCCP to be spoken of. Unlike historic conduct unrelated to the purposes of the zones, recent and contemporary conduct should be taken into account in the first place. Existing patterns of exploitation of minerals and fisheries should be considered *ex officio* as much as surface-related aspects. This does not amount to solutions merely reflecting a status quo, since the principle is only one among others to be taken into account. Status quo may be produced if legal requirements of historic

---

[278] Ibid., paras. 124–5.   [279] See Chapter 2(II).   [280] See Chapter 2(III).

rights, estoppel or acquiescence are fulfilled. But that is a different normative level and not part of equity. An equitable principle of recent and contemporary conduct (short of independent legal entitlement in customary law or general principles of law) gives adequate expression to the idea of effectiveness within the concept of equity. Moreover, it is in line with findings on the location of resources. While resources as such may not be taken into account as a relevant circumstance, some weight should be given to them if they are already under exploitation as evidenced by the conduct and activities of a party.

3. Conclusions

The legal situation with respect to the relevance of patterns of conduct is still a grey area and is not yet sufficiently clear in law. While estoppel and acquiescence are conceptually settled and well established, both their application and the existing tension between the marine revolution and historic conduct led to diverging views in jurisprudence as to whether, and to what extent, there is a place for historic rights at all. The more so, it is unclear as to what extent, short of fulfilling legal requirements of historic rights, estoppel and acquiescence, conduct is to be taken into account. The cases do not yet show any clear lines, but there is a trend toward a more extensive relevance of conduct under the fundamental rule of equity in maritime boundary delimitation than in general international law. It is submitted that historic conduct, dating back to long before the legal shelf and EEZ emerged, is relevant to the extent that is supported by clear evidence and that it does not fundamentally alter boundaries arrived at on the basis of geographical allocation. Recent and contemporary conduct within the time span from the emergence of the shelf and the EEZ, respectively, in customary law to the time during which a dispute arose is more important, since it reflects actual economic interests which are important for a solution to be acceptable. Such conduct, of course, has to be equally supported by unequivocal evidence, which in most cases will not be a problem to present. As a modified *Grisbadarna* principle, RCCP exerts a prime impact on delimitation as an equitable principle among other standards, and may therefore exert a considerable influence.

B. Social and economic standards

A glance at the history and the underlying purposes of the maritime revolution readily reveals the inherent economic functions of the new zones. From the very beginning, coastal states developed legal concepts in order to secure national access to resources, either directly or indirectly by means of licensing agreements and to protect national industries, in particular in fisheries.[281]

Given the essentially economic background of the maritime revolution, it is necessary to study the potential impact of social and economic interests as much as geography in the context of delimitation. Equity does not operate in a vacuum. It relates to a background and underlying ideas, and discussion of human conduct already shows that delimitation is not merely a matter of principles and circumstances related to surface geography. Indeed, delimitation can exert considerable influence on the national economies of the states concerned. The question therefore arises whether and to what extent social and economic standards exist and have to be taken into account during the process of delimitation in order to achieve an equitable result.

It is submitted that there are two major groups of economic considerations, which should be distinguished and treated separately. The first relates to general, the second to specific, economic interests within the window of delimitation.

1. General social and economic interests

Politically, the recent allocation of marine space and resources is a unique opportunity to use the newly nationalized marine territories adjacent to shores and land in order to improve and diversify national economies and thereby reinforce long-term viability and sustainable development, in particular of weaker and economically disadvantaged nations. Equally, there is a potential for the improved management and conservation of marine resources, prosperity, balance of powers, and therefore stability of global regions, could be enhanced by wise and far-sighted marine policies. The *Jan Mayen* conciliation[282] and a number of agreements[283] show that such considerations can and should be taken into account as a matter of sound long-term policies in the process of delimitation in order to realize goals of global, or at least regional, distributive justice or equity.

Contrasting with such overall policy goals, the case law has shown a decreasing emphasis on economic considerations in the process of delimitation. Germany, which was economically the strongest party in the *North Sea* dispute, was not in a position to make arguments of

---

[281] See Chapter 2(III)(A) et passim.   [282] See Chapter 6(III)(B).
[283] See in particular the Arab Gulf agreements. Chapter 5(III).

compensatory allocation on economic grounds. Instead, arguments focused on distributive justice. Despite the Court's rejection of this school of thought, the shares allocated under equity in fact increased the economic wealth of Germany – showing that delimitation is not 'a kind of Robin Hood justice'.[284]

The *Anglo-French Channel* arbitration paid little heed to the economic and constitutional status of the Channel Islands 'as clearly territorial and political units which have their own separate existence',[285] though they were under British sovereignty and not semi-independent states.[286] Neither was attention given to the islands' possible aspirations to extended shelf areas, which would naturally be in the interest of these islands in order to sustain their economic prosperity. Between France and the United Kingdom, and not parties to the dispute, the islands were merely allocated a 12 nm continental shelf zone,[287] far below ordinary extensions in customary law.

The 1982 *Tunisia* v. *Libya* Court did not straightforwardly reject economic considerations presented *in extenso* by Tunisia in the case, to show her relative poverty vis-à-vis oil-rich Libya.[288] Yet the Court held that such data could not be taken into account due to its inherent instability and an evolution at variance with the stability sought by a boundary:

> The Court is, however, of the view that these economic considerations cannot be taken into account. They are virtually extraneous factors since they are variables which unpredictable national fortune or calamity, as the case may be, might at any time cause to tilt the scale one way or the other. A country may be poor today and become rich tomorrow as a result of an event such as the discovery of valuable economic resources.[289]

This judicial policy also prevailed in subsequent cases. Socio-economically related considerations and alleged factors, including data concerning

---

[284] As Wolfgang Friedmann said: 'It cannot even be said that the correction of this particular accident of nature [the concavity of coasts] was a kind of Robin Hood justice. For the Court's delimitation benefited, as it happened, the biggest and wealthiest of the three States concerned', 'The North Sea Continental Shelf Cases – A Critique' (1970) 64 *American Journal of International Law*, 229 at 240. See also Monconduit, n. 239, 243–4, who made the point that the argument of fair and equal sharing of resources could well have justified a strict application of equidistance (and a smaller segment for Germany) due to the relative strength of the German economy.
[285] N 54 at 89 (441), para. 184. [286] Ibid., at 90 (442), para. 186.
[287] Ibid., at 95 (444), para. 202. See also Bowett, n. 56, p. 17.
[288] N. 20 at 65, para. 81 (the Court 'has to give due consideration ... to a number of economic considerations').
[289] Ibid., 77, para. 107.

population, employment, wealth and poverty, as well as industrial activities, were also held to be irrelevant by the consultants on inter-US continental shelf boundary delimitation.[290] Except for the regional economic concerns of fishing industries, discussed below, general socio-economic arguments were not put forth in the *Gulf of Maine* case. But the Chamber's exclusive reliance on surface-related standards for the construction of the boundary *a fortiori* excluded such broad considerations in a legal operation without decision-making *ex aequo et bono*.[291] The *Guinea/Guinea-Bissau* arbitration refused consideration of general economic levels following the *Tunisia/Libya* Court, and reverted parties to mutually advantageous co-operation in order to promote developmental needs.[292] The ICJ finally closed the door on any further attempts to bring developmental needs, lack of resources and fishing activities into play in exclusive shelf delimitation when it held such considerations to be totally unrelated to the shelf concept:

> The Court does not however consider that a delimitation should be influenced by the relative economic position of the two States in question, in such a way that the area of continental shelf regarded as appertaining to the less rich of the two States would be somewhat increased in order to compensate for its inferiority in economic resources. Such considerations are totally unrelated to the underlying intention of the applicable rules of international law. It is clear that neither the rules determining the validity of legal entitlement to the continental shelf, nor those concerning delimitation between neighbouring countries, leave room for any consideration of economic development of the States in question. While the concept of the exclusive economic zone has, from the outset, included special provisions for the benefit of developing States, those provisions have not related to the extent of such areas nor to their delimitation between neighbouring States, but merely to the exploitation of their resources.[293]

It has to be conceded that the strict case law is fully in line with what was found to be the partly inequitable concept of the shelf which, by its very definition, privileges large coastal states independently of their economic situation at the expense of smaller coastal states, and even more so of geographically disadvantaged and land-locked states. The case law reflects the fact that, what from a perspective of global welfare is an inequitable system, cannot be remedied during boundary delimitation between adjacent or opposite coastal states. From this point of view, the complete exclusion of general socio-economic factors is logical, and it is

---

[290] Charney, n. 57 at 53. [291] ICJ Reports 1984, p. 278, para. 59.
[292] N 268 at 301–2, paras. 121, 122. [293] ICJ Reports 1985, p. 41, para. 50.

no surprise that this is strongly supported by the school of equidistance and a purely geographical approach to delimitation.[294] Yet, the question arises whether the case law, as it stands, is not too strict and absolute on the issue. It is submitted that the final test should be sought in the justiciability of economic factors. From this angle, extensive realization of resources based on need, and therefore the concept of global equity, is at variance with the underlying philosophy and legal foundation of the shelf and the EEZ. Moreover, it also leaves the provinces of the courts behind and what may be reasonably expected from them in international dispute settlement. Courts are not fit to decree and implement major programs of redistribution successfully. This is true in a domestic context,[295] and even more so in international relations. But Courts do and may deal well with complex economic matters such as anti-trust or trade remedy cases or with issues of specific local interests. There is no reason to decline justiciability in economic matters in general terms. Also, the argument that economic situations may change and that boundaries drawn on the basis of particular circumstances may be outdated and therefore would not provide for stable boundaries[296] is not really convincing. Changes occur over long periods of time, and mineral resources in particular are not expected to last for a very long period anyway. As to fisheries and nutritional patterns, developments may instead take a very long time.

The true limitation of justiciability lies in two areas. Firstly, the consideration of a wide-open range of economic factors, as proposed by McDougal and Burke,[297] inherently ends up in decision-making

---

[294] See dissenting opinion of Judge Oda, ICJ Reports 1985, p. 141, para. 34 ff.; ICJ Reports 1985, p. 159, para. 65, and in particular ICJ Reports 1985, p. 159, para. 66 (irrelevance of world social justice) and ICJ Reports 1985, p. 160, para. 67. Elisabeth Zoller objected to the fact that economic factors were even considered *obiter dictum* by the 1982 Court and construed the reference in terms of a procedural duty to deal with all arguments submitted by the parties, 'Recherches sur les méthodes de délimitation du plateau continental: à propos de l'affaire Tunisie-Libye' (1982) 86 *Revue Générale de Droit Internationale Public*, 645, 658. On the background of these views see Chapter 8(I)(E).

[295] See Jörg Paul Müller, *Soziale Grundrechte in der Verfassung* (Basel: Helbing und Lichtenhahn, 1981).

[296] E.g., S. P. Sharma, 'Relevance of Economic Factors to the Law of Maritime Delimitation between Neighbouring States', Paper presented at 19th Annual Conference of the Law of the Sea Institute, Cardiff, July 1985 (on file with author).

[297] Myres McDougal and William T. Burke in the early 1960s suggested a wide-open method of taking into account a great number of factors, such as demography (increased rate of population), economic structure, availability of capital, labour, investment, resource consumption and needs, technological development in communication and transport, scientific knowledge in oceanography, living customs and traditions, historic patterns of claimed authority, and military positions and requirements,

ex aequo et bono and is difficult to reconcile with a legal approach. Secondly, space and resource allocation became a major political issue, which governments now could hardly put in the hands of an international court. To the extent, however, that economic factors remain within the realm of a legal operation and do not fundamentally change allocation based on equitable principles discussed, there is no reason why needs cannot be taken into account. *De lege ferenda*, Bowett suggested using existing margins of discretion to the benefit of the comparatively poorer state, the one that has the larger population dependent on the economic benefits of offshore resources, and which has no, or very few, land-based resources, or which is independent, as against a territory that is able to rely upon economic support from a larger wealthier state.[298] Such considerations do not impair the principle that equity cannot fundamentally alter the accidents of nature. But at the same time, they allow for the realization that a concept of global equity and allocation according to need can contribute to the new maritime zones in judicial dispute settlement.

But foremost, this door, even if minimal, avoids a fundamental rift between judicial settlement and what may and should be aspired to during political, negotiated settlements. It should be recalled that states are not limited to a particular set of equitable principles and relevant circumstances in negotiated settlement.[299] The number of agreements already mentioned show that far-sighted policies taking into account socio-economic development, and therefore long-term prosperity and peace in a region, are possible in maritime boundary law. Moreover, states may ask a court by way of special agreement to take into account such needs, as the *Jan Mayen* conciliation shows. Limits in general law to economic factors are not a matter of strict principle, as the present case law suggests, but

---

Myres McDougal and William T. Burke, *The Public Order of the Oceans* (New Haven CT, London: Yale University Press, 1962), p. 580. It seems that early authors linked considerable expectations to resource realization among nations on the basis of socio-economic factors such as population ratios. See Jose Luis de Azcarraga y de Bustamante, *La Plataforma Submarina y el Derecho Internacional* (Madrid: Instituto 'Francisco de Vitoria', Consejo Superior de Investigaciones Cientificas, Ministerio de Marina, 1952) (quoted by Marcus L. Jewett, 'The Legal Regime of the Continental Shelf' (1984) 22 *Canadian Yearbook of International Law*, 53, 174).

[298] Derek W. Bowett, 'The Economic Factor in Maritime Delimitation Cases' in P. Ziccardi (ed.), *International Law at the Time of its Codification, Essays in Honour of Roberto Ago* (Milan: Guiffre, 1987), vol. II, pp. 45, 62–3.

[299] See ICJ Reports 1969, p. 51, para. 93; ICJ Reports 1985, p. 40, para. 47 ('there may be no legal limit to the considerations which States may take into account of').

rather a matter of degree due to the problem of the limited justiciability of these issues. The general law as such has to be framed in a way that allows and encourages the parties to take general economic considerations into account and to pursue a functional approach, just as much as it is necessary to achieve solutions which assure reasonable management and conservation of resources. There is neither the need nor the interest to aggravate the inherent inequities of the shelf and EEZ concepts. Again, in many instances, solutions could and should result in schemes of joint zones. The present law, even if parties need not follow established principles in negotiations, does not encourage such approaches.

Although comprehensible from a point of view of judicial policy, the absolute exclusion of general socio-economic considerations is too broad, and should be refined, as Bowett suggested. At any rate, it is unlikely that broad economic interests remain without at least implicit influence and practical impact on the court, given the political environment of each case. States will therefore not refrain from submitting economic arguments in the psychological context of a trial. Yet, again, why should this be left to a hidden agenda? To improve acceptability and transparency, an open and rational discussion of economic interests should take place, with the courts making it clear when they refrain from considering such factors due to lack of justiciability of the matter.

2. Specifically related economic interests, in particular to the EEZ, and the principle of viability (VP)

It is important to distinguish between general and more specific socio-economic interests, the latter being directly linked to the very purposes of the shelf or the EEZ and inherent to these protectionist concepts. In practice, these interests have played a major role in fisheries, while the shelf remained within general socio-economic interests, except for pearl and sponge fishing. This may be due to the fact that drilling operations are mainly undertaken either on a national basis or by licensing agreements that provide revenues to the state in general. It is difficult to find interests that are more specifically related to coastal economies and the interests of coastal populations, and arguments put forth in their favour in shelf cases tend to relate to general economic interests including fisheries.[300] On the other hand, the EEZ often involves historic fishing

---

[300] E.g., Judge Schwebel did not rely on aspects particularly related to the shelf, but argued on the basis of the ancient and sustained fishing and maritime traditions of the population of the island of Kerkennah in order to support his disagreement with giving only half-effect to the island by the Court, ICJ Reports 1982, p. 99 (dissenting opinion).

patterns and local fishing industries, which are particularly affected by and interested in the matter of delimitation,[301] and these interests are also clearly dominant in all-purpose boundary cases covering both the shelf and the EEZ.[302] Specific economic interests are therefore more prominent in the EEZ context, and the difference shows why economic interests need further development in the EEZ. The case law as developed with respect to the shelf cannot be simply transferred.

These differences are highlighted by the fact that economic interests have played a significant role in the delimitation of fisheries. In the context of the territorial sea and the establishment of base lines, the relevance of economic interests has been well established in international law since the *Grisbadarna* Arbitration and the 1951 *Anglo-Norwegian Fisheries* case, which, in fact, brought about the legitimacy of expanded fishing zones based on economic needs and implied equity.[303] The economic factor was introduced in subsequent codifications as a legitimate concern to be taken into account.[304] But foremost, the 1974 *Fisheries Jurisdiction* case strongly relied upon economic interests. Indeed, such interests emerged as the decisive factor of the case. The Court's refusal to declare the unilateral Icelandic extension of the existing 12 nm zone to a 50 nm exclusive fishing zone invalid – well before the 200 nm EEZ emerged – was essentially based on considerations of the extensive economic dependency of Iceland on fishing.[305] The obligation of parties to seek 'in good faith for an equitable solution of their

---

[301] See also Collins and Rogoff, n. 54 (difference arises from historic fishing rights and economic dependencies, subjected to exploitation for centuries).
[302] In the *Gulf of Maine* case, the economic interests articulated all dealt with fisheries, and not oil and gas exploitation. See ICJ Reports 1984, p. 277, para. 58; ICJ Reports 1984, pp. 340–1, paras. 233, 234.
[303] See Chapter 8(II)(A).
[304] See Art. 4(4) of the Convention on the Territorial Sea and Contiguous Zone, 516 *United Nations Treaty Series*, p. 205.
[305] The underlying facts of the case were that Icelandic waters were seriously endangered by overfishing, particularly by British and West German vessels. According to Judge Dillard, Iceland, Britain and West Germany accounted for 96–97% of all catches (1952–1972) while fishing amounted to 83% of Icelandic exports, ICJ Reports 1974, p. 54, note 1 (separate opinion). See also Ondolf Rojahn, 'Die Fischereigrenze Islands vom 1. September 1972 im Lichte maritimer Abgrenzungsprinzipien des Internationalen Gerichtshofes' (1974) 16 *Archiv für Völkerrecht*, 37. For a partisan view, see Hannes Jonsson, *Friends in Conflict: The Anglo-Icelandic Cod Wars and the Law of the Sea* (London: C. Hurst, 1982); for a critical review, see E. Langavant and O. Pirotte, 'L'Affaire des Pêcheries Islandaises, l'arrêt de la Cour Internationale de Justice du 25 juillet 1974' (1976) 80 *Revue Générale de Droit International Public*, 55–103.

differences'[306] within the expanded area beyond the traditional zone was expected to be implemented largely on the basis of economic considerations relating to the fishing industries of both parties, but clearly contained an element of reverse discrimination to the benefit of Iceland and its viability in the light of the country's essential reliance and dependence on the fishing industry.[307]

It may be argued that these cases have to be distinguished from maritime boundary delimitation between adjacent and opposite states on several grounds. However, it is submitted that the underlying problems are the same, whether it is a matter of setting seaward boundaries by stretching base lines or the determination of the outer limits of a zone. In all configurations, similar interests and patterns of conduct are involved, for which equitable solutions need to be found. One would therefore expect that specific economic interests play an equally significant role in EEZ delimitations. Yet on the surface, the *Gulf of Maine* case could not be more of a contrast. The Chamber refused to consider socio-economic interests in the matrix of equitable principles. They appear to be absent in the surface-related geographical approach of the Chamber. Constructive involvement of economic considerations on fisheries, amply provided by both parties, was considered beyond the realm of legal decision-making and as belonging to the province of *ex aequo et bono*.[308] What was said before in relation to conduct also applies to economic interests. The Chamber acknowledged the relevance of socio-economic fishing interests in the context of its final test of arbitrariness. It is in this context that the Chamber acknowledged the relevance of the 'human and economic geography' as a potentially corrective factor:

> It might well appear that other circumstances ought properly to be taken into consideration in assessing the equitable character of the result produced by this portion of the delimitation line, which is destined to divide the riches of the waters and shelf of this Bank between the two neighbouring countries. These other circumstances may be summed up by what the Parties have presented as the data provided by human and economic geography, and they are thus circumstances which, though in the Chamber's opinion ineligible for consideration as criteria to be applied in the delimitation process itself, may – as indicated in Section II, paragraph 59, above – be relevant to assessment of the equitable character of a

[306] ICJ Reports 1974, p. 35, para. 79(3).
[307] See ICJ Reports 1974, p. 28, para. 62, p. 30, paras. 69, 70; ICJ Reports 1974, pp. 30–1, para. 71.
[308] ICJ Reports 1984, p. 278, para. 59.

delimitation first established on the basis borrowed from physical and political geography.[309]

Such consideration *ex post* was then further qualified. The Chamber was prepared to consider socio-economic considerations only to the extent that results produced on the basis of surface-related principles are likely to produce catastrophic repercussions for the livelihood and economic well being of the populations of the countries concerned:

> What the Chamber would regard as a legitimate scruple lies rather in concern lest the overall result, even though achieved through the application of equitable criteria and the use of appropriate methods for giving them concrete effect, should unexpectedly be revealed as radically inequitable, that is to say, as likely to entail catastrophic repercussions for the livelihood and economic well-being of the population of the countries concerned.[310]

Not surprisingly, the Chamber found itself in a position to assure that, 'fortunately', no such fears would materialize. It therefore saw no need to take corrective socio-economic circumstances into account under the particular facts of the case.[311] It is beyond the scope of this study to assess whether such conclusions were appropriate. The general implication of this approach, however, is highly relevant: the Chamber agrees that delimitation on the basis of surface-related, geographical principles and circumstances may well affect related industries and even create catastrophic repercussion for the livelihood of industries and populations. The *ex post* test indicates the importance of socio-economic aspects as an overriding final test, against which a geographical delimitation has to stand in order to qualify as an equitable result. It implies that geographic equity can turn out to neglect such interests and therefore can be inequitable. In other words, geographic principles are not sufficiently reliable per se.

The Court in *Jan Mayen* treated fishing as a factor relevant to the delimitation.[312] The Court noted the importance of fishing to both parties' respective economies and their conflict over access to fishery resources.[313] The Court held that in the light of the *Gulf of Maine* case and the 'catastrophic repercussions' test it, had to consider whether any shifting or adjustment of the median line, as a fishery zone boundary, would be required to ensure equitable access to the capelin fishery

---

[309] ICJ Reports 1984, p. 340, para. 232.   [310] ICJ Reports 1984 p. 342, para. 237.
[311] ICJ Reports 1984, p. 343, para. 238.
[312] *Denmark v. Norway (Jan Mayen)*, paras. 72, 73.   [313] Ibid., paras. 73, 74, 75.

resources for the vulnerable fishing communities concerned.[314] The Court held that the delimitation of the fishery zone should reflect the fact that the seasonal migration pattern of the capelin centres on the southern part of the area of overlapping claims.[315] It appeared to the Court that the median line would have been too far to the west for Denmark to be assured of an equitable access to the capelin stock, since it would have attribute to Norway the whole of the area of overlapping claims. Accordingly, the Court shifted the median line eastward so as to attribute a larger area of maritime spaces to Denmark.[316]

After liberal application of the *Gulf of Maine* exception of 'catastrophic repercussions' by the *Jan Mayen* judgment with regard to fisheries factors, the 1999 *Eritrea* v.*Yemen* award 'marks in particular a detour to more restrictive treatment of this exception, as originally effected in the *Gulf of Maine* Judgment'.[317] The Tribunal in *Eritrea* v. *Yemen* noted that neither party had succeeded in demonstrating that the line of delimitation proposed by the other would produce a catastrophic or inequitable effect on the fishing activity of its nationals or detrimental effects on fishing communities and economic dislocation of its nationals.[318]

Moreover, the Tribunal recalled that the whole point of its 1998 holding on 'the perpetuation of the traditional fishing regime' was that 'such traditional fishing activity has already been adjudged by the Tribunal to be important to each Party and to their nationals on both sides of the Red Sea'.[319] The Tribunal held that precisely because of this mutual importance, the fishing practices of the parties were now not germane to the task of equitable maritime boundary delimitation.[320]

The Tribunal could find no relevant effect upon the delimitation line that would be 'appropriate under international law in order to produce an equitable solution'[321] based on the evidence and arguments advanced by the parties with respect to general past fishing practice, the potential deprivation of fishing areas or access to fishing resources, or based on nutritional or other grounds.[322]

---

[314] Ibid., para. 75. [315] Ibid., para. 76. [316] Ibid., paras. 76, 90.
[317] Barbara Kwiatowska, 'The *Eritrea* v. *Yemen* Arbitration: Landmark Progress in the Acquisition of Territorial Sovereignty and Equitable Maritime Boundary Delimitation' (2001) 32 *Ocean Development & International Law*, 1–25, updated as of 27 March 2003, p. 37.
[318] *Eritrea* v. *Yemen*, n. 63 para. 72.
[319] Eritrea-Yemen Arbitration (First stage: Territorial Sovereignty and Scope of Dispute), (9 October 1998) (2001) 40 ILM 983–1019, para. 526 and ruling para. VI
[320] *Eritrea* v. *Yemen*, n. 63, para. 63. [321] Ibid., para. 74. [322] Ibid., para. 73.

The 2006 Tribunal in *Barbados* v. *Trinidad and Tobago* recognized that some 190 ice boats owned and manned by Barbados nationals could not at the time fish off Tobago as they had done previously. It noted that:

> this deprivation is profoundly significant for them, their families, and their livelihoods, and that its deleterious effects are felt in the economy of Barbados. But injury does not equate with catastrophe. Nor is injury in the course of international economic relations treated as sufficient legal ground for border adjustment.[323]

The Tribunal accordingly refused to adjust the equidistance line in the relevant sector.[324] It held that even if Barbados had proven its core factual contention (century-old flying fish fishery practice off Tobago, 'catastrophic repercussions'), it does not follow that, as a matter of law, its case for adjustment would be conclusive:

> Determining an international maritime boundary between two States on the basis of traditional fishing on the high seas by nationals of one of those States is altogether exceptional. Support for such a principle in customary and conventional international law is largely lacking. Support is most notably found in speculations of the late eminent jurist, Sir Gerald Fitzmaurice, and in the singular circumstances of the judgment of the International Court of Justice in the *Jan Mayen* case (I.C.J. Reports 1993, p. 38). That is insufficient to establish a rule of international law.[325]

Socio-economic interests are difficult to bring into operation. The test is difficult to meet. The impact is extremely limited and requires the likelihood of grave and severe, even catastrophic repercussions. Such effects are difficult to anticipate and demonstrate in court and, moreover, are unlikely to take place in most cases, provided that there is sufficient room for structural adjustments of the affected industries. One explanation for this restriction in acknowledging economic interests at stake is that they have played a significant role in the discourse relating to the precedents cited above, and no convincing arguments were made as to why their impact should be differently assessed in EEZ delimitations. Also, it is submitted that the minimal, *ex post* test does not sufficiently reflect the true impact of economic interests inherent to the very protective and conservationist purposes and underlying values of the EEZ.[326] It is not an accident that the Chamber found itself in a position to deny fundamental repercussions. Finally, throughout the judicial process, and given the political environment of the case, judges have been aware of such

---

[323] *Barbados* v. *Trinidad and Tobago*, n. 146, para. 267. [324] Ibid., para. 270.
[325] Ibid., para. 269. [326] See Chapters 2(III) and 9(II).

interests and have taken them implicitly into account on a hidden agenda when geometric constructions are being developed and adopted, often without inherent logic. The problem is similar to the relevance of conduct: it is necessary to find an expression of socio-economic interests which are able to reflect the true and underlying importance of them in what, after all, the courts themselves consider to be a legal-political operation.[327] If results assuring the viability of populations are inherent to an equitable result, it is difficult to see why such fundamental aspects of equity cannot be taken into overt consideration in the first place. Again, this is also necessary and advisable for improving the transparency of the process and thereby the acceptability of the results.

It is therefore submitted that, parallel to a principle of recent and contemporary conduct (RCCP), an equitable principle of viability should be introduced into the methodology of the fundamental rule. Unlike the *ex post* test of the *Gulf of Maine* Chamber, the principle would relate to coastal populations and fishing industries, and not to the population of parties at large. The principle of viability (VP) would be taken into account and balanced in the first place with surface-related principles, rather than being considered only in the second step of the delimitation exercise. Often the principle will coincide, and be compatible with, the principle of recent and contemporary conduct, since conduct essentially relies on the realization of economic or other interests. Yet there may be circumstances where an independent impact exists. Complex delimitations, in particular those requiring considerations of third party rights, may require going beyond conduct-proven interests in order to achieve an overall equitable result.

3. The circumstance of cultural and ethnological interests

VP will often equally serve the preservation and improvement of inherited cultural or ethnological identity of coastal populations in EEZ delimitations. In particular with regard to ethnic minorities of coastal or insular populations, it could be that economic viability itself is not enough to assure preservation of cultural identity, such as if particular needs exist with respect to particular lifestyles and fishing methods. Beyond economic viability, such requirements may seldom arise. In the case law, such circumstances, so far, have rarely materialized, as treatment of the Channel Islands shows.[328] But considerations of such circumstances in the Torres Strait Agreement by the creation of a

[327] ICJ Reports 1984, p. 277, para. 56.   [328] Above n. 54.

protective zone for the purposes of preserving the habitat of the Torres Strait islanders, a population which is distinct from the Papua New Guineans, shows that there has to be room for cultural and ethnological considerations, which should be taken into account as a relevant circumstance in order to achieve an equitable result.[329] A similar case in point, albeit of a more economic nature, is the 'perpetuation of traditional fishing rights' by the *Eritrea/Yemen* award[330] that entitles fishermen of both parties to engage in artisanal fishing around the islands which were attributed to Yemen.[331] The emerging law of protecting the cultural heritage of indigenous populations will further support such considerations within the fundamental rule of equity.

C. National security interests

National security has been of paramount interest in marine policies, as the evolution and gradual extension of the territorial sea concept shows. With increasing offshore distances, such interests may become less important, whilst the importance of economic interests grows;[332] but they remain alive in closed seas and among neighbours in unfriendly co-existence or in hostile relationships. It should be noted that international law does not know the concept of peacetime security zones,[333] nor is it possible to achieve similar effects by means of the shelf and the EEZ, except for the prevention of military installations of weapons of mass destruction.[334]

---

[329] See Chapter 5(III)(D).
[330] 1998 *Eritrea* v. *Yemen* Award on Sovereignty, n. 319, operative para. 527(vi) and paras. 525–6, as reaffirmed by the 1999 Award paras. 62–9 and 87–112.
[331] *Eritrea* v. *Yemen*, n. 63, para. 103. The Tribunal noted that:
[the] factual situation reflected deeply rooted common legal traditions which prevailed during several centuries among the populations of both coasts of the Red Sea, which were until the latter part of the nineteenth century under the direct or indirect rule of the Ottoman Empire. The basic Islamic concept by virtue of which all humans are 'stewards of God' on earth, with an inherent right to sustain their nutritional needs through fishing from coast to coast with free access to fish on either side and to trade the surplus, remained vivid in the collective mind of Dankhalis and Yemenites alike (*Eritrea* v. *Yemen*, para. 92).
[332] See Robert W. Smith, 'A Geographical Primer to Maritime Boundary-Making' (1983) 12 *Ocean Development & International Law*, pp. 1, 6.
[333] See Choon-Ho Park, 'The 50 Mile Military Boundary of North Korea' (1978) 72 *American Journal of International Law*, 866.
[334] Treaty on the Prohibition of the Emplacement of Nuclear Weapons and other Weapons of Mass Destruction on the Seabed on Ocean Floor, ILM 10(1971) p. 145, entered into force 18 May 1972.

The concept of horizontally shared jurisdiction does not allow the impairment of free communications under the law of the high seas.

To a large extent, the geographical principles of non-encroachment and non-cutting-off (NEP, NCP) bring about adequate assurances in terms of security interests. Adequate distances of shelf areas generally allow nations to preserve their security interests. Drilling and fishing operations may be granted in such a way that naval operations are not impaired and foreign powers are inhibited from establishing military installations, such as listening devices or even weapons systems, close to a neighbour's coast. Nevertheless, geographical principles may not be sufficient. Drilling and fishing operations may impair the naval operations of the neighbouring state or third nations, in particular that of submarines, without amounting to a violation of navigational freedoms.[335] Moreover, it is not settled whether and to what extent coastal states have an obligation to tolerate military installations such as sonic detection and navigational devices.[336] The more customary law moves toward a comprehensive jurisdiction of the coastal state over the EEZ, combining shelf and water column, the more security interests will affect delimitation itself if vital interests can no longer be preserved in large sea areas appertaining to another state.

In maritime boundary negotiations, security interests sometimes play a significant, even decisive, role. Nineteen years of negotiations between Sweden and the Soviet Union were concluded only after adequate solutions were found to protect Swedish security interests in the Baltic Sea.[337] Equally, security interests have been of paramount importance in the Soviet–Norwegian dispute over the Barents Sea. No agreement on the basis of equidistance was reached, because such a line, beside economic interests, was not acceptable to the former Soviet Union with regard to its major strategic interests on the Kola peninsula (naval base) and the Barents Sea as a missile-launching area for Delta Class submarines.[338] These bases also indirectly played an important role in the Iceland 'Cod' War, since

---

[335] LOS Convention, see n. 304, Arts. 87, 58(1), 78(2).
[336] For controversial views on the topic see Tullio Treves, 'Military Installations, Structures and Devices on the Seabed' (1980) 74 *American Journal of International Law*, 831 (affirming such rights subject to non-interference with economic activities); Rex J. Zedalis, 'Military Installations, Structures and Devices on the Continental Shelf' (1981) 75 *American Journal of International Law*, 926 (excluding such rights of third states within the shelf and the EEZ); see also Winrich Kühne, *Das Völkerrecht und die militärische Nutzung des Meeresbodens* (Leiden: Sijthoff, 1975).
[337] Neue Zürcher Zeitung, 13 January 1988, p. 1.
[338] See Kim Traavik and Willy Ostreng, 'Security and Ocean Law: Norway and the Soviet Union in the Barents Sea' (1977) 4 *Ocean Development & International Law*, 343, 349, 351.

Iceland threatened to renounce agreements establishing the NATO Keflavik base, which would serve as a check on the Soviet Kola bases, if Britain did not respect the 200 nm zone. Only in 2010 did immediate economic interests in fossil resources finally became strong enough not only to overturn old security concerns but also to bring about a compromise between the sector approach claimed by Russia and the equidistance method claimed by Norway. Security interests and the Icelandic bargaining chip were instrumental also for Norwegian willingness to accept preferential agreements in the *Jan Mayen* conciliation.[339]

Such interests often play a more or less open role in negotiations and should not preclude judicial settlement, if the case may arise. Security interests, therefore, should be included among equitable standards to be taken into account under the particular facts of a case. So far, none have been decisive, but the courts did not rule out considerations of this kind. The 1977 *Channel Arbitration* discussed, but rejected, French contentions of security interests relating to the shelf as being 'without pertinence'.[340] France argued that British sovereignty over the Hurd Deep (Fosse Central) would involve serious inconvenience and risks for French submarines operating from Cherbourg.[341] The Court therefore considered security interests as a potential relevant circumstance, and established that such criteria may become important in cases between coastal states with difficult and tense security relationships.

Beyond the principles of NCP and NEP, security interests are therefore the subject of relevant standards within the rule of equity. Should it even amount to an equitable principle? The Court in the 2009 *Romania/ Ukraine* case held that its equidistance line fully respected the legitimate security interests of either party. It thus merely observed that 'legitimate security considerations of the parties may play a role in determining the final delimitation line'.[342] Since the purposes and underlying goals of both the shelf and the EEZ are not directly linked to security, but to economic interests (except for a prohibition on stationing weapons of mass destruction), security does not amount to an inherent element

---

[339] See Willy Ostreng, *International Exploitation of 'National' Ocean Minerals*, (Oslo: The Fridtjof Nansen Institute, Studie R:007, Ocean Mining Project Report No. 5, 1983), pp. 16–22.
[340] *Channel Arbitration*, n. 54, p. 87(440), para. 175.
[341] Ibid. p. 81(437), para. 161, p. 87(440), para. 176, 91(442), para. 161; see also p. 82(438), para. 163.
[342] ICJ Reports 2009, p. 61, para. 204. The Court referred to the judgment in *Libya* v. *Malta* which, in turn, merely said that '[s]ecurity considerations are of course not unrelated to the concept of the continental shelf' (ICJ Reports 1985, p. 13, para. 51).

which should be the subject of a prime principle.[343] Instead, it is an aspect of a factual nature, which has to be considered, as the case may be, as a relevant circumstance in order to achieve an equitable solution responding to the needs of acceptability.

D. Toward a principle of third generational rights

Principles and equitable circumstances discussed so far all serve the purpose of achieving an equitable result with respect to allocation of spaces and resources for contemporary use and exploitation. Geography, conduct, socio-economics, cultural identity and security interests essentially rely on the needs of existing generations. Indeed, the marine revolution of the post-World War II era has focused on such perspectives, and equity, or equitable results, are measured in state practice and case law against the ability of solutions achieved to comply with such goals. At the same time, the shelf, and even more so the EEZ, also comprise goals of prudent conservation and management. The zones were established with a view to protecting marine resources from over-exploitation.[344] It should be recalled that fears of excessive foreign exploitation were an important factor leading up to the Truman Proclamation.[345] More important than fears were the hard facts of over-fishing in inducing the movement toward exclusive fishing zones and finally to the adoption of the EEZ in customary international law.[346]

Therefore, inherent to the shelf and EEZ are elements which contemporary doctrine and legal theory – under the heading of equity – qualify as third generational rights.[347] An avant-garde has argued in favour of the rights of nature itself, which would provide the basis for better

---

[343] See, however, n. 342.
[344] For underlying objectives and values see below Chapter 2.   [345] Chapter 2(II).
[346] Chapter 2(III).
[347] See e.g. Edith Brown Weiss, *In Fairness to Future Generations: International Law, Common Patrimony and Intergenerational Equity* (Irvington NY: Transnational Publishers Inc., 1989); Edith Brown Weiss, 'The Planetary Trust: Conservation and Intergenerational Equity' (1984) 11 *Ecology Law Quarterly*, 495; Anthony D'Amato, 'Do We Owe a Duty to Future Generations to Preserve the Global Environment' (1990) 84 *American Journal of International Law*, 190–8; Edith Brown Weiss, 'Our Rights and Obligations to Future Generations for the Environment' (1990) 84 *American Journal of International Law*, 198–207; Lothar Gündling, 'Our Responsibility to Future Generations' in 'Agora: What Obligations Does Our Generation Owe to the Next? An Approach to Global Environmental Responsibility' (1990) 84AJIL, 190–212; Rosemary Rayfuse, 'The Challenge of Sustainable High Seas Fisheries' in Nico Schrijver and Friedl Weiss (eds.), *International Law and Sustainable Development: Principles and Practice* (Leiden, Boston MA: Martinus Nijhoff Publishers, 2004) pp. 467–99; Anja von

protection of ecological interests and give standing to organizations defending them.[348] Importantly, the concept of equity is once more heading to challenge established and deeply enshrined patterns of the legal order, with a view to responding to new needs and bringing about respect for resources for tomorrow's generation. In the law of the sea, the concept of common heritage of mankind, as applied to the Area, still belongs to the generation of distributive equity among nations, in particular among industrialized and developing countries. It was not great as the concern to preserve the rights of future generations, but exploitation of deep seabed resources and perhaps other marine resources will be a matter for them.

Sustainable development in the law of the sea mainly relates to the management of fisheries and minerals, and to trade issues, but has not been extended to maritime boundary delimitation. The question therefore arises as to what extent third generational rights should become, *de lege ferenda*, part of equitable standards within the fundamental rule of equity. Such rights, it is submitted, would equally take care of the idea of rights of nature and entitlement to protection itself. It was seen that ecological systems, as much as other natural features of a geological nature, are hardly able to settle maritime boundary disputes. Quite apart from problems of evidence, the idea of natural boundaries is difficult to reconcile with the underlying perception of delimitation as a legal–political process. But the practical exclusion of natural boundaries does not imply that ecology and aspects of prudent management and conservation of resources cannot and should not be taken into account as an equitable standard, either as a principle or as a relevant circumstance, to be measured and balanced with the standards discussed so far. Provided it can be shown that a particular line arrived at on the basis of established standards relating to needs of contemporary society is detrimental to prudent conservation and management, it is difficult to see why adjustments may not be undertaken in order to improve that situation for the benefit of future generations.

To what extent such modifications, short of natural boundaries established by alleged ecosystems, can be helpful, cannot be assessed *in abstracto*. Further research is required and general attitudes and

---

Moltke (ed.), *Fisheries Subsidies, Sustainable Development and the WTO* (London: Earthscan, 2011). See also Introduction to this book on equity and sustainable development, section II(A).

[348] See J. Leimbacher, *Die Rechte der Natur* (Basel, Frankfurt am Main: Helbing und Lichtenhahn, 1988); see also Christopher D. Stone, *Should Trees Have Standing?* (New York: Oxford University Press, 2010).

perceptions need to develop toward more functional approaches to marine management and delimitation.[349] Within the existing concepts of the shelf and the EEZ it is and remains a matter to be examined on a case-by-case basis, taking into account the specificities of the ecological configuration of the shelf and the water column. The absence of sufficient data to that effect at the present time does not exclude suggesting an equitable standard to reflect the inherent and explicit ecological concern of the shelf and EEZ concepts. Such a standard is necessary to bring these concerns to an operational level in future delimitation cases. Without it, third generational rights and interests simply are not taken into account when delimitation is effected on the basis of standards discussed so far.

It is therefore submitted that the set of equitable standards needs to be amended. In order to reflect the ecological goals of the zones, the fundamental rule needs to comprise a principle of prudent conservation and management (PCMP). It largely corresponds to the principles of sustainable development, seeking a balance between ecological, social and economic interests.[350] The principle is to be taken into account in the first place, competing with traditional equitable standards. Solutions need to be favoured that best serve that goal, and thereby also the interests of future generations, balanced with the traditional distributional objectives and values of the zones. Such a balance may be difficult to achieve. One of the main problems is, of course, that whatever boundary is drawn, interest in prudent management and conservation may be impaired by the very fact of drawing a line and splitting jurisdiction over shared resources. Whatever the impact of the principle of prudent management and conservation, its very purpose may be frustrated by the concept of delimitation. The *North Sea Continental Shelf* cases established a need for joint exploration and exploitation of common deposits, without impairing the boundary line drawn across such deposits. With movable

---

[349] For an impressive debate over contemporary constraints of *realpolitik*, which flow from existing perceptions and attitudes by constituencies to optimize contemporary – not future – access to resources, and a more functional, third generational approach to joint management and conservation, see workshop discussions by, inter alia, Colson, Johnston, LeGault, Pietrowski and Robinson, in L. Alexander (ed.), *The Gulf of Maine Case: An International Discussion*, Studies in Transational Legal Policy vol. 3 (ASIL: Washington, 1988), pp. 63–101.

[350] See generally Nico Schriever and Friedl Weiss (eds.), *International Law and Sustainable Development: Principles and Practice* (Leiden, Boston MA: Martinus Nijhoff Publishers, 2004). The legal foundations and methodology of sustainable development, balancing ecological, social and economic concern, are carefully expounded by Katia Gehne, *Nachhaltige Entwicklung als Rechtsprinzip* (Tübingen: Mohr Siebeck, 2011).

resources, the problem is aggravated, since stocks under exploitation may travel across human boundaries and therefore be subject to excessive exploitation overall. In the final analysis, it is doubtful whether sharing arrangements and a principle of prudent management and conservation can be sufficiently realized under the present concept of national jurisdictions.[351] The limits of what delimitation can achieve for third generations will soon be reached, and it will be seen that new and more functional approaches are necessary to achieve equitable solutions for third generations and nature. PCMP is yet another element that points to the need for common zones to replace the traditional concepts of delimitation from a long-term perspective. The problem, however, also indicates how important it is to induce the evolution of maritime boundary law by means of agreements establishing joint zones. In the process of equity, they may substantially promote the introduction of new, third generational aspects into maritime boundary law.

IV. Ad hoc concretization of equity by way of special agreement (compromis)

The preceding discussion of equitable principles and relevant circumstances inherent to customary law or submitted *de lege ferenda* now allow the indication of the potential elements which, in addition, may become part of equity by way of *ad hoc* concretization in special agreements or compromises which establish jurisdiction of a court of law or panel of conciliation. The relevance and importance of these agreements for the legal environment of equity has been discussed before, and its implications need not be restated.[352]

So far, most cases asking for delimitation or relevant principles of delimitation have been submitted on the basis of special agreement or compromis. Such agreements, it was seen, vary considerably and reflect the diverging results achieved in negotiations.[353] After the discussion of equitable principles and relevant circumstances, it may now be possible to evaluate which elements may be reasonably introduced or particularly emphasized, and thereby amend the body of general law for the purpose of a particular delimitation. Further, limitations to that effect may also be more readily seen.

---

[351] Johnston, n. 349, pp. 63, 66–7 ff. ('I can't imagine any other logic than the logic of putting sharing arrangements first and ocean delimitation and the dispositive resolutive sense a good bit farther down in the pecking order').
[352] Chapter 6(IV)(B).   [353] Chapter 6.

There is scope for further specifications which could assist a court of law. This is part of the possibility of approaching delimitation in conjunction with negotiations and legal third party dispute settlement, ever since the *North Sea* cases and explicitly affirmed by the Court in the 1985 *Tunisia* v. *Libya* revision case.[354] In light of existing principles and relevant circumstances, agreements providing for a single boundary line (*Gulf of Maine*,[355] *Qatar* v. *Bahrain*[356]), and particular emphasis on the economic interests of a party (*Jan Mayen*), a conceptual separation of equitable principles and relevant circumstances (*Tunisia* v. *Libya*), indication of target areas for the boundary to be met (*Gulf of Maine*), are compatible with the general law. Definition of the relevant window of delimitation by the parties, if possible, is an important clarification. Special agreements may furthermore include, inter alia, particular emphasis of historic rights and conduct, recent and contemporary conduct, special economic interests particularly relating to fishing industries, cultural identity, security interests, the location of resources to the extent known or a mandate to particularly take into account ecological needs for conservation and prudent management, taking into account the need for sustainable development. Courts or panels may be instructed to take such additional standards into account in a manner that grants them preferred positions in the process of balancing equitable principles and relevant circumstances. Parties may rely on an equidistance–median line, if they can agree, and direct the Court to settle the problem of deviations without the use of completely different approaches under the fundamental rule. Moreover,

---

[354] ICJ Reports 1985, p. 218, para. 47 ('It is always open to the parties to a dispute to have recourse to a conjunction of judicial determination and settlement by agreement').

[355] The Chamber did not question the lawfulness of its task, as requested by the parties, to draw a single maritime boundary line, with the practical effect that the scope of relevant principles and circumstances was limited to those applicable to both the shelf and the EEZ. See ICJ Reports 1984, pp. 326–7, paras. 192–4. Judge Gros, on the other hand, dissented, inter alia, on grounds that the request to draw a single line cannot be treated as a given fact, but is a legal issue to be decided. ICJ Reports 1984, pp. 363–4, para. 6 (dissenting opinion) (referring to *Nottebohm*, Preliminary Objections, Judgment, ICJ Reports 1963, p. 122 ('The seisin of the Court is one thing, the administration of justice is another. The latter is governed by the Statute, and by the Rules')). Given the clear language of the compromise ('What is the course of the single maritime boundary that divides the continental shelf and fisheries zones of Canada and the United States of America', ibid. 253 Art. II), the issues as to whether a single maritime boundary is legally possible has been agreed by the parties and clearly forms part of the legal environment of the case, notwithstanding the fact that it would have been interesting to obtain a legal precedent on this issue of general importance.

[356] *Qatar* v. *Bahrain*, n. 30, paras. 67–9.

parties may go entirely new ways in judicial settlement and agree to instruct a third party settlement to establish joint zones of management, exploration and exploitation within parts of, or in the entire window of, delimitation.

On the other hand, there are clauses and concretizations parties should not undertake to include in special agreements. The *Tunisia* v. *Libya* or the *Malta* v. *Libya* experience shows that it is advisable either to request the setting out of general principles and relevant circumstances upon which parties should then proceed to delimitation or, preferably, to request a determination of a final boundary line. Leaving the issue ambiguous as to whether or not the court should define a boundary should be avoided; otherwise differences as to the interpretation of the special agreement have to be settled on the basis of wording and must take into account the pleadings of the parties[357] and differences as to the scope of a judgment are more likely to arise, as the 1985 *Tunisia* v. *Libya* revision case shows.[358] Conflicts may be protracted at great financial and political cost. Experience shows that it is difficult to conclusively indicate relevant equitable principles and relevant circumstances without suggesting concrete boundary lines. Even if not legally binding, such lines exert a factual and authoritative impact on successive negotiations. They can hardly be ignored without the consent of both parties concerned, and their undefined legal nature may again bring about roadblocks along the way to settling the dispute.

Optimally, parties will agree to ask the court or panel to draw the boundary on the basis of the fundamental rule of equity, i.e. international law, equitable principles and relevant circumstances, as possibly amended and specified by particular emphasis on particular principles and relevant circumstances. Parties remain free to renegotiate an adjudicated boundary – the binding force of a judgment does not impair their ability to consensually reopen the issue. The parties are bound to a judgment and its guidance to, or lines of, delimitation on the basis of *res judicata*, in accordance with Article 94 of the UN Charter and Article 59 of the Statute of the Court,[359] as long as, and only as long as, they do not supersede the compromis by a new agreement. The Court clarified this issue in the 1985 *Tunisia* v. *Libya* revision case as follows:

---

[357] See ICJ Reports 1982, pp. 39–40, paras. 25–30; see also ICJ Reports 1982, p. 101, para. 5 (separate opinion Aréchaga).
[358] ICJ Reports 1985, p. 192.
[359] International Court of Justice, *Acts and Documents Concerning the Organisation of the Court*, No. 1 (May 1947).

While the Parties requested the Court to indicate 'what principles and rules of international law may be applied for the delimitation of the area of the continental shelf', they may of course still reach mutual agreement upon a delimitation that does not correspond to that decision. Nevertheless, it must be understood that in such circumstances their accord will constitute an instrument superseding their Special Agreement. What should be emphasised is that, failing such mutual agreement; the terms of the Court's Judgment are definitive and binding. In any event moreover, they stand, not as something proposed to the Parties by the Court, but as something established by the Court.[360]

To achieve additional flexibility for a combined political and legal approach to delimitation, it might also be worth examining whether the use of advisory opinions should be introduced for international disputes among states,[361] which is currently excluded under Article 96 UN Charter, much as it exists for international organizations. Parties, however, are free today to agree to submit a case to an *ad hoc* court of arbitration with a mandate limited to fact finding[362] or to providing an advisory opinion to help parties achieve a negotiated settlement.

Experience with special agreements also shows that formulations should remain based on the fundamental rule of equity. Taking into account 'new trends' and other concepts of similar vagueness creates considerable confusion and impedes the evolution of case law. In general, special agreements should not deviate from established principles or relevant circumstances in law. They should primarily rely upon general principles and rules of international law (e.g. *Libya v. Malta*). They may, however, highlight certain elements or add new aspects which the parties agree are pertinent in the dispute but are not yet established or that are still controversial in law. Finally, limitations already discussed are confirmed: third party rights and claims are to be respected and cannot be disposed of by special agreement among parties, as much as this cannot be done by delimitation agreements. Whatever principles and circumstances parties choose to emphasize or add, solutions achievable under such instructions need to meet the requirement of an equitable solution both under the LOS Convention and, arguably, also under customary law.

---

[360] ICJ Reports 1985, pp. 192, 219, para. 49.

[361] See Paul C. Szaz, 'Enhancing the Advisory Competence of the World Court' in L. Gross (ed.), *The Future of the International Court of Justice* (New York: Oceans Publications, 1976), vol. II, pp. 499, 515.

[362] This is also provided for under the special arbitration procedures under the LOS Convention, Art. 5, Annex VIII LOS Convention.

Given the considerable room under the fundamental rule of equity to direct a court of law or panel of conciliation under the particularities of a case, the question arises whether there are inherent limits to such instruction. While parties may, by way of agreement, waive pre-existing rights based on treaty, historic rights, estoppel or acquiescence, there is a clear limitation on interference with third party claims or rights. It is conceivable that two parties would instruct a court in a way which would lead to the impairment of such claims or rights. In such a case, the court is bound to respect such rights and the special agreement cannot be respected. Since customary maritime boundary law is not, even in its main principles, a matter of *jus cogens*, no formal limits exist under customary law on dispositions agreed by both parties, provided that the agreement was entered into in good faith and without duress.[363] Moreover, it is submitted that the special agreement needs to allow a court to adopt what it considers to be an equitable result in line with the underlying purposes and inherent values of the shelf and the EEZ. Even if not part of *jus cogens*, this part of the fundamental rule, it is submitted, cannot be at the disposition of the parties.

Arguably, more limitations exist under the LOS Convention. Given the constitutional nature of the treaty,[364] special agreements entailing instructions contrary to provisions of that agreement cannot be respected by a court of law which has to apply the Convention. Since states are not likely to forfeit their entitlement to equitable solutions in special agreements, the problem is of a somewhat academic nature. Yet it is conceivable that special agreements will be concluded that do not respect equitable principles concretizing the respective provisions of the Convention. At any rate, achieving an equitable solution clearly is a mandatory requirement under the Convention, and state parties cannot escape this obligation by either maritime boundary agreements or by special agreements.

Special agreements, in sum, are an important instrument for parties to specify shared perceptions and to instruct the court or panel of conciliation as to the specific normative aspects of the case. Foremost, it provides an opportunity to emphasize particular principles or relevant circumstances, and allows the introduction of new ideas and criteria into the process and concept of equity. However, parties should seek to rely upon the basic principles elaborated in case law without fundamentally deviating from the body of law that exists in customary law or that which

---

[363] See Art. 52 Vienna Convention on the Law of Treaties.   [364] Chapter 1(II)(B).

will be developed in the future under the provisions of the LOS Convention. Special requirements should be additional elements, consistent with general rules. In particular, special agreements offer an opportunity for parties to request the definition of joint zones of management and conservation. In general, such additional elements should not jeopardize further evolution of case law and make it more complicated than necessary by the use of unclear concepts or ambiguous language. Both under customary law and the LOS Convention, parties have to respect third party rights and the requirement to achieve an overall equitable solution.

11

The methodology of judicial boundary delimitation

I. Competing schools of jurisprudence

A. Introduction

The essence and virtue of any legal concept and process, consisting of a principled and reasoned approach to problems of life, is no different in maritime boundary delimitation and the allocation of marine space from any other field of the law. In Chapter 10, a principled approach was considered to be an essential requirement for satisfying legitimate expectations, political predictability and acceptance of results. Abstract approaches by the courts to this effect have evolved over the last fifty years through a pendulum development and a process of trial and error – away from an emphasis on rule-orientation and towards result-orientation, then backagain to delimitation primarily based on equitable principles, and finally towards a combination of a result-oriented and a rule-oriented approach emphasizing the method of equidistance and taking into account special circumstances and proportionality on the basis of a three-step approach with equitable principles largely operating in the background.[1] Whatever the practical differences of these various approaches and the submitted return to an approach based upon equitable principles in this book, there is no disagreement that delimitation based upon equity pursues the ambition of being a legal and rule-based concept, relying upon principles and relevant circumstances, the specification of which should result in an overall equitable apportionment. Whether delimitation based on the rule of equity is in fact a legal operation, or one of *ex aequo et bono* settlement in disguise, much depends on the methodology and the consistency with which it is applied in a particular case.[2] By and large, the results of cases so far have implicitly complied with the requirements of equitable solutions under the standards of political predictability and legitimate expectations, and the compromises achieved have been equitable in that

---

[1] See Chapter 8(II)(B).   [2] See Chapter 8(I).

sense. They were all politically accepted. But, all too often, they have not been achieved in a sufficiently principled manner.[3]

At the outset, before turning to the proper methodology of delimitation, it might be appropriate to revive the discussion over jurisprudence that was briefly introduced when attitudes to the model of equity and equitable principles were analysed and explained. The two competing schools of thought, equidistance and equity, were seen not only to reflect different sets of national interests on the political level, but also different concepts of jurisprudence and theoretical underpinnings.[4]

In the final analysis, the concept of equidistance–special circumstances, as is the case for any model that consists of a rule plus exceptions, still adheres to models of jurisprudence which in principle draw a clear distinction between law-making and law-applying, the latter being perceived as a logical operation of the subsumption of facts to a particular rule. Equidistance adheres to the ideal and model of legal syllogism.[5] A rule properly construed is applied to a particular set of facts (coastal configuration, islands and base points) and the result inevitably and logically follows without any further value judgments. However, the very need to make exceptions in order to remedy what is superficially called a distortion highlights the need to make recourse to underlying values.[6] This situation is merely one example of a more general problem, which caused western jurisprudence and legal theory to turn to a more fact- and value-oriented approach over a long period of time.[7] Indeed, the equidistance school provides a classic example to illustrate what Pound said in *Law and Morals* in 1924:

---

[3] This has been the main thrust of criticism voiced by Judge Gros, see ICJ Reports 1982, p. 147, para. 9 ('I find myself in disagreement with the judgement in respect of the *way* in which the Court set about the search for an equitable delimitation'); see also ICJ Reports 1982 (dissenting opinion); ICJ Reports 1984, p. 386, para. 42 etc.; André Gros, 'La Recherche du consensus dans les décisions de la Cour Internationale de Justice' in R. Bernhardt et al. (eds.), *Völkerrecht als Rechtsordnung, Internationale Gerichtsbarkeit, Menschenrechte: Festschrift für Hermann Mosler* (Berlin: Springer, 1983), p. 351.

[4] See Chapter 4(III).

[5] On the premises and logic and deductive operation of the classic syllogism and its assumption of a single correct conclusion see e.g. John H. Farrar and Anthony M. Dugdale, *Introduction to Legal Method* (London: Sweet & Maxwell, 1984), p. 74; René A. Rhinow, *Rechtsetzung und Methodik: Rechtstheoretische Untersuchung zum gegenseitigen Verhältnis von Rechtsetzung und Rechtsanwendung* (Basel/Stuttgart: Helbing und Lichtenhahn, 1979), pp. 17–20 with further references.

[6] See Chapter 8(I)E et passim.

[7] For an excellent assessment of this process see Rhinow, n. 5, pp. 17–30 ('Vom Justizsyllogismus zur Wertungsjurisprudenz').

A legal science that refuses to look beyond formal legal precepts ... misses more than half of what goes to make up the law.[8]

There is of course no single established theory among the many schools dealing with the problem of facts and values beyond positivism and logic reasoning, from which the problem of boundary delimitation could draw authoritatively. As in national law, there is no uniform legal theory in international law. It reflects a wide tradition of different schools in different legal systems, in particular civil and common law. Widely shared standards of jurisprudence may best be found in the doctrine of international law sources (e.g. Article 38 of the ICJ Statute) and rules on treaty interpretation of the Vienna Convention on the Law of Treaties (VCLT), although the emphasis given to textual interpretation in Article 31 VCLT no longer reflects a common and shared basis in international jurisprudence.[9] Beyond that, jurists draw from their national traditions and systems, and considerable differences in underlying perceptions of law in these traditions perhaps led to the absence of a commonly shared international legal theory. There exists a predominance of implicit and often not deeply reflected mainstream approaches, apart from well-developed particular schools which have not received general acceptance but have nevertheless exerted a considerable influence in an implied manner, such as the New Haven School of policy oriented jurisprudence.[10] Evolutions of legal theory in the pragmatic world of international relations occur here and there, rather haphazardly, and language

---

[8] Roscoe Pound, *Law and Morals* (Chapel Hill NC: University of North Carolina Press, 1924), p. 88, quoted from Ralph A. Newman, 'The General Principles of Equity' in Ralph A. Newman (ed.), *Equity in the World's Legal Systems: A Comparative Study* (Brussels: Bruylant, 1973), p. 595.
[9] See in particular criticism by Myres S. McDougal, 'The International Law Commission's Draft upon Interpretation: Textuality "Redivivus"' (1967) 61 *American Journal of International Law*, 992, 997; for discussion see also Jörg Paul Müller, *Vertrauensschutz im Völkerrecht* (Cologne, Berlin, Bonn: Heymann, 1971), pp. 119–24.
[10] See in particular Myres S. McDougal, Harold D. Lasswell and W. Michael Reisman, 'Theories About International Law: Prologue to a Configurative Jurisprudence' (1968) 8 *Virginia Journal of International Law*, 188–299; Myres S. McDougal, Harold D. Lasswell and W. Michael Reisman, 'The World Constitutive Process of Authoritative Decision' (1967) 19 *Journal of Legal Education*, 253–300, 403–37, reprinted in Cyril E. Black and Richard A. Falk (eds.), *The Future of the International Legal Order* (Princeton University Press, 1969), vol. I, p. 73; Harold D. Lasswell and Myres S. McDougal, 'Jurisprudence in Policy-Oriented Perpectives' (1966/67) 10 *University of Florida Law Review*, 468–514; Myres S. McDougal and W. Michael Reisman, 'The Changing Structure of International Law' (1965) 65 *Columbia Law Review*, 810–35. For an assessment see Christoph H. Schreuer, 'New Haven Approach und Völkerrecht' in Christoph H. Schreuer (ed.), *Autorität und Internationale Ordnung, Aufsätze zum Völkerrecht* (Berlin: Duncker & Humblot, 1979),

barriers often impair fruitful interaction. The results do not draw directly from a shared concept; rather the new concepts may be gradually reflected, discovered and identified as the law proceeds in practical life.

Thus, it would be wrong to say that the different schools of thought and approaches to maritime boundary law stem from particular legal theories. Yet, as much as equidistance reflects logical and purely normative concepts, it may equally be submitted that delimitation based on equity reflects the basic premises of the fact- and value-oriented schools, and one of them seems particularly appropriate to assist in the present context.

B. Topical jurisprudence

It is not an accident that in the 1969 *North Sea* cases, counsels for Germany submitted that delimitation should be effected on the basis of a number of factors. The approach reflects what in German schools has been called 'Topik', or topism, referring to a topical and problem-oriented approach. Among other value-oriented schools, this approach was a response to the predominantly positivist, logical, and deductive concepts of law and the failure of formal positivism to challenge the erosion and violation of human dignity and to cope with the tensions of reality and underlying values. It is a response to the dogmatism, deduction, and closed conceptual systems of methodology which had allowed such deteriorations.

According to Viehweg, the founding theorist in civil law,[11] topism consists of solving legal problems by looking at them in the light of generally accepted considerations, issues and aspects which are called topoi, and by discussing and encircling the problem on the basis of such topoi without engaging in any logical and deductive reasoning. In essence, the topical approach can be characterized by the interpretation of rules, principles, and decision-making on the basis of an assessment and discussion of all relevant issues and aspects (topics) to a case, weighing and balancing the impact of such aspects, and then reasoning the decision on the basis of such a process. Joseph Esser summarized the method as follows:

<blockquote>
pp. 63–85. The theory has been of particular importance to the issue of assessing international obligations and the problem of soft law, see Oscar Schachter, 'Towards a Theory of International Obligation' in Stephen M. Schwebel (ed.), *The Effectiveness of International Decisions* (Leiden, Dobbs Ferry NY: Oceana Publications, 1971), pp. 9–31; Oscar Schachter, 'The Twilight Existence of Nonbinding International Agreements' (1977) 71 *American Journal of International Law*, 296. For an impact on assessing 'nonbinding' acts of political planning see Thomas Cottier, 'Die Rechtsnatur 'unverbindlicher' Entwicklungspläne' (1984) 103 *Zeitschrift für schweizerisches Recht II*, 386.
</blockquote>

[11] Theodor Viehweg, *Topik und Jurisprudenz* (Munich: C. H. Beck Verlag, 1974).

> Topical reasoning can and should afford to justify results not following
> logically and inevitably from established principles, but to present them
> intelligibly out of the matter (*aus der Sache einsichtig darstellen*). While, in
> dogmatic deduction, the reduction of complexity to logically relevant
> aspects becomes a technique, things are different here: The situation
> needs to be assessed in all of its complexity, in order to discuss all
> problems with a view to achieving an ideal solution (*das Lösungsideal
> 'problematisieren'*). Encompassing all the complexities of competing legal
> interests has to replace the depreciation of problems in deductive logical
> systems and all formal considerations in order to discover convincing
> reasons.[12]

In theory, the process of topism entails two different stages.[13] Firstly, as in daily life, a problem is approached by discussing it on the basis of aspects that come to mind more or less accidentally and at random. A second stage, however, entails a process of building catalogues of topoi, which are relevant and suitable in the context of a particular problem. Such catalogues are open-ended, are not systematic, and may take any form. Beyond topoi of a general nature, particular fields of law develop specific aspects that may be contained in generally accepted propositions, principles, precedents, or guidelines, which leave the notion of legal topoi rather vague and open to various perceptions.[14] Topism, therefore, is more of a general approach than a precise methodology, and it can be perceived in different ways. In its most radical perception, the methodology transgresses statutory law even where textually fairly clear. This of course may create problems of judicial subjectivism and undermine democratic rule and legal security and predictability.[15]

More moderate views recognize inherent limitations to topism in the sense that the method needs to work within decisions taken by the legislature and the scope of interpretation available. Moreover, it is generally accepted that topism does not exclude a systematic approach as long as the system remains open for further considerations and topoi which may eventually evolve in a particular context. There is room for the historical process of building the body of law in a process of assessing

---

[12] Josef Esser, *Vorverständnis und Methodenwahl* (Frankfurt am Main: Athenäum-Fischer-Taschenbuch-Verlag, 1972), pp. 157–8 (translation by this author).
[13] Viehweg, n. 11, pp. 29, 36, 38 ff.
[14] See also Karl Larenz, *Methodenlehre der Rechtswissenschaft* (Berlin, Heidelberg, New York: Springer, 1975), p. 141 (including a summary description of the approach).
[15] This perception has been the main cause of criticism from the point of view of legal security, but also from a democratic perspective, see Larenz, n. 14, pp. 142–4; in particular Friedrich Müller, *Juristische Methodik* (Berlin: Duncker und Humblot, 2002), p. 70 ff.

problems and developing principles and their conceptualization in a systematic manner.[16] In this more moderate sense, the basic idea of topism stands for the proposition of an inductive, problem-oriented approach to jurisprudence. The school has been particularly influential in constitutional law, which is often called upon to construe and concretize broadly textured rules and principles with extensive scope for interpretation.[17] Binding precedents assume an important role in offering the foundations and context for future topical decisions.[18] Moreover, the school characterizes fields of economic law which are closely intertwined with economic analysis, such as competition law. Based upon broad principles, economic analysis and factors are introduced to define normative concepts such as relevant markets or dominant positions. The analysis of courts and authorities is strongly influenced not only by underlying economics, but primarily the realities of the market place. The same is true for international trade regulation. The case law of the adjucative bodies of the WTO, of panels and the Appellate Body, essentially follow a topical approach in interpreting and applying the relevant principles and rules enshrined in the WTO Agreements in accordance with the principles of interpretation of Article 31 and 32 of the VCLT.[19]

Whatever the nuances, it is evident from this summary that topical jurisprudence particularly relies upon, or at least takes into account, the context and the realities of a case in the process of interpretation and seeks to achieve justice in an inductive manner. To the extent that it operates with normative topoi, interpretation goes back and forth from norm to reality (in an often-cited term coined by Engisch: *Hin und Her Wandern des Blicks*[20]); in other words, interpretation takes into account the social ambiance.[21] Norm and reality are therefore found in a dialectical process of interaction. The more openly norms are textured, the more facts and interests are taken

---

[16] Josef Esser, *Grundsatz und Norm in der richterlichen Fortbildung des Privatrechts* (Tübingen: Mohr, 1990), p. 7.
[17] See Martin Kriele, *Theorie der Rechtsgewinnung entwickelt am Problem der Verfassungsinterpretation* (Berlin: Duncker und Humblot, 1976).
[18] Ibid., pp. 243–309.
[19] Thomas Cottier and Matthias Oesch, *International Trade Regulation: Law and Policy in the WTO, the European Union and Switzerland* (Bern: Stämpfli, 2005), pp. 108–18 ff.
[20] Karl Engisch, *Logische Studien zur Gesetzesanwendung* (Heidelberg: Winter, 1963), p. 15.
[21] Swiss theorist Dietrich Schindler snr. formulated this idea in 1931. Dietrich Schindler, *Verfassungsrecht und soziale Struktur* (Zurich: Schulthess, 1970), p. 92 ff. The academic environment in Zurich also informed the thinking of Judge Max Huber, who in 1928 published the foundations of a sociological school of international law long before the New Haven School; see Max Huber, *Die soziologischen Grundlagen des Völkerrechts* (Berlin: Rothschild, 1928): cf. Daniel Thürer, 'Max Huber: A Portrait in Outline', (2007) 18 European Journal of International Law 69–80.

into account. Strict rules, on the other hand, containing a high degree of abstract decision, leave less room for individual assessment. It goes beyond the province of this book to study the relationship and interaction of topical jurisprudence to the schools of American realism and pragmatism and the New Haven school of policy-oriented jurisprudence. Yet, it seems they share a common concern for arriving at conclusions on the basis of extensive assessment, evaluation of facts, interests and underlying values as well as on the effect decisions and results may have on reality.

It is submitted that maritime boundary law in the courts has been considerably influenced by these schools' broad lines of thinking without explicitly referring to them. Given the fact that the law following the maritime revolution had to be built from a largely clean slate, the concept of equity was particularly suitable and inviting to work on the basis of a topical method of jurisprudence.[22] The separate opinion of Judge Jessup in the *North Sea* cases with its detailed assessment is perhaps the most important piece of evidence to that effect.[23] It is mirrored by the criticism voiced mainly by European continental scholars at the time, reflecting more traditional perceptions of jurisprudence based upon subsumption, syllogism and law-applying as opposed to law-making.[24] Yet, even the assessment of relevant circumstances within the alleged rule of equidistance is characterized by a dialectic process of norm and reality under these traditional perceptions. This is particularly true for delimitation on the basis of equity, or regulation by equity, and the concept of

---

[22] It should be noted in this context that the distinction of legal issues and issues of equity in the present analysis does not mean that fundamentally different methodologies apply. The doctrine of topism is meant to apply in all fields of law. It is not something limited to equity or other very broad legal concepts, although it is evident that here there is more leeway to apply a problem-oriented approach than under rules of international law to the extent that they are more precise than equitable principles. For example, if the matter is one of construing a given agreement which defines a boundary in terms of precise cartographic points, there is virtually no room for interpretation. The relationship of strict rules and topism, indeed, has been the subject of extensive discussions. It would go beyond the scope of this study to consider to what extent it could, and does, apply in the process of interpretation of strict international law. In this context, it suffices to emphasize its potential for the concretization and interpretation of broad standards as found under the rule of equity. Differences between law and equity here are of a gradual nature.

[23] See ICJ Reports 1969, pp. 67 ff. and 83 ('I am quite cognisant of the fact that the general economy of the Court's Judgment did not conduce to the inclusion of the detailed, and largely factual analysis which I have considered it appropriate to set forth in this separate opinion, but I believe that what is stated here, even if it is not considered to reveal an emerging rule of international law, may at least be regarded as an elaboration of factors to be taken into account in the negotiations now to be undertaken by the Parties').

[24] See Chapter 8(I)(D).

equitable standards, i.e. principles and relevant circumstances. Indeed, the reluctance of courts to define equitable principles and a preference to consider them merely as factors or criteria without making a distinction between norms and factually relevant circumstances may be considered a paradigm of topism. It also shows, at the same time, the risks and difficulties of subjectivism and discretionism and the result-orientation of realist concepts devoid of substantive normativity. Efforts throughout this study to shape and systematize the notion of equitable principles, relevant circumstances and the functions of equitable results in somewhat clearer terms are an attempt to cope with such difficulties by bringing them into an open system, which is able to strike a proper balance between normativity and factual interests.

Refining the balance of norms and facts, however, does not change the characteristics of the methodology. Maritime boundaries should be assessed and defined, and marine spaces allocated, in a dialectical process taking into account all relevant normative and factual elements, whether competing or concordant. It is important to reach conclusions on the basis of an open and transparent discussion of all the problems involved on the basis of normative and factual elements. The ideal solution, of course, is the one able to solve all the problems. Since it is in the nature of disputes that not all problems can be settled ideally, it is important to reason and explain transparently within the available normative framework why some problems were settled at the expense of others, and why some interests were given priority.

While courts may learn from jurisprudence to cope with practical problems, jurisprudence and legal theory also learn from practical experience and complexity. The methodology of maritime boundary delimitation depicts how a problem-oriented approach may be structured and developed in case law. Indeed, maritime boundary delimitation is one of the few fields, and in fact the only one before the ICJ, where, in a process of trial and error, jurisprudence was able to gradually build in a series of cases and over a period of around half a century. No other field except international trade and investment, both essentially dealt with outside the ICJ, offers a remotely comparable stream of case law. It is from this experience that we can learn about modern methodology in international law relating to the allocation of natural resources and thus relating to distributive justice. As much as the law of the sea is at the origin of international law, so its case law is bound to exert a wide ranging influence upon other fields of international relations. Many of them show comparable complexities, and all of them are obliged to respond to the precepts of justice and equity in order to achieve legitimacy and thus acceptance. Doctrine can also learn from this with a view to further shaping the theory of legal methodology and interpretation beyond the nineteenth-century concepts enshrined in the rules on sources and interpretation. It is from this experience that the real functions of equity, beyond the classical and rarely operational doctrines of equity *infra*, *praeter* and *contra legem*, can be assessed and equally put to operation and use in other areas of international law.

The following affirms the insight that a topical approach is by no means inconsistent with the concept of an open system and legal framework proceeding on different levels and at successive stages. Topism and a structured methodology are by no means mutually exclusive, as is sometimes suggested, but rather a necessary pairing in legal reasoning.[25] Moreover, the effort to define equitable principles and a number of relevant circumstances shows that identifying legal topics is closely linked to the underlying legal concepts, values and purposes of maritime boundary delimitation. These needed to be identified before legal topoi can be assessed; they are not identical with the mere and actual interests that parties may have in a particular case. Finally, maritime boundary law also indicates that there are some limits to generalizing legal methodology. Particular fields may require particular approaches.

II. The programme of delimitation

It follows from the examination of the legal environment and the many legal issues besides equity that are possibly involved that the methodology of delimitation entails a fundamental two-step approach, as is reflected in the two subheadings that follow. Delimitation first should deal with the legal issues arising *outside* of the fundamental rule of equity. To the extent that the solution of these issues does not yet settle the dispute (which rarely is the case), it then becomes necessary to turn to the rule of equity. Our main interest lies in this latter field, and the examination will ultimately also provide the basis for drawing conclusions as to the impact of islands which are of major importance in the process of delimitation.

The following programme should be considered within an open system. It does not provide a checklist. Different cases raise different issues, and courts will only decide them to the extent necessary. Moreover, it should be recalled that the following methodology primarily aims at judicial dispute settlement under the rule of equity of what are

---

[25] See also Rhinow, n. 5, p. 151.

necessarily complex and contentious configurations in situations where negotiations based on equidistance or any other method have failed. It is not designed to deal primarily with appropriate and simplified approaches in negotiations. These will be dealt with briefly in Chapter 12. Finally, delimitations bound to the model of rule-exception of Article 6 of the 1958 Shelf Convention may only partially rely upon the following methodology, particularly with regard to preliminary legal issues and the examination of relevant circumstances. They provide the basis for deviation from the median or equidistance line, based on recourse to underlying equitable principles.

A. Adjudication of legal issues outside the realm of equity

All cases of maritime boundary delimitation are likely to entail a number of legal issues outside the realm of equity. These were addressed in Chapter 10. It is recalled that some of the cases discussed so far, like the El *Salvador/Honduras* case or the *Maritime Dispute* between Peru and Chile, show a considerable and even predominant number of such legal issues. Others, such as the *Gulf of Maine* case, were mainly concerned with equity. While some of the legal issues outside equity are naturally dealt with in advance, such as matters relating to the existence and interpretation of relevant treaties, others remain closely related to equity. They could be approached in a more systematic and separate manner. Experience indicates a number of issues that need to be dealt with before the stage of equitable principles is reached. Of course, any further case may add issues not thought of here, given the variety of facts in real life, and the sequence may vary according to the particularities of the case in accordance with the perception of an open system. Yet, the following methodology should cover the essential steps in most cases before a court of law or body of conciliation. The main substance of these steps has already been described in the previous chapters. A brief summary is sufficient at this stage.

B. Defining the window of delimitation

1. Courts generally and with good reason start their investigations with a geographical description of the relevant area in dispute as claimed by the parties.
2. Going beyond description, this primary step should also entail an examination of whether the expanses of the overlapping claims of the

parties are sufficiently justified on the conceptual bases of the continental shelf and the EEZ. This is a legal issue. In general, it should not create major difficulties, although it may be that parties include areas that are not covered by the shelf or the EEZ. Such marine expanses have to be excluded at the outset. For example, the shelf shows considerable discontinuity and the dispute therefore is not entirely amongst adjacent or opposite coastal states appurtenant to the same shelf. This issue naturally does not arise where the Court is called upon to delimit a single all-purpose boundary. But it shows that the issue of, and arguments surrounding, natural boundaries should in fact appear at an early stage and be disposed of before a court of law deals with equitable principles.

3. More important in practical terms is the potential need to assess and adjudicate third party claims and rights.[26] It is an essential step in defining the proper window of delimitation. It needs to be undertaken *ex officio* with or without formal intervention and hearing of third parties. Given the regional implication of any judicial settlement, the area of delimitation cannot legally extend to areas which belong to, or may reasonably be claimed by, third parties. In many instances, such as the 1985 *Libya/Malta* case, this may limit the scope of the window of delimitation considerably, also affecting the relevant coastal configurations that eventually must be taken into account. Third party claims, actual and potential, cause a practical dilemma. Such states, per se, are not parties to the dispute. Hearing these parties has been one solution that has been used, albeit it comes at great procedural cost in effort and time.[27] Experience of state practice may teach that there are techniques that allow these rights to be safeguarded without necessarily impairing the possibility of settling the case. Colson, examining state practice, found essentially five groups of approaches to the problem:

(a) leaving the issue open by defining a line 'until the jurisdiction of a third state is reached';
(b) selecting a point presumed to be a tri-point (with a risk of dissent and challenge, as in the North Sea configuration leading to the 1969 *North Sea Continental Shelf* cases);
(c) tri-point agreements;
(d) stopping a boundary short of a tri-point, stating that it is without prejudice to the continuation of the boundary until the jurisdiction of the third state is reached;

---

[26] See Chapter 9(III)(D).   [27] See Chapter 9(III)(D)(2).

(e) extending the line well beyond the point, but expressly subject to third party rights.

These techniques, with the exceptions of (b) and (c), may equally be used in judicial proceedings without prejudice to third party rights. Parties may assist the court by ordering these issues in the special agreement, without overly limiting the window of delimitation.[28]

C. *Adjudication of rights and obligations stemming from treaty law, historical rights, estoppel and acquiescence or any other legal title*

Next to defining the window of delimitation, potential rights and obligations stemming from international law other than equity should be considered. This stage includes the examination of alleged rights and obligations in treaty law, either bilateral or multilateral or a pre-existing judgment deploying effects of *res judicata*. It also entails the examination of historical rights claimed, obligations based on *uti possidetis*; or human conduct (estoppel and acquiesence). Adjudication of these issues may settle the dispute in one way or another before the following stage of the fundamental rule of equity is reached. Yet, they can only do so if the parties to the agreement enjoy jurisdiction over the matter, i.e. entitlement is based on the concepts of the shelf and the EEZ, and third party rights and potential claims are being respected. Experience shows that the case can rarely be disposed of and closed on the basis such claims. Often, existing agreements, court rulings or historical conduct may settle issues relating to coastal areas where jurisdiction has long been established by means of internal waters and a gradually expanding territorial sea. Long-distance maritime boundaries, however, have been established too recently to benefit at this point in time from established legal titles by means of agreement, historical rights or conduct. Indeed, as was previously noted, the relevance of existing patterns of conduct rather emerges within the concept of equity, short of establishing legal titles, but to be taken into account as a relevant factor.

---

[28] David A. Colson, 'The Legal Regime of Maritime Boundary Agreements' in Jonathan I. Charney et al., 'Introduction' in Charney et al. (eds.), *International Maritime Boundaries*, 5 vols. (The Hague: Martinus Nijhoff Publishers, 1993–2005), vols. I and II (Charney and Alexander (eds.), 1993), vol. III (Charney and Alexander (eds.), 1998), vol. IV (Charney and Smith (eds.), 2002), vol. V (Colson and Smith (eds.), 2005); vol. I (Charney and Alexander), p. 41, pp. 47, 61–3.

D. Adjudication of territorial jurisdiction

To the extent that the boundary has not yet been settled at this stage, it may now be appropriate to assess base points and base lines within the window of delimitation. This is undertaken with a view to defining internal waters and the beginning of the continental shelf and EEZ zones.

The next stage involves adjudication of jurisdiction over territory and islands, and therefore may entail a comprehensive and detailed analysis of territorial claims and land boundaries as a prerequisite to the concretization of equitable principles. Legally speaking, however, defining the territorial jurisdiction of parties belongs to the setting of the stage and to matters strictly related to the international law of the sea outside the realm of equity.[29]

III. The proper methodology of equity

Once the preceding issues have been dealt with and adjudicated to the extent necessary on the basis of international law, as referred to within the fundamental rule (but often without disposing the case), the case now turns to the process and concept of equity and equitable standards. Besides the analysis and the distinction of equitable principles and relevant circumstances, the proper methodology of equity is at the very heart of the matter and the key to understanding the particular and new function which the concept of equity has assumed in the present field of international law. It entails a number of difficult but fundamental issues of legal theory, and an attempt is made to deal with them at the respective stages of the operation. Before doing so, the beginnings of this process in case law should be reviewed.

A. The beginnings in the courts: the idea of weighing and balancing factors

The elaboration of a proper methodology of equity in the context of maritime boundary delimitation is still in its infancy, even more than four decades after the *North Sea* cases. It is still somewhat at the other end of the method of equidistance, which was seen to be too rigid in many cases but offers the advantage of a clear and precise approach in

---

[29] Courts do not always respect such sequencing. In *Maritime Delimitation and Territorial Questions between Qatar and Bahrain (Qatar v. Bahrain)*, Merits, Judgment, ICJ Reports 2001, p. 40, para. 220, the court awarded sovereignty over one of the islands based on its position on the Qatari side only after the court had drawn its equitable boundary line based on a half-effect method, para. 220.

the first stage. Indeed, the amount of criticism in the literature discussed in Chapter 8(III)(E) and beyond which has considered decisions rendered so far by the ICJ and courts of arbitration arguably pertaining to the realm of decision-making ex *aequo et bono* reflects this situation. The analysis of rulings reveals that key results often are not arrived at in a transparent manner. The length of an opinion is not a guarantee that crucial conclusions are arrived at in a well-reasoned manner. For example, the *Anglo-French Channel* arbitration states no reasons why the various factors stated by the tribunal led to the adoption of a 12-nm, rather than a 6 or 18 nm, continental shelf enclave of the Channel Islands, or why the Scilly Islands and the island of Ushant were given only half-effect.[30] Similarly, there is a lack of reasoning for giving half-effect to Kerkennah Island in the *Tunisia/ Libya* case,[31] or the Seal Islands off the coast of Nova Scotia in the *Gulf of Maine* case,[32] or why some islands off the coast in the *Guinea/ Guinea-Bissau* arbitration were taken into account and others not.[33] Again, no reasoning can be found why the Island of Fifla was not taken into account in the *Libya/Malta* case when a provisional median line was established.[34] When it mitigated the disproportionate effect of the small island of Qit'at Jaradah, the Court in *Qatar v. Bahrain* merely referred to the case law, including the case of *Libya v. Malta*.[35] Likewise, the Court in *Romania v. Ukraine* relied on the case law when it disregarded Serpent's Island for the choice of base points due to its distance from the coast – with reference to the treatment of the Island of Fifla in the *Libya v. Malta* case.[36] The ITLOS Tribunal, in turn, referred to the ICJ in *Romania v. Ukraine* when it ignored the island of St. Martin for its 'distorting effect' upon the single

---

[30] See also Derek W. Bowett, 'The Arbitration between the United Kingdom and France concerning the Continental Shelf Boundary in the English Channel and South-Western Approaches' (1978) 49 *British Yearbook of International Law*, 1, 9; Elihu Lauterpacht, 'Equity, Evasion, Equivocation and Evolution in International Law' (1977–1978), *Proceedings and Commentaries Report of the American Branch of the International Law Association*, p. 1 ff., 11.
[31] See ICJ Reports 1982, p. 89, para. 129.
[32] See ICJ Reports 1984, p. 337, para 222 (except from stating that full effect would be 'excessive').
[33] Arbitration Tribunal for the Delimitation of the Maritime Boundary between Guinea and Guinea-Bissau, Award of 14 February 1985, transl. in (1986) ILM 292, para. 97. *Tribunal Arbitral pour la délimitation de la frontière maritime Guinée/Guinée-Bissau, Sentence du 14 Février 1985*, reprinted in French (the only authentic text) in (1985) 89 RGDIP 484.
[34] ICJ Reports 1985, p. 48, para. 64.   [35] *Qatar v. Bahrain*, n. 29, para. 219.
[36] *Maritime Delimitation in the Black Sea (Romania v. Ukraine)*, Judgment, ICJ Reports 2009, p. 61, para. 149, referring to the treatment of the Island of Fifla in *Continental Shelf (Libyan Arab Jamahiriya v. Malta)*, Judgment, ICJ Reports 1985, p. 13.

maritime boundary between Bangladesh and Myanmar.[37] Finally, the Court in *Nicaragua v. Colombia* disregarded the insular feature of Quitaseño for the construction of the median line – again with reference to its own practice in the case of *Romania v. Ukraine*. It placed no base point on Low Cay, either, with the sole reasoning that the feature is 'small and uninhabited'.[38] In *Qatar v. Bahrain*, the Court, without further reasoning, drew two hypothetical equidistance lines because it had not determined whether the maritime feature of Fasht al Azm was part of the Island of Sitrah or a low-tide elevation.[39] The resulting position of the maritime feature of Fasht ad Dibal on the Qatari side under both these hypothetical lines was subsequently considered by the Court to be reason enough for awarding sovereignty over Fasht ad Dibal to Qatar.[40] The Court in *Nicaragua v. Honduras* completely disregarded the offshore islands for the task of delimitation between the mainland coasts and treated delimitation around the islands as a separate task – granting each island only a claim to a 12 nm territorial sea.[41] In fact, the wide absence of thorough reasoning with regard to the treatment of islands, being one of the most difficult and controversial problems, reflects a rather poor state of legal methodology in many opinions produced so far.

The practical difficulties and failure to come to grips with a methodology of delimitation under equity, however, does not mean that the Courts would not have started to develop, at least *in abstracto*, the beginnings of a methodology which so far characterizes the very essence of the concept of equity in the present context: the weighing and balancing of diverging interests.

In 1969, the *North Sea Continental Shelf* cases laid down the following methodological foundations, when it held that in most cases the computation of a boundary line is the result of the balancing of all open-ended considerations:

> In fact, there is no legal limit to the considerations that States may take into account for the purpose of making sure that they apply equitable procedures, and more often than not it is the balancing-up of all such

---

[37] *Dispute concerning Delimitation of the Maritime Boundary between Bangladesh and Myanmar in the Bay of Bengal (Bangladesh v. Myanmar)*, Judgement, International Tribunal for the Law of the Sea, 14 March 2012, Case No. 16, para 265., para. 265.
[38] *Territorial and Maritime Dispute (Nicaragua v. Colombia)*, Judgment, ICJ Reports 2012, p. 624, para. 202.
[39] *Qatar v. Bahrain*, n. 29, paras. 190, 216.   [40] Ibid., para. 220.
[41] *Territorial and Maritime Dispute between Nicaragua and Honduras in the Caribbean Sea (Nicaragua v. Honduras)*, Judgment, ICJ Reports 2007, p. 659, paras. 299–305.

considerations that will produce this result, rather than reliance on one to the exclusion of all others. The problem of the relative weight to be accorded to different considerations naturally varies with the circumstances.[42]

The 1977 *Anglo-French Channel* arbitration endorsed the approach and spoke of 'balancing the equities of the [Channel islands'] region',[43] yet it did not provide further clarification on the underlying methodological issues or make the operation more transparent. Despite its emphasis on result-orientation and therefore discretion, it is the 1982 *Tunisia v. Libya* case that contains the first, more systematic, statement of the approach sought by the Court. For the first time, equitable principles are used synonymously with the term of considerations or elements. The Court stated that:

> it is bound to apply equitable principles as part of international law, and to balance up the various considerations which it regards as relevant in order to produce an equitable result. While it is clear that no rigid rules exist as to the exact weight to be attached to each element in the case, this is very far from being an exercise of discretion or conciliation; nor is it an operation of distributive justice.[44]

There has been no linear evolution of this thinking. The *Gulf of Maine* Chamber, it seems, was much more reluctant to endorse the balancing approach, and no corresponding statement of the method can be found. Instead, the fundamental rule emphasized the application of equitable criteria[45] without defining their mutual relationship in methodological terms. Nevertheless, the application of a balancing test may be seen in the final overall examination of the result in the light of economic factors.[46] The *Guinea v. Guinea-Bissau* arbitration does not contain explicit statements on a balancing test. It seems that the Court, relying upon an extensive result-oriented approach, discussed the matter on the basis of alternative models and geometry. But again, a balancing test may be seen in the final examination of the boundary in light of the other circumstances invoked by the parties.[47]

---

[42] *North Sea Continental Shelf (Federal Republic of Germany v. Denmark, Federal Republic v. Netherlands)*, Judgment, ICJ Reports 1969, p. 51, para. 93.
[43] 'Arbitration between the United Kingdom of Great Britain and Northern Ireland and the French Republic on the Delimitation of the Continental Shelf' 18 ILM (1979), pp. 397, 442, para. 187.
[44] *Continental Shelf (Tunisia v. Libyan Arab Jamahiriya)* Judgment, ICJ Reports 1982, p. 60, para 71; see also p. 78, para 107.
[45] ICJ Reports 1984, p. 300, para 112(2).   [46] ICJ Reports 1984, p. 339, para. 230 ff.
[47] See n. 33 *Delimitation of the Maritime Boundary in the Gulf of Maine Area (Canada v. United States)* Judgment, paras. 108–25.

After the *Gulf of Maine* case, it is perhaps no coincidence that the 1985 *Libya/Malta* Court restated the methodology initiated in the *North Sea* cases.[48] In line with the move away from a predominantly result-oriented approach, the Court refined the methodology when it limited considerations to be taken into account in the balancing test. Unlike in 1969 and even 1982, considerations eligible in court, unlike those in negotiations, were explicitly limited to those pertinent to the respective type of zone. For the first time also, the Court affirmed the normative nature of equitable principles in law:

> Yet, although there may be no legal limit to the considerations that States may take into account, this can hardly be true for a court applying equitable procedures. For a court, although there is assuredly no closed list of considerations, it is evident that only those that are pertinent to the institution of the continental shelf as it has developed within the law, and to the application of equitable principles to its delimitation, will qualify for inclusion. Otherwise, the legal concept of the continental shelf could itself be fundamentally changed by the introduction of considerations strange to its nature.[49]

The Court also set forth in clear terms the method for proceeding in different stages. Upon establishment of a prima facie line (here equidistance), a second step entails balancing all of the relevant circumstances which may lead, in a third step, to adjustments of the provisional line:

> In applying the equitable principles thus elicited, within the limits defined above, and in the light of the relevant circumstances, the Court intends to proceed by stages: thus, it will first make a provisional delimitation by using a criterion and a method both of which are clearly destined to play an important role in producing the final result; it will then examine this provisional solution in the light of the requirement derived from other criteria, which may call for correction of this initial result.[50]

The Court also held that:

> for the purposes of achieving an equitable result in a situation in which the equidistance line is prima facie the appropriate method, all relevant circumstances must be examined, since they may have a weight in the assessment of the equities of the case which it would be proper to take into account and to reflect in an adjustment of the equidistance line.[51]

---

[48] *Continental Shelf (Libyan Arab Jamahiriya v. Malta)*, Judgment, ICJ Reports 1985, p. 40, para 48.
[49] Ibid., 40, para. 48.   [50] Ibid., p. 46, para. 60.   [51] Ibid., p. 48, para. 65.

Importantly, the Court also stated that the process of balancing the equities is not a mathematical process, which emphasizes the perception of a balancing test. It cannot be reduced to infallible figures:

> Weighing up these several considerations in the present kind of situation is not a process that can infallibly be reduced to a formula expressed in actual figures.[52]

In the *Jan Mayen* case, the ICJ followed the method it had set up in the *Libya/Malta* case. The Court found it proper to begin the process of delimitation by drawing a provisional line corresponding to the median line. The Court then went to the next stage:

> The Court is now called upon to examine every particular factor of the case which might suggest an adjustment or shifting of the median line provisionally drawn. The aim in each and every situation must be to achieve 'equitable result'.[53]

The Tribunal in the 2007 *Guyana/Suriname* arbitration was able to pronounce on the consolidation of the two-step approach, consistently taken since the *Jan Mayen* case:

> In the course of the last two decades international courts and tribunals dealing with disputes concerning the delimitation of the continental shelf and the exclusive economic zone have come to embrace a clear role for equidistance. The process of delimitation is divided into two stages. First the court or tribunal posits a provisional equidistance line which may then be adjusted to reflect special or relevant circumstances.[54]

The Tribunal recalled the *Anglo-French Channel* arbitration and held that the notion of special circumstances generally refers to equitable considerations rather than a notion of defined or limited categories of circumstances. It recalled the Court in the *Libya/Malta* case that there is 'assuredly no closed list of considerations' and the Court in *Jan Mayen* case, that it was 'called upon to examine every particular factor of the case which might suggest an adjustment or shifting of the median line provisionally drawn' and that it 'will consult not only "the

---

[52] Ibid., p. 52, para. 73.
[53] *Maritime Delimitation in the area between Greenland and Jan Mayen (Denmark v. Norway)* Judgment, ICJ Reports 1993, p. 62, para. 54.
[54] *Arbitral Tribunal Constituted Pursuant to Article 287, and in Accordance with Annex VII, of the United Nations Convention on the Law of the Sea in the Matter of an Arbitration between Guyana and Suriname*, Award of 17 September 2007 p. 108 para 335, www.pca-cpa.org/showfile.asp?fil_id=664 (last accessed 18 Feburary 2012), para. 302.

circumstances of the case" but also previous decided cases and the practice of States'.[55] The Tribunal then said that:

> [It] agrees that special circumstances that may affect a delimitation are to be assessed on a case-by-case basis, with reference to international jurisprudence and State practice.[56]

The Court in *Romania* v. *Ukraine* confirmed the validity of the two-step approach, which the ICJ had for the first time broadly explained in the *Libya* v. *Malta* case and consistently applied since the *Jan Mayen* case. The Court stated that the two-step approach has in recent decades been specified with precision and reflects settled jurisprudence.[57] It noted that once the provisional equidistance line has been drawn in the first stage, it shall then consider in the second stage 'whether there are factors calling for the adjustment or shifting of that line in order to achieve an "equitable result"'.[58] The Court continued that:

> Such factors have usually been referred to in the jurisprudence of the Court, since the *North Sea Continental Shelf* ... cases, as the relevant circumstances (*Judgment, I.C.J. Reports 1969*, p. 53, para. 53). Their function is to verify that the provisional equidistance line, drawn by the geometrical method from the determined base points on the coasts of the Parties is not, in light of the particular circumstances of the case, perceived as inequitable. If such would be the case, the Court should adjust the line in order to achieve the 'equitable solution' as required by Articles 74, paragraph 1, and 83, paragraph 1, of UNCLOS.[59]

The ICJ has since confirmed his approach, stating that it 'has made clear on a number of occasions' that it proceeds in three steps.[60] It recalled that in the second step, it considers if there are any relevant circumstances that necessitate adjusting the provisional equidistance line so as to achieve an equitable result and that if 'it concludes that such circumstances are present, it establishes a different boundary'.[61]

Rendering its first judgment in a maritime delimitation case, the ITLOS confirmed the approach as developed in arbitral awards and ICJ judgments. With extensive reference to the Court in *Romania* v. *Ukraine*, it endorsed the three-step methodology and likewise referred to it as the

---

[55] Ibid., paras. 301–2.   [56] Ibid., para. 303.
[57] *Romania* v. *Ukraine*, n. 36, paras. 116, 118.
[58] Ibid., paras. 120–1 and 155, citing *Land and Maritime Boundary between Cameroon and Nigeria (Cameroon* v. *Nigeria: Equatorial Guinea intervening)*, Judgment, ICJ Reports 2002, p. 303, para. 288.
[59] ICJ Reports 2009, p. 61, para. 155.   [60] ICJ Reports 2012, p. 624, para. 191.
[61] Ibid., para. 192.

equidistance–relevant circumstances method.[62] The Tribunal stated that in applying this method it takes into account the jurisprudence of international courts and tribunals. It noted at the outset that, if it finds 'any relevant circumstances requiring adjustment of the provisional equidistance line ... it will make an adjustment that produces an equitable result'.[63] Turning to the delimitation exercise, it stated similarly that it would now 'consider whether there are factors in the present case that may be considered relevant circumstances, calling for an adjustment of that line with a view to achieving an equitable solution'.[64]

It is one thing to define a methodology, but it is quite another to apply and realize it under the complex facts of a particular case. Lip service has often been paid to balancing, but rarely acted upon.[65] The reasoning of the courts does not necessarily follow an abstract programme set out in a systematic and methodological manner. Or, at least written opinions do not fully reflect such an intellectual process. There is a shared perception that equities, considerations, criteria, interests, factors and equitable principles need to be balanced, but the process of doing so is not yet fully developed. It is telling and somewhat paradoxical that a more systematic and coherent statement can be found in the *Tunisia/Libya* case than in the *North Sea* cases, although the former case stands, at the same time, for the proposition of an eminently result-oriented approach. There has been no clear relationship between the fundamental approach of rule- or result-orientation and efforts to develop a methodology in case law. Different cases show different approaches, and it seems that methodologies were chosen which best seemed to suit the courts and tribunals under the facts of the cases.

All this may be explained by a number of reasons. Firstly, it has never been the province of international courts and case law to expound in great detail on methodological issues. Judges are primarily concerned with deciding specific cases, and diverging views and backgrounds within a court on methods add to the reluctance to dwell on matters of jurisprudence and legal theory. Secondly, it is partly also due to the relative infant stage of the field and to prudent reluctance of the courts to make commitments on rules, principles and methodology in a new area of the law of the sea where 'ideas age very quickly'.[66] But finally, it is

---

[62] *Bangladesh v. Myanmar*, n. 37, paras. 233, 239.   [63] Ibid., para. 240.
[64] Ibid., para. 275.
[65] See also Jonathan I. Charney, 'Ocean Boundaries Between Nations: A Theory for Progress' (1984) 78 *American Journal of International Law*, 582, 593, 596.
[66] ICJ Reports 1984, p. 334, para. 160.

due to the fact that no elaborate methodology can be developed without further clarification of the relationship of equitable principles, relevant circumstances, considerations, factors, criteria or any other term used to depict elements to be taken into account, weighed and balanced. And this, so far, has not been properly developed in case law.

B. Toward a topical, problem-oriented methodology of equity

It is submitted that the conceptualization and clarification of equitable standards, of equitable principles, their normativity and relationship to the factually relevant circumstances and the normative objectives of equitable results undertaken in previous chapters allows, at this stage, further elaboration on the methodology of equity. There is ample room to render the concept and process of equity somewhat more systematic, transparent and rational, and to achieve a careful balance of rule-oriented and discretionary elements. Recalling that equidistance is not in a position to settle a complex case, the two-step approach practised by the ICJ merely postpones the problem to the level of relevant circumstances. Instead, recourse to the underlying equitable principles expounded in Chapter 10 should take place from the outset. Maritime boundary delimitation thus amounts to computation of a boundary line entailing the operation of both equitable principles and relevant circumstances. It does not exclude recourse, inter alia, to the method of equidistance in the process.

While most of the methodological debate has focused on a fundamental dichotomy of basic approaches in the context of the equidistance versus equity dispute, interesting efforts to bring about a more systematic operation within the rule of equity were proposed. Perhaps the most elaborate scheme has been submitted by the late Jonathan Charney. Overall, he suggested proceeding in a five-step operation, which may best be summarized in his own words:

(1) The functions served by coastal state jurisdiction in the specific ocean zone to be delimited should be identified.
(2) All the facts concerning the instant boundary area that reflect the functions to be served by the zone should be identified.
(3) To the extent possible, each piece of information identified in the prior paragraph should be used to construct a line or range of lines that best suits the function to which it relates.
(4) These alternative lines and previously identified factors should be studied and weighed according to their importance. In a process that

might even approach vector analysis, a line that best reflects all the relevant factors in light of their importance to the zone should be sought.
(5) A cartographical method should be selected to describe the line accurately and reliably.[67]

Many of the elements corresponding to points (1) and (2) have already been dealt with in the context of legal issues discussed before. The following proposals basically rely upon the approach expressed in points (3) to (5) and seek further refinement in light of the view expressed before that a methodological distinction should and can be drawn between equitable principles as such and relevant circumstances. Overall, it is submitted that the operation of equity entails a number of sequential steps, although the particularities of any case may require deviation from the programme set out below. Essentially, the concept and process exhibit three different stages.

Firstly, a preliminary boundary line or different lines for different zones are established and computed on the basis of equitable principles. This operation itself will consist of different methodological steps. Secondly, the preliminary result is reviewed from the perspective of relevant circumstances as factual elements which may exert a corrective effect and establish a revised version of the line in the light of the overall objective to reach an equitable result, i.e. to honour legitimate expectations. Finally, technical methods are used for the purpose of a cartographic and legally binding fixation of the result. This step may involve further simplifications of the boundary line for administrative ease. Yet, before all these steps are taken, it is important to clarify the precise mandate of the court on the basis of the special agreement or compromis.

1. Assessing the type of boundary required or permitted

While in terms of substance the special agreement was dealt with toward the end of Chapter 10,[68] it should be discussed here at the very outset. Indeed, detailed analysis and determination of the scope and leeway of a court as to the application of equitable principles and relevant circumstances are crucial. Perhaps the very first question for clarification on the basis of the special agreement or subsequent agreement by the parties relates to the issue of whether the court is bound to establish an all-purpose boundary line for both the shelf and the EEZ, as in the

[67] Charney, 'Ocean Boundaries Between Nations', n. 65, p. 579.   [68] Chapter 10(IV).

1984 *Gulf of Maine* case,[69] the *St. Pierre and Miquelon* arbitration,[70] the *Qatar/Bahrain* case,[71] the *Cameroon/Nigeria* case (albeit agreement was reached here only during written and oral pleadings),[72] the *Guyana/Suriname* case,[73] the *Nicaragua/Honduras* case,[74] the *Romania/Ukraine* case[75] and the *Bangladesh/Myanmar* case.[76] An obligation to establish a single boundary considerably limits the range of equitable principles and, in particular, of relevant circumstances to those related to surface geography. Where the court is free to adopt diverging boundaries, the examination of equitable principles and relevant circumstances has to be split for both the shelf and the EEZ or any other type of zone.[77] The analysis may well lead to a single boundary line in accordance with established presumptions. But it may lead in other cases to the adoption of diverging boundary lines for the shelf and the EEZ if the assessment of the various equitable principles and relevant circumstances, in particular those related to human conduct, produces considerably diverging results.

Similarly, the court should assess at this stage whether or not it is in a position to create common areas of joint operation for one or each of the different zones. Again, the mandate given the parties is disposing. The absence of any explicit exclusion of such an approach, or the implicit inclusion, considerably enlarges the scope for consideration of different principles and circumstances in terms of a delegation of power to the court.

At each subsequent step, it is evident that the court has to examine the special agreement in similar terms as to what extent the parties agreed to put particular emphasis on particular principles or circumstances. Such agreement may considerably influence the result. For further discussions, no such specialities are assumed, but it should be made clear that they may be introduced by the will of the parties at any stage of the following operations. They may deviate from the general concept and methodology of equity, provided that it still allows for an overall equitable

---

[69] ICJ Reports 1984, p. 263, Special Agreement Art. II(1).
[70] See Ted McDorman, 'The Canada–France Maritime Boundary Case: Drawing a Line around St. Pierre and Miquelon' (1990) 84 *American Journal of International Law*, 157, 166 ff., Compromis Art 2(1).
[71] *Qatar* v. *Bahrain*, n. 29, para. 67.   [72] ICJ Reports 2002, p. 303, para. 286.
[73] *Guyana* v. *Suriname* Award, n. 54, paras. 213, 218.
[74] ICJ Reports 2007, p. 659, paras. 72, 73.   [75] ICJ Reports 2003, p. 61, paras. 11, 12.
[76] *Bangladesh* v. *Myanmar*, n. 37, paras. 179–81.
[77] On this issue, see Malcolm D. Evans, 'Delimitation and the Common Maritime Boundary' (1993) 64 *British Yearbook of International Law*, 283–332.

apportionment. For the purpose of the present methodological discussion, it is assumed that no such requirements exist.

2. Assessment and adjudication of equitable principles

An equitable maritime boundary is characterized by compliance with the equitable principles developed and set forth in the previous chapters. Ideally, all principles can be served and respected. In reality, this will rarely be the case, and the essence of what is called the balance of equities consists of drawing lines which make them compatible with these principles as far as possible. Before such efforts at co-ordination and co-existence of principles can be made, it is necessary to concretize each of the relevant principles.

3. Specification and visualization of principles

The first step of the operation consists of the specification of the principles to the facts of the individual case. Courts have done so explicitly with some of the principles, in particular proportionality and the principle of non-cutting-off, in particular in the *Guinea/Guinea-Bissau* case and in the *St. Pierre and Miquelon* arbitration.[78] However, no systematic specification and visualization of either the lines that ideally reflect each of these principles, or of the problems such lines would solve (or create), has been made available to parties and the public at large. As Charney proposed, it would seem appropriate to draw optimal tentative lines for each of the surface-related principles. These principles include the following: the principles of non-encroachment (NEP) and non-cutting-off (NCP); the principle of equal division of marine space within the window of delimitation (EDP); and the principle of fair and reasonable proportionality (FRPP) discussed in Chapter 10.

The process of concretizing principles, however, does not stop at this point. It was also seen in Chapter 10 that equitable principles are not limited to surface geography. They also include a number of principles related to human conduct: the principle of recent and contemporary conduct (RCCP); the principle of viability relating to fisheries (VP); and the principle of prudent conservation and management (PCMP) expressing third generational concerns. Unlike relevant circumstances,

---

[78] *Guinea v. Guinea-Bissau*, n. 33, paras. 118–20; *Court of Arbitration for the Delimitation of Maritime Areas between Canada and France, Case concerning the Delimitation of Maritime Areas between Canada and the French Republic* (1992) 31 ILM 1145, paras 66–74.

discussed shortly, these principles should also be included in this first stage. As for surface-related geographic principles, tentative boundary lines and perhaps even joint zones should be drawn that best serve these interests in a particular case.

4. Vector analysis and co-ordination of boundary lines

Inevitably, these tentative surface boundary lines vary, and the question arises how to eliminate such differences. The process is not simply one of balancing interests, but of achieving the co-ordination of normative principles. Any true operation of balancing assumes that different factors or criteria of various levels of importance are at stake. Balancing essentially entails the weighing of interests according to the importance attached to them in a particular case. Yet, things are different with regard to normative principles. They are not subject to balancing in that broad sense. It is submitted that, firstly, all of the equitable principles defined above enjoy a similar level of importance (unless otherwise defined by special agreement). They need to be co-ordinated. The problem of hierarchy and preferred position will only emerge in relation to the level of relevant circumstances. The process of balancing interests entails the possibility of excluding one aspect at the expense of another. It is for such reasons that, for example, the field of determination of extraterritorial jurisdiction in international law relies upon an assessment and balancing of factual interests and is not suitable for governance by rules and principles.[79] Given the normative nature of equitable principles, the situation is the inverse of the present context. It follows from the normative equality of all equitable principles that none of them can be completely excluded at the advantage of full realization of another.

Delimitation should therefore proceed by establishing vectors among the different lines as visualized. The process gives more weight to a scenario where a group of lines close to each other can be identified. It seems evident that where there are two or more lines that were each arrived at through the specification of an equitable principle, the common line would be closer than where lines deviate considerably and are found to run in a different direction. Yet, it is not simply a

---

[79] See Derek W. Bowett, 'Jurisdiction: Changing Patterns of Authority over Activities and Resources' in R. St. J. Macdonald and D. M. Johnston (eds.), *The Structure and Process of International Law: Essays in Legal Philosophy, Doctrine and Theory* (Dordrecht: Martinus Nijhoff Publishers, 1983), pp. 555, 573; see also Jean Nicolas Druey, 'Interessenabwägung – eine Methode?' in *Beiträge zur Methode des Rechts, St. Galler Festgabe zum schweizerischen Juristentag 1981* (Bern: Haupt, 1981), p. 131.

matter of eliminating such lines; as stated, equitable principles, being normative principles, cannot simply be ignored for the convenience of others. The problem is comparable, although of a different quality, to human rights, where limitation is still needed to preserve the core content and cannot lead to a total erosion of the right in competition with other rights or public interests running in the opposite direction.[80] Lines outside such groups therefore still exert some influence, leading to further adjustment. That aside, it is nevertheless legitimate that overall they are given less weight. The process may entail difficult decisions at this stage, and this is where an analysis as to the effect of different solutions should take place. The practical effects of alternative vector lines need to be examined at this stage, and a final assessment has to be made in full knowledge of the problems at stake, caused as well as solved by such alternatives. Again, it is important to reiterate the fact that delimitation is not a mathematical operation, but rather necessarily entails value judgments. This is inherent to creative delimitation. It is in this context that balancing enters the stage. But there is a difference whether final judgments are merely made implicitly by some broad balance of interests, or whether discussions take place on the basis of vector analysis and reasons are stated explicitly.

---

[80] Except for a number of absolute rights, such as the freedom from torture, slavery and imprisonment for debt, human rights in international instruments are, in one way or another, subject to restrictions. Generally, such restrictions need to be necessary and prescribed by law; for a survey see Paul Sieghart, *The International Law of Human Rights* (Oxford University Press, 1983), pp. 85–103. While the case law in international protection is gradually building, in particular within the European Convention on Human Rights, constitutional courts have developed different techniques and methods to avoid total erosion of constitutional rights, such as the doctrines of strict scrutiny, of substantive due process (past and present), including the requirement of a compelling state interest, the contract clause, or the clear and present danger test in freedom of speech in the US, or the general doctrine of *Wesensgehalt* (essential content) in Germany, or the doctrine of *Kerngehalt* (core content) in Swiss law. Beyond balancing interests and requiring that means do not go beyond necessary restriction (proportionality test), these latter doctrines share in common the concern that the enjoyment of fundamental rights must not be completely restricted, although absolute and core elements of rights are extremely difficult to define in general terms; for US law see e.g. Kathleen M. Sullivan and Gerald Gunther, *United States Constitutional Law – Cases and Materials* (Mineola NY: The Foundation Press, 15th edn., 2004), pp. 885–970; for German Law see e.g. Konrad Hesse, *Grundzüge des Verfassungsrechts der Bundesrepublik Deutschland* (Heidelberg: C. F. Müller, 1999), pp. 147–53; for Swiss law see Jörg Paul Müller, *Elemente einer schweizerischen Grundrechtstheorie* (Bern: Stämpfli, 1982); Jörg Paul Müller, *Die Grundrechte der schweizerischen Bundesverfassung* (Bern: Stämpfli, 1991).

5. The corrective impact of relevant circumstances and of the requirement of an equitable result

The fundamental rule not only requires delimitation on the basis of equitable principles, it also requires taking into account relevant circumstances in order to achieve an equitable result. Once a tentative boundary line is reached on the basis of equitable principles, the process should turn to the problem of relevant circumstances. It was submitted that, unlike principles, these circumstances are of a factual nature. They do not have a normative content, but they may exert an impact by virtue of the obligation to reach an overall equitable result. And according to these criteria, an open-ended number of relevant circumstances were described on the basis of the aforementioned case law. They relate to a number of interests in the context of resource allocation (unity of deposits, existing wells and concessions, potential ecological factors), as well as a range of factors related to human geography (historical conduct prior to the establishment of the zones, cultural and ethnological interests, and national security interests beyond NCP).

With regard to these and perhaps further (but non-macroeconomic) circumstances, it is submitted that three steps are required. Firstly, it is necessary to assess the relevance of the interests invoked by the parties. Since the circumstance is considered by the submitting party to be relevant, relevance can hardly be denied, except in cases where the argument obviously does not bear any relation to the facts. More important is that the invocation of circumstances needs to rely upon sufficient and conclusive evidence, and this hurdle can be difficult to overcome. The *Gulf of Maine* case showed this with regard to ecological circumstances. In most cases, however, the process will focus on the assessment of the relative importance of the circumstance. This determination provides the basis for the next steps. It is conceivable that the parties submit similar or different circumstances that may compete with one another. It is here that the court now has to undertake an operation of balancing these interests and of determining the extent to which one or the other prevails, or whether they offset each other. For example, parties may invoke security interests, and/or ecological arguments, and/or circumstances related to historic conduct (short of historical title). If such arguments are conflicting, a determination has to be made as to which of them prevails, or whether they exert a mutually neutralizing effect. The second step may on that basis be to eliminate the relevance of some circumstances. The courts need to be able to decide *proprio motu* upon hearing the parties, without necessarily being bound by, and limited to, circumstances submitted by them.

Unchallenged or prevailing relevant circumstances enter the third stage of the operation. So far, they have not been exposed to the tentative boundary lines established on the basis of equitable principles in the first place. The court now has to examine whether and to what extent a relevant circumstance may exert its impact on the tentative line.

Again, it might be thought that the following operation consists of balancing the equities. However, it is submitted that the process is more correctly characterized as one of assessing the potential corrective effects of factual circumstances. As stated, equitable principles, and therefore also the resulting combined vector line of their computation, are not of the same normative value as any relevant circumstance. For the following operation it is important to recall that equitable principles enjoy, vis-à-vis relevant circumstances, a preferred position. This is well established by 'the coast dominates the sea' principle (CDS), and it is often said that delimitation is not a matter of totally or completely refashioning nature or compensating for the inequalities of nature.[81] *De lege ferenda*, this is also true for equitable principles related to human conduct. Their recognition as fundamental principles is important if the shortcomings of a purely geographical approach are to be overcome. Relevant circumstances, on the other hand, and again, are interests of a factual nature, and they cannot be placed on an equal footing with principles.

It follows from this relationship that relevant circumstances need to represent overriding or compelling interests in order to modify a boundary line computed on the basis of combined equitable principles. Relevant circumstances of a factual nature amount to a corrective, rather than a constitutive function. This perception, it is submitted, adequately reflects a reasonable position of an open-ended number of such circumstances. Within a topical model, they insert additional flexibility. At the same time, the requirements of overriding or compelling interests also avoid deterioration into unprincipled adjudication. Moreover, it also reflects the reluctance of courts to give effect to such circumstances in the existing case law.

In result, the operation at this stage much more resembles the model of rule-exception than it amounts to a balancing of the equities. While the

---

[81] See Chapter 10(II)(A)(1).

main tentative line is computed on the basis of equitable principles (and not on a technical method such as equidistance), the assessment of corrections to that line may follow the same methodology as was found and applied in Article 5 of the 1958 Shelf Convention. Close analysis therefore reveals that the differences between the two main schools of thought, i.e. of equity and of equidistance, can be eliminated with regard to the treatment and impact of relevant circumstances. They follow the pattern of corrective equity *contra legem*. Starting from the tentative boundary line and its assessment of the importance of the relevant circumstance, the court makes adjustments of the line to the extent necessary to satisfy fully or partly the concerns lying behind the relevant circumstance as accepted in substance by the court.

C. The methodological impact of the goal of an equitable apportionment

Since the normative impact of factual circumstances of any kind in a particular case relies upon the normative requirement of achieving an overall equitable apportionment, it is submitted that defining such relevance and the assessment of a compelling nature has to be made, in the final analysis, in the light of legitimate expectations.

Legitimate expectations, it was seen, primarily rely on the underlying equitable principles and their probable specification. They primarily define the range of solutions still falling within such expectations. But in complex cases, they may not be able to reflect them appropriately, and the neglect of factual circumstances cannot provide equitable apportionment. It is here where they are compelling. The problem is that the range of legitimate expectations cannot be defined in precise terms. They are very much a matter of 'look and feel', and the judge will regularly look back and forth, not only when assessing special circumstances, but also equitable principles, to determine whether an emerging solution still lies within the range which he or she considers satisfies legitimate expectations. This dialectical process involves psychological and political sensibility; and these ingredients of wise judgments are often difficult to articulate in words. It is at this point that skill and methodology end and art, experience and wisdom come into play to the benefit of dispute settlement. Looking back and forth from standards to reality and the political environment of equity is an essential element of topism and does not render the operation one of *ex aequo et bono* decision-making.

D. Role of technical methods and geometrical constructions

Finally, the methodology of equity turns to technical methods. Unlike in negotiations, where technical methods, in particular equidistance and median lines, serve as a useful starting point, technical methods are used under the fundamental rule of equity at the very end in order to determine with cartographic precision the results achieved in the dialectical process of assessing equitable principles and the corrective impact of relevant circumstances. Technical methods basically do not have any intrinsic normative value.[82] The variety of different models and the ingenuity of courts in constructing boundary lines in the case suggests that this is also the prevailing perception in case law, even though some technical methods, such as giving half-effect to islands or modification of closing lines in proportion to the comparative coastal lengths, have been used in a normative and apparently self-evident manner, without relying upon a transparent process of assessing equitable principles and relevant circumstances.

In many instances it will be appropriate to define the final lines in terms of geographical co-ordinates of longitude and latitude listed in the operative part of the judgment. Sometimes it is possible to apply other technical methods described above.[83] This stage of the operation may also serve to further simplify the results achieved and bring about final solutions which will be suitable for the purpose of convenience and practicability in terms of navigation, conservation or exploitation. Still, such adjustments cannot deviate substantially from the lines established previously by the application of equitable standards through a transparent process.

E. Iura novit curia *and the need for structural pairing of substance and procedure*

The methodology set forth should also clarify two further aspects. Firstly, all equitable principles and relevant circumstances, having effects on vectors and therefore on the finding of a final line, need to enjoy a similar normative status within their respective groups, albeit that some are more common in practice than others. This is important in terms of burden of proof. None of the standards enjoys a privileged position in that respect. None of the parties should be under an obligation to bear the

---

[82] See Chapter 4(II).   [83] Ibid.

burden of proof in order to influence vector analysis. The 1977 *Anglo-French Channel* Court of Arbitration refuted British arguments to that effect in the context of the equidistance–special circumstances rule.[84] The more so, this is true in the context of the rule of equity. The second point is closely linked to this. The courts need to be in a position to make a judgment *proprio motu*, and independently of the arguments and assessments made by the parties. Lack of argument or defence does not impair a court's undertaking of the appropriate and full vector analysis. In all cases, arguments have been used which were not necessarily proposed by one of the parties, e.g. with regard to giving half-effect to islands or to the assessment of conduct *(iura novit curia)*.[85] The *Gulf of Maine* Chamber confirmed this principle when it held that 'it must formulate its own solution independently of the proposals made by the Parties'.[86]

The application of this principle, however, may lead to situations where courts are relying upon *de novo* arguments and reasoning upon which the parties did not have an opportunity to comment. This problem arose during the *Anglo-French Channel* arbitration, when the Court gave the Scilly Islands half-effect even though neither of the parties had argued for this. In the *St. Pierre and Miquelon* award, the question may be asked if the Court of Arbitration, in allocating an area not claimed by the French, in fact ruled *ultra petita*. In such situations, it is important in due process to submit such proposals to the parties before a final judgment is rendered. Firstly, it is only with the full view of the parties that the court can make a fully informed judgment. Moreover, hearing the parties is essential for practical acceptance and compliance with the judgment. Bowett therefore suggested the introduction of a second round of hearings,[87] and Lauterpacht, emphasizing the crucial importance of debate and discourse among the parties and the court, equally called for new types of procedures in recourse to equity:

> The court is not applying the law; it is creating the law for the parties. The court may not have enough knowledge adequately to discharge this task without the specific assistance of the parties. There is a real need for

---

[84] Above n. 43, para. 67.
[85] See Bowett, n. 30, at 21 ('It is difficult to sustain the argument that an international tribunal is restricted to giving a judgment based on the legal arguments of the Parties').
[86] ICJ Reports. 1984, p. 325, para. 190 in fine; see also the decision of the Court of Arbitration in the *St. Pierre and Miquelon* case not to retain any of the solutions proposed by the parties and to formulate its own solution, 31 ILM 1169, paras. 64–5 (1992).
[87] Bowett, n. 30, pp. 20–1.

debate, not only between the parties but also between the parties and the court. At the very least, the court should not decide such a case by reference to points which have not been precisely argued and elaborated before it. And the better still, it should go through a process of discussing such points in detail with the parties. This approach suggests that there is a strong case for the introduction in this kind of case of a two-stage procedure which involves not only the traditional techniques of written and oral pleadings but also a preliminary assessment by the court of the main elements of the case which, in its judgment, are going to affect its decision. And that preliminary assessment could be conveyed privately to the parties. They could be given an opportunity for further argument specifically related to the issues which appear likely to control the court's decision. Then, and only then will the court be sufficiently informed to decide on the equities of the matter... If a suggestion of this kind is novel, it is because the problem is novel. We have not been faced by it before. We are faced by it now. We must grapple with it now. And we must be ready to introduce innovations in our procedures.[88]

The problem of adjudication *proprio motu* shows the importance of adequate structural pairing of substance and procedures in maritime boundary law. Sir Hersch Lauterpacht seems to assume that the rule of equity is a special case and different from legal adjudication. It is submitted that we are faced with a general problem which simply may be more acute here than elsewhere. Going back and forth in assessment and argument, testing possible solutions and their implications, is a problem of a general nature in all legal adjudication based on a problem-oriented, topical approach. It is inherent to all adjudication based on broad principles and open-textured norms. And it is important to compensate for the inherent vagueness or complexity of substance with appropriate procedural rules. The argument of structural pairing of substance and procedure and the need to compensate by procedures for open norms has been discussed in constitutional law.[89] However, it is clearly of a general nature and the relationship also applies to international law.[90] In fact, cases are reported where courts of arbitration

---

[88] Lauterpacht, n. 30, pp. 13–14.
[89] See the concept of structural due process in Laurence Tribe, 'Structural Due Process' (1975) 10 *Harvard Civil Rights–Civil Liberties Law Rev*, 269; Thomas Cottier, *Die Verfassung und das Erfordernis der gesetzlichen Grundlage* (Ruegger: Diessenhofen, 2nd edn., 1991), pp. 206–15.
[90] Thomas Cottier, 'Constitutional Trade Regulation in National and International Law: Structure-Substance Pairings in the EFTA Experience' in Meinhard Hilf and Ernst-Ulrich Petersmann (eds.), *National Constitutions and International Economic Law* (Deventer: Kluwer, 1993), p. 409; also in Thomas Cottier, *The Challenge of WTO Law: Collected Essays* (London: Cameron May, 2007), pp. 471–505.

have adopted more flexible and informal procedures and granted exceptions by taking recourse to equity.[91] Additional hearings have also been admitted in maritime boundary law.[92] It should also be noted that Article 52 of the ICJ Statute does not preclude the court from hearing the parties in subsequent terms. There is no obligation to refuse further oral or written evidence after hearings have been concluded. The court and chambers are therefore free to introduce a two-stage process.

What might be new and should be examined in the light of the optimal structural pairing of substance and procedure are procedures developed in the GATT and further refined in the Uruguay Round negotiations and the WTO. While parties have long been entitled to review the factual parts of the judgment, they are now also in a position to comment in the interim review on the arguments and rationales made by the panel for a period prior to opening the report to the contracting parties. The Panel may resume further discussions and debate in a further meeting, or disregard the arguments raised. The procedure not only allows for final adjustments to be made, but also provides an opportunity to hear parties *ex post* where the judgment is arrived at on the basis of arguments not submitted by one of the parties.

Finally, attention should be drawn to the possibility that parties may prescribe special procedures in the compromise which obliges the court to come back to them in case it pursues its reasoning on new arguments which have not (or have not sufficiently) been under consideration and debate among the parties before the court. The approach tested in GATT may also be suitable to break new ground in maritime boundary adjudication to achieve equitable apportionment and successful dispute settlement.

F. *Conclusions*

No amount of refinement of the methodology of equity can solve the intrinsic difficulty that maritime boundary delimitation entails at all stages of the operation; the need to make value judgments and decisions.

---

[91] See Vladimir-Đuro Degan, *L'Équité et le droit international* (La Haye: Martinus Nijhoff, 1970), p. 181 ff.; Charles de Visscher, *De L'Équité dans le règlement arbitral ou judiciaire des litiges de droit international public* (Paris: Editions A. Pedone, 1972), pp. 55, 93.
[92] See Bowett, n. 30, p. 21, note 1, where it is said that written observations on Eddystone Rock (a base point issue) were made and hearings held after closing main hearings.

It cannot replace what has previously been found to be essentially a truly creative legal operation and act. But methodology helps to structure the process in a rational, well-reasoned, transparent and therefore persuasive manner. Equitable principles and relevant circumstances, shaped on the basis of underlying concepts, goals and objectives of the different zones, do help to reduce valuational difficulties, but they cannot replace the need for a creative judgment process and selection from a variety of possible solutions within the concept of equity. It may be argued that this is an intrinsic weakness of the concept and the very reason why the concept of equity essentially remains in the realm of decision-making *ex aequo et bono* in substantive terms. Yet, it is submitted that the inherent openness of principles and the considerable amount of discretion that goes with them does not disqualify equity as a legal process if it is applied by means of a transparent and rational process. The quality of the methodology is the test of whether decisions are made in equity or *ex aequo et bono*. Delimitation of marine boundaries is the art of creating and doing justice in a convincing manner. It is not different from shaping the contours of broadly textured human rights, such as human dignity.

IV. The problem and impact of islands

A. *Introduction*

It is only at this point that we are ready to deal with the difficult issue of the impact of islands on the delimitation process. Upon setting out the methodology, we can approach this issue, being one of the most delicate problems in the field of maritime boundary delimitation. In fact, islands often give rise to controversy, and most of the contentious cases reaching the courts have entailed major problems and divergences of views as to the proper impact of islands. In fact, major disputes, such as in the *Aegean Shelf*, the *Libya/Malta* case, the *St. Pierre and Miquelon* arbitration, the *Jan Mayen* case, the *Eritrea/Yemen* Arbitration, the *Qatar/Bahrain* case or the *Nicaragua/Colombia* case and the *Newfoundland, Labrador and Nova Scotia* arbitration, essentially focused on islands. The problems in such cases are by no means exceptional. Islands are a common feature, found scattered all over the seas and often in the vicinity of mainland coasts. Finding an adequate method of dealing with the problem of islands is crucial. The manner it is dealt with in terms of equitable principles, relevant circumstances and methodology is determining whether the operation is one of law and equity, or whether it truly remains in the realm of discretionary decision-making *ex aequo et bono*. Moreover, it may not only be a matter of allocating maritime space to islands. Sovereignty over the islands themselves is often contentious, further complicating the dispute, as in cases where the land boundary is unsettled. Sometimes maritime boundary negotiations have succeeded in settling the sovereignty issue.[93] Methods that ignore islands are also legitimate possibilities unless one claim impinges on another.[94]

The legal regime of islands with regard to delimitation of the continental shelf and the EEZ is less settled in law and equity than other aspects of the problem. Efforts at UNCLOS III to deal with the problem failed due to the multitude of configurations and national interests at stake, and no particular provisions on delimitations involving islands found their way into the Convention. Extensive studies reveal some common tendencies found in state practice, but these fall short of establishing any particular principles or rules related to islands. State practice reveals that islands have been generally taken into account as relevant base points for the application of equidistance. In 1979, Bowett published a number of propositions reflecting state practice.[95] He came to the general conclusion that the impact of islands diminishes under the model of equidistance the further they are from the coast of the mainland in cases of opposite configurations.

As to adjacent configurations, state practice at the time was less abundant but has shown several tendencies according to Bowett. Where close inshore, islands have been both ignored and counted for boundary purposes; where they belong to different states, they may be subject to a 'trade-off' so as to produce a local median line; and the more remote from the mainland the islands are, the less effect they will have on the boundary.[96] In a survey of state practice published in 1993, Bowett was more cautious, only attempting a rough categorization, accepting that exceptional configurations may not fit into such categorization.[97] He suggests the following categories of islands:

---

[93] See Colson, n. 28, pp. 47, 63–7 with cases; see also Derek W. Bowett, 'Islands, Rocks, Reefs, and Low-Tide Elevations in Maritime Boundary Delimitations' in Charney et al., *International Maritime Boundaries*, n. 28, vol. I (Charney and Alexander), pp. 130, 136.
[94] Bowett, ibid., p. 151.
[95] Derek W. Bowett, *The Legal Regime of Islands in International Law* (Alphen aan den Rijn, Dobbs Ferry NY: Sijthoff and Noordhoff, Oceana, 1979). See also Dipla Haritini, *Le régime juridique des îles dans le droit international de la mer* (Paris: Presses Universitaires de France ; Geneva: Institut universitaire de hautes études internationales, 1984).
[96] Bowett, ibid., p. 182.   [97] Ibid., p. 132.

'(a) Islands as the sole unit of entitlement.' State practice provides many examples of islands being given full effect as against mainland coasts.[98] Where the claim of the island impinges upon the claim of another territorial unit as in the *Libya/Malta* case, 'the area to which the island is entitled will depend upon, primarily, comparisons of coastal lengths abutting from the other claimant, the political status of the island ..., population, and economic self-sufficiency'.[99]

'(b) Islands entitled in conjunction with the entitlement of a larger territorial unit under the same sovereignty, to which they are proximate.' In such configurations, state practice reveals a great diversity. Islands have either had no influence due to the delimitation method used (adjacent constellations), or they have been deliberately ignored because their sovereignty is disputed, or they have even been given full effect despite being close to a mainland. Practice, therefore, suggests that islands will be used in conjunction with the equidistance method and given full effect where they will not 'distort' an equidistant line so that it ceases to reflect the overall geographical relationship.[100]

'(c) Islands mid-way between two principal coasts subject to delimitation.' According to their proximity to the mainland, islands will have more or less effect on the delimitation.

'(d) Islands proximate to a mainland coast under a different sovereignty.' Despite remote location, such islands may be given full or partial effect. They may also be partially or wholly enclaved, or awarded an area which will not impinge on a neighbouring claim.

Derek Bowett was not the only one to study the structure of the legal regime of islands. Other more elaborate and interesting models as to the methodology were designed, also based on analyses of state practice. Donald E. Karl suggested a model that reflects reverse proportionality of distance and impact of islands in geometrical and even mathematical terms.[101] These propositions and models are designed under the model of equidistance and deviations are suggested in order to avoid distortions. But, this begs the question: distortions of what? The problem, again, shows that this crucial question cannot be resolved without recourse to the underlying values and principles of delimitation. The weakness of descriptive propositions and models based on state practice perhaps lies in the fact that such values are assumed and have remained highly unclear. The

---

[98] Ibid., pp. 132–3.   [99] Bowett, n. 79, p. 151.   [100] Bowett, n. 93, pp. 138–9.
[101] Donald E. Karl, 'Islands and the Delimitation of the Continental Shelf: A Framework for Analysis' (1977) 71 AJIL, 642.

courts, finding it difficult to explain why islands were treated in one way or another in order to achieve a particular result, often chose to remain silent or eventually referred to the prior case law. In fact, treatment of islands discussed in Section III(A) above shows a wide variety of different approaches which hardly allow finding common methods let alone rules at a technical level: disregard of islands to secure a median line in the *Anglo-French Channel* arbitration; enclavement of islands to retain general course of the bisector line in *Nicaragua* v. *Honduras*; giving half-effect to islands in the *Dubai/Sharjah* arbitration or partial effect in the *Qatar/Bahrain* case and the *Nicaragua/Colombia* case; giving half-effect to an archipelago in the *Tunisia/Libya* case; giving reduced effect to achieve a proportional closing line in the *Gulf of Maine* case; giving partial consideration of islands to compute the coastal lengths in the *Guinea/Guinea-Bissau* arbitration and the *Nicaragua/Colombia* case; disregarding islands for base points in the *Romania/Ukraine* case, the *Nicaragua/Colombia* case and the *Bangladesh/Myanmar* case; disregarding for base points and the computation of coastal lengths in *Libya* v. *Malta* and *Romania* v. *Ukraine*; and ignoring the uninhabited islands in the CEIP delimitation and of Sable Island in the *Newfoundland, Labrador and Nova Scotia* arbitration.

Yet, it is particularly important to approach the impact of islands on delimitation on the basis of underlying principles. Again, inference from technical methods in state practice may not be enough to cope with the problem of distortions in more complex and contentious cases. Instead, the problem of islands should be addressed on the basis of the equitable standards and the methodology set out above. Here, as elsewhere, it is important to distinguish strictly legal issues from the rule of equity.

B. Legal issues

Delimitation may entail a number of issues related to the status of islands, which are pure questions of international law and need to be dealt with before applying the methodology of equity. Some particular issues may be briefly addressed in addition.

1. Basic entitlement to shelf and EEZ

It has been generally accepted in customary law and stated in *Quatar* v. *Bahrain* that islands are entitled to a shelf to the same extent that mainland territory is.[102] The rule is expressed in Article 121, paragraph 2, of

---

[102] ICJ Reports 2001, p. 40, para. 185.

the LOS Convention, which states that islands, regardless of their size, generate the same maritime rights as other land territory. This was one of the principles invoked by France to claim extensive maritime areas around the two tiny islands of St. Pierre and Miquelon.[103] Basic entitlement builds upon recognition of the physical fact of the continental shelf and has been evidenced by Article 1 of the 1958 Shelf Convention. From here, the regime was expanded to the EEZ due to increasing convergence of the zone, although the physical rationale cannot be used here. Today, under Article 121(2) of the LOS Convention, the territorial sea, the contiguous zone, the continental shelf and the EEZ of an island are to be determined in accordance with the provisions applicable to land territory. This implies that the effective amount of entitlement within a region of competing claims in most cases depends, as with all territories, upon equity, unless the expanses of the zones are defined by virtue of natural boundaries (e.g. *thalweg*, discontinuity of shelves).

The assimilation of mainland and islands also implies that there is no fundamental difference between independent and dependent territories. The argument has been made that dependent territories should, *a priori*, be given less weight than independent islands[104] which enjoy the principle of sovereign equality and therefore always require full effect to be given. This distinction does not exist with respect to entitlement on the basis of land territories. Nor can it exist in law in the context of islands.[105] Whether or not rights to a shelf or an EEZ are exercised by an independent government or a metropolitan power does not alter the basic entitlement of the island vis-à-vis third states, to the same extent as the island territory is entitled as such to all rights under international law such as territorial integrity and the ensuing right to self-defence. A special regime may affect the internal allocation of resources attributed to the territory between the local populations, in particular with regard to fisheries. The issue entails complex aspects, and it is not clear as to what extent the matter is governed by

---

[103] Bowett, n. 79, p. 140. 'Court of Arbitration for the Delimitation of Maritime Areas between Canada and France, Case concerning de Delimitation of Maritime Areas between Canada and the French Republic' (1992) 31 ILM 1164, para. 43 (hereinafter *St. Pierre and Miquelon Arbitration*).

[104] Bowett, ibid., para. 48.

[105] *St. Pierre and Miquelon Arbitration*, n. 103, para. 49: 'In the view of this Court there are no grounds for contending that the extent of the maritime rights of an island depends on its political status.'

international law. Yet, it will be seen that the principle of viability (VP) exerts a certain amount of influence under equity.

At this stage, particular factual problems may arise as to whether the legal qualifications of an island are met, being 'a naturally formed area of land, surrounded by water, which is above water at high tide', or whether entitlement is denied. Article 121(3) of the LOS Convention excludes insular features from entitlement both to the shelf and the EEZ, which cannot sustain human habitation or economic life of their own. The Court in *Romania v. Ukraine* did not need to consider whether Serpents' Island falls under paragraphs 2 or 3 of Article 121 of UNCLOS nor their relevance to the case. It does not provide guidance on this much-debated question, because, in the case at hand, any maritime entitlement potentially generated by Serpents' Island would in any case have been fully subsumed by other maritime entitlements of Ukraine.[106]

State practice has excluded small islands from a point of view of equitable delimitation, and the legal question might arise whether or not Article 121(3) of the LOS Convention has become part of general international law at the outset, or whether entitlement exists but may be denied in the context of equitable delimitation.[107] Moreover, it might be controversial whether an island denied of entitlement may still be used as a base point for delimitation by a technical method, in particular equidistance. While the island cannot influence delimitation short of entitlement, it may still be referred to as part of the relevant coast determining the base line, which is equally used to define territorial waters, continental shelf and EEZ in a seaward direction.[108]

Finally, it should be recalled that, of course, jurisdiction over the islands entails a classical legal issue. With a view to their entitlement for shelf and EEZ rights, islands remote and thus hitherto removed from attention have become contested, and the problem may therefore be more frequent than with respect to jurisdiction over land boundaries. But determination of sovereignty does not require any particular rules. It relies upon all sources of law available (existence and interpretation of agreements; effectiveness, historical rights; inter-temporal law; conduct (acquiescence and estoppel)) and does not pose a particular problem to the legal regime of islands.

---

[106] ICJ Reports 2009, p. 61, para. 187. [107] On this issue, see Bowett, n. 79, p. 131.
[108] See Bowett, n. 95, note 3 p. 194 (Eddy Rock).

2. Two categories of islands: constitutive and accessory entitlement

The basic entitlement of all islands alike qualifying for the respective zones seems to suggest that all islands enjoy the same legal position in the process of delimitation. Moreover, it was submitted that there is no fundamental difference between dependent and independent islands as to the basic entitlement. State practice, case law and doctrine have not attempted to work out different types or groups of islands. It is submitted that, at the outset, and based upon legal reflection relating to the concepts of the shelf and the EEZ, two categories exist, which enjoy different treatment in delimitation in accordance with the fundamental rule.

Islands may be part of a delimitation between coastal states, either adjacent or opposite, or a combination of both. Within the window of delimitation, the basic overlapping entitlement of each coastal state primarily relies upon entitlement stemming from the coastal facade and its quality as a coastal state. Although islands within this window enjoy entitlement of their own, the point is that such entitlement is not the only constitutive source, but an additional, and therefore accessory, title where islands belong to a coastal state.

The situation is different for islands whose entitlement is the sole and constitutive source of rights. This is true for independent islands off the coast of one or more third coastal states. Malta offers a typical example. Or, it is also typical for overseas islands under the jurisdiction of a metropolitan state that may or may not enjoy jurisdiction over a different shelf or EEZ disconnected with the island overseas.[109] The constitutive entitlement of these islands is equal to the entitlement based on land territory. Therefore, with the exception of minor features, such as protrusions, it cannot be fully or partially disregarded independent of the location or size of the island in order to achieve an equitable result. In other words, the function of islands in the process of delimitation is a different one, depending upon whether they merely establish additional entitlement on the same continental shelf or within the same EEZ of the coastal state or whether they are independent constituencies or dependencies lying further afield. The two form different configurations of accessory or constitutive islands and are therefore treated separately.

---

[109] See e.g. the *St. Pierre and Miquelon* arbitration, n. 103, Chapter 6(I)(H).

C. Assessment and adjudication of equitable principles

1. The impact of additive islands: ignoring locations

Whenever states have failed to reach agreement on the basis of the method of equidistance and adjustments in order to bring about a solution that is compatible with equitable principles and relevant circumstances, the methodology outlined earlier could proceed in the following manner.

Upon definition of the window of delimitation, including all coastal configurations and islands concerned, tentative lines should be drawn for each of the principles without regard to the additive islands. The step reflects the basic principles that the coast dominates the sea (CDS) and equal division (EDS) in opposite configurations. A computed tentative line co-ordinating the different principles to the utmost possible in vector analysis would therefore produce a boundary that satisfies the principles, including those relating to human conduct.

Additive islands could then be considered during a second step. Unlike equidistance, the approach would ignore the difficult question of the impact of the position of the islands at this stage, but would first deal with the impact of their size. The total coastal lengths of the islands or the archipelago concerned should be measured. The tentative line established could then be moved in such a way as to comply with proportionality of coastal length and marine spaces in accordance with FRP. Coastal states with islands under their jurisdiction would therefore increase spaces.

The new line then has to be checked again with other equitable principles and, if necessary, further adjusted in order to satisfy the principles of non-encroachment (NEP), non-cutting-off (NCP) and of recent and contemporary conduct (RCCP) and NEP, NCP and the RCCP. These principles, of course, also have to be applied to the islands. They will either lead to adjustments of the line where intersecting an island or in the vicinity of it, or to the establishment of enclaves where they lie beyond the tentative line. Such enclaving should be measured in order to satisfy the principle of economic viability (VP) of reasonable and fair proportionality (FRP), in particular with regard to fisheries, of the island concerned. At least, the enclave amounts to the territorial sea or equal division where distances to the mainland do not allow for such expanses.

A next step would check the line with existing relevant circumstances of a factual nature. Finally, the line achieved needs to be defined in precise cartographic terms.

Perhaps the advantage of the methodology proposed is that it attempts to ignore the difficult problem of the positioning of islands. Moreover, it helps to deal with islands within disputed jurisdictions. Existence within the window of delimitation suffices to exert an impact. But what, in the final analysis, despite mathematical efforts, can only be a gradual decrease of impact of additive islands as a function of their distance from the mainland, and which is responsible for the often unreasoned use of full or half-effect, or even ignorance of islands, can be avoided. The approach does not give as much prominence to the position of islands. It therefore deviates from successfully concluded agreements in state practice which have relied upon equidistance in opposite configurations. It is submitted that the results achieved in case law may well be explained or even improved in terms of equity by this method. Applied to future state practice, it is likely to bring about increased enclaving in complex cases, in particular where islands are situated 'on the wrong side', as the *Anglo-French Channel* arbitration stated. Yet, this is not inconsistent with the model of equitable principles, which reduces the predominance and impact of equidistance and the excessive impact of small islands on the allocation of marine space that goes with it.

The proposed method gives more weight to proportionality than the ICJ was prepared to give to Malta, in light of state practice, in the *Libya/Malta* case. *Ex post* adjustments of the median line were motivated, but not effected, on the basis of coastal lengths. Using more precise ratios of coastal lengths, as was done by the *Gulf of Maine* Chamber, however, does not necessarily prevent an equitable result, if it is clearly considered to be one principle among others and subject to further co-ordination of all vectors drawn. Moreover, it is submitted that in the case of Malta the situation was different, since the island is constitutive and not additive to the entitlement of the shelf and the EEZ. The proposed method would have also brought more clarity into the treatment of St. Martin's island in *Bangladesh* v. *Myanmar*, where the island was granted an influence on the territorial sea but not further seaward. Therefore, the island was ignored in the selection of base points as well as in the consideration of equitable principles for the delimitation of the EEZ and continental shelf – both times with the same reasoning that its effect would be exaggerated there.[110] Yet, the island had been considered in the territorial sea where its full effect upon the boundary was considered not to be a special circumstance requiring adjustment of the equidistance line.[111] To achieve this differential treatment, the Tribunal partitioned its Award into separate parts dealing with the territorial sea, the single maritime boundary and the extended continental shelf. Since the methodology of maritime

---

[110] *Bangladesh* v. *Myanmar*, n. 37, paras. 265, 318.   [111] Ibid., paras. 151–2.

delimitation in the territorial sea and up to 200 nm – or even beyond, as this case showed[112] – is today closely assimilated,[113] there was no need to partition the Award but for the varying impact of St. Martin's Island. With the method proposed here, the issue of St. Martin's Island could have been consolidated in one place instead of dealing with it in various places but with recurring reasoning.

2. Constitutive islands

Apparently, the methodology of delimitation between coastal states and constitutive islands resembles the standard methodology much more closely. Upon definition of the window, again, tentative lines are drawn satisfying each of the equitable principles involved to the utmost extent in vector analysis. The main difficulty, again, lies with the principle of fair and reasonable proportionality (RFP). Major disputes arise because the use of equidistance projects major shadows of small islands off the main coast in a seaward direction, allocating enormous space at the expense of the coastal state. As a matter of fact, the result is a considerable disproportion of coastal lengths and marine spaces allocated. While rejecting the application of strict proportionality in such cases, which would, in reverse, often drastically reduce space to the constitutive island, the Courts in *Libya v. Malta* and *Nicaragua v. Colombia* undertook to reduce disproportionality only to a limited extent. In effect, the principle applies to a limited degree and therefore tends to reduce spaces otherwise allocated to the coastal state under equidistance. *De lege ferenda*, it is submitted that proportionality could again apply in more precise terms, provided that other principles, in particular NCP, NEP and the principles related to human conduct (RCCP) are applied, preventing a predominant impact of proportionality in balancing the different equitable principles.

3. Special circumstances and geometric fixation

Finally, a tentative, co-ordinated line should be examined from the point of view of the relevant circumstances identified, and, if necessary, be further adjusted before geometric fixation takes place.

---

[112] Ibid., paras. 454–5.   [113] See section III(A) above and Chapter 8(II)(F).

12

The role of equity in negotiations

I. Introduction

The prime and most frequent and cost-effective mode of settling maritime boundaries, as in any other business in international relations, is and remains diplomatic negotiations. Most boundaries have and will be successfully settled this way. Chapter 5 reflects the account of state practice and the many agreements achieved over more than half a century of long-distance maritime boundary delimitation. There are far more agreements than settlements by courts. In the sample period alone from 1942 to 1992 (Appendix I), 120 maritime boundaries were settled by agreement while merely 20 cases (16.6 per cent) reached the courts and arbitration in that period. Judicial and costly third party settlement is by all means a subsidiary remedy. It applies in protracted cases where negotiations failed to settle the matter in the negotiating process.

The question thus arises whether and to what extent the legal framework based upon the fundamental rule of equity and the methodology developed in judicial settlement is, or ought to be, relevant and guiding the process of negotiations. The question is of general interest in assessing the role of equity in international law and diplomacy. Recourse to equity and equitable principles is essentially a judge-made concept, developed for the purpose of deciding complex and protracted cases. Balancing a variety of principles and factors, while excluding others, with a blind and impartial view, is not necessarily suitable for the diplomatic process. It requires authoritative decision-making in the very end – a feature absent in the process of negotiations and the quest for agreement and consent. It may be argued that the diplomatic process is not primarily interested in law and legal arguments. It focuses on interests and shows little concern for theory.[1] Thus, governments are mainly interested in resource allocation,

---

[1] John R. Prescott, a leading authority in political boundary making, writes in his preface to *The Maritime Political Boundaries of the World* (London: Methuen, 2004), xiv: 'This is an essential practical book. There is no attempt to develop a theory of ocean boundary-making

rather than maritime space, the principle object and reference point for judicial settlement. Power-oriented approaches play an important role in finding arrangements, and negotiations may be linked with other issues, related or unrelated to the allocation of marine space and resources. Powerful nations enjoy an advantage, while smaller nations may need to consider extraneous factors at the negotiating table.

At the same time, real life is more complicated than power politics seems to suggest, and the role of law and legal principles is often underestimated, in particular by *realpolitik* thinking. In practical terms, substantive law and judicial precedents provide important guidance in informing negotiating positions and arguments in discussions. And vice versa, negotiations impress legal developments and shape future law, by treaties and customary law alike.[2] Moreover, it may be argued that it is particularly during negotiations that the expounded principles should apply, for the simple reason that most boundaries are and can be settled this way, and it is only by respecting the law that lasting and fair solutions will be found. It is not an accident that a considerable number of agreements were found which explicitly refer to the ideals of equity.[3]

As a matter of fact, and albeit we lack hard evidence on behind-the-door talks, it is fair to say that the existing body of law is likely to influence negotiations. Parties using international lawyers will use precedents in order to sustain their interests and arguments. The threat to take recourse to third party dispute settlement at least requires taking into account the law in assessing negotiating positions from the very beginning. Proposals running counter to existing case law, practices or other agreed settlements run the risk of being rejected out of hand, knowing that they cannot be successfully sustained before a court of law. Of course, they will use the law and cases in advocacy, extracting favourable arguments, and leaving others aside. Yet, as both parties similarly engage in such an exercise, the full range of arguments will be presented, facilitating an

---

because in my experience of observing and sometimes working with governments, theoretical considerations have no place in developing policies and strategies. In every case policies and strategies have been selected because they are perceived to be the best way of serving national self-interest.'

[2] As William Bishop put it: 'agreement is reached in a mutual process of give-and-take. Such solution of troubles may be based upon existing rules of international law and go toward the establishment of practices which may become a part of what the parties regard as customary law', William Bishop (ed.), *International Law: Cases and Materials* (Boston MA: Little Brown & Co., 1971), p. 63.

[3] See Appendix I and the discussion of treaties in Chapter 5.

open and structured debate. While diplomats will dominate, there is clearly room for supporting legal advice and lawyers at the negotiating table. This description relies upon traditional precepts that law merely plays an auxiliary and argumentative role in negotiations. Two interesting issues, however, arise during the next stage of analysis:

Firstly, are negotiators obliged, as a matter of international law, to follow the basic rule of taking equity and equitable principles into account? The matter is far from clear in terms of legal obligations. Is maritime boundary law a special and innovative field where legal requirements need to be taken into account as a matter of obligation? In other words, to what extent should the fundamental rule of equity and equitable principles, including its methodology, be a *mandatory* prescription to be followed and respected in negotiations? To what extent, on the other hand, do states remain free to find any settlement by agreement, irrespective of such principles?

Secondly, and in contrast to substantive rules, are states under a legal obligation to negotiate maritime boundary delimitations? In other words, are there procedural obligations which may be based upon, and informed by, the precepts of equity? If yes, to what extent, and how do they relate to judicial dispute settlement?

This issue is of particular interest, both from the perspective of judge-made law, as well as with regard to Articles 74(1) and 83(1) of the LOS Convention. These provisions require parties to effect delimitation 'by agreement on the basis of international law'. This formulation not only addresses the relevance of substantive standards. It also addresses the question of the extent to which the parties are under an obligation to negotiate. Both are closely related and cannot be separated. We turn firstly to an analysis of the nature of these requirements and then later to the equitable duty to negotiate in this particular field of law.

II. The rule of equity and equitable principles in negotiated settlements

A. *Mandatory or residual rules?*

Article 6 of the 1958 Continental Shelf Convention applies the classical model of residual rules. Parties to the Convention remain free to adopt any solution by agreement. The combined equidistance–special circumstances rule becomes applicable, as a matter of law, only in case of judicial third party settlement. Of course, and for the reasons indicated above, the rule is not without influence in diplomacy. It will often determine the outcome of negotiations. As a matter of law, however, it was only the *North Sea* cases which introduced the rule of equity as a mandatory approach and method. The obligation was established not only between the parties in dispute. It was conceived as a general rule – 'that is to say, rules binding upon all States for all delimitations' – based upon the underlying 'ideas' of continental shelf law.[4] This was a fundamental departure from previous case law, which merely recommended the negotiation of equitable solutions.[5] The understanding of mandatory compliance with rules set forth equally prevailed throughout UNCLOS III. Despite explicit proposals to introduce residual rules,[6] both schools of thought operated under a widely unchallenged assumption that the treaty was to establish mandatory standards of delimitation, either based upon equitable principles or a rule of equidistance. The wording of the compromise that was finally adopted leaves little doubt that Articles 74(1) and 83(1) of the LOS Convention are intended to make the standards, evolving throughout case law and state practice, binding upon the parties. The provisions state that delimitations '*shall* be effected by agreement on the basis of international law, as referred to in Article 38 of the Statute of the International Court of Justice, in order to achieve an equitable solution'.[7]

With the debate at UNCLOS III focusing entirely on finding a compromise formula between the two schools of thought, it is, however, not entirely clear whether there was full awareness of the problems relating to a mandatory rule. The records do not show evidence of a substantial discussion of this conceptually important point.[8] In

---

[4] *North Sea Continental Shelf (Republic of Germany v. Denmark, Republic of Germany v. Netherlands)*, Judgment, ICJ Reports 1969, p. 47, para. 85. See Chapter 8.

[5] See *Société Commerciale de Belgique* case [1939] PCIJ, Series A/B No. 78, at 178; *Serbian Loans* case [1929] PCIJ, Series A No. 20 at 39; *Exchange of Greek and Turkish Population* advisory opinion [1925] PCIJ, Series B No. 20 at 24; see also Tomas Rothpfeffer, 'Equity in the North Sea Continental Shelf Cases' (1972) 42 *Nordisk Tidskrift for International Ret*, 81, 90.

[6] See e.g. the proposal by Israel, NG 7/28, and statement by the Second Committee, Summary Reports, 57th Mtg. (1979), reprinted in Renate Platzoeder (ed.), *The United Nations Conference on the Law of the Sea*, 4 vols. (Dobbs Ferry NY: Oceana Publications, 1982–85) (hereinafter Platzoeder), p. 474, para. 50, and see n. 8 below.

[7] Emphasis added.

[8] See the Reports of the Chairman of Negotiating Group 7, Doc. NG 7/24 (14 September 1978), *Official Records* vol. X, pp. 170–2, Doc NG 7/45 (22 August 1979), *Official Records* vol. XII, pp. 107–8, Doc. A/CONF.62/L.47 (24 March 1980), *Official Records* vol. VIII, pp.

particular, the relationship between paragraphs 1 and 4 of the two provisions remained, as it seems, undefined in Negotiating Group 7. In identical language, paragraphs 4 of Articles 74 and 83 reserve delimitation according to agreements in force between states concerned.[9] The scope and impact of these provisions is by no means clear. Are they mere provisions of inter-temporal law? Or, do they effectively transform paragraphs 1 into residual provisions, as Rainer Lagoni seems to suggest?[10]

Traditionally, states are free to adopt any solution by mutual agreement, provided it does not violate *jus cogens* or third party rights. Moreover, existing agreements can be altered by subsequent agreement with the latter prevailing over the former. From this contractual point of view, it is possible to argue that the parties to the LOS Convention remain free to adopt any delimitation of their respective zones, even if inconsistent with general or customary international law. After all, such agreements themselves form part of international law, as referred to by Articles 74(1) and 83(1) of the LOS Convention.

Such a view, however, is hardly compatible with the very essence of multilateral law-making treaties. The aforementioned provisions oblige parties to achieve, or at least seek in good faith the achievement of, an equitable solution on the basis of international law of their maritime boundary problem. This entails an obligation to negotiate. It also entails the obligation to achieve an overall equitable solution in accordance with international law. These requirements apply, in my view, to all attempts at settlement. Furthermore, reference to 'the basis of international law' in Articles 74(1) and 83(1) incorporates the judge-made law of the ICJ, which contains both the obligation to apply the rule of equity and to seek a settlement. These obligations do not leave paragraphs 4 without particular meaning and function. Firstly, as the texts indicate, they are rules

---

76–8, and the general debate of the Second Committee, Summary Reports 57th Mtg. (1979), pp. 470–81.

[9] Arts. 74(4) and 83(4) LOS Convention read:
    4. Where there is an agreement in force between the States concerned, questions relating to the delimitation of the exclusive economic zone [the continental shelf] shall be determined in accordance with the provisions of that agreement.

[10] Rainer Lagoni, 'Interim Measures Pending Maritime Boundary Delimitation Agreements' (1984) 78 *American Journal of International Law*, 345, 348–9. ('Paragraph 4 makes clear that, as a rule, the states concerned are to choose the methods of drawing the boundary. Only if there is no agreement in force between them is one referred by paragraph 1 to the principles and rules of delimitation of international law.')

grandfathering[11] existing delimitation agreements concluded prior to the entry into force of the LOS Convention in 1994. Secondly, they allow parties to define particular methods of delimitation in a preliminary agreement.[12] An agreement or compromis may set forth relevant factors and circumstances to be taken into account. It may also be guiding and binding upon a court of law which is mandated to effect the boundary delimitation, or require the court to establish joint zones of co-operation instead of a final delimitation.

Agreements under Articles 74(4) and 83(4) LOS Convention are, in other words, a special *ad hoc* concretization of the rule of equity. They are only fully compatible with international law and thus paragraphs 1 of Articles 74 and 83 so long as they do not jeopardize and contravene the basic requirement of an overall equitable solution. An agreement establishing apparently unfair apportionment of marine spaces and resources cannot be defended under Articles 74(4) and 83(4) of the LOS Convention. These provisions do not turn the fundamental rule of equity, established as a mandatory rule in the *North Sea* cases, into a mere residual rule. The concept of equity is not *à prendre ou à laisser* in the business of long-distance maritime boundary delimitation.

---

[11] The term was coined in the law of GATT. It was used to mark permissible historical trade preferences and exceptions entered into prior to the adoption of the Protocol of Provisional Application, or subsequent protocols of Accession to the GATT 1947. Typically, grandfather legislation is only allowed to continue until it is revised; subsequent legislation falls under the respective rules and disciplines, see generally John H. Jackson, *World Trade and the Law of GATT* (Indianapolis IN: Bobbs-Merrill Co., 1969) 28, pp. 264–70. The law of the WTO no longer recognizes grandfathering, except for specifically negotiated exemptions, for example derogations of most-favoured nation treatment in the General Agreement on Services, see Art. II: 2 and Annex to Art. II.

[12] It seems that authority to choose alternative methods of delimitation was the prime goal of the provision which has remained unchanged since the 1975 ISTN which required the employment of the median or equidistance line 'where appropriate', Art. 61(1)(6), Art. 70(1)(6) ISNT, Doc A/CONF.62/WP.8 Part II (7 May 1975), reprinted in Platzoeder, n. 6, vol. I, pp. 30–2. Provision 83 of the 1974 Main Trends expressed a rule similar to Art. 74(4) and 83(4) LOS Convention. It followed after the models of delimitation in Provision 82, which either referred to equidistance (Formula A and C, respectively) or equitable principles (Formula B), UN Doc. A/CONF.62/C.2./W.P.1 (15 October 1975), reprinted in Platzoeder, n. 6, vol. IV, pp. 3, 42–4. Since Art. 74(1) and 83(1) LOS Convention no longer indicates any particular method of delimitation, the original function of para. 4 is no longer apparent. In the existing framework, the provisions can serve the purpose of allowing members to the Convention to define particular methods as starting points for negotiations or for legal dispute settlement. The common choice of a particular method, however, does not affect the overall obligation to seek an equitable solution.

The obligation of the parties to seek agreement on the basis of standards of substantive law is, as a matter of legal theory, a highly significant development of recent origin. It reflects, beyond the doctrine of *jus cogens*, a movement towards a constitutional concept and framework of international law. An implementing agreement has to be in line with an underlying multilateral framework agreement. Similarly, agreements implementing decisions of the court, such as subsequent agreements between Germany, the Netherlands and Denmark following the *North Sea* ruling,[13] or the technical delimitation effected by the agreement between Tunisia and Libya following the 1982 judgment of the Court,[14] can be seen as *implementing agreements*. The law of maritime boundary delimitation, both under the LOS Convention and case law, therefore implies some sort of a hierarchy of agreements for which classical international law does not offer an explanation. It is perhaps an irony that Articles 74(1) and 83(1) of the LOS Convention refer to the canon of sources of international law under the Statute of the ICJ, which inherently leaves the notion behind that all international agreements are on an equal level and not subject to any higher rules, except for *jus cogens*.[15] The law of maritime boundary delimitation entails a first step towards the establishment of such meaningful hierarchies in international law sources. The rule of equity demonstrates that it is no longer sufficient to distinguish merely two categories: of *jus cogens* (as fundamental minimal standards of world public order), and *jus dispositivum*. The multilateral framework of the LOS Convention occupies a new middle ground.

The analysis here reflects the finding that the LOS Convention inherently entails what may tentatively be called a constitutional structure, with prescriptive rules for subsequent negotiations among states. A similar structure can be found in the law of the WTO. Rules defining conditions and qualifications for free trade agreements, customs unions and regional integration both in GATT Article XXIV and GATS Article V prescribe conditions to be met by WTO members in shaping their bilateral or regional agreements.[16] Non-compliance with these rules does

---

[13] See Chapter 6(II)(A). [14] See Chapter 6(II)(D).
[15] See Godefridus J. H. van Hoof, *Rethinking the Sources of International Law* (Deventer: Kluwer, 1983), pp. 151–69.
[16] See Thomas Cottier and Matthias Oesch, *International Trade Regulation: The Law and Policy of the WTO, The European Union and Switzerland* (Bern: Stämpfli, 2005), p. 370–81, with further references; Thomas Cottier and Marina Foltea, 'Constitutional Functions of the WTO and Regional Trade Agreements' in Lorand Bartels, and Federico Ortino (eds.), *Regional Trade Agreements and the WTO Legal System* (Oxford University Press, 2006), pp. 43–76.

not annul such agreements, but gives rise to 'most favoured nation' claims, compensation or, eventually, the withdrawal of market access rights (concessions) and thus authorized sanctions. The constitutional structure effectively depends on efficient dispute settlement. Indeed, a system of compulsory legal third party settlement, as in the WTO, effectively improves the impact of law and legal thinking during the negotiating process. The risk of being challenged by a third party in dispute settlement arguably reinforces the rule of law in negotiations, despite the fact that a majority of existing free trade agreements are not fully compatible with the requirements of WTO law.

Like the WTO Agreement, the LOS Convention thus would greatly benefit from effective dispute settlement. It would assist in preventing unfair apportionment of marine space and resources by 'agreement' among states of unequal bargaining powers. Yet, this was not achieved at UNCLOS III. The failure to reach a system of compulsory dispute settlement in maritime boundaries and to allow parties to opt out of compulsory dispute settlement under Part XV Section 2 of the Convention[17] in what emerged as one of the most important areas of the law of the sea in the last century, withdrew an important incentive to foster the rule of law in the process of delimitation. The achievement of compulsory, albeit non-binding, conciliation is in itself a first step toward progress. But given the (widespread) lack of accepted *ex ante* jurisdiction for compulsory judicial dispute settlement, major incentives to emphasize the law through negotiations are still absent. The Commission on the Limits of the Continental Shelf (CLCS) was not given any obvious powers by the Convention to influence maritime boundary delimitation.[18] Considerations of policy, national interests and bargaining are likely to prevail in most cases, even under the mandatory rule of equity.

---

[17] Art. 298(a)(i) LOS Convention.

[18] See LOS Convention Annex II. The task of the Commission is limited to recommendations in defining the outer limits of the shelf in accordance with Art. 76(8) of the Convention. Art. 9 of the Annex reads: 'The actions of the Commission shall not prejudice matters relating to the delimitation of boundaries between States with opposite and adjacent coasts.' Rule 44 and Annex I to the Rules of Procedure of the Commission on the Limits of the Continental Shelf, adopted 1998 (CLCS/3/Rev.2), limits obligations of states to inform the Commission on disputes and to ensure, to the extent possible, that submissions on the outer limit do not prejudice matters relating to the delimitation between states; see Chris M. Carleton, 'Delimitation Issues' in P. J. Cook and C. M. Carleton (eds.), *Continental Shelf Limits: The Scientific and Legal Interface* (Oxford University Press, 2000), pp. 312, 314.

B. Law and policy in the negotiating process

The legal validity and mandatory nature of the rule of equity itself does not depend on compliance in negotiations. But whether or not the fundamental conceptual shift towards a constitutional framework with implementing agreements based on a fundamental rule will show practical significance largely depends on the practical and effective impact which mandatory rules exert in the arena of international negotiations. The role of the law in this arena, of course, cannot be assessed in general terms. Albeit it is conceivable that negotiations are approached in a thoroughly lawyerly manner, they are generally dominated and characterized to a much greater extent, as was noted in the introduction to this chapter, by political and economic interest, goodwill or distrust (the ambiance of negotiations) and a process of *do ut des, quid pro quo* and extra-legal trade-offs, on the basis of bargaining chips that the parties are able to mobilize.

This characterization equally applies to the business of long-distance maritime boundary delimitation, given the economic interests regularly at stake.[19] As was observed at the outset, legal arguments are not missing in negotiations. Governments closely monitor the developments in case law.[20] Its evolution can induce changes in an existing bargaining position.[21] But, in a negotiating context, parties only address the law to the extent that it serves their interests. It is utilized and referred to in order to foster strategies that are not primarily determined by legal analysis and considerations. As noted above, the great practical importance of equidistance in state practice is not likely to be much of an expression of *opinio juris*, nor of an application of Article 6 of the 1958

---

[19] See the various reports on the negotiating process of maritime boundary delimitation in Chapter 5.

[20] This fact is also illustrated by the interests of states in obtaining early access to materials and pleadings before the court pursuant to Art. 51(1) of the Statute, such as requested by Argentina, Canada, Malta, the Netherlands, the United States and Venezuela in the *Tunisia/Libya* case (*Continental Shelf (Tunisia v. Libyan Arab Jamahiriya*)), Judgment, ICJ Reports 1982, para. 14, or of Canada and the United Kingdom in the *Gulf of Maine* case (*Delimitation of the Marine Boundary in the Gulf of Maine Area (Canada v. United States*)), Judgments, ICJ Reports 1984, para. 11.

[21] For example, the 1977 Channel arbitration induced Canada to change its bargaining position in the *Gulf of Maine* negotiations with the United States. Relying on the Court's findings in the Southern Approaches (half-effect to Scilly Islands, see Chapters 4(II)(A)(1)(c) and 6(II)(B), Canada claimed an 'exceptionally' long peninsula of Cape Cod and the islands of Nantucket and Martha's Vineyard to be special circumstances, modifying a strict line of equidistance adhered to before, see *Gulf of Maine* case, ICJ Reports 1984, para. 71.

Shelf Convention.[22] The frequent use of this method is more likely to be due to the fact that it often happens to reflect middle-of-the road compromises that are politically acceptable to both parties and their interests. To refer to Oscar Schachter's three-storey house, bilateral negotiations over maritime boundary delimitations mainly take place on the first floor of 'subjectivities' (demands, purposes and expectations) expressing national policies.[23] This reflects traditional residual rules that leave freedom of contract entirely between the parties to a dispute.

Given the weak level of constitutionalization in the LOS Convention, states enjoy considerable leeway during negotiations. From this perspective, it may be argued that there is no point in further examining the question of whether the rule of equity and equitable standards and principles can be effectively used in negotiated settlement. On the other hand, the prohibition of unilateral settlement and the power to leave the table and seek arbitration or a court decision may not leave the judge-made law without effect in negotiations.

C. Equity and the methodology of negotiations

1. The role of equitable standards

Given the realities described, what normative role may the rule of equity and the concept of equitable standards and principles play in the process of negotiations? It will hardly be sufficient to invoke the mandatory character of equity in general terms, and to remind states of their obligation to seek agreement in accordance with the law and the principles set forth in general international law on maritime boundary delimitation. Not all of the principles, components and relevant circumstances developed in case law are of equal importance. Some may be more important than others and enjoy stronger attention than in judicial settlement, for example considerations concerning the location of resources or ecosystems. The very nature of negotiations is likely to require a different approach and methodology in the use of equitable principles.

The single most important mandatory message of the rule of equity is that, at the end of the day, the parties are obliged to achieve an overall fair

---

[22] Chapter 8(I).
[23] Oscar Schachter, 'Towards A Theory of International Obligations' in St. M. Schwebel (ed.), *The Effectiveness of International Decisions* (Leiden: Sijthoff, 1971), pp. 9, 27–30. Although Schachter does not use the term policy for his ground floor, it may well be used if restricted to national policy.

apportionment of the disputed marine spaces and resources. This is the essence of Articles 74(1) and 83(1) of the Law of the Sea Convention and of the case law analysed previously. In order to achieve such a result, the various equitable standards provide important and valuable guidelines and the broad framework for negotiations. This is particularly true for the geographic principles of the coast dominates the sea (CDS), equal division of marine space (EDS), non-cutting-off (NCP), non-encroachment (NEP) and reasonable and fair proportionality (RFP).[24] Due consideration given to the location of resources and, in respect to the EEZ, the criteria of regional economic viability, will provide further assistance.[25] Other criteria discussed in Chapter 10 are of less importance to the negotiating process. Claims to historic rights will often be controversial and require, as much as the criteria relating to the conduct of parties, an impartial third party decision. The very breadth of equitable principles confers both advantages and disadvantages. Paradoxically, the very vagueness of all these principles may improve probable compliance, because it leaves ample room for the bargaining process and does not bind parties *a priori* into a legal framework that is too narrow, as a strict rule of equidistance would. On the other hand, the inherent vagueness of these principles renders them completely unsuitable as starting points for negotiations. Unlike equidistance, they cannot by themselves provide a line of delimitation in the bargaining process. Identical or different criteria, as argued by the delegations, may set each other off. And additional factors, unknown so far in case law, may cause further complications. It is important to realize that equitable principles cannot assume similar methodological functions in the judicial and negotiating process.

2. The proper methodology of delimitation in negotiations

It is submitted that the different nature of the negotiating process and the judicial approach have not been sufficiently reflected in the extensive discussion of the law of maritime boundary delimitation. It is generally assumed that the law and its methodology of delimitation apply to negotiations and dispute settlement alike. Rules are shaped primarily with a view to being applied in negotiations and subsequently to judicial settlement. After all, the unity of law demands this. Yet, differences exist. Some indication of these differences can be found in the case law. Given the nature of the negotiating process, the Court was correct in stating, during the *North Sea* cases, that 'there is no legal limit to the considerations which states may take into account in making sure that they apply

---

[24] Chapter 10(II)(A). [25] Chapter10(III)(B)(2).

equitable procedures'.[26] The proposition was clearly framed with a view towards further negotiations. It is, however, contrary to the legal methodology applied in a court of law, which has to search for a contained number of relevant principles and factors in the process of law-making. This difference was indicated in the 1977 *Anglo-French Channel* arbitration, when the Court rejected the French reference to the aforementioned statement of the ICJ on the following grounds:

> But in those cases, the Parties had retained the actual delimitation of the boundary in their own hands for further negotiations in the light of the principles and rules to be stated by the International Court of Justice.[27]

Apart from these indications, however, the differences of methodology and approaches between negotiations and judicial settlement are hardly reflected. The *North Sea* cases reflect the traces of an eminently judicial methodology, which is hardly appropriate for application, *tel quel*, in further negotiations. This is particularly true in respect to the process of balancing different factors and interests. Balancing interests is an eminently judicial approach to a problem. It requires an independent third party, who is in a position not only to analyse, but also to weigh, conflicting values and factors. It requires impartiality. It is therefore difficult to see how states and their representatives can fruitfully engage in such an operation, which is more than trading and bargaining interests and equities.

Due consideration of these differences may further help in explaining much of the controversy between the champions of equitable principles and the combined rule of equidistance–special circumstances.[28] What is debated at the level of substantive rules is, in fact and upon close examination, actually a dispute about methodology. In substance, both avenues merged in the 1977 *Anglo-French Channel* arbitration and the Court correctly pointed out that: 'the different ways in which the requirements of "equitable principles" or the effects of "special circumstances" are put reflect differences of approach and terminology rather than of substance'.[29] It very much depends on whether the problem is looked at from a perspective of negotiations or of the judicial process. Commentators often failed to make this distinction. Many lawyers, almost by instinct, think of judicial proceedings whilst suggesting rules

---

[26] ICJ Reports 1969, p. 50, para. 93.
[27] *Arbitration between the United Kingdom of Great Britain and Northern Ireland and the French Republic on the Delimitation of the Continental Shelf* (Judgments of 30 June 1977 and 14 March 1978) para. 245, reprinted in (1979) 18 ILM 397.
[28] See Chapter 8.   [29] (1979) *Channel Arbitration*, n. 27, para. 148.

THE ROLE OF EQUITY IN NEGOTIATIONS 657

that may be equally applicable to negotiations. Diplomats, at the same time, may consider it necessary to work with the same methodology as courts, thus facing a lack of clear guidelines for negotiations.[30] The two fields need to be separated in terms of methodology.

The model of equitable standards expounded throughout this book is an inherently judicial approach; it is indispensable for the solution of complex and protracted cases, as we argued before in justifying the fundamental rule of equity.[31] The model of equidistance–special circumstances, on the other hand, primarily suits the negotiating process and offers an excellent starting point in most cases.[32] The great number of successfully concluded agreements under review formed on the basis of equidistance (40 per cent) and modified equidistance (20 per cent)[33] proves this method to be a valuable starting point, as many have pointed out since the term was first used by Lauterpacht in 1950: 'the delimitation can properly be effected by reference to equitable considerations, and any formula based on a system of median and lateral lines ought to be no more than the starting point of an equitable solution.'[34] There is a considerable chance that negotiations based upon equidistance can successfully accommodate the mutual interests of parties in a great number of cases. Difficulties may be overcome by balanced acknowledgement of special circumstances and modification of pure equidistance during the bargaining process. A similar approach may also be undertaken on the basis of any other technical method of delimitation, whether it be a perpendicular to the general coastline, prolongation of the general direction of the common land boundary, or a parallel of latitude or longitude, i.e. all the other starting points which led to successful results in some 40 per cent of all the agreements concluded in the period reviewed.

The essential point is that negotiations, unlike a judicial settlement, should start from a specific technical method and try, first of all, to reach agreement on that basis. Unlike before a court of law, the discussion of equitable principles and relevant circumstances primarily serves the purpose

---

[30] See Prescott, n. 1, p. 90 ('It is the lack of restriction on arguments which might be raised that accounts for the wide range of circumstances which might create complications for boundary negotiations').

[31] See Chapter 8.

[32] See also Prescott, n. 1, p. 95 ('In practical terms, the concept of equidistance will always be accorded a higher rank by a number of countries, and in many negotiations the nub of the disagreement will continue to be the use of an equidistant line versus the use of a boundary based on some other principles').

[33] See Appendix I and Chapter 5.

[34] Hersch Lauterpacht, 'Sovereignty over Submarine Areas' (1950) 27 *British Yearbook of International Law*, 569, note 37.

of negotiating and assessing proposed modifications to the line agreed upon as a starting point in the bargaining process in justifying and rationalizing departing claims and counterclaims, finally leading to compromise. It may well be that the principles expounded by case law can provide the basis of a settlement. Failure to achieve agreement indicates that the starting point chosen by the parties does not provide sufficient sophistication. It is at this stage that the case is likely to become protracted. Submission of the problem to full or partial third party procedures for partial or full settlement of the dispute opens the door to the more complex methodology of analysing and balancing factors and equities on the sole basis of equitable standards in order to achieve the line of delimitation. Because negotiations failed on the basis of equidistance (or any other technical method), the court or any other third party is not advised to rely upon that particular approach, but will instead construct a line based upon the results of the balancing process. This is not a contradiction to the methodology proposed for negotiations, but rather provides a complementary alternative, should negotiations fail because the standard methods fail.

Evidence of diplomatic negotiations is anecdotal. While it is in the nature of courts to justify each and every step in reasoning and thus acquire legitimacy and acceptance of results, the negotiating process remains without public record. It merely presents its results. It is therefore impossible to analyse and draw from previous experience and use this as a basis for recommendations. From what has previously been discussed throughout this book, the following elements can be suggested for the negotiating process:

1. Seek agreement on the relevant geographical area under discussion and the window of delimitation. Third party interests and potential rights need to be clarified. If necessary, inclusion and participation of third parties should be sought in order to bring about viable and acceptable results. The principle of *pactum tertiis nec prosunt nec nocent* applies, and there is no interest in reaching an agreement which may subsequently be challenged by a third party.
2. Explore whether a boundary should be established or whether there is a potential for a joint zone. Difficulties in finding a boundary may be overcome by focusing upon economic interests and resources. State practice shows that joint exploitation and co-operation is useful, not only if and where the specific location of resources is still unclear.[35]

---

[35] See Chapter 5(III). But see also Prescott, n. 1, p. 86, who clearly prefers delimitation to joint zones and considers them second best only in order to avoid unfriendly relations.

It is also a promising concept with regard to environmental management of overlapping areas and complex ecological systems. Of course, this philosophy or policy requires good neighbourly relations: it cannot work among hostile states where boundaries remain the sole and primary tool of international relations based upon mere co-existence.
3. Seek agreement on the methodology that should be used to provide a starting line, in particular equidistance, median, perpendiculars, prolongation of land boundaries *et al.* Such agreement also needs to define relevant base points and base lines.
4. Negotiating proposals to deviate from the starting line should be based upon the equitable principles and relevant circumstances discussed in Chapter 10, the impact of which should be visualized. The relevance of these standards should be based on case law, but is not necessarily limited to it. Negotiations should focus on discussing competing factors and interests.
5. Assess domestic needs and margins and define bottom lines that need to be kept in order to obtain domestic support and acceptance of a future agreement.
6. Negotiations need to focus on learning about the other party's political and economic needs. Accommodation should be sought by possibly revising starting proposals in the light of accommodating such needs. Linkages to other areas of interest may be made and trade-offs achieved within and without the delimitation.

In this process, the impact of power will inevitably be felt. Taking the law into account avoids losing sight of the boundaries of power play and discourages the other party from leaving the table, opting for judicial settlement in order to protect its own rights and interests. Results achieved need political justification with a view to obtaining support and acceptance by relevant constituencies. The law may be supportive, but not necessarily the main line of reasoning. As results of allocation of marine spaces (either by joint operation or through drawing a boundary) are defined by technical methods, the legal justification of how these definitions are achieved is not of primary importance.

Throughout negotiations, parties reserve their rights in light of potential dispute settlement, should negotiations fail. Arguments and concessions made will not necessarily be the same as those made before a court of law in the case of failed negotiations.

D. Conclusion

Regardless of which method of delimitation the parties apply, the rule of equity obliges them to achieve an overall fair apportionment of marine space and resources. This is the only message of the law of a truly mandatory nature. Equitable standards provide an important framework and guidelines for argumentation and negotiations to this effect. Due to the realities and particularities of the international negotiating process, it is essential to realize that a different methodology from judicial settlement is required. The substantive law is based upon equity and equitable standards. It is sufficiently nuanced to cope with complex cases. During negotiations, however, equitable standards can hardly provide and define a boundary line in practical terms. Unlike the situation that occurs in judicial analysis, it is recommended that the starting point should be a preliminarily agreed upon, provisional and negotiable line of delimitation. Such a line can often be based upon equidistance, but any method or ad hoc construction may be used. Parties should then, guided by equitable principles and recognized relevant circumstances, seek the achievement of mutual modification through a bargaining process. Failure to make progress on such a basis indicates that the complexity of the case may best be solved by third party legal settlement, now based upon the methodology of equitable standards. As a matter of substantive law, the rule of equity cannot provide more than a broad and flexible framework for negotiations. To some extent, the second and procedural mainstay of the rule of equity, the procedural obligation to negotiate, mitigates such inherent deficiencies. What cannot be compensated for in terms of normativity will be compensated for by procedural requirements.

III. The equitable obligation to negotiate

A. A new dimension of law

For a long time, the field of international negotiations has been almost exclusively the domain of diplomacy and the academic discipline of international relations. Although international lawyers are often involved in the negotiating process, the discipline of international law, it seems, was not primarily interested in exploring the law and process of negotiations. Instead – shaped by the traditions of national law (both civil and common law) and jurisprudence – the main focus has been, and still is, on substance, doctrine and case law. The practice of courts attracts more interest from international lawyers than the process of how agreements are reached and treaties concluded. The law of treaties contains an important body of law dealing with formal and substantive issues of treaty making. The law of international organizations mainly deals with procedures and with decision-making. However, a similar code relating to the very process of negotiations, conduct and procedures during this process does not exist beyond the pertinent rules of the Vienna Convention on the Law of Treaties (VCLT). The matter is mainly left to the extra-legal disciplines of diplomacy, convention, custom and legal craftsmanship, and to political science and psychology.[36] We still lack a proper and comprehensive interdisciplinary doctrine of international negotiations and representation.[37] We are still at the beginning of what may emerge as an important chapter in the process of the constitutionalization of international law. Yet again, it is the law of the sea that has induced new interest into this field. The multilateral complexity of UNCLOS III and the departure from rather formal conference diplomacy on the basis of well-prepared ILC drafts in the UN, the adoption of package deal approaches, and consensus, has brought the importance of the negotiating process to the discipline of international law.[38] Indeed,

---

[36] E.g. Roger Fisher, William Ury and Bruce Patton, *Getting to Yes: Negotiating an Agreement without Giving In*, (New York: Pinguin, 3rd edn., 2011); William Zartman and Maureen R. Bergman, *The Practical Negotiator* (New Haven CT: Yale University Press, 1982), I. William Zartman, *Negotiation and Conflict Management: Essays on Theory and Practice* (Milton Park: Routledge, 2008); Bying-il Choi and Brendam M. Howe, *International Negotiations: Theory and Practice* (Seoul: Ewha Womens University Press, 2007).

[37] See generally Wolfgang Graf Vitzthum, 'Verfahrensgerechtigkeit im Völkerrecht. Zu den Erfolgsbedingungen internationaler Rechtsschöpfungskonferenzen' in Ingo von Münch (ed.), *Staatsrecht – Völkerrecht – Europarecht, Festschrift für Hans-Jürgen Schlochauer* (Berlin, New York: de Gruyter, 1981), pp. 738, 751, note 33 (still unclear as to whether conference diplomacy is part of international law). Earlier writings on the subject include Wilfried Jenks, 'Craftsmanship in International Law' (1956) 50 *American Journal of International Law*, 32, 54; Manley Hudson, 'The Prospects of International Law in the Twentieth Century' (1925) 10 *Cornell Law Quarterly*, 349–440; Philip C. Jessup, 'Parliamentary Diplomacy' (1958) *Recueil des Cours*, 181. A more systematic attention to negotiation research started only twenty or so years ago, see Oscar Schachter et al., *Towards Wider Acceptance of UN Treaties*, UNITAR Study (New York: Arno Press, 1971); ILC, 'Review of the Multilateral Treaty-Making Process', A/CN4/325 (23 July 1979).

[38] See Robert Jennings, 'Law-Making and Package Deal' in A. Strati, M. G. and N. Skourtos (eds.), *Mélanges offertes à Paul Reuter* (Paris: Editions A. Pedone, 1981), p. 347; Guy de Lacharrière, 'La Réforme du droit de la mer et le rôle de la conférence des Nations Unis' (1980) 84 *Revue Générale de Droit International Public*, 216–52; Bernhard Zuleta, 'The Law of the Sea after Montego Bay' (1983) 20 *San Diego Law Review*, 475, 478–80 (package deal), M. C. W. Pinto, 'Modern Conference Techniques: Insights from Social Psychology'

the very provisions of the LOS Convention that relate to long-distance maritime boundary delimitation, amongst many others, cannot be addressed on the basis of substance alone. They entail important procedural issues, as a settlement must be reached by agreement in the first place.

The obligation to bring about maritime boundaries in Articles 74(1) and 83(1) LOS Convention by agreement based on international law implies a proper obligation to negotiate. It goes beyond a mere obligation to consult. What does this obligation amount to? Firstly, the rule implies the fundamental principle that maritime boundaries must not be determined unilaterally. Unilateral proclamations are therefore not valid. Secondly, the concerned parties are obliged to interact. What are the legal requirements informing this obligation? When it is complied with, when is an effort to negotiate insufficient? The Convention does not address these questions, except for its explicit reference to the principle of good faith in Article 300, which is, of course, a mainstay of all human interaction and is thus a prime pillar of the law of negotiations.

The obligation to negotiate maritime boundaries in the treaty was largely informed by state practice. The substantial body of successfully concluded delimitation agreements amounts to some 75 per cent of delimitations.[39] Yet, the duty was mainly induced and informed by the case law and the procedural requirements expounded by the ICJ. Again, it is the law of the sea relating to fisheries and maritime boundaries which took the lead in the shaping and forming of procedural requirements and pairings of substance, process and structure, which is of importance way beyond this province of the law. As a foundation, equity plays an important part in defining procedural obligations in the process of delimitation. An analysis of the case law and precedents may well assist in defining procedural obligations under the LOS Convention and in general international law. It is interesting to observe that the procedural dimension of equity and equitable standards has

---

in R. St. J. McDonald and D. M. Johnston (eds.), *The Structure and Process of International Law* (The Hague, Boston MA: Martinus Nijhoff, 1983), pp. 305, 309 ('While the ad hoc and sporadic nature of the international legislative process remains, there seems little doubt that the community is moving, albeit hesitant and faltering steps, towards a more integrated and systemic approach to the making of international law through multilateral treaties negotiated at conferences convened under the auspices of the United Nations'); see also Bruno Simma, 'Consent: Strains in the Treaty System', see above McDonald and Johnston, *The Structure and Process of International Law*, pp. 485.

[39] See Chapter 5.

attracted much less attention than its aspects of substantive law and judicial methodology.

B. The duty to negotiate maritime boundary delimitations

1. The scope of obligation

In expounding the fundamental principles of equity and equitable principles of maritime boundary delimitation, the 1969 *Continental Shelf* Court, the very first one to pronounce on a set of equitable principles, established the duty to negotiate and to seek an agreement. The Court stated:

> the parties are under an obligation to enter into negotiations with a view to arriving at an agreement, and not merely to go through a formal process of negotiation as a sort of prior condition for the automatic application of a certain method of delimitation in the absence of agreement; they are under an obligation so to conduct themselves that the negotiations are meaningful, which will not be the case when either of them insists upon its own position without contemplating any modification of it.[40]

This duty was further elaborated upon within the fundamental rule of delimitation by the 1984 *Gulf of Maine* ruling. It linked the obligation to the principle of good faith. The Chamber of the ICJ held:

> No maritime delimitation between States with opposite or adjacent coasts may be effected unilaterally by one of those States. Such delimitation must be sought and effected by means of an agreement, following negotiations conducted in good faith and with the genuine intention of achieving a positive result. Where, however, such agreement cannot be achieved, delimitation should be effected by recourse to a third party possessing the necessary competence.[41]

The Court in the 2002 *Cameroon v. Nigeria* case confirmed the duty to negotiate in good faith in a case where the LOS Convention formed the applicable law. Having confirmed that negotiations between the parties concerning maritime delimitation in the area were conducted as far back as the 1970s, the Court stated:

---

[40] ICJ Reports 1969, p. 47, para. 85(a). In the operational part of the judgment, the duty was not explicitly restated but taken for granted in the light of Art. 1(2) of the special agreement which in itself obliged the parties to undertake further negotiations on the basis of the judgment, ICJ Reports 1969, pp. 10 and 53, para. 101(D).

[41] ICJ Reports 1984, p. 57, para. 112(1).

These negotiations did not lead to an agreement. However, Articles 74 and 83 of the United Nations Law of the Sea Convention do not require that delimitation negotiations should be successful; like all similar obligations to negotiate in international law, the negotiations have to be conducted in good faith.[42]

The obligation to negotiate in good faith thus is an implied part of the rule that maritime boundaries cannot be defined unilaterally in law. Short of acquiescence by the states affected, such delimitation is not valid in law. Action based on unilateral determination, such as exploration and exploitation of resources, seizure of ships or imposing fines, is not lawful. Instead, determination is subject to negotiations in good faith and, failing such negotiations, to third party settlement.

The obligation to negotiate not only imposes formal negotiations, but also obliges a party to adopt and work in good faith on the basis of constructive and flexible attitudes. President Bustamante y Rivero considered that the principles set forth in paragraphs 85(a) and (b) of the *North Sea* ruling reflect, inter alia, 'the need to introduce into the negotiations on the continental shelf, complex in themselves, and frequently full of unforeseen factors, that factor of good faith and flexibility which equity constitutes and which reconciles the needs of peaceful neighbourly relations with the rigidity of the law'.[43] In the context of maritime boundary delimitation, this implies a willingness to work in a creative manner and spirit towards a mutually acceptable compromise solution, in the absence of any aspiration of maximizing gains in an all-winning and all-losing outcome by insistence on a particular method of delimitation. The Dutch and Danish negotiating positions, insisting on equidistance in the *North Sea* negotiations, were explicitly held not to comply with the obligation to negotiate in a sufficiently flexible manner with a view to achieving a settlement.[44]

The duty to negotiate is an obligation to seek agreement. It is an *obligatio de negotiando*, and not an *obligatio de contrahendo*. It does not imply, as sometimes feared,[45] an obligation to reach agreement at any cost. Long before the era of maritime boundary delimitation, this was established by the PCIJ in its Advisory Opinion in the case of *Railway*

---

[42] *Land and Maritime Boundary between Cameroon and Nigeria (Cameroon v. Nigeria: Equatorial Guinea intervening)*, Judgment, ICJ Reports 2002, p. 303, para. 244.
[43] ICJ Reports 1969, separate opinion, p. 58. [44] ICJ Reports 1969, p. 48, para. 87.
[45] See ICJ Reports 1969, separate opinion Ammoun, p. 147, dissenting opinion Lachs, p. 220 (addressing the issue in the context of Art. 6 of the 1958 Shelf Convention); Judge Dillard conceived the duty to negotiate as an obligation to respond to a request for negotiations, rather than as a duty to initiate negotiations, sooner or later, *Fisheries Jurisdiction* case, ICJ Reports 1974, p. 67 (separate opinion).

Traffic between Lithuania and Poland, which said that an obligation to negotiate did not imply an obligation to reach agreement.[46] In the present context, Judge Gros' dissenting opinion may be considered the *locus classicus* on this point:

> The limits of the obligation [to negotiate] is simple: to negotiate in a reasonable manner and in good faith in order to achieve a result acceptable to both Parties, but without being obliged to reach agreement at any price.[47]

Any other, more far-reaching content of the obligation to negotiate (*obligatio de negotiando*) in international law would not be compatible with the basic precepts of the law and legal system, and particularly the overall system of international dispute resolution under Article 33 of the UN Charter and the principles of the Friendly Relations Declaration of the United Nations General Assembly.[48] These instruments oblige parties to take recourse to *peaceful* means of dispute settlement while leaving the choice of means to states. An obligation to reach agreement *à tout prix* would render obsolete all recourse to forms of third party settlement which, of course, are made available primarily for the very reason of remedying failed negotiations.[49]

2. The impact of good faith and legitimate expectations

The principle of conduct in good faith is perhaps the sole, most important and common principle in all legal systems and legal orders. Respect for, and legal protection of, legitimate expectations induced by human conduct provide the very foundations, upon which the law is built. The same is true in international law. The 1970 Friendly Relations Declaration captures

---

[46] [1935] PCIJ, Series A/B No. 42, p. 31, referred to in ICJ Reports 1969, p. 48, para. 87. But see also the interpretation of the ICJ of Art. 80(2) of the UN Charter in the International Status of South-West Africa Advisory Opinion, where the Court denied 'an obligation to negotiate without any obligation to conclude an agreement' – a view hardly sustainable in the light of contemporary views, ICJ Reports 1950, pp. 128, 140.

[47] ICJ Reports 1982, pp. 144–5, para. 3 (dissenting opinion).

[48] Declaration on Principles of International Law Concerning Friendly Relations and Co-operation among States in Accordance with the Charter of the United Nations, GA Res. 2665, 25 GOAR, Supp. 28, UN Doc. A/8028 at 121 (adopted without a vote, 24 October 1970).

[49] Ibid., in particular the second principle: 'The Parties to a dispute have the duty, in the event of failure to reach a solution by any one of the above peaceful means [inter alia: negotiations, inquiry, mediation, conciliation, arbitration, judicial settlement] to continue to seek a settlement of the dispute by peaceful means agreed upon by them.' See also Art. 280 LOS Convention (right of states to agree to settle disputes 'by any peaceful means of their own choice').

the essence of it by stating: 'Every State has the duty to fulfil in good faith its obligations under the generally recognised principles and rules of international law.'[50] There is thus a requirement that negotiations be conducted on the basis of good faith. This is equally true in the business of maritime boundary delimitation. The *Gulf of Maine* Chamber explicitly expressed this fundamental principle. In a broad and generic sense, it first of all stands for the proposition and obligation to conduct open-minded and honest bargaining and negotiations without a hidden agenda and without *arrières pensées*. This attitude is essential to building a climate of mutual trust and confidence based upon which meaningful negotiations can be conducted.

The theory of negotiations emphasizes the importance of these qualities.[51] It is submitted that good faith also implies transparent negotiations. Relevant facts and circumstances need to be put on the table. Negotiations in good faith first of all require an opportunity to fully understand the interests and problems of the negotiating partner. Based upon that understanding, and with all relevant facts having been made available, a process of mutually approaching a common denominator then becomes a possibility. If all pertinent information is not provided, this may lead to *culpa in contrahendo*, and thus to the nullification of the agreement that was reached based on incomplete or misleading information.

3. The prohibition of acts frustrating negotiations

Besides these general precepts of good faith negotiations, international law has developed some more specific connotations in the context of the negotiating process. It may be recalled that the ILC draft articles on the law of treaties of 1966 proposed an obligation 'to refrain from acts tending to frustrate the object of the treaty', once agreement to negotiate was achieved.[52] While the majority of delegations rejected the proposals as being too far-reaching and limiting explicit obligations to avoid

---

[50] Principle 7, para 2, Declaration on Principles of International Law concerning Friendly Relations and Co-operation among States in accordance with the Charter of the United Nations, GA Res. 2625, 25 GAOR, Supp. 28, UN Doc. A/8028, at 121 1970).

[51] See e.g. Raymond Saner, *The Expert Negotiator* (Leiden: Martinus Nijhoff, 4th edn., 2012).

[52] Art. 15 ILC draft read as follows: 'A State is obliged to refrain from acts tending to frustrate the object of a proposed treaty when: (a) It has agreed to enter into negotiations for the conclusion of the treaty, while these negotiations are in progress', 'Draft articles on the law of treaties and commentary' (1966) 2 *Yearbook of International Law*, p. 202, UN Doc. A./CN3/SER.A/1966/Add.1.

frustration upon the signature of the agreement,[53] the *travaux préparatoires* nevertheless show strong support for good faith obligations during the negotiating process.[54] Sir Humprey Waldock coined the term of 'a minimum of fair dealing'.[55] The scope of such a standard, of course, remains unclear, and constitutes a grey area. The matter is not susceptible to strict rule-making. A careful balance has to be achieved between the needs of flexibility, opportunities and the protection of legitimate expectations flowing from the conduct of a party. In the light of the 1968/9 Conference materials, protection may not extend to acts that merely may, or tend to, frustrate the objective of negotiations. But it is submitted that it possibly includes acts that clearly frustrate the objective and run counter to the goals of the negotiations at stake and the treaty in the making. Waldock (as expert consultant to the Conference) illustrated the obligation of minimum fair dealing with an example of particular interest in this context: if a coastal state, during the process of negotiations on the delimitation of territorial waters, following the discovery of natural resources, accelerates the exhaustion of such resources, the obligation of minimum fair dealing is violated. The statement remained unchallenged.[56]

Whilst this is quite a clear example, an issue of much greater practical importance is whether a similar conclusion is justified in the case of mere exploration or continued exploitation of non-living resources during negotiations, despite the negotiating partner's protests.

Since the entry into force of the LOS Convention, the Tribunal in *Guyana v. Suriname* had the opportunity to pronounce on the issue. The arbitration proceedings were initiated by Guyana under Part XV, Section 2 of the LOS Convention in February 2004, following unsuccessful negotiation triggered by the so-called CGX incident. The CGX incident occurred in June 2000. An oil exploration fleet on behalf of the

---

[53] Art. 18(a) Vienna Convention on the Law of Treaties (1969), entered into force 27 January 1980. It was doubtful whether this provision codifies prior customary law or was a new provision, and, more importantly, whether it is opposable to non-members to the Convention. There is authority in support of customary law, but a proper perception of Art. 18 considers it to be an expression and concretization of good faith, see Jörg Paul Müller, *Vertrauensschutz im Völkerrecht, Beiträge zum ausländischen öffentlichen Recht und Völkerrecht* (Cologne, Berlin, Bonn: Heymann, 1971), pp. 162-4; Rudolf Bernhardt, 'Völkerrechtliche Bindungen in den Vorstadien des Vertragsschlusses' (1958) 18 *Zeitschrift für ausländisches öffentliches Recht und Völkerrecht*, 652, 654.

[54] See in particular statements by delegations refuting draft Art. 15, UN Conference on the Law of Treaties, 1 *Official Records* 97, 99, 103-6 (UK, Guinea, Uruguay, Cyprus, Chile). For an analysis see Müller, n. 53, p. 160.

[55] United Nations Conference on the Law of Treaties, 1 *Offical Records* 104.

[56] 1 *Official Records* 194, Müller, n. 53, p. 160.

Canadian company, CGX Resources Inc. and operating under a Guyanese concession was ordered by the Surinamese navy to leave the disputed maritime area and was escorted away by two Surinamese patrol boats.[57] In this respect the Tribunal considered the parties' obligations under LOS Convention Articles 74(3) and 83(3) with respect to negotiations appending delimitation of the EEZ and the continental shelf. Articles 83(3) and 74(3) LOS Convention read as follows:

> Pending agreement as provided for in paragraph 1, the States concerned, in a spirit of understanding and co-operation, shall make every effort to enter into provisional arrangements of a practical nature, and, during this transitional period, not to jeopardise or hamper the reaching of the final agreement. Such arrangements shall be without prejudice to the final delimitation.

Both parties claimed that the other had breached its obligations under LOS Convention Articles 74(3) and 83(3) to make 'every effort to enter into provisional arrangements of a practical nature', pending a final delimitation. Guyana also claimed that Suriname jeopardized or hampered the reaching of a final agreement by its conduct in the CGX incident. Suriname made the same claim in respect of Guyana's authorization of its concessionary CGX to undertake exploratory drilling in the disputed area.[58]

The Tribunal held that the first obligation contained in Articles 74(3) and 83(3) LOS Convention is designed to promote interim regimes and practical measures that could pave the way for provisional utilization of disputed areas pending delimitation. It added that this obligation imposes on the parties 'a duty to negotiate in good faith'.[59] The Tribunal held that this obligation was violated by Suriname with its conduct in the CGX incident.[60] Suriname should have actively attempted to engage Guyana in a dialogue, but instead resorted to self-help in threatening the CGX oil-rig.[61] Guyana had also violated that obligation by not seeking to engage Suriname in discussions concerning the drilling at an earlier stage, 'in a spirit of cooperation'.[62]

---

[57] *Arbitral Tribunal Constituted Pursuant to Article 287, and in Accordance with Annex VII, of the United Nations Convention on the Law of the Sea in the Matter of an Arbitration between Guyana and Suriname*, Award of 17 September 2007 (*Guyana v. Suriname* Award) www.pca-cpa.org/showfile.asp?fil_id=664 (last accessed 18 Feburary 2012), paras. 150–1.
[58] Ibid., para. 453.   [59] Ibid., para. 460.
[60] Ibid., para. 474, referring to Suriname's conduct after 8 August 1998 (the date of entry into force of the LOS Convention between the parties).
[61] Ibid., para. 476.   [62] Ibid., para. 477.

With regard to the second obligation of making every effort not to hamper or jeopardize the achievement of a final agreement, the Tribunal held that: '[a] distinction [has] to be made between activities of the kind that lead to a permanent physical change, such as exploitation of oil and gas reserves, and those that do not, such as seismic exploration.'[63] The Tribunal noted that the distinction thus adopted is consistent with the jurisprudence of international courts and tribunals on interim measures – referring to the ICJ's decision in the *Aegean Sea* case between Greece and Turkey, which distinguished between activities of a transitory character and activities that risk irreparable prejudice to the position of the other party.[64] According to the Tribunal, the exploratory drilling in the disputed area as licensed by Guyana fell into the class of permanent physical damage and thus violated the obligation.[65] In Suriname's case, the Tribunal noted that the use of force was not a substitute for the pursuit of peaceful means of dispute settlement and 'if bilateral negotiations failed to resolve the issue, a remedy is set out in the options for peaceful settlement envisaged by Part XV and Annex VII of the Convention'.[66] In this respect, the Tribunal held that Suriname's threat of the use of force in a disputed area threatened international peace and security and jeopardized the reaching of a final delimitation agreement.[67] The Tribunal found that both Guyana and Suriname violated their obligations under Articles 74(3) and 83(3) of the Convention to make every effort to enter into provisional arrangements of a practical nature, and to make every effort not to jeopardize or hamper the reaching of a final delimitation agreement.[68]

Prior to the entry into force of the LOS Convention, the situation was more complicated. For example, did unilateral explorations by Turkey in disputed areas, following formal negotiations in 1976, amount to a violation of minimum fair dealing?[69] A similar question may be raised with regard to Canadian authorizations of explorations in the Georges Bank and the refusal to adopt a moratorium after an agreement to negotiate with

---

[63] Ibid., para. 467.   [64] Ibid., para. 468.   [65] Ibid., para. 477.   [66] Ibid., para. 482.
[67] Ibid., para. 484. See generally in this context Nikolas Stürchler, *The Threat of Use of Force in International Law*, (Cambridge University Press, 2007).
[68] *Guyana v. Suriname* Award, n. 57, para. 486.
[69] For the facts see *Aegean Continental Shelf Case (Greece v. Turkey)*, Judgment of 19 December 1978, ICJ Reports 1978, pp. 3, 9 paras. 19–22. Unfortunately, this issue was neither addressed in the case nor in the order relating to the Greek request for interim measures, see *Aegean Continental Shelf Case (Greece v. Turkey)*, Request for the Indication of Interim Measures for Protection, 1976 ICJ Rep 3. For discussion of the case see section III(D)(3) below.

the United States had been reached.[70] A comparable case arose in 1983 between Sweden and Denmark with respect to Danish explorations in the Kattegatt.[71] It is important to note that in all three cases, exploration pending negotiations and agreement considerably aggravated the dispute. It triggered the Greek application to the ICJ and the Security Council in 1976.[72] The Chamber of the ICJ considered Canadian conduct one of the starting points of the *Gulf of Maine* case.[73] In the Kattegatt, the sea only calmed due to the fact that the exploration did not find any commercially exploitable resources in the disputed zone.[74]

It is doubtful whether conduct in these cases amounted to a violation of minimal fair dealing in negotiations, as envisaged by Article 15(a) of the ILC draft on the law of treaties. Subsequent developments, however, indicate that the idea of this provision subsequently developed beyond a mere minimal standard. The 1970 Friendly Relations Declaration, adopted by consensus without a vote, expresses a duty to the effect that 'States parties to an international dispute, as well as other States, shall refrain from any action which may aggravate the situation so as to endanger the maintenance of international peace and security'.[75] Whenever conduct may escalate a major crisis of this magnitude (such as in relations between Turkey and Greece), a standard that is higher than a minimum requirement applies. More specifically, UNCLOS III adopted special obligations in the context of maritime boundary delimitation on which a Tribunal ruled in the above-mentioned *Guyana* v. *Suriname* Award.[76] Articles 83(3) and 74 (3) LOS Convention require parties to seek interim arrangements pending negotiations which, at the same time, do not prejudice final outcomes:

> Pending agreement as provided for in paragraph 1, the States concerned, in a spirit of understanding and co-operation, shall make every effort to enter into provisional arrangements of a practical nature, and, during this

---

[70] For the facts see ICJ Reports 1984 paras. 64–7, Chapter 6(II)(E). Again, the issue was not addressed. Arguments of estoppel and acquiescence relating to the alleged acceptance in negotiations of equidistance, however, were refused, ICJ Reports 1984, paras. 126–49.
[71] See Lagoni, n. 10, 363–4.   [72] Above n. 69, para 22.
[73] ICJ Reports 1984, para. 64 ('The Chamber considers that it was at this stage – i.e. after the American diplomatic note of 5 November 1969 refusing to acquiesce in any authorization given by Canada to explore or exploit the natural resources of Georges Bank, and after Canada's reply of 1 December 1969, refusing inter alia to agree to any kind of moratorium – that the existence of the dispute became clearly established.').
[74] Lagoni, n. 10, 364.   [75] Above n. 48.
[76] *Guyana* v. *Suriname* Award, n. 57, paras. 453–86.

transitional period, not to jeopardise or hamper the reaching of the final agreement. Such arrangements shall be without prejudice to the final delimitation.

The obligation is based upon an initial proposal submitted by India, Iraq and Morocco.[77] A closed group convened by the Chairman, including the former Soviet Union, further revised the text.[78] Informal negotiations brought about the formula that states 'shall make every effort'. At the outset, a separate sentence stated that states '[a]ccordingly ... shall refrain from activities or measures which may aggravate the situation and thus hamper in any way the reaching of the final arrangement'.[79] For reasons unknown, the two sentences were eventually merged with the effect of extending the soft formula ('shall make every effort') to the entire provisions of Articles 74(3) and 83(3) of the Convention. The term 'make any effort' is fully compatible with the principles relating to the obligation to negotiate which does not entail an obligation to reach agreement. It expresses an obligation to negotiate interim arrangements in a spirit of understanding and co-operation and reflects the case law developed by the courts. However, provisional arrangements can only be sought if parties refrain from unilateral action in disputed areas. Neither successful provisional arrangements nor final solutions can possibly be reached without an obligation to refrain from unilateral exploration and exploitation. In light of the Friendly Relations Declaration and the purpose and context of the provision, duties to refrain from actions which may hamper or jeopardize an equitable, final solution therefore must be considered mandatory and of strict law in their very nature. Lagoni concluded that these obligations operate as soon as claims overlap.[80] A reading that renders these obligations operational only upon signing an interim agreement (in accordance with Article 18 VCLT) cannot fulfil essential peacekeeping functions. The materials, as far as they are available, seem to support such a view, albeit that they do not extend to the idea of a moratorium.[81] The aggravations witnessed in state practice following unilateral exploitation and exploration of resources

---

[77] Conf. Doc. NG7/32 (5 April 1979), quoted from Lagoni, n. 10, 353. See also report of the Chairman on the work of the Negotiating Group 7, NG7/39 (20 April 1979) reprinted in Platzoeder, n. 6, vol. II, pp. 681–2.
[78] Suggested Compromise Formula for Articles 74(3) and 83(3), prepared by a private group convened by the chairman of NG 7, CONF.Doc. NG7/39 (17 April 1979).
[79] Report of the Chairman, Platzoeder, n. 6, vol. II, p. 683.   [80] Lagoni, see n. 10, 364.
[81] With a view to improving and clarifying the provision on Arts. 83(3) and 74(3) ICNT on interim arrangements, the Chairman of NG 7 indicated plans to amend the provisions which would exclude a moratorium, but prevent measures only which aggravate the

conclusively demonstrate the need for early legal protection with a view to support successful dispute resolution in due course.

This conclusion is equally supported by an analogous principle developed in case law relating to a pending legal dispute. The PCIJ held in 1939 that 'Parties to a judicial settlement must abstain from any measure capable of exercising a prejudicial effect in regard to the execution of the decision to be given, and in general, not to allow any steps of any kind to be taken which aggravate or extend the dispute'.[82] The more the process of diplomatic negotiations is part of a legally structured process, such established principles of damage prevention in judicial settlement become equally relevant in the context of negotiations. Even more so than legal and adversarial dispute resolution, negotiations depend on a climate of mutual trust and good faith. Obligations to refrain from frustrating actions are *a fortiori* imperative.

C. Foundations of the duty to negotiate

1. Issues

Exploration of obligations to negotiate raises the question of the legal foundations of such obligations. They may rely upon different and multiple sources, ranging from specific provisions to the Charter of the UN, customary law, good faith and equity. The following sections describe different sources and conclude that the obligation to negotiate maritime boundary delimitation and the corollary of banning unilateral determinations was primarily based upon equity. Even before adoption of the rule in the LOS Convention, it was established by the Court, and there is judge-made law.

2. Specific foundations

None of the cases prior to the *North Sea Continental* shelf ruling that imposed a duty to negotiate relied upon a general obligation to negotiate

---

dispute, Statement by the Chairman, made at the 28th Mtg. of NG 7 prepared for the last series of negotiations of the Group, NG7/27 (26 March 1979) reprinted in Platzoeder, n. 6, vol. II, pp. 645, 647. A compromise proposal took into account criticism by states which opposed a moratorium and the compromise solution was finally restricted to an obligation to 'refrain from aggravating the situation or hampering in any way the reaching of the final agreement', see Report of the Chairman, Platzoeder, n. 6, vol. II, p. 683. The obligation, for reasons unknown, was not included and is limited to best efforts in the wording of the text.

[82] *Electricity Company of Sofia and Bulgaria* case [1939] PCIJ, Series A/B, No. 778, p. 199. But see also discussion of the *Aegean Continental Shelf* case at section III(D)(3) below.

in international law. This is sometimes not sufficiently considered when reference is being made to case law.[83] These cases all show more specific sources. The obligation in *Railway Traffic* relied upon an accepted recommendation of the Executive Council of the League of Nations.[84] Interestingly, the Court spoke of an obligation despite the non-binding nature of this recommendation. In *Société Commercial de Belgique*, the Court denied a general obligation to renegotiate debts:[85] 'it is certain that the Court is not entitled to oblige the Belgian Government ... to enter into negotiations with the Greek Government with a view to a friendly arrangement regarding the execution of the arbitral awards which that government recognises to be binding.'[86] Instead, it relied upon a unilateral declaration by the Belgian Government:

> This declaration, made after the Greek Government had presented its final submissions, is in a general way in line with the Greek submissions. It enables the Court to declare that the two Governments are, in principle, agreed in contemplating the possibility of negotiations with a view to a friendly settlement, in which regard would be had, amongst other things, to Greece's capacity to pay. Such a settlement is highly desirable.[87]

Similarly, the obligation of Peru and Chile to negotiate a framework for a plebiscite in the *Tacua–Arica* arbitration[88] relied upon Article 3 of the 1883 Andean Pact Treaty and was therefore based upon an agreement, as is generally the case. Other cases demonstrate by negative implication that no general obligation to negotiate existed. The *Free Zone* case[89] merely invited the parties to undertake negotiations (which finally failed). The matter was later settled by arbitration. The *International Status of South-West Africa* Advisory Opinion[90] held that the provision of the international Trusteeship System – under Chapter XII of the UN Charter – did not create a mandatory obligation for states to enter into negotiations for Trusteeship agreements:

> it was expected that the mandatory States would follow the normal course indicated by the Charter, namely, conclude Trusteeship Agreements. The Court is, however, unable to deduce from these general considerations

---

[83] See Rainer Lagoni, 'Oil and Gas Deposits across National Frontiers' (1979) 73 *American Journal of International Law*, 215, 235; ibid., n. 10 at 355.
[84] [1935] PCIJ, Series A/B No. 42, p. 108.   [85] [1939] PCIJ, Series A/B No. 78, p. 160.
[86] Ibid., p. 177.   [87] Ibid., p. 178.
[88] 'Tacua–Arica Arbitration' (1925) 19 *American Journal of International Law*, 393.
[89] *Free Zones of Upper Savoy and the District of Gex* [1929] PCIJ, Series A No. 22.
[90] Advisory Opinion of 11 July 1950, ICJ Reports 1950, p. 128.

any legal obligation mandatory for States to conclude or to negotiate such agreements. It is not for the Court to pronounce on the political or moral duties which these considerations may involve.[91]

The UN Charter explicitly requires that 'the terms of trusteeship for each territory ... shall be agreed upon by States directly concerned' (Article 79). The Court rejected a duty to negotiate with a view to reaching agreement on the argument that Article 80(2) of the UN Charter does imply a duty to conclude an agreement. Such an interpretation of the Charter is no longer sustainable. The changes brought about by the *North Sea* cases could not be emphasized in a better way.

3. UN Charter?

In the *North Sea Continental Shelf* cases, the ICJ relied upon the underlying ideas of the continental shelf title enshrined in the 1945 Truman Proclamation[92] and a general principle of the UN Charter. According to the Court, the duty to negotiate 'merely constitutes a special application of a principle which underlies all international relations, and which is moreover recognised in Article 33 of the Charter of the United Nations as one of the methods for the peaceful settlement of international disputes'.[93] A similar foundation was relied upon in the 1974 *Fisheries Jurisdiction* case.[94] Interestingly, the Court did not rely upon specific contractual obligations of the parties under Article 1(2) of the Special Agreement in the *North Sea* cases.[95] The language seems to suggest the existence of a general duty of states to negotiate the settlement of disputes under the UN Charter. Yet, this seems to be overly broad. Article 33 of the Charter, as well as Article 2(3) and (4), establish the principles of peaceful settlement of disputes. These provisions do not include a general obligation to negotiate the settlement of a dispute. The same is true under the LOS Convention. Article 279 of the Convention obliges parties to settle disputes by peaceful means, which includes other forms and avenues, including conciliation and judicial settlement. It would therefore go too far to say that Article 33 of the UN Charter entails and supports a general obligation to settle disputes by way of negotiations. Similarly, proposals made in the doctrine of the former Soviet Union suggesting that there is an obligation to settle all international disputes by means of negotiations cannot be supported by

---

[91] Ibid., p. 140.   [92] ICJ Reports 1969, p. 47, para. 85.   [93] ICJ Reports 1969, para. 86.
[94] *Fisheries Jurisdiction (United Kingdom v. Iceland)*, Judgment, ICJ Reports 1974, p. 32, para. 75.
[95] See ICJ Reports 1969, pp. 4, 6, 7.

evidence.[96] Moreover, such a general rule should not be envisaged. Convincing as it may sound in the first place, such a rule would be equally directed against other forms of dispute resolution, in particular third party settlement by way of arbitration or judicial decision. This cannot be the goal of Article 33 UN Charter. Other foundations need to be sought and found.

4. Customary law: prior consultation

It is important to distinguish duties to negotiate both from duties to co-operate and of prior consultation. For the latter, customary law foundations can be found. A view on state practice, precedents and doctrine shows that duties to co-operate by information, prior consultation and negotiations do exist on the basis of specific foundations. They are subject-related and applicable in particular fields of law, mainly based upon treaty obligations. In an extensive survey of state practice and treaties, Kirgis found that the rules on prior consultation and negotiations were most developed in specific areas of international law.[97] These areas mainly relate to the use of natural resources and the environment. They encompass the law of maritime zones, transnational air pollution, activities in outer space and international economic regulations (and particularly the imposition of trade barriers under GATT law at the time). Since most of these obligations relate to the use of natural resources, the author was able to conclude that there exists a general 'consultation duty in shared-use situations'.[98] Evidence shows that in these areas, duties to consult developed, and are developing, from a consensual basis into customary law, on the basis of state practice. It seems fair to say and possible to conclude that Article 3 of Chapter II of the UN Charter of Economic Rights and Duties of States has emerged as a rule of customary law on international consultations:

---

[96] See John N. Hazard, book review of D. B Levin, 'Printsip miruogo razresheneniia mezhduanarodnykh sporor' (The principle of peaceful settlement of international disputes (1977)) (1979) 72 AJIL, 151.
[97] Frederic L. Kirgis Jr., *Prior Consultation in International Law: A Study of State Practice* (Charlottesville VA: University Press of Virginia, 1983). See also Judo Umarto Kusumowidagdo, *Consultation Clauses as Means of Providing for Treaty Obedience: A Study in the Law of Treaties* (Stockholm: Almqvist & Wiksell International, 1981). The author reaches comparable results, focusing on what he calls treaties of common interests and apportionment of rights.
[98] Kirgis, ibid., p. 196.

In the exploration of natural resources shared by two or more countries, each state must co-operate on the basis of a system of information and prior consultation in order to achieve optimum use of such resources without causing damage to the legitimate interests of others.[99]

While in the field of use of natural resources and environmental law, duties to prior consultation are founded in emerging customary law, the same is not necessarily true for the duty to negotiate. It is important to distinguish the two. Prior consultation may include elements of negotiation; it nevertheless primarily applies to areas open to unilateral action by governments. Unilateral exploitation of common resource deposits, for instance, is probably not prohibited by customary international law.[100] The very purpose of prior consultation or prior consent is to provide assurances that unilateral action taken by a government is not taken without due consideration of the needs and interests of the other state concerned. Duties to negotiate, however, relate to areas and fields subject to bilateral or multilateral action. It relates to areas where unilateral action is essentially barred and both states need to agree in order to define legal relations. The emerging doctrine of customary law of prior consultation cannot sufficiently support a general duty to negotiate. Not only is it much rarer in practice than consultation, it also has a different object and purpose. Customary law, as much as the UN Charter, does not provide an appropriate foundation.

5. Equity

It is submitted that the prime foundation of obligations to negotiate in areas necessarily subject to bilateral action relies upon the concept of equity. It may be confirmed by treaty law, such as Articles 74(1) and 83(1) LOS Convention. The duty to negotiate is most advanced in areas that necessarily require bilateral settlement, such as the exploitation of natural resources overlapping the boundary, boundary delimitation and the allocation of resources. It is interesting to observe that early Arab proclamations on the shelf, declaring unilateral delimitation after consultation, were, in practice, all settled by means of negotiations, leaving unilateral determinations a rare exception.[101] The duty to

---

[99] GA Res. 3281 (XXIX), adopted 12 December 1974, 29 UN GAOR Supp (No. 31) 50.
[100] Cissé Yacouba and Donald McRae, 'The Legal Regime of Maritime Boundary Agreements' in Jonathan I. Charney et al. (eds.), *International Maritime Boundaries*, 5 vols. (The Hague: Martinus Nijhoff Publishers, 1993–2005), vol. V (Colson and Smith), pp. 3281, 3293.
[101] See Chapter 5(I)(A).

negotiate inherently follows from a need and duty to bilateral settlement and the corresponding exclusion of unilateral determination of maritime boundaries. Bilateral settlement implies a need and duty to negotiate. The obligation to seek bilateral settlement is based upon equity. And so is the corresponding duty to negotiate.

The ICJ referred to the very same foundations both for procedural and substantive obligations in the *North Sea Continental Shelf* cases: both rely upon the application of 'equitable principles in accordance with ideas which have always underlain the development of the legal régime of the continental shelf'.[102] Neither substantive nor procedural rules are relied upon simply as a concept of abstract justice, but as applying proper rules of law based upon equity.

The rule of equity, with all its vagueness and elusiveness, is a coin with two sides. Substantive law, based upon the fundamental rule, is inherently accompanied by procedural rules. There is a necessary interrelation, and the vagueness of substantive law is compensated for by procedural and collateral obligations and safeguards of a procedural nature. Judge Morelli expressed the view that equity and equitable principles are not substantive rules, but merely provide an instrumental rule, which contemplates a certain way of creating a material rule.[103] Without reaching the same conclusion on the substance of equity, the view highlights the realization that equity inherently depends upon negotiations or third party settlement. Process, therefore, is an inherent element of the fundamental rule.[104]

The foundations of the duty to negotiate in the 1974 *Fisheries Jurisdiction* case can best be explained in these terms. Due to unilateral application of the measure, the imposed obligation to negotiate an equitable apportionment of fish stocks could not be based upon consent. The Court primarily relied upon the very nature of the rights of the parties:

> It is implicit in the concept of preferential rights that negotiations are required in order to define or delimit the extent of those rights ...[105] The obligation to negotiate flows from the very nature of the respective rights of the Parties.[106]

The fact that these rights are not absolute and have to be balanced by compromise in order to achieve an equitable apportionment[107] indicates

---

[102] ICJ Reports 1969, p. 47, para. 85.
[103] ICJ Reports 1969, p. 215 (dissenting opinion). [104] See also Rothpfeffer, n. 5, 111.
[105] ICJ Reports 1974, p. 32, para. 74. [106] ICJ Reports 1974, p. 32, para 75.
[107] ICJ Reports 1974, p. 32, para. 71, pp. 34–5, para. 79(4).

that the duty to negotiate is directly related to the concept of equity and its implementation and realization. Judge Nagendra Singh expressed the relationship in the following terms:

> negotiations are also indicated by the nature of the law which has to be applied, whether it be [treaty law requiring negotiations] or whether it be *reliance on considerations of equity*.[108]

It is submitted that the same considerations are valid in maritime boundary law and, indeed, in all fields regulated on the basis of equity. Regulation by equity inherently triggers an obligation to negotiate *ratione materiae* as an additional foundation of the obligation, which exists independently of customary or treaty law. States opting for equity regulation imply corollary duties to negotiate in good faith with a view to seeking an agreement. Wherever the court approaches and regulates a field on the basis of equity as a matter of judicial legislation, it has to be prepared to allocate collateral procedural rights and obligation of states to negotiate a settlement in the first place. Moreover, it is submitted that equity not only serves as a basis of the obligation to negotiate, but it also implies the duty to negotiate in a flexible manner with a view to achieving a compromise, as expounded in the *North Sea Continental Shelf* cases and before the 1974 *Fisheries Jurisdiction* cases.

Although equity and good faith and the protection of legitimate expectations are closely related, it is equity itself which requires a flexible bargaining attitude within the framework of equitable principles and additional considerations which parties may invoke in structuring the bargaining process. Unlike equity in the present context, good faith does not in itself require the adoption of specific attitudes in negotiations. In matters ruled by strict law, good faith does not prevent a party taking a tough line and insisting on the application of the rules. The minimal requirement of good faith negotiations (applicable to all negotiations including those under the umbrella of the principle of equity) under the standard of minimal fair dealing amounts to an obligation not to frustrate the objective of the agreement sought. It does not necessarily imply standards and attitudes of flexibility as required in this context by the principle and foundation of equity.

---

[108] Declaration by Judge Singh, ICJ Reports 1974, p. 42 (emphasis added).

D. *Legal effects of violations of the duty to negotiate*

1. Compliance and possible reprisals

The procedural duties to consultations and negotiations primarily depend on, and find their practical importance in voluntary compliance by states. They share an underlying mutual interest to communicate. As in many other areas, the law depends on respect rather than *ex post* implementation and enforcement. It is difficult to imagine sensible negotiations taking place without the willingness of the requested government to engage in talks. They cannot be imposed and it is exactly this factor that prohibits the adoption of too broad a notion of obligations to negotiate in international law. Nevertheless, the obligation, if taken seriously, is not necessarily soft, weak and toothless. Failure to honour obligations to negotiate amounts to violation of international law and may be made subject to sanctions. The Court of Arbitration in the Lake Lanoux case held to this effect:

> Sanctions can be applied in the event, for example, of an unjustified breaking off of the discussions, abnormal delays, disregard of the agreed procedures, systematic refusal to take into consideration adverse proposals or interests, and, more generally, in cases of violation of the rules of good faith.[109]

Whether or not the threat or use of sanctions is appropriate and helpful for the promotion of further negotiations and settlement is primarily a matter of political and diplomatic judgment, which needs to be made under the specific circumstances of the configuration. More often, such action will widen rather than close the gaps between the parties and thus may not be appropriate.[110] Sanctions tend to make the matter worse and amount to a crisis in the international process.[111] The goal may better be served by taking recourse to measures of persuasion, incentives, and possibly measures improving and restoring mutual trust and

---

[109] 'Sentence du Tribunal Arbitral Franco-Espagnol en date du 16 novembre 1957 dans L'affaire de l'utilisation des eaux du Lac Lanoux' (1958) 62 *Revue Générale de Droit International Public*, 79, transl. (1961) 24 ILR 101, 128.

[110] See generally Eiichi Fukatsu, 'Coercion and the Theory of Sanctions in International Law' in MacDonald and Johnston, n. 38, p. 1187; Michael Reisman, 'Sanctions and Enforcement' (1981), in Myres S. McDougal and W. Michael Reisman (eds.), *International Law Essays* (Foundation Press, 1981), pp. 381–437.

[111] Simma, n. 38, pp. 485, 497–504. ('Law enforcement by sanctions is, in general, extremely difficult to achieve and as experience shows, full of pitfalls and boomerangs. It may even be more so with regard to enforcing procedural obligations of States.')

confidence.[112] If sanctions are taken, rather than constructive attitudes, the primary avenue will be to seek compliance by reliance on world public attention, either by recourse to protest or to the UN Security Council. Recourse to other means of peaceful dispute settlement, in particular to third party dispute settlement, is open, and must not be considered an unfriendly act or even a measure of retaliation.[113] In WTO law, failure to engage in informal negotiations triggers the right to ask for formal consultations, which, upon failure, may lead to the establishment of a panel under the Understanding on Dispute Settlement (DSU).[114] It is explicitly considered not to amount to an unfriendly act and conduct.[115]

Besides such measures, recourse to measures of reprisal may be taken in an appropriate field, provided that prior calls upon compliance with procedural obligations have failed, and the measures taken remain proportionate to the goals[116] and do not infringe upon *jus cogens*. Thus, it may be appropriate to suspend negotiations in another field of interest to the party concerned or suspend the operation of a treaty obligation for the time being. While it is clear that recourse to the use of force is unlawful in this context,[117] appropriate economic sanctions cannot be ruled out, particularly if vital interests are at stake and the other state shows a persistent resistance to negotiation, or to negotiate flexibly towards a meaningful compromise solution. The major problem always will consist of finding appropriate measures in this context which provide some effectiveness and which are not in result counterproductive. The goal may best be achieved, if at all, by recourse to subject-related matters

---

[112] See also Fukatsu, n. 110.

[113] '[R]ecourse to judicial settlement of legal disputes, particularly referral to the International Court of Justice, should not be considered an unfriendly act between States', GA Res. 3232 (XXIX) para. 6, quoting Judge Lachs, separate opinion, *Aegean Continental Shelf* case, ICJ Reports 1978, pp. 52–3.

[114] Understanding on Rules and Procedures Governing the Settlement of Disputes (DSU), Arts. 4 and 6, in *The Results of the Uruguay Round of Multilateral Trade Negotiations, the Legal Texts* (WTO, reprinted 1995), pp. 404, 407, 410.

[115] 'It is understood that requests for conciliation and the use of the dispute settlement procedures should not be intended or considered as contentious acts and that, if a dispute arises, all Members will engage in these procedures in good faith in an effort to resolve the dispute. It is also understood that complaints and counter-complaints in regard to distinct matters should not be linked', ibid., Art. 3 para. 10 DSU.

[116] See *Naulilaa Arbitration (Portugal v. Germany)*, RIAA II 1024 (31 July 1928).

[117] See also Michael Reisman, 'Coercion and Self-Determination: Construing Charter Article 2(4)' (1984) 78 *American Journal of International Law*, 642; Oscar Schachter, 'The Legality of Pro-Democratic Invasion' (1984) 78 *American Journal of International Law*, 645.

(e.g. the threat to impose an embargo in fishery products during a dispute on the EEZ) and thus targeting the very interested group of actors who may have been influential in denying meaningful negotiations on the subject. Effective sanctions without the risk of boomerang effects remain a general problem, and may be even more troublesome with regard to enforcing procedural requirements.

2. The impact in court proceedings

While the use of reprisals remains problematic here and elsewhere, it is important to explore the potential effects of violations of the duty to negotiate on court proceedings. Given the fact that court cases occur upon the failure to find an appropriate settlement by the parties, the question arises over the extent to which courts should be entitled to examine whether the obligation to negotiate had been sufficiently respected. What is the legal impact of a lack of sufficiently serious and flexible negotiations conducted in good faith on standing and the right to bring a complaint? For obvious reasons, the quality of negotiations can have no direct legal effect in cases where the matter is brought by consensus on the basis of a *special agreement* or by consent of the defendant party concerned. The court, or a commission of conciliation, will be obliged to examine the matter based upon a joint mandate of the parties to the dispute. The framework of the third party settlement is tailored according the compromis. It is an element of an overall negotiating process. Dismissing a case for further negotiations would be contrary to the special agreement. It would put parties back at square one and almost certainly frustrate the overall goal of achieving a peaceful solution of the dispute.

The situation, however, is different in cases of unilateral application for third party settlement under the compulsory jurisdiction of the ICJ or any other court of law having jurisdiction. Firstly, as indicated previously, unilateral application to the ICJ may serve the purpose of attracting world public attention to the case, and expose a state's persistent violation of its duties to negotiate flexibly and in good faith. Although the respondent may not appear in court, the threat of, or the actual application and the prospects of, an explicit statement of its violation of its duties to negotiate, or even an imposed settlement on the merits, may encourage a state to take up and pursue meaningful negotiations in the first place. The applicant state remains free to withdraw the case and the court may even take into account *proprio motu* contemporary conduct of a state, in particular a promise to negotiate and settle the matter by negotiations.[118] Judicial proceedings may then be discontinued on the merits, provided that simultaneous negotiations result in the settlement of the dispute.[119]

Secondly, it is submitted that the duty to negotiate flexibly and in good faith has an essential and important effect of avoiding premature judgment on the merits, i.e. before the applicant state has engaged in meaningful negotiations that remained without success. According to the standards which lead either to agreement or a stadium of protraction, it is only at this point in time that the defendant state may become interested and be prepared to lose full control over the dispute and thus to participate in third party settlement. Waiting for this point in time is an important condition for the prospect of successful compliance and implementation of the ruling. If such a ruling occurs before the avenue is exhausted from the point of view of the defendant, he is not likely to accept the legitimacy of the judgment. Courts should therefore examine, as a preliminary matter, whether the complainant party did comply with its obligations to negotiate before the merits of the case are addressed. However, this is not established in case law.

3. The 1978 *Aegean Continental Shelf* case: an opportunity missed

The *Aegean Continental Shelf* case[120] shows all the signs and problems of a premature application to the Court by Greece in 1976. At the time, the case was not ripe for judicial settlement, and the Court's policy, quite clearly, was to avoid a judgment on the merits. The ruling was a

---

[118] See *Nuclear Tests Cases (Australia v. France) (New Zealand v. France)*, ICJ Reports 1974, pp. 253, 457.
[119] See *Trial of Pakistani Prisoners of War*, ICJ Reports 1973, p. 347, restated in *Aegean Continental Shelf*, ICJ Reports 1978, pp. 3, 12, para. 29.
[120] *Aegean Continental Shelf (Greece v. Turkey)*, Judgment of 19 December 1978, ICJ Reports 1978, pp. 3. See also Request for the Indication of Interim Measures of Protection, Order of 11 September 1976, ICJ Reports 1976, p. 3. See generally Ulf Dieter Klemm, 'Der Streit um den Festlandsockel in der Aegais' (1975), 21 *Recht der internationalen Wirtschaft*, 568; Emmanuel Gounaris, *Die völkerrechtliche und aussenpolitische Bedeutung der Kontinentalshelf-Doktrin in der Staatenpraxis Griechenlands und der Bundesrepublik Deutschland und der Deutschen Demokratischen Republik* (Frankfurt am Main, Bern, Las Vegas LA: Lang, 1979); Rudolf Bernhardt, 'Das Urteil des Internationalen Gerichtshofs im Aegais-Streit' in von Münch, n. 37, p. 167; Karin Oellers-Fram, 'Die Entscheidung des internationalen Gerichtshofes im griechisch--türkischen Streit um den Festlandsockel der Aegais' (1980) 18 *Archiv des Völkerrechts*, 377; Leo Gross, 'The Dispute between Greece and Turkey Concerning the Continental Shelf in the Aegaen' (1977) 71 *American Journal of International Law*, 31.

missed opportunity to set forth and develop the obligation to negotiate in the context of maritime boundary delimitation which the Court had emphasized so much, *in abstracto*, in the 1969 *North Sea* Cases and the 1974 *Fisheries Jurisdiction* cases a few years before. Even on the Court's own assessment of the facts,[121] there is reason to believe that the Greek application in 1976, both to the Court and the Security Council, occurred before the parties had fully engaged in serious and flexible negotiations in good faith beyond primarily procedural discussions.[122] This process was, at the time, still developing. From the beginning of the dispute, it would seem that Greece favoured third party settlement over negotiations on the basis of a special agreement.[123] Turkey, on the other hand, insisted on negotiations having priority.[124] A gradual approach towards procedural compromise, expressed in the 1975 Brussels Communiqué,[125] and even suggestions for a joint operation and exploitation,[126] were destroyed by further unilateral exploitations by the Turkish vessel Sismik I, which were unilaterally undertaken without consulting Greece in the disputed areas in July 1976.[127] These research activities prompted Greece's application to the Court and the Security Council on 10 August 1976.[128] Negotiations were resumed, as urged by the Security Council Resolution 395 (1976)[129] and Article 1 of the Bern Agreement of 11 November 1976, pledging that 'negotiations shall be frank, thoroughgoing and pursued in good faith with a view to reach an agreement'.[130] Greece even suggested the postponement of the oral hearing,[131] and Turkey expressed the opinion that the removal of the case would be more conducive to the creation of a favourable political climate for an agreed settlement.[132] In a letter to the Court, Turkey

---

[121] See ICJ Reports 1978, pp. 8-13, paras. 16-31.
[122] But see also Leo Gross, n. 120, p. 32.   [123] ICJ Reports 1978, p. 9, para. 18.
[124] ICJ Reports 1978, pp. 8, 9, 12, paras. 17, 18, 20, 21, 28.
[125] ICJ Reports 1978, pp. 19, and 39, para. 95 ff. The essential part says that the Prime Ministers 'ont décidé que les problèmes doivent être résolues pacifiquement par la voie des négotiations et concernant le plateau continental de la mer Egée par la Cour international de la Haye', ibid., pp. 39-40, para. 97.
[126] ICJ Reports 1978, p. 57, para. 103.   [127] ICJ Reports 1978, p. 10, para. 22.
[128] ICJ Reports 1978.
[129] ICJ Reports 1978, p. 10, para. 23. For full text see 'United Nations: Security Council Resolution on the Dispute between Greece and Turkey over the Aegean Sea Continental Shelf' (1976) 15 ILM 1235.
[130] ICJ Reports 1978, para. 27. For full text see (1977) 16 ILM 13.
[131] ICJ Reports 1978, p. 12, para. 28.
[132] ICJ Reports 1978, p. 12, para. 28, note verbale to the Greek Government of 29 September 1978.

argued that Greece had refused to participate in meaningful negotiations. Later on, it expressed the view that 'the application was filed although the two Governments had not yet begun negotiations on the substantive issue'.[133] The counsel for Greece 'correctly stated that there is in fact a double dispute between the parties', namely as to the method by which the dispute should be settled 'whether by negotiations alone or by submission to a tribunal competent to exercise jurisdiction in the matter, either following upon negotiations or even in the absence of them'.[134]

The Court actually decided the case on narrow and formal grounds of jurisdiction.[135] The reasoning of the Court in this case raises important issues that are of no concern in this context. In particular, it remains to be seen whether its dynamic and extensive interpretation of the 1931 Greek reservation to the 1928 General Act for the Pacific Settlement of International Disputes[136] will not effect, as a precedent, further and self-inflicted setbacks to the concept of compulsory jurisdiction in international law. There were good reasons and arguments for affirming the court's jurisdiction. A traditionally restrictive interpretation of reservations could have equally led to the affirmation of jurisdiction.[137] Moreover, it is doubtful whether the continental shelf containing shared and horizontal jurisdiction amounts to a full territorial concept falling under this reservation. Furthermore, the matter raises issues of inter-temporal law and it is doubtful whether the reservation should apply to legal concepts which emerged only decades after the reservation was made.[138] Finally, we note that there was the Treaty of

---

[133] ICJ Reports 1978, p. 11, para. 27, Letter to the Registrar of 24 April 1978. A similar statement had already been made in 1976, see Observation of the Turkish Government on the Request of the Government of Greece for provisional measures, dated 10 August 1976: 'Greece had refused to participate in meaningful negotiations, even in attempts to define the area in dispute', ICJ Pleadings (*Aegean Continental Shelf* case), pp. 69–70, para. 10, see also ICJ Reports 1976, p. 5, para. 8.

[134] Ibid., pp. 12–13 para. 30.   [135] See ICJ Reports 1978, pp. 13–37, paras. 32–90.

[136] The Greek reservation of 1931 in its instrument of accession to the Act excluded, inter alia, disputes 'ayant trait au statut territorial de la Grèce, y compris ceux relatif à ses droits de souveraineté sur les parts et ses voies de communication', see ICJ Reports 1978, p. 20, para. 48. From a historical perspective, the reservation was directed in particular against mainland claims by Bulgaria after World War I for access to the Agean Sea (see ICJ Reports 1978, p. 25, paras. 60, 63, 69 ff.). See finally Judge Castro, who remarked in his dissenting opinion: 'It may also be added that the effect of the accession by States to the General Act was to create ties of co-operation', ibid., p. 71 in fine.

[137] See Judge de Castro, dissenting opinion, ICJ Reports 1987, p. 62 ff.

[138] See Taslim Olawale Elias, 'The Doctrine of Intertemporal Law'(1980) 74 *American Journal of International Law*, 285, 296–302.

Friendship, Neutrality, Conciliation and Arbitration in force between the two parties, which was likely to establish jurisdiction of the Court. Greece did not invoke that Treaty, but the Court had the power to consider it *ex officio*.[139]

Assuming jurisdiction, the Court could have disposed the case on the basis of the equitable obligation to negotiate in good faith and to seek agreement. This is a matter of substantive-procedural law, not jurisdiction.[140] In the present case, the duty did not only arise from the 1969 *North Sea* and the 1974 *Fisheries Jurisdiction* cases, but today also from the fundamental rule of equity first expounded in the 1984 *Gulf of Maine* case and the LOS Convention. It could equally have relied upon the Brussels Communiqué and the Bern Agreement.[141] In accordance with the Turkish defense, but also *proprio motu*, the Court was bound to examine whether or not one of the parties had failed, so far, to comply with their duties to negotiate and consult prior to the first exploration until the day of the judgment. Such examination was not new and the matter is fully justiciable. The *Tacna/Arica* case is a precedent in point.[142] The matter is justiciable. It is possible to decide whether or not the

---

[139] ICJ Reports 1978, p. 38, para. 91–3. See *Certain Norwegian Loans*, ICJ Reports 1957, p. 57, quoted by Judge Tarazi, separate opinion at p. 60. See also ICJ Reports 1957, p. 18, paras. 41–3 of the judgment where the Court rightly adopted an informal view with regard to formal deficiencies in the objections of Greek reservations; see also Bernhardt, n. 119, pp. 171–2 and Judge Singh, separate opinion, p. 48; but see also Judge Strassinopolous, dissenting opinion at p. 74.

[140] It is important to note that the duty to negotiate does not affect jurisdiction of the Court under Art. 36(2) ICJ Statute. In order to establish a 'legal dispute', only minimal diplomatic interaction is required under customary law, although the Court did not set uniform standards to this effect. Whether or not parties have sufficiently exhausted the avenue of negotiations is a matter of substantive law. The notion of jurisdiction does not depend on duties to negotiate, and the establishment of special jurisdictional standards would not be accurate. The question, therefore, is one of a procedural aspect of the merits.

[141] The Court correctly concluded that the Joint Communiqué cannot be read as an immediate, unconditional commitment establishing jurisdiction of the Court, ICJ Reports 1978, pp. 38–44, paras. 94–107. From its purely procedural perspective the Court refrained from elaborating other legal effects of the document, ICJ Reports 1978, p. 44, para. 108. However, it acknowledged the possibility of the Communiqué being an informal, binding agreement, ICJ Reports 1978, p. 39, para. 96. The evidence before the Court leaves no doubt that the Communiqué was a binding soft law agreement, obliging both parties to pursue negotiations and to seek jointly a special agreement. See also separate opinion of Judge Tarazi, ICJ Reports 1978, pp. 55–6, Judge Singh, ICJ Reports 1978, p. 47, and, in particular, Judge Lachs, ICJ Reports 1978, pp. 51–2 ('In general, I find that an obligation to negotiate has been established').

[142] 'The Tacna and Arica Case' (1925) 19 *American Journal of International Law*, 393.

dispute is still in an early stage of negotiations, which are far from having explored all possible modes of settlement, or, conversely, whether the lack of agreement is due to continued and persistent divergencies. Under the facts of the *Aegean* case, the Court was in a position to reason that the duty to negotiate had not been sufficiently complied with. It could have disposed the case on this procedural ground, making an important contribution to the international law of negotiations.

In the light of interrelated, judicial and negotiating procedures, the task of establishing and promoting a favourable climate for dispute settlement, it is doubtful whether the Court's rejection of interim measures against further scientific exploration and military measures in the disputed area by Turkey (and without Greece's consent) in 1976[143] was an appropriate exercise of its wide discretionary powers under Article 41 ICJ Statute. The Court acknowledged that exploration might constitute an infringement of Greek rights,[144] but held that acquired scientific research, if established, 'might be capable of reparation by appropriate means', and therefore no irreparable prejudice to the alleged rights of Greece was established.[145] The Court by no means explained how reparation could materialize of such immaterial information.

In the light of contemporary principles set forth earlier, unilateral exploration amounts to a violation of the duty to negotiate in good faith. The imposition of interim measures may have contributed to the creation of a more suitable climate for negotiation. The measures could have served to accelerate the negotiating process. None of the parties is interested in unilaterally and voluntarily abstaining from undertaking such an exploration. A prohibition of unilateral exploration was likely to promote the achievement of an interim arrangement, now provided for by Articles 74(3) and 84(3) LOS Convention, or even a final settlement. Even if the Court is not going to decide the matter on the merits, interim measures according to Article 41 of the ICJ Statute provide an important safeguard against the prejudicing of rights in subsequent negotiations.[146]

---

[143] *Aegean Continental Shelf* case (Order of 11 September 1976), ICJ Reports 1976, p. 3.
[144] Ibid., p. 11, para. 31.   [145] Ibid., p. 11, para. 33.
[146] See also Jerome B. Elkind, *Interim Protection: A Functional Approach* (The Hague: Martinus Nijhoff, 1981), pp. 211-19; Jerome B. Elkind, 'The Aegan Sea Case and Article 41 of the Statute of the International Court of Justice' (1979) 32 *Révue Héllenique de Droit International*, 285-345; see also Jerzy Sztucki, 'Interim Measures in the Hague Court: An Attempt at a Scrutiny' (1983), reviewed in 77 *American Journal of International Law*, 673.

The Court, it seems, relied solely on expectations exerted by Resolution 395(1976) of the Security Council as a political tool aimed at encouraging the negotiating process.[147] But one is left with the uneasy feeling that the Court, by its line of argument, merely intended to avoid the essential and controversial issue of *prima facie* jurisdiction (yet another missed opportunity). Judge Lachs argued in favour, spelling out the legal consequences of the Security Council Resolution, obliging the parties to exercise restraint in support of a 'positive contribution to the solution of the dispute'.[148] A court of law must decide a case on its narrowest appropriate basis and avoid unrelated dicta. However, this does not allow the avoidance of addressing the crucial issues and sailing around these cliffs, at the expense of the necessary development of international law by the primary judicial body of the United Nations.

4. Ordering negotiations

In the 1974 *Fisheries Jurisdiction* case, the Court particularly emphasized negotiations 'clearly' to be 'the most appropriate method' of achieving a solution to the dispute and peaceful settlement.[149] The procedural approach chosen is to be welcomed.[150] This statement is equally valid and suitable for maritime boundary delimitation at such an early stage of the conflict. The fundamental rule of the *Gulf of Maine* case equally

---

[147] ICJ Reports 1976, p. 13, para. 41.
[148] ICJ Reports 1976, p. 19 (separate opinion). See also Judge Elias who was only prepared to follow the majority of the Court due to its practical emphasis on the parties' duty to negotiate under SC Res. 395 (1976), ICJ Reports 1976, p. 29.
[149] ICJ Reports 1974, p. 31, para. 73, see also p. 32, para. 76.
[150] See also Vitzthum, n. 37, p. 752 ('Dieser Verweis auf eine 'obligation to negotiate' bedeutet keine Schwächung des Urteils, keine Rechtsverweigerung'). But see Judge Gros who argued that the Court had not complied with its task to settle the dispute: 'Répondre à un différend sur une prétension exclusive de jurisdiction exclusives par des directives pour un accord de conservation n'était pas accomplir la mission de la Cour. L'échec de la solution proposé par la Cour est connu', 'La recherche du consensus dans les décisions de la Cour International de Justice' in R. Bernhardt, W. K. Geck, G. Jaenicke and H. Steinberger (eds.), *Völkerrecht als Rechtsordnung, internationale Gerichtsbarkeit, Menschenrechte, Festschrift für Hermann Mosler* (Berlin, Heidelberg, New York: Springer Verlag, 1983), pp. 351, 357. There is good reason to believe that the judicial determination or rejection of exclusive fishing rights would, at the time, have met considerable problems of compliance. It was a matter of great political importance going beyond the provinces of the Court. Moreover, it is important to note that solutions require considerable technical expertise which can better be brought to effect in negotiations than in judicial dispute settlement.

stressed the priority of settlement by agreement and urged, quite naturally, third party settlement 'where such agreement cannot be achieved'.[151]

Meaningful negotiations are, of course, the natural and most cost-efficient avenue before proceeding before a court of law, or any other third party settlement is called upon. Negotiations can even continue or restart during judicial proceedings, and vice versa. Judicial proceedings neither pre-empt negotiations, nor pre-empt the avenue of the court's jurisdiction. Parties can pursue strategies and techniques of combined and interrelated procedures, both applying negotiations and judicial settlement. As Judge Lachs pointed out in his separate opinion in the 1978 *Aegean Continental Shelf* case:

> There are obviously some disputes which can be resolved only by negotiations, because there is no alternative in view of the character of the subject-matter involved and the measures envisaged. But there are many other disputes in which a combination of methods would facilitate their resolution. The frequently unorthodox nature of the problems facing States today require as many tools to be used and as many avenues to be opened as possible, in order to resolve the intricate and frequently multi-dimensional issues involved. It is sometimes desirable to apply several methods at the same time or successively. Thus no incompatibility should be seen between the various instruments and fora to which States may resort, for all are mutually complementary. Notwithstanding the interdependence of issues, some may be isolated, given priority and their solution sought in a separate forum. In this way it may be possible to prevent the aggravation of a dispute, its degeneration in to a conflict.[152]

Considering the delicate balance of power, and given the only relative importance of the international judiciary function (and in particular the ICJ) in international relations and politics, being fully dependent on voluntary compliance and acceptance, it is essential to recognize that the courts can sometimes contribute a more acceptable step towards a negotiated solution rather than insisting on, and trying to bring about, a final settlement, which may be unacceptable to one of the parties. The *North Sea* cases are examples in point of such an intermediate step by the Court, and, for similar reasons, the outcome of the 1974 *Fisheries* cases is to be welcomed. They were necessarily followed by further negotiations,

---

[151] ICJ Reports 1984, p. 299, para. 112(1). The Court carefully refrained from framing a mandatory rule of judicial settlement ('should be effected by recourse to a third party possessing the necessary competence'). It takes into account that, as already discussed, no regime of compulsory judicial settlement was achieved at UNCLOS III with regard to the settlement of maritime boundaries of the continental shelf and the EEZ.

[152] ICJ Reports 1978, p. 52.

based upon guidance provided by the Court. Earlier, the Court refrained from imposing a final solution in the *Haya de la Torre* case, hoping that its findings will support parties in finding a practical solution.[153] Equally, the Court in the 2007 *Nicaragua* v. *Honduras* case found that 'the Parties must negotiate in good faith with a view to agreeing on the course of the delimitation line' of that portion of the territorial sea which the Court left un-delimited, between the endpoint of the land boundary and the starting-point of the single maritime boundary as determined by the Court.[154]

It is submitted that the duty to negotiate, where existing either as an obligation under equity or under treaty law, offers an important tool to the court in order to structure the interrelationship of negotiations and third party settlement in legal terms. It refines the basic equality and availability of all avenues of peaceful dispute settlement (Article 33 UN charter and Friendly Relations Declaration) by establishing, with regard to multilateral applications, a *legally binding sequence of negotiations* prior to a third party settlement on the merits of the case. A court is not supposed to deal with the merits before the avenue of negotiations has been – to borrow the term – reasonably exhausted, i.e. before flexible, good faith negotiations fail to show non-negotiable remaining legal issues. Not as a matter of jurisdiction, but rather as a matter of substantive law, the court should only address the merits after the negotiations of the parties have 'reached a deadlock', as the Court required in the *Interhandel* case.[155]

It is no longer accurate to say under the rule of equity that 'judicial settlement in the final analysis is simply an alternative to direct and friendly negotiations'.[156] It should be seen and perceived as a sequence

---

[153] *Haya de la Torre Case (Colombia v. Peru)*, Judgment, ICJ Reports 1951, p. 83.
[154] *Territorial and Maritime Dispute between Nicaragua and Honduras in the Caribbean Sea (Nicaragua v. Honduras)*, Judgment, ICJ Reports 2007, p. 659, para. 321(4), para. 321(4).
[155] *Interhandel Case (Switzerland v. United States)*, Judgment, ICJ Reports 1959, p. 21.
[156] ICJ Reports 1984, p. 266, para. 22 in fine, a statement made in the context of bilateral submissions. It remains valid in the sense that simultaneous negotiations do not exclude jurisdiction of the Court. See also to this effect *Free Zones and Upper Savoy and the District of Gex* case, PCIJ, Series A No. 22 at 13 (Order of 19 August 1929); 1974 *Fisheries Jurisdiction* case, ICJ Reports 1974, p. 19, para. 38 and Order, ICJ Reports 1973, p. 303, para. 7 (concerning an interim agreement), see also Judge Sing, separate opinion, ICJ Reports 1974, p. 41, Judge Lachs, separate opinion, ICJ Reports 1978, n. 68 at p. 52. Equally, the statement does not question that recourse to judicial settlement as an alternative does not constitute an unfriendly act, GA Res. 3232 (XXIX) para. 6, quoted by Lachs, ICJ Reports 1978, pp. 52–3.

and possibly a matter of interaction. This refinement is, in accordance with the relationship set out above by Judge Lachs, by no means to the disadvantage of the overall system of dispute settlement. On the contrary, it possibly strengthens commitments to timely, meaningful negotiations, without delay, detour and tactics. It saves the Court from handling the dilemma of a premature judgment, which, in a context of interrelated avenues of dispute settlement, is not only unlikely to be accepted and implemented. Even worse, it jeopardizes, rather than promotes, the recreation of ambiance and a climate that is favourable for successive negotiations. But foremost, declining to deal with the merits and ordering parties back to negotiations has important preventive effects: to take seriously the procedural obligations to negotiate and to seek a peaceful settlement under the rule of equity in the very first place.

Appendix I

Table A.1 *Maritime boundary agreements 1942–1992*

No.	Agreements	Method of delimitation			Source
	Chronology (Sig.)	Method indicated in Agreement	Effective method	Reference Doc.
	MB: Maritime boundary CS: Continental shelf EEZ: excl econ. zone APB: all purpose boundary (CS & EEZ) A: Adjacent coast O:: Opposite coast	1: None 2: Equidistance 3: Median line (+/-) 4: Parallel of latitude 5: Straight line / azimuth 6: Perpendicular to coastal line 7: Equity 8: Other	1: Equidistance (strict or simplified) 2: Modified equidistance 3: Non-equidistant	1: ICJ, *Gulf of Maine* case, Annexes submitted by Canada, Vol. I (1983) 2: ASIL (1993) 3: Other

No	Agreement	1	2	3	4	5	6	7	8	Note	1	2	3	Note	Source
1	Trinidad & Tobago UK/ Venezuela 26.2.1942 CS-O	•											•		1: No. 1 at 63 2: I 2–13(1) at 639 3: 205 LNTS 122

2	Chile/Peru 18.8.1952 MB-A-APB		•			1: No. 2 at 69 2: I 3–5 at 793 3: Limits No. 86
3	Equador/Peru 18.8.1952 MB-A-APB		•			1: No. 3 at 73 2: I 3–9 at 829 3: Limits No. 88
4	Chile/Equador/ Peru 4.12.1954 MB (Special Z ext. 10 m. on either side)		•			3: Atlante at 200
5	Norway/USSR 15.2.57 CS-OA			•	+/− 'Median Point'	1: No. 4 at 77 2: II 9–6 at 1781 3. Limits No. 17
6	Saudi Arabia/ Bahrain 22.2.1958 CS-OA			•		1: No. 5 at 83 2: II 7–3 at 1489 3: St/LEG/SER. B 16 p.409

Table A.1 (*cont.*)

No.	Agreements	Method of delimitation							Source
7	Senegal/Guinea-Bissau 26.4.1960 CS-OA			•					1: No. 6 at 89 3: Limits No. 68
8	Netherlands/Federal Republic of Germany 1.12.1964 CS-A	•				•	small area only		1: No. 7 at 95 2: II 9–11 at 1835 3: 550 UNTS 123
9	Sharjah/Umm al Qaiwain undated 1964 CS-OA			•					1: No. 8 at 99 2: II 7–10 at 1549
10	Norway/UK 10.3.1965 CS-O-APB		•			•	median		1: No. 9 at 103 2: II 9–15 at 1879 3: 551 UNTS 214
11	Finland/USSR (Gulf of Finland) 20.5.1965 CS-O-APB				•	•			1: No. 10 at 107 2: II 10–4(1) at 1959 3: 566 UNTS 37

12	Denmark/FRG (North Sea) 9.6.1965 CS-O	•				•		1: No. 11 at 113 2: II 9–8 at 1801 3: 570 UNTS 91
13	Denmark/FRG Baltic Sea CS-OA	•				•		1: No. 12 at 117 2: II 10–1 at 1915 3: 570 UNTS 91
14	Netherlands/UK 6.11.1965 amended 25.11.1974 CS-OA-APB	•				•	short line	1: No. 13 at 123 2: II 9–13 at 1859 3: 595 UNTS 113
15	Denmark/ Norway (North Sea) 8.12.1965 amended 24.4.1968 CS-OA-APB	•				•		1: No. 14 at 129 2: II 9–9 at 1815 3: 634 UNTS 71 as amended: ST/LEG/SER.B/16 at 412
16	UK/Denmark 3.3.1966 amended 25.11.1971 CS-O-APB				•	•		1: No. 15 at 135 2: II 9–10 at 1825 3: 592 UNTS 209

Table A.1 (cont.)

No.	Agreements	Method of delimitation			Source
17	Finland/USSR (Baltic Sea, Gulf of Finland ext) 5.4.1967 CS-O-APB	•			1: No. 16 at 141 2: II 10–4(2) at 1971 3: 640 UNTS 111
18	Italy/Yugoslavia 8.1.1968 CS-O	•		quite significant deviations and half-effect	1: No. 17 at 145 2: II 8–7(1) at 1627 3: Limits No. 9
19	Abu Dhabi/Dubai 18.2.1968 CS-A		• parallelogram	•	1: No. 18 at 151 2: II 7–1 at 1475 3: New Directions V at 214
20	Sweden/Norway 24.7.1968 CS-O-APB	•	+/−		1: No. 19 at 155 2: II 9–14 at 1871 3: St/LEG/SER.B/ 16 at 413

21	Saudi Arabia/Iran 24.10.1968 CS-O	•			•		'just and accurate manner'			1: No. 20 at 159 2: II 7-7 at 1519 3: 696 UNTS 189
22	Poland/German Democratic Republic 29.19.1968 CS-OA-APB	•				•				1: No. 21 at 169 3: 768 UNTS 253
23	Quatar/Abu Dhabi 30.3.1969 CS-OA	•			•					1: No. 22 175 2.II 7-9 at 1541 3: St/LEG/SER. B/ at 16, 403
24	Poland/USSR 28.8.1969 CS-A-APB	•				•	+/-			1: No. 23 at 179 3: 769 UNTS 75
25	Iran/Qatar 20.9.1969 CS-A			•				•		1: No. 24 at 185 2: II 7-6 at 1511 3: 787 UNTS 165

Table A.1 (*cont.*)

No.	Agreements	Method of delimitation			Source
26	Malaysia/ Indonesia 27.10.1969 CS-OA	•		1: median 2: half-effect	1: No. 25 at 189 2: I 5–9(1) at 1019 3: ST/LEG/SER.B/ 16 at 417
27	FRG/Denmark (North Sea) 28.1.1971 CS-A	•	Ref. to ICJ Rep.		1: No. 26 at 195 2: II 9–8 at 1801 3: ST/LEG/SER.B/ 16 at 424
28	Netherlands/FRG 28.1.1971 CS-A	•	Ref. to ICJ Rep.		1: No. 27 at 201 2: II 9–11 at 1835 3: SF/LEG/SER.B/ 16 at 419

29	Australia/ Indonesia (Timor and Arafwa; Pacific Ocean) 18.5.1971 CS-AO	•		1: Arafwa/ Timor 2. Pacific	•	2: half-effect	1: No. 28 at 209 2: II 6–2(1) at 1195 3: New Directions IV at 91
30	Iran/Bahrain 17.6.1971 CS-O		•	'Just, equitable and precise manner'	•		1: No. 29 at 217 2: II 7–2 at 1481 3: 826 UNTS 227
31	Italy/Tunisia 20.8.1971 CS-O		•	except islands	•	substantial modification	1: No. 30 at 221 2: II 8–6 at 1611 3: ST/LEG/SER. B/ 18 at 437
32	FRG/UK 25.11.1971 CS-O	•		very short line	•		1: No. 31 at 231 2: II 9–12 at 1851 3: 880 UNTS185

Table A.1 (*cont.*)

No.	Agreements	Method of delimitation			Source
33	Thailand/ Indonesia 17.12.1971 CS-O	•			1: No. 32 at 235 2: II 6–12 at 1455 3: ST/LEG/SER.B/ 18 at 437
34	Malaysia/ Indonesia/ Thailand (Malacca Strait ext.) 21.12.1971 CS-O	•		•	1: No. 33 at 239 2: II 6–13(I) at 1443 3: id.429
35	Malaysia/ Thailand (Andaman Sea) 21.12 1971 CS-OA-APB	•		•	1: No. 34 at 243 2: II 6–13(I) at 1455 3: id 429
36	Uruguay/Brazil 21.7.1972 MB-A-APB		•	•	1: No. 35 at 247 2: I 3–4 at 785 3: Limits at 73

37	Finland/Sweden 29.9.1972 CS-O-P		•					•		+/-				1: No. 36 at 255 2: II 10-3 at 1945 3: ST/LEG/SER. B/ 18 at 439
38	Australia/ Indonesia (Arafwa; Timor Sea ext.) 9.10 1972 CS-O-P	•											•	1: No. 37 at 261 2: II 6-2(2) at 1207 3: id 441
39	Australia/ Indonesia (Arafwa Sea ext.) 12.2.1973 MB-A	•							•						1: No. 38 at 267 2: II 6-2(3) at 1219 3: id 444
40	Argentina/ Uruguay 19.11.1973 MB-OA-APB			•					•						1: No. 39 at 273 2: I 3-2 at 757 3: Government of Argentina
41	Denmark/Canada 17.12.1973 CS-O-APB						adjacent			•					1: No. 40 at 307 2: I 1-1 at 371 3: ST/LEG/SER. B/ 18 at 447

Table A.1 (cont.)

No.	Agreements	Method of delimitation							Source
42	Spain/France 29.1.1974 CS-O-A-P	•	•				•	Proportionality of coastlines	1: No. 41 at 315 2: II 9–2 at 1719 3: ST/LEG/SER. B/ 19 at 445
43	Japan/Korea 5.2.1974 CS-O	•				•		development zone in unresolved area	1: No. 42 at 323 2: I 5–12 at 1057 3: Government of Japan
44	Italy/Spain 19.2.1974 CS-O		•			•			1: No. 43 at 357 2: II 8–5 at 1601 3: Limits No. 90
45	Sudan/Saudi Arabia 16.5.1974 CS-O			•			•		3: 952 UNTS 193
46	India/Sri Lanka 26./28.6.1974 MB-O				•		•	historic waters	2: II 6–10(1) at 1409 3: Limits No. 66
47	FRG/GDR 29.6.1974 MB-O-A Fishing zone	•					•		2: II 10–5 at 1997 3: Limits No. 74 (5.10.1976)

48	Iran/Oman 25.7.1974 CS-O				•									1: No. 44 at 363 2: II 7–5 at 1503 3: ST/LEG/SER. B/ 19 at 450
49	India/Indonesia 8.8.1974 CS-O	•					•							1: No. 45 at 367 2: II 6–6(1) at 1363 3: Limits No. 62
50	Iran/United Arab Emirates 13.8.1974 CS-O				•			•						1: No. 46 at 373 2: II 7–8 at 1533 3: id 63
51	Senegal/Gambia 4.6.1975 MB-A-APB									•		•		1: No. 47 at 377 2: I 4–2 at 849 3: id 85
52	Colombia/ Ecuador 23.8.1975 MB-A-APB									•		•		1: No. 48 at 381 2: I 3–7 at 809 3: ST/LEG/SER. B/ 19 at 398

Table A.1 (*cont.*)

No.	Agreements	Method of delimitation									Source
53	Indonesia/ Thailand 11.12.1975 CS-O	•									1: No. 49 at 385 2: II 6–13 at 1465 3: U.S. Dept. of State, Office of the Geographer
54	Portugal/Spain 12.2.1976 CS-A-APB					•			•		1: No. 50 at 391 2: II 9–7 at 1791 3: Government of Spain
55	India/Sri Lanka (extension of No. 46 above) MB-O	•						•			1: No. 51 at 395 2: II 6–10(2) at 1419 3: ST/LEG/SER. B/ 19 at 402
56	Mauritania/ Morocco 14.4.1976 CS-A					•			•		1: No. 52 at 403 2. I 4–6 at 885 3: Government of Marocco

57	Kenya and Tanzania 9.7.1976 MB-OA-APB		•				•	1: No. 53 at 407 2: I 4–5 at 875 3: Limits No. 92
58	Cuba/Mexico 26.7.1976 MB-OA-EEZ	•			•			1: No. 54 at 413 2: I 2–8 at 565 3: Government of Mexiko
59	Colombia/Panama 20.11.1976 MB-OA		•		•	+/− between methods	•	1: No. 55 at 417 2: I 2–5 at 519 3: Limits No. 79
60	India/Maldives 28.12.1976 MB-OA	•			•		full effect islands	1: No. 56 at 425 2: II 6–8 at 1389 3: id 78
61	India/Indonesia 14.1.1977 CS-OA	•			•		full effect islands	1: No. 57 at 431 2: II 6–6(2) at 1371 3: Government of India

Table A.1 (cont.)

No.	Agreements	Method of delimitation		Source
62	USA/USSR Jan./Feb. 1977 MB-O-P Fishing zone	• historic treaty boundary		1: No. 58 at 437 2: 1216 ASIL 75 (1987) 729 3: 11 TIAS (Bevans)
63	Colombia/Costa Rica 17.3.1977 MB-O-P		• •	1: No. 59 at 443 2: I 2–1 at 463 3: Government of Colombia
64	Italy/Greece 24.5.1977 CS-O	•	•	1: No. 60 at 449 2: II 8–4 at 1591 3: Government of Greece
65	Haiti/Cuba 27.10.1977 MB-O	• 'On the basis of the principle of equidistance or equity, as the case requires.' Art. 1	•	1: No. 61 at 455 2: I 2–7 at 551 3: New Directions vol. VIII at 69

66	USA/Cuba 16.12.1977 MB-O-APB	•				see ASIL 75 at 746 (1981)		parties used a third intermediate equidist line	1: No. 62 at 465 2: I 1–4 at 417 3: US State Department, Office of the Geographer
67	Colombia/ Dominican Republic 13.1.1978 MB-O-APB		•		•			common zone for research and fishing	1: No. 63 at 473 2: I 2–2 at 477 3: Government of Columbia
68	Colombia/Haiti 13.2.1978 MB-O-APB-EEZ		•				•	Island disregarded	1: No. 64 at 481 2: I 2–3 at 491 3: Government of Columbia
69	Venezuela/USA 28.3.1978 MB-O-APB			•		'conscious of the need to establish precise and equitable maritime limits'			1: No. 65 at 487 2: I 2–14 at 691 3: US State Department; Office of the Geographer

Table A.1 (cont.)

No.	Agreements											Method of delimitation		Source
70	Venezuela/ Netherlands 31.3.1978 CS-MB-O(Saba/ Aves Islands)- OA(Caribbean Sea)-APB		•								•	'Animados del propósito de deliminar de manera justa, precisa y en base a princi- pos equitativos las árenas marinas y submarinas entre las Antillas Neerlandesas y Venezuela'		1: No. 66 at 49 (recte: 31.3.1978) 2: I 2–12 at 615 3: Tractatenblad van Het Koninrijk der Hollanden Jahrgang 1978 No. 61.
71	USA/Mexico 4.5.1978 MB-CS-OA-APB	•									•	Recognizes that lines adopted in 1976 agreement are equitable	cf. ASIL 75 743 (1981)	1: No. 67 at 507 2: I 1–5 at 427 3: US State Department, Office of the Geographer
72	India/Thailand 22.6.1978 CS-O	•									•			1: No. 68 at 513 2: II 6–11 at 1433 3: cf. Limits No. 93 at 5 (17.8.1981) Government of India

73	India/Indonesia/ Thailand 22.6.1978 CS-O	•	Tripoint agreement	•	2: II 6–7 at 1379 3: Limits No. 93 at 5 (17.8.1981)
74	Sweden/GDR 22.6.1978 MB-O-P-CS Fishing zone	•		•	1: No. 69 at 517 2: II 10–7 at 2029 3: Government of Sweden
75	Turkey/USSR 23.6.1978 CS-OA		'Agreeing that the demarcation of the continental shelf in the Black Sea should be based on equitable principles'	•	1: No. 70 at 523 2: II 8–10(2) at 1693 3: Government of Turkey
76	Australia/Papua New Guinea 18.12.1978 CS-MB-O	•		•	1: No. 71 at 529 2: I 5–3 at 929 3: Government of Australia

Table A.1 (*cont.*)

No.	Agreements	Method of delimitation							Source
77	Norway/UK 22.12.1978 CS-O-APB	•							1: No. 72 at 593 2: II 9–15 at 1879 3: Atlas of the Seabed Boundaries p. 30
78	Venezuela/ Dominican Republic 3.3.1979 MB-O			•	equitable principles		•	Third states used as base points	1: No. 73 at 597 2: I 2–9 at 577 3: Government of Venezuela
79	Denmark/ Norway (Faeros) 15.6.1979 MB-O-APB			•			•		1: No. 74 at 603 2: II 9–1 at 1711 3: Government of Denmark
80	Malaysia/ Thailand CS-A-APB		•					•	1: No. 75 at 607 3: Government of Malaysia

81	France/Tonga 11.1.1980 MB-OA-EEZ-APB	•		equidistance principes équitables	•		1: No. 76 at 621 2. I 5–8 at 1011
82	Costa Rica/Panama 2.2.1980 MB-A		•	despite median rather a perpendicular coastline	•	results to perpendicular	1: No. 77 at 625 2: I 2–6 at 537 3: US State Department, the Office of the Geographer
83	Mauritius/France 2.4.1980 MB-O-APB		•	Equidistance as equitable	•		1: No. 78 at 631 2: II 6–5 at 1353 3: Government of France
84	USA/Cook Islands 11.6.1980 MB-O-APB	•			•		1: No. 79 at 635 2: I 5–5 at 985 3: Government of New Zealand

Table A.1 (*cont.*)

No.	Agreements					Method of delimitation		Source
85	Venezuela/France 17.7.1980 MB-O-APB		•			4: meridian 7: Ref. to int. law and work of UNCLOS	• meridian	1: No. 30 at 643 2: I 2–11 at 603 3: Journal officiel de la République Française
86	Burma/Thailand 25.7.1980 MB-OA			•			•	1: No. 81 at 647 2: II 6–4 at 1341 3: Government of Thailand
87	New Zeland/USA (Tokelau) 2.12.1980 MB-OA-APB	•					•	1: No. 82 at 653 2: I 5–14 at 1125 3: Government New Zealand
88	Indonesia/Papua New Guinea 13.12.1980 MB-OA			•		by reference to former agreement	•	1: No. 83 at 661 2: I 5–10 at 1039 3: Government of Australia
89	France/Brazil 30.1.1981 MB-A-APB				•			1: No. 84 at 669 2: I 3–3 at 777 3: Government of Brazil

90	St. Lucia/France 4.3.1981 O-APB		•		equidist.=equitable in case	•		1. No. 85 at 675 2: I 2–10 at 591 3: Government of St. Lucia
91	Norway/Iceland (Jan Mayen) 22.11.1981 CS-MB-O	•			based on conciliation		•	1: No. 76 at 681 2: II 9–4 at 1755 3: p. 71 joint development zone
92	France/Australia 4.1.1982 MB-O-CS-APB		•		reference to international law and UNCLOS	•		Method difficult to establish No reference was made to equidistance Full effect to islands	1: No. 87 at 689 2. I 5–1 at 905 3. Government of Australia
93	France/UK 24.6.1982 CS-O	•				•			1. No. 88 at 697 2: II 9–3 at 1735 3: UK Government

Table A.1 (cont.)

No.	Agreements	Method of delimitation							Source
94	France/UK (Pacific Islands; Ardupeloso, Tuamotu, Pitcairn, Henderson, Dulie, Oeno Islands) 25.10.1983 EEZ-FZ-O-P	'précise et équitable'				•			1: 131 2: I 5–7 at 1003
95	France/Monaco 6.12.1984 MB-A-APB	5: impact		•				•	1: 17 2: II 8–3 at 1581
96	Argentina/Chile 29.11.1984 CS-EEZ-A-APB	based on Holy Sea		•				•	1: 213 2: I 3–1 at 719
97	Finland/USSR 5.3 1985 O-APB-P		•			•			1: 10–4 (4) 2: II at 1989
98	Costa Rica/ Equador 12.3.1985 MB-OA			•		•			1: 3–8 2: I at 819

99	USSR/North Korea 22.1.1986 MB-A		•					•	1: 5–15(2) 2: I at 1145
100	Colombia/ Honduras 2.8.1986 OA-MB			•		•			1: 2–4 2: I at 503
101	Burma/India (Andaman Sea, Coco Channel and Bay of Bengal) 23.12.1986		•				3: 14–16	•	1: 6–3 2: II at 1329
102	Dominica/France (Guadeloupe and Martinique) 7.9.1987 MB-O				•	First delimitation based 'on the rules and principles of international law as they are expressed in the United Nations Convention on the Law of the sea'	1: 40%	•	1: 2–15 2: I at 705

Table A.1 (*cont.*)

No.	Agreements	Method of delimitation						Source
103	Sweden/USSR 18.4.1988 CS-FB-MB-O-APB		•				75/25% Joint zone	1: 10–9 2: II at 2057
104	Australia/ Solomon Islands 13.9.1988 EEZ-CS-MB-O	•			•	reference to Loscan venture		1: 5–4 2: I at 977
105	Denmark/GDR 14.9.1988 CS/Fishz.-MB-O-P		•		•		1: (I) 2: (ii)	1: 10–11 2: II at 2087
106	Ireland/UK 7.11.1988 (parallels of latitude and meridians of longitudes) CS-O			•			•	1: 9–5 2: II at 1767

107	Tanzania/ Mozambique 28.12.1988 MB-A-APB							1: 4–7 2: I at 893
108	Papua New Guinea/ Solomon Islands 25.1.1989 MB-O Srg LOS both	•				• •		1: 5–16 2: I at 1155
109	Poland/Sweden 10.2.1989 CS-MB-O-APB Fishing zone				25/75% in favour of Sweden; General recognized principles of int. law	•		1: 10-10 2: II at 2077
110	GDR/Poland 22.4.1989 CS-EEZ-A-P FGR 14.11.1990				General recognized principles of int. law	•	•	1: 10–6(1) 10–6(2) 2: II at 2005 II at 2023

Table A.1 (*cont.*)

No.	Agreements	Method of delimitation	Source
111	Poland/Sweden/ USSR 30.6.1989 OA-P-MB	• Tripoint agreement completing bilateral agreements	1: 10–12 2: II at 2097
112	Trinidad and Tobago/ Venezuela 4.8.1989 and 18.4.1990 Parties MB-O	• precise and equitable maritime boundary	1: 2–13(2) 2–13(3) 2: I at 655 I at 675
113	Australia/ Indonesia 11.12.1989 Timor gap CS-O Co-operation zone	• co-operation zone	1: 6–2(5) 2: II at 1245 3: co-operation zone

114	Trinidad and Tobago/ Venezuela 18.4.1990 MB-OA-APB Eastern part		•					1: 2–13(3) 2: I at 675
115	USA/USSR 1.6.1990 MB-O-P-APB	•				longest existing boundary in the world 1600 nm based on 1867 convention		•	1: 1–6 2: I at 447
116	Cook Islands/ France 3.8.1990 MB-O			•			•		1: 5–18 2: I at 1175
117	Belgium/France 8.10–1990 CS-A-APB Reservations by France				•			•	1: 9–16 2: II at 1891
118	France (New Caledonia)/ Solomon Islands 12.11.1990 MB-O			•				•	1: 5–17 2: I at 1167

Table A.1 (*cont.*)

No.	Agreements	Method of delimitation			Source
119	Belgium/UK 29.5.1991 CS-O-P	•	Belgium invoked equity		1: 9–17 2: II at 1901
120	UK/France 25.7.1991 CS-O-P Reservation by France	•	linking to French–Belgian boundary	• 2: unclear	1: 9–3 2: I at 1735

Appendix II General maps

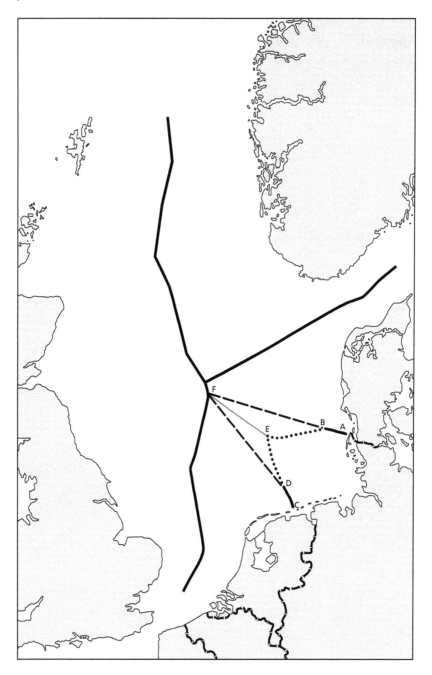

Map 1: *North Sea Continental Shelf (Federal Republic of Germany v. Denmark; Federal Republic of Germany v. Netherlands)* Judgment, ICJ Reports 1969, p. 3 at p. 15. A–B: German–Danish Agreement, 9.6.65; C–D: German–Dutch Agreement, 1.12.1964; E–F: Dutch–Danish Agreement, 31.3. 1966, contested by the Federal Republic of Germany. The Court produced guiding principles of delimitation. It was not asked to draw a boundary line.

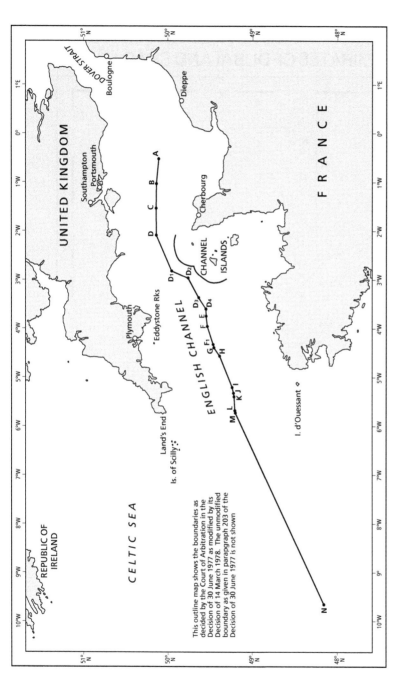

Map 2: *Arbitration Between the United Kingdom of Great Britain and Northern Ireland and the French Republic on the Delimitation of the Continental Shelf*, Decisions of the Court of Arbitration dated 30 June 1977 and 14 March 1978, Command Paper 7438, March 1979, reprinted in 18 ILM, p. 397 at 494.

700   COURT OF ARBITRATION (DUBAI/SHARJAH)

In the matter of an arbitration concerning the border between

THE EMIRATES OF DUBAI AND SHARJAH, 1981

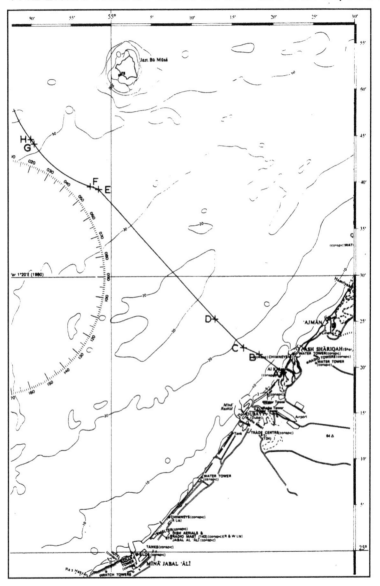

Map 3: *The 1981 Arbitration concerning the Border between the Emirates of Dubai and Sharjah*, E. Lauterpacht and C. J. Greenwood (eds.), *International Law Reports*, vol. 91 (Cambridge University Press, 1993), p. 700.

APPENDIX II: GENERAL MAPS 725

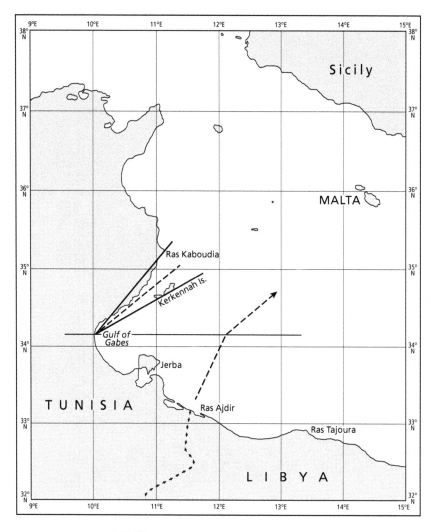

Map 4: *Continental Shelf (Tunisia v. Libyan Arab Jamahiriya)*, Judgment, ICJ Reports 1982, p. 18 at p. 90.

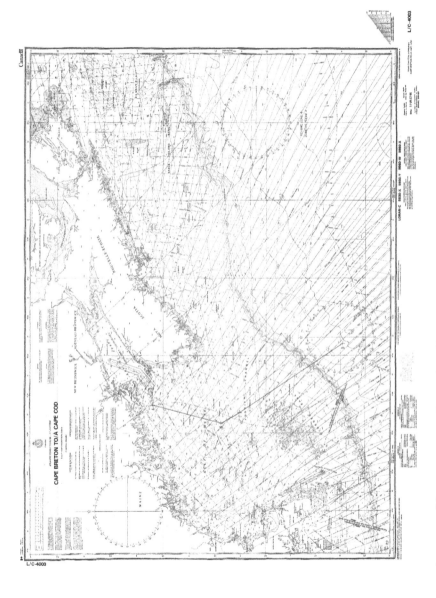

Map 5: *Delimitation of the Maritime Boundary in the Gulf of Maine Area (Canada v. United States of America)*, Judgment, ICJ Reports 1984, p. 246 at p. 346.

APPENDIX II: GENERAL MAPS 727

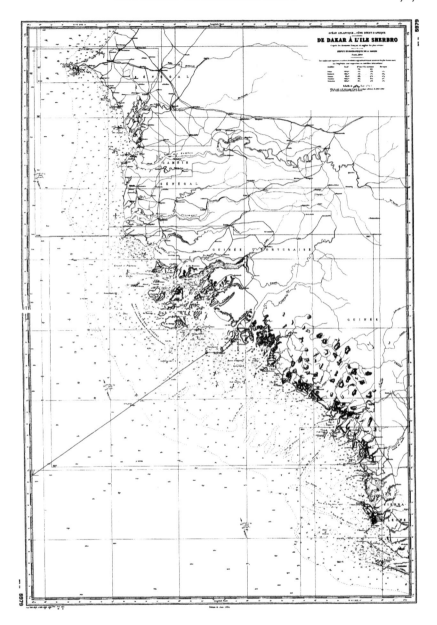

Map 6: *Arbitration Tribunal for the Delimitation of the Maritime Boundary Between Guinea and Guinea-Bissau*, Award of 14 February 1985, transl. in (1986) 25 ILM, p. 251 at p. 307.

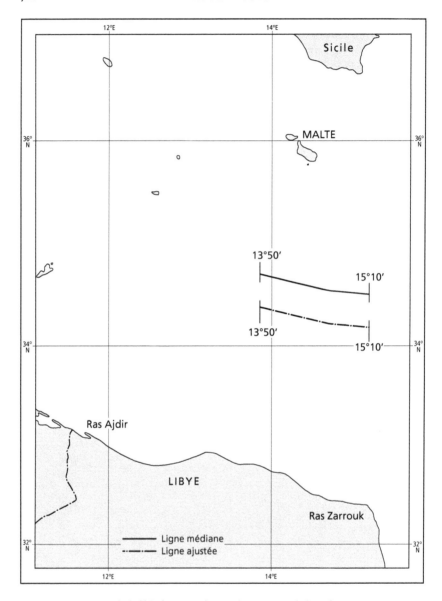

Map 7: *Continental Shelf (Libyan Arab Jamahiriya v. Malta)*, Judgment, ICJ Reports 1985, p. 13 at p. 54.

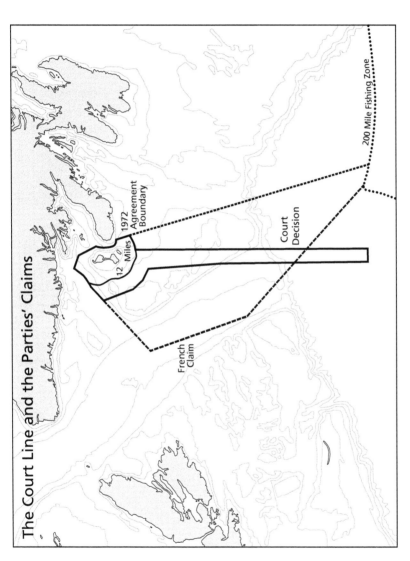

Map 8: Court of Arbitration for the Delimitation of Maritime Areas between Canada and France, *Case concerning de Delimitation of Maritime Areas between Canada and the French Republic* (1992) 31 ILM p. 1145 at p. 1148.

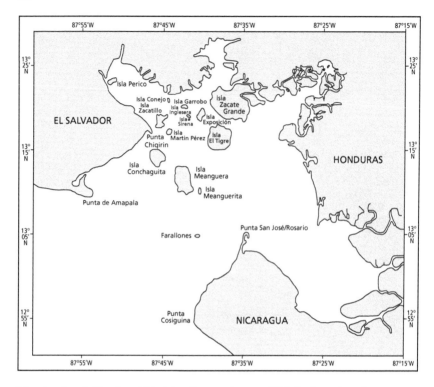

Map 9: *Land, Island and Maritime Frontier Dispute (El Salvador v. Honduras: Nicaragua intervening)*, Judgment, ICJ Reports 1992, p. 351 at p. 587; the map illustrates the Gulf of Fonseca, in the judgment no delimitation of the disputed maritime spaces, whether within or outside the Gulf were made.

APPENDIX II: GENERAL MAPS 731

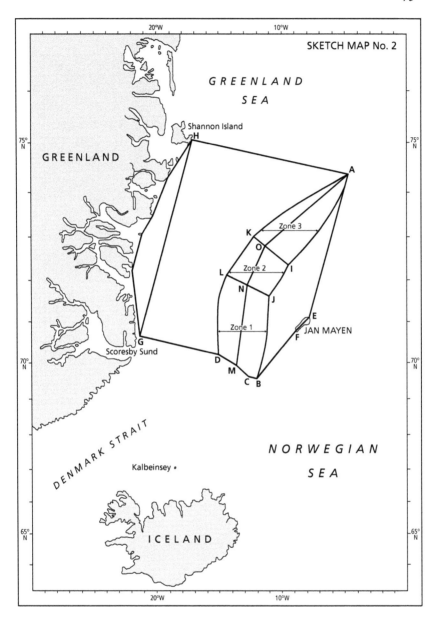

Map 10: *Maritime Delimitation in the Area between Greenland and Jan Mayen (Denmark v. Norway)*, Judgment, ICJ Reports 1993, p. 38 at p.80.

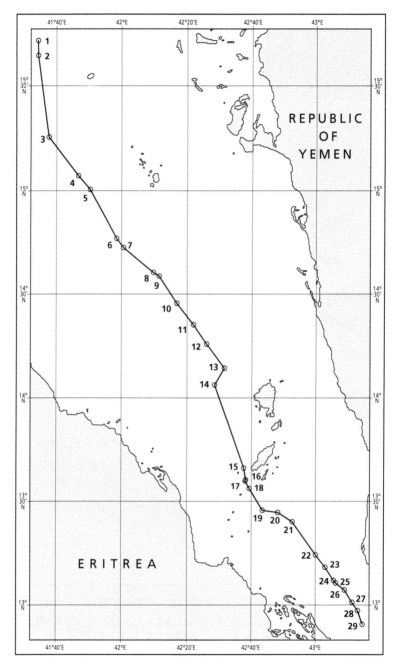

Map 11: *Permanent Court of Arbitration (PCA): Eritrea–Yemen Arbitration* (Second Stage: Maritime Delimitation) (17 December 1999), www.pca-cpa.org/showpage.asp?pag_id=1160 (last accessed 27 March 2014).

MARITIME DELIMITATION AND TERRITORIAL QUESTIONS (JUDGMENT) 105

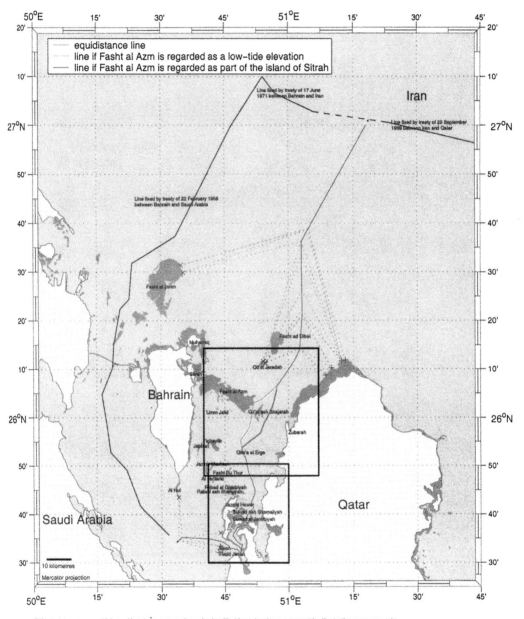

Map 12.1: *Maritime Delimitation and Territorial Questions between Qatar and Bahrain*, Merits, Judgment, ICJ Reports 2001, p. 40 at p. 105.

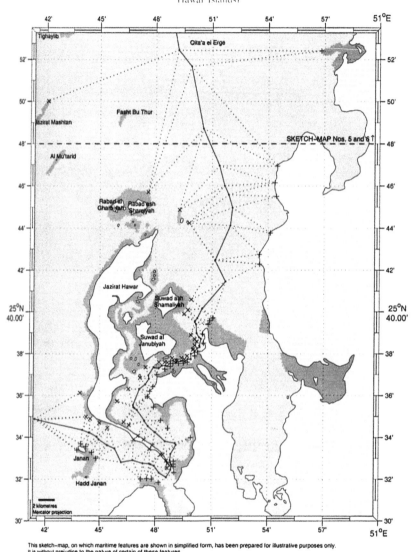

Map 12.2 (Enlargement of Map 12.1): *Maritime Delimitation and Territorial Questions between Qatar and Bahrain,* Merits, Judgment, ICJ Reports 2001, p. 40 at p. 106.

APPENDIX II: GENERAL MAPS 735

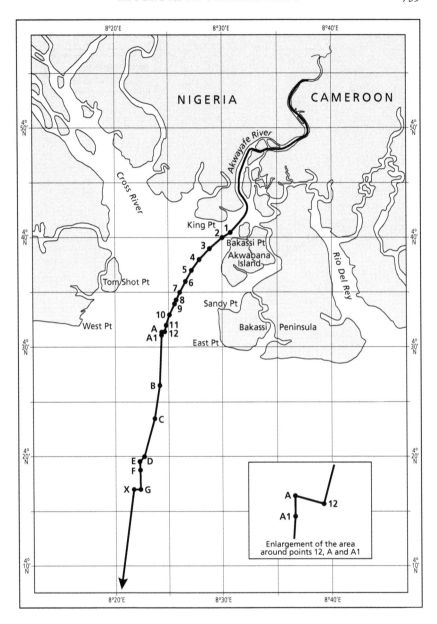

Map 13: *Land and Maritime Boundary between Cameroon and Nigeria (Cameroon v. Nigeria: Equatorial Guinea intervening),* Judgment, ICJ Reports 2002, p. 303 at p. 449.

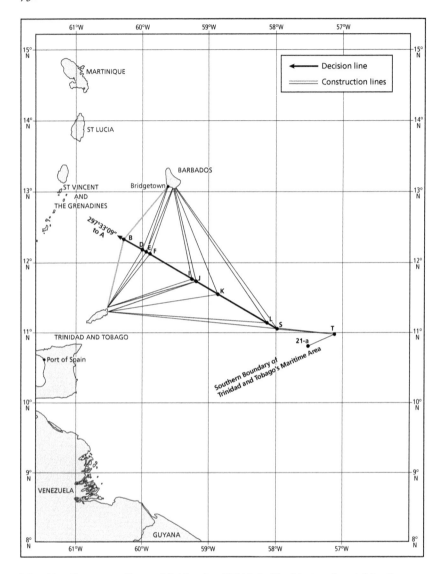

Map 14: *Permanent Court of Arbitration (PCA): In The Matter of an Arbitration between Barbados and the Republic of Trinidad and Tobago* (11 April 2006) (2006) 45 ILM, p. 800 at p. 869.

APPENDIX II: GENERAL MAPS 737

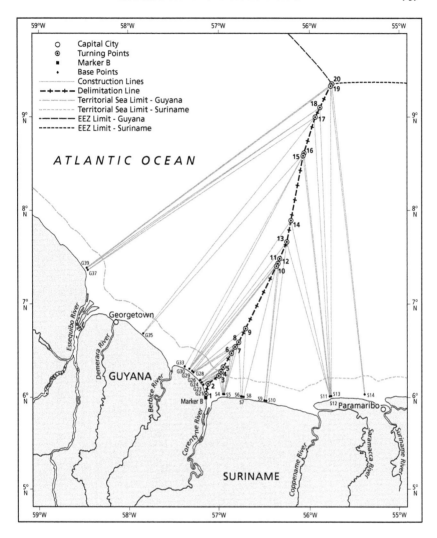

Map 15: *Arbitral Tribunal Constituted Pursuant to Article 287, and in Accordance with Annex VII, of the United Nations Convention on the Law of the Sea in the Matter of an Arbitration between Guyana and Suriname*, Award of 17 September 2007, A-5.

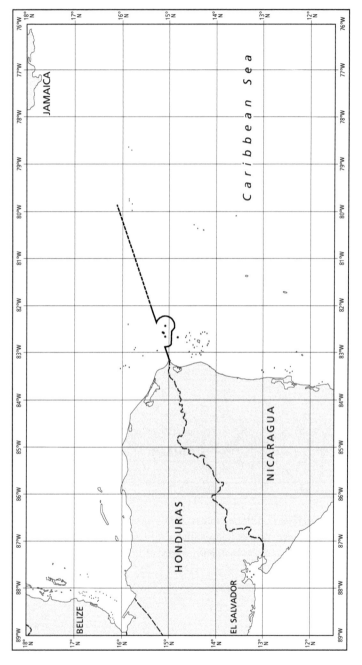

Map 16.1: Territorial and Maritime Dispute between Nicaragua and Honduras in the Caribbean Sea (Nicaragua v. Honduras), Judgment, ICJ Reports 2007, p. 659 at p.761.

APPENDIX II: GENERAL MAPS

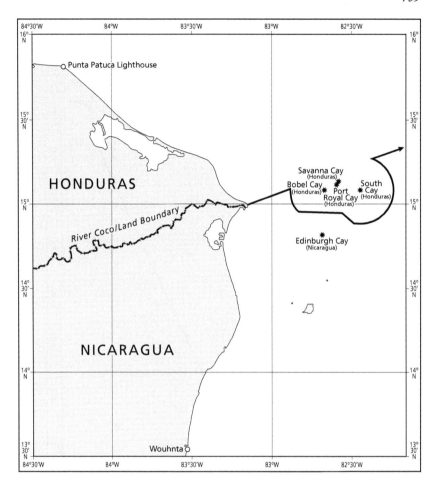

Map 16.2 (Enlargement of Map 16.1): *Territorial and Maritime Dispute between Nicaragua and Honduras in the Caribbean Sea (Nicaragua v. Honduras),* Judgment, ICJ Reports 2007, p. 659 at p. 762.

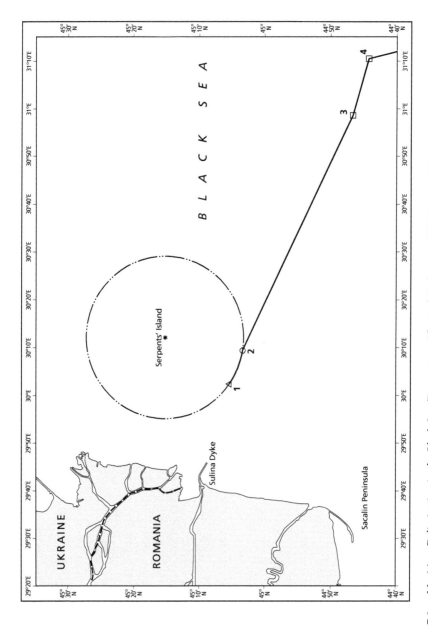

Map 17.1: *Maritime Delimitation in the Black Sea (Romania v. Ukraine)*, Judgment, ICJ Reports 2009, p. 61 at p. 132.

APPENDIX II: GENERAL MAPS 741

Map 17.2: *Maritime Delimitation in the Black Sea (Romania v. Ukraine),* Judgment, ICJ Reports 2009, p. 61 at p. 133.

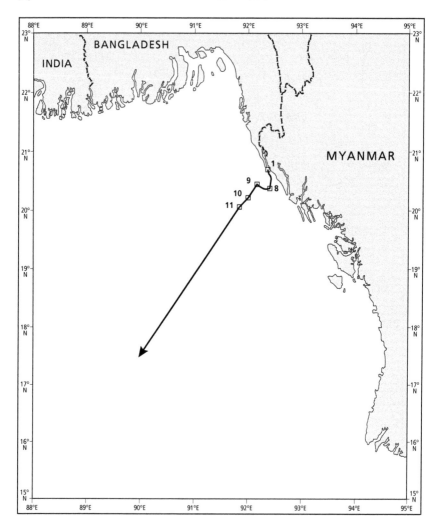

Map 18: *Delimitation of the Maritime Boundary in the Bay of Bengal (Bangladesh v. Myanmar)*, Judgment, ITLOS Reports 2012, p. 4 at p. 129.

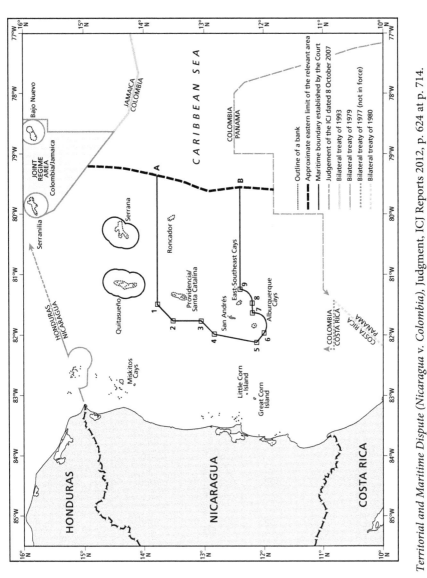

Map 19: *Territorial and Maritime Dispute (Nicaragua v. Colombia)*, Judgment, ICJ Reports 2012, p. 624 at p. 714.

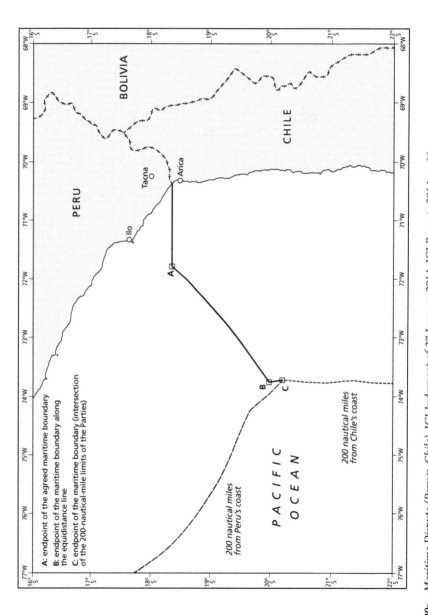

Map 20: *Maritime Dispute (Peru v. Chile)*, ICJ Judgment of 27 January 2014, ICJ Reports 2014, p. 66.

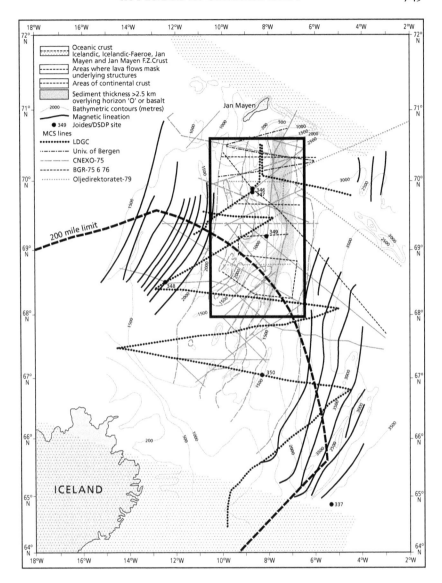

Map 21: *Conciliation Commission on the Continental Shelf Area between Iceland and Jan Mayen: Report and Recommendations to the Governments of Iceland and Norway*, Report and Recommendations to the Governments of Iceland and Norway of the Conciliation Commission on the Continental Shelf Area between Iceland and Jan Mayen (1981) 20 ILM, p. 797 at p. 828.

746 APPENDICES

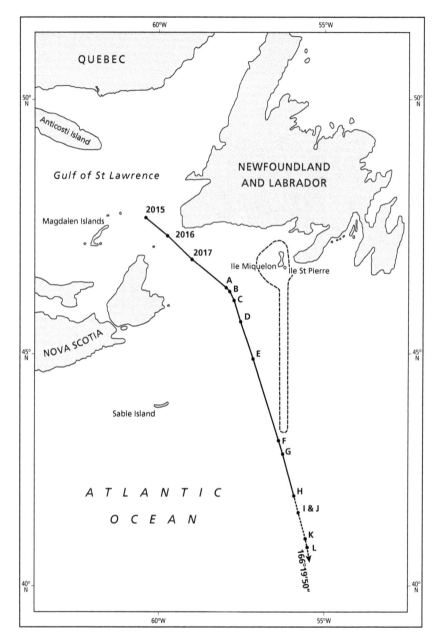

Map 22: Arbitration between Newfoundland and Labrador and Nova Scotia Concerning Portions of the Limits of Their Offshore Areas as defined in the Canada-Nova Scotia Offshore Petroleum Resources Accord Implementation Act and the Canada-Newfoundland and Atlantic Accord Implementation Act, Award of the Tribunal in the Second Phase, Ottawa, 26 March 2002, p. 96.

BIBLIOGRAPHY

Aasen, Pal Jakob, *The Law of Maritime Delimitation and the Russian-Norwegian Maritime Boundary Dispute*. FNI Report 1/2010. Lysaker, FNI, 2010, 77.

Adede, A. O., 'Prolegomena to the Dispute Settlement Part of the Law of the Sea Convention' (1977) 10 N.Y.U. Journal of international Law and Politics, 253.

Akehurst, Michael, 'Equity and General Principles of Law' (1976) 25 International and Comparative Law Quarterly, 801.

Alexander, Lewis M., 'The Gulf of Maine Case: An International Discussion, Studies in Transnational Legal Policy No 21' (1988) American Society of International Law.

'The Ocean Enclosure Movement' (1983) 20 San Diego Law Review, 561.

Allott, Philip, 'Power Sharing in the Law of the Sea' (1983) 77 American Journal of International Law, 1.

American Society of International Law, 'Workshop on ICJ Decision in the Libya-Tunisia Continental Shelf Case' (1982) 76 The American Society of International Law, Proceedings 150.

Amin, S. H., 'Law of Continental Shelf Delimitation: The Gulf Example' (1980) 27 Netherlands International Law Review 335.

Anand, Ram P., 'Freedom of the Sea: Past, Present and Future' in Rafael Cutiérrez Giradotet et al. (eds.), *New Directions in International Law: Essays in Honour of Wolfgang Abendroth: Festschrift zu seinem 75. Geburtstag* (Frankfurt am Main: Campus Verlag, 1982), p. 215.

Origin and Development of the Law of the Sea, Publications on Ocean Development, vol. VII (The Hague: Martinus Nijhoff Publishers, 1983).

(ed.), *The Law of the Sea: Caracas and Beyond* (The Hague: Martinus Nijhoff Publishers, 1980).

'The Politics of a New Legal Order for Fisheries' (1982) 11 Ocean Development & International Law, 265.

Anderson, David, 'Developments in Maritime Boundary Law and Practice' in Jonathan I. Charney et al. (eds.), *International Maritime Boundaries*, 5 vols. (Dordrecht: Martinus Nijhoff Publishers, 1993–2005), vol. V (Colson and Smith), 3197.

Modern Law of the Sea, Selected Essays (The Hague: Martinus Nijhoff Publishers, 2008).

Strategies for Dispute Resolution: Negotiating Joint Agreements, in Gerald H. Blake et al. (eds.) *Boundaries and Energy: Problems and Prospects* (London: Kluwer, 1998), 473.
Apollis, Gilbert, *L'Emprise martitime de l'Etat côtier* (Paris: Editions A. Pedone, 1981).
Arbour, Jean Maurice, 'L'Affaire du Chalutier-Usine 'La Bretagne' ou les droits de l'Etat côtier dans sa zone économique exclusive' (1986) 24 Canadian Yearbook of International Law, 61.
Attard, David J., *The Exclusive Economic Zone in International Law* (Oxford: Clarendon Press, 1987).
Auburn, F. M., 'The North Sea Continental Shelf Boundary Settlement'(1973) 16 Archiv des Völkerrechts, 28.
Auburn, F. M., *Antarctic Law and Politics* (London: C. Hurst & Co., 1982).
Azcarraga de Bustamante, Luis de, 'España suscribe, con Francia e Italia, Dos Convenios sobre Delimitación de sus Plataformas Submarinales Comunas' (1985) 28 Rivista Española de Derecho Internacional, 131.
La Plataforma Submarina y el Derecho Internacional (Madrid: Instituto 'Francisco de Vitoria', Consejo Superior de Investigaciones Cientificas, Ministerio de Marina, 1952).
Bardonnet, Daniel and Virally, Michel (eds.), *Le Nouveau droit international de la mer* (Paris: Editions A. Pedone, 1983).
Barmeyer, Patricia T., 'Litigation of State Maritime Boundary Disputes' in L. De Vorsey and D.G. Dallmeyer (eds.), *Rights to Oceanic Resources* (Dordrecht: Martinus Nijhoff Publishers, 1989), 53.
Barnes, James N., 'The Emerging Convention on the Conservation of Antarctic Marine Living Resources: An Attempt to Meet the New Realities of the Resource Exploitation in the Southern Oceans' in: Jonathan I. Charney (ed.), *The New Nationalism and the Use of Common Spaces* (Totowa NJ: Allanheld, Osmun, 1982), 239.
Barston, Ronald P. and Birnie, Patricia (eds.), *The Maritime Dimension* (London, Boston MA: Allen & Unwin, 1980).
Bath, Richard C., 'Book Review: El Nuevo Derecho del Mar: El Peru y las 200 Millas. By Eduardo Ferrero Costa' (1982) 76 American Journal of International Law, 690.
Bedermann, David J., 'The Old Isolationism and the New Law of the Sea: Reflections on Advice and Consent for UNCLOS', 49 Harvard International Law Journal Online, 22.
Bello, Emmanuel G., 'International Equity and the Law of the Sea: New Perspectives for Developing Countries' (1980) 13 Verfassung und Recht in Uebersee, 201.
Bentwisch, Norman ET AL. 'Justice and Equity in the International Sphere' in *The New Commonwealth Institute Monographs*, Series B. N. 1 (London: Constable, 1936).

Berkowitz, Leonard and Walster, Elaine (eds.), *Equity Theory: Toward a General Theory of Social Interaction* (New York: Academic Press, 1976).

Bermejo, Romualdo, 'Les Principes équitables et les délimitations des zones maritimes: analyse des affaires Tunisie/Jamahariya Arabe Libyenne et du Golfe du Maine' (1988) 1 Hague Yearbook of International Law, 59.

Bernhardt, Rudolf, 'Das Urteil des internationalen Gerichtshofs im Ägäis-Streit' in Ingo von Münch/Hans-Joachim Schlochauer (eds.), *Staatsrecht-Völkerrecht-Europarecht: Festschrift für Hans-Jürgen Schlochauer zum 75. Geburtstag am 28. März 1981* (Berlin, New York: Walter de Gruyter, 1981), 167.

Beurier, Jean Pierre and Cadenat, Patrick, 'Le Contenu économique des normes juridiques dans le droit de la mer contemporain' (1974) 78 Revue Générale de Droit International Public, 575.

Bilge, S., 'Le Nouveau rôle des principes équitables en droit international' in E. Diez et al. (eds.), *Festschrift für R. Bindschedler, Botschafter, Professor Dr. iur., zum 65. Geburtstag am 8. Juli 1980* (Bern: Stämpfli, 1980), 105.

Blake, Gerhald H. (ed.), *Maritime Boundaries, World Boundaries*, vol. V (New York: Routledge, 1994).

Blecher, M. D., 'Equitable Delimitation of Continental Shelf' (1979) 73 American Journal of International Law, 60.

Bleicher, Samuel L., 'The Law Governing Exploitation of Polymetallic Sulfide Deposits from the Seabed' in T. Buergenthal (ed.), *Contemporary Issues in International Law, Essays in Honor of Louis B. John* (Kehl, Strasbourg: N. P. Engel Publisher, 1984).

Blumann, Claude, 'Frontières et limites' (1980) in Société française de droit international colloque de Poitiers, *La Frontière* (Paris: Editions A. Pedone, 1980), 3.

Boczek, Boleslav A., *The Transfer of Marine Technology to Developing Nations in International Law* (The Law of the Sea Institute, Occasional Paper 32, 1982).

Bothe, Rainer, 'Zusammenarbeit statt Grenzziehung: Neue Wege zur 'Lösung' von Grenzstreitigkeiten', in R. Bernhardt (ed.), *Deutsche Landesreferate zum öffentlichen Recht und Völkerrecht* (Heidelberg: Müller, 1982).

Bowett, Derek W., 'Islands, Rocks, Reefs, and Low-Tide Elevations in Maritime Boundary Delimitations', in Jonathan I. Charney et al. (eds.), *International Maritime Boundaries*, 5 vols. (Dordrecht: Martinus Nijhoff Publishers, 1993–2005), vol. I (Charney and Alexander), 130.

'Jurisdiction: Changing Patterns of Authority over Activities and Resources' in R. St. J. Macdonald and D. M. Johnston (eds.), *The Structure and Process of International Law: Essays in Legal Philosophy, Doctrine and Theory* (Dordrecht: Martinus Nijhoff Publishers, 1983), 555.

'The Arbitration between the United Kingdom and France concerning the Continental Shelf Boundary in the English Channel and South Western Approaches' (1979) 49 British Yearbook of International Law, 1.

'The Economic Factor in Maritime Delimitation Cases' in P. Ziccardi (ed.), *International Law at the Time of its Codification, Essays in Honour of Roberto Ago* (Milan: Guiffre, 1987), vol. II, 45.

The Law of International Institutions (London: Steven & Sons, 1982).

The Legal Regime of Islands in International Law (Alphen aan den Rijn, Dobbs Ferry NY,Sijthoff and Noordhoff, Oceana, 1979).

Boyer, Georges, 'La Notion d'équité et son rôle dans la jurisprudence des Parlements' in *Mélanges offerts à Jacques Maury, tome II droit comparé, théorie générale du droit et droit privé* (Paris: Librairie Dalloz et Sirey, 1960).

Brown Weiss, Edith, *In Fairness to Future Generations: International Law, Common Patrimony and Intergenerational Equity* (Tokyo: The United Nations University, 1989).

'Our Rights and Obligations to Future Generations for the Environment' (1990) 84 American Journal of International Law, 198.

'The Planetary Trust: Conservation and Intergenerational Equity' (1984) 11 Ecology Law Quarterly, 495.

Brown, Edward Duncan, 'Freedom of the High Seas versus the Common Heritage of Mankind: Fundamental Principles in Conflict' (1983) 20 San Diego Law Review, 521.

Seabed Energy and Minerals: The International Legal Regime, 2 vols. (The Hague: Martinus Nijhoff Publishers, 2001), vol. I: The Continental Shelf.

'The Anglo-French Continental Shelf Case' (1979) 16 San Diego Law Review, 461.

'The Impact of Unilateral Legislation on the Future Legal Regime of Deep-Sea Mining' (1982) 20 Archiv des Völkerrechts, 148.

The International Law of the Sea, 2 vols. (Aldershot: Dartmouth Publishing, 1994).

The Legal Regime of Hydrospace (London: Stevens for the London Institute of World Affairs, 1971).

'The Libya-Malta Continental Shelf Case (1985)' in Bin Cheng and E. D. Brown (eds.), *Contemporary Problems of International Law: Essays in Honour of G. Schwarzenberger on his Eightieth Birthday* (London: Stevens, 1988), 3.

'The North Sea Continental Shelf Cases' (1970) 23 Current Legal Problems, 187.

The Tunisia/Libya Continental Shelf Case: A Missed Opportunity' (1983) 7 Marine Policy, 142.

Brownlie Ian, 'Legal Status of Natural Resources in International Law'(1979) 162 Recueil des cours, I, 245.

Bubier, Jill L., 'International Management of Atlantic Salmon: Equitable Sharing and Building Consensus' (1988) 19 Ocean Development & International Law, 35.

Buderi, Charles L. O. and Caron, David D. (eds.), *Perspectives on U.S. Policy Toward the Law of the Sea: Prelude to the Final Session of the Third U.N. Conference on the Law of the Sea*, Proceedings of a Symposium held in 1982, The Law of the Sea Institute Occasional Paper No. 35 (Honolulu: Law of the Sea Institute, University of Hawaii, 1985).

Burke, William T., 'Exclusive Fisheries Zones and Freedom of Navigation' (1983) 20 San Diego Law Review, 595.

The New International Law of Fisheries: UNCLOS 1982 and Beyond (Oxford: Clarendon Press, 1994).

'U.S. Fishery Management and the New Law of the Sea' (1982) 76 American Journal of International Law, 24.

Burmester, Henry, 'The Torres Strait Treaty: Ocean Boundary Delimitation by Agreement'(1982) 76 American Journal of International Law, 321.

Buzan, Barry, 'Negotiation by Consensus: Developments in Technique at the United Nations Conference on the Law of the Sea' (1981) 75 American Journal of International Law, 324.

Caflisch, Lucius, 'La Révision du droit international de la mer' (1973) 29 Schweizerisches Jahrbuch für Internationales Recht, 49.

'Les Zones maritimes sous juridiction nationale, leurs limites et leurs délimitations'(1980) 84 Revue Générale de Droit International Public, 68.

'Vers une nationalisation ou une internationalisation des espaces marins?' (1990) 61 Relations Internationales, 59.

Caminos, Hugo (ed.), *Law of the Sea* (Aldershot: Ashgate/Dartmouth, 2001).

'Sources of the Law of the Sea', in René-Jean Dupuy and Daniel Vignes (eds.), *A Handbook of the New Law of the Sea*, 2 vols. (Dordrecht: Martinus Nijhoff Publishers 1991), vol. I, 29.

Caron, David D., 'Climate Change, Sea Level Rise and the Coming Uncertainty in Oceanic Boundaries: A Proposal to Avoid Conflict' in Seoung-Yong Hong and Jon Van Dyke (eds.), *Maritime Boundary Disputes, Settlement Processes, and the Law of the Sea* (Leiden, Boston MA: Martinus Nijhoff Publishers, 2009), 1.

Caron, David D. and Scheiber, Harry N. (eds.), *Bringing New Law to Ocean Waters* (Leiden: Martinus Nijhoff Publishers, 2004).

Carroz, Jean E., 'Institutional Aspects of Fishery Management under the New Regime of the Oceans' (1984) 21 San Diego Law Review, 513.

'Les Problèmes de la pêche à la Conférence sur le droit de la mer et dans la pratique des Etats' (1980) 84 Revue Générale de Droit International Public, 705.

and Savini, Michel, 'Les Accords de pêches conclus par les Etats africains riverains de l'Atlantique' (1983) 23 Annuaire Français de Droit International, 675.

and Savini, Michel, *The Practice of Coastal States Regarding Foreign Access to Fisheries Resources,* FAO Fisheries Report No. 293 (Rome: 1983).

Castañeda, Jorge, 'La Conférence des Nations Unis sur le droit de la mer et l'avenir de la diplomatie multilaterale' in A. Migliazza et al. (eds.),

International Law at the Time of its Codification: Essays in Honour of Roberto Ago, 4 vols. (Milan: Giuffrè, 1987), vol. II.

Cellamore, Giovanni, 'Intervento in causa davanti alle Corte internazionale di giustizia e lien jurisdictionel tra interveniente e parti originale del processo' 66 Rivista di diritto internazionale, 291.

Charney, Jonathan 'Progressive Development of Public International Law through International Conferences' in C. Buderi and D. Caron (eds.), Perspectives on U.S. Policy Toward the Law of the Sea: Prelude to the Final Session of the Third U.N. Conference on the Law of the Sea, Proceedings of a Symposium held in 1982, The Law of the Sea Institute Occasional Paper No. 35 (Honolulu: Law of the Sea Institute, University of Hawaii, 1985), 88.

Charney, Jonathan I. et al. (eds.), *International Maritime Boundaries*, 5 vols. (The Hague: Martinus Nijhoff Publishers, 1993–2005) vols. I and II (Charney and Alexander (eds.), 1993), vol. III (Charney and Alexander (eds.), 1998), vol. IV (Charney and Smith (eds.), 2002), vol. V (Colson and Smith (eds.), 2005).

Charney, Jonathan I., 'International Maritime Boundaries for the Continental Shelf: The Relevance of Natural Prolongation' in Ando, Nisuke, McWhinney, Edward and Wolfrum, Rüdiger (eds.), *Liber Amicorum Judge Shigeru Oda* (The Hague: Kluwer Law International 2002), 1011.

'Introduction', in Jonathan I. Charney et al. (eds.), *International Maritime Boundaries*, 5 vols. (Dordrecht: Martinus Nijhoff Publishers, 1993–2005), vol. I (Charney and Alexander), xxvii.

'Ocean Boundaries Between Nations: A Theory for Progress' (1984) 78 American Journal of International Law, 582.

'Progress in International Maritime Boundary Delimitation Law' (1994) 88 American Journal of International Law, 227.

'Technology and International Negotiations' (1982) 76 American Journal of International Law, 78.

'The Delimitation of Lateral Seaward Boundaries between States in a Domestic Context' (1981) 75 American Journal of International Law, 12.

'The Delimitation of Ocean Boundaries', in L. De Vorsey and D. Dallmeyer (eds.), *Rights to Oceanic Resources* (Dordrecht: Martinus Nijhoff Publishers, 1989), 25.

Chinkin, Christine, *Third Parties in International Law* (Oxford University Press, 1993).

Christie, Donna R., 'Coastal Energy Impact Program Boundaries on the Atlantic Coast: A Study of the Law Applicable to Lateral Seaward Boundaries' (1979) 19 Virginia Journal of International Law, 841.

'From the Shoals of the Ras Kaboudia to the Shores of Tripoli: The Tunisia/Libya Continental Shelf Boundary Delimitation' (1983) 13 Georgia Journal of International and Comparative Law, 1.

Christy, Francis T. and Scott, Anthony, *The Common Wealth in Ocean Fisheries* (Baltimore MD: Johns Hopkins Press, London: Oxford University Press, 1965).

Churchill, Robin R., 'Maritime Delimitation in the Jan Mayen Area' (1985) 9 Marine Policy, 16.

'The Greenland-Jan Mayen Case and its Significance for the International Law of Maritime Boundary Delimitation' (1994) 9 International Journal of Marine and Coastal Law, 1.

Clain, L. E., 'Gulf of Maine – A Disappointing First in the Delimitation of a Single Maritime Boundary' (1985) 25 Virginia Journal of International Law, 521.

Collins, Edward Jr. and Rogoff, Martin A., 'The International Law of Maritime Boundary Delimitation' (1982) 34 Maine Law Review, 1.

Colson, David A., 'Litigating Maritime Boundary Disputes at the International Level – One Perspective' in Dorinda G. Dallmeyer and Louis De Vorsey (eds.), *Rights to Oceanic Resources* (Dordrecht: Martinus Nijhoff Publishers, 1989).

'The Legal Regime of Maritime Boundary Agreements' in Jonathan I. Charney et al. (eds.), *International Maritime Boundaries*, 5 vols.(The Hague: Martinus Nijhoff Publishers, 1993–2005), vol. I (Charney and Alexander), 41.

'The United Kingdom-France Continental Shelf Arbitration' (1978) 72 American Journal of International Law, 95.

'The Maritime Boundary of the United States' (1981) 75 American Journal of International Law, 729.

'The United Kingdom-France Continental Shelf Arbitration: Interpretative Decision of March 1978' (1979) 73 American Journal of International Law, 112.

Combacau, Jean, *Le Droit international de la mer* (Paris: Presses Universitaires de France, 1985).

Conforti, Benedetto, 'L'Arrêt de la Cour internationale de justice dans l'affaire de la délimitation du plateau continental entre la Libye et Malte' (1986) Revue Générale de droit international public, 313.

and Francalanci, Giampiero (eds.), *Atlante dei Confini Sottomarini – Atlas of the Seabed Boundaries*, Part I (Milan: Giuffrè, 1979).

et al. (eds.), *Atlante dei Confini Sottomarini – Atlas of the Seabed Boundaries*, Part II (Milan: Giuffrè, 1987).

Cook, Peter J. and Carleton, Chris M. (eds.), *Continental Shelf Limits: The Scientific and Legal Interface* (Oxford University Press, 2000).

Cooper, John, 'Delimitation of the Maritime Boundary in the Gulf of Maine Area' (1986) 16 Ocean Development & International Law, 59.

Cosford, E. J., 'The Continental Shelf 1910–1945' (1958) 4 McGill Law Journal 245.

Dallmeyer, Dorinda G. and De Vorsey, Louis (eds.), *Rights to Oceanic Resources* (Dordrecht: Martinus Nijhoff Publishers, 1989).

De Aréchaga, Jiménez, 'The Conception of Equity in Maritime Delimitation', in Università di Genova et al. (eds.), *II International Law at the Time of its Codification, Essays in Honour of Roberto Ago* (Milan: Giuffré, 1987), 229.

De Lacharrière, Guy, 'La Loi française sur l'exploration des ressources minerales des grands fonds marin' (1981) 27 Annuaire Français de Droit International, 673.

Decaux, Emmanuel, 'L'Affaire de la délimitation maritime dans la région située entre le Groënland et Jan Mayen (Danemark c. Norvège) arrêt de la C.I.J. du 14 juin 1993' (1993) 39 Annuaire Français de Droit International, 495.

'L'Arrêt de la Chambre de La Cour Internationale de Justice sur l'affaire de la délimitation de la frontière maritime dans le Golfe du Maine (Canada/Etats-Unis)' (1984) 19 Annuaire Français de Droit International, 304.

'L'Arrêt de la Cour internationale de justice dans l'affaire du plateau continental (Tunisie/Libye)' (1982) 28 Annuaire Français de Droit International, 357.

'L'Arrêt de la Cour internationale de justice sur la requête de l'Italie à fin d'intervention dans l'affaire du Plateau continental entre la Libye et Malte' (1984) 29 Annuaire Français de Droit International, 282.

Degan, Vladimir-Duro, *L'Equité et le droit international* (La Haye: Martinus Nijhoff Publishers, 1970).

Deschenaux, Henri, 'Le Traitement de l'équité en droit Suisse' in M. Bridel (ed.), Recueil des travaux suisses présentés au VIIIe Congrès international de droit comparé (Basel: Verlag Helbing & Lichtenhahn, 1970), 27.

'Richterliches Ermessen' in Max Gutzwiller (ed.), *Einleitung und Personenrecht* (Basel: Helbling Lichtenhahn, 1967), 130.

Dipla, Haritini, 'La Sentence arbitrale du 10 juin 1992 en l'affaire de la délimitation des espaces maritimes entre le Canada et la France'(1994) Journal du droit international, 653.

Le Régime jruidique des îles dans le droit international de la mer (Paris: Presses Universitaires de France. Geneva: Institut universitaire de hautes études internationales: 1984).

Donges, Jürgen B., *The Economics of Deep-Sea Mining* (Berlin: Springer-Verlag, 1984).

Druey, Jean Nicolas, 'Interessenabwägung – eine Methode?' in *Beiträge zur Methode des Rechts, St. Galler Festgabe zum schweizerischen Juristentag 1981* (Bern: Haupt, 1981), 131.

Dupuy, René-Jean, 'Droit de la mer et communauté internationale' in D. Bardonnet (ed.), *Mélanges offerts à Paul Reuter: le droit international: unité et diversité* (Paris: Editions A. Pedone, 1981), 221.

L'Océan partagé (Paris: Editions A. Pedone, 1979).

The Law of the Sea: Current Problems (Dobbs Ferry NY: Oceana Publications Inc.; Leiden: Sijthoff, 1974).

(ed.), *The Management of Humanity's Resources: The Law of the Sea*, Workshop 29–31 October 1981, Hague Academy of International Law (The Hague, Boston MA: Martinus Nijhoff Publishers, 1982).

'The Sea under National Competence' in René-Jean Dupuy and Daniel Vignes (eds.), *A Handbook on the New Law of the Sea*, 2 vols. (Dordrecht: Martinus Nijhoff Publishers, 1991), vol. I, 247.

and Vignes, Daniel (eds.), *A Handbook of the New Law of the Sea* (Dordrecht: Martinus Nijhoff Publishers, 1991).

and Vignes, Daniel (eds.), *Traité du nouveau droit de la mer* (Paris: Editions Economica, 1985).

Eckert, Ross D., *The Enclosure of Ocean Resources: Economics and the Law of the Sea* (Stanford CA: Hoover Institution Press, 1979).

Eitel, Tono, 'Seerechtsreform und internationale Politik' (1982) 107 Archiv des oeffentlichen Rechts, 216.

Elferink, Alex G. Oude, 'Third Stats in Maritime Boundary Delimitation Cases: Too Big a Role, Too Small a Role, or Both?' in Aldo Chirop, Ted L. Dorman and Susan J., Rolston (eds.), The Future of Ocean Regime Building: Essays in Tribute of Douglas M. Johnston (Leiden: Martinus Nijhoff Publishers 200) 611.

El-Hakim, Ali A., *The Middle Eastern States and the Law of the Sea* (Manchester University Press, 1979).

Elias, Taslim Olawale, 'The Doctrine of Intertemporal Law' (1980) 74 American Journal of International Law, 285.

'The Limits of the Right of Intervention in a Case Before the International Court of Justice' in Bernhardt, Rudolf (ed.), *Völkerrecht als Rechtsordnung – Internationale Gerichtsbarkeit – Menschenrechte: Festschrift für Hermann Mosler* (Berlin, Heidelberg, New York: Springer, 1983), 159.

Elkind, Jerome B., 'The Aegan Sea Case and Article 41 of the Statute of the International Court of Justice' (1979) 32 Révue Héllenique de Droit International, 285.

Interim Protection: A Functional Approach (The Hague: Martinus Nijhoff Publishers, 1981), 211.

Engisch, Karl, *Logische Studien zur Gesetzesanwendung*, (Heidelberg: Carl Winter Universitätsverlag, 1963).

Espiell, Héctor Gros, 'The Right of Development as a Human Right' (1981)16 Texas International Law Journal, 189.

Esser, Josef, Grundsatz und Norm in der richterlichen Fortbildung des Privatrechts, 4th edn. (Tübingen: Mohr, 1990).

Vorverständnis und Methodenwahl in der Rechtsfindung: Rationalitätsgrundlagen richterlicher Entscheidungspraxis, 2nd edn. (Frankfurt am Main: Athenäum-Fischer-Taschenbuch-Verlag, 1972).

'Wandlungen von Billigkeit und Billigkeitsrechtssprechung im modernen Privatrecht' in University of Tübingen, Law Faculty, *Summum Ius Summa Iniuria: Individualgerechtigkeit und der Schutz allgemeiner Werte im Rechtsleben* (Tübingen: Mohr, 1963), 22.

Evans, Malcolm D., 'Case Concerning Maritime Delimitation in the Area between Greenland and Jan Mayen (Denmark v. Norway)' (1994) 43 International and Comparative Law Quarterly, 697.

'Delimitation and the Common Maritime Boundary' (1993) 64 British Yearbook of International Law, 283.

Evensen, Jens, 'La Délimitation du plateau continental entre le Norvège et l'Islande dans le secteur de Jan Mayen' (1983) 27 Annuaire Français de Droit International, 738.

'The United Nations Convention on the Law of the Seas of December 10, 1982: Its Political and Legal Impact – Present and Future' (1982) 38 Revue égyptienne de droit international public, 11.

Extavour, Winston Conrad, *The Exclusive Economic Zone: A Study of the Evolution and Progressive Development of the International Law of the Sea* (Geneva: Institut universitaire de hautes études internationales, 1978).

Farrar, John H. and Dugdale, Anthony M., *Introduction to Legal Method* (London: Sweet & Maxwell 1984).

Feldman, Mark B., 'The Tunisia-Libya Continental Shelf Case: Geographic Justice or Judicial Compromise?' (1983) 77 American Journal of International Law, 219.

Ferrero Costa, Eduardo, *El Nuevo derecho del mar: el Perú y las 200 millas* (Lima: Pontificia Universidad Católica del Perú, 1979).

Fietta, Stephen, 'Guyana/Suriname Award' (2008) 102(1) American Journal of International Law, 119.

Fox, Hazel et al. (ed.), *Joint Development of Offshore Oil and Gas: A Model Agreement for States for Joint Development with Explanatory Commentary* (London: British Institute of International and Comparative Law, 1989).

François Eustache, 'L'Affaire du plateau continental de la mer du Nord' (1970) 74 Revue Générale de Droit International Public, 591.

Franck, Thomas M., *Fairness in International Law and Institutions* (Oxford: Clarendon Press, 1995).

Frankx, Erik, 'Baltic Sea Boundaries' in Jonathan I. Charney et al. (eds.), *International Maritime Boundaries*, 5 vols.(Dordrecht: Martinus Nijhoff Publishers, 1993–2005), vol. V (Colson and Smith), 3197.

Freestone, David et al. (eds.), *The Law of the Sea: Progress and Prospects* (Oxford University Press, 2006).

Friedheim, Robert L., 'A Proper Order for the Oceans: An Agenda for the New Century' in Davor Vidas and Willy Østreng (eds.), *Order for the Oceans at the Turn of the Century* (The Hague: Kluwer, 1999).

Friedmann, Wolfgang, *Legal Theory* (New York: Columbia University Press, 1967).

'The Contribution of English Equity to the Idea of an International Equity Tribunal' in *The New Commonwealth Institute Monographs* Series B. N. 5 (London: Constable, 1935).

'The North Sea Continental Shelf Cases – A Critique' (1970) 64 American Journal of International Law, 229.

Fritzemeyer, Wolfgang, *Die Intervention vor dem internationalen Gerichtshof: Eine internationale verfahrensrechtliche Untersuchung auf rechtsvergleichender Grundlage* (Baden-Baden: Nomos Verlagsgesellschaft, 1984).

García-Amador, F. V., 'The Origins of the Concept of an Exclusive Economic Zone: Latin American Practice and Legislation' in Francisco Orrego Vicuña (ed.), *The Exclusive Economic Zone: A Latin American Perspective* (Boulder CO: Westview Press, 1984), 7.

García-Amador, Francisco., 'The Latin American Contribution to the Development of the Law of the Sea' (1974) 68 American Journal of International Law, 33.

Gaster Jens-Lienhard, *Der Meeresbodenbergbau unter der hohen See: Neuland des Seevölkerrechts und der nationalen Gesetzgebung* (Cologne: Carl Heymanns Verlag, 1987).

Gavouneli, Maria, *Functional Jurisdiction in the Law of the Sea* (Leiden: Martinus Nijhoff Publishers, 2007).

Gehe, Katja, *Nchhaltige Entwicklung als Rechtsprinzip* (Tübingen: Mohr Siebeck 2011).

Gehring Markus W., Cordonier Segger, Marie Claire (eds.), Sustainable Development in World Trade Law (The Hague: Kluwer Law International, 2005).

Gernhuber, Joachim, 'Die Billigkeit und ihr Preis' in University of Tübingen, Law Faculty, *Summum Ius Summa Iniuria: Individualgerechtigkeit und der Schutz allgemeiner Werte im Rechtsleben* (Tübingen: Mohr, 1963).

Die Integrierte Billigkeit' in Joachim Gernhuber (ed.), *Tradition und Fortschritt im Recht, Festschrift zum 500-jährigen Bestehen der Tübinger Juristenfakultät* (Tübingen: Mohr, 1977).

Gidel, Gilbert, Le Droit international public de la mer, 3 vols. (Chateauroux: Mellottée, 1932–1934, repr. 1981), vol. III.

Gotlieb, Allan E., 'The Impact of Technology on the Development of International Law' (1981) 170(I) Recueil des cours, 115.

Gounaris, Emmanuel, 'Die Aufteilung des Festlandsockels unter dem Adriatischen und Ionischen Meer zwischen Griechenland und Italien vom 24.5.1977 und die Internationale Praxis' (1978) 31 Revue hellénique de droit international, 191.

'Die völkerrechtliche und aussenpolitische Bedeutung der Kontinental-Shelf-Doktrin in der Staatenpraxis Griechenlands, der Bundesrepublik Deutschland und der Deutschen Demokratischen Republik', in Günther Doeker, *Völkerrecht und internationale Politik*, 7 vols. (Frankfurt am Main, Bern, Las Vegas LA: Peter Lang, 1979), vol. I, 261.

'The Delimitation of the Continental Shelf of Islands: Some Observations' (1980), 33 Revue hellénique de droit international, 111.

'The Delimitation of the Continental Shelf of Jan Mayen' (1983) 24 Archiv des Völkerechts 492.

'The Extension and Delimitation of Sea Areas under the Sovereignty, Sovereign Rights and Jurisdiction of Coastal States' in B. Vukas (ed.), Essays on the New Law of the Sea (University of Zagreb, 1985), 85.

Grahl-Madsen, Erik A., 'Økonomisk sone rundt Jan Mayen?' (1980) 49 Nordisk tidsskrift for international ret, 3.

Grisel, Etienne, 'The Lateral Boundaries of the Continental Shelf and the Judgment of the International Court of Justice in the North Sea Continental Shelf Cases' (1970) 64 American Journal of International Law, 526.

Gros, André, 'La Recherche du consensus dans les décisions de la Cour Internationale de Justice' in R. Berhardt et al. (eds.), *Völkerrecht als Rechtsordnung, Internationale Gerichtsbarkeit, Menschenrechte: Festschrift für Hermann Mosler* (Berlin: Springer, 1983), 351.

Gross, Leo, 'The Dispute between Greece and Turkey Concerning the Continental Shelf in the Aegaen' (1977) 71 American Journal of International Law, 31.

Gündling, Lothar, *Die Zweihundert-Seemeilen Wirtschaftszone: Entstehung eines neuen Regimes des Meeresvölkerrechts* (Berlin, New York: Springer, 1983).

'Our Responsibility to Future Generations' in Anthony D'Amato, Edith Brown Weiss and Lothar Gündling, 'Agora: What Obligations Does Our Generation Owe to the Next? An Approach to Global Environmental Responsibility' (1990) 84 American Journal of International Law, 190.

Habicht, Max, 'The Power of the Judge to Give A Decision *Ex Aequo et Bono*', *The New Commonwealth Institute, Monographs* Series B No. 2 (London: Constable, 1935).

Hanbury, Harold G. in Jill E. Martin (ed.), *Hanbury & Martin: Modern Equity* (London: Thomson, Sweet and Maxwell, 2009).

Henchonz, Alain-Denis, *Réglementations nationales et internationales de l'exploration et de l'exploitation des grands fonds marins* (Zurich: Schulthess Polygraphischer Verlag, 1992).

Herman, Lawrence L., 'The Court Giveth and the Court Taketh Away: An Analysis of the Tunisia-Libya Continental Shelf Case' (1984) 33 International and Comparative Law Quarterly, 825.

'The New Foundland Offshore Mineral Rights References: An Imperfect Mingling of International and Municipal Law' (1984) 22 Canadian Yearbook of International Law, 194.

Hodgson, Robert D. and Cooper, E. John, 'The Technical Delimitation of a Modern Equidistant Boundary' (1976) 3 Ocean Development & International Law Journal, 361.
Hollick, Ann L., 'U.S. Foreign Policy and the Law of the Sea' (1981) 17 Virginia Journal of International Law, 196.
  'U.S. Ocean Policy: The Truman Proclamation' (1981) 17 Virginia Journal of International Law, 23.
Hong, Seoung-Yong and Van Dyke, Jon M. (eds.), *Maritime Boundary Disputes, Settlement Processes, and the Law of the Sea* (Leiden: Martinus Nijhoff Publishers, 2009).
Howard, Matthew, 'The Convention on the Conservation of Antarctic Marine Living Resources: A Five-Year Review' (1989) 38 International & Comparative Law Quarterly 104.
Hughes, Valerie, 'Nova Scotia – Newfoundland Dispute over Offshore Areas: The Delimitation Phase' (2002) XK Canadian Yearbook of International Law, 373.
Hurst, Sir Cecil, 'Whose is the Bed of the Sea' (1923) 4 British Yearbook of International Law, 42.
Hussein, Kamal, *Legal Aspects of the New International Economic Order* (Law of the Sea and NIEO) (London, New York: Pinter, 1980).
Hutchinson, D. N., 'The Seaward Limit to the Continental Shelf Jurisdiction in Customary International Law' (1986) 56 British Yearbook of International Law, 111.
Institute of Public International Law and Relations (ed.), *The Law of the Sea with Emphasis on the Mediterranean Issues, Thesaurus Acroasium*, vol. XVII (Thessaloniki: Sakkoulas Publications, 1991).
Institute of Public International Law and Relations (ed.), *The Law of the Sea, Thesaurus Acroasium*, vol. VII (Thessaloniki: Sakkoulas Publications, 1977).
Jackson, John H., *Sovereignty, WTO, and Changing Fundamentals of International Law* (Cambridge University Press, 2006).
Jenks, Wilfried, 'Craftsmanship in International Law' (1956) 50 American Journal of International Law, 32.
  'Equity as a part of the law applied by the Permanent Court of International Justice' (1937) 53 Law Quarterly Review, 519–524.
  The Prospects of International Adjudication (London: Stevens, 1964), 316.
Jennings, Robert, 'Law-Making and Package Deal' in Anastasia Strati, Maria Gavouneli and Nikolaos Skourtos (eds.), *Mélanges offertes à Paul Reuter* (Paris: Editions A. Pedone, 1981), 347.
  'The Principles Governing Marine Boundaries' in Kay Hailbronner (ed.), *Staat und Völkerrechtsordnung, Festschrift für Karl Doering* (Berlin, Heidelberg, New York, London, Tokyo, Hong Kong: Springer,1989) 397.
Jennings, Robert Y., 'A Changing Law of the Sea' (1972) 31 Cambridge Law Journal, 32.

'The Limits of the Continental Shelf Jurisdiction: Some Possible Implications of the North Sea Case' (1969) 19 International and Comparative Law Quarterly, 819.

Jessup, Philip C., 'Intervention in the International Court of Justice' (1981) 75 American Journal of International Law, 903.

Jewett, Marcus L., 'The Evolution of the Legal Regime of the Continental Shelf' (1984) 22 Canadian Yearbook of International Law, 157.

Jiménez de Azcárraga, Eduardo 'La sentencia del Tribunal Internacional de Justicia sobre los casos de la plataforma continental del Mar del Norte' (1969) 21 Revista Española de Derecho Internacional, 349.

Jiménez de Azcárraga, Eduardo, 'Intervention under Article 62 of the Statute of the International Court of Justice' in Rudolf Bernhardt (eds.), *Völkerrecht als Rechtsordnung – Internationale Gerichtsbarkeit – Menschenrechte: Festschrift für Hermann Mosler* (Berlin, Heidelberg, New York: Springer, 1983), p. 453.

Jonsson, Hannes, *Friends in Conflict: The Anglo Icelandic Cod Wars and the Law of the Sea* (London: C. Hurst; Hamden CT: Archon, 1982).

Johnston, Douglas M., *The International Law of Fisheries: A Framework for Policy-Oriented Inquiries* (New Haven CT, London: Yale University Press, 1965).

The Theory and History of Ocean Boundary-Making (Montreal: McGill–Queen's University Press, 1988).

Juda, Lawrence, 'World Marine Fish Catch in the Age of Exclusive Economic Zones and Exclusive Fishery Zones' (1991) 22 Ocean Development & International Law, 1.

Kerrest, Armel, 'Note sur la Sentence du Tribunal Arbitral pour la délimitation de la frontière maritime Guinée/Guinée/Bissau' (1988) 3 Espaces et Ressources Maritimes, 175.

Kewening, Wilhelm A., 'Common Heritage of Mankind – politischer Slogan oder völkerrrechtlicher Schlüsselbegriff?' in Ingo von Münch (ed.), *Staatsrecht, Völkerrecht, Europarecht* (Berlin, New York: de Gruyter, 1981).

Kim, Sun Pyo, *Maritime Delimitation and Interim Arrangements in North East Asia* (Dordrecht: Martinus Nijhoff, 2004).

Kimminich, Otto, 'Das Völkerrecht und die Neue Weltwirtschaftsordnung', (1982) 20 Archiv für Völkerrecht, 2.

Kirchhof, Paul, 'Gesetz und Billigkeit im Abgaberecht' in Norbert Achterberg et al. (eds.), *Recht und Staat im sozialen Wandel, Festschrift für Hans Ulrich Scupin zum 80. Geburtstag* (Berlin: Dunker & Humblot, 1983).

Kirgis, Frederic L. Jr., *Prior Consultation in International Law: A Study of State Practice* (Charlottesville VA: University Press of Virginia, 1983).

Kiss, Alexandre, 'La Frontière-coopération' in Société française de droit international colloque de Poitiers, La Frontière (Paris: Editions A. Pedone, 1980), 183.

'La Notion du patrimoine commun de l'humanité' (1982) 175 Recueil des cours, 99.
Klabbers, Jan, Peters, Anne and Ulfstein, Geir (eds.), *The Constitutionalization of International Law* (Oxford University Press, 2009).
Klee, Hans, *Grotius, Hugo and Selden, Johannes: Von den geistigen Ursprüngen des Kampfes um die Meeresfreiheit* (Bern: Paul Haupt, 1946).
Klemm, Ulf-Dieter, 'Die seewärtige Grenze des Festlandsockels. Geschichte, Entwicklung und lex lata eines seevölkerrechtlichen Grundproblems' in H. Mosler/R. Bernhardt (eds.), *Beiträge zum ausländischen öffentlichen Recht und Völkerrecht* (Berlin, Heidelberg, New York: Springer, 1976), vol. LXVIII, 285.
'Der Streit um den Festlandsockel in der Aegais' (1975) 21 Recht der internationalen Wirtschaft, 568.
Knight, H. Gary, *The Life and Works of Hugo Grotius* (London: Sweet & Maxwell, 1925).
Kock, Karl-Hermann, 'Fishing and Conservation in Southern Waters' (1994) 30 Polar Record, 3.
Koers, Albert W., *International Regulation of Marine Fisheries: A Study of Regional Fisheries Organizations* (West Byfleet: Fishing News Books, 1973).
'The External Authority of the EEC in regard to Marine Fisheries' (1977) 14 Common Market Law Review, 269.
Koh, Tommy T. B., 'Negotiating a New World Order for the Sea' (1984) 24 Virginia Journal of International Law, 761.
Kolb, Robert, *Case Law on Equitable Maritime Delimitation / Jurisprudence sur les délimitations maritimes selon l'équité. Digest and Commentaries / Répertoire et commentaires* (The Hague: Martinus Nijhoff Publishers, 2003).
La Bonne foi en droit international public: Contribution à l'étude des principes généraux de droit (Paris: Presse Universitaire de France, 2000).
Koskenniemi, Martti, *From Apology to Utopia: The Structure of International Legal Argument, Reissue with a new epilogue* (Cambridge University Press, 2005).
Kozyris, Phaedon John, 'Lifting the Veils of Equity in Maritime Entitlement: Equidistance with Proportionality around Islands' (1998) 26 Denver Journal of Law and Policy, 319.
Kriele, Martin, *Theorie der Rechtsgewinnung entwickelt am Problem der Verfassungsinterpretation*, 2nd edn. (Berlin: Duncker und Humblot, 1976).
Kronmiller, Theodore G., *The Lawfulness of Deep Seabed Mining*, 2 vols. (Dobbs Ferry NY: Oceana Publications, 1980).
Krueger, Robert B. and Nordquist, Myron H., 'The Evolution of the 200 mile Exclusive Economic Zone: State Practice in the Pacific Basin' (1979) 19 Virginia Journal of International Law, 321.
Kühne, Winrich, *Das Völkerrecht und die militärische Nutzung des Meeresbodens* (Leiden: Sijthoff, 1975).

Kwiatkowska, Barbara, 'Economic and Environmental Considerations in Maritime Boundary Delimitations' in Jonathan I. Charney et al. (eds.), *International Maritime Boundaries*, 5 vols. (Dordrecht, Boston MA: Martinus Nijhoff Publishers, 1993–2005), vol. I (Charney and Alexander), 75.

'Maritime Boundary Delimitation between Opposite and Adjacent States in the New Law of the Sea – Some Implications for the Aegean' in *The Aegean Issues, Problems and Prospects* (Ankara: Foreign Policy Institute, 1989) 181, 203.

'New Soviet Legislation on the 200 Mile Economic Zone and Certain Problems of Evolution of Customary Law' (1986) 33 Netherlands International Law Review 24.

The Eritrea v. Yemen Arbitration: Landwork Progress in the Acquisition of Territorial Sovereignty and Equitable Boundary Delimitation (2001) 32 Ocean Development & International Law 1–25.

'The 2006 Barbados/Trinidad and Tobago Maritime Delimitation (Jurisdiction and Merits) Award', in Tafsir Malick Ndiaye/Rüdiger Wolfrum (eds.), *The Law of the Sea, Environmental Law and Settlement of Disputes: Liber Amicorum Judge Thomas A. Mensah* (Leiden: Martinus Nijhoff Publishers, 2007), 946.

Lagoni, Rainer, 'Antarctica: German Activities and Problems of Jurisdiction of Marine Areas' (1980) 23 German Yearbook of International Law, 392.

'Interim Measures Pending Maritime Boundary Delimitation Agreements' (1984) 78 American Journal of International Law, 345.

'Oil and Gas Deposits across National Frontiers' (1979) 73 American Journal of International Law, 215.

and Vignes, Daniel, *Maritime Delimitation* (Leiden: Martinus Nijhoff Publishers, 2006).

and Vignes, Daniel, 'Report on Joint Development of Non-Living Resources in the Exclusive Economic Zone' in ILA, Report of the Sixty-Third Conference (Warsaw, 1988).

Lang, Jack, *Le Plateau continental de la mer du Nord: l'arrêt de la Cour de Justice, 20 février 1969* (Paris: Collection Bibliothéque de droit international, LGDJ, 1988).

Langavant, E. and Pirotte O., 'L'Affaire des Pêcheries Islandaises, l'arrêt de la Cour Internationale de Justice du 25 juillet 1974' (1976) Revue Générale de Droit Internationale Public, 55–103.

Larson, David L., 'The Reagan Administration and the Law of the Sea' (1982) 11 Ocean Development & International Law.

'When will the UN Convention on the Law of the Sea come into Effect?' (1989) 20 Ocean Development & International Law, 175.

Lasswell, Harold D. and McDougal, Myres S., 'Jurisprudence in Policy-Oriented Perpectives' (1966/67) 10 University of Florida Law Review, 468.

Lathrop, Coalter G., 'Newfoundland and Labrador – Nova Scotia: The Latest "International" Maritime Boundary' (10 April 2002) 34 Ocean Development & International Law, 83.

'Tripoint Issues in Maritime Boundary Delimitation' in Jonathan I. Charney et. al. (eds.), *International Maritime Boundaries*, 5 vols. (Dordrecht: Martinus Nijhoff Publishers, 1993–2005), vol. V (Colson and Smith).

Lauterpacht, Elihu,'Equity, Evasion, Equivocation and Evolution in International Law' (1977–1978), Proceedings and Commentaries Report of the American Branch of the International Law Association, 1.

Lauterpacht, Hersch, 'International Law' in E. Lauterpacht (ed.), *Collected Papers of Hersch Lauterpacht* (Cambridge University Press, 1970), 257.

'Sovereignty over Submarine Areas' (1950) 27 British Yearbook of International Law, 376.

The Development of International Law by the International Court (London: Stevens & Sons, 1958, reprinted 1982).

Lazarev, Marklen I. (ed.), *Modernes Seevölkerrecht* (Berlin: Duncker & Humblot, 1987).

Leanza, Umberto, 'La controversia tra Libia, Malta ed Italia sulla delimitazione della piattaforma continentale nel Mediterraneo centrale' in Umberto Leanza (ed.), *Nuovi saggi di diritto del mare* (Turin: Giapricelli impr., 1988).

Legault, L. H. and Hankey, Blair, 'From Sea to Seabed: The Single Maritime Boundary in the Gulf of Maine Case' (1984) 22 Canadian Yearbook of International Law 267.

'Method, Oppositeness and Adjacency, and Proportionality in Maritime Boundary Delimitation' in Jonathan I. Charney et al. (eds.), *International Maritime Boundaries* (Dordrecht/Boston: Martinus Nijhoff Publishers, 1993–2005), vol. I (Charney and Alexander), 203.

Lévy, Jean-Pierre, *La Conférences des Nations Unies sur le droit de la mer: Histoire d'une négociation singulière* (Paris: Editions A. Pedone, 1983).

Limpert, Martin, Verfahren und Völkerrecht: Völkerrechtliche Probleme des Verfahrens von Kodifikationskonferenzen der Vereinten Nationen (Berlin: Duncker und Humblot, 1985), 104–21, 160 et seq.

Lowe, Alan V., 'Reflections on the Waters Changing Conceptions of Property Rights in the Law of the Sea' (1986) 1 International Journal of Estuarine and Coastal Law, 1.

'The Development of the Concept of the Contiguous Zone' (1981) 52 British Yearbook of International Law, 109.

'The International Seabed: A Legacy of Mistrust' (1981) 5 Marine Policy, 205.

The Law of the Sea (Manchester University Press, 1983).

Lucchini, Laurent, 'L'Arrêt de Chambre de la CIJ dans le différend Honduras/Salvador. Aspects insulaires et maritimes' (1992) Annuaire Français de Droit International, 427.

Lumb, Richard D., 'The Delimitation of Maritime Boundaries in the Timor Sea' (1981) Australian Yearbook of International Law, 72.

Lupinacci, Julio César, 'The Legal Status of the Exclusive Economic Zone in the 1982 Convention on the Law of the Sea' in Francisco Orrego Vicuña (ed.), *The Exclusive Economic Zone: A Latin American Perspective* (Boulder CO: Westview Press, 1984), 75.

Maine, Henry, 'Ancient Law' in Ernest Rhys (ed.), *Everyman's Library: History: [no. 734]* (London et. al.: Dent, 1917 (reprinted 1977)).

Makhdoom, Ali Khan, 'The Juridical Concept of the Continental Shelf' (1985) 38 Pakistan Horizon, 21.

Malick Ndiaye, Tafsir and Wolfrum, Rüdiger (eds.), *Law of the Sea, Environmental Law and Settlement of Disputes: Liber Amicorum Judge Thomas A. Mensah* (Leiden: Martinus Nijhoff Publishers, 2007).

Manin, Philippe, 'Le Juge international et la règle générale' (1976) 80 Revue Générale de Droit International Public, 7.

Mann-Borgese, Elisabeth, *The Future of the Oceans: A Report to the Club of Rome* (Montreal: Harvest House, 1986).

'The New International Economic Order and the Law of the Sea' (1977) 14 San Diego Law Review, 584.

et al. (eds.), *Ocean Yearbook* (University of Chicago Press Journals, 1989), vol. VIII.

Marek, Krystyna, 'Le Problème des sources du droit international dans l'arrêt sur le plateau continental de la mer du Nord' (1970) 6 Revue Belge de Droit International, 44.

Marques Antunes and Nuno Sérgio, *Towards the Conceptualisation of Maritime Delimitation, Legal and Technical Aspects of a Political Process* (Leiden: Martinus Nijhoff Publishers, 2003).

Marston, Geoffrey, 'Federal Disputes over Offshore Submerged Lands' (1977) 11 Journal of World Trade Law, 184.

'The Newfoundland Offshore Jurisdictional Dispute' (1984) 18 Journal of World Trade Law 335–341.

McDorman, Ted, et al. (eds.), *Maritime Boundary Delimitation: An Annotated Bibliography* (Boston MA: Lexington Press, 1983).

'The Canada-France Maritime Boundary Case: Drawing a Line around St. Pierre and Miquelon' (1990) 84 American Journal of International Law, 157.

'The Libya-Malta Case: Opposite States Confront the Court' (1986) 24 Canadian. Yearbook of International Law, 335.

McDougal, Myres S., 'The Hydrogen Bomb Tests and the International Law of the Sea' (1955) 49 American Journal of International Law, 356.

and Burke, William T., *The Public Order of the Oceans* (New Haven CT, London: New Haven Press, 1987).

and Reisman, W. Michael 'The Changing Structure of International Law' (1965) 65 Columbia Law Review, 810.

McLlarky, K. A., 'Guinea/Guinea-Bissau: Disputes Concerning Delimitation of Maritime Boundary, February 14, 1985' (1987) Maryland Journal of International Law, 93.

McRae, Donald M., 'Adjudication of Maritime Boundary in the Gulf of Maine' (1979) 17 Canadian Yearbook of International Law, 292.

'Proportionality and the Gulf of Maine Maritime Boundary Dispute' (1981) 19 Canadian Yearbook of International Law, 287.

'The Gulf of Maine Case: The Written Proceedings' (1983) 21 Canadian Yearbook of International Law, 266.

McWhinney, Edward, *The World Court and the Contemporary International Law Making Process* (Alphen aan den Rijn: Sithoff & Noordhoff, 1979).

Meier-Hayoz, Arthur (ed.), *Berner Kommentar zum schweizerischen Privatrecht* (Bern : Stämpfli, 1966).

Mengozzi, Paolo, 'The International Court of Justice. The United Nations Conference and the Law of the Sea' (1972) 3 Italian Yearbook of International Law, 92.

Mensah, Thomas, 'Joint Development Zones as an Alternative Dispute Settlement Approach in Maritime Boundary Delimitation', in Rainer Lagoni and Daniel Vignes (Eds.), *Maritime Delimitation* (Leiden: Martinus Nijhoff 2006).

Menzel, Eberhard, 'Der Festlandsockel der Bundesrepublik Deutschland und das Urteil des Internationalen Gerichtshofes vom 20. Februar 1969' (1969) 14 Jahrbuch für Internationales Recht, 13.

Merills, J. G., 'The United Kingdom-France Continental Shelf Arbitration' (1980) 10 California Western International Law Journal, 314.

Miller, John T., 'Intervention in Proceedings before the International Court of Justice' in Leo Gross (ed.), *The Future of The International Court of Justice*, (Dobbs Ferry NY: Oceana Publications, 1976), vol. II, 550.

Monconduit, François, 'Affaire du plateau continental de la mer du Nord' (1969) 15 Annuaire Français de Droit International, 213.

Monnier, Jean, 'La Troisième Conference des Nations Unies sur le droit de la mer' (1983) 39 Schweizerisches Jahrbuch für Internationales Recht, 1.

Morelli, V., 'Note sull' intervento nel processo internazionale '(1982) 67 Rivista di diritto internazionale, 805.

Morison, W. L., 'The Schools Revisited' in R. St. J. MacDonald and D. M. Johnston (eds.), *The Structure and Process of International Law* (The Hague, Boston MA: Martinus Nijhoff Publishers, 1983), 131.

Morris, Michael A., 'Maritime Geopolitics in Latin America' (1986) 5(1) Political Geography Quarterly.

Müller, Friedrich, *Juristische Methodik* (Berlin: Duncker und Humblot, 1971).

Müller, Jörg Paul, *Vertrauensschutz im Völkerrecht, Beiträge zum ausländischen öffentlichen Recht und Völkerrecht* (Cologne, Berlin, Bonn: Heymann, 1971).

Müller, Jörg Paul and Wildhaber, Luzius, *Praxis des Völkerrechts*, 3rd edn. (Bern: Stämpfli, 2001).

Münch, F., 'Das Urteil des IGH vom 20.2.1969 über den deutschen Anteil am Festlandsockel der Nordsee' (1969) 29 Zeitschrift für ausländisches öffentliches Recht und Völkerrecht, 455.

Nandan, Satya N., 'The 1982 UN Convention on the Law of the Sea: At a Crossroad' (1989) 20 Ocean Development & International Law, 515.

Nef, Urs, *Das Recht zum Abbau mineralischer Rohstoffe vom Meeresgrund und Meeresuntergrund unter besonderer Berücksichtigung der Stellung der Schweiz* (Zurich: Schulthess Polygraphischer Verlag, 1974).

Nelson, L. D. M., 'The Patrimonial Sea' (1973) 22 International Comparative Law Quarterly, 668.

Newman, Ralph A. (ed.), *Equity in the World's Legal Systems: A Comparative Study* (Brussels: Bruylant, 1972).

Nordquist, M. H. (ed.), *United Nations Convention on the Law of the Sea, 1982: A Commentary.* vol. I (Dordrecht: Martinus Nijhoff Publishers, 1985).

(ed.), *United Nations Convention on the Law of the Sea, 1982: A Commentary.* vol. II (Dordrecht: Martinus Nijhoff Publishers, 1993).

(ed.), *United Nations Convention on the Law of the Sea, 1982: A Commentary.* vol. V. (Dordrecht: Martinus Nijhoff Publishers, 1989).

Novakovic, Stojan, 'Could we have Provided for a better United Nations Convention on the Law of the Sea?' in B. Vukas, *Essays on the New Law of the Sea* (University of Zagreb, 1985).

Noyes, John E., 'Judicial and Arbitral Proceedings and the Outer Limits of the Continental Shelf' (2009) 42 Vanderbilt Journal of Transnational Law, 1211.

Oda, Shigeru, 'Fisheries under the United Nations Convention on the Law of the Sea' (1983) 77 American Journal of International Law, 739.

International Law of the Resources of the Sea, rev. edn. (Alphen aan den Rijn: Sijthoff & Noordhoff, 1979).

'Proposals for Revising the Convention on the Continental Shelf' (1968) 7 Columbia Journal of Transnational Law, 1.

Oellers-Fram, Karin, 'Die Entscheidung des IGH zur Abgrenzung des Festlandsockels zwischen Tunesien und Libyen: eine Abkehr von der bisherigen Rechtssprechung?' (1982) 42 Zeitschrift für ausländisches öffentliches Recht und Völkerrecht, 804.

'Die Entscheidung des internationalen Gerichtshofes im griechisch-türkischen Streit um den Festlandsockel der Aegais' (1980) 18 Archiv des Völkerrechts, 377.

Ogley, Roderick C., *Internationalizing the Seabed* (Aldershot: Gower, 1985).

Ong, David M., 'Joint Development of Common Offshore Oil and Gas Deposits: Mere' State Practice or Customary International Law?' (1999) 93 American Journal of International Law, 771.

Onorato, William T., 'Apportionment of an International Common Petroleum Deposit' (1968) 17 International and Comparative Law Quarterly, 85.
Orfield, Lester B., 'Equity as a Concept of International Law' (1930) 18 Kentucky Law Journal, 31.
Orrego Vicuña, Francisco, 'La Zone économique exclusive: regime et nature juridique dans le droit international' (1986/IV) 199 Recueil des cours 9.
Ostreng, Willy, *International Exploitation of 'National' Ocean Minerals* (Oslo: The Fridtjof Nansen Institute, Studie R:007, Ocean Mining Project Report No. 5, 1983).
  'Norwegen und die Sowjetunion in der Barentsee' (1980) 35 Europa Archiv, 711.
  'Regional Delimitation Arrangements in the Arctic Seas: Cases of Precedence?' (1986) 10 Marine Policy, 132.
Oude Elferink, Alex G. and Rothwell, Donald R. (eds.), *Oceans Management in the 21st Century: Institutional Frameworks and Responses* (Leiden: Martinus Nijhoff Publishers, 2004).
Oxman, Bernhard H., 'Interests in Transportation, Energy and Environment', in C. Buderi and David D. Caron (eds.), *Perspectives on U.S. Policy Toward the Law of the Sea: Prelude to the Final Session of the Third U.N. Conference on the Law of the Sea*, Proceedings of a Symposium held in 1982, The Law of the Sea Institute Occasional Paper No. 35 (Honolulu: Law of the Sea Institute, University of Hawaii, 1985).
  'The Third United Nations Conference on the Law of the Sea: The 1974 Caracas Session' (1975) 69 American Journal of International Law, 763.
  'The Third United Nations Conference on the Law of the Sea: The 1976 New York Session' (1977) 71 American Journal of International Law, 247.
  'The Third United Nations Conference on the Law of the Sea: The 1977 New York Session' (1978) 72 American Journal of International Law, 57.
  'The Third United Nations Conference on the Law of the Sea: The Seventh Session (1978)' (1979) 73 American Journal of International Law, 1.
  'The Third United Nations Conference on the Law of the Sea: The Eighth Session (1979)' (1980) 74 American Journal of International Law, 211.
  'The Third United Nations Conference on the Law of the Sea: The Ninth Session (1980)' (1981) 75 American Journal of International Law, 227.
  'Political, Strategic and Historic Consideration' in Jonathan I. Charney (ed.) *International Maritime Boundaries*, 5 vols. (The Hague: Martinus Nijhoff Publishers, 1993–2005).
  'The Territorial Temptation: A Siren Song at Sea' (2006) 100 American Journal of International Law Centennial Essays, 830.
  'The Third United Nations Conference on the Law of the Sea' in René-Jean Dupuy and Daniel Vignes (eds.), *A Handbook on the New Law of the Sea* (Dordrecht: Kluwer Academic Publishers, 1991), 163.

Pannatier, Serge, *L'Antarctique et la protection internationale de l'environnement* (Zurich: Schulthess, 1994).

Papadakis, Nikos, *International Law of the Sea: A Bibliography* (Dordrecht: Kluwer Academic Publishers, 1980).

Pardo Arvid, 'An Opportunity Lost', in C. Buderi and D. Caron (eds.), *Perspectives on U.S. Policy Toward the Law of the Sea: Prelude to the Final Session of the Third U.N. Conference on the Law of the Sea*, Proceedings of a Symposium held in 1982, The Law of the Sea Institute Occasional Paper No. 35 (Honolulu: Law of the Sea Institute, University of Hawaii, 1985), 68.

'The Convention on the Law of the Sea: A Preliminary Appraisal', (1983) 20 San Diego Law Review, 489.

'Whose is the Bed of the Sea?', (1968) 62 American Society of International Law Proceed, 216.

Park, Choon-Ho, 'The 50 Mile Military Boundary of North Korea' (1978) 72 American Journal of International Law, 866.

Paulsen, Majorie B. (ed.), *Law of the Sea* (New York: Nova Science Publishers Inc, 2007).

Petersmann, Ernst U., 'Rechtsprobleme der deutschen Interimsgesetzgebung für den Tiefseebergbau' (1981) 41 Zeitschrift für ausländisches öffentliches Recht und Völkerrecht, 257.

Peyroux, Evelyne, 'Les Etats africains face aux questions actuelles du droit de la mer' (1974) 78 Revue Générale de Droit International Public, 623.

Pharand, Donat, 'The Law of the Sea: An Overview' in Donat Pharand and Umberto Leanza (eds.), *The Continental Shelf and the Exclusive Economic Zone* (The Hague: Martinus Nijhoff, 1993), 5.

Pinto, M. C. M., 'Modern Conference Techniques: Insights from Social Psychology and Anthropology', in R. Maconald and D. Johnston (eds.), *The Structure and Process of International Law: Essays in Legal Philosophy, Doctrine and Theory* (The Hague: Nijhoff, 1983), 305.

Platzoeder, Renate (ed.), *Dokumente der Dritten Seerechtskonferenz, 1979 Geneva Session*, 3 vols. (Materialiensammlung der Stiftung Wissensschaft und Politik, 1977).

Platzoeder, Renate (ed.), *Third United Nations Conference on the Law of the Sea: Documents*, 4 vols. (Dobbs Ferry, NY: Oceana Publications Inc., 1982–1985).

Pohl, Reynaldo Galindo, 'The Exclusive Economic Zone in the Light of Negotiations of the Third United Nations Conference on the Law of the Sea' in Francisco Orrego Vicuña (ed.), *The Exclusive Economic Zone: A Latin American Perspective* (Boulder CO: Westview Press, 1984), 31.

Pontecorvo, Giulio, 'The Economics of the Resources of Antarctica' in Jonathan I. Charney (ed.), *The New Nationalism and the Use of Common Spaces* (Totowa NJ: Allanheld, Osmun, 1982).

Posner, Eric and Sykes, Alan O., 'Economic Foundations of the Law of the Sea' (16 December 2009) University of Chicago Law & Economics, Olin Working Paper No. 504 (available at SSRN: http://ssrn.com/abstract=1524274).

Post, Alexandra M., *Deep Sea Mining and the Law of the Sea* (The Hague: Martinus Nijhoff Publishers, 1983).

Pound, Roscoe, *Law and Morals* (University of North Carolina Press, 1924), p. 88, quoted from Ralph A. Newman, 'The General Principles of Equity', in Ralph A. Newman (ed.), *Equity in the World's Legal Systems: A Comparative Study* (Brussels: Bruylant, 1973), 595.

'The Decadence of Equity' (1905) 5 Columbia Law Review, 20.

Prescott, John R. V., *Political Frontiers and Boundaries* (London: Routledge, 1990).

The Maritime Political Boundaries of the World (London: Methuen, 1985).

Pulvenis, Jean-François, 'The Continental Shelf Definition and Rules Applicable to Resources' in René-Jean Dupuy and Daniel Vignes (eds.), *A Handbook on the New Law of the Sea*, 2 vols. (Dordrecht: Martinus Nijhoff, 1991), vol. I, 315.

Quéneudec, Jean-Pierre, 'L'Affaire de la délimitation du plateau continental entre la France et le Royaume Uni' (1979) 83 Revue Générale de Droit International Public, 53.

'Les Incertitudes de la nouvelle Convention sur le droit de la mer' in Budislav Vukas (ed.), *Essays on the New Law of the Sea* (University of Zagreb, Faculty of Law, 1985), 47.

'Les Rapports entre zone de pêche et zone économique exclusive' (1989) 32 German Yearbook of International Law, 138.

'Note sur l'arrêt de la Cour internationale de justice relatif à la délimitation du plateau continental entre la Tunisie et la Libye' (1981) 27 Annuaire Français de Droit International, 203.

Rangel, Vicente M., 'Le Plateau Continental dans la Convention de 1982 sur le Droit de la Mer' (1985) 194 Recueil des cours, 267.

Rao, S. Rawa, 'EEZ Concept under the New Law of the Sea Convention: Basic Framework for another Approach' (1984) 24 Indian Journal of International Law, 102.

Ratiner, Leigh S., 'The Deep Seabed Mining Controversy: A Rejoinder', in C. Buderi and D. Caron (eds.), *Perspectives on U.S. Policy Toward the Law of the Sea: Prelude to the Final Session of the Third U.N. Conference on the Law of the Sea*, Proceedings of a Symposium held in 1982, The Law of the Sea Institute Occasional Paper No. 35 (Honolulu: Law of the Sea Institute, University of Hawaii, 1985).

Reed, Michael W., 'Litigating Maritime Boundary Disputes: The Federal Perspective' in L. De Vorsey and D.G. Dallmeyer (eds.), *Rights to Oceanic Resources* (Dordrecht: Martinus Nijhoff Publishers 1989), 61.

Reid, Robert S., 'Gulf of Maine – A Disappointing First in the Delimitation of a Single Maritime Boundary' (1985) 25 Virginia Journal of International Law, 521.

'Petroleum Development in Areas of International Seabed Boundary Disputes: Means for Resolution' (1984/5) 3 Oil & Gas L. & Taxation Rev, 214.

Reisman, W. Michael, 'Coercion and Self-Determination: Construing Charter Article 2(4)' (1984) 78 American Journal of International Law, 642.

Eritrea-Yemen Arbitration (Award, Phase II: Maritime Delimitation)' (2000) 94 American Journal of International Law, 721.

Reynaud, André, *Les Différends du plateau continental de la mer du Nord devant la Cour internationale de justice: La volonté, la nature, et le droit* (Paris: LGDJ/ Montchrestien, 1975).

Rhee, Sang-Myon, 'Equitable Solutions to the Maritime Boundary Dispute between the United States and Canada in the Gulf of Maine' (1981) 75 American Journal of International Law, 590.

'Sea Boundary Delimitation between States Before World War II' (1982) 76 American Journal of International Law, 555.

'The Application of Equitable Principles to Resolve the United States – Canada Dispute over East Coast Fishery Resources'(1980) 21 Harvard International Law Journal, 667.

Richardson, Elliot L., 'Dispute Settlement under the Convention on the Law of the Sea' in T. Buergenthal (ed.), *Contemporary Issues in International Law, Essays in Honor of Louis B. John* (Kehl, Strasbourg: N. P. Engel Publisher, 1984).

'Jan Mayen in Perspective' (1988) 82 American Journal of International Law, 443.

Rigaldies, Francis, 'La Délimitation du plateau continental entre Etats voisins' (1976) 14 Canadian Yearbook of International Law, 141.

Roach, J. Ashley and Smith, Robert W., *United States Responses to Excessive Maritime Claims*, 2nd edn. (The Hague: Martinus Nijhoff Publishers, 1996).

Rojahn, Ondolf, 'Die Fischereigrenze Islands vom 1. September 1972 im Lichte maritimer Abgrenzungsprinzipien des Internationalen Gerichtshofes' (1974) 16 Archiv für Völkerrecht, 37.

Rothpfeffer, Tomas, 'Equity in the North Sea Continental Shelf Cases' (1972) 42 Nordisk Tidskrift for International Ret, 93.

Rotoni, Mario, 'Considerations sur la fonction de l'équité dans un système de droit positif écrit' in *Aspects Nouveaux de la Pensée Juridique, Recueil d'études en hommage à Marc Ancel, vol. I, Etudes de droit privé, de droit public et de droit comparé* (Paris: Editions A. Pedone, 1975).

Rudolf, Davorin, 'Some Remarks about the Provisions Concerning the Continental Shelf in the UN Convention on the Law of the Sea' in Budislav Vukas (ed.), *Essays on the New Law of the Sea* (University of Zagreb, 1985), 141.

Ruiz-Fabri, Hélène, 'Sur la délimitation des espaces maritimes entre le Canada et la France. Sentence arbitrale du 10 juin 1992' (1993) 97 Revue Générale de Droit International Public, 67.

Rümelin, Max, *Die Billigkeit im Recht* (Tübingen: Mohr Paul Siebeck, 1921).

Rüster, Bernd, 'Das britisch-französische Schiedsverfahren über die Abgrenzung des Festlandsockels: Die Entscheidungen vom 30. Juni 1977 und vom 14. März 1978' (1978) 40 Zeitschrift für ausländisches öffentliches Recht und Völkerrecht, 803.

Die Rechtsordnung des Festlandsockels (Berlin: Duncker und Humblot, 1977).

Sadursky, Wojciech, *Giving Desert its Due: Social Justice and Legal Theory* (Dordrecht: D. Reidel Publishing, 1985).

Sahurie, Emilio J., *The International Law of Antarctica* (New Haven Press, Dordrecht: Martinus Nijhoff Publishers, 1992).

Saladin, Peter and Zenger, Christoph, *Rechte Künftiger Generationen* (Basel, Frankfurt am Main: Helbing & Lichtenhahn, 1988).

Sanger, Clyde, *Ordering the Oceans: The Making of the Laws of the Sea* (London: Zed Books, 1986).

Sarin, Manohar Lal, 'Reflections on the Progress made by the Third United Nations Conference in Developing the Law of the Sea' in Rafael G. Girardot et al. (eds.), *New Directions in International Law: Essays in Honour of Wolfgang Abendroth: Festschrift zu seinem 75. Geburtstag* (Frankfurt a. M., New York: Campus Verlag, 1982), 278.

Schachter, Oscar, 'Creativity and Objectivity in International Tribunals' in R. Bernhardt, W. K. Geck, G. Jaenicke and H. Steinberger (eds.), *Völkerrecht als Rechtsordnung, internationale Gerichtsbarkeit, Menschenrechte, Festschrift für Hermann Mosler* (Berlin, Heidelberg, New York: Springer Verlag, 1983).

Sharing the World's Resources (New York: Columbia University Press, 1977).

Schenk, Dedo von, 'Die Verträge zur Abgrenzung des Festlandsockels unter der Nordsee zwischen der Bundesrepublik Deutschland, Dänemark und den Niederlanden nach dem Urteil des Internationalen Gerichtshofes vom 20. Februar 1969' (1970) Jahrbuch für Internationales Recht, 379.

Schmidt, Markus G., Common Heritage or Common Burden? The United States Position on the Development of a Regime for Deep Seabed Mining in the Law of the Sea Convention (Oxford: Clarendon Press, 2001).

Schneider, Jan, 'The Gulf of Maine Case: The Nature of an Equitable Result' (1985) 79 American Journal of International Law, 539.

Schreiber, Arias, 'The Exclusive Economic Zone: Its Legal Nature and the Problem of Military Uses' in Francisco Orrego Vicuña (ed.), *The Exclusive Economic Zone: A Latin American Perspective* (Boulder CO: Westview Press, 1984), 123.

Schrijver, Nico and Weiss, Friedl (ed.), International Law and Sustainable Development: Principles and Practice (Leiden, Boston MA: Martinus Nijhoff Publishers, 2004).

Schücking, Walter (ed.), *Das Werk vom Haag, Der Staatenverband der Haager Konferenzen* (Munich, Leipzig: Duncker & Humblot, 1917).

Schwarzenberger, Georg, 'Equity in International Law' (1972) The Yearbook of World Affairs, 346.

and Ladd, William, 'An Examination of an American Proposal for an International Equity Tribunal' in *The New Commonwealth Institute Monographs* Series B. No. 3, (London: Constable, 1936).
Scott, S. V., 'The Inclusion of Sedentary Fisheries within the Continental Shelf Doctrine' (1992) 41 International and Comparative Law Quarterly, 788.
Scovazzi, Tullio, The Evolution of International Law of the Sea: New Issues, New Challenges (2000) 286 Recueil des cours (Académie de Droit International), 39.
Sebenius, James K., *Negotiating the Law of the Sea* (Harvard University Press, 1984).
Shalowitz, L. and Reed, Michael W., *Shore and Sea Boundaries*, 3 vols. (Washington, DC: Office of Coeast Survey, National Oceanic and Atmospheric Administration, 1962), vol. I.
Shaw, Malcolm N., 'Case Concerning the Land, Island and Maritime Frontier Dispute (El Salvador/Honduras: Nicaragua Intervening), Judgment of 11 September 1992' (1993) 42 International and Comparative Law Quarterly, 929.
Shearer, Ivan A. (ed.), *The International Law of the Sea*, 2 vols. (Oxford: Clarendon Press, 1982–84).
Shigeru, Oda, 'Intervention in the International Court of Justice' in Rudolf Bernhardt (eds.), *Völkerrecht als Rechtsordnung – Internationale Gerichtsbarkeit – Menschenrechte: Festschrift für Hermann Mosler* (Berlin, Heidelberg, New York: Springer, 1983), 629.
Shusterich, Kurt M., *Resource Management and the Oceans: The Political Economy of Deep Seabed Mining* (Boulder CO: Westview Press, 1982).
Shyam, Manjula R., *Metals from the Seabed: Prospects for Mining Polymetallic Nodules by India* (New Delhi: Oxford and IBM, 1982).
Simmonds, Kenneth R., 'The Community's Declaration upon Signature of the U.N. Convention on the Law of the Sea' (1986) 23 Common Market Law Review, 521.
Singh, Nagendra, 'Codification and Progressive Development of International Law: The Role of the International Court of Justice' (1978) 18 American Journal of International Law, 1.
Sinjela, A. Mpai, 'Land-locked States Rights in the Exclusive Economic Zone from the Perspective of the UN Convention on the Law of the Sea: A Historical Evaluation' (1989) 20(1) Ocean Development & International Law 63.
Slouka, Zdenek J., *International Custom and the Continental Shelf* (The Hague: Martinus Nijhoff Publishers, 1968).
Smith, Robert W., 'A Geographical Primer to Maritime Boundary-Making' (1983) Ocean Development & International Law, 1.
  'Global Maritime Claims'(1989) 20 Ocean Development & International Law, 83.

Sohn, Louis B., 'Exploring New Potentials in Maritime Boundary Dispute Settlement' in L. De Vorsey and D. Dallmeyer (eds.), *Rights to Oceanic Resources* (Dordrecht: Martinus Nijhoff Publishers, 1989), 153.
and Gustafson, Kristen, *Law of the Sea in a Nutshell* (St. Paul MN: West Group, 2010).
Soons, Alfred H.A., *Marine Scientific Research and the Law of the Sea* (Deventer, Boston MA: Kluwer Law and Taxation Publishers, 1982).
'The Position of the EEC towards the LOS Convention', Proceedings of the 84th Annual Meeting (1990) American Society of International Law, 278.
Stern, Brigitte, 'Chronique de la Cour internationale de justice' (1993) Journal de droit international, 684.
Stevenson, John R. and Oxman, Bernard H., 'The Preparations for the Law of the Sea Conference' (1974) 68 American Journal of International Law, 1.
'The Third United Nations Conference on the Law of the Sea: The 1974 Caracas Session' (1975) 69 American Journal of International Law, 763.
Stocker, Werner, *Das Prinzip des Common Heritage of Mankind als Ausdruck des Staatengemeinschaftsinteresses im Völkerrecht* (Zurich: Schulthess, 1993).
Stone, Julius, 'Approaches to the Notion of Justice of International Justice' in Richard A. Falk and Cyril E. Black (eds.), *The Future of the International Legal Order: Trends and Patterns*, vol. 1 (Princeton University Press, 1969).
Strati, Anastasia, Govouneli Maria and Skourtos Nikolaos (eds.), *Unresolved Issues and New Challenges to the Law of the Sea: Time Before and Time after* (Leiden, Boston MA: Martinus Nijhoff Publishers, 2006).
Strupp, Karl, 'Das Recht des internationalen Richters, nach Billigkeit zu entscheiden' in F. Giese and K. Strupp (eds.) (1930) 20 Frankfurter Abhandlungen zum Völkerrecht.
'Der Streitfall zwischen Schweden und Norwegen' in W. Schücking (ed.), *Das Werk vom Haag, die gerichtlichen Entscheidungen* (Munich, Leipzig: Duncker & Humblot 1917), 124.
'Le Droit du juge international de statuer selon l'équité' (1930) 33 Recueil des cours de l'Académie de Droit International.
'Proposals for an International Equity Tribunal' in *The New Commonwealth Institute Monographs*, Series B. N. 4 (London: Constable, 1935).
Studier, Alphons (ed.), *Seerechtskonferenz und Dritte Welt* (Munich: Weltforum Verlag, 1980).
Suarez, Suzette V., *The Outer Limits of the Continental Shelf: Legal Aspects of their Establishment* (Berlin: Springer, 2008).
Subedi, Surya Prasad, 'The Marine Fishery Rights of Land-locked States with particular Reference to the EEZ' (1987) 2 International Journal of Estuary and Coastal Law, Issue 4, 227.
Swan, Peter N., *Ocean Oil and Gas Drilling and the Law* (Dobbs Ferry NY: Peter N. Swan Oceans Publications, 1979).

Symmons, Clive R., 'The Canadian 200 mile Fishery Limit and the Delimitation of Maritime Zones around St. Pierre and Miquelon' (1980) 12 Ottawa Law Review, 145.

Szaz, Paul C., 'Enhancing the Advisory Competence of the World Court' in Leo Gross (ed.), *The Future of the International Court of Justice*, vol. II (New York: Oceans Publications, 1976), 499.

Sztucki, Jerzey, 'Interim Measures in the Hague Court: An Attempt at a Scrutiny' (1983) 77 American Journal of International Law, 673.

Tanaka, Yoshifumi, *A Dual Approach to Ocean Governance: The Cases of Zonal and Integrated Management in International Law of the Sea* (Farnham: Ashgate Publishing Ltd., 2008).

Predictability and Flexibility in the Law of Maritime Delimitation (Oxford: Hart, 2006).

Theutenberger, Bo Johnson, *The Evolution of the Law of the Sea* (Dublin: Tycooly International Publishing, 1984).

Thirlway, H. W. A., 'The Law and Procedure of the International Court of Justice: Part Five' (1994) 64 British Yearbook of International Law, 41.

Tomuschat, Christian, Neuhold, Hanspeter and Kropholler, Jan, *Voelkerrechtlicher Vertrag und Drittstaaten (Treaties and Third States): Referate und Thesen mit Diskussion with English summaries of the reports* (Heidelberg: Müller, 1988).

Traavik, Kim and Ostreng, Willy, 'Security and Ocean Law: Norway and the Soviet Union in the Barents Sea' (1977) Ocean Development & International Law Journal, 343.

Treves, Tullio, 'Military Installations, Structures and Devices on the Seabed' (1980) 74 American Journal of International Law, 831.

'Une Nouvelle technique de la codification du droit international: Le comité de rédaction dans la conférence sur le droit de la mer' (1981) 27 Annuaire Français de Droit International Public, 65.

Ulfstein, Geir, '200 Mile Zones and Fisheries Management' (1983) 52 Nordisk Tidsskrift for International Ret, 3.

UNFAO (ed.), *The Law of the Sea: Essays in Memory of Jean Carroz* (Rome: UNFAO, 1987).

Vallat, F. A., 'The Continental Shelf' (1946) 23 British Yearbook of International Law, 333.

Vallée, Charles, *Le Plateau Continental dans le droit positif actuel* (Paris: Editions A. Pedone, 1971).

Van der Zwaag, David, *The Fish Feud: The U.S. and Canadian Boundary Dispute* (Lexington, Toronto: Lexington Books, 1983).

Van Dijk, P., 'Nature and Function of Equity in International Economic Law' (1986) 7 Grotiana New Series, 5.

Van Dyke, Jon M. (ed.), *Consensus and Confrontation: The United States and the Law of the Sea Convention* (Honolulu HI: The Law of the Sea Institute, University of Hawaii, 1984).

Van Wie Davis, Elizabeth, *China and the Law of the Sea Convention* (Lewiston MA: Edwin Mellen Press, 1995).

Vargas, Jorge, 'The Legal Nature of the Patrimonial Sea: A First Step towards the Definition of the Exclusive Economic Zone' (1979) 22 German Yearbook of International Law, 142.

Vasciannie, Stephen C., *Land Locked and Geographically Disadvantaged States in the International Law of the Sea* (Oxford: Clarendon Press, 1990).

Vicuña, Francisco Orrego, *The Changing International Law of High Seas Fisheries* (Cambridge University Press, 1999).

Vidas, Davor and Østreng, Willy (eds.), *Order for the Oceans at the Turn of the Century* (The Hague: Kluwer Law International, 1999).

Viehweg, Theodor, *Topik und Jurisprudenz*, 5th edn. (C.H. Beck Verlag, 1974).

Vignes, Daniel, 'La Création dans la Communauté au cours de l'automne 1976 et de l'hiver 1977, d'une zone de pêche s'étendant jusqu'à deux cent milles' in Mélanges F. Dehousse (ed.), *La Construction Européenne*, 2 vols. (Paris: F. Nathan, 1979), vol. II, 323.

'Will the Third Conference on the Law of the Sea Work According to the Consensus Rule?' (1975) 69 American Journal of International Law, 119.

Vignes, Jacques, *Le Rôle des intérêts économiques dans l'évolution du droit de la mer* (Geneva: Institut universitaire de hautes études internationales, 1971).

Villani, U., 'Gli interessi dell'Italia sulla piattaforma continentale del Mediterraneo centrale e la controversia tra Libia e Malta' (1984) Studi marittimi, 85.

Virally, Michel, 'Review Essay: Good Faith in Public International Law' (1983) 77 American Journal of International Law, 130.

Visscher, Charles de, *De l'équité dans le règlement arbitral ou judiciaire des litiges en droit international public* (Paris: Editions A. Pedone, 1972).

Vitzthum, Wolfgang Graf, 'Auf dem Wege zu einem neuen Meeresvölkerrecht: Zur Rechtslage vor der dritten Seerechtskonferenz' (1973) 16 Jahrbuch für internationales Recht, 229.

'Verfahrensgerechtigkeit im Völkerrecht. Zu den Erfolgsbedingungen internationaler Rechtsschöpfungskonferenzen' in Ingo von Münch (ed.), *Staatsrecht–Völkerrecht–Europarecht, Festschrift für Hans-Jürgen Schlochauer* (Berlin, New York: de Gruyter, 1981), 738.

Vitzthum, Wolfgang Graf, *Die Plünderung der Meere: Ein gemeinsames Erbe wird zerstückelt* (Frankfurt: Fischer Verlag, 1981).

Von Münch, Ingo, *Internationales Seerecht: Seerechtliche Abhandlungen 1958–1982 mit einer Einführung in das internationale Seerecht* (Heidelberg: R. v. Decker Verlag, 1985).

Vratusa, Anton, 'Convention on the Law of the Sea in the Light of the Struggle for the New International Economic Order' in B. Vukas (ed.), *Essays on the New Law of the Sea* (University of Zagreb, Faculty of Law, 1985), 17.
Vukas, Budislav (ed.), *Essays on the Law of the Sea* (University of Zagreb, Faculty of Law, 1985).
  The Law of the Sea: Selected Writings (Leiden, Boston MA: Martinus Nijhoff Publishers, 2004).
Wani, Ibrahim J., 'An Evaluation of the Convention on the Law of the Sea from the Perspective of the Landlocked States' (1982) 22 Virginia Journal of International Law, 627.
Watts, Sir Arthur, *International Law and the Antarctic Treaty System* (Cambridge: Grotius Publications Ltd, 1992).
Weil, Prosper, 'A Propos du Droit Coutumier en Matière de Délimitation Maritime' in Università di Genova et al. (eds.), *II International Law at the Time of its Codification, Essays in Honour of Roberto Ago* (Milan: Giuffré, 1987), 535.
  'Des espaces maritimes aux territoires maritimes: vers une conception territorialiste de la délimitation maritime' in *Droit international au service de la paix, de la justice et du développement: Mélanges Michel Virally* (Paris: Editions A. Pedone, 1991), 501.
  'Geographic Considerations in Maritime Delimitation' in Jonathan I. Charney et al. (eds.), *International Maritime Boundaries*, 5 vols. (Dordrecht: Martinus Nijhoff Publishers, 1993–2005), vol. I (Charney and Alexander), 115.
  Perspectives du droit de la délimitation maritime (Paris: Editions A. Pedone, 1988).
Weiss, Norman, *Hugo Grotius: Mare Liberum, Zur Aktualität eines Klassikertextes*, (Potsdam: Universitätverlag, 2009).
Wengler, Wilhelm, 'Die Abgrenzung des Festlandsockels zwischen benachbarten Staaten' (1969) 22 Neue Juristische Wochenschrift, 965.
Wengler, Wilhelm, 'Der internationale Gerichtshof und die Angrenzung des Meeresbodens im Mittelmeer' (1982) Neue Juristische Wochenschrift, 1198.
Whittemore Boggs, S., 'Delimitation of Seaward Areas under National Jurisdiction' (1951) 45 American Journal of International Law, 240.
Wijkmann, Per Magnus, 'UNCLOS and the redistribution of Ocean Wealth' (1982) 16 Journal of World Trade Law, *reprinted in* Richard Falk et al. (eds.), International Law: A Contemporary Perspective (Boulder CO: Westview Press, 1985), 598.
Windley, David W., 'International Practice Regarding Traditional Fishing Privileges of Foreign Fishermen in Zones of Extended Maritime Jurisdiction' (1969) 63 American Journal of International Law, 490.
Wolf, Klaus Dieter, *Die Dritte Seerechtskonferenz der Vereinten Nationen* (Baden-Baden: Nomos Verlagsgesellschaft, 1981).

Wolfrum, Rüdiger, 'Die UN-Seerechtskonvention in der Perspective der Neuen Weltwirtschaftsordnung' in Jost Delbrück (ed.), *Das neue Seerecht. Internationale und nationale Perspektiven* (Berlin: Duncker & Humblot, 1984).

Woodliffe, J. C., 'International Unitisation of an Offshore Gas Field' (1977) 25 The International and Comparative Law Quarterly, 338.

Wright, Quincy, 'The Stimson Note of January 7, 1932'(1932) 26 American Journal of International Law, 342.

Yacouba, Cissé and McRae, Donald, 'The Legal Regime of Maritime Boundary Agreements' in Jonathan I. Charney et. al. (eds.), *International Maritime Boundaries*, 5 vols.(Dordrecht: Martinus Nijhoff Publishers, 1993–2005), vol. V (Colson and Smith), 3281.

Yanagida, Joy A., 'The Pacific Salmon Treaty' (1987) 81 American Journal of International Law, 577.

Zedalis, Rex J., 'Military Installations, Structures and Devices on the Continental Shelf' (1981) 75 American Journal of International Law, 926.

Zoller, Elisabeth, 'L'Affaire de la délimitation du plateau continental entre la République française et le Royaume-Uni de Grande-Bretagne et d'Irlande du Nord' (1977) 28 Annuaire Français de Droit International, 359.

La Bonne foi en droit international public (Paris: Editions A. Pedone, 1977).

'La Première constitution d'une Chambre spéciale par la Cour internationale de justice, Observations sur l'ordonnance du 20 janvier 1982'(1982) 86 Revue Générale de Droit International Public, 305.

'Recherches sur les méthodes de délimitation du plateau continental: à propos de l'affaire Tunisie-Libye' (1982) 86 Revue Générale de Droit International Public, 645.

Zuleta, Bernhard, 'The Law of the Sea after Montego Bay' (1983) 20 San Diego Law Review, 475.

INDEX

Abu Dhabi, co-operation agreements of, 257
accessory entitlement of islands, 641
acquiescence, principle of, 489–90, 568–73, 613
ad hoc geometrical constructions in judicial and conciliatory settlements, 352
additive islands, in adjudication process, 642–4
Aegean Continental Shelf case (*Greece* v. *Turkey*; ICJ, 1978), 682–7. *See also Table of Cases, for more detailed references*
Agenda 21, 24, 166, 168
Ago, Roberto, 567
agreed equitable model, 213–33, 365–7
Alexander, L. M., 360
Algerian Group of 32, 361
allocation of marine spaces. *See* maritime boundary delimitation
Allott, Philip, 53, 68
American realism, 608
American Society of International Law (ASIL), 248, 250
amicus curiae, 504–10
Ammoun, Judge, 425, 426
Anderson, David H., 242, 366
Anglo-French Channel arbitration (1977/78), 275–9, 403. *See also Table of Cases, for more detailed references*
Anglo-Norwegian Fisheries case (ICJ, 1951), 398–403. *See also Table of Cases, for more detailed references*
Anglo-Saxon law, equity in, 10, 11, 13
Antarctica: CCAMLR (Convention on the Conservation of Antarctic Marine Living Resources; 1980), 164, 165, 166; fishing operations in, 159, 164, 166
Antunes, Nuno S., 366
aquaculture. *See* fisheries and aquaculture
Arabian Gulf States: co-operation agreements, 252; *Dubai* v. *Sharjah Emirates* arbitration (1981), 279–80; unilateral acts by, 238. *See also specific states*
arbitration. *See* judicial and conciliatory settlements
Arctic Ocean: climate change and accessibility of, 179; contemporary interest in governance of, 65
the Area, 48, 55, 59, 67, 92, 130
Aréchaga, H. E. Eduardo Jiminez de, 201, 378, 465
Argentina: co-operation agreements, 263; Falklands/Malvinas War (1982), 110, 132
Aristotle, *Nicomachean Ethics*, 8, 29
ASIL (American Society of International Law), 248, 250
Australia: co-operation agreements, 257, 261, 263–6; Timor Trough and, 200, 202, 463
Austria, on mineral rights of LLCs and GDCs, 144
autonomous or corrective equity, 375–8

Bahamas, state practice of, 241
Bahrain: co-operation agreements, 257; maritime delimitation and territorial questions, case with Qatar concerning (ICJ, 2001), 311–15, 415

INDEX

Bangladesh, in *Bay of Bengal* case (with Myanmar; ITLOS, 2012), 332–5. See also Table of Cases, for more detailed references
Barbados: state practice of, 240; *Trinidad and Tobago v. Barbados* arbitration award (2006), 318–21, 415–17
Barents Sea boundaries and national security interests, 591
base points: determining, 185–8; modification of, 189
Bay of Bengal case (*Bangladesh v. Myanmar*; ITLOS, 2012), 332–5. See also Table of Cases, for more detailed references
bilateral access agreements, 138
bisector method, 191–5
Bishop, William W., Jr., 78, 207, 646
Black Sea case (*Romania v. Ukraine*; ICJ, 2009), 327–32, 413–14. See also Table of Cases, for more detailed references
Bluntschli, J. C., 261
Boggs, Whittemore, 184
boundaries, maritime. See maritime boundary delimitation
Bourgois, M., 496
Bowett, Derek W., 101, 468, 632, 636–7
BP Deepwater Horizon oil spill (2010), 132
Briggs, Judge, 383
Britain. See United Kingdom
Brown, Edward Duncan, 377
Brunei, in Spratly Islands dispute, 132
Bull, Hedley, 175
burden of proof, 631
Burke, William T., 581
Burmester, Henry, 266
Bustamante, A. S. de, 18

Cameroon v. Nigeria case (ICJ, 2002), 315–18, 415–16. See also Table of Cases, for more detailed references
Canada: co-operation agreements, 260, 261, 267, 269; *Gulf of Maine* case (ICJ, 1984), 285–90, 406–8; *Newfoundland/Labrador/Nova Scotia* arbitration (2002), 346–8; *St. Pierre and Miquelon* arbitration (1992), 297–300, 411; state practice of, 239, 248, 251
Caney, Simon, 172
cannon ball rule (traditional 3-mile territorial limit), 46, 526
case law. See judicial and conciliatory settlements, and separate Table of Cases for more detailed references to case law
CCAMLR (Convention on the Conservation of Antarctic Marine Living Resources; 1980), 164, 165, 166
CDS (the coast dominates the sea) principle, 525–38, 542, 557, 629
CEIP (Coastal Energy Impact Program), US (1979), 341–4
CGX incident (2000), 667
Channel Islands, 589
Charney, Jonathan I., 360, 364, 402, 622
CHF (Common Heritage Fund), 144
Chile: EEZs, establishment of, 108; maritime dispute with Peru (ICJ, 2014), 338–41, 415
China: fisheries, market share of, 154, 155, 160; Spratly Islands dispute, 132
civil law, codification of, 12–13
Clairon-Clipperton Zone, 57
close relationship of offshore spaces to coastal state: as conceptual doctrine, 472–3; continental shelf zones and, 95–101; EEZs and, 114; proportionality principle and, 542
closure of the seas. see maritime boundary delimitation
CMZ (continental margin zone), 71; the coast dominates the sea (CDS) principle, 525–38, 542, 557, 629
coastal and island states: justiciable standards related to conduct of, 569–77; as main beneficiaries of maritime boundary delimitation, 140–3; natural prolongation of

territory of, 77–92, 199, 463, 467–70, 542. *See also* close relationship of offshore spaces to coastal state; permanent sovereignty over natural resources
Coastal Energy Impact Program (CEIP), US (1979), 341–4
Cod War, 591
co-existence. *See* law of co-existence
Colombia v. Nigeria territorial and maritime dispute (ICJ, 2012), 336–8. *See also Table of Cases, for more detailed references*
colonialism and equity, 21–2
Colson, David A., 126–7, 202, 253, 470, 510, 612
Common Heritage Fund (CHF), 144
Comoros, state practice of, 240
compromis (special agreement): *ad hoc* concretization of justiciable standards in, 596–601; importance of, 349–50; inherent limitations, 600; in judicial boundary delimitation, 623–5; legal environmental of equity and, 482–5; LOS Convention and, 600; negotiations, quality of, 681; resource allocation, as means of improving, 567–8; third party rights and, 484
conceptual and contextual issues, 440–514; basic conceptual problems, 451–3; close relationship doctrine, 472–3; importance of context in equity cases, 39; judicial and conciliatory settlements, context and specificity in, 348–9; natural boundaries, 462–72; object of delimitation, as marine resource or marine space, 456–8; political environment of equity, 510–12; process of conceptualization and concretization in case law, 442–51; relational nature of equity and equitable standards, 453–6, 542, 557; underlying values and principles, impact of, 473–5; window of delimitation, 459–61. *See also* legal environment of equity

conciliation. *See* judicial and conciliatory settlements
concretization: *ad hoc* concretization of justiciable standards in *compromis*, 596–601; in case law, 442–51; of permanent sovereignty over natural resources, 475; of principles to facts of case, 625–6
conduct: historical, 571–4, 628; RCC (recent and contemporary), 574–7, 589, 625
Congo, multilateral fisheries development agreement, 153
conservation. *See* natural resources and resource allocation
constitutionalization of international law: decline of equity and, 14; LOS Convention as constitution, 60, 227–33, 485, 651; multilayered governance, encouraging perception of, 172; WTO and, 172, 651
constitutive entitlement of islands, 641
constitutive islands, adjudication process for, 644
context. *See* conceptual and contextual issues
Continental law, equity in, 12–13
continental margin zone (CMZ), 71
continental rise, 71
continental shelf (properly speaking), 71
continental shelf zones, 70–104; close relationship of offshore spaces to coastal state, 95–101; conceptual framework for, 102–3; convergence toward single homogeneous zone with EEZ, 122–8, 219; in customary law, 81–4, 91, 359–69; defined and described, 70–4; distance-related criteria, 92–5; distributive justice and, 132–4; divergences between EEZs and, 121–2; economic interests in, 583–9; within EEZ, 79; emergence of doctrine, 1–7, 46; establishing limits and settling disputes over, 86–91; exploitability test, 85–6, 92–5; geography, moving beyond, 98–9; historical conduct prior to creation

of, 571–4; as horizontally shared, quasi-territorial zones, 67–70; ICJ decisions and, 78, 103–4; islands' basic entitlement to, 638–40; legal foundations and nature of, 77–101; natural law *(ipso iure)* arguments for, 77–81; as natural prolongation of territory of coastal state, 77–92, 199, 463, 467–70, 542; permanent sovereignty over natural resources and, 100; relationship with EEZ, 92, 100, 121–9; scope of shelf rights, 74–7; state unilateral acts regarding, 236–8; territorial expansion, limiting, 85–6

continental slope, 71

Convention on the Conservation of Antarctic Marine Living Resources (CCAMLR; 1980), 164–165, 166

co-operation agreements, 252–70; advantages and limitations of, 453–6; common zones under joint administration, 261–6; for economic regions, 256; equidistance issues, 270; long-lasting zones overlapping a boundary line, 259–61; models for, 254–6; revenue sharing and compensation model, 257–8; shared jurisdiction pending exploration model, 258–9

co-operation, customary duty of, 367–9, 675–6

co-ordination of boundary lines, 626–7

corrective or autonomous equity, 375–8

corridors (parallel lines) method, 197

court proceedings. *See* judicial and conciliatory settlements

CRT (Closest Relation Test). *See* close relationship of offshore spaces to coastal state

cultural and ethnological interests, 589–90, 628

customary law, 354–72; absence of specific customary rules for maritime delimitation, 359–69; agreed equitable model in, 365–7; continental shelf zones in, 81–4, 91, 359–69; EEZs in, 114–18, 359–69; equidistance or median line in, 369–72; equitable principles model in, 363–5; explicit evidence of, 356; on maritime boundary delimitation, 59–63; mutual co-operation, obligation of, 367–9, 675–6; negotiation and, 358–9, 675–6; *opinio juris* and, 356–7; prior consultation, 675–6; requirements for existence of rule in, 355–7; residual rules and exceptions model (equidistance–special circumstances) in, 359–63; state practice and, 355, 365; subsequent codification of, 354; unilateral delimitation prohibited by, 357–8

Cyprus, Greek-Turkish dispute over, 270

Decaux, Emmanuel, 389

decolonization and equity, 21–2

deep seabed mining: continental shelf doctrine used to limit territorial expansion for purposes of, 85–6; UNCLOS III/LOS Convention on, 52–8; unilateral appropriation of sites in national legislation, 91

Degan, Vladimir, 18

Denmark: co-operation agreements, 269; *Grisbadarna* arbitration (1909), 394–8; *Jan Mayen* case (ICJ, 1993), 303–6, 411; *North Sea Continental Shelf* cases (ICJ, 1969), 272–5, 403–4, 420–1, 423–6; state practice of, 240, 250

development: differential and preferential treatment for less-developed countries under UNCLOS III/LOS Convention, 54; Doha Development Agenda, WTO, 138; equity and, 23, 26; global equity, LDC quest for, 130–40; LIFDCs, 154, 158, 160; LLCs and GDCs, 143–53; main beneficiaries of maritime boundary delimitation and, 140; market share and production in

fisheries and agriculture, 153–61; Non-Aligned Movement of LDCs, 50
dialectical process accounting for normative and factual elements, judicial boundary delimitation as, 608–9
discretionary determination, 405–8
disproportionality test: cases applying, 331, 335, 338, 340, 341; EDS (equal division of marine space) principle and, 541; in historical development and evolution of equity, 416; specification, problem of, 545, 550, 551, 552, 553
distributive justice, 130–75; beneficiaries of maritime boundary delimitation, 140–3; conservation and management of fisheries, 161–70; continental shelf zones and, 132–4; EEZs and, 130, 134–40; enclosure movement and, 3, 49; equitable surplus allocation, 146–53; equity as broad synonym for, 30, 31; in fisheries and aquaculture, 134–40, 146–70; global equity, quest for, 130–40; for LLCs and GDCs, 143–53; market share in fisheries, 153–61; mixed results of enclosure movement for, 161; in oil and gas deposits, 132; permanent sovereignty of coastal states over natural marine resources, concept of, 2; rebirth of equity and, 28; in renewable energy production, 133; structural limitations on, 170–5
Doha Development Agenda, WTO, 138
domestic practice. *See* state practice
Dubai v. *Sharjah Emirates* arbitration (1981), 279–80. *See also Table of Cases, for more detailed references*
duty to negotiate, 647, 660–90; *Aegean Continental Shelf* case (*Greece* v. *Turkey*; ICJ, 1978), 682–7; compliance with, 679–81; court proceedings affected by violations of, 681–2; equity as primary foundation for, 676–8; foundations of, 672–8; jurisdiction of ICJ not affected by, 685; legal effects of, 679–90; sanctions and reprisals to enforce, 679–81; scope of, 663–5
Dworkin, Ronald, 520, 679

East Timor's co-operation agreement with Australia, 263
eco-geographical criteria, as relevant circumstances, 563–4, 628
ecological methods, 199–203, 470–2
ecology. *See* natural resources and resource allocation
economic interests: as justiciable standards of equity, 577–90; negotiations considering, 659
Ecuador, establishment of EEZs by, 108
EDS (equal division of marine space), 538–41, 625
EEZs. *See* exclusive economic zones
El Salvador v. *Honduras* dispute (ICJ, 1992), 300–3. *See also Table of Cases, for more detailed references*
enclaving, 197–8, 642
enclosure movement. *See* maritime boundary delimitation
Engisch, Karl, 607
England. *See* United Kingdom
English law, equity in, 10, 11, 13
environment. *See* natural resources and resource allocation
equal division of marine space (EDS), 538–41, 625
Equatorial Guinea: land and maritime boundary, case concerning (*Cameroon* v. *Nigeria*; ICJ, 2002), 315–18; multilateral fisheries development agreement, 153
equidistance or median line, 184–91, 208, 210; advantages and limitations of, 369–72; co-operation agreements and, 270; in customary law, 369–72; equity versus, 375–92, 603–10; in judicial and conciliatory settlements, 350–1; in state agreements, 242–52; in unilateral state practice, 236
equidistance–special circumstances. *See* residual rules and exceptions model

equitable principles model, as legal approach to boundary delimitation, 206–8, 363–5
equitable solution: international law and goal of, 226–7; justiciable standards of equity and, 525; third party rights and, 224–6; in UNCLOS III/LOS Convention, 217, 224–6
equitable surplus allocation, 146–53
equity, xxv, 1–41, 375–439; ambiguity and multiplicity of meanings of, 31–4; appropriateness of, 392–3; conceptual and contextual issues, 440–514 (*See also* conceptual and contextual issues); corrective or autonomous, 375–8; decline of, 8–16; decolonization and, 21–2; defined and described, 8–9; development and, 23, 26; in different legal schools of thought, 34–9; distributive justice, as broad synonym for, 30, 31 (*See also* distributive justice); equidistance versus, 375–92, 603–10; global, 26–7, 28–9, 130–40, 453–6; historical development and evolution, 9–14, 394–418 (*See also* historical development and evolution of equity); intergenerational, 23, 162; *ius gentium* and natural law brought together in, 10; judicial and conciliatory settlements, as common factor in, 352; jurisdiction and legal theory, questions of, 389–92; justiciable standards of, 515–601 (*See also* justiciable standards of equity); legal nature of, 28–39; maritime boundary delimitation leading to renaissance of, 1–8; methodological insights, 40; multiple normative levels of, 28–9; natural justice and, 15; natural resources, rebirth in law of, 18–21; negotiation, relevance to, 645–7 (*See also* negotiation); new legal principles arising from, 29–31; NIEO linking sovereign equality and, 169; normative levels of, 381; operational, 28–9; political environment of, 510–12;

programmatic function of, 22–4; proper methodology of, 614–35; public international law and rebirth of, 16–18; residual rules and exceptions (equidistance–special circumstances) model versus, 375–92, 603–10 (*See also* residual rules and exceptions model); self-determination and, 25–8; structural limitations on, 170–5
Eritrea v. Yemen arbitration award (1999), 306–10. See also *Table of Cases*, for more detailed references
Esser, Joseph, 605
Estonia, market share of fisheries in, 159
estoppel (preclusion), 489–90, 568–73, 613
ethnological and cultural interests, 589–90, 628
European law, equity in, 12–13
European Union: co-operation agreements, importance of, 256; fisheries, market share of, 155; international law shaped by, 25
Evensen, Jens, 389
evolution of equity. See historical development and evolution of equity
ex aequo et bono: ICJ decision-making based on, 8, 17, 205; legal foundations of equity and, 430–5; legal model of juridical vacuum, 205–6
exclusive economic zones (EEZs), 104–21; close relationship of offshore spaces to coastal state and, 114; continental shelf zones within, 79; convergence toward single homogeneous zone with continental shelf zone, 122–8, 219; in customary law, 114–18, 359–69; defined and described, 104–11; distributive justice and, 130, 134–40; divergences between continental shelf zones and, 121–2; economic interests in, 583–9; emergence of doctrine, 1–7, 48; fisheries and aquaculture in, 105–8,

110; historical conduct prior to creation of, 571–4; as horizontally shared, quasi-territorial zones, 67–70; ICJ and, 109, 114–16; islands' basic entitlement to, 638–40; legal foundations and nature of, 111–16; LLCs and GDCs, 143–53; market share and production of fisheries in, 153–61; NIEO and, 130; patrimonialist approach to, 109, 147; permanent sovereignty over natural resources and, 112–14; relationship with continental shelf zones, 92, 100, 121–9; renewable energy platforms in, 133; scope of EEZ rights, 116–21; in state practice, 116–18, 238–41; territorialist approach to, 109, 118; UNCLOS III/LOS Convention and, 110, 118–21
exploitability test, 85–6, 92–5
exploratory drilling on continental shelf zones, 76
extrapolation of the land boundary method, 196–7

failure to negotiate: court proceedings affected by, 681–2; sanctions and reprisals for, 679–81
fair and reasonable proportionality (FRP). *See* proportionality principle
Falk, Richard A., 169, 171, 172
Falklands/Malvinas War (1982), 110, 132
FAO (Food and Agriculture Organization), 138, 139, 161, 166–8
Fiji, state practice of, 239
Finlay, Luke W., 86
fisheries and aquaculture: in Antarctica, 159; conservation and management issues, 161–70; continental shelf zone rights to, 75; distributive justice and, 134–40, 146–70; EEZs and, 105–8, 110; equitable surplus allocation for LLCs and GDCs, 146–53; intergenerational/third generational rights, 593–6; market share and production in, 153–61; regional co-ordination of, 107; as specific economic interest, 583–9; in state practice, 238–41; TAC (total allowable catches), 138, 165
Fitzmaurice, Sir Gerald, 211
flexible residual rules, 209
Food and Agriculture Organization (FAO), 138, 139, 161, 166–8
France: *Anglo-French Channel* arbitration (1977/78), 275–9, 404–5; co-operation agreements, 260, 267; *St. Pierre and Miquelon* arbitration (1992), 297–300, 411; state practice of, 238, 251
Franck, Thomas, 30
'freedom of the high seas', 45, 64
Friedmann, Wolfgang, 18, 579
FRP (fair and reasonable proportionality). *See* proportionality principle
frustration of negotiations, prohibition of, 666–72

Gabon, multilateral fisheries development agreement, 153
gas. *See* oil and gas deposits
GDCs (geographically disadvantaged countries), 143–53
General Agreement on Tariffs and Trade (GATT): global equity and, 26; MFN principle, 138; structural pairing of substance and procedures in, 634; Uruguay Round, xxvi, 51, 133, 634; gatt I; WTO founded on basis of, 26
Geneva Continental Shelf Convention (1958), 49, 105, 245–6, 488. *See also* *Table of Main Multilateral Agreements and Selected Instruments, for more detailed references*
geodesic lines, 198, 199, 278
geographically disadvantaged countries (GDCs), 143–53
geography: continental shelf zone understanding moving beyond,

98–9; eco-geographical criteria, as relevant circumstances, 563–4, 628; justiciable standards related to human conduct and human geography, 568–96, 628, 629; justiciable standards related to physical geography, 525–68; methods of maritime boundary delimitation based on, 183–99 (*See also* methods and approaches to boundary delimitation); negotiation, determining relevant geographic area in, 658; surface coastal configuration, principles of, 525–38
geological and ecological (natural boundaries) methods, 199–203
geometrical methods of maritime boundary delimitation, 183–99 *See also* methods and approaches to boundary delimitation
Georges Bank, as ecological system, 200, 201, 285–90, 471–2
Georgia, market share of fisheries in, 159
Germany: on equidistance, 382; fair and equitable sharing, introduction of doctrine of, 543, 565; *North Sea Continental Shelf* cases (ICJ, 1969), 272–5, 403–4, 420–1, 423–6; state practice of, 237, 238, 240; topism or topical method in, 605; UNCLOS III/ LOS Convention and, 56–7; *Wesensgehalt* (essential content) in, 627
Gibbs, Sir Harry (Australian Chief Justice), 83
global equity, 26–7, 28–9, 130–40, 453–6
global mobility, 69
Goldsmith, Jack L., 170
good faith: in negotiations, 665–6; in *North Sea Continental Shelf* cases (1969), 423–6
Gounaris, Emmanuel, 247
Great Britain. *See* United Kingdom
Greece: *Aegean Continental Shelf* case (with Turkey; ICJ, 1978), 682–7; co-operation agreement with Turkey,

possibility of, 269; Cyprus, dispute over, 270; state practice of, 250
Grisbadarna arbitration (1909), 394–8. *See also Table of Cases, for more detailed references*
Gros, André, 389, 431, 603, 665, 687
Grotius, Hugo, *Mare Liberum*, 63, 64
Group of 77, 48, 50, 147
Guinea v. *Guinea-Bissau* arbitration (1985), 290–3, 408. *See also Table of Cases, for more detailed references*
Gulf of Maine basin, as ecological system, 200, 471
Gulf of Maine case (*Canada* v. *US*; ICJ, 1984), 285–90, 406–8. *See also Table of Cases, for more detailed references*
Guyana: state practice of, 240; *Suriname* v. *Guyana* arbitration award (2007), 321–4, 415

Habicht, Max, 17
half effect to islands, 189
Hankey, Blair, 248, 459–61, 555
Helsinki Rules, 19
Henkin, Louis, 38, 86
historical conduct, as relevant circumstance, 571–4, 628
historical development and evolution of equity, 9–14, 394–418; definition of fundamental rule and factors (1969), 403–4; discretionary determination, victory of (1982 and 1984), 405–8; *ex aequo et bono* decision-making and, 430–5; ILC and, 421–2; judicial activism involved in, 426–9; judicial boundary delimitation, proper methodology of equity in, 614–22; justice, good faith, and equity, 423–6; legal foundations, 418–39; in LOS Convention, 437–8; more principled and less discretionary approach, efforts to find (1985), 409–13; *North Sea Continental Shelf* cases (ICJ, 1969) and, 453–6, 420–1; paramount source of maritime boundary law in equity before LOS Convention, 435–7; peaceful settlement of

disputes principle in UN Charter, 422–3; reduction of rule (1977), 404–5; roots of fundamental rule, establishment of (1909), 394–8; roots of fundamental rule, establishment of (1951), 398–403; rule-oriented versus result-oriented approaches, shifts between, 394; set of independent equitable principles for maritime boundary law, 438–9; Truman Proclamation (1945) and, 393, 404–5, 421–2; two-step and three-step approaches, development of (1999-2014), 413–17
historical rights to maritime boundaries, 485–8, 568–73, 613
Holmes, Oliver Wendell, 32
Honduras: *Land, Island, and Maritime Frontier Dispute* (ICJ, 1992), 300–3; territorial and maritime dispute with Nicaragua (ICJ, 2007), 324–7
horizontally shared zones: EEZs and continental shelf zones as, 67–70; national security interests and, 591
Huber, Judge, 487
human conduct and human geography, justiciable standards related to, 568–96, 628, 629
human rights, marine boundary delimitation compared to, 627

Iceland: Cod War, 591; co-operation agreements, 260; economic importance of fisheries to, 584; Jan Mayen Ridge conciliation with Norway (1981), 344–6; state practice of, 240
ICJ. *See* International Court of Justice
idealism, equity in, 34
ILC. *See* International Law Commission
India: on negotiation, 671; state practice of, 240; UNCLOS III/LOS Convention and, 58
indigenous peoples, interests of, 589–90
Indonesia: co-operation agreement with Australia, 257, 263, 266; Timor Trough and, 200, 202, 463

intergenerational/third generational rights, 23, 162, 593–6, 625
International Court of Justice (ICJ): conceptualization process of, 443–51; on continental shelf zones, 78, 103–4; on convergence toward single homogeneous boundary, 127; on customary law criteria, 355; decision-making *ex aequo et bono* and reliance on equitable principles in, 8, 17, 205; on EEZs, 109, 114–16; on geometrical and geographic methods of boundary delimitation, 183; horizontally-shared zones, concept of, 68; jurisdiction not affected by duty to negotiate, 685; Koskenniemi's reference to case law of, 38; maritime boundary delimitation case law in, 4, 59–63; negotiations ordered by, 687–90; on relationship between continental shelf zones and EEZs, 121; on scientific evidence of ecological facts, 201; unilateral application to, 681 *See also* judicial and conciliatory settlements
international law: equitable solution, relationship to goal of, 226–7; human rights in, 627; judicial activism in, 426–9; UNCLOS III/ LOS Convention requiring application of, 217, 221–4 *See also* constitutionalization of international law
International Law Association: on decision-making *ex aequo et bono*, 206; Helsinki Rules adopted by, 19; on sustainable development, 23
International Law Commission (ILC): Geneva Conventions on Law of the Sea developed by, 49; on geometrical and geographic methods of boundary delimitation, 183; Helsinki Rules adopted by, 19; legal foundations of equity and, 421–2; on prohibition of acts frustrating negotiation, 666

international law of the seas, boundaries in. *See* maritime boundary delimitation
International Plan of Action for the Management of Fishing Capacity (1999), 167
International Tribunal for the Law of the Sea (ITLOS): *Bay of Bengal* case (*Bangladesh* v. *Myanmar*, 2012), 332–5; three-step approach adopted by, 450
ipso iure title to continental shelf zones, 77–81
Iraq: on negotiation, 671; unilateral acts by, 237, 238
Ireland, co-operation agreements of, 269
Irish Formula, 93
island states. *See* coastal and island states
islands, 635–44; accessory entitlement of, 641; additive, adjudication process for, 642–4; basic entitlement to shelf and EEZ, 638–40; case law on, 635, 638; categorical schemes and models for, 636–7, 641; constitutive, adjudication process for, 644; constitutive entitlement of, 641; dependent versus independent, 641; enclaving, 197–8, 642; half effect to, 189; judicial boundary delimitation for, 642–4; legal issues, 638–41; relevant circumstances, considering, 644; state practice regarding, 636–7; UNCLOS III/LOS Convention on, 636, 639
Italy, unilateral acts by, 237
ITLOS. *See* International Tribunal for the Law of the Sea
iura novit curia, 631–4
ius gentium and natural law brought together in equity, 10

Jagota, S. P., 248
Jan Mayen case (*Denmark* v. *Norway*; ICJ, 1993), 303–6, 411. *See also* Table of Cases, for more detailed references

Jan Mayen Ridge conciliation (*Iceland* v. *Norway*; 1981), 344–6. *See also* Table of Cases, for more detailed references
Japan: Antarctica, fishing operations in, 159, 165; co-operation agreements, 262; fisheries, market share of, 155, 159; state practice of, 240
Jay Treaty (1794), 16
Jenks, Wilfried, 18
Jennings, Sir Robert, 50, 402, 493
Jessup, Philip C., 457, 608
Jewett, Marcus L., 80
Johnston, Douglas M., 106
joint development agreements. *See* co-operation agreements
judicial activism involved in legal foundations of equity, 426–9
judicial and conciliatory settlements: *ad hoc* geometrical constructions in, 352; *Aegean Continental Shelf* case (*Greece* v. *Turkey*; ICJ, 1978), 682–7; *Anglo-French Channel* arbitration (1977/78), 275–9, 404–5; *Anglo-Norwegian Fisheries* case (ICJ, 1951), 398–403; *Barbados* v. *Trinidad and Tobago* arbitration award (2006), 318–21, 415–17; *Bay of Bengal* case (*Bangladesh* v. *Myanmar*; ITLOS, 2012), 332–5; *Black Sea* case (*Romania* v. *Ukraine*; ICJ, 2009), 327–32, 413–14; *Cameroon* v. *Nigeria* case concerning land and maritime boundary (ICJ, 2002), 315–18, 415–16; *compromis* (special agreement), importance of, 349–50; context and specificity in, 348–9; domestic and quasi-judicial proceedings, 341–8; *Dubai* v. *Sharjah Emirates* arbitration (1981), 279–80; *El Salvador* v. *Honduras land, island, and maritime frontier dispute* (ICJ, 1992), 300–3; equidistance or median line in, 350–1; equity as common factor in, 352; *Eritrea* v. *Yemen* arbitration award (1999), 306–10; failure to negotiate affecting,

681-2; *Grisbadarna* arbitration (*Norway* v. *Denmark*; 1909), 394-8; *Guinea* v. *Guinea-Bissau* arbitration (1985), 290-3, 408; *Gulf of Maine* case (*Canada* v. *US*; ICJ, 1984), 285-90, 406-8; *Guyana* v. *Suriname* arbitration award (2007), 321-4, 415; international legal proceedings, 272-341; on islands, 635, 638; *Jan Mayen* case (*Denmark* v. *Norway*; ICJ, 1993), 303-6, 411; *Jan Mayen Ridge* conciliation (*Iceland* v. *Norway*; 1981), 344-6; *Malta* v. *Libya Continental Shelf* case (ICJ, 1985), 294-7, 409-13; negotiation during, 688; negotiation versus, 687-90; Newfoundland/Labrador/Nova Scotia arbitration (2002), 346-8; *Nicaragua* v. *Colombia territorial and maritime dispute* (ICJ, 2012), 336-8; *Nicaragua* v. *Honduras territorial and maritime dispute* (ICJ, 2007), 324-7; *North Sea Continental Shelf* cases (Denmark/Germany/Netherlands; ICJ, 1969), 272-5, 403-4, 420-1, 423-6; *Peru* v. *Chile* maritime dispute (ICJ, 2014), 338-41, 415; political environment of equity and, 511; process of conceptualization and concretization in case law, 442-51; proper methodology of equity, evolution of, 614-22; *Qatar* v. *Bahrain* case concerning maritime delimitation and territorial questions (ICJ, 2001), 311-15, 415; *St. Pierre and Miquelon* arbitration (*France* v. *Canada*; 1992), 297-300, 411; third party rights, lack of jurisdiction over, 492-3; *Tunisia* v. *Libya Continental Shelf* cases (ICJ, 1982 and 1985), 281-5, 405; UNCLOS III/LOS Convention not establishing compulsory requirements for, 219; unilateral settlement, exclusion of, 219-20; US CEIP program (1979), 341-4. *See also separate Table of Cases for more detailed references to case law*

judicial boundary delimitation, 602-44; burden of proof, 631; case law evolution of, 614-22; *compromis* (special agreement), dealing with, 623-5; concretization and visualization of principles to facts of case, 625-6; as dialectical process accounting for normative and factual elements, 608-9; equidistance versus equity and, 603-10; equitable principles, assessing and adjudicating, 625; equity, proper methodology of, 614-35; international law other than equity, adjudicating rights and obligations under, 613; for islands, 642-4; *iura novit curia*/judgement *proprio motu*, 631-4; legal issues outside realm of equity, adjudicating, 611; legitimate expectations of goal of equitable apportionment, 630; relevant circumstances, corrective impact of, 628-30; structural pairing of substance and procedures in, 633-4; technical methods in methodology of equity, role of, 631; territorial jurisdiction, adjudicating, 614; topism or topical method, 603-10, 622-30; type of boundary required or permitted, assessing, 623-5; vector analysis and co-ordination of boundary lines, 626-7; window of delimitation, defining, 611-13

juridical vacuum (*ex aequo et bono*), 205-6

jus cogens, 229, 485, 600, 680

justice, distributive. *See* distributive justice

justice, good faith, and equity in *North Sea Continental Shelf* cases (1969), 423-6

justiciable standards of equity, 515-601; *ad hoc* concretization in *compromis* (special agreements), 596-601; CDS (coast dominates the sea) principle, 525-38, 542, 557, 629; coastal and island states, conduct of, 569-77; cultural and ethnological interests,

589–90; equitable principles for purposes of, 518–22; equitable solution and, 525; historical conduct, 571–4; human conduct and human geography, related to, 568–96, 628–9; natural security interests, 590–3; NCP (non cutting-off) principle, 530–8; NEP (non-encroachment) principle, 530–8; PCM (Prudent Conservation and Management Principle), 593, 595; physical geography, related to, 525–68; RCC (recent and contemporary conduct), 574–7, 589; requirement of justiciability, 515–18; social and economic interests, 577–90; space allocation (EDS or equal division of marine space), related to, 538–41; surface coastal configuration, related to, 525–38; third generational/ intergenerational rights, 593–6; vicinity, as essential criterion of NEP and NCP, 536–8; VP (viability principle), 589 See also proportionality principle; relevant circumstances,

Karl, Donald E., 637
Kenya: EEZs, establishment of, 109, 112; state practice of, 239
Kissinger, Henry, 50
Kolb, Robert, 30
Koskenniemi, Martti, 20, 36–9
Kothari, Rajni, 174
Kwiatkowska, Barbara, 255

Lachs, Manfred, 533, 687, 688, 690
land boundary, extrapolation of, 196–7
land-locked countries (LLCs), 143–53
Latvia, market share of fisheries in, 159
Lauterpacht, Elihu, 419
Lauterpacht, Hersch, 80, 370, 632–3
law of co-existence: co-operation agreements and, 254; customary duty of co-operation and prior consultation, 254; maritime boundary delimitation as paradigm of, 5–7; mutual co-operation, customary obligation of, 367–9; peaceful settlement of disputes principle in UN Charter, 422–3
Law of the Sea (LOS) Convention. See United Nations Conference on the Law of the Sea (UNCLOS) III/Law of the Sea (LOS) Convention
law of the seas. See maritime boundary delimitation
least-developed countries (LDCs). See development
legal approaches to boundary delimitation, 204–33; agreed equitable model, 213–33, 365–7; equitable principles model, 206–8, 363–5; juridical vacuum *(ex aequo et bono)* model, 205–6; mandatory versus residual rules, 220–1; natural boundaries, 202–3; negotiated agreement requirement, 217 See also residual rules and exceptions model
legal environment of equity, 475–510; *compromis* (special agreement), 349–50, 482–5; estoppel (preclusion) and acquiescence, 489–90, 568–73, 613; historical rights, 485–8, 568–73, 613; *pacta sunt servanda*, 476–85; *uti possidetis juris*, 479–82, 613 See also third party rights
legal positivism, 35, 605
legal realism, 35, 608
Legault, Leonard, 248, 459–61, 555
legitimate expectations: of goal of equitable apportionment, 630; in negotiations, 665–6
Libya: EEZ claims rejected by US, 108; *Malta v. Libya Continental Shelf* case (ICJ, 1985), 294–7, 409–13; *Tunisia v. Libya Continental Shelf* cases (ICJ, 1982 and 1985), 281–5, 405
LIFDCs (Low-Income Food-Deficit Countries), 154, 158, 160
Lima Declaration, 112
Lithuania, market share of fisheries in, 159
LOS (Law of the Sea) Convention. See United Nations Conference on the Law of the Sea (UNCLOS) III/Law of the Sea (LOS) Convention

Low-Income Food-Deficit Countries (LIFDCs), 154, 158, 160
loxodromes, 198, 199, 278

Macdonald, J., 170
Maine, Sir Henry, 10, 20
Malaysia, in Spratly Islands dispute, 132
Maldives, state practice of, 239
Mali, multilateral fisheries development agreement, 153
Malta: constitutive entitlement of, 641; *Libya v. Malta Continental Shelf* case (ICJ, 1985), 294–7, 409–13
Malvinas/Falklands War (1982), 110, 132
Mandelbrot, Benoît, 141
mare clausum. See maritime boundary delimitation
mare liberum ('freedom of the high seas'), 45, 64
marine resources. *See* natural resources and resource allocation
maritime boundary delimitation, 45–66; 'the Area', concept of, 48, 55, 59, 67, 92, 130; beneficiaries of, 140–3; as classical field of international law, 5; Conferences and Conventions regarding, 49–59; continental shelf zones, 70–104 (*See also* continental shelf zones); convergence toward single homogeneous boundary, 122–5, 126–7; customary and case law on, 59–63; in customary law, 354–72 (*See also* customary law); distributive justice and, 130–75 (*See also* distributive justice); EEZs, 104–21 (*See also* exclusive economic zones); environmental conservation and, 2; 'freedom of the high seas' and, 45; historical perspective on, 63–6; historical rights, 485–8, 568–73, 613; human rights compared to, 627; increasing number of boundaries, 179; judicial and conciliatory settlements, 271–353 (*See also* judicial and conciliatory settlements); judicial methodology of, 602–44 (*See also* judicial boundary delimitation); methods and approaches, 179–235 (*See also* methods and approaches to boundary delimitation); negotiating, 645–90 (*See also* negotiation); object of delimitation, as marine resource or marine space, 456–8; as paradigm of law of co-existence, 5–7; permanent sovereignty of coastal states over natural marine resources, concept of, 2 (*See also* permanent sovereignty over natural resources); state practice regarding, 236–70 (*See also* state practice); territorial appropriation and, 5–7; traditional three-mile territorial limit (cannon ball rule), 46, 526; tragedy of the commons and, 2, 137, 170; twentieth-century enclosure of seas, 1–8, 45–9
MBaye, Judge, 464
McDougal, Myres S., 581
McNair, Judge, 400
McRae, Donald, 127, 255
median line. *See* equidistance or median line
methods and approaches to boundary delimitation, 179–235; ad hoc geometrical constructions in judicial and conciliatory settlements, 352; base points, determining, 185–8; base points, modifying, 189; bisector method, 191–5; competing interests and goals complicating efforts to formulate general rules, 179–82; definition of method, 182; enclaving, 197–8, 642; extrapolation of the land boundary method, 196–7; Geneva Continental Shelf Convention (1958) equidistance–special circumstances rule, 245–6; geodesic lines, 198, 199, 278; geological and ecological (natural boundaries) methods, 199–203; geometrical and geographic methods, 183–99; half effect to islands, 189; loxodromes, 198, 199, 278; negotiation, methodology of, 654–9; parallel lines

(corridors) method, 197; perpendicular to the general direction of the coastline method, 195–6; ratio of coastal lengths, projecting, 190–1; role of technical methods in methodology of equity, 631; scale distortions and errors, 141, 198–9; scientific evidence, what constitutes, 200–2; state agreements indicating specific methods and models, 243–4; state application of specific methods and models, 244–5; straight base lines, 106, 307, 312, 398, 401, 526; technical and scientific methods, 182–203; tectonics, delimitations based on, 200, 201, 463–7, 470; theoretical aspects, 202–3. *See also* equidistance or median line; judicial boundary delimitation, ; legal approaches to boundary delimitation,
Mexico, state practice of, 238, 239, 247
MFN (most favoured nation) treatment, 138
mining and mineral rights: continental shelf zone rights to, 75; existing wells and concessions, 561–3, 564, 628; exploratory drilling on continental shelf zones, 76; intergenerational/third generational rights, 593–6; for LLCs and GDCs, 144–6; unity of deposits in area of delimitation, 560, 564, 628. *See also* deep seabed mining; oil and gas deposits,
mobility, global, 69
Monconduit, François, 385
Monroe doctrine, 73
Morocco: on negotiation, 671; state practice of, 239
most favoured nation (MFN) treatment, 138
Müller, Jörg Paul, 30, 356
mutual co-operation, customary obligation of, 367–9, 675–6
Myanmar, *Bay of Bengal* case (with Bangladesh; ITLOS, 2012), 332–5. *See also* Table of Cases, for more detailed references

NASCO (North Atlantic Salmon Conservation Organization), 143
national practices. *See* state practice
national security interests, 456, 536, 590–3, 628
NATO (North American Treaty Organization), 269, 591
Natuna Islands, 65
natural boundaries: as conceptual issue, 462–72; doctrine of natural prolongation, 77–92, 199, 463, 467–70, 542; ecological methods of determining, 199–203, 470–2; geological methods of determining, 199–203; plate tectonics, 200, 201, 463–7, 470
natural gas. *See* oil and gas deposits
natural justice and equity, 15
natural law: continental shelf zones and, 77–81; equity bringing together *ius gentium* and, 10; equity in, 34
natural resources and resource allocation: eco-geographical criteria regarding, 563–4, 628; enclosure movement and conservation of, 2; existing oil wells and concessions, effect of, 561–3, 564, 628; intergenerational/third generational rights, 23, 162, 593–6, 625; limitations of allocation of, as general law of delimitation, 564–7; negotiation and *compromis*, improving allocation by, 567–8; as object of delimitation, 456–8; PCM (Prudent Conservation and Management) Principle, 559–68; programmatic function of equity and, 23–4; rebirth of equity in law of, 18–21; relevant circumstances related to allocation of, 559–68, 628; unity of deposits in area of delimitation, 560, 564, 628. *See also* permanent sovereignty over natural resources; *specific resources, e.g.* fisheries and aquaculture,
NCP (non cutting-off principle), 530–8, 625

Negotiating Group 7 (NG 7), 213–17, 649, 671
negotiation, 645–90; *Aegean Continental Shelf* case (*Greece v. Turkey*; ICJ, 1978), 682–7; boundary establishment versus joint zone, 658; customary law and, 358–9, 675–6; deviations from starting line, 659; domestic needs, accounting for, 659; good faith and legitimate expectations in, 665–6; during judicial and conciliatory settlements, 688; judicial and conciliatory settlements versus, 687–90; law and policy in, 653–4; mandatory versus residual rules of, 647–52; methodology of, 654–9; normative role of equitable standards and principles in, 654–9; obligation to follow equitable principles in, 647–60; political and economic needs, meeting, 659; prohibition of acts frustrating, 666–72; proper delimitation methodology in, 655–9; relevance of equity to, 645–7; relevant geographic area, determining, 658; resource allocation, improving, 567–8; starting line, determining, 659; state practice in difficult and protracted negotiations, 250–2; UN Charter on, 674–5; UNCLOS III/LOS Convention on, 217, 647–52, 661–2, 668, 670; unilateral settlement, exclusion of, 219–20. *See also* duty to negotiate; failure to negotiate,
neo-positivism, equity in, 35
NEP (non-encroachment principle), 530–8, 625
Nepal, on mineral rights of LLCs and GDCs, 144
Netherlands, in *North Sea Continental Shelf* cases (ICJ, 1969), 272–5, 403–4, 420–1, 423–6. *See also Table of Cases, for more detailed references*
New Haven School, 35, 608
New International Economic Order (NEIO): absence of law of the sea from early discussions and documents, 131; distributive justice and, 130, 169; enclosure movement and, 55; programmatic function of equity and, 23, 24
New Zealand, state practice of, 239
Newman, Ralph A., 9, 32
NG 7 (Negotiating Group 7), 213–17, 649, 671
Nicaragua: territorial and maritime dispute with Colombia (ICJ, 2012), 336–8; territorial and maritime dispute with Honduras (ICJ, 2007), 324–7
NIEO. *See* New International Economic Order
Niger, multilateral fisheries development agreement, 153
Nigeria: land and maritime boundary, case with Cameroon concerning (ICJ, 2002), 315–18, 415–16; state practice of, 240
non-cutting-off principle (NCP), 530–8, 625
Non-Aligned Movement of LDCs, 50
non-encroachment principle (NEP), 530–8, 625
non-interference with third party rights, as principle, 491
North American Treaty Organization (NATO), 269, 591
North Atlantic Salmon Conservation Organization (NASCO), 143
North Sea Continental Shelf cases (Denmark/Germany/Netherlands; ICJ, 1969), 272–5, 403–4, 420–1, 423–6. *See also Table of Cases, for more detailed references*
North–South debate, 21, 140
Norway: *Anglo-Norwegian Fisheries* case (ICJ, 1951), 398–403; co-operation agreements, 258, 260; *Grisbadarna* arbitration (1909), 394–8; *Jan Mayen* case (ICJ, 1993), 303–6, 411; *Jan Mayen Ridge* conciliation with Iceland (1981), 344–6; national security interests,

591; state practice of, 239; unilateral acts by, 237

OAU (Organization of African Unity), 232, 479
O'Connell, Daniel P., 64
Oda, Shigeru, 381, 382, 389, 431
oil and gas deposits: continental shelf zone rights to, 75, 132; distributive justice and, 132; existing oil wells and concessions, 561–3, 564, 628; exploratory drilling on continental shelf zones, 76; unity of deposits in area of delimitation, 560, 564, 628
Ong, David M., 254, 368
operational equity, 28–9
opinio juris and customary law, 356–7
Orfield, L. B., 17
Organization of African Unity (OAU), 232, 479
Oxman, Bernhard H., 6, 228, 360

pacta sunt servanda, 476–85
Papua New Guinea's co-operation agreement with Australia, 261, 266
Paracel Islands, 65
parallel lines (corridors) method, 197
Pardo, Arvid, 153
partial jurisdiction, EEZs and continental shelf zones as zones of, 67–8
patrimonialist approach to EEZs, 109, 147
PCM (Prudent Conservation and Management) Principle, 593, 595, 625
peaceful settlement of disputes principle in UN Charter, 422–3
permanent sovereignty over natural resources, 2; conceptualization and concretization of, 475; continental shelf zones and, 100; EEZs and, 112–14; proportionality principle and, 542; self-determination and, 25
perpendicular to the general direction of the coastline method, 195–6
Peru: EEZs, establishment of, 108; fisheries, market share of, 154; maritime dispute with Chile (ICJ, 2014), 338–41, 415
Philippines: *Spratly Islands* dispute, 132; unilateral acts by, 238
physical geography. *See* geography
Pinto, M. C. W., 661
plate tectonics, 200, 201, 463–7, 470
Plumley, Frank, 1
Poland, state practice of, 250
political environment of equity, 510–12
political needs of negotiating parties, 659
Portugal, state practice of, 240
positivism, legal, 35, 605
Posner, Eric A., 170
Pound, Roscoe, 16, 34, 603
pragmatism, 608
precautionary approach, 166
preclusion (estoppel), 489–90, 568–73, 613
Prescott, John R. V., 269, 645, 657
principles, concept of, 518–22
prior consultation, 675–6
programmatic function of equity, 22–4
proportionality principle, 541–59; additive islands, adjudicative process for, 643; as broad notion, 557–9; coastal lengths and, 542–3; conceptualization of equity and, 450, 475; concretization and visualization of, 625; equal division as basis for, 541–59; field of application, 556–7; NEP and NCP compared, 531; related principles, 542; specification, problem of, 543–55. *See also* disproportionality test
proprio motu judgement, 631–4
Prudent Conservation and Management (PCM) Principle, 593, 595, 625

Qatar: co-operation agreements, 257; maritime delimitation and territorial questions, case with Bahrain concerning (ICJ, 2001), 311–15, 415
quasi-judicial proceedings, 341–8
quasi-territoriality of EEZs and continental shelf zones, 67–70
Quéneudec, Jean-Pierre, 54, 389

ratio of coastal lengths, projecting, 190–1
Rawls, John, 171
RCCP (principle of recent and contemporary conduct), 574–7, 589, 625
Reagan, Ronald, and Reagan Proclamation (1983), 56, 170, 241, 429
realism, legal, 35, 608
relational nature of equity and equitable standards, 453–6, 542, 557
relevant circumstances: corrective impact of, 628–30; historical conduct, 571–4, 628; of islands, 644; legal nature of, 522–5; resource allocation and, 559–68, 628
renewable energy production, 133, 456
reprisals for failure to negotiate, 679–81
res judicata, 613
residual rules and exceptions model (equidistance–special circumstances): clarity and simplicity attributed to, 382–4; in customary law, 359–63; equity versus, 375–92, 603–10; flexible residual rules, 209; jurisdiction and legal theory, questions of, 389–92; as legal model, 208–12; limitations and shortcomings of, 386–8; mandatory rules versus, 220–1; in negotiation, 647–52; NG 7 and UNCLOS III Conference restating, 213; normative levels of, 381; predictability and stability attributed to, 385–6; strict residual rules, 208–9; underlying concept of, 379–80
resource allocation. *See* natural resources and resource allocation
Richardson, Elliott L., 267, 269
Rio Declaration (1992), 113, 166
Rivero, Y., 564
Roman law, *Aequitas* in, 10
Romania, in *Black Sea* case (with Ukraine; ICJ, 2009), 327–32, 413–14.

See also Table of Cases, for more detailed references
Rome Consensus, 166, 168
Roosevelt, Franklin Delano, 78
Rossi, Christopher, 20
Ruester, Bernd Peter, 247
Russian Federation: Antarctica, fishing operations in, 165; co-operation agreements, 269; fisheries, market share of, 159; on negotiation, 671; state practice of, 250. *See also* Soviet Union

St. Pierre and Miquelon arbitration (*France v. Canada*; 1992), 297–300, 411. *See also Table of Cases, for more detailed references*
sanctions enforcing duty to negotiate, 679–81
Sao Tome e Principe, multilateral fisheries development agreement, 153
Saudi Arabia, co-operation agreements of, 257, 262
scale distortions and errors, 141, 198–9
Schachter, Oscar, 15, 22, 30, 356, 654
Schwarzenberger, Georg, 18
Schwebel, Stephen M., 377, 556, 583
scientific and technical methods, 182–203. see also methods and approaches to boundary delimitation
scientific evidence, what constitutes, 200–2
Scotian shelf, as ecological system, 200, 471
seas, law of. *See* maritime boundary delimitation
Selden, John, 31
self-determination and equitable principles, 25–8
Seychelles, state practice of, 239
Shalowitz, Aaron L., 185
Sharjah/Dubai Emirates arbitration (1981), 279–80. *See also Table of Cases, for more detailed references*

single maritime boundary: convergence toward, 122–8, 219; state practice, concept stemming from, 124, 242, 567
social and economic interests, as justiciable standards of equity, 577–90
social psychology, theory of equity in, 33
Sohn, Louis B., 353
solar energy, 456
Sørenson, Judge, 385, 392, 564
South China Sea: co-operation agreements in, 254; maritime boundary disputes in, 65, 132, 269
South Korea, co-operation agreements of, 262
sovereignty: NIEO linking equity and, 169; programmatic function of equity and, 22–4; self-determination, principle of, 25–8; states, sovereign equality of, 475. *See also* permanent sovereignty over natural resources
Soviet Union: additional boundaries arising from breakup of, 179; fisheries, market share of, 159; national security interests, 591; state practice of, 239; UNCLOS III/LOS Convention and, 58. *See also* Russian Federation
space: equal division of, 538–41, 625; justiciable standards of equity related to allocation of, 538–41; object of delimitation as resource or, 456–8
Spain: co-operation agreement with France, 267; state practice of, 240; special agreement. *See compromis*
Spratly Islands, 65, 132, 269
state national security interests, 456, 536, 590–3
state practice, 236–70; applications of specific models and methods, 244–5; continental shelf zones and, 236–8; customary law and, 355, 365; in difficult and protracted negotiations, 250–2; domestic and quasi-judicial proceedings, 341–8; EEZs in, 116–18, 238–41; fisheries and, 238–41; Geneva Continental Shelf Convention (1958), impact of,

245–6; indications of specific models and methods to be used, 243–4; on islands, 636–7; literature review on state agreements, 246–50; maritime boundary delimitation agreements, 242–52; mutual co-operation, customary obligation of, 368; single maritime boundary concept stemming from, 124, 242, 567; on third party rights, 612; unilateral acts (proclamations and legislation), 236. *See also* co-operation agreements
Stockholm Principles (1972), 113
Stone, Julius, 22, 170
Straddling Stocks Agreement, 166–8
See also Table of Main Multilateral Agreements and Selected Instruments, for more detailed references
straight base lines, 106, 307, 312, 398, 401, 526
strict residual rules, 208–9
structural pairing of substance and procedures, 633–4
Strupp, Karl, 17, 18, 397
Sudan, co-operation agreements of, 262
Suriname/Guyana arbitration award (2007), 321–4, 415. *See also Table of Cases, for more detailed references*
sustainable development and equity, 23–4. *See* development; natural resources and resource allocation
Sweden: *Grisbadarna* arbitration (1909), 394–8; national security interests, 591; state practice of, 250
Switzerland: Civil Code of 1907, 12; *Kerngehalt* (core content) in, 627

TAC (total allowable catches), 138, 165
Taiwan, in *Spratly Islands* dispute, 132
Tanaka, Yoshifumi, 248, 430
technical and scientific methods, 182–203. *See also* methods and approaches to boundary delimitation
tectonics, 200, 201, 463–7, 470
territorial appropriation and expansion: continental shelf zone

doctrine limiting, 85–6; maritime boundary delimitation and, 5–7
territorial jurisdiction, adjudicating, 614
territorialist approach to EEZs, 109, 118
thalweg, 199, 538, 639
third generational/intergenerational rights, 23, 162, 593–6, 625
third party rights, 491–510; *amicus curiae* concept and, 504–10; *compromis* (special agreements) and, 484; Courts lacking jurisdiction over, 492–3; equitable solution requirement and, 224–6; intervention/participation of third parties, 494–510; non-interference principle, 491; state practice regarding, 612; state responsibility rules, invocation of, 231; substantive claims of, 491–4; window of delimitation and, 612
three-mile territorial limit (cannon ball rule), 46, 526
three-step approach, 413–17
tidal energy, 133, 456
Timor Trough, 200, 202, 463
topism or topical method, 605–10, 622–30
Torres Strait Agreement, 589
total allowable catches (TAC), 138, 165
tragedy of the commons, 2, 137, 170
Trinidad and Tobago v. *Barbados* arbitration award (2006), 318–21, 415–17. *See also Table of Cases, for more detailed references*
Truman Proclamation (1945): continental shelf zones and, 72, 77, 80, 83, 97, 100; EEZs and, 107, 112; in historical development and evolution of equity, 393, 404–5, 421–2; legal model of equitable principles and, 206, 221; Reagan Proclamation (1983) reaffirming, 241; underlying policy of, 536, 593; as unilateral act, 237
Tunisia v. *Libya Continental Shelf* cases (ICJ, 1982 and 1985), 281–5, 405. *See also Table of Cases, for more detailed references*
Turkey: *Aegean Continental Shelf* case (with Greece; ICJ, 1978), 682–7; co-operation agreement with Greece, possibility of, 269; Cyprus, dispute over, 270; state practice of, 250
two-step approach, 413–17, 448–50

Ukraine: *Black Sea* case (with Romania; ICJ, 2009), 327–32, 413–14; fisheries, market share of, 159
UNCLOS. *See also* entries at United Nations Conference on the Law of the Sea
underlying values and principles: impact of, 473–5; need for, 379–80; of residual rules and exceptions model (equidistance–special circumstances), 379–80
unilateral acts (proclamations and legislation) of states, 236
unilateral application for third party settlement, 681
unilateral delimitation: customary law prohibiting, 357–8; UNCLOS III/LOS Convention excluding, 219–20
United Kingdom: *Anglo-French Channel* arbitration (1977/78), 275–9, 404–5; *Anglo-Norwegian Fisheries* case (ICJ, 1951), 398–403; co-operation agreements, 258, 269; Falklands/Malvinas War (1982), 110, 132; Iceland Cod War, 591; UNCLOS III/LOS Convention and, 56–7
United Nations Charter: on duty to negotiate, 674–5; peaceful settlement of disputes principle in, 422–3
United Nations Conference on the Law of the Sea (UNCLOS) I, 49, 105. *See also Table of Main Multilateral Agreements and Selected Instruments, for more detailed references*
United Nations Conference on the Law of the Sea (UNCLOS) II, 50, 105. *See also Table of Main Multilateral Agreements and Selected*

Instruments, for more detailed references
United Nations Conference on the Law of the Sea (UNCLOS) III/Law of the Sea (LOS) Convention, 50–9; agreed equitable model, as legal approach to boundary delimitation, 213–33; *compromis* (special agreement) and, 600; constitution, LOS Convention viewed as type of, 60, 227–33, 485, 651; distributive justice and, 130, 153; EEZs and, 110, 118–21; equitable solution requirement, 217, 224–6; historical background of articles 74 and 83, 213–17; historical rights, lack of reference to, 488; international law, requirement to apply, 217, 221–4; interpretation of articles 74(1) and 83(1), 217–18; on islands, 636, 639; legal foundations of equity in, 437–8; LLCs and GDCs, rights of, 143, 144, 146–7; on negotiation, 217, 647–52, 661–2, 668, 670; relationship between international law requirement and goal of equitable solution, 226–7; on residual versus mandatory rules, 220–1, 647–52; third party rights, requirement to respect, 224–6, 231; uniform concept of continental shelf and EEZ in, 219; unilateral settlement excluded by, 219–20. *See also Table of Main Multilateral Agreements and Selected Instruments, for more detailed references*
United Nations FAO (Food and Agriculture Organization), 138, 139, 161, 166–8
United States: CEIP program (1979), 341–4; on continental shelf zones, 72; co-operation agreements, 260, 261, 267, 269; fisheries, market share of, 155; *Gulf of Maine* case (ICJ, 1984), 285–90, 406–8; Libyan EEZ claims rejected by, 108; Reagan, Ronald, and Reagan Proclamation (1983), 56, 170, 241, 429; state practice of, 239, 241, 247; UNCLOS III/LOS Convention and, 54–9; wind energy potential, offshore, 133. *See also* Truman Proclamation
unity of deposits in area of delimitation, 560, 564, 628
Uruguay, co-operation agreements of, 263
Uruguay Round of GATT, 51, 133, 581, 634
uti possidetis juris, 479–82, 613

Vasciannie, Stephen C., 25
Vattel, Emmerich de, 36
vector analysis, 626–7
Venezuela, state practice of, 238
viability principle (VP), 589, 625
vicinity, as essential criterion of NEP and NCP, 536–8
Viehweg, Theodor, 605
Vietnam: Spratly Islands dispute, 132; state practice of, 241
Visscher, Charles De, 18, 397
Vitzthum, Wolfgang Graf, 687
VP (viability principle), 589, 625

Waldock, Sir Humphrey, 667
water column, ecology of, 199–203, 470–2
wave energy, 133, 456
Weil, Prosper, 360, 361, 432
Weiss, Edith Brown, 23
wind energy, 133, 456
window of delimitation: concept of, 459–61; judicial definition of, 611–13
Wolff, Christian, 36
WOMP (World Order Model Project), 171
World Bank, 26, 135
World Charter for Nature, 162
World Trade Organization (WTO): Agreement on Agriculture, 133; constitutionalization of international

law and, 172, 651; distributive justice and, 136; Doha Development Agenda, 138; equitable principles of, 26; failure to negotiate in, 680; law of co-existence and WTO-1, 5; non-discrimination principles, reinforcing WTO-2, 15; structural pairing of substance and procedures in, 634; UNCLOS III compared, 51
Wright, Quincy, 174
WTO. *See* World Trade Organization

Yacouba, Cissé, 127, 255
Yemen: Eritrea/Yemen arbitration award (1999), 306–10; state practice of, 240
Young, Margaret, 138
Yugoslavia, former, on flexible residual rules, 211

Zaire, multilateral fisheries development agreement, 153
Zoller, Elisabeth, 249, 390, 391, 468, 581

For EU product safety concerns, contact us at Calle de José Abascal, 56–1°, 28003 Madrid, Spain or eugpsr@cambridge.org.

www.ingramcontent.com/pod-product-compliance
Ingram Content Group UK Ltd.
Pitfield, Milton Keynes, MK11 3LW, UK
UKHW020347060825
461487UK00008B/556